The READER'S COMPANION to U.S. WOMEN'S HISTORY

EDITORS

Wilma Mankiller

Gwendolyn Mink

Marysa Navarro

Barbara Smith

Gloria Steinem

HOUGHTON MIFFLIN COMPANY ▪ **BOSTON** ▪ **NEW YORK**

The READER'S COMPANION to U.S. WOMEN'S HISTORY

For information about permission to reproduce selections from this book,
write to Permissions, Houghton Mifflin Company, 215 Park Avenue South,
New York, New York 10003.

Library of Congress Cataloging-in-Publication Data
The reader's companion to U.S. women's history.
    p.   cm.
  Edited by Wilma Mankiller and others.
  Includes index.
  ISBN 0-395-67173-6   ISBN 0-618-00182-4 (pbk.)
    1. Women—United States—History—Sources. 2. Women—United
States—Social conditions.   3. Feminism—United States—History.
I. Mankiller, Wilma Pearl, 1945– .
HQ1410.R43   1998
305.4'0973—dc21   97-39923
                    CIP

Printed in the United States of America
QUM 10 9 8 7 6 5 4 3 2 1

Title page illustration: Cherokee Young Ladies' Seminary,
Denver Public Library, Western History Collection

CONTENTS

ADVISORY BOARD

CONTRIBUTORS

Stephanie Aaronson
Washington, D.C.

Mimi Abramovitz
City University of New York

Bella Abzug
*Women's Environment and
Development Organization*

Martha Ackelsberg
Smith College

Ally Acker
Reel Women Trust Foundation

Edna Acosta-Belén
State University of New York at Albany

Margot Adler
New York, New York

Sara Alpern
Texas A & M University

Nawal H. Ammar
Kent State University

Teresa L. Amott
Bucknell University

Margo A. Anderson
University of Wisconsin at Milwaukee

Joyce Antler
Brandeis University

Linda Apodaca
*California State University,
Stanislaus*

Bettina Aptheker
University of California, Santa Cruz

Jeannette C. Armstrong
En'owkin Centre

Betsy Aron
Cambridge, Massachusetts

Marilou Awiakta
Memphis, Tennessee

Judith A. Baer
Texas A & M University

Barbara Bair
Santa Cruz, California

Lois W. Banner
University of Southern California

Kathleen Barry
Pennsylvania State University

Bess Beatty
Oregon State University

Evelyn Torton Beck
University of Maryland at College Park

Martha N. Beck
Phoenix, Arizona

Susan E. Bell
Bowdoin College

Janet Benshoof
Center for Reproductive Law and Policy

Claudia Bepko
Brunswick, Maine

Jane Bernard-Powers
San Francisco State University

Alma R. Berson
Jamaica Plain, Massachusetts

Caroline Bird
Palmetto, Florida

Joan E. Biren
Takoma Park, Maryland

Karen J. Blair
Central Washington University

Kathleen M. Blee
University of Kentucky

Linda M. Blum
University of Michigan

Janet K. Boles
Marquette University

Patricia Bonica
The Union Institute

Eileen Boris
Howard University

Nan Alamilla Boyd
University of Colorado at Boulder

Ellen Bravo
Nine to Five

Wini Breines
Northeastern University

Janet Farrell Brodie
Claremont Graduate School

Rita Mae Brown
Charlottesville, Virginia

Jean Gould Bryant
Florida State University

Charlotte Bunch
Center for Women's Global Leadership

Julie Burton
Voters for Choice

Susan K. Cahn
State University of New York at Buffalo

Emily Card
Santa Monica, California

Mina Carson
Oregon State University

Antonia I. Castañeda
San Antonio, Texas

Lucie Cheng
University of California, Los Angeles

Brenda Child
University of Minnesota

Sally Cline
University of Cambridge

Catherine Clinton
Harvard University

Johnnetta B. Cole
Spelman College

Sophia Collier
Citizens' Trust

Bettye Collier-Thomas
Temple University

Blanche Wiesen Cook
East Hampton, New York

Katsi Cook
Cornell University

Clare Coss
East Hampton, New York

Anne N. Costain
University of Colorado at Boulder

Vicki Crawford
University of North Carolina at Charlotte

Elizabeth C. Cromley
State University of New York at Buffalo

Helen Damon-Moore
Cornell College

Patricia D'Antonio
University of Pennsylvania School of Nursing

Nora Marks Dauenhauer
Sealaska Heritage Foundation

Angela Y. Davis
San Francisco, California

Martha F. Davis
National Organization for Women Legal Defense and Education Fund

Martha L. Deed
State University of New York at Buffalo

Anselma Dell'Olio
Rome, Italy

Ileen A. DeVault
Cornell University School of Industrial and Labor Relations

Janice L. Dewey
University of Arizona

Jane Dolkart
Southern Methodist University Law School

Carol Downer
Los Angeles, California

Virginia G. Drachman
Tufts University

Ellen Carol DuBois
University of California, Los Angeles

Roxanne Dunbar
San Francisco, California

Andrea Dworkin
Brooklyn, New York

Zillah Eisenstein
Ithaca College

Cynthia Enloe
Clark University

Sara M. Evans
University of Minnesota

Candace Falk
University of California, Berkeley

Elizabeth Feder
Colorado College

Peggy A. Feerick
Takoma Park, Maryland

Roslyn L. Feldberg
Massachusetts Nurses' Association

Martha Albertson Fineman
Columbia University School of Law

Maureen Fitzgerald
University of Arizona

Yvette G. Flores-Ortiz
University of California, Davis

Dana Frank
University of California, Santa Cruz

Marge Frantz
University of California, Santa Cruz

Carla Freccero
University of California, Santa Cruz

Estelle B. Freedman
Stanford University

Jo Freeman
Brooklyn, New York

Marilyn French
New York, New York

Adriane Fugh-Berman
Washington, D.C.

Theresa Funiciello
Woodstock, New York

Nancy F. Gabin
Purdue University

Alma M. García
Santa Clara University

Linda J. Gesling
Evanston, Illinois

Marcia Gillespie
Ms. Magazine

Leslie Friedman Goldstein
University of Delaware

Linda Gordon
University of Wisconsin, Madison

Lynn D. Gordon
University of Rochester

Janice Gould
University of Colorado, Greeley

Sara K. Gould
Ms. Foundation for Women

Jaime M. Grant
The Union Institute

Carol Green-Devens
Central Michigan University

Rita M. Gross
University of Wisconsin—Eau Claire

Camille Guerin-Gonzales
University of California, Los Angeles

Beverly Guy-Sheftall
Spelman College

Pamela Haag
Yale University

Lisbeth Haas
University of California, Santa Cruz

Barbara Haber
The Schlesinger Library

Elizabeth Amelia Hadley Freydberg
Simmons College

Kay Leigh Hagan
Santa Fe, New Mexico

Shirlee Taylor Haizlip
Los Angeles, California

Shelley P. Haley
Hamilton College

Jean A. Hamilton
Duke University

Evelynn M. Hammonds
Massachusetts Institute of Technology

Susan Harding
University of California, Santa Cruz

Jean V. Hardisty
*Political Research Associates,
Cambridge, Massachsetts*

Joy Harjo
Albuquerque, New Mexico

Maxine Harris
Community Connections, Washington, D.C.

Cynthia Harrison
George Washington University

Daphne Duval Harrison
Columbia, Maryland

Holly Hartman
Boston, Massachusetts

Heidi Hartmann
Washington, D.C.

Leah Haus
New York University

Diana L. Hayes
Georgetown University

Lois Rita Helmbold
San Jose State University

Karen Henry
Middle East Education Project

Susannah Heschel
Case Western Reserve University

Nancy A. Hewitt
Duke University

Lisa Beth Hill
The American University

Darlene Clark Hine
Michigan State University

Martha Hodes
New York University

Beatrix Hoffman
Rutgers University

Judith Hole
CBS News

Helen Bequaert Holmes
*Center for Genetics, Ethics, and Women,
Amherst, Masssachusetts*

Akasha (Gloria) Hull
University of California, Santa Cruz

Tera W. Hunter
University of North Carolina, Chapel Hill

Aída Hurtado
University of California, Santa Cruz

H. Patricia Hynes
Boston University School of Public Health

Patricia Ireland
National Organization for Women

Janice M. Irvine
University of Massachusetts at Amherst

Ruth Harriet Jacobs
*Wellesley College Center for Research
on Women*

Sylvia M. Jacobs
North Carolina Central University

Naomi Jaffe
Troy, New York

Gladys M. Jiménez-Muñoz
State University of New York at Oneonta

Susan Lee Johnson
University of Colorado at Boulder

Adrienne Lash Jones
Oberlin College

Ann Jones
New York, New York

Teresa Jordan
Deeth, Nevada

Suad Joseph
University of California, Davis

Lani Ka'ahumanu
San Francisco, California

Peggy Kahn
University of Michigan—Flint

Wendy Kaminer
Radcliffe Public Policy Institute

Temma Kaplan
State University of New York at Stony Brook

Debra Renee Kaufman
Northeastern University

Mim Kelber
*Women's Environment and
Development Organization*

Elizabeth Lapovsky Kennedy
State University of New York at Buffalo

Madhulika S. Khandelwal
Queens College

Nazli Kibria
Boston University

Clara Sue Kidwell
National Museum of the American Indian

Wilma King
Michigan State University

Ynestra King
New York, New York

Frances Kissling
Catholics for a Free Choice

Rebecca E. Klatch
University of California, San Diego

Kathryn Kolbert
Center for Reproductive Rights

Anne Kornhauser
New York, New York

Virginia Sánchez Korrol
City University of New York

Jo-Ann Krestan
Brunswick, Maine

Molly Ladd-Taylor
York University

Robin Tolmach Lakoff
University of California, Berkeley

Joan B. Landes
Pennsylvania State University

Cassandra Langer
New York, New York

Sylvia A. Law
New York University School of Law

Laura J. Lederer
University of Minnesota Law School

Charlotte Libov
Bethlehem, Connecticut

Marilee Lindemann
Takoma Park, Maryland

Susan Lynn
Portland Community College

Catharine A. MacKinnon
University of Michigan

Patricia Mainardi
City University of New York

Irena S. M. Makarushka
Bowdoin College

Wilma Mankiller
Park Hill, Oklahoma

Henrietta Mann
Haskell Indian Nations University

Isabel Marcus
State University of New York at Buffalo School of Law

Valerie Matsumoto
University of California, Los Angeles

Julie Matthaei
Wellesley College

Glenna Matthews
Berkeley, California

Sucheta Mazumdar
Duke University

Carole R. McCann
University of Maryland

Kathleen D. McCarthy
City University of New York

Carolyn D. McCreesh
Powder Springs, Georgia

Davianna Pomaika'i McGregor
University of Hawaii

Nellie Y. McKay
University of Wisconsin—Madison

Beatrice Medicine
Wakpala, South Dakota

Suzanne B. Mettler
Syracuse University

Ruth Meyerowitz
State University of New York at Buffalo

Sonya Michel
University of Illinois, Urbana—Champaign

Ruth Milkman
University of California, Los Angeles

Andrea Miller
Center for Reproductive Rights

Kay Mills
Santa Monica, California

Gwendolyn Mink
University of California, Santa Cruz

Patsy T. Mink
U. S. Congress

Elizabeth Kamarck Minnich
The Union School

Regina Morantz-Sanchez
University of Michigan

Priscilla Murolo
Sarah Lawrence College

Nancy A. Naples
University of California, Irvine

Vasudha Narayanan
University of Florida

Marysa Navarro
Dartmouth College

Cynthia Neverdon-Morton
Coppin State College

Carolyn Moore Newberger
Harvard Medical School

Vivien W. Ng
State University of New York at Albany

Gail M. Nomura
University of Michigan

Mary Beth Norton
Cornell University

Karen Nussbaum
Washington, D.C.

Bernadette Nye
Union College

Karen O'Connor
The American University

Ann Shola Orloff
University of Wisconsin—Madison

Cynthia E. Orozco
University of Texas

Grey Osterud
San Jose State University

Sharon Parker
The Union Institute

Kathy Peiss
University of Massachusetts at Amherst

Kathy A. Perkins
University of Illinois at Urbana—Champaign

Susan L. Phillips
*United Food and Commercial Workers
International Union*

Letty Cottin Pogrebin
New York, New York

Valerie Polakow
Eastern Michigan University

Barbara M. Posadas
Northern Illinois University

Marie Luise Proeller
New York, New York

Laura M. Purdy
Wells College

Jill Quadagno
Florida State University

Margaret Randall
Albuquerque, New Mexico

Gerda W. Ray
University of Missouri — St. Louis

Maureen T. Reddy
Providence, Rhode Island

Linda Reed
University of Houston

Melissa Riley
San Francisco Public Library

Trina Robbins
San Francisco, California

Belinda Robnett
University of California, Davis

Ruthann Robson
*City University of New York
School of Law*

Helen Rodriguez-Trias
Brookdale, California

Jessie M. Rodrique
Boston, Massachusetts

Mary Romero
Arizona State University

Margaret Rose
*California State University,
Bakersfield*

Phyllis Rosser
Holmdel, New Jersey

Rachel Roth
Yale University

Barbara Katz Rothman
City University of New York

Kate Rounds
Ms. Magazine

Harilyn Rousso
*Disabilities Unlimited Counseling Service,
New York, New York*

Judith M. Roy
Century College

Charlotte Streifer Rubinstein
San Diego, California

Rosemary Radford Ruether
Garrett Theological Seminary

Vicki L. Ruiz
Arizona State University

Leila J. Rupp
Ohio State University

Diana E. H. Russell
Mills College

Dalee Sambo Dorough
Vancouver, British Columbia

Judith Schwarz
Wynnewood, Pennsylvania

Anne Firor Scott
Duke University

Carol Seajay
Feminist Bookstore News

Barbara Seaman
New York, New York

Mab Segrest
Durham, North Carolina

Stephanie J. Shaw
Ohio State University

Christine Marie Sierra
University of New Mexico

Helene Silverberg
University of California, Santa Barbara

Kathryn Kish Sklar
State University of New York at Binghamton

Margaret Sloan-Hunter
Oakland, California

Barbara Smith
Albany, New York

Martha Nell Smith
Takoma Park, Maryland

Nancy B. Smith
Ms. Magazine

Carroll Smith-Rosenberg
University of Pennsylvania

Geneva Smitherman
Michigan State University

Rickie Solinger
Boulder, Colorado

Adaljiza Sosa-Riddell
University of California, Davis

Judith Stacey
University of California, Davis

Amy Dru Stanley
University of Chicago

Gloria Steinem
Ms. Magazine

Catharine R. Stimpson
MacArthur Foundation

Wendy Stock
Pacific Graduate School of Psychology

Nancy E. Stoller
University of California, Santa Cruz

Sharon Hartman Strom
University of Rhode Island

Nadine Strossen
American Civil Liberties Union

Norma Swenson
Newton Centre, Massachusetts

Amy Swerdlow
Sarah Lawrence College

Dana Y. Takagi
University of California, Santa Cruz

Tani Takagi
Ms. Foundation for Women

Gayle T. Tate
Rutgers University

Verta Taylor
Ohio State University

Mary Thom
New York, New York

Sue Thomas
Georgetown University

Becky W. Thompson
Middletown, Connecticut

Barrie Thorne
University of Southern California

Rochella Thorpe
Binghamton University

Veronica E. Velarde Tiller
Albuquerque, New Mexico

Sheila Tobias
Tucson, Arizona

Andrea Tone
Georgia Institute of Technology

Emily Toth
Louisiana State University

E. Kay Trimberger
Sonoma State University

Denise Troutman-Robinson
Michigan State University

Kathleen Underwood
University of Texas at Arlington

Antonia Villaseñor
Los Angeles, California

Mary Jo Wagner
Denver, Colorado

Helen Walker-Hill
Laramie, Wyoming

Skye Ward
Berkeley, California

Naomi Weisstein
New York, New York

Dorothy Wertz
The Shriver Center

Candace West
University of California, Santa Cruz

Marilyn J. Westerkamp
University of California, Santa Cruz

Julie Wheelwright
University of London

Deborah Gray White
Rutgers University

Katie Kinnard White
Tennessee State University

Lillian Serece Williams
State University of New York at Albany

Susan M. Williams
Albuquerque, New Mexico

Marie Wilson
Ms. Foundation for Women

Deborah Woo
University of California, Santa Cruz

Jennifer Wriggins
University of Maine School of Law

Lynn Yaeger
The Village Voice

Alice Yang Murray
University of California, Santa Cruz

Shirley J. Yee
University of Washington—Seattle

Susan M. Yohn
Hofstra University

Tricia Henry Young
Florida State University

Judy Yung
University of California, Santa Cruz

Beth Zemsky
University of Minnesota

Min Zhou
University of California, Los Angeles

Helen Zia
Oakland, California

EDITORS' NOTE

■ WILMA MANKILLER

When Gloria Steinem called to ask if I would join her and Marysa Navarro as a coeditor of a women's history reference book, I did not hesitate to accept this honor. It had been part of Gloria's original discussions with Houghton Mifflin that at least four other contributing editors would participate, representing diverse strands of women's experience; later we welcomed Wendy Mink and Barbara Smith. Indeed, it has been an honor to work with this wonderfully strong team of women. From the outset we felt connected to one another by our friendship and by our individual and collective commitment to produce a volume that would provide the reader with new and comprehensive information about women's history.

I once participated in a tribal ceremony (not Cherokee) in which I was doctored by a traditional medicine man to "speak for those who cannot speak for themselves." In the course of reviewing dozens of pieces for the book, I tried to uphold this principle.

As *The Reader's Companion to U.S. Women's History* evolved, it became clear that even the most committed feminist scholars knew little about contemporary Native American women or our history. But then who can blame them when Native American people, women in particular, are not even a blip on the national screen? Because there is so little accurate information about Native American women in either educational institutions or the popular culture, stereotypes are pervasive. Most people are genuinely surprised to learn that in some tribes women have held and still hold powerful leadership positions. The editors were dedicated to working with the writers to do as much as possible to eliminate stereotypes about all women.

I hope the reader will be as inspired as I was by these pieces. Most of all I hope *The Reader's Companion* is useful and will encourage the reader to learn more about women's history.

Working on this book was kind of like sitting with four other women to weave a basket over a long period of time. During that time all of our lives changed, some profoundly. We shared our stories with one another, drew strength from encouraging other women to tell their stories, and stayed focused on the weaving. In the end, like a communal basket, the book is the product of many hours of labor by a great many people. It will now take on a life of its own. The spirits of all the women who contributed and all the women for whom they speak will be with it wherever it goes.

■ GWENDOLYN MINK

The Reader's Companion to U.S. Women's History is a part of women's history as much as it presents the history of U.S. women. It is the first reference work to provide information and interpretation to a wide audience about women's diverse experiences across the centuries. It is the first such work devoted to exploring moments, topics, and events in U.S. history as they affected, and were affected by, women. It is the only work I know of that lets women who have made history showcase their own ideas, accomplishments, and expertise:

scholars who have blazed trails constituting and reconstituting the field of women's history; activists who have generated agendas and strategies for social change; practitioners who have exposed problems of race, class, and gender inequality to better view.

The Reader's Companion also makes history in the way that it asks readers to think about the history of U.S. women. The articles invite readers to ask "which women?" whenever "women" are referred to in the text; to wonder how claims and gains made by middle-class white women—so often the feminist subject—affected women of other classes and races; to view the lives and struggles of less visible or less powerful women as foundational to U.S. history; and to consider the ways in which differences among women have interacted with differences between the genders to complicate and enrich women's varied contributions to the development of U.S. society.

My hope for The Reader's Companion was that it would follow the best work in women's history to make race, class, and sexuality analytically pivotal to how we understand our gendered past. Women's history—and feminism—have come a long way in thirty years: it is a rare scholar or activist who consciously insists that the experiences of middle-class white women stand for the experiences of all. However, in women's history and across feminism, the goal of inclusion often has been forwarded by purely additive means.

The addition of different groups' stories to the tableau of women's history has been tremendously important, for it has broadened the very category "U.S. women" to include women whose identities have been erased by the dominant culture or whose communities have been treated as irrelevant to the central plot of U.S. history. Still, the incorporation of more women's stories has not always altered the way we think. The incorporation of untold histories has not immunized us from exoticizing, "othering," these histories, for example. Nor has it necessarily moved us beyond a mere enumeration of diversity to recon-struct visions and agendas because of that diversity.

Taken together, the articles in this volume complicate what we mean by "women's history" and so advance approaches that make differences the starting point of historical analysis rather than the afterthought to white women's stories. The articles do much more than give less privileged women an equal but separate place on the stage of U.S. history. They suggest that women's diversity runs to the core of U.S. women's collective history. Each article bears the imprint of its author, of course, so none fits a singular mold or speaks from a singular perspective. However, I think most authors honored our mission and have helped to construct a pathbreaking narrative.

Inventing The Reader's Companion and shepherding it to its final form has been a labor-intensive, sometimes frustration-filled, endeavor: thousands of manuscript pages to review, hundreds of galleys to proof and edit, my own essays to write, and sticky issues to settle. But every aspect of our work and collaboration has been instructive and rewarding to me. Some of our knottiest disagreements have been about lived differences—underscoring the importance of foregrounding distinctions of privilege and experience even as we commonly celebrate the history of U.S. women. All of our work gave me opportunities to learn for which I will always be grateful—about painting, dance, Woodlands Indians, and other subjects about which I know far less than I should. I only wish that readers could read each article as many times as I have!

I am indebted to the many authors who changed their schedules and personal agendas to develop the several hundred articles contained in The Reader's Companion. They make this volume —and it is one of which they, and I, can be proud. I am particularly indebted to Dana Frank, whose own contributions to the volume improved its quality and upon whose encyclopedic knowledge of women's history and labor history I have come to depend. My mother, Patsy Takemoto Mink, let me rant and moan about the various obstacles I encountered along the way and always gave judicious advice. Although Theodore J. Lowi did not choose this role, he provided sage feminist counsel when I was unsure of how to proceed and showed me how political science (after all) could offer solutions to dilemmas of both history and feminism.

■ MARYSA NAVARRO

The idea of participating in *The Reader's Companion to U.S. Women's History* was irresistible from the first moment Gloria Steinem mentioned it to me. We were going to be working together in a project that would involve the widest possible array of feminists—Native Americans, Latinas, African Americans, Asian Americans, old, young, early visionaries, guerrilla actresses, labor organizers, lesbian and gay leaders, activists of all kinds, and scholars. Our purpose would be to write a book that would tell the different histories of U.S. women, histories shaped by their race and ethnic origin, sexual orientation, and class. It would also include the history of ideas about women at present and in the past. It would encompass the history of Cherokee and Pueblo women, Kongo- and Yoruba-speaking slaves, English-speaking indentured servants and mill workers, Spanish-speaking Hispanas, and young brides in Chinatown.

I have never regretted saying yes, despite the mountain of articles piled on my desk every so often, the endless conference calls, and at times tense discussions. My enthusiasm for this project was generously nurtured by the people at Houghton Mifflin, by my fellow editors, and by the extraordinary commitment of the writers who believed in the effort as much as we did.

We were inclusive, but this does not mean we were able to do everything. Very early on, for example, we agreed that we would exclude biographies and that certain subjects would receive greater emphasis than others. The women's health movement has been an important component of the women's movement, so this book contains many entries covering health issues. Readers are directed to such subjects as birth control, breast cancer, the Boston Women's Health Book Collective, and mental health.

The knowledge, activism, and information produced by U.S. women and represented in *The Reader's Companion* are truly dazzling. *The Reader's Companion* has nineteen different articles on feminism—twenty, when we include the piece on womanism. There are more than a dozen entries on specific labor unions, numerous articles on immigration, legislation, and religion, with entries on Buddhism, fundamentalism, and Wicca, among others.

Some articles provide information about subjects where the research is limited or where the cross-cultural perspective has been lacking or is dispersed among various scholarly articles. The essay "Images of Women," for example, required the culling of information from multiple sources. There are long interpretive essays written by scholars, practitioners, or activists. Some topics are traditional, but the interpretation is new. The general overview article on literature does not simply provide information about women's contribution to this field, although it does mention the names of women who have distinguished themselves in particular genres. It also discusses how literature has been defined and, from a cross-cultural perspective, it seeks to explain what literature has meant in the lives of women, how it has been affected by their writing, and its relationship to the women's movement. *The Reader's Companion* is a unique reference work because it represents much of what U.S. women have written about themselves at the close of the twentieth century.

■ BARBARA SMITH

When I was invited in 1992 to be one of the five general editors of *The Reader's Companion to U.S. Women's History*, I was of course intrigued, but I also had serious questions. Because I was aware of significant political differences among the potential editors, I wondered if it would be possible for us to work together and to shape a volume that would be true to each of our visions of feminist activism, theory, and scholarship. After much soul-searching and stimulating, productive discussions at our first meeting in January 1993, I decided to commit to the project.

All of my previous work as a writer and editor has been shaped by my various identities and by my political activism in liberation movements that I see as fundamentally connected to one another. I am an African American woman from a working-class family, born into segregation in 1946. I am a Black feminist, socialist, and lesbian, and it is these perspectives that I have tried to bring to this book.

When I was still in graduate school in the early 1970s and teaching courses in African American literature and Black women writers, I often thought how fascinating and useful it would be to teach so-called American literature (that is European American authors) from a Black and feminist perspective. Such a course would not merely add a few token people of color and women to the syllabus, but would actually interrogate the white male literary canon, which would inevitably reveal oppressive ironies that are as integral to the formation of "American" literature as themes such as the quest for identity, autonomy, and freedom in a "new" land. I never had the opportunity to teach this course, but I was excited that work on *The Reader's Companion* would be an opportunity to do something similar, to redefine an area of knowledge.

It was not enough to have specific entries about women of color, lesbians, and working-class women, but material about women of color, lesbians, and working-class women needed to be addressed in every article whose subject matter would logically encompass their experiences. I think that attempting this level of inclusiveness was the most difficult challenge of the project and

also what makes this history of U.S. women so unique.

In our guidelines for contributors we gave the following instructions: "The scope of each article should provide a multicultural and inclusive perspective, including information on race, ethnicity, class, social status, sexuality, religion, and politics as relevant to the understanding of the subject matter." I regret that this statement did not also mention disability and age. Those omissions indicate that working toward inclusiveness has been a challenge for us as editors as well. Some of the contributors were already used to thinking about the implications of their subject areas for all women, but for many more our expectations were quite new. In one case a historian was assigned to write specifically about a group of European American women but refused to discuss their race and class privilege, instead treating European American women's experience as generic. We reassigned the entry. In contrast, Ruth Harriet Jacobs points out in her article, "Aging," how race, class, and sexual orientation affect different women's experiences of growing older. Ellen Bravo's entry, "Clerical Work," describes how racism excluded women of color from this predominantly female occupation until the civil rights era.

Although I participated in countless hours of telephone conference calls to arrive at our entries and assignments and read and edited thousands of pages of manuscripts and galleys, the most arduous task by far was trying to make sure that no racism, elitism, or heterosexism either by exclusion or by factual or interpretive distortion appeared in this book. Fortunately, the majority of contributors were open to expanding the coverage in their articles.

As comprehensive as we have tried to be, which to me is one of the book's most appealing strengths, some gaps remain. Early on, we chose to exclude biographical entries because of space limitations. There are entries that we tried very hard to obtain but frustratingly could not. The political differences that had concerned me at the outset did not, for the most part, prevent our effectively working together. Not surprisingly, the article on capitalism and socialism and what developed into two different articles on feminism were focal points for significant disagreement.

Despite these many challenges, I am very glad that I signed on to the project. I hope that *The Reader's Companion* will make a unique and useful contribution for years to come to our understandings of the diverse communities of women who have shaped the history of this land.

▪ GLORIA STEINEM

This book has many mothers, but the first was Liz Kubik, who believed that readers deserved a guide to the newly emerging history of the female half of the country. As editorial director of reference at Houghton Mifflin, she had seen the old definition of an encyclopedia — a reference work with alphabetically arranged articles on a variety of topics — expand to encompass good writing, conceptual thinking, and new popularity. She decided to create *The Reader's Companion to U.S. Women's History*.

When Liz suggested that I become the outside editor that each such Companion has had, her enthusiasm was contagious. For one thing, I, too, love the format of short descriptive entries and longer evaluative essays. It rewards the researcher, invites the reader, and offers all of us the serendipitous pleasure of discovering unexpected treasures on the way to whatever we started out to find. For another, I had been hoping to find ways of getting women's history out of the classroom and into everyday life. As someone from the days before Women's History, African American History, and other courses best described as Remedial History, I was painfully aware of how difficult it was to find this knowledge off campus, and how crucial to a view of the country *as if women mattered.*

In other words, I wanted *The Reader's Compan-*

ion to exist. I just couldn't imagine trying it by myself.

Secure in my knowledge that my suggestion wasn't possible within the Companion format, I said I couldn't imagine attempting such a task as an individual. One of the few advantages of exclusion from history is the determination to end exclusion; thus women's history has tended to be more inclusive by race, ethnicity, class, sexuality, religion, ability, and region that other histories. Even to symbolize the diversity of women's experience on this subcontinent would take a group of editors.

"All right," Liz said gamely. "We can have a group of editors."

Still looking for an out, I added that such a Companion would have to begin with the first nations on this land, not with the arrival of the first Europeans. After all, many Native American cultures were based on the idea of balance between males and females, a prepatriarchal past that could help give us faith in the possibility of a post-patriarchal future. Though the political limits of scholarship would make this enlarging of the American canvas difficult, it also would make us conscious of blank spaces and perhaps turn up new parts of the big picture. Liz agreed.

I got to musing about the redefinition of categories — for example, expanding "work" to include the labor of homemakers, or "art" to include what has been called "crafts" if created by women. I knew I was hooked; there was no way I could resist this adventure.

After that first meeting in early 1993, Wilma Mankiller, Wendy Mink, Marysa Navarro, Barbara Smith, and I formed the editorial group. You are meeting each one in her own words here, but all said yes with courage and generosity. Together, I think we've disproved the theory that "there has to be one boss." We've done collectively what none of us could have done alone.

There were many moments when I wondered what I had got myself into. Computer printouts of entries and essays could have felled a small forest.

Telephone conferences went on for so long that separating the phone from my ear seemed to require surgery. Reading and commenting on manuscripts took unexpected amounts of time, and scheduling meetings of busy women required almost as much energy—especially on the part of the Houghton Mifflin staff—as did the meetings themselves. When different experiences and viewpoints created tension, I had to have faith that encompassing difference would create a broader viewpoint and benefit readers.

There have been epiphanies of learning from our group of editors, advisers, and more than three hundred contributors. Each has been part of the labor of birth. I doubt that such a diverse collection of scholars, activists, and writers has ever tried to cover so much new territory in such a concentrated form. As a wider view of history began to emerge, I remembered the breadth of Liz's early instruction to "redirect history." But like all mothers who watch their young one go off into the world, I know this is a beginning, not an end. Because the message of this project goes beyond the past: We are all forces of history.

Acknowledgments

Many people were involved in the creation of *The Reader's Companion to U.S. Women's History*. In the editorial department at Houghton Mifflin, editorial director Elizabeth Kubik's bold vision and generous support got the project off the ground. With Elizabeth Kubik, assistant editor Amy Smith Bell coordinated the early and formative work among the coeditors, facilitating editorial decisions and communications with the contributors. Senior editor Borgna Brunner saw the project through some critical transitions. Assistant editor Holly Hartman, who also researched and selected the illustrations, guided the volume through its demanding final stages. Her erudition and attention to detail eased the coeditors' burdens and unquestionably improved the book. Special thanks are extended to designer Melodie Wertelet, proofreaders Kathleen Roos and Susan Innes, and manuscript editor Deborah Sosin, who, for the project's duration, edited hundreds of articles with great care and intelligence.

The READER'S COMPANION to U.S. WOMEN'S HISTORY

≋ Abolitionist Movement

In 1852 Frances Ellen Watkins Harper (1825–1911), a Black abolitionist, teacher, and poet, wrote: "The conditions of our people, the wants of our children, and the welfare of our race demand the aid of every helping hand." Several years later, Lucretia Coffin Mott (1793–1880), a white abolitionist, emphasized that the ultimate focus of the abolitionist movement was to destroy slavery "root and branch." The U.S. abolitionist movement, led by both Black and white men and women, fought for the immediate end of slavery and racism. Efforts to end racial oppression, begun through the resistance of slaves themselves since the beginning of bondage in the seventeenth century, found organized voices among free-born and freed Blacks in the North as well as among sympathetic whites by the late eighteenth century.

The visions of "abolition" by Harper and Mott, two dedicated activists, illuminate the existence of diverging definitions of the movement to abolish slavery between 1817 and 1860. Women, across racial and class lines, had participated in organized abolition since 1817, when Black women and men met in Philadelphia to lodge a formal, public protest against the white-led colonization movement, which proposed to send Blacks "back" to Africa. Black women abolitionists and Black men shared the view that abolition meant more than simply eliminating the institution of slavery but required obtaining political, social, and economic equality as well. Many Black women abolitionists were also teachers and community activists. Black women's participation in this expanded notion of abolition illustrates that the immediate end of slavery was only one goal of the movement. The continuous participation of Black women and men since the eighteenth century also belies the assumption that "radical" abolition began with the appearance in 1831 of white abolitionist William Lloyd Garrison and his newspaper, *The Liberator*.

Abolitionist women formed both formal and informal networks that sometimes crossed gender, race, and class boundaries. Perhaps the best-known woman abolitionist was Harriet Tubman (1820?–1911), an escaped slave from a Maryland plantation who returned to the South at least nineteen times to rescue approximately three hundred slaves. Black abolitionist Sarah Douglass (1806–82), whose mother, Grace Bustill Douglass (1782–1842), helped organize the Philadelphia Female Anti-Slavery Society (PFASS), devoted forty years to Black education. Early in her teaching career, Douglass operated a school for Black children and adults through PFASS, from which she derived both spiritual and financial support. Although she eventually ran her school independently of the organization, she built and maintained important personal and professional ties with the women of the Philadelphia abolitionist community. Female abolitionists also routinely worked with male colleagues. Lucretia and James Mott, for instance, were active in antislavery organizations and helped lead the Free Produce Movement, which boycotted slave-produced goods from the South, particularly cotton.

The organization of female antislavery societies reflected the conventional organizational structure present in social reform organizations, in which men formed the leadership and headed the state and national societies, while women were expected to form separate, auxiliary societies. The function of female antislavery societies was similar to that of other female reform organizations of the period, namely, to raise money to support the movement's lecturers and its official newspapers.

The composition of the female societies varied. In some cases women followed prevailing social conventions of racial separation by forming segregated antislavery societies. Others, such as the women in Boston and Philadelphia, struggled to break down racial barriers by organizing racially integrated societies. Historians believe that these societies were biracial as opposed to multiracial.

Harriet Tubman (far left), with former slaves she helped to freedom via the Underground Railroad. The best known of the Railroad's "conductors," Tubman made an estimated nineteen trips to the South to free family members and hundreds of other slaves.

The issue of challenging the custom of race segregation sometimes erupted into heated public debates among men and women in the movement. In Fall River, Massachusetts, for instance, the predominantly white female antislavery society nearly disbanded when white abolitionist sisters Elizabeth Buffum Chace (1809–99) and Lucy Buffum Lovell (n.d.) invited "a few very respectable young colored women" to join as members. A number of white members threatened to quit, arguing that while the Black women could sit in on meetings, to offer them membership implied that they were the social equals of white women in the society.

The debates among white women about admitting Black women into the female antislavery societies illustrated that discourses on racial equality within the movement also implicated gender. Northern abolitionist women constructed a rhetoric of sisterhood that placed Black women, especially slaves, into abolitionist discourse by emphasizing the common bonds of womanhood, particularly motherhood, in order to gain the sympathies of Southern white women. The slogan "Am I Not a Woman and a Sister?" which paralleled the earlier antislavery rallying cry "Am I Not a Man and a Brother?" became the rhetorical link between slave women of the South and free women of the North.

Unlike other reform movements of the time, including temperance and antiprostitution groups, in which such questions rarely arose, by the mid-1830s abolitionist men and women furiously debated the "proper" role of women in public reform movements. The fact that abolitionists were already wrestling with the issue of racial equality as a goal of the movement created a climate ripe for discussions about equality between the sexes. During the 1830s a few women abolitionists began to step outside the boundaries of "proper" female activities by engaging in traditionally male domains, such as political writing and public speaking. Maria Miller Stewart, a free-born Black from New England, delivered public speeches in Boston between 1831 and 1833 on antislavery and the improvement of economic and educational opportunities for Black women and men. Angelina and Sarah Grimké, white sisters from South Carolina, traveled throughout the Northeast, delivering public addresses condemning slavery. Both Stewart and the Grimké sisters received mixed responses from those who questioned the propriety of women taking the podium and assuming a position of authority. A "Pastoral Letter," circulated by a group of New England ministers, condemned the Grimkés' actions.

The "Woman Question" contributed to a formal split in the American Anti-Slavery Society (AAS) in 1841 after Abigail Kelley Foster, a white abolitionist from Massachusetts, was elected as the first woman to sit on the executive board. Garrison, the acknowledged leader of the AAS, was a vocal supporter of women's rights and had backed the election of Kelley Foster. Those who had opposed her election to the executive board defected from the AAS to form the American and Foreign Anti-Slavery Society (AFAS).

Some women abolitionists pushed the boundaries of acceptable behavior in public reform by stepping into male domains and expanding discussions about "equality" in the movement. In so doing, this generation of women activists forged a collective legacy for subsequent movements for sexual and racial equality in U.S. society. More important, however, their participation in aboli-

tion and women's rights also foretold the continuing struggle over racism, classism, and sexism both within the movements themselves and in society at large.

Blanch Glassman Hersh, *Slavery of Sex: Feminist-Abolitionists in America* (Urbana: University of Illinois, 1978); Shirley J. Yee, *Black Women Abolitionists: A Study in Activism, 1828–60* (Knoxville: University of Tennessee Press, 1992); Jean Fagan Yellin, *Women and Sisters: The Antislavery Feminists in American Culture* (New Haven: Yale University Press, 1989).

• SHIRLEY J. YEE

SEE ALSO Constitution and Amendments: Emancipation Proclamation and Thirteenth Amendment; Slavery.

≋ Abortion

Abortion refers to the purposeful termination of a pregnancy. Millions of girls and women have sought and received abortions during the two eras when the procedure was legal (eighteenth century to mid–nineteenth century, and 1973 to the present), and during the criminal era (mid–nineteenth century to 1973). Legislative, medical, judicial, religious, political, and popular responses to abortion have constrained or enabled access to abortion services in both legal and criminal eras. Across the history of the United States, females have obtained abortions in very large numbers, no matter what the prevailing legal status and public attitudes toward the procedure. For example, during the 1950s, when abortion was illegal, U.S. public-health experts estimated that as many as one million criminal abortions were performed each year.

In the first decades of nationhood, the legal status of the procedure was governed by British common law that viewed abortion before quickening as a legal act. ("Quickening" referred to the sensation of fetal movement felt and reported by the pregnant woman.) After quickening, destruction of the fetus without cause was considered a crime. Many women of that era were aware of and employed herbal and other remedies that caused abortion, sometimes with the assistance of midwives or physicians who consented to remove "menstrual blockages." Enslaved African American women used abortion to resist coerced reproduction and slavery itself, employing the knowledge of African-based midwifery culture and folk medicine.

Connecticut was the first state to criminalize abortion, in 1821. This legislation was apparently concerned in part with protecting women from dangerous substances and techniques associated with pregnancy termination. The early state laws were not enacted in response to popular objections to abortion. Rather, they were expressions of an innovative collaboration between legislators and physicians interested in consolidating the authority of university-trained medical doctors ("regulars") in the area of obstetrics.

Over the course of the nineteenth century, as women's lives were shaped by urbanization, industrialization, and the experiences of migration and immigration, abortion became more common and more visible. By midcentury, observers estimated that 20 to 25 percent of all pregnancies ended in abortion. The combined growth of urban newspapers and advertising enabled broad dissemination of information about abortion providers and abortifacients. Young white women beginning to enter the work force and married women concerned about adjusting family size to urban settings took advantage of this information. While leaders of the emergent women's rights movement publicly expressed negative views of abortion, it is likely that the new visibility of abortion, combined with the feminists' goal of controlled conception (through "voluntary motherhood," or sexual abstinence), encouraged many white, native-born women to use abortion to resist traditional reproductive experiences, including serial childbearing.

Having worked successfully with a number of state legislatures to enact antiabortion laws, medical doctors intensified their campaign after the founding of the American Medical Association in 1847. Dr. Horatio Robinson Storer led efforts that resulted in antiabortion statutes in every state by the end of the nineteenth century. The new laws were a triumph for physicians now fully invested with scientific authority; midwives and "irregular" doctors were excluded as legitimate abortion practitioners, and the women-centered "quickening" doctrine was abandoned. The new laws were sharply moralistic; for example, they deepened the stigma attached to abortion by associating it with "obscenity." In addition, the laws reflected a triumph for sexual conservatism and medical doctors' determination to block middle-class women from employing abortion as a tool for resisting traditional roles and facilitating new ones. Despite the criminalization of abortion, however, many women of every class and race, married and unmarried, continued to use abortion to limit their childbearing.

In the early twentieth century, women found midwives, physicians, and various lay practitioners to perform illegal abortions. Increasingly, cities and towns were home to abortion providers who had full-time abortion practices, worked semi-openly, and were highly proficient. These practitioners probably rarely caused complications or deaths, which usually occurred in the case of self-induced abortions or abortions performed by the relatively small number of untrained lay practitioners who exploited some pregnant women's desperation.

Periodically, journalists and police forces in this era, often in league with politicians and medical doctors, orchestrated local exposés of abortion practices. The exposés typically targeted and tainted midwives—who chiefly served immigrant women and women of color—but not physicians. Antiabortion campaigns combined a mix of agendas, all of which were incorporated into antiabortion rhetoric. They championed medical prerogatives, demanded female sexual purity and conformity, opposed women's rights, and enforced eugenic and demographic goals.

Many contemporary observers and historians have noted that these campaigns did not halt the practice of abortion, nor did they stir public indifference to the crime of abortion, although the salacious content of raids and trials did engage the newspaper-buying public. Nevertheless, the campaigns effectively promoted the agendas noted above and successfully warned all women of the dangers that could beset any woman who tried with abortion to control her own fertility.

Interestingly, during the Great Depression of the 1930s, a massive number of women who could not afford babies obtained abortions, but the number of exposés and prosecutions of abortion providers declined. In this era, doctors spent more time debating which conditions warranted therapeutic abortions than they spent collaborating with police and politicians to stamp out abortion. Poor women and women without information or other resources continued to resort to self-induced abortions. One study in the early 1930s showed that 76 percent of these involved complications.

The response to abortion changed in the World War II and postwar era. After some years of unofficial tolerance, in which most law enforcement entities employed the principle of "no death, no prosecution," politicians and police forces once again engaged in exposés, arrests, and trials more frequently than before, even in cases where there was no evidence of abortion-related damage or death. Historians have argued that this crackdown was similar to, or a feature of, the postwar anti-Communist fervor. It aimed to eradicate "the enemy within," to demonstrate that the United States was a vigilant, virtuous country, and to enforce a conforming, conservative code of female sexual behavior, just as the seeds of "the sexual revolution" and the women's liberation movement were beginning to sprout.

At the same time, medical doctors began to construct hospital abortion boards charged with implementing group decision making regarding which women applying to the boards to end their pregnancies would be granted permission and on the basis of which physical symptoms. These committees were antithetical to women's interests. They reinforced medical authority and forged a protective, fraternal relationship between doctors and a legal system that acknowledged only board-sanctioned abortions as legitimate. They also significantly reduced the number of in-hospital abortions. This situation, coupled with the effects of the antiabortion crackdown, increased many pregnant women's desperation. Many women without the resources to leave the country to obtain an abortion or to pay a private U.S. physician willing to perform an illegal procedure resorted to self-abortion. Not surprisingly, this era saw a rise in abortion complications and death, particularly among poor women and women of color.

Abortion boards did permit some women to obtain an abortion. For example, women seeking abortions, together with psychiatrists, constructed the "psychiatric indication" for abortion, which forced some women to define themselves as suicide-prone or unfit to be a mother in order to get board permission.

By the 1960s, many observers acknowledged that antiabortion statutes could not be enforced. Moreover, the conditions of women's lives were changing in ways that intensified their need for fertility control, including access to safe and legal abortion. For example, female labor-force participation and college attendance rates were increasing; age at first marriage was rising. Many liberal physicians, clergy, academics, and others, recognizing the inevitability of abortion, began to advocate abortion reform.

In addition, politicians concerned about welfare expenditures and "ghetto unrest," and population controllers worried about the "population bomb," spoke out in favor of abortion reform. The American Law Institute published guidelines for reform in 1960, and the American Medical Association endorsed reform in 1967, a year in which one study indicated that 87 percent of physicians favored liberalization. The National Association for the Repeal of Abortion Laws was formed in 1969.

Some leading African American activists in the late 1960s and early 1970s opposed abortion reform, associating abortion with other white-sponsored attempts to limit or otherwise control the fertility of African American women. Over time, as African American women used abortion in their own interests, and Black feminists supported reproductive rights, their outspoken opposition abated.

Small groups around the country formed, each with a specific focus: The Society for Humane Abortion, in California, claimed that abortion was a woman's right, fought for the repeal of antiabortion statutes, and educated women about their bodies and abortion. Carol Downer and Lorraine Rothman's project in Los Angeles taught women how to perform "menstrual extraction." The Jane Collective, in Chicago, helped women contract with doctors to provide illegal abortions and later to perform abortions on their own. Some "doctors of conscience" around the country performed abortions and referred patients to others because they were convinced that women should have access to this service.

By the mid- to late 1960s, national feminist leaders and grassroots feminist organizations were focusing on abortion as the key to women's liberation. The Redstockings, a feminist group in New York City, held the country's first "speak out" on abortion in 1969, during which women publicly described their experiences obtaining illegal abortions. In following years, several state legislatures, including those of New York, Colorado, and North Carolina, liberalized their abortion statutes.

These developments—demographic trends, the rise of the population-control movement, the emergence of feminism and grassroots support of abortion reform, the persistence of abortion, the

actions of a few state legislatures, and the climate of the era that supported "rights" claims—pushed the medical and legal communities to support formal legalization. *Roe v. Wade*, the 1973 Supreme Court decision legalizing abortion, was, in part, a pragmatic response to this complex range of developments.

The years since legalization have been marked by millions of women obtaining safe abortions. These years have also been marked by unemployment, a rise in female labor-force participation and wages, changes in family composition, and other economic and cultural shifts that sparked the rise of the New Right and the antiabortion movement. Using demonstrations, clinic blockades, legislative strategies, judicial appointments and legal challenges, and violent tactics such as clinic bombings and even murder of abortion practitioners and their colleagues, various segments of the antiabortion movement have significantly reshaped the abortion arena.

At the end of the century, abortion is still legal, but access to services is more limited than in the 1970s as a result of such legislated obstacles as the Hyde Amendment, which denies Medicaid funding for abortion, and parental notification provisions for teenagers, and because the number of practitioners has dwindled. The successes of the antiabortion movement have sharply constrained access of poor women and young women to safe abortion. Middle-class women are still able to exercise "choice" relatively unimpeded, although abortion rights proponents have had to assume a defensive stance. The Supreme Court seems committed at this time to sustaining legal abortion, but significant numbers in the U.S. Congress and state legislatures are determined to pass laws further reducing access and constraining rights, despite the fact that a majority of Americans support "a woman's right to choose."

Marlene G. Fried, ed. *From Abortion to Reproductive Freedom: Transforming a Movement* (Boston: South End Press, 1990); Laura Kaplan, *The Story of Jane: The Legendary Underground Feminist Abortion Service* (New York:

Pantheon, 1995); Rickie Solinger, *The Abortionist: A Woman Against the Law* (New York: The Free Press, 1994); Rickie Solinger, ed. *Abortion Wars: Fifty Years of Struggle, 1950–2000* (Berkeley: University of California Press, 1997).

■ RICKIE SOLINGER

SEE ALSO Abortion Self-Help Movement; Pro-Choice and Antiabortion Movements; Reproductive Rights; *Roe v. Wade.*

≋ Abortion Self-Help Movement

The abortion self-help movement has spanned more than twenty-five years. Its early perspective was influenced heavily by repressive abortion laws, in particular the 1967 California Therapeutic Abortion Act, which stated that abortion was available only in an accredited hospital, only up to twenty weeks, and was subject to approval by a panel of doctors. Women's access to abortion was also severely limited by class, race, and age. Although adult white women with money could obtain abortion (the painful dilation and curettage), young women, poor women, and women of color—those women with least access to institutional medical care—were often forced to turn to illegal abortionists or self-induced abortions.

California women suffered under the restrictions of the Therapeutic Abortion Act. After observing abortions being performed at a local illegal clinic that used a new, less traumatic method utilizing suction to extract the contents of the uterus through a plastic tube attached to a syringe, some decided to learn to do abortions themselves.

The first "self-help clinic" meeting took place in Los Angeles on April 7, 1971. The leaders, including this author, shared information about nontraumatic suction abortion and self-abortion methods and also demonstrated vaginal self-ex-

amination using a speculum, mirror, and light. One attendee, Lorraine Rothman, returned to the next meeting with the prototype of a device called the Del'em that made it possible for women with minimal training to perform either menstrual extraction or early abortion. After observation, training, and improvements in the Del'em, the small group successfully performed early abortions and menstrual extractions in private homes.

Starting in 1970, these women traveled around the country to hold "self-help clinic" meetings, sharing information about vaginal self-examination, menstrual extraction, and improved abortion methods. The response was overwhelming. Self-help clinic groups sprung up in their wake. When abortion became legal in January, 1973, some of these groups formed the nuclei of women-controlled abortion clinics.

The collective, which became formally organized as the Federation of Feminist Women's Health Centers, studied the history of abortion and birth control and learned about population control. The philosophy of the population control movement rested on three assumptions. First, rapid population growth in developing countries is the cause of hunger, disease, and underdevelopment. Second, women cannot be trusted to use birth control and abortion and so should be sterilized, whether or not they want to be. Third, without Western intervention, the Third World will not be able to stabilize its birthrate.

At first the population control movement took approving notice of the self-help movement. The Federation of Feminist Women's Health Centers was tentatively approached by foundations about grants for research into menstrual extraction. But women in the self-help movement refused to participate in any program that forced sterilization on women of color while simultaneously espousing support of women's reproductive rights.

■ CAROL DOWNER

SEE ALSO Abortion; Women's Health Movement.

≋ Advertising

In 1886 *Ladies' Home Journal* editor Louisa Knapp complained about men teasing women who read advertisements. Knapp's complaint reflected the special relationship between advertising and femininity that had developed in the United States by the late 1880s, was consolidated at the turn of the last century, and has persisted with some variations until the present day.

The nineteenth-century United States saw the Industrial Revolution paralleled by a consumer revolution, which coalesced in the 1880s when mass production expanded rapidly, transportation networks improved, and national markets grew. A number of the earliest mass-produced items, such as cereals, canned goods, and cleaning powders, were assumed to be of interest to women because of their domestic role, and therefore a significant proportion of early advertising was targeted specifically to women. As markets became national, gender-related assumptions provided a language through which advertisers could reach a specific yet sizable audience. Thus, advertisers sacrificed a potentially broader audience—both women and men—for the narrower gender-targeted audience.

In the 1880s magazines such as the *Ladies' Home Journal* replaced newspapers as the primary forum for commercial messages. These magazines sold for as little as a nickel, supplementing their rock-bottom subscription prices with advertisements that filled one-quarter to one-third of their pages. The magazines promoted advertisements by placing them in careful proximity to relevant editorial copy; by "ad-stripping," where editorial copy was continued to the back of the magazine and surrounded by advertisements; and by leaving editorial pages uncut (the reader had to detach each page from the next) but carefully cutting those pages featuring the most advertising.

Magazine editors believed that reading and attending to commercial messages would benefit women, since increased consuming would be a legitimate route to power and autonomy within marriage. This belief fueled the evolution in these years from advocating that women *could* be consumers to identifying women as properly, and even primarily, consumers.

The first products advertised to women were household items. Beauty products entered the market and proliferated in the early twentieth century. Women from this point on were often objectified in and targeted by advertising. The changing portrayal of women in beauty advertising paralleled the evolution in the image of women as consumers, moving from the position that women *can* be beautiful to the message that women *must* be beautiful. The solution again, according to the commercial media, was for women to buy more products.

However, women did not blindly or unthinkingly buy all the products pitched to them. They supported some commercial messages, for mainstream products like Pearline Washing Powder, and not others, like the more risqué Rose Blush (which was "guaranteed to draw the men"), and they enjoyed purchasing particular goods when they had the means. They actively confronted the commercialized media, deciding what to read, listen to, and watch, and whether to purchase a given product.

In addition, women did not make choices uniformly as a gender group. Historically, advertising has been targeted to segmented audiences, known variously as "class," "mass," or "ethnic" audiences. The class market represented higher-priced lines sold to wealthy white women in department stores and salons and advertised in fashion magazines such as *Vogue*. "Mass" cosmetics were sold in pharmacies and discount stores and marketed in women's magazines catering mainly to white middle-class and upwardly mobile working-class women. The ethnic market consisted primarily of the African American beauty industry, although it also included Hispanic Americans, Asian Americans, and other women of color. Advertisers created desires across the economic spectrum from the turn of the century until after World War I, although some women were better positioned to satisfy those desires.

Some advertisers focused their energies in a different direction in the 1940s, working with media producers and the government to create an elaborate propaganda campaign aimed at convincing women to support the war effort. Advertising messages again targeted different classes and ethnicities. White, middle-class women were pictured and addressed as people in control of their destiny who could triumph over obstacles to fulfill their wartime role of self-sacrificing martyr. Working-class white women, in contrast, were portrayed as highly dependent upon male authority, responding to the call to work because they lacked other options. Images of women of color were virtually nonexistent in advertisements, despite the fact that women of color were breaking barriers in some areas of the United States to perform critically needed war work.

Whatever the nature of their portrayal in wartime commercial propaganda, all women were treated similarly as the war drew to a close. Their contributions to the war effort were downplayed, and many women's interest in and need to continue working were summarily dismissed in the media. Some women did remain in the work force, but they disappeared from public view and were replaced almost completely in advertising and the commercial media by images of happy homemakers and sexy seductresses. Advertising previously limited to the print media profoundly affected the new media, first radio and then television. Critics, from Betty Friedan (*The Feminine Mystique*, 1963) to Erving Goffman, pioneer of analyzing advertisements for stereotyping and sexism (1970s), to Gloria Steinem ("Sex, Lies and Advertising," 1990), have protested advertising's power to shape as well as to embody gender construction ever since.

Attending to such critics and becoming critics ourselves is central to strengthening women's position vis-à-vis commercial media. It is critical that we teach media literacy; boycott offensive materi-

A 1920s *advertisement assures the female consumer that ScotTissue is "the choice of discriminating women everywhere."*

als; support women in advertising and positive, women-centered advertising campaigns; and support ad-free media such as *Ms.* Above all, it is crucial to separate the construction of gender roles from the realm of commerce, if we are ever to break the link forged between advertising and womanhood over a century ago.

William Leach, *Land of Desire: Merchants, Power, and the Rise of a New America* (New York: Pantheon, 1993); Kathy Peiss, "Making Faces: The Cosmetics Industry and the Cultural Construction of Gender, 1890–1930," *GENDERS* 7 (spring 1990): 143–169; Michael Schudson, *Advertising, the Uneasy Persuasion: Its Dubious Impact on American Society* (New York: Basic, 1984).

■ HELEN DAMON-MOORE

SEE ALSO Beauty Culture; Consumerism and Consumption; Images of Women.

≋ Affirmative Action

Affirmative action began in the mid-1960s as a supplement to the Civil Rights Act's promise to end race discrimination in employment. It applied a principle announced by President Lyndon Johnson at Howard University on June 4, 1965: "We seek . . . not just equality as a right and a theory but equality as a fact and equality as a result." Concerned that ending formal discrimination would not by itself eliminate racism in employment decisions, President Johnson issued Executive Order 11246 in September 1965, calling upon employers who received federal contracts to take extra steps to integrate their work forces.

Under the executive order, which is still in effect, federal contractors were required to search aggressively for qualified people of color to apply for job vacancies. Following appeals from U.S. Women's Bureau chief Esther Peterson and from women's groups, President Johnson added gender to the executive order in 1967. Also in 1967, the U.S. Department of Health, Education, and Welfare (HEW) included race-based affirmative action in higher education in its enforcement plan for Title VI of the Civil Rights Act. With passage of Title IX of the Education Act Amendments of 1972, HEW (now the Department of Education) began to monitor college and university hiring and admissions practices affecting women.

Affirmative action is a means, not an end. It is primarily a recruitment mechanism to incorporate people of color and white women into the social institutions that historically have excluded them. Affirmative action establishes the expectation that employers and educational institutions will open consideration for hiring and admissions to all qualified applicants and will encourage applications from members of underrepresented groups. Some schools and employers engage in affirmative action voluntarily because it promotes academic freedom, is good for business, or shows a good-faith interest in preventing discrimination.

Government also may enforce affirmative action by making it a condition of federal funding. For example, under Executive Order 11246, private businesses that contract with the federal government must demonstrate an effort to attract representative applicant pools for jobs created by their federal contracts. This form of required affirmative action emphasizes procedures rather than results: training for potential applicants, wide advertising, open searches. Affirmative action procedures also include treating the race and/or gender of qualified applicants from underrepresented groups as factors in employment or university admissions decisions.

Affirmative action does not require an employer to hire a woman for a specific job; and it does not require a college to admit a person of color because of her race. Affirmative action does not usually require particular outcomes. Exceptions have been "set-aside" programs for small businesses contracting in the public sector, incentive subsidies to encourage primary contractors to subcontract with minority businesses, and affirmative action plans imposed by courts to remedy individual employer violations of the Civil Rights Act. In most cases, however, affirmative action plans spell out voluntary goals and timetables for integrating workers and students from underrepresented groups into workplaces and schools. Goals and timetables give employers and universities a framework to develop recruitment strategies, adding race and gender to the mix of considerations that determine hiring and admissions decisions.

Set-asides, incentive subsidies, and court-ordered affirmative action plans have been constitutionally challenged since the mid-1970s. In 1978, a divided Supreme Court ruled in *Regents of the University of California* v. *Bakke* that racial quotas are impermissible in public higher education. However, the Court went on to say that affirmative action programs to promote diversity are valid. Through the 1980s, the Court upheld all forms of federal affirmative action programs. But in 1989, it found a local program in violation of the equal protection clause of the Constitution *(City of Richmond v. Croson)*.

During the 1980s and 1990s, affirmative action became a volatile political issue, as many whites came to view *any* effort to expand opportunities available to people of color as a cap on their own opportunities. Debates raged about whether it is ever acceptable to take into account race and/or gender in deciding among qualified applicants. In 1995, the Supreme Court brought all race-conscious affirmative action under heightened judicial suspicion in a case challenging a federal incentive program for disadvantaged minority-owned businesses. *Adarand v. Pena* announced a new constitutional presumption that remedial race-consciousness is as offensive as oppressive race-consciousness—that both represent invidious discrimination. The Court did not discuss whether or how its new approach will apply to gender-conscious affirmative action.

The decision has fueled a roiling political controversy over race- and gender-conscious affirmative action. Now under special scrutiny are programs based on goals and timetables rather than set-asides and incentives, particularly in education. To critics, affirmative action destroys the rule of merit. In their view, merit is properly measured by the numerical rating of applicants through standardized test scores and grades, or, in the case of businesses, through competitive bidding. Affirmative action foes believe that when numerical rankings are balanced against social factors, unqualified or less qualified individuals steal college admission from "the best" students, good jobs from deserving workers, and business contracts from the lowest bidder. They argue that opportunity must be color- and gender-blind to be truly equal whether or not white and male prejudices, habits, and institutional practices continue to circumscribe the life chances of people of color and women.

Advocates for affirmative action do not slight the value of merit but do disagree that merit alone should determine the distribution of entry-level opportunity. According to its advocates, affirmative action is necessary to ensure that people with power over hiring and admissions do not disregard the merits of white women and people of color. Advocates also want to expand the meaning of merit to include the ways life's struggles—against sexism and racism—modulate ability and enrich each individual's contribution to her job, school, or community.

Affirmative action has been an effective instrument of opportunity. It has offered both white women and women and men of color a foot in the door to social and economic institutions from which they were barred either by habit or design only a generation ago. It has recognized and cultivated role models for hope and aspiration in younger generations. It has provided the tools for white women and people of color to seek entry into workplaces previously monopolized by white men.

Although originally conceived as a remedy for the effects of past discrimination, affirmative action counters the effects of and works to prevent continuing racism and sexism. For example, in the employment arena, Executive Order 11246 requires firms with federal contracts to develop plans for creating a more representative work force, to develop plans for achieving their goals, and to report annually on their progress. This keeps employers aware of the prejudices and practices that continue to exclude underrepresented groups from due consideration and encourages employers to struggle self-consciously against them.

Affirmative action is changing police forces, fire departments, and industrial employment. It is changing the face of the professions. In 1980, 13 percent of all doctors and 14 percent of all lawyers were women; in 1996, the numbers were 23 percent and 31 percent. It is changing the face of managerial jobs. In 1980, white men occupied 65 percent of all management jobs; in 1996, they occupied 50 percent. Affirmative action is not by itself a prescription for equality, nor is it self-enforcing. Affirmative action's success has depended upon the goodwill of the people who make employment and admissions decisions. But affirmative action has opened doors to white men's world, thereby beginning the slow process of democratizing opportunity in the United States.

· GWENDOLYN MINK

SEE ALSO Civil Rights Act of 1964; Civil Rights Movement.

≋ African American Women

The history of Black women in the United States began with the forced migration of millions of African women from the interior to the west coast of Africa, where waiting ships transported human cargo across the Atlantic Ocean to plantations in the West Indies. The horrors of the tortuous and often deadly "middle passage," as scholars refer to that leg of the journey, were mediated only by the strong bonds formed among shipmates. This bonding became one of the most durable and significant dimensions of African women's lives and enabled captive women to endure brutalization on slave ships and the Caribbean "seasoning"—the process designed to subdue and transform captive Africans into obedient slaves. Because women historically are culture bearers, their captors employed special efforts aimed at undermining, if not destroying completely, all vestiges of traditional African culture. The enslaved Africans then were sold to European immigrant colonies on the North American mainland. Regional location determined where Africans worked, either as agricultural laborers on plantations and farms in the South or in the homes and shops of northern colonialists.

In 1619 the first three African women to be taken to an English-speaking colony arrived in Jamestown, Virginia. Their initial status was like that of indentured servants, who received freedom after laboring for a number of years. Within a generation, however, the status of enslaved Africans worsened as Maryland and Virginia's colonial authorities enacted measures to ensure lifelong enslavement. As "African" and "slave" became conflated, new legislation dictated that, contrary to British law and custom, an African child would inherit the status of the mother. This measure underscored a distinct difference in the treatment of African women as compared with that accorded European immigrant women.

African women never acquiesced passively to their enslavement. Even on the ships, they participated in mutinies and rebellions. Second and third generations of women slaves developed more complex forms of resistance. Historian Deborah Gray White argues that survival was a form of resistance and that enslaved women resisted by bearing and nurturing future generations of African Americans. At the other end of the adaptation/resistance continuum, some slave women challenged slave masters' efforts to control their reproductive capacities by abortion, sexual abstinence, or infanticide. The majority, however, occupied a middle ground of passive resistance, including feigning illness, ignorance, or ineptness. Others occasionally engaged in more active tactics such as arson, poisoning, mutilation of farm animals, destruction of property, and even running away. Less obvious, but perhaps even more effective resistance focused on creating a sense of community, preserving and transmitting to their children African-based cultural practices and beliefs as revealed in music making, quilting, storytelling, naming of children, and sustaining traditional marriage practices.

Even as slaves, African women attempted to shape the "peculiar institution" in ways that allowed them to preserve their dignity and affirm their humanity. During the era of the American Revolution, many northern states abolished slavery or made arrangements for gradual emancipation. As a result of increased rates of manumission, rising rates of reproduction, and larger numbers of runaways, the free African women's population grew and many free Black women engaged actively in the abolition movement. From the 1830s to the onset of the Civil War they formed societies, supported abolitionist newspapers, lectured, wrote books, served on vigilante committees, and worked within the Underground Railroad system. For over three decades women such as Maria Stewart, Sojourner Truth, and Francis Ellen Watkins Harper raised their voices and wrote against the tyranny of slavery.

Harriet Tubman delivered a frontal assault against the institution of slavery. General Tubman, as she was sometimes called, made over a dozen forays into the South after her own escape from slavery in 1849. Fearless and bold in her determination to destroy slavery, she freed over three hundred slaves, secretly leading them along various routes and using different disguises. She carried doses of paregoric to silence crying babies and a pistol to discourage any fugitive from thoughts of disembarking the freedom train. Only illness prevented her from joining John Brown's aborted raid on Harper's Ferry. After the Civil War began, Tubman served as a spy for the Union army in South Carolina as well as a nurse, along with Susie King Taylor, for wounded Black soldiers.

Oppressed people historically find ways to express and preserve their humanity. To ensure survival, slave women, like their free sisters in the North, also developed supportive and empowering female networks, nurtured extended families, and embraced Christian teachings. Simultaneously, slave women worked hard in the fields alongside the men or in the plantation household under the mistress's watchful scrutiny. Indeed, they often worked double shifts, for they would return to the cabin at dusk to do the housework.

After the Civil War, Black women began the daunting challenge of infusing meaning into their recently acquired freedom. Although the 1868

AFRICAN AMERICAN WOMEN

For more on the history of African American women, see the following entries:

Abolitionist Movement
Atlanta Washerwomen's Strike
Black Clubwomen's Movement
Black Nationalism
Black Sororities
Black Women's Language
Civil Rights Movement
Constitution and Amendments: Emancipation
    Proclamation and Thirteenth Amendment
Feminism, Black
Free Black Women
Garveyism
Harlem Renaissance
Interracial Cooperation Movement
Lesbians, Black
Lynching
Miscegenation
Missionaries, Black
Mississippi Freedom Democratic Party
Mississippi Freedom Summer
Montgomery Bus Boycott
National Association for the Advancement
    of Colored People
National Association of Colored Women
National Black Feminist Organization
National Council of Negro Women
National Urban League
Pedestal
Phyllis Wheatley Clubs and Homes
Plantation System
Slavery
Student Non-Violent Coordinating Committee
Women's Colleges, Black

Fourteenth and the 1870 Fifteenth Amendments to the Constitution conferred citizenship and suffrage to men only, Black women nevertheless played a significant behind-the-scenes political role. They encouraged Black men to support the politicians and the legislation that would protect them and ensure a measure of economic autonomy. When possible they reconstituted families, legalized marriages, and fought against long-term apprenticeships of their children.

The collapse of Reconstruction in 1877 signaled the return to power of ex-Confederate elites, now determined to nullify the Reconstruction amendments. Accompanying the loss of political rights was the rebirth of the Ku Klux Klan, widespread white terrorism, lynching, rapes, and murders. The indifference of Northern whites and the entrenchment of Jim Crow racial segregation forced Black men and women to develop strategies that ranged from accommodation to protest, as represented by Booker T. Washington of Tuskegee, Alabama, and the Harvard University–educated W.E.B. Du Bois.

Black women perfected their own culture of dissemblance that enabled them to appear open but actually to preserve their interior lives from whites, and even from Black men and children. Behind a cult of secrecy and within a politics of respectability, this culture of dissemblance was revealed most powerfully in the national women's club movement that flourished at the turn of the century. Black clubwomen organized clinics and nurses' training schools, collected and distributed food and clothing to the needy, founded orphanages and homes for the elderly, launched mutual aid societies to provide funeral benefits, and sustained churches through fund-raising activities. Dissemblance, secrecy, and silence appealed to some Black women and proved powerful instruments of resisting dehumanization and multilayered exploitation and oppression.

Newspaper editor Ida B. Wells spoke out against the lynching of Black men; she shattered white male rationalizations of such brutality under the guise of protecting the sanctity of white womanhood. In 1892 Wells launched the first phase of the antilynching movement with articles and editorials in the Memphis *Free Speech* and the *New York Age,* and in the publication of her pamphlet, *Southern Horrors.* Following her exile from Memphis, Wells settled in Chicago, married Ferdinand Barnett, launched a Black women's political club, established a settlement house, and fought for woman suffrage. Wells-Barnett joined

forces in 1909 with W.E.B. Du Bois and other white and Black radicals to form the National Association for the Advancement of Colored People (NAACP).

The closing decade of the nineteenth century had witnessed a flowering of Black women's activism and organizational development. One of the most portentous events in Black women's history occurred in 1896 with the merger of the League of Colored Women, a coalition of 113 organizations, and the National Federation of Afro-American Women, a combination of 85 organizations, to form the National Association of Colored Women (NACW), with Oberlin College graduate Mary Church Terrell as its first president. Under the leadership of Terrell, Josephine St. Pierre Ruffin, and Margaret Murray Washington, the NACW grew at a phenomenal rate. By 1914 it had a membership of fifty thousand and had become the strong voice championing Black women. Terrell declared, "We proclaim to the world that the women of our race have become partners in the great firm of progress and reform. . . . We refer to the fact that this is an association of colored women, because our peculiar status in this country . . . seems to demand that we stand by ourselves."

Although political engagement and club activism consumed the lives of Wells-Barnett, Terrell, Fannie Barrier Williams, Mary Talbert, and other middle-class Black women, the vast majority were more concerned with the day-to-day struggle of earning a living and securing a measure of economic independence while simultaneously existing in the grips of an exploitive capitalist patriarchy. For most Black women agricultural work and domestic servitude were their only economic options.

Out of this bleak economic landscape appeared the astounding accomplishments of Madam C. J. Walker, a washerwoman from Delta, Louisiana, who, by the time of her death in 1919, had parlayed a hair-and-scalp-treatment formula into a million-dollar enterprise. Born Sarah Breedlove in 1867, Walker created a network of beauty schools and a manufacturing and marketing system that allowed thousands of Black women to become independent operators of beauty shops and thus escape the drudgery of exhausting, low-status, underpaid household labor.

Migration was another way to define or give meaning to freedom. To escape racial discrimination, sexual exploitation, and poverty, hundreds of thousands of African American women migrated to northern urban areas. What began as a trickle escalated with the advent of World War I and the cessation of European immigration into a full-scale flood of human movement. Between 1914 and 1925 the Great Migration witnessed the resettlement of 1.5 million African American men, women, and children. Harlem, New York, became the Black mecca and Chicago, Illinois, the Black metropolis. Black women followed a different migratory pattern than did Black men. Most Black women moved directly from the South to the North, foregoing the strategy of working one's way up to the "promised land" in a series of stops. Black women also usually had a family member at the final destination who would provide food, shelter, and protection as well as leads to jobs that would facilitate her adaptation to the new environment.

Although Black women eagerly sought employment in industries, shops, department stores, and the array of newly sex-stereotyped jobs, such as secretaries or sales clerks, they quickly crashed into the wall of Jim Crow. Most of these jobs were reserved for white women. There were never as many industrial job opportunities for Black women in the urban centers as there were for Black men. Few employers would hire Black women in the food-processing or automobile industries except for the most undesirable positions. Even those Black women who were lucky enough to secure positions outside of domestic service during World War I lost out when employers fired them to make way for the returning male veterans.

During the 1920s and 1930s, Black women writers and poets such as Nella Larsen, Jessie Redmon Fauset, Alice Dunbar Nelson, and Zora Neale Hurston participated in the artistic flowering known as the Harlem Renaissance. Amy Jacques Garvey assisted her husband Marcus Garvey in the creation and growth of the nationalist organization, the Universal Negro Improvement Association, and urged Black women to envision new definitions of Black beauty and purposefulness. Black women singers, especially blues women Bessie Smith and Billie Holiday, sang of the frustrations many of their sisters felt during the disillusioning decades between world wars. The advent of the Great Depression during the 1930s gave them even more reason to sing the blues.

The Great Depression was one of the most catastrophic periods in U.S. history. But the majority of Black women had little time to stay in sorrow's kitchen. They had children to feed, families to nurture, and communities to mobilize for self-help. In southern cities some Black women participated in sharecropping unions and Communist Party–led struggles within the steel industries. In northern areas Black women developed programs of economic nationalism and formed consumer action groups such as the Housewives' League of Detroit. Established in 1930, the Housewives' League had as one of its mottos "Stabilize the economic status of the Negro through directed spending." For the next thirty years, members of the league pledged to patronize all organized Negro businesses; to patronize "stores that employ Negroes in varied capacities and that do not discriminate in types of work offered"; to support and encourage institutions training Negro youth for trades and commercial activities; to teach "Negro youth that no work done well is menial"; and to conduct "education campaigns to teach the Negro the value of his spending." The directed-spending campaigns, or boycotts of neighborhood all-white stores, spread to other cities and secured an estimated seventy-five thousand new jobs for Blacks.

Black urban women employed a variety of strategies to ward off economic devastation and political powerlessness. In 1935 Mary McLeod Bethune, a prominent member of Roosevelt's New Deal, founded the National Council of Negro Women (NCNW). The NCNW declared as its purpose the collecting, interpreting, and disseminating of information concerning the activities of Black women. Its leaders, including Mary Church Terrell and Estelle Massey Riddle, wished "to develop competent and courageous leadership among Negro women and effect their integration and that of all Negro people into the political, economic, educational, cultural, and social life of their communities and the nation."

The advent of any war usually results in an improvement in women's status. As men are drafted to foreign locations, women usually are expected to take up the slack and fulfill those jobs that during peacetime are considered "men's work." While some Black women got jobs in nontraditional occupations as welders, workers in defense plants, or instructors of aviation, the majority remained in domestic service and agricultural labor. Even Black women nurses were engaged in struggles against exclusionary practices and quotas that restricted their right to serve in the Armed Forces Nurse Corps. Mabel K. Staupers, executive secretary of the National Association of Colored Graduate Nurses, won recognition for Black nurses to serve in the Nurse Corps near the end of World War II, to fight against fascism and Nazism. On January 25, 1945, the Navy Nurses' Corps was opened to Black women. A few weeks later Phyllis Dailey became the first Black nurse to be inducted.

Recent investigation into the roles of Black women in the civil rights movement has demonstrated connections between the communal institution-building work of earlier generations of clubwomen and the successful activism of the 1950s and 1960s. Ella Baker was a key player both in the Southern Christian Leadership Conference and the Student Non-Violent Coordinating Committee. According to Jo Ann Gibson Robinson's memoirs, women were the ones who initiated the Montgomery bus boycott that led to the overthrow of Jim Crow transportation laws across the South and signaled the beginning of the modern civil rights movement. Following Rosa Parks's arrest in December 1955, Robinson, a professor of English at Alabama State College and president of the Women's Political Council of Montgomery, mimeographed and distributed thirty thousand leaflets advising the Black citizens of Montgomery to stay off the buses. The bus-riding population, consisting as it did mainly of Black women, heeded her call—and Jim Crow's days were numbered.

In more recent decades Black women have amassed outstanding achievements. In politics, Carol Moseley-Braun won election to the U.S. Senate in 1992. Mae Jemison became the first Black woman astronaut, and Toni Morrison won the 1993 Nobel Prize for literature, the first African American, male or female, to do so. Julie Dash in 1992 directed and produced a unique Black women's film, *Daughters of the Dusk*. Today, over half of all Black undergraduate students are women, and employed Black women have steadily reduced the gap between their income and that of white women. These achievements are the outgrowth of the new Black women's consciousness that was forged in the immediate aftermath of the civil rights movement's passage of the Voting Rights Act of 1965.

This new consciousness dates back to the 1970 publication of Toni Cade's *The Black Woman: An Anthology*. This anthology was the first of its kind and its influence continues to resonate. In 1974 the Combahee River Collective was launched as the Boston chapter of the National Black Feminist Organization. The collective's first priority was to raise Black women's consciousness and to define issues of concern, such as sexual harassment, class oppression, and homophobia. According to Barbara Smith, the collective, during its six-year existence, also defined itself as anticapitalist, socialist, and revolutionary. The Combahee River Collective Statement inspired Black women's mobilization during the 1980s and 1990s.

Three additional markers heralded the rise of a new Black woman's creative activism. Michele Wallace's controversial *Black Macho and the Myth of the Superwoman* (1978), Ntozake Shange's explosive Broadway play, *For Colored Girls Who Have Considered Suicide When the Rainbow Is Enuf* (1975), and Alice Walker's powerful and provocative novel, *The Color Purple* (1982), which included a positive portrayal of a lesbian relationship between two Black women, all unveiled the reality of sexism within the Black community. These works allowed Black women across age, class, color, and occupational backgrounds to address those issues relevant to them, which the civil rights and women's liberation movements had overlooked.

By the early 1990s the achievements against the odds by a significant number of Black women, as well as the attention accorded their accomplishments, threatened to obscure the degradation and intransigence of poverty, sexual harassment, domestic violence, the ravages of life-threatening illnesses, the demonization of welfare recipients, the rise of female-headed households, and the lack of support for education and skills training. Negative stereotypes of Black women as welfare queens or oversexed moral wantons resurfaced in new guises. Yet the centuries-long spirit of resistance and culture of struggle remains a vital force, ensuring the ultimate coherence and survival of Black women in the United States.

Paula Giddings, *When and Where I Enter: The Impact of Black Women on Race and Sex in America* (New York: Morrow, 1984); Darlene Clark Hine, Elsa Barkley Brown, and Rosalyn Terborg Penn, eds., *Black Women in America: An Historical Encyclopedia* (New York: Carlson Publishers, 1993); Darlene Clark Hine, Wilma King, and Linda Reed, eds., *We Specialize in the Wholly Impossible: A Reader in Black Women's History* (New York: Carlson Publishing, 1995).

▪ DARLENE CLARK HINE

≋ Aging

The world of the old, and especially of the very old, is predominately female. One of the most important differences between men and women in the United States is that of longevity. As yet unproven explanations for this phenomenon include genetic factors, male life stresses, male war casualties, women's greater utilization of health care, and the purported biological weakness of males when compared with females.

On average, women live seven years longer than men in the United States and have a substantially lower rate of death at any age. Life expectancy at birth is 71.5 years for men and 78.3 years for women. For those who survive until 65, men can expect to live on the average 14.9 more years and women 18.6.

The gender imbalance in aging is accelerating. In 1960 there were 82 U.S. men per 100 women over 65. By the year 2000 there will be 65 men per 100 women over the age of 65. In the 85-plus age group, there were 67 men per 100 women in 1960. By the year 2000 there will be 38 men per 100 women who are over 85. The gender imbalance is even greater for Black women, Latinas, Asian Pacific women, and Native American women.

Black women have a lower life expectancy than white women because they suffer more poverty and poorer health care. Black women live on the average 73.6 years as compared with white women, who live 79.4 years. The Indian Health Service in Rockville, Maryland, has two figures on life expectancy for Native American women, both from 1990. One is 78.8 years for twelve areas and another of 74.7 for some remaining areas. However, this longevity may be inflated by the fact that funeral directors may be recording Native American women who die younger under the categories of other ethnicities because of their non-Indian names and dress, while older Native American women who are more traditional are more often recorded at death as Native Americans.

By 2025 15 percent of U.S. old are expected to be nonwhite. In the culture of many nonwhite and recent immigrant groups, older women are more respected and utilized than in mainstream United States. Generations more often live together, as in Native American cultures, and grandmothers play a needed and valued childcare role. This can be a burden rather than a blessing.

Ironically, though women fear aging because of internal and external ageism, older women are one of the most rapidly growing categories in the United States in terms of percentage. In 1990 people over 65 composed 12.5 percent of the population, but by 2050 that figure is expected to be 22.9 percent. Women now represent 60 percent of the 32 million Americans aged 65 and over. The so-called baby boomer women, born between 1946 and 1964, are now at midlife and considered older women by a society that labels women old before they do men.

Because men generally marry women younger than themselves, women experience even more years of widowhood than differential gender longevity alone would indicate. At age 65, 36 percent of U.S. women are already widows. Women widowed between ages 45 and 54 have only a 22 percent remarriage rate after 15 years. Among women who divorce between ages 45 and 54, only 59 percent remarry after 15 years. The remarriage rates are much higher for widowed and divorced men. After age 65 there is one widower for every four widows. Over age 65, more than three-fourths of men are married and more than half of women are widows.

There are no accurate statistics for the number of old lesbian women but estimates are about 10 percent of the older women population. Some lesbians who are now old have remained celibate or closeted because of discrimination while others have been out all along. Because of today's more accepting climate, some lesbians come out late in life. Some women who were married to men in their youth come out as lesbians in old age because of formerly suppressed orientation.

In the past several decades, the number of national organizations for lesbians has increased. Local groups have also sprung up around the country. They provide support and advocacy and confront ageism in the gay, lesbian, and mainstream communities. There are few bereavement support groups for lesbians who have lost lifetime partners because the many widows' support groups often are not accepting of lesbians.

In addition to the aging world being predominately female, more women than men work in the gerontology field, a field that does not pay well but does appeal to nurturing women. With few exceptions, women are the nurses, assisted-living attendants, paid homemakers, home health aides, social workers, recreational workers, senior center directors, psychologists, physicians, occupational and physical therapists, and volunteers who work with the old. Family caregiving of frail elders is also usually done by wives, daughters, daughters-in-law, and other women relatives.

Not surprisingly, a recent book on older women was titled *Women on the Front Lines: Meeting the Challenge of an Aging America*. Women are on the front lines of aging for other reasons than their numbers and employment in the field. Old women are also poorer than old men, with lower savings and social security and fewer pensions. Women have generally worked for substantially lower wages than men and took time from paid work for childbearing, raising children, and caring for aged family members. Displaced homemakers have difficulty reentering the work force, especially for good wages. In 1990 only 24 percent of retired women received pensions compared with 46 percent of men. Women's pensions were also lower.

Women make up 71 percent of the elderly poor. This poverty is clustered among older women living alone, and those never married, separated, divorced, or widowed. One in four women past 65 living alone is poor. A third of women past 65 have

The New York Gray Panthers demonstrate in New York City, August 26, 1980. Founder Maggie Kuhn (wearing hat) displays the banner.

incomes close to the poverty line. Black women compose 23 percent of the female elderly poor even though they now constitute only 9 percent of elderly women. Over 40 percent of elderly Latinas are also poor. About three-quarters of those receiving SSI (Supplemental Security Income) because they do not have enough earnings are women. The base SSI payment is slightly over $400 monthly; that is the sole income for numerous old women.

The health care for many older women is not good. Cancer and heart disease rates are high, as are arthritis and other chronic illnesses. Although Medicare is available to most women over 65, the average out-of-pocket expense for women past 65 was $4,000 a year in 1990. Many women cannot afford supplementary Medicare insurance or out-of-pocket payments and go without health care or use it only in a crisis. In addition, women from 45 to 65 often have no health insurance at all because they had been covered by the insurance of a deceased or divorced spouse or their health insurance had been tied to a job now lost.

Two now-deceased California women, Tish Sommers, a divorcée, and Laurie Shields, a widow, started the Older Women's League in the 1970s to fight for medical insurance for uninsured older women. Their efforts have been largely unsuccessful.

Married women often exhaust savings to care for a husband during his final illness and have no financial cushion for their own health care or other needs. Nursing homes are primarily occupied by never-married or currently uncoupled old women.

Although younger women hope their finances and health care will be better in old age, women's wages are still lower today than men's. Women today often still move in and out of the labor market, work part-time, or subordinate their careers to accommodate their husband's. Therefore, it is likely that poverty and insufficient health care insurance will continue to affect substantial numbers of old women. In 1993 67 percent of women aged 45 to 64, compared with 54 percent of men, reported in a survey that they worry about retirement finances.

Despite the somewhat gloomy situation depicted above, there is good news about women and aging. Amazing numbers of old women are redefining old age by carving out new roles for themselves and learning how to survive and thrive despite limited financial resources. They find late-life jobs, volunteer, become politically active, advocate, and express themselves through the arts. They enroll in college, attend Elderhostels and Senior Venture programs, travel using American Youth Hostels, write poetry, enhance their spirituality, and inspire younger women not to fear aging. They walk outdoors in good weather and in malls in bad weather, take up sports, and exercise.

There has been both a national and a grassroots movement to encourage older women to engage in active lifestyles and to empower them. Maggie Kuhn's Gray Panthers have advocated for older women for over twenty years. In 1990 the American Association of Retired Persons' Women's Initiative published, with the International Federation on Ageing, a sixty-page booklet, *Empowering Older Women.*

Many advice books for older women were published in the 1990s. Old women have also developed their own magazines as vehicles for expression, information, and inspiration. Unfortunately, in 1993, after twenty years, the pioneering *Broom-* *stick* magazine from Oakland, California, folded for lack of funds.

Still flourishing is *Hot Flash*, a newsletter for midlife and older women started in 1981 by the National Action Forum for Midlife and Older Women in Stony Brook, New York. *Hot Flash's* founder and editor in chief, Jane Porcino, has been active in the movement to help older women seek housing alternatives, since housing is usually the greatest expense for the 36 percent of older women who live alone. In 1988 a scholarly journal, *Women and Aging*, was started by J. Dianne Garner, D.S.W., and continues under her editorship.

Friendship networks are strong among many old women. Older women are also the chief consumers of programs at senior centers. Many love the poem "When I Am an Old Woman I Will Wear Purple," by Jenny Joseph, from the book by that name, edited by Sandra Martz. The book has sold over one million copies since its first printing in 1987. Wearing purple T-shirts, women from sixty on up are having a good time, working for their causes, and staying out of rocking chairs and kitchens. But frail women in nursing homes and poor women who need help should not be neglected.

Organizations working for aging women and providing resources include: Older Women's League (OWL), Washington, DC; Gray Panthers, Washington, DC; Senior Action in a Gay Environment (SAGE), New York, NY; National Association for Lesbian and Gay Gerontology, San Francisco, CA; National Caucus and Center on the Black Aged, Washington, DC; Women's Initiative of the American Association of Retired Persons (AARP), Washington, DC; Associacion Nacional Pro Peronanas Mayores (National Association for Hispanic Elderly), Los Angeles, CA; National Asian Pacific Center on Aging, Seattle, WA; Old Lesbian Organizing Committee (OLOC), Houston, TX; Families International, Inc., Milwaukee, WI.

Jessie Allen and Alan Pifer, eds., *Women on the Front Lines* (Washington, D.C.: The Urban Institute Press, 1993); Paula B. Doress-Worters and Diana Laskin Siegal, in cooperation with the Boston Women's Health Book Collective, *The New Ourselves, Growing Older* (New York: Simon and Schuster, 1994); Ruth Harriet Jacobs, *Be An Outrageous Older Woman: A R.A.S.P.* [Remarkable Aging Smart Person] (Manchester, Conn.: K.I.T. Press, 1993).

■ RUTH HARRIET JACOBS

SEE ALSO Stereotypes, Age.

≋ Agriculture

The history of women in U.S. agriculture reveals a fundamental contradiction: women's work has always been integral to farming, yet women have been excluded from controlling farms. Farm women's ambivalence about their situation reflects this contradiction. In the early twentieth century, some farm women complained that men were reluctant to invest in household improvements, such as running water, and that men seldom assisted with the physically heaviest domestic chores. Many women worked alongside men, preferring the seasonal cycle of outdoor tasks to the repetition and confinement of housework, taking pride in their strength and skill, and enjoying the companionship of shared labor.

Native American women alone enjoyed a social status commensurate with their centrality to the economy. Before the European invasion, farming yielded the bulk of most peoples' subsistence. Women cultivated corn, beans, and squash, crops known as the "three sisters." Women usually worked together and controlled both access to land and the distribution of produce. Men helped to clear new fields and participated in rituals to ensure the soil's fertility.

European settlers brought different systems of farming, property holding, and gender relations to North America. Agriculture was based on animal husbandry as well as the cultivation of crops; adult men owned, bought, and sold land as a commodity; women were subsumed within male-headed families. Most European Americans divided agricultural tasks relatively clearly between men and women, although the allocation of specific tasks by sex varied based on the peoples' places of origin and settlement. Men were responsible for the field crops and woodlot, women were responsible for the garden and poultry, and men and women shared responsibility for the cattle. At planting, haying, and harvest, women "helped" men in the fields. When men were away or disabled, women took over men's customary tasks.

Enslaved African American women who labored on plantations producing crops sold on the world market had different experiences from white women who worked on family farms. Planters required women to labor as field hands, regardless of whether they were pregnant, nursing, young, or old. Sometimes women worked together, but often they worked in mixed groups. Many women could keep pace with men in the tobacco, rice, and cotton fields.

Emancipation led to significant changes in African American women's work, although the Southern economy was still based on plantation agriculture, and ex-slaves were not granted the "forty acres and a mule" that they believed would bring economic independence. Refusing contracts that required them to do wage labor in gangs, African Americans insisted on farming in family groups as tenants and sharecroppers. Freedwomen spent more time raising food for their families and less time cultivating staple crops than enslaved women did.

The U.S. agricultural economy underwent a profound transformation during the nineteenth century. Despite uneven development and considerable resistance, farmers became integrated into capitalist systems of production and distribu-

Women picking cotton, Tallulah, Louisana, 1924 or 1925. Before the 1930s, the South had the highest percentage of women agricultural workers, many of them Black.

tion. In the early stages of commercialization, expanding markets for butter, cheese, and poultry enlarged the economic opportunities available to farm women. Eventually, however, women became marginal to many commercial farm operations, producing the family's subsistence instead.

In the twentieth century, women of color have been employed by corporate agribusiness as seasonal wage laborers. In the West, Native Americans, Asian Americans, and Mexican Americans harvested crops, but racial discrimination prevented many families of color from owning land.

Rural women have actively resisted threats to family farming as a way of life. In the late nineteenth and early twentieth centuries, women joined farm organizations such as the Grange and the Farmers' Alliance and gained experience in political debate. The Grange extended membership to women on an equal basis with men and, after persistent lobbying, supported women's suffrage; women also served as traveling speakers in the Farmers' Alliance. In the early twentieth century, farmers' pressure on the government and land-grant universities led to the formation of the Farm and Home Bureaus and the Extension Service. In contrast to the mixed groups that farmers themselves controlled, government-sponsored agencies dealt with rural women and men separately. Only 4-H, the youth organization, was gender integrated.

Joan M. Jensen, *With These Hands: Women Working on the Land* (Old Westbury, N.Y.: Feminist Press, McGraw-Hill, 1981); Nancy Grey Osterud and Joan M. Jensen, eds., *American Rural and Farm Women in Historical Perspective* (Washington, D.C.: The Agricultural History Society, 1994); Rachel Ann Rosenfeld, *Farm Women: Work, Farm, and Family in the United States* (Chapel Hill: University of North Carolina Press, 1985).

■ GREY OSTERUD

See also Labor Unions: United Farm Workers; Native American Cultures; Native American Women; Plantation System.

≋ AIDS

Although statistics can never reflect well enough the impact AIDS has had on women, three "facts" frame women's experience with AIDS: 1) in 1990 women represented 10 percent of all AIDS cases in the United States; 2) over 70 percent of women with AIDS in the United States are women of color, compared to 40 percent of men with AIDS; and 3) women diagnosed with AIDS have a lower survival rate than men diagnosed with AIDS. These statistics, based on AIDS cases reported to the Center for Disease Control (CDC) in 1990, are not unrelated. Access to health care directly determines survival time, and in a society structured by race, class, and gender hierarchies, health care has become a privilege, not a right. As a result, women and people of color who have less access to preventive health care or good health insurance suffer more and die faster from AIDS.

AIDS is a diagnostic category characterized by a set of specific opportunistic infections that are understood to be a response to an individual's exposure to the human immunodeficiency virus, or HIV. Although a lab can clinically test for HIV antibodies, indicating with relative certainty the presence of the virus in the body, AIDS itself is not a virus or a disease but a syndrome, a pattern of symptoms, such as a lower T-cell count or diseases such as Kaposi's sarcoma or PCP, *pneumocystis carinii* pneumonia. In other words, a person may contract HIV (be "HIV-positive") but may not develop infections or diseases (be "asymptomatic"). In such cases, a person is not diagnosed with AIDS. A person with HIV may live for years without developing the opportunistic diseases that translate into an AIDS diagnosis, and many people (women in particular) live with and die from HIV-related infections without ever being diagnosed with AIDS.

The history of AIDS remains hinged to its social context. Because HIV-related opportunistic infections first surfaced among gay men, the virus was initially stigmatized as a "gay disease." Although what was once called GRID (Gay-Related Immune Deficiency) was renamed AIDS (Acquired Immune Deficiency Syndrome) in 1982, the syndrome continues to carry a number of stigmas that hinder both its social control and the humane treatment of those affected by the virus. For instance, scientific research remains underfunded because bisexuals and homosexuals, the perceived targets and "victims" of the virus, are devalued socially, and the rhetoric of "risk groups" rather than risky behaviors perpetuates ignorance about transmission of HIV. Women remain peripheral to AIDS research and education (except as mothers-to-be who may expose their fetus or child to HIV). In fact, it is often difficult for women to get tested for HIV, and because many clinical trials exclude women from their research samples, HIV-positive women have less access to experimental or innovative drug treatments.

Women in the AIDS crisis have fewer resources and greater responsibilities. Women on average earn less than men and therefore have less access to expensive health care or good health insurance, and women of color have even less access to health care than white women: approximately 30 percent of Latinos in the United States reported having no health insurance compared to 12 percent for whites. HIV-positive women like Lisa Tiger, Creek/Seminole, are working to inform poor women of their special risk factors. Poor women also tend to have more dependents, as they are often the primary caretakers for children, the elderly, and the disabled. Women also consistently negotiate sexual relationships and interactions that leave them responsible for both birth control and safer sex practices. Given all these factors, women with HIV are more likely to be held responsible for contracting and transmitting the virus. CDC guidelines remain narrowly defined and women still are less likely to be diagnosed with AIDS, thus perpetuating the invisibility of women with AIDS. Finally, because women are often underdiagnosed or misdiagnosed, medical knowledge about how women's bodies respond to HIV continues to be a severely unexplored and unarticulated area of research.

Women have been at the forefront of AIDS activism, however, fighting for greater attention from scientists and health care workers. In 1986 New York's chapter of ACT UP (AIDS Coalition to Unleash Power) formed a women's caucus that initiated an informational campaign directed at doctors, drug companies, and women themselves. In 1988 they demonstrated against misinformation at the offices of *Cosmopolitan* magazine because an article reassured heterosexual women that they were not at risk for exposure to HIV through "normal heterosexual intercourse." Another action pressured drug companies to print warnings on yeast-infection medicines to indicate that persistent infections can point to the possible presence of HIV in women. An ongoing ACT UP campaign also targets misinformation about lesbians and AIDS, insisting that scientists study woman-to-woman transmission and that lesbians practice safer sex despite CDC assertions that lesbians remain at low risk. Finally, the recent production of AIDS documentaries as well as erotic videos by and for women provides vital information about safer sex in a world all too silent about female sexuality. With few advocates but themselves, women have organized to translate invisibility into effective political action.

The ACT UP/NY Women & AIDS Book Group, *Women, AIDS & Activism* (Boston: South End Press, 1990).

■ NAN ALAMILLA BOYD

≋ Alcoholism

The history of women's relationship with alcohol constitutes a profound commentary on U.S. cultural attitudes about gender and power. Women who don't drink traditionally have been viewed as "good," "moral," "women of sterling virtue," but those who do have been stigmatized as sick, evil corrupters of men and children. For men, out-of-control behavior associated with drinking historically has been accepted and even encouraged. But the alcoholic woman is both a victim of her addiction and victimized as a result. The social concern at issue is control—who has it and who doesn't.

The double standard applied to women's drinking has its roots deep in the history of Western culture. In first-century Rome, drinking by women was a crime. A woman suspected of drinking was assumed to have betrayed her husband sexually and could be put to death.

U.S. attitudes toward female alcoholics were prefigured by England's. For ladies of the upper classes, drinking was considered a refined and elegant pastime. But in the 1750s, when Parliament lifted restrictions on selling gin to raise local revenues, the impoverished who drank to make their lives in the slums of London more bearable died of disease in record numbers. Public outrage at this "gin epidemic" focused on women because they were considered to be abusing their children.

During the U.S. colonial era alcohol was regarded as a medicinal tool and an economic mainstay—women brewed and sold beer to supplement household income. Women ran taverns.

Women could drink but not too much. Those who did could be forced to wear a large letter *D*.

By the early 1800s, women had begun to organize to fight the effects of male drunkenness. Alcohol was viewed as an "evil force" that undermined the purity and sanctity of the home and family. But the real danger of male drinking involved the random violence and abuse of women and children that accompanied it. Women frequently were abandoned and left in poverty by drinking husbands.

The subtleties of the societal struggles for control also were being fought on other levels. While the somewhat ridiculed members of the Woman's Christian Temperance Union (WCTU) struggled to bring about Prohibition, some were unknowingly becoming addicted to the patent medicines of the era, which contained at least 50 percent alcohol and often opium, heroin, or cocaine. Women were encouraged to buy these elixirs to improve their moods and to treat the "weaknesses" of womanhood. "Good" women could be drugged for economic gain and could be the silent victims of men's alcohol abuse, but they could not overtly drink to excess—or have the right to vote.

Prohibition was passed and repealed. Women won the vote. After World War I, women reacted to the double standards that controlled their behavior. Prohibition created a backlash in which women drank more rather than less. Women ran speakeasies, much as they had run taverns in colonial times. But by the end of World War II, women were returned to the home. And just as the women of the WCTU had unwittingly taken to patent medicines to temper their unrest, the housewives of the 1950s became one more wave of victims of the medical establishment, which plied them with prescription tranquilizers and sedatives. Over the next three decades, women's increased drinking was viewed as an outcome of their attempts to adopt male roles.

In the 1990s it is estimated that almost six million women suffer from alcohol abuse or addiction. The double standard regarding control still applies. Society takes punitive measures against women who abuse alcohol during pregnancy. Women are still viewed as promiscuous when they drink, even though the research increasingly shows that alcohol use makes women more vulnerable to sexual abuse by males. Women have less access to treatment programs than men because of inadequate access to child care. Women typically participate in the treatment of spouses, but the same is not true of males whose wives are affected by alcohol. Men are much more likely to leave alcoholic wives than women are to leave alcoholic husbands. Women alcoholics have higher rates of suicide and prescription-drug overdose than do males and higher rates of depression. Lesbians, who face social stigma and must often depend on bar culture for social contact, have higher rates of alcoholism than do women in the general population. African American women abstain from drinking more than other groups but tend to drink more when they do drink. Latinas are less likely to be heavy drinkers than women of other ethnic groups, and Native American women tend to have higher rates of alcohol-related deaths. Rates of alcohol use among Asian American women increase relative to their assimilation into "American" culture. The heaviest drinking rates tend to be among women who are divorced, separated, or never married. Among women who abuse alcohol, between 60 and 70 percent have been sexually or physically abused or have experienced family violence as children.

In this modern, medically controlled culture, women who drink are considered sicker than men who drink. And a woman affected by a man's drinking is labeled "codependent," although "overresponsible" behavior is sanctioned, considered central to a woman's role. Women, who are often only too ready to adopt the label, pathologize themselves. Feminist critics challenge the concept of codependency as the woman-blaming label that it can be. They question the patriarchal bias of twelve-step programs and the concept of accepting that they are "powerless" as part of their recovery. Increasingly, feminist mental health workers advocate approaches to addiction treatment that take into account women's special needs and the shaming impact of the double standard.

Drinking is a multilevel phenomenon—a function of genetic and emotional vulnerability, as well as social conditioning. But the realities of alcohol abuse in this country are a testament to women's continued oppression. The effects on their bodies and emotions are poorly researched except when children are involved. The ways that male violence, sexual exploitation, racism, homophobia, and economic exploitation are implicated in women's addictions are rarely discussed. Attitudes toward alcohol abuse leave one more extremely negative mark in the annals of U.S. women's history, one that calls for both political and health care attention as well as the continued fight for female rights.

Claudia Bepko, ed., *Feminism and Addiction* (New York: Haworth Press, 1991); Jo-Ann Krestan, "The Baby and the Bathwater," in *Women and Power: Perspectives for Family Therapy*, edited by T. J. Goodrich (New York: W. W. Norton, 1991); Marian Sandmaier, *The Invisible Alcoholics: Women and Alcohol*, 2nd edition (Blue Ridge Summit, Penn.: TAB Books, 1992).

▪ CLAUDIA BEPKO
and JO-ANN KRESTAN

SEE ALSO Prohibition and Temperance.

≋ Alternative Healing

Through history, Western medicine has focused on the study of disease rather than on health or healing. Only in recent decades has the importance of the patient's own defense mechanisms (including the mind) been recognized; research in this area is only in its infancy, and findings have not yet been widely applied to the practice of medicine in this country.

Excessive medical and surgical interventions on women are a tradition in U.S. medicine. Only one hundred years ago it was thought that a physiological basis for female insanity existed in the reproductive organs and that the obvious solution was surgery. For example, women underwent hysterectomies for "calming" purposes; the word "hysteria" is derived from the Greek word for uterus.

Although U.S. doctors no longer believe that women's reproductive organs cause mental illness, women still are treated very differently than are men. Thousands of prophylactic mastectomies (removal of healthy breasts to prevent the development of breast cancer) are performed in this country annually. One-third of U.S. women have had a hysterectomy before menopause; after menopause the number rises to one-half. Women are prescribed drugs more frequently than are men: some of the more overused drugs include hormones, tranquilizers, diet drugs, lactation suppressants, and drugs for premenstrual symptoms.

Preventive medicine also has become more interventionist: current research emphasizes using potent drugs to decrease the risk of one disease although they may cause another; the field has moved from disease prevention to disease substitution.

Normal processes such as menopause and childbirth have been heavily medicalized. The chronic use of hormone replacement therapy (HRT), even in women who do not need the therapy to treat hot flashes or vaginal dryness, has been heavily promoted to prevent heart disease and osteoporosis, although evidence is skimpy for these claims, and hormone replacement therapy appears to increase the risk of breast cancer.

Great strides have been made in reducing interventions in childbirth (women are no longer shaved, denied food during labor, or put under general anesthesia). Obstetricians are trained to view childbirth as a process fraught with potential problems. Fetal monitoring, for instance, is widely used, although studies show no difference in the outcomes of normal labors that are electronically monitored (usually with a belt around the woman's body that restricts movement) and those that are intermittently monitored by stethoscope.

Midwifery, which treats childbirth as a normal event with rare complications, is an example of health care, as opposed to disease care. Unlike obstetricians, midwives are trained to see childbirth as a normal process.

The women's health movement sprouted in the early 1970s with the publication of *Our Bodies, Ourselves* and the creation of the National Women's Health Network. Both were key in helping women to take control of their own health, battle unnecessary and dangerous medical interventions, and fight for better health care.

Birth control and abortion rights always have been a key part of the women's health movement. When abortion was illegal, feminists in Chicago organized the Jane Collective, a sophisticated network that allowed women to get safe abortions. Feminists also created self-help groups, where women learned cervical self-exam and menstrual extraction, a low-tech technique of early pregnancy termination.

A Harvard study found that one of three U.S. consumers surveyed had used some kind of alternative therapy (excluding exercise and prayer) in 1990. Consumers spent $13.7 billion on alternative medicine, which is more than the annual out-of-pocket amount spent on hospitalizations. Relaxation techniques were the most commonly used therapies, followed by chiropractic and massage. A survey distributed through *Prevention* magazine found that the use of alternative therapies was quite high among menopausal women.

More women than men visit alternative practitioners (or use alternative therapies on their own); however, practitioners of alternative medicine who have achieved media prominence are predominately white men, who rarely give credit to the African, Asian, Native American, and other cultures that spawned these forms of treatment. The only alternative fields dominated by women are therapeutic touch and massage. Women have long practiced herbalism, and, interestingly, in chiropractics, three of the first "Fifteen Disciples" of D. D. Palmer's Chiropractic School and Cure were women. One of these women was Minora Paxson, who coauthored the first textbook in the profession. By the 1920s between one-third and one-half of chiropractors were women. A backlash against women followed World War II; female admissions dropped precipitously and never recovered. In 1986 only 10 percent of chiropractors were women.

True health is not only the absence of disease but the optimum functioning of body, mind, and spirit. The presence of love, work, and meaning in women's lives is vital to health. Many alternative practitioners emphasize preventive medicine and stress reduction, including changes in diet, lifestyle, and exercise patterns. Concepts such as balancing energy or using tonic herbs to strengthen organs and prevent illness still are ideas guaranteed to elicit blank stares from most traditional physicians. As unconventional medicine is increasingly accepted and practiced, we can look forward to research on health as well as disease, to true partnerships between consumers and health care practitioners, and to the use of the most benign (instead of the most drastic) therapies for any given condition.

Boston Women's Health Book Collective, *The New Our Bodies, Ourselves* (New York: Simon and Schuster, 1992); Barbara Ehrenreich and Deirdre English, *For Her Own Good: 150 Years of the Experts' Advice to Women* (Garden City, New York: Doubleday, 1979); Barbara Katz Rothman, *Giving Birth: Alternatives in Childbirth* (New York: Penguin, 1982).

■ ADRIANE FUGH-BERMAN

SEE ALSO Women's Health Movement.

≋ Amendments, Constitutional

SEE Constitution and Amendments.

≋ Americanization

Twenty-three million Southern and Eastern Europeans immigrated to the United States between 1890 and 1920. Some were exiles from religious persecution and others were stimulated by global conditions of economic modernization to seek opportunities in a country rich in the lore of opportunity.

Many of the personal encounters through which immigrants redefined U.S. culture transpired through "Americanization" campaigns sponsored by federal, local, and private organizations in the 1910s. The Americanization movement encompassed thousands of local civic organizations, English language classes, a national committee, settlement houses, domestic science classes, and immigrant protective services sponsored by organizations such as the YWCA. Although explicitly racist, exclusionist sentiments that argued for the racial unassimilability of non-white people diminished the movement by the 1920s, its governing, assimilationist objectives in the 1910s were to "reeducate" the native-born American, to interpret America to the immigrant and the immigrant to America, to elicit a voluntary consent to citizenship from the newcomer, and to cultivate in the immigrant thereafter patriotic loyalty.

Well-educated, white, middle-class women such as Lillian Wald and Jane Addams, who lived in immigrant community settlement houses—hubs for the effort to Americanize the female immigrant—or who volunteered to teach language, civics, and housekeeping classes, helped to devise an Americanization program that hinged in many respects on the immigrant woman. Female social workers engrossed in urban life argued that since immigrant women would raise the next generation of citizens it was imperative that she be inculcated as a family conduit in America's way of life. Although topically diverse, Americanization programs consistently endeavored to replace what appeared to be antimodern, Old World customs with more efficient, modern habits. Classes, conducted in English, included food preparation, home sanitation, civics, hygiene, child rearing, and other family topics. Americanization programs often reversed traditional power relations between husbands and wives or parents and children. Because they tended to speak English and become "Americanized" faster, children became "authorities" on America before their parents did.

What would it have meant to be an Americanized immigrant woman, and did middle-class apostles succeed in their efforts to instill nebulous U.S. values? These questions have generated a familiar mythology among scholars, typically centered on the male immigrant and his "rags-to-riches" heroic assimilation into U.S. culture or, by other historians' accounts, on his triumphant *resistance* to assimilation and his preservation of an indigenous culture against the intrusions of the condescending, meddlesome Americanization officer. The substance and outcome of Americanization were undoubtedly more complex than these myths allow. First, Americanization efforts balanced crucially not on individual assimilation but on the diffusion of modern, *heterosexual* norms among immigrant populations, often by female Americanization officers.

Second, the American culture of native-born, middle-class women involved in immigrant life did not remain a static reference point for the immigrant woman to either embrace or reject. Instead, native-born women reinvented gender and sexual relations for *themselves* along modern lines through interpreting America to the immigrant. Immigrant cultures, in turn, reinvented themselves through reference to the modern life promised by America. Hence the appropriate metaphor for the encounter between immigrant and native-born women is perhaps not the "melting pot" but "alchemy," the creation of a new cultural, female identity partially through interactive Americanization programs.

This alchemy—and the central role of sexuality in the modernization of the United States in the 1910s—is most obvious in one of the compositional staples of both the immigrant woman's autobiography and the female social worker's musings on immigrant life: arranged marriage and romantic love. Asian and Southeastern Europeans, who composed the majority of immigrants in the early 1900s, were more familiar culturally with customs of arranged marriage (families would negotiate marriages through dowry exchange and formal contracts for their daughters), than the ambiguous and decidedly modern enticements of the "true-love" match that appeared central to the American way of life.

Social workers joined other modern immigrant women in criticizing arranged marriage customs as antimodern and un-American in their denial of sexual choice. They also questioned arranged marriage as a violation of both heterosexual intimacy and privacy, certainly the soul of modern American rights to conduct social relations free of tyranny. In the context of legal restrictions on the importation of women for prostitution, immigration officers and, in a subtler way, caseworkers at Edith and Grace Abbott's Immigrant Protective League, in Chicago, for example, tended to link arranged marriage to coercion or to economic sexual bargains. One caseworker in 1922 intervened on behalf of an eighteen-year-old Syrian girl, Rachel Badad, who had been detained on Ellis Island. Rachel had been detained because authorities refused to believe that her second cousin, David, who was born in Chicago, was her affianced. She was excluded because she supposedly lacked a "genuine" bond to her fiancé. The social worker checked the home conditions in Chicago and followed up on character references. She could only secure admission for Rachel if the family "agreed to postpone the proposed marriage till the young people got to know each other better." She explained, "When the family learned what a shocking thing such [an arrangement] seemed to us in this country, they were willing to be very American and to allow her a choice" of marrying either David or one of his brothers.

On the West Coast, the Japanese and Korean immigrant practices of procuring brides through proxy by the exchange of pictures and letters were discontinued by the Japanese as a result of public protest and consequent pressure from the Japanese American business community in 1920. In Japanese and Korean cultures, marriage had always been a matter of family negotiation for which the betrothed needn't be present. As a consul explained in 1907, the woman became "not only a wife but an internal part of [the husband's] family. . . . The social unit is not the individual, but the family." Precisely because "picture brides" married for family interests, they appeared to immigration workers to be like merchandise rather than modern U.S. individuals with free choice in social and sexual relations.

Settlement workers, more empathetic to the antimodern family networks of immigrant life, championed privacy as the remedy to women's servile condition. Social worker Ruth True condemned the confounding of economic and personal relations in the immigrant family, citing the girl's expected economic contributions as a diminution of her freedom and humanity. Another observer of immigrant life, Florence Kitchelt, recorded a triumphant story of a German immigrant who fell in love with and married an Irish Catholic against her parents' wishes. "To free herself from their yoke . . . she had to choose between her parents or him," Kitchelt concluded. "She chose—the choice every woman makes when it comes to final issue. She returned to her husband and they lived happily ever after."

It is crucial to recognize that as confidently as Kitchelt pronounced that the romantic couple lived happily ever after, her concepts of privacy and personal freedom were hardly timelessly American values: marital choices in Victorian American middle-class culture, while not arranged, typically entailed some consideration of pragmatic, familial, and economic concerns. U.S. citizenship and freedom were hardly defined by romantic love and choice in the 1800s. Educated, native-born women involved in Americanization, then, refined or perhaps created their own standards of heterosexual modernity through attempting to uplift presumably antimodern immigrant cultures.

For their part, immigrants often resisted true love as a seduction of an individualist culture that ironically enslaved its citizens in their impetuous longings by casting them adrift from extended familial networks in a country with exaggerated standards of personal choice. As one unpublished autobiography recalls, "My daughter calls me old fashioned but I laughed from her. To be so a slave to a man would I never be. One makes one self cheap to give [oneself] away to husband.... Where Julia loves she cares not for herself. She says, 'Take what I have, your life it is all but I, I am a nothing.' A Lower-East-Side matchmaker, put out of business by modernity, would have agreed. "[Immigrants] have learned how to start their own love affairs from the Americans," he lamented, "and it is one of the worst things they have picked up.... The love which they have learned to put so much faith in dribbles out in trips to Coney [Island]. In a month they are finding ways of getting rid of each other."

However ambiguous the course of modern heterosexual love, it is important to recognize, in any event, that sexual choices for the immigrant woman bore a crucial relation to her concept of true U.S. citizenship. Immigrants aspired to become sexually modern or resisted the advances of sexual modernity in conversation with the idea of U.S. citizenship. So, too, did female Americanization officers redefine their own values through immigrant culture. They attempted to interpret the United States to the immigrants, but in the process they inevitably reinterpreted and reinvented U.S. sexual roles for themselves along demonstrably modern lines.

Elizabeth Ewen, *Immigrant Women in the Land of Dollars: Life and Culture of the Lower East Side, 1890–1925* (New York: Monthly Review Press, 1985); Sydney Stahl Weinberg, *The World of Our Mothers* (Chapel Hill: University of North Carolina Press, 1988); Anzia Yezierska, *Breadgivers* (New York: Persea Books, 1925).

▪ PAMELA HAAG

SEE ALSO Immigration; Settlement House Movement.

≋ Anarchism

Anarchism is the philosophy of social affiliation unrestricted by law, government, or hierarchies of power, in which free groupings of women and men join together for the common good. Its vision includes equitable distribution of wealth and liberation from internalized barriers to personal freedom. Its tactics for change range from philosophical writings to direct action.

The backlash against anarchists has thwarted anarchism's power as a mass movement and continues to obscure its historical contribution to free speech. It was a strong conceptual current in the turn-of-the-century U.S. labor movement and integral to the emergent critique of the suffrage movement as the best way to achieve women's freedom.

Anarchist influence on public discourse about reproductive and sexual freedom, however, continued to evolve between 1870 and 1920. Anarchist women, including Emma Goldman, Voltairine de Cleyre, and Margaret Anderson, formed a vocal subculture with socialists, radicals, and bohemians. Their early crusade for autonomy in private life was echoed in the resurgent women's movement of the 1960s and 1970s and its hallmark slogan, *the personal is political.*

Anarchism's tradition pervades U.S. cultural and political radicalism, especially in feminists' demand for freedom and equality in all aspects of life and in its implicit critique of social conventions that subordinate women—demands that have spurred profound changes both in social custom and in the guarantee of basic human rights.

• CANDACE FALK

SEE ALSO Radicalism.

≋ Anticommunism

Anticommunism has been the dominant ideological weapon of the power elites in the United States and the major determinant of foreign and domestic policy since World War II. The communist specter emerged after the Paris Commune of 1871, when class conflict gripped the newly industrialized United States and the "red menace" proved an effective tool against labor and agrarian radicals. During and after World War I and the Bolshevik revolution, the red scare, with its accompanying xenophobia, grew tremendously and targeted among others the women's suffrage campaign and first-wave feminists.

Anticommunism took center stage after World War II, driven by the need to win popular support for a new cold war foreign policy and the desire of the right to destroy the New Deal coalition. A purge of government employees, congressional investigating committees, FBI harassment, new repressive legislation, federal and state prosecutions, and deportations victimized men and women on the Left, as well as gays and lesbians and their associates. A climate of intense fear, censorship, and conformity paralyzed social activism and labor militancy, undermined the First Amendment, and contributed to the power of family-centered ideology and the rigidly defined gender roles that were so oppressive to women in the 1950s.

Senator Joseph McCarthy was but an opportunistic latecomer to the scene, though he bequeathed it his name. "McCarthyism" was a misleading name, however, because by 1950 anticommunism *already* had become the ruling national ideology, and the nation's top leaders and law enforcement authorities, not McCarthy, were responsible. Anticommunism defined U.S. foreign policy, fueling an unprecedented military buildup directed at the USSR and at insurgent movements worldwide.

By 1960 the civil rights movement began to weaken the orthodoxy of the 1950s, belatedly aided by the Supreme Court and popular resistance, markedly that of Women Strike for Peace members who effectively used ridicule to undermine McCarthyism's power. The national security state and the age of surveillance remain a part of our society, threatening the civil liberties of leftists, militant environmentalists, and groups working for social change abroad.

• MARGE FRANTZ

SEE ALSO Conservatism and the Right Wing.

≋ Antifeminism

Throughout U.S. history, there has been an undercurrent of opposition to any measures that might advance gender equality. As early as the 1790s, Mary Wollstonecraft's famous treatise, *Vindication of the Rights of Women*, was met with a hailstorm of criticism for suggesting that women had a rightful place outside the home. Similarly, Francis Wright, a renowned lecturer who advocated for equal education and enhanced legal rights for women in the 1820s, was denounced as a proponent of atheism and free love. Only during periods of sustained agitation in support of expanded rights for women, however, has anti–women's rights sentiment crystallized into organized antifeminist politics. Thus, the two major waves of antifeminist activity coincide with the two waves of the women's rights movement: the campaign to secure female suffrage in the late nineteenth and early twentieth centuries, and the feminist movement of the late twentieth century. In both periods, those holding a traditional view of women's place in the home and family tried to advance their cause by joining with other conservative groups to forestall efforts to extend women's rights.

A campaign of opposition began almost as soon as the doors closed on the first national women's rights convention in 1848. Calls for marital equality and improved educational opportunities, better working conditions, and additional legal rights for women were met with a flurry of publications, sermons, and lectures denouncing such demands as a repudiation of women's natural place as domestic caretakers and submissive wives. By the 1870s, as the battle for the vote became a centerpiece of women's rights agitation, those opposed to extending the franchise to women also became organized and public. Often headed by the wives of socially prominent politicians and business leaders, committees against female suffrage worked actively to block state and municipal suffrage efforts by testifying at legislative hearings, distributing pamphlets, and deluging newspapers with letters expressing opposition to women's right to vote.

In 1911 state antisuffrage associations formed the National Association Opposed to Woman Suffrage (NAOWS). At its height in the years 1911 to 1916, the NAOWS claimed a membership of 350,000 devoted to home and national defense against women's suffrage, feminism, and socialism. Antisuffragists maintained that extending the vote to women would reduce the special protections and routes of influence available to women, destroy the family, and increase the number of socialist-leaning voters. These sentiments dovetailed with the fears of many Southern whites that female suffrage would undermine the Jim Crow

restrictions that had effectively disenfranchised African American voters in the South and the apprehension of industrial and business leaders, especially brewers, that women would vote in favor of social and political reform and for prohibiting the sale of liquor.

With the passage of the Woman's Suffrage Amendment in 1920, women's rights agitation, and thus antifeminist counteractivity, sharply declined. Nearly fifty years later, antifeminist organizers resurfaced, as a new wave of feminism began to challenge the second-class status of women in law, education, politics, family, and the work force. Antifeminists in this period primarily organized in opposition to two feminist demands: passage of the Equal Rights Amendment (ERA) to the U.S. Constitution, and the legalization of abortion.

The major vehicle through which antifeminists organized to oppose passage of the ERA was STOP-ERA, a nationwide group headed by longtime conservative leader Phyllis Schlafly. The organized effort to defeat the ERA bore many similarities to the fight against women's vote earlier in the century. Like the antisuffragists, Schlafly and her followers deluged state legislators and the media with visits, letters, and pamphlets warning that dire consequences would result if the U.S. Constitution was amended to accord equality to women. Many of the arguments wielded against the ERA were also reminiscent of those used by antisuffragist forces. According to its opponents, the ERA would erode the duty of men to support their wives and children financially, prohibit sex-segregated restrooms, allow women to be drafted into military service, sanction homosexual marriage, and generally threaten the family. Schlafly and others paradoxically also argued that the ERA was unnecessary since women had been granted legal protection and equal rights through earlier statutes and judicial decisions.

If their tactics were similar, the constituencies of anti-ERA forces differed significantly from those of the antisuffrage movement a half-century earlier. While the antisuffrage movement was composed largely of the wives of wealthy and socially prominent men, the typical rank-and-file member of STOP-ERA was a white middle-aged rural and religiously devout housewife married to a working- or lower-middle-class man. In contrast, many anti-ERA leaders, including Schlafly, were upper-middle-class career women or were men with professional occupations. Just as antisuffragists were supported by people with business and political interests who feared women's votes, so did the anti-ERA movement find common cause with corporate leaders and others who worried about the financial consequences of gender equality.

The other major focus of modern organized antifeminist sentiment has been manifest in opposition to feminist demands for abortion rights. In 1973 the U.S. Supreme Court issued a decision in the *Roe* v. *Wade* case that greatly limited the ability of states to restrict abortions. Antifeminist groups reacted immediately and strongly, insisting that legalized abortion, like the ERA, would undermine respect for women's traditional roles as homemakers and mothers. Antifeminists thus allied with conservative religious leaders who opposed abortion on moral grounds and right-wing politicians who wanted to protect traditional patriarchal family arrangements. The efforts of antiabortion forces to overturn the Supreme Court decision have been unsuccessful to date. Constant, intense pressure on legislators and judges— together with both violent and nonviolent harassment of abortion clinics and their personnel and clients—has, however, resulted in legal and financial repercussions that have made abortion inaccessible to many women.

Cynthia D. Kinnard, *Antifeminism in American Thought: An Annotated Bibliography* (Boston: G. K. Hall & Co., 1986); Jane J. Mansbridge, *Why We Lost the ERA* (Chicago: University of Chicago Press, 1986).

▪ KATHLEEN M. BLEE

SEE ALSO Conservatism and the Right Wing.

≋ Antipornography Activism

Antipornography activism has been basic to the contemporary women's movement from its beginnings in the 1960s, with protests against dehumanizing and objectifying women, judging and exploiting women as sexual commodities, and promoting rape. As activists learned more about violence against women, they learned more about the coercion of women into pornography and the use of pornography in sexual abuse. The focus has always been on harm to women, not on the regulation of morals. Strategies have included marches and demonstrations; slide shows, writing, and education; civil disobedience and vandalism; and civil rights legislation.

Foreshadowing later decades of activism and analysis, in 1963 in *Show* magazine, Gloria Steinem published "A Bunny's Story," a two-part journalistic exposé of the shabby economic exploitation of waitresses in Hugh Hefner's Playboy clubs. In the early 1970s many activists participated in raucous demonstrations outside the clubs. In an in-house memo (subsequently quoted in *Glamour* in 1971) Hefner wrote: "These chicks are our natural enemy. It is time to do battle with them."

The first national action of the U.S. women's movement was a 1968 demonstration in Atlantic City opposing the Miss America Pageant. Two hundred women protested the use of women's bodies for entertainment and noted in a flier (reprinted in *Sisterhood Is Powerful*) that "Miss America and Playboy's centerfold are sisters over the skin."

Grassroots organizing against beauty pageants continued, including a 1975 protest in Dallas at which feminist agitator Nikki Craft threw pieces of meat onto the stage. A decade of actions, starting in 1980, against California's qualifying pageant for the Miss America crown, included demonstrations using performance art and participants committing acts of civil disobedience.

In 1970 feminists occupied the offices of Grove Press to protest its publication of pornography as sexual liberation and the economic exploitation of its female employees. In the same year feminists seized the left-wing underground rag *Rat*, because it published pornography, this time as revolution.

In the early 1970s groups called Women Against Violence Against Women formed independently in many cities to protest pornography on billboards and record-album covers as well as in advertising and fashion photography that featured the brutalizing of women.

In 1974 Robin Morgan articulated the principle (reprinted in *Going Too Far*) that "pornography is the theory, and rape the practice." That same year Susan Brownmiller, in *Against Our Will*, identified pornography as the "undiluted essence of antifemale propaganda" and exposed its use to promote mass rape as a military tactic in the 1971 Bangladesh war, and argued that domestic pornography promoted rape as well. Also in 1974 this author published *Woman Hating*, which showed that pornography sexualized the same sex-role stereotypes found in children's fairy tales.

In November 1978 Women Against Violence in Media and Pornography in San Francisco organized the first feminist conference on pornography and also a Take Back the Night march. Over three thousand women shut down the sex-industry district.

In 1979 Brownmiller founded Women Against Pornography (WAP), which opened an office in Times Square. WAP took women on tours of pornography stores and live sex shows in Times Square and developed the first slide show to take to college campuses. An October 1979 WAP-sponsored march on Times Square included over five thousand supporters.

Mass demonstrations began in 1976 with pickets and marches against *Snuff*, a film purporting to show the evisceration of a woman. After 1978, Take Back the Night marches, which linked pornography with date rape, incest, and battery, became annual events, first in cities, then on campuses.

In 1980 two books advanced the struggle: *Take Back the Night*, an anthology, persuasively defining pornography as a form of violence; and *Ordeal*, by the former Linda Lovelace, who told of her coercion into prostitution and pornography. In 1981 this author published *Pornography: Men Possessing Women*, which analyzed the dynamics of dehumanization, force, and domination.

Acts of vandalism ranged from spray painting cinemas, to destroying *Hustler* magazines in 1981–82 in Southern California, to overturning and despoiling all the stock in adult bookstores at various locations in Ohio, Minnesota, and Massachusetts.

Civil disobedience included unfurling banners in front of theaters showing pornography films, screaming in the audience whenever a woman was hurt on film, pouring blood over pornography in stores, staging sit-ins, and tearing up copies of *Penthouse* in cities throughout the Midwest.

In 1983 this author cowrote with Catharine A. MacKinnon a civil rights bill—vetoed by the Minneapolis mayor, passed then stopped in other cities—that recognized pornography as a form of sex discrimination. Under this law, individual plaintiffs could bring civil suits (thus no police enforcement or prior restraint is involved) against pornographers and traffickers for the harms consistently and systematically associated with pornography: the civil inequality that results from the bigotry and aggression created by pornography; coercion into pornography; forcing pornography on a person (for instance, using pornography to make a work environment hostile to women); or attack or physical injury caused by pornography. Legislative hearings allowed women hurt in and by pornography to testify about the role of pornography in rape, incest, battery, prostitution, and sexual harassment. The struggle to pass this law and have it upheld continues, as do conferences, marches, writing, and demonstrations.

Andrea Dworkin, *Letters from a War Zone* (New York: Lawrence Hill Books, 1993); Catharine A. MacKinnon, *Only Words* (Cambridge, Mass.: Harvard University Press, 1994); John Stoltenberg, *What Makes Pornography "Sexy"?* (Minneapolis: Milkweed Editions, 1994).

• ANDREA DWORKIN

SEE ALSO Censorship; Pornography; Take Back the Night.

≋ Arab American Women

Arab Americans represent a wide spectrum of diversity historically and politically as well as religiously, racially, and ethnically. Of 212 million Arabs worldwide, approximately three million live in the United States, nearly half of whom are women. Arab Americans come from small villages and cosmopolitan cities spanning northern Africa and western Asia. They share a common culture and language and in recent years have experienced a growing unity in the face of anti-Arab and anti-Muslim bias in the United States. Arab Americans' entrepreneurial spirit and work ethic have helped them to assimilate culturally and they are now represented in most areas of employment throughout the United States. They are primarily Christian, Muslim, and Druze and are among the most highly educated of America's ethnic groups.

Early Arab American women immigrants faced a particular challenge: to adapt to the United States and maintain their cultural identity while creating a home environment that made this balancing act look effortless. The first wave of Arab immigrants who came in the late 1800s was composed primarily of Christian men who worked as peddlers and found it easier to assimilate than did the Muslims who arrived later. A surprising number of women arrived alone during this period. Among them was Kamila Gibran, the mother of poet Khalil Gibran, who arrived in 1895 with her four children and began peddling in Boston. Women were often successful peddlers; rural dwellers were more comfortable letting women rather than men into their homes to show their merchandise, which included yard goods, needles and thread, ribbons, lace, and toys. Through peddling, the women learned language and values, easing their adaptation to a new society.

Many women came to the United States after World War II to join their families. They were often well educated or seeking to further their education; some came to escape political turmoil after the creation of the state of Israel in 1948. Muslim women immigrants arrived in greater numbers than Christians and had the additional challenge of adjusting to a society that did not understand their religion. Some Muslim women wore the *hijab*, a head covering, and were perceived as particularly foreign by U.S. society. Newer immigrants (those arriving after 1965) came with a sense of nationalism and pride in their heritage because they had lived in independent Arab states; the generations born in the United States sometimes felt little connection to their Arab roots. Even with divergent ethnic, religious, and political identifications, Arab women worked hard to integrate their heritage into their new lives in America. They organized committees and raised funds to build churches, mosques, and community centers—places that kept their culture alive and created opportunities to socialize. They also joined PTAs, played school sports, and served on local councils as they embraced the wider community.

Women historically preserve tradition, and Arab women were expected to keep Arab culture alive in their homes. The strong bonds of Arab women's friendships were a source of strength during periods of adjustment. In *Muslim Families in North America*, anthropologist Barbara Aswad writes that "sisterhood is an organizational strategy brought from the Middle East, and it is used extensively to adapt to a new environment."

Even though Arab women were entering the public domain, an area previously reserved exclusively for men, they also remained in charge of the private domain. In Arab culture, a family's honor is judged by how its daughters are raised. Arab girls are expected to be virtuous, to conduct themselves decorously, to be good students, and to help out at home. Arab boys are shown preference and given more freedom than girls since males traditionally hold the dominant role. In some instances the gender inequality is changing as women articulate the need for sexual justice in and out of the home.

The U.S. government's Middle East policy in recent decades has had a profound effect on Arab Americans. Loyal to the United States and proud of their heritage, Arab Americans have sometimes felt alienated by the U.S. government's anti-Arab bias and by a society that seems hostile to their presence. Arabs, especially Muslims, have been disparagingly stereotyped by the U.S. government and media alike. The 1991 bombing of Iraq by the United States generated a patriotic euphoria that discounted the lives of the Arabs who died or were injured. Arab Americans felt marginalized and were left trying to explain this racism to their children.

Arab women are often absent in news coverage. Palestinian women struggling against an occupier as well as gender bias in their own communities have been largely invisible in media reporting. Negative images of Arabs are reinforced on television, in movies, textbooks, comic books, and in the language used to describe them. The Arab as dangerous terrorist or exotic foreigner is an alienating and inaccurate description. Arab women are often perceived as either heavily veiled, austere Muslims or as sexually available belly dancers. Arab women are working to dismantle the stereotypes and to educate Americans about Arab culture and politics. They are writing political analyses and sharing their heritage of poetry. They are writing children's books that portray Arabs in real and interesting ways. Conferences and workshops

are held all over the United States, offering educational tools for understanding early and recent Arab contributions to civilization. Arab art, museum displays, theater, and dance are beginning to flourish throughout the country. And perhaps most important, Arab American women are proudly identifying themselves as Arab American.

As Arab women in the Middle East become more prominent politically, get published more often, and talk openly of a feminist agenda, Arab American women become more public with their concerns. Arab American women's groups can be found on college campuses and in many communities. They are discussing and writing about geopolitics, the environment, and how Arab women fit into the American feminist movement. Arab American women are talking about women's status, economics, education, violence against women, lesbian and gay issues, health concerns, family planning, Islamic law, and color, race, and ethnicity. Women understand that their bodies are viewed simultaneously as sacred and profane and that this perception makes it harder for them to be accepted as full members of society. Many believe that sexism, racism, and other forms of oppression must be fought concurrently in order for true liberation to evolve.

Early economic and cultural assimilation of Arabs into U.S. society resulted in a loss of cultural heritage, but Arab American women are now working to incorporate Arab identity and tradition into their lives in the United States. They want to keep the Arab sense of kinship, the value Arabs place on old people, the intimacy of female friendships, and many of the social traditions. They also expect to be valued as participants in the political, social, economic, and cultural life of the United States.

Louise Cainkar, "Palestinian Women in the United States: Coping with Tradition, Change, and Alienation" (Ph.D. diss., Northwestern University, 1988); Elsa Marston Harik, *The Lebanese in America* (Minneapolis: Lerner Publication Company, 1987); Earle H. Waugh, Sharon M. Abu-Laban, and Regula B. Qureshi, eds., *Mus-*

lim Families in North America (Burlingame: University of Alberta Press, 1991).

■ KAREN HENRY

SEE ALSO Feminism, Arab American.

≋ Architecture

Women's role in U.S. architecture can be seen from several perspectives: women are homemakers, and women are members of the architecture and design professions; women construct transitory gardens and shelters, and they commission or produce permanent buildings and landscape designs.

The architecture profession in the United States has its roots in the nineteenth century, when it was solely a male pursuit. The first architecture schools were storefront operations for carpenters, such as Asher Benjamin's New Hampshire school of the 1790s. Universities did not include architecture departments until after the Civil War. MIT did admit women to its architecture program as early as the 1880s, but Harvard's was closed to women until 1942. In 1915 the Cambridge (Massachusetts) School of Architecture and Landscape Architecture was founded to train women; Eleanor Raymond, a student there from 1917 to 1919, enjoyed a successful forty-five-year career in Boston.

After World War II more U.S. architecture schools admitted and trained women. Civil rights legislation of the 1960s and feminist analyses of the 1970s encouraged some architecture schools to adopt a policy of admitting 50 percent women; schools without such policies average about 30 percent women students and 10 percent women faculty. Salaries for women professional architects were about 50 percent of equally trained men's salaries in the 1960s and increased to about 85 percent of men's by 1993. Only 8.91 percent of AIA members are women, and only 0.64 percent of them are people of color.

Women have been recognized since the nineteenth century as key contributors to domestic architecture, especially to interior design. Nineteenth-century authors claimed that women had the best ideas for house design, since the house is traditionally a woman's workplace as well as her home. Women's nineteenth- and early-twentieth-century contributions to making house architecture more functionally successful are exemplified in Dolores Hayden's *Grand Domestic Revolution*. Attributed with special talent for the interior, professional women thus became specialists in residential architecture or interiors. Some, like Patricia Conway, head of interior design at a major architectural firm, applied their talents to office interiors for skyscrapers of the 1980s.

Nonprofessional women have made informal, "folk," or transitory architecture in diverse settings. Mollie Jenson built "Art Exhibit," a series of outdoor monuments, beginning in the 1930s. She worked in concrete and covered her surfaces with broken shards of ceramics, glass, and other colorful materials from her farm near River Falls, Wisconsin. A 1980s homeless woman, Pixie, erected a tent, flower vase, doll bed, and doll to ornament her appropriated empty-lot garden on Eighth Street, in New York City.

Today there are more well-known professional women architects than ever before in U.S. history: Susanna Torre, Diana Agrest, Sharon Sutton, and Adele Santos provide role models for women entering the profession. Professional landscape architects such as Diana Balmori and Martha Schwartz carry on a tradition dating back to turn-of-the-century women landscape designers such as Beatrix Farrand. Since the 1960s these women have run their own professional practices, served as deans of architecture schools, written important books and essays, and produced a new generation of designs.

■ ELIZABETH C. CROMLEY

SEE ALSO Housing; Suburbanization; Urbanization.

≋ Armed Forces

American women have participated in military operations since the American Revolution, although sometimes in disguise, often without uniforms, and they typically were dismissed once the war was over. In some Native American tribes, women accompanied men to war. White women were allowed inside the regular ranks of the U.S. government's military only in World War I. The WACs, WAVEs, and SPARs of World War II were disbanded in the 1970s. In the mid-1990s women compose a high percentage of the U.S. military's total uniformed personnel during peacetime— 11.8 percent in 1993.

The armed forces also include a high proportion of women of color. While women of all ethnic and racial backgrounds have participated in the armed forces in the past, the 1990s mark the first time that tens of thousands of African American, Latina, Asian American, and Native American women wear the U.S. military uniform, follow orders, and give orders. By 1993 Hispanic women made up 5.2 percent of all women in all three branches on active duty, while Asian American and Native American women together composed 4.4 percent of the women in all three branches. Notably, the Defense Department's 1993 figures about African American women showed that they compose 33.6 percent of all active-duty women and 48 percent of the total 59,668 enlisted women serving in the army. This is a stunning figure to consider, when in the U.S. population, African American women constitute only 12 percent of all women.

The year 1972 marked the turning point for women's entry into the military, particularly women of color. Beginning that year the numbers and percentages of women soldiers on active duty began to climb steadily upward. Also beginning that year African American women began to enlist in especially high numbers. At first glance, one might think that the cause was the second wave of the U.S. women's movement, because the 1970s saw a new national mobilization of women advocating equal rights. But assigning too much weight to this coincidence may tempt one to underestimate the military's own strategies. It also eludes the question of whether women's increasing participation in the military was a sign of genuine liberation for all U.S. women. Some historical background may shed light on the subject.

In 1972 the U.S. government surrendered in Vietnam. While thousands of U.S. women, especially military nurses, had fought in that war, a legal ceiling on the percentage of women who could be accepted as volunteers meant that most U.S. soldiers in Vietnam were young male draftees. In the early 1970s there was a public call for the end of the draft. But continued cold-war ideology presumed that the U.S. military would have to remain large. In this atmosphere Congress and the Defense Department lifted the ceiling on women, calling for more recruits.

Male civilian and military policymakers saw the expanded recruitment of women volunteers as a way to reconcile their desire for a large, educated superpower military force with their political need to end the male draft. They did not give much thought to racial politics regarding women soldiers. The next twenty years' steep rise in the proportion of African American women among all military women went virtually unnoticed by the Pentagon, by Congress, by white feminists, by feminists of color, and by the civil rights and Black nationalist movements. Black women's motivations for enlisting varied, though some speculate that the obstacles facing young poor and working-class African American women in a discriminatory civilian work force were a principal factor.

Even after the draft ended, men were still required to register on their eighteenth birthdays. In *Rostker* v. *Goldberg*, the Supreme Court upheld the government's decision to keep a male-only military registration system. The National Organization for Women objected to this all-male system, arguing that because many Americans thought military service was the touchstone of patriotism, male-only draft registration deprived women of first-class citizenship. Conservative women such as Phyllis Schlafly opposed NOW's position, stating that national well-being depended on a firm division between feminine and masculine public duties. Many progressive women, especially those who had become feminists in the 1960s' antiwar and civil rights movements, were either unaware of *Rostker* v. *Goldberg* as central to women's liberation or explicitly disagreed that women's registration for potential future military conscription would be a step toward first-class citizenship.

Over the next two decades the divisions among women's rights activists persisted. Nonetheless, conservatives in the Pentagon, the White House, Congress, or veterans' organizations sought to restrict military women's duties to traditional noncombat medical and administrative jobs. Feminist representatives in the House of Representatives, particularly Patricia Schroeder, Barbara Boxer, and Beverly Byron, launched successful efforts in the 1980s and early 1990s to dismantle the masculinized "combat" barrier that had prevented so many women from rising to senior ranks in the military. When parts of the formidable conservative alliance tried to cover up sexual harassment perpetrated by Navy pilots during their 1991 Tailhook Convention, a broad alliance of feminists backed Senator Boxer and her colleagues as they pressed defense officials to treat sexual harassment seriously. They and others noted that women soldiers had reported rapes and sexual harassment by their fellow male soldiers for decades without those complaints being taken seriously. "Tailhook '91" was a scandal but not an anomaly.

When President Bill Clinton proposed in 1993 to end the ban on gays and lesbians in the military, his action provoked a national debate. Heretofore women military personnel had been more likely than men to be investigated on charges of homosexuality, perhaps because service commanders wielded the "gay ban" as a misogynist weapon against all women in uniform.

Despite feminists' antisexism consensus, there remains a profound ambivalence toward women's role as soldiers. Should the post–cold war era expect feminists to roll back U.S. militarism in all its forms—including the presumption that being a soldier is the best way to prove one's patriotism and gain first-class citizenship? Some committed women's advocates were not convinced. They believed that militarism wasn't the issue; masculinism was. They began to lobby to keep the reduction in military personnel from providing an excuse for cutting women out of the military. They also saw the declining interest among young men of all races to enlist as a chance for women to enter all four military branches. Their efforts bore fruit: 1993 figures showed that as the military was being "downsized," the trend for women soldiers was heading upward.

The 1990s are a time when U.S. women's roles in the military pose international, not simply domestic, political questions. The 1995 United Nations Conference on Women, in Beijing, was the site of an international debate between advocates who saw women's increased participation at all levels of military service to be a step toward the "demasculinization" of public life and advocates who saw militarism as violent imperialism and thus concluded that pride in soldiering is an essential building block of patriarchy, even when it is women who feel that soldierly pride.

Amanda Maisels and Patricia M. Gormley, *Women in the Military: Where They Stand* (Washington, D.C.: Women's Research and Education Institute, 1994); Office of the Inspector General, U.S. Department of Defense, *The Tailhook Report* (New York: St. Martin's Press, 1993); Rand Corporation, *Sexual Orientation and U.S. Military Personnel Policy: Options and Assessment* (Santa Monica, Calif.: Rand Corporation, 1993).

• CYNTHIA ENLOE

SEE ALSO Aviation; Wars: 1900 to the Present.

≋ Art and Crafts

The contributions by U.S. women to the fields of art and crafts have been significant. Throughout our country's history, women artists have been innovators of style and leaders of movements, blazing a trail for others to follow. Though they often have faced societal disapproval, inadequate educational opportunities, and exclusion by art historians, their determination has only been strengthened by these obstacles, making their achievements all the more meaningful.

Early U.S. society allowed few women outlets for personal expression; therefore most women turned to crafts as the only accepted means of creative expression. These women, largely anonymous, still left us a window into their world. Since no written history ever focused on the lives and experiences of women, crafts became a communication of sorts, through which women told their personal stories.

Hundreds of years before European settlers arrived in this land, Native American women had been creating striking examples of art and crafts: ceramic pottery for storage, woven basket trays for religious ceremonies, intricate embroidery for clothing, and blankets for warmth. Their bold use of color and abstract design is still appreciated and appropriated today.

For the first European settlers, a woman's craftwork meant the very survival of her family. All were dependent on the woman of the house to weave fabric, spin and dye yarn, sew clothes and blankets, knit stockings and scarves—all by hand—to keep them warm and clothed. These items were so valuable that they were used until they literally wore out, the scraps saved to make pieced quilts.

African American women relied on their craftwork as well, not only as a means of personal survival but for the survival of their heritage. Robbed of their homeland and their freedom, slaves fought to keep their African roots alive through songs, narratives, crafts, and so on. Though their craftwork for the plantation households mimicked European styles, the items slave women made for their own personal use had a strong African design sense. Motifs and techniques used in the creation of textiles, quilts, and baskets remained close to the African traditions. Even today, African American basket weaving in South Carolina differs little from original African examples.

As the United States began to grow and prosper, a demand for art grew out of the desire of merchants and landowners to have a tangible record of their wealth. Women artists were active in both portrait styles of the day. One style, adhering to formal European aesthetics, was represented by artists such as Henrietta Johnston; the other, a naive country style, unaware of art theory altogether, can be seen in the charming watercolors of Eunice Pinney, Mary Ann Willson, and of Deborah Goldsmith—one of the few itinerant women artists.

Crafts at this time also mirrored the country's increasing wealth. Women of the upper classes now had leisure time to create intricately embroidered bed hangings, petticoats, and seat cushions, as well as woven coverlets and stitched quilts.

The greatest challenge facing women artists as they entered the nineteenth century was the lack of proper education. Young ladies' academies, where craft skills such as embroidery were taught, flourished at this time, but true art education for women was not equal to that available to men. Not surprisingly many women who had become successful artists up until that time were related to well-known male artists.

Society considered it unthinkable for women to draw from the nude figure, as it would undoubtedly endanger their delicate sensibilities. As the century progressed art schools such as the Pennsylvania Academy of Fine Arts and the National Academy of Design opened their doors to women students. In 1868 women were allowed to draw from the female nude; in 1877, the male nude. It was not until well into the twentieth century, however, that drawing classes became coeducational.

Despite these drawbacks women artists made great strides during this period. Ann Hall, known for her delicate miniature paintings, was the first woman to become a full member of the National Academy of Design. Sarah Miriam Peale was a leading portraitist in Baltimore and St. Louis, forgoing marriage and motherhood to dedicate herself to her craft. Of African and Native ancestry, Edmonia Lewis became the first Black sculptor to receive white recognition and joined a group of U.S. women sculptors in Rome, where Ulysses S. Grant posed for her.

The late nineteenth century was an exciting time both for art and for crafts. Traveling abroad became an option chosen by more women art students, such as May Alcott, sister of Louisa May Alcott, an academic painter who exhibited in the Paris Salon and even wrote a guidebook for U.S. women interested in studying in Paris. Mary Cassatt became our nation's first impressionist, working alongside the leading men in the movement. Women such as Alice Austen even ventured into the new and relatively unknown world of photography.

The arts and crafts movement, started in England during the 1870s, helped lift crafts to the level of art for the first time in the modern world. The movement, a reaction to the aesthetic void created by the Industrial Revolution, sought to return to the days when items were skillfully and lovingly made by hand. Socially prominent women, seeing this not only as a chance to support the arts but also as a way to advance women's causes, brought the theories of the arts and crafts movement to the United States. Upper-class, middle-class, rural, and immigrant women were recruited to put their craft skills to use in any number of the many women's industries that sprang up around the country (for example, the Cincinnati Women's Pottery Club, the Providence Handicraft Club, and the Society of Decorative Art of New York City). The arts and crafts movement ul-

Sampler worked by Anne Anthony at age ten in 1786, Newport, Rhode Island. The design — featuring a house with figures, the alphabet, and floral motifs — is typical of the genre.

timately came to an end in the early twentieth century when it could no longer compete with more affordable manufactured items, but the legitimacy it brought to crafts would endure.

The twentieth century was a time of great change, for the country, the art world, and the lives of women. The success of the suffrage movement, as well as increased work and educational opportunities, indicates the changing role of women in U.S. society. A new artistic freedom arose as the strict aesthetic ideals of the nineteenth century faded. Painter Georgia O'Keeffe, whose career spanned most of the century, signified this new freedom by creating a style all her own. Margaret Bourke-White, Dorothea Lange, and Diane Arbus became strong new voices in the field of photography. And a revival in the interest of Native American crafts brought to light the work of craftswomen such as Pueblo potters Maria Montoya Martinez and Helen Cordero, the inventor of the storyteller figure.

Hawaii became a U.S. territory in 1900 and Hawaiian traditional craftwork gained greater notice on the mainland. Intricately woven mats and baskets were appreciated for their fine workmanship, while the Hawaiian women's unique twist on quilting—bright, cut-out patterns appliquéd onto a white top—created a distinctive style.

The 1930s was an incredibly active time for artists and craftspeople in the United States and a period unique in U.S. history for its opportunities for women. Federally funded arts programs such as the Federal Art Project and the Works Progress Administration (WPA) had strict equal opportunity hiring standards so women artists were fairly represented. Women, in numbers unheard of up until this time, were commissioned to create public murals, sculptures, and mosaics, and hired to lead administrative and decision-making groups. African American sculptor Augusta Savage served as the director of the Harlem Community Art Center, one of the largest of the many community art centers set up around the country under the WPA.

The decades following World War II saw the decline of these federally funded art projects, and with them the equal opportunities for women artists. But these years were also some of the most exciting times in terms of art. The United States became the center of the art world as leading international artists fled turmoil in their own countries. Women artists seized the opportunity to study with artists such as Arshile Gorky, Hans Hofmann, and Anni Albers, the famous Bauhaus weaver whose abstract works first hinted at the future of fiber art. Lee Krasner and Elaine de Kooning were active in the abstract expressionist movement, while Louise Nevelson and Louise Bourgeois helped redefine U.S. sculpture.

The feminist movement of the 1960s and 1970s brought to light injustices against women in all walks of life; the art world was no exception. Though women historically had been active participants in all major art movements, they were rarely mentioned in art history texts or included in museum exhibitions.

Women artists joined together, demanding their fair share of gallery and museum space as well as critical evaluation of their work. Colleges, such as the California Institute of the Arts, began teaching courses on women's art. Women's art journals and cooperative galleries flourished.

Feminist artists turned the male-dominated art world on its ear, challenging all its established formulas. Painter Sylvia Sleigh reversed the traditional roles of "clothed male painter, female nude model," and instead painted a series of lounging nude males. Artists such as Judy Chicago and Miriam Schapiro adopted a female "language" by incorporating traditional craft materials such as fabric, thread, and ceramics into their art.

This use of craft materials brought about a revival of crafts as art. Innovative fiber artists such as Lenore Tawney and Sheila Hicks wove, twisted, and tied fabric into large sculptural forms. Potters Toshiko Takaezu and Karen Karnes turned clay into sensuous forms, covered in slips of glaze, opaque, transparent or iridescent. Black women artists were creating powerful, politically charged artwork at this time, though they received only limited support from both the feminist movement, because of racism, and the civil rights movement, because of sexism.

The strong artistic legacy of sculptor Edmonia Lewis of the nineteenth century was followed by the twentieth-century work of painter Lois Mailou Jones and sculptor Augusta Savage of the Harlem Renaissance, as well as color field artist Alma Thomas. These women paved the way for sculptors Elizabeth Catlett and Barbara Chase-Riboud, assemblage artist Betye Saar, and Faith Ringgold, whose own use of craft materials spoke of both Black and female experience.

Ethnic pride as a subject matter in modern art spread as Latina artists also began to examine their roots and reclaim their artistic heritage. Muralists Judith Baca and Judithe Hernandez and printmakers Carmen Lomas Garza and Linda Vallejo drew upon experiences in their communities and created images of hope for the future.

The feminist art movement made a difference. In today's art world—known as *postmodern*—art is no longer a mere examination of aesthetic questions but an evaluation of society. Art is an opinion; the art world is the forum. Women artists use their work to fight discrimination against women, people of color, lesbians, and gays.

The acceptable means of expression have grown dramatically. Dolls, lipstick, even chocolate, are used in collages, installations, and performance art. Sexist images in popular culture are confronted in Cindy Sherman's photographs and Barbara Kruger's thought-provoking text laid over black-and-white images. And activist groups such as Guerrilla Girls post statistics in exhibition spaces and on the streets documenting the sexism and racism still prevalent in the art culture.

Film and video art is another popular medium for women artists today. This medium allows women a more direct way to illustrate their visions, tell their personal stories, or starkly portray the prejudice they may have encountered throughout their lives. Active contemporary filmmakers include Asian Americans Shu Lea Cheang and Christine Chang, African American Julie Dash, Mexican American Lourdes Portillo, lesbian Sadie Benning, and African American lesbians Michelle Parkerson and Cheryl Dunyé.

Increased research and scholarship in women's art and crafts are another important result of the feminist art movement. In the past women artists and craftspeople were rarely mentioned in relevant art books. Today libraries and research centers abound. Courses on women's art are taught regularly in art history departments of major universities around the country. The American Craft Museum and the American Craft Council, both in New York City, are dedicated to the further study and appreciation of U.S. crafts.

Finally, after years of hard work and self-sacrifice, the monumental achievements of women artists and craftspeople are being acknowledged. The stories of this country's talented mothers, daughters, and sisters will continue to inspire generations of creative women to come.

Eileen Boris, "Crossing Boundaries: The Gendered Meaning of the Arts and Crafts," in *The Ideal Home 1900–1920: The History of 20th Century American Craft* (New York: Harry N. Abrams, Inc., 1993); Charlotte Streifer Rubinstein, *American Women Artists from Early Indian Times to the Present* (Boston: G. K. Hall & Co., 1982).

▪ MARIE LUISE PROELLER

SEE ALSO Art Criticism; Decorative Arts; Film; Guerrilla Girls; Painting; Photography; Quilting; Sculpture.

≋ Art Criticism

A rt students and art historians are taught that good art is not supposed to have a sex. But the field of art criticism reveals underlying patterns of gender discrimination that compel readers to take a harder, more skeptical look at the sexual politics of the discipline, which is rooted in patriarchal attitudes.

Feminist art criticism, as its name implies, is criticism with a cause. It is about transforming institutions, not just interpreting art, but changing how one sees culture and its relationship to images. During the 1970s, running counter to the mainstream, women critics (and a few good men) forged a new feminist art criticism based on the work of artists who struggled to redefine themselves within the "art-for-art's-sake" tradition. Women artists rebelled against participating in culture on male terms, choosing instead subjects including birth, motherhood, rape, household imagery, menstruation, autobiography, family and friends, and organic abstractions inspired by real women's experiences.

Feminist artists and critics inveighed against the sheer foolishness of a social system that excluded at least half its finest potential leaders, making them mere handmaidens to culture. It was still common practice to disregard women, to strip them of self-confidence, to refer to a married woman or a mother as a dilettante, and to treat women as sex objects. Self-consciousness of femaleness and its position in patriarchal culture opened new contexts in which to see and evaluate art.

In the 1970s Lucy Lippard's widely read *From the Center* expanded the audience for and dialogue about feminist criticism. Mainstream trade journals such as *Art in America*, *Arts*, and *Artforum* felt obliged to include a few articles on women. Alternative magazines founded by women included *The Feminist Art Journal* (1972–77), *Womanspace Journal* (1973), *Womanart* (1976–78), *Chrysalis* (1977–80), *Women Artists News* (1975–91), *Heresies* (1977 to the present), and *Woman's Art Journal*, which survives the current backlash against feminism.

During the decade of the 1980s and into the 1990s, the death of modern art ushered in a new movement known as postmodernism. In this period, women of color and lesbians reoriented feminism. Debates about pornography and censorship divided feminists. Much late-1980s feminist art criticism dissolved into a male-dominated postmodernist view focusing on theory. Simultaneously, artists and critics moved back to upholding male supremacy, again making the male a normative standard of "serious" art and criticism.

Today major differences of opinion among feminist artists and critics about how best to achieve goals as well as questions about what those goals are continue to expand feminist discourse.

                                        • CASSANDRA LANGER

SEE ALSO Art and Crafts; Guerrilla Girls.

≋ Asian Immigrant Women Advocates

Founded in November 1983 by women workers, activists, and community organizers, Asian Immigrant Women Advocates (AIWA) began as an Oakland-based organization to address working conditions in the San Francisco–Oakland Bay Area. Many of these workers, who are not unionized, work in the apparel industry, which employs twenty thousand seamstresses, 85 percent of whom are Asian immigrant women. AIWA has also worked with women in other industries—hotel, restaurant, janitorial, nursing home, and electronics. In 1990 AIWA opened a second office in San Jose to reach electronics assemblers in Santa Clara County's "Silicon Valley." At present, the organization has a membership base of over eight hundred and an active worker membership board.

Sensitive to the fact that Asian immigrant women face multiple barriers to organizing (cultural and social history in Asia, fears of retribution from employers, and language barriers), AIWA's organizing strategies have been diverse and above all community-based. AIWA is guided by a grassroots approach that seeks to empower women in their workplace and democratize leadership through popular education. Over its history, women have been educated about wage laws, occupational health and safety issues, and other issues related to workers' rights. Workplace English literacy classes, which have included Chinese, Korean, and Vietnamese women, have been an important component of the organizing mission. Instruction is designed to help women directly address problems in the workplace.

In addition, AIWA's advocacy work has also assumed a more broad-based approach, challenging each targeted industry's unfair or illegal practices, through boycotts, media campaigns, and legislative reform. Finally, as a multiethnic, multioccupational organization, AIWA has also formed alliances with other worker groups across the nation—Asian, Latino/a, and African American. With the globalization of industry in search of cheap labor, these linkages have further extended to include workers in countries such as Hong Kong, Korea, and Mexico.

• DEBORAH WOO

≋ Asian Law Alliance

Modeled after the Asian Law Caucus, the Asian Law Alliance (ALA) was founded by University of Santa Clara law students in 1975 to provide individual legal assistance, educational programs, and community advocacy for Asian Americans in the San Jose, California, area. The ALA specializes in civil rights, housing, labor, and immigration issues. Primarily serving low-income clients, the ALA handles approximately three hundred fifty cases and fifteen hundred consultations per year. Multilingual pamphlets and community workshops also inform Asian Americans of their legal rights.

The ALA has helped vacate the convictions of Japanese Americans who contested World War II curfew and internment orders; lobbied for enhanced penalties for hate crimes; and campaigned against the elimination of bilingual services. Since 1980 the ALA has exchanged legal resources and planned joint educational activities with the Asian Law Caucus and La Raza Centro Legal to protect the rights of legal immigrants and undocumented residents.

In 1995 five of the ALA's eight staff members were women. Women constitute between 60 and 70 percent of all ALA clients. Many of these female clients seek ALA advice or representation in cases of housing and employment discrimination. The ALA also has developed services specifically for women who are victims of domestic violence. Multilingual pamphlets inform battered women of their legal rights and the availability of ALA legal services. The ALA represents battered spouses in divorce and child custody cases and helps victims of domestic violence obtain restraining orders against abusive partners. The ALA also lobbied for a provision in the Violence Against Women Act to grant battered spouses the right to file petitions for permanent residency.

• ALICE YANG MURRAY

≋ Asian Law Caucus

The first legal organization to focus on Asian American community problems, the Asian Law Caucus (ALC) primarily services low-income residents in the San Francisco area. It was founded in 1972 by a small group of lawyers representing Asian Americans who were conscientious objectors during the Vietnam War. Often representing recent immigrants and refugees who lack English language skills, the ALC handles an average of five hundred cases and more than one thousand consultations annually. Caucus attorneys specialize in litigation and public education on civil rights, landlord-tenant, employment, and immigration issues. Between 1983 and 1986, caucus lawyers helped vacate the convictions of Japanese Americans who challenged World War II curfew and internment orders. Working with Latino/a activists, the caucus also mounted unsuccessful campaigns against the 1986 "English-only" amendment to the California State Constitution and against California's 1994 Proposition 187, aimed at denying government health and educational services to illegal immigrants.

In 1995 three out of four full-time ALC staff members were women. These staff members have helped male and female clients protest substandard housing, unfair evictions, and employment discrimination. Women constitute most of the ALC clients in cases involving garment workers and victims of domestic violence. In a 1993 landmark California case, ALC attorney Lora Jo Foo successfully represented fourteen female garment workers who sued a clothing manufacturer, Moviestar Garments, for wages owed by its subcontractor. ALC also successfully lobbied for a provision in the Violence Against Women Act to grant battered spouses the right to file petitions for permanent residency.

▪ ALICE YANG MURRAY

≋ Asian Pacific Women

Between 1800 and 1920, approximately half a million Asians, predominantly from China and Japan but also from Korea, the Philippines, and India, came to the United States. Three common experiences mark the history of these early immigrants. Unlike the majority of their compatriots who went to Southeast Asia, Latin America, and the Caribbean, Asian immigrants to the United States were mostly male and, with the exception of Japan, migrated from colonized countries. The history of Asian immigration to the United States prior to World War II was contoured by various types of immigration legislation designed to restrict and prevent large-scale Asian immigration. Many of these restrictions applied specifically to the immigration of women and consequently slowed family formation and the development of the second generation.

The first Asians to arrive in the United States came to the East Coast in the early nineteenth century. Records exist of at least one Indian man in Philadelphia who was brought as a servant by an American trader and sold as a slave around 1804. The first U.S. envoy to China came back with one Malay and five Chinese servants in 1798. The first Chinese community in the United States emerged in New York in the 1840s and 1850s, when some Chinese merchants and sailors settled there and married Irish women. The first recorded Asian woman in the United States was Afong Moy. Between 1834 and 1847, she sat every day surrounded with Chinese lanterns, vases, and Asian artifacts at the American Museum, the Brooklyn Institute, and other New York locations. She talked and counted in Chinese and ate with chopsticks to entertain the thousands who lined up to see her. Barnum's Chinese Museum later brought over Miss Pwan-ye-koo and her maidservant with great fanfare. The small, bound feet of both women were a prime attraction. This objectification of Asian women and their portrayal as alien and exotic creatures is one dimension of American popular culture that has endured until the contemporary period.

More Chinese women began to arrive on the West Coast. Maria Seise went to work in Hawaii for an American family in 1837 and was brought as a domestic by her missionary employer to San Francisco in 1848. Ah Choi (sometimes called Ah Toy) arrived soon after and became a legendary beauty and the owner of her own brothel. Such Chinese immigrant women were few; between 1848 and 1854, only sixteen women arrived from China while the number of men arriving totaled 45,000. By 1870, 58,625 Chinese men and 4,574 Chinese women had arrived in the United States.

Initially, California, much like the rest of the U.S. West, had a predominantly male population, among not only the Chinese but all immigrants. In 1850, there were twelve men for every woman in San Francisco, regardless of race; even in 1880, men outnumbered women in California three to one. The imbalance in gender ratio, the gold-rush economy, and frontier conditions made prostitution a booming industry. Chinese prostitution, organized by Chinese Mafia-like business associations, proliferated. Ah Choi, as an independent operator, was the exception. Of the 1,769 Chinese women over the age of fifteen found living in San Francisco in 1870, as many as 1,452 worked as prostitutes; the vast majority were bonded sex workers. Some women managed to complete their terms of indenture and married Chinese men once free.

As the cult of domesticity and motherhood increasingly defined the female ideal of the Anglo-American middle classes, moral issues like prostitution and unwed motherhood captured public attention. The dismal conditions of Chinese prostitution were singled out for special opprobrium by the denizens of California and by the nation as a whole. Moral politics directed toward the Chinese also addressed polygamy, concubinage, female infanticide, foot binding, and the sale of girls and women. Reformers and nativists criticized victimization of Chinese women and labeled a people who treated their women so poorly "unassimilable." The Page Act, introduced in California in 1870 and passed by Congress in 1875, was entitled "An Act to Prevent the Kidnapping and Importation of Mongolian, Chinese and Japanese Females for Demoralizing Purposes." The law assumed that all Asian women entering the country were doing so for "criminal and demoralizing purposes" unless proven otherwise. This effectively ended the immigration of unmarried Asian women to the United States.

The relative ease with which this legislation was passed indicated the strength of the anti-Chinese movement. In 1882, on the heels of the Page Act, the Chinese Exclusion Act became the first federal exclusion law directed at a specific nationality. The law suspended Chinese labor immigration and prohibited all Chinese, other than merchants, students, diplomats, and visitors, from entering the country.

With restrictions on Chinese labor immigration, agribusiness interests turned to Japanese and Korean sources to help develop Californian and Hawaiian agriculture. The penetration of capitalism and the political economy of sugar had altered the Hawaiian economy by the end of the nineteenth century. Queen Lili'uokalani was deposed in 1893 and the islands were formally annexed by the United States in 1898. As increasing

---

ASIAN PACIFIC WOMEN

For more on the history of Asian American women, see the following entries:

Asian Immigrant Women Advocates
Asian Law Alliance
Asian Law Caucus
Chinatowns
Chinese American Women
Chinese Exclusion Act
Feminism, Asian American
Filipinas
Japanese American Citizens League
Japanese American Internment
Japanese American Women
Korean American Women
Lesbians, Asian American
Picture Brides
South Asian American Women
Vietnamese American Women

---

numbers of the indigenous Hawaiian people succumbed to diseases against which they had no immunity, the sugar planters turned to Asia for labor. In 1865 the recruiters brought 521 Chinese, including ninety-five women and thirteen children, to Hawaii. The recruiters turned to Japan, Korea, and the Philippines for more laborers. Japanese immigration to Hawaii and the mainland began in significant numbers in the 1890s. By 1920 the Japanese population of Hawaii was almost 110,000, with 21,000 Filipinos and close to 5,000 Koreans. Unlike the Chinese situation, the Japanese government supervised its citizens' emigration. Plantation owners and the Meiji government considered women a stabilizing social influence and recruiters from Hawaii actively sought couples. Women were brought as contract laborers to work in the cane fields, and as cooks, laundresses, and seamstresses.

Under pressure from anti-Asian nativists, Japanese immigration to Hawaii and the mainland, as well as Korean immigration, was curtailed by the Gentlemen's Agreement of 1907. Other labor emigration, such as from India to the West Coast, was also closed off by the passage of the Asiatic Barred Zone Act of 1917, which excluded all entrants except merchants, students, and diplomats from regions lying to the east of an imaginary line drawn from the Ural Mountains to the Red Sea, dividing the continent of Asia.

The 1924 National Origins Act firmly terminated further immigration from Japan and the Asian mainland. Filipinos, who could emigrate as U.S. nationals after annexation in 1898, were declared aliens and subjected to restrictive immigration laws under the Tydings-McDuffie Act of 1934. For Asians residing in the United States, hostile laws restricted opportunity and mobility.

Between 1913 and 1923, several states enacted measures preventing Asian immigrants from owning land. Under the Naturalization Acts of 1790 and 1870, which limited naturalized citizenship to "free whites" and "persons of African nativity or descent," Asians could not become U.S. citizens.

Anti-Asian sentiment focused especially on Asian women. For example, there were three Indian wives in California by 1910. When the fourth one arrived, newspaper headlines declared, "Hindu women next swarm to California." Only the Japanese American community was able to establish families with anything approaching a balanced gender ratio. Under the terms of the Gentlemen's Agreement, those men already married could send for their wives or, if unmarried, bachelors could send for wives through arranged marriages validated by an exchange of photographs, giving rise to the term *picture brides*. Koreans, as colonial subjects of Japan after 1910, were also able to send for picture brides. However, in most of the Asian communities gender ratios remained extremely uneven until the 1940s.

The presence of women seemingly had a "steadying influence" on the workers. But the labor activism of Japanese women in a 1909 strike convinced Hawaiian plantation owners recruiting Filipinos that there was little advantage in having female immigrants. Filipinos could not hope for conditions permitting family emigration like the

Japanese. Antimiscegenation laws in California and Washington prevented Asians from marrying whites. Some Indian and Filipino men married Mexican American women. A few Indians and Filipinos married African American women in California, as did several Chinese men in Illinois and in Mississippi. Marginalized politically, barred from naturalization, and subject to the laws of segregated schooling and housing, the different Asian communities in the United States all faced a struggle for survival.

Life for the first generation of Asian American women varied enormously based on their class and their location within the American economy. Chinese American communities were located primarily in urban centers, where the majority of women worked as laundresses, seamstresses, housekeepers, clerks, storekeepers, and gardeners. The wives of wealthier Chinese merchants living in the Chinatowns of San Francisco and Los Angeles prior to 1900 did not work outside the home, usually had bound feet, and did not appear in public except for special occasions.

After 1900, as the revolutionary sentiments of the anti-Manchu Republican Nationalist movement found supporters among the overseas Chinese, the reformist agendas of this movement regarding the status of women also began to change Chinatowns. American-born Chinese daughters as well as sons attended schools. By 1910 over 64 percent of the Chinese American women were native born, and by 1940, American-born women represented over 72 percent of the community's women. Several Chinese American women trained as doctors, teachers, and dentists prior to World War II. But until the late 1930s and the 1940s, when antagonism toward Chinese Americans decreased, most found that professional careers in the majority white community were closed to them.

The invasion of China by Japan in 1937 marked the beginning of World War II in the Pacific. When the United States entered World War II following the bombing of Pearl Harbor, it became a military ally of the Chinese. The 120,000 people of Japanese ancestry living on the West Coast were deemed potential traitors and President Roosevelt ordered their internment. For the Chinese American community, however, the status of China as an ally and the general expansion of the American economy in the interwar years provided opportunities for integration into the mainstream. Chinese American women took production jobs in the defense industry and clerical jobs in the U.S. bureaucracy.

When Madame Chiang Kai-shek, the Wellesley College–educated wife of the Chinese political leader, addressed the U.S. House and Senate in 1943 as an American ally, the issues of Chinese exclusion and denial of citizenship through naturalization were embarrassing to the U.S. government. The Chinese Exclusion Act of 1882 was repealed and Chinese immigrants became eligible for citizenship through naturalization. By 1952 naturalization rights were extended to Asians generally. That year, immigration from Asia was also opened up on a quota basis for between 100 and 120 immigrants annually from each Asian group. The intense military activity in the Pacific and the dislocation of local economies through the entry and then withdrawal of U.S. naval bases also led to migration from Guam and Samoa to Hawaii and California. The traditional gender imbalance within the Asian American communities changed under the War Brides Act in the late 1940s.

Although the Asian American community increased in the postwar period, the approximately two million Asian Americans in the country by 1970 formed an almost insignificant minority group, politically visible only in California, Washington, and Hawaii. The economy's expansion in the U.S. West enabled many to move into white-collar and pink-collar jobs. For example, compared to the almost 30 percent of Chinese American women in domestic service and 8 percent in professional categories in 1940, 17 percent were in professional categories and 38 percent in clerical and sales by 1960. By contrast, Native Hawaiian women and Filipino men earned far less than Chinese or Japanese men and women in Hawaii in 1970.

Urbanization, the dispersal of communities and increased contact with the majority culture, led to outmarriage, beginning with the second generation in several communities. But resurgent ethnic identity politics also fostered tighter links in some communities, where interracial dating and marriage remained taboo down through the 1960s.

Like the rest of the country, Asian America was changed by the events and activism of the late 1960s and early 1970s. The involvement of Asian Americans in the civil rights movement, the antiwar movement, and campus activism for ethnic studies and curricular changes brought forth a new generation of women activists. Organizations such as the Nisei Women's Forum began consciousness-raising meetings that also reopened discussions about the internment camp experience. University of California, Berkeley, students organized International Women's Day celebrations in San Francisco's Chinatown. Several women in Los Angeles, San Francisco, and Honolulu led community efforts to resist real-estate developers who sought to demolish old Asian American neighborhoods and housing for the elderly. Others traveled to Canada to meet North Vietnamese women and began speaking out against the Vietnam War.

The Asian American community also radically changed as a result of expanded immigration from Asia, which emerged with new immigration legislation in 1965. These immigrants, many from different national backgrounds in Asia than those of earlier arrivals, are overwhelmingly from the urban, educated middle classes. Their experiences in the U.S. economy are thus unlike those of earlier generations of immigrants. The challenges women in these recent immigrant communities face and the opportunities open to them are different from the issues confronting nineteenth- and early-twentieth-century immigrants.

■ SUCHETA MAZUMDAR

≋ Atlanta Washerwomen's Strike

In July 1881 African American washerwomen in Atlanta formalized the Washing Society and launched a strike to protect their autonomy and demand higher fees for their services. The initial organizers expanded their ranks from twenty to three thousand and generated broad support within the Black community by canvassing houses from door to door. Churches provided sanctuaries for meetings and disseminated information. White employers and city authorities arrested the strikers for "disorderly conduct," threatened to levy an exorbitant business tax on each member of the Washing Society, and proposed building a competing laundry facility to minimize the leverage of the women's monopoly. Undaunted, the women wrote a defiant open letter to the mayor outlining their grievances and demanding respect for their labor.

There is no conclusive evidence about the strike's resolution. But even the *Atlanta Constitution*, the opposition's unofficial mouthpiece, admitted that the women were effectively organized. Moreover, the strike was symbolically meaningful. The laundry workers' protest sharply contrasted with the image of docile southern workers depicted by the city's business and political elite. The washerwomen demonstrated an astute political consciousness by making domestic labor a public issue in a city where white households relied on Black women's labor as laundresses, cooks, maids, or child nurses. Their action was a pointed reminder to the city that African American women's labor was vital to the political economy of the New South.

■ TERA W. HUNTER

SEE ALSO Strikes.

≋ Autobiography

When Europeans arrived on U.S. shores in the seventeenth century, they began recording their experiences of their new country. Since then, autobiography has become perhaps the preeminent form of U.S. writing. Critics note that qualities in autobiography, such as the valorization of individualism and focus on success, suit our national character. Readers respond to the personal authority in autobiography that suggests direct contact between writers and readers. Young people find role models in the stories of women and men who overcome obstacles and achieve successes. The popularity of autobiographies of U.S. sports figures and entertainment personalities indicates an identification with those writers. Today, thanks to the civil rights and feminist movements of the 1960s and 1970s, more white women as well as women and men of various racial and ethnic groups write and publish autobiography for popular audiences and scholars. In academia, research on and teaching about women's lives bring the history of women's autobiography to the general public.

White teenage girls and well-to-do white women who kept diaries and journals contributed to the earliest U.S. autobiography—the mostly religious and spiritual Puritan tradition of the seventeenth and eighteenth centuries. Most other colonial women had neither the leisure nor the literacy to participate. Extant documents from that period include religious and secular accounts of domestic life and travel. Anne Dudley Bradstreet (1612–72), the first recognized U.S. woman writer, honored for her 1650 poetic work *Tenth Muse Lately Sprung up in America*, included autobiography in these domestic poems. And in 1660, an ill Bradstreet wrote a short autobiographical prose narrative, "To My Dear Children," which reviewed her life, questioned providence, and encouraged her children in piety. But the most distinctive women's self-stories of the period were those by white women in captivity: the U.S.'s first unique autobiographical form. The writings were religious narratives by white women captured by Native Americans during times of unrest between settlers and Native peoples and later released. The most celebrated is Mary Rolandson's 1682 work, *A True History of the Captivity and Restoration of Mrs. Mary Rolandson, a Minister's Wife in New England*. The subject matter of women's and men's autobiographies during the seventeenth century was similar; female perspectives on those times made major contributions to the tradition.

Puritan autobiography continued in the nineteenth century, and increases in literacy permitted women to expand the boundaries of the domestic autobiography with stories of unhappy childhoods and marriages; of experiences in prisons, mental institutions, or convents; and of women who assumed disguises in search of adventure, escape, or to enter military service. During the "American Renaissance" (1820–ca. 1850), when a large number of popular women novelists flourished, one of the most interesting women's autobiographies was the unfinished *Memoirs* of Margaret Fuller. In the second half of the century, pioneer women going west as missionaries or accompanying their families in search of better economic conditions wrote journals, letters, and other forms of narrative that addressed women's isolation, fears of childbearing, and other privations. Toward the end of the century, improvements in women's social, political, and economic conditions led to the emergence of reform minded and feminist women (mostly white and middle class), including the suffragists, who wrote seriously of women's lives and careers. Women from this group included Frances Elizabeth Willard, temperance movement activist; Elizabeth Blackwell, first woman to graduate from a U.S. medical school; and Elizabeth Cady Stanton, a major intellectual figure of the women's movement in that era.

While white citizens struggled to shape their identity from the seventeenth through much of the nineteenth century, in their writing and in other ways they denied almost entirely the humanity of African slaves, their descendants, and free Black people. Except in abolitionist literature, there is little mention of Blacks in writings of the period. But slaves and Black nonslaves alike, rejecting dehumanization, struggled for almost two hundred years to liberate themselves from the physical and psychological chains of their treatment. Writing about the self was a weapon of struggle. By the end of the eighteenth century the Black spiritual narrative and the slave narrative — the latter the predominant genre in early Black writing as well as the second of the two unique forms of U.S. autobiography — emerged from this community. Spiritual narrators claimed selfhood through access to the love and forgiveness of a Black-appropriated Christian God. Slave narrators, aiming their words toward Northern white sympathizers, used personal experiences in direct, immediate voices to develop the most persuasive antislavery literature of the century. For women slave narrators, their written quest articulated the twin wrongs of racial and gender oppression. The most renowned of these is Harriet Jacobs's 1861 story, *Incidents in the Life of a Slave Girl*, published under the pseudonym Linda Brent. The first Black slave woman to make her own written plea against the sexual tyranny of slavery, Jacobs wrote of early-childhood circumstances that shielded her from the horrors of slavery, of her coming-to-awareness of her condition, and her determination to be free. After hiding for seven years in a crawlspace under the roof of her grandmother's house, she escaped a lascivious master and concluded her story with a superb feminist analysis of the meaning of freedom for Black women.

U.S. women's autobiography in the twentieth century has flourished, with an astonishing diversity that blends the voices of Native American, Latina, Asian American women, and women of different classes, educational backgrounds, and sexual orientations, with those of Black and white women who founded this tradition. Women's narratives, once neglected for their differences from conventional male autobiography, now self-assuredly engage brilliant experiments in textual self-creation. For example, Maxine Hong Kingston's *The Woman Warrior: Memories of a Childhood Among Ghosts* combines the mythical world of her Chinese heritage with the realism of her adopted world in the United States; Kim Chernin's *In My Mother's House* brings together autobiography, biography, history, and fiction; Maya Angelou almost entirely fictionalizes *I Know Why the Caged Bird Sings*; and Cherríe Moraga skillfully combines languages and genres in *Loving in the War Years*. Women's autobiography, in its great medley today, celebrates women's lives and, to borrow from critic Margo Culley, offers splendid "fea(s)ts of reading."

Joanne M. Braxton, *Black Women Writing Autobiography: A Tradition Within a Tradition* (Philadelphia: Temple University Press, 1989); Margo Culley, *American Women's Autobiography: Fea(s)ts of Memory* (Madison: University of Wisconsin Press, 1992); Estelle C. Jelinek, *The Tradition of Women's Autobiography: From Antiquity to the Present* (Boston: G. K. Hall & Company, 1986).

▪ NELLIE Y. MCKAY

SEE ALSO Literature.

≋ Aviation

W omen in aviation, like most women who entered the public realm of society designated solely for men, had a precarious beginning. Men did not believe that women were emotionally stable enough to pilot airplanes. Some women succeeded in piloting their own planes and others eventually procured pilots' licenses, irrespective of prevailing chauvinistic attitudes. Indeed, several women convinced some of the most intransigent pioneering male aviators to train them. They were white, usually upper class, and were permitted to purchase private planes.

Women entered aviation as entertainers by way of barnstorming. Blanche Stuart Scott (1889–1970) from Rochester, New York, became the first U.S. aviatrix in 1910. Harriet Quimby (1875–1912) was the first woman to fly across the English Channel. Ruth Law, the first woman to fly at night, set a non-stop distance record in 1916 for both men and women by performing sixteen consecutive loops. Her expert stunt flying earned her the reputation as a daredevil of the sky; she won many honors for breaking and establishing flight records and is credited with launching nighttime airmail between Chicago and New York. Katherine Stinson, the first woman airmail carrier (1913), a stunt flyer and also a pioneering skywriter, studied with Maximillian Theodore Liljestrand (Max Lillie). Marjorie, her younger sister, graduated from the Wright School of Aviation in Dayton, Ohio, in 1914. She was the youngest licensed pilot in the United States and in 1915 became the only woman inducted into the U.S. Aviation Reserve. The same year their mother, Emma, established the Stinson Aviation Company in San Antonio, Texas, where during the war the three women trained Canadian pilots for the British Air Force.

Perhaps the most renowned aviatrix, Amelia Earhart (1898–1937), the first woman to fly solo across the Atlantic (1937), was trained by Netta Snooks, who had difficulty gaining entrance into aviation school because males excluded her. By 1921, however, when she acquired Earhart as a pupil, Snooks had attended two different aviation schools. Another name synonymous with aviation is Charles Lindbergh, whose wife, Anne Morrow Lindbergh (b. 1907), was a skilled aviatrix who assisted him on many flights as copilot, navigator, radio operator, and photographer.

If men were predisposed to excluding women from aviation, many white aviators, whose views were reinforced by segregation laws in every sector of U.S. society, advocated exclusion of African Americans from this field predicated entirely on racist attitudes and beliefs, such as Charles Lindbergh's, that African Americans were mentally incapable of piloting an airplane.

Bessie Coleman (1896–1926), an African American, like some of her white counterparts, utilized barnstorming to gain a foothold in aviation. When her efforts to enroll in a U.S. aviation school proved futile, she enrolled in France, where she received her international pilot's license in 1921. She was the first American to be awarded this type of license, which permitted her to fly anywhere in the world. Coleman chose, however, to return to the United States to establish an aviation school and use her barnstorming skills in exhibition flights to convince other African Americans to pursue a career in aviation. She was hailed by airmen and aircraft engineers in France, Germany, Holland, and Switzerland as the "greatest aviatrix in the world, even surpassing the marvelous record made by the famous Ruth Law."

Coleman's flight activities bolstered the confidence of other African Americans to undertake aviation, but prevailing racism continued to curtail African American involvement in the field. When Janet Harmon Bragg (née Waterford, 1907–93), a registered nurse and licensed aviatrix, answered a recruitment telegram for women pilots in 1943 to transport military aircraft across the country and to England, she was rejected by Ethel Sheehy, vice president of the Ninety-Nines and the WFTD (Women's Flying Training Detachment) executive officer, because "she did not know what to do with colored girls." Through writing newspaper columns and lecturing nationally at churches, schools, museums, and civic organizations, Bragg continued for the remainder of her life actively encouraging African Americans to undertake aviation careers.

Willa Brown (Chappell) (1906–92), also inspired by Coleman's valor, received her private pilot's license in 1938 with a score of 96 percent, the highest grade ever received by an African American woman. Brown successfully advocated for the

A handbill from the early 1920s advertises the tour of celebrated aviator Bessie Coleman.

inclusion of African Americans in the Civilian Pilot Training Program (CPTP), a government-funded aviation training program initiated in 1939 to prepare a reserve supply of in civilian pilots who could be called upon in the event of a national emergency. Brown was awarded contracts to train African American pilots, and as director of the Coffey School of Aeronautics, she administered large federal contracts. Lieutenant Brown was also the first African American officer in the Civil Air Patrol (CAP). In 1943 she was the only woman in the United States simultaneously holding a mechanic's license and a commercial license and was employed as president of a large aviation corporation. She was instrumental in racially integrating the aviation industry and trained some of the most celebrated African American pilots of World War II. Several of the men she trained in aviation mechanics became members of the now legendary Tuskegee Airmen of the 99th Pursuit Squadron, the military's first African American pilots.

Ida Van Smith Dunn (b. 1917) is an African and Native American whose love for airplanes began when she was a child. Her father would take her to the airfield in their hometown of Lumberton, North Carolina, where she was delighted by barnstorming exhibitions performed by pilots and by the women performing wing-walking stunts on the airplanes. At age fifty, Ida Van became an instrument-rated licensed pilot (she could fly during inclement weather) and ground instructor. She founded the Ida Van Smith Flight Clubs in 1967 to introduce youngsters ages three to nineteen to the variety of careers in aviation and space.

The women mentioned here represent an extensive roster of women flyers who, inside and outside the cockpit, cleared the obstacle-strewn runways for contemporary aviatrixes. Their courage made opportunities in aviation possible for Mae Carol Jemison, M.D., the first African American woman astronaut, a physician and engineer who designed and conducted scientific experiments on the space shuttle *Endeavour* in September 1992; Sally Ride, Ph.D., the first U.S. woman in space (1978); Kathryn Sullivan, Ph.D., the first woman to walk in space (1984); and for women pilots presently assigned to combat airplanes in the U.S. armed forces. Women pilots moved a wing closer to equality when the Defense Department abolished gender-based restrictions in the armed services in January 1994, making it possible for the first time in U.S. history for women to pilot combat aircraft.

Deborah G. Douglas, *United States Women in Aviation: 1940–1985* (Washington, D.C.: Smithsonian Institution Press, 1991); Betty Kaplan Gubert, *Invisible Wings: An Annotated Bibliography on Blacks in Aviation, 1916–1993* (Westport, Conn.: Greenwood Press, 1994); Elizabeth Amelia Hadley Freydberg, *Bessie Coleman: The Brownskin Lady Bird* (New York: Garland Publishing, 1994).

• ELIZABETH AMELIA HADLEY FREYDBERG

SEE ALSO Armed Forces.

≣ Banking and Credit

Women in the United States have faced a long history of economic discrimination. In colonial times, when women married they ceased to exist as legal entities and lacked independent rights to own or control property. Nineteenth-century reformers sought married women's property acts and earnings laws to give women control of their own wages. These reforms did not, however, make women fully equal, independent participants in financial matters.

Women made some inroads in the banking field during the early twentieth century. Maggie Lena Walker, an African American, established a bank in Richmond, Virginia, in 1903 and served as its president until 1930. Some women became banking professionals during World War I. Following the war, in their capacity as heads of many banks' newly created women's departments, women advised other working women about financial investments.

However, many women suffered from the denial of access to credit in the woman's own name. Thus, women have been discriminated against as consumers and as entrepreneurs. Often women of color experienced both racial and sexual barriers to credit.

Women's equal access to credit is a relatively recent phenomenon. Attention to this issue has surfaced along with concern about other sex and race discrimination issues since the late 1960s. Actions to ameliorate credit discrimination came from individual state laws and from federal legislation. The 1968 Truth in Lending Act and the 1968 Consumer Credit Protection Act were amended to include protection without regard to sex or marital status. Congress also passed an Equal Credit Opportunity Act in 1974, which allowed married women to obtain independent credit, without their husband's signature.

• SARA ALPERN

SEE ALSO Equal Credit Opportunity Act.

≋ El Barrio

The *barrio* has multiple meanings that embrace the historical and regional differences within the neighborhoods and city quarters to which the term refers. The barrio is also a concept addressed by artists and writers and explored in youth culture.

The designation "El Barrio" refers to the oldest Puerto Rican neighborhood in New York City. Puerto Ricans began to live in this area (also known as Spanish Harlem) around 1916, when most of its residents were Jewish and Italian. El Barrio grew rapidly with the large migration from Puerto Rico after World War II. In the Southwest (from Texas to California), barrios formed after 1848, usually in the heart of former Mexican pueblos and mission towns, where Mexicans retained some land after the significant loss of property and goods they sustained as a result of the Mexican War (1846–48). The number of Mexican barrios grew significantly during the twentieth century, when some also formed outside the southwest region. During the 1970s many Mexican, Puerto Rican, and Cuban barrios began to develop ethnically diverse Latina/Latino populations drawn from the Caribbean, South and Central America, and Mexico.

The barrio is a highly contested social and symbolic space. The origins of barrios are usually traced to the politics of territorial expansion and racial segregation. Barrios are frequently devalued as neighborhoods by city governments, and many have been reduced in size or destroyed during redevelopment and urban renewal projects. In response, barrio residents have formed grassroots urban movements to defend their communities and to define publicly the importance of the barrio as a historical, family, and community space. Latinas frequently organize and lead these movements, seeking greater representation for barrio residents in urban politics and planning. Barrios are often identified by scholars and residents as places where significant cultural innovation takes place and close ties of friendship and fictive kinship are forged distinctly by women and men.

• LISBETH HAAS

SEE ALSO Urbanization.

≋ Beauty Culture

Beauty culture developed in the United States as a commercial endeavor and social ritual in the late nineteenth century and emerged as a mass consumer industry after World War I. Before that time, a small number of hairdressers, perfumers, and druggists dispensed some beauty goods and services, mainly to prosperous Americans. Victorian gender ideology taught the middle class that beauty was the duty of white middle-class women, while fashion plates and such women's magazines as *Godey's Ladies Book* depicted idealized female images. Much of the prescriptive literature of the period, however, decried external and artificial beauty, preferring instead to encourage cleanliness and moral living as keys to better appearance. Nonetheless, many women knew how to make simple skin and hair preparations and passed on their knowledge by word of mouth, in handwritten recipe books, and through published household manuals. Farm wives, immigrants, indigenous women, and enslaved women alike drew upon their own therapeutic traditions, using herbs, berries, and other natural substances to heal, soften, and improve their skin.

By the 1880s a web of establishments—chemists, perfumers, beauty salons, drugstores, mail-order houses, and department stores—began to establish a profit-making infrastructure for new notions of beauty. At first eschewing makeup and artifice for "natural" methods, after World War I the nascent cosmetics industry promoted rouge, powder, and eyebrow pencils as "necessary arti-

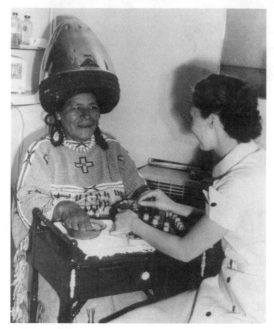

Red Cloud woman in a beauty shop in the Dakotas, 1941.

fice." Its dominant message, that every woman could achieve beauty, reached rural and urban dwellers, European immigrants, Latinas, African Americans, young working women, and middle-class housewives. In this sense, the cosmetics industry democratized beauty culture.

The view that beauty was a feminine pursuit opened an array of economic opportunities for women as sales agents, cosmetologists, advertising writers, "beauty experts," and inventors. Female entrepreneurs strongly influenced the development of commercial beauty culture, more so than in any other line of business in the country. Often coming from marginal social and economic backgrounds, they not only built business empires and fortunes but also played a crucial role in creating twentieth-century norms for women's appearance. Elizabeth Arden and Helena Rubinstein were immigrants from relatively poor families and worked in low-paying jobs before achieving suc-

cess. They initially based their trade in exclusive beauty salons, providing skin treatments and makeup to an elite clientele. African American entrepreneurs such as Madame C. J. Walker and Annie Turnbo Malone promoted beauty products and hair-care techniques to Black women through door-to-door sales agents and salon operatives. Women in the beauty business tended to work through the everyday networks of sociability—clubs, churches, and informal gatherings—that women had already established. These provided alternative routes of distribution for women who could not afford or were not permitted to sell through drugstores and department stores.

The growth of a cosmetics and hair-care industry went hand in hand with cultural changes that placed a greater emphasis on uniform standards of physical beauty. Celebrity photographs, rotogravure magazines, motion pictures, and advertisements created a visual culture that widely circulated idealized images. Cosmetics manufacturers were second only to food purveyors in purchasing advertising space in women's magazines after 1920. Beautiful women had posed in nineteenth-century *tableaux vivants*, theater spectacles, and May Day celebrations. The first Miss America pageant, held in 1921, drew upon and codified these traditions.

By the 1920s many women had embraced beauty culture as an aspect of modernity. They believed that tasteful appearance was necessary in the job market, especially in the clerical and service sector. New dating patterns, mixed-sex leisure, and companionate marriage reinforced the advertisers' messages. Immigrant and second-generation women frequently turned to beauty culture as a way to represent themselves as "American." For African American women, beauty culture offered a vision of Black female modernity, albeit a highly controversial one. The sale of skin bleaches and hair straighteners prompted contentious debate in the African American press over white emulation and status differences based on skin tones and hair texture.

In the post–World War II period, the beauty industry increasingly marketed products to girls in their teens and preteens. Companies worked with schools, clubs, and mass-circulation magazines to train girls in grooming and makeup applications, teaching that beautifying was essential to achieving femininity and a sexual image. Revlon's famous "Fire and Ice" advertising campaign of 1952, featuring a sophisticated and sensual woman, marked a turning point in cosmetics advertising.

Since the late nineteenth century, vocal critics of commercial beauty culture have included women's organizations, consumer advocates, physicians, and animal-rights activists. Charges of deceptive advertising, hazardous products, and overpriced merchandise resulted in the inclusion of cosmetics under the Food and Drug Administration's mandate in 1938. It was not until the 1960s, however, that feminists offered a systematic critique of beauty culture, targeting the widespread commercialization and objectification of women's appearance. Significantly, the first public action of the radical women's movement was a demonstration against the Miss America pageant in 1968. In the same period, African Americans denounced the dominance of white beauty images, a critique expressed in the slogan "Black is beautiful." While these challenges have in some ways expanded the images of beauty available to women, they did not fundamentally threaten commercial beauty culture. If anything, challenges to the beauty industry resulted in the creation of new markets, appealing to diverse populations with products designed along racial-ethnic, generational, and class lines.

Lois W. Banner, *American Beauty* (Chicago: University of Chicago Press, 1983); Kathy Peiss, "Making Faces: The Cosmetics Industry and the Cultural Construction of Gender, 1890–1930," in *Unequal Sisters*, edited by Ellen DuBois and Vicki Ruiz, 2d ed. (New York: Routledge, 1994).

▪ KATHY PEISS

SEE ALSO Advertising; Fashion and Style.

≋ Bill of Rights

SEE Constitution and Amendments.

≋ Birth Control

Contraception and abortion have had tangled meanings in U.S. history. Many factors can affect birthrates (physiological sterility, the age at which women marry, customs affecting the timing and frequency of sexual intercourse), but most cultures have had methods purported to prevent conception or induce miscarriage. In colonial days such actions were illicit, associated with fornication or adultery. In the mid-eighteenth century some married couples—Quakers for example—deliberately began to have smaller families. Between 1800 and 1900 marital birthrates among white, native-born women fell dramatically as couples in both urban and rural areas restricted family size. First-generation European immigrants maintained higher fertility than native-born whites, with considerable variation by group and with reduced fertility levels by the second generation.

Women in the United States began to practice family limitation earlier than women in any nation except France. Assessing people's motivation to practice reproductive control is especially complex. Women in the United States appear to have wanted smaller families for a variety of reasons: concerns about mothers' health, the changing costs (monetary and emotional) of child raising, concerns about the well-being of children already born, and concerns about land distribution and children's inheritance.

Two important threads run through the modern history of birth control in the United States. Its potential for increasing personal liberty has held great appeal but it has also generated vehement opposition, because reproductive control

A display table of the National Committee on Federal Legislation for Birth Control during the early 1940s. Birth-control information of the time—such as A Marriage Manual: A Practical Guide-book to Sex and Marriage, *among those shown here—emphasized family security rather than personal freedom.*

challenged established family, gender, and social relationships. A second thread has been the linkage of reproductive control with broader social change. From the neo-Malthusians of the mid–nineteenth century, who promoted contraception as a cure for class divisions and poverty, to the eugenicists, who deplored the "race suicide" of the "better classes," to the population-control advocates of the mid–twentieth century, reformers across the political spectrum have viewed birth control as a means to achieve their goals of social betterment.

Certain contraceptive and abortive methods have been known since antiquity, including one formerly called the "crime of Onan," coitus interruptus (withdrawal of the penis from the vagina before emission). In 1710 a Massachusetts woman

accused her husband of "Onan's abominable sin," and in another case, a Massachusetts man denied being the father of a bastard infant because he had "always minded [his] pullbacks." Most early reproductive-control methods, however, were chosen by women rather than men. Some women prolonged breast-feeding, hoping to prevent conception or induce miscarriage.

Women have also sought to control fertility through abortion. Inducing miscarriage before "quickening" was not regarded in early U.S. common law or social custom as immoral or unethical. Women sought miscarriages by doing strenuous exercise or by ingesting botanical remedies known in folklore as abortifacients, including savin, tansy, rue, pennyroyal, cottonroot, ergot, black cohosh, and blue cohosh. When commercial abortive preparations became available in U.S. cities and by mail order after 1840, these remedies continued to be the chief ingredients of the well-advertised "medicines for ladies." Once quickening occurred some women ceased their efforts and accepted the pregnancy, but others intensified the drug dosages, or exercised more vigorously, or turned to more drastic solutions (insertion of slippery elm bark into the cervix) or sought the services of "professional abortionists."

Historically Native American tribes used abortion, infanticide, and contraception to restrict fertility. Women in some tribes knew of plants, herbs, and medicines effective in preventing pregnancy or inducing miscarriage, although such knowledge was not universally known. Many Indian women also affected fertility by prolonging breast-feeding. Birth control among Native Americans in the twentieth century has been controversial, including accusations in the 1970s that public-health officials forced sterilizations.

Slaves had a high birthrate, although slaves' fertility levels varied depending on the decade, geographic area, and the economy. Despite high levels of reproduction, slave owners and white physicians believed that slaves held secret knowledge that enabled them to induce miscarriages. Such reports, however, did not specify what methods the slaves used. Slaves from Africa and the Caribbean brought to North America an abundance of medical lore, some of which included contraceptives from plants and abortifacients. Slave women did not necessarily share the attitudes of freewomen toward reproduction; although fecundity offered slave women some hope against being sold, they also recognized that their children would be in lifetime bondage.

Between 1840 and 1880 birth-control information, products, and services became more widely available. Safer, cheaper, and more effective techniques were broadly distributed among the urban workers and middle classes, and via mail order to rural residents.

Women gained greater control over reproduc-tion by using douches; spermicides; and barrier contraceptive devices such as the vaginal sponge, an early version of the cervical cap, and the diaphragm. Experts promoted ideas about a rhythm method, which was often ineffective. But women believed firmly that they had a discernible "sterile period" every month, which encouraged hopes of controlling fertility.

Men, too, were urged by activists, lecturers, and writers to take part in reproductive control by letting wives determine when and how often to have sexual intercourse. Other than cooperation with a woman's birth-control practices, the only methods available to men were withdrawal and condoms. Condoms, long associated with prostitution, began to be used for family limitation.

Until the nineteenth century abortion was almost never punished as a crime in the United States if it occurred before quickening; even after quickening only the abortionist might be charged with a high misdemeanor if the woman died. From 1829 to 1860 states revised their statutory codes and in the process—not always intentionally—tightened restrictions against abortion. Even then prosecutors found it difficult to win abortion cases and state supreme courts upheld the common-law tradition of tolerating abortions.

From the 1860s through the 1880s states passed more intentionally restrictive abortion laws, instigated by a handful of physicians who belonged to the new and ambitious American Medical Association, a group of men who wanted greater professionalism in medicine. Until the 1960s state laws governing abortion were a confusing patchwork. Women continued to have abortions but, driven underground, abortion became a criminal act—expensive and dangerous to a woman's physical and psychological health. The class differential intensified, too. Middle- and upper-class women, who had better access to private physicians, could more easily—although not always—obtain "therapeutic" abortions; the poor and the unmarried had fewer and more dangerous choices. The criminalization of abortion lasted until the 1960s, when sixteen states liberalized their laws. In 1973 the U.S. Supreme Court ruled in *Roe* v. *Wade* that a woman's right to privacy allows abortions during the first trimester. Even in the *Roe* decision, however, the Court upheld the right of the state to restrict abortion once fetal viability was determined unless a woman's life was at stake.

The legal climate with respect to both contraception and abortion had changed in 1873 when Congress, with virtually no debate and little public interest, tightened the existing law against obscenity and specified that birth-control information and items could not be mailed or imported. Named for Anthony Comstock, a self-appointed vice hunter and sponsor of the bill, this federal law, although mitigated by court decisions in the 1930s, remained on the statute books until overturned by Supreme Court decisions in the 1960s and 1970s. One serious consequence of the federal law was its stimulation of far more sweeping state laws, some of which forbade citizens from asking or giving information about birth control or even using it. Reproductive-control information and services continued to be available, but the literature that offered the best advice disappeared and was replaced by inferior and confusing tracts. Products continued to be available, but at a higher cost and from fewer and less respectable sources. Legions of social-purity reformers and public acquiescence overrode a generation of commercialization and public discourse, which drove reproductive control, if not totally underground, into a netherworld of back-fence gossip and back-alley abortions. With the Comstock laws, class barriers widened. Impoverished, single, and rural women had less access to the better and safer methods. The growing momentum of women's reproductive rights was temporarily derailed.

In the twentieth century the politics surrounding birth control were manifest in more open contestations over power, world-views, gender roles, social change, and social status. Advocates of reproductive control founded organizations to lobby for legal changes and to provide birth control via private and public-sector clinics and organized networks. From Margaret Sanger's crusade and from her American Birth Control Association—an organization that worked to legitimize "family limitation" from World War I to World War II—to Planned Parenthood from the 1950s to the present, physicians and other professionals with status have taken prominent roles in promoting contraception. Individuals within these movements promoted birth control for diverse reasons: some for "family planning"; some out of anxieties about high birthrates among the "unfit," poor, and people of color; some for "population control" in developing countries. Native Americans and African Americans in particular have criticized government-sponsored birth-control organizations for their programs of forced sterilization and for testing new birth-control products primarily on poor women and women of color.

In the late 1960s the women's movement gave rise to a reproductive rights movement whose goals encompassed legalizing abortion, promoting easier and safer contraception, and fighting racist and classist birth-control programs. The vibrancy and successes of that reproductive rights movement, as well as its broad attack on traditional gender roles, stimulated the backlash politics of the New Right. From the 1970s to the present, coalition groups of the New Right have sought to overturn the *Roe* v. *Wade* decision, restrict access to contraception, and restore traditional patriarchal values.

Another characteristic of twentieth-century birth control has been the continuing search for improved methods, primarily for women. Little research has focused on men's methods, nor have there been marked successes for either sex. The anovulent pill, introduced in 1960 and marketed to millions of women in that decade, continues to arouse debate over its alleged associated risks of vascular disease, breast cancer, and ovarian cysts. IUDs, also invented and sold on the mass market in the early 1960s, have fared even more poorly. In spite of wide hopes that IUDs would prove to be cheap, safe, and reliable contraceptives, their use declined after the mid-1970s, when the Dalkon Shield—the most aggressively marketed and widely used of all the contraceptive IUDs—was found to have caused over twenty deaths, life-threatening pelvic infections, and septic abortions. Poorly designed, inadequately tested, and deceptively marketed, the Dalkon Shield had been inserted into nearly four million women between 1970 and 1973, before it was recalled and its manufacturer prosecuted in numerous class-action lawsuits.

Two birth-control drugs stirred controversy in the 1990s. RU486, labeled by antiabortionists as an abortifacient "morning-after pill," blocks production of the hormone progesterone, normal in pregnancy, thus allowing the breakdown of the uterine lining and the expulsion of any new embryo. Although by 1991 RU486 had been widely used in Europe and Great Britain, the U.S. Food and Drug Administration banned its importation and the Supreme Court upheld the ban in a July 1992 decision. At the time of this writing, however, the FDA has permitted the Population Council to begin planning distribution.

Norplant, another contested invention of the 1990s, is a hormonal birth-control drug implanted as matchstick-sized capsules under a woman's skin, usually in the upper arm. Hailed as a "dream contraceptive" for its safety and five-year effectiveness, it was approved by the FDA in 1990 and used in government-funded clinics. By 1992, however, women across the country filed class-action lawsuits against Norplant charging that insertion and removal caused pain, scarring, excessive bleeding, tumors, and depression. Its use aroused even more controversy when medical, judicial, and governmental authorities advocated mandatory insertion of the drug as a way to reduce illegitimate births and to lower welfare rolls.

Controversial and complex, the history of reproductive empowerment has had enormous significance in the lives of U.S. women. Not a history of progressive improvement in knowledge, access, or practice, even less a history of simplified gender, sexual, and marital politics, reproductive control in the U.S. has shaped the consciousness, power, and actions and changed the lives of countless women and men.

▪ JANET FARRELL BRODIE

SEE ALSO Abortion; Eugenics; Planned Parenthood; Reproductive Rights.

≋ Bisexuality

Bisexuality is the capacity for emotional, romantic, and/or physical attraction to more than one gender. A bisexual identity affirms complexity and acknowledges a reality beyond the dualistic paradigms of heterosexism. Bisexuals are a part of as well as apart from heterosexual society and the lesbian and gay community.

In the early 1970s bisexuals began organizing social and support groups across the United States. Individual bisexual people and some bisexual groups worked with and publicly aligned themselves with the gay, lesbian, people-of-color, and feminist movements. Bisexual political action groups formed in the early to mid-1980s to combat stereotypes and to give bisexual people a means to voice their issues.

Bisexuals were among those first and most severely affected by AIDS. HIV/AIDS exposed the fluid nature of sexuality and the difference between hetero- and homosexual identity categories and behavior. Because bisexuality is outside these either-or categories, bisexually identified people have been told they don't exist and have been scapegoated as carriers of HIV. In response to these defamations, the early bisexual politic emphasized visibility, inclusion, and pride.

A national bisexual movement was conceived at the 1987 March on Washington for Gay and Lesbian Rights; and BiNet USA, an educational and civil rights organization, was founded. Six years later, at the 1993 March on Washington for

Lesbian, Gay, and Bi Equal Rights and Liberation, the movement came of age by successfully campaigning for inclusion in the march title and program.

• LANI KA'AHUMANU

SEE ALSO Sexuality.

≋ Black Clubwomen's Movement

In the summer of 1896 members of the four-year-old Colored Women's League and the one-year-old National Federation of Afro-American Women held conventions in Washington, D.C. During the course of the meetings, seven members from each group convened to determine whether their goals were similar enough to unite as one organization in order to have a stronger foundation. The National Association of Colored Women (NACW) thus was born—with 198 member clubs, whose participants would devote their energies to improving the homes and home life of African Americans, advocating for their civil and political rights, and, in particular, working to improve the plight of women and children.

Black women had for generations recognized the advantages of association. Members of the Colored Female Religious and Moral Society of Salem, Massachusetts, from its inception in 1818, for example, promised, among other things, "to be charitably watchful over each other." By 1830, Philadelphia alone had some twenty-seven female mutual aid societies. One of them, the Daughters of Africa, an organization of two hundred working-class women, "bought groceries and supplies for the needy, paid sick benefits, and lent money to society members in emergency situations." The Ladies Benevolent Society of Detroit was created in 1867 to provide sick and death benefits to its members. Twenty years later in the same city, the Willing Workers made and sold quilts, using the proceeds to provide baby clothes and general care for Detroit's poor children.

Although technically, beneficial societies functioned primarily for the advantage of their members, and benevolent societies worked to provide for "the needy," few African American women's associations functioned exclusively as one or the other.

In the postemancipation period, Black women's associations flourished. Many of these organizations were connected to churches, and their members worked to address the needs of freedpeople that were not adequately met by Reconstruction governments. One such organization, the Daughters of Zion, founded in 1867 in Memphis, Tennessee, was an interclass organization of more than three hundred women who provided financial relief for those who needed it, employed a physician to manage the health of church members without charge, and undertook a variety of other health and educational missions.

By the 1890s organized Black women branched out and extended their activities to institution building, or community development. For example, the first project of the Woman's League, founded in Kansas City in 1893, was to establish "an industrial home and school for teaching cooking, sewing, and other useful employments." The clearest evidence of institution building among clubwomen, however, came after the creation of the NACW. Members organized mothers' clubs throughout the country, in which they taught domestic science, child care, and health classes. They financed, organized, and maintained kindergartens, old folks' homes, orphanages, hospitals, settlement houses, and other "public" institutions that African Americans needed but could not get from their local governments. They organized girls' clubs, where they taught a variety of classes and provided educational scholarships and interest-free loans to African American girls. Although NACW clubs were involved in many activities designed to advance the causes of "the race," the NACW was the umbrella organization for hundreds of clubs and its leaders spoke in one powerful voice for thousands of African American women on all the issues important to them.

The NACW provided a powerful impetus for further organization among women, and NACW work reflected the members' interests in self-determination, self-improvement, and community development. They saw themselves neither as helpless nor as total victims. As Josephine Saint Pierre Ruffin noted in her address to the 1895 conference that preceded the creation of the NACW, "Our woman's movement is . . . led and directed by women for the good of women and men, for the benefit of all humanity . . . [W]e are not alienating or withdrawing, we are only coming to the front . . ."

Although social clubs and literary societies also were a part of this club movement, Black women in associations had long been in the forefront of movements to provide insurance—illness, death, and burial insurance—for their members. They led efforts to furnish food, shelter, fuel, and clothing to their neighbors in need. All of these activities helped establish Black women as community leaders.

● STEPHANIE J. SHAW

SEE ALSO Black Sororities; National Association of Colored Women; National Council of Negro Women; Phyllis Wheatley Clubs and Homes.

≋ Black Nationalism

Black nationalism is a body of social and political thought that reflects the collective aspirations of African Americans seeking political, economic, and cultural autonomy in U.S. society. Although Black nationalism is shared to some degree by all Blacks, its variety of themes and ideological components leave considerable room for interpretation. In the late eighteenth and early nineteenth centuries, separatism and emigrationism were the dominant themes of Black nationalism. In the twentieth century it has often been identified with Pan-Africanism, which advocated an international political agenda for liberation.

Despite historical and political variations, four features of Black nationalism have remained constant. The principal feature is racial solidarity, whereby African Americans collectively pursue social and political change. Religious separatism is the second feature, evinced in the establishment of Black Christian and non-Christian houses of worship. The third feature is cultural history, which promises the reemergence of African greatness and racial pride. Self-determination is the fourth unifying element, emphasizing autonomy for Blacks.

In 1835 Maria W. Stewart's *Productions of Mrs. Maria W. Stewart* placed Black women in the center of Black nationalism. Stewart argued that moral rectitude, educational achievements, and business acumen combined with persistent political activism would restore Black women's dignity and provide a legacy for future generations.

Black nationalism developed further after the failure of Reconstruction and the rise of Jim Crow in the South. It established all-Black institutions, all-Black towns, and back-to-Africa movements. By the 1880s economic nationalism experienced a resurgence. In the early twentieth century, Black nationalists stressed Pan-Africanism as well as economic, religious, and cultural autonomy. W.E.B. Du Bois revived Pan-Africanism. Marcus Garvey transported Black nationalism into the twentieth century by founding the Universal Negro Improvement Association (UNIA).

Women played varied roles in the UNIA, particularly in the Black Cross Nurses, who provided the unemployed with food and housing. Amy Jacques Garvey, editor of the *Negro World*, was the most influential woman in the Garvey movement.

By the 1950s the Nation of Islam, under Elijah Muhammad and its most eloquent spokesman, El Hajj Malik El-Shabazz (Malcolm X), emerged with a nationalism based on the tenets of the Islamic faith. Malcolm X espoused a philosophy of racial pride, knowledge of Black history, and self-determination that led to the Black Power movement. Women in the movement, however, played a subordinate role because of pervasive male chauvinism. These women focused on traditional female domestic roles. Following the death of Elijah Muhammad in 1975, the Nation of Islam split into two groups. One, under Minister Louis Farrakhan, has retained the traditional tenets of the Nation of Islam; the World Community of Islam in the West, by contrast, led by Wallace Muhammad, has merged into the larger worldwide Islamic movement and stresses more progressive roles for African American women.

Since the 1960s nationalist organizations have been common. Founded in 1966, the Black Panther Party, espousing revolutionary Black nationalism, captured the attention of Black youth. Although sexism shaped the party's structure, women played important roles within it. Assata Shakur (JoAnne Chesimard), Angela Davis, Kathleen Neal Cleaver, Elaine Brown, and Ericka Huggins participated in the community survival programs as well as the party's internal leadership. In the 1990s Black nationalism is clearly dominated by the Nation of Islam's emphasis on cultural, economic, and spiritual development. The Nation's limitations are its Black male domination/female subordination relationship and extreme homophobia.

■ GAYLE T. TATE

See also Garveyism.

≋ Black Sororities

Black sororities are unique civic and social organizations, whose focus is on service to the Black community. Long before women and/or Blacks began to be accepted into mainstream society, Black sororities supported the cultural development and leadership of Black women.

Three of the first four Black sororities, Alpha Kappa Alpha, Delta Sigma Theta, and Zeta Phi Beta, were founded at Howard University (a Black institution) between 1908 and 1920. Sigma Gamma Rho was established at Butler University (a predominantly white institution) in 1922. These groups were committed to expanding opportunities for women's academic pursuits and providing services to the disadvantaged.

The sororities, along with other community organizations, sponsored activities for the development and benefit of the disenfranchised. Services ranged from feeding and housing the homeless to establishing and supervising federally funded projects.

Since the 1960s' activist movements, Black sororities have become racially integrated although the majority of their membership is Black women. All have foreign chapters, funds or foundations to foster education and research, and programs that support community uplift and economic empowerment. The service hallmark of Black sororities includes basic improvements in urban U.S. ghettos as well as global initiatives. These initiatives provide hope for the less fortunate; more significantly, financial support and hands-on assistance (for example, with young parents or job seekers) help citizens to identify and access community services and opportunities to raise their standard of living.

Some regard Black sororities as "elitist" because they restrict membership to college women. However, the sororities' worth is well established. Black sororities continue to offer service programs throughout the world.

■ KATIE KINNARD WHITE

See also Black Clubwomen's Movement.

≋ Black Women

See African American Women.

≋ Black Women's Language

Language research traditionally has focused on the grammar and speaking styles of European American males. During the era of explosive rhetoric and militant political activism by African Americans during the 1960s, language research broadened to include African Americans, but that research also focused exclusively on the grammar and speaking styles of males. Pioneering studies of "language and woman's place" have been conducted, but these studies have generally not addressed language patterns representative of a cross-section of women. Rather, the work on women's speech behavior has concentrated on the language of European American, middle-class speakers, thus conveying the false impression that all women use language in the same ways, regardless of race, class, ethnicity, or age. Linguistic data on African American women "are essential if we are to understand how the community expresses its reality, because women historically have been responsible for the language development of their children and therefore their community," according to Marcia Morgan.

Black women researchers such as Marsha Houston Stanback and Gwendolyn Etter-Lewis have launched an important beginning in the study of African American women's language. Based on this work, it is possible to identify four key features of Black women's talk: 1) signifyin, 2) reading dialect, 3) culturally toned diminutives, and 4) bold speech, or "smart talk."

Signifyin is a form of ritualized insult in which a speaker puts down, talks about, needles—signifies on—the listener. This discourse practice is a culturally accepted method of talking about another person, who is present in the speech situation, through the use of "indirection." The signifier always employs humor, which is a face-saving strategy for the person being signified on. In addition, a speaker may signify by talking about the targeted person's mother, or occasionally about relatives of the target. For example, Betty signifies on Linda in the following:

> *Linda:* Girl, what up with that head? [referring to her friend's hairstyle]
> *Betty:* Ask yo momma.
> *Linda:* Oh, so you going there, huh?

Instead of answering Linda's question directly, Betty chooses to inform Linda that her hairstyle is none of Linda's business by responding with "Ask yo momma." Betty's response is taken humorously by Linda and any others present. Since the normal expectation in a conversation is that a speaker's question will be answered honestly and sincerely, the unexpected indirection ("Ask yo momma") produces laughter. Linda clearly recognizes Betty's entry into the realm of ritualized insult, as indicated by her response, "Oh, so you going there, huh?"

Reading dialect is a way of making a point by contrasting the Black community's two languages, Black English and Euro-American English, through the use of words, sentences, or discourse structures. Speakers select a contrasting feature in the two speaking styles to "read" a conversational partner, that is, to denigrate that person verbally, or to tell her off. Among African American women, a common way of reading dialect is through use of the expression "Miss Thang." In order to communicate dissatisfaction, one person may refer to another as "Miss Thang": "We were doing all right until Miss Thang decided she didn't want to go along with the program." The expression "Miss Thang" among African American women is a direct put-down, conveyed by use of the Black vernacular form "thang." The broader African American speech community, as well as the African American women's speech community, interprets "thang" negatively, since a thing is an object, lacking an identity or other human qualities.

Culturally toned diminutives are a major conversational feature resonant in African American women's speech. These forms are used to show solidarity, although in other communities they might be perceived as terms that diminish a person. For generations, African American women have used diminutives, such as *girl, honey, child, baby*, and so on, to refer to someone who is likeable, loveable, or a social intimate. The diminutive "girl," for example, is a highly popular word used by African American females to show solidarity in all spheres of existence, public or private, and among all age groups. An African American five-year-old may say to her eight-year-old sister, "Girl, you bed' stop dat" or "Girl, you crazy." The same expressions can be used by adult Black females, and the females involved do not have to be blood relatives. They may be neighbors, classmates, playmates, church members, club members, or colleagues. In contemporary times, *girl* has even expanded to *girlfriend*.

Both "girl" and "girlfriend" are words that establish solidarity and may be used to bridge social distance, even when the females engaged in a conversation are strangers. Both terms are in current and frequent use. One exception is the case of African American women over the age of sixty-five who will use "girl," but not "girlfriend." These women have a long history of saying "girl" and may not be prone to using the new term. Their reticence about using the new term is similar to the linguistic practice of older African Americans, male and female, who continue to use "Negro" (or even "Colored") rather than "Black" or "African American" as their term of racial identification.

"*Smart talk*" is an overall characteristic of African American women's speech. Black women use language in an assertive, bold, outspoken manner. In a conversation among three women friends, one woman remarked, "I'm glad I don't have a man around 'cause I can do whatever the hell I want to do." Terry McMillan, in her 1992 novel *Waiting to Exhale*, creates authenticity in her women characters by the use of "smart talk." McMillan's main character, Savannah, punctuates her sentences with this style of speech from

the novel's beginning: "Sheila, my baby sister, insisted on giving me his [Lionel's] phone number because he lives here in Denver and her simple-ass husband played basketball with him eleven years ago at the University of Washington." This feature of Black women's discourse departs from the so-called "code of feminine politeness" characteristic of European American women. Instead of Marilyn Frye's depiction of women who "live in cages," that is, women who know their "place," African American women boldly assert their right to define their place in the world through the use of smart talk.

Gwendolyn Etter-Lewis, *My Soul Is My Own: Oral Narratives of African American Women in the Professions* (New York: Routledge, 1993); Marilyn Frye, "Oppression," in *The Politics of Reality*, edited by Marilyn Frye (Freedom, Calif.: Crossing Press, 1983); Marsha Houston Stanback, "Language and Black Woman's Place: Evidence from the Black Middle Class," in *For Alma Mater: Theory and Practice in Feminist Scholarship*, edited by P. A. Treichler et al. (Chicago: University of Illinois Press, 1985); Marcia Morgan, "Indirectness and Interpretation in African American Women's Discourse," *Pragmatics*, 1, no. 4 (1991): 421–52.

■ GENEVA SMITHERMAN and
DENISE TROUTMAN-ROBINSON

≋ Boston Women's Health Book Collective

The Boston Women's Health Book Collective authored *Our Bodies, Ourselves* (OBOS), the first and still the most comprehensive book to provide information about women's health and sexuality. Since 1970 more than three and a half million copies of OBOS have been printed in twelve different languages. The book (retitled *The New Our Bodies, Ourselves* in 1984) has gained almost legendary status because it has revolutionized the way a generation of women think about their bodies.

The Collective seeks to challenge the medicalization of normal life events such as pregnancy and menopause, to bring a feminist perspective to health care debates, to improve health options for women, to help women be full partners in their own health care, and to create a more just society. All book royalties go to women's health projects, especially its own Women's Health Information Center, a resource to women by phone, fax, or in person, at its office in Somerville, Massachusetts. It networks with organizations with similar goals throughout the world.

The Collective began in 1969, when twelve young white feminists in the Boston area prepared a series of women's health and sexuality courses. It has since created a more diverse board of directors that attempts to represent different sectors of the women's community, such as women with disabilities, women of color, and lesbians. Members of the Collective also have written *Ourselves and Our Children* (1978), *Changing Bodies, Changing Lives: A Book for Teens* (1980), *Talking with Your Teenager: A Book for Parents* (1984), and *Ourselves, Growing Older* (1987, 1994).

■ SUSAN E. BELL

SEE ALSO Women's Health Movement.

≋ Breast Cancer

Some people believe we are winning the war on breast cancer. But in the United States, there are 184,000 new cases a year, up from 67,000 in 1965.

According to the National Women's Health Network, the breast cancer incidence for Latinas is lower than for white or African American women. In any one year, 70 out of every 100,000 Latinas are diagnosed with breast cancer, compared with 112 out of every 100,000 whites and 95 out of every 100,000 African Americans. African Americans have an overall lower rate of breast cancer than whites, but their rate is higher up to age forty. The overall mortality rate for African Americans is higher than for white women or Latinas, and appears to be increasing. Breast cancer incidence for Native American women varies depending on region, but for most it is lower than for whites, African Americans, and Latinas. However, for those Native Americans who receive this diagnosis, the five-year survival rate is lower than for all other ethnic and racial groups in the United States. Asian Pacific women are the least likely to have an annual gynecological exam or to ever have had a mammogram. Yet, their mortality rate from breast cancer is the lowest of the main ethnic populations in the United States. The specific breast cancer incidence in the Asian Pacific subgroups ranges from a low of 29 per 100,000 for Koreans to 106 per 100,000 for Native Hawaiians.

According to Katherine O'Hanlan, M.D., cancer surgeon and former president of the Gay and Lesbian Medical Association, lesbians may have more risk factors for breast cancer than heterosexual women. For example, she says, they are less likely to conceive children and more likely to be obese. However, they are also less likely to have had exposure to pharmaceutical hormones— from oral contraceptives or DES. An analysis by Suzanne Haynes, Ph.D., suggests that lesbians *do* get more breast cancer. Stimulated by her preliminary work, confirming studies are under way but are not complete. Many lesbians are alienated from the medical establishment and go for few checkups and screening tests. One reason for the alienation may be that lesbians often encounter physician insensitivity or lack of awareness ("What? You don't use birth control?!"). Thus, it is argued, lesbians are apt to be diagnosed later rather than sooner. Lesbians are also more likely to live on low incomes and to lack health insurance and other "perks" that heterosexuals may receive through marriage. Why staying out of the doctor's office is correlated with lower breast cancer rates in Asian Pacific women and higher in lesbians has yet to be explained.

Devra Lee Davis, Ph.D., author of the *Scientific American* article, "Can Environmental Estrogens Cause Breast Cancer?" answers questions about her personal history with, "No, I haven't had breast cancer *yet.*" Since the 1940s, when pharmaceutical estrogens were introduced, and xenoestrogens, especially in the form of pesticides, fuels, and plastics, were dispersed into our environment, a woman's lifetime chances of breast cancer have nearly tripled, while age-specific death rates have remained almost unchanged. Nonetheless, one adage says "more people live by cancer than die by cancer." The cancer industry, as Ralph Moss titled his disturbing book on the subject, remains indifferent to activist demands for accountability or increased research into prevention.

A "message of hope" and early detection ("see your doctor at the slightest hint of trouble") have been major themes of cancer education campaigns since 1913. But when the Women's Community Cancer Project, a grassroots group in Cambridge, Massachusetts, challenged the American Cancer Society (ACS) in 1992 to defend its exaggerated claim that early breast cancer detection through mammography would result in a cure "nearly 100 percent of the time," an ACS director of professional education responded, "When you make an advertisement, you just say what you can to get women in the door. You exaggerate a point . . . because advertising people do that." As Maryann Napoli observes in *Health Facts*, the newsletter of the Center for Medical Consumers in New York, "The overselling of mammography has led many women to view a mammogram as the only thing that stands between them and an imminent death from breast cancer." Thus, many members of the large, enthusiastic audience who gathered on September 26, 1994, to hear Gloria Steinem speak at a New

York Hospital–Cornell Women's Health Symposium seemed bewildered and perplexed when she recounted her own experience: "I wasn't aware that mammograms are inaccurate in at least 15 percent of cases. Having a mammogram kept me from getting treatment for a year."

Mammography screening ads cannot promise a "nearly 100 percent" cure, not even for CIS (carcinoma in situ), which is classified as Stage Zero disease. Eighty-five percent of women with Stage One breast cancer (a small lump, no more than three-quarters of an inch, no evidence of any spread) are still living five years later, but 15 percent are not. Ninety percent of women with Stage Four metastatic cancer, which many doctors deem incurable and untreatable, die within the five-year time frame, but 10 percent survive, some in excellent health. Five-year survival for Stage Two breast cancer is 66 percent, and for Stage Three it is 41 percent. Of course, the odds can never predict what will happen to a given woman, nor do doctors normally reveal how little gain there may be from "piling on" aggressive treatments. There is little if any funding for research into lifestyle differences between longer- and shorter-surviving breast cancer patients, even though psychiatrist David Spiegel has shown that joining a support group increases survival by almost two years.

It is essential to bring an advocate or knowledgeable friend to help you question and evaluate any cancer diagnosis or treatment plan. Cancer activist Ann Fonfa has written, "Many patients say they couldn't hear anything else after the word cancer. It is a paralyzing diagnosis." Dr. Susan Love—North America's most trusted cancer surgeon—adds, "The diagnosis of breast cancer is not an emergency. Anybody who tries to rush you, you have to say, 'Wait a second.' Catch your breath, get the shock over with, and start to investigate. Sometimes you can find out more than they know. You have to get a second opinion, to read, to explore."

The National Cancer Institute (NCI) offered some hopeful news in the mid-1990s. At nineteen years, 52 percent of breast cancer patients are still alive, up from 48 percent. Some may credit the identification of estrogen receptors and the use of tamoxifen, others may credit mammography, but it is likely that breast cancer activists of the mid-1970s had a profound effect. It's no coincidence that the survival rates improved as significant numbers of women began to take treatment decisions into their own hands.

One such activist was journalist Rose Kushner, diagnosed in 1974, who opened her Women's Breast Cancer Advisory Center in 1975, the same year that the National Women's Health Network, for which she chaired the Breast Cancer Task Force, was founded. Kushner was so brash, so brilliant, and so driven, that, in an unprecedented move, President Carter appointed her, a "mere patient," to the national Cancer Advisory Board, where she defended informed consent, exposed the fallacies in poor-quality research, and stirred up much controversy. Her books include *Why Me?*, which she later retitled *Alternatives*, presumably to convey her growing regard for them.

Paving the way for Kushner was the publication in 1973 of the first trade edition of (the formerly underground) *Our Bodies, Ourselves*. The book's section on breast cancer concludes on a note that might seem humdrum to younger readers, but at the time was nothing less than a call to revolution: "Remember: you have a choice about having your breast removed. You don't have to choose between immediate, painful death and breastlessness when you first discover a lump."

The Halsted radical mastectomy has been called "the greatest standardized surgical error of the twentieth century." Introduced in the 1880s by William Halsted, a surgeon at Johns Hopkins, it was debilitating, even crippling, and based on Halsted's unproven conviction that breast cancer was a local disease that could be fully—if brutally—excised before it spread. The Halsted radical was exacting. The woman was anesthetized and the doctor performed a "quick-section" biopsy. If the biopsy was positive, the doctor, with-

out waking the patient, began his incision at the shoulder and removed the breast as well as the lymph glands, the muscles of the chest wall, and all the fat under the skin. The patient was left with a loss of feeling on that side of her body, a sunken chest, restricted movement, and probably some degree of "milk arm," the chronic and painful condition in which lymph fluid can no longer circulate properly and thus accumulates.

Halsted's followers effectively brainwashed many other doctors and patients into believing that his procedure was an absolute cure. In a 1989 lecture, the ACS's Arthur Hollub, a surgical oncologist, recalled that when he started his internship in the 1940s, "the Halsted radical mastectomy was unquestioned. A failure to cure was usually attributed to a woman's delay or a non-alert family physician who did not get the woman to a surgeon quickly enough." In fact, the quick-section biopsy, so terrifying and demeaning to the patient, was medically unreliable as well. Some false positives of old frozen sections were uncovered in the 1980s at NCI. The National Women's Health Network tried, without success, to convince NCI of its absolute obligation to notify the patients, who'd proceeded through life believing they'd survived breast cancer when, in fact, they never had it. It seems puzzling that a government institution would use taxpayer money to do research and then fail to inform the directly affected taxpayers of the results. For all the good that NCI may do, it urgently needs a large infusion of consumer advocates at policy levels.

In 1954 Terese ("Ted") Lasser, founder of Reach to Recovery, become the first militant advocate for radical mastectomy patients. Recalling the Halsted radical she had in 1952, she said, "You awake to find yourself wrapped in bandages from midriff to neck—bound like a mummy in surgical gauze, somewhere deep inside you a switch is thrown and your mind goes blank. You do not know what to think, you do not want to guess, you do not want to know." Lasser, the soignée, energetic (and imperious) matriarch in an affluent and well-connected family (J. K. Lasser, her husband, was author of the perennially popular *Your Income Tax*), was not accustomed to being patronized or hustled and had not been prepared for this drastic result. Nor did her surgeon (whom she described as a "brilliant but very busy man"), or anyone else at Memorial Hospital, give her the specific advice she craved on arm exercises, if, when, or how to resume sex relations with her husband, what to tell her children, or even how to shop for a prosthesis. Her epiphany occurred when she showed up at the department store where she normally bought brassieres, and the saleswoman screamed and fled, crying "People like us shouldn't have to wait on people like you."

As soon as Lasser discovered how to cope with all these matters, a compulsion came over her to teach what she knew. She slipped into the hospital rooms of "mastectomees," bearing gift boxes with: 1) a starter "falsie" to pin on the inside of their nightgowns, 2) a ball, string, and instructions, which she demonstrated, for the painful but effective arm-restoring exercises that she herself had devised out of her desperation and genius, and 3) perhaps most daring, her famous "Letter to Husbands" about sex. Lasser maintained a pretense that she made these calls only at the request of the patient's doctors or family. According to Hollub, however, she was often "escorted out of the front door of Memorial Hospital when she was found visiting patients at random and without the consent of the responsible surgeon."

Reach to Recovery (R2R) drew its name from the stretch exercise that "Ted" Lasser flogged her mastectomees to perform from the moment they could rise up from their hospital beds: to lean their foreheads against the nearest wall and crawl the fingers of their affected arms up the wall until they screamed in pain. Lasser marked each day's progress with a pencil, as in measuring a child's height. For those who had the stamina to persevere, the exercises were often "miraculously" effective. Lasser herself regained the full use of her affected arm and so did thousands of the patients she (or her lieutenants) counseled.

By the late 1960s, R2R had chapters in twenty-five foreign countries, as well as in many U.S. cities. Lasser remained dissatisfied, recognizing that she alone would never command the womanpower to achieve her goal of offering support services and rehabilitation to every last mastectomee on earth. In 1969, she merged forces with ACS, which had over three thousand grassroots units, and reached small community hospitals as well as the large urban medical centers. By the 1990s, ACS boasted thirteen thousand trained volunteers who visit up to one hundred thousand breast cancer patients every year. The drawback, in some people's view, is that what was once a proactive and subversive enterprise became mainstream, even conventional. Indeed, in her brilliant 1994 book on the politics of breast cancer, *Patient No More*, Sharon Batt concludes that certain attitudes of ACS have even made R2R an "object of anger and ridicule among women with cancer." In a Canadian case that prompted widespread resignations from R2R, a well-loved volunteer visitor was dismissed because she refused to wear falsies. "We like our volunteers to look normal," her supervisor explained. Or, as Vermont activist Ginny Soffa complains, "Organizations in the so-called cancer business want to take us [grassroots groups] by the hand and get us to be more sedate."

One consistent message from breast cancer activists has been that when cancer cells are "growing wild" inside, some sense of outer autonomy becomes imperative, even life-saving, for the woman. M. Vera Peters, M.D., thought so, and is said to have treated her patients accordingly, from the time she graduated from medical school in Toronto in 1934. A world-class radiotherapist/oncologist, before she reached the age of forty she'd made a major contribution to the treatment of Hodgkin's disease. She argued for an aggressive approach; but regarding her second major interest, breast cancer, the evidence led her in the opposite direction.

Peters worked at a Toronto facility that admitted 7,261 patients for treatment of breast cancer between 1935 and 1960. On April 10, 1967, she published a paper in the *Journal of the American Medical Association* that reported the outcome for 825 of these women, including 200 who had only lumpectomies with radiation. All of the patients in the three other treatment groups had had some combination of mastectomy and radiation, but in only one group was the mastectomy performed immediately after a "quick-section" biopsy, eliminating patient choice.

Lumpectomy patients with Stages One and Two breast cancer survived fully as well, at five years, as those who had had mastectomies. Peters already considered this fact proven in the world medical literature (although few North American women knew it at the time). Of greater urgency to her was the chance to present evidence against the scourge of quick-section biopsies. Her article begins:

> Concern for the patients' morale as well as their physical well-being has prompted me. . . . Technical progress has not altered the survival rate in breast cancer, as it is reflected in the constant mortality rate for several decades . . . the curability of the individual patient . . . may be predetermined by host influences and not by the method of treatment employed to eradicate the tumor. . . . It behooves us as cancer therapists to[find methods] which will not harm the self-respect and good will of the patient. With quick-section biopsy . . . the patients feel that they have been deprived of an opportunity to think positively about their treatment because the diagnosis had not been confirmed preoperatively. They approach the operation hopefully and in spite of lurking doubt, the shock after the one-stage operation is profound. . . . If a preliminary local incision . . . were carried out routinely, the more radical treatment could then be discussed with the patient and the final decision in favor of either surgery or irradiation could safely be influenced by the patient's "special" fears.

Upon her retirement in 1976, Vera Peters was appointed to the Order of Canada, in recognition of her extraordinary contributions to the treat-

ment of Hodgkin's disease and breast cancer, just as patients all over the world were beginning to seize their newfound opportunities to "think positively" and for themselves.

> ■ BARBARA SEAMAN

SEE ALSO Cancer; Medical Research.

≋ Buddhism

Buddhism in the United States is far more pluralistic than in its Asian homeland because immigrants from all parts of the Asian Buddhist world have settled in the United States, where they have closer contact than was possible in Asia. Since the 1970s Buddhism also has become the religion of choice for many Caucasians and some African Americans.

Converts to Buddhism and those born into Buddhist ethnic groups, however, often have little contact with one another. Their separation is a reflection of the two very different ways that Buddhism first entered the United States in the nineteenth century. On the one hand, nominally Buddhist immigrants, mainly from China and Japan, came to the United States in search of economic opportunity but did not emphasize Buddhism either among themselves or to outsiders. On the other hand, after Chicago's 1893 World Parliament of Religions, a small group of Asian Buddhist teachers came to the United States specifically to teach Buddhism to Caucasians. This small stream of mainly Japanese men grew to a torrent by the 1970s, as teachers from all Asian Buddhist countries, especially Tibet, welcomed the opportunity to spread Buddhism among eager North American converts.

Women's participation in the spread of Buddhism in the United States is largely untold among Asian immigrants. Buddhism's view of women is ambiguous. Some Buddhists strongly emphasize the irrelevance of gender but others claim that women should strive to be reborn as men because women's capacities are limited. As is the case with all major world religions, Buddhism's institutions are patriarchal. None of the early teachers sent to minister to Chinese or Japanese communities or to teach Caucasians were women. However, Buddhism is important in the religious lives of Asian women, and women are crucial supporters of Buddhism in all Asian Buddhist countries. These patterns continue among Asian Americans. Caucasian women were receptive to Buddhist teachers and worked hard to establish Buddhist centers in North America. The response of these women lends credibility to a common thesis about U.S. religious history: women, more than men, are drawn to alternative religions because they can more easily act as leaders and teachers than in most Christian denominations. One woman, Ruth Fuller Everett Sasaki (d. 1967), first studied Buddhism in Japan in the 1930s. In the late 1930s she became a major supporter and teacher for the Buddhist Society of America, one of the first Zen groups in the United States. She continued to help lead this group for the rest of her life. She married her Japanese teacher in an internment camp in 1944; after World War II she returned to Japan and in 1958 became the first foreigner ordained as a Zen priest in Japan. During her last years she oversaw the translation of classic Zen texts.

The most dramatic events in the history of Buddhism in the United States occurred during the 1970s, when the number of Asians teaching Buddhism in the United States increased dramatically. Buddhism, like all religions practiced in the United States, was deeply affected by the second wave of feminism. The result is the most egalitarian form of Buddhism thus far in its long and varied history—a strong, international Buddhist women's movement involving women from all sects of Buddhism, and the beginnings of a feminist transformation of Buddhism that parallels feminist transformations of other world religions. In Zen Buddhism many women have received "dharma transmission," the highest achievement,

meaning that they can become independent teachers. Many women hold leadership positions in all sects of Buddhism. Feminist Buddhists have begun to reconceptualize Buddhism in feminist ways.

▪ RITA M. GROSS

SEE ALSO Religion.

≋ Businesswomen and Corporations

In 1992 women in the United States represented 41.5 percent of all persons employed in managerial, executive, and administrative occupations, indicating an increase from 26.5 percent in 1978. These gains are also reflected in the dramatic increase in the number of women receiving bachelor's and master's degrees in business management over the last two decades. In 1970–71 women earned 9.1 percent of the bachelor's and 3.9 percent of the master's degrees awarded. In 1989–90 they earned 46.7 percent of the bachelor's degrees and 34 percent of the master's degrees. Much of this significant gain can be attributed to the women's movement, affirmative action, and the passage in 1972 of Title IX of the education amendments. These amendments legally recognized and prohibited sex discrimination in institutions of higher education.

Despite these real gains, closer inspection of women's distribution within the corporate world reveals some disturbing patterns common to all women aspiring to prestigious, high-paying, and male-dominated professions. Korn Ferry, a leading executive recruiting firm, notes that women and all people of color composed virtually the same percentage of officials with ranks of vice president or higher as they did a decade ago. Of the jobs at the vice-presidential level or higher within the nation's largest corporations, only 2.6 percent were held by women.

In their article on women managers in the United States, Ellen Fagenson and Janice Jackson reported the following: In 1992 12 percent of white and slightly more than 7 percent of Black and Latina women were managers. Annual earnings differ among women, but the largest inequities are still between men and women. The annual median income of women managers in 1992 represents 65 percent of the income of white male managers and 66 percent of all male managers. Latina women, compared with both other women and men, reflected the weakest distribution within the management ranks and the poorest earnings. Their annual median income represented 93 percent of white women managers' salaries, 76 percent of their Latino male counterparts' wages, 60 percent of white male managers' earnings, and 61 percent of all male managers' salaries.

What accounts for such differences between men and women in the corporate setting? As outright discriminatory practices and policies recede in the face of legal and social changes, other less obvious but equally powerful forces still persist. Despite significant increases in the numbers of women in the corporate setting, the model for those in the world of business remains based on male personality and behavioral characteristics. Research has clearly shown that traits associated with femininity are not as highly valued in our culture as those associated with men. Furthermore, although the scientific data show that the overlap between the sexes on most personality and behavioral measures is extensive, gender-role stereotypes continue, leaving women at a disadvantage in the workplace.

Unlike earlier studies, which showed that male managers and administrators held uniformly more negative perceptions of women compared to men regarding aptitude, motivation, temperament, and work habits, more recent research shows that negative correlations about women supervisors are weaker among women, well-educated males, and workers with female bosses. Although positive changes have occurred, other barriers for women, deeply embedded in the very organization of corporate life itself, still exist. Perhaps among the most critical are those that exclude women from the "old boy" networks, which are vital to individual advancement. When excluded from the key arena where the ongoing dynamics of professional life are carried out, women are rendered invisible when important professional decisions and judgments are made. When women are denied access to this component of corporate life (even if they have formed their own networks), they are left out of the profession's power centers. Their exclusion often prevents the male oriented corporate culture from seeing beyond myths about women's professional work habits, attitudes, and commitment.

Even when women have been able to achieve high-paying, high-prestige positions within a corporation, the costs have been high. Many have had to give up or delay marriage, children, and significant relationships. Those with a family have had to add to career commitments the demands of managing home and child-care. U.S. society must change its view of a "woman's place" both within the professions and within the home in order to balance and equalize the demands and rewards that men currently experience. It is important that feminists continue to question the "corporate success ethic" as defined by the prevailing traits, behavioral characteristics, and timing of white men's lives.

Ellen Fagenson and Janice Jackson, "The Status of Women Managers in the United States," in *Competitive Frontiers*, edited by Nancy Adler and Dafna Izraeli (Cambridge, Mass.: Basil Blackwell Ltd., 1994); Rosabeth Kanter, *The Challenge of Organizational Change* (New York: Maxwell MacMillan International, 1992); Debra Kaufman, "Professional Women: How Real the Recent Gains?" in *Women: A Feminist Perspective*, edited by Jo Freeman (Mountain View, Calif.: Mayfield Publishing Company, 1994).

■ DEBRA RENEE KAUFMAN

SEE ALSO Entrepreneurs; National Federation of Business and Professional Women.

≋ Cancer

More questions than answers exist about all types of cancer, particularly cancer in women. Cancer, however, was a "women's issue" long before the twentieth century. Attitudes, medical theories, and techniques related to cancer in women developed in the nineteenth century and continue to influence the treatment of women with gynecological cancers today.

From the days of classical Greece to the last quarter of the nineteenth century, society considered cancer primarily a woman's disease, probably because of the visible nature of some "women's cancers" such as those of the breast, vulva, and cervix, which led to more frequent diagnoses. As a result, the female reproductive system appeared predisposed to cancerous growths and, consequently, women felt particularly vulnerable to a disease that attacked the most intimate parts of their body. Tumors in these accessible parts of the body could be excised; records of mammectomies exist as far back as ancient Grecian times. The surgeries were performed without anesthesia. This naturally terrified women and in addition "desexed" them by removing body parts they identified with their womanhood. One symptom most feared by postmenopausal women was a bloody discharge, which often prefigured a painful death from uterine cancer. German women in the eighteenth century even had special terms for this type of bleeding, calling it "the clumps" or "the blight." Until the advent of abdominal surgery in the late nineteenth century, women with these symptoms turned to traditional therapies such as bloodletting, purging, and blistering, or tonics and herbs to build strength or relieve pain. None of these treatments changed their belief that cancer was a hopeless, killing disease that attacked women far more often than men.

In the United States a deep-seated cultural fear of cancer as a major threat to men as well as women emerged during the second half of the nineteenth century, when doctors reported an alarming increase in cancer rates among men. Physicians put forward several reasons to account for this: medical advances, such as microscopic examination and more frequent autopsies, revealed many previously hidden cancers as the actual cause of death in men as well as women; a gradual increase in the life span of both men and women allowed more cancers to develop; and environmental factors, such as urbanization and the stress of modern life, might have weakened the body.

The new fears intensified attempts to find cancer cures and, significantly, some of the first new procedures focused on gynecological cancers. Surgical gynecology appeared as a new medical specialty in the 1850s. By the 1860s a surgical model was created to treat virtually all female complaints. It is important to note that the vast majority of these "woman's surgeons" were male, since prejudice made it very difficult for any woman to obtain medical training, and surgery in particular remained a male bastion. Even women trained at women's medical colleges or abroad found it almost impossible to obtain hospital appointments. Thus, this most "female" of medical specialties internalized a male bias from its inception.

Several important cultural assumptions and myths about the nature of women reflected this male bias and became part of the medical logic of the new specialty. First, women were the weaker sex, with more delicate physical and emotional systems. Many medical pronouncements contained a strong paternalistic element, stressing the duty of the stronger male physician to guide his weaker female patient. Equally important in dictating the kind of health care available to women was the belief that the reproductive system dominated a woman's entire body and that any dysfunction could ruin her physical and mental health. The popular "nerve force" theory, frequently mentioned in Victorian medical journals, claimed that the most important organs in the human body required most of the body's energy resources. In men, the brain was the highest-ranked organ, while in women the womb took precedence. If women diverted necessary nerve force from the womb to some other area, such as the brain, their reproductive organs purportedly could not develop or function properly. Further, the supersensitive female nervous system could then "broadcast" these pathological conditions throughout the body and even the mind. These ideas fostered a sense of inevitability about the necessity for medical intervention at some point in a woman's gynecological life.

Even before the advent of successful antiseptic techniques in the 1880s, gynecological surgeons aggressively expanded the scope of their operations into the abdominal cavity itself, establishing themselves as pioneers in high-risk abdominal surgery at a time when most surgeons avoided it. During the late 1850s, for example, mortality rates for ovariotomies to remove ovarian tumors and cysts were as high as 75 percent. Mortality rates fell into the 20 percent range by the end of the 1870s although some surgeons achieved much lower rates. Surgical observations supported the theory that cancer first developed in a specific area and, if located early enough, surgeons could remove the abnormal cells, leaving healthy tissue behind. Surgical gynecologists, therefore, played an important role in establishing surgery as the primary, and, until recently, only successful treatment for cancer in general.

How can women's experiences with the new surgical procedures such as ovariotomy be evaluated? The individual voices of most women patients of the past remain hidden, but hospital case histories offer a sense of women's personal experiences. For example, an 1869 case book for Woman's Hospital of New York records information about Mrs. Fannie L., fifty-eight. By the time she entered the hospital, she was debilitated from over five years of pain, uterine bleeding, and harsh medical treatment with caustics. The surgeon re-

moved a large cancerous tumor from her uterus and she received liberal doses of morphine and opium for pain.

Significantly, Mrs. L. waited at least three years before consulting a doctor about her symptoms. Even today many women dread a pelvic examination, but Victorian prescriptions for female modesty made the thought of exposing yourself to a man who was not your husband nearly impossible. Since women doctors were relatively scarce, social standards of modesty and propriety kept many women from seeking help until their pain overcame their inhibitions.

In addition to modesty, poor women faced special obstacles in getting treatment. Mrs. L. occupied a free or very low-cost bed, which she had obtained by qualifying as "respectable poor" and submitting a letter of recommendation from one of the wealthy sponsors of charity beds. Only women judged worthy by the standards of the benefactors received their "lines," women who could prove their moral character as well as their medical need. These women also needed the means, strength, and time to travel about the city to the homes of sponsors to petition for these letters. Given the racism of the time, women of color had little chance of receiving a recommendation. The vast majority of poor women, especially women of color, remained outpatients, making do with cursory treatment by an overworked dispensary physician.

Once admitted to the hospital, cancer patients often endured a particular stigma. In 1871 the Lady Managers of Woman's Hospital, the women who raised funds and oversaw the daily running of the hospital, insisted that no cancer patients be admitted to the hospital in the future. They maintained that the fetid odor emanating from cancer patients (this was especially true in cases of uterine cancer) offended other women patients and the mere presence of cancer cases frightened them. This would lead to financial disaster, since the Lady Managers argued that the women most likely to leave the hospital would be paying patients from the middle class, whose fees accounted for half the annual income of the hospital. The logic of this argument stemmed in part from the common belief that genteel women were more delicate than poor women, with nervous systems that were more vulnerable to physical or emotional stress. Doctors as well as the lay community adhered to this class bias and adapted medical treatments accordingly. Wealthy women could arrange for care at home, but poor women who were rejected by a hospital rarely received further treatment.

Nonetheless, the pursuit of surgical cures for cancers continued, and surgery continued to be the primary mode of treatment even after it was combined with radiation and chemotherapy in the twentieth century. As we have seen, poor urban women did not have the same access to cancer surgery as middle-class women. Poor rural women, including Native American women on reservations, had even less access, since they would need to travel to urban centers, where the specialists and hospitals were usually located. Hospitalized women of color endured the double burden of poverty and racism. The statistical tables for gynecological cases from 1892 to 1911 at Johns Hopkins Hospital in Baltimore show separate "white" and "colored" listings. The table for white gynecological cases, including many types of cancer cases, is seven pages long with an extremely detailed list of diseases and diagnoses. The table for women of color, however, is only two pages long and consists of a generic list of body areas and the total number of benign and malignant tumors. This in itself reflects the relative status and quality of care accorded each type of patient. Women of color rarely gained admission at all, and then received substandard treatment in segregated wards.

The marketing of cancer surgery to women also reflected a middle-class bias. Since early detection was key, doctors urged women to consult them at the first signs of symptoms and to get regular check-ups, both of which required money. Nothing, it seemed, could be done to *prevent* can-

cer in women. In fact a 1908 commentary in the *British Medical Journal* noted that surgeons had no time for researching the causes of gynecological cancer and lacked the necessary scientific training. The article also stated, however, that neither scientist nor surgeon had studied the living habits of women over time and that this needed to be redressed in the future.

Some gynecologists developed general theories about why certain cancers developed in certain women based on their personal observations. For example, many doctors linked uterine cancer with change of life and some believed cervical cancer developed only in sexually active women. A common explanation for malignancies in younger women, such as ovarian cancer, was their unmarried status or sterility. Without concerted research activity, however, these theories remained speculative. One might ask if the underlying theories of female physiology discussed above delayed further research. After all, why look beyond the notion that the female reproductive system was somehow *predisposed* to morbidity?

The methods and attitudes developed by the medical community to treat and investigate women's cancers in the nineteenth century persisted into the late twentieth century.

Medical bias has remained white, middle-class, and heterosexual. Neither women of color nor lesbians have been the focus of major medical research, and quality of care has been problematic for both groups. For example, very few medical studies have addressed the interaction of racism, economic disadvantage, and genetics that has contributed to increasing rates of cancer in African American women.

Lesbians run higher risks of breast and uterine cancer because they bear fewer children than heterosexual women. Furthermore, many lesbians do not get regular gynecological exams, in part because they do not use contraceptives, which would require such exams, but more often because of the homophobic attitudes they encounter. As with women of color, there is inadequate information on lesbian health.

Feminist activists continue to campaign for more basic research and improved access to care for all women. One positive development has been the Women's Health Care Initiative, a long-term NIH study of women's health launched in 1991 by then-director Dr. Bernadette Healy. Expansion of these efforts, however, is endangered by political backlash and severe cuts in funding.

Change has been slow. The feminist activism of the past two decades has created a climate for supporting women's health care research, but as Australian feminist Germaine Greer wrote in *The Change*, "[W]e do not know enough about the well woman to understand what has gone wrong with the sick one."

James Patterson, *The Dread Disease: Cancer and Modern American Culture* (Cambridge, Mass.: Harvard University Press, 1987); Sue V. Rosser, *Women's Health—Missing From U.S. Medicine* (Bloomington: Indiana University Press, 1994).

■ JUDITH M. ROY

SEE ALSO Breast Cancer; Medical Research.

≋ Catholicism

The Roman Catholic Church in North America emerged from two distinct and contradictory aspects of Catholic political history. The church triumphant is exemplified by the fifteenth- and sixteenth-century Spanish adventurers and their priests, who worked for the conquest and conversion of the native peoples of the Americas from Patagonia to California. The concept of the church persecuted, on the other hand, manifested itself in the English colonies of North America. Catholic colonists had emigrated in pursuit of religious freedom but were often objects of deep suspicion, intolerance, and discrimination.

From those beginnings emerged today's church: the largest single religious denomination in the United States, claiming almost fifty-four million members (about 25 percent of the population). The church is a major provider of social services throughout the United States, a recipient of billions of government dollars, and a powerful player in national and state social policymaking.

Given the profoundly patriarchal and sexist nature of church governance and hierarchical perspectives on theology, Catholic women worldwide have had difficulty achieving recognition of their moral competency and equality with men. In the United States, the Catholic bishops' advocacy against both women's rights and measures to enhance sexual well-being and reproductive health has impeded women's progress.

To understand the U.S. bishops' political agenda, one must understand the origins of Christian social thought. Early Christianity was characterized by distrust of women's nature and by fear and loathing of the body and sexuality. No example could be more telling than the role model the church offers young women: Mary, the Virgin Mother—and, unable to be both virgins and mothers, women must be one or the other. The major shapers of church teaching, from the early period through the age of high scholasticism to the current pope, sound this theme repeatedly in their writings.

The litany of antiwoman statements is long: Paul announced in the First Letter to Timothy (2:12): "I permit no woman to teach or have authority over men; she is to keep silent." Clement of Alexandria noted that among women "the very consciousness of their own nature must evoke feelings of shame." Augustine mused that nothing "drags the mind of a man down from its elevation so much as the caresses of a woman." In the thirteenth century, Aquinas held that women are at best imperfect men corresponding to "nature's second intention [to such things as] decay, deformity, and the weakness of age." Odo of Cluny said "to embrace a woman is to embrace a sack of manure."

Antifemale thinking was and is reinforced by the exclusion of women from the priesthood and the prohibition of marriage for priests. This thinking perpetuates the pre-Enlightenment views of women and sex that are still held up in today's church as appropriate models of female thought and behavior. In May 1994, for example, Pope John Paul II held up two role models of Christian womanhood by his beatification (a significant rung on the ladder to sainthood) of two women. The first was an Italian pediatrician who, in her fourth pregnancy, was diagnosed with uterine cancer and refused treatment that would have saved her life but cost that of the fetus. She died shortly after delivering a daughter. The second was a nineteenth-century Italian battered woman who was beatified because she honored the sacrament of matrimony and remained in the marriage, enduring abuse.

"Indicating these women as models of Christian perfection," the pope said, "we wish to pay homage to all courageous mothers who devote themselves totally to their own family, who suffer in giving birth to their children, and are willing to accept all weariness, all sacrifice, in order to give them the best of themselves."

Current church positions still claim that women cannot be ordained as priests because they do not physically resemble Jesus and that sex is permissible only in a lifelong, monogamous, heterosexual marriage. Control of reproductive decisions that seriously affect women's participation in society is an especially active area of church intervention. The list of the "forbidden" is long and unrelenting: masturbation, homosexual activity, all contraceptive devices and medications, most methods of assisted reproduction, and all abortions, even those performed to save a woman's life.

U.S. church leaders have worked throughout the twentieth century to promote legislation that would limit women's freedom and rights. They have opposed proposals to liberalize divorce, legalize contraceptives for married couples, amend the Constitution to affirm equal rights for women, legalize abortion, provide funding for abortions for poor women, and foster gay civil rights.

Beginning in the 1970s an overtly feminist movement developed within the Roman Catholic Church. Catholic women were influenced by both the secular women's movement and by a growing international Catholic movement for social justice. They were attracted to a new Latin American liberation theology that not only held that the church should stand with the poor and oppressed but also applied a Marxist analysis of the state to the governance of the church. U.S. Catholic women created grassroots and national organizations that are struggling for a voice and for change in church and public policy. The Women's Ordination Conference works for a more egalitarian priesthood. The Conference of Catholic Lesbians serves as a support network and advocacy group for Catholic lesbians. Catholics for a Free Choice seeks the recognition of the moral agency of women as decision makers about reproduction. African American and Hispanic women have formed organizations and developed distinctive theologies—called *womanist* and *mujerista*, respectively—to address questions of race as well as gender. A diverse base of Catholic women's groups has gathered in a coalition called the Women-Church Convergence to enhance women's rights in the church and in civil society. Some groups have adopted a "post-Catholic" posture: rather than try to change the church, they create models of church and worship that are distinctly feminist.

While church leaders at various times have criticized all these groups, condemning their "exaggerated secular feminism," the groups are growing. Catholic feminist scholars and theologians have developed a rich feminist Catholic literature that aims to recover the lost history of women's roles in the church and to develop a feminist theology and ethic rooted in women's experience rather than in patriarchal abstraction.

■ FRANCES KISSLING

SEE ALSO Nuns; Religion.

≋ Celibacy

Fifty years ago it took courage for a woman to admit she was enjoying a genitally active sex life. Today it takes courage to admit she is not. Our society assumes that women in particular should be eager consumers of preferably heterosexual activity which, along with beauty products, diets, low wages, and violence, is part of the contemporary culture that aims to limit women's power. In researching *Women, Passion and Celibacy*, this author found that women of all ages, races, and sexual orientations are expected to buy into the "genital myth," which prescribes genitally active behavior.

Despite celibacy's ancient and honorable tradition that historically has been seen as a more elevated male ideal than genital activity, celibate women are labeled asexual or frigid. Female celibacy has been defined by the patriarchy as total genital abstention. But women are redefining their behavior and identity as essentially sexual. Differences exist between "ascetic celibates," who eschew any form of genital intimacy and much sensual expression, and "sensual celibates," who feel free to touch and who enjoy masturbation and affectionate physical intimacy.

Celibacy is a form of female sexuality, a choice to be without a sexual partner for positive reasons of personal, political, or spiritual growth and independence. It is a sexual singlehood that allows women to define themselves autonomously while still retaining a network of connections. It is a form of sexual practice without the power struggles of a genitally active relationship.

Although historically nuns' celibacy has been required, today's celibates make choices for other positive reasons, as a search for autonomy. Celibacy constitutes passion without possession, in which genital abstention is not the determining feature. Women turn to celibacy for many reasons, including platonic companionship, spiritual growth, time for careers, fear of violence, dislike of penetration, antipathy to the unequal power dimension inherent in genital relationships, sexual anxiety, an after-effect of child sexual abuse, fear of AIDS, dislike of possessiveness, widowhood, illness, disability, lack of communication with partners, a search for passion, or the need for solitude. Many celibate women see men as friends rather than as lovers or enemies. Lesbian women in partnerships report less pressure about being celibate than do heterosexual women. Those *in* couples find it harder than do single women to state openly that they are celibate for fear of hurting partners.

If celibacy can be seen as a form of sexuality, even when what celibate women do is not generally described as sexual activity, then a philosophical change could occur in understanding the word. Celibacy can include masturbation, intimate touching, and a high degree of physical affection, but it is *not* about relating to other people; it focuses on women's personal development and illustrates a cultural shift in the perception of celibacy. In the area of sexuality, women are breaking new ground, linguistically, philosophically, and practically.

▪ SALLY CLINE

SEE ALSO Sexuality.

≋ Censorship

Throughout history, the anticensorship cause has been integrally connected to the women's rights cause. All censorship measures have been used disproportionately against relatively powerless individuals and relatively unpopular ideas. Accordingly, along with other oppressed groups and reformers, women and feminists have borne the brunt of censorship and have had the greatest stake in defending freedom of speech.

The suppression of speech that is especially important for women has been accomplished primarily through measures aimed at sexual expression. For example, in 1839 Massachusetts prosecuted the author of the first U.S. medical work about contraception, under its antiobscenity law. Important feminist works that recently have been attacked as obscene or pornographic include Betty Friedan's landmark *The Feminine Mystique*; the classic book on women's health and sexuality, *Our Bodies, Ourselves*; and *Ms.* magazine.

During the first wave of the U.S. women's movement, beginning in the nineteenth century, a central goal was reproductive freedom. But the first major U.S. censorship law was repeatedly used to silence pioneering advocates of women's reproductive rights. This 1873 statute, called the "Comstock Law" after antiobscenity crusader Anthony Comstock, made it a serious crime to mail material concerning contraception or abortion. Most states enacted their own versions of this legislation, outlawing publications about contraceptives and abortifacients.

Pathbreaking feminists and birth-control advocates such as Margaret Sanger were constantly plagued by Comstockian censorship. Sanger was twice imprisoned for distributing birth-control information. In 1912 postal officials barred one of her first newspaper articles, even though it contained no contraceptive information, because of her discussion of venereal disease. Her 1917 movie "Birth Control," dramatizing her family planning work, was censored in New York. Until the 1950s New York censors continued to ban films concerning subjects of particular interest to women and feminists, including abortion, birth control, divorce, illegitimacy, interracial marriage, pregnancy, prostitution, and venereal disease.

Until the 1930s the Comstock Law and its state counterparts were regularly used against feminists and health experts who published information about women's sexuality and reproductive options. More recently, other legal tools have been used for the same purposes. The "gag rule"—in effect from 1988 until 1993 and, since 1994, threatened to be reinstated by congressional Republicans—prohibits personnel at federally funded family planning clinics from providing any information about abortion. In 1990 an American Civil Liberties Union lawyer was charged with a misdemeanor under Guam's newly passed antiabortion law when she told Guamanian women that they could still get legal abortions in Hawaii.

Most recently, as part of the Communications Decency Act (CDA) passed in February 1996, Congress extended the Comstock Law into cyberspace, criminalizing on-line communications about abortion. The CDA's additional sweeping bans on "indecent" and "patently offensive" cybercommunications also endangered much expression of particular value to women's rights, including information about birth control, sexually transmitted diseases, sexual abuse, and violence against women. In 1997 the Supreme Court found the CDA to be unconstitutional.

Along with advocates of women's reproductive freedom, other women and feminists who have been special targets of censorship—with antiobscenity laws again the major weapons—are those who have advocated lesbian rights or even just described lesbian relationships. In 1929 a New York magistrate held that Radclyffe Hall's pathbreaking novel, *The Well of Loneliness*, was obscene.

To this day, obscenity prosecutions and other censorial tools are used disproportionately against lesbians. Illustrative are the recent political attacks on the National Endowment for the Arts (NEA). As a federal judge noted in ruling that some NEA cutbacks amounted to unconstitutional censorship, "[T]he NEA has been the target of congressional critics . . . for funding works . . . that express women's anger over male dominance in the realm of sexuality or which endorse equal legitimacy for homosexual and heterosexual practices."

In light of this long history of censorship measures—in particular, those aimed at sexually-oriented expression—being used to suppress expression that is particularly important to the women's rights cause, many feminists have opposed antipornography laws that other feminists have advocated since the early 1980s. These laws define illegal pornography as sexually explicit words or images that are "subordinating" to women.

While the feminists who advocate this form of censorship secured the passage of antipornography laws in one U.S. jurisdiction, which the Supreme Court struck down as unconstitutional, their efforts have also spawned an influential feminist anticensorship movement. Several women's organizations have been founded specifically to counter the notion that censoring pornography would promote women's rights and safety. In 1984, when the first antipornography law advocated by some feminists was passed in Minneapolis, a brief opposing it was filed by the Feminist Anti-Censorship Taskforce, or FACT. FACT argued that, far from advancing women's interests, the law violated women's equality rights.

That antipornography laws advocated by some feminists would do particular damage to women's rights has been confirmed by the experience in Canada, which since 1992 has criminalized sexual expression that is "degrading" or "dehumanizing" to women. Under this law, too, along with all other censorship measures throughout U.S. history, major targets have been feminist and lesbian and gay expression. The historical (and contemporary) lesson is clear: the fight against censorship is an essential element in the fight for women's rights.

Margaret A. Blanchard, "The American Urge to Censor: Freedom of Expression versus the Desire to Sanitize Society—From Anthony Comstock to 2 Live Crew," *William and Mary Law Review* 33 (1992): 741–851; Nadine Strossen, *Defending Pornography: Free Speech, Sex, and the Fight for Women's Rights* (New York: Scribner, 1995).

▪ NADINE STROSSEN

SEE ALSO Antipornography Activism; Obscenity; Pornography.

≋ Census

A census is a complete count of a population conducted by house to house or mail enumeration. The area covered is generally a political jurisdiction, such as a county, city, state, or the country. The United States has conducted a constitutionally mandated decennial census since 1790.

Both the surviving manuscript records of the enumerations and the resulting census reports provide information about family structure, fertility and mortality patterns, race and ethnic composition, the nature of work, and economic status. As such, census information is the ground on which much basic knowledge about women—and all Americans in the last two centuries—stands.

Census records and publications are also embedded in the ideological constructions of the existing society—particularly in the official state classifications and categories for work, family, race, and "normal" household forms. Until the twentieth century, most census takers were men. The questions asked about women and the answers considered credible and important enough to tabulate and publish are viewed as inadequate from a modern feminist perspective. In particular, women's unpaid household labor has not been included in the accounts of occupations and the labor force. Until the practice changed in 1980, the U.S. Census Bureau defined the oldest adult male in the household as the "head," even if the woman claimed headship.

Recently, feminist scholars have begun to retabulate manuscript and public-use sample census data to provide a more realistic and diverse picture of women's experiences and situations in the past.

▪ MARGO A. ANDERSON

≋ Chicana Civil Rights Organizations

Chicana civil rights activists have faced serious obstacles within male-dominated political organizations. Beginning in the 1960s Chicanas formed numerous regional and national civil rights organizations. In 1970 a group of Chicanas in California founded the Comision Femenil Nacional (National Feminist Commission), which addressed a wide range of issues affecting Chicanas. The Comision Femenil promoted the formulation of public policies that would address the specific needs of Chicanas. This organization would become the model for subsequent organizations due to its emphasis on developing leadership roles and organizational skills among its members.

Similarly, the Mexican American Women's National Association (MANA)—a major national organization established in 1974—worked toward the advancement of Mexican American women by promoting leadership and facilitating a national communication network among Chicanas from all socioeconomic backgrounds and political ideologies. MANA was organized by Chicanas living in Washington, D.C., and soon after its founding had members in sixteen states. MANA promoted the establishment of regional chapters throughout the United States. MANA's main priorities included organizing a yearly national leadership training conference, publishing position papers on Chicana issues, and representing Chicanas at national conferences dealing with Hispanic issues. MANA representatives participated actively in U.S. Hispanic organizations in order to put Chicana issues on their national agendas.

A key Chicana civil rights activist and feminist, Francisca Flores, founded the California League of Mexican American Women, a southern Californian organization that worked at the local and regional level for women's rights. The Chicana National Welfare Rights Organization was created by Alicia Escalante, who later, with Francisca Flores, established the Chicana Service Action Center. Chicanas in these groups developed skills as community leaders and organizers. Both groups organized workshops, conferences, and other community activities that addressed Chicana concerns, such as education, immigration, child care, and reproductive rights.

In 1981 a group of Chicana academics formed Mujeres Activas en Letras y Cambio Social (MALCS—Women Active in Letters and Social Change). This organization aimed to restructure universities by recruiting and retaining more Chicana faculty and students, revising the curriculum, and supporting academic research that contributes directly to the improvement of Chicanas in the United States.

■ ALMA M. GARCÍA

SEE ALSO Mujeres Activas en Letras y Cambio Social (MALCS).

≋ Chicanas and Mexican American Women

Beginning with the Coronado expedition of 1540, Spanish-speaking women migrated to what is now the United States. In efforts to secure its territorial claims, the Spanish crown offered inducements to those willing to undertake the arduous and frequently perilous journey. Subsidies given to a band of settlers headed for Texas included not only food and livestock but also petticoats and stockings. Although some settlers claimed "Spanish" blood, the majority were mestizo (Spanish/Indian), and some were of African descent.

Few women ventured to the Mexican north as widows or orphans; most arrived as the wives or

The Amador family women, circa 1910, New Mexico.

daughters of soldiers, farmers, and artisans. Over three centuries, they raised families on the frontier and worked alongside their fathers or husbands, herding cattle and tending crops. Furthermore, the Franciscans recruited Mexican American women into their service as teachers, midwives, doctors, cooks, seamstresses, and supply managers.

Women's networks, based on ties of blood and kinship, were central to the settlement of the Mexican frontier. At times women settlers acted as midwives to mission Indians and also baptized sickly or stillborn babies. As godmothers for these infants, they established bonds between Native American and Spanish/Mexican women. However, exploitation took place among women. For those in domestic service, racial and class hierarchies undermined the pretense of sisterhood. In San Antonio, Texas, in 1735, Antonía Lusgardia Ernandes, a mulatta, sued her former employer for custody of their son. Admitting paternity, the man claimed that his former servant had relinquished the child to his wife because his wife had

baptized the child: the court, however, granted Ernandes custody. Although the godparent relationship could foster ties between colonists and Native Americans, elites used baptism as a venue of social control. Indentured servitude, for instance, was prevalent on the colonial frontier well into the nineteenth century.

Spanish/Mexican settlement has been shrouded in myth. Walt Disney's film *Zorro*, for example, epitomized the notion of a romantic California controlled by fun-loving, swashbuckling rancheros. As only 3 percent of California's Mexican population could be considered rancheros in 1850, most women did not preside over large estates but helped to manage small family farms. In addition to performing traditional female tasks, Mexican women were accomplished *vaqueras*, or cowgirls. Like their Anglo counterparts, they encountered a duality in frontier expectations. On the one hand they were placed on a pedestal as delicate "ladies"; on the other hand they were responsible for a variety of strenuous chores.

Married women on the Mexican frontier had certain legal advantages not afforded their Anglo peers. Under English common law, when women married they became *feme covert* (or "dead" in the eyes of the legal system) and could not own property separately from their husbands. Conversely, Spanish/Mexican women retained control of their land after marriage and held one-half interest in the community property they shared with their spouses.

Life for Mexicans changed dramatically in 1848 with the conclusion of the Mexican War, the discovery of gold in California, and the Treaty of Guadalupe Hidalgo. Mexicans on the U.S. side of the border became second-class citizens, divested of their property, political power, and cultural entitlement. Their world turned upside down. Segregated from the Anglo population, Mexican Americans in the barrios of Southwest cities and towns sustained their sense of identity and cherished their traditions. With little opportunity for advancement, Mexicans were concentrated in lower echelon industrial, service, and agricultural jobs. This period of conquest and marginalization, both physical and ideological, did not occur in a dispassionate environment. Stereotypes affected rich and poor alike, with Mexicans commonly described as lazy, sneaky, and greasy. In Anglo journals, novels, and travelogues, Spanish-speaking women were frequently depicted as flashy, morally deficient sirens.

At times these images had tragic results. On July 5, 1851, a Mexican woman swung from the gallows, the only woman lynched during the California gold rush. Josefa Segovia (also known as Juanita of Downieville) was tried, convicted, and hanged on the same day she had killed an Anglo miner, a man who the day before had assaulted her.

Some historians have asserted that elite families believed they had a greater chance of retaining their land if they acquired an Anglo son-in-law. Intermarriage, however, was no insurance policy. In 1849 María Amparo Ruiz married Lieutenant Colonel Henry S. Burton and five years later the couple purchased Rancho Jamul, a sprawling property of over five hundred thousand acres. When Henry Burton died in 1869, the ownership of Rancho Jamul came into question. After seven years of litigation, the court awarded his widow only 8,926 acres. Even this amount was challenged by squatters and she would continue to lose acreage in the years that followed. Chronicling her experiences, Ruiz de Burton, probably the first Spanish/Mexican woman writer in the Southwest, wrote *The Squatter and the Don* (1885), a fictionalized account of the decline of the ranching class.

Nineteenth-century Spanish-language newspapers provided insight into community life and offered ample information on social mores. Newspaper editors upheld the double standard. Women were to be cloistered and protected to the extent that some residents of New Mexico protested the establishment of coeducational public schools. In 1877 Father Gasparri of *La revista católica* editorialized that women's suffrage would destroy the family. Despite prevailing conventions, large numbers of Mexican women, as a result of economic circumstances wrought by political and social disenfranchisement, sought employment for wages. Whether in cities or on farms, family members pooled their earnings to put food on the table. Women worked at home taking in laundry, housing boarders, and sewing, while others worked in the fields, or in restaurants, hotels, canneries, and laundries.

In 1900 over four hundred thousand Mexicans lived in the Southwest. By 1930 this figure would more than double as over one million Mexicanos, pushed out by revolution and lured in by prospective jobs, came to the United States. They settled in existing barrios and forged new communities both in the Southwest and the Midwest. Like their foremothers, women usually journeyed north as wives and daughters. Some, however, crossed the border alone or as single mothers. As before, women's wage earnings proved essential to family survival. They worked in canneries and garment plants as well as in the service sector. Entire families labored in the fields and received their wages in a single check made out to the head of the household. Few have pleasant memories of their work experiences. Julia Luna Mount remembered peeling chilies by hand all day long while Grace Luna related how women would scale ladders with one hundred pounds of cotton on their backs; some had to "carry their kids on top of their picking sacks!"

Exploitation in pay and working conditions prompted attempts at unionization. Through Mexican mutual aid societies and progressive trade unions, Mexican women proved tenacious activists. In 1933 alone thirty-seven major agricultural strikes occurred in California, with twenty-four led by the Cannery and Agricultural Workers Industrial Union (CAWIU). The Los Angeles Dressmakers' Strike (1933), the San Antonio Pecan Shellers Strike (1938), and the California Sanitary Canning Company Strike (1939) are examples of urban activism.

Like the daughters of European immigrants, young Mexican women experienced the lure of consumer culture. Considerable intergenerational conflict emerged as adolescents wanted to dress and perhaps behave like their Anglo peers at work or like the heroines they encountered in movies and magazines. Evading traditional chaperonage became a major preoccupation for youth. However, they and their kin faced the specter of deportation. From 1931 to 1934 over one-third of the Mexican population in the United States (more than five hundred thousand people) were deported or repatriated. Discrimination and segregation in housing, employment, schools, and public recreation further served to remind youth of their second-class citizenship. In María Arredondo's words, "I remember . . . signs all over that read 'no Mexicans allowed.'"

Operating small barrio businesses, the Mexican middle class at times allied themselves with their working-class customers and at times strived for social distance. The League of United Latin American Citizens (LULAC) did both simultaneously. An important civil rights organization, with women's active participation, LULAC confronted segregation through the courts; however, only U.S. citizens could join. Conversely, El Congreso de Pueblos de Habla Española stressed immigrant rights.

After World War II, Mexican women were involved in a gamut of political organizations, from the American G.I. Forum to the Community Service Organization (CSO). An Alinsky-style group, CSO stressed local issues and voter registration. Two CSO leaders, Cesar Chávez and Dolores Huerta, would forge the United Farm Workers (UFW) during the early 1960s, he as president, she as vice president. A principal negotiator, lobbyist, and strategist, Huerta relied on extended kin and women friends in the union to care for her eleven children during her absences. Although criticized for putting the union first, Dolores Huerta has had few regrets. As she told historian Margaret Rose, "But now that I've seen how good they [her children] turned out, I don't feel so guilty." Family activism has characterized UFW organizing.

As part of global student movements of the late 1960s, Mexican American youth joined together to address continuing problems of discrimination, particularly in their educational and political representation. Embracing the mantle of cultural nationalism, they transformed the pejorative barrio term "Chicano" into a symbol of pride. "Chicano/Chicana" implies a commitment to social justice and to social change. A graduate student in history at UCLA, Magdalena Mora not only wrote about trade union struggles but participated in them as well. She organized cannery workers in Richmond, California, and participated in CASA, a national immigrant rights group. An activist since high school, she died in 1981 of a brain tumor at the age of twenty-nine. The informal credo of the Chicano student movement was to return to the community after a college education.

Sexism permeated gender relations within Chicano organizations, yet the class orientation and racism within "mainstream" feminist groups precluded coalition building. Ana Nieto Gómez called this being caught between the "paternal and the maternal" movements. In forming their own agenda, Chicanas looked to the histories of their mothers and grandmothers and to role models of the past—Sor Juana Inés de la Cruz (the Mexican poet), and labor leaders Sara Estela Ramírez, Emma Tenayucca, and Luisa Moreno. Elizabeth Martínez's *450 Years of Chicano History* brought to light these legacies. Marta Cotera, Ana Nieto Gómez, and Carmen Tafolla began to articulate a feminism that was distinctly Chicana.

Chicana lesbians often found themselves isolated from Chicanos and heterosexual Chicanas. It was not until 1992 that the Lesbian Caucus was established at the National Association of Chicano Studies. The works of Gloria Anzaldúa, Cherríe Moraga, and their compañeras bring out their pain and isolation, but more importantly their joys, self-respect, and dignity. Lesbian writers such as Chela Sandoval remain at the heart of Chicana feminist theory.

A layering of generations exists among Mexicans in the United States from seventh-generation New Mexicans to recent immigrants. This layering provides a vibrant cultural dynamic. Artists Amalia Mesa Bains, Judy Baca, and Carmen Lomas Garza, and poets Sandra Cisneros, Pat Mora, and Alicia Gaspar de Alba (to name a few) articulate the multiple identities inhabiting the borderlands of Chicana culture. Across generations, women have come together for collective action. Communities Organized for Public Service (San Antonio) and Mothers of East LA (Los Angeles) exemplify how parish networks become channels for social change. Former student activists María Varela and María Elena Durazo remain committed to issues of economic justice—Varela through the New Mexico rural cooperative Los Ganados del Valle and Durazo as president of Local 11 of L.A.'s Hotel and Restaurant Employees Union. Whether they live in Chicago or El Paso, Mexican women share legacies of resistance. As Varela related, "I learned . . . that it is not enough to pray over an injustice or protest it or research it to death, but that you have to take concrete action to solve it."

Adela de la Torre and Beatríz M. Pesquera, eds., *Building with Our Hands: New Directions in Chicana Studies* (Berkeley: University of California Press, 1993); Adelaida R. Del Castillo, ed., *Between Borders: Essays on Mexicana/Chicana History* (Los Angeles: Floricanto Press, 1990); Vicki L. Ruiz, *From Out of the Shadows: A History of Mexican Women in the United States* (New Haven: Yale University Press, 1997).

▪ VICKI L. RUIZ

SEE ALSO Chicana Civil Rights Organizations; Community Service Organization (CSO); Feminism, Chicana; La Raza; Latina/Chicana Migration; Latinas; League of United Latin American Citizens; Lesbians, Latina; Mujeres Activas en Letras y Cambio Social (MALCS); Witchcraft on the Spanish-Mexican Borderlands.

≋ Child Abuse

In the United States in the 1960s, a new protectiveness toward children emerged, stimulated in part by the civil rights and women's movements, which created a growing awareness of other groups' vulnerabilities and needs. In 1962 pediatrician C. Henry Kempe published "The Battered Child Syndrome." This influential article paved the way for the modern child protection system. Within ten years, every state in the nation had passed laws requiring professionals who are responsible for the care of children to report—usually to state departments of social service or welfare—situations in which they believe a child could be at risk for abuse.

The definition of child abuse has expanded over the years from physical injury to physical assault, neglect, emotional abuse, and sexual activity that is coercive or that occurs with someone older than the child. This broadening definition of child abuse, increasing public awareness, and—more arguably—intensifying pressures on the family have combined to rocket child abuse reports from around six to seven thousand a year in the late 1960s to between two and three million a year by the 1990s. Abuse reports, however, do not necessarily reflect the actual incidence of child abuse. No one knows with certainty how many children are abused; most agencies mandated to protect children are overburdened and underfunded, and children and families are all too often poorly served.

Child abuse is one of the five leading causes of childhood death in the United States today and has serious physical, emotional, and behavioral consequences for the child, including, in some cases, a tendency toward aggression and violence. The prevailing theory in the 1960s about the reasons for child abuse was that parents who abused their children were mentally disturbed (and the designated "sick" parent was typically the mother). The focus on parental psychopathology led to "talking" cures—psychotherapy or counseling—or to removing children from the home. The theory ignored the extraordinary stresses many parents of abused children endure.

Although research findings have helped to debunk the "crazy-parent" theory, much of the focus on child abuse still suffers from methodological problems that limit its usefulness. For example, studies show that professionals are more likely to report child abuse if the family is of color, poor, or headed by a single woman. As a consequence, some researchers wrongly concluded that child abuse is a problem among people of color, the poor, and single women. In fact, child abuse is found in every population and at every economic level in U.S. society.

No single theory or causal agent is sufficient to explain child abuse. Several well-designed longitudinal studies, however, have identified factors that contribute to the *risk* of abuse, including being the child of a parent who grew up in an abusive home; being the child of a teenage or single mother; or experiencing poverty, family conflict, dangerous neighborhoods, social isolation, and substance abuse. A particularly troubling finding is that the majority of mothers of abused children also are battered by their male partners. Protective services may view a woman as unprotective and remove her children, even though the abusive man may be victimizing both the mother and children. As a result, women are often blamed for their children's abuse or neglect.

It is important to realize that risk factors do not *create* abuse; rather, they increase the likelihood of abuse. Some theorists propose an ecological view, recognizing that child abuse is not caused by any single factor but more typically occurs when risk factors converge. This viewpoint underscores the importance of looking at child abuse in a social and family context and not—as is often the case—as maternal failure or malfeasance.

Common sense dictates that the most appropriate approach to child abuse be ecological and multifaceted, including both prevention and intervention. This rarely happens. Once cases are recognized, a flexible and compassionate family assessment is the ideal first step toward identifying where the problems are and finding ways to alleviate them, including a combination of advocacy, counseling, and family support. A movement exists among those responsible for child protection to keep at-risk or abused children within their homes and to provide services to strengthen their families. Programs that support this type of intervention are woefully underfunded, however, leading child protection workers to remove children from their families because such family support services are unavailable. Furthermore, poorly trained workers often believe that mothers deliberately set out to harm their children. This blaming of mothers reflects a historical and deep-rooted prejudice against women whose children are at risk. For example, for decades psychiatrists erroneously held mothers responsible if their children were schizophrenic or autistic. Efforts to improve child protective services must include attention to the way professionals treat mothers as well as children.

In addition to interventions to treat abused children and their families, other programs are designed to prevent child abuse from occurring in the first place. A worrisome trend is the use of interviews and checklists designed to screen new parents to determine whose children are most at risk of being abused. The problem with screening is that professionals don't know precisely which factors cause child abuse, and labeling families can stigmatize them. Another preventive approach is home visiting, where trained specialists visit new parents, usually those who are very young or are single mothers. The best programs, which offer comprehensive educational, social, and medical services, appear to reduce reported incidents of child abuse, although—as with all child abuse interventions—more evaluation is needed to determine what is most effective and for whom.

Vulnerable families need more and better treatment and prevention services. Yet for service providers to make meaningful inroads against child abuse, they must address the fundamental aspects of society that erode the family. Particularly noxious is the feminization of poverty and the extent to which women and children live in circumstances that do not support a productive, nurturing family life. Minimally, women who must work outside the home need good, affordable child care and reasonable assurance that their children are well cared for; opportunities for satisfying jobs with incomes that allow for at least the basic necessities of life; safe and affordable housing; and access to health care, including mental health care.

Child abuse is not an isolated phenomenon that happens to other people; it affects everyone and can happen in all families. It is part of the culture and reflects the values and commitments of contemporary society.

Dante Cicchetti and Vicki Carlson, eds., *Child Maltreatment: Theory and Research on the Causes and Consequences of Child Abuse and Neglect* (Cambridge, England/New York: Cambridge University Press, 1989); David Finkelhor and Jennifer Dziuba-Leatherman, "Victimization of Children," *American Psychologist* Vol. 49 (1994): 173–83; Robert Hampton and Eli Newberger, "Child Abuse Reporting by Hospitals: Significance of Severity, Class, and Race," *American Journal of Public Health* Vol. 75 (1985): 56–60.

■ CAROLYN MOORE NEWBERGER

SEE ALSO Violence Against Women: Incest.

≋ Childbirth

The United States uses more technology related to childbirth than any other developed nation. About 99 percent of U.S. births take place in hospitals, attended by doctors. Most women receive medication for pain, an episiotomy (a four-inch surgical cut in the vaginal opening to allow the baby's head to emerge), and electronic monitoring of the baby's heartbeat during labor. About 25 percent of U.S. women give birth by caesarean section. Despite advanced technology, the United States ranks twenty-first worldwide in newborn mortality, a standing that has changed little in eighty years. Unequal distribution of health care accounts for this low ranking. The mortality rate for African American mothers is over three times that for white mothers, a gap that has remained the same since 1913, when national reporting started. Data on Hispanic mothers, whose mortality rates are one-and-one-half times the rate for whites, began only in 1985. African American mothers have twice the rate of low-birthweight babies and neonatal deaths as whites. Native Americans, Asians, and Hispanics have rates slightly above those for whites, but rates vary, depending on socioeconomic status and early prenatal care. Japanese, Cuban, Chinese, or Filipina women are more likely than white women to receive early prenatal care, while Mexican, Puerto Rican, Central or South American, Native American, or African American women are less likely to receive early care.

Birth in the United States has undergone two profound transformations: the shift from midwives to doctors in the mid–nineteenth century, and the move from homes to hospitals in the early twentieth century. Women took active roles in both transformations.

The seventeenth century was the era of "social childbirth." Women relatives, friends, and neighbors attended the birth, which always took place at home, and cared for the new mother's house and other children during her six- to eight-week period of recovery, or "lying-in." At the end of this period, the mother gave a "groaning party" for the many women who had helped her. In the North, midwives, who attended all births, were women from the same community and social class as the mother. Anne Hutchinson, a founder of Rhode Island, and Mary Dyer, later hanged on Boston Common for her Quaker beliefs, were both midwives. In the South, midwifery sometimes crossed racial lines, with white plantation owners using particularly skilled slave midwives. Midwives had no formal training; they learned by attending neighbors' births. Men, even husbands, rarely witnessed births, except on the frontier (then western Massachusetts or Virginia) in cases when no midwife or woman neighbor was available.

By the latter half of the eighteenth century, the reciprocal ties that fostered social childbirth had weakened. Middle- and upper-class families paid workers to care for mother and child instead of depending on neighbors. They also began to ask male doctors—"man-midwives" or "accoucheurs"—to attend deliveries. These doctors had a new instrument, the forceps, which could help to deliver a live baby.

In the North American colonies no midwives arose to defend articulately their profession as the upper and middle classes began to turn to male doctors. Doctors were rare in the colonies; doctors with a medical education (as opposed to apprenticeship) were even rarer. Therefore a university-educated doctor could receive high fees from his well-to-do patients. For some patients, having a doctor present in the home at the time of a birth was a sign that the family had "arrived" socially, even if the doctor played cards with the husband while a midwife delivered the baby.

Doctors regarded midwives as potentially serious competitors. In the entrepreneurial climate of nineteenth-century U.S. medicine, orthodox physicians already faced competition from other sources: unorthodox doctors; Thomsonian botanists, who appealed to the lower and middle classes in the South and West; homeopaths, who appealed to the upper classes in the East; and eclectics, hydrotherapists, and outright quacks. Under Jacksonian democracy, already-weak state licensure laws were repealed and virtually anyone could practice medicine. To keep women out of medicine, it was necessary to convince the middle classes that men were superior birth attendants. Midwifery came under attack. In 1820 a noted Boston physician argued in an anonymous pamphlet that women were too sympathetic with patients, too irrational, and too affected by their monthly flux of hormones to make the calm, detached, rational decisions required at births. The author also pointed out that midwives were of a lower social class than the women they attended and might use the language of the streets. A "lady" would ostensibly prefer to be attended by a male physician of her own class. By 1830 no middle-class midwives remained in Boston. By midcentury midwives attended mainly rural or African American women or immigrants from their own social groups.

When women finally succeeded in entering medical schools, starting with Elizabeth Blackwell in 1847, their practice, like that of midwives, was confined mainly to serving the poor—thus women doctors would not compete with males. Even in the 1890s, when women composed almost 20 percent of physicians and often established and headed their own hospitals, their practice had little effect on the increasing technologizing of the birth process.

By the mid-1800s male doctors were attending most middle-class urban births. Obstetrician—literally "one who stands before" the birthing woman—replaced the term man-midwife, which sounded too feminine. Births still occurred in the home; husbands did not attend. Women's health appeared to decline and childbirth became more difficult. Doctors' poor medical education compounded women's health problems. Until mid-century, most doctors had no college education, only two years of medical education, and no clinical training.

An infection called puerperal fever often killed women and infants several days after the baby's birth. For much of the nineteenth century, the infection's source baffled doctors. Some thought it came from foul air (miasma); most others blamed the cause of infection on the "dirty living habits" of patients from the slums, and some even attributed the problem to unwed mothers' despondency over their "immorality." In 1880 Louis Pasteur discovered that streptococcal bacteria caused both puerperal fever and infections of battlefield wounds. Postpartum women were seen as "wounded women" who had small tears in the tissues. It took another thirty years for the medical profession to adopt rigorous aseptic procedures. As late as 1910, some texts suggested sterilizing a needle by running it through a bar of soap.

The United States escaped the massive epidemics of puerperal fever that ravaged European hospitals, largely because few U.S. women gave birth in hospitals. Most medical procedures continued to be performed in the home. In the nineteenth century, only poor, typically unmarried women gave birth in "lying-in" hospitals. These hospitals, established by private charities, had a

moral mission—to reclaim otherwise virtuous women who had been "seduced." Most hospitals accepted only women having a *first* illegitimate child. Those pregnant out of wedlock a second time were considered incorrigible and had to give birth in a public almshouse. Many poor women paid for their deliveries by staying on in the hospital for several months as unpaid cleaning staff. But nineteenth-century hospitals were dangerous places because of puerperal fever; no woman who had a home would consider the hospital a fit place for birth. By 1900, however, hospitals had become safer, and the occasional middle-class woman requested hospital delivery. Thus began the hospital administrators' campaign to entice paying patients. They built private wings with furnishings similar to the luxury homes of the day. They advertised a safe, sterile environment; twenty-four-hour nursing service; modern equipment, such as x-ray machines; and specialists in obstetrics. Many women regarded hospitals as hotels with room service, at a time when servants were becoming scarce.

The "generation gap" of the early twentieth century contributed to the rise in hospital births. The "modern woman" took her pregnancy out of "confinement" and showed herself during daylight hours in maternity clothes. Modern women often preferred to give birth in the hospital. Doctors, in turn, wished to centralize their activities rather than traveling to women's homes.

A new method of analgesia that required constant monitoring also greatly influenced the move to the hospital. Developed in Freiburg, Germany, in 1914, "Twilight Sleep" used a combination of scopolamine, an amnesiac, and morphine, a painkiller, to remove all memory of birth. Women in Germany waxed ecstatic about this method; they reported going to sleep and awakening to find their beautiful baby lying in a bassinet. So compelling were accounts in women's magazines that upper-class U.S. women traveled to Germany to give birth, approximately at the outbreak of World War I. Early feminists supported Twilight Sleep as promoting faster recovery from birth and thus helping to equalize the sexes in public life. Conservatives thought it was the answer to "race suicide," the failure of Anglo-Saxon women to have enough babies to outnumber immigrants from eastern and southern Europe. If childbirth were totally painless, then Anglo-Saxon women "should" want to have large families. From about 1930 to 1960, Twilight Sleep was the preferred analgesic in U.S. hospitals.

Doctors had launched a renewed attack against the remaining midwives who, by the 1920s, were primarily African Americans or recent immigrants. Racial and ethnic slurs highlighted the doctors' attacks, even though investigating agencies found that midwives had had higher rates of successful deliveries than did general practitioners. Some states licensed midwives who had received rudimentary training in sterile procedures. First-generation immigrants preferred following the "American way"—hospital birth—over using their own midwives.

By 1930 most urban births took place with doctors, in hospitals, and by the beginning of World War II, almost all women gave birth in hospitals. Insurance companies aided in this transition by paying for hospital but not home births. At the beginning of the war, new mothers' traditional two-week hospital stays were reduced to five to seven days because many hospital staff members were at the battlefront. Discharge after one day became the norm in the 1990s as a result of insurance company policies. In 1996 Congress enacted legislation requiring forty-eight hours of hospital care for new mothers.

One technique—the Lamaze method—is the foundation of most natural childbirth today. Ferdinand Lamaze, an obstetrician at a Parisian metalworkers' clinic, traveled to Russia to learn "psychoprophylaxis," a painkilling technique derived from Pavlovian psychology and from midwives' folk practices. The method diverted the brain's attention from pain impulses through controlled, rapid breathing, which also supplied extra oxygen to the contracting uterus. Marjorie Karmel, an American who gave birth at Lamaze's clinic, popularized the method in the United States in 1959. The Lamaze method did not challenge doctors' authority; the woman gave birth, but the doctor coached and directed her. Birth was an event at which she had to succeed. Lamaze method admirers tended to be middle class and well educated, and have remained so.

"Natural childbirth" has acquired so many meanings that it is now applied to virtually any birth except caesarean section. The Lamaze breathing technique has been incorporated into a host of birth-related interventions that include routine analgesia, spinal or epidural anesthesia, the "lithotomy position" (flat on the back, feet raised in stirrups), pubic shaving, enema, fetal heart monitoring with a machine that immobilizes the woman, transfer from a labor room to a delivery room, and episiotomy. Most modern women do not complain about these interventions because they have achieved now what they have most wanted—the presence of a sympathetic person during labor and delivery, usually the baby's father, a historic first.

Although most women are now conscious during childbirth, hospitals use more rather than less technology. Caesarean section rates in the United States are so high (about 25 percent, as compared, for example, with 4 percent in Ireland) that public-health officials and feminist activists have begun to investigate. Alternative options such as freestanding birth centers, home births, or independent (lay) midwives have attracted less than 1 percent of birthing women, despite much media attention over a period of twenty years. Most nurse-midwives serve the poor in inner-city hospitals.

In 1920 women of all social groups organized around making childbirth safe. The efforts resulted in passage of the first federal legislation to promote safe prenatal and maternity care, the Sheppard-Towner Act, which was later repealed. Such a widespread, concerted social effort has not been repeated. The United States has relied on high technology in the birth process to try to overcome social problems that lead to poor outcomes.

Robbie E. Davis-Floyd, *Birth as an American Rite of Passage* (Berkeley: University of California Press, 1992); Judith Walzer Leavitt, *Brought to Bed: Childbearing in America: 1750–1950* (New York: Oxford University Press, 1986); Richard W. Wertz and Dorothy C. Wertz, *Lying-In: A History of Childbirth in America*, expanded edition (New Haven and London: Yale University Press, 1989).

■ DOROTHY WERTZ

SEE ALSO Midwifery; Pregnancy; Sheppard-Towner Maternity and Infancy Protection Act.

≋ Child Care

Child care refers to the care of children by a person or persons other than their parents during hours when parents are working, attending school, or pursuing another ongoing, nonleisure activity. In the United States, child care has taken many forms, both informal and formal or institutional, private and public. Unlike many advanced industrial societies, this country has no comprehensive government-supported system. Attitudes toward child care and the development of public child-care policy have been closely linked to values concerning motherhood and maternal employment and to changing concepts of childhood—who requires care, what type, and for how long.

Colonial Americans regarded women as economic producers as well as mothers. To complete their productive tasks and keep children out of harm's way, mothers confined toddlers in a variety of devices including "standing stools" and "gogins." They also assigned child-rearing duties to kin, servants, or slaves; sent young children to live in other households; or placed them in local "dame schools" which, for a small fee, offered rudimentary education and daily supervision. Children as young as seven were expected to perform household tasks.

The onset of industrialization and the market economy in the late eighteenth century changed European American women's economic and social roles. Production sped up and began to shift from home to factory, making it difficult for mothers to combine productive and reproductive labor. At the same time motherhood gained new value, with child rearing increasingly seen as women's primary duty. Many mothers, however, were compelled to do wage work, either because husbands were absent or families could not survive solely on men's wages. To address such dilemmas, Philadelphia Quaker women established the first formal child-care institution in the United States, the House of Industry. It included a workroom where widows spun or wove for wages while one or two elderly women looked after their children in a nursery. By midcentury charitable "day nurseries" had been established in other cities as well. The middle-class women who founded these nurseries, adhering to the male breadwinner ideal, claimed that their services were intended only as temporary help to mothers in crisis (because of their husbands' death, illness, disappearance, or disability).

African American slave mothers had little choice in the matter of child care. Masters, seeking to extract maximal labor from all slaves regardless of sex as well as protect their "property," usually arranged supervision for slave children from infancy onward. On larger plantations elderly slaves and older slave children were placed in charge of the "baby house"; on smaller farms, white mistresses looked after slave children, training them to assume tasks and field work as early as possible.

Nineteenth-century utopian communities set up communal nurseries to free women from exclusive responsibility for children and at the same time inculcate group values and behavior. Though these experimental communities operated on the principle of gender equality, their marginal status barred them from influencing mainstream thinking about child care. Instead, the philanthropic model became predominant.

By the late nineteenth century approximately two hundred charitable nurseries were operating nationwide, but more were needed. To expand their base, child-care philanthropists set up a "model day nursery" at the 1893 World's Columbian Exhibition in Chicago and then formed the National Federation of Day Nurseries (NFDN), whose purpose was to modernize nurseries and raise their standards. Though forward-looking in some respects, the NFDN failed to keep up with progressive ideas about educating and protecting young children. The Progressive Era proved decisive for the child-care movement, as reformers withdrew their support for day nurseries in favor of state-funded mothers' pensions or mothers' aid, which allowed mothers to remain at home to care for their own children. With access to public funding blocked, day nurseries' growth and quality stagnated. Under the 1930s New Deal, the federal government established the first nationwide program for young children, the Emergency Nursery Schools, which emphasized the educational benefits of group care but carried the stigma of "relief."

Federally supported child care materialized briefly during World War II. The Lanham Act program ran more than 3,100 nurseries caring for nearly 130,000 pre-school children, while Extended School Services served up to 320,000 schoolchildren. Withdrawal of federal funds at the war's end shut down most of these facilities.

Despite the postwar emphasis on domesticity, maternal employment continued and even increased during the 1950s. Federal surveys found that the lack of child care put many children at risk, but Congress, committed to restoring the male-headed household, took no action. Attitudes began to change in the early 1960s, when Congress decided to push welfare mothers into the work force by supporting targeted child care through block grants to states. Funding remained sparse, however, because of continuing ambivalence over maternal employment. Meanwhile, attempts to legislate universal child-care provisions supported by a coalition of feminists, labor, and children's professionals were rebuffed, most notably the Comprehensive Child Development Act of 1971, which was vetoed by President Nixon.

Presidential opposition to child care persisted through the 1980s, but maternal employment continued to increase. Commercial, voluntary, cooperative, and family-based child care moved to fill the vacuum; businesses employing large numbers of women set up resource and referral services or on-site day-care centers. Expense, availability, and quality remained key issues. Scandals over the alleged sexual abuse of children in day-care centers spawned public suspicion but did not improve regulation and oversight. High-income families often hired nannies, many of whom were undocumented workers.

In the context of welfare reform, the Family Support Act of 1988 required recipients to work or participate in federally funded job training programs, while states were to guarantee child care. Fewer than half ultimately complied. Seizing the opportunity to reopen the child-care issue, the Alliance for Better Child Care, a coalition of feminists and children's advocates, called for federal funding to expand and improve services for all families. In 1990 a compromise measure, the Child Care and Development Block Grant, benefiting mainly low-income families was signed into law, but child care remained an issue in the debates over welfare reform of the mid-1990s.

Throughout U.S. history, public provision of child care has been linked to other issues such as national crisis or welfare reform, but seldom advocated—except by feminists—as a right for women. Employed mothers meanwhile have made do with a variety of provisions, many of them costly and unsatisfactory. Currently, the possibility of a universal, government-supported system seems more remote than ever.

Mary Frances Berry, *The Politics of Parenthood: Child Care, Women's Rights, and the Myth of the Good Mother* (New York: Viking, 1993); Sonya Michel, *Children's Interests/Mothers' Rights: The Shaping of American Child Care Policy* (New Haven: Yale University Press, 1996); Geraldine Youcha, *Minding the Children: Child Care in America from Colonial Times to the Present* (New York: Scribner, 1995).

■ SONYA MICHEL

SEE ALSO Mothers' Pensions; Welfare and Public Relief.

≋ Children's Bureau

The Children's Bureau, established in 1912 in the Department of Commerce and Labor, represented women's first inclusion in the national state. Directed initially by Julia Lathrop, the bureau was staffed primarily by elite Anglo-American women who, like Lathrop, were highly educated, worked in settlements, and promoted professional opportunities for women in social work, nursing, and home economics. Congressional support of the bureau also established that children's and mothers' well-being were rightfully governmental concerns.

The bureau's history illustrates both the potential for women's cross-class and cross-racial/ethnic alliances and the dangers of promoting elite women's power over poor women. Children's Bureau activists believed that science and other means could mitigate the social problems of industrial America, and that women could best work toward this goal.

Of the two primary Children's Bureau campaigns in the 1910s and 1920s—infant and maternal mortality and child labor—nonelite women judged the former more successful. The bureau focused on new scientific knowledge about relevant hygiene, nutrition, and medical practice through publishing and distributing pamphlets. Though the bureau often deemed immigrant, African American, and Native American mothering and midwifery practices "inferior," women from all classes and cultures sought out the pamphlets and embraced the notion that infant and maternal mortality were preventable.

The bureau successfully lobbied for the Sheppard-Towner Act in 1921, establishing state programs for maternal and infant protection. This initiative succumbed to opposition to the act's renewal in 1927. Right-wing groups objected to the fact that the act encouraged women's mounting sense of entitlement to state-sponsored health care, while the American Medical Association held that the program undermined doctors' authority and control over medical knowledge.

The bureau encountered considerable resistance from nonelite women when it attained funding and authority to enforce the 1916 Keating-Owen Act, which prohibited children under fourteen from mill, quarry, and factory work, and children under sixteen from laboring at night or more than eight hours per day. The bureau's campaign to abolish child labor reflected its belief that child labor represented egregious exploitation. Poor mothers complained that losing children's wages would impoverish them further or necessitate women's increased wage work, but their protests went unheeded.

Although the Children's Bureau drafted legislation creating the New Deal program Aid to Dependent Children (ADC), and attempted through the 1930s to include African American women and children as recipients, the bureau's influence waned substantially after the administration of ADC was assigned to the Social Security Board in 1935. The bureau's reluctance to support wage work or day care for mothers during 1940s' war mobilization signaled a final rift between the bureau's maternalist politics and the politics of most working women.

■ MAUREEN FITZGERALD

SEE ALSO Sheppard-Towner Maternity and Infancy Protection Act.

≋ Chinatowns

Historically, immigrant Chinese have clustered in "Chinatowns" in a few large cities in California and New York. Chinatowns in San Francisco and the Lower East Side of Manhattan, New York, are probably the oldest and largest Chinese communities in the United States. The emergence of Chinatowns involved both involuntary and voluntary processes. Before World War II legal and institutional exclusion and discrimination forced immigrant Chinese to develop insulated enclaves for self-protection. At the same time, many Chinese old-timers, mostly men, wanted communities of their own because they had little desire to assimilate and because immigration laws impeded family formation.

Old Chinatown was essentially a bachelor's society with a highly skewed gender ratio. At the turn of the century the gender ratio was eight women per one hundred men in San Francisco's Chinatown and only two women per one hundred men in New York's Chinatown. For these workers, Chinatown was the only place they could speak their own language, eat their own food, play their own games, exchange news from home, and share common experiences.

After World War II the bachelor's society in Chinatowns began to dissolve as Chinese women were allowed into the United States to join their husbands and families. As a result of the repeal of the Chinese Exclusion Act and passage of the War Bride Act, immigrant Chinese women composed more than half of the postwar arrivals from China. However, the number of Chinese immigrants entering the United States each year was quite small because the annual quota was set at 105. It was only after 1965, when Congress amended the immigration law abolishing the national origins quota system, that Chinatowns changed dramatically into family-oriented communities.

Since 1965 Chinatowns have expanded in all directions, taking over decaying neighborhoods and giving rise to "satellite" and suburban Chinatowns in many parts of the country. New Chinatowns function not only to help immigrant Chinese to sustain a sense of identity, community, and self-esteem and to shield them from racial discrimination, but also to mobilize resources for economic and institutional development oriented toward the goal of "making it in America."

During the 1930s and 1940s, most of Chinatowns' economies were highly concentrated in restaurant and laundry businesses. By the 1970s the garment industry emerged as one of the backbone industries in Chinatowns. New York City Chinatowns, for example, have more than five hundred Chinese-owned garment factories, providing jobs for more than twenty thousand immigrant Chinese, mostly women. The restaurant business, another core industry in Chinatowns, has continued to grow and prosper. Restaurants run by Chinese in New York City grew from 304 in 1958 to 781 in 1988, employing at least fifteen thousand immigrant Chinese workers. These ethnic enterprises and services have created job opportunities for immigrant Chinese and provided convenient and easy ways to meet ethnically specific demands.

Chinatowns' strong ethnic economies along with their well-organized community-based service systems and positive cultural orientation provide an adaptive advantage for immigrant Chinese and their children.

▪ MIN ZHOU

SEE ALSO Chinese American Women.

≋ Chinese American Women

Few women were among the first wave of Chinese immigrants to the United States in the mid–nineteenth century. Driven overseas by war and poverty at home, young Chinese men who intended to strike it rich and return home did not bring their families with them. Cultural restrictions at home, lack of traveling funds, and anti-Chinese violence in the U.S. West further discouraged the immigration of women. In 1882, at the height of the anti-Chinese movement, Congress passed the Chinese Exclusion Act, which further barred the entry of Chinese laborers and their families. Only the merchant class, which made up less than 5 percent of the Chinese immigrant population in the late nineteenth century, was exempt from the Exclusion Act and could afford to have families in America. As a result, the numbers of Chinese women in the United States remained low throughout the nineteenth century, never exceeding 8 percent of the total Chinese population.

This sexual imbalance, combined with antimiscegenation attitudes and laws that prevented Chinese men from marrying white women, created a demand for prostitution. Although most white prostitutes were independent professionals or worked in brothels for wages, Chinese prostitutes, who formed an estimated 85 percent of the Chinese female population in San Francisco in 1860 and 71 percent in 1870, were uniquely indentured servants who had been kidnapped, lured, or purchased from poor parents in China and resold in the United States for high profits. Treated as chattel and subjected to physical and mental abuse, the average prostitute did not outlive her contract term of four to five years. Some were redeemed by wealthy clients; others sought refuge at Protestant mission homes and later married Chinese Christians. By 1920 organized prostitution had declined due to antiprostitution laws, the Chinese Exclusion Act, and successful rescue raids by Protestant missionaries.

Aside from prostitutes, most of the remaining Chinese women were wives who lived in urban Chinatowns or in remote rural areas where their husbands could find work. Following Chinese decorum, Chinatown wives seldom left their homes, where, in addition to doing housework

and caring for their children, they often worked for low wages—sewing, washing, rolling cigars, and making slippers and brooms. In rural areas, Chinese wives also tended livestock and vegetable gardens, hauled in the catch and dried seafood for export, or took in boarders to help with the family income. Regardless of their husbands' social status, Chinese immigrant wives led hard-working lives and remained subordinate to their husbands and confined to the domestic sphere.

As China continued to be torn by internal upheaval and foreign aggression, Chinese immigrants continued to enter the United States primarily by impersonating members of classes exempt from the Exclusion Act—merchants and derivative U.S. citizens. In this way, women were able to join their husbands and establish family life in the United States. Many settled in cities and small towns where jobs were more plentiful and the Chinese presence was tolerated. Even so, because they lacked English and marketable job skills, were saddled with child-care responsibilities, and faced race and sex discrimination in the labor market, most women worked at menial jobs in garment shops, canneries, or fruit orchards, or they helped their husbands operate small laundries, restaurants, or grocery stores. Life for Chinese immigrant women in the early twentieth century focused on survival through hard work. Their one consolation was a newfound freedom from traditional social constraints and the satisfaction of being able to provide a better future for their children.

Like other immigrant children, most second-generation Chinese American girls who grew up in the early 1900s were torn between their cultural upbringing at home and the larger society's values. They led sheltered lives at home, following Chinese traditions and assuming heavier household responsibilities and receiving less education than their brothers. However, as they became exposed to U.S. ways of thinking and behavior through public schools, churches, and the popular media, many began to adopt Western ways and

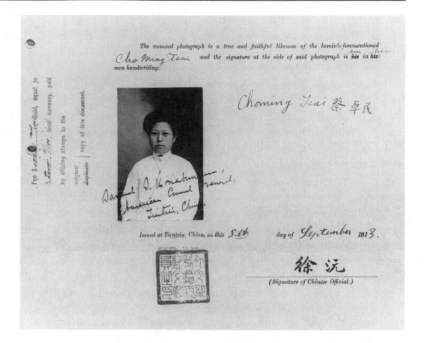

The annexed photograph is a true and faithful likeness of the hereinbeforementioned
Cho Ming Tsai and the signature at the side of said photograph is true after in his own handwriting.

Choming Tsai 蔡卓民

Samuel S. Knabenshue,
American Consul general,
Tientsin, China

Issued at Tientsin, China, on this 8th day of September 1913.

徐 沅
(Signature of Chinese Official.)

*Immigration document,
September 1913.*

to challenge traditional gender roles at home. But despite their ability to speak English, educational attainment, and Western orientation, second-generation women were limited to low-paying jobs and excluded from participating in mainstream society because of discrimination. Nevertheless, unlike women of their mothers' generation, U.S.-born Chinese women were able to move into clerical and professional jobs, break out of the custom of arranged marriages, and become active in social and political affairs. Women's organizations for charitable and political causes proliferated in the 1920s and 1930s, and Chinese women participated actively in the 1938 garment workers' strike in San Francisco, and contributed to Chinese nationalism and the war effort in China.

World War II heralded profound changes in the lives of Chinese American women, providing them with unprecedented opportunities to attain high-paying jobs in defense factories and in the private sector as well as to participate in the national war effort. While some enlisted in the armed services, many contributed in the areas of fundraising, civil defense, and Red Cross work on the homefront. Because of China's allied relationship to the United States, the Exclusion Act was repealed in 1943 and naturalization rights were granted to the Chinese. Following the war and the civil rights movement, other immigration restrictions were eased and anti-Chinese laws revoked, resulting in increased immigration of women and families, improved educational and employment opportunities, and the beginning of Chinese integration into U.S. society. In 1980 the Chinese male-to-female ratio finally approached parity.

Contrary to the monolithic image of the successful "model-minority" projected by the mass media, Chinese American women today have diverse backgrounds and problems, although they share certain common concerns. Some have college degrees and professional training, while others are less educated and without English or marketable job skills. The primary concerns of the latter continue to be cultural adjustment and finding gainful employment beyond low-wage, menial jobs in the garment, hotel, and electronic industries. In contrast, college-educated immigrant and U.S.-born Chinese American women form a middle-class population either employed in the technical/sales job sector or having careers in professional fields such as education, medicine, and law. They are concerned with assimilation and socioeconomic success.

While overall conditions have improved for Chinese American women since World War II, they still must contend with race, class, and gender oppression. In many households women are still expected to assume all the domestic responsibilities regardless of whether they hold jobs outside the home, while at work they often receive less pay than men and than other women doing the same work, and they are passed up for promotion despite merit. Added to these problems are rising incidents of domestic violence at home and sexual harassment at work. But learning from the lessons of their past and inspired by the current wave of social activism, Chinese American women are more adept than were their predecessors at dealing with the conflicts and challenges of U.S. life.

Chinese Historical Society of Southern California, *Linking Our Lives: Chinese American Women of Los Angeles* (Los Angeles: Chinese Historical Society of Southern California, 1984); Lucie Cheng Hirata, "Chinese Immigrant Women in Nineteenth-Century California," in *Women of America*, edited by C. R. Berkin and M. B. Norton, 223–44 (Boston: Houghton Mifflin, 1979); Judy Yung, *Chinese Women of America: A Pictorial History* (Seattle: University of Washington Press, 1986).

• JUDY YUNG

SEE ALSO Asian Pacific Women; Chinatowns; Chinese Exclusion Act.

≋ Chinese Exclusion Act

In 1882, at the height of the anti-Chinese movement in the U.S. West, Congress—under siege from white labor and politicians—passed the Chinese Exclusion Act, which suspended the immigration of Chinese laborers for ten years and denied Chinese residents the right to naturalization. It was the first time in U.S. history that a specific group of people was excluded from immigrating on the basis of race and class. The underlying premise for the act was to eliminate Chinese competition for jobs during a time of economic depression and to discourage the permanent settlement of Chinese in the United States. Only Chinese officials, teachers, students, merchants, visitors, and derivative citizens were exempt. The act was extended for another decade in 1892 and made permanent in 1904. It was not repealed until 1943, as a goodwill gesture to China, an ally of the United States during World War II.

Although not specifically mentioned in the Chinese Exclusion Act, female laborers and wives of laborers were barred by implication, as the federal court ruled in two separate cases in 1884. Women of the exempt classes only were allowed entry; however, wives of U.S. citizens were later barred entry by the Immigration Act of 1924. The Exclusion Act succeeded in keeping Chinese women out of the country and separated from their husbands, sometimes for decades, thus creating undue hardships for family members on both sides of the ocean. In turn, the absence of women resulted in a skewed sex ratio, a delay of the second generation, and an unstable bachelor society vulnerable to the social vices of drugs, gambling, prostitution, and internecine violence. The Chinese male/female ratio was 18 to 1 in 1900 and did not approach parity until 1980.

• JUDY YUNG

SEE ALSO Chinese American Women; Immigration.

≋ Church of Jesus Christ of Latter-Day Saints

SEE Mormons.

≋ Cities

SEE Urbanization.

≋ Citizenship

The Fourteenth and Fifteenth Amendments created a *national* definition of citizenship for the first time. Until then, the due-process guarantee did not apply to the states and qualifications for voting had been set by the states. Nevertheless, it was not until 1920 that women were guaranteed the right to vote by the ratification of the Nineteenth Amendment. Native American Indians born in the United States were formally admitted to full citizenship in 1924. The rights of African Americans to vote were not protected in any effective way until the passage of the Voting Rights Act of 1965. Even in the 1990s, legislation to guarantee equal protection for gays and lesbians is being challenged in many jurisdictions, and struggles for equal representation and equal protection by gender and race/ethnicity continue at both federal and local levels.

In theory and in practice, the rights and responsibilities associated with citizenship have changed markedly in the United States over the course of the past two hundred years. Citizenship has referred to those who are considered to have "standing" to make claims against the state—for the protection of life, liberty, and property—commonly called *civil* rights, and to those who have the right to participate in decision making, commonly referred to as *political rights*. Since at least the late nineteenth century in the United States, there have been struggles, many of them led by women reformers, both white and Black, to extend the meaning of citizenship to include rights to the provision of necessities, such as social insurance or unemployment benefits, sometimes referred to as *social* rights. In the United States, these three types of rights have not always been distinguished as such, nor has there been any necessary connection among them.

The status of citizen (in the political sense) has been accorded to those deemed worthy of the state's protection. Originally, that meant free, propertied men and their families. With the passage of the Reconstruction Amendments, the rights of citizenship were formally extended to Black men and their families; but, in many areas of the country, violence, poll taxes, and economic threats combined to deny to most African American and many immigrant men full exercise of civil and political citizenship rights. Until the passage of the Nineteenth Amendment in 1920, women were considered citizens, but not independent citizens. Denied political rights and many civil rights, women lacked equal protection of the law, especially regarding rights to own property, to sue in courts, to engage in professional work, and otherwise to determine the direction of their lives.

Full citizenship has been granted to those perceived as self-supporting, or "independent," and ready to engage in public service. Throughout much of U.S. history, each of these measures had built-in assumptions about gender, race, and class. At first, for example, in virtually all states, manual laborers and others who supported themselves by wage work were excluded from full political rights on the grounds that they "depended" on others for wages, thus were not self-supporting. By the mid–nineteenth century, however, state-based extensions of suffrage to all free-born white males incorporated wage laborers into the citizen body on the basis of their "productive" role in society. This left intact assumptions about the relationship between citizenship and self-support —assumptions that denied political rights to women, slaves, sharecroppers, and so on. When women won the right to vote in 1920, they did so largely on the grounds of women's *difference* from men: in effect, dependency was deemed compatible with citizenship *only* for women.

The introduction of some notion of social citizenship rights, through the efforts of (largely female) social reformers during the late nineteenth and early twentieth centuries, reinforced assumptions about the relationship among gender, race, class, and citizenship. Newly developing programs to address the poverty and inequality that accompanied the growth of industrial capitalism ignored able-bodied male workers and focused instead on the needs of those dependent *on* such men—or, worse, those who were without a man on whom to depend—e.g., families of disabled or unemployed workers, widows, mothers with no means of support for their children, or female and child laborers. The programs were not extended in practice to any African Americans until many decades later. Roosevelt's New Deal social programs offered the beginnings of a social safety net to the wage-earning white population. But universal social citizenship rights (including rights to health care, minimal economic support, and housing) are still unmet goals for all U.S. citizens. Meanwhile the effect of the so-called Contract with America offered by Republican members of the 104th Congress is to place many of those "rights" under much more serious threat.

Linda Gordon, ed., *Women, the State, and Welfare* (Madison: University of Wisconsin Press, 1990); Carole Pateman, *The Sexual Contract* (Stanford, Calif.: Stanford University Press, 1988); Kathryn Kish Sklar, "The Social Bases of Women's Power in the Construction of the Welfare State, 1830–1920," in *Mothers of a New World*, edited by Seth Koven and Sonya Michel (New York: Routledge, 1993).

■ MARTHA ACKELSBERG

SEE ALSO Citizenship and Nationality; Constitution and Amendments; Legal Status.

≋ Citizenship and Nationality

One meaning of citizenship is membership in a national political community. Such membership is ordinarily the precondition for the rights and obligations that confer political personhood to citizens. In the United States, nationality or passport citizenship can be acquired in three ways. The primary determinant for U.S. nationality is territorial birthright: by virtue of being born on U.S. soil (*jus soli*), one is automatically an American citizen. Persons born abroad are also born into U.S. citizenship if either parent is a U.S. citizen. A third path to citizenship is through naturalization.

Throughout most of the nineteenth and early twentieth centuries, these principles did not apply equally to all persons. Under the naturalization laws of the early Republic, naturalization was available only to whites. Under mid-nineteenth-century naturalization policy, foreign-born white women who married U.S. citizens were automatically naturalized, whether or not they wanted to be U.S. citizens. Under the naturalization law of 1907, U.S.-born women of all races *lost* their nationality citizenship when they married noncitizens. Also, from 1855 to the 1930s, children born overseas to U.S.-born women did not automatically acquire U.S. citizenship; those children enjoyed automatic U.S. citizenship at birth only if their *father* was a U.S. citizen.

Race and marriage mediated women's nationality status until the 1930s. From the constitutional Founding through the Civil War, African, Indian, and Asian women and men could not be naturalized. Mexicans in the Southwest could become naturalized after the mid-nineteenth-century U.S. conquest of Mexican territory, and Africans were permitted naturalization under post–Civil War legislation. Except for those Indians whose tribal treaties with the U.S. government provided naturalization rights, Indians were excluded from naturalization until 1924. Until 1952,

Asian immigrants were deemed "ineligible for citizenship."

Racial barriers to U.S. citizenship interacted with the legal and ideological subordination of women to men in marriage to deprive even U.S.-born white women of secure and independent nationality citizenship. Although early-nineteenth-century judicial decisions considered women's nationality status to be independently determined by the territorial condition of their birth, by the mid–nineteenth century, women's nationality was tied to that of their husbands. Following the family law doctrine of coverture, according to which married women assumed the state or domicile citizenship of their husbands, the Naturalization Act of 1855 imposed citizenship on foreign-born white women who married U.S. citizens. This assigned political consequences to women's marriage decisions; it also reinforced the idea that by consenting to marriage, women consented to multiple forms of dependency on and subordination to men.

The 1907 naturalization policy added a punitive dimension to women's derivative citizenship by revoking the nationality status of U.S.-born women who married men from other countries. Reform of nationality rules affecting women rose to the top of the post-suffrage feminist agenda. Led by the Women's Joint Congressional Committee, a lobbying group consisting of the heads of many women's organizations, feminists pressed for independent nationality citizenship for women. In 1922, a nativist Congress intent on restricting immigration and immigrant participation in U.S. political life passed the Cable Act, which ended the automatic naturalization of foreign-born (non-Asian) women who married U.S. citizens.

Although not fully satisfied with the new law, feminists saw it as a shift toward independent citizenship, because the Cable Act required foreign-born married women from races eligible for citizenship to go through the naturalization process as independent individuals and because it ended

U.S.-born women's automatic loss of citizenship when they married noncitizen men, unless the men were Asian. The Cable Act retained loss of citizenship provisions for U.S.-born women who married "aliens ineligible for citizenship" — Asians. This meant that U.S.-born women who chose to marry Asia-born men would continue to pay for their decision with their nationality. This was especially burdensome for Asian American women who chose to marry immigrant men within their own cultures.

During the nineteenth century, nationality law repeated family law and gender ideology, strengthening the rule of U.S.-born white husbands and fathers and declaring their families American. After 1907, nationality law worked simultaneously to regulate women's marital decisions and to enforce racist and nativist goals. However, by the early 1930s, under pressure from women's groups and as a result of women's changed political status, Congress removed the barriers to independent nationality citizenship, at least for women deemed "eligible for citizenship."

▪ GWENDOLYN MINK

SEE ALSO Citizenship; Immigration; Legal Status.

≋ Civil Rights Act of 1964

The first major federal legislative response to the civil rights movement, the Civil Rights Act of 1964 prohibited discrimination on the basis of race, national origin, and religion in several important arenas, including public accommodations, education, and employment. The employment provision (Title VII) also barred discrimination on the basis of sex. No provision of the Civil Rights Act prohibited discrimination on the basis of sexual orientation.

The authors of the Civil Rights Act did not intend to include sex discrimination in any of its provisions. Sex discrimination was introduced into the civil rights debate by southern opponents of the measure who sought to flummox its supporters and kill it through ridicule.

Congressional majorities shrugged off early efforts by southern men to add "sex" to the bill's provisions. But white women's rights advocates in the House of Representatives were incited by the laughter that greeted the motion to bar sex-based discrimination in employment. Congresswoman Martha Griffiths led the fight to take the employment amendment seriously. She argued "as a white woman" concerned that "when this bill is passed . . . white women will be last at the hiring gate." Griffiths warned her male colleagues that a vote against the sex discrimination amendment would be a vote against their own wives and daughters. In language recalling the racist appeals of white suffragists during Reconstruction, Griffiths charged, "It would be incredible . . . that white men would be willing to place white women at such a disadvantage except that white men have done this before . . . your greatgrandfathers were willing as prisoners of their own prejudice to permit ex-slaves to vote, but not their own white wives."

Not all women policy activists shared Griffiths's position. The president's Commission on the Status of Women and the U.S. Women's Bureau opposed an unqualified ban on sex-based employment practices. Key men in the House tried to use the division of opinion among women leaders to defeat the amendment. With eleven of the twelve women in the House speaking in favor of the amendment, however, it passed.

Congresswoman Griffiths, along with the National Organization for Women (NOW), women's unions, and individual women, struggled to ensure that the new Equal Employment Opportunity Commission (EEOC) would enforce the sex-discrimination provision. Many women also pursued Title VII claims through the courts, winning landmark decisions that removed sex-based restrictions on occupational choice;

changed hiring, promotion, and benefits practices that disadvantaged women; and brought sexual harassment within the jurisdiction of discrimination law.

Although Native Americans subject to tribal authority were not covered by the Civil Rights Act, Congress extended equal protection principles to Indians in relation to tribal governments in the Indian Civil Rights Act of 1968. This permitted Native American women to sue tribal governments for gender discrimination (e.g., *Santa Clara Pueblo* v. *Martinez*). Because of the concept of tribal sovereignty, however, the measure has been difficult to enforce.

How powerful a legal weapon Title VII can be depends on the EEOC and the courts. During the 1980s an increasingly conservative Court eviscerated Title VII in both gender and race decisions. To correct the Court, Congress enacted the Civil Rights Act of 1991. The new measure restored key precedents of the 1970s (e.g., *Griggs* v. *Duke Power*).

The Civil Rights Act of 1991 also broadened the remedies available to women under Title VII. Under the 1964 act, remedies in sex discrimination complaints were limited to back pay, reinstatement, and other job-specific claims. Because a nineteenth-century statute permitted damage claims in race discrimination cases, successful race cases could impose severe financial burdens on employers. Many women felt that sex discrimination was, therefore, an unequal sister in the structure of employment law. This point was brought to light by sexual harassment victims/survivors for whom back pay offered only token remedy and for whom reinstatement alongside harassers offered no remedy at all.

In the aftermath of Anita Hill's brave testimony against Supreme Court nominee Clarence Thomas in 1991, Congress ushered a strengthened Civil Rights Act toward passage. However, while the new law provided for damages in sex discrimination cases, it placed a ceiling on damages available to women and calibrated the ceiling according to the size of employer. In the realm of remedies for proven discrimination—the "stick" that encourages employers to comply with the law—women with sex discrimination claims remain second-class citizens.

• GWENDOLYN MINK

SEE ALSO Title VII.

≋ Civil Rights Movement

The success of the civil rights movement of the 1950s and 1960s was in large part a result of the crucial role that women played in propelling and sustaining mass action. Women in communities throughout the South acted as leaders, organizers, and members of the rank and file from the movement's beginnings. African American women already had begun organizing and protesting the discriminatory treatment of Blacks in urban transportation systems. Civil rights activist Rosa Parks refused to give up her seat on a segregated bus in Montgomery, Alabama, and was arrested on December 1, 1955. Parks's action was not coincidental, but rather a response to years of organizing experience in the National Association for the Advancement of Colored People (NAACP).

In 1949, six years prior to the Montgomery Bus Boycott, a group of Montgomery African American women organized the Women's Political Council (WPC). Led by college professors Jo Ann Gibson Robinson and Mary Fair Burks, WPC initially focused on voter registration and citizenship education with the intent of mobilizing Blacks to protest segregation. Following Parks's arrest, when the newly formed Montgomery Improvement Association (MIA) organized a yearlong bus boycott, WPC communicated the strategy and tactics essential for mass mobilization. Widespread support of the boycott was enabled not only by WPC members, who provided transportation alterna-

tives to city buses, but also by the large number of working-class African American women who refrained from using the bus system to travel to jobs as domestic workers in white homes.

The boycott had its southern white supporters as well, though few in number. Virginia Foster Durr was an outspoken Alabama activist who opposed segregation in the 1940s, as did her husband Clifford Durr, a civil rights attorney who later represented Mrs. Parks after her arrest. Durr and another southern-born white woman, Anne Braden, remained active in the movement throughout the 1950s and 1960s. A native of Alabama, Braden became radicalized in the mid-1950s when she and her husband, Carl, purchased a home in Kentucky and later sold it to a Black friend. Outraged southern whites labeled them "communist agitators," which compelled Braden to become involved in a range of civil and other human rights causes since that time.

Across the South, African American women were at the forefront of social change. In South Carolina, Septima Poinsette Clark struggled for racial justice before the 1960s. As a young schoolteacher in the 1920s, Clark's political consciousness was shaped by witnessing the extreme poverty of residents on John's Island, South Carolina. She conducted workshops there on literacy and health issues, which laid the foundation for more extensive activism in subsequent years. Later, after teaching for several years in the public schools of Charleston, Clark protested the unfair practice of paying Black teachers less than their white counterparts. The equalization of teachers' salaries became law in 1945 as a result of Clark's and others' activism. After forty years of teaching, Clark was fired from her job in 1956 for refusing to comply with a state law that banned any city employee from joining a civil rights organization. Undeterred, Clark went to work at the Highlander Folk School in Monteagle, Tennessee, an interracial training school for labor organizers and community activists, and worked alongside Rosa Parks and her niece, Bernice Robinson, to develop a program of adult literacy and citizenship education.

Although the *Brown* decision outlawed segregated schools in 1954, it was not until years later that public schools in the South were forced to comply. Massive white resistance escalated amidst attempts to desegregate schools and colleges in the region. In 1957 Autherine Lucy became the first Black student to attend the University of Alabama at Tuscaloosa. By her side was NAACP regional director Ruby Hurley, one of the few women to hold a national position in the organization. In 1955 Hurley had traveled to Mississippi to investigate firsthand the murder of fourteen-year-old Emmett Till, a Black youth who was killed for allegedly talking back to a white woman. Other Black women desegregated southern schools that year—Charlayne Hunter at the University of Georgia and Vivian Malone Jones at the University of Alabama at Birmingham.

By the end of the 1950s, white resistance in the South made no appeal to reason or legality. On February 1, 1960, the southern civil rights movement gained momentum with the lunch-counter sit-in led by students from North Carolina Agricultural and Technical State University in Greensboro. Following this action, veteran activist Ella Baker called upon student leaders from universities across the nation to participate in the Southwide Student Leadership Conference in April 1960, at Shaw University in Raleigh, North Carolina. The Student Non-Violent Coordinating Committee (SNCC) was founded here. Baker had worked in New York during the 1930s and 1940s organizing domestic workers and advocating cooperative buying campaigns before she served as a field secretary and later president of the New York City branch of the NAACP. Through her experience with the NAACP and later participation in the Southern Christian Leadership Conference (SCLC), Baker developed a critique of bureaucratic, hierarchical leadership, a style favored by the predominantly male leadership in both organizations. Instead, she ad-

vocated a group-centered approach to decision making that would involve all organization members. She believed that "strong people don't need strong leaders."

From its inception, the interracial SNCC was largely influenced by Baker's egalitarian vision and emphasis on participatory democracy. SNCC successfully increased voter registration in the most rural and impoverished communities in the Deep South. Among the young activists whom Baker influenced were two African American women who held key leadership positions within SNCC—Ruby Doris Smith Robinson, a Spelman College student from Atlanta, and Diane Nash of Fisk University. White college students were equally influenced by Baker. SNCC members Mary King, Casey Hayden, Jane Stembridge, and Dorothy Dawson, for example, came from strongly religious backgrounds. They followed in the tradition of an earlier generation of activist white women, including Virginia Durr and Anne Braden.

Sandra Casey Hayden, known as "Casey," grew up in Austin, Texas, where she became politicized through work with the YWCA and the Christian Faith and Life Community, the only interracial student group at the University of Texas. She was recruited by Connie Curry, another white activist, to work with the United States National Student Association, where she met Ella Baker and went to work for SNCC. Hayden, along with Mary King, worked out of SNCC's headquarters and developed news releases, pamphlets, and other communication. They remained with SNCC until 1964, when the organization shifted its emphasis from interracialism to advocacy of Black power and Black self-determination.

Although both King and Hayden recognized the importance of this shift in focus, they had begun to consider how women's experiences paralleled those of Blacks. At a pivotal staff retreat on the future of SNCC held in November 1964 at Waveland, Mississippi, King and Hayden wrote a controversial position paper, "Women in the

September 6, 1957. Elizabeth Eckford, age fifteen, is harassed by a hostile white mob as she walks through a line of National Guardsmen to Central High School in Little Rock, Arkansas. Her admission and that of eight other Black students had been ordered by a federal court following legal action taken by the Little Rock NAACP.

Movement." Circulated anonymously, the paper argued that the position of women within SNCC had been analogous to the historical discriminatory treatment of African Americans. Because of gender, wrote King and Hayden, women had been denied leadership positions within SNCC and relegated to second-class status.

Even before Waveland, 1964 was a watershed year in the history of the civil rights movement.

SNCC was immersed in organizing throughout the South. Along with other civil rights organizations, SNCC launched a full-scale cooperative effort to break open the racial caste system in Mississippi, the most oppressive of southern states. The Mississippi Summer Project was implemented to attract thousands of college students and young people from across the nation to register voters in the Deep South.

On the eve of the freedom summer, white resistance to the mass organizing effort resulted in the murder of three civil rights workers. James Chaney, a Black Mississippian, and two white organizers from the North, Michael Schwerner and Andrew Goodman, were found buried beneath eighteen feet of clay in the burned-out station wagon they had been driving. Yet, this violent incident did not prevent the project from proceeding. Controversial from the outset, the project had some successes, such as the innovative "freedom schools," which taught Black history and citizenship skills to local Black residents.

Another important development in the summer of 1964 was the establishment of the Mississippi Freedom Democratic Party (MFDP). Created as a grassroots, independent third party, the MFDP challenged the unconstitutional representation of the state's all-white, Democratic electorate, which excluded Mississippi's majority of Black voters. The leadership and rank and file of MFDP were decidedly working class. The party's national representatives were three Black women—Fannie Lou Hamer, Annie Belle Robinson Devine, and Victoria Gray. Fannie Lou Hamer's role and political influence within the party were critical to the effectiveness of the organization from the outset. In 1963 Hamer had suffered a brutal beating in a Winona, Mississippi, jail cell after attending a voter registration workshop.

At the 1964 Democratic National Convention in Atlantic City, New Jersey, MFDP party delegates sought to unseat the all-white Mississippi delegation. The contingent drew nationwide attention when Fannie Lou Hamer gave compelling televised testimony, exposing the violence and poverty suffered by Mississippi's Black citizens. She asked, "Is this America? The land of the free and the home of the brave?" The MFDP ultimately was unsuccessful in unseating the regular Mississippi delegates. In a political maneuver orchestrated by the Democratic Party's top national leadership, the MFDP was offered a compromise of two at-large seats, which they refused to accept.

Mrs. Hamer eloquently captured the party's commitment to full equality, which, on principle, they were unwilling to relinquish. She remarked, "We didn't come all this way for no two seats."

Hamer's remarkable courage and strength evolved from her experience living with the extremes of Mississippi racism. She was born as the twentieth child of sharecroppers in Sunflower County, Mississippi, where her family barely survived poverty and deprivation. The turning point in Hamer's life occurred following the arrival of young SNCC workers in the state. After attending a voter registration workshop in 1962, she returned to the plantation where she had worked for eighteen years, only to be told that she and her husband were fired. Hamer then became relentlessly committed to dismantling Mississippi's system of racial apartheid. She delivered powerful speeches, registered voters, and infused the movement with her gift of singing, which often galvanized the masses at civil rights meetings. Her extraordinary leadership derived from a deep spirituality and religious faith. Without the benefits of formal education, Hamer relied on biblical teachings to articulate the suffering and injustice of Black people. She confronted leadership, both Black and white, and was exceptional in her understanding of the interconnections of race, class, and gender in the United States. Remarking that "I am sick and tired of being sick and tired," Hamer realized that the plight of poor Blacks in Mississippi was not solely the result of racism but of economic injustice as well.

Like Ella Baker, Mrs. Hamer had a strong impact on younger leaders and provided a generational bridge between their activism and her own. Unita Blackwell was a personal friend whose own activism was influenced by Hamer. Blackwell, too, was the daughter of Mississippi sharecroppers. Blackwell later worked for SNCC, organizing counties around voter registration and working tirelessly to challenge oppression. In 1976 she became the first Black woman mayor in the state of Mississippi, in the rural, delta town where only years earlier she had been denied the right to vote.

Blackwell became involved in housing and economic development, working jointly with the National Council of Negro Women (NCNW) to tackle the severe problem of rural poverty. In 1965 she initiated one of the most successful desegregation lawsuits in the state, *Blackwell* v. *Issaquena County Board of Education.*

As Ella Baker commented, "the civil rights movement of the 1950s and 1960s was largely carried by women" whose organizing skills and political consciousness evolved from years of unflagging involvement in social change. The success of the Black freedom struggle was a result of the courageous leadership and selfless commitment of women who dedicated their lives to the vision of a free and just society.

Vicki Crawford, Jacqueline Rouse, and Barbara Woods, eds., *Women in the Civil Rights Movement: Trailblazers and Torchbearers, 1941–1965* (Bloomington: Indiana University Press, 1993); Sara Evans, *Personal Politics: The Roots of Women's Liberation in the Civil Rights Movement and the New Left* (New York: Alfred Knopf, 1979); Kay Mills, *This Little Light of Mine: The Life of Fannie Lou Hamer* (New York: Dutton, 1993).

▪ VICKI CRAWFORD

SEE ALSO Black Nationalism; Civil Rights Act of 1964; Mississippi Freedom Democratic Party; Mississippi Freedom Summer; Montgomery Bus Boycott; National Association for the Advancement of Colored People (NAACP); Student Non-Violent Coordinating Committee (SNCC).

≋ Civil War

SEE Wars: Colonization to 1900.

≋ Class

Analyzing class in women's history is difficult because most theories of class either have left out women altogether or assumed women's class position to be identical to that of men. Approaches to class analysis, moreover, vary widely. Some focus on the cultural sphere, distinguishing classes on the basis of divergent access to cultural resources such as education. Others define class as social status, arguing that an agreed upon hierarchy demarcates higher- from lower-status groups. More prominent theories define class in economic terms, distinguishing different classes according to income, wealth, or property ownership. Classic Marxist theory, in this vein, defines class in capitalist society according to a person's relationship to the means of production.

These various approaches implicitly assume that women's class status derives from the men to whom they are related through ties of kinship or marriage. Indeed, women's relationship to wealth and power—owning the means of production, for example—usually has been mediated through men. Gender oppression has meant that women have never been equal to the men of their equivalent class position.

Historians of women have not yet completely met the challenge of constructing a feminist interpretation of the history of class or of fully analyzing the class dynamics of women's experiences. Some historians do acknowledge differences among women depending on their access to wealth, their status in the labor market, or their cultural and intellectual attributes. This sort of analysis might point out, for example, that in the United States middle-class women reformers had a greater amount of leisure time available to pursue politics. Many studies of these women acknowledge the class status of their subjects, note that the conclusions of their studies are class-specific, but do not necessarily analyze further the ways in which class shaped their subjects' lives.

Class does not merely demarcate differences between women. Class, rather, as E. P. Thompson put it, is a relationship—one of power, domination, and, often, exploitation. Some women have directly employed other women, as domestic servants most commonly, or as laborers on farms, or at firms they own. They have profited from such relationships with both increased leisure time and monetary rewards. Other women have benefited from class domination more indirectly, through family ties or marriage. Their husbands might have managed or owned plantations or factories, owned stock in any range of profit-producing enterprises benefiting from the exploitation of slaves or wage workers, or participated in lucrative speculative endeavors that left others bankrupt. Conversely, enslaved or working-class women have spent much of their daily lives laboring to produce the wealth enjoyed by those above them yet have been denied the products of their own toil.

Christine Stansell's study of antebellum New York City, *City of Women*, offers a glimpse into the complexities of class relationships among women. Middle- and upper-class white women, she found, deplored the morality of poor women and sought to help alleviate the poverty of those deemed respectable. Yet the same middle-class women wore dresses, hats, and shoes produced at less-than-subsistence wages by the very working-class women they wanted to "help." When they returned home, their houses had been cleaned and their suppers cooked by female domestics working six-and-a-half-day weeks. The husbands of these middle-class women went off to work each day to build the industrial capitalist edifices that would institutionalize the political and economic power of the upper classes, producing further impoverishment—while at the same time providing the funds to buy lavish dresses and hats.

U.S. women's history is just beginning to explore such complex relationships. Studies of middle-class women face the task of sorting out the position of women cut off from much power because of their gender status and subservience to the rich, who nonetheless gained economically from their husbands' or fathers' relatively privileged positions as managers, technicians, or small-business owners. A clearer distinction needs to be made among such middle-class women and those above them. Many studies of white women re-

formers at the turn of the century have lumped together elite women with the wives of small-town businessmen under the rubric "middle class." Historians of working-class women, meanwhile, are still in the process of defining the working class in terms that include women and all their labors.

Since the seventeenth-century conquest of the eastern seaboard by Europeans, class dynamics in women's history have been deeply racialized. Most women of color have been working class, in part because of the heritage of slavery, in part because of the conquest of Spanish, Mexican, and Native America, and in part because people of color often have been allowed to immigrate only to perform the most menial jobs. Ideologies of racial hierarchy have played a central role in legitimating class domination and blocking the upward mobility of people of color. Apologists for slavery codified theories of the inferiority of African peoples, for example, to justify their enslavement. More recently, the "underclass" debate conceptualizes poverty entirely in racial terms. Such concepts continue to obscure the power of class dynamics in U.S. history by deflecting complex gender, class, and racial politics onto race alone.

Not all women of color in U.S. history have been working class, however. Small African American middle-class communities have struggled to survive in both the North and South since the antebellum period. A Latino elite evolved throughout the Southwest in the early nineteenth century, its original landowning status eventually destroyed by Anglo conquest. Within communities of color, class relationships have marked relationships among women. Women of the Chinese immigrant merchant class in early-twentieth-century San Francisco, for example, imported indentured "slave girls" from China to perform household labor. Middle-class women of color have often sought to manage the working classes of their own communities as did African American women active in the early-twentieth-century women's club movement, who sought to reform the moral character of poor African American women while training them for employment considered appropriate to their station in life.

Class analysis, if central to women's history, has its limits. The class position of many women is by no means simple to assess. Where, for example, do we place the impoverished white tenant farm women depicted in Margaret Hagood's 1939 study *Mothers of the South*? They fit no easy Marxist categories. They were near starvation, often dominated by abusive husbands; and yet they could still afford occasionally to hire African American women to help them after childbirth or when ill. Their example illustrates the ways in which race privilege has sharply divided white women of a given class from those of the same ostensible class position who have been marked as racially inferior.

The history of Native American women further illustrates the limits of easy class analysis. The multiple systems of internal organization within tribal communities do not fit European-derived understandings of class, which evolved to explain the dominant capitalist society. Historically, when Native American women have entered the wage labor market it has been at the bottom only, as racism, U.S. federal policies of forced assimilation into the bottom of the class structure, and the economic strangulation of land-based communities have combined to bar most indigenous peoples from the wealth or employment that would allow them entry into the dominant society's middle class.

Nonetheless, to attempt a class-neutral approach or to give only lip service to class dynamics merely obscures the power dynamics underlying women's experiences. The history of the women's movement offers a clear lesson. Middle- and upper-class white women, both in the early twentieth century and in the period since the 1960s, have usually defined "feminism" in a manner designed to liberate them to be equal to the men of their class and race, while still leaving in place the larger structure of racialized class domination—and their position at its top. White working-class women, by contrast, have refused to separate women's equality from the advancement or liberation of working-class men and women alike, while women of color have defined the liberation of their people from racial domination as central to the emancipation of women—indeed as its goal. The lesson is not to place class analysis over race or gender but to see how class inequalities have been central to both.

▪ DANA FRANK

≋ Classical Music

Whether on the concert stage or as composers, women in classical music have long been on the frontiers of the struggle for equality. The question "Why have there been no great women composers?" perennially appears in print, ignoring the many who have been the equals of the "masters." Until the twentieth century, females as professional musicians in the public sphere were rare in the United States. The nineteenth-century ideology of domesticity encouraged women to cultivate music in the home. Ladies' seminaries offered lessons in harp, guitar, piano, and voice, alongside embroidery and other domestic skills. Toward the end of the century, as more young women turned to careers in teaching and the professions, normal schools and music conservatories were established, many by women. Clara Baur founded the Cincinnati Conservatory in 1867, and Jeanette Thurber opened the National Conservatory of Music in New York in 1886. Crane Normal Institute of Music of Potsdam, New York, was founded in 1886 by Julia Ettie Crane.

Women organists, choir directors, and singers were the first to enter the concert stage. Sophia Hewitt (1799–1846) was invited to fill the position of organist for Boston's prestigious Handel and

Haydn Society when she was only seventeen. In the 1840s and 1850s, singers Eliza Ostinelli Biscaccianti (1824–96) and soprano Elizabeth Taylor Greenfield (1809–76), the "Black Swan" and a former slave, pursued concert careers. Clara Louise Kellogg (1842–1916); Sissieretta Jones (1869–1933), the "Black Patti"; Emma Eames (1865–1952); the African American Hyers sisters Anna and Emma; Mary Garden (1874–1967); and Lillian Russell (1861–1922) were among the many successful operatic, vaudeville, and musical comedy performers. Maria Callas (1923–77) and African Americans Marian Anderson (1902–94) and Leontyne Price (b. 1927) are among the most celebrated divas of this century.

In the instrumental realm, women performers' public visibility emerged more gradually. Pianists Julie Rivé-King (1854–1937) and Fannie Bloomfield Zeisler (1863–1927) toured in the 1870s and 1880s, and violinist Maud Powell (1867–1920) played with leading orchestras in Europe and the United States. In the twentieth century, pianists Rosalyn Tureck (b. 1914) and Ruth Slenczynski (b. 1925) have enjoyed illustrious careers. The late cellist Jacqueline duPré was active in the 1960s and early 1970s, and violinist Nadja Salerno-Sonnenberg has been prominent since the 1980s.

Female choruses began in the women's music clubs of the 1870s. Some, such as the St. Cecilia Society of New York and the Rubenstein Club of Cleveland, gave ambitious and highly polished concerts. All-women orchestras began to flourish in the 1880s. Caroline B. Nichols founded the long-lasting Boston Fadette Lady Orchestra in 1888, performing classical music and vaudeville acts. By 1908 some thirty all-women orchestras catered to popular demand for this novelty. Although women substituted in "regular" orchestras during the world wars, they gave up their jobs when the men returned. Not until the 1960s did major orchestras include women players. Meanwhile, all-women orchestras in many cities have continued to train both conductors and instrumentalists, from the Los Angeles Woman's Or-

chestra and Chicago Woman's Symphony Orchestra to the Bay Area Women's Philharmonic. In 1925 Ethel Leginska (1886–1970) became the first woman to conduct the New York Symphony Orchestra. Frédérique Petrides (1903–83) and Antonia Brico (1902–89) formed their own orchestras. Women conductors such as Sarah Caldwell, Margaret Hillis, JoAnne Falletta, Marin Alsop, and Afro-Cuban Tania León are at last entering the predominantly male world of major and community orchestras.

If women conductors have struggled for acceptance in roles of authority, composers have had to combat the widely held prejudice that women are incapable of the complex, abstract thought necessary to create "serious" music. Nevertheless, by 1900 at least 230 U.S.-born women composers were active, and by 1985 their number exceeded two thousand. The earliest compositions by U.S. women were published anonymously, often by "a lady." By the 1830s a few allowed their names to be used in women's journals such as *Godey's Ladies' Book*. The greatest flowering of nineteenth-century women composers took place in Boston. Mrs. H.H.A. Beach (1867–1944), a self-taught prodigious talent, was particularly well known; her "Gaelic Symphony" (1897) was the first symphony by a U.S. woman to be performed anywhere. No doubt the young Florence Price (1887–1953), studying at the New England Conservatory in 1902, heard Beach's works. Price's Symphony in E Minor, performed in 1933 at the Chicago World's Fair, was the first symphony to be composed by a Black woman. Marion Bauer (1897–1955) was among the first Americans to study in Paris with the great pedagogue Nadia Boulanger. She and Mary Howe (1882–1964), one of the founders of the Association of American Women Composers, wrote orchestral tone poems and piano pieces.

Ruth Crawford Seeger's life and work (1901–53) took two paths: during the 1920s and 1930s her ultramodern compositions earned her the first Guggenheim Fellowship for composition awarded to a woman. On her return from Europe, she joined husband Charles Seeger and stepson Pete Seeger on another path, collecting and publishing folksongs.

Boulanger protegée Louise Talma (b. 1906) employed twelve-tone techniques freely, permitting her exuberant rhythmic vitality and open, bell-like sounds to dominate her piano works. Barbara Kolb (b. 1939) and Joan Tower (b. 1938) also combine twelve-tone techniques with a focus on one or more other elements: sonority, rhythm, texture, timbre, and performance improvisation. Tower received the 1990 Grawemeyer Award for her orchestral work *Silver Ladders* (1985). Nancy Van de Vate (b. 1930) founded the International League of Women Composers in 1975; her *Chernobyl* (1987) for orchestra evokes impending disaster through dense sound clusters. Julia Perry (1924–79) was the first Black woman to win the Guggenheim Fellowship for composition.

New concepts in sound and performance are being explored by Annea Lockwood in her works using sounds in nature; Priscilla McLean in processed whale sounds; Lucia Dlugoszewski in her newly invented percussion instruments; Joan La Barbara in radically new vocal techniques; and Meredith Monk in her total-art-experience pieces. Electronic music is favored by many women composers, from pioneer Bebe Barron, who founded the earliest electronic music studio with her husband in 1951, to Jean Eichelberger Ivy, Joyce Mekeel, and Beth Anderson.

A pioneer in performance experiments, Pauline Oliveros explores theatricality, humor, feminism, meditation, electronic music (including tones outside the range of human hearing), the accordion (her favorite instrument), and audience participation. Laurie Anderson combines music, storytelling, humor, and the visual arts — video, slides, lighting effects — in evening(s)-long concerts.

Amidst this new technology and experimentation, some composers continue to explore traditional forms: Miriam Gideon was the first woman to receive a commission for a complete synagogue service, *Sacred Service for Sabbath Morning* (1970). Neoclassicist Ellen Taafe Zwilich was the first woman to receive a Pulitzer Prize in music, for her Symphony No. 1 (1982). Her chamber works and orchestral works employ established developmental principles. This brief survey of women in U.S. classical music history highlights only a few of the many composers, performers, and works deserving attention.

Christine Ammer, *Unsung: A History of Women in American Music* (Westport, Conn.: Greenwood Press, 1980); J. Michelle Edwards and Leslie Lassetter, "North America since 1920," in *Women and Music: A History*, edited by Karin Pendle (Bloomington: Indiana University Press, 1991).

▪ HELEN WALKER-HILL

SEE ALSO Music.

≋ Clerical Work

Soon after being appointed secretary of labor by President Clinton, Robert Reich abolished the executive dining room and joined employees in the cafeteria. While in line, he struck up a conversation with the woman next to him. "And what do you do?" the woman asked. "I'm the secretary," replied Reich. "Oh," said the woman, "whose secretary are you?"

Today people laugh at a member of the president's cabinet being mistaken for a secretary. But his title reminds us that the job of secretary was once to serve as trusted adviser to the top person in an organization. The position was a steppingstone to management, requiring a high level of skill and responsibility and conferring a commensurate level of status and pay. In 1870 only 1 percent of the nonagricultural work force was engaged in clerical work; 97.5 percent of those employees were males.

Sixty years later, clerical work itself had changed dramatically—and so had the makeup of

Students in a typewriting class at Emma Ransom House in Harlem, New York, in the 1920s.

those who performed it. By 1930 nearly 10 percent of all nonagricultural jobs were clerical, and more than 50 percent of clerical workers were female.

White women first worked in offices during the labor shortage that occurred as a result of the Civil War. To hire women to clip currency for the U.S. Treasury in the 1860s, the government first had to pass a statute creating the job category "female clerk." Supporters in Congress praised the practical education and industriousness of certain women, not to mention the fact that women could be hired for substantially lower salaries than men commanded. The rate for "female clerk" was established at one-half the rate for males.

By 1900 30 percent of clerical jobs were performed by women. By the end of World War I, nearly one in four women workers was employed in office work. Technological advances—including the typewriter, telephone, tabulators, and pneumatic tubes—meant that clerical positions were more mechanized and more routine. Numerous factors contributed to the feminization of this sector of the U.S. work force. More women were available for work, and the growth in high school education prepared them with the necessary skills. Women's purported "nimble fingers" were considered well suited for the job. Just as discriminatory wages made them more attractive to employers, barriers based on gender kept women out of many other occupations.

The overwhelming majority of women employed in clerical positions were white and native-born. Those African American women (and men) who made gains as clericals did so mainly in Black-owned businesses. Strict segregation excluded most African American women from positions in white-owned firms until the 1960s, with some exceptions for short periods during the first and second world wars. The greatest inroads for women of color occurred in the public sector.

Although clerical work paid more than factory or domestic jobs in the early part of the century, the status and pay declined as the jobs expanded. The office worker, rather than being a trusted adviser, was seen as a subordinate. One employer, quoted in a *Ladies' Home Journal* article in 1916, attributed more than half of the value of a good stenographer to submissiveness: "I expect from my stenographer the same service I get from the sun, with this exception: the sun often goes on a strike and it is necessary for me to use artificial light, but I pay my stenographer to work six days out of every seven and I expect her all the while to radiate my office with sunshine and sympathetic interest in the things I am trying to do."

Clerical jobs expanded with the growth in business services. In 1994 25.9 percent of all working women, including 26 percent of African American women and 29 percent of Latinas, held administrative support or clerical jobs. Ninety-eight percent of secretaries and stenographers are female.

Technological advances in the last fifteen years have increased productivity greatly but without accompanying increases in pay. Two trends coexist: in a minority of businesses, work has been reorganized into a high-performance model. There secretaries may serve as part of managerial teams, with more opportunities for training and decision making. At the same time, many firms have contracted out clerical work or "outsourced" it to suppliers in other countries who pay very low wages. Women in clerical jobs also have been affected by the sharp increase in part-time and temporary positions, which generally pay less and offer fewer or no benefits. Unionized women office workers earn 21 percent more, on average, than unaffiliated clericals, but only 16 percent of women in these jobs belong to a union.

■ ELLEN BRAVO

SEE ALSO Labor Unions: Nine to Five (District 925 of SEIU); Pink Collar Ghetto.

≋ Coalition of Labor Union Women (CLUW)

Founded in 1974, the Coalition of Labor Union Women (CLUW) identified several goals: 1) to organize women workers and to make unions more responsive to their needs; 2) to promote affirmative action in the workplace; 3) to strengthen women's role in unions, especially as leaders; 4) to raise policy issues concerning work and family, the minimum wage, child and elder care, family leave, the right to a job, and health and safety; and 5) to create links between the women's movement and organized labor.

CLUW has supported women as workers, mothers, and family members by promoting policies and contract language to make wages and salaries adequate to support families, to achieve pay equity and equal opportunity, and to encourage practices that respect both the workers' employment and family responsibilities. CLUW consistently has emphasized the family needs of women wage earners. Its 1977 study of child care in Israel, Sweden, and France led to a call for child-care policy and for union contracts that would support parents' family obligations.

Priorities for the 1990s include union contracts that broaden the definition of "family" to serve all varieties of U.S. families.

CLUW continues to raise gender issues in the workplace, to work for a progressive labor program, and to ally working women with the feminist movement. CLUW's achievements include the introduction of women's issues into collective bargaining, passage of the Family and Medical Leave Act in 1993, and an increased leadership role for union women.

■ RUTH MEYEROWITZ

SEE ALSO Labor Movement; Labor Unions.

≋ Colleges

SEE Education; Women's Colleges.

≋ Colonial Period

Although few histories of the European settlements in North America in the seventeenth and eighteenth centuries have acknowledged it, women played a key role in the development of the North American colonies. The first European outposts (St. Augustine, Jamestown, Quebec, Montreal, New Amsterdam) were composed exclusively or primarily of men. Since these settlements were envisioned as military or trading ventures, that fact is hardly surprising, but the absence of a substantial number of European women among the first settlers had a lasting impact on those societies' subsequent histories.

In colonies such as New France, where European men lived in close contact with large numbers of Native Americans, sexual liaisons between white men and Indian women were common. These unions gave rise to the métis, mixed-race people who became cultural, political, and economic mediators between Europeans and natives. In other colonies, however, the absence of European women meant that migrants had great difficulty sustaining their societies. Either those colonies fell to stronger powers, as New Netherland did to England in 1665; or they required constant infusions of immigrants to survive, as did Virginia and Maryland, where demographic problems caused by the absence of women were compounded by high mortality rates.

By contrast, the European settlements that included large proportions of women from their beginnings—New England, Pennsylvania, New York, and New Jersey—quickly reproduced themselves through natural increase. They did not need continued migration from Europe to sustain or expand their settlements, in part because New England and the middle colonies were very healthy places to live by seventeenth-century standards. Thus marriages were long and fertility rates higher than in either England or the Chesapeake.

For Native American women, the arrival of Europeans was devastating to their culture and society. In much of eastern North America, women had been the agriculturalists, responsible for planting and tending crops. But English settlers refused to acknowledge Natives' claims to the soil, and their farms and plantations intruded onto Indian women's fields. Smallpox and other diseases such as dysentery and influenza decimated the populations of many villages. Catholic priests and nuns in New France and New Spain pressed Indian women and men to convert to Christianity (the Protestants of English America were less energetic in this regard), enforcing new ideas of morality—for example, condemning the premarital sexual freedom common in many Indian cultures—while at the same time offering female Indian converts the role model of the Virgin Mary, which many of them found inspiring. Europeans also encouraged Native women to adopt "proper" (i.e., European) gender roles by confining their activities to cooking, child care, and other "feminine" tasks such as spinning, rather than continuing to work in the fields. By 1800 the remaining Native American women in the eastern third of the continent had largely succumbed to these pressures, primarily because it was impossible for Indian people to sustain traditional ways of life—which involved expansive hunting territories and seasonal migrations—in the midst of European settlements.

After about 1680, African women were also essential to the success of the colonies. Enslaved women provided invaluable field labor to the tobacco and rice plantations of the mainland and to the sugar plantations of the Caribbean islands. The conditions of slavery were so harsh and the sex ratio so skewed (men composed the vast majority of slaves) that only after about 1740 and then only in the Chesapeake colonies did the African American population expand through natural increase rather than repeated importations.

In European households during this period, white women were the chief manufacturers of goods for consumption or sale; men provided the raw materials, women processed those components into useful commodities—clothing, butter and cheese, cured meats, and other foodstuffs. The sexual division of labor was so pronounced that when households lacked female members, those tasks were not accomplished.

Historians once regarded the colonial period as a "golden age" for white women because of their significant contributions to the economy and their employment as widows in a wide variety of occupations, but this interpretation ignored women's lack of access to education, dependent legal status in marriage, and lives of hard work, frequent childbearing, and—especially in the Chesapeake—early death. Now historians assess white women's lives more realistically, recognizing that their labor contributions did not necessarily translate into control over resources and that most of their lives were spent as subordinates to fathers or husbands. Moreover, the older interpretation overlooked the experiences of female Africans, who endured lives of brutality and exploitation, and Native Americans, who suffered the destruction of their ancient ways of life.

Karen Anderson, *Chain Her by One Foot: The Subjugation of Women in Seventeenth-Century New France* (London: Routledge, 1991); Mary Beth Norton, "The Evolution of White Women's Experience in Early America," *American Historical Review* Vol. 89 (1984): 593–619; Carole Shammas, "Black Women's Work and the Evolution of Plantation Society in Virginia," *Labor History* Vol. 26 (1985): 5–28.

■ MARY BETH NORTON

SEE ALSO Explorers; Indentured Servitude; Native American Cultures; Plantation System; Slavery.

≋ Colorism

Colorism is a form of intragroup stratification generally associated with Black people in the United States but present among all peoples of color. Colorism subjectively ranks individuals according to the perceived color tones of their skin. People who "look white" receive preferential or prejudicial treatment both within and between races. Social status, marriage desirability, economic and educational attainment often have been historically related to light skin tones.

Colorism is a poisonous legacy of slavery and reflects the persistent Eurocentric bias in U.S. culture. Black people with lighter skin tones were born as a result of various forms of miscegenation since colonial times. They were the country's earliest multiracial inhabitants, along with children of Native American–white unions.

Tension sometimes occurs in Native American tribes with mixed-blood populations between the light-skinned mixed-bloods and "full-blood" Native people. They debate about whether one is really a tribal person if he or she is not "identifiably Native." Furthermore, Native people sometimes identify themselves by the degree of Indian blood they possess.

Contrary to popular myth, no evidence exists to support the notion that lighter-skinned slaves were chosen as house servants or concubines. They worked in the fields alongside their darker brothers and sisters, but they were given preferential emancipation from servitude—both indentureship and slavery. Freedom was often granted to the offspring of interracial unions after a specified term of servitude if the mother was white; some were manumitted by a white father.

European Americans attempted to recognize distinctions among Blacks by creating various census categories. In each census year from 1850 to 1920, except 1880 and 1900, efforts were made to differentiate Blacks and mulattos. Different states had different percentage rules to determine who was Black. Therefore methods for racial determination were imprecise, subjective, and primarily based on visual observation, which yielded an undercount of Black Americans.

Colorism has varied in intensity regionally and historically. Emphasis on light skin, straight hair, and sharp features allowed some individuals to attempt to distance themselves from the "typical" image of Blacks. Color consciousness manifested its most extreme form in urban areas, where elite groups called "blue vein" societies developed. Light skin was the primary qualification for membership, although education, sobriety, manners, dress, wealth, and proper elocution were also essential attributes. Thus the number of members was small and select.

Some of the historically Black colleges, such as Howard and Fisk Universities, became bastions for multiracial elites. Churches, literary clubs, and social organizations also reflected color preferences. During the Black consciousness movement of the 1960s as well as the 1970s' Black arts renaissance, colorism was submerged. It re-emerged strongly in the 1980s and 1990s in the media's images of light-skinned women in music videos, Black films, television shows, and commercials.

People who practiced colorism were casualties of the deeper racial oppression embedded in U.S. society. By internalizing oppression, victims of racism themselves became perpetrators of a divisive and pernicious system. In 1983 author Alice Walker observed, "Unless the question of Colorism . . . is addressed in our communities and definitely in our black 'sisterhoods,' we cannot, as a people, progress."

• SHIRLEE TAYLOR HAIZLIP

SEE ALSO Miscegenation; Whiteness.

≋ Commissions on the Status of Women

The most important proposals for commissions on the status of women emerged out of the conflict over the Equal Rights Amendment (ERA). As early as 1947 the U.S. Women's Bureau proposed a commission to study the economic, civil, social, and political status of U.S. women in an effort to counter growing support for the amendment. The commission's task was to support policies or legislation that prohibited sex discrimination but permitted differentiation on "reasonable" grounds, thereby preserving special labor legislation for women. But the bill generated little support in Congress.

Similar concerns about the ERA led the U.S. Women's Bureau to persuade President John F. Kennedy to establish the President's Commission on the Status of Women (1961–63). Chaired by Eleanor Roosevelt, the twenty-six member commission helped to forge a compromise on the ERA and catapulted the issue of women's status to national prominence. The commission rejected the formal equality of the ERA and recommended litigation under the Fourteenth Amendment. The commission also rejected any similarity between race and sex discrimination and opposed the inclusion of sex in executive orders and laws that barred discrimination on the basis of race. They regarded differential treatment in employment on the basis of sex as warranted under some circumstances because of women's familial obligations. Passage of the Civil Rights Act of 1964, however, made these recommendations irrelevant.

The commission's most enduring contribution was its role in helping to launch the contemporary feminist movement. Through the creation of state commissions on the status of women, the president's commission fostered a national network of primarily white, middle-class women concerned with these issues. It was at the 1966 national gathering of state commissioners that the National Organization for Women was founded.

■ HELENE SILVERBERG

SEE ALSO Civil Rights Act of 1964; Women's Bureau.

≋ Communism

Communist theories and movements emerged in Europe during the second half of the nineteenth century largely as a response to the works of Karl Marx and Friedrich Engels. Like the socialist movements that preceded them, they embraced collective ownership and control of the means of economic production. What distinguished communism from socialism, however, was the theory that such collective ownership could not be instituted without the overthrow of the capitalist system. Because communist parties advocated the establishment of socialism as a step toward the creation of a communist society without class distinctions and economic inequality, the terms communism and socialism are often used interchangeably.

Communist movements and women's rights movements have unfolded along parallel and often intersecting trajectories. The women's rights convention organized by Elizabeth Cady Stanton and Lucretia Mott in Seneca Falls, New York, took place in 1848, the same year the *Communist Manifesto* was published. Although supporters of the demand for women's suffrage often equated political equality with women's emancipation, women who advocated socialist transformation argued that political equality for women would not independently guarantee economic equality for working-class people, regardless of gender. During the ten years immediately preceding the passage of the Nineteenth Amendment, increasing numbers of women emerged as activists in work-ing-class and socialist movements, thus reconceptualizing the battle for the vote. Many of these women were Jewish immigrants from Eastern Europe, often carrying on revolutionary legacies rooted in their native working-class struggles.

European women like Rosa Luxemburg, Clara Zetkin, and Emma Goldman (the Jewish, Russian-born anarchist whose critiques of socialist politics have a striking contemporary relevance) have left an important body of theoretical literature. Others, like Alexandra Kollontai (a member of Lenin's first Revolutionary Council), U.S. labor organizers Ella Reeve Boor and Elizabeth Gurley Flynn, international organizer and activist Peggy Dennis, and U.S. communist leader Dorothy Healey, have produced autobiographical works that explain how they evaluate their own contributions to organizing socialist and communist movements. Their perspectives often reflect complicated historical contexts, which led some of them to sever their organizational ties to the parties with which they were affiliated, while negotiating new ways of expressing their socialist commitment. Others remained loyal to their parties throughout their lives.

Vast numbers of women who have devoted their lives to organizing for revolutionary socialist transformation have left neither theoretical nor autobiographical works. Some, like Lucy Gonzales Parsons and Claudia Jones, have become subjects of important biographies. Of the many women of color associated with socialist and communist organizing, Parsons is one of the few whose lives have been carefully documented. Hers was a long and rich life in which she variously represented herself as Mexican and Black and became active in the Socialist Labor Party as early as 1877. An active organizer for the Chicago Working Women's Union, she often focused her work on women. Along with "Mother" Mary Jones, another well-known labor activist of the late nineteenth century, Parsons was one of the first women to join the International Workers of the World (IWW), the radical syndicalist organi-

Communist Party supporters parade on May Day 1930, in Union Square, New York. The group's popularity grew during the 1930s, joining forces with other leftist organizations to work for Black civil rights, labor and unions, and relief for the unemployed.

zation. During the 1905 founding convention of the IWW, she and Mother Jones took their places on the podium alongside Eugene Debs and Big Bill Haywood. Parsons' was a lifetime of struggle, much of which was devoted to campaigns to free political prisoners—from her husband Albert Parsons (arrested and eventually executed in connection with the 1886 massacre at Chicago's Haymarket Square), to the Scottsboro Nine, and the young Black communist Angelo Herndon.

Claudia Jones immigrated to the United States from Trinidad as a child and became an international socialist activist. Born in 1915 into a poor family and raised in the nucleus of Black America

at the time, Harlem, Jones had a lifelong commitment to social change that led her to become active in the Communist Party. During her impressive career, she published a number of articles in *Political Affairs*, some of which make stunning observations about the intersection of race, class, and gender long before the concept of "intersectionality" was formulated. After being arrested and deported to Britain during the McCarthy period, she became a prominent spokesperson for London's Black communities. A collection of her writings was published and Jones's image has become an important part of Black political culture in London.

Although most of the communist women activists were involved at one time or another in the party, membership has not been a prerequisite for women's significant interventions in the development of communist theories and practices. Many women who have worked within other socialist and communist formations continue to engage in important political organizing projects today, such as the Line of March Party and the Committees of Correspondence, a network of individuals committed to the ongoing possibility of socialism and democracy.

Carolyn Asbaugh, *Lucy Parsons: American Revolutionary* (Chicago: Charles H. Kerr Publishing Co., 1976); Elizabeth Gurley Flynn, *The Rebel Girl: An Autobiography* (New York: International Publishers, 1973); Alix Kates Shulman, ed., *Red Emma Speaks: Selected Writings & Speeches by Emma Goldman* (New York: Random House, 1972).

▪ ANGELA Y. DAVIS

SEE ALSO Feminism, Marxist; Radicalism; Socialism.

≋ Community Service Organization (CSO)

Community Service Organization (CSO) came into existence in post–World War II Los Angeles. Reeling from the euphoria of democratic victory, the Mexican American community of East Los Angeles and Boyle Heights was also still healing from the infamous Zoot Suit riots and the Sleepy Lagoon case. The organization was founded in 1947 out of a long tradition of Mexican American community organizations. These organizations, called *mutualistas*, were a crucial step in Mexican American self-reliance, providing a variety of services including loans, low-cost medical and life insurance, legal aid, job search and referral, and advocacy for educating children of Mexican descent.

A century after the rise of *mutualistas*, the postwar generation took a different and explicitly political stand in their organizing efforts: U.S. citizens were exercising their civil rights. CSO became an umbrella group addressing civil rights issues in East Los Angeles, including neighborhood improvement, educational equity, labor support committees, citizenship education, race relations committees, and credit unions. CSO was active in the massive voter registration of the Mexican American community and in the election of Edward R. Roybal to the ninth district of the Los Angeles City Council.

Mexican American women were involved in all these activities. Lupe Morales, Lucille Roybal, Lucy Rios, Maria Duran, Margarita Duran, and Enriqueta Villaesquesa took leadership roles in organizing home meetings, fundraising, door-to-door voter registration, research projects related to education, housing, and civil rights.

Some of these women used the skills they acquired in organizing CSO to develop careers in political campaigns, become project directors for Planned Parenthood, form grassroots organizations in Panama, initiate mental health programs for Los Angeles County, and create Services for Senior Citizens. Dolores Huerta, the vice president of the United Farm Workers Union, got her start in grassroots organizing through the CSO. The Los Angeles CSO still exists, under the direction of Rosario (Rosie) Vasquez.

▪ LINDA APODACA

≋ Comparable Worth

In the 1980s in the state of Minnesota, women clerk stenographers earned nearly $400 per month less than men laborers; in Illinois, licensed practical nurses, nearly all female, earned less than half what electricians, nearly all male, in state employment earned; and in Washington State, female laundry operators were paid seventeen pay grades below male farm equipment operators. These cases illustrate two tenacious facts of the U.S. economy: 1) most workers are employed in jobs that have been and continue to be sex-segregated, and 2) wages for jobs in which women predominate are substantially lower than those paid for male-dominated jobs. Comparable worth — also referred to as pay equity — is one proposed remedy for this injustice. Comparable worth doctrine proposes that within organizations, female-dominated jobs should be rewarded comparably to male-dominated jobs judged similar in skills, effort, responsibility, and working conditions.

The notion that wages for sex-segregated jobs should be set by a standard of equivalent or comparable value was implicit in the earliest calls for "equal pay for equal work." As early as 1908, women of the Bookkeepers and Accountants Union Local 1 of New York demanded "equal pay" and compared themselves to higher-paid male hod-carriers. In Western Europe at this time, proponents prevailed upon the International Labor Organization (ILO) to adopt standards broad enough to benefit women in sex-segregated jobs. In the United States, trade union women agitated for this standard in national equal pay legislation for nearly twenty years, but only when narrowed to the strict "equal work" standard did the Equal Pay Act finally pass in 1963.

The limited reach of the Equal Pay Act, together with the social and political changes affecting U.S. women, led to the resurfacing of the issue of comparable worth in the 1970s and 1980s. The feminist movement had resurged, women's participation in the labor force had increased, and families had become more dependent on women's earnings because of the decline in good salaries for men's jobs and the rise in single-mother-headed households — yet full-time women workers were still earning only sixty-five cents for every dollar earned by white men.

Comparable worth action emerged across the country. Efforts in Washington State were among the earliest: the public sector workers' union, American Federation of State, County, and Municipal Employees (AFSCME), along with women political leaders claimed that lower wages for women's jobs were discriminatory. They filed a suit against the state (*AFSCME* v. *State of Washington*) which, among others, attempted to extend Title VII of the 1964 Civil Rights Act, prohibiting race and sex discrimination in employment, to include equal pay for work of equivalent value. The Washington State employees' initially favorable verdict was overturned, however, by the Court of Appeal, which argued that if employers followed prevailing "market" rates, it was not illegal. Eventually AFSCME reached an out-of-court settlement to implement comparable worth in Washington State, but this decision came about because of strong public support for the union's case. Other lawsuits brought under Title VII have failed despite compelling arguments that prevailing "market" wages represent the institutionalization of past discriminatory practices.

Even without a national legal standard, many local and state cases have succeeded through legislative and collective bargaining routes. For example, in 1981 city workers in San Jose, California, won the right to comparable worth wages after predominantly female clerical, library, and recreation workers went on strike. In 1984 newly unionized women clerical and technical workers at Yale University went on a ten-week strike, using the issue of comparable worth to win substantial wage increases.

Other efforts, such as those directed at state employment in New York, Oregon, and Michigan, have not involved similar grassroots participation. The job evaluation studies used to compare tasks, demands, and wages of male- and female-dominated jobs in these large organizations employ technical procedures and statistical methods. Therefore, state officials and management consultants have dominated wage-adjustment processes, limiting not only employee involvement but also the possibility of far-reaching transformation of wage structures.

Comparable worth agitation in the United States has occurred primarily among unionized government or public sector workers. Although proponents argue that pay equity will reach the private sector eventually, the only strong model existing is in Ontario, Canada, where all companies employing ten or more workers must implement pay equity. Fewer workers, however, are unionized in the U.S. private sector; they lack the power to fight for such reforms, and such proposals would provoke vigorous opposition from U.S. businesses. Vocal employer opposition was particularly influential during the pro-business Reagan administration; the director of the Civil Rights Commission, Clarence Pendleton, called comparable worth "the looniest idea since Looney Tunes."

In early actions, comparable worth proponents often ignored race discrimination in the labor market, and some women of color viewed comparable worth as a white women's issue. By the mid-1980s, however, some comparable worth cases included race in pay equity studies and policies. In fact African American women (and to some extent men), who are disproportionately employed in public sector jobs, have a direct stake in achieving comparable worth; the policies benefit people employed as food service workers and entry-level clerks as well as those who are college educated. However, many women of color as well as many white women are employed in jobs and sectors of the economy that would not be affected by comparable worth policies that are geared toward large and stable bureaucratic organizations. Domestic workers, temporary or contingent electronics assembly workers, or garment workers—jobs that employ many women of color—will require more relevant reforms. Comparable worth is an important policy aimed at guaranteeing all working women and their families a decent standard of living, but it does not yet adequately address the needs of women of color.

Linda M. Blum, *Between Labor and Feminism: The Significance of the Comparable Worth Movement* (Berkeley: University of California Press, 1991); Michael W. McCann, *Rights at Work: Pay Equity Reform and the Politics of Legal Mobilization* (Chicago: University of Chicago Press, 1994); Donald J. Treiman and Heidi I. Hartmann, eds., *Women, Work, and Wages: Equal Pay for Jobs of Equal Value* (Washington, D.C.: National Academy Press, 1981).

■ LINDA M. BLUM
and PEGGY KAHN

SEE ALSO Equal Pay Act; Labor Movement; Labor Unions; Wage Gap.

≋ Confederate Women

The formation of the Confederate States of America, commencing with the inauguration of Jefferson Davis as president in 1861 and ending with the surrender at Appomattox in 1865, demanded the loyalty and absorbed the energies of most white women in the eleven seceding states. Women of the planter class formed voluntary societies, enlisting yeoman sisters as well, to collect food, supply clothing, and establish medical facilities. The resourceful Sally Tompkins, who ran the Robertson Hospital in Richmond, the Confederate capital, was the only woman awarded the rank of captain in the Confederate army. Other women took on more daring challenges, such as spies Belle Boyd, Belle Edmondson, and former society belle Rose Greenhow. An unknown number of Confederate women assumed male identities to become soldiers, including the intrepid Amy Clarke, who served by her husband's side as he was killed at Shiloh, and was discovered to be a woman by Union captors only after being wounded. Exploits such as these were rare, but it was not uncommon for Confederate women of every class to sacrifice a son, a husband, a brother—at times all three—to the war effort.

Under threat of Union invasion, hundreds of thousands of Confederate women became refugees, including First Lady Varina Davis. Following surrender, white war widows memorialized the Lost Cause and launched crusades to honor veterans and the war dead that culminated in the formation of the United Daughters of the Confederacy in 1894, an organization that sought to celebrate and perpetuate Confederate values of honor, chivalry, and white supremacy.

▪ CATHERINE CLINTON

SEE ALSO Wars: Colonization to 1900.

≋ El Congreso de Pueblos de Habla Española

El Congreso de Pueblos de Habla Española (the Spanish-speaking Peoples Congress) was the first national civil rights assembly for Latinas-Latinos. The approximately one thousand delegates representing 128 organizations assembled in Los Angeles on April 28–30, 1939, to address issues of jobs, housing, education, health, and immigrant rights. Veteran labor leader Luisa Moreno, the principal organizer, drew upon her contacts with labor unions, mutualistas, and Workers' Alliance chapters in order to ensure a truly national conference. Los Angeles activists Josefina Fierro de Bright, Eduardo Quevedo, and Bert Corona would also assume leadership roles in El Congreso. Although the majority of the delegates hailed from California and the Southwest, women and men traveled from such distances as Montana, Illinois, New York, and Florida to attend the convention.

Congreso delegates drafted a comprehensive platform, including political representation, immigrant rights, and bilingual education. El Congreso called for an end to segregation in public facilities, housing, schools, and workplaces, and for an end to discrimination in the disbursement of public assistance. Immigrant rights included the rights to live and work in the United States, to vote, and to hold public office. Delegates emphasized the importance of preserving Latina-Latino cultures and called upon universities to create departments in Latino studies. Despite the promise of the first convention, a national network of local branches never developed and red-baiting would later take its toll among fledgling chapters in California.

▪ VICKI L. RUIZ

≋ Congress

In 1917, three years before a constitutional amendment guaranteed U.S. women the right to vote, Jeannette Rankin took her place as the first woman member of Congress. A progressive Republican from Montana, Rankin proved to be the archetype for women who followed. She came to Congress after conducting reform and political work at the local level, continued to advocate for women throughout her tenure, and remained conspicuous because of her gender. Rankin introduced the first infant and maternal health bill, which passed in 1921, and led the House debate for a federal woman's suffrage amendment. Like subsequent women members of Congress, Rankin was also an advocate for peace. With fifty-six other members, she voted against U.S. entry into World War I. Rankin lost her seat as a result of redistricting but returned to Congress again in 1941, when she cast another vote against the U.S. entry into another world war. After her defeat in the next election, Rankin devoted herself to work for peace.

For six decades the number of women who succeeded Rankin in Congress was small. In the thirty years following national enfranchisement for women, no more than eleven women sat in Congress at any one time. In 1961 twenty women sat in both houses, a record that was sustained for twenty years. The roster of women increased slowly through the 1980s to a high of thirty-three in the 102d Congress (1991–93), and the 1992 election brought a singular leap: in the 103d Congress, fifty-four women took the oath of office. By 1997 the number of women in Congress had risen to sixty.

In the early years "widow's succession" seemed to be the most reliable entrée to Congress for women candidates. Of the twenty-two women elected to Congress during the first twenty years after suffrage, nine were widows; three other widows were appointed seats. Even the redoubtable Margaret Chase Smith (R., Maine) originally succeeded her husband in the House of Representatives but went on to serve four full terms in the Senate—elected in her own right. In 1978 Nancy Kassebaum (R., Kansas) became the first woman who had not been married previously to a congressional member to win a Senate seat. As women's political participation grew more routine, widowhood played less of a role; of all the women in the 105th Congress none entered office initially by succeeding her husband. (Susan Molinari [R., N.Y.] had succeeded her father in 1990.) Most women members had come to Congress after holding public office on the state or local level.

Of the 187 women members of Congress serving from 1917 to 1997, the majority have been white (164) and members of the Democratic Party (107). According to data collected by the Center for the American Woman and Politics, at Rutgers University, twenty-three women of color (twenty-one Democrats and two Republicans) have included seventeen African Americans, four Latinas, and two Asian/Pacific Americans. The first woman of color, Patsy Takemoto Mink (D., Hawaii), joined the House in 1965. Shirley Chisholm (D., N.Y.), the first African American representative, served from 1969 to 1983. Ileana Ros-Lehtinen (R., Fla.), who won her seat in a special election in August 1989, was the first Latina in Congress. Only one woman of color has served in the U.S. Senate, Carol Moseley Braun (D., Ill.), who was elected in 1992. In 1992 Menominee tribe member Ada Deer ran for Congress in Wisconsin. Although she won the Democratic primary but lost the general election, her campaign brought her to President Clinton's attention; he named her as the first woman to head the Bureau of Indian Affairs (BIA).

Women activists have always viewed women in Congress, no matter how small their numbers, as special representatives of women's interests. Even before a grassroots women's movement emerged in the 1960s, congresswomen protected women's interests. Edith Nourse Rogers (R., Mass.), whose career in Congress spanned from 1925 to 1960, introduced the legislation that authorized women's military service in World War II. Katharine St. George (R., N.Y.), who served from 1947 to 1965, was the principal advocate of the Equal Rights Amendment; Edith Green (D., Oreg.), a member from 1955 to 1974, authored an equal pay bill and later ensured that women were included in the Job Corps, part of President Lyndon Johnson's "Great Society" initiative. Martha Griffiths (D., Mich., 1955–74) became a feminist heroine because of her insistence on the inclusion of "sex" in Title VII of the 1964 Civil Rights Act, the primary legal protection against discrimination toward working women. Shirley Chisholm fought for federal funds for day care and a guaranteed family income. Patsy Mink introduced the first comprehensive childcare initiative in 1967 and saved Title IX from near defeat in 1975.

The visible and potent women's movement empowered women in Congress, who heeded the calls of feminists. In 1970 Martha Griffiths moved the Equal Rights Amendment in the House after a nearly fifty-year stalemate. Bella Abzug (D., N.Y., 1971–77) fashioned an all-purpose amendment prohibiting sex discrimination, which was incorporated into numerous pieces of legislation.

Yvonne Braithwaite Burke (D., Calif., 1973–79) introduced the Displaced Homemakers Act in 1977 to help women reentering the paid labor force.

In 1977, when the women in the House of Representatives tallied eighteen, they formed the Congresswomen's Caucus, a bipartisan group to promote women's legislative interests. The Caucus led the successful movement to extend the ratification deadline for the Equal Rights Amendment. By 1982 the newly named Congressional Caucus on Women's Issues (CCWI) admitted male as well as female members. In 1993 the CCWI included forty-three of the forty-eight women House members and 117 male House members. Their agenda included health, economic equity, and protection for women against violence. With the opening of the 104th Congress (1995–96), however, the newly elected Republican majority abolished all twenty-eight legislative service organizations, including the CCWI, eliminating budget and staff. Thirty-eight of the forty-eight women House members reorganized as an informal group with the same name.

Congressional staff women also benefited from the women's movement and the increasing numbers of women in Congress. Early in her career, Republican Representative Lynn Martin (Ill., 1981–91) publicized the inequity in the pay rates for men and women staffers: in 1983 80 percent of staff earning over $40,000 were men and 80 percent of those earning less than $20,000 were women. Notorious for its arbitrary treatment of staff, Congress had routinely exempted itself from the antidiscrimination requirements imposed on private employers, such as the Civil Rights Act of 1964 and the Family and Medical Leave Act. In 1988 the House created an office of fair employment practices; the Senate followed suit in 1992. But a 1993 poll conducted by the *Washington Post* disclosed that one-third of the women staff reported that they had been sexually harassed by coworkers, supervisors, lobbyists, or members of Congress. In January 1995 the Congressional Ac-

countability Act extended to congressional staff the protections of the wage, safety, and equal opportunity legislation that already applied to workers in the private sector.

In 1997 a conservative Republican majority in Congress continued to target abortion rights, equality laws, and social spending. Women in Congress thus retained an important role in speaking on behalf of equity for women both inside Congress and out and to those social issues that historically have been the focus of women's concerns.

Mildred L. Amer, *Women in the United States Congress* (CRS Report for Congress, Congressional Research Service, Library of Congress, October 18, 1989); Cynthia Harrison, *On Account of Sex: The Politics of Women's Issues, 1945–1960* (Berkeley: University of California Press, 1988); Office of the Historian, U.S. House of Representatives, *Women in Congress, 1917–1990* (House Doc. 101-238, 101/2, Washington, D.C.: Government Printing Office, 1991).

• CYNTHIA HARRISON

SEE ALSO Politicians.

≋ Consciousness Raising

During the second wave of U.S. feminism in the 1960s, small-group discussions—consciousness-raising groups—were begun by white women to identify the connecting links among their individual and collective experiences. The groups provided women with "rooms of their own," where they discovered that the "personal was political." An analysis of women's personal lives produced an understanding of women's collective oppression and became a cornerstone for feminist political action.

Women of color engaged in consciousness raising through sharing personal experiences, problems, grievances, and developing strategies to eliminate sexism. Women of color, however, rarely used the term consciousness raising because of its direct association with the white femi-

Members of a consciousness-raising group, 1970. Because of their informal structure, these groups could be easily organized and the participants evolved into an activist network that helped galvanize the second wave of the women's movement.

nist movement, which was also largely identified as a middle-class movement. Chicana feminists, for example, were often labeled *vendidas* (sell-outs) by the Chicano nationalist political organizations of the 1960s and 1970s. Many women of color struggled to legitimize their feminist concerns within a broader social protest movement, maintaining that as women they experienced multiple sources of oppression: racism, classism, and sexism.

As a result of pressure from women university students since the 1960s, courses on women were added to many curricula. Women professors taught the courses, which quickly became centers for feminist activities and forums for women to analyze the contradictions in their personal lives. Consciousness-raising groups contributed directly to the political transformation of large numbers of women as they gained an understanding of the collective struggle to identify the personal as political.

▪ ALMA M. GARCÍA

SEE ALSO Feminism and Feminisms.

≋ Conservatism and the Right Wing

Although right-wing movements have existed since colonial times in the United States, the majority of studies on the subject have focused on either what is termed the "Old Right" of the 1950s or the "New Right," formed during the mid-1970s and 1980s. Historically, right-wing movements in the United States have been based on a crucial marriage of interests between two groups: 1) Members of less-educated, lower economic strata who are highly religious and drawn to the noneconomic issues of right-wing movements; this sector is intolerant of ethnic and religious minorities and expresses particular antagonism toward Blacks and immigrants. In the past, their antagonism was directed against Catholics and Jews and, more recently, Mexicans and Asians. 2) Those rooted in a more highly educated, higher-income strata who are less religious, tolerant of people of color, and committed above all to economic conservatism.

The Old Right of the 1950s combined these two sectors, one consisting of a devoutly religious and less-educated, lower-middle-class following, fearful of communism due to strong evangelical and fundamentalist beliefs, and the other comprised of more affluent economic conservatives, particularly those reacting to the expansion of government implemented by President Franklin D. Roosevelt during the New Deal of the 1930s. Anticommunism held together the Old Right, spearheaded by the campaigns of Senator Joseph McCarthy.

It is not clear whether the lack of attention to women in the Old Right was the result of the small number of female participants in the movement or to the male bias of the researchers. The vast majority of studies of the Old Right make no mention at all of female activists. Therefore, it is impossible to assess how women of the Old and New Right compare in terms of number of participants, degree of involvement, or social background.

Social and ideological distinctions within the popular movements of the Right in the United States are also evident in the conservative intellectual movement, which is composed of three main groups. First are classical liberals or libertarians who promote the free market, private property, limited government, self-reliance, and laissez faire, and resist the threat of the ever expanding state to liberty and free enterprise. Second are traditionalists who are dismayed by the erosion of values and by the emergence of a secular society. This group calls for a return to traditional religious and ethical absolutes. Third are the militant anticommunists, ex-radicals disillusioned by the Left and alarmed during the cold war by the despotism of the Soviet Union. With the emergence of the New Right, this third strand also includes "neoconservatives," primarily academics and writers who rejected the politics of the Democratic Party during the late 1960s. Converts from the Left, neoconservatives are disillusioned liberals drawn heavily from Jewish intellectual circles of the East Coast. As with mass right-wing movements, anticommunism has acted as the glue holding together the conservative intellectual movement.

Although nearly all of the influential conservative intellectuals are male, libertarian author Ayn Rand has had a profound impact on generations of right-wing adherents. In novels such as *The Fountainhead* and *Atlas Shrugged*, Rand introduced the philosophy of objectivism and celebrated unbridled individualism, rationalism, and laissez-faire capitalism.

Like the Old Right, the New Right that arose in the mid-1970s and 1980s also incorporated two distinct constituencies: social conservatives who are devoutly religious and primarily concerned about moral issues and protecting the traditional family; and laissez-faire conservatives or libertarians who aim to protect the economic and political liberty of individuals. And like the Old Right, the New Right is unified in its virulent opposition to communism.

The New Right is distinct, however, in the visibility of its female participants and leaders. Increasingly, women have taken a more active and visible leadership role in right-wing politics. Phyllis Schlafly, who led the fight to defeat the Equal

Rights Amendment (ERA), typifies the social conservative movement, and Jeane Kirkpatrick, a professor of government, former United Nations ambassador, and newspaper columnist, embodies laissez-faire beliefs. But although women remain active participants in the New Right the vast majority of leaders are not women; the New Right is still dominated by male leadership.

Women of the New Right, like their male counterparts, are not a homogeneous entity (although the majority are white). Social conservative women tend to be devoutly religious, primarily Catholic or Protestant fundamentalist, married with children (some are full-time homemakers), and somewhat less educated than laissez-faire women. Laissez-faire women tend to be younger, more secular in orientation, and have more postgraduate degrees and professional careers. In fact, laissez-faire women resemble mainstream feminist women in terms of social background.

Women of the New Right also have contrasting beliefs regarding gender. Social conservatives believe in a strict division of gender roles, deemed to be divinely ordained, in which men are the spiritual leaders and decision makers in the family and women exist to help men in their positions of higher authority. By contrast, laissez-faire women reject any notion of male authority, female submission, or women's so-called natural orientation toward helping others. Instead, they see both women and men as capable of individual self-reliance and free will.

And while social conservatives view feminism as one of the primary forces of the moral decay considered responsible for America's decline, laissez-faire women actually adhere to part of the feminist vision. Social conservative activism is a direct countermovement to the feminist movement of the 1960s and 1970s, as well as to the changes brought on by the civil rights, student, and lesbian and gay movements. Social conservatives blame feminists for attacking the status of the homemaker and for promoting issues such as the ERA, abortion, lesbian and gay rights, and child care, all of which are viewed as eroding traditional notions of gender and the family. They call themselves the "pro-family" movement, and the group's social conservative opposition to these very issues tops its political agenda. Laissez-faire women, on the other hand, support lesbian and gay rights, a woman's right to abortion, and day care, seeing them as private matters that should not be legislated by the state. Laissez-faire women depart from many feminists, however, in the way they view the means to achieve women's equality. While feminists call for federal support to address women's needs, laissez-faire women oppose any reliance on big government, including government funding of day care or abortion. Further, the top priority of laissez-faire women is not addressing women's inequality; rather, issues related to the economy and defense remain the objectives of these women.

Women of the New Right are not only *not* monolithic but in no way are social conservative women "brainwashed" or lackeys of men, as some commentators assume. Ironically, despite the fact that laissez-faire women are ideologically closer to feminists, it is actually the social conservative woman who acts in her own interest. Far from suffering from false consciousness, the social conservative woman is well aware of her status *as a woman* and acts to defend that status. She acts to defend the *traditional* role of women and, in particular, women's role as homemaker. Thus, the social conservative woman's view of women's interests is at odds with any such feminist view.

To borrow a phrase from Marx, social conservative women act as women *for themselves*, while laissez-faire women remain women *in themselves*. Gender identity is central to the political involvement of social conservative women; recognizing their commonality with other traditional women, they seek to protect women's place as a group. In contrast, laissez-faire women act in defense of their self-interest in the marketplace, not to protect their interests as women within the family.

Rebecca E. Klatch, *Women of the New Right* (Philadelphia: Temple University Press, 1987); Kristin Luker, *Abortion and the Politics of Motherhood* (Berkeley: University of California Press, 1984).

▪ REBECCA E. KLATCH

SEE ALSO Anticommunism; Antifeminism; Fundamentalism.

≋ Constitution and Amendments

Constitution

W omen are not mentioned in the text of the original U.S. constitution. The white men, ranging in number from thirty-nine to fifty-five, who met in Philadelphia's Independence Hall in the summer of 1787, produced a document whose few references to race are mostly indirect, and whose references to gender are nonexistent. Male dominance was so deeply embedded in the political culture that the exclusion of women required no legal reinforcement. The Constitution's omission made it a white man's law for a white man's country. Those who were not white or male — Blacks, Native Americans, and women of all races — were disenfranchised and barred from full citizenship. Even as the Thirteenth, Fourteenth, and Fifteenth Amendments brought former slaves closer to equality after the Civil War, statutes subjected Asian aliens to special restrictions. The Constitution reflected and reinforced white male supremacy. But, paradoxically, the Constitution's words ultimately helped to create the conditions that would make change possible.

After the Revolutionary War each state determined the legal status of its residents: who was a free person, who was a citizen, who had rights, and what those rights were. In slave states, female slaves were treated as property, like male slaves. The status of free women depended on their mar-

ital and class status. All states followed the common-law doctrine of *coverture*, which gave a husband control of his wife's person and property. Most women, married or single, were denied the right to vote; but until 1806 a few communities enfranchised all property owners, of either sex.

The original Constitution affirmed the states' powers to make these decisions. It allowed the states to import slaves for twenty years without federal regulation and obliged every state to return all runaway slaves. It left common law in force and provided that the people eligible to vote in national elections "shall have the qualifications requisite for electors of the most numerous branch of the state legislature." The document mentioned few rights for anyone. The commitment to equality proclaimed in the Declaration of Independence eleven years earlier is reflected nowhere in the Constitution's text. The "Bill of Rights," the first ten amendments, was designed not so much to protect individual freedom as to protect state power by limiting the powers of the national government.

There was never any chance that the new Constitution would give women the vote or establish a constitutional right to equality. If the issue was raised at all in Philadelphia, no written record survives. Unlike slavery, which by 1787 had its critics, women's rights was not yet a political issue in the United States. No one had ever gone so far as to publicly advocate *sexual* equality. Not even the best-educated Americans were familiar with the writings of their English contemporary Mary Wollstonecraft; and the first feminist tract in the United States, Judith Sargent Murray's *On the Equality of the Sexes*, would not appear in print until 1790.

If any white women held office or exercised significant political power at the time the Constitution was adopted, their stories are lost to us. But women were far from silent or apathetic on public issues. Although fewer girls attended school than did boys, women were not kept illiterate or ignorant. Many were active supporters of the revolutionary effort. They served as spies, engaged in boycotts, raised money for the troops, and took over farms and trades while their male relatives fought.

The notion that a "woman's place is in the home," familiar from antisuffrage rhetoric of the nineteenth century, did not fit the reality of life in the eighteenth. The home was women's responsibility but not their only responsibility. Like most agrarian societies, early America did not make a sharp distinction between home and work. The transition to industrial capitalism, which later highlighted that distinction, had begun by the 1780s. But while economic changes were shrinking women's role outside the home, the Revolution fostered a new role for women that combined the public and the private. Tracts and sermons exhorted mothers to train their children in civic virtue, a task that required women to be well informed.

Privileged women did not lack opinions or the opportunity to express them. Mercy Otis Warren of Massachusetts, for example, was an anti-Federalist (an opponent of strong central government), whose published criticism of the draft Constitution so dismayed its supporters that they attacked her arguments in print. Similar to Abigail Adams, her sometime friend and sometime enemy, Warren was an early, albeit private, feminist. She opposed coverture, while Adams admonished her husband, John, to "remember the ladies" when he attended the Second Continental Congress in 1776. Feminist ideas were not a part of eighteenth-century U.S. political discourse, but women used their minds to read, analyze, and question everything, including their own position. And, perhaps without intending to, the Constitution that left the status quo in force also gave women access to the means of effecting change.

The original Constitution speaks not of "men," but of "persons." For example, no "person" under the age of thirty-five may be elected president; and the right of habeas corpus "shall not be suspended." In Anglo-American law, "man" is almost always used in the generic sense to mean "human being" rather than "adult male." But the fact that the Constitution consistently uses the word "person" has made it impossible, not merely difficult, for anyone to claim that constitutional rights do not apply to women or that women may not run for office.

The First Amendment freedoms of expression and association, which are essential for any sort of political activity, have been available to women who wished to promote change. The neutral language of the Constitution presumed women's eligibility for the offices that would give them power to pursue their goals. Several constitutional amendments have enhanced women's rights—most explicitly the Nineteenth (1920), which gave women the vote, but also the equal protection clause of the Fourteenth Amendment. Although the proposed Equal Rights Amendment fell short of ratification in the 1980s, women continue to use their rights to improve their status. Thus, even though the original Constitution was silent on the issue of sexual equality, its language, its recognition of individual rights, and the amending process helped empower women to effect change.

Judith A. Baer, *Women in American Law* Vol. 2 (New York: Holmes & Meier Publishers, 1991); Mercy Otis Warren, *Observations on the New Constitution, and on the Federal and State Conventions* (New York: Thomas Greenleaf, 1788); Marlene Stein Wortman, ed., Women in American Law Vol. 1 (New York: Holmes & Meier Publishers, 1985).

■ JUDITH A. BAER

SEE ALSO Equal Rights Amendment (ERA); Legal Status.

Bill of Rights

The Bill of Rights contains the first ten amendments to the U.S. Constitution; they were ratified as a block by 1791. Beginning with the words "Congress shall make no law . . . ," these amendments limited only the power of the federal (not the state) governments. Not until well into the twentieth century did the U.S. Supreme Court eventually incorporate, piecemeal, most protections from the first eight amendments into the "due process of law" requirement that the Fourteenth Amendment imposes on state governments. These protect all of the following: freedom of speech and press; the right to assemble peaceably and petition government (and by implication freedom of association); freedom to exercise religion as well as freedom from the establishment of religion; the right as members of state militias to keep and bear arms; the right to keep soldiers out of one's home in peacetime; the right to be secure in one's person, house, papers, and effects against unreasonable (or warrantless) searches and arrests; and the right to a variety of procedural protections for persons accused of a crime (for example, the right to counsel, jury trial, and so on). None of the amendments refers specifically to women, or to men.

Unlike the Fourteenth Amendment, which limits the state governments, the Bill of Rights has no clause that guarantees "the equal protection of the laws." However, in race discrimination cases, beginning with the 1944 case of *Korematsu* v. *U.S.*, the Supreme Court ruled that the Fifth Amendment clause, "no person shall be deprived of life, liberty, or property without due process of law," implies also the idea of equal protection. Thus, when the equal protection clause was interpreted to forbid most state governmental gender discrimination in the 1970s, the federal government also became so restricted by the Fifth Amendment. This amendment was then used to eliminate certain gender discriminations in the social security system (for example, *Weinberger* v. *Wiesenfeld*, 1975), and in federal employee spouse benefits (*Frontiero* v. *Richardson*, 1973). Not until 1975 (*Taylor* v. *Louisiana*) did the Court rule that the Sixth Amendment right to trial by jury meant that juries could not systematically exempt women.

The Ninth Amendment acknowledges that there are rights not enumerated in the Consti-

tution. Some judges wanted to ground rights to abortion and contraception here, but the Supreme Court chose instead to use the word "liberty" in the due process clauses.

The Constitution leaves most of the powers of everyday governance to the individual states, where laws on such matters as marriage, divorce, and rape are made. The Tenth Amendment reaffirms this power arrangement.

■ LESLIE FRIEDMAN GOLDSTEIN

Emancipation Proclamation and Thirteenth Amendment

Entirely apart from the military defeat of the Confederacy and the political battle to make slavery rather than secession the goal of Union mobilization, slavery had to be legally abolished and emancipation constitutionally enshrined. Decades of Supreme Court decisions, the most notorious being the 1857 *Dred Scott* case, had established the constitutionality of slavery. Abolitionists, unable to contend that the Constitution did not authorize slavery, were forced to argue that slavery violated a higher moral law. But how then to dismantle slavery without uprooting the Constitution itself, without turning a partial rebellion into a complete revolution?

The Emancipation Proclamation, issued by President Lincoln on January 1, 1863, began this process in a small way. The Emancipation Proclamation, which was defended before Congress and the U.S. people as a "military necessity," declared free only those slaves who lived under Confederate rule. In order not to alienate border states such as Maryland and Tennessee, whose commitment to the Confederacy was wavering, these states were exempted from the proclamation's coverage. Thus, it would be easy to read the Emancipation Proclamation as a meaningless act, "freeing" only those men and women whom the authority of the U.S. government could not reach. But this was not entirely the case; the Emancipation Proclamation clearly communicated to the enslaved people of the South that the federal government and the Union army recognized them as free people. The steady stream of southern Black people, running away from the farms and plantations of their owners to the lines of the Union army, now became a growing flood. In this way the Emancipation Proclamation was a "military necessity": it worked to deprive the slave South of its vital labor force by convincing Black workers that the army of the North would regard them as people, not property. The Emancipation Proclamation began the process not only of federal commitment to the abolition of slavery but also of self-emancipation by African Americans themselves. It became the basis of Jubilee, the folk holiday still celebrated in southern Black communities, commemorating the end of slavery.

The legal eradication of slavery was completed by the ratification of the Thirteenth Amendment, in December 1865, after the military defeat of the Confederacy. The Thirteenth Amendment's brevity and simplicity belie the profound change it represented. It abolished in a stroke a major form of property and wealth (the ownership of slaves) and prohibited forever "slavery [and] involuntary servitude . . . within the United States or any place subject to its jurisdiction." Americans then and now can appreciate the radical quality of the Thirteenth Amendment, but they must also acknowledge its limits. After its enactment, slavery was still tolerated in various forms, including practices of sexual slavery among Chinese immigrants in nineteenth-century California and slave-labor conditions in U.S. territories such as the Philippines. Also, the adoption of the Thirteenth Amendment left undefined the status of the ex-slaves and the content of their new "freedom." Freed men and women were unable to secure any monetary compensation for their generations of uncompensated labor. Even the political dimensions of freedom, especially the right to vote, were extremely hard won after slavery was abolished. Finally, the passage of the Thirteenth Amendment, while it released African American women

from the clutches of slavery, in many ways legally intensified the subordinate status of women with respect to citizenship and enfranchisement.

This was ironic inasmuch as the amendment's passage was agitated for by a women's political movement. The National Women's Loyal League was an organization of some Black, but mostly white, women who worked for two years gathering hundreds of thousands of signatures of U.S. citizens on behalf of the constitutional abolition of slavery. It was formed by women's rights leaders Susan B. Anthony and Elizabeth Cady Stanton out of a conviction that chattel slavery and women's subordination were closely linked, and that once slavery was abolished, the way would be paved for a universal declaration of citizenship and enfranchisement for *all* freed people and all women alike. But while Radical Republican senators such as Charles Sumner relied on women's petitions to push the cause of abolition forward, when Congress debated the next proposed constitutional act—the Fourteenth Amendment, which would establish universal citizenship—the distinction of sex entered the Constitution and replaced the status of slave as a legal barrier to full and equal citizenship rights.

Ira Berlin, et al., eds., *Freedom at Last: A Documentary History of Slavery, Freedom and the Civil War* (New York: New Press, 1992); W.E.B. Du Bois, *Black Reconstruction* (New York: Harcourt, Brace and Co., 1935); Eric Foner, *Nothing but Freedom: Emancipation and Its Legacy* (Baton Rouge: Louisiana State University Press, 1983).

■ ELLEN CAROL DUBOIS

SEE ALSO Slavery.

Fourteenth and Fifteenth Amendments

The Fourteenth and Fifteenth Amendments to the U.S. Constitution, ratified in 1867 and 1869 respectively, set in motion the woman suffrage movement for the next half-century. Both amendments sought to resolve the legal status of former slaves emancipated by the Thirteenth Amendment. The Fourteenth Amendment established the universality of U.S. citizenship for "all persons born or naturalized in the United States," and then set up penalties against states that denied the right to vote to significant numbers of adult male citizens. Inasmuch as women were included by the Fourteenth Amendment's broad definition of citizenship but excluded by its narrow definition of the electorate, U.S. women's rights advocates began to agitate for an equally universal gender-inclusive definition of voting rights. As Elizabeth Cady Stanton said, it was time to "bury the woman and the freedman in the citizen."

When it became clear that the Fourteenth Amendment would be insufficient to force the rebel states of the Confederacy to grant votes to freedmen, the Fifteenth Amendment was introduced. It authorized congressional action to guard against disfranchisements by the states on the basis of "race, color or previous condition of servitude." Once again, women were excluded. The women's rights movement was divided over whether or not to oppose the Fifteenth Amendment because of its limitations. Nonetheless, the entire woman suffrage movement agreed on the necessity of securing another constitutional amendment for women, patterned after the Fifteenth Amendment.

▪ ELLEN CAROL DUBOIS

SEE ALSO Citizenship; Suffrage Movement.

Nineteenth Amendment

The Nineteenth Amendment to the Constitution is brief: "The right of citizens of the United States to vote shall not be denied or abridged by the United States or by any state on account of sex. The Congress shall have power, by appropriate legislation, to enforce the provisions of this article."

Seventy-two years passed between women's first formal demand for the right to vote in 1848 until the ratification of the amendment in August 1920. This apparently simple demand for equal rights for women encountered formidable resistance. After the Civil War the drive for suffrage became the focus of the growing women's rights movement. As women gained more opportunities for higher education the movement became more sophisticated and effective.

Under the leadership of Carrie Chapman Catt, the National American Woman Suffrage Association organized to support suffrage amendments to state constitutions and set up a powerful lobbying operation in Washington, D.C., focused on the passage of the federal amendment. The Woman's Party, headed by Alice Paul, depended on confrontation, modeled on what had been done by English suffragettes, to push for the federal amendment. As a consequence of their combined efforts and the growing number of congressmen who came from suffrage states, the amendment was at last adopted by both houses of Congress and ratified by the necessary number of states. On August 26, 1920, the secretary of state issued the proclamation: everywhere in the United States white women were now entitled to vote.

▪ ANNE FIROR SCOTT

SEE ALSO Suffrage Movement.

≋ Consumerism and Consumption

Within the sexual division of labor in U.S. society, consumption has been uniquely assigned to women, and the politics of consumption and consumerism are deeply gendered. Consumer society, however, is a relatively recent development. While some historians argue that a consumer society was born in the eighteenth century, only in the late nineteenth century did mass-production techniques make mass consumption available to the middle class. By the turn of the century new cultures of consumption emerged, epitomized by department stores, "palaces of consumption," in which white middle-class women found creative expression through shopping. By the early twentieth century the U.S. had become dependent upon a high-production, high-consumption economy. Through labor struggles, meanwhile, some sectors of the white working class were able to achieve access to greater levels of consumption.

With the triumph of the U.S. as a dominant power in global markets, in the 1950s a broad sector of U.S. society began to participate in mass consumption. Yet large numbers of Americans, including most people of African, Mexican, or Native American descent, along with significant sectors of the white working class and many Asian Americans, remained excluded from the fruits of consumer prosperity.

Many theorists of consumer society, especially sociologists, have argued that a rise in "consumerist" ideologies accompanied these structural changes in the economy. Pointing in particular to the 1920s, they argue that mass-market advertising campaigns proffered fulfillment through a new glorification of consumption that transformed U.S. culture. In the process, advertising set new standards of womanhood—including both proper sexuality and the performance of domestic labor—which women were exhorted to achieve through increased shopping.

In the emerging division of labor in this new consumer society, most (if not all) consumption activities were assigned to women as part of the sexual division of labor in the home. Men, in theory, earned; women transformed those earnings into well-decorated homes and bodies, mouthwatering meals, and well-developed children. If the model ignored women's rising labor-force participation, it did capture the essence of consumption as women's work. Consumption, for women, was a job—the "other side of the paycheck," to use Amy Bridges and Batya Weinbaum's phrase.

The activities often lumped together as "consumption" in fact break down into two distinct categories: on the one hand, leisure; and on the other, labors of consumption that reproduce daily life through housework, food purchases, or child rearing. Spending money at an amusement park, for example, is quite different from buying a new washing machine. While the one might indicate a playful expenditure of discretionary income, the other is anything but play, but rather serves to alleviate household labors. Yet an enormous conceptual gray area lies between the two. A young woman who spends money on ostensibly "frivolous" clothes to wear to an amusement park might have done so in order to attract a man, whose wages she needed to support herself. A feminist approach to the history of consumption needs not only to view consumption as work but also to acknowledge the intermixture of work and leisure in women's lives.

Although sociologists have argued that mass consumption and consumerism inculcated women into dominant capitalist ideologies, many historians now argue that consumption has instead been a sphere of resistance. Not only have women been savvy shoppers, well aware of manipulative marketing practices, but they also have consciously shaped their consumption habits for a wide range of political ends, developing creative consumer tactics through which to apply political pressure from within the sexual division of labor African American women, for example, in the "Don't Shop Where You Can't Work" campaigns of the 1930s used boycotts to combat racism. Working-class women similarly employed boycotts, union-label promotion, and cooperatives to support the labor movement. Chinese American women in 1930s San Francisco campaigned against the purchase of products from Japan to protest Japanese imperialism in China. Middle-class white women organized the turn-of-the-century Consumers' League to protest sweatshop labor.

These activities demonstrate that women have by no means been the uncritical, duped victims of mass-market advertising. Similarly, consumerism, the alleged ideological effects of high levels of consumption, needs to be distinguished sharply from consumption, the act of buying goods and services. If the first remains to be proven, the second needs to be understood as not just frivolous but integral to the labors of women's—and many men's—daily lives.

■ DANA FRANK

SEE ALSO Advertising.

≋ Contingent Work

Contingent work is often defined in comparison to what it is not: full-time permanent employment with a single employer. Most part-time work is usually considered contingent as is migrant, seasonal, and contract work; work performed by multiple-job holders; and work arranged through temporary services agencies. Contingent work is also characterized by relatively low wages and lack of benefits. Women are more likely than men to be employed as contingent workers, as are the young and elderly.

Short-term employment has always existed in the United States although perhaps not in the same forms as today. Agricultural work, the primary occupation of Americans until this century, is seasonal. As land became less available, the proportion of individuals working as contingent seasonal laborers likely grew. Some early industries in which women were employed, such as canning, also required seasonal labor. This type of contingent work grew with industrialization. Temporary employment through temporary help services firms is a relatively new type of labor arrangement. More informal temporary arrange-

ments, such as on-call agreements between employers and employees, and short-term direct hires, may be of longer standing. Since 1982, when the Bureau of Labor Statistics began to keep records, the number of employees hired by temporary help services firms has increased almost three times as fast as overall employment. Still these are probably the minority of all temporary arrangements.

Paid part-time work has become increasingly common. In the late nineteenth and early twentieth centuries paid part-time work was uncommon. Women who performed this work received less daily and probably less hourly pay than did women working full-time. The 1940 census reported that 18 percent of all female employees were working part-time. Part-time work did not become commonplace until the 1950s. By 1970 the proportion of the female labor force working part-time had risen to 31 percent. Between 1970 and 1990 contingent work as measured by both part-time and temporary work grew faster than overall employment, with most of the jobs concentrated in lower-paying occupations such as sales and clerical support.

During peaks in the demand for specific types of labor, the U.S. government has encouraged contingent work by allowing foreign workers to enter the country on a temporary basis. This policy affects both immigrants, who face insecure employment opportunities, as well as U.S. workers, who face suppressed wages. Mexican workers were allowed into the country during the tight labor markets of World War I and throughout the 1920s until the Great Depression, when many were deported. More recently, Filipina nurses were allowed into the country to alleviate a nursing shortage, provided that they return to the Philippines after two years.

Contingent workers face less job security, lower pay, and fewer benefits than those who work in full-time permanent positions. The median hourly wage for a part-time worker in 1990 was $5.06 compared to $8.09 for a full-time worker.

Similarly, the average hourly wage for a worker in temporary help services was $8.08 in 1990 compared to $10.03 for nonsupervisory and production employees. Whereas women working at full-time full-year jobs received health insurance for nine out of twelve months on average in 1990, part-time workers employed for a full year with one employer received health insurance for only four months. Self-employed or wage and salary workers with less regular schedules received insurance for fewer than two months. Contingent workers are also less likely to receive sick and vacation leave, pension contributions, or job training.

Is the increase in contingent work driven by the demands of the employers or by the desires of employees? For women who can afford it, part-time and contingent work may provide the flexibility required to balance household responsibilities with paid employment. Between 1920 and 1940 the number of women seeking part-time employment rose, increasing the supply of part-time workers; at the same time, the number of single women available to work full-time decreased, increasing the demand for part-time workers. The increase in contingent work in the latter part of the twentieth century seems to be demand-driven: the proportion of workers employed part-time voluntarily increased by 2.3 percent between 1970 and 1990, while involuntary part-time work increased 45 percent. The increased demand for certain categories of contingent workers may be a result of a number of factors. Structural changes in the economy have strengthened industries in which contingent workers were already common. Contingent workers are also cheaper to employ than are full-time permanent workers since they receive lower wages and fewer benefits and because they offer employers greater flexibility.

Teresa L. Amott and Julie A. Matthaei, *Race, Gender, and Work* (Boston: South End Press, 1991); Polly Callaghan and Heidi Hartmann, *Contingent Work: A Chart Book on Part-Time and Temporary Employment* (Washington, D.C.: Economic Policy Institute, 1991); Claudia Goldin,

Understanding the Gender Gap: An Economic History of American Women (New York: Oxford University Press, 1990).

■ STEPHANIE AARONSON
and HEIDI HARTMANN

SEE ALSO Work.

≋ Contraception

SEE Birth Control.

≋ Cooking

Like language, food can reveal information about individuals and groups. Just as a speaker's choice of words or her accent or dialect can tell us something about her origins and training, so can a prepared meal, with its selection of ingredients, dishes, and the menu itself, which may disclose the background of the cook. Because food is a common part of family and cultural rituals, an awareness of its meaning can provide insights into the lives of a given group. For example, within current Native American traditions, the Iroquois open and close ceremonial gatherings with an address that gives thanks to the food sources provided by the Earth Mother, food plants, fish, animals, and birds. Such a thanksgiving acknowledges the interdependence of all living things and expresses gratitude for each gift of creation.

The connection between food choices and culture was certainly known to U.S. reformers, who, in the late nineteenth and early twentieth centuries attempted to speed along the assimilation of immigrant groups by influencing their eating customs. Home economists, social workers, and visit-

A January 1923 column, "What's Cooking," in the Yiddish journal Froyer Zhurnal *informs readers about American cooking. Note the modern appliances and organization of the kitchen space. By this time, it was typical that one adult woman in a household would manage the kitchen alone, often reliant on the advice of home economists.*

ing nurses were convinced that by changing what people ate, they would change the very nature of the people themselves. By establishing the New England Kitchen in Boston, where simple prepared foods could be purchased at low cost, well-meaning reformers hoped to standardize U.S. eating habits and lure immigrants into accepting such Yankee dishes as codfish cakes and rice pudding in place of the heavy stews and garlicky dishes of their homelands.

Such attempts at cultural imperialism failed, for Italians and other European newcomers to the United States opened their own bakeries and developed new systems for distributing produce so that the fruits and vegetables they remembered from their homelands could be shipped to eastern

cities from California. This illustrates the profound importance of human dietary habits and the lengths to which people will go to acquire their accustomed foods.

It would follow then that cooking and all of the customs that surround the selection and consumption of foods are important avenues for understanding human behavior. For feminists, asking such simple questions as "who cooks and who eats" can lead directly into examining gender arrangements within a family, revealing that women have been the traditional providers of meals and that male family members often have been served the largest and best portions of a dish. Some historians of women are also beginning to realize the importance of Black women's cooking to the evolution of U.S. cuisine. Although we know that African American women have worked in kitchens from the time of slavery, they have not been given credit for the invention of dishes that fill the pages of U.S. cookbooks. Just as feminist literary scholars searched for and discovered the lost voices of women writers, so can culinary historians enrich our knowledge by looking for the lost voices of women cooks.

■ BARBARA HABER

SEE ALSO Americanization.

≋ Cosmetics

SEE Beauty Culture.

≋ Coverture

Under the common law of England and in the states following the common law in the United States, a single woman, or feme sole, became known upon her marriage as a feme covert.

During the period of her marriage (or coverture), she lost many of her rights to ownership and control of property. The husband became the owner of all personal property owned by the wife before marriage or acquired by her thereafter; he also had the right to control her real property and all of her earnings. The wife had no power to contract, to sue, or even to be sued in her own name. Coverture was based on the patronizing and discriminatory notion that, because of their "natural" and "proper" timidity and delicacy, married women needed to be protected.

Beginning in Mississippi in 1839, some states began to make statutory changes in the common law of coverture by granting married women increased legal rights. New York's 1848 married women's statute, which limited the scope of coverture, was the first law to gain widespread attention. Eventually coverture was abolished in all states. However, the reforms were not part of a coherent program to grant equal rights to married women. As recently as 1975 one of the remaining vestiges of coverture was eliminated when several state and federal laws were enacted to ensure equal credit opportunity. The abolition of coverture helped achieve formal but not substantive equality for married women. Married women had a formal legal identity. It paved the way for their suffrage, but did not give women equal opportunity in employment or admission to professions.

• ISABEL MARCUS

SEE ALSO Citizenship; Legal Status; Marriage.

≋ Cowgirls

The term *cowgirl* is problematic. In its purest form, *cowboy* refers to a hired hand who works with cattle and horses. Cowgirl originally referred only to women who performed in Wild West shows or competed in rodeos. Rodeo still provides the most common use; few women who work on ranches, as hired hands or owners, call themselves cowgirls.

Starting in the 1880s Wild West shows and rodeos offered athletic careers for women. By 1930 bronco and trick riders such as Tad Lucas and Alice Greenough were world famous. After World War II, major rodeos replaced the more thrilling events for women with barrel racing, and in 1990 Charmayne Rodman became the first barrel racer to break the one-million-dollar mark for career winnings. Unfortunately, other women's events, such as bronco and bull riding, were ghettoized in all-women rodeos, which offered little pay. In 1993 world champion bareback bronco rider Vickie Crawford won less than $2,600.

Outside of rodeo, Native American, Latina, African American, and European American women have worked with cattle and horses for as long as the animals have been in North America. In the early eighteenth century, María Bentacour and Doña Rose Hinojosa de Balli were among the first ranchers in what is now Texas. Sally Skull, a divorced mother of two, supported her family by trading horses in Texas and Mexico in the mid-1800s. Lizzie Johnson followed her own cattle up the Chisholm Trail in the 1880s. Around the same time, Middy Morgan, an Irish immigrant, earned fame in Montana as a cattle buyer. "Yes, it was my grandmother," wrote contemporary Navajo poet Luci Tapahonso about a more recent ancestor, "who trained wild horses for pleasure and pay."

Today, women work in every aspect of the cattle business. The number of women who work as hired hands, cattle buyers, horse trainers, professors of animal science, herd veterinarians, and in related occupations increases each year. One study suggests that by the year 2000, women will be sole owners of 25 percent of the ranches in Texas and will co-own, with their families, another 60 percent.

• TERESA JORDAN

SEE ALSO Western Women.

Frances Clalin, a soldier with Federal forces in Missouri, was one of hundreds of women who cross-dressed in order to serve in the Civil War.

≋ Crafts

SEE Arts and Crafts.

≋ Cross-Dressing

Throughout U.S. history women of all races have lived and worked as men for various reasons. For many it was a way of gaining access to the social, financial, and sexual privileges denied

them as women. By the eighteenth century, Anglo-American balladry abounded with tales of women who swapped skirts for trousers to follow their true love to war. Newspaper reports reveal, however, that many more dressed as men to enter "masculine" occupations. Elsa Jane Guerin, the illegitimate daughter of a plantation owner, was born in Louisiana about 1837. She married a river pilot at the age of twelve and when he died three years later, Elsa Jane became "Mountain Charley," working aboard steamships traveling between St. Louis and New Orleans. She was later employed as a brakeman on the Illinois Central

Railroad and then headed west to become a gold prospector. She may also have served in the Iowa cavalry during the Civil War, along with an estimated four hundred other women soldiers. Sarah Emma Edmonds, who became a Union soldier after her career as Bible-salesman Franklin Thompson, wrote a best-selling book about her experiences and received a full military pension. Lesbians have also "passed," working in occupations ranging from politics to journalism, mining, and the theater. By the 1950s "passing" women protected themselves from prosecution for transvestism by wearing the legal requirement of at least three items of female clothing. The tradition has persisted; as recently as 1988, a Spokane jazz musician, Billy Tipton, who was married with three adopted sons, was revealed to be a female cross-dresser upon "his" death.

▪ JULIE WHEELWRIGHT

≋ Cult of Domesticity

The Cult of Domesticity (or the Cult of True Womanhood) had its roots in the emerging bourgeois literature of eighteenth-century England: conduct books, religious tracts, and sentimental novels. By the early nineteenth century, the cult had taken hold in the United States, disseminated through novels, religious writings, and advice books written by and for the emerging U.S. urban middle classes. The cult imposed a highly restrictive series of roles on the new white middle-class woman. To be a True Woman, she must be tender and submissive, self-sacrificing, deeply religious, and untouched by sexual desire. She must be confined to the home, devoted to husband and children, and eschew productive labor and the political arena. African American women, poor women, and immigrant women, compelled by poverty to work, could not be True Women; they

and their families were considered unnatural, unfeeling, and sexually depraved.

The restrictions and responsibilities the cult placed upon the middle-class woman put her in a double bind. Required to be sexually ignorant and devoid of sexual desire, she was to spend her life conceiving, bearing, and nursing children. Submissive and dependent, she was still to control her husband's and children's spiritual and sexual behavior.

But the cult also empowered middle-class women. Representing themselves as soldiers in Christ's army against lechery, sin, and injustice, True Women joined moral reform organizations. They campaigned against prostitution, the double standard, intemperance, and espoused radical abolitionism to support their enslaved sisters. Thus the cult could be used to subvert the patriarchal, political, social, and domestic order it sought to erect.

▪ CARROLL SMITH-ROSENBERG

SEE ALSO Moral Reform.

≋ "Culture of Poverty"

The term "culture of poverty" was introduced by anthropologist Oscar Lewis, most prominently in his 1966 book, *La Vida: A Puerto Rican Family in the Culture of Poverty, San Juan and New York*. In the somewhat liberalized political climate of the 1960s, Lewis and other social analysts intended to render "the poor" as legitimate, interesting subjects whose lives were battered by poverty, and to reveal that poverty itself generated a way of life that constituted a unique "culture of poverty." This was a liberal, innovative perspective, since "the poor" had previously been construed as lacking culture.

Despite this intention, policy analysts and others read accounts of the culture of poverty as evidence that the folkways of the poor were crude and irresponsibly self-indulgent. The poor, it was argued, were poor because they perpetually misbehaved. Their disorganized hedonism (sometimes called a "deficit culture") was both a mark of poverty and the reason that the poor were chained to poverty, generation after generation.

Between the 1960s and the end of the century, this interpretation of the culture of poverty became a cornerstone of conservative politics and became racialized: people of color are poor not only because they "misbehave" but also because they refuse to adopt the middle-class values and goals that would lead them out of poverty. Culture of poverty theories particularly targeted women of color, labeling them sexually wanton and maternally irresponsible. Analysts denied the roles of racism, colonialism, substandard housing, education, medical care, and job opportunities in creating and sustaining poverty. Thus, poverty and the culture it allegedly spawns were seen as the offspring of individual and group irresponsibility. According to politicians and policymakers, then, it is futile and wasteful to mount public policy initiatives to ameliorate the lives of the poor because the culture (or the race) of poor people themselves mandates endemic and enduring poverty. On the contrary, culture of poverty theorists argue that public policy should have a punitive thrust: poor women should be forced to use birth control and denied benefits if they become pregnant while receiving public assistance.

■ RICKIE SOLINGER

SEE ALSO Poverty; Welfare and Public Relief.

≋ Dance

The role of women in dance is influenced by a complex set of historical and cultural issues. In the United States, the field of dance is characterized by great cultural diversity and is found in many contexts.

Dance cultures of Native American women comprise the earliest female dance traditions in the United States and remain vital in the twentieth century. In many contemporary Native American cultures, women participate in sacred, social, and concert dance. In the early nineteenth century, in response to increasing pressures from invading European Americans, the Pan-Indian powwow—from the Algonquian word to "rekindle"—became an important unifying tool and expression of cultural identity. Dances from many Native American cultures are represented in the numerous powwows held throughout the country, which often include women and specifically female dances such as the Buckskin Dance, Cloth Dance, Fancy Shawl, and Jingle Dress. Today, powwows recall ancestral traditions and cultivate pride in Native American culture among new generations. Native American concert dance companies, notably the American Indian Dance Theatre, founded in 1987 by Barbara Schwei and Hanay Geiogamah, perform works based on traditional Native American dance forms and reflect in their repertories the distinct but equally valued roles of male and female dancers.

European colonists placed emphasis primarily on social and theatrical dance traditions. By the beginning of the nineteenth century, social dancing was popular in the United States among the elite and middle classes. In major urban cultural centers, where emulation of European styles thrived, dancing was associated with an aristocratic upbringing. Women were active in ballroom dancing in gender-specific roles that reinforced their expected role in society, that is, literally following the male lead.

Africans enslaved by the European colonists brought dance traditions from their homelands. Stripped of everything but the body and memory, they used dance as a vital communicative and adaptive tool. Traditional African dance existed in religious contexts; men and women participated with equal status but danced in same-sex configurations. Because slave dances were often put into secular guise to hide their religious purpose, male-female roles were influenced by European mixed-couple social dancing. From the mid-nineteenth-century Cake Walk to twentieth-century dances such as the Charleston, Lindy Hop, and Disco, mixed-gender dancing has been a dominant trend. In turn, African American social dance has had a profound influence on white social dance and gender identity as mainstream white culture has appropriated and assimilated Black dances. The Charleston, for example, originating in the Black community and popular in the late 1910s and early 1920s with both Black and white dancers, became a symbol of liberated women who cut their hair, bound their breasts, wore straight, figure-camouflaging shifts, and smoked in public. A woman danced independent of her partner—neither following his lead nor held in his embrace.

In the nineteenth century, minstrel and variety shows were performed primarily for male audiences. In the 1880s and 1890s, however, promoters sought to refine variety shows by banning obscene gestures and suggestive words. Now known as vaudeville, the shows were considered wholesome family entertainment and their ticket sales significantly increased by appealing to women. The new female audiences influenced popular theatrical tastes, brought women to the stage in greater numbers, and greatly affected the evolution of dance in the United States as it became a serious art form.

Classical ballet, with its origins in the courts of Renaissance Europe, had long held a central place among the cultural institutions of Europe. In the United States, however, audiences were largely unfamiliar with ballet until the nineteenth century. When Europe's solo romantic ballerinas, most notably Fanny Elssler, began touring the United States in the 1840s, Americans were unaware that ballet involved a highly complex system of training and had an aristocratic history.

Audiences were fascinated with the dancers more as exotic curiosities and for their titillating show of legs than as serious artists. Gradually, however, interest in ballet as a serious art began to grow and by the 1880s more training was available. Although a few nineteenth-century ballerinas acquired some social and financial autonomy, and the repertory from this era showcased the female dancer, the view that women dominated the field is misleading. The ballerina was the performer rather than the creator of the work. Ballet was a male construct; men usually trained the dancers, wrote the librettos, choreographed the dances, composed the music, designed the settings, selected the performers, and composed the majority of audiences. The ballerina embodied white male concepts of Victorian womanhood in the roles created for her: She was either the virginal, submissive, and lovely ideal or the vindictive, controlling, and malevolent nemesis.

By the 1930s, ballet was firmly established in the United States and a new generation of home-grown dancers, choreographers, and directors emerged. Among the many notable American ballerinas are Suzanne Farrell, Cynthia Gregory, Lisa Bradley, and Melissa Hayden. Equally influential and famous dancers of Native American and Latin American descent include Maria Tallchief, Marjorie Tallchief, Yvonne Chouteau, Rosella Hightower, Moscelyne Larkin, and Carmelita Maracci. Few women in ballet have had widespread influence beyond their roles as performers; those few exceptions in the United States include Lucia Chase, cofounder of American Ballet Theatre; Ruth Page, choreographer and director of several ballet companies in Chicago and her own Ruth Page International Ballet; Agnes De Mille, choreographer for ballet and musical theater; and Rebekah Harkness, a composer and important benefactress of American ballet. African Americans have had a far more difficult time establishing careers in ballet; women of color suffer a double oppression. Ballet companies and academies in the United States have historically been segregated by law or tradition. Although there is a regrettable lack of documentation of their careers, a number of African American women have made inroads into classical ballet as performers, teachers, and company directors. Notable ballerinas include Janet Collins, Raven Wilkinson, Sara Yarborough, Debra Austin, and Virginia Johnson. Doris Jones and Claire Haywood founded the Capitol Ballet in Washington, D.C., in 1961. Dance Theatre of Harlem, founded by Arthur Mitchell in 1968, was another pioneer in presentation of Black classical dancers. Black ballet dancers, however, continue to suffer prejudicial treatment in traditionally white companies, often excluded from leading roles or relegated to "exotic" or "specialty" roles. Many African American dancers, such as Judith Jamison, were trained in ballet but turned to the more inclusive genre of modern dance. Jamison, for example, performed for many years with the Alvin Ailey American Dance Theatre and currently serves as its director.

A dearth of choreographers in the ballet idiom in the past twenty years has prompted many ballet companies to hire modern-dance choreographers, many of whom are women, to create repertory for their companies. The presence of women in such positions of influence is beginning, slowly, to diversify women's roles in ballet both on- and offstage.

Modern dance, pioneered by U.S. women at the turn of the twentieth century, began as a rebellion against the aristocratic ideals of European ballet and as an exploration of personal expression. In the 1890s, a series of young performers, including Loie Fuller, Isadora Duncan, and Ruth St. Denis, began presenting dances that departed significantly from both classical ballet and dance in the popular theater. Strong-willed, independent-minded women, they sought to create a new art form that would raise the respectability of dance and reflect the sensibilities of the modern American woman. This new dance embodied in a single form issues that had been engaging reform-

ers and feminists for decades, including dress reform, physical activity, and artistic expression. Often as rebellious in their social lives as in their artistic ones, these pioneers championed women's right to both artistic and social freedoms. Indeed, the modern dancer became a prime symbol of the liberated woman. Invented and initially practiced solely by women, modern dance provided opportunities unavailable in the patriarchal paradigm of ballet: Female dancers created and taught their own techniques and choreography, founded their own companies (often named for themselves), and controlled all aspects of artistic direction. Beginning in the 1930s, Martha Graham, Doris Humphrey, and Hanya Holm developed their own techniques and repertories and inspired subsequent generations of dancers to do the same. Because early modern dancers came from varied religious, national, and racial backgrounds and represented many aesthetic, social, and political perspectives, modern dance has included a more multicultural population and eclectic aesthetic than has ballet. In the 1940s Pearl Primus and Katherine Dunham began presenting work, which was influenced by their studies of African and Caribbean dance forms, encouraging further exploration of traditional forms within the concert-dance idiom. Dunham also founded her own company and developed a technique combining elements of ballet, modern, African, and Caribbean dance forms. Jawole Willa Jo Zollar, who founded the all-female dance company Urban Bushwomen in 1984, combines African American folk and spiritual traditions with contemporary styles. Another all-female company, the Wallflower Order was founded in 1975 with the goal of expressing social and historical themes in women's lives. In ballet and modern dance, many performers retire from the stage by the age of thirty-five. Rejecting stereotypes of youthful beauty and limited notions about what constitutes technical virtuosity, groups such as the Liz Lerman Dance Exchange, founded in 1976, present work made for multigenerational companies. A number of modern-dance companies have recently begun presenting works made by and for "older" women.

Women have also been instrumental in the histories of other twentieth-century theatrical dance forms in the United States, including tap, musical theater, and movie musicals. The growing industry of music videos since the late 1970s has brought popular dance to a wide audience, and women are making significant contributions as choreographers and performers in this genre. Representing a range of cultural identities and aesthetic influences, female artists include Janet Jackson, Paula Abdul, Rosie Perez, and Madonna.

Christie Adair, *Women and Dance* (New York: New York University Press, 1992); Lynne Fauley Emery, *Black Dance from 1619 to Today* (Princeton, N.J.: Dance Horizons, 1988); Elizabeth Kendall, *Where She Danced: The Birth of American Art-Dance* (New York: Knopf, 1979).

■ TRICIA HENRY YOUNG

≣ Decorative Arts

The category "decorative arts" usually includes those things that furnish interiors—the fittings that make rooms into usable and beautiful spaces. The decorative arts include furniture, textiles, lighting, clocks, bronzes, porcelain, and glass. Women have had many roles in the decorative arts: women design and make objects, write books and articles on the decoration of houses and other interiors, become professional interior designers and decorators, and take responsibility for the purchase and arrangement of a home's contents.

Women active in designing and creating objects have been recorded in Alice I. Prather-Moses's *International Dictionary of Women Workers in the Decorative Arts*. She lists women from Renaissance times to the modern era, in Europe, England, Japan, and the United States, such as Marinda Cheeney, who was active in

1843 as an upholsterer in Nashua, New Hampshire; and Betsy Ross, famous for designing the U.S. flag, who was also reputed to have been an upholsterer. While some women worked in the furniture trades, the greatest number worked as painters of ceramic and glass objects. Centers of ceramics production, such as Rookwood in Cincinnati, founded by Maria Longworth Nichols, and Newcomb College Pottery in New Orleans, trained women in art-pottery production at the turn of the century. Such work is now collected by museums. In addition, Native American pots, baskets, rugs, and other items, once necessary to everyday life, are now classified as decorative arts. Exquisite Pomo basketry, for example, has become a collector's item, although some Native Americans continue to use baskets to gather seaweed along the Pacific Coast. Both functional and aesthetic, quilts, pottery, and baskets made by slaves in the nineteenth century are now used by collectors as decoration. On the more commercial side, Fannie Handel ran Handel and Co., in Meriden, Connecticut, from 1914 to the late 1920s after her husband, who founded the company, had died. Several women painters were employed to produce "art items for domestic use," such as lamp bases, shades, and globes.

Women brought a reform spirit to the decorative arts during the arts and crafts movement, turning to simplicity of form and using materials in their natural colors and textures. They participated professionally in this movement as ceramicists, embroiderers, and furniture designers. Notable women in furniture design include Lucia Kleinhans Mathews (1870–1955), who was active in California's arts and crafts movement, where she and her husband operated The Furniture Shop from 1906 to 1920. They did furnishings and interiors; she did painted ornament, while he was "chief designer." Also active in California arts and crafts, Margery Wheelock was known for her furniture design in the 1910s. She was affiliated with the California College of Arts and Crafts in San

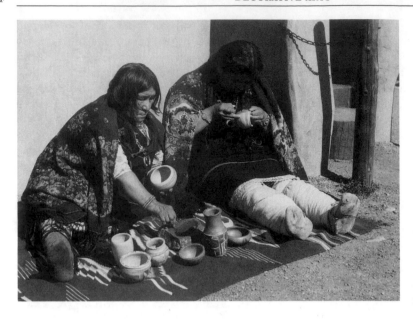

Hopi women decorate pottery in New Mexico.

Francisco, where artificers executed her artistic plans for custom-made chairs, tables, and cabinets. The arts and crafts ethic resurfaced in modern design in the work of Florence Knoll and her husband. They opened the Knoll furniture company in the 1950s, specializing in contract furniture disseminated to architects working in the modern style.

The profession of interior decoration began at the end of the nineteenth century and was promoted by women such as Candace Wheeler (1827–1923). She started out as an embroiderer, designing tapestries, then ran the textiles and embroidery division of the Associated Artists partnership (later the Tiffany firm). Her influence on the decorative arts increased through the popularity of her books *Household Art* in 1893 and *Principles of Home Decoration* in 1908. Novelist Edith Wharton (1862–1937) also influenced interior design in her 1898 book *The Decoration of Houses.* Other early women professional decorators include Elsie DeWolfe, whose 1913 *The House in Good Taste* promoted an airy anti-Victorian aesthetic. Many women have entered this field suc-

cessfully since these female predecessors claimed the terrain.

Nonprofessional women have also played an important role in the decorative arts. Starting in the late eighteenth century, women were taught skills in the decorative arts as part of their educations at academies such as that of Susanna Rowson. She taught embroidery, watercolor, drawing, and painting to young ladies in Boston from 1797 to 1822. Her students produced flower subjects and landscape painting on tabletops, quilt designs, and framed pictures in several media. These skills were badges of gentility—part of every educated woman's repertoire.

The expectation that women would ornament their own homes was reinforced by magazines directed toward women, which provided instruction on needlework and other kinds of crafts and fancy-work. Patterns were printed in nineteenth-century periodicals, including *Godey's Ladies' Book*, which offered middle-class women the newest ideas for parlor embellishments. The responsibility for home decoration today continues to be mainly the work of women—both as purchasers of furnishings and as crafters of ornament—and is reinforced by innumerable magazines such as *Ladies' Home Journal* or *Better Homes and Gardens,* advice books by authors such as Martha Stewart, and instructional television programs.

Lamia Doumato, *Candace Wheeler and Elsie DeWolfe, Decorators: A Bibliography* (Monticello, Ill.: Vance Bibliographies, 1989); Alice I. Prather-Moses, *The International Dictionary of Women Workers in the Decorative Arts* (Metuchen and London: Scarecrow Press, 1981); Paula Chiarmonte, ed., *Women Artists in the United States—A Selective Bibliography on the Fine and Decorative Arts* (Boston: G. K. Hall, 1990).

■ ELIZABETH C. CROMLEY

SEE ALSO Art and Crafts.

≋ Democracy

Democratic institutions existed among native peoples in North America (most notably the Iroquois) for centuries before the colonies formed. Both the meaning and the practice of democracy in the United States have since been fraught with contradictions and conflicts. Democracy commonly refers to "government by the people," and, in this respect, is closely related to "republicanism." It may also refer to a condition of *social* equality and the consequences of that equality for political practice. Finally, disagreement continues over whether "democracy" is properly understood as a characteristic of *institutions,* or as a characterization of a broader political culture. Beyond these definitional differences lies a more serious problem: a great gap between the promise, or ideal, of democracy and the reality of unequal power and participation in U.S. society.

"Government by the people" has proven to be an ambiguous and elusive goal. One might even argue that U.S. history has been characterized by ongoing conflicts over who is to be included in the body known as "the people"; over what sorts of decisions "the people" should exercise control; and over how that control should be expressed and/or limited.

Perhaps the most dramatic conflicts have focused on the question of who constitutes "the people." During colonization and the early years of the Republic, indigenous peoples were not only *not* considered to be among "the people," they were largely annihilated by European settlers. Africans, imported as slaves, were denied the status of full persons (the Constitution mandated that a slave count as three-fifths of a person for census purposes), and the political rights that accompanied such status, until well into the twentieth century. None of the colonies took democracy to include equal participation by women (a right not won at the national level until 1920 and still not effectively achieved in practice).

Different *forms* of government also reflected different understandings of "the people" and their role. Thus, many of the New England colonies (and the states that developed from them) were governed by town meetings, in which every free male (or, until the 1820s, those with minimal property holdings) participated in making decisions about local governance. In New York, Virginia, and many of the southern colonies (and states), on the contrary, a more deferential and elitist politics tended to be the norm, and local decision making was in the hands of the so-called *best men* of the community.

Over the longer term, conflicts have centered on inclusions and exclusions on the basis of class, race, ethnicity, and gender. "Mechanics" and other laboring men agitated in the early Republic for representation and a voice in the political process. Although full membership in the citizen body was primarily accorded to those deemed economically independent, working people struggled to demonstrate that their dependence on wages ought not disqualify them from full membership in "the people." African Americans and women achieved full participation only with the passage of the Civil Rights Amendments of 1868–70, the Woman's Suffrage Amendment of 1920, and the Voting Rights Act of 1965. Native Americans did not gain citizenship rights until 1924; and Asian immigrants achieved rights to full participation only after World War II.

In practice, directly participatory town-meeting democracy has been replaced virtually everywhere by representative democracy, in which "the people" vote for *representatives* who are elected for specific terms of office and make decisions in the name of the entire community. Those elected to such positions have tended *not* to be "representative" of the larger body in the strict sense: they are, on average, male, middle-aged, white, Christian, and relatively wealthy. Women and people of color have fought great struggles, not only for the right to vote but also for the right to hold office.

The growth of the economic and political power of the United States also has resulted in increasingly strict limits over the range of local decision-making power. The shift from the Articles of Confederation to the Constitution meant that the democratic power of local communities over certain economic matters (such as tariffs) was severely limited, if not eliminated. Democracy, in the sense of local economic controls, came to be identified with anarchy, and limitations on democracy were seen as necessary for successful governance. In the contemporary period, the ever increasing power of multinational corporations has meant that fewer decisions of economic importance are effectively included on the democratic political agenda at the local or the national level.

Limits on the absolute power of the majority have also come to be recognized as necessary to preserve democracy itself. For example, the Bill of Rights guarantees freedoms of speech, press, and assembly, as well as other individual protections. In recent years the civil rights movement struggled to assert that white people cannot pass laws limiting the freedom and participation of African Americans, and feminists have insisted that women ought not be denied access to political positions. In short, democracy now includes protection for people of color and for women's rights — basic "democratic norms" that may theoretically limit democracy.

These questions of *who* exercises control, and in what manner, also are related to another meaning of democracy: democracy as social equality, or, in the words of Alexis de Tocqueville, the mid-nineteenth-century French commentator on U.S. society, "equality of conditions." As it was first used, this term referred to the difference between political communities based on patriarchally organized hereditary classes, which would be reflected not only in social but also in political power, and those in which social and political positions were, at least formally, open to all. Complete "equality of conditions" was far from the reality in the United States in de Tocqueville's time, and has not yet been achieved in our own: inequalities of class, race, ethnicity, sexuality, and gender undergird some of the most basic social and political institutions and practices.

Democracy, in this sense, also connotes the *ideal* toward which we strive as a society: that no one be assigned a place, or political or social power, on the basis of ascribed characteristics. The ideal of democracy has come to be identified with meritocracy: equal access by all to positions of authority in the political system, or to respect in society, regardless of heritage or gender. Again, it must be emphasized that this vision of democracy is more ideal than reality: the overwhelming majority of those who hold positions of authority are white, wealthy, and male, and most public policy effectively reinforces existing social inequalities. Nevertheless, struggles continue — ranging from the civil rights movement to the feminist movement to the welfare rights movement, and to the lesbian and gay rights movement — to open positions to all citizens on a truly equal basis.

Finally, ought democracy refer only to the structure and workings of formal political institutions, or can it be used to characterize popular practices more broadly? In recent years political commentators have attended increasingly to "civil society," that complex of organizations and activities that may affect the public business, but that takes place outside of, or apart from, formal representative (or nonrepresentative!) political institutions. This country has a long history of such activities.

For many of those excluded from formal participation in politics, "democracy" has meant participation in organizations and activities based less on geographic proximity than on shared interests and concerns, activities in which women typically play a disproportionate role. In the nineteenth century, for example, workers formed labor unions and other organizations through which they fought for improved economic and social conditions. Men and women, both whites and free Blacks, participated in organizations to abolish slavery and end lynching (a form of "mob democracy") and to enfranchise women. Other activists addressed the injustices of the newly developing industrial society, particularly as they affected women and children, establishing "moral reform societies," public charities, schools, societies for the prevention of cruelty to children, temperance organizations, and settlement houses. During much of the nineteenth and early twentieth centuries, the "political" participation of both white and African American women, and of many African American males, was expressed almost entirely in such "nonpolitical" forms. Nevertheless, as Paula Baker and others have noted, those activities, undertaken largely by women, and usually outside the formal institutions of politics, effectively challenged mainstream views of politics and helped to broaden the agenda of "democratic" institutions.

Efforts aimed at democratizing U.S. society and politics continue. In the face of an increasingly global economy and the constraints that globalization places on decision making by individual national political bodies, struggles over democracy likely will be both more local and more international in the years to come.

Paula Baker, "The Domestication of American Politics: Women and American Political Society, 1780–1920," *American Historical Review* Vol. 89 (June 1984): 620–49; Nancy Hewitt and Suzanne Lebsock, eds., *Visible Women: New Essays on American Activism* (Urbana and Chicago: University of Illinois Press, 1993); Alexis de Tocqueville, *Democracy in America* (New York: Harper and Row, 1969).

■ MARTHA ACKELSBERG

SEE ALSO Citizenship; Constitution and Amendments.

≋ Depression

Depression is a major public-health problem. Although most people experience sadness at one time or another, in the United States between 8 and 26 percent of the population meet the psychiatric criteria for clinical depression. Depression is characterized by a cluster of symptoms, including crying spells, loss of interest in daily activities, fatigue with or without agitation, difficulties with concentration, sleep disturbances, sexual withdrawal, changes in appetite with concomitant weight loss, feelings of hopelessness and despair, and suicidal thoughts and tendencies. Most persons experience multiple symptoms; in addition, the symptoms must be present for at least two weeks for a diagnosis to be made.

Studies conducted around the world indicate that women have considerably higher rates of depression than men. These higher rates are evident across age groups, but particularly marked among married women who do not work outside the home. While marriage appears to protect men from depression, the data suggest the opposite for women.

Early psychoanalytic studies of female depression focused on women's "neurotic character" and what was believed to be their biological predisposition to emotional instability. More recent attempts to understand the gender difference in rates of depression have focused on studying the role of biological markers in a woman's life: menstruation, childbirth, and menopause. Although biochemical changes may affect women's moods and women may be more susceptible to depression after childbirth, research findings indicate that biological changes alone do not explain the prevalence of depression in women.

Unlike other mental illnesses, depression appears more tied to fundamental conditions of inequality in society and the family: socioeconomic status, sexism, heterosexism and homophobia, and racism. The evidence that most convincingly accounts for higher rates of depression in women points to their position in society and their gender roles within the family, their role as wives, their patterns of problem solving, and their attributional style.

Women tend to blame themselves for their misfortunes and credit luck for their successes, as part of the cultural script they learn about being female. Men, on the other hand, generally attribute their failures to external factors and their successes to internal ones.

Women's internal attributional style, coupled with traditional gender roles, create a context ripe for mental illness. The traditional gender roles ascribed to women emphasize the cultural assumptions that women should be the heart of the family, responsible for nurturing and the transmission of family traditions. A woman's success as a human being typically is measured in terms of her fulfillment of cultural expectations and the well-being of her family members. If her marriage does not work or her children have problems, a woman is likely to blame herself and experience depression.

A woman's expected loyalty to family precludes her complaining about injustices she may experience in her family life. Furthermore, women who adhere to traditional gender roles are not expected even to acknowledge their own unfulfilled needs.

Thus women more likely will internalize the problem, not challenge or confront the situation directly, and accept the blame for circumstances over which they may have little control.

Women who work outside the home show lower levels of depression when compared with housewives. However, the struggle to balance the often conflicting role demands of employment and traditional roles is reflected in higher levels of depression among married working women when compared with single working women. Thus role strain is a factor that influences the relationship of work, marriage, and depression among women. In addition, women of all backgrounds who experienced family violence in their childhood, particularly sexual abuse, have been found to suffer from depression to a greater extent than women who did not suffer abuse in the family.

Most studies of depressed women find a strong relationship between onset of depression and family and marital problems, including evidence that when marital difficulties are unresolved symptoms remain or worsen, despite treatment, or return even if medication has diminished the symptoms.

Likewise, lesbians, who do not conform to heterosexist ideals of traditional marriage and motherhood, may experience depression because of social rejection or ostracism as a function of homophobia or heterosexism. The social positioning of lesbians and other women who do not conform as "others" can lead to feelings of marginality and isolation that can cause depression. Gender roles, the impact of marital problems, and a number of other stressors also have been identified as precursors of depression. Central among these are low socioeconomic status and conditions of social inequality among women of color. Compared with European American women, women of color, particularly African Americans, Native Americans, and Latinas, evidence significantly higher rates of depression. Studies of Mexican American women, for example, find more depressive symptoms when compared with Mexican American men and European American women even when the effects of age, education, and income are controlled for.

For immigrant women, age at migration, stresses related to adjustment to a new social and cultural context, disruptions in family relationships, and other losses experienced as a function of the migration all contribute to the development of depression. The older the migrant, the more disrupted are her family relations; the more discrimination she experiences in the new country, the greater the likelihood she will experience feelings of marginality and a perceived inability to perform successfully her culturally mandated roles. An additional factor is the extent to which her migration was voluntary. Women who migrate to follow a man, or who are forced into migration by economic problems, political upheavals, or other family pressures, are at greater risk of depression after the migration.

Depression is a mental disorder grounded in the social realities and expectations that women of all ethnicities, races, sexual orientations, and social classes have to face by virtue of their gender. Although a biological predisposition to depression may explain in part the incidence of depression in women, the prevalence of the disorder can be understood, treated, and prevented only if the fundamental conditions of inequality faced by all women are addressed.

Lois Braverman, "The Depressed Woman in Context: A Feminist Family Therapist's Analysis," in *Women and Family Therapy*, edited by Marianne Ault-Riche, 90–99. (Rockville, Md.: Aspen Publications, 1986); Yvette Flores-Ortiz, "Levels of Acculturation, Marital Satisfaction, and Depression among Chicana Workers: A Psychological Perspective," *Aztlan: A Journal of Chicano Studies*, 20, nos. 1, 2 (1991): 151–75; V. Nelly Salgado de Snyder, "Factors Associated with Acculturative Stress and Depressive Symptomatology Among Married Mexican Immigrant Women," *Psychology of Women Quarterly*, Vol. 11 (1987): 475–88.

▪ YVETTE G. FLORES-ORTIZ

SEE ALSO Mental Health and Illness.

≋ Diethylstilbestrol (DES)

DES, discovered in 1938, is the first synthetic estrogen widely used to treat women's reproductive health problems, notably menopause and threatened miscarriage. Scientific research has shown that DES does not prevent miscarriage and it is a transplacental carcinogen. Women exposed to it prenatally, "DES daughters," have a greater risk (1/1000) than do nonexposed women of developing vaginal or cervical cancer. Before the distribution of DES, clear-cell adenocarcinoma was diagnosed only in postmenopausal women, but research now shows that DES daughters are most likely to be diagnosed with cancer between the ages of fifteen and twenty-seven. The upper age limit for developing the cancer is unknown. Cases continue to be diagnosed in the 1990s. DES daughters who conceive have a greater risk than do nonexposed women of having ectopic pregnancy, miscarriage, premature birth, or stillbirth. DES mothers have a slightly greater risk of breast cancer than do nonexposed women. DES sons are more likely to have genital abnormalities and may have a greater risk of infertility than nonexposed men.

Published reports of DES's carcinogenic effects in animals appeared as early as 1939. Political, economic, and cultural factors after the New Deal combined to prevent the Food and Drug Administration (FDA) from heeding the warnings in its premarketing review of DES. These factors included pressure to market a cheap substitute for natural estrogens; excitement about controlling the level of hormones in women's bodies; and uncertainty about the meaning of science in medicine. In 1941 FDA officials decided that DES could safely be prescribed to treat menopausal symptoms, vaginitis, and juvenile gonorrheal vaginitis, and to suppress lactation in non-nursing mothers. At the time DES was approved, drugs had to be proven *safe* but did not have to be proven *effective* before they could be marketed.

DES was never officially approved for use during pregnancy, but until the early 1970s, U.S. physicians prescribed DES to between 2 million and 4.8 million pregnant women, most often white and middle class, because they believed it could prevent miscarriage. In the 1950s controlled clinical trials showed that DES was ineffective in preventing miscarriages, but its use during pregnancy was not banned by the FDA until 1971, when it was identified as the first transplacental carcinogen. DES-exposed persons and their families have since filed hundreds of lawsuits. They have also founded DES Action, the DES Cancer Network, and the DES Sons' Network to distribute information about DES and change the institution of medicine. Congressional passage of H.R. 4178 in 1992, which allocated funds for scientific research about DES, reflects their collective efforts.

DES is still marketed in the United States to treat advanced breast and prostate cancer. In developing countries DES is used to suppress lactation as well as to prevent miscarriage. Although DES does not prevent miscarriage, regulatory decisions and the interpretation of scientific evidence regarding drug use do not necessarily cross borders, and many drugs can still be marketed internationally. The case of DES provides a powerful lesson of how medical mistakes can happen and why people must work collectively to provide remedies for past mistakes and to prevent future ones.

■ SUSAN E. BELL

≋ Disability

Women and girls with disabilities are a large, diverse group, 26 million strong, according to 1991–92 census data. Combined with the 23 million men and boys with disabilities in the United States, they compose 19.4 percent of the total population. Women with disabilities are older than nondisabled women—the prevalence of disability increases with age—and are more likely to live in poverty. Disability also cuts across all racial and ethnic lines.

Definitions of disability vary, sometimes contradictory and often broad, encompassing diverse roles and functions, which suggests that disability status is as much a function of culture as biology. The Americans with Disabilities Act (1990), a landmark civil rights law prohibiting discrimination against people with disabilities, defines a person with a disability as:

1. Someone with a mental or physical impairment that substantially limits one or more major life activities, such as walking, talking or seeing.
2. A person with a record of such an impairment, such as a history of heart disease or cancer.
3. A person who is regarded as having a disability, such as someone misperceived as having AIDS because of weight loss.

What binds together the people identified as "disabled" is not the nature of their impairments, which can be vastly different, but rather the widespread discrimination and second-class status they face. While the nature of discrimination varies among people with different types of disability, there are enough similarities in the prejudices to warrant a single set of disability rights laws and a single disability rights movement.

Women with disabilities face double discrimination based on disability and gender. Women with disabilities fare considerably worse than men with disabilities or women without disabilities on most measures of success in our culture: education and income levels, employment rates, rates of marriage and other types of long-term relationships, and levels of self-esteem. Disabled women of color and disabled lesbians confront additional levels of discrimination. For example, as reported in the *New York Times* on August 16, 1989, in 1988 the full-time employment rate for women with

Disability activists demonstrate in the streets of New York City.

disabilities was 13.1 percent, compared to 23.4 percent for men with disabilities and 47.1 percent for nondisabled women. In 1987 the average annual income for women workers with disabilities was $8,075, compared to $13,000 for all women workers, $15,497 for male workers with disabilities, and $24,095 for all male workers. According to a 1988 study by Adrienne Asch and Michelle Fine, who analyzed data on the economic status of persons with work disabilities in the early 1980s, for every dollar earned by a white nondisabled man, a disabled African American woman earned twenty-two cents.

Pervasive negative stereotypes underlie discrim-inatory policies and practices. Women with disabilities are often perceived as sick, helpless, childlike, asexual, incompetent, and unable to perform adult roles. These stereotypes persist despite the growing number of women with disabilities who have responsible jobs, social and political commitments, lovers, partners, and children.

At a time when the women's movement is seeking to expand women's options, women with disabilities face limited access to even the most traditional female roles of wife and mother. Studies show that women with disabilities are less likely to marry, more likely to marry later, more likely to be divorced, and less likely to have intimate partners than nondisabled women or disabled men. One explanation is that women continue to be chosen, at least in heterosexual relationships, on the basis of their ability to meet cultural norms of physical attractiveness and beauty; women with visible disabilities, with differently shaped bodies and adaptive devices, may be perceived as too far removed from the norms to be valued as partners. Also, to the extent that men may choose women to nurture and take care of them, they may perceive women with disabilities as needing too much care themselves to nurture others. While research on the social lives of lesbians with disabilities is lacking, anecdotal information suggests that they too face considerable hurdles in finding partners.

The exclusion of women with disabilities from the social scene starts early. Studies of girls with physical or sensory disabilities suggest that they have their first date, kiss, and sexual encounters later than their nondisabled peers, not by choice but rather lack of opportunity. These girls pay a price for their social exclusion: heightened self-doubts in a culture that continues to value women on the basis of their capacity to "catch" a man.

Myths about sexuality contribute to the difficulties women with disabilities face not only in finding partners but also in becoming mothers. Women with disabilities, particularly those with visible physical disabilities, are often viewed as asexual. Perceived as undesirable, they are assumed to lack sexual desire. Because of her disability, a woman's capacity to give and receive sexual pleasure in traditional ways is also called into question. A disability, as well as disability-related medications and treatments, can have physiological effects on sexual desire, lubrication, orgasmic capacity, and fertility. The physical aspects of a disability can also affect spontaneity, types of foreplay, positioning, and communication styles between partners. The age of onset of the disability can further influence sexual functioning. Women who become disabled as adults may have to adjust to a changing body, body image, and social status, whereas women disabled since childhood may

have to confront a lifetime of negative socialization. Through creative problem solving, open communication, support networks, and an expansive definition of sexuality, every woman regardless of disability can create ways to express herself sexually. Eliminating negative assumptions about her sexuality from the hearts and minds of potential partners is a far greater challenge.

Coexisting with the assumption of asexuality is the myth that women with disabilities, particularly those with less visible disabilities that affect intellectual, cognitive, or emotional functioning, have excessive sexual desire or are unable to control their sexuality. This myth then perpetuates false assumptions about the childbearing capacities of disabled women, including the fear that they will bear disabled or "defective" children or that they will do harm to any child they bear, disabled or not, because of inadequate mothering abilities. Such assumptions have led to laws and practices designed to keep the sexuality of, and particularly childbearing by, women with disabilities in check. Historically, women with intellectual disabilities have been institutionalized and/or forced to submit to involuntary sterilization. And reproductive health and family planning services, to the extent that they have been available to women with disabilities, have focused on preventing these women from having children, often against their will or knowledge, through abortions, sterilization, or hormonal treatments. Many states have laws forbidding marriage for people with certain disabilities (to prevent procreation), and some have intrusive policies designed to separate children from parents with disabilities. Women with disabilities are also at high risk for losing their children in custody cases resulting from divorce. Such elaborate restrictions contradict existing facts and violate civil rights. There is no evidence that women with disabilities are any less capable of rearing children, particularly when they have access to adaptive equipment and supports. Also, it is more the exception than the rule for women with disabilities to bear children with disabilities. Regardless of whether a disability is hereditary, women with disabilities should have the right to biological motherhood—to deny them the right to bear children is a throwback to the eugenics movement, in which only the "best" genes could be perpetuated.

Myths that seek to limit the sexual expression and fulfillment of women with disabilities do not protect them from sexual harassment and abuse, encounters that have to do more with power than sexual desire. Women with disabilities are perceived as less able to resist and less likely to report attacks than nondisabled women. Indeed, research suggests that women and girls with disabilities experience higher rates of sexual and physical abuse than do their nondisabled counterparts, and also face more barriers to reporting abuse and obtaining safety. Police stations, crisis centers, and shelters are often inaccessible, and officials and counselors sometimes doubt the credibility of women whom they may perceive as incompetent and asexual.

Women with disabilities have responded to the limited roles, negative stereotypes, and heightened vulnerability they face in myriad ways. The multiple barriers can lower self-esteem and cause depression, but not invariably so. Some women pursue paths of individual achievement or engage in collective action despite (or to spite) the barriers. Notable disabled women have included Annie Jump Cannon, a nineteenth-century astronomer who classified more than three hundred thousand stars; Elizabeth Blackwell, the first U.S. woman to receive her medical degree, in 1849; and Harriet Tubman, fugitive slave and leader of the Underground Railroad movement. In recent times, women with disabilities have been active participants in the disability rights movement. Judy Heumann sued the New York City Board of Education for refusing to grant her a teaching license because she used a wheelchair; until her successful lawsuit, no wheelchair user had been allowed to teach in that public school system. She went on to become a founder of the independent living movement, spawning a national network of independent living centers, organizations run by and for people with disabilities.

Feminists with disabilities have sought to find their place in the women's movement, but not without a struggle. Nondisabled feminists fighting the image of women as sex objects sometimes fail to understand that the sexless image is also damaging. At times, members of the pro-choice movement have used fears about having a disabled child to justify access to abortion, failing to see how the "life not worth living" view devalues the lives of women and men with disabilities. Nonetheless, the issues and contributions of women with disabilities are gaining recognition as the women's movement seeks strength through an appreciation of diversity.

Adrienne Asch and Michelle Fine, "Introduction: Beyond Pedestals," in *Women with Disabilities: Essays in Psychology, Culture and Politics,* edited by Michelle Fine and Adrienne Asch. 1–37. (Philadelphia: Temple University Press, 1988); Marsha Saxton and Florence Howe, eds., *With Wings: An Anthology of Literature by and About Women with Disabilities* (New York: The Feminist Press at CUNY, 1987); Barbara Faye Waxman, "Up Against Eugenics: Disabled Women Challenge to Receive Reproductive Health Services," *Sexuality and Disability* Vol. 12 (Summer 1994): 155–71.

• HARILYN ROUSSO

SEE ALSO Stereotypes: Disability.

≋ Divorce and Custody

Marriage is a legal status and spouses must have the state's agreement to dissolve a marriage. Prerevolutionary divorce laws in the United States followed England's ecclesiastical courts, which viewed marriages as indissolvable. Annulment was a possibility in rare cases, while a "divorce from bed and board" allowed separation without dissolving the legal status of wives as chattel, or the duty of husbands to provide financially for their wives.

After 1776, a court-administered "fault" divorce system evolved. If a judge found that one spouse had committed dire offenses while the petitioning spouse remained "innocent," divorce was granted. If the wife was the innocent spouse, her right to financial support theoretically continued and could be satisfied through the award of alimony or by property division.

Adultery and desertion were the most frequent grounds for divorce. Some states were liberal, defining transgressions flexibly, such as Vermont's "intolerable severity" or Rhode Island's "gross misbehavior and wickedness." Court processes gave judges control, in contrast to the more restrictive and exclusive parliamentary divorce in Britain as well as legislative divorce, which was prevalent in the South well into the eighteenth century.

During the twentieth century, changing mores and a legal profession increasingly willing to ignore obvious fabrication of evidence eventually led to what has been termed a "dual system" of divorce. Laws officially remained strict, but collusion between spouses (often with the assistance of attorneys) made it easy to divorce. Widespread dissatisfaction with the disparity between the formal law and hypocritical tactics used in its interpretation prompted a wave of "no-fault" divorce reform beginning in the 1960s.

By 1985, every state had changed its divorce laws to reflect the no-fault philosophy: divorce was no one person's fault; it resulted from irreconcilable differences. The accepted wisdom among reformers was that an unhappy spouse should be able to sever marital ties and "start over." Many states retained their original laws, merely placing a no-fault option alongside the traditional grounds.

No-fault changes were accompanied for additional social reasons by a rapid increase in the rate of divorce. It more than doubled between the early 1960s and mid-1970s. The rate continues to hover around 50 percent for newly contracted unions. Some predict that three in five first marriages will end in divorce, with the rate for second marriages even higher.

Divorce reformers also turned their attention to property division, alimony, and child custody and support. They argued that fault in the conduct of the marriage should be irrelevant in determining what each spouse receives at divorce. The idea that each spouse made important (even if different) contributions to the marriage resulted in the metaphor of marriage as a "partnership." The notion of equality ushered in reforms such as presumptions that marital property should be divided equally regardless of who was financially responsible, the replacement of permanent alimony (viewed as demeaning and also condoning dependency) with temporary or "rehabilitative maintenance" for spouses who had to retool for market work, and vigorous arguments for "shared parenting."

Historically, fathers had the right to custody and control of their children. This right complemented the father's obligation to support and discipline the child and stemmed from the original assertion that wives and children were men's property. The father custody rule was attacked in the latter part of the nineteenth century by feminists and social welfare advocates who urged placing the child's interests above paternal privilege. Maternal custody became practical only when the system considered paternal financial obligations to be appropriately fulfilled through the institution of child support payments. The primary judicial inquiry as to custody thus became what was "in the best interest of the child."

Courts quickly evolved rules to assist in making the best-interest determination. Fit mothers were given custody of children under the age of seven or so and the "same-sex" preference dictated that preparation for adult roles mandated older boys went with their fathers while girls remained with mothers.

For most of this century, maternal custody has been the norm, with over 85 percent of children residing with their mothers after divorce. Patterns of division of labor within households typically made mothers the caretakers during the marriage and that pattern voluntarily continued after divorce. Even in the small percentage of cases where it is an initial issue, custody usually has not been litigated.

Negotiation and compromise are the predominant modes for resolving this and other issues arising from divorce. Formal rules affect this process, however, since rights and entitlements represent power within the context of bargaining. The rules also have a powerful symbolic content and are often the site of real contention.

In recent years, fathers' rights groups have sprung up to argue forcefully that men are discriminated against in the custody context. They blame maternal bias for such widespread paternal practices as the refusal to pay child support or to visit with children after divorce. The changes that have resulted from fathers' agitation have destabilized the system, raising custody issues in many more divorce cases.

Many practicing attorneys and judges believe that the acrimony inevitably associated with divorce has now been relocated from a determination of who was at fault to the issue of who is the better parent. Others worry that women will lose the economic gains they won from divorce law property reforms, since mothers will often trade alimony and child support and property entitlements to prevent the possibility of losing custody of their children.

                    ▪ MARTHA ALBERTSON FINEMAN

SEE ALSO Families; Marriage.

≋ Domestic Science

Originating with the cult of domesticity around the turn of the century, domestic science (also known as home economics, household administration, euthenics, and domestic economy) aimed to professionalize the status of housewife and upgrade the household arts. The new discipline, founded by Ellen Richards, applied principles to the home borrowed from economics, chemistry, horticulture, and the emerging ideologies of domesticity and scientific management. Tradition, common sense, and personal taste were replaced by expert knowledge of rationalized household processes. The goal was to set the highest level of sanitation, nutrition, and efficiency and to establish standards for all aspects of the domestic sphere, including cooking, child care, sewing, housecleaning, laundry, table setting, and home decorating.

Domestic science was a major component in "Americanization programs." Many European immigrant women and women of color became the targets of zealous teachers proselytizing about nutrition, hygiene, and U.S. middle-class values. Vocational and industrial education programs dominated by a domestic science curriculum trained young girls for homemaking and for employment in domestic service. Among the poor and working class, the introduction of "American" standards functioned to expand homemaking activity and redesign the family around consumption. Adult courses and training in home economics later became major components of programs developed for women during the New Deal, including the Works Progress Administration and the National Youth Administration. The Bureau of Home Economics, the first federal agency devoted to home economics, made domestic science into government policy.

                            ▪ MARY ROMERO

SEE ALSO Americanization; Cooking; Cult of Domesticity.

≋ Domestic Work

SEE Household Workers.

≋ Double-Day

The concept of the double-day refers to women taking on two jobs: a paid job in the labor force as well as the unpaid job of homemaking for her family. Although this practice came to society's attention in the post–World War II period, the double-day has a long history in the United States. A striking example is seen in the work lives of enslaved African American women, who were forced to labor long hours for their owners, usually doing backbreaking fieldwork alongside their partners and children. At the end of their long day, they then performed domestic chores. This experience of the double-day under slavery helps explain the higher labor-force participation rates of married African American women after abolition, which were eight times those of U.S.-born married white women. Husbands' lower incomes also contributed to the higher prevalence of the double-day among African American families, as among all poorer families.

The overall share of married women working the double-day—that is, who were in the paid labor force—rose dramatically in the course of the twentieth century from 5.6 percent in 1900 to 59.2 percent in 1992. Indeed, women are often expected to be "superwomen," excelling both in the "masculine" labor-market competition as well as in the "feminine" duties of wife- and motherhood. This gradual but significant expansion in women's work responsibilities has brought pressure on the traditional marital division of labor. In many marriages, employed wives have maintained almost total responsibility for women's traditional work in the home in an attempt to shore up their femininity, or as a result of their husbands' resistance to doing "women's work." However, more and more couples are experimenting with "symmetrical marriages," in which the partners play similar rather than the traditional complementary roles. In such relationships, partners share the housework and child care and each holds down a paid job.

■ JULIE MATTHAEI

SEE ALSO Household Workers, Unpaid.

≋ Dress Reform

Sheer, empire-waisted dresses covered only by flimsy gauze shawls; thin-soled slippers worn in the wettest weather; huge hoop skirts that frequently caught fire, leaving their wearers disfigured or dead; corsets and stays so tight they damaged the internal organs of the legions who wore them—all this and more fed the movement for dress reform that began in the early 1800s and grew throughout the nineteenth century. Feminists meeting in Seneca Falls took up the struggle for dress reform and in 1852 introduced the bloomer dress, so named because it was endorsed by Elizabeth Cady Stanton and her comrade Amelia Bloomer. Unfortunately, the bloomer costume, though originally greeted with cautious enthusiasm, was defeated by a wildly popular reactionary press that mercilessly lampooned the style as ungainly, unfeminine, and indicative of sympathy for the dangerous notion of "free love."

Nevertheless, incremental improvements began to emerge—first, ankle-baring skirts, rapidly followed by the introduction of the shirtwaist. This garment, really a feminized version of a man's white shirt, could be combined with a plain skirt to provide a sartorial solution for trodding muddy streets and ten-hour working days. Of course the issue of dress reform had far more impact upon women of the middle and upper classes. For poor women, working-class women, and slaves, obtaining decent clothing of any kind was a much more pressing concern.

Vast social changes in the early years of the twentieth century—more women in the work

The bloomer costume was developed in the 1850s by women's rights advocates Amelia Bloomer and Elizabeth Cady Stanton in an effort to give women practical, nonrestrictive clothing. It was considered sexually provocative, however, and never gained wide appeal.

force, an increasing enthusiasm for sports, and a growing suffrage movement—brought about radical changes in dress far beyond the modest dreams of the early bloomer wearers. Corsets disappeared, hems rose, and not only ankles but nude limbs were seen on the streets by the mid-1920s.

■ LYNN YAEGER

SEE ALSO Fashion and Style.

≋ Drugs

Since the 1950s women have increasingly used legal and illegal drugs. The 1988 National Household Survey conducted by the National Institute on Drug Abuse found that 9 percent of the sixty million U.S. women of childbearing age (between fifteen and forty-four) had used illicit drugs in the prior month. Women now compose about one-third of addicts in treatment; the figures for unrecognized and untreated female drug users are estimated to be much higher.

During the last decade drug use by white men has remained stable or declined but increased among adolescents, white women, and people of color. In addition, cocaine and crack use has reached epidemic proportions, particularly among African American urban women. While the precise number of pregnant women who use drugs and the number of drug exposed babies are unknown, a congressional survey of eighteen urban and suburban hospitals found three to four times as many drug-exposed births in 1989 as in 1985. These figures continued to rise in the early 1990s.

The public health cost of addiction in the United States is estimated to be over $1 billion per year, not including the long-term consequences of addiction: academic failure, chronic underemployment, health problems, including HIV or AIDS infection, fetal damage, and neurological impairment of some babies born to drug-addicted mothers. Furthermore, the increase in female criminality and rise in the numbers of female inmates have been associated with drug use and drug-related criminal activity.

The understanding, prevention, and treatment of female drug addiction have been impacted by sexism and racism. Women have been invisible alcoholics and addicts for a number of reasons. First, traditional gendered perceptions of women have contributed to a lower detection of female alcoholics and other addicts. Second, until the crack cocaine epidemic affected women of all social classes, female addicts were regarded as "hard-core" members of lower economic status groups and/or disenfranchised minority populations. Third, the majority of women addicts became addicts as a result of dependence on legally prescribed pain killers, tranquilizers, mood enhancers, or diet pills.

The historical perception of women as homemakers, nurturers, and providers of the moral basis of family life has influenced policies that study drug abuse. Until recent legislation mandated inclusion of women in federally funded studies, few women participated in clinical trials or epidemiological studies of drug abuse. The erroneous and stereotypic perception that few women abuse drugs such as heroin, cocaine, or hallucinogens has also contributed to their invisibility in prevention and treatment programs.

Tax dollars for drug research, prevention, and treatment are tied to epidemiological studies. Data collection sources that document the extent of the problem rely largely on information about addicts in treatment, emergency-room admissions, and criminal justice data. Since the majority of addicts in or out of treatment and prison inmates are male, most prevention and treatment programs have targeted and benefited men. In fact, drug treatment programs specifically for women are a recent development.

People of color historically have been shut out of research studies. Until very recently, data collection sources did not identify racial or ethnic categories, with the exception of African Americans. Consequently, the extent of the problem of drug abuse among the general population of Latinas, Asians, Pacific Islanders, and Native American women is determined only on the basis of patient data, maternal drug use, and, more recently, HIV infection rates. These figures tend to provide a skewed profile, which feeds into negative stereotypes.

Moreover, as most illegal drug users are young and poor, African American, Latina, and Native American women who are predominantly young and working class are likely to be overrepresented in this category. White women who, prior to the crack cocaine epidemic, used primarily marijuana and prescribed drugs may not be suspected of being addicts. Women of color, however, are especially likely to be suspected because the patient data suggests they are overrepresented in drug-use figures and HIV infection rates. This overrepresentation, however, has not translated necessarily into the development of culturally specific or sensitive prevention or treatment efforts. Thus racism may render addicted women of color more visible yet less likely to be treated.

Women are the primary consumers of mental health services. Psychiatry has a long history of addressing the gender and emotional needs of women by misdiagnosing their symptoms as "hysterical" or "depressive" syndromes, which are then treated with psychopharmacological agents. Women's history of addiction to Valium is an example of how psychiatry attempted to treat the problems of women by ignoring their larger social and gender context.

The normalization of prescribed addiction is reflected in the absence of data regarding the specific numbers of women addicted to legal drugs. Furthermore, the medical profession often treats the addictive power of prescribed drugs as an inevitable side effect of an otherwise useful agent.

A major barrier to treatment of addicted women is the punitive social response to female addicts, particularly those who are mothers. Pregnant addicts often lose custody if the child is born drug-exposed. Women addicts may also lose custody of any other children, whereas male addicts do not typically lose custody. In addition, few residential treatment programs house children, forcing mother-child separation. Unless the addicted woman has a supportive family system, she may need to place her children in foster care. Often women experience difficulties regaining custody once they have surrendered it, even if the reason for foster placement was to enter drug treatment.

In addition, not enough beds are available for in-patient treatment, and long waiting lists exist for those seeking outpatient services.

Sexism, classism, and racial discrimination have affected the documentation of women addicts and generated prevention and treatment policies that until recently ignored the health and social needs of women. Recent legislation has attempted to sensitize researchers and practitioners to women's needs in order to address more effectively and humanely this serious health crisis.

Barbara Bloom and David Steinhart, *Why Punish the Children?: A Reappraisal of the Children of Incarcerated Mothers in America* (National Council on Crime and Delinquency, 1993); Drug Abuse Services Research Series, No. 1. *Background Papers on Drug Abuse Financing and Services Research* (National Institute on Drug Abuse, U.S. Department of Health and Human Services, 1991); National Corrections Reporting Program, *Bureau of Justice Statistics*, 1991, 1994.

- YVETTE G. FLORES-ORTIZ

≋ Eating Disorders

"**E**ating disorders" is the umbrella term for a number of eating problems including bulimia, anorexia nervosa, and pica. Pica is a craving for nonfood substances (such as dirt, paint, and clay) and is unrelated to anorexia and bulimia. Bulimia involves recurrent episodes of binge eating usually followed by self-induced vomiting, laxative abuse, and/or rigorous dieting. The long-term medical complications of bulimia can include stomach rupture, tooth decay, dehydration, and, in a few instances, death (resulting from the depletion of electrolytes, which can lead to cardiac arrhythmias). Anorexia nervosa includes severe weight loss to below one's minimally healthy body weight, intense fear of gaining weight, and poor self-image. The effects of anorexia include weakness and sickness caused by malnutrition, distorted body image, and depression. In a small percentage of diagnosed cases, death by starvation results. Although anorexia and bulimia are considered separate diagnostic categories there is much overlap between the two. Many bulimics have a prior history of anorexia. In addition, while compulsive eating (bingeing for emotional rather than nutritional reasons) typically is considered a symptom of bulimia, compulsive eating is increasingly recognized as an independent problem, which is associated with eating to the point of great physical discomfort, losing control over eating during an episode, and feeling depressed or guilty after overeating.

Although instances of food refusal can be traced to at least the thirteenth century, the first medical use of the term *anorexia* dates back to the 1870s. Bulimia also has a long history, but it was not included in the psychiatric diagnostic manual until 1980. The prevalence of anorexia and bulimia is difficult to determine because secrecy is a common component of the problem, studies have accounted effectively for racial and ethnic diversity, and variations exist in the definitions of the terms. Until the 1960s both bulimia and anorexia were considered rare. Since that time, the reported incidence of both has risen significantly. Estimates of the incidence of bulimia range from about 2 to 13 percent of women (depending on the criteria used); between 1 and 2 percent of women are thought to be anorexic. Among college-aged women, as many as one in five are bulimic and between 5 and 10 percent have symptoms of anorexia. Many studies have also documented a dramatic rise in dieting in the last twenty years, which often begins even before girls reach puberty.

Increasing evidence shows that long-term dieting may be implicated in the onset of bulimia and anorexia. Approximately 90 percent of people who go on diets gain back the lost weight. Further, long-term food restriction may slow the metabolism, making it more rather than less difficult to lose weight or maintain weight loss. Cycles of weight loss and weight gain can make people especially vulnerable to taking more drastic steps to lose weight, including purging, fasting for extended periods, taking appetite suppressants, and/or exercising compulsively. For this reason, health professionals now understand that the prevention of eating problems must include educating people about the possible dangers of long-term dieting.

In the past two decades, research on eating disorders has pointed to a significant emphasis on thinness and has examined why the vast majority of people with eating problems are women. Attempts to control women's bodies are certainly not new given the history of restrictions on women's reproduction, attempts to limit women's athletic development, and the use of corsets and other restrictive clothing. However, the promotion of a "drop-dead" thin woman's body size that has been widely encouraged since the 1960s is unprecedented. Many feminists have argued that at a historical period when increasing numbers of women are seeking economic, legal, and sexual power, one form of patriarchal backlash is to define the "ideal" female body size as childlike and thin. In the United States this image is upheld by interlocking institutional powers: a $33 billion weight-reduction industry, most of whose consumers are women; medical professionals who maintain the dubious assumption that fat is by definition unhealthy and ought to be eliminated; multibillion dollar advertising and pornography industries that promote demeaning images of women; a job market in which women who do not fit narrow beauty standards face discrimination; and an insurance industry that upholds medically prescribed standards of what constitutes a healthy body size. The cultural emphasis on dieting robs women of crucial energy—both physical and psychic—and undermines their ability to control their appetites and bodies. In fact, scientific research on the body's "set point"—a physiologically programmed weight level that the body defends—indicates that, in reality, body weight

may be similar to height or foot size. Attempts to change one's "set point" may be akin to trying to make oneself taller or smaller-footed. Institutionally supported imperatives to sculpt one's body size—through dieting, intestinal bypass surgery, or liposuction—typically backfire as physiological mechanisms return the body to its preprogrammed weight.

While feminists have spearheaded research on why eating problems predominate among women, until recently there has been little attention to issues of race, religion, class, and sexuality. Since anorexia was first recognized in the nineteenth century, it has been considered a "golden girl's" illness, associated with white, middle- and upper-class girls. Almost all of the medical and psychological research on eating disorders has focused on this group of women. As a consequence, an extraordinarily diverse group of women of color—Asian American, African American, Native American, and Latina women—has been categorically ignored. Regarding eating problems as "white concerns" has been based on the assumption that women of color are somehow separate from and can protect themselves from dominant images of beauty and weight. In a society where virtually everyone has a television and the media permeates even the most remote areas of the country, it makes little sense to assume that women of color can escape cultural imperatives about thinness.

Working-class women were thought not to develop anorexia presumably because they do not have time to be weight-conscious, or they are one step away from hunger and therefore not susceptible to developing eating problems. These stereotypes have slowed the delivery of badly needed attention to how the stress of poverty or being overworked may be involved in the development of eating problems. Similarly, the lack of attention to lesbians with eating problems reflects the biased notion that they are as a group disinterested in or unaffected by dominant heterosexual beauty standards and therefore would not be at risk.

The research findings on eating problems among white, middle- and upper-class heterosexual women are also most likely reflective of the locations where studies have been conducted historically (e.g., private girls' schools, suburbs, and private hospitals) rather than of actual prevalence. This narrow focus has also stemmed from the tendency to view anorexia and bulimia as largely appearance-based disorders developed by women who are especially self-absorbed, vain, and obsessively fashion conscious. While anorexia and bulimia are certainly encouraged by the diet, fashion, and insurance industries, there are additional stresses that may make women vulnerable to developing eating disorders. Increasing evidence points to bingeing, starving, and purging as coping mechanisms that girls and women first develop in response to one or more traumas, including sexual abuse, poverty, homophobia, racism, and the stress of acculturation. When faced with injustices that undermine a girl's or woman's ability to control her body or to feel safe in the world, bingeing or refusing food may be a logical method of attempting to take care of herself. Some feminist researchers accordingly refuse to use the term eating disorder to label what may begin as an orderly behavioral solution to highly disordered circumstances.

A multicultural picture of eating problems also illuminates reasons why those historically left out of the frame of focus may be especially vulnerable to eating problems. For example, being one of only a few African American, Latina, or Asian American women in overwhelmingly white schools, neighborhoods, or work environments may cause stress that women may cope with by bingeing or starving. Women who recently immigrated to the United States may be particularly vulnerable to bingeing, purging, or dieting as a means of coping with culture shock and discrimination. The processes of exclusion facing many lesbian and gay youth may lead them to turn to (or away from) food as a means of comfort and companionship.

Historically, medical treatment of anorexia and bulimia has ranged from hospitalization and regulated feeding to outpatient therapy that emphasizes behavior modification, family counseling, and psychoeducational treatment. The high financial cost of inpatient treatment programs or outpatient therapy with specialists has severely restricted access to professional help for countless women. Self-help groups (such as Overeaters Anonymous and the community-based support-group model developed by the National Black Women's Health Project) have provided no-cost, conveniently located assistance for women. The link between eating problems and socially induced trauma (caused by sexism, homophobia, sexual abuse, and racism) underscores why the prevention of bulimia and anorexia rests not simply with individual healing but also with changing the underlying social conditions that may cause the problems. Ultimately the prevention of eating problems depends on women's access to economic, cultural, racial, political, social, and sexual justice.

Lisa Schoenfielder and Barb Wieser, eds., *Shadow on a Tightrope: Writings by Women on Fat Oppression* (Iowa City: Aunt Lute, 1983); Becky Thompson, *A Hunger So Wide and So Deep: American Women Speak Out on Eating Problems* (Minneapolis: University of Minnesota, 1994); Evelyn C. White, *The Black Women's Health Book: Speaking for Ourselves* (Seattle: Seal Press, 1994).

▪ BECKY W. THOMPSON

≋ Economic Empowerment/ Autonomy

In the early 1980s five battered women's shelters around the United States participated in a special project sponsored by the National Coalition Against Domestic Violence. These five programs received assistance in starting businesses that could employ battered women, enabling them to earn sufficient income to permanently leave their batterers. This project illustrates the transition made subsequently by many women-serving organizations as they realized that a root cause of problems facing their clients was economic.

In 1983 the first of a new generation of organizations opened its doors in St. Paul, Minnesota. The Women's Economic Development Corporation (WEDCO) led to the development of numerous self-employment programs offering the same essential benefit: a welcoming system of resources and encouragement that women—particularly low-income white women and women of color from all economic groups—seldom experienced in the traditional business world.

Cooperatives were another job-creation model well suited to women's needs and to transforming a woman from a worker to a worker-owner or member. Watermark Association of Artisans, a craft-marketing cooperative in northeastern North Carolina, provides income-generating opportunities for its members and advocates on behalf of low-income women at the city, county, and national levels. Cooperative Home Care Associates (CHCA), in the South Bronx, uses cooperative ownership as a tool to turn the usually dismal job of a home-health aide into a higher-paying, full-time job with benefits and annual dividends. CHCA's 300 worker-owners are active in leadership positions throughout the company, including the majority of its board of directors.

▪ SARA K. GOULD

≋ Economic Growth

I n conventional economic theory, expansion is an economy's productive capacity over time, creating rising standards of living. Growth occurs as the factors of production (resources such as labor and the capital stock) grow through population increase and investment in the capital stock. In addition, growth occurs as labor and the capital stock become more productive, through advances in knowledge, economies of scale (greater efficiency through mass production methods), and improvements in resource allocation (for example, when people move from lower productivity jobs in agriculture to higher productivity jobs in manufacturing). Over the long run, growth rates generally depend on factors such as technical progress, savings, investment, and population growth.

In the short run, economic growth fluctuates over the business cycle, with periods of recession followed by periods of recovery. Periods of more rapid economic growth typically are accompanied by expansions in labor market opportunities for women. For the United States, wartime periods have been accompanied by rapid economic growth, creating new labor market opportunities for women. Women have held jobs vacated by men who are engaged in war, and wartime spending stimulates demand for goods and services and leads to increased production of goods and services. Rapid economic growth appears to provide relatively greater opportunities for disadvantaged groups such as working-class women and people of color, while periods of slower growth disproportionately harm these groups.

Growth is usually measured by the rate of growth of per capita gross domestic product (GDP, or the value of goods and services produced and sold in a nation). Industrialized economies typically experience growth rates of a few percentage points per year. In the United States, per capita real GDP grew at slightly less than 2 percent per year over the past one hundred years, leading to a doubling of the average material standard of living approximately every forty years. Some economists believe that growth occurs in cycles that are triggered by technological change; others believe that capitalist economies necessarily suffer periods of stagnation caused by overproduction, underconsumption, or failures in the political or social institutions that support economic growth. The slowdown in U.S. economic growth that began in the early 1970s has caused stagnation in real wage growth and is thought to be responsible for rising social problems such as unemployment.

Since GDP measures only the value of goods and services produced and sold in a market, women's unpaid labor, such as child rearing, cooking, cleaning, and volunteer work, does not count. Thus, women's contributions to economic growth, including the production and reproduction of the labor force, are typically undervalued by conventional measurements. The process of economic growth in capitalist countries typically involves the movement of labor out of nonmarket sites such as the home, where work is not counted, into the market, where work takes on monetary value. As a result, GDP-based measures of economic growth can overstate the extent of the rise in living standards accompanying market-based economic growth.

■ TERESA L. AMOTT

SEE ALSO Poverty; Wealth and Its Distribution; Work.

≋ Education

Education is the means by which information about human communities is kept alive, challenged, and transformed through the generations. Usually, "education" refers to formal, institutionalized schooling that also certifies its graduates in culturally legitimized ways. It therefore serves various processes of selectivity—cultural, religious, economic, social. Informal education takes place in the ways that adults prepare girls and boys for societal roles. Sometimes, too, as in the Freedom Schools in the South during the civil rights movement, education is insurgent, designed to counter and oppose formal and/or informal education. Insurgent education has also developed to subvert progressive schooling: for example, anti-integrationist white Christian schools sprang up throughout the South in the 1960s.

The many strands of the history of women's education tell us how cultural, economic, and governance systems have established at differing times what is "right" and "proper" for females, and how women have worked both with and against those prescriptions. The stories of sex/gender in education also implicate other groupings of humans—by racial categories, socioeconomic class, ethnicities, traditions, religions, sexualities, and definitions of "normality," physical or psychological. Throughout history, education for women and girls has been shaped by complex prescriptions of what is "natural" and "appropriate" for their gender. In 1837 Oberlin College in Ohio was the first to admit to higher education women and men of all races. Oberlin students were required to work as well as study; one could speculate that one reason Oberlin admitted women was that they would take care of domestic chores for the males who worked on the college farm. In the early Republic, white women's education focused on preparing females to be beacons of enlightened morality for their families and better companions for their husbands. In addition, many women were trained to be teachers as well as other caretakers, such as nurses and social workers. Well into the twentieth century, girls were raised and women were more formally educated to do the unpaid or underpaid work that boys and men did not think they should do. Some women turned these assigned roles and professions into opportunities to subvert as well as serve society.

Education has also been culturally prescriptive. In some Native American tribes, notably the Iroquois, women held positions of power. This gender equality was hardly admired by colonialists or European male explorers. At the first Anglo-American representative assembly in Jamestown, the burgesses pronounced that settlements should

The 1855 graduating class of Oberlin College, Ohio. In 1837 Oberlin College became the first U.S. college to accept women, who were enrolled in a "female department" and received separate degrees.

educate a "certaine number of the natives' children . . . in the true religion and civile course of life." "Infidels" also were "corrected" as to their faith and ways of life, including gender prescriptions, in the mission boarding schools to which many Native American children were later sent.

Education has maintained hierarchical divisions among people by converting and training them for (less powerful) "appropriate" roles and jobs and by excluding them from others. Gender prescriptions have paralleled other hierarchies. In 1850, for example, two Black men were admitted to Harvard Medical School with the stipulation that they would practice medicine only in Africa. Even with that racist condition, their admission led to complaints that the "intermixing" of the races would follow from *any* equalizing: ultimately, admission was rescinded.

The tension between the idea that learning is proper only for select men and the belief that a democracy requires an educated general citizenry intensified as justice movements and federal actions produced a more inclusive citizenship. In an early democratic move, the 1862 Morrill Act established coeducational state universities and land grant colleges that emphasized "practical" as well as liberal arts education. Gender informed the curriculum; for example, home economics was developed for women, while agricultural and mechanical studies were developed for men. Race also structured educational opportunity: "separate but equal" was the rule.

Throughout the 1800s, women's opportunities in formal education expanded. Female academies begun in the revolutionary era grew in the 1820s and 1830s. As more girls were formally educated, provisions for the higher levels of education were created. Women's education was constrained by gender ideology, however. Offering the same curriculum for women of all races as was offered at prestigious white male private schools was considered both desirable and risky. Some also feared

The 1875 graduating class of the Cherokee Young Ladies' Seminary, which was modeled after Mt. Holyoke College.

that "too much" learning would harm female reproductive systems: females thinking for themselves must be "unnatural."

The debate at both private and public institutions concerned whether to offer courses of study "appropriate" to females or to offer the same curriculum offered to white males. This was similar to the debate about the education of Black people: should it be "appropriate," "practical," or "the best"? By 1870, 30 percent of colleges were coeducational. The elite—private, expensive, white male—schools, however, tended instead to establish independently funded coordinate colleges for women: Harvard, Columbia, and Brown Universities followed that path.

Nevertheless, by the early 1900s, 70 percent of higher education institutions were coeducational, and about 30 percent of the total student body comprised females studying in diverse public and private institutions, including post–Civil War schools for Southern Black people, normal schools, and Catholic- and Protestant-affiliated mission schools. In the 1920s and 1930s, the Progressive education movement spawned Sarah Lawrence, Bennington, and Scripps Colleges for women, giving a few women the chance to benefit from education that emphasized student independence, experimentation, the arts, and creativity. At the same time, the junior college movement stressing vocational goals led to the establishment of two-year colleges for women. However, less than 4 percent of the college-age population was enrolled in higher education, which remained primarily dedicated to preparing men in agriculture and mechanical arts, teaching, or, for the privileged few, ministry, law, and medicine.

Although increasing numbers of women received formal education, colleges and universities enforced gender hierarchies through quotas. In 1892 women composed 24 percent of the student body at the University of Chicago; by 1902, the number was 52 percent. In 1901, at Stanford University, 102 males and 98 females graduated, with more women than men winning awards and honors. Although women's educational performance disproved old theories about education being "bad for females," universities feared that "good" education would be "feminized," or distorted. Across higher education, quotas restricted women's access. Under Stanford's quota system, three males were accepted for every female. Histories of higher education reveal other uses of quotas. For many years there were quotas for Jews. Jewish women faced an at least double barrier, gender and religion, as did white ethnic working-class women who were not only limited by gender and poverty but in some cases also by their Catholicism. Even when prestigious private men's universities opened doors to women, admissions quotas were again set (as at Yale in 1969).

During the first half of the twentieth century, economic upheavals and large-scale wars expanded women's education. After World War II, the G.I. Bill led to a rise in male enrollments at the cost of female students. By 1950 women, who had made up 41 percent of student bodies in 1940, comprised only 24 percent and did not regain prewar levels until the 1970s. In the early 1960s, women applicants still often had to be better qualified than men to be admitted. In addition, many colleges and universities restricted enrollment by married women and part-time students.

By the late 1960s and early 1970s, the federal government responded to organized pressure with antidiscrimination laws, with the student loan program, and with other forms of financial assistance for education at all levels. Among the most important governmental actions were congressional efforts to end gender tracking in vocational education and enactment of the landmark Title IX, a provision of the Education Act Amendments of 1972. Title IX requires all educational institutions that use federal funds to treat boys and girls, men and women, equally.

Curricular changes arose as a result of expanded educational opportunities. Girls and women, as well as men from excluded groups, demanded courses about their own heritages and issues. The fruits of informal educational traditions and of insurgent educational movements were enriched by renewed scholarship. Black studies began against often fierce opposition, and women's studies soon followed, creating new fields of knowledge, differing pedagogies, and safe spaces on hostile campuses. Once launched, critiques of the supposedly "best" curricula, along with new fields, were developed to counter old prejudices. On the elementary level, for example, 1930s readers featuring the white, suburban family of Dick, Jane, Baby Sally, Mom, Dad, Spot (the dog), and Puff (the cat) were, with some encouragement from Congress, discarded. New texts were created to represent differing groups (although sometimes superficially, and rarely inclusive of lesbians and gays), and the fruits of the new scholarship that drew on but also corrected and transformed many fields began to spread to all levels of education.

In 1966 Native Americans, who had long struggled against the schools that stole their children, saw, for example, the establishment under Native control of Rough Rock School on the Navajo reservation. There, Navajo children learned English as a second language, studied their traditions, and were encouraged to visit their homes frequently (boarding schools remain common because of the distances covered).

It became evident that a "benign neutrality" would not suffice to undo systems of knowledge and institutional practices premised on exclusion and cultural conformity. Executive Order 11375 expanded federal affirmative action, adding sex discrimination to race, color, religion, and national origin. Section 504 of the 1973 Rehabilitation Act, which mandated accessibility for people with disabilities, also encouraged curricular developments, such as disability studies, to undo exclusions and devaluations.

Additional tools for educational equity developed since the 1970s include sexual harassment and hate speech policies. Offensive, exploitive, and intimidating speech and acts are considered suspicious and actionable. The legal aspects and policy implications of recognizing the harm of many kinds of harassment remain murky and contested, but there is a growing body of public policy and law where once there was nothing but the silencing effects of denial, threat, and ridicule.

In the 1990s a backlash has developed, putting many of the important equity-supporting provisions in jeopardy. Affirmative action and special supports for people of color and some ethnic groups—such as scholarship funds, dual-language instruction, and classes designed for the children of migrant workers—have been found by a few state bodies and courts to be unacceptable. The Civil Rights Act of 1991, however, extended the right to sue for punitive damages in cases of intentional sex discrimination. The backlash is also reanimating student movements, and many educational institutions are strongly reaffirming their commitment to diversity as an educational as well as equity issue crucial to a democratic nation. Nevertheless, the increase in college enrollment of people of color in the 1970s slowed in the 1980s: only Asian Americans have steadily increased their gains (but not equally for each of the culturally distinct groups that make up Asian America). Both the number and proportion of Black students actually declined; the number of Latino students increased slightly, while remaining incommensurate with their growing proportion of the population. And while there are now supports for lesbians and gay men in education, homophobia persists.

Women's studies is flourishing, along with other fields that the new academy created in relation to justice movements in the past thirty years. It is estimated that there are more than thirty thousand women's studies courses across the country. Recent decades have also seen the establishment of women's caucuses in almost all of the professional academic associations. Some six hundred women's centers continue their work bridging scholarship and activism, although on some campuses, a rift between scholarship and activism exists. Continuing education programs now welcome returning women. Some women's colleges, such as Spelman, Mt. Holyoke, Bennett, Smith and Mills are thriving. Women are moving into virtually all fields, including academia, where they constitute about 30 percent of the professoriate and a comparable proportion of administrators, albeit at lower levels and salaries.

In the future, broad economic and social changes will continue to affect educational opportunities for all women. At the same time, education will remain a crucial precondition of change that benefits women.

• ELIZABETH KAMARCK MINNICH

SEE ALSO History and Historians; Mississippi Freedom Summer; Multiculturalism; Science and Gender; Standardized Testing; Teaching Profession; Title IX; Vocational Education Act (1917); Women's Colleges; Women's Educational Equity Act (WEEA); Women's Studies.

⚞ Eighteenth Amendment

SEE Constitution and Amendments; Prohibition and Temperance.

≋ Electoral Politics

U ntil Congress and state legislatures extended
suffrage to U.S. women through the Nineteenth Amendment in 1920, women had little involvement in electoral politics. The major
woman suffrage organizations adopted the tactic
of blaming whichever political party was currently
in power for women's lack of a vote. By intentionally shifting support to a party that was out of office and power, suffragists used an unconventional means of pressuring politicians, which may
have lengthened the time needed to gain the vote.

By contrast, some Native American nations
have always given women a formal role in their
governments. When some tribal governments
adopted an elective system of governance, a few,
including the Cherokee, guaranteed women the
right to vote.

When women's voting in federal elections was
imminent in the late 1910s and early 1920s, analyses of the political scene hypothesized that
women's votes would revolutionize politics, shifting the balance of power from entrenched urban
political machines to a more liberal and progressive politics. Journalists also anticipated that the
expanded electorate might replace male officeholders with women. However, by the end of the
1920s, like the dog in Sherlock Holmes whose failure to bark yields an important clue, the search to
explain why there was *no* bloc of women's votes
overwhelmed speculation about how women voters would change politics. By the 1950s and 1960s
social scientists had constructed an explanation of
women's insignificance to electoral politics both
as voters and candidates.

Part of their theory focused on differences in
the socialization of boys and girls toward politics.
Researchers found that elementary school girls
were less interested in politics than were boys.
This finding "explained" adult women's lower
rate of voting and their poorer performance on national surveys regarding political questions. Many

assumptions in this research were seriously
flawed. The researchers equated boys' preference
for war toys, such as guns, with political interest,
and attached significance to the greater appearance of political figures on the boys' most-ad-
mired Americans list (as contrasted with movie
actresses, who appeared on girls' lists). They ignored the strong same-sex attraction that children
have for role models. Yet, during the 1950s and
1960s women across all racial and socioeconomic
groups voted less, ran for political office less, and
demonstrated less substantive knowledge of politics than men.

The early socialization research was buttressed
by findings that married women typically held the
same political party preference and voted the
same way as did their husband. Political scientists
constructed a world in which girls from an early
age had little political interest compared with
boys. As women, they were thought to take political cues first from their fathers, then their husbands. The fact that few women ran for or were
elected to political office between 1920 and 1960
reinforced the perception that electoral politics
was a man's game.

Even in the 1950s women voters' party preferences differed from men's, particularly in presidential races. Female voters supported Dwight
Eisenhower by a 5- to 6-percentage point greater
margin than men in the 1952 and 1956 elections.
John Kennedy won many of the Democratic primaries in 1959 with the aid of significant female support when compared with rivals Hubert Humphrey and Lyndon Johnson. The early
polls showed that Kennedy's Republican opponent Richard Nixon was running better among
women. Kennedy responded by using his energetic mother and many sisters to spread his message to women. He also established the first
women's presidential campaign committee for a
major party. He won an extremely narrow victory
over Nixon in the presidential election. The Democratic presidents after Kennedy continued to
court support among women by appointing

women to political posts and by proposing and passing reforms that would target discrimination against women. The emergence and activism of the women's movement in the late 1960s heightened the political focus on women's concerns. Issues of legal equality and fair treatment in the workplace arose as national priorities.

Until Ronald Reagan's nomination as the Republican Party's presidential candidate in 1980, the major parties competed closely for women's votes. Although Democratic women officeholders outnumbered Republicans, the Republican Party had long advocated legal equality for women through its support for an equal rights amendment. When candidate and then president Reagan ushered in a "conservative revolution," he changed the positioning of the parties relative to women. Republicans removed support for an equal rights amendment from the party's platform in 1980, while supporting the repeal of *Roe* v. *Wade*, the Supreme Court opinion that legalized abortion. Women voted in greater numbers than men (59.4 percent versus 59.1 percent) for the first time in the 1980 election. Nine percent fewer women than men voted for Reagan. Since 1980 both a "turnout gap" and a "gender gap" in party preference have increased the importance of women's vote. For presidential elections, gender gaps of around 6 percent, with women favoring the Democratic candidate, are normal.

In response to the electoral gender gap, both the Democratic and Republican parties are renewing their efforts to recruit women candidates and to provide financial support for potentially strong contenders. A consistent nationwide picture emerges of more women, of all races and ethnicities, winning electoral office, with the greatest numbers at local levels and the fewest in the most powerful political offices.

Unlike the picture of the United States in the 1950s, when women were less interested or engaged in politics than men and shared their spouse's preferences, today the average woman is somewhat more active politically than her spouse

and far less likely to share his political preferences. In the 1990s the Republican and Democratic parties have been forced to acknowledge a reality in which well-educated, middle-class white men and women (particularly those under thirty) may share a marriage and a house but not party or candidate preferences. By contrast, African American couples are divided by a much smaller gap. The two parties stand at opposite sides of this split, with the Republican Party in danger of becoming the white men's party, while the Democrats strain to broaden their appeal beyond women and people of color. The gendering of politics takes place as women's participation increases in unprecedented numbers.

Joni Lovenduski and Pippa Norris, eds., *Gender and Party Politics* (Thousand Oaks, Calif.: Sage, 1993); Carol Mueller, ed., *The Politics of the Gender Gap* (Beverly Hills, Calif.: Sage, 1987).

• ANNE N. COSTAIN

SEE ALSO Gender Gap; Political Parties; Politicians.

≋ Emancipation Proclamation

SEE Constitution and Amendments.

≋ EMILY's List

EMILY's List ("Early Money Is Like Yeast") was created in 1985 as a donor network to elect pro-choice Democratic women to national office. Its founder and president, Ellen Malcolm, pursued the goal of making women candidates as competitive in fundraising as their male counterparts.

Since its inception EMILY's List has become the largest financial network for women candidates. In 1992 its members contributed $6.2 million to fifty-five candidates. Among those recommended were Senators Barbara Boxer, Dianne Feinstein, Patty Murray, Carol Moseley-Braun, and Barbara Mikulski. During each election cycle, network staff determine which women candidates meet the basic criteria for consideration, run well-organized campaigns, and have strong chances of victory. Candidates who fit the requirements are recommended for support to the 24,000 members of EMILY's List.

Members of EMILY's List pay $100 to join and then commit to contributing at least another $100 to a minimum of two candidates per election cycle. While members write checks directly to the campaigns of their chosen candidates, the money is channeled through EMILY's List—a practice known as bundling.

As of 1995 women held forty-eight seats in the U.S. House of Representatives and eight seats in the U.S. Senate, or 10 percent of the total seats. In contrast, in 1985 women held only 5 percent of congressional seats and almost all of them were in the House of Representatives. This doubling of representation is by no means attributable solely to the effects of EMILY's List; however, to say the network has had a significant impact would not be an overstatement. EMILY's List also has become the model for other networks for women candidates. During the 1992 election, for example, WISH List (Women in the Senate and House), which funds pro-choice Republican women, was created.

▪ SUE THOMAS

≋ Entrepreneurs

T oday women-owned businesses in the United States contribute $1.6 trillion to the economy and employ one out of five workers nationwide. Prior to twenty-five years ago, however, women-owned businesses were relatively rare and re-

ceived little support. Only in 1979 did the Small Business Administration begin to recognize women's businesses.

The success stories of early women business owners are therefore particularly inspiring. Katherine Mary Goddard, the only printer in Baltimore, printed the original Declaration of Independence in 1777. Benjamin Franklin later appointed her to be Baltimore's postmaster, making her the first woman to hold a federal position.

In 1905 Sarah Breedlove Walker, later known as Madame C. J. Walker, became the first female African American millionaire in the United States. A former washer woman, she developed a highly successful hair straightening product and her business eventually employed over three thousand people.

In 1951 Bette Nesmith Graham developed "Liquid Paper" in her blender. Failing to sell the formula to IBM, she began distributing it through her own business and in 1979 sold her company for $48 million.

The pace of women's enterprise increased significantly in the 1970s and 1980s—the result of women's increasing recognition that economic self-sufficiency is a critical part of self-determination. Muriel Siebert founded her own investment firm in 1967 and became the first woman member of the New York Stock Exchange. She went on to become a pioneer in discount brokerage, a marketing strategy that has redefined the investment industry.

In 1982 Patricia Gallup was only looking to start a business that would allow her to stay in the tiny New Hampshire town where she lived. Now, as chairman and CEO of PC Connection, Inc., she heads the nation's most highly regarded mail-order computer company, with 1995 sales estimated at more than $250 million.

Not all women entrepreneurs have had to form their own corporations to succeed. Linda Wachner engineered a buy-out of the clothing manufacturer Warnaco, and as CEO is now the only woman to head a Fortune 500 company. And

Katharine Graham will be remembered not only for her business acumen but also for her role in U.S. history. As publisher of the *Washington Post,* in the early 1970s she took on a story other newspapers wouldn't touch, and went on to expose Richard Nixon's crooked presidency.

• SOPHIA COLLIER

SEE ALSO Businesswomen and Corporations.

≋ Environmentalism

Historians have dedicated only a few pages in the annals of the U.S. ecology movement to the significance of women. This is not for lack of women's participation or significant legacy but rather because many women conservationists of the nineteenth and early twentieth centuries lived and worked as assistants to and in the shadow of "great" men. Moreover, male chroniclers, accustomed to seeking a singular, heroic male as "father" of a new trend in environmentalism, have taken little note of women's environmental work. Thus, the small number of women cited in mainstream texts on environmental history belies both the large number of women who are active in the environmental movement and also the incommensurate impact of those few whose contributions have been recorded.

Women currently constitute some 60 to 80 percent of the mainstream environmental organizations and about 80 percent of grassroots environmental and animal rights groups in the United States. An international survey of public attitude about the environment, commissioned by the United Nations Environment Programme, found that women across the world, in industrial and third-world countries alike, express more concern over the state of the environment than do men. They also favor more stringent environmental laws and more public spending for environmental

protection than do men. Thus, by membership, by degree of activism, and by their political stands, women are the major social force in the environmental movement.

What of women's role as thinkers and strategists? There are none more responsible for the scope and force of the modern U.S. environmental movement than three women: a turn-of-the-century chemist, Ellen Swallow; a midcentury biologist and nature writer, Rachel Carson; and a late-twentieth-century blue-collar housewife and mother-turned-environmental-activist, Lois Gibbs. The future of U.S. environmentalism is presently being forged by the emerging and dynamic environmental justice movement, a broad network of community activists and scholars with roots both in the civil rights movement and the Native American tradition of holism. The majority of this movement are women of color.

Ellen Swallow was the first woman student (graduated in 1873) and instructor (from 1876 to 1911) at the Massachusetts Institute of Technology (MIT), where she pioneered the world's first environmental science curriculum that integrated the chemistry of soil, air, and water, as well as bacteriology and public health, with the scientific study of the home environment. She initiated standard setting for pure food, public drinking water supplies, and wastewater treatment. As specialization overtook science, Swallow and her interdisciplinary curriculum were dismissed from MIT. Her students emerged as "fathers" of their respective disciplines, while Swallow was tokenized as "mother of home economics."

Rachel Carson published *Silent Spring* in 1962, a book that swept through the U.S. public and government, widening and deepening the stream of modern environmental consciousness. By 1970 the federal government created its first comprehensive environmental agency, the Environmental Protection Agency (EPA). In the same decade, Congress passed a rapid succession of environmental legislation, including the Clean Water Act; the Safe Drinking Water Act; and laws governing hazardous waste, pesticides, toxic substances, and air pollution. Carson raised the specter of cancer and genetic mutations resulting from exposure to pesticides; she was challenged by industry but never refuted. Her prescience is further affirmed in the recent studies that link breast cancer in women and reproductive toxicity in animals with exposure to chlorinated hydrocarbons and estrogen-mimicking compounds.

In 1978 Lois Gibbs, at twenty-six, was elected president of the Love Canal Homeowners' Association. With other housewives and mothers, she organized a successful protest to have families relocated from a neighborhood that had been built adjacent to a mile-long trench filled with industrial waste. High school educated women devised and conducted a health survey of their neighborhood, held EPA officials hostage, conducted press conferences, and learned the fundamentals of environmental science and toxicology. Their action launched modern grassroots environmentalism based on "popular science," citizen protest, and making links between health and environmental pollution.

In the mid-1980s an African American community in Warren County, North Carolina, protested EPA's siting of a national landfill for the disposal of polychlorinated biphenyls (PCBs) in their community. This event sparked a sequence of studies of and protests against the deliberate siting of waste facilities and "dirty" industry in poor communities of color, identifying the practice as *environmental racism*. This movement for environmental justice has challenged government and mainstream environmental organizations to include people of color in their organizations and to integrate issues of race and economic justice into their analyses and decision making. Further, community-based organizations, such as the West Harlem Environmental Action Coalition, founded by Vernice Miller and Peggy Shepard, and the People for Community Recovery in Chicago, founded by Hazel and Cheryl Johnson, organized in their neighborhoods to defeat

planned incinerators, to stop "midnight dumping," to attract "clean" industry, and to turn vacant lots into community gardens.

The common ground shared by the diverse women who have shaped and are shaping U.S. environmental history is precisely a new understanding of environment, which dominant white male perspectives have not offered. Environment is not solely or primarily Thoreau's and John Muir's wilderness without people, or Gifford Pinchot's utility for human use, or the EPA's aggregate of air, water, and soil. Rather, environment is, foremost, the *lived* reality of a community: the nexus of housing, neighborhood, safety, social well-being, and the quality of the community's air, water, soil, wildlife, and health.

Robert Bullard, *Dumping in Dixie: Race, Class and Environmental Quality* (Boulder, Colo.: Westview Press, 1992); H. Patricia Hynes, *The Recurring Silent Spring* (New York: Teachers College, 1989); Joni Seager, *Earth Follies: Coming to Feminist Terms with the Global Environmental Crisis* (New York: Routledge, 1993).

▪ H. PATRICIA HYNES

SEE ALSO Feminism and Feminisms: Ecofeminism; Women's Environment and Development Organization.

≋ Equal Credit Opportunity Act

Before passage of the Equal Credit Opportunity Act (ECOA) in October 1974, most women had difficulty obtaining credit without a male cosigner. In the 1960s, as women increasingly entered the work force, they demanded individual access to consumer credit. The 1968 Consumer Credit Protection Act paved the way for ECOA by providing consumers access to their credit reports and by requiring lenders to reveal actual interest rates.

As late as 1968, women still were denied credit access. In 1972 the National Commission on Consumer Credit held hearings. At Congresswoman Bella Abzug's (D., N.Y.) insistence, that commission included testimony about the need for women's credit access but did not recommend federal action, and none was taken.

As a Senate Fellow in 1973 serving Senator Bill Brock (R., Tenn.), this author set out to create a legislative environment to introduce and pass ECOA. With Senator Brock as chief sponsor, the act passed the Senate in July 1973 and went to the House. The act became law in October 1974; it prohibited discrimination in credit access on the basis of sex or marital status, and later was amended to include race, religion, national origin, or age.

Statistics show that enormous changes resulted from ECOA. Until 1970 women's mortgage activity wasn't tracked; now women are a major force in the home-buying market. In 1972 women-owned businesses constituted 4.6 percent of all small businesses. Now that number is nearing 40 percent. Of those, 75 percent are started with women's personal credit. The next step is to ensure women adequate access to capital so that they won't have to rely solely on credit cards to underwrite their entrepreneurial dreams.

• EMILY CARD

SEE ALSO Banking and Credit.

≋ Equal Employment Opportunity Commission (EEOC)

The EEOC was established to enforce the 1964 Civil Rights Act's Title VII prohibitions against discrimination, including sex discrimination, in employment. Its capacity and commitment, however, have varied over time amid changing political contexts.

The EEOC originally was authorized to investigate and resolve individual complaints of employment discrimination. In 1972 Congress authorized the EEOC to initiate lawsuits against employers and extended the jurisdiction of the EEOC to federal, state, county, and municipal workplaces, where disproportionate numbers of African American as well as white women worked.

The first EEOC commissioners did not regard equality of women's employment opportunity as their mandate. The commission declined to attack protective labor laws and sex-segregated employment advertising. The National Organization for Women was founded partly because of the outraged response to EEOC laxity. The pressure of activists, including complaints filed by women working in the airline and garment industries, forced EEOC policy changes.

Under the leadership of Eleanor Holmes Norton during the Carter years, the EEOC virtually eliminated its backlog of sex-discrimination cases by encouraging settlements. It also began to undertake legal actions against large-scale patterns of discrimination, to explore the relationship between wage discrimination and job segregation, and to examine the doctrine of comparable worth. In 1980 the EEOC issued regulations defining sexual harassment as illegal.

Following President Ronald Reagan's appointment of Clarence Thomas as EEOC chair and Michael Connolly as general counsel in 1982, the agency reduced its rate of litigation, abandoning class-action suits and pattern and practice cases. Many areas of law that were of interest to women—such as sexual harassment, comparable worth, and equal pay—became low priorities. Following Anita Hill's widely publicized 1991 charges against Clarence Thomas, sexual harassment complaints filed with the EEOC increased steeply. Passage of the 1991 Civil Rights Act also increased the visibility of the agency. In October 1994 the Clinton administration appointed Gilbert Casellas as the commission's chair. He initiated an ambitious campaign to revitalize the agency, which nonetheless continues to face an enormous backlog of cases and severe budgetary constraints.

■ PEGGY KAHN

SEE ALSO Civil Rights Act of 1964; Title VII.

≋ Equality and Difference

Do men and women naturally differ—not just biologically but in terms of character, cognition, temperament, and moral sensibility? Should law account for presumed gender differences, establishing different rights, responsibilities, and entitlements for men and women? Should women be drafted? Should men have equal claims to custody of young children? Feminists have long been divided about these fundamental questions of gender and law. The drive for equal rights, which focuses on what the sexes share—intelligence and a capacity for self-determination—has always been countered by a drive for special protections, which focuses on how the sexes differ. Those who favor protective laws stress the emotional strengths and physical weaknesses presumed to be visited upon women by motherhood.

A preoccupation with sex and gender differences and the demands of motherhood underlay one of the most important and problematic turn-of-the-century Progressive reforms for women, namely, protective labor laws. Maximum-hour laws and laws prohibiting women from night work or manual labor helped alleviate some hardships for wage-earning women, especially mothers who bore the double burden of paid work and child care. The labor laws also established a precedent for government regulation of the marketplace aimed at protecting the health and safety of male and female workers and mandating a minimum wage. But these benefits came at the cost of sex-typing jobs, excluding women from higher-paying

occupations considered more suitable for men and maintaining the dual labor market. The benefits of protective labor laws were also distributed unequally among women, serving primarily industrial and sales workers and effectively excluding African Americans (who were relegated to agriculture and domestic service) as well as white domestic workers. Focusing on how women differed from men, protectionism failed to acknowledge how women differed from one another.

Traditional labor protections for women were invalidated by Title VII of the 1964 Civil Rights Act and Supreme Court decisions applying Fourteenth Amendment guarantees of equal protection in instances of sex discrimination. But by the 1980s, having achieved a good measure of legal equality, feminists began confronting practical barriers to actual equality—notably motherhood and traditional divisions of labor within the home. At the same time, feminism's focus on female autonomy and women's ability to perform men's jobs gave way to a resurgent belief in women's need for connectedness and the emotional wisdom implicit in their "different" voice. Some feminists argued that applying the same rules to male and female workers universalized male models of behavior and effectively penalized motherhood. Feminists argued about the benefits of "mommy tracking" and the preferential treatment of pregnant workers.

The conflict for contemporary feminists over equality and protectionism in the workplace is exemplified in the 1987 case *California Federal Savings and Loan Association v. Guerra*, which involved a state law extending special benefits to pregnant women. California law provided four months' disability leave and guaranteed job reinstatement to pregnant female workers. Male workers disabled by prostate surgery enjoyed no comparable benefits. Feminists were sorely divided by this case. Advocates of the California law argued that it protected pregnant women from discrimination in the workplace. Feminist opponents of the law argued that it harked back to turn-of-the-century protective legislation that perpetuated notions of women's weakness and a sex-segregated job market. They did not argue that the law should be invalidated (as did the Reagan administration) but they did argue that its benefits should be extended to male workers as well.

The Supreme Court upheld the law, without requiring its extension to men. Still, the Court managed to satisfy feminists on both sides of the debate—a rare achievement. Justice Thurgood Marshall likened the California law to affirmative action, suggesting that it was not based on "archaic or stereotypical" beliefs in women's weaknesses presumed to be mandated by nature but on the historic discrimination against wage-earning mothers attributable to culture.

Can women's sexual vulnerability be blamed on culture as well? Or does nature demand that criminal laws establish different standards of sexual behavior for men and women as well as different rules in the workplace? The Supreme Court confronted this question in a 1981 case, *Michael M. v. Superior Court*, which challenged California's statutory rape law for discriminating against men. The law criminalized sexual intercourse between males and underage females, imposing sanctions only on the male. (No comparable sanctions were imposed on women or men who had sex with underage males.) *Michael M.* involved the criminal prosecution of a seventeen-year-old boy for engaging in apparently consensual intercourse with a sixteen-year-old girl.

The state of California argued that its statutory rape law was intended to prevent teenage pregnancy, and the Supreme Court accepted this rationale and upheld the law. It reasoned that the risk of pregnancy serves as a natural "sanction" for sexually active females (presuming that women ought to be punished for engaging in sex outside of marriage); statutory rape laws, imposing criminal sanctions on men, simply "'equalizes' the deterrents."

But, as the dissent in this case observed, statu-tory rape laws were not conceived as teenage pregnancy prevention measures; they were conceived in deference to double standards of sexuality, which the Court was perpetuating by upholding double standards of criminal liability for men and women. If the Cal Fed case illustrated the benefits of protectionism, *Michael M.* dramatized its perils.

• WENDY KAMINER

SEE ALSO Legal Status; *Muller* v. *Oregon*; Protective Labor Legislation; Title VII.

≋ Equal Pay Act

The United States passed the Equal Pay Act in 1963. The campaign to enact this principle, however, began in the late nineteenth century as a demand of male trade unionists to prevent wage cutting by women in unregulated labor markets and was supported by several federal agencies during the First World War. The principle received its most important endorsement during the Second World War when the National War Labor Board, under General Order No. 16, embraced as its national policy equal pay for "comparable quality and quantity of work." Hoping to build on this wartime precedent, the U.S. Women's Bureau campaigned unsuccessfully for equal pay legislation throughout the postwar period. However, twelve states enacted equal pay laws, and 17 percent of collective bargaining agreements included equal pay clauses by the mid-1950s.

During the Kennedy administration, the Women's Bureau resumed its campaign. To win congressional approval of the equal pay principle, supporters substituted "equal work" for "comparable work" in a provision added to the Fair Labor Standards Act of 1937. These compromises significantly limited the reach of the law. The equal pay guarantee reached only the wage and salary occupations covered by the FLSA. Jobs held primarily by women, and especially women of color, were thus excluded. Moreover, the language of equal pay for equal work has proved too narrow to address the problem of wage inequity in an economy characterized by a high level of occupational segregation by both sex and race. The absence of men from many workplaces has made it difficult to undertake the comparison required to prove pay discrimination. Feminists have developed the ideas of "comparable worth" or "pay equity" to overcome these limitations of the Equal Pay Act.

■ HELENE SILVERBERG

SEE ALSO Comparable Worth.

≡ Equal Rights Amendment (ERA)

When it was first introduced into Congress in 1923, the Equal Rights Amendment to the U.S. Constitution read: "Men and women shall have equal rights throughout the United States and every place subject to its jurisdiction." The wording of the ERA when passed by Congress and sent to the states for ratification almost fifty years later in 1972 was similar: "Equality of rights under the law shall not be denied or abridged by the United States or by any State on account of sex." Thus for more than fifty years the key concept behind the ERA was the notion that women were individuals whose rights should be equal to those of men and who should be treated equally by public agencies.

The group most responsible for the development of the ERA in 1921 and for its steady advance during the half century before 1972 was the National Woman's Party (NWP). Formed by Alice Paul and a small coterie of her supporters as a vehicle for advancing women's rights beyond the achievement of suffrage, the NWP developed the ERA to draw attention to and eliminate the many

inequalities that deprived women of equal citizenship, such as the exclusion of women from juries and from political office.

The ERA came close to being adopted as a constitutional amendment. In 1972 Congress sent it to the states for ratification and it received an overwhelmingly positive vote: 354 to 23 in the House and 84 to 8 in the Senate. Ratification required the endorsement of at least thirty-eight states by June 30, 1982. Within one year thirty states had approved the ERA; by 1977 supporting states numbered thirty-five. Opposing states lay primarily in the South and the Rocky Mountain regions. The only non-ERA state outside these regions, Illinois, became the seat of a titanic struggle in 1981–82; but even if Illinois had ratified the ERA, passage in another state seemed unlikely at the time. By 1980 the tide had turned against the amendment.

Why did such a seemingly innocuous constitutional amendment fail? One answer may lie with the nature of U.S. political culture itself and the implications of gender- and class-related issues. It took fifty years from 1921 to 1972 for the ERA to be accepted by most politically active women—those who, one might think, would have been its most likely supporters. Their opposition, which ranged from fervent to ferocious during the 1920s and 1930s, arose from many political women's commitment to gender-specific strategies to achieve social justice. Between 1923 and the mid-1960s, women activists on the left of the political spectrum viewed the ERA as antilabor because it benefited professional women at the expense of wage-earning women, and because it called into question three decades of hard-won social and labor legislation for women. By 1972 opponents of the ERA, on the right of the spectrum, viewed the ERA as pro-labor because it would benefit wage-earning women and because it conflicted with the New Right's strategy of limiting governmental intervention regarding issues of social justice. Thus, when women activists on the left unified behind the amendment, activists on the right organized against it.

Wage-earning women were central to this contextual shift in the history of the ERA. The campaign for its passage lasted long enough to reflect the profound changes that occurred in women's labor-force participation in the twentieth century. In 1921 the ERA was overwhelmingly opposed by trade union women, but by 1972 most trade union women supported it. During that half century, the conditions of women's work, public-policy needs related to women's work, and the population of women wage-earners themselves changed dramatically. For example, Title VII of the 1964 Civil Rights Act provided new forms of protection against labor-force discrimination and supplanted older protective laws. In the context of women's wage earning, then, the ERA became the friend rather than the enemy of working women.

In 1921 the great majority of wage-earning women were young and poorly paid. Between 1890 and 1920, politically active middle-class women became deeply committed to the passage of statutes designed to aid young and poorly paid women workers, such as state-imposed maximum hours and minimum wage laws. These laws were female-specific because laissez-faire attitudes on the part of U.S. courts opposed such legislation for men. However, laws for women were part of a general strategy by Progressive women reformers to extend such legislation to men—a strategy that finally succeeded with the passage of the Fair Labor Standards Act in 1938. By 1970 the average age of women workers was similar to that of the female population as a whole, and the average wages of year-round full-time employed women could for the first time support a woman and two children. Women workers no longer needed protective legislation; they needed equal opportunity.

This shift helps to explain why the ERA's chief opponents changed from women on the political left to women on the political right. Both in 1921 and in 1981, opponents of the ERA were better organized than its proponents.

Kept alive between 1921 and 1972 by organizations of professional women, especially the National Federation of Business and Professional Women's Clubs, as well as by the National Woman's Party, the campaign for the ERA was revitalized by the women's movement in the late 1960s. With the founding of the National Organization for Women (NOW) in 1966, the campaign torch was passed on. Opposition to the ERA by left-leaning women activists was swept away by the renewed wave of feminism. Yet by 1980 the New Right had targeted the ERA. Phyllis Schlafly, author of books about the communist conspiracy and the Russian threat in the 1960s, led the assault. She and others raised new questions about the potentially negative effects of the ERA and successfully misrepresented issues surrounding the ERA's purpose. Would women be subject to the draft? Would they lose child care or alimony support upon divorce? Would husbands no longer be required to support their families? Leaders of NOW and other pro-ERA organizations were too loosely organized to respond effectively to these fears. Moreover, the extension of the Fourteenth Amendment to women by the U.S. Supreme Court during the 1970s obscured the amendment's positive potential.

Ultimately, however, the ERA's passage was blocked by a coalition of right-wing Christian fundamentalists. Although white, middle-class Protestants dominated the pro-ERA leadership, polls in the early 1980s showed substantial grassroots support for the ERA among Catholics, African Americans and working-class people. Schlafly's forces mobilized Christian fundamentalists to counter this extensive support.

Hindsight shows that the ERA would not have been the panacea that its advocates often envisioned, but it might have served as a helpful focal point for legal and social discussions about how best to promote women's full and equal citizenship.

Joan Hoff-Wilson, ed., *Rights of Passage: The Past and Future of the ERA* (Bloomington: Indiana University Press, 1986); Jane J. Mansbridge, *Why We Lost the ERA* (Chicago: University of Chicago Press, 1986); Donald G.

Mathews and Jane S. De Hart, *Sex, Gender, and the Politics of ERA: A State and the Nation* (New York: Oxford University Press, 1991).

▪ KATHRYN KISH SKLAR

SEE ALSO Legal Status; National Woman's Party.

≋ Etiquette

SEE Manners and Etiquette.

≋ Eugenics

Eugenics was formulated in 1883 by British statistician Francis Galton. Entranced with the new science of heredity, Galton—a distant cousin of Charles Darwin—believed that eugenics could augment the evolutionary process of natural selection. Galton believed that, like the horse-breeder's practice of selectively mating specimens with desired traits, eugenics—selective breeding based on scientific principles of heredity—would improve the biological quality of humanity and thus hasten so-called "racial progress."

In the context of increasing ethnic diversity and class struggle that shook the United States in the early twentieth century, eugenics appealed to a variety of white social reformers. Many Progressives saw it as a means for enhancing human nature through social reform. Yet eugenics essentially gave scientific legitimacy to traditional elitism and racism in the United States. It offered two main strategies for achieving racial progress: positive eugenics—encouraging reproduction among the fit—and negative eugenics—discouraging reproduction among the unfit. Fitness was demonstrated by social status; poverty was thought to indicate biological inferiority. Likewise, eugenicists

claimed that racial differences were biologically determined. Their taxonomies of the races placed Northern and Western Europeans at the apex of human evolution, because only they carried both the instinct for democracy and the full capacity for reason.

Although African American women rejected eugenics and avoided using its rhetoric, white women used it to argue for expanding women's rights. If the political character of a nation depended upon the biological character of its people, then the United States was dependent on women, who bore and reared the next generation of citizens. Women were, therefore, as important to U.S. politics as were men, and they deserved the same rights. White feminists across the political spectrum, including Emma Goldman and Charlotte Perkins Gilman, appropriated eugenics to their causes. But eugenics was particularly important to the birth-control movement: it provided a scientific language with which to discuss the otherwise vulgar topic of sexual reproduction. Moreover, it bolstered the argument for women's right to contraception. Only women who could control their fertility would be able to produce high-quality children. Despite this argument, fear of unrestrained growth among the poor and ethnic masses dominated U.S. population policy.

Anxious about the declining birthrates of "old-stock Americans," eugenicists exhorted white, middle-class women to stop committing "race suicide" and bear more "naturally superior" children. Concurrently, eugenicists sponsored laws to restrict immigration and to require the compulsory sterilization of insane, criminal, and mentally retarded persons. In 1921 and 1924 Congress restricted immigration on the basis of ethnic origin. Compulsory sterilization received approval from the Supreme Court in its 1927 *Buck* v. *Bell* decision. Contraception and abortion were still illegal when the Court ruled that in order to protect public health against the spread of the hereditary taint of feeblemindedness, a state could sterilize a woman against her will. In effect, the Court gave the government the right to determine which women were competent to become mothers. Although Carrie Buck, the woman in the case, was poor and white, the Court's decision implicitly endorsed elitism *and* racism. It sanctioned the eugenic logic behind sterilization laws that defined fitness by class and race as much as by intelligence or character. Eugenics was eventually discredited by disclosures about Nazi racial policies, but U.S. immigration restrictions and compulsory sterilization laws were not eased until the mid-1960s.

▪ CAROLE R. McCANN

SEE ALSO Birth Control; Sterilization and Sterilization Abuse.

≋ Evangelicalism

A frican American and European American women have been involved in U.S. evangelical movements since the revivals of the 1790s through 1840s. Initially, clergy selected women to bring the gospel into families and communities. Women soon worked to mold evangelicalism to serve women's needs nationally and globally. Evangelical men divided over women's proper place in the movement, and the issue is still unresolved in the 1990s.

Women had first participated as missionary wives, but by the 1830s single European American and African American women were assistant missionaries in Asia, Africa, Hawaii, and the U.S. West. By 1868 women missionaries began working among urban poor and on reservations, where Native American women also served as lay missionaries.

Women also publicly evangelized, although they were not licensed to do so until after the Civil War. Jarena Lee, of the First African Methodist Episcopal Church, preached throughout the 1830s and 1840s; by the 1850s, Methodist women also preached. Most churches did not ordain women but did support women using their skills to spread the gospel, and by the late nineteenth century, women were lay leaders. Women-only organizations created networks among evangelical women and gave them experience in planning and administration. Some of these women moved on to work toward social reform in the 1890s, as an extension of their evangelical mission.

When evangelicalism moved toward fundamentalism in the early twentieth century, a decrease in society's openness to women's public ministry occurred although women's foreign mission efforts remained strong until the 1930s. Male conservative evangelical leaders increasingly believed women's ministry challenged scriptural order. Institutions that previously accepted women soon excluded them and the percentage of women pastors declined from 20 to 30 percent in the 1920s to 3 to 6 percent by 1950. By the 1960s some neoevangelical women contested these limitations and espoused a new vision of women's roles, based on social justice and equality of the sexes. The issue of women's ordination and ministry, however, remains controversial.

▪ CAROL GREEN-DEVENS

SEE ALSO Missionaries; Protestantism; Religion.

≋ Explorers

T he exploration of the continents that came to be called the Americas was largely the work of European men driven by a lust for wealth and knowledge. They were intrigued with the mysterious and unknown that was the legacy of Greek skepticism. The native peoples of those continents were farmers and hunters who defined their homelands quite clearly by both tradition and use.

They valued a sense of place and settledness. Their traditions often included stories of the dangers that people encountered when they ventured into unknown places. When Europeans encountered the native people of new worlds, these ideas and perceptions clashed, resulting in misunderstanding and, often, conflict.

Women played important roles in many of these early encounters. Men needed guides and translators, functions that women could serve. Marriage or alliances with native women created relationships that smoothed the way for white men. Dona Marina, also known as La Malinche, was crucial in Hernando Cortez's conquest of the Aztec empire. Although her actions helped the Spanish, she had no vested interest in preserving native culture from Spanish invasion. She had been sold as a slave by her own people to another tribe, who in turn had given her to Cortez on his march to the Aztec capital of Tenochtitlán. She warned him of a plot against him. She spoke Nahautl and a dialect of Mayan and could translate through a Mayan-speaking Spaniard in Cortez's party. She bore Cortez a son, thus setting a precedent for the mixing of Indian and Spanish blood and the evolution of new cultures.

When Juan de Oñate and his forces marched to the Southwest to establish a Spanish capital at Santa Fe, they were accompanied by Dona Inés, a woman who had been kidnapped from the Panthamba Pueblo by Gaspar Castaño de Sosa during an expedition into New Mexico in 1590. When Oñate obtained permission to colonize the area, he demanded that she accompany him.

In the Southeast in 1541 Hernando de Soto's party was greeted in northern Georgia by the "Lady of Cofitachequi," a young woman who had the trappings of privilege and who gave de Soto her own string of pearls as a sign of good will. The Spaniards, however, met with active resistance in later encounters with native villagers.

In the first recorded encounter with native people along the coast of California in June 1579, Sir Francis Drake reported that men, women, and children appeared with gifts of feathers, and that the women wailed loudly and gashed their faces and bodies with their fingernails in some ritual that the English never understood. Later the women appeared with baskets of food as gifts.

When Jacques Cartier's ships were frozen fast in the ice of the St. Lawrence River in February of 1536, he and his men suffered dreadfully from scurvy. They were rapidly cured when the chieftain Domagaya sent two women with Cartier to gather the branches of a tree (arborvitae) whose juice and bark he told them to drink and rub on their bodies. Before Cartier returned to France in the spring, he kidnapped another chief, his two sons, and two of his followers. He took them, along with two young girls who had been given to him as gifts, to demonstrate his accomplishment to the French king. All the captives died in Europe.

John Smith and his followers were able to establish their settlement at Jamestown because Pocahontas, daughter of Powhatan, the chief of the local Indian confederacy, saved Smith's life. She did it in the presence of her father and her older female relatives in order to adopt him, thereby asserting a right exercised by female lineages of tribes on the East Coast to make war captives members of their tribes.

The Lewis and Clark expedition benefited from the knowledge of Sacagawea, the Shoshone wife of a Frenchman who had bought her from the Mintarees before he joined the expedition in Montana in 1805. She gave birth to a son and carried him with her on the expedition. She did not lead the expedition but rather recognized certain landmarks in the Bitterroot mountains and told what lay ahead. She interpreted in encounters with Shoshone bands, one of whose leaders was her brother Cameahwait, who gave the expedition horses and led them part of the way over the mountains to the west. She did not stay with her tribe since most of her relatives were dead. Her presence in the expedition reassured the tribes they met that their intent was peaceful, since Indian tribes did not usually take women on war parties.

If European exploration of the Western Hemisphere was a peculiarly male preoccupation, native women played active roles as mediators as the explorers entered their lands.

Ella E. Clark and Margot Edmonds, *Sacagawea of the Lewis and Clark Expedition* (Berkeley: University of California Press, 1979); Ramon A. Gutierrez, *When Jesus Came, the Corn Mothers Went Away: Marriage, Sexuality, and Power in New Mexico, 1550–1846* (Stanford: Stanford University Press, 1991); Rachel Phillips, "Marina/Malinche: Masks and Shadows," in *Women in Hispanic Literature: Icons and Fallen Idols*, edited by Beth Miller, 97–114. (Berkeley: University of California Press, 1983).

▪ CLARA SUE KIDWELL

SEE ALSO Colonial Period.

≋ Fair Employment Practices Committee

The Fair Employment Practices Committee (FEPC) was established by President Franklin D. Roosevelt on June 25, 1941, to investigate discrimination in the national defense program on the basis of race, creed, color, and national origin. The exclusion of sex from the executive order, though it had been included in the federal government's antidiscrimination statement the previous year, helped to establish the pattern of viewing race and sex as competing categories. Despite the failure to include the issue of sex, however, approximately 30 percent of FEPC complaints were filed by women. In 1945 a hostile Congress dominated by southern Democrats terminated the committee's funding and it went out of existence the following year. During the Truman administration, liberal Democratic members of Congress pursued a vigorous but unsuccessful campaign for national fair employment practices legislation. Eight states established fair employment practices committees by 1950, though none of them covered discrimination on the basis of sex.

During the Kennedy administration liberal members of Congress resumed the campaign for what was now called equal employment opportunity legislation. In 1962 Representative James Roosevelt (D., Calif.), son of Franklin and Eleanor, introduced a pioneering comprehensive bill to prohibit discrimination in employment on the basis of sex, race, religion, and national origin. But the Departments of Justice and Labor, as well as the NAACP, opposed the inclusion of women because they did not consider discrimination on the basis of sex to be as important. They also believed it would make passage and enforcement more difficult. The provision was omitted by the House Committee on Education and Labor. The Fair Employment principles were revived and extended to include sex in Title VII of the 1964 Civil Rights Act. The Equal Employment Opportunity Commission was established in 1964 to enforce Title VII and remains the most important federal agency in the area of equal employment opportunity.

▪ HELENE SILVERBERG

SEE ALSO Civil Rights Act of 1964; Equal Employment Opportunity Commission (EEOC); Title VII.

≋ Fair Labor Standards Act

After decades of struggle by women reformers, New Dealers enacted enduring national minimum wage and maximum hours regulations in the Fair Labor Standards Act of 1938 (FLSA). Previously the courts had opposed national labor standards, and individual states achieved reform only in the guise of "protective" labor laws for women. The constitutional revolution of the New Deal allowed policymakers to base wage and hours legislation on the seemingly gender-neutral commerce clause, newly interpreted to permit

Congress to regulate the economy quite broadly. The potential scope of the FLSA was narrowed severely, however, as the Roosevelt administration tried to appease the Supreme Court and the factions of the New Deal Democratic Party, including male-dominated organized labor and southern planters.

Women workers in the garment and textile trades composed a large share of the million or so who the Department of Labor estimated would gain higher wages under the FLSA in its early years. While equal portions of the male and female work forces were exempt from the FLSA, excluded women were twice as likely as men to earn wages below minimum standards. Occupational segregation kept women in low-paying positions in service, retail, and clerical work, sectors largely circumvented by the FLSA. At least nine-tenths of Black women were excluded from coverage through the exemption of domestic and agricultural workers. Similarly, Latinas were denied coverage of the law through the omission of canneries and food processing plants, as well as agriculture.

Congress later amended FLSA to include broader categories of workers, though not until 1966 were agricultural workers included; most retail and service workers did not gain coverage until 1974. In 1993 women workers still figured disproportionately among those earning at or below the prevailing hourly minimum wage of $4.25.

■ SUZANNE B. METTLER

SEE ALSO Industrial Homework; New Deal; Protective Labor Legislation.

≋ **Families**

"**F**amily" . . . "families" . . . "the family." These minor twists of language open issues basic to this area of history. No one has come up with a definition that can adequately grasp this elusive subject; indeed, the word "family" did not even enter the English language until the fifteenth century, and then it was used to denote a household with servants. Today, family is most often used to refer to a particular set of people related by blood or marriage. But just who counts as family varies widely and may not be limited by ties of marriage, biology, or adoption. Other definitions emphasize sentiments of love and activities of caregiving, especially across generations. But families may be sites of violence and neglect, while nurturing, including the care of children, also takes place in other contexts. Finally, the word "family" evokes images of households, of people living together and pooling resources. But those who call one another family do not always live in the same household or share material goods. And members of some households do not pool resources.

Whether focusing on kinship, sentiments, or households, most scholars agree that throughout U.S. history, family arrangements have always been diverse and changing. The plural word, "families," suggests this variety, whereas the widely used, monolithic terminology, "the family," incorrectly implies that there is one natural form—a fixed, bounded unit of father, mother, and children. This moralizing ideology persists, but there is ample evidence that families are social, not biological, groupings and that their composition, size, boundaries, sentiments, and material activities vary by culture and change along with economic and social conditions.

Such variation was sharply evident in the seventeenth-century United States. Native American cultures organized kinship and residence in a variety of ways. All had marriage rituals and parental ties to children, but they did not give marriage primary significance, and nuclear families were not set apart from larger kinship and household groups. Among the Iroquois, eight to ten conjugal families lived together in longhouses, and older women organized the growth and distribution of corn and exercised strong influence over the all-male tribal council. There was no private ownership of land or resources, no distinction between "domestic" and "public."

European settlers established families based on private property, which reproduced social-class hierarchies. Although more bounded than those of Native Americans, early colonial families were also enmeshed in larger communities; village and church officials governed many activities, including sexual conduct and the behavior of disobedient children. Households were primary sites of economic activity, social welfare, education, and religious instruction. While strongly patriarchal, households varied in size and composition. Some consisted of a married couple and their children. Some included servants, who did not have separate family households, and children as young as seven who were "sent out" by their own families to learn a trade or to perform housework in another home. Because death and remarriage rates were high, many households contained blended families, with children from previous marriages.

With the spread of slavery in the eighteenth and nineteenth centuries, the range of families became even more complex. Slave traders brought Africans to the United States as commodities and deliberately severed the Africans' family ties to prevent revolt. Enslaved parents often were compelled to live separately from each other, and spouses and children were sold to other, sometimes geographically distant, owners. Although they could not legally marry, slaves created their own marriage rituals and actively worked to develop networks of kin, some not related by blood or marriage but nonetheless regarding one another as family. In patterns that have continued to the present, African Americans relied upon broad, women-centered kinship networks and a more collective approach to child rearing to sustain a sense of human dignity and to survive in harsh circumstances.

During the nineteenth century the process of industrialization gradually shifted production from households to wage labor. More and more men, and some women, left their households to work in factories, which altered the dynamics and meaning of family life. The notion of separate spheres, of a division between public (associated with male breadwinners and masculinity) and private (associated with wives, mothers, and femininity), took hold as an ideal, especially among the white and affluent. Middle-class families began to ritualize everyday practices such as family meals and to turn the anniversaries of their members' births and marriages into celebratory occasions. The family became a sentimentalized concept, idealized as a haven from the marketplace.

Government officials, social workers, teachers, ministers, and missionaries worked to impose this middle-class ideal upon the increasing waves of immigrants from southern and eastern Europe, working-class people, and surviving Native Americans. But crowded living conditions, the dependence of the impoverished on whatever additional earnings women and children could contribute to their precarious subsistence, and the persistence of alternative cultural notions of family (e.g., emphasis on extended kin among Native Americans and among Italian immigrants) sustained wide variation in the forms and meanings of family. Exploitive labor practices, often tied to racism, disrupted the cultures and families not only of African Americans but also of conquered Mexicans and immigrants from China and Mexico. In a labor and family pattern that continues in parts of the United States, Chinese and Mexican men migrated to the United States to build railroads or to work in mining or agriculture. Their parents, wives, children, and other kin often remained in the country of origin, in part because of overtly racist U.S. immigration policies. These "sojourner families" maintained split households that crossed national boundaries.

"The family" reached its most monolithic and idealized status during the 1950s cold war period. Television shows such as *The Adventures of Ozzie and Harriet* celebrated breadwinner fathers, full-time mothers, and their children living harmoniously in single-family, suburban houses. Contemporary North Americans often nostalgically call this model the "traditional" American family, but it was, in fact, a historical and cross-cultural anomaly. In the United States and throughout the world, few cultures have defined marriage and motherhood as the totality of adult women's identities, in part because women have so actively contributed to economic survival. And family forms and meanings have always been diverse. Even while many working-class families achieved the Ozzie-and-Harriet form in the 1950s, family diversity continued. Economic hardship and the absence of other employment opportunities pressed many Japanese American women in California and Hawaii, African American women in the South and in northern cities, and Mexican American women in the Southwest to do paid domestic work in white households or to work in low-paying agricultural or service jobs. Even when they had their own children, these women were neither expected nor allowed to be full-time mothers. Popular images of the family also obscured high rates of poverty (at the end of the 1950s up to one-third of U.S. children lived in poverty) and government subsidies—G.I. benefits, federal housing loans, and the construction of highways used by commuters—that facilitated the apparent self-sufficiency of more affluent suburban households.

In the late 1960s the pace of family change began to accelerate, with dramatic increases in the paid employment of women and in rates of divorce. In 1950 three-fifths of U.S. households contained male breadwinners and full-time female homemakers, with or without children, but by 1990 more than three-fifths of mothers with children younger than six were in the labor force. By the late 1970s divorce surpassed death as the major source of marital dissolution, generating a complex array of familial arrangements. No one family form has achieved statistical or cultural dominance under the "postmodern" conditions of family life, in which a patchwork of diverse, and often incompatible, family ideologies and practices coexist uneasily, even within individual fam-

ilies. For example, even many evangelical Christian families include divorced adults and make use of new reproductive technologies.

Since the 1960s "family" has become a debated concept, and talk of "family crisis" has become an idiom for passionate social conflicts over gender, sexual, racial, and welfare politics. In 1965 Daniel Moynihan ignited the first of these family-crisis debates when he argued that rising rates of single motherhood among African Americans represented a "tangle of pathology." Soon after, the women's liberation movement began to challenge the ideology and power relations of the "normal" family, calling attention to inequalities in the division of household labor and resources, gendered patterns of domestic violence, and the discontent of many full-time homemakers. The movement also named the feminization of poverty as a social problem, one that is especially prevalent among families without a male wage earner. This problem has worsened over time; in 1993, 38 percent of families headed by women who lost the benefits of a male's income through divorce lived below the poverty line, as did a startling 66 percent of families headed by women who had never married.

During the 1970s the lesbian and gay movement also began to challenge prevailing family ideologies that made heterosexuality seem inevitable and defined other sexual identities as sinful, deviant, and even criminal. By the 1980s many lesbian and gay activists began to demand not only civil rights but also familial rights, including domestic partner legislation and full and equal access to child custody, adoption, and new reproductive technologies. Increasingly, lesbians and gay men are using the discourse of "family" to describe their intimate ties and many are now campaigning to legalize lesbian or gay marriages.

In the late 1970s the New Right waged a full-scale backlash campaign against feminists and homosexuals, whom they portrayed as "antifamily." So successful was this backlash that politicians and social movements across the political spectrum have come to speak in the name of "the family" ever since. In the late 1980s some mainstream social scientists joined middle-of-the-road politicians, such as Moynihan, to wage a secular campaign for "family values." This group blames "family breakdown," especially divorce and single mothers supported by welfare, for everything from poverty to crime and violence. The rhetoric of moral failure deflects attention from the real sources of contemporary poverty, especially global economic restructuring, racism, and the widening gap between rich and poor during the 1980s. More realistic social policies would recognize these deep-seated structural problems, acknowledge the diverse realities of American family life, and seek to enhance the basic well-being of all families, whether single, coupled, extended; lesbian, gay, or straight; or endowed with one parent, two, or more.

The United States approaches a new millennium with a proliferating diversity of family forms and values. Moreover, astonishing new reproductive technologies, which allow wombs for hire, sperm for purchase, fertility for postmenopausal women, lactation for men, and which promise (or threaten) to remove test-tube babies from the realm of science fiction, should lay to rest any simply biological or universalistic definitions of "the family." Nevertheless, it seems likely that heated debates over relations and meanings of gender, generation, sexuality, race, and economic justice will continue well into the next century.

Stephanie Coontz, *The Social Origins of Private Life: A History of American Families, 1600–1900* (London: Verso, 1988); Evelyn Nakano Glenn, Grace Chang, and Linda Rennie Forcey, eds., *Mothering: Ideology, Experience, and Agency* (New York: Routledge, 1994); Barrie Thorne, with Marilyn Yalom, eds., *Rethinking the Family: Some Feminist Questions* rev. ed. (Boston: Northeastern University Press, 1993).

■ BARRIE THORNE and JUDITH STACEY

SEE ALSO Divorce and Custody; Marriage; Motherhood.

≋ Farming

SEE Agriculture.

≋ Fashion and Style

Until recently, fashion historians assumed that prior to the twentieth century, U.S. clothing styles were imported from and imposed by the European ruling classes; more recent scholarship acknowledges that throughout its history, U.S. fashion has reflected the dynamic relationship among early colonists, immigrant settlers, persons who arrived in bondage from Africa, and Native Americans.

The first European women to arrive in North America brought with them the cumbersome clothing of the late-Renaissance—puffy skirts; capes; tight-laced, low-cut bodices—clothing that was particularly unsuited to the rigors of a settler's life in colonial America. Native American women wore mantles and aprons of animal skins, moccasins, and elaborate pendants and earrings. Gradually, the European settlers adopted some of the Indians' clothing, for example, fur capes and soft shoes. And Native Americans acquired, through barter, some of the exotic apparel of the European settlers.

By the end of the seventeenth century, relative prosperity allowed many people to expand their wardrobes: wealthier women imported intricate clothing (long skirts, full sleeves with lace ruffles, wide collars) from England; poorer women sewed wardrobes from homespun fabrics like linsy-woolsy. Clothing was used to delineate individuality and status. In the Puritan colonies of New England, sumptuary laws were imposed, but women continually flouted them, indulging in forbidden hoods, silks, and short sleeves.

For most of the eighteenth century, fabric remained a precious commodity. (In the early 1700s, an appraisal of a burned house considered the value of the fabrics lost to be more important

Anna Held in a wasp waist gown, circa 1900. The gown's corset created a broad bosom and wide hips, considered indications of prosperity, while the tiny waist confined the wearer.

than the building itself.) Though women continued to covet expensive European clothing, the revolutionary consciousness sweeping the world was reflected in some apparel — notably empire gowns (plain, sheer, high-waisted) made popular by revolutionary women in France. (For Americans, these dresses may also have been evocative of ancient Greece and Rome.)

Perhaps the greatest degree of cultural, economic, and political change in the history of the United States took place over the course of the nineteenth century. Though denied political rights, Caucasian women in the colonies enjoyed a degree of freedom unknown in Europe. By midcentury, many women were working outside the

home — often in the textile industry. (And in the South, the cotton industry was dependent on the labor of slave women.) A growing immigrant population, willing to do piecework in their homes, provided a vital link between the spheres of homemade and industrial manufacturing. More employment of women had a direct effect on the fashion philosophies of the time — by midcentury, the dress-reform movement was loudly decrying impossibly uncomfortable horsehair petticoats, hoops, bustles, tight corsets, and hems so long they dragged in the unpaved streets. It took the impetus of women's involvement in the work force during the Civil War to introduce mannish skirt suits, slightly shorter hems, and waterproof cloaks and boots.

Though clothing continued to be made at home, as the nineteenth century progressed there was increasing competition from retail venues. Even women who never bought ready-made clothes began buying fabric by the yard at dry-goods stores rather than spinning it themselves. The midcentury introduction of paper dress patterns not only made home sewing easier but also standardized and made available the latest fashions to residents of distant rural areas.

The love of sports, and a new emphasis on fitness, also influenced women's dress in the latter part of the nineteenth century. U.S. women could not resist the lure of the golf course and the bicycle, and though the bloomer costume was considered too radical to gain acceptance in the 1850s, plainer, more comfortable tailored sports costumes began to be worn by women who viewed themselves, despite Victorian strictures, as healthy and active. (It should, however, be noted that complete sartorial rebels were not unknown in the nineteenth century. Dr. Mary Edwards Walker, a Civil War volunteer and the first woman permitted to work as a surgeon in the field, always wore men's trousers and frock coats though this was illegal. Congress eventually passed special legislation granting her the legal right to dress this way.) By the end of the century, white women clad in shirtwaists (made by piece-work and sold in stores) and tailored ankle-baring skirts were working for wages in stores, offices, and factories from Maine to California. Black women, though prohibited from this employment, wore the same styles.

If the nineteenth century saw the most intense cultural and social changes in U.S. history, the twentieth century witnessed the most profound changes in fashion. In the two decades between the turn of the century and the end of the First World War, U.S. women discarded virtually all of the fashion remnants left from one hundred years of constricting Victoriana undergarments, cumbersome hats, sweeping skirts, high collars, and so on. The silhouette of the 1920s became the silhouette of the twentieth century—shortened (sometimes above the knee) lengths, simple lingerie, and a general diminution in the use of excessive trims, beading, and the other furbelows that had decorated women's clothing for centuries. The introduction of the homogeneous "little black dress"—a simple, accessible garment enthusiastically embraced by women of all races, ethnic backgrounds, and social and economic classes—was emblematic of the democratization of fashion that was to continue throughout the rest of the century. Political movements and increasing racial and ethnic pride also have had an impact upon clothing styles. From the 1960s on, many African American women and men chose to wear African and African-inspired clothing, jewelry, and hairstyles in response to growing Black consciousness and political militancy. Some European Americans adopted these styles as well.

Until World War II, "high" fashion was still thought to emanate from the couture houses of Europe, but after the collapse of the French fashion industry during the Nazi occupation, a long overdue recognition was finally granted to U.S.-born designers. These American clothes were noted for their simplicity, their sense of modernity, and their understated, comfortable lines. In the postwar years, U.S.-designed clothing found its way back across the Atlantic, and currently the blue jeans, polo shirts, and plain lines of American clothing are ascendant in the streets of major cities all over the world.

Lois W. Banner, *American Beauty* (New York: Alfred A. Knopf, 1983); Lee Hall, *Common Threads* (Boston: Little, Brown and Company, 1992).

▪ LYNN YAEGER

SEE ALSO Beauty Culture; Dress Reform.

≋ Feminism and Feminisms

Feminism

Feminism—the belief in the full economic, political, and social equality of males and females—is usually seen as a modern movement to transform the male-dominant past and create an egalitarian future. On this and other continents, however, feminism is also history and even memory.

As Paula Gunn Allen wrote in *The Sacred Hoop: Recovering the Feminine in American Indian Traditions*, "Feminists too often believe that no one has ever experienced the kind of society that empowered women and made that empowerment the basis of rules and civilization. The price the feminist community must pay because it is not aware of the recent presence of gynarchical societies on this continent is necessary confusion, division, and much lost time."

The suffragist and modern waves of U.S. feminism usually have been traced to their beginnings in the abolitionist and civil rights movements—and to ideas in European women's writings, from Mary Wollstonecraft's *A Vindication of the Rights of Woman* to Simone de Beauvoir's *The Second Sex*—but there is also an indigenous source of lived feminism. By studying oral traditions, evaluating the patriarchal assumptions of official records, and researching women's early writings, scholars are rediscovering the history of women in the five hundred tribes that flourished on this continent before Columbus arrived. This history can begin to be incorporated into the history of feminism, as illustrated by the following examples.

The Iroquois Confederacy, a system of self-government evolved by the six major northeastern tribes, inspired the structure of the U.S. Constitution, a fact only recently acknowledged in legal history. It also guaranteed the social and political power of women. Clan Mothers nominated the Chief of each tribe, who then served on the Grand Council of all the tribes. They continued as advisers, making sure council decisions met the traditional standard of serving the welfare of seven future generations, and also retained the power to warn or remove Chiefs, decide when young men should go into battle, determine the fate of captives, and dictate the terms of peace agreements. In addition, they controlled food production, participated in discussions at tribal meetings, and were consulted in all matters of importance to the community and the Confederacy. Early treaties between the Iroquois Confederacy and the U.S. Government were signed not only by the Sachema or Principal Chief, but also by the Principal Women of the Six Nations.

Sally Roesch Wagner, a historian who has pioneered the discovery of the Iroquois influence on women's rights activists in the U.S., points to evidence such as that of a report by Alice Fletcher, a suffragist and ethnographer who lived among Iroquoian tribes. Fletcher told an 1888 International Council of Women that "the man owns his own ponies and other belongings which he has personally acquired; the woman owns her horses, dogs, and all the lodge equipments; children own their own articles; and parents do not control the possessions of their children. . . . A wife is as independent as the most independent man in our midst." The concept of illegitimacy did not exist. Each child had a place within the matrilocal

group composed of the child's mother, her sisters, and the men they married. "As an Indian woman," Fletcher quoted one informant as saying, "I was free. I owned my own home, my person, the work of my own hands, and my children could never forget me. I was better as an Indian woman than under white law." An Indian man said, "Your laws show how little your men care for their women. The wife is nothing of herself."

In Georgia, the traditional land of the Cherokees, a written constitution built on principles of reciprocity and consensus allowed Clan Mothers to choose the Chief. This thriving republic guaranteed equal education for boys and girls. Even after the U.S. Government had forcibly removed them to Oklahoma on the Trail of Tears, a march so long and cruel that a quarter of the population perished, the Cherokees set up seminaries that served men and women equally. In 1885 Senator Henry Dawes wrote an official report on the Cherokee Nation, conceding that they had achieved a literacy rate higher than that in the surrounding population and a system of sharing so effective that "there was not a pauper in that nation."

In addition, there is the silent testimony of girls and women taken prisoner by Indian tribes who sometimes chose to remain, though the reverse was rarely true. There are also condemnations of Indian women as unchaste because they could divorce and could control their own fertility through a combination of timing, extended nursing, and herbal abortifacients. Even the Quakers, who often championed the Indian cause, tried to persuade Indian women to leave the fields and stay home.

According to many Native American creation myths, the earth and all living things were created by a female spirit. She had many names: Changing Woman, Earth Mother, Corn Mother, Spider Woman, and Turtle Grandmother. The worship of female as well as male deities symbolized the balance of power between men and women. After the U.S. Government had outlawed Native spiritual practices for more than two centuries, these female images had largely been demonized or relegated to the memories of a few elders. Though the stereotypes of the merciless warrior and the downtrodden woman had been used to justify violence and assimilation, there remained ancient and powerful female spirits that symbolizes not only women's strength but respect for all living things.

Perhaps the strongest written testimony to the indigenous roots of U.S. feminism comes from the suffragists who had contact with Native people before the apartheid-like reservation system was completed around 1900. Elizabeth Cady Stanton and Matilda Joslyn Gage, two influential leaders of the radical wing of the suffrage movement, lived in the Iroquois country of upstate New York. Like Frances Wright, Lucretia Mott, and Susan B. Anthony, they knew and learned from women in the surrounding tribes. Gage and other European American suffragists called the Iroquois' matrilineal and matrilocal system "The Matriarchate," perhaps because its balance of power was so unlike their own situation.

Nonetheless, biases can cause scholars to overlook this influence. As Wagner wrote after twenty years of studying the writings of early U.S. women's rights activists, "I realized I had been skimming over the source of their inspiration. . . . My own unconscious white supremacy had kept me from recognizing what these prototypical feminists kept insisting in their writings: They caught a glimpse of the possibility of freedom because they knew women who lived liberated lives."

In addition, most early white suffragists were abolitionists who knew that runaway slaves found refuge with Native groups. Free Black women who were abolitionists and suffragists often knew Native cultures through intermarriage. Whether due to this contact or similarities between Native and African traditions—both often made women the primary agriculturalists with considerable spiritual and community power—nineteenth-century African American women's views often sounded much like those of Native women. In

1893 Anna Julia Cooper, a feminist educator and human rights advocate whose mother had been a slave, said "woman's cause" was universal, "not the white woman's nor the black woman's nor the red woman's."

In *The History of Woman Suffrage*, Matilda Gage cited Native cultures as her inspiration for a "regenerated world." Stanton also took positions that seemed inspired by her Seneca neighbors. For instance, she insisted on women's right to divorce, a position so radical that she eventually was forced to abandon it. Even conservative suffragist Reverend Anna Garland Spencer said in a speech at an 1899 suffrage convention that "when we tried to divide 'in severalty' the lands of the American Indian, we did violence to all his own sense of justice and cooperative feeling when we failed to recognize the women of the tribes in the distribution. We then and there gave the Indian the worst of the white man's relationship to his wife." Wagner tracked down the fact that Stanton's young cousin, Elizabeth Smith Miller—who often saw Oneida women at the family dinner table—adapted the Oneida costume of a soft tunic over loose trousers as an alternative to tight corsets and heavy skirts. Later named "Bloomers" after Amelia Bloomer, the editor who popularized Miller's adaptation, this style freed women from corset-induced fainting spells and even allowed them to bicycle, a means of transport and liberation advocated by suffragists.

In addition, Wagner notes that some Native men tried to extend equality beyond their own cultures. Two nineteenth-century Tuscarora historians testified to the rarity of rape in their societies—including rape of white women prisoners—and called on white men to follow suit. One of them, J. N. B. Hewitt, confirmed that the Iroquois Confederacy, to which the Tuscarora belonged, entrusted power to "a representative body of men and women chosen by the mothers of the community . . . not . . . a hereditary body, nor to a purely democratic body, nor even to a body of religious leaders." In 1866 newspapers reported a speech by Seneca Chief Dr. Peter Wilson, urging white men to adopt universal suffrage, "even of the women, as in his nation."

Lesbian scholars often have led the way in research into feminism's indigenous roots. They discovered that in many indigenous cultures lesbian, gay, bisexual, or cross-gendered people were accepted as "twin-spirited" and given honorable roles such as healers, teachers, namers, and seers—functions that required both male and female wisdom. Poet and lesbian/gay cultural historian Judy Grahn wrote in 1984, "What Americans call Gayness not only has distinct cultural characteristics, its participants have long held positions of social power in history and ritual among people all over the globe."

In summing up the meaning of U.S. feminism's indigenous origins, Cherokee writer and scholar Rayna Green wrote, "A feminist revolution here would simply honor American tradition, not overthrow it."

Of course, women have come here from every continent and many have brought feminist hopes or memories with them. In the Hausa creation story of West Africa, for example, a female Moses led her people out of the wilderness and into a promised land. It could have presaged the courage of Harriet Tubman, the fugitive slave who became known as a Black Moses for her daring raids that freed hundreds of slaves. Many enslaved African women kept female-honoring traditions, from ancient spiritual practices to the covert use of abortifacients.

During most of the colonial period, European women's imported healing skills allowed them to outnumber men in medicine until persecution and restrictive licensing turned medicine into a male profession. Emma Goldman's feminist ideas began in her girlhood as a Russian anarchist. Polish-born Ernestine Rose used her European socialist experience to organize for the Married Woman's Property Act of 1848. Spanish-speaking women arrived with heroines such as Flora Tristan of Peru and Malintzin and Sor Juana Ines de la Cruz of Mexico.

Chinese American novelist Maxine Hong Kingston addressed the rarely recorded history of many women when she spoke about her 1976 novel, *The Woman Warrior*. She had assumed this warrior who comes down from the hills to rescue her people was unique fiction in "the peasant talk-story Cantonese tradition" but discovered when she traveled through Asia that woman warriors are legends told and lived everywhere.

Nonetheless, the great majority of men and women who conquered or settled this country came from Europe at its most male-supremacist and racist. From the fifteenth to the seventeenth centuries the effort to stamp out female-dominated pagan religions resulted in the death of countless witches, leaving some villages with few females. In that period and beyond, imperialism and colonialism were justified by a desire to Christianize other peoples.

Against this backdrop, British and Northern European women and girls came with their families to New England, seeking freedom to worship. Single women arrived in the Virginia colonies, often fleeing poverty, jail sentences for theft or prostitution, or forced marriage.

Since there were three times more white men than white women in the colonies, importing brides became a high priority—methods varied from emptying jails to kidnapping girls off the streets of London to offering unmarried women free land in Maryland. Women also came as indentured workers and women of all classes were used as a source of cheap or free labor and as the means of reproduction. Of 144 marriageable women brought by a sea captain to Virginia in 1619, only 35 were still alive six years later; such was the result of hard work, disease, and pressure to populate this "new" country. On the frontier, the average white family had two mothers: one who died in childbirth and another who took care of her predecessor's children while producing more. However, these hardships were far surpassed by the sufferings of female slaves.

Fanny Kemble, who left her slaveholder husband in opposition to slavery, recorded the conditions of slave women, who experienced the body-invasion of rapes and forced pregnancies. Kemble noted ruptured uteruses, dropped wombs, abscesses, epilepsy, internal tumors, injured backs, and temporary insanity—all among women who also labored in the fields. In 1861 former slave Harriet Jacobs stated, "slavery is terrible for men; but it is far more terrible for women . . . *they* have wrongs, and sufferings, and mortifications peculiarly their own." Many slave women rebelled by such sabotage as setting fires, and a few chose infanticide or suicide as the only alternative to enriching and pleasuring their enslavers.

Gradually, U.S. feminism became less a lived tradition and more one of resistance and hope for the future. Amid competing loyalties to men and families, and diverse realities of servitude, marital status, race, class, culture, and sexuality, feminism also became a struggle to come together for mutual interest. Broadly shared goals included ending any status as chattel; the freedom to bear or not to bear children; unlinking sexuality from reproduction; the right to self-determination and participation at all levels of government; equality of work, property, and income in and out of the home; democratic family structures and laws to enforce them; cultural and spiritual practices that honor females; women's culture and leadership as a source of diminished violence; and ending hierarchies based on race, class, ethnicity, and sexuality, not only because they penalize and divide females but also because they necessitate female oppression. This struggle does not always succeed, but always recurs.

For example, the history of slavery in the United States includes the most intimate betrayals of Black women by white women and also the most revolutionary alliance between abolitionists and suffragists. Encompassing women such as the white Southern wife who was described as "the chiefest slave in the harem" and the Black abolitionist and suffragist Sojourner Truth, this alliance was dedicated to ending any human status as chattel and achieving universal adult suffrage. In Stanton's words, "The Negro's skin and the woman's sex are both [used as] *prima facie* evidence that they were intended to be in subjection to the white Saxon man." Angelina Grimké explained, "I rejoice exceedingly that our resolution should combine us with the Negro." Later, Frederick Douglass wrote in his autobiography, "When the true history of the antislavery cause shall be written, women will occupy a large space in its pages, for the cause of the slave has been peculiarly women's cause." This race/sex alliance came together, split apart, and then resurfaced in the civil rights movement and modern feminism.

After the Civil War, white male abolitionists divided the alliance by supporting the vote only for its smallest segment, Negro males. Black male abolitionists agreed that this was "the Negro's hour," as did such prominent Black female abolitionists and feminists as Frances E. W. Harper, and also some white feminists. They feared that linking woman suffrage to Negro male suffrage would jeopardize its chance for success. Sojourner Truth disagreed: "There is a great stir about colored men getting their rights, but not a word about colored women . . . So I am for keeping the thing going . . . " Stanton and Anthony protested "male" being put in the Constitution for the first time and argued that the white women's vote was necessary to balance the "uneducated" votes of immigrant and Black men. This type of racist argument became even more virulent as white women who had never been abolitionists joined the suffrage cause. Meanwhile, many Black women carried on the fight for woman suffrage in comparative obscurity. Once won, the ballot power of Negro men was soon limited by poll taxes and impossible literacy tests, barriers that were still in place when women of all races finally won the vote fifty years later and that were defeated only by the civil rights movement of the 1960s.

However, the memory of this alliance—and the price of its division—could have saved the civil rights and feminist movements much pain and added to their strength. White women who identified with other oppressed groups could have found their tradition in history, as could Black women suffering from what historian Beverly Guy-Sheftall has called "This tendency to ignore long years of political struggle aimed at eradicating the multiple oppressions that black women experience [and the] erroneous notions about the relevance of feminism to the black community." Nonetheless, the modern women's movement covers more diversity of race, class, sexuality, ethnicity, and ability than any other U.S. movement. It has also created a laboratory for self-discovery, friendship, and struggle that often helps bridge similar divisions elsewhere.

Both successes and failures show the importance of feminism in self-determined and culturally diverse forms, from reforms inside patriarchal institutions to experimental structures outside; from balance between males and females to the goal of achieving the full range of human qualities within each person. As Guy-Sheftall has written, "The history of American feminism has been primarily a narrative about the heroic deeds of white women." Only broadening that history will reveal a feminism that belongs to all women, that frees men from the prison of gender, and that reconnects what has been divided by dualism and hierarchy.

There is a growing hope that the history of U.S. feminism will no longer be lost and rediscovered, lost again and again rediscovered. In Paula Gunn Allen's words, "the root of oppression is the loss of memory."

■ WILMA MANKILLER,
MARYSA NAVARRO,
and GLORIA STEINEM

Feminisms

AUTHOR'S NOTE: *Some feminist histories stress what might have been, others examine what was. Some accounts begin and end with the story of* white feminists. Some attribute all of women's varied oppressions to male power. Others treat feminism as a history of struggle among women, as well as between women and men. The following article presents the history of feminism not simply as a history of women mobilizing on their own behalf, but also as a history of race, culture, class, and sexuality. Such an approach gives visibility not only to feminist solidarities, but to differences among feminists; it also holds feminists accountable for their actions. In this view, feminism is not where differences among women disappear, although generations of feminists have certainly tried to erase or deny them. Nor is feminism a singular history, for as individuals and members of groups we have forged distinctive paths toward gender justice.*

Feminism articulates political opposition to the subordination of women as women, whether that subordiniation is ascribed by law, imposed by social convention, or inflicted by individual men and women. Feminism also offers alternatives to existing unequal relations of gender power, and these alternatives have formed the agendas for feminist movements. Some feminists may borrow or claim other women's oppression and empowerment as their own, but feminism generally springs from each woman's own lived experience. Such experiences vary enormously, as some women's burdens are other women's privileges: gender roles, expectations, and limitations are not the same for Black women and white, for poor women and rich, for lesbians and straight women. Feminism thus challenges women to respect differences among us and to honor, rather than appropriate, other women's triumphs and tragedies. Yet feminism also challenges women to navigate across differences to build coalitions for social change.

Women have acted collectively to contest their subordination throughout U.S. history. Whether through community activism, broad-based mobilization, policy advocacy—or through a variety of other means—women have pursued social, political, and legal change to improve their lives, choices, and opportunities. But as our circumstances and ideologies have varied, so too have our goals, strategies, and relations to one another. Within the history of feminism in the United States have been many feminisms—many voices claiming respect, dignity, and freedom for women.

Feminists have commonly fought for the advancement of women, though we have not always agreed on how that could best be accomplished. We have been at odds over the meaning of equality, over the relevance of our racial, cultural, class, and sexual differences, and over methods of political action. During the late nineteenth and early twentieth centuries, for example, many activists argued that women should enjoy the same rights as men did in the public sphere, and they challenged laws and practices that treated women and men differently. But many others defended the legal and political differentiation of women from men and claimed greater power and respect for women in the domestic sphere.

Debates over goals and strategies have made for a robust and changing feminist history. Nineteenth-century activists pursued many paths, from moral reform through abolition to Seneca Falls during the first half of the century, to the suffrage movement and social welfare work during the second half. For many Anglo-American women, the context for activism was the home. From women's role as mothers and as their children's first teachers, some women derived claims to educational opportunities. Pointing to women's caretaking and nurturing experiences, some women argued for a public role in guiding the moral quality of the Republic. But for many other Anglo-American activists, it was less women's responsibilities in the home than their subordinate condition there that propelled their activism. From Seneca Falls through the Civil War, these women invoked the rights of universal humanity to advance demands for a voice in public life as well as for an end to legal discrimination against women in marriage.

Inspired to claim rights for themselves by their participation in the abolition movement, mid-nineteenth-century women's rights activists forged their agenda primarily around their needs as Anglo-American upper- and middle-class women. Their early consciousness framed by their experience of oppression in marriage, they sought rights in relation to marriage—divorce, custody, and property rights, as well as the right to vote alongside, rather than through, their husbands. These rights have become fundamental elements of all women's legal and political personhood. However, in their day, such rights claims had limited appeal for women struggling against bondage or for economic survival—enslaved women whose marriages were not legally recognized and working-class women whose most pressing concerns were labor conditions and fair wages.

Women's rights activism, already weakened by the silences of the middle-class agenda, became deranged by racism following the Civil War. Denouncing the exclusion of women from the Fifteenth Amendment, many Anglo-American suffragists resorted to racial arguments. Elizabeth Cady Stanton warned, for example, that electoral participation by emancipated African American men and immigrant men would "degrade" the Republic if not offset by white women's vote; and Susan B. Anthony charged that the new amendment cast white women "under the heel of the lowest orders of manhood."

The sacrifice of racial justice for Anglo-American women's goals plagued feminist history into the twentieth century. Discrimination against African American women by many Anglo-American women's organizations throughout the nineteenth and early twentieth centuries created distrust and resentment among African American women, as did many white suffragists' accommodation to lynch law and Jim Crow. This impeded feminist unity. Nevertheless, feminisms continued to grow.

From the late nineteenth century forward, many working-class women became labor activists, fighting for decent working conditions for themselves and for other women. African American women of all classes organized against lynching, while middle-class African American women established social services and formed club movements based on the philosophy that women of their race should "lift as they climb." Chinese American women began to question foot binding and arranged marriage, and to call for women's education.

Although the suffrage issue held center stage until 1920, between 1900 and 1945 new feminist visions also competed in political and social life. African American and Mexican American women conducted boycotts, deploying women's buying power against racist businesses. Both built mutual aid networks and civil rights organizations to defend their communities against economic and political exploitation. The activism of these women opened possibilities for later feminisms moved not by the singularity of gender oppression but by the weight of its interaction with the multiple systems of inequality that affect women's lives.

Aside from the women's rights advocates associated with the suffrage campaign, the most visible activists during the early decades of this century were Anglo-American social reformers devoted to improving the conditions facing poor, mostly immigrant women in cities such as Chicago and New York. Unlike the suffragists, who sought to empower themselves through rights, these activists worked to protect, nurture, and assimilate other women, women remote from the reformers' own social and cultural station. Emphasizing the political significance of woman's sphere, and most especially of motherhood, these "maternalist" reformers asserted government's obligation to support poor and working-class mothers. They won protective labor policies, pensions for widowed mothers, maternity and infancy services, and educational initiatives to speed the Americanization of immigrant children and their mothers and to mitigate the effects of poverty.

Where Anglo-American women's rights advocates spoke for themselves, maternalists spoke about and to other women. Rights advocates often alienated or excluded women whose social status and political needs were different from their own. Meanwhile, maternalist reformers directed their attention to women outside the Anglo-American middle class—chiefly southern and eastern European immigrants—prescribing their "uplift" and conformity to the cultural and economic norms of the Anglo-American family. Both rights advocates and maternalists fought for suffrage and other public rights, particularly in relation to marriage: during the 1920s, for example, they commonly campaigned for married women's independent nationality citizenship. But where women's rights advocates demanded legal and political parity with men, maternalists sought social and political recognition for themselves and other women based upon their gender difference. Thus, while rights advocates championed public equality—under law, in politics, and in the market—maternalists developed gender-specific policies to control the deleterious effects of wage work on motherhood and to Americanize material and cultural conditions in the home.

The philosophical divide among Anglo-American feminists erupted into conflict over the Equal Rights Amendment (ERA) to the Constitution during the 1920s and 1930s. At issue were differing feminist understandings of the roots of women's subordination as well as of the strategies for overcoming it. For the National Women's Party, the chief proponent of the ERA, constitutional equality promised to secure for women equal treatment with men in the public sphere. For maternalist reformers, it threatened social policy gains won in the name of women's domestic role.

This conflict debilitated the first ERA but did not debilitate feminisms. Into World War II, maternalists played a crucial role developing policies for women in the emerging welfare state.

Equality advocates, meanwhile, stood firm in their defense of principle, sometimes joining the reformers to contest discriminations against women under the New Deal, sometimes working alone to press the political parties to embrace equality for women.

Despite a century of feminist struggle, by the 1950s, advances were few and social and cultural expectations regarding women's roles remained generally conservative and limiting. Although they had participated in the work force in record numbers during World War II, middle-class Anglo-American women were once again expected to be contented wives, homemakers, and mothers. But in reality, their roles were in flux. Some 29 percent of white women worked outside the home in 1950. By 1960, 34 percent of white women participated in the outside labor market, along with 43 percent of women of color. Approximately 75 percent of white women had completed high school and 17 percent were college graduates.

By the mid-1960s, some women's dissatisfaction with their relegation to the domestic sphere began to ignite. Betty Friedan captured that dissatisfaction in her groundbreaking book *The Feminine Mystique*, which explored the frustrations of bright and educated white women who were limited to working in the home. Coming together in the new National Organization for Women, some middle-class feminists mobilized to secure public rights for women, especially the employment rights promised by the Civil Rights Act of 1964. The Black civil rights, student, and growing anti–Vietnam War movements provided fertile contexts in which women could be politically active and also question basic assumptions about traditional social and power relationships in society as a whole. By the late 1960s, young women who were active in various liberation movements, often in roles subordinate to their male counterparts, began to question their position as women and to express the necessity of organizing for their own liberation.

Across the country thousands of women came together in small consciousness-raising (C.R.) groups to talk about and to analyze the content of their daily lives. C.R. groups provided direct validation for the pervasive but often invisible oppression that women experienced. These groups often gave birth to grassroots women's political organizations concerned with an array of issues such as rape, reproductive freedom, health care, and economic injustice. The women's movement soon built thoroughgoing critiques of women's oppression in every facet of U.S. life, from violence against women to sexist language to the exclusion of women athletes from most organized sports.

In 1968 feminists staged a protest in Atlantic City at the Miss America Pageant, and from then on, despite its frequently ridiculing tone, the media helped spread the word that vital movements for women's liberation were taking root all over the country. From the late 1960s through the 1970s, gender-conscious women's activism brought about pervasive changes in almost every aspect of U.S. life. In the private sphere, expectations for relations between the sexes altered. Many women, even if they were not actively involved in feminist organizations, demanded to be treated as equals in both sexual and nonsexual interactions with men. In the public sphere, middle-class white women began to enter the work force in unprecedented numbers and soon began to organize for pay equity; access to professional, managerial, and nontraditional jobs; and fair consideration for advancement and promotion. Women's many stories and frustrations made it clear that all U.S. institutions—the economy, law, medicine, schools, the media, the arts, religion, and the family—discriminated against women and girls. These institutions and others became the focus of feminist organizing.

Despite a broadly shared commitment to ending the subordination of women, the late-twentieth-century women's movement was an eclectic mix of varying theories, politics, and strategies. A multiplicity of feminisms flourished during the 1970s, reflecting the diversity of U.S. women.

Radical feminists developed an incisive critique of sexual politics under patriarchy. Often deploying irreverent tactics such as zaps, street theater, and speak-outs, radical feminists illuminated how violence against women, lack of access to safe and legal abortions, pornography, and demeaning media images all contributed to keeping women powerless.

Socialist feminists who had been active in the New Left and who often maintained at least ideological links to leftist politics maintained that women's freedom could not be achieved under the current capitalist system because the successful profiteering of the ruling class required permanent hierarchical patterns of class, race, and gender exploitation. Socialist feminists also looked at women's situation globally and linked U.S. women's liberation to women's struggles for national liberation in the Third World.

Carrying forward the women's rights emphasis of many earlier feminists, liberal feminists worked to secure institutional and policy change through the courts, Congress, and constitutional amendment. These activists campaigned to elect women to public office; challenged laws, employment practices, and schooling that discriminated against women; and argued for child-care, pregnancy, and parental leave legislation to facilitate women's participation in the public sphere and to open opportunities to them. With other feminists, liberal feminists also fought to defend abortion rights as *Roe* v. *Wade* came under assault beginning in the mid-1970s.

Lesbian feminists were among the most active participants in the burgeoning women's movement, but because of homophobia, many lesbians formed their own groups and developed an analysis of how virulent heterosexism and homophobia were linked to sexism and all women's confinement in traditional gender roles within the nuclear family. Lesbian feminists were responsible for building numerous institutions, especially cultural outlets such as women's bookstores, presses, record companies, and women's concert circuits.

Many, but not all, cultural feminists were also lesbians. These women wanted to build a widespread women's culture in which women redefined and determined every aspect of their own daily lives, free of male rules and values. Making a women's culture meant transforming traditional art forms, as well as creating autonomous women's spaces, including women's land, and formulating new women-centered spiritual practices.

By the early 1970s, feminists of color began to build autonomous groups that stressed the impact of racial and economic oppression upon the political situation of women of color. Their examination of the nexus among race, class, and gender subordination supplied a groundbreaking multi-issue, antiracist feminist analysis, which had far-reaching ideological impact not only upon feminist movements but upon many struggles for political and social change. Feminists of color also wanted to connect their feminisms to their various cultures, languages, and communities of origin.

Working-class feminists formed organizations beginning in the mid-1970s as well. Nine to Five and the Coalition of Labor Union Women (CLUW) addressed the workplace and economic issues of the majority of employed women who held lower-paying blue-, pink-, and white-collar positions. Raising gender-based wage, benefit, job-opportunity, and job-security concerns, union women broadened the agendas of both feminist organizations and unions.

Although the various feminisms that emerged during the 1960s and 1970s were each ideologically and strategically distinctive, much overlap existed in memberships, participation, and coalition building. For example, some of the most visible feminists of color were also lesbian feminists. Socialist feminists, radical feminists, feminists of color, and lesbian feminists sometimes worked together on particular issues, such as reproductive rights or violence against women. Women of color and lesbians also worked in the National Organization for Women and other women's rights groups. All varieties of feminists participated in feminist protests, marches, conferences, and cultural events.

Still, the differences among feminisms and among the women who support each perspective sometimes have led to outright conflicts, confrontations, and splits. There have been gulfs, for example, between women who believe in electoral and legislative strategies for reform and those committed to grassroots organizing and sweeping political change. Advocates of gender-neutral laws have clashed with feminists who believe that women's differences from men, whether inherent or socially constructed, warrant legal and institutional recognition. Meanwhile, in their methods and analyses, white, middle-class, heterosexual feminists across the ideological spectrum often slighted concerns of women of color, poor and working-class women, and lesbians. For example, as they narrowed reproductive freedom struggles to a defense of abortion rights, many white feminists marginalized issues of particular importance to poor women and women of color, such as sterilization abuse, universal access to quality health care, economic security for children, and genocidal population-control measures directed against communities of color.

Conflicts that have expressed feminists' various racial, sexual, and class identities and perspectives have caused some bitter divisions. But conflict has also been productive, stimulating successful autonomous organizing by diverse groups of women, encouraging coalition work around common goals, and broadening movement agendas. Interventions by women of color around racism in the women's movement during the late 1970s, in particular, helped open up rich dialogues about anti-Semitism, ableism, ageism, fat oppression, and other issues and identities.

During the 1980s, feminists attained some of their goals. For example, the Supreme Court recognized sexual harassment as a form of sex discrimination in violation of the Civil Rights Act and validated gender-based affirmative action in employment. But the conservative Reagan-Bush administrations and the country's overall move to the right also undermined feminist achievements, pitting gender equality against conservative mantras such as "family values" and states' rights. With the anti-abortion movement's violent tactics and the Right's assault on reproductive freedom, welfare, lesbian and gay rights, immigration, crime, and affirmative action, the 1990s became a time of demoralizing retrenchment.

Not surprisingly, the media frequently demeaned feminism during this period, claiming that it was irrelevant, outdated, or even that it no longer existed. Feminists also witnessed attacks from within by women who said they were feminists yet dismissed critical human rights issues such as rape, sexual harassment, and women's and children's poverty as mere "victim" feminism.

Despite these setbacks, feminism has also enjoyed recent advances. In 1991 the Anita Hill/Clarence Thomas hearings provided a major catalyst not only for organizing against sexual harassment but also for women's greater empowerment in many contexts. In 1992 record numbers of women were elected to the U.S. Congress, where they have successfully pressed for parental leave and domestic violence legislation. Meanwhile, young women, some who are junior and senior high school students, continue to join the movement and to form their own feminist networks and organizations. And, although they may not call themselves feminists, most women (77 percent according to a 1992 poll) credit the women's movement for improving their lives. As the twenty-first century approaches, feminism continues to be a necessary and vital force for political and economic justice and for social change.

■ GWENDOLYN MINK
and BARBARA SMITH

American Indian Feminism

Feminism is not a word found in tribal languages, though tribal societies have long provided for a uniquely women's expression in both secular and religious forums.

Tribal feminism is a multisphered concept with the family as the center, surrounded by clan identification, then tribe and tribal relationships, which can mean relationships with state and federal governments and those with other tribal and international governments. Crucial to this tribal context are land and history as well as the belief that nothing is possible without the female and the power of the female to harbor and sustain creation. The female is sacred, as is the male. Both female and male energies are found in all life and these aspects coexist equally in a balanced universe. In recognition of the importance of women in sustaining tribal cultures, community takes precedence over individual women's rights yet conversely there are no human rights until femaleness is respected and venerated. These mandates in tribal social and religious thought form the backbone of tribal cultures that have lived in this country since time immemorial.

Over five hundred federally recognized tribes exist in the United States today. Both the federal government and the tribal governments have broad sovereign powers over the reservation territories. The tribal governments' sovereignty and property rights, primarily regarding water in this era, are under severe legal and political attack from state governments and from non-Indians who reside on or near reservations. The issues facing these parties admittedly are complex, and they are exacerbated by racial tensions. Thus, the political and legal dynamic for the many Indian women who are members of tribes or who live on the reservations is heavily influenced in these struggles. For example, federal deference to tribal governments may have the effect of denying Indian women certain property rights under ancient tribal laws. In these circumstances, Indian women must make their claims in tribal legal and political forums. Nascent concerns about discrimination against Indian women often are overshadowed by the need of all tribal members to band together against political and legal attacks.

Feminist activities by American Indian women, both mainstream and tribal, are occurring throughout the country. In urban Indian communities, the national feminist movement has had its greatest impact. For example, in the late 1970s, the National Institute for Women of Color was founded by a group of Indian, Black, Asian Pacific, and Hispanic women who became disillusioned with the National Organization for Women (NOW). They claimed that NOW exhibited insufficient understanding of the concerns of nonmainstream communities and therefore the unique character of their feminism. OHOYO (Choctaw for "sister") was founded soon after by Owanah Andersen, a Texas-based Indian woman, to promote national understanding of the unique problems facing American Indian women.

Urban American Indian women's response to the feminist movement was recounted by Paula Gunn Allen in her landmark book *The Sacred Hoop*, which recast feminist premises through indigenous native cultures, particularly her own Laguna Pueblo tribal culture. Two notable anthologies of Indian women's writing were released in the crucible of the late 1970s and early 1980s, both still in print: *A Gathering of Spirit*, edited by Beth Brant; and Rayna Green's *That's What She Said*. Some Native women continue to be active in national feminist organizations, yet for the most part they remain outside the national feminist movement.

On the reservations, women seemingly have continued the traditions of banding together to accomplish particular tasks. For example, Women of All Red Nations was founded to broaden dialogue and participation in land-rights battles. More recently, the Indigenous Women's Network, an international Native women's network, formed. This group is concerned with land rights, economic development, and welfare of tribal traditional areas. This and other Indian women's groups are increasingly participating, as a group, in defending tribal sovereignty in the multiple battles facing their tribes.

Other Native women have taken their place within traditional tribal structures that have excluded women from all-male theocratic governments. Verna Williamson, in the early 1990s, became the first Isleta Pueblo female governer in the known history of the tribe. Wilma Mankiller became the first woman to be chief of the Cherokee tribe in recent history, since the establishment of Christianity in the tribe (when women no longer held positions of respect and power due to the insecurity of the men). She follows in the path of other Beloved Women of her tribe, such as Nancy Ward, whose advice and counsel were sought and respected. Today, many American Indian women are the elected leaders of their tribal governments. Many are from tribes that have always treated men and women as equally sacred, a mandate that is indeed a universal truth.

▪ SUSAN M. WILLIAMS
and JOY HARJO

SEE ALSO Native American Women.

Arab American Feminism

The building of a female Arab American identity leading to Arab American feminism accelerated in the 1970s as a result of: first, the political awakening of Arab Americans following the defeat of Arab nations in the 1967 war with Israel; second, the immigration of more educated and politicized Arabs after 1967; third, the civil rights, student, and women's movements, which stimulated gender, race, and ethnic activism in the 1970s. Arab American feminists face the dual tasks of constructing both their Arab American identities and their feminism. Many Arab countries have changed borders, names, and national identities several times in this century; thus most Arab Americans have only recently come to create organizations and institutions as Arab Americans. Christians accounted for most of the Arab immigrants to the United States until the 1960s, by which time Muslim Arab immigrants outnumbered Christians. Differences of religion, nationality, ethnicity, education, class, and the individual character at the time of immigration all have factored into the complex and fluid construction of Arab American identity. Additionally, the U.S. media's conflation of Arabs with Iranians and Turks, as well as political conflicts in the Arab world, have led to divisions among Arab Americans.

Arab American identity has been facilitated, however, by the externally imposed unifying definition of "Arab American" in U.S. ethnic discourses, which dissolved national origin through the spread of pan-Arab nationalism in the 1960s. In addition, Arab American identity was further established externally by the rise of Islamic fundamentalism in the late 1970s, in the wake of the Iranian revolution and its supranational appeal. Arab American feminists have faced the challenge of bridging these lines.

Academic meetings have been central sites for constructing Arab American feminism. The Middle East Studies Association organized its first plenary on women in 1984, leading to the founding of the Association for Middle East Women's Studies and *Amews News* in 1985. In the early 1980s feminist conferences, such as the Berkshire Women's History Conference, began soliciting panels on Middle Eastern women. Meetings such as those held by the American Anthropological Association and those organized by research centers increasingly focused on Arab women. Recent Arab feminist expatriates, dual citizens, or feminists retaining their natal citizenship have been central leaders in the construction of Arab American feminism in academia.

Arab American feminists have made inroads into Arab American organizations such as the Association for Arab American University Graduates and the Arab American Anti-Discrimination Committee. They have also founded their own organizations such as the Feminist Arab American Network.

Some women's organizations in the Arab world have active counterparts in the United States. The Union of Palestinian Women's Association in North America, stimulated by the General Union of Palestinian Women, is active in many large urban areas with a significant Palestinian population. The Arab Women's Union, founded in Egypt in the 1980s and shut down by the Egyptian government, spurred Arab American feminist activism through the founding of the Arab Women Solidarity Association, North American Chapter, which has consultative status with the United Nations. Noted Arab feminists, such as Fatima Mernissi and Nawal el Saadawi, frequently visit the United States, translate their writings, and work with Arab American feminists for unified causes.

Arab American feminists organized the first major exhibit of Arab women's art in the United States in 1993, at the National Museum of Women in the Arts in Washington, D.C. The works of some Arab American feminist novelists and poets, such as Etel Adnan, are used in mainstream college courses. The first two volumes of writings by Arab American feminists have been published in the 1990s.

Religious institutions are another site for the emergence of Arab American feminism. Within the Islamic fundamentalist movement, many Arab American women have identified and organized as Islamic feminists. Feminists within Islam are working to reinterpret the Koran and religious traditions. These Muslim feminists argue that women are equal before Allah and Islamic law but that the Prophet's words have been distorted by men and by corrupt states. Christian Arab feminists have generally identified with and organized in either non-Arab feminist movements or with feminists in their churches.

Family, as the center of Arab and Arab American society, is beginning to receive critical feminist attention. Religious issues, particularly contestations over Islamic fundamentalism, have occupied Arab American feminists. National struggles (Palestinian, Lebanese, Yemenite) and the Gulf War fallout are of great concern to Arab American feminists.

Finally, Arab American feminists often struggle with divided loyalties. Many feel the need to defend their cultures, nations of origin, and religions from hostile media and political affronts in the United States. Yet they are committed to feminist criticism of the Arab American culture, working to integrate Arab American feminist struggles within the larger U.S. and global women's movements. The pressures of cultural loyalty have silenced some Arab American feminist criticism. However, other Arab American feminists consider their cause to be a matter of life and death for their people. Regardless of the issues or sites of contestation, Arab Americans are increasingly bringing gender issues into their battles and Arab American feminists are emerging as central players in the struggles within Arab American communities.

▪ SUAD JOSEPH

SEE ALSO Arab American Women.

Asian American Feminism

The aim of female education is perfect submission, not cultivation and the development of the mind.
　　　　　　　　　　　　　—Confucius

All the fuss about Bobbitt! It's the standard thing in the Philippines. If you have someone who's fooling around, you cut off his penis! Talk about different cultural perspectives.
　　　　　　—Ninotchka Rosca, in A. Magazine

Offering a rich array of immigrant and U.S.-born women's experience, Asian American feminists extend their activism from East Asia, South Asia, Southeast Asia, and the Pacific Islands across to the Americas. With cultural and family ties to Asia still strong, Asian American women challenge practices common in Asia, such as arranged marriages, sex trafficking, female infanticide, and *purdah* (social seclusion), while making their own imprint on U.S. feminism. As the two quotes illustrate, the impressions can be widely divergent.

The very presence of Asian women in the Americas reflects the courage and defiance of foremothers who endured great hardship to begin new lives in U.S. society, where racial hostility toward Asian émigrés has dominated. Poverty and economic turmoil in Asia drove men into indentured labor markets building the railroads and working the fields on the U.S. mainland and Hawaii. Outnumbered by men more than twenty to one in the late 1800s, Asian women came to the United States most commonly as Japanese picture brides, wedded to husbands they had met only once, if ever; as farm, hotel, and domestic laborers; and as sex workers in brothels for unmarried Asian men. Asian immigrant women and men have been demonized as "immoral, depraved heathens" and subjected to lynchings, beatings, and riots; Asian women, and Chinese women in particular, have been targeted in antiprostitution campaigns and depicted as the "sexually subservient 'Oriental' female."

Such portrayals remain and are integral to the experience of Asian American women. The popular image of the "exotic, erotic, docile, and submissive" Asian female, still perpetuated by the mass media, has radicalized many Asian American women, who have experienced racial and sexual affronts on college campuses, at places of employment, and in the course of daily life. Many cases of sexual harassment that have reached the nation's highest courts have been brought by Asian American women. Asian American feminists scored a victory with the federal Violence Against Women Act of 1994 by securing protections for battered immigrant women who previously risked deportation for leaving abusive rela-

tionships. Asian American feminists have been active in establishing domestic violence services for Asian women, bringing women's issues to the attention of the Asian community and Asian issues to the women's movement. The works of feminist writers such as Maxine Hong Kingston and Janice Mirikitani also have helped to define a new sense of Asian womanhood.

The use of the word "feminist" is a matter of some debate among Asian American women activists. Many Asian women are less than comfortable with a label so closely linked to the mainstream women's movement, where issues of race and racism loom. Yet Asian American feminists are active participants in women's organizations and have played significant leadership roles, for example, Irene Natividad, who was head of the National Women's Political Caucus from 1985 to 1989.

Regardless of how they describe themselves, Asian American activists tackle both gender and race issues and in doing so are a vital part of the multicultural women's movement. Labor organizers struggle to overcome stratification by race and immigration status, even at women-owned designer companies such as Jessica McClintock's. Asian American women's health organizations have been founded to ensure that Asian priorities are met. Asian American lesbians are creating visibility for Asian lesbians, gays, and bisexuals. Civil rights activists have drawn attention to the issue of hate violence against Asian women and other women of color.

International women's coalitions bridge the distance between Asian and Asian American feminists, taking on the mail-order bride business in the United States as well as sex trafficking and the sex tourism industry around U.S. military bases and in countries like Thailand. These groups reach across the diaspora of Filipinas, who are forced to seek work around the globe to support their families; they bring attention to tragedies of war, from the sexual enslavement of Korean "comfort women" to the *hibakusha* survivors of the nuclear bombings of Hiroshima and Na-gasaki. They protest human rights violations ex-emplified in the dowry deaths of Indian women, female infanticide in China, and the selective abortion of female fetuses throughout Asia. In linking these issues to struggles of women every-where, Asian American women activists deepen the understanding and spirit of feminism for all women.

Asian American Women: Special Issue, A. *Magazine* (New York: Metro East Publications, 1994); Asian Women United of California, *Making Waves* (Boston: Beacon Press, 1989).

▪ HELEN ZIA

SEE ALSO Asian Pacific Women.

Black Feminism

Women of African origin in the United States have always been keenly aware of the im-pact of race, class, and gender oppression upon their lives. Since slavery, they have struggled indi-vidually and in groups, spontaneously and in for-mal organizations, to eradicate the multiple injus-tices that they and their communities face.

The term *Black feminism* was not widely used until the inception of the contemporary Black women's movement in the 1970s. However, Black feminist scholars frequently apply it to a variety of Black women's survival strategies and actions in the past. It is used to characterize Black women's tradition of courage, independence, and pragma-tism under the brutal conditions of slavery and in-stitutionalized racism. Black women's widespread employment outside of the home has sometimes been cited as evidence of their feminist goals, al-though economic necessity has been a more likely motive. Black women's activism, which has focused upon a range of issues, has been de-scribed as feminist, especially when it has oc-curred in all-female groupings. Black feminism has of course been used to define political theory and practice that explicitly addresses gender and sexual oppression in Black women's lives.

What most clearly distinguishes Black femi-nism from the politics of mainstream European American feminism is its focus upon the simul-taneity of oppressions that affect Black and other women of color, especially racism, sexism, class oppression, and homophobia. Issues of particular concern to Black women, such as lynching or sterilization abuse, cannot be solely attributed to gender discrimination. Issues that affect all women, for example, battering, are simultane-ously shaped by racial identity, class status, and sexual orientation as well as by gender.

African American women began to express concern publicly about their situation as women in the nineteenth century. In the early 1800s, most Black women were enslaved, but free Black women participated in the abolitionist cause. Some, like Maria Stewart, Frances E. W. Harper, and Sojourner Truth, spoke out about Black women's rights. Sojourner Truth was active in the women's rights movement, and her oft-quoted 1851 "Ain't I a Woman" speech (which may have been inaccurately transcribed) nevertheless illus-trates how gender oppression has unique reper-cussions for Black women living under a racist, economically exploitive system.

The struggle to pass the Fifteenth Amendment, which extended the voting franchise to Black males (at least on paper), caused splits between Black and white women. Most Black women agreed with Frederick Douglass, a staunch advo-cate of women's rights, that it was critical to win the vote for at least some of the Black population at that time, even if it meant delaying universal suffrage for women. The woman suffrage move-ment continued to be undermined by racism, for example, when white women appealed to white supremacist males to add more white voters to the electorate by supporting votes for women.

By the end of the nineteenth century, Black women had organized their own network of clubs.

These groups supported woman suffrage but prioritized a range of social and political issues that affected Black communities as well as Black women specifically. Antilynching activism, brought to national attention by journalist and activist Ida B. Wells-Barnett, not only challenged racist terrorism but also the sexual stereotyping of Black women as immoral in contrast to pure white women, whom lynching supposedly avenged. The National Association of Colored Women, formed in 1896, brought together more than one hundred Black women's clubs. Leaders in the Black women's club movement such as Josephine St. Pierre Ruffin, Mary Church Terrell, and Anna Julia Cooper, author of *A Voice from the South by a Black Woman of the South*, were outspoken about the needs of Black women and girls, although they did not describe themselves as feminists.

During the first half of the twentieth century, Black women's activism focused primarily on challenging racism and the demoralizing social and economic problems that it spawned. Gender issues could still be raised in this context. Amy Jacques Garvey wrote about women's rights as editor of the women's page of *The Negro World*, the weekly newspaper of the United Negro Improvement Association. She expressed concern about Black women's situation in the Americas and, as a Pan-Africanist, demonstrated an internationalist perspective about women of color around the world. In 1947, novelist Ann Petry published an article in the widely circulated *Negro Digest* entitled, "What's Wrong with Negro Men?" which criticized sexism within the Black community.

Black women's participation in the civil rights movement during the 1950s and 1960s was crucial, although few were recognized for their leadership. In fact, frustration with male dominance in the civil rights and Black nationalist movements as well as dissatisfaction with the narrowness of white feminists' agendas were among the reasons that Black women began to confront the impact of gender oppression in their own lives.

In 1970, writer Toni Cade Bambara edited a collection entitled *The Black Woman*. Although not uniformly feminist in perspective, the contributors did examine what it meant to be simultaneously Black and female and opened up a dialogue that continues today. In 1973, a group of Black feminists in New York formed the National Black Feminist Organization (NBFO) and held a conference that drew hundreds of Black feminists from all over the country.

As the decade continued, more and more Black women began to question for the first time the reality of sexual oppression within the Black community as well as how the sexism of the society as a whole impacted them as Black women. The work of Black feminist writers and theorists, most notably Alice Walker, Ntozake Shange, and Michele Wallace, led to national debates about sexual politics in the Black community.

In 1977, the Combahee River Collective, a grassroots Black feminist organization in Boston, which had begun as a chapter of NBFO, issued a position paper that analyzed the intersection of oppression in Black women's lives and asserted the legitimacy of feminist organizing by Black women. The Collective's work broke significant new ground because it was explicitly socialist, addressed homophobia, and called for sisterhood among Black women of various sexual orientations. In fact, the early commitment of Black lesbian feminists such as Audre Lorde, Pat Parker, Margaret Sloan, and Barbara Smith was crucial to building the movement in the 1970s, when many heterosexual Black women were reluctant to identify themselves as feminists.

Black feminists' autonomous organizing began to influence strongly other parts of the women's movement in the 1980s. They challenged white feminists to eradicate racism, to broaden the scope of what they defined as women's issues, to integrate their organizations, and to share leadership with women of color.

In the 1990s, Black feminism has had a positive effect on many aspects of the Black community. It has been a particularly successful catalyst in the growth of Black women's studies. In 1991, a grass-roots effort, African American Women in Defense of Ourselves, gathered more than sixteen hundred signatures for a widely circulated ad in response to the Anita Hill–Clarence Thomas hearings. In 1995, amid controversy, Black feminists spoke out about the patriarchal assumptions of the male-only Million Man March. However contested, Black feminism, rooted in the struggles of generations of Black women, continues to play a vital role in the sociopolitical life of the United States.

Patricia Hill Collins, *Black Feminist Thought* (Boston: Unwin Hyman, 1990); Beverly Guy-Sheftall, ed., *Words of Fire: An Anthology of African-American Feminist Thought* (New York: New Press, 1995); Barbara Smith, ed., *Home Girls: A Black Feminist Anthology* (New York: Kitchen Table Press, 1983).

■ BARBARA SMITH

SEE ALSO African American Women; Black Club-women's Movement; National Black Feminist Organization; Womanism.

Chicana Feminism

Beginning in the 1960s a Chicana feminist movement developed that addressed the specific issues affecting Chicanas as women of color in the United States. Through their political organizations, activities, and writings, Chicana feminists assessed their participation in the larger Chicano social protest movement. In the same way that Chicano males were analyzing their unequal status in U.S. society, Chicanas examined the forces shaping their own life circumstances as women.

Chicana feminists published their writings in newsletters, pamphlets, and feminist newspapers. In the first issue of the Chicana newspaper, published in 1971, *Hijas de Cuauhtemoc* (Daughters

of Cuauhtemoc), Anna Nieto Gomez called for an elimination of sexism in Chicano families, communities, and in the male-dominated Chicano movement. Similarly, Bernice Rincon, another voice of Chicana feminism, argued in her magazine/newsletter, *Regeneracion*, that Chicanas could no longer be relegated to a subservient status. Chicanas needed to have access to key leadership positions. Enriqueta Longeaux y Vasquez, founder of the New Mexico–based Chicana newspaper *El Grito*, wrote numerous articles calling on Chicanas to challenge sexism within their communities and racism in the larger society. Her articles addressed a variety of issues facing Chicanas. She examined a woman's role in the family, her experiences with discrimination in education and the workplace, her economic circumstances, and the development of survival strategies.

The publication of Chicana feminist newspapers and newsletters provided a basis for the development of a feminist communication network for Chicanas. As in other feminist movements, activity within the Chicana community was facilitated by the rise of a feminist press. Other publications that raised consciousness among Chicanas included *Encuentro Femenil*, *La Comadre*, and *Hembra*. By the 1980s a small group of Chicanas had entered universities and colleges and started to produce research studies on Chicanas. A direct connection exists between the development of Chicana feminist thought and the rise of Chicana studies as an academic field. This scholarship has challenged many of the assumptions inherent in both ethnic studies and women's studies by emphasizing the interconnectedness of race, class, and gender.

Chicana feminists have organized numerous regional and national conferences to address their concerns. These meetings were designed to draw attention to the most pressing needs of Chicanas, such as welfare rights, reproductive rights, health care, poverty, immigration, and education. Chicana feminist groups placed demands on many national Chicano organizations. As early as 1972 a group of Chicanas exerted pressure on the leaders of the National Chicano Political Conference, meeting in San Jose, California, in order to have their needs addressed by the entire organization. Similarly, in 1982 a Chicana feminist group organized by students from the University of California at Berkeley called for the National Association for Chicano Studies (NACS) to address their concerns. In 1984 women in NACS formed a Chicana caucus within the organization and succeeded in changing the theme for the national conference to "Voces de la Mujer" (Voices of Women).

Chicana feminist lesbians struggled against the sources of oppression facing other Chicana feminists but, in addition, they fought against homophobia within their Chicano communities. Chicano cultural nationalists viewed a Chicana feminist lesbian movement as an extreme form of feminism. The writings of Cherríe Moraga and Gloria Andzaldúa address the impact of homophobia on their daily lives. Chicana lesbians adopted a variety of organizational strategies including joining Chicana feminist groups, forming lesbian coalitions across racial and ethnic lines, and developing separate Chicana lesbian groups. All strategies represented a response to the discrimination and marginalization experienced by Chicana lesbians.

All Chicana feminists continue to examine the intersection of race, class, and gender in their daily lives. They emphasize that Chicanas have made few gains in comparison to white men and women and to Chicano men in terms of every socioeconomic indicator. Over the last forty years, for example, they have made only small occupational moves from low-paying unskilled or service jobs to higher-paying clerical or professional positions. The 1990 census shows that about 66 percent of all Chicanas remain occupationally segregated in service, sales, clerical, and factory work. Less than 15 percent have entered the occupational ranks of professionals, administrators, and

business managers. Poverty levels among both Chicanas and Chicanos have reached three times that of the white population. Chicana feminists point out that the persistently low educational attainment levels of Chicanas underscore the negative consequences of race, class, and gender stratification.

Chicana feminist discourse has also focused on the persistence of exclusionary practices within feminist movements. A major theme within Chicana feminism involves the origins, nature, and consequences of exclusionary practices. Chicana feminists have joined the voices of other feminist women of color in criticizing the movement's limited attention to differences among women on the basis of race, ethnicity, class, and sexual orientation. Chicana feminists are critical of any feminist analysis that treats race/ethnicity as a secondary source of oppression. Chicana feminist voices call for a reformulation of feminist theory and practice in order to establish a more inclusive framework for analyzing the experiences of all women and for bringing about meaningful political change.

Alma M. García, "The Development of Chicana Feminist Discourse, 1980," *Gender & Society*, 3, no. 2 (1989): 217–38.

■ ALMA M. GARCÍA

SEE ALSO Chicanas and Mexican American Women; Feminism, Latina.

Cultural Feminism

Cultural feminism refers to the multiracial, multicultural movement of women's expressive art that arose with and deeply influenced the women's movement begun in the 1970s. The flowering of a specifically lesbian culture and the sharing of lesbian life and experience were crucial aspects of this artistic revival. Within this broader movement lesbian separatism gained its first expression. Not all cultural works produced by women in this period were self-consciously women-centered or committed to women's liberation, but they benefited from the strength of an explicitly feminist community.

A women's cultural renaissance swept the United States and many parts of Europe, Asia, Latin America, the Middle East, and Africa in the 1970s and 1980s. Writers, artists, poets, musicians, photographers, journalists, and performers shared in a wellspring of energies released after centuries of suppression, erasure, and marginalization. Influenced by the liberation movements of peoples of color and formerly colonized peoples in the United States and abroad, women were inspired both by the struggles of their respective communities and by their affinity with the women's movement.

In the United States, Native, Asian, African, Latin, and Euro-American women produced a marvel of works from Ntozake Shange's choreopoem, *For colored girls who have considered suicide when the rainbow is enuf*, to Judy Chicago's cathedral-like celebration of women's history in her artistic panorama, "The Dinner Party," to Marge Piercy's epoch of Jewish women's resistance during the Holocaust, *Gone to Soldiers*, to the evocation of slavery in Toni Morrison's ancestral homage, *Beloved*. The resurrection of the goddess was portrayed in Mayumi Oda's artistic pantheon of Buddhist compassion and wisdom, the harmonious chorus of the Southwest pueblos was depicted in the intricately layered paintings of Native American artist Helen Hardin, the portraiture of daily life was shown in the barrio of Sandra Cisneros's *House on Mango Street*, and breathtaking healing manifested in Leslie Marmon Silko's *Ceremony*.

Women's music festivals became annual events, drawing thousands. Poetry readings, concerts, dance recitals, repertory theatre, and art exhibits begun in obscurity burgeoned into major events. Women's philharmonic orchestras were founded and the works of classical women composers performed. The work of lesser-known artists and writ-

ers such as the German graphic artist Käthe Kollwitz, the Mexican self-portraitist Frida Kahlo, the African American sculptor Elizabeth Catlett, and white, working-class writers including Meridel LeSueur and Tillie Olsen was reclaimed. Similarly, traditional female art forms like quilting, needlework, and tapestry were newly recognized. Women's oral histories revised the historical record, and women's spirituality reclaimed ancient Wicca and goddess traditions on the one hand, while challenging the patriarchal conventions of established religions on the other.

Lesbian feminists including Audre Lorde, Adrienne Rich, Barbara Smith, Irena Klepfisz, Gloria Anzaldúa, Cherríe Moraga, Estela Trujillo, Meg Christian, Holly Near, Cris Williamson, Kitty Tsui, Rita Mae Brown, Susan Griffin, Judy Grahn, Michelle Cliff, Paula Gunn Allen, Charlotte Bunch, and Lillian Faderman produced a veritable avalanche of poetry, essays, plays, music, comedy, and scholarship that transformed both lesbian and feminist ideas. Giving voice to a multiracial and multicultural lesbian experience, these women presented a new understanding of how heterosexuality is sanctioned and privileged in a male-dominated culture. Likewise, lesbian literature offered one of the first sustained analyses of the simultaneous and intersecting structures that enforce race, class, gender, and sexual oppressions.

From this outpouring a feminist scholarship arose that accorded this cultural renaissance a more overarching theoretical significance. It defined culture as the ordered system of meaning in terms of which people explain their world, express their feelings, and make their judgments. From this definition feminist scholars claimed that women produce distinct cultures, different from those produced by men.

These cultures arise as a result of women's experiences that come from both a sexual division of labor in which women do specific work not usually performed by men and by the oppression of women (by men) and its consequent inequality. All women do not have the same culture or share the same beliefs; but women of each particular race, ethnicity, or group have a consciousness, a way of seeing that is common among them.

To give examples of women's cultures, to look at women's poems, stories, paintings, music, and quilts from this point of view is to make women's actions and beliefs intelligible on their own terms. It is to recognize women's strategies for coping, surviving, shaping, and changing the parameters of their lives, and it is to recognize the authenticity of women's historical achievement. The women's cultural renaissance of the 1970s and 1980s made this visible. Once seen, our whole understanding of women's lives and their works changed from being a mere addendum to men's accomplishment to being coequals in the struggles and triumphs of humanity.

Bettina Aptheker, *Tapestries of Life: Women's Work, Women's Consciousness and the Meaning of Daily Existence* (Amherst: University of Massachusetts Press, 1989); Mary Belenky, et al., *Women's Ways of Knowing: The Development of Self, Voice and Mind* (New York: Basic Books, 1988); Alice Walker, "In Search of Our Mothers' Gardens," in her book of the same title (New York: Harcourt Brace Jovanovich, 1984).

▪ BETTINA APTHEKER

Ecofeminism

Ecofeminism is an international, multicultural, antihierarchical movement that is still evolving. The term *ecofeminism* was coined by French theorist Francoise d'Eaubonne in 1974. The first self-identified ecofeminist political gathering was a 1980 conference in Amherst, Massachusetts, called "Women and Life on Earth: Ecofeminism in the 1980s," attended by over one thousand women. Ecofeminist theory synthesizes an ecological critique of modern Western science with its mechanistic and dualistic nature philosophy and technologies of domination with a radical feminist critique of gender-based and dualistic hierarchies. Politically, ecofeminists oppose all hierarchical forms of ownership, power, privilege, and

agency; support nature-friendly science, technology, and democracy; and celebrate diversity in nature and culture. While the principal focus is on gender hierarchies, whether in values or political power structures, ecofeminists recognize all forms of oppression as interrelated and work at demonstrating relationships and making connections between movements for nature and movements for human freedom. For ecofeminists, the configuration of modern Western science and technology and capitalism and Eurocentric masculinist culture together pose a threat to the continuation of life on earth. Politically, this critique is reflected in the strong commitment by ecofeminists to multiculturalism and transnationalism.

Ecofeminists are also committed to the recognition and protection of fertility as the source of life and wealth, and to preserving species diversity and cultural diversity as the basis of a healthy living world. Ecofeminists advocate nonviolent direct action as a form of opposition to the modern state and are leading activists in the peace movement, women's and reproductive rights movements, environmental struggles, and animal advocacy. They oppose unnecessary and dangerous technologies such as bovine growth hormone and genetic engineering as well as contemporary consumerism and the inequitable division of wealth worldwide. Ecofeminism is a utopian movement, engaged in a process of resistance and revision. It represents the possibility of a nontotalitarian, whole world. Many artists identify as ecofeminists and are presenting visionary and critical work as writers, painters, performance artists, playwrights, and musicians.

▪ YNESTRA KING

Electoral Feminism

The suffragists who finally secured women's right to vote in 1920 thought women's enfranchisement would give them more power to win political victories for their women's rights agenda. Winning theoretical representation by men, however, did not mean winning real political power.

The second wave of feminism in the late 1960s gave birth to a number of new organizations that use overtly political strategies to confront age-old challenges. Some feminists argued that moving more women's rights supporters into public office would do little to change inherently unjust economic, political, and social systems. However, most of the new feminist organizations began to engage in electoral politics in addition to other strategies to create legal as well as cultural change. In the early years after its founding in 1966, the National Organization for Women (NOW) challenged men in power through court cases, protests, and legislative work on issues such as job discrimination, the Equal Rights Amendment (ERA), and abortion rights. The National Women's Political Caucus formed in 1971 as an electoral arm of the feminist movement. The group continues to support women candidates, organize women at state and local levels, and influence both parties to support women. Rutgers University established the Center for the American Woman and Politics in 1971 to track, analyze, and encourage women's political participation. The Women's Campaign Fund, set up in 1974, offers financial support and technical assistance to candidates of both parties. After 1977 reforms in political action committee (PAC) laws, NOW established a PAC that requires the candidates it endorses to support not only ERA and abortion rights but also lesbian rights, civil rights, and poor women's rights.

In the 1970s, noting that women legislators championed ERA and other women's rights issues more than men did, feminists changed their strategy from influencing the people in power to becoming the people in power. When the time limit ran out on ratification of the ERA in June 1982, feminists vowed, "We'll remember in November." The gender gap—the difference in male-female voting patterns—showed up in races nationwide that year, as 53 percent of women voted Democratic and 47 percent Republican; the numbers were

exactly the reverse among men. NOW's intensive campaigns to recruit and field candidates doubled the number of women serving in the senates of both Florida and Illinois, two of the states that had not supported ERA's ratification.

In the face of the antifeminist politics of the Reagan-Bush era in the 1980s, women's electoral activity surged. The YWCA joined more overtly political groups to offer training not just for women candidates but also for campaign managers, staff members, and volunteers. After a concerted effort by feminists, Democrats in 1984 nominated New York attorney Geraldine Ferraro for vice president, a first for one of the two major political parties. The same year, "EMILY's List" (an acronym for "Early Money Is Like Yeast," that is, it rises) initiated the breakthrough technique of "bundling," or gathering campaign contributions directly payable to pro-choice Democratic women in key races. Several years later pro-choice Republican women formed a similar group, the "WISH List," which stands for "Women in the Senate and House." When U.S. Representative Patricia Schroeder (D., Colo.) announced her presidential bid at a 1988 NOW conference, activists pledged hundreds of thousands of dollars to support her campaign.

By the early 1990s several factors turned feminist electoral activism into front-page news. Presidents Reagan and Bush stacked the U.S. Supreme Court with conservative judges, thus posing a threat to abortion rights legislation. Clarence Thomas won confirmation to the Court, even though law professor Anita Hill had accused him of sexual harassment. Feminist groups organized a record-breaking 750,000 people to march on Washington in support of abortion rights in April 1992. In the November 1992 elections sweep, which headlines dubbed the "Year of the Woman," women doubled their numbers in Congress to nearly 11 percent. In sharp contrast to their male counterparts, one-third of the women who served in the 103d Congress were women of color, roughly the same proportion as their representation among women in the general population. Two years later Republicans won control of the House and Senate in an upset that pundits called the "revenge of the angry white men." Today organizers continue to focus on electing feminist women to shape public policy on women's rights.

• PATRICIA IRELAND

SEE ALSO Electoral Politics; EMILY's List; Gender Gap; National Organization for Women (NOW); National Women's Political Caucus; Voters for Choice.

International Feminism

Since its beginnings in the nineteenth century, feminism has been committed to international solidarity, cooperation, and the creation of institutions to advance these objectives. The international expansion of feminist ideas was aided not only by contacts with élite women who had the means to travel but also by organizations such as the Second Socialist International and new organizations committed to support the struggles for woman suffrage in different countries.

The first international women's organization, the World's Woman's Christian Temperance Union, was founded in 1884 by Frances Willard as part of the U.S. WCTU. In 1888 the U.S. National Suffrage Association organized the first International Congress of Women. Held in Washington, D.C., it resulted in the founding of the International Council of Women, a federation of national councils concerned with women's issues, which eventually established headquarters in Zurich, Switzerland.

In February 1902, at an international suffrage conference sponsored by the National American Woman Suffrage Association, with Susan B. Anthony presiding and delegates from ten countries, another international body was created: the International Woman Suffrage Alliance. This new group was composed of organizations committed to obtaining woman suffrage and sought "to secure the enfranchisement of the women of all nations, and to unite the friends of women's suffrage throughout the world in organized co-operation and fraternal helpfulness." It met for the first time in Berlin in 1904 and elected Carrie Chapman Catt president. The meeting was attended by representatives from eleven countries, including the founder and first president of the National Association of Colored Women, Mary Church Terrell, the only U.S. delegate who addressed the assembly in fluent German. By the eve of World War I, the Alliance, which met every two years, had member groups in twenty European countries. Its meetings provided a crucial forum for discussions, especially when the English suffragists began their militant tactics of hunger strikes and acts of civil disobedience.

Feminists also created International Women's Day. Since 1909 U.S. socialist women had celebrated National Woman's Day on the last Sunday of February by holding demonstrations in favor of woman suffrage. In 1910 the International Conference of Socialist Women met in Copenhagen, Denmark, and declared Woman's Day an international celebration. German delegate Clara Zetkin proposed that socialist women hold demonstrations throughout the world on the same day, but no date was officially adopted. The first International Woman's Day was celebrated on March 18, 1911, the anniversary of the Paris Commune. Over one million women and men took to the streets in Austria, Denmark, Germany, and Switzerland in support of women's rights. The marches spread to other countries but in the United States socialist women continued to celebrate Woman's Day in February.

After World War I Russia's new Bolshevik government adopted as International Woman's Day March 8 (the day the 1917 Revolution was begun by women and children protesting the lack of food). The holiday gradually became an exclusively Communist observance, and by the

1950s ceased entirely. The resurgence of feminism in the 1960s revived the observance of International Women's Day on March 8 throughout the world.

Feminists also introduced the issue of women's continuing second-class status into the post–World War II international agenda, beginning with the United Nations proclamation of the International Woman's Year (1975) and the world conference in Mexico City, where 125 nations adopted recommendations designed to ensure equal participation of women in all facets of society. That same year the United Nations General Assembly established the U.N. Decade for Women (1975–1985), later extended to a second decade under the theme "Equality, Development and Peace."

In the late 1960s feminism expanded rapidly in the United States and in a few European countries; but in countries still attempting to overcome the effects of colonialism, racism, nationalism, and imperialism, its growth was much slower. In a world divided by the cold war, uneven development, apartheid, and the Palestinian-Israeli conflict, interaction in the first three world conferences on women was at times heated. Nevertheless, since 1975, when women first created a tribune of nongovernmental organizations to parallel the official meeting, gatherings created a space for direct contact, exchange of information and experiences, and the gradual creation of international networks. By the end of the cold war, despite historical and cultural differences, racial and ethnic inequalities, and socioeconomic disparities, women organized globally to act effectively in the international arena. They succeeded in redefining women's rights as human rights in the 1993 Vienna Conference on human rights. They also shaped the program on environment and development adopted at the 1992 Rio de Janeiro Conference, the recommendations on population voted on at the 1994 Cairo Conference on Population and Development, and the economic and social platform resulting from the 1995 Copenhagen World Summit for Social Development. In the world women's conference

held in September 1995, in China, thirty thousand women attended the Non-Governmental Organizations (NGO) Forum in Huairou and 16,921 persons participated in the official U.N. conference in Beijing. The Platform for Action that was developed is a comprehensive plan recommending action in twelve areas considered obstacles to women's advancement, including poverty, violence, economic structures, power sharing, and the media. The platform incorporates earlier recommendations and addresses women's health, education, and training; their marital and sexual rights; and their political, economic, and social empowerment.

　　　　　　　　　　　　　▪ MARYSA NAVARRO

SEE ALSO International Women's Day.

Jewish Feminism

Jewish feminists have a double agenda. We monitor anti-Semitism in society, including in the women's movement, but our greatest challenge is to fight sexism within Judaism. As such, ours is the doctrine of unmitigated *chutzpah*.

"The world cannot be without sons and daughters," said Rabbi Judah the Prince, who compiled the *Mishnah* (the Oral Law, redacted in the fourth century), "yet happy is he who has sons and woe to him who has daughters." The ancient tradition of son preference continues to this day: nearly 92 percent of American Jewish couples say they want their first-born to be a boy. To Jewish feminists, this rudimentary sexism is symptomatic of a world in need of repair.

Indeed, we believe that Judaism's core mandate *tikkun olam*—to repair the world—is a commandment every Jew must take seriously, and we try to fulfill it by dismantling patriarchy with the text of Jewish ethics and the equity blueprints of feminism.

We also take seriously the commandment to do *tzedakah*—the Hebrew word for charity, caring, and "right action," whose linguistic root, *tzedek*, means justice. The difference between Jewish feminists and other Jews is that we apply that mandate to gender. We believe that the biblical injunction to "pursue justice" should lead every Jew to challenge the gender double standard and refuse to accept tradition as an excuse for inequality or oppression.

Jewish feminists believe that women should not only perform *tzedakah* but also receive it. We ask that the Jewish community, which is so generous to the poor and hungry, also be generous to women who are spiritually impoverished and hungry for power over their own lives. We argue that the long history of Jewish suffering demands that women be made strong for themselves *and* for the sake of Jewish communal survival. To achieve its diverse goals, Jewish feminism takes many forms: Religious feminists target injustice in the synagogue, promoting women's ordination, feminist theology, and gender-inclusive God-language, liturgy, and rituals.

Some Jewish feminists concentrate on secular issues, be it disarmament, the environment, the sanctuary movement, lesbian and gay rights, child care, or women's health initiatives. Others work against hunger, racism, poverty, violence, or sexual harassment in coalition with other grassroots groups and political constituencies, organizing, writing, and speaking out for social and economic justice. Still others choose to focus on Jewish institutions, struggling to establish nonsexist child-care centers, parenting classes, support groups, and social programs, or to organize lectures, films, and courses that promote feminist perspectives, whether on marriage, political representation, or peace in the Middle East.

Jewish feminists introduce nonsexist books into Hebrew schools. We collect oral histories so that women's reality will be part of the bedrock Jewish narrative. We support projects that specifically benefit women—such as *Lilith*, the magazine of Jewish feminism; or the Israel Women's Network, a feminist advocacy group; or battered women's shelters here and in Israel. Many of us are pioneers in intergroup dialogue with women of color and solidarity efforts with Arab women.

Finally, Jewish feminists are complainers. We protest when Jewish men treat women's issues as peripheral to the main battles of the community, or when white Christian women treat ethnic, religious, or racial issues as peripheral to feminism. We complain when Jewish organizations worry about the impact of affirmative action on Jewish *men* and ignore the fact that many Jewish women have benefited from affirmative action. We monitor Jewish agencies, more than half of whose staffs are women but only 2 percent of whose executive directors are women. We protest when the Jewish establishment makes politically pragmatic alliances with evangelical Christians and right-wing conservatives.

In the personal sphere, we insist that girl and boy babies be greeted as equally precious new lives. We attack whoever buys into the "Jewish American Princess" stereotype, gentile or Jew. We talk back. We are not always polite. Sometimes we confound other Jews and other feminists and make them uncomfortable. But what we want is clear and simple: equality as women with men, as Jews with gentiles, as Jews with Jews. We want to be seen and heard. We want to be valued not just because we are devoted wives or mothers of the Jewish people but because we ourselves *are* half the Jewish people, half its history, and half its destiny.

- LETTY COTTIN POGREBIN

SEE ALSO Jewish Women.

Latina Feminism

I come from a long line of eloquent illiterates whose history reveals what words don't say.
—Lorna D. Cervantes

The history of Latina feminism has gone largely undocumented. However, as Lorna D. Cervantes's poem indicates, this lack of documentation does not mean a lack of action by Latina feminists on behalf of women's issues. But first, what is meant by "Latinas"? The Latino population in the United States uses different ethnic labels—Chicana, Mexican American, Cuban American, Puerto Rican American, Central American, and so on. Most recently, however, the ethnic term Latina/Latino is used as the most inclusive. It refers to any person of Latin American ancestry residing in the United States. Latino also connotes identification with Indo-American heritage rather than Spanish European. Consequently, Latina feminists have felt a strong allegiance with feminists of color in the United States. Some Latinas are recent immigrants and others are descendants of the original Mexicans who resided in the Southwest since 1848, when the Treaty of Guadalupe Hidalgo ended the Mexican War and Mexico lost over 50 percent of its territory to the United States. Most Latinas reside in the five southwestern states (California, Texas, Arizona, New Mexico, and Colorado). However, sizable numbers of Latinas of Puerto Rican descent reside in New York, of Cuban descent in Miami, and of Mexican and Puerto Rican descent in Chicago.

Historically the Latino community has always had strong women leaders, from Emma Tenayuca, a famous labor leader in Texas, to María Mercedes Barbudo, who was jailed in 1824 in Puerto Rico for conspiring against the Spanish colonizers, to *las soldaderas*, who fought in the Mexican Revolution of 1910. "Soldadera" literally means female soldier. Soldaderas helped democratize Mexico from a feudal country to one where land was distributed among peasants. Marta Cotera documents that among the victims of social injustice were such women as Juanita, of Downiesville, California, who was lynched in 1851; Chipita Rodriguez, who was the only woman ever to be executed in Texas; and countless other Chicanas who were killed by Texas Rangers during their raids on communities.

Latinas in the United States have been forced to resist gender subordination within their own communities as well as gender, class, and race/ethnic discrimination in society at large. Latinas' "triple" oppression has resulted in their earning less, receiving less education, and having more children to support than whites or than men in their own group. The core concerns of Latina feminists are material conditions such as employment, poverty, education, health, child care, and reproductive rights. Their political mobilization historically has revolved not only around these material conditions, issues that affect them disproportionately, but also has involved political empowerment for themselves and their communities. A model of this type of leadership is exhibited by Antonia Pantoja, founder of the Puerto Rican Association for Community Affairs, who emphasizes collective decision making, the development of new leaders, especially among the youth, and the good of the group over the personal gain of the individual. Latina feminists' concerns always have been intimately tied to those of their communities. Many Latinas have fought side by side in revolutionary struggles in Cuba, Nicaragua, and El Salvador, and they have worked to unionize miners and farm workers in the Southwest as well as garment workers in the Northeast. From Emma Tenayuca in Texas to Dolores Huerta in California, one of the foremost leaders of the United Farm Workers Union, to Esperanza Martell, cofounder of the Latin Women's Collective in New York City, their political efforts on behalf of women's issues have been embedded in their political activities.

Currently there is a flurry of academic and artistic production from Latina feminists who are making connections with Latina activists in the United States and in the rest of the Americas. Some of the most exciting work is being created by Latina feminists who are questioning the heterosexism of Latino culture and are beginning to document the lives of Latina lesbians. These scholars are also working with Latina feminists and women of color to form domestic and international alliances around women's issues. In the domestic arena are such organizations as the Women of Color Resource Center, which is committed to creating inclusive political agendas to span ethnic and cultural differences.

International alliances have been built among Latinas in the United States and Latin America through scholarly conferences, political mobilization along the U.S.-Mexico border, and with Latinas residing on the mainland who are cultivating cultural and political alliances with Latinas residing in Puerto Rico.

Gloria Anzaldua, ed., *Making Face, Making Soul/Haciendo Caras* (San Francisco: Aunt Lute Foundation, 1990); Marta Cotera, *Chicana Feminism* (Austin, Tex.: Information System Development, 1977); Adela de la Torre and Beatríz M. Pesquera, eds., *Building with Our Hands: New Directions in Chicana Studies* (Berkeley: University of California Press, 1993).

■ AÍDA HURTADO

SEE ALSO Feminism, Chicana; Feminism, Puerto Rican; Latinas.

Lesbian Feminism

Although lesbian and feminist communities have overlapped throughout U.S. history, the 1960s saw the development of an unabashedly proud connection between the two. By the mid-1970s lesbian feminism had become perhaps the most assertive arm of the feminist movement, espousing a politic that encouraged feminists to turn their energies toward other women in every aspect of their lives. Lesbianism had become the political shorthand for a radical woman's complete dedication to feminism.

After decades of relative inactivity, organized feminism resurfaced in the 1960s with women's involvement in civil rights, antiwar, and New Left organizations. Although these movements encouraged women's political participation, women

nevertheless tended to play subordinate roles, and they were often locked out of leadership or decision-making positions. As a result, by the mid-1960s women began to meet separately, and some feminists suggested that women's fight against male supremacy was more important than fighting "the system" within leftist organizations such as SDS (Students for a Democratic Society) or CORE (Congress for Racial Equality). Women's liberation organizations such as New York Radical Women (NYRW) and, later, the Redstockings emerged. Focused entirely on gender inequity, radical feminists developed nuanced critiques of social institutions such as marriage and the family. They also developed political action coalitions to strengthen the laws concerning rape and end restrictions on abortion. With the hippie movement and its assertion of free love, unisex clothing, and assertive nonconformity as a backdrop, young, college-educated women pushed a new era of feminist organizing and activism into the public eye.

At the same time, homosexual movements similarly matured from the politics of conformity and assimilation to a more aggressive and positive philosophy of social change. The Stonewall Riots in June 1969 framed the transition from "homophile" activism, which saw no cultural difference between homosexuals and heterosexuals and sought acceptance from the larger society, to the lesbian and gay liberation movement, which saw homosexuals as a distinct social minority and sought equality rather than acceptance. While the lesbian and gay liberation movement popularized the slogan *Gay is good*, radical feminists began to declare that *the personal is political*, asserting critiques of male supremacy.

As women split off from political organizations that refused to address feminist concerns, the committees they forged often took the form of small consciousness-raising groups in which women met to discuss and analyze the sexism they faced. More radical members began to refuse any complicity with patriarchal institutions. This combination of radical feminist politics and women's separatism led to lesbian feminism and lesbian separatism. Of course, many lesbian feminists were lesbians before lesbian feminist philosophies emerged. The separatist lesbian feminists saw gender inequity as the primary site for struggle in contemporary society, and viewed sexuality as a choice. They learned through consciousness-raising groups that "women-identified women" put women first in all ways even if they had previously led heterosexual lives. They encouraged feminists to love other women sexually and argued that if women directed all their energies toward other women, they would not only strengthen feminism but destabilize patriarchal institutions. As they severed their relationships with men, lesbian feminists hoped to construct a new society that valued women and to forge a new culture based on women's values. Although not all feminists who are lesbians subscribed to lesbian feminist ideologies, in the 1970s lesbianism became the political tool that framed a feminist cultural revolution.

Lesbian feminism, however, alienated many women and men. Older or working-class lesbians who felt that they did not choose their sexuality were put off by the political rhetoric that seemed to devalue their lifelong sexual attraction to women. Butch-femme lesbians came under fire from lesbian feminists for seemingly perpetuating oppressive gender roles. Straight, gay, and bisexual men were uneasy or unwanted allies, and by the mid-1970s coalitions between lesbian feminists and lesbian and gay liberation activists seemed to break down completely. Finally, feminists and lesbians of color often rejected lesbian feminism because it did not address pressing issues facing communities of color (such as racist violence or access to health care) and because lesbian separatism left feminists of color socially and culturally alienated from communities of color. Over time these shortcomings limited lesbian feminism's appeal to a very specific and narrow group of women; as separatists, many lesbian

feminist communities have become socially and culturally withdrawn. However, lesbian feminism remains an influential part of lesbian and feminist politics. Its strengths lie in the practical demand that women put women first, and, ideologically, lesbian feminism continues to assert the vital connection between gender and sexual politics.

> Alice Echols, *Daring to Be Bad: Radical Feminism in America 1967–1975* (Minneapolis: Minnesota University Press, 1989); Lillian Faderman, "'Not a Public Relations Movement': Lesbian Revolutions in the 1960s through 1970s," in *Odd Girls and Twilight Lovers: A History of Lesbian Life in Twentieth-Century America* (New York: Columbia University Press, 1991).

▪ NAN ALAMILLA BOYD

SEE ALSO Lesbians.

Marxist Feminism

Marxist feminism as a theoretical construct is a hybrid born of the women's liberation movement in the late 1960s. Before that time, Marxist theorists, to the extent that they were concerned with the situation of women, addressed what they termed "the woman question" and concluded that the "emancipation" of women would occur only with the destruction of capitalism and the construction of socialism, in which women would be freed from dependency on men and be involved in "productive" labor.

Marxist feminism is not monolithic or even unified. With the advent of the women's liberation movement, a few women Marxists began using Marxist theory as a grid to accommodate their own consciousness as newly born feminists without abandoning their fundamental Marxist principles. However, Marxist women who were affiliated with formal organizations, the largest of which were the Communist Party and the Socialist Workers Party, did not stray far from party doctrine, focusing on working class and working women and posing capitalism as the enemy of women's emancipation.

On the other hand, key founders of the early women's liberation groups had worked in the southern civil rights movement; some were already Marxists or were drawn to Marxist theory to understand the relationship of race, class, and gender. As historians Sara Evans, in *Personal Politics*, and Alice Echols, in *Daring to Be Bad*, argue, those "New Left" women brought with them the civil rights movement's idea and practice of "the personal is political," which became the unifying base of the women's liberation movement, whatever other differences emerged. Yet the personal as political essentially contradicted traditional Marxist theory and practice.

Independent Marxists who were not tied to Marxist organizations were less hesitant than party-bound Marxists to reinterpret Marxism in light of their new feminist consciousness. A number of those women were already wrestling in the mid-1960s with reinterpreting Marxism to accommodate the nationalist movements of African Americans, Chicanas/Chicanos, Puerto Ricans, and Native Americans. Frances M. Beal, New York coordinator of the Black Women's Liberation Committee of the Student Nonviolent Coordinating Committee, stated in *Sisterhood Is Powerful*: "If the white groups do not realize that they are in fact fighting capitalism and racism, we do not have common bonds." That view was echoed and applied by other feminists of color, for instance, by Elizabeth Sutherland Martinez to the Chicana/Chicano movement.

Marxist feminists, although small in number, have been highly influential in developing feminist theory. Even feminist theorists who rejected Marxism as applicable to women's liberation, such as Shulamith Firestone, in *The Dialectic of Sex*, and lesbian leader Rita Mae Brown, in *Class and Feminism*, and more recently Catharine MacKinnon, in *Toward a Feminist Theory of the State*, among many others, argued with Marxism

to reach their conclusions that women constituted an oppressed class *as women*.

Marxist theory attracted many new feminists of the late 1960s because it addressed the origin of the suppression of women and related the condition of women to the capitalist system under which they experienced oppression. In their 1846 work, *The German Ideology*, Marx and Engels theorized that the original division of labor was based on division of labor in the family; they concluded that the wife and children were the slaves of the husband and formed the "first property," marking the first instance of a group of people gaining the power to dispose of the "labor-power" of others, the very crux of capitalist development.

After Marx's death, Friedrich Engels in 1884 attempted to trace what he termed "the historical downfall of the female sex" in *The Origin of the Family, Private Property and the State*. In her 1972 introduction to the republication of Engels's text, Marxist-feminist anthropologist Eleanor Leacock wrote, ". . . it is crucial to the organization of women for their liberation to understand that it is the monogamous family as an economic unit, at the heart of class society, that is basic to their subjugation."

Simone de Beauvoir, following Engels, had made the same point based on her 1949 study, *The Second Sex*, which was revived during the 1960s' women's liberation movement and became one of its fundamental texts.

The significant and continuing contribution of Marxist feminism is its identification of women's institutionalized and historic oppression with the system of capitalism.

Angela Y. Davis, *Women, Race and Class* (New York: Random House, 1981); Juliet Mitchell, *Women's Estate* (New York: Random House, 1971); Margaret Randall, *Gathering Rage: The Failure of 20th Century Revolutions to Develop a Feminist Agenda* (New York: Monthly Review Press, 1992).

■ ROXANNE DUNBAR

See also Communism; Feminism, Socialist.

Puerto Rican Feminism

In Puerto Rico during the second half of the nineteenth century an agenda for progress and nation building addressed the status of the rural population, including women, among whom illiteracy was common. Women's efforts secured the first schools for girls in Puerto Rico. Educated women also began to play a more visible and assertive role in Puerto Rican politics. One group of women, members of the privileged creole *hacendado* class of proprietors, actively participated in the separatist movement against Spanish colonial rule. Women such as Mariana Bracetti (1825–1903) and Lola Rodríguez de Tió (1843–1924) are well known for their political defense of Puerto Rican independence.

After the U.S. invasion and occupation of Puerto Rico in 1898, many U.S. sugar and tobacco companies and other industries, such as needlework, were established. Some of the former and most of the latter employed primarily women.

These early-twentieth-century changes coincided with the emergence of a feminist movement. Two major trends characterized the movement: the petit bourgeois and the proletarian. Each developed in a parallel fashion but functioned at distinct and separate social levels. The suffragist leaders were educated women who were primarily concerned with improving women's education and obtaining the right to vote. Organizations such as the Puerto Rican Feminine League and the Puerto Rican Association of Women Suffragists, founded in 1917 and 1925 respectively, played a leading role in this effort. The work and activism of Ana Roqué de Duprey (1853–1933), Isabel Andreu de Aguilar (1887–1948), and Mercedes Solá (1879–1923), among others, helped bring about the passage of the suffrage bill. Solá's essay *Feminismo* (1922) stands today as a legacy and inspiration to the contemporary feminist movement. The efforts of the suffragists culminated in 1929 when a bill was finally approved that granted literate women the right to vote. In 1932

women participated for the first time in legislative elections. Universal suffrage was not approved by the Puerto Rican legislature until 1936.

The proletarian feminist movement developed as an integral part of the organized labor movement. The vanguard of the women's emancipation movement existed within the ranks of the socialist Free Federation of Labor [Federación Libre de Trabajadores, FLT], which also waged legal battles in favor of universal suffrage, better working conditions, and against the economic exploitation of all workers.

One of the most extraordinary women labor leaders of the first decades of the twentieth century was Luisa Capetillo (1880–1922), a socialist labor organizer and a writer who argued on behalf of equal rights for women, free love, and human emancipation. She was a crusader who tried to raise the consciousness of workers through her activities and public challenges to social convention. Capetillo's writings were well ahead of her time. For example, in her book *Mi opinión sobre las libertades, derechos y deberes de la mujer (My Opinion about Women's Freedom, Rights, and Duties)* (1911), she exhorts women to fight for justice and social equality. Other women leaders in the Puerto Rican labor movement included Concepción (Concha) Torres, who, in 1902, became the first woman to give a speech at a public rally; Juana Colón (1875–1971), known as the "Joan of Arc of Comerío," a leader and an active organizer of the tobacco strippers; Genara Pagán and Emilia Hernández, who presided over the Women's Organization Committee of the FLT; and Franca de Armiño, who led the Popular Feminist Association [Asociación Feminista Popular], founded in 1920.

The rapid industrialization of the 1950s and the transformation of the Puerto Rican agrarian economy to an industrial one challenged traditional Puerto Rican values and institutions as well as the role of women. Industrialization opened up new occupations for women; their increasing visibility in the job market was often interpreted as Puerto

Rican patriarchal values succumbing to Americanization. Intellectual and political elites at the time defended cultural traditions and values, even those oppressive to women. This partially explains why the contemporary feminist movement has developed apart from the Puerto Rican independence struggle. Political parties in Puerto Rico have downplayed the issue of feminism and women's liberation. Despite the dramatic changes experienced in Puerto Rico since industrialization and modernization, sexism and male chauvinism ingrained in the concept of *machismo* are still deeply rooted in cultural and social patterns and in institutions; these attitudes continue to deprive women of true equality.

Since the resurgence of a worldwide feminist movement in the 1970s, many grassroots and professional women's and feminist organizations have emerged in Puerto Rico, while academic courses and research and documentation centers have been introduced in the curriculum at most universities. Major issues related to the experience of Puerto Rican women, in both the island and the United States, are now a major focus of research and public policy.

Edna Acosta-Belén, ed., *The Puerto Rican Woman: Perspectives on Culture, History, and Society* (New York: Praeger, 1986); Yamila Azize, ed., *La mujer en Puerto Rico* (Río Piedras, P.R.: Ediciones Huracán, 1987).

▪ EDNA ACOSTA-BELÉN

SEE ALSO Feminism, Latina; Puerto Rican Women

Radical Feminism

R adical feminism confronts women's oppression with a revolutionary analysis (as distinguished from reform) that goes to the root causes of male domination, defines men as responsible for and gaining from women's subordination, and focuses on sisterhood and women's bonding. The personal politics of radical feminism, which emphasizes sexual and reproductive exploitation of women, focuses on the commonality of women's condition across class and race as well as cultures and national boundaries. In the beginning it was criticized for making women's issues a priority over all other issues. Later in the movement, racism took the form of theories that did not effectively address different racial conditions of women and practices that subordinated or excluded women of color.

In the United States in 1967, radical feminism launched the "Women's Liberation Movement" through consciousness-raising groups (CR). In small group meetings women found commonality in their experiences of subordination; and from a feminist critique of power, they produced the critical awareness that "the personal is political." Radical feminism championed controversial or silenced issues, such as women's experiences of botched or denied abortions, rape, and wife abuse, which newly organized commissions for women's economic and political equality would not address. Lesbian feminism helped to deepen the radical feminist critique. Women's health organizing efforts added control of one's body to the issues that feminists prioritized. Guerrilla theater, zap-action protests, wet-ins for child care, demonstrations at the Miss America Pageant, and disruption of bridal parties were among the early forms of conveying the message and politics of radical feminism. Speakouts on rape and testimony on forced pregnancy enabled women to give public voice and political context to those experiences that had been treated as only individual. These actions led to demands for changes in law and law enforcement.

Radical (autonomous) feminism, based on the commonality of women's oppression, spans the globe, arising from its own indigenous conditions in one country after another. In the United States women came to the movement out of the "male-dominated Left," the civil rights movement, academia, their homes, and declared autonomy and self-determination. Groups like Redstockings;

WITCH (Women's International Terrorist Conspiracy from Hell); The Feminists; and Cell 16, which published "No More Fun and Games," were identified particularly with women's autonomy. Many women who remained in the New Left challenged radical feminism's prioritization of women's issues across classes and founded their own movement of socialist feminism.

Shulamith Firestone turned Marxism on its head in 1970 with her analysis of historical materialism in *The Dialectics of Sex*. Kate Millett's *Sexual Politics*, also from 1970, critiqued the patriarchal family as an institutional foundation of male domination. Both authors simultaneously reflected and advanced the critique of the growing radical feminist movement, which pushed women's oppression, and consequently a woman's revolution, to the top of any agenda for social change. Phyllis Chesler's *Women and Madness* turned Freudian psychology of women into a political analysis of personal exploitation. Ti Grace Atkinson, among others, challenged Freud's determination that "anatomy is destiny." Valerie Solanos's notable essay that fired the anger if not the politics of radical feminists in the SCUM (Society for Cutting Up Men) Manifesto satirically observed that while it takes two X chromosomes to produce a female, the X-Y male combination is flawed because the Y is an incomplete X, making men incomplete females or "a biological accident." The Fourth World Manifesto, published by a CR group of radical feminists in Detroit, denounced the male Left for its attempts to co-opt the women's movement and set out the theory that women are the first colonized class—the territory colonized is women's bodies and proposed feminist solidarity and female culture are its antidote.

Radical in its analysis, revolutionary in its politics, radical feminism, still the target of attacks from an increasingly conservative society since the 1970s, continues to be reflected in current theory, politics, and action in the women's movement, global feminism, the reproductive rights movements, and the feminist confrontation of sexual exploitation in prostitution, pornography, and marriage.

                                    ▪ KATHLEEN BARRY

SEE ALSO Radicalism.

Socialist Feminism

Socialist feminism criticizes the system of capitalism for being exploitive of women. Socialist feminists use *and* critique traditional Marxism to uncover the complex nature of women's oppression, especially as it relates to economics.

Socialist feminism focuses on the economic class aspects of women's oppression. Much debate has occurred within socialist feminist circles about the exact relationship between sexual, economic class, and racial oppression. Some, usually termed Marxist-feminists, claim that economic class causes oppression. Although they recognize women's oppression as part of a complicated nexus of male dominance, they view it always through its capitalist foundations.

Other feminists see patriarchy and capitalism as mutually dependent systems, interwoven, with no single core. Women are recognized as both mother and worker, reproducer and producer, homemaker and wage earner, consumer and employee.

Some socialist feminists name society's system of male privilege "masculinist"; others term it patriarchy. Whatever the nuances, all socialist feminists recognize that capitalism—the exchange of one's labor for wages to create someone else's profit—is particularly problematic for women. However, the particular relationship between patriarchy as a semi-independent system of masculinist privilege and capitalism remains controversial.

Early forms of twentieth-century Western as well as third-world socialist feminism grew out of traditional Marxist theory. Women's oppression was equated with their position in the economic class structure: working-class women were oppressed by their exploitation; that is, their labor was not paid for in wages equal to the value of their work. Few people recognized that women were exploited at a higher rate than men (e.g., women are paid a smaller percentage than men for doing the same work) simply because they were women. There was, and sometimes still is, little recognition that women, despite class differences, have common interests (abortion, day care, maternity leave).

During the second wave of the U.S. women's movement, which began around 1969, socialist feminist ideology began to shift. From the mid-1970s through the mid-1980s more acknowledgment was given to the semiautonomy of patriarchal privilege by socialist feminists such as Sheila Rowbotham, Zillah Eisenstein, Heidi Hartmann, and Juliet Mitchell. They argued that the system of capitalist patriarchy, not just capitalism, defined the problem of women's oppression; that patriarchal privilege was as central to society as its economic structure. They also viewed capitalist patriarchy as fundamentally racist in its treatment of women of color.

In this period socialist feminism focused on the ways the patriarchal organization of traditional heterosexual families institutionalized sexual hierarchy between men and women. Women were defined as mothers and wives and therefore were primarily responsible for the domestic labor of the home and child rearing. Women were either excluded from the marketplace as full-time, unpaid housewives or hired at lower wages than men because their primary responsibility was considered to be home and family.

Socialist feminists, along with feminist women of color, criticized the even greater exploitation of women of color, who were usually paid less than white women in the labor force although they worked in greater numbers as domestics, maids, and the like—often for white women.

Today, socialist feminists give priority to the economic side of women's oppression. They believe that the economic class aspects of women's lives define their life choices and that these differences between women must be addressed before women can understand one another's needs. This understanding led to abortion-rights work, which demanded access for poor women, not just for middle-class women who could afford to pay for it.

Events of the 1980s, the Reagan-Bush decade, had a great impact on the U.S. women's movement. Its posture became defensive against an increasing right-wing, antifeminist onslaught. U.S. leftist and socialist feminists had less of a forum. The language of socialism seemed more and more foreign. Then came the anti-Communist Eastern European revolutions of 1989. By the early 1990s socialist feminism had become a problematic political identity in most Western societies. Communist statism, and socialism along with it, became discredited ideologies throughout eastern and central Europe. Feminism seemed better served by an independent and autonomous discourse.

How will socialist feminism develop in the twenty-first century? As the global capitalist web develops and new forms of women's exploitation are institutionalized in first-world nations as well as in factories throughout the world, there may be a new focus on the need for an anticapitalist, feminist politics. Whether those politics are named socialist feminism remains to be seen.

Zillah Eisenstein, ed., *Capitalist Patriarchy and the Case for Socialist Feminism* (New York: Monthly Review Press, 1979); Sonia Kruks, Rayna Rapp, and Marilyn Young, eds., *Promissory Notes, Women in the Transition to Socialism* (New York: Monthly Review Press, 1989); Lydia Sargent, ed., *Women and Revolution, A Discussion of the Unhappy Marriage of Marxism and Feminism* (Boston: South End Press, 1981).

▪ ZILLAH EISENSTEIN

SEE ALSO Feminism, Marxist; Socialism.

Working-Class Feminism

Working-class feminism has not been a formally articulated ideology or a clearly marked social movement. Instead, it has most often emerged through working-class women's practical struggles to combat gender inequality as it has been interlaced with class and racial oppression. Understanding working-class feminism thus involves more than identifying working-class women's "special burdens," it also includes acknowledging that it is an entirely different approach to feminism.

Historically, working-class women — both wage earners and the wives of working-class men — have not had to worry about expectations for them to be homebound shrinking violets; they have had little choice but to be strong. They have struggled individually with patriarchal expectations in their families and in balancing the demands of the double day of housework and waged work. Whereas many women of higher class backgrounds have eschewed full-time work in the home, many working-class women have viewed it as a desirable ideal that they cannot afford, preferable to the dead-end, dangerous, monotonous, and ill-paid waged work to which they have been limited. Restricted to the bottom of the employment ladder, they have challenged gender barriers in employment by knocking on doors; filing legal suits; cross-dressing; or hiding their marital status, sexual orientation, or pregnancies. By the 1970s, working-class women had breached gender walls in a range of traditionally all-male lucrative trades such as coal mining, plumbing, or aircraft mechanics. Often, though, their goal was not consciously to tear down gender barriers but, rather, to survive. As Evelyn Luna, a Navajo miner, put it: "Women on the reservation want jobs [as miners] not to be equal with men but just to have enough money to live."

When they have organized collectively, working-class women have framed their politics less in terms of equal rights for individuals than in terms of collective advancement for working-class women and men both. Since the 1830s, wage-earning women have founded and joined a variety of trade unions through which to combat women's exploitation in employment. Through these unions they have fought for feminist demands such as equal pay for equal work, child care, or an end to sexual harassment.

Usually it has been necessary to struggle with men within the movement to achieve equal access to union power and to define the labor movement in terms that address women's concerns. Working-class women have formed women's solidarity groups within the labor movement, such as the Coalition of Labor Union Women (CLUW) in the 1970, or formed their own, independent unions such as African American women's locals of the Knights of Labor in the 1880s. Trade unions have not been the only form, however, of working-class women's collective action that merges feminism and class concerns. Welfare rights activists in the 1960s and 1970s, for example, organized to force the federal government to validate poor women's unwaged labor in the home.

Historically, most women of color have been working-class, and both racism and class oppression have shaped their struggles against gender inequality. In the strike made famous in the 1950s film *Salt of the Earth*, for example, Chicana wives of copper miners had to fight mine owners' unequal treatment of Chicano miners as well as their general exploitation of Anglo and Chicano miners. At the same time, the women had to battle with their menfolk over equal rights to fight the owners and over the inclusion of women's demand that sanitation be upgraded.

Working-class feminists have had to defend themselves against charges, often racialized, that because of their activism they weren't "respectable," that they were "bad girls" or prostitutes. African American laundry workers in Chicago in the 1930s, for example, had to defend their moral integrity simply to protest; white women textile organizers in North Carolina in the 1920s had to defend themselves against accusations that they were sleeping around. Both lesbians and straight women have had to confront the homophobia with which men have greeted women's forays into nontraditional employment.

Working-class feminism is distinct, therefore, from white middle-class feminism. Less individualistic in some ways, it embeds struggles for gender equality in larger struggles against racism and economic exploitation. As Dorothy Sue Cobble described waitresses' union activism in the 1940s, "Upward mobility for the few did not seem as important as the economic advancement of the many."

Working-class women have not necessarily opposed middle-class women's access to high-powered professional jobs, political office, or public visibility. Rather, they haven't had the luxury of expecting they could leap alone over the barriers of class and race as well as gender. Instead, they have tried either to join hands with their working-class sisters—and sometimes brothers—to climb over such barriers together or, sometimes, tried to tear them down altogether.

▪ DANA FRANK

SEE ALSO Coalition of Labor Union Women (CLUW); Labor Movement; Labor Unions; National Welfare Rights Organization.

≋ Feminist Jurisprudence

Women were not present or represented when the U.S. laws were written and the legal institutions designed under which women as well as men live. To Abigail Adams's plea to John Adams to "remember the ladies" in founding the United States, for example, he replied, "We know better than to repeal our Masculine systems." With the passage of the Nineteenth Amendment in 1920, U.S. women were granted the right to vote, but full citizenship and equal rights have continued to be withheld. Women from every walk of life have resisted and dissented from law's collaboration in women's subjection, but nothing has changed it. The task of the legal arm of the women's movement from 1970 to the present has been to change it.

As a term for this aspiration, *feminist jurisprudence* first appeared in print in 1978 in the inaugural issue of the *Harvard Women's Law Journal*. Since then, women's organizing and activism for social equality through legal equality have produced substantial initiatives in political activism, legislation and case law, theoretical and practical literature, law journals in the United States and abroad, legal associations, litigating organizations, policy foundations, judicial education drives, casebooks, courses, and clinics. Since the late 1970s women went from being a tiny percentage of law students to nearly half, yet remain a far smaller percentage of the legal profession as a whole. The increase in women's presence in elite positions as partners in firms, law professors, legislators, and judges has also been significant, although still falling far short of substantial representation. But while there is no substitute for women being everywhere, shifting gender demographics among elites does not change women's status as such.

Jurisprudence refers to the relation between life and law, as well as a body of particular judicial interpretation and application of law. Feminism seeks to end the subordination of women. Feminist jurisprudence thus pioneers a relation between life and law through which women's unequal social reality will be legally confronted and transformed.

To reframe women's exclusion from, and subordination within, life and law, a new, larger picture has to be drawn. Rather than do this in the abstract, feminist projects have been grounded in the concreteness of particular women's experiences, embracing women's diversity and specificity, and stressing actual outcomes over theoretical ones.

For example, in the law of equality, substantive equality has been stressed over the abstraction of equal treatment, producing a new vision of equal protection of the laws; in the law of rape, the real rape rate, and the comparatively tiny percentage of rape convictions, have impelled critical examination of the law against rape, as has its use for racist ends; race, class, age, and sexual orientation have been included with gender as inequalities that must be addressed if sex equality is to have any real meaning. All areas of law, from tort, contract, and corporate law to criminal, constitutional, and international law, have been interrogated. Direct accountability to victims and survivors—often clients who seek rights in hostile situations—has been the basic principle of this work.

Crisis intervention, policy formation, legislation, litigation, and scholarship have flourished, expanding women's rights. Subjects of particularly creative scrutiny include pregnancy, wife beating, rape (including rape in marriage), athletics, abortion, incest, gay and lesbian rights, prostitution, and pornography. Legal doctrines of equality, obscenity, privacy, self-defense, education, hate crime, even justice itself have been reenvisioned. Whole new legal doctrines, such as sexual harassment, have been invented. Global organizing and international conventions against trafficking women as sex-based exploitation, transnational litigation against genocide and war crimes as sex and ethnic violation, and new policy approaches to economic development have emerged.

This movement in the practice of law for women has always been diverse, drawing on the insights and energies of activists, organizers, advocates, legal workers, and grassroots lawyers of every race and class, infusing work for all women with a clear awareness of hierarchy among women. The academic theory of this movement, by contrast, has often lagged behind, reflecting neither the diversity of practice, the subtlety of innovations, nor the understanding of power and the necessity of its redistribution that those who work hands-on have made routine, if not solved.

Academic writings by women of color in the past decade have done much to rectify this situation.

Can law be remade in the image of women's perspectives and experiences? Can it see women's human face? Perhaps law itself will need to be remade in new, nonhierarchical forms. So long as law is a form social power takes, an avenue for relief of injury, a right of citizenship, a lever for social legitimacy, and a force in women's lives, feminist jurisprudence will seek to make law respond to women as well as to men.

Catharine A. MacKinnon, *Toward a Feminist Theory of the State* (Cambridge, Mass., and London: Harvard University Press, 1989); Mari Matsuda, "When the First Quail Calls: Multiple Consciousness as Jurisprudential Method," 11, *Women's Rights Law Reporter* 7 (1987).

▪ CATHARINE A. MacKINNON

SEE ALSO Legal Status.

≋ Feminist Literary Criticism

Feminist literary criticism can be defined as the study of literature by women, or the interpretation of any text written with an attention to gender dynamics or a focus on female characters. Many would date the beginnings of U.S. feminist literary criticism to the 1929 work of British writer Virginia Woolf in *A Room of One's Own*. Woolf was white, economically privileged, and married (though bisexual); she celebrated a European literary tradition and high cultural aesthetic values. One of her concepts, however, "a room of one's own"—the necessary material precondition for a woman's creativity—has been used by feminist literary critics across the spectrum to describe the material obstacles to women's literary aspirations.

Author and critic Alice Walker, who coined the term womanist to describe the specificity of African American women's feminism, rewrote

Woolf's exclusive focus on gender in the 1983 book *In Search of Our Mothers' Gardens*. Walker emphasizes both race and gender as determinants of women's achievement. She also revises the female literary tradition celebrated by Woolf, centering her discussion instead on women artists of the past who were African American, such as the eighteenth-century poet and emancipated slave Phillis Wheatley and the early-twentieth-century anthropologist and novelist Zora Neale Hurston. Many of the histories of feminist literary criticism by womanist or feminist critics of color are often less individualist in their focus. They argue for communal continuity across time. Some stress oral traditions of storytelling transmitted from mother to daughter as the point of origin for a woman-centered perspective on the world and its fictions.

Feminist literary criticism depends on universities and publishing houses for its existence. Thus feminist literary criticism typically has been practiced by educated women with rooms of their own, recent and hard won though they be. During World War II, women of all races entered the wage-labor force in unprecedented numbers, a move that brought with it upheavals in the social relations of gender and, later (as a result in part of mass migrations of African Americans to the North and the burgeoning civil rights movement), of race. With the demographic expansion of colleges and universities after World War II (spurred on in part by cold-war competitiveness) and the modest gains in educational opportunity produced by the civil rights movement, working- and middle-class women began entering graduate schools.

Feminism's second wave in the United States — initially a reflection of the civil rights movement of the 1950s and 1960s and the subsequent women's liberation movements of the 1960s and 1970s — is primarily responsible for spawning feminist literary criticism. The economic and racial privilege that permitted some women to attain institutional footholds during these years marked the divisions that came to characterize debates in feminist literary criticism in the late 1970s and 1980s, when numerous anthologies appeared defining a feminist literary criticism of color critical of and sometimes in opposition to Anglo-centered feminist literary criticism.

At the same time, in response to the political pressures of identity politics (as the new struggles for civil rights by the disenfranchised in the United States have come to be known), women writers of color in the United States — at first African American women, later Chicanas, Asian American women, Latinas, and Native American women — began to receive unprecedented national attention. Many of these creative writers became what Cornel West, following Gramsci, termed the new "organic intellectuals," using their prominent roles as distinguished writers of fiction to write criticism and to facilitate the growth of feminist literary criticism by and about women of color within the academy. Indeed, until recently one of the differences between Anglo-centered feminist literary criticism and feminist literary criticism by women of color in the United States was that while many practitioners of the former were most often university professors in literature departments, many womanist/feminist-of-color literary critics were often published creative writers themselves, such as Paula Gunn Allen, Alice Walker, Toni Morrison, Gloria Anzaldúa, and Cherríe Moraga. Academic women-of-color literary critics, such as Barbara Christian, Deborah MacDowell, Norma Alarcón, Gloria T. Hull, Mary Helen Washington, and Barbara Smith, were also defining the field. Some of these women also played a major role in shaping the field of lesbian feminist literary criticism.

The enormous growth of feminist literary criticism in the 1980s and its current multiracial character coincide ironically with a decade of governmental rollbacks in progressive social policy that arose in the 1960s and 1970s. Although this development might be viewed as a "retreat" from frustrating political arenas of social change to the less resistant domain of culture, cultural movements nevertheless often, if not always, accompany struggles for social and political change. Feminist and womanist literary criticism provides critiques of gender, racial, sexual, and class domination in the United States. They have also begun to alter the canon of literature and literary history to include not only a significant number of female fiction writers and poets whose works will be read by future generations of students but also female literary traditions whose roots extend backward in time and across continents.

Gloria Anzaldúa, ed., *Making Face, Making Soul/Haciendo Caras: Creative and Critical Perspectives by Women of Color* (San Francisco: Aunt Lute Foundation Books, 1990); Jane Gallop, *Around 1981: Academic Feminist Literary Theory* (New York: Routledge, 1992); Alice Walker, *In Search of Our Mothers' Gardens: Womanist Prose* (New York: Harcourt Brace Jovanovich, 1984).

▪ CARLA FRECCERO

SEE ALSO Literature.

≋ Feminist Presses, Publications, and Bookstores

The second wave of the women's movement burst into public consciousness at the end of the 1960s and the early 1970s. It was accompanied by, and propelled by, an enormous need to know: to know what other women were discovering, thinking, doing.

Following in the footsteps of the anti- (Viet Nam) war movement and the civil rights movement, as well as the earlier women's movement and the abolition movement and social movements since the invention of the printing press, feminists of the 1970s wrote and published pamphlets and started newspapers and magazines defining, debating, clarifying and inventing their ideas. Organizations such as KNOW and the al-ready-existing New England Free Press published and circulated thousands of copies of one-article pamphlets. Publications such as *Notes from the First (Second, and Third) Year(s)* collected these articles into staple-bound, newsprint anthologies. Women in Montreal published *The Birth Control Handbook* and the Boston Women's Health Collective published *Our Bodies, Ourselves* (named for the popular abortion-rights slogan, "Our bodies, our selves, our right to decide."). *OBOS* initially sold for thirty-five cents per copy. The price was later reduced to twenty-five cents because of their political conviction that it was wrong to make a profit off women.

Women's newsletters, newspapers, magazines, and journals sprang up in hundreds of cities. Publications ranged from brief calendars of local events to full-fledged newspapers and journals with national and international circulations. Women's liberationists got articles in publications, published special issues of magazines (*Motive*), took over entire magazines and turned them into feminist publications (*LibeRATion*), and started their own magazines with names such as *The Furies, It Ain't Me Babe, Ain't I A Woman, Lavender Woman,* and *off our backs.* Journals such as *The Second Wave, Women: A Journal of Liberation, Amazon Quarterly,* and *Lesbian Tide* sprang up nationwide. *Ms.* magazine, founded in 1972, elbowed its way into the nation's magazine racks and became a household word virtually overnight.

Consciousness demanded action and women organized women's liberation conferences and women's centers in towns and universities across the country. Information tables featuring pamphlets and anthologies published by women's liberation groups and the small handful of relevant books from mainstream publishers (*Sisterhood Is Powerful, Sexual Politics, Lesbian/Woman*) were a vital part of every feminist conference. Between conferences the book and information tables moved into corners of women's centers. As funding for women's centers diminished, women in many parts of the country realized that selling hard-to-find books and pamphlets from the emerging feminist publishers (and some mainstream publishers) could help pay the rent.

Women's bookstores, a wonderfully contagious idea, emerged as quickly as women could organize them: ICI (Information Center Incorporated)–A Woman's Place (Oakland, California); Amazon (Minneapolis); Labyris and Womanbooks (New York City); First Things First and Lammas (Washington, D.C.); Charis (Atlanta); and Sisterhood (Los Angeles). These bookstores usually also functioned as women's centers, complete with bulletin boards, housing referrals, and support for battered women. Initially, stores were run on volunteer labor, donations, and fundraisers. Many stores opened and closed over the years but eventually the demand for books by and about women as well as the increase in the number of books available made it possible for feminist bookstores to become self-supporting. There are, or have been, women's bookstores in all but five U.S. states. At the time of this writing, approximately one hundred twenty feminist bookstores provide books for women in the United States and Canada and challenge mainstream publishers and the aggressively competing chain stores to provide a decent selection of women's books.

Feminist bookstores and feminist publishers were supported at their beginnings with volunteer labor, political passion, fundraising, and the belief that the information they could provide would radically change women's lives. Many of these early bookstores and publishers closed because of the burnout or disillusionment that often accompanies this kind of organizing. Nevertheless, they helped to create and sustain a vision of feminist publishing and book distribution until enough books and magazines could be published and sold so that the stores could survive financially and make that vision a reality. Achieving financial viability has been a long process that faces new challenges today as national chain stores and multi-national corporations begin to dominate mainstream bookselling and publishing industries and to com-

pete with even specialty stores such as feminist and other politically-based bookstores.

Feminist publishing started with pamphlets and periodicals. The Women's Press Collective published an anthology of women's poetry; a collection of poetry, prose, and art, *Lesbians Speak Out*; and work by women of color and working-class women. Diana Press published two sets of three anthologies, each consisting of articles and fiction originally published by *The Furies* and *The Ladder*, as well as other books, including early poetry by Rita Mae Brown, while functioning as a job shop (printing as needed for a wide variety of customers). Seal Press started as a women's letter press and became one of the strongest and most diverse of today's feminist publishers. New Victoria Press also started as a job shop and initially published books as a sideline. Daughters took the New York publishing world by surprise with their experimental women's fiction, including *Rubyfruit Jungle*. The Feminist Press was organized to reclaim and republish works by lost women writers for both classroom use and a general readership. Naiad's initial goal remains the same—publishing lesbian fiction. Kitchen Table: Women of Color Press was the first U.S. publisher run by and for women of color.

Many early publishers such as Long Haul and Shameless Hussy have long since recycled into other endeavors. Some were simply one-book or one-author publishers. Some focused on poetry in an era when many feminist ideas first were expressed by the movement's poets. Some survived a shift to nonfiction and novels. Feminist publishers challenged the book world by inventing and popularizing anthologies of previously unpublished and largely political works.

Printers such as the Iowa City Women's Press (which also published books as well as printing them for other publishers) were founded when male-owned/controlled printers and publishers refused to print feminist publications and called them "indecent" or "pornographic." The Iowa City Women's Press, in its heyday, shared a building with a woman-run bindery and a woman-run typesetting shop, so that women could control the entire means of production, in association with women's distribution companies (such as Women in Distribution and Old Lady Blue Jeans) and women's bookstores. This was an era when men could not tell women that their ideas and work were unpublishable and silence them by refusing to print (or bind or typeset) it.

The second wave of the women's movement blossomed into book publishing—forty-six feminist publishers published 129 books in the fall 1993 publishing season alone, almost all focusing on areas underserved by mainstream publishing— lesbian, women of color, older women, cutting-edge and not-yet-popular theory and ideas. Women also took the idea of distributing the books ourselves to new heights by establishing a network of feminist bookstores that sell books from feminist presses as well as the best of what is published by mainstream, university, and independent small presses. These women's bookstores fuel mainstream feminist publishing by proving, with their sales, that the interest in women's books is not a "fad," it's not "over," and that it is, in fact, growing both in terms of the dollar value of the books sold and in terms of the interest in new (and more familiar) ideas and directions. Women's bookstores and feminist publishers have kept the women's movement visible and accessible through shifting political climates for twenty-five years.

                                        ▪ CAROL SEAJAY

See also Magazines; Newspapers.

≋ Feminist Theology

F eminist theology is a recently recognized type of theological reflection whose major development has taken place in the United States, although it is becoming increasingly global and multifaith. Feminist theology is not primarily re-flection on special "feminine" themes in theology and does not intend to create a special subcategory of theology relevant primarily to women. Rather, feminist theology arises from a recognition that traditional theology in Christianity (and other major religions) has been created almost exclusively by males.

Women, until recently, have been excluded from theological study and ordained ministry. Theology has functioned in a way that has justified this exclusion and subordination of women. Males have been assumed to be the normative humans and representatives of God. Women have been defined as both inferior by nature and more prone to evil. Christianity particularly has scapegoated women, blaming them for the origin of sin. These teachings reinforce women's social subordination by claiming that this is the way women must pay for having caused evil to come into the world.

Feminist theology arises as a critical response to these male-centered and antiwoman biases in classical theology. These biases are recognized as systemic, pervading the tradition during its whole development, not just the odd views of a few individuals. Thus feminist theology calls for a thoroughgoing revision of all the symbols and precepts of the tradition.

Feminist theology develops through a three-stage dialectic. First, women recognize the male-centered and antiwoman biases in the tradition and begin to analyze these patterns throughout its history. They develop articles and books documenting this bias, showing how extensive it is, revealing its underlying assumptions, and denouncing it as wrong. In short they identify this bias as a serious ethical and theological error, not a verity to be accepted. Mary Daly's 1968 book, *The Church and the Second Sex*, is an example of this first stage of feminist theology.

In the second stage of feminist theology women search for alternative traditions that provide positive symbols to affirm women. The quest for alternatives draws feminist theologians in different directions. Some feminists interested in theology conclude that the classical tradition of Christianity (or Judaism or Islam) is incapable of affirming women as equals of men. The tradition itself is a religious reflection of patriarchy and cannot be significantly reformed. Mary Daly came to this conclusion in her thought, beginning with *Beyond God the Father*, in 1973.

Other feminists remain committed to their historical religious communities and believe that the original or essential message of the religion affirms women as equals of men, but the message has been distorted by its social context in patriarchal societies. These feminist theologians engage in a historical quest to surface the alternative traditions within the early beginnings and the wider development of the tradition to show these affirmative themes. The 1982 book by New Testament scholar Elisabeth Schüssler Fiorenza, *In Memory of Her: A Feminist Theological Reconstruction of Christian Origins*, belongs in this second stage of feminist theology.

Having searched out what they see as the authentic teachings of the tradition, separate from the cultural misogyny, feminist theologians begin a third stage of constructing a new theological system, reinterpreting the theological symbols of divinity, human nature, the origins of the world, good and evil, revelation, salvation, and redemptive community in ways that not only affirm women's full participation but also call for a transformation of the religion and society as integral to the redemptive mission of the religious faith. This author's 1983 book, *Sexism and God-talk: Toward a Feminist Theology*, reflects this third stage of feminist theology.

Other feminist theologians who may have left Christianity or Judaism in search of more feminist religions also move toward a presentation of their options for new communities of faith and practice. Rita Gross, who moved from Christianity to Judaism to Buddhism in search of a more woman-positive religion, has presented her reconstruction of Buddhism in 1993 in *Buddhism After Patriarchy*. Starhawk, of Jewish background, has been a leader in developing Goddess religion, beginning with her 1979 work, *The Spiral Dance: A Rebirth of the Ancient Religion of the Great Goddess*.

Although feminist theology has developed its major work since the late 1960s, efforts of women to critique and revise religious teachings to be more affirmative of women can be found in earlier centuries, such as the seventeenth-century writing by the woman cofounder of the Society of Friends, Margaret Fell. But it has only been since the 1960s, as more and more women could be ordained and began to teach in theological schools in the Christian or Jewish traditions, that there has been a large enough number of theologically trained woman able to find not only an audience for their writings but also to incorporate feminist theology into theological education.

In addition to the increasing feminist reflection across traditional religions, Christianity, Judaism, Islam, and Buddhism, and new alternatives to historic religions in Goddess worship, Black, Latina, Native American, and Asian American women are also contextualizing feminist theology in their racial/ethnic community's experience. African American women speak of their distinct feminism as "womanist theology," while Latinas speak of "Mujerista theology." Asian American women are finding their distinct voice, apart from their particular national communities. Native American women also are reclaiming women-centered traditions within their communal religious worldviews and practices.

Thus feminist theology is no longer only white and Christian; it is reflecting the increasing pluralism of U.S. religiosity, as well as ethnic cultures.

Ada Maria Isaisi-Diaz, *En La Lucha: A Hispanic Woman's Liberation Theology* (Minneapolis: Fortress Press, 1993); Judith Plaskow, *Standing Again at Sinai: Judaism from a Feminist Perspective* (San Francisco: Harper and Row, 1990); Delores Williams, *Sisters in the Wilderness: The Challenge of Womanist God-talk* (Maryknoll, N.Y.: Orbis Press, 1993).

■ ROSEMARY RADFORD RUETHER

SEE ALSO Religion.

≋ Fetal Rights

The notion of fetal rights is most familiar in the context of abortion debates, where opponents of legal abortion assert the fetus's absolute right to life. However, in the years since the Supreme Court recognized women's constitutional right to have an abortion (*Roe* v. *Wade*, 1973), the concept of fetal rights has gained currency outside the abortion context. Women who will continue their pregnancies and give birth and women who are not pregnant but merely fertile both become objects of regulation when they engage in actions that might harm an actual or potential fetus. In a backlash against women's increasing independence, proponents of fetal rights have successfully restricted women's access to jobs, autonomy in medical decisions, and justice in the courts, undermining women's prospects for self-determination.

Until recently, the legal system has considered the fetus to be part of the pregnant woman herself. The concept of "fetal rights" provides new grounds for the old practice of treating all women as potential mothers and subordinating women's interests and needs to those attributed to unborn children or society. In the 1908 case *Muller* v. *Oregon*, the Supreme Court upheld a law limiting the number of hours women could work each day because, the Court claimed, women are the guardians of the race and must protect their health, rather than because workers are entitled to occupational safety.

Throughout U.S. history and culture, women have been assigned this role of guardian over the well-being of fetuses and children. When women violate this norm, however, society's *enforcement* of the responsibility is quite selective. Race, class, and religion help determine which women will be punished for failing to live up to their assigned duties, and poor women of color are the most frequent targets.

Conflicts over women's reproductive self-determination and fetal rights are played out daily in legislatures, courts, welfare offices, factories, hospitals, bars, and television shows. Pregnant women endure harassment ranging from a waiter's admonition against drinking alcohol to the violence of caesarean sections performed against their will.

Typically, the justification for treating women in these ways is that fetuses have rights that conflict with the woman's and somehow a balance must be struck. For instance, since the 1970s many companies have barred all women of childbearing age from jobs exposing them to toxins that might harm a fetus, keeping women out of relatively high-paying blue-collar jobs. A conflict is posed between a fetus's right to health and a woman's right to employment opportunity—despite the fact that no fetus need exist since fertility, not actual pregnancy, is the factor that excludes women.

Instead of cleaning up the workplace or providing alternative work for women (and men) planning to have children, companies burden women with concerns about fetal safety (and about liability from workers' lawsuits). The Supreme Court invalidated one of the most egregious of these "fetal protection policies" in *United Auto Workers* v. *Johnson Controls* (1991), in which a group of workers and their union challenged a company policy keeping all women up to age seventy out of jobs working with lead (as well as jobs from which women could be promoted to one involving lead) unless they could provide medical proof that they could not become pregnant. The Court ruled that the way Johnson Controls singled out women workers for exclusion violated their civil rights. Other companies may still use less sweeping policies that could gain judicial approval, jeopardizing women's access to some fifteen to twenty million industrial jobs.

During the 1980s a second fetal rights trend emerged. In at least twenty-five states across the nation, women have been arrested, prosecuted, and jailed for using drugs or alcohol while pregnant. Here, the conflict is cast as a fetus's right to health versus a woman's right to pleasure, engendering little sympathy for a pregnant woman's addiction problems and little tolerance for a woman's occasional drug use, which may not impair the fetus. This conflictual model results in women facing criminal penalties for using drugs that men and other women never face. In addition, women might lose their children without the benefit of a proper investigation into their actual parenting abilities. These events happen in a context of inadequate government services in which the vast majority of pregnant women cannot get drug treatment or sometimes even basic prenatal care.

The women punished for substance use during pregnancy are disproportionately poor Black and Latina women, those who have the fewest resources to sustain a healthy pregnancy in the first place. Native American women living on reservations also experience unusual penalties. Some women have been "detained" during their pregnancies by tribal authorities to try to prevent Fetal Alcohol Syndrome. Not surprisingly, jail is a terrible place to be pregnant and doesn't guarantee that a healthy baby will be born. As with employment discrimination, society's solution is to burden women with all the concerns about fetal safety, locking them away from potential hazards rather than providing resources that can address the roots of their problems.

Cynthia Daniels, *At Women's Expense: State Power and the Politics of Fetal Rights* (Cambridge, Mass.: Harvard University Press, 1993); Janna Merrick and Robert Blank, eds., *The Politics of Pregnancy: Policy Dilemmas in the Maternal-Fetal Relationship* (New York: Haworth Press, 1993); Katha Pollitt, " 'Fetal Rights': A New Assault on Feminism," *The Nation* Vol. 250 (March 1990): 409–18.

▪ RACHEL ROTH

SEE ALSO *Muller* v. *Oregon*; Reproductive Rights.

≋ Fifteenth Amendment

SEE Constitution and Amendments.

≋ The Fifties

Betty Friedan's *The Feminine Mystique* became a bestseller in 1963. She argued that in the postwar period, rigid gender norms restricted middle-class, suburban white women's options and aspirations to full-time wifedom and motherhood. The roles of women were contradictory: more middle-class white women than ever before had opportunities for education, work, and autonomy, but the culture punished the women who pursued them. Discrimination, scorn, and characterizations of professional women as old maids, unfeminine, or negligent mothers, functioned to keep women in the home, literally and psychologically.

The 1950s are best known as a time of prosperity and optimism; obsessive anticommunism, which led to the cold war; narrow gender expectations for women; and a glorification of the "normal" nuclear family. In fact the 1950s are an aberrant decade in the twentieth century in that after the Great Depression and World War II, most Americans wanted to settle down. The number of young people who married rose precipitously; age at the time of marriage and childbearing dropped; and the birthrate increased significantly, a trend termed the *baby boom*. Premarital virginity for white women and traditionally male-dominant heterosexual families (with men as the breadwinner and head of the household and women at home) were universally promoted. Institutions and goods expanded rapidly in postwar America: corporations; the military; advertising and media; suburbs; highways; and consumerism and consumer products, particularly housing, automobiles, household appliances, and televisions. The decade is often remembered fondly as a time of abundance, optimism, and safety.

At the same time currents of discontent and anxiety arose. Black people, especially in the South, were angry and the national struggle for civil rights intensified. The 1950s are punctuated with important race-related events, such as the 1954 Supreme Court decision against segregated schools, the Montgomery Bus Boycott, the Emmett Till case, and the Little Rock Central High School integration struggle. Many of the heroes of these events were Black women.

Black music (and its imitators) was popular among teenagers, who formed a demographic category unto themselves, especially from a market perspective. Thousands of teenagers had money and time to spend on records, magazines, clothes, and makeup—they created a new youth culture. Parents worried about losing control of young people, most visible in the national concern over juvenile delinquency. The Beat writers, known for their rejection of mainstream American values and their embrace of bohemian existence, attracted many young whites. Homophobia was apparent in the glorification of the "nuclear" family and in the campaigns against lesbians and gays that linked them to crime and communist activities. In addition, anxiety over the atom bomb and nuclear war permeated the culture.

Unknown to most suburban whites, there were many poor people in this country. In fact the United States was deeply divided by race and class, a realization that galvanized young Blacks and whites in the 1960s. The cities were becoming underfunded sites of Black and Latino/Latina neighborhoods as whites moved to the segregated suburbs. The migration of Blacks out of the South, and the influx of people from Puerto Rico and Mexico into the United States, changed racial and ethnic urban demographics. For Native American women and communities, the 1950s saw the emergence of two very damaging federal policies—the era of termination of tribal life and the Bureau of Indian Affairs (BIA) Relocation Program. These policies were designed to "mainstream" Native Americans so they could be "just like everyone else" in the 1950s. The policies added to Native American urban migration. In contrast to the upward mobility of many white women, women of color struggled to survive.

The 1950s were a paradoxical time, then, when American society seemed stable and contained. Underneath the facade, however, African Americans and other people of color, youth, women, lesbians, and gays were gathering force to expose its contradictions.

▪ WINI BREINES

≋ Filipinas

Women of Filipino heritage have likely been present in what is now the United States since the last decades of the eighteenth century, when the Philippines, their fathers' homeland, was a Spanish colony and Filipino seamen manned the galleon trade between the Islands and Mexico. Some jumped ship in Mexican ports and ultimately settled in Louisiana, where their anonymous daughters by women of other ethnicities became the first Filipina Americans, part of a relatively small community that took shape during the nineteenth century in New Orleans and in several southeastern Louisiana fishing villages.

Shortly after 1900, following U.S. acquisition of the Islands, Philippine-born women began to arrive. As U.S. nationals, they were permitted unrestricted entry into the States before 1935. But Filipinas made the voyage across the Pacific less frequently than did men. Although married Filipinas traditionally exercised considerable power within their own households, social mores dictated strict supervision of unmarried Filipinas, thus precluding their independent travel. Additionally, because Filipino men usually intended a temporary stay, wives and sweethearts did not typically join them abroad.

Nonetheless a daring few did venture to the United States, their motives similar to those of men in their socioeconomic class. Prosperous and aspiring Filipinos viewed education in the United

States as a sure route to success in the Philippines. By 1904 five Filipinas were among approximately one hundred fifty *pensionados* sent at government expense to U.S. schools. Other Filipinas came to U.S. universities with family funds, under the auspices of later *pensionado* programs, or on private scholarships, such as the University of Michigan's Barbour Scholarship for "deserving Oriental women." Unlike the many self-supporting Filipinos who ultimately failed in the attempt to combine school and work in the 1920s and early 1930s and remained in the United States, Filipinas, who enjoyed the financial support necessary to achieve their academic goals, usually returned to the Philippines after graduation.

Poorer Filipinos, and some Filipinas, came to earn money. The Hawaiian Sugar Planters Association recruited Filipino contract laborers and, especially in the aftermath of labor unrest among the bachelors, financed the importation of Filipinas. Nonetheless, of 103,544 Filipinos who entered Hawaii between 1909 and 1934, only 8,952 were women. These Filipinas were eagerly sought as marriage partners, as were their daughters, who frequently became the young wives of much older Filipinos. On the mainland, the sex ratio was even more skewed. By 1930 in California, where 67.4 percent of Filipinos in the continental United States lived, men numbered 28,625; women, 1,845, or 6.1 percent.

Little additional immigration from the Philippines took place between passage of the Tydings-McDuffie Act (1934), which limited Filipino immigration to a fifty-per-year quota, and the end of World War II. Yet, during these years, Filipina American girls—citizens all, unlike their Philippine-born parents—were born to Filipina women or to women of other groups who had married Filipino men. Although they shared a visible presence as non-Caucasian, the extent of their ethnic consciousness remains unclear, likely dependent upon the importance of Filipino heritage and identity to their parents and to the communities where they grew to maturity.

After World War II the Philippines gained independence and a one-hundred-per-year quota. Yet Filipino immigration accelerated. After unmarried Filipinos already in the United States won the right to naturalization in 1946, many returned temporarily to the Philippines to find wives. Other Filipinas who came as students or visitors remained permanently. Newly formed families added second-generation Filipino Americans. The 1960 census recorded 67,435 Filipinas—37.1 percent of the Filipino population in the United States.

In 1965 immigration law changed drastically. Quotas were scrapped in favor of preferences based largely on two goals: achieving family reunification and relieving occupational shortages. Dominated most visibly by health professionals, Filipino immigration surged. By 1984 approximately 26,000 Philippine-trained nurses had arrived. As the numbers grew, the sex ratio evened: in 1970, Filipinas totaled 153,556, or 45.6 percent; in 1980, 400,461, or 51.7 percent; in 1990, 762,946, or 53.7 percent, of whom 67.8 percent were foreign born.

Educationally, Filipinas constitute a diverse group today. Among those over twenty-five in 1990, 18.6 percent had not completed high school; 15.6 percent held a high school diploma; 24.2 percent had done some college work; 34.6 percent held a bachelor's degree; and 7 percent held postgraduate degrees. Filipinas have also achieved distinction in the United States, including 1948 Olympic springboard and platform-diving gold medalist Victoria Manalo Draves; Dorothy Laigo Cordova, cofounder of the Filipino American National Historical Society; fashion designer Josefina Cruz Natori; novelist Jessica Hagedorn; actress Lea Salonga; and classical pianist Cecile Licad. As individuals, partners, wives, and mothers, as paid and unpaid workers, as entrepreneurs and businesswomen, and as community participants and leaders, Filipinas contribute daily in an increasingly diverse nation.

Fred Cordova, *Filipinos: Forgotten Asian Americans, A Pictorial Essay/1763–circa 1963* (Dubuque, Iowa: Kendall/ Hunt, 1983); Marina E. Espina, *Filipinos in Louisiana* (New Orleans: A. F. Laborde & Sons, 1988); Harry H. L. Kitano and Roger Daniels, *Asian Americans: Emerging Minorities* (Englewood Cliffs, N.J.: Prentice-Hall, 1988).

■ BARBARA M. POSADAS

SEE ALSO Asian Pacific Women.

≋ Film

Bette Davis, Katharine Hepburn, Gloria Swanson, and countless famous on-screen women all had the upper hand in creating their movies. If they didn't think it would ruin their public image (as with Mary Pickford, whose public refused to accept her as anyone other than the twelve-year-old "Little Mary"), these actresses would also have taken the on-screen credit of "producer." Powerful actors forming their own production firms in order to gain control over their careers is among cinema's oldest traditions.

More women worked in influential positions behind the scenes in motion pictures *before* 1920 than at any other time in history. Scores of female filmmakers who were not established actresses played vital roles as directors, producers, screenwriters, editors, and studio owners in the industry's formative years. Lois Weber became the highest-paid director of the silent era. Screen comedienne Mabel Normand taught Charlie Chaplin many of his early routines and directed without credit many of the "Keystone" comedies. Helen Keller produced and starred in a 1919 docudrama about her life.

Before film became big business, anyone who had energy, desire, and enthusiasm could participate. The more people to churn out the hundreds of one-reelers produced each week, the better. "The most exciting place to be on a Sunday was

the studio," said actress Lillian Gish, who directed her own feature in 1921. "You didn't care if you were getting paid or not." This attitude of tremulous excitement for the new medium of celluloid drew people from all walks of life, regardless of their sex.

In 1896, when Alice Guy Blaché, a secretary to photo-equipment salesman Leon Gaumont, suggested they shoot a film sample that would demonstrate how the new motion-picture projector worked, his response was, "Knock yourself out. It's only a toy." That weekend, Guy Blaché shot *La Fee aux Choux (The Cabbage Fairy)*, the first narrative film ever created. Guy Blaché's experiment proved so successful, Gaumont created a production arm for the company and put Guy Blaché in charge. By the end of her career she had directed over three hundred films.

It wasn't until the emergence of the studio system in the 1920s, when film became big business, that women were no longer welcome. The new all-male, nepotistic unions quickly ousted women from the top ranks. Female producers and directors who did not have the additional skill of acting were suddenly out of a job.

By the 1940s the once-powerful women were no longer in the forefront and were often forgotten. However, the facts reveal a proud heritage of women participating in every cinematic craft. Between 1913 and 1927, twenty-six women directed in Hollywood; between 1949 and 1979 that number had dropped to seven. But even in these slower eras, the assumption that Hollywood's glamor divas were the only women calling the shots was simply a myth.

Frances Marion won the second and third Oscars ever awarded for screenwriting. Both Marion and *Gentlemen Prefer Blondes* author Anita Loos have many screen credits in their fifty-year careers.

Dorothy Arzner, the only woman directing in the Hollywood of the 1930s and 1940s (and with a strong, distinctively female eye), also invented the boom microphone and the movie crane. She was the only director of the day to work with all the major female stars: Katharine Hepburn, Lucille Ball, Rosalind Russell, Clara Bow, Claudette Colbert, and Joan Crawford.

Mae West, the show-stopping queen of sexual innuendo, is less well remembered as the genius comedy writer who penned all of her own material. Few are aware that British screen star Ida Lupino was also a prolific director, with seven features and hundreds of television episodes filmed before her 1995 death.

In the mid-1940s, screenwriter Virginia Van Upp catapulted the career of Rita Hayworth by placing her in a daring striptease scene (Hayworth essentially removed her gloves) in *Gilda*. The risk won Van Upp the vice presidency of Columbia Pictures (over nine male producers) in 1945. Characteristic of Van Upp's screenplays were women portrayed in positions of social power, including Irene Dunne as a mayor of a small town (*Together Again*, 1944) and Rosalind Russell as a successful psychiatrist (*She Wouldn't Say Yes*, 1945). Yet by the end of these two films, each woman marries, retreating forever from public life.

It is both fascinating and sadly typical of the times that the industry did not accept the portrayal of successful women on the screen. Van Upp was unable to pen a story such as the one she was living unless her characters saw the "error of their ways" and went back to a "more fulfilling" life of children and anonymity.

By the mid-1970s the film world was changing. Female filmmakers no longer waited to be granted entrance to Hollywood's court before making celluloid statements about the truth of their lives. Now they raised money and did independent films. In 1978, with *Girlfriends*, Claudia Weill dared to make friendships among women a crucial topic for the big screen. Directors of color, such as Euzhan Palcy (*A Dry White Season*, 1989) and Julie Dash (*Daughters of the Dust*, 1992), challenged the rules of an all-white industry. Their films debunked false stereotypes, creating

Famous as "America's sweetheart," Mary Pickford was also a director, shown here behind the camera in 1920.

new cinematic truths for people of color. They followed the courageous lead of Kathleen Collins Prettyman (1942–1988), the first Black woman to direct feature films.

Dede Allen, one of the industry's top-paid film editors, is also the first editor to have achieved solo screen credit for editing. Elaine May also helped open the doors for women to direct, with *A New Leaf* (1971). In 1980 Sherry Lansing became the first woman since Mary Pickford (1921) to be named president of a major studio. And in 1987 Dawn Steel rose in rank at Columbia Pictures Corporation, where she was not only responsible for production but for distribution and marketing as well.

Although by 1995 only 10 percent of Holly-wood's Directors Guild of America members were women, evidence is clear that the numbers will steadily increase. The result of both the inde-pendents as well as the women entering a pre-dominantly patriarchal Hollywood is the transfor-mation of *all* people on the screen. From Dorothy Arzner's bold female aviator (*Christopher Strong*, 1933) to Ida Lupino's novel vision of male bond-ing (*The Hitchhiker*, 1953) to Margarethe von Trotta's revolutionary view of child care (*The Sec-ond Awakening of Christa Klagas*, 1977) to Donna Deitch's fulfilling tale of lesbian love (*Desert Hearts*, 1985), women filmmakers have perma-nently and undeniably transformed the stereo-types of their sisters behind and in front of the camera forever.

Ally Acker, *Reel Women: Pioneers of the Cinema, 1896 to the Present*, (New York: Continuum, 1993); also see *Film-makers on Film*, ten-part video documentary series on women filmmakers, directed by Ally Acker, distributed by Reel Women Videos, 8 Hayloft Lane, Roslyn Heights, NY 11577; *Premiere*, "Women in Hollywood" (special issue, 1993).

▪ ALLY ACKER

SEE ALSO Art and Crafts.

≋ Fourteenth Amendment

SEE Constitution and Amendments.

≋ Free Black Women

Women made up a large percentage of "freed-persons" of African ancestry—individuals free born, or who purchased their liberty, or gained it through private and public manumis-sions—in antebellum America. The 1790 census listed the free Black population as 59,466, con-centrated primarily in the urban North and South. Subsequently, the growth rate declined. Whites abhorred the unsettling idea of freedper-sons living among the bondservants because the slaveholders believed the presence of freedper-sons raised the slaves' aspirations of also gaining their freedom. An increasingly systematic defense of bondage persuaded many whites that slavery was positive. Nevertheless, between 1820 and 1860 the number of free Black women grew from 120,790 to 253,951.

A woman's legal status determined that of her offspring; however, increases in births account for only part of the growth. At the Revolutionary War's end, northern states had either abolished slavery or provided for gradual emancipation. In-dividual owners' wills and deeds manumitted oth-ers. Some women bought their liberty, but they had fewer opportunities than men to become arti-sans and earn money through extra work. In all probability, childbearing prevented access to trades for female slaves since it would interrupt work that could not be completed by unskilled substitute workers.

Runaways also boosted the free population; however, women appeared infrequently in adver-tisements for fugitives. When traveling alone, they attracted more attention and were captured more quickly. Slave mothers were not likely to run away because of the extra hazards of taking along children, and because they were unwilling to leave their children behind.

Maryland-born slave Harriet Tubman freed herself by running away in 1849. Afterwards, she repeatedly returned to the South and brought hundreds of others out of bondage. She fi-nanced the trips, in part, with money earned as a domestic. By contrast, Polly Crockett, a kid-napped free-born woman, removed herself from slavery by suing for her freedom and that of her daughter, Lucy Delaney. Crockett had spared no opportunity to tell her children to seek lib-erty. Delaney chronicles their fight for freedom in a narrative. Despite the obstacles, women were among the runaways who gained their freedom.

Society's rigid gender roles limited women's duties to those of wife and mother. Economic deprivation forced most free Black women to work outside the home; yet most occupations were closed to them because of race and gender bias. Some did earn meager wages for long hours of toil as domestics, cooks, peddlers, shopkeepers, teachers, and nurses. When circumstances demanded, they worked at home as laundresses, seamstresses, and hairdressers. Still others turned their humble abodes into boardinghouses. As a last resort, some women became prostitutes.

All free Black women did not live in dire economic circumstances. Many in the lower South were more likely to enjoy economic advantages than their northern counterparts. Among the free property owners in Savannah, Georgia, women commonly dominated in the category of assessed values at $1,000 or more in 1820. Of the freedwomen in the planter class, most benefited from direct association with whites.

A few southern freedwomen owned slaves. Some state laws required freedpersons to relocate or risk reenslavement; therefore, relatives sometimes held title to their kin to prevent separations. Persons held by their kin enjoyed "virtual" freedom in the sense that they did not have the legal documentation declaring their freedom, yet they were unfettered by bondage and at liberty to make decisions for themselves and their children. Otherwise, free Black women did not differ from other slaveholders, some of whom were brutal while others were benevolent.

Regardless of their role or level of income, free Black women also were caregivers and helpmates. During their leisure time, they enjoyed social activities and devoted attention to improving their lives and those of others. Benevolent organizations and literary societies among freedwomen date back to the early nineteenth century. Monies collected by the Afric-American Female Intelligence Society of Boston benefited sick members and defrayed the cost of books.

The founding of schools and the dedication of their teachers, including Maria W. Stewart, Margaretta Forten, and Sarah Mapps Douglass, reflect a keen interest in the intellectual development of African Americans. After the 1831 Nat Turner rebellion, some southern states forbade teaching Blacks to read and write. Mary Peake, a Black resident of Hampton, Virginia, ignored prohibitions and continued teaching in Tidewater, Virginia, until her death in 1862. Peake was not alone in such efforts. As a result, an estimated 5 percent of the Black population was literate by 1860.

The Normal School for Colored Girls, in Washington, D.C., and Ohio's Wilberforce University and Oberlin College, were among the institutions where free Black women could receive higher education. Most women at Oberlin enrolled in the "Ladies' Course," which, unlike the college department, did not require courses in Latin, Greek, or higher mathematics. Female education in the nineteenth century often emphasized moral and religious education, domestic science, and teacher training. Lucy Stanton, the first Black woman to complete the program, graduated in 1850. Between 1851 and 1861, ten more Black women graduated. They, like Stanton, became teachers.

Women rarely sought professional training in law or medicine because of racism and gender bias. Similarly, few women sought leadership roles in organized churches. The spiritual autobiographies of Jarena Lee, Julia A. J. Foote, and Zilpah Elaw reveal their struggles for entry and acceptance in a career ordinarily closed to women.

Among female abolitionist lecturers were the free-born Sarah Remond, Mary Ann Shadd Cary, and the ex-slave Sojourner Truth. Truth's well-known May 1851 "Ar'n't I a Woman?" speech linked the abolitionist cause to the women's rights issue. The address presented a clear challenge to white women and men both for their racism and their sexism.

Frances E. W. Harper, a regular contributor to abolitionist newspapers, employed poetry in *Poems on Miscellaneous Subjects* (1854) to protest slavery. Sarah Forten's essays and poems also indicted bondage. Harriet Jacobs wrote *Incidents in the Life of a Slave Girl* (1861), a chronicle of her resistance to and triumph over enslavement, to sway Northern women against chattel slavery and white racism.

Aside from speeches and publications, free Black women fought slavery in other ways. For example, the wife of William Parker, an ex-slave, helped defy the stringent 1850 fugitive slave act by protecting four alleged runaways from slave catchers.

Such actions suggest that the women would not be content with their own liberty until all African Americans were freed. The Thirteenth Amendment (1865), which erased legal distinctions between slaves and freedpersons, emancipated nearly four million bondservants. Many women from the antebellum free class continued working for the social and economic improvement of all African Americans.

Adele Logan Alexander, *Ambiguous Lives: Free Women of Color in Rural Georgia, 1789–1879* (Fayetteville: University of Arkansas Press, 1991); Nell Irvin Painter, "Sojourner Truth in Life and Memory: Writing the Biography of an American Exotic," *Gender & History* Vol. 2 (Spring 1990): 3–16; Loren Schweninger, "Property-Owning Free African-American Women in the South, 1800–1870," *Journal of Women's History* Vol. 1 (Winter 1990): 14–44.

▪ WILMA KING

SEE ALSO Abolitionist Movement; African American Women.

≋ Freedom Summer

SEE Mississippi Freedom Summer.

≋ Fundamentalism

Certain conservative Protestants, predominantly Calvinists, began to call themselves "fundamentalists" in the 1920s to describe their adherence to "fundamental" doctrines that supernaturalize the Bible and the life and death of Jesus Christ. This group protested early feminist reforms as well as the teaching of evolution and modern Biblical criticism. After the 1925 Scopes Trial, they largely withdrew from the public arena until the late 1970s. Then, allied with other conservative Protestants and Catholics, they launched a "pro-family" political and cultural movement. The movement has not succeeded in passing its major legislative reforms, but it has blocked many others and established itself as a powerful voice in the public arena.

Fundamentalists oppose affirmative action, welfare, "secular humanism," sex education, feminist reforms, and lesbian and gay rights. They support school prayer, a constitutional amendment that would criminalize abortion, censorship in the arts and literature, and the teaching of creationism in the public schools. These positions are justified by "pro-family" rhetorics that divinely sanction gender stratification ("male headship" and "female submission"), proscribe all sex outside marriage, and render pregnancy an act of God.

"Fundamentalist" is most often applied to politically active evangelical (or "born-again") Protestants. Since 1979 (the Iranian Revolution and the founding of the Moral Majority), the term is commonly used by secular observers to include politically mobilized orthodox Muslims and Jews as well as Christians. The rhetoric traditionalizing family relations is as strong in these communities as it is among U.S. fundamentalist Protestants.

▪ SUSAN HARDING

SEE ALSO Conservatism and the Right Wing; Evangelicalism; Religion.

≋ Garveyism

Garveyism, a Black nationalist social and political movement and Pan-African philosophy that emerged through Marcus Garvey's Universal Negro Improvement Association (UNIA) between the world wars, is often viewed as part of the "New Negro" manhood politics that transfused Black radical culture and intellectual life in that period. Garveyism was equally a new womanhood movement. Structures of leadership and membership activity in the UNIA mirrored those of the Black church: women formed the backbone of the benevolent and community service functions of the organization and of its female auxiliaries, including the Black Cross Nurses corps, and men dominated the status roles and policy-making aspects of UNIA affairs.

Women also held key positions as organizers, orators, editors, and writers. An exceptional few women gained access to top power and policy positions typically reserved for men. These included African American actress Henrietta Vinton Davis; Nicaraguan-born M.L.T. De Mena; and the primary propagandist of the movement and editor of the UNIA newspaper's women's page, Jamaican-born Amy Jacques Garvey. These outstanding women were joined on the local level by scores of women activists who were leaders in their communities, delegates to UNIA conventions, and contributors to ongoing internal debates about gender and the roles of women and men within the nationalist cause.

Jacques Garvey's women's page served as a forum for news and discussion on women's issues, including women in revolutionary movements and party politics, businesses and the professions, relationships and the family. The page represented a range of political positions, from advocacy of equity feminism—or the argument that women have the same abilities as men and should have access to the same opportunities for development and expression—to domestic feminism, to special protection or cultural difference standpoints, in which women's entry into greater political influence was seen as a method of purifying and reforming the public sphere. The "race-first" platform of the UNIA also emphasized women's roles as protectors of Black children and supporters of Black men in the face of continued white racism and oppression. The UNIA was important as a training ground for young women, who were politicized by their membership. When the UNIA dwindled in the late 1920s, those women went on to apply the principles of Garveyism to other causes.

While many leaders in the UNIA were professionals and members of the middle class, the majority of Garveyites were working- and lower-class people, members of the migrations from the Caribbean and Central America and from the rural south to industrial and urban centers of the north. Little overlap existed between women in the UNIA and in the more elite Black women's club movement. Garveyite women embraced a radical vision of society, including separatist economic and cultural development, pride in being Black, and the liberation of Africa from white colonial rule.

■ BARBARA BAIR

SEE ALSO Black Nationalism.

≋ Gay, Lesbian, and Bisexual Organizations

National political advocacy organizations serving the lesbian and gay community have sprung up in great numbers since the 1969 Stonewall Rebellion, widely acknowledged as the starting point of the modern gay rights movement. After Stonewall a new gay and lesbian consciousness of resistance moved beyond the acceptance-seeking character of the earliest gay organizations, the Mattachine Society and the Daughters of Bilitis, which courageously grew up in the hidden, isolated gay life of the virulently homophobic 1950s. Beyond acceptance, these new organizations moved to secure civil rights protections for its members, drawing upon the strategies and successes of the Black civil rights and women's liberation movements of the 1960s and 70s.

Three organizations claim to be the oldest national lesbian and gay political advocacy organizations in the United States: Lambda Legal Defense and Education Fund (LLDEF), the National Gay and Lesbian Task Force (NGLTF—founded as the National Gay Task Force), and the National Center for Lesbian Rights (NCLR), all founded in 1973. LLDEF was founded in the tradition of the NAACP Legal Defense and Education Fund and other movement-based legal defense funds. Their mission is to undertake definitive legal battles to build a positive legal history for lesbians and gays in civil rights and family law. NGLTF at first focused on operating a national hotline and on depathologizing homosexuality in the medical and psychological establishments. In the 1980s the group served as the movement's key lobbyist on AIDS issues and a definitive voice on antigay violence. Today, NGLTF stands as the movement's premier grassroots organizing and media advocacy group. NCLR, like LLDEF, undertakes precedent-setting legal cases but focuses on lesbians, with particular attention to reproductive and adoption rights, and employment and benefits discrimination.

Other key national groups from the late 1970s include the Lesbian Herstory Archives, which began in 1974. The Archives, housed in Brooklyn, New York, serve as the national repository of lesbian social, cultural, and political life in the United States and beyond. The Seattle-based Mothers' National Defense Fund also began in 1974. Now the Lavender Families Resource Network, its mission was to provide advocacy, information, and referrals for lesbian and bisexual women around custody, visitation, child-rearing, donor insemination, and adoption issues. Gay American Indians, an all-volunteer, national network of gay and lesbian Native activists, emerged in 1975. Known today as Gay American Indians, Indian AIDS Project, GAIIAP offers educational, social, and cultural programming for the Native lesbian/gay/bisexual/transgender community in San Francisco. GAIIAP also advocates on tribal issues affecting its members. The National Coalition of Black Lesbians and Gays (originally the National Coalition of Black Gays) was founded in 1978 and drew to its ranks and nurtured some of the most significant African American lesbian and gay activists of the post-Stonewall era. NCBLG had chapters nationwide and was at the forefront of Black and other people-of-color organizing for more than ten years.

Following the 1979 march on Washington for lesbian and gay rights, the movement's first such national mobilization, a number of new groups formed. National Gay Rights Advocates (NGRA) was founded in Los Angeles in 1979 and, like LLDEF, took up legal causes, specifically around immigration issues for lesbians and gay men, until its closing in 1991. In 1979, the D.C.-based Gay and Lesbian Parents Coalition was founded to provide support, education, and advocacy to gay and lesbian parents, prospective parents, and those functioning in a parental role. Today, GLPC has one-hundred chapters internationally.

In addition, the Human Rights Campaign Fund was established in 1980 and funds gay and pro-gay candidates for office and mobilizes grassroots responses to federal initiatives.

The National Association of Black and White Men Together, founded in 1980, is the oldest multiracial U.S. gay organization. The organization has grown from its early social focus into a chapter-based advocacy and educational group built on crosscultural alliances. Men of All Colors Together has expanded work to include men of all racial and ethnic groups.

Further, the Gay and Lesbian Medical Association (GLMA) was founded as the American Association of Physicians for Human Rights (AAPHR) in 1981. Its two-pronged mission is to combat homophobia in the medical profession while promoting the best possible care for lesbian/gay/bisexual/transgendered patients. The National Coalition of Lesbian and Feminist Cancer Projects was founded in 1991 to bring attention to lesbian-specific risks around cancer.

Kitchen Table: Women of Color Press was founded in 1981 by leading lesbian feminists of color to disseminate through its books the analyses and vision of women of color. The press has remained this country's only national advocacy organization founded and led by lesbians of color.

The Gay and Lesbian Alliance Against Defamation was founded in 1985 in the tradition of other national media watchdog groups to protest media coverage of the AIDS crisis by the *New York Post*. Recently, its members have intensified their efforts, working in Los Angeles, targeting the film and television industry's representation of gay and lesbian people.

The AIDS Coalition to Unleash Power (ACT-UP) was founded in early 1987 to take action against massive government indifference to the deaths of thousands of gay men (and others) as a result of AIDS. ACT-UP became the vanguard of gay activism in the late 1980s, drawing upon a history of lesbian feminist direct action among key members and utilizing extensive gay male media contacts to publicize well-organized actions.

National organizing among transgendered activists came to fruition in the 1987 founding of Renaissance, a national educational organization on transgender issues. Renaissance's chapters are based largely in Pennsylvania and southern New Jersey.

The 1987 march on Washington for lesbian and gay rights marked the largest political mobilization of gay, lesbian, and bisexual people in U.S. history. A groundswell of grassroots activism followed, and an enormous number of new national organizations emerged. Many of them focused upon workplace organizing, including, to mention a few, a national gay and lesbian teachers' organization, a national lawyers' association, and the Association for Lesbian and Gay Journalists. Generally, these organizations have advocated for equity for their gay, bisexual, and lesbian members, while pushing their respective disciplines to take pro-gay stances on federal, state, and local initiatives affecting gay, lesbian, and bisexual people.

October 11 was designated as National Coming Out Day (NCOD), an annual date for members of the community to "take the next step" in coming out. The largest organization formed after the march was LLEGO, the National Latino/a Lesbian and Gay Organization, which works to strengthen the Latino/a gay and lesbian communities through local grassroots projects and by providing a national lesbian/gay Latino/a voice in Washington. In addition, BiNet USA: National Bisexual Network represents and supports bisexual activists and organizations nationally.

The Black Gay and Lesbian Leadership Forum, founded in 1988, is supported by the Black gay leadership of the AIDS service movement in Los Angeles. BGLLF produces an annual national conference for African American lesbians and gays.

In 1991 the Gay and Lesbian Victory Fund was created as a political action committee geared to funding openly gay candidates. It already has raised over $1 million to fund directly over twenty successful gay or lesbian candidates for state and local offices.

In 1992 several lesbians from ACT-UP formed the Lesbian Avengers, which immediately spread out in several major cities. The group is committed to expanding activism and visibility concerning lesbian issues.

TransSisters, founded in 1993, was established to provide information, education, and a national journal addressing transsexuality from a feminist perspective.

In 1994 the National Advocacy Coalition on Youth and Sexual Orientation (NACYSO) was founded after two years of meetings by youth advocates from across the country. NACYSO works as an advocacy voice for queer youth in Washington, D.C. and as an educator about queer youth issues.

       ▪ JAIME M. GRANT
with PATRICIA BONICA

SEE ALSO Lesbian Organizations.

≋ Gay Women's Alternative

Gay Women's Alternative (GWA), founded in 1973, was originally conceived as a congenial place for lesbians to meet as an alternative to the bars they frequented in New York City. The founders who included Batya Bauman, Jean Powers, and Roz Lipps, at first had difficulty finding a location. The homophobia of that time slammed all the doors shut. Jean Powers, a member of the Unitarian-Universalist Church in Manhattan, prevailed upon her congregation to take a principled stand. The church provided space for weekly meetings at a reduced fee and has continued to be supportive.

Until her death in 1985, Isaaca Siegel headed the steering committee and devoted herself fulltime to GWA. She is considered the guiding light and nurturer of the organization. In the past ten years Marge Barton, active with GWA since its inception, has run the organization with Vivian Clemmons and Pat Woods, keeping it a vital and vibrant part of the ever growing lesbian community.

Gay Women's Alternative presents a speaker at each meeting, followed by discussion and social hour. The founders wanted a place just for women that wouldn't be eclipsed, co-opted, or taken over by men. For a nominal charge that helps pay for rent and nonalcoholic refreshments, all women are welcome to enter a consistently warm social atmosphere. Surplus income is contributed to organizations such as the Lesbian Switchboard, Senior Action in a Gay Environment (SAGE), Sisterhood in Support of Sisters in South Africa (SISA), and the Lesbian Herstory Archives (LHA).

Since its inception thousands of women have enjoyed a wide range of cultural and political programs that inform, entertain, and enrich the lives of all present. Speakers, who generously donate their time, include women on the cutting edge of lesbian, lesbian-feminist, and feminist activity.

Gay Women's Alternative met weekly until 1991, when the number of meetings was reduced to once a month because of the vast number of organizations now serving the lesbian community. The founders chose to meet on Thursdays because in the days of the closet, gay girls wore green on Thursdays.

       ▪ CLARE COSS

SEE ALSO Lesbian Organizations.

≋ Gender

Gender, according to the 1993 *American Heritage College Dictionary*, is "sexual identity, esp[ecially] in relation to society or culture." This entry, hinting at the distinction between biological "sex" and socially constructed "gender," recognizes a neologism and thereby expresses the influence and transformation in social thought generated by the women's movement of the last two decades.

Some first-wave feminists, from Mary Wollstonecraft to Charlotte Perkins Gilman, distinguished between biological and "secondary" sex characteristics in order to challenge conventional norms about what women were "naturally" suited for. But they did not name this distinction and it was not universally accepted—indeed, some feminists opposed it because they sought advancement for women on the basis of uniquely feminine qualities they did not wish to challenge. Only second-wave feminism succeeded in communicating broadly the notion that masculinity and femininity are largely created by culture, not by biology.

The new feminist definition of "gender," now part of the vernacular, derives from the work of anthropologists such as Margaret Mead, who described socially constructed masculine and feminine patterns of behavior, emotion, and intellect as distinct from biological characteristics. Yet lack of clarity in usage and disagreements about goals continue to divide feminists. First, "gender" and "sex" can never be definitively separated because we do not know all the biological components of male/female differentiation and because "gender" is not an arbitrary construct but a set of meanings given to sex. Second, "gender" has developed in the context of dominant heterosexuality, which is being challenged now as never before. Third, feminists remain deeply divided about what the future of gender should be: one stream calls for the transcendence of gender entirely and aspires to androgyny; another celebrates female/male difference and emphasizes the value, even superiority, of female patterns. Moreover just as some first-wave feminists challenged assumptions about universal sex differences, so some second-wave feminists now challenge the class and racial biases in the assumption that there are universal, transhistorical gender patterns and emphasize instead multiple gender systems in different cultures and historical periods.

■ LINDA GORDON

SEE ALSO Sexuality.

≋ Gender Gap

The "gender gap" refers to the differences in voting patterns of U.S. women and men, which first emerged in the 1980 presidential election. While 54 percent of all male voters chose Republican Ronald Reagan over Democrat Jimmy Carter, only 46 percent of women voters did. This gender gap of 8 percent was the largest difference between male and female voters since the Gallup organization began compiling such data in 1952. Only 37 percent of men voted for Carter, compared with 45 percent of women. Third-party candidate John Anderson received 7 percent of the vote from each sex.

The electoral gender gap narrowed slightly in 1984, when Reagan won reelection with 62 percent of the male vote and 56 percent of the female vote. In the 1988 Bush-Dukakis contest, men voted 57 percent for the Republican and 41 percent for the Democrat, with women splitting 50 percent for Bush and 49 percent for Dukakis.

Male-female voting patterns differed in the 1992 presidential race. Bill Clinton received 45 percent of the overall vote, incumbent George Bush received 38 percent, and Ross Perot 19 percent. Clinton won 46 percent of the women's vote and 41 percent of the male vote. Clinton led Bush among women in every age and educational category except among homemakers, who favored Bush by 45 percent to 36 percent. Clinton's highest percentage of support (86 percent) came from African American women. There was also a 7 percent gender gap in party identification: 41 percent of women identified themselves as Democrats, compared with 34 percent of men; 34 percent of women and 36 percent of men identified themselves as Republicans, and 26 percent of women and 30 percent of men called themselves independents.

The gender gap reappeared in the 1994 congressional elections, but a reduced turnout of women voters contributed to the GOP's electoral sweep. In the 1996 presidential race, Bill Clinton won 49 percent of the overall vote and Bob Dole won 41 percent. Although Clinton and Dole each received 44 percent of the male vote, Clinton won 54 percent of the female vote while Dole won 38 percent of the female vote.

These and other polling data sustain the view that a majority of women's votes provide core support for policies and candidates committed to preserving peace, attending to the needs of others, promoting the economic and social well-being of their families, and protecting the environment.

▪ MIM KELBER

SEE ALSO Electoral Politics; Political Parties.

≋ General Federation of Women's Clubs

The General Federation of Women's Clubs, an alliance of women's literary clubs and civic reform societies, was formed in 1890. It quickly grew to become one of the largest and most influential women's organizations in turn-of-the-century America. Established in New York City at the instigation of Sorosis, an early women's cultural association, it united forward-thinking women who met regularly in small towns and major cities to discuss history, literature, and current events.

Although there were a few exceptions, members tended to be white, middle-class Protestant wives of business and professional men, whose children were in school. The first clubwomen sometimes were criticized for diverting attention from their domestic responsibilities, but club activity grew respectable and members used the clubs to exercise a strong voice regarding public affairs.

The federation's founder was journalist Jane Cunningham Croly and its first president was Charlotte Emerson Brown. The organization grew from an initial meeting of delegates from sixty-one clubs to 475,000 U.S. women from 2,865 clubs in the mid-1920s to a peak of 830,000 women in 1955. The General Federation of Women's Clubs supplied its members with newsletters, study guides, bibliographies, speakers, touring collections of art pottery, and conventions. It united members behind a broad range of municipal reforms designed to improve the quality of life for women, children, and for the community. Among the reform issues members addressed were child labor, clean milk, recreation, public libraries, sanitation and street lighting, conservation, and maternal and infant health care. In wartime members dedicated themselves to relief programs, and in 1914 the organization endorsed women's suffrage.

In the early 1920s the group's leadership acquired a national headquarters in Washington, D.C., where it is still located. Today the organization has declined in size and influence, but it continues to alert its membership to vital social problems and invite study, discussion, and lobbying on local, state, and national levels to support a variety of civic reforms.

▪ KAREN J. BLAIR

≋ Girls' Socialization

Following a decade of women's political activism, the 1980s finally produced a sustained scientific inquiry into girls' social and psychological development. Before this time, all major theories of development were based on samples of men and boys—women were considered deviant from a male norm. Researchers in girls' development found that, in a paradox of progress, just as they are perceived to be entering a world filled with opportunities, adolescent girls as a group suffer more psychological distress than do their male peers. In a rush to deal with the girls' problems, researchers' most promising new data have been largely ignored—data that describe girls' preadolescent health and resilience and point toward ways to bolster that resilience.

Confidence, directness, and power characterize girls' early and middle childhood. Sigmund Freud was so struck by how different young girls were from the feminine ideal of his time that he thought of them as little men. Indeed, between the ages of three and five, little girls are "princesses of power," potent creatures, eager to explore the world around them. Even as they dress and coif the current feminine ideal represented by the Barbie doll, studies indicate that they are actually playing "power Barbie"—games in which the long-legged beauty is in control and victorious in her domestic encounters with Ken. Girls are also fascinated with Barbie because she accentuates gender differences—breasts, long hair, shapely legs—areas of their femininity that they are just beginning to explore. When they are between three and five, girls begin to understand that gender is a constant factor and that they will grow up to be women. Consequently, they are curious about the women in their lives—particularly their mothers—and about male-female differences.

During this period girls identify with their mother and (usually) her role as primary caretaker, learning that nurturing activities often are essentially female work. Girls actually get a developmental boost since they don't have to disconnect from Mommy or her role to realize their femaleness as little boys have had to do in early childhood to discover their maleness.

This fierce connection to mother and to the women who predominate their childhood world provides a psychological safety net. Even in homes where gender dynamics are traditional and girls are exposed to the power compromises the world demands of women, young girls (who have not been abused) are secure during these early years. Buoyed by these connections, girls enter grade school ahead of or equal to boys on almost every standardized measure of achievement and psychological well-being.

By the age of eight, girls become keen observers of gender and confidently question the imbalance of power between men and women that they observe: "Why did you give in to Daddy about dinner when it wasn't what you wanted?" "Why didn't you keep your own name?" These questions often make adult women uncomfortable and tempt them to silence girls. Little by little, girls are shocked as the women they saw as all-powerful sometimes behave in ways they perceive to be subservient and weak.

But the very passivity girls question in adult women is now often reinforced in their own daily encounters with teachers and in texts that show boys in action while girls watch. In classroom interactions boys call out and are called on with greater frequency than girls. Research conducted in over one hundred classrooms found that boys are more likely to be praised, corrected, helped, and constructively criticized by teachers. Eventually, girls' early show of independence and self-worth erodes and their grade-school promise is short-circuited. And to make matters worse, since girls get better grades by being quieter and more conforming, their actual decline is masked by the general impression that they are doing well. By the end of elementary school, at the edge of adolescence, little girls who have been silenced now know to silence themselves or to discount institutions that demand their silence. Not speaking, not knowing, not feeling seem safer than raising open disagreements that might lead to isolation or violence.

At adolescence, girls begin to perceive the differences in ideals, standards, and expectations for each gender, as well as for different races, ethnic groups, and social classes. Sexual comments, jokes, and threats become more intimidating as girls develop an understanding of sexuality and as boys, on average, become physically bigger and stronger than girls. From the media and advertising, girls learn how women's looks are used to market products. As girls' minds and bodies develop, they begin to recognize that good looks are necessary for certain kinds of success, and that good looks lead to being looked at, which for young adolescent girls can seem threatening.

Adolescent girls realize the role that boys and men will play in their lives and recognize the tightrope of sexuality that they must walk. As a result, girls often have difficulty creating an identity because of the varied demands different groups make on their loyalty and love.

Far from complete, current research nevertheless offers clues as to how various demands and loyalties shape this developmental crossroad for girls: In order to be loved, white, middle-class girls try in vain to become the "perfect girl." They suppress bad thoughts or feelings from themselves. Increasingly, they stop trusting what they know, and the phrase "I don't know" gluts their language. These girls suffer a dramatic dip (33 percent) in real self-esteem as compared to boys. Latinas tend to hold on to their sense of self longer, but once their self-esteem drops, the drop is greater (38 percent) than in any other group. During the year in which the American Association of University Women (AAUW) conducted its survey *Shortchanging Girls, Shortchanging America*, urban Latinas left school at a greater rate than any other group, male or female. African American girls don't suffer the dramatic drops in self-esteem (7 percent) but are more likely to be pessimistic about their teachers and their schoolwork than are other girls, or they simply give up on the institutions they sense have given up on them.

Asian American girls may struggle to cope with traditional, male-oriented Asian cultures as well as the stereotype of the "model minority." Research from the University of Minnesota finds that Native American female adolescents exhibit a pro-

gressive increase of self-injurious behaviors from seventh to twelfth grade. Girls with disabilities contend with the punishment inflicted on any person whose characteristics are likely to place them outside society's standards of perfection. At a time when opportunities to explore competence and sexuality are essential, these girls are often denied both. Young lesbians identify themselves only at risk of losing their family and freedom, and are more likely to attempt suicide than are heterosexual girls.

Researchers and practitioners are beginning to examine the factors that could prevent some of the unnecessary losses of adolescence and sustain girls' resilience. Some are exploring the powerful relationships girls have had with mothers, families, and other caring adults as sources for continued psychological health.

Transforming the powerful relationships between daughters and mothers offers one opportunity for building girls' preadolescent resilience and for sustaining their self-esteem into womanhood. The strategy is to enlist women in general, and mothers in particular, to support young girls in what Carol Gilligan and her team at Harvard have observed as the "healthy resistance" girls put up to the losses of adolescence. In this context, resistance refers to what the *Ms.* Foundation has called "an ability to take action, to mobilize oneself—and potentially others—against physical or psychological threat to one's well-being, integrity and relationships, even when doing so risks conflict." For instance, rather than silencing them, adult women could help girls explore truthfully and assess realistically their behavioral options when faced with injustice. This would empower girls and forge a better alliance between adult women and girls and in girls' relationships to themselves.

Adults can also be allies to girls by assisting them in developing certain competencies, a known aid to loss of self-esteem. For instance, studies show that girls who excel in math and science are less concerned with their appearance. Participation in sports has also been proven to shore up self-esteem among certain groups of girls.

In research conducted at the University of Minnesota, increased "family connectedness," which is usually sustained with sons more than with daughters at adolescence, acts as a positive factor in retaining self-esteem. Practitioners are exploring ways in which other institutions can supply this connection. Schools where faculty and staff take on aspects of the parental role may offer possible ways to boost self-esteem and functioning.

Engaging in action within one's community in a "resistance for liberation" is a strategy that has particular salience for girls of color. This resistance builds on collective history as a context for current action. For instance, a girl could be encouraged to respond to racism in the school's curriculum by taking action that challenges the school or offers a remedy for other students of color.

Signithia Fordham found that African American girls in a Washington, D.C., high school took on the achievement standards of white society and exhibited the conforming characteristics associated with middle-class white girls. For the African American girls, Fordham posits this as a "resistance by conforming" adopted by girls who refuse to recognize their "designated place" in a predominantly white world.

Each of these strategies comes with a cost, and most of them cost the resister. As girls resist the pressure to conform to narrow definitions of femininity and to question injustice, adults have a responsibility to stand beside them and work to change schools, workplaces, and government.

Finally, the recent emphasis on the value of "emotional intelligence," which relies on the relational skills that girls learn (and then come to devalue), could offer an instant dose of self-worth to girls. If adolescent girls' knowledge can be generalized to the society and community, then girls, who are the little justice seekers of the universe, may attain justice and thrive after all.

Elizabeth Debold, Marie Wilson, and Idelisse Malavé, *Mother Daughter Revolution: From Good Girls to Great Women* (New York: Bantam Books, 1994); Carol Gilligan, Annie G. Rogers, and Deborah L. Tolman, eds., *Women, Girls and Psychotherapy* (Binghamton, N.Y.: Haworth Press, 1991); Wellesley College Center for Research on Women, *The AAUW Report: How Schools Shortchange Girls* (Washington, D.C.: AAUW Educational Foundation, 1992).

■ MARIE WILSON

SEE ALSO Education; Standardized Testing; Title IX.

≋ Great Depression

At the nadir of the depression in 1933, one-third of the nation's people were "ill-housed, ill-clad, and ill-nourished," in the words of President Roosevelt. The worst economic crisis that the country ever experienced elicited women's resourcefulness and creativity to ensure that they and their loved ones survived. Women held on to jobs or found paid employment for the first time, expanded their housework and caregiving, and volunteered in union struggles and community organizations. But their efforts were not uniformly successful—long-standing racism and sexism influenced their strategies, their triumphs, and their defeats.

Sex segregation of the labor force both protected and harmed women workers. Unemployment decimated the jobs of men in the skilled trades, in manufacturing, and at unskilled labor, while women clerical workers lost comparatively fewer jobs, because paperwork continued when production ceased. Female employees in restaurants, hotels, laundries, and other women's homes, on the other hand, suffered enormous joblessness, because consumers could not afford these services; women industrial workers also sustained high unemployment. If they lost their jobs, women scrambled to stay employed and moved down the ladder of desirable occupations in order to find work. Elementary school teachers became secretaries, secretaries took jobs as waitresses, waitresses moved into laundries, and laundry operatives became domestic workers. Some wives and mothers sought jobs for the first time, and women of every occupational background took domestic jobs. Fewer jobs, increased competition, and downward mobility ensured that young, white, single, attractive, Christian women had the best opportunities for employment, while older, Black women were the most likely to be pushed out of the work force. The women on the bottom rung of the ladder of job desirability lost the most.

In their homes, urban women compensated for lost wages by returning to subsistence production when they lacked cash to consume goods and services. They planted gardens, canned fruits and vegetables, sewed and repaired clothing, and created comfort and cleanliness. They built wood fires and heated water for bathing and laundry when they moved into poorer housing that lacked modern conveniences. Many rural women never knew the luxury of electricity or indoor plumbing, and migrant women did housework under the sun and stars. Women sacrificed their possessions and security for the future: furniture, life insurance, and even their homes.

To comfort unemployed men and to keep their families intact, women took on greater emotional burdens as well. Relatives and friends doubled up, while young women postponed marriage and the birthrate dropped precipitously. Cooperation surged and conflict swelled as lack of money, sagging hopes, and overcrowded living conditions sparked tensions between parents and children, wives and husbands, and among relatives. Outside their families, women relied on female friends for meals, loans of clothing, and a place to stay when they were evicted. Women on their own frequently shared rented rooms just as families doubled up.

When their employment, subsistence, familial, and friendship strategies proved inadequate, women reluctantly considered accepting government relief. So severe was the stigma that women literally died of hunger and cold to avoid asking for help. If they did apply, they received grocery vouchers, used clothing, or a small amount of coal in the early 1930s. After the inauguration of the New Deal (1933), direct cash payments provided the margin for survival, but usually only heads of families were eligible and the amounts remained inadequate. Women were required to meet both means and motherhood tests to receive assistance.

New Deal opportunities disproportionately benefited white men, and political tensions reflected white male dominance of the social fabric. Newly legislated minimum wage and maximum hour protections in the National Industrial Recovery Act excluded domestic and agricultural workers, among them most Black women and many Black men. Public works projects hired men in far larger proportions than women. Local administration of federal programs allowed white southerners to maintain racial segregation and wage differentials. Scapegoating resulted in mass deportation and repatriation of roughly one-third of the Mexican American population. Public sentiment blamed the depression on married women's employment and sometimes excluded wives from jobs.

Despite the harshness of unemployment, poverty, and fear, women created hope through their community activities. Chicana cannery workers in Los Angeles, for example, provided union leadership. Black and white wives of autoworkers and women operatives militantly supported sit-down strikes, like the one in Flint, Michigan. Southern women struck textile mills throughout the Piedmont region. Women joined political organizations such as the Communist Party and its affiliates, marched in unemployment demonstrations, moved evicted families back into their homes, boycotted grocers, and supported the Scottsboro boys. Charitable and religious organizations relied on women's volun-

Migrant family, November 1940. Photograph by Dorothea Lange, whose images of agricultural workers during the Great Depression documented these families' plight and helped garner support for the New Deal.

teer labor to feed the hungry and distribute clothing.

A small number of elite women, many with roots in the suffrage movement of the 1910s, forged government policy to right the wrongs of the depression. Eleanor Roosevelt captured the nation with her activist outlook and actions, and lesser-known women organized within the Democratic Party and in New Deal agencies. Frances Perkins, secretary of labor, led the effort to pass the Social Security Act in 1935, which inaugurated unemployment insurance, aid to dependent children, and old-age insurance. Mary McLeod Bethune, a Black educator, clubwoman, and activist, directed minority affairs in the National Youth Administration and led Roosevelt's unofficial Black cabinet. Artists such as photographer Dorothea Lange, working for the Farm Security Administration, shaped our visual images of the era.

People often mistakenly believe that the depression had little effect on women because they were housewives. Not all women were housewives; those who were expanded their daily labor, practically and emotionally, and some entered the labor force. Racial and class discrimination disproportionately harmed women of color in employment and eligibility for government-sponsored work and relief. Almost all women suffered emotional and economic depression, but they exercised their ingenuity in their homes, jobs, and communities to create the best possible lives they could imagine.

Lois Rita Helmbold, *Making Choices, Making Do: Survival Strategies of Black and White Working-Class Women during the Great Depression* (Urbana: University of Illinois Press, 1997); Richard Lowitt and Maurine Beasley, eds., *One Third of a Nation: Lorena Hickok Reports on the Great Depression* (Urbana: University of Illinois Press, 1981); Charlotte Nekola and Paula Rabinowitz, eds., *Writing Red: An Anthology of American Women Writers, 1930–1940* (New York: Feminist Press, 1987).

■ LOIS RITA HELMBOLD

SEE ALSO New Deal; Welfare and Public Relief.

≋ Great Society/War on Poverty

The Great Society is a term used to describe antipoverty legislation passed during President Lyndon Johnson's administration. Johnson's Great Society extended President John F. Kennedy's New Frontier initiatives, which operated under the assumption that by expanding access to health care, education, employment, and training opportunities, the poor could benefit from the then-projected growth of the U.S. economy.

Michael Harrington's influential book *The Other America* (1962), the civil rights movement, and urban unrest of the 1960s exposed the need for legislation to address economic and social problems faced by the elderly, unemployed, and others living in poverty, as well as to protect the civil rights of women and racial minorities. Great Society legislation targeted poor communities and individuals living in poverty as well as educational and employment practices.

One of the most significant pieces of legislation to pass during this period was Title VII of the 1964 Civil Rights Act, which prohibited discrimination in employment on the basis of race and sex. Programs that targeted poor communities included the Area Redevelopment Act of 1961 and the Economic Development Act of 1965, both designed to encourage new industries to move into economically depressed areas. Housing and community development programs included the 1965 rent supplement program and the 1966 Demonstration (Model) Cities and Metropolitan Development Act. The 1962 Manpower Development and Training Act offered retraining for displaced workers, and the Food Stamp Act of 1964 provided eligible individuals and families with cash vouchers to purchase basic food and related items. Education measures included the Elementary and Secondary Education Act of 1965 and the Higher Education Act of 1965.

Among other key programs associated with the Great Society were the 1965 Title XVIII (Medicare) and Title XIX (Medicaid) amendments to the Social Security Act. Because Medicare was provided as a universal health care program for the elderly, it did not carry the stigma that was attached to Medicaid, which was designated for those who met the low-income requirements. However, since women were overrepresented among the elderly and among the poor generally, they benefited from both programs.

In his 1964 State of the Union Address, President Johnson called for a "War on Poverty." The resulting legislation, the Economic Opportunity Act (EOA), became one of the most hotly contested legislative innovations of the Great Society. The EOA offered the first government-sponsored attempt to involve the poor directly and formally in decision making, advocacy, and service provision in their own communities.

Early reports on the War on Poverty ignored women's contributions as paid workers, despite the fact that the majority of positions such as community aide, community worker, and parent aide were filled by women. In keeping with the traditional view of women's work as unpaid, the Office of Economic Opportunity (OEO), established by the EOA, defined women's role in the War on Poverty as that of volunteer. Strategies for preventing poverty emphasized expanding employment opportunities for poor men; this marginalized women's employment needs as well as their actual contributions as staff members and administrators of antipoverty programs.

Policymakers, along with African American male and Latino community leaders who parlayed antipoverty experiences into political careers or built large welfare bureaucracies, are treated in most written accounts as the primary beneficiaries of the War on Poverty. Although many of the extensive reports on the Community Action Programs (CAPs) mentioned that women were in the majority at the lower-level positions, few detailed the important leadership roles that women played in these programs.

EOA's framers and implementers were unprepared for the challenge the CAPs in low-income communities of color posed to the political establishments in different locales. In less than two years, political pressures from mayors, other local officials, and traditional social service organizations had already circumscribed the federal government's commitment to maximum feasible participation of the poor. Furthermore, funds available for the War on Poverty quickly subsided as costs for the Vietnam War escalated.

Funding was initially provided in a lump sum with specific programmatic decisions to be made at the local level. To circumscribe local discretion over program design, the 1968 amendments targeted specific programs to be funded such as Head Start, legal services, and emergency food and medical services. As funds were cut back, local communities had little money remaining for other program initiatives. The comprehensive, multiservice approach to fighting poverty that marked the initial efforts was further undermined as the specific programs were delegated to other government agencies. By 1970, community action and Volunteers in Service to America (VISTA) were the only programs operated by OEO.

Under pressure from President Nixon, OEO was disbanded, and the remaining CAPs were coordinated by the newly established Community Services Administration (CSA) of the Department of Health and Human Services. CSA received little support from President Carter and was finally dismantled by the Reagan administration in 1981.

The classification of community action positions as paraprofessional helped expand jobs in health and social welfare organizations but hastened the deskilling of certain forms of work in the health, legal, and social work professions. Many of these positions were filled by women, so this deskilling process also furthered the gender segregation in these occupations. Women of color were disproportionately represented in these positions and therefore disproportionately affected by the cutbacks in social services.

Many observers point out that the War on Poverty's attention to Black America created the grounds for the backlash that began in the 1970s. The perception by the white middle class that it was footing the bill for ever-increasing services to the poor led to diminished support for welfare state programs, especially those that targeted specific groups and neighborhoods. Many whites viewed Great Society programs as supporting the economic and social needs of low-income urban minorities; they lost sympathy, especially as the economy declined during the 1970s.

Of the many Great Society programs, more support remains for Medicare, which serves the elderly, and for Head Start, which serves the youngest of the poor, than for housing subsidies and other transfer payments for families living in poverty or low-income communities. The basic assumption of the Great Society, that government must take an active role to reduce poverty, has been replaced by the 1990s assertion that government support for the poor leads to dependency and undermines the work ethic. Whereas the Great Society emphasized the structural roots of poverty, contemporary poverty policy focuses on the individual behaviors and choices of people who are poor.

Numerous critics of the War on Poverty, representing a range of political perspectives, emphasized the limits of maximum feasible participation as a strategy to enhance democratic practice. Others criticized the programs for undermining progressive efforts to develop a national unemployment policy and for increasing local infighting among people of color in poor communities. Many also argued that inexperienced and greedy program administrators misspent and misappropriated funds. However, from the vantage point of women hired by antipoverty programs, the War on Poverty contributed to their personal and political empowerment. It also transformed the unpaid work they were already performing for their communities into paid work. The skills they gained in struggling against insensitive and ineffective public agencies in efforts to address the economic and social needs of their communities enhanced their political efficacy on behalf of themselves, their families, and their community.

Michael Harrington, *The Other America: Poverty in the United States* (New York: Macmillan, 1962); Nancy A. Naples, *Grassroots Warriors: Activist Mothers, Community Work, and the War on Poverty* (New York: Routledge, forthcoming); Jill Quadagno and Catherine Fobes. "The Welfare State and the Cultural Reproduction of Gender: Making Good Girls and Boys in the Job Corps," *Social Problems*, 42 no. 2 (1995): 171–90.

▪ NANCY A. NAPLES

SEE ALSO Civil Rights Act of 1964; Poverty; Welfare State.

≋ Guerrilla Girls

T he Guerrilla Girls are an anonymous group of women who work to expose and challenge the sexism and racism in the art world, while wearing gorilla masks to hide their identities.

Angered into action by the Museum of Modern Art's 1985 "International Survey of Contemporary Art," which included only nineteen works by women and none by people of color among its 165 artists, the Guerrilla Girls first gained attention for the posters they plastered around New York City. Beautifully simple, the posters listed statistics on discrimination in New York galleries and museums along with witty, often sarcastic commentary. "Do women have to be naked to get into the Metropolitan Museum?" read a typical headline, followed by the percentages of women artists (5) and female nudes (85) in the Metropolitan Museum of Art's modern art sections. Not surprisingly, the press tuned in to these mysterious masked women and the group members soon became spokeswomen—lecturing, appearing on talk shows, and exhibiting their posters internationally.

The Guerrilla Girls also have pursued other forms of publishing. In 1992 they received an NEA grant to produce four single-subject issues of a journal, *Hotflashes,* and in 1995 published *Confessions of the Guerrilla Girls,* a "how-to" book for women on organizing and activism.

The Guerrilla Girls maintain anonymity to focus attention on facts instead of personalities. Some admit to being involved in the New York City art scene as curators, directors, and visual and performance artists. The Guerrilla Girls' identities are the subject of endless speculation within the art world.

▪ NANCY B. SMITH

SEE ALSO Art Criticism.

≋ Harlem Renaissance

During the Harlem Renaissance—that fabled outpouring of artistic creativity sandwiched between World War I and the Great Depression—African American women became more visible to themselves and to the larger world. Centered in the flourishing Black community of New York City, the movement was fueled by migrations from other parts of the United States and from the Caribbean. It embodied a "new negro" mood of racial assertiveness, pan-Africanist consciousness, greater participation in electoral politics, increased publication of newspapers and magazines for Blacks, and the liberal and expansive atmosphere of the Jazz Age, the Roaring Twenties. Despite gender discrimination, Black women achieved representation and status that they would not enjoy again until the 1980s. These relatively flamboyant cultural occurrences took place at a time when a foundation of "ordinary" women—single mothers, small-business owners, teachers, cooks, nurses, domestics, housewives, church sisters, and clubwomen—lived away from the teeming in-group center. The women who participated most directly in the Renaissance were salon keepers, promoters, writers, and performers.

Ethel Ray Nance was Charles Johnson's influential secretary at the Urban League's *Opportunity* magazine. Regina Anderson was assistant librarian at the Harlem branch library; she read new books by Black writers and wrote helpful digests of them. The two shared quarters in Sugar Hill, an area that became a gathering center for Zora Neale Hurston, Eric Walrond, and others. Dorothy Peterson, teacher and cultural activist, turned her father's Brooklyn home into a literary salon. Later, with her brother, she kept an apartment haven on the East Side for budding writers. Jessie Fauset's more pervasive influence gave her an impresario status equal to that of Renaissance "midwife" Alain Locke. As literary editor of the NAACP's *Crisis* magazine, Fauset first published

Langston Hughes's work and encouraged Countee Cullen and Jean Toomer. She also wrote standard-setting articles and four well-received novels and presided over intellectual soirees at her home.

As writers, women contributed in all genres, sometimes fettered by literary and social conventions but often forging, like their male counterparts, new forms and idioms. The most famous, Zora Neale Hurston, devised a participant-observer narrative for her folklore collections and, in her stories and later signature novel, *Their Eyes Were Watching God*, depicted earthy, ultimately independent heroines. Nella Larsen's two psychological novels, *Quicksand* and *Passing* (1928, 1929), feature mixed-blood, middle-class women who struggle unsuccessfully to navigate gender and racial turbulence. Poets abounded, the most prominent being Georgia Douglas Johnson, Angelina Weld Grimké, Anne Spencer, and Helene Johnson. G. D. Johnson sang "the heart of a woman" and penned prize-winning folk plays; Grimké's output was compromised by her need to cloak lesbian longing; Spencer wrote about beloved nature but had "no civilized articulation" for racist horrors; and H. Johnson wrote boldly in the fresh, popular slang. Poet-journalist-diarist Alice Dunbar-Nelson and newspaperwoman Geraldyn Dismond arbitered the era.

Along with the tan, high-brown, and yellow chorus girls who startled Broadway by simultaneously dancing and singing, the likes of Florence Mills and Ethel Waters entertained audiences on stage and in fashionable nightclubs. Blues singers such as Bessie and Clara Smith, Ida Cox, and Gladys Bentley freely expressed themes of sexuality, including lesbian and bisexual, in their punning, explicit lyrics, and unabashed female presence. For many, they typify the era, but it was all of the women, in their many lines of creativity, who asserted their genius to make up the Harlem Renaissance glory.

▪ AKASHA (GLORIA) HULL

SEE ALSO Literature.

≋ Health

SEE Alternative Healing; Medical Research; Women's Health Movement.

≋ Heart Disease

It is well known that coronary heart disease is the biggest killer of American men, but the fact that it is the greatest disease cause of death in women was ignored by the medical profession, public education campaigns, and the media for most of this century. The myth that "women don't get heart disease" has prevailed even though, in 1908, heart disease surpassed childbirth as the biggest health hazard faced by women. In the early 1990s, studies demonstrated that men were twice as likely as women to receive state-of-the-art cardiac treatment. The problem that many doctors, mostly women, had fought to bring to the forefront for years finally gained more widespread attention.

Cardiovascular disease (heart disease and stroke) results in about 479,000 female deaths annually, nearly double the number who die from all forms of cancer combined. Cardiovascular disease is also the leading disease cause of death for women of color, causing 42.5 percent of the deaths for Blacks, 34 percent for Latinas, 39.7 percent for Asian and Pacific Islanders, and 31.7 percent for Native American women. Despite these grim statistics, a 1995 Gallup survey found that four out of five women, and one in three of their doctors, do not perceive heart disease as a threat to women. There is little research regarding the difference in heart disease rates among women of color; there is little research on women in general.

The myth that "women don't get heart disease" became rooted for three reasons. First, the vast majority of medical research was performed using men. Second, early results of the Framingham Heart Study, which included women and shaped many of society's views on heart disease, were mis-interpreted. Initially, this study looked at middle-aged people and found heart disease common in men but not women. As the years passed and the participants aged, more women did become ill, but the earlier results had already shaped medical opinion. Third, women tend to be stricken later in life, when they are more socially isolated, less economically visible, and, as a group, easier for society to ignore. The result? Too often women were misdiagnosed, their cardiac symptoms ascribed to "nerves" or "hysteria," sometimes with tragic results. Furthermore, while women were instructed to make their husbands' lifestyles more heart-healthy, they weren't alerted to the importance of caring for themselves, too.

The definitive cause of atherosclerosis, the disease process that results in coronary heart disease, is not known, but several risk factors are associated. Since less research has been done with women, whether they have other risk factors is unknown. There is evidence that the same risk factors that affect men play a role, including family medical history, high blood pressure, obesity, abnormal cholesterol patterns, diabetes, smoking, and a sedentary lifestyle. Therefore, controlling blood pressure and diabetes, quitting smoking, and exercising regularly are believed protective for women as well. Some also believe that hormone replacement therapy (HRT) may reduce heart disease risk.

In studies of subgroups of women of color, African American women have been the research subjects in most of the few studies conducted. Research shows that African American women are more likely to have some of the risk factors at early ages, most notably high blood pressure, diabetes, and high cholesterol level. In addition, they have the lowest reported rates of exercise. It is not known how sociological factors, including lack of access to medical care, influence the cardiac risks for African American women.

Stress is thought to have an impact but studies conflict. The assumption is often made that women are at increased risk as a result of their growing role in the corporate workplace. Not only is there no evidence to support this, but the research to date shows the opposite—women employed in high-level, satisfying jobs are at less risk than their counterparts who hold low-level jobs with little autonomy.

Among the important differences in how heart disease affects men and women is age. Usually, women develop heart disease ten to fifteen years later than men, a benefit generally ascribed to the estrogen women's bodies naturally produce before menopause. Such factors as a strong family history of heart disease, diabetes, and/or smoking can erase this "gender protection." Furthermore, smokers who take oral contraceptives have a higher risk of heart disease.

Heart disease is more difficult to diagnose in women. Symptoms typically associated with heart disease in men, such as severe chest pain, can occur, but manifest themselves more subtly in women, who tend to complain of difficulty breathing, nausea, or fatigue.

Another problem is that cardiac tests and treatments were designed for men. The commonly done exercise stress test, in which a treadmill or stationary bicycle is used to put stress on the heart, is less accurate in women. Testing can be improved if this test is performed in conjunction with a technique known as "cardiac perfusion imaging." A "stress echo," which is a combination of an exercise stress test and an echocardiogram, also improves results in women.

Cardiac treatments, developed and tested on men, are generally effective on women, but they can pose some problems. Cardiac drugs prescribed for women were largely tested among male research subjects. Although the mortality rate for coronary bypass surgery is tiny, the death rate is higher for women. When balloon angioplasty, a surgical alternative, was first developed, the female death rate was higher because the balloon used in the procedure was too large for a woman's smaller arteries. This technique has since improved. Cardiac rehabilitation programs, designed to meet the needs of middle-aged men, often fail to take into account the needs of older women.

More research is needed in the future. Because heart disease is often diagnosed later in women, they are likely to be sicker, require more emergency surgery, and suffer a higher death rate. Techniques are needed to diagnose heart disease earlier in women. There is little understanding about the role that hormones play in heart disease, or whether more appropriate treatments can be developed. More education and awareness campaigns are needed to underscore the importance of this health problem in women.

Bernadine Healy, M.D., *A New Prescription for Women's Health: Getting the Best Medical Care in a Man's World* (New York: Viking Penguin, 1995); Leslie Laurence and Beth Weinhouse, *Outrageous Practices: The Alarming Truth About How Medicine Mistreats Women* (New York: Fawcett Columbine, 1994); Fredric J. Pashkow, M.D., and Charlotte Libov, *The Woman's Heart Book: The Complete Guide to Keeping a Healthy Heart and What to Do If Things Go Wrong* (New York: Plume, 1994).

■ CHARLOTTE LIBOV

≋ Heterodoxy

"There was a club called Heterodoxy for unorthodox women, women who did things and did them openly," wrote Mabel Dodge Luhan. Founded in 1912 by Unitarian minister Marie Jenney Howe in New York City's Greenwich Village, Heterodoxy was a unique gathering place for feminists, radicals, labor organizers, and professional women. Thirty to fifty women of the one hundred twenty known members usually met every other Saturday from September to May at Village restaurants until 1940 to debate such issues as women's rights, pacifism, birth control, revolutionary politics, and civil rights. Historian Nancy Cott reported that meetings focused on "themes of deprivations and rebellions felt in common by women of various sorts."

Members ranged in age from their twenties to their early sixties. Most were Anglo-Americans; one member was African American, and several members were Jewish or Irish. The women ranged from nudists and free-love advocates to lesbian couples, from oft-married heterosexuals to monogamous wives in lifelong relationships.

What held this "little band of willful women, the most unruly and individualistic females" together for thirty years was their pride in the group's enormous range of personalities, interests, and occupations, and their common belief in suffrage. As Inez Haynes Irwin noted, the members "possessed minds startlingly free of prejudice. They were at home with ideas. All could talk; all could argue; all could listen." Rose Young said, "To me feminism means that woman wants . . . to push on to the finest, fullest, freest expression of herself. . . . It means the finding of her own soul."

• JUDITH SCHWARZ

≋ Heterosexism

Heterosexism is a term adopted by feminists in the early 1970s to describe the institutional and ideological domination of heterosexuality as the only "legitimate" expression of sexuality and familial partnership. Modeled after the concepts of racism and sexism, the term does not imply that heterosexuality is innately bad (as white racism does not mean the white race is inherently evil). Rather, it refers to the structural and attitudinal ways in which one form of sexuality has dominated and distorted others (as the domination of one race or sex has oppressed others).

The primary victims of heterosexism are lesbians and gay men, who suffer innumerable types of discrimination in everyday life, from social ostracism to hate violence to job discrimination. Heterosexism takes both attitudinal forms—expressions of bigotry or homophobia—and structural forms, such as exclusion from the partner-

ship rights of marriage, inheritance, health insurance, immigration status, and so on.

Feminist analysis of heterosexism shows that it also maintains male supremacy and works against the freedom of all women. Society's institutions are based on the heterosexist assumption that every woman either is or wants to be individually bonded to one man both economically and emotionally. Discrimination against a woman in the workplace, then, is justified by the rationale that her job is not a primary vocation since she can ostensibly rely on a male as the primary breadwinner in the family. Heterosexism also promotes the idea that sexuality is "either/or"—lesbian or straight, perverse or normal—and thereby constrains women's sexual freedom.

Heterosexism is maintained by compulsory heterosexuality and the punishment not only of lesbians but also of any woman or man who departs from assigned gender roles. Witness the most common slurs used against gender-role deviation: sissy, faggot, butch, dyke. If anyone—gay or straight—fails to take action or say something out of fear of these homophobic labels, heterosexism has prevailed. Such labels are not just name-calling. Behind each label is the implicit threat of social, economic, or physical reprisal—the denial of life-supporting systems or even life itself if one steps too far out of line.

Heterosexism thus works to keep women subordinate; it seeks to deny straight women their independence and strength and to keep lesbians in the closet. The power of heterosexism as a tool to control women will be defused only when women refuse to fear the lesbian label and defend the rights of those outside heterosexism's approved territory: lesbians, gay men, transsexuals, and bisexuals.

Understanding the importance of heterosexism to the oppression of women was pioneered by lesbian feminists in the 1970s. When the women's movement was lesbian-baited and some leaders sought to purge open lesbians, lesbian feminist groups began to form, such as Radicalesbians in New York, The Lesbian Tide in Los Angeles, and

The Furies in Washington, D.C. Although their politics varied, the groups' demands for open discussion of lesbianism and heterosexism as political issues led over time to growing acceptance of lesbian rights. This culminated in 1977 at the National Women's Conference in Houston, when a prolesbian sexual preference plank was accepted as part of the twenty-five agreed-upon points in the national women's platform.

Since the 1970s more analysis of heterosexism and the construction of sexuality has developed, including significant work regarding the interface among race, class, culture, and sexuality. Women from diverse cultures internationally also are beginning to break the silence of how heterosexism functions in their lives.

> • CHARLOTTE BUNCH

SEE ALSO Homophobia.

≋ Heterosexuality

During more than 350 years of U.S. history, the meaning and place of heterosexuality have changed from family-oriented reproduction in the colonies, to a romantic and conflicted sexuality in nineteenth-century marriage, and to a more public and commercialized twentieth-century sexuality, the supposed source of personal identity and individual happiness.

The concept of heterosexuality is a historical creation, first articulated in the United States in the 1890s in medical books and journals as a response to the conceptualization of homosexuality. Hetero- and homo- sexuality are thus interdependent, "unnatural" cultural creations linking gender to sexuality and connecting both to one's personal and social identity. Although various acts, feelings, and relationships that are now labeled "heterosexual" or "homosexual" existed earlier, they likely did not carry the same meaning to the participants or to other members of society as they do in the twentieth century.

Thus sexuality is not private, but is political and related to power. "Compulsory heterosexuality" is part of a power structure benefiting heterosexual males at the expense of women and homosexuals. This inequity is justified by an ideology that sees heterosexuality as natural, universal, and biologically necessary, and homosexuality as the opposite. The system also is reinforced by legal sanctions and violence against women (rape, battering, incest, and murder) and against lesbians, gays, and transgendered persons (verbal harassment, physical assault, and murder).

If our sexuality is socially constructed it can also be de- and reconstructed. In theory, postmodernists fight against binary labels for gender and for sexuality. In practice, many seek to separate sexual choice and pleasure from sexism and oppression.

> • E. KAY TRIMBERGER

SEE ALSO Heterosexism; Sexuality.

≋ Hinduism

A woman's fertility is usually celebrated by the Hindu tradition, but her ascetic practices, scholarship, and patronage of temple rituals have largely been ignored both by androcentric Sanskrit texts as well as by two centuries of Western scholarship that has relied on these texts for information on Hindu culture. Classical Hindu literature portrays women as servants and goddesses, strumpets and saints, protected daughters and powerful matriarchs, shunned widows and worshiped wives. The ideal woman in androcentric literature is a woman whose husband is alive—a *sumangali* or "auspicious." This ideal has been weakened considerably for Hindu women in the diaspora.

Hindu women have been both empowered and subjugated by religious tradition over the centuries. The Brahminical Hindu tradition has been marked by sanctions against women and the so-called lower castes. Power is not based on gender alone; caste, age, and economic status are equally important in determining hierarchies. Caste is a prominent factor, and historically child marriages, abuses against widows, prohibition against divorce, and sanctions against widow remarriage were predominant in the "higher" castes. Lower-caste women had greater freedom in many areas but were discriminated against by the higher-caste men and women. Traditional stigmas associated with divorce and widowhood have been declining among Hindu women in the United States, but vestiges of caste consciousness linger among the Indians.

Discrimination against women within the Hindu tradition in India exists in many domains, including cultural norms, received ideologies, and texts of religious law. Many Hindu women in the diaspora still refrain from worship at the family shrine and at the temple during their menstruation, even though notions of pollution and social isolation have almost completely disappeared in the West. Conservative Hindu women from parts of northern India perform the rituals of *karva chauth* and *hoi ashtami* (October–November) at home for the welfare of husbands and sons, although not for daughters. Women also play important roles in creating and managing Hindu temples in the United States; the president of the Hindu Temple Society of North America in Queens, New York, is female.

There are women poets in the Vedas (1500 B.C.), theoretically the most important scriptures of Brahminical Hinduism, but the most prominent ones came after the seventh century. In India and North America, women sing and choreograph the songs of Antal and Mira. Through the words and passion of such poets, women approach God directly, rather than through the intermediary (male) priests.

The opportunities that some women created for themselves in the twentieth century straddle domains not traditionally considered to be religion in Western cultures. For example, acting, music, and dance are ways to achieve salvation within Hin-

duism. Despite this religious connection, for several centuries high-class and caste women were prevented from public performance. Only in this century have women of all castes appropriated Bharata Natyam dancing. Women play a prominent part in musical performances in the United States and dominate the arena of dance. Schools of classical dance are popular in all major U.S. metropolitan areas; devotional dances are prominent.

■ VASUDHA NARAYANAN

SEE ALSO Religion.

≋ Hispanic Women

SEE Latinas.

≋ History and Historians

The history of the Americas is a product of Europeans' intrigue with the unknown and reflects their intellectual heritage—logic, skepticism, and belief in the primacy of a particular view of reality. Intrigue led historians to begin describing the people of the New World. By the second half of the nineteenth century, the professionalization of history and its establishment as an academic discipline emerged with the work of Leopold von Ranke. Von Ranke initiated the process of defining an absolute historical reality that could be uncovered by careful, methodical research—the gathering and assembling of facts. History thus acquired the trappings of scientific objectivity, assuming that cause-and-effect relationships held true in both natural processes and human affairs.

The development of historical thinking also coincided with the rise of nationalism throughout Europe and America, focusing on the affairs of states and the motives of the men who carried them out. History has thus been concerned primarily with public events; and human action, primarily white male action, has been perceived as the driving force in political change. Frederick Jackson Turner's frontier thesis, for instance, postulated that the response of men to the challenges of environment and hostile Indians shaped a peculiarly American civilization.

In the first quarter of the twentieth century, Carl Becker and Charles and Mary Beard challenged the absolutism inspired by von Ranke. Becker's "Everyman His Own Historian" was a statement of historical relativism that asserted that history was a creation of time and place, based upon men's perceptions of events. The term *Everyman* was apt, since history remained a male-dominated profession.

While Becker and others thought about history as influenced by social forces rather than strictly by the record of those forces, Marxist historians interjected theory into history by using class struggle as an analytic framework. White women could be included in studies of labor because they had entered the labor force during the early years of the nineteenth-century Industrial Revolution as factory girls in the textile mills of Lowell, Massachusetts, and in the garment industry. During the Civil War, they represented a significant proportion of the national labor force.

Most U.S. history texts, however, continued to ignore women. In 1922 Arthur Schlesinger noted that historians' silence about women made it appear that half of the U.S. population had played no role in the country's history. "Any consideration of woman's part in American history must include the protracted struggle of the sex for larger rights and opportunities, a story that in itself is one of the noblest chapters in the history of American democracy," wrote Schlesinger in 1935. Women's place in history became a struggle for acceptance by a male-dominated society. Women's history, in Schlesinger's view, focused on legal and political issues of rights and their attempts to gain entry into male realms.

Feminist historians found new ways of examining social relationships, the condition of women workers to public attention during the first decade of the twentieth century. Mary Van Kleek, Sophonisba Breckinridge, and Josephine Goldmark contributed to investigations of women's status in the labor force, giving visibility to women in the public sphere.

The history of women emerged as a distinctive area of the discipline during the late 1960s. Much of women's history began in order to tell "women's stories." One of the pioneers of women's history is Abbie Graham, whose *Ladies in Revolt*, published in 1934, chronicles the women's rights movement. Rose Schneiderman, in *All for One*, published in 1967, wrote about the early history of the Women's Trade Union League as well as her own experiences. Gerda Lerner's *The Grimké Sisters of South Carolina*, published in 1967, established the place of women in the Civil War era and her own position as a founder of women's history. Caroll Smith-Rosenberg made explicit the place of sexuality in women's history in *Disorderly Conduct: Visions of Gender in Victorian America*, published in 1985.

Feminist scholarship contributed to and was fostered by the emergence of an important new interest in social history. The universalist ideal that historians could determine the true cause of events that affected all people changed to emphasize the importance of classes of people who had thus far been overlooked in historical narrative. During the 1960s historians turned their attention increasingly toward the study of social groups outside the mainstream — people of color, working class people, and women — and explored the activities of everyday life.

Historians used anthropological and sociological methods to analyze data from court records and studied census data to supplement other evidence. This interdisciplinary approach was used to understand the larger scale of human actions in history. Studies of populations, rather than battles and elections, became a way to learn about large-scale changes in society. The roles of women, Blacks, Native Americans, and people of Hispanic and Asian origin were finally recognized as factors that shaped U.S. history.

Family historians approached the study of social change through examining the lives of ordinary families. Demography played an important role in analyzing patterns of birth, death, marriage, and divorce. "Ordinary" people were viewed as actors in as well as subjects of social change.

Feminist critiques—as well as theories such as deconstructionism—that question the meaning of language have also influenced historical inquiry. The analysis of women's roles by Marxist historians presaged the discussion of women's roles in relationships of power. By the late 1960s Michel Foucault was attempting to destabilize notions of historical truth. Foucault, as Becker had done before, stressed the discontinuities of history, but Foucault moved the analysis of those discontinuities into the realm of language and discourse. He called for a total reconceptualization of knowledge as relationships of power between those who control information and those who depend upon it. Hayden White took the analysis of historical discourse into the literary realm to attempt a reconstruction of knowledge based on similarities of linguistic structure.

Beginning in the early 1960s historians and anthropologists explored the meaning of relations between the scholarly inquirer and "the other," the culturally different subject of study. Ethnohistory emerged as a field of study that explicitly addressed issues of culture in different historical contexts. Using anthropological methods to analyze historical meaning, ethnohistorians examined the relationships between native people in the Americas and the European conquerors and colonists who met them there. They also challenged U.S. historians to confront the idea that the European colonizers of the eighteenth century were as culturally different from contemporary Americans as they were from Native people. Ethnohistorians contributed to the discussion of meaning and intent in human action.

The idea of history as linear progress is a peculiar product of Western civilization. Various scholars claim to have absolute, universal knowledge,

but they have been questioned by other scholars on many grounds. As the discipline of history has focused on social and cultural factors rather than on politics and war, women of various social groups and ethnic identities have gained prominence. The subjects of historical study have come to include prostitutes on the Western frontier, women moving west across the continent, women in public life, and women in science. Family history deals with the demographics of family relationships and how women's roles establish the structure of social relations. As in other disciplines that impact historical inquiry, literary theory questions the meaning of written language and authorial intent—the basis of historical inquiry—and gives voice to women and people of different cultures. Anthropologists examine the nature of meaning, and thus ideas of history, among people of different cultural backgrounds. The discipline of history is changing, and women's voices have been an important force in that change. History becomes "herstory," questioning the male domination of language in historical studies.

Although the number of women historians declined dramatically after the Second World War, it rose substantially during the 1960s. The civil rights movement of the 1960s, like the earlier women's rights movement in the 1850s, has given women opportunities and voices previously denied them. Women have become subjects of, actors in, and writers of history as part of the growth of the discipline. The Berkshire conferences of women historians, begun in the 1930s and revived in the 1970s, provide a new forum for women scholars. Although women have felt constrained to establish their own forums within the profession, they are increasingly taking leadership roles. As the scholarly debate within the history profession continues, women's voices are now essential.

Mabel E. Deutrich and Virginia C. Purdy, eds., *Clio Was a Woman: Studies in the History of American Women* (Washington, D.C.: Howard University Press, 1980) [National Archives Conference, April 22–23, 1976]; Eleanor Flexner, *Century of Struggle: The Woman's Rights Movement in the United States* (New York: Atheneum, 1970);

Arthur M. Schlesinger, "The Role of Women in American History," in *New Viewpoints in American History* (New York: Macmillan, 1935).

■ CLARA SUE KIDWELL

SEE ALSO Education; Women's Studies.

≋ Homophobia

Homophobia is defined as the irrational fear and hatred of lesbians, gay men, bisexuals, and of homosexuality in general. The term *homophobia* has its roots in Wainright Churchill's 1967 study of attitudes toward homosexuals, in which "homoerotophobia" was used to describe a pervasive cultural fear of erotic or sexual contact between members of the same sex. In 1971 Kenneth Smith used the term homophobia in the development of a personality profile of individuals who had negative or fearful reactions to homosexuals. The term homophobia was popularized by George Weinberg in his 1972 book *Society and the Healthy Homosexual*, which played a significant role in shifting the focus from studying homosexuality as a deviancy to examining homophobia as a social issue. Weinberg is often credited with developing the concept of homophobia.

Homophobia is a complex prejudice with three components: First, homophobia, much like other forms of oppression, has xenophobic qualities (that is, it reflects a deep-seated fear of people who are perceived to be different from the dominant culture).

Second, erotophobia, or the fear of excessive sexuality, is also important in relation to homophobia. Erotophobia reinforces stereotypes of gay men, lesbians, and bisexuals as hypersexual or as sexual predators. Hypersexuality is a common stereotypical representation of many marginalized groups, such as people of color, ethnic minorities, women, religious minorities, poor or working-class people, and sexual minorities. In addition, erotophobia contributes to a profound aversion to homoerotic feelings. The Kinsey report revealed that approximately half of the general population experiences some same-sex sexual feelings or fantasies. However, cultural negativity about sexuality has led many to despise homoerotic sexuality despite its prevalence.

Third, research on homophobia has consistently revealed that an aversion to perceived violations of sex-role stereotypes underlies much of people's hatred toward gay men, lesbians, and bisexuals. Gay men are stereotypically perceived as effeminate and female sex-role typed, while lesbians are thought to be "butch" and male sex-role typed. Conversely, anyone who acts in these cross-gender typed ways is thought to be gay or lesbian regardless of their sexual behavior. Thus, homophobia serves to reinforce the entrenched sexism of our culture by labeling any men or women who deviate from rigidly defined traditional sex roles as "queer."

Lesbian baiting, a particular manifestation of homophobia, is often used in an effort to discredit individual women or the feminist movement in general. By attempting to stigmatize independent, assertive, and self-determined women as "lesbian," lesbian baiting has been utilized to control women, regardless of their sexual orientation. In addition, lesbian baiting has led to divisiveness within feminist organizations as some women have tried to distance themselves from the taint of "queerness."

The institutionalization of homophobia in social, religious, legal, and medical systems is known as heterosexism. Heterosexism is the belief in the superiority of heterosexuality and heterosexual relationships. Heterosexism creates the conditions for homophobia by institutionally reinforcing the power and privilege of heterosexuality as the norm.

Together, homophobia and heterosexism often produce devastating political, social, and legal consequences for gay men, lesbians, and bisexuals. For instance, in all but eight states in 1995, there is no legal protection against discrimination associated with sexual orientation in housing, employment, and public accommodations. In addition, numerous antigay initiatives have been placed on ballots in jurisdictions across the country to legalize differential and discriminatory treatment of lesbians, gay men, and bisexuals. Sodomy laws, used selectively to stigmatize and criminalize same-sex sexual behavior, still exist in twenty-four states. These laws are often used to justify denying lesbian, gay, and bisexual parents custody of their children. Hate crimes, harassment, and violence against persons perceived to be gay, lesbian, or bisexual have been increasing. The U.S. Justice Department now identifies these groups as the most likely victims of hate crimes.

• BETH ZEMSKY

SEE ALSO Heterosexism.

≋ Household Workers

Paid Household Workers

The occupation of domestic service has roots in both slave and feudal economies. Under feudalism, the aristocracy developed elaborate divisions of household labor, including coachmen, cooks, bakers, butlers, nursemaids, chambermaids, scullery maids, valets, gardeners, and laundresses. Although they were based on specialized household tasks, the various divisions of domestic labor reproduced gender divisions in society. The traditional paternalistic relationships between masters and servants were exported from Europe to the colonies. Indentured servants, male and female, first dominated the ranks of domestic service in the U.S. colonies, but in the South, Black slaves eventually replaced the indenture system. Before the Civil War unpaid domestic service was a major occupation for both male and female slaves in the South. House servants were commonly isolated from their family and the community of other slaves and subjected to two degradations: domination by the male head of household

in a form of feudalistic paternalism and the brutalities of chattel slavery.

Racial and gendered stratification in domestic service continued long after emancipation, transforming Black women from domestic slaves to low-wage servants and marking Black women as analogous to maids. Following the American Revolution, native-born white women were frequently hired as "help" or "hired girls" to work side by side with housewives. Here, as on the continent, "feminization" of domestic service occurred as women were hired to fill gaps created when men turned to other occupations during transitional phases of industrialization, while free white laborers replaced indentured servants in the North.

A household industrial revolution of sorts began in the mid–nineteenth century. Middle-class women professionalized homemaking activity under the ideology of the "cult of domesticity." Acting as employers, mistresses applied principles of scientific management to the home and adopted the modern employer-employee relationship, which emphasized both benevolent and entrepreneurial versions of supervision. Unlike the aristocracy, the middle class hired fewer workers and most domestics eventually became "maids-of-all-work," who toiled alone in the employers' homes. The change resulted in deskilling household labor and the allocation of the most menial and physical tasks to the worker.

After the Civil War, as the first wave of massive immigration began, household service developed a reputation as a beneficial apprenticeship for young immigrants or rural women migrating to urban areas. By 1900 60 percent of Irish-born, 62 percent of Scandinavian-born, and 43 percent of German-born women were employed as domestic servants. Combining the influences of domestic science and the cult of domesticity, the supervision of immigrant women became a form of moral entrepreneurship for employers, a reforming vocation aimed at changing morals and imposing middle-class standards of cleanliness. Efforts to induce immigrant and rural women to conform to middle-class culture, develop work

The workers of a single household in Black River Falls, Wisconsin, circa 1890, hold props that indicate their individual responsibilities.

habits similar to those demanded at factories, inculcate proper feminine deportment, and aspire to middle-class consumption patterns resulted in restrictions for the servants that governed even such things as their choice of clothes and leisure activities. Domestic service was held out to Northern or Western European immigrants as a "bridging" occupation to assist them in the adjustment to U.S. life and to learn skills for social mobility.

Movement toward the professionalization of homemaking and the elevation of supervision to a vocation occurred simultaneously with the shortage of household workers brought about by the industrial expansion of the late nineteenth century. At this time domestic science was also introducing new standards of cleanliness that replaced regular maintenance with labor-intensive "ritual cleaning." The magnitude of the servant shortage can be seen in the fact that in 1870, half of employed women were servants and washerwomen. By the turn of the century only a third of working women were in the servant category. During peri-

ods of labor shortage, training and certification were frequently offered as incentives and solutions to the low status ascribed to the occupation. As part of the professionalization movement, and unlike previous generations of Anglo-Saxon native-born "help," European immigrant household workers were increasingly treated separately from the employer's family and community. The use of the livery became more common, and separate living quarters were arranged within the house. Attempts at professionalizing domestic service have seldom been successful, in part because the "personalism" of the mistress-maid relation is seen by workers as a mark of servitude and a major drawback. Workers instead argue for the establishment of formal contractual relations resembling other paid work in society.

In the nineteenth century, patterns of employment in the North revolved around seasonal needs (harvest) or household crises (illness or childbirth), but in the twentieth century labor arrangements throughout the country increasingly were made on the basis of time rather than task. After the turn of the century, immigration from southern or eastern Europe predominated and many women moved directly into factory work. The percentage of Black women in domestic service increased in northern households, from 9 percent in 1910 to 19 percent in 1920. By 1930 Black women dominated the occupation in northern cities. A similar pattern was reproduced in the West and Southwest, with different people of color forced into structurally equivalent positions. Racial discrimination against Mexicans and Mexican Americans throughout the West and Southwest, and Asians in California and the Pacific Northwest, left the most vulnerable workers no other options. Dual wage systems and racial stratification were enforced further by imposing school curricula and creating vocational and training programs in home economics. Again, domestic service figured in Americanization campaigns and job opportunities created by the New Deal. In 1930 45 percent of all employed Mexican women were domestics, and they dominated the occupation in Southwestern cities like El Paso. In the Southwest, Mexican American and Mexican immigrants gained access to higher-paying and higher-status domestic jobs only when native-born white women moved on to clerical, sales, and teaching positions.

Domestic service attracted, and continues to attract, women with few other employment options. People of color and immigrants have dominated domestic service since the colonial period. Since the 1980s Latina immigrant women have constituted the largest category of women entering the occupation.

Prior to the turn of the century, live-in situations dominated the occupation and U.S. homes were built with spatial deference separating the domestics' working and living quarters from the employers' family areas. The use of separate entrances, passageways, and rooms allowed the employee to move "invisibly" around the house. The kitchen was usually the only room where the employee sat. Live-in working conditions were marked by long hours, extreme isolation and loneliness, and the most severe cases of exploitation (rape, withholding pay). Traditionally Sunday was assigned as the day off, along with one afternoon during the week. Live-in situations today are increasingly common among Latina or other immigrant women who are undocumented workers or are applying for residency.

While live-in working conditions have remained the same, labor shortages have resulted in a significant change in the occupation: the shift to day work. Day work changed the structure of domestic service by eliminating employee dependency on working for room and board, increasing autonomy and opportunities to leave jobs with oppressive employers, and establishing a trend toward an eight-hour day. Day work for a single employer eventually gave way to the practice of workers dividing their work week among numerous employers. In some cases smaller homes and apartments have even made it possible to clean more than one place a day. Nonetheless, domestic service retains many undesirable aspects, not the least of which is that the occupation is seen as a low-status occupation carrying the mark of servitude. Most of the work is physically demanding, pay and labor arrangements are irregular and often unpredictable, and domestic workers are almost universally expected to perform curious kinds of emotional labor, for example, ritual deference to affirm and enhance the employer's sense of self-worth. Domestics are often required to do a wide range of tasks outside the sphere of housecleaning, including laundry, child care, cooking, nursing, running errands, and gardening. Despite the attempts to commercialize the occupation through agencies acting as intermediaries, domestic service operates increasingly in the underground economy, ignoring minimum-wage and social security legislation. Large numbers of undocumented immigrants continue to work in domestic jobs.

In 1993 "Nannygate" represented the first national scandal over household labor. Zoe Baird, a corporate lawyer with Aetna Life and Casualty Company, was nominated by President Clinton for U.S. attorney general. She was forced to withdraw from consideration because of the controversy that emerged over the fact that she had hired an undocumented Peruvian housekeeper and for failing to pay the woman's social security tax or unemployment insurance. Since then, federal nominees are questioned about their employment of household workers. Nannygate involved two issues: 1) the hiring of an undocumented worker during a period when it was illegal for an employer to do so, and 2) the failure to pay social security and taxes. These issues remain in the political arena. In the 1994 elections candidates smeared one another with accusations of hiring undocumented immigrants. The scandal served to expose routine practices of the middle classes who hire undocumented household workers at the lowest possible wage scale. Unfortunately, the issue is increasingly framed as an immigration issue rather than as a work issue.

Although social scientists a generation ago forecast the disappearance of domestic service from the modern economy, the demand for household workers continues to increase in response to middle- and upper-class women working outside the home. Ironically their entry into the work force as a result of the second wave of feminism has been made possible by the exploitation of poor women of color.

Faye E. Dudden, *Serving Women, Household Service in Nineteenth-Century America* (Middletown, Conn.: Wesleyan University Press, 1983); David Katzman, *Seven Days a Week: Women and Domestic Service in Industrializing America* (Chicago: University of Illinois Press, 1981); Mary Romero, *Maid in the U.S.A.* (New York: Routledge, 1992).

▪ MARY ROMERO

SEE ALSO Work.

Unpaid Household Workers

The view of child care and housework as unpaid work arose with the rise of paid work, which accompanied the development of a capitalist, market economy. In most societies, a sexual division of labor generally has assigned females to intrahousehold, reproductive, familial activities, while giving males a greater role in interhousehold and political activities. This separation of spheres has contributed to the construction of separate "genders"—feminine, family-centered women, and masculine, public-oriented men—who need one another to be complete. Hence, it helps to provide an imperative for heterosexual marriage.

The distinction between unpaid and paid home and market work arose gradually over the course of U.S. history and across racial-ethnic and class groups. The Native American nations who inhabited this continent before Europeans arrived lived in subsistence economies; in many of these, women's assignment to the reproductive work did not confer an inferior social status. However, when colonists journeyed from Europe, where private property and markets were developing, to the New World, they brought with them these fledgling institutions and the associated striving for income and wealth. They viewed the accumulation of wealth as masculine and denied the married women among them (as well as the peoples they displaced or used as slaves) property rights.

In spite of this market focus among the European colonists, wage labor—what we view as "paid work"—was scarce. Property-owning European families set up family businesses or farms, using the labor of family members, indentured servants, slaves, or, occasionally, hired hands. All of these individuals' efforts contributed to the production of goods and services for the market and hence to earning income—including, for example, women's work of feeding and caring for the household's "workers." However, no one other than the hired hands was actually paid a wage for working—the others simply received their subsistence. Thus, although white, male property owners had power over their wives, children, and workers, wives' and homemakers' work did not, then, stand out as "unpaid."

It was with the rise of wage labor and capitalist production that women's household work began to be clearly differentiated from market-oriented work, because the latter gradually moved out of the household domain into that of the capitalist firm. Those who produced commodities for sale in the market were no longer family members, or unfree laborers, but rather wage earners. By 1890 there were twice as many people working for wages or salaries as there were self-employed workers; by 1970 there were nine times as many.

The movement of commodity production out of the household did not empty the home and family of their content. Rather, women's traditional reproductive work—childbearing, child rearing, feeding, clothing, and caring for family members—stayed within the sphere of the family, and women as wives and mothers retained the primary responsibility for those tasks. A division between husband as wage earner or "breadwinner" and the wife as homemaker emerged as households were unevenly drawn into the capitalist economy.

In this process, family life began to emerge as a distinct arena of social relationships, one assigned specifically to women, and one whose relationships of sharing, nurturing, and love stood in stark contrast to the competitive self-seeking of the economy. In the nineteenth century a "cult of domesticity" arose among the upper and middle classes, particularly but not exclusively among European Americans, which elaborated and glorified women's family responsibilities. The "cult" argued that women's traditional reproductive work was a "career" equally important to men's workplace careers. Mothering, it proposed, was not simply physical drudgery, just as easily done by a wet nurse or slave. On the contrary, it was a supremely social task that shaped the character of the child and determined his or her future success. Further, women as homemakers were viewed as possessing a special, caring morality—a necessary, humanizing complement to men's individualistic and aggressive natures.

This homemaking career, as elaborated by the cult of domesticity, was seen to be a full-time one that precluded labor-force participation. Married women were, if at all possible, to eschew participation in gainful employment so as to dedicate themselves to their domestic duties. If additional income was needed to make ends meet, families usually sent their children into the labor force; conversely, young women and men postponed marriage until the prospective husband earned enough to support a full-time homemaker. Thus, in 1890, only 4.5 percent of all married women were "gainfully employed," compared with 40.5 percent of single women. Many employers adhered to the cult of domesticity by establishing "marriage bars," implicit or explicit policies that barred married women from employment (and required firing single women employees once they married). The cult also helped to justify sex-typing of jobs, in which women's jobs were paid much less than men's, given that men had families to support.

The prevalence of domesticity among married women varied according to class: the higher the husband's income, the more the family could afford the wife's domesticity. Further, there were significant differences in the extent of domesticity among racial-ethnic groups; whereas only 6.5 percent of married European American women were gainfully employed in 1920, 18.5 percent of married Asian American women and 32.5 percent of married African American women were so employed.

The actual content of women's domestic work also varied greatly across class. Among the middle and upper classes, proper homemaking was thought to require the aid of one or more paid domestic servants (usually women, but sometimes men of color). Such privileged homemakers spent their time supervising their servants and children, and they often also entered the public sphere to do "social homemaking" for the needy. In sharp contrast, poor and working-class wives could not afford domestic servants. For them, homemaking involved a good deal of arduous physical work, such as carting water and scrubbing clothing, as well as efforts to "make ends meet" by bargain shopping, scavenging, taking in boarders, or doing odd jobs in their homes.

The cult of domesticity's confinement of women to unpaid domestic work imposed high economic costs on women. The ideal marital division of labor between full-time homemaker and breadwinning husband created a clear power inequality between the two. Women were totally financially dependent upon their husbands for their survival, and, indeed, their job was to serve their husbands. This specialization in domestic work proved economically disastrous when full-time homemakers lost their husbands through death or desertion and were forced to fend for themselves and their children. The flip side of the primacy of women's domestic careers was the view that, for women, wage earning was at most an adolescent stage that ended at the time of marriage. Thus, employed women were either adolescents (immature women) or "spinsters" (unmarried and hence failed women). This view then translated into the segregation of employed women and girls into jobs that did not pay living wages. Even though women of color exhibited a greater labor-force commitment than did white women, they were restricted as women to jobs that fit the white-defined "cult of domesticity," and as people of color to jobs that were lower paid and lower status than those to which white women had access.

In the twentieth century there have been some major changes in the organization of women's unpaid household work. First, technological and product innovation have changed the face of household work for all U.S. citizens. Between 1880 and 1930 a number of new, household labor-saving goods and services appeared on the market: electricity, furnaces, running water, running hot water, plumbing, electric appliances (including toasters, irons, vacuum cleaners, washing machines), telephones, refrigerators, automobiles, and more. Rising real wages for workers allowed the rapid diffusion of these products among households, and the drudgery work involved in homemaking was reduced substantially. However, homemaking remained time-consuming, as standards of cleanliness rose, the availability and use of domestic servants fell, and the focus on mothering responsibilities intensified; as a result, homemaking responsibilities expanded to fill the time available.

A second and crucial influence on married women's unpaid work has been their growing entrance into the labor force. Ironically, much of the impetus behind this movement out of the domestic sphere seems to have come from the cult of domesticity itself. First, numbers of middle- and upper-class women pursued higher education in the late nineteenth and early twentieth centuries, with the goal of becoming better mothers; however, achieving this goal backfired as, once educated, growing numbers of women decided to utilize their skills in labor-force careers and, increasingly, tried to combine their careers with marriage. Second, as the homemaker's job of filling her family's needs became increasingly one of purchasing and using store-bought goods, entering the labor force became a more common and accepted way of doing women's work of filling family needs. These trends combined with the rapid growth of women's jobs, particularly office work, to produce a dramatic increase in married women's labor-force participation rates from 5.6 percent in 1900, to 23 percent in 1950, to 59.2 percent in 1992. While this increase was most pronounced among European American women, it was significant for all racial-ethnic groups.

The growing labor-force participation rates of women of all classes, including the pressuring of privileged and educated women for entrance into the top, male-dominated jobs, have changed the face of women's unpaid work. Employed married women, especially those who are mothers, are now working a "double day" of paid and unpaid work. While growing numbers of women in dual-career couples have begun to pressure their husbands to take on a greater share of the unpaid domestic work, studies still show that employed women, on average, do two to three times more unpaid work than do their husbands. Families have responded to women's double day by increasing the use of household labor-saving goods and services, including child care, restaurant or prepared meals, and elderly care.

Now that most women, including the most class-privileged, are participating in the paid labor force, and some in high-powered, prestigious jobs, full-time homemakers find themselves and their work increasingly devalued. Rather than representing the ideal career for a woman, full-time homemaking is viewed more as simply work, and unpaid work at that. The full-time homemaker is now "just a housewife." Thus, the mothering and caretaking activities that are crucial to social survival have not only been squeezed into less time but have also been devalued.

Teresa Amott and Julie Matthaei, *Race, Gender & Work: A Multicultural Economic History of Women in the United States* (Boston: South End, 1991); Julie Matthaei, *An Economic History of Women in America: Women's Work, the Sexual Division of Labor, and the Development of Capitalism* (New York: Schocken Books, 1982); U.S. Department of Commerce, Bureau of the Census, *Statistical Abstract of the United States*, 1993.

■ JULIE MATTHAEI

SEE ALSO Cult of Domesticity; Domestic Science; Double-Day.

≋ House of Representatives

SEE Congress.

≋ Housing

The term *housing* has two connotations in the United States. Housing can mean all the dwellings—both publicly and privately initiated—which, taken together, provide shelter for people of all classes. More often housing refers to all dwellings built by state, federal, and charitable agencies to house people who cannot afford market-rate shelter. Women are generally assigned the responsibilities of nurturing, feeding, and clothing their children, and need a safe and healthy environment; therefore housing is a primary concern for women.

The normal market-rate private house may have been paid for by men historically but has long been the province of women. In the nineteenth century, bourgeois women undertook to domesticate their houses with interior decoration and by acquiring utilities to keep their families comfortable. Middle-class houses in the Victorian era contained numerous rooms on several floors; housekeeping was strenuous work for women both as servants and as mistresses of households. Although women were not often granted mortgages to purchase such houses independently from men until the 1970s, they maintained the value of their husbands' houses through keeping the home in good repair. When banks finally changed mortgage policies to include women, their redlining practices excluded African Americans.

In the late nineteenth century, specialized housing appeared for women. In New York, department-store magnate A. T. Stewart built the Home for Working Women, where his store employees could rent a private room, dine in a communal dining room, and sign up to use a limited number of private parlors to entertain guests. The YWCA followed this model in the early twentieth century, offering safe and respectable rooms for white women to rent.

Families of the working class, often immigrants and people of color, found shelter in the tenements of nineteenth-century cities. "Tenements" implied all that was bad in housing: cramped rooms, no corridors, little ventilation or sunlight, no running water, and no bathtubs or indoor toilets. Tenement districts gained a deserved reputation for breeding diseases. By the turn of the century, new forms of housing remedied some of these problems. Testimony from tenement dwellers along with reforms proposed by designers helped to formulate legislation in U.S. cities that guaranteed minimum room sizes, private toilets and water supply, external windows in each room, and separate hallways. Tenements with sizable courtyards and modern kitchens, developed first by charitable organizations and later by trade unions, were available at affordable rents for the working class.

Middle-class women's abilities to keep house in the twentieth century were improved by living in smaller, compact homes. Usually one-floor designs, the houses reduced distances between rooms and cut down on stair climbing. Electricity finally enabled women to use small household machines, such as vacuum cleaners, refrigerators, and washers, to mechanize the house.

Public housing built by government agencies occasionally in the early twentieth century and widely after World War II has also been of particular concern to women. Housing activists Edith Elmer Wood and Catherine Bauer Wurster promoted public involvement in housing reforms in the 1920s and 1930s. Today women are often heads of households, but many are unable to meet market-rate rents or mortgage payments due to poverty, so they turn to public housing. Because of racism, the poor are disproportionately people of color. High-rise towers favored by 1960s planners become barriers to women's family caretaking. Mothers, separated in the upper-floor apartments from their children playing below, cannot oversee their activities or get to know their neighbors, which impedes the formation of communities. However, women in low-rise housing form support networks because residents close to the ground can communicate easily, help one another, and keep an eye on community space.

Suburban single-family housing has been criticized by Susan Saegert, Marsha Ritzdorf, and others because of the way it segregates women. Suburban spatial structures can isolate women and children who are located far from public transportation, day-care centers, and workplaces.

Housing for groups with special needs arose in the late twentieth century, including group homes created for women addicted to drugs, young single mothers, the elderly, or women battling mental illness. The fact that a multiple dwelling collects many persons under one roof allows group services to develop, such as a resident social worker or a day-care center—an advantage unavailable to people in single-family houses. While neighbors often resist such special housing in the planning stages, once in place these housing complexes have been quite successful.

Inadequate housing has often placed constraints on women's abilities to shelter and nurture their families, but women have also been active in articulating and exposing problems. Women's needs have helped to shape the interior spaces, the locations, and the special services available in a variety of current housing types.

Karen Franck and Sherry Ahrentzen, eds., *New Households, New Housing* (New York: Van Nostrand-Reinhold, 1989); Joan Forrester Sprague, *More Than Housing: Lifeboats for Women and Children* (Boston: Butterworth Architecture, 1991).

■ ELIZABETH C. CROMLEY

SEE ALSO Architecture; Suburbanization; Urbanization.

≋ Hull House

SEE Settlement House Movement.

≋ Humor

Can women be great comedians? Many believe they can't. A group of male comics recently watched in stony silence as their aspiring female counterparts tried, first cheerfully, then tearfully, to get them to laugh. "Bitches ain't funny," they sneered.

Funny women performers, with endlessly inventive schtick, have romped through all types of media, from standup and sketch comics to comic actresses and singers, including vaudeville's Fanny Brice; radio's Gracie Allen; television's Lucille Ball, Imogene Coca, and Lily Tomlin; cinema's Mabel Normand and Bette Midler; and nightclubs' Joan Rivers and Marsha Warfield.

"Bimbos" often have been played with grace, wit, and intelligence. One recalls Marilyn Monroe's airhead bombshell in *Some Like It Hot* and *The Seven Year Itch,* or Goldie Hawn's endearing character in *Cactus Flower.*

Why then are women considered not funny? Is it because, until recently, comic actresses usually have played culturally stereotyped bubbleheads? Or is it because women comics so frequently have played the straight "man" to the presumably funnier male and thus aren't recognized for their humor?

Professional comedy imitates life. Women set up the comedy and keep it going. Men get the payoffs. Little girls are known to giggle incessantly among themselves. When girls are socialized into becoming "little women," their laughter becomes more covert, more pointed. Erma Bombeck's accommodationist sniping, Molly Ivins's cheerful obscenity—their followers quip, laugh, and smile both to avert male rage and to survive what frequently are unbearable situations.

The belief that bitches ain't funny is not entirely explained by women being cast in ditsy or subordinate roles. Many great female comics have overwhelmed their male partners. In *She Done Him Wrong,* Mae West upended the funny man/straight woman routine. "Come up and see me sometime," she insinuates at Cary Grant. "Wednesday night is amateur night." "I can't, Mae, it's Lent," says Cary. Mae gives him a cool, diagnostic glance. Pause. "Well, when you get it back, come up and see me."

Society's expanded notions of women's work, endless permutations of family structures, openness about sexual preference, the mainstreaming of profanity, and, most important, women's resistance to being typecast have produced a diversity of female comics. Breaking the iron lock (with a few exceptions) of straight nice gorgeous white bimbo, women now can be fat (Carrie Snow), plain (Roseanne), Black (Whoopi Goldberg, Thea Vidale, and Simply Marvelous), nerdy (Margaret Smith), or lesbian (Kate Clinton, Lea DeLaria, and Marga Gomez).

Have these developments smashed the idea that women are humorless? No and yes. No, because patriarchal beliefs in the ubiquitous inferiority of women border on the religious and generally do not vanish with evidence. Each counterexample is treated as an exception. According to the sexist world-view, Mae West was a female impersonator.

One also could argue yes, because the same forces that have led to so many changes in the contemporary world may finally make it possible to acknowledge the comic genius of women. What has made this possible is—here's the "F" word—feminism. One cannot account for the demographic and cultural changes mentioned above without recognizing the sea change brought about by thirty years of second-wave feminism. Feminism opened up the workplace and challenged the patriarchal family. It ridiculed the notion that women should be sweet, submissive, and decorous. Feminism changed society's consciousness about who women are and what they can do and wiped clear the lenses through which women have been viewed.

If feminism survives, women will be known as great comics. If feminism fails, the standing patriarchal order will again deny female humor, courage, brilliance, and creativity. With feminism, women are great comics. Without feminism, bitches ain't funny.

■ NAOMI WEISSTEIN

≋ "Illegitimacy"/Single Pregnancy

In the United States, the term "illegitimacy" historically has referred to children born to unmarried females; single pregnancy refers to unmarried, pregnant girls and women. The social, cultural, and political significance of these terms has varied in this country according to the race (and often the class) of the women and children involved.

In the seventeenth and eighteenth centuries, illegitimacy rates among white colonists varied over time and among colonies but generally remained low, reflecting the strength of community and religious control over sexual and marital norms. Despite civil and religious punishment of fornicators, evidence from New England colonies at least shows that females who became pregnant outside marriage, and their children, stayed within their families of origin, and the women eventually married.

In the early nineteenth century, illegitimacy rates remained low as emergent norms of Victorian womanhood were strictly enforced. In these same decades, laws in slave-holding states proscribed marriage for African Americans, and slave owners regularly mandated and coerced female slaves to procreate in order to increase owners' investments. Slave owners frequently accomplished this end by impregnating their female slaves by rape. According to civil and church law, then, all slave children were "illegitimate," yet they were recognized and valued within their own communities. After the Civil War, white rates of illegitimacy began to rise partly due to urbanization and industrialization, both of which often caused women to live outside of the family and community sphere. Among the white poor and working class the incidence of illegitimacy was similar to African American rates. In 1880, between 66 and 75 percent of Black children lived with both a mother and a father.

Despite this similarity and the fact that most Black women eventually married, African American unmarried motherhood became a symbol of Black degeneracy to white politicians and social commentators. Moreover, contrary to white myths, definitive data indicate that northern migration between 1880 and 1920 did not shatter the Black family; four out of five African American children in northern urban communities lived in households where the father was present.

In the early decades of the twentieth century, single pregnancy gradually became a public policy obsession. As the family, not the community, became the locus of social and sexual control, the newly atomized family was regularly accused of policing its daughters poorly. Also in these decades, public policy experts and "reformers" used Euro-American, Victorian definitions of "family" in support of their efforts to undermine Native American tribal integrity. Thus, the children of unmarried mothers, for example, were targeted for removal to schools off the reservations, where they could be "Americanized." In sum, single pregnancy became a proxy for anxiety about urbanization, immigration, and industrialization. Single pregnancy and illegitimacy were cast as environmental diseases.

Beginning in the late 1930s, Black and white single pregnancy were treated as two distinct phenomena. As the children of some African American women became eligible for Aid to Dependent Children grants, the white tax-paying public's attitude toward these expenditures became increasingly hostile. In succeeding decades, with the emergence of the civil rights movement, politicians and others in every region mounted campaigns of resistance against unmarried Black childbearing women and their children. The attacks cited "suitable home" laws, which established that unmarried women could not, by definition, provide such an environment for their children.

In those same years, white, unmarried pregnancy was redefined as proof of the mother's neurosis. The psychological explanation moved the "cause" from the mother's body to her mind and claimed that the neurosis could be cured. This innovative perspective allowed unmarried pregnant women to resume "normal" lives after the "cure," which mandated relinquishment of the child. By midcentury, it was more important for a white woman to appear sexually pure, whatever her real history, than to be so. The white illegitimate baby was redefined as well, cleared of the biologically based taint associated with the bastard child, and thus rendered a valuable commodity on the emergent adoption market.

The political perception of illegitimacy remained racialized for the remainder of the twentieth century, even though substantial data exist demonstrating that class is more closely associated than race in the case of out-of-wedlock births. The endurance of race-based political responses to single pregnancy shows that politicians and others in the United States have been using women's bodies and their reproductive capacity for the better part of the century to promote political agendas hostile to female autonomy and racial equality.

By the end of the century less than 3 percent of white unwed mothers were giving up their babies for adoption, a dramatic decrease from midcentury. The change revealed that white unwed mothers were determined to define for themselves who was a legitimate mother and what was a legitimate mother-child dyad. Unmarried pregnant women of color, who had usually kept their children, continued to be the target of politicians explicitly engaged since 1980 in developing policy to erode gains in the areas of civil rights, welfare, taxes, education, contraception, abortion, health care, job training, and housing.

Herbert Gutman, *The Black Family in Slavery and Freedom, 1750-1925* (New York: Vintage, 1976); Regina Kunzel, *Fallen Women, Problem Girls: Unmarried Mothers and the Professionalization of Social Work, 1890–1945* (New Haven: Yale University Press, 1993); Rickie Solinger, *Wake Up Little Susie: Single Pregnancy and Race Before Roe v. Wade* (New York: Routledge, 1992).

■ RICKIE SOLINGER

SEE ALSO Single Motherhood.

≋ Images of Women

Two images of women have been dominant throughout U.S. history. The first is one of innocence and spirituality, in line with the "Virgin Mary" or madonna figure of Christian belief. The second is one of sexuality and evil, in line with the "Eve" figure of Judeo-Christian belief or the Pandora of classical mythology. (In the Garden of Eden story, Eve took the apple from the serpent and persuaded Adam to eat it. In the Pandora tale, Pandora opened the jar that unleashed evil upon the world.) A third image is one of women as devoted wives and housekeepers, in keeping with the medieval "patient Griselda," who endured an abusive husband without complaint, or the more active "Betsy Ross" of the American Revolution, who demonstrated loyalty to home and country by sewing the nation's flag.

The virgin/whore dichotomy is an example of the tendency of Euro-American thought toward dualistic categorization (good/evil, beauty/ugliness, man/woman, black/white). The spirituality/sexuality dualism also reflects Western hierarchies of class, race, and gender, which have been connected with the venerable "double standard" of sexual behavior. (Under the "double standard," men are allowed a sexual freedom denied "proper" women.) This gender differentiation has often linked female purity to male honor as the primary guarantee of patrimony, while until the late nineteenth century, women were catalogued as the property of fathers and husbands. Thus the "fallen woman" historically was beyond respectability, women were held responsible for rapes perpetrated on them, and prostitution was considered necessary to service male sexual needs.

Nineteenth-century Victorianism reversed prevailing belief to designate women as asexual. Its corresponding image of heightened spirituality for mainstream women undergirded an ethic of inferiority, dependency, and femininity. These qualities were reflected in the period's cult of thinness for women and its confining dress, which included long skirts, tightly bound waists, and a bell-shaped body outline. But stigmatizing sexuality only provoked its return sub rosa. Thus prostitution flourished, while burlesque and music-hall actresses with large hips and bosoms became symbols of ideal beauty. The preference among immigrant and upwardly mobile groups for plumpness in women as an indication of prosperity combined with the campaign of doctors against extreme thinness and tight-lacing corsets to make weight fashionable among women by the mid–nineteenth century. For a time, fat was considered beautiful.

By 1920 women's increasing participation in education, the professions, and sports undermined Victorianism, creating both new freedoms and restrictions. Sexuality became more open and clothing more comfortable; the virgin/whore dichotomy blurred somewhat. Concurrently, advertising and the consumer culture replaced Victorianism as a primary means of control. The advertising industry found avenues for female objectification through images in magazines, the movies, and other media. It created public demand through arousing both sexual desires for products and personal insecurities about such matters as status and appearance. Thus thinness came back in vogue, and women took up wearing cosmetics, previously associated with prostitution.

Social class played a role in defining the image of beauty for women in the 1920s, especially with the vogue for tanned skin. For centuries darkened skin had been negatively associated with laborers and peasants working out of doors. In the eighteenth century fashionable European women painted their skin white, while in the nineteenth century they wore bonnets and carried parasols to avoid the sun. The pallor representative of those who worked in mines, factories, and office buildings undermined the association between darkened skin and low social rank. Widely publicized accounts of well-to-do people tanning themselves on beaches delivered the final blow. Yet some historians contend that the trend of tanning resulted from the popularity of Black entertainer Josephine Baker and the general fascination with Blacks engendered by the popularity of Harlem nightclubs and jazz joints during the 1920s.

Despite the tanning vogue, "black" and "white" designations of skin color were sharply dichotomized. This continues to be the case even though the sexual exploitation of Black women in the South produced a large mulatto population, as did that of Spaniards with Indians as a result of the conquest of Latin America. In Hawaii, where whites are a minority, distinctions based on skin color have been reduced. In Puerto Rico, with a large mixed population, categories of browns and Indians also exist.

In terms of image, the dominant culture has often sexualized the "other," seeing a perverse exoticism in persons of differing classes, nationalities, and races. In addition, the stringent work ethic of middle-class capitalism, with its implicit disapproval of pleasure, contributed to redefining those outside its confines as possessed by an appealing—or appalling—freedom in lifestyle. This sexual stereotyping has been applied to ethnic and racial minorities primarily as a means of denigration and control. Thus Black women were catalogued as Sapphires, as slavewomen consumed by lust, even after the Civil War brought emancipation. Asian women have been viewed in terms of "Tokyo Rose," the shadowy figure who broadcast undermining sexual innuendos to U.S. troops during the Second World War. For Latin American and Mexican women, the figure of the dancing "Carmen" flinging her body as the prostitute/bar girl with hot "Latin" blood was the degraded sexualized image. The image for Native American women was the "squaw," a woman so driven by her sexuality that she freely cohabited with white men.

The obverse of these sexualized images has not been one of spirituality: the virgin/whore dichotomy breaks down when applied to women of color. The absence of the claim to spirituality has caused problems for women attempting to assert respectability in a middle-class world where morality matters. Rather, the spiritual side of the divide has been replaced by an image of submission. For Black women, beside Sapphire stands the "mammy" of Southern slavery and the Aunt Jemima figure of the modern age. These rotund, simple, and motherly images have greater loyalty to the white families they serve than to their own race. Recent historians contend that the slave mammy was a fiction invented by the white South to justify slavery. Aunt Jemima was an advertiser's creation to sell a pancake mix. All historical studies of domestic servants, Southern or Northern, conclude that they were grossly exploited.

Among women of color, the image of Native American women has upon occasion involved spirituality, in an extension of the eighteenth-century "noble savage" typology. This image emerged when Northern Europeans first encountered the North American continent and visualized its Indian inhabitants as exemplars of the purity of the natural man, untouched by the corruptions of civilization. This image was perpetuated by the story of Pocahontas, the noble Native American woman who supposedly rescued John Smith from death in colonial Virginia. Correspondingly, Native American tribal groups hold to a more spiritualized concept of beauty in women, in line with their connection to the natural world.

Mexican and Latin American women, predominantly Catholic, had their own virgin/whore dichotomy in the Virgin of Guadalupe, the mother protector and symbol of female virtue, and La Malinche, the Aztec noblewoman who was given to Cortés as a slave and who became his lover. Although La Malinche has traditionally been denigrated as the mother-whore who created a mixed Spanish race, Latina and Mexican feminist revisionists are redefining her as a woman who survived through using her strength and cunning.

Throughout U.S. history, the idealized mainstream images of women have often been young, representing the stage of life associated with purity, innocence, and sexuality. In the twentieth century, the young woman has been a symbol used by advertisers to promote cosmetic products that have no intrinsic value aside from adornment and to create consumer identifications with brand names of otherwise indistinguishable products.

Correspondingly, aging women have been demonized as witches and menopausal hags, trivialized as grandmothers baking cookies and crocheting, and stylized as laughable figures clutching to lost youth. By the early twentieth century, however, such overriding images of aging women were contested because women were living longer and were healthier than men. Advances in life expectancy, in addition to women's movement into public and reform activity, contributed to what was widely viewed by the second decade of the twentieth century as a "renaissance" of aging women. Public individuals such as Jane Addams, Eleanor Roosevelt, and Margaret Mead, whose vigor and achievements in later life were praised and publicized, also helped to undermine the negative stereotype.

Still, the wisdom of aging women, prized in traditional cultures, has historically been dismissed as "old wives' tales." It is still not widely known that women and men in both Asian and Native American cultures will add years to their life span when asked their age, so prized is the wisdom and strength of age in these cultures.

Images of women also reflect homophobia. Until the late nineteenth century, no category of gender identification named "lesbian" existed, since before then, sex was considered impossible without a phallic component. Late-nineteenth-century sexologists refuted this view but defined lesbians as men in women's bodies. This contributed to the common stereotyping of lesbians as "dykes," creatures with no claim to femininity or spirituality. Still, lesbians themselves often took on the identity of a masculinized "butch" or a feminized "femme"—whether to mimic or to satirize dominant cultural attitudes. More recent generations of lesbians, living in a less repressive climate, have tended toward less stylized behaviors.

The radical movements of the 1960s, explicitly countercultural in dress and behavior, contested many stereotypes of women. In response, recycled images of women that drew from old categorizations resurfaced. The emaciated, childlike "Twiggy" was the 1960s supermodel, and her appearance created a fad of extreme thinness that has lasted to the present. It has brought in its wake an epidemic of anorexia nervosa and bulimia, as young women strive to be ever thinner. Moreover, as much as women may exercise to achieve strong bodies, in line with feminist ideals of appearance, they also reshape those bodies surgically to achieve large bosoms and thin waists. In the process they resort to such medical procedures as breast implants and liposuction (the removal of fatty deposits by a vacuum suction surgical method).

What has this meant for physically challenged women, a group historically shunned by mainstream culture as outside normal womanhood? Vigorous lobbying on their part has brought laws according them equal access to public space. Through athletic contests and some sympathetic television portrayals, they have gained public recognition. But these successes have not translated into public acceptance as personal and sexual equals.

Among Western binary categorizations of women, a primary one has been between beauty (associated with youth, innocence, and perfection) and ugliness (associated with what is different and "imperfect"). The recent trend toward reshaping bodies according to an image of "perfection" not only reinforces the "beauty/ugliness" duality but also poses a special threat to physically challenged women and to all women who choose to retain their natural appearance.

The old dichotomy between women as madonnas or whores may have broken down, only to be replaced by a new one directly based on physical appearance. This new dualism is furthered not only by advertisers but also by doctors seeking profits in the consumer-oriented culture of the United States in the late 1990s. Generational conflict has also surfaced, as young women define themselves as "postfeminist" and exert the right to define their own appearance, even if the media both manipulate and control it.

What do we make of a youth icon such as the singer-actress Madonna? On the one hand, by flaunting her sexuality in the context of lesbian and interracial images, she seems to defy centuries of sexist stereotyping and to validate trends affirming positive images of all women. On the other hand, defining freedom as primarily sexual hardly addresses issues of race, class, and economic oppression for women that are still endemic in the United States today.

■ LOIS W. BANNER

SEE ALSO Stereotypes.

≋ Immigration

Other than Native American Indians, Mexicans, and Hawaiians, whose land was incorporated into the United States as the result of U.S. military expansion or annexation, and Blacks who were brought forcibly to serve as slaves, the entire population of the United States consists of immigrants or their descendants. Since Jamestown in 1607, U.S. history has been one of relations between established peoples and newcomers. Attitudes toward immigrants have varied from enthusiastic welcoming to indifferent tolerance to strong opposition and exclusion, on the basis of race or national origin, class, and gender of both immigrants and the established peoples.

Europeans dominated the first one hundred years of immigration. Escaping from economic deprivation as well as religious and political persecution, white men and women came as colonizers and free workers. Africans were brought by slave traders and eventually were forced to care for their masters' land and children. Latinos and Asians first came to labor in the mines, fields, and railway construction projects and later to work in occupations that ranged from unskilled to professional and technical. The Chinese experienced an erratic pattern of growth and decline because of exclusionary and severely restrictive immigration policies. Others, including refugees such as the Vietnamese and Hmongs, are recent migrants, with no history of immigration to the United States. These groups have been sorted into a racial ethnic hierarchy that has only recently begun to show signs of crumbling.

The British government maintained an Anglocentric immigration policy for its colony. In the nineteenth century the newly independent United States generally favored immigrants from Europe, especially Western Europe. Before 1881 U.S. immigration policies were left up to individual states. The new federal government expressed faith that out of diversity would emerge a national unity and identity but assumed such diversity would be confined to "free white persons."

Although the 1882 Chinese Exclusion Act, which barred the entry of Chinese laborers, is commonly regarded as the first major shift in immigration policy from decentralization to centralization and from unrestrictive to restrictive, it was actually Chinese women who were the first target of federal discriminatory legislation. The Page Law of 1875 singled out potential Chinese women immigrants and discouraged their coming. Policies discriminating against Chinese women from the 1870s to the early 1940s postponed the emergence of a native-born Chinese American generation.

Even though Chinese, and later other Asians, were declared "ineligible for citizenship" and their laboring class was refused entry, the influx of Southern and Eastern Europeans regarded as "incapable of becoming Americans" by Anglo-Americans was the impetus for the Immigration Acts of 1917, 1921, and 1924. These policies rank ordered eligible immigrants, favoring national groups thought to be most assimilable. The 1917 literacy test was especially unfavorable to both working peasants and women, who were educationally disadvantaged.

It was not until 1965 that numerical quotas based on national origin were removed. Subse-quently, a preference and a point system were adopted that emphasized personal characteristics of potential immigrants, including, among others, family ties and specific occupational skills. The former resulted in a change of the sex ratio of immigrants in favor of women, while the latter gave employers an opportunity to bring relatively cheap immigrant women labor to fill specific labor-market needs.

U.S. participation in World War II and the cold war led to many special acts and provisions that brought refugees from many countries. However, not all refugees were welcome. Those displaced by communist revolutions fared best. The differential treatment of refugees from Haiti and Cuba is perhaps the most glaring example of discrimination. The War Brides Act of 1945 facilitated exclusively the immigration of women.

Males outnumbered females in legal immigration before 1930. Between 1930 and the 1980s, the number of females arriving each year exceeded that of males, in some years reaching 60 percent of the total. The proportion of female immigrants declined somewhat in the early 1980s but has since remained about half of all immigrants, except in 1990 and 1991, when the percentage dropped to 47 and then to a low of 34, respectively. By 1992 immigrants of both sexes were about equal in proportion. Women dominated most immigration from Europe, Southeast Asia, Australia, New Zealand, and nearly all countries in the Western Hemisphere. Although the specific reasons for this variation may differ, in general, the overall increase of female immigration since the 1930s has been attributed to four major factors.

First, U.S. males have been far more likely than females to marry abroad. With more people, mostly men, traveling and working in foreign countries, their wives gained the right to entry under family reunification provisions. In addition, the resurgence of "picture brides" and its commodified equivalent, "mail-order brides," has contributed to the increase of women immigrants.

Second, U.S. military involvement abroad clearly contributed to the increase in female im-

Immigrants in a naturalization class, 1924.

migrants. Countless young servicemen assigned to Europe and Asia married foreign brides. The War Brides Act of 1945 and the family reunification policy brought them to the United States.

Third, the adoption of family reunification as a principle in immigration policy also corrected the predominance of males in earlier immigration streams. Women now were able to join their husbands who had migrated years ago. This policy resulted in more female immigration for several reasons: the relative longevity of women compared with men; the fact that widows were more inclined than widowers to join their children and grandchildren; and the fact that female babies were more available and preferred as adoptees by U.S. parents.

Finally, the almost universal increase in women's education and relaxation of patriarchal control, combined with the changing human resource needs of the United States and increasing global inequality, made it possible and often desirable for women to immigrate independent of men. The influxes of foreign female nurses, medical technicians, and domestics are examples. Among the immigrants were also women, including lesbians, who sought individual freedom from family and community control.

The tremendous disparity in the sex ratio during the early years of immigrant settlement has led to its characterization as a "bachelor society," and among the few women who came regardless of national origin, many worked as prostitutes to serve immigrant men.

Although many immigrants came to the United States to escape economic, political, and religious oppression at home, women also came to escape from oppression unique to them, such as sexual harassment and other discriminatory treatment. Euro-American women, despite great hardships, had a smoother transition than did women of color. The latter suffered not only from U.S. discriminatory treatment but their governments of origin also participated in discrimination against them. For example, the Japanese government prohibited male Japanese immigrant laborers in the United States from sending for their wives before 1915 if they could not prove their ability to support a family.

The prolonged shortage of women among certain non-European immigrant groups as a result of discriminatory practices postponed family formation and the emergence of a native-born generation. So too did antimiscegenation laws in many states, which prohibited interracial marriages, as well as the policy depriving U.S.-born women of their citizenship when they married Asians who were "ineligible for citizenship."

Most immigrant women became wives and mothers. Burdened with housework, pregnancy, childbirth, and child-care responsibilities in an alien environment, they formed networks to share their work with other women and often were the first to establish interethnic social ties. They had a stabilizing effect on the family, played an important consolidating role, and provided an anchor for the group.

Married immigrant women often were required to produce income to make ends meet. Unequal access to education between immigrant men and women and gender discrimination in employment limited the channels of mobility for women immigrants in general, but the fact that few women of color were found in higher status and better-paid "feminine" occupations such as teaching underlined the effect of race. Educated immigrant women of color, unable to obtain suitable work outside, carved out a niche in their own ethnic communities, often as employees in white businesses. Two exceptions worth noting are the deliberate recruitment of immigrant women to fill specific temporary shortages (such as nursing in the 1970s), and the availability of jobs in regions where there is no visible concentration of a particular ethnic group.

Most immigrant women, however, have always been unskilled or semiskilled workers found in the more labor-intensive and backward sectors of industries or domestic services. Faced with language barriers, racism, nativism, class prejudice, and sexism, these immigrant women are similar to their male counterparts and are often trapped in low-wage, undesirable jobs.

Some research studies have focused on the pain and hardship suffered by immigrant women, but recent ethnic and feminist movements since the 1960s have produced new scholarship that emphasizes their resourcefulness, adaptability, and activism. Immigrant women's participation in social movements and labor strikes only recently has become known. The names of Emma Goldman, Mother Jones, and Amy Jacques Garvey, among others, are now familiar.

Pierrette Hondagneu-Sotelo, *Gendered Transitions: Mexican Experiences of Immigration* (Berkeley: University of California Press, 1994); Karen Hossfeld, *Small, Foreign, and Female: Immigrant Women Workers in Silicon Valley* (Berkeley: University of California Press, 1992); Maxine Schwartz Seller, ed., *Immigrant Women* 2d ed. (Philadelphia: Temple University Press, 1995).

▪ LUCIE CHENG

SEE ALSO Chinese Exclusion Act; Citizenship and Nationality; Indentured Servitude; Latina/Chicana Migration; National Origins Act; Nativism.

≋ Incest

SEE Violence Against Women.

≋ Indentured Servitude

Indentured servitude was a form of bound labor common in British North America. Although all of the British colonies, including those in the Caribbean, employed indentured servants at one time or another, these laborers were particularly numerous in the Chesapeake colonies of Virginia and Maryland during the seventeenth century and the middle colonies of Pennsylvania, New Jersey, and New York during the eighteenth. In exchange for paid passage to the colonies, a servant would bind him or herself to an indenture, or labor contract, of four to seven years. Some laborers negotiated directly with potential masters or their agents, but many seeking transport to the colonies negotiated with a ship's captain who would, upon arrival, sell the contracts. Servants were recruited from England, Scotland, Ireland, and Germany.

Male servants outnumbered females by approximately three to one. Most men worked as agricultural laborers and women as household servants. Freed servants hoped for quick upward mobility. Men became wage laborers, tenants,

Convicted of perjury, Elizabeth Canning receives her sentence of indentured servitude. She embarked for Philadelphia on the Myrtilda *on August 7, 1754.*

and sometimes landowners. Women looked toward marriage, and until the eighteenth century, the poorest of female servants could marry well.

Although British laborers had known servitude in England, the colonial system was particularly exploitive. Many servants experienced excessive brutality and found little protection under the law. Female servants were particularly vulnerable to sexual exploitation, and a female servant who became pregnant was required to compensate her master for work time lost. Labor contracts were no longer personal agreements but commodities that could be bought, sold, and traded without the consent of servants. Some historians see this commodification of labor as an early step toward the institution of chattel slavery.

- MARILYN J. WESTERKAMP

SEE ALSO Colonial Period.

≋ Indian Women

SEE Native American Women.

≋ Industrial Homework

Industrial homework, or waged labor performed at home, emerged at the time of industrialization in the late eighteenth century and came to characterize the garment industry and other undercapitalized, seasonal trades well into the twentieth century. Under the homework system, manufacturers and contractors paid by the number of pieces finished and saved on overhead and materials by requiring the maker to supply her own tools and workroom. Without permanent workers, employers gained greater flexibility. They depended upon the sexual division of labor within the household and between the household and the larger community to obtain cheap labor. Homeworkers were married women with small children, whose husbands earned inadequate wages and whose cultural traditions or family responsibilities kept them homebound. Such mothers contributed a fourth of the family income, while squeezing household labor and child care into days—and nights—dominated by piecework. The elderly, disabled, children, and older daughters in rural regions, without other employment, also became homeworkers.

Industrial homework grew among the people living in urban tenements during the massive emigration from eastern and southern Europe in the late nineteenth century. The location of the labor, its intermittent quality, and often illegal status hampered adequate remuneration. In 1910 at least 250,000 New York City homeworkers were licensed to manufacture one hundred items. Seventy percent of home finishers in major cities earned $3.49 or less a week, whereas over 75 percent of comparable shop workers earned more. Piece rates remained arbitrary, with contractors assigning the same kind of work at varying rates. In 1925 homework apparently increased in the Northeast, spreading to small towns and suburbs. It also existed in Appalachia, Puerto Rico, and southern mill towns. Fashion and mechanization changed which items were produced; slack times eliminated homework because growth depended on the overall health of the garment trades. But the economic collapse of 1929 intensified the exploitation of homeworkers. The median hourly wage of Chicago homeworkers in 1934 was nine cents; nearly a quarter of workers were forced to resort to relief. The existence of homeworkers also undermined labor standards and hampered unionization.

Since the 1890s states had regulated the sanitary conditions of tenement homework, but courts blocked outright bans as interference with the right to contract. Women reformers attacked homework for mocking motherhood and destroying children's lives, offering the family wage, mothers' pensions, and minimum wages for women as alternatives. While the federal government prohibited homework on army uniforms during World War I, not until the New Deal did it institute broader restrictions, initially through the National Recovery Administration and then through the Fair Labor Standards Act (FLSA) of 1937. During World War II the wage and hour administrator ended homework in seven garment industries in order to sustain FLSA. In the 1980s the Reagan administration lifted most of these bans. Though New York City had over fifty thousand underground garment workers in 1982, the woman at the keyboard replaced the tenement mother as the new icon of homework. While some found homework a solution to the work and family dilemma of

the time, others thought homework encouraged a return to the era of the sweatshop.

• EILEEN BORIS

SEE ALSO Industrial Revolution; Needle Trades.

≋ Industrial Revolution

The Industrial Revolution transformed women's lives. A worldwide economic and social revolution, industrialization in the United States began in New England in the 1790s and integrated women into an emergent industrial capitalist society.

Industrialization in the antebellum era occurred as the result of two distinct processes. The first, the rise of the factory system, had its greatest impact on northern textile manufacture. The second, the development of the more labor-intensive sweating system, which kept production decentralized in households and small shops, was vital to the growth of the garment, hat, box, glove, and flower industries.

In preindustrial America, women and girls performed much of the labor necessary for family survival, including the household manufacture of yarn, cloth, candles, and food. By 1790 the availability of water-powered machinery such as spinning frames and carding machines enabled businessmen to substitute power tools for women's hand labor in the manufacture of cloth. In December 1790 the first water-powered spinning mill opened its doors in Pawtucket, Rhode Island; by 1813, 175 other cotton and wool spinning mills, employing entire families, punctuated the river-rich New England landscape.

Ironically, early mills increased the market value of women's household labor. Mechanizing only some of the most labor-intensive steps of textile production, spinning mills paid women at home to weave factory-manufactured yarn into marketable cloth. (The arrangement whereby labor was contracted out to women by local merchants, manufacturers, or middlemen was, and continues to be, known as "outwork" or the "putting out system.") As late as 1820, two-thirds of all cloth manufactured in the United States was produced by women working at home.

The importance of outwork to textile manufacture declined after the first fully integrated textile factory began operations in Waltham, Massachusetts, in 1814. The success of the Waltham model, which centralized under one roof all of the steps necessary for producing cloth, facilitated the rise of both an urban working class and a network of single-industry textile towns. The most famous of these was Lowell, Massachusetts, by 1860 the leading textile center in the nation. In the 1830s and 1840s Lowell attracted international attention as an industrial utopia that had dodged the hazards of English industrialization, particularly the creation of a permanent, "debased" working class. Until the immigration wave of the 1840s, Lowell's factory workers were single, white, native-born women recruited from middle-class New England farms. Symbolically virtuous because of their youth, class background, and race, Lowell workers ostensibly remained pure because of the mills' stringent behavioral rules and the expectation that women workers would leave after a brief period of employment. The reality was less glamorous than propagandists claimed. Lowell's female factory hands worked over seventy hours a week at substandard wages. In 1834 and 1836 they went on strike, challenging the depiction of female fulfillment and passivity in this "model" factory town.

Women's experiences as factory workers varied according to ethnicity, race, and class, and differed from those of men. An occupational hierarchy among women prevailed in which Yankee women enjoyed greatest access to the best-paying women's jobs; daughters of immigrants concentrated in semiskilled positions; and immigrant women worked in the least skilled, most poorly remunerated occupations. As a rule, free African American women were excluded from factory employment. The cleavages that distinguished women's work from men's were equal in impor-

tance to those existing among wome[...] der-based occupational segregation[...] even the highest-paid, most senior f[...] worker could expect to receive les[...] employed in the same establishment. Although by the 1840s women represented 50 percent of factory workers in the shoe and textile industries, they rarely worked alongside men. Instead, they held jobs reserved exclusively for women, jobs whose low wages affirmed the belief that women's work was less skilled than men's and less important to family survival.

Most women holding factory jobs in the first decades of industrialization were single. Immigrant and working-class wives and mothers were more likely to participate in the wage-based labor market as outworkers. In New York City, the foremost manufacturing center of the antebellum period, outwork was the dominant form of female employment. It was also one of the most exploitive. Outwork enabled women confined to their homes to contribute to the family economy while still performing tasks as wives and mothers. But merchants took advantage of women's limited mobility and bargaining power by withholding and cutting wages. Already doubly burdened by society's expectations of them as wives and wage earners, female outworkers coped with their precarious financial status by accepting more contracted jobs to make ends meet. Converting households into workshops, outwork meshed gender roles with the most exploitive features of industrial capitalism.

Although upper- and middle-class white women were typically spared the long hours and low wages that characterized both factory labor and outwork, they were nevertheless forced to contend with the ideological devaluation of homework that industrialization spawned. As "real" labor became more closely identified with work that had a concrete market value, women lost out. Childbearing, child rearing, cooking, cleaning, and other traditionally female tasks, whether performed by elite women, working-class women, or a growing number of domestic servants, were demeaned. The household, increasingly perceived in opposition to a male-dominated market as a feminized space, came to be viewed as a site of leisure and consumption rather than labor and production.

Thomas Dublin, *Transforming Women's Work: New England Lives in the Industrial Revolution* (Ithaca, N.Y.: Cornell University Press, 1994); Bruce Laurie, *Artisans into Workers: Labor in Nineteenth-Century America* (New York: Noonday Press, 1989); Christine Stansell, "The Origins of the Sweatshop: Women and Early Industrialization in New York City," *Working-Class America: Essays on Labor, Community, and American Society*, edited by Michael H. Frisch and Daniel J. Walkowitz (Urbana: University of Illinois Press, 1983).

• ANDREA TONE

SEE ALSO Industrial Homework; Labor Movement; Needle Trades; Sweatshops.

≣ Industrial Workers of the World

SEE Labor Unions.

≣ Infertility

"Give me children or I die," the words of Rachel in the Old Testament, remind us that infertility has been a source of anguish for women through the ages. Until the technological advances of the late 1970s and early 1980s, medical treatment was practically nonexistent and adoption provided the only possibility of parenthood. For most of the twentieth century in the United States, the prevailing assumption was that female intrapsychic conflict caused infertility, and thus women routinely were referred to psychiatrists. The development of the laparoscope made possible the identification of biological problems, such as endometriosis, a problem located in the reproductive tract rather than in the psyche. Ensuing diagnostic advances have allowed us to identify a still growing number of obstacles to fertility. In addition to proving that infertility is rarely, if ever, a byproduct of neurosis, science has shown that men are just as likely as women to have a physical problem that makes them unable to produce offspring.

Though the assisted reproductive technologies now offer realistic hope to the infertile, success rates are only 15 to 20 percent for the most common high-tech treatment, in vitro fertilization, which costs as much as ten thousand dollars per attempt. Such state-of-the-art medical treatments, while within reach of wealthier Americans, are usually unattainable for the rest.

The threat to biological parenthood strikes at the core of a woman's inner assumptive life. Fantasies of motherhood and the pregnancy experience are common for girls, who assume that they will be able to choose whether to have children in adulthood. Later, vital decisions about careers and partners are often linked with the wish for and expectation of motherhood. Fulfilling her reproductive potential—and the roles of mother and provider of grandchildren—is integral to most heterosexual women's lives.

Nature and nurture conspire to make femininity and reproductive capacity virtually inextricable. The diagnosis of infertility can precipitate a major crisis. A woman's sense of self is rocked at its foundation, and every aspect of her life can be affected. Her relationships with family and friends become stressed by a variety of factors including feelings of being damaged goods due to her inability to procreate and feelings of guilt about not being able to provide a child for her husband or grandchildren for her parents. If she pursues treatment, her body can feel like a battleground on which the war for a baby is fought, even if it is her partner who has the medical problem. She may have exploratory surgery, routine biopsies, daily injections, extreme hormonal fluctuations, and worries about the largely unknown long-term effects of infertility drugs, some of which have been linked to ovarian cancer. The harsh realities of the biological clock push women to take serious and often inadvisable risks in order to achieve pregnancy before time and money run out. Women also must take into account available insurance coverage as well as anticipated treatment imperatives when making career choices and employment decisions. It comes as no surprise that infertile women can become isolated and withdrawn and are at increased risk for emotional depression.

When infertility is protracted, young women are catapulted into dealing with developmental tasks of midlife before they have had the opportunity to master the tasks of their own life stage. The threat to genetic continuity ends the illusion of a timeless future far earlier than it does for fertile women and sets into motion heightened concerns about mortality, legacies, and meaning. Like many "empty-nest" middle-aged women, the infertile young adult may feel socially invisible. Like her midlife counterpart, she may be preoccupied with the variety of feelings and social stigma related to reproductive loss.

Cultural factors make the infertility experience far worse for some women than for others. In a number of contemporary cultures, a man may leave his wife if she cannot bear children. People around the world—from Czech and Polish peasants to Oceanic Islanders—still believe women are responsible for infertility. This persistent notion has a primitive logic: indeed it *is* always the woman who fails to get pregnant. Americans, many of whose standard of living allows them access to cutting-edge science and technology, often view infertility as a woman's fault also.

Even as the infertile face immense social pressure to reproduce, they are often confronted with equally strong pressure to forego using assisted reproductive technologies (ARTs), which provide their best and often only hope of biological parenthood. Religion is one common source of conflict. For example, Catholic and Orthodox Jewish women face doctrinal opposition to the ARTs even as they cope with the mandate to "be fruitful

and multiply." Some feminists object to what they see as the shifting of control over conception and birth from the bodies of women to the hands of doctors, scientists, and the state. For many, the ARTs are a sign of a fearsome "brave new world" in which people are dehumanized; for others, they symbolize struggles over sexuality, reproduction, gender, and family that lie at the center of contemporary society. For the infertile, the ARTs are simply the best chance of having children.

The late twentieth century has yielded reproductive options—and ethical and moral questions—that were, not long ago, almost beyond imagination. Social questions about economic barriers to equality of access sit alongside others such as whether sixty-year-old women should be enabled to produce babies using the new technologies. At least temporarily, the lightning speed of science has outstripped our ability to keep up with the many emotional, social, and financial dilemmas that infertility poses.

Susan L. Cooper and Ellen S. Glazer, *Beyond Infertility: The New Paths to Parenthood* (New York: Lexington Books, 1994); Arthur L. Griel, *Not Yet Pregnant: Infertile Couples in Contemporary America* (New Brunswick, N.J.: Rutgers University Press, 1991); Barbara Eck Menning, *Infertility: A Guide for the Childless Couple*, 2d ed. (New York: Prentice-Hall, 1988).

■ ALMA R. BERSON

SEE ALSO Reproductive Technology.

≋ International Women's Day

Clara Zetkin, longtime German socialist leader and advocate for working women, first proposed a holiday honoring working women in 1907. Because of her efforts, socialists throughout Europe began holding symbolic, day-long general strikes for women's economic equality in 1911, calling the celebration International Woman's Day (IWD). In the United States socialist women declared February 23, 1909, as the first National Woman's Day. At lectures and demonstrations they focused on winning women's suffrage as well as improving working conditions for women and children.

Under Zetkin's direction the holiday became linked with issues of peace. On International Woman's Day in 1915 she led women from opposing sides of World War I to demonstrate in Bern, Switzerland, for world peace. The war had already claimed over one million lives in Russia alone; Russian women decided to organize a general strike calling for "Bread and Peace" on the date of IWD, thus launching the February Revolution in 1917. When Lenin organized the Third International in 1922, Zetkin persuaded him to establish March 8, the day the Russian women struck, as an official holiday.

By the 1930s the celebration had died out in the United States, though it provided an occasion for women to oppose fascism and authoritarianism in Europe, China, and Latin America. After 1955 women around the world demonstrated on International Woman's Day against open-air nuclear testing. Since 1967 feminists in the United States have revived the celebration as International Women's Day, demonstrating for peace and justice as well as fighting to achieve improved health care, education, and human rights for women.

• TEMMA KAPLAN

SEE ALSO Feminism, International.

≋ Interracial Cooperation Movement

The Commission on Interracial Cooperation (CIC) was founded in Atlanta, Georgia, in 1918, to study and develop programs to address the "Negro problem." During the summer of 1920, male staff organized eight hundred state and local interracial committees throughout the south. With a membership of largely reform-minded professional white men—white women joined as central committee members in 1920—CIC spent its first decade informing the public of Black achievements, opposing the Ku Klux Klan, and denouncing lynching.

In 1920 the female leadership of CIC and the National Association of Colored Women met to discuss Black women's issues and concerns, including lynching, suffrage, child welfare, education, and protection of Black girls. At subsequent meetings and in publications, the women focused on lynching.

CIC established the Southern Commission on the Study of Lynching in 1930. Jessie Daniel Ames, director of the CIC Woman's Department, established the Association of Southern Women for the Prevention of Lynching (ASWPL) in 1932. By 1939 forty thousand women and men were reported as members. Because Ames did not encourage passage of the 1940 federal antilynching bill, ASWPL lost support from both African Americans and CIC leadership.

Disenchanted with selected programs and what some labeled as the paternalistic approach of CIC toward African Americans, in 1944 leading citizens established a new interracial activist organization, the Southern Regional Council (SRC). CIC merged with SRC, losing its identity as the South's premier interracial organization. Nevertheless, CIC is credited with formulating public policy and programs that enabled whites and African Americans to effect positive change collectively in the south.

• CYNTHIA NEVERDON-MORTON

SEE ALSO Lynching.

≋ Iroquois Confederacy

The seed for the Iroquois Confederacy was planted long before European contact when five nations of Iroquoian-speaking people formed an alliance to prevent feuding among the Cayuga,

Mohawk, Oneida, Onondaga, and Seneca. The Five Nations were joined by the Tuscarora in the 1700s. The Mohawks, Senecas, and Onondagas are referred to as the elder brothers of the Confederacy.

The Iroquois, or People of the Long House, are noted for many accomplishments, in particular their democratic system of government and egalitarian treatment of women, children, and elders. One early historian referred to the Iroquois as the "Romans of the Western World." This is an interesting analogy in view of the fact that Iroquois democracy was more advanced than that of the Romans. The laws of the Iroquois Confederacy spoke to issues of sharing of resources among the people; the rights of all people; unity; and the importance of alliances between nations. The Iroquois system of governance deeply influenced the founders of the U.S. Constitution, but unfortunately not when it came to women's rights.

In the matrilineal system of Iroquois government, the clan mother played an important role in the political and social life of each of the Six Nations. Clan mothers selected the representatives to speak at tribal meetings.

The Iroquois women nominated the Chiefs and removed them if they failed to perform their duties. They also controlled food production and the land, and decided the fate of captives. Women participated in discussions at tribal meetings and were consulted in all matters of importance to the community and the Confederacy.

Iroquois women enjoyed a relatively higher status than their newly arrived European sisters. One criminal law of the Iroquois Confederacy is indicative of the value of women. When a murder was committed, the family of the murderer was required to give twenty strings of shells to the victim's family. But if the victim was a woman, the family of the murderer was required to give thirty strings of shells to the victim's family.

As we approach the twenty-first century, the Iroquois Confederacy continues its historical alliance. Women play a significant role in all aspects of Iroquois life, such as teaching humane values to the young and speaking out on Iroquois sovereignty in global political forums.

Oren Lyons, et al., *Exiled in the Land of the Free* (Santa Fe, N.M.: Clear Light Publishers, 1994); Lillian Ackerman and Laura Klein, *Women and Power in Native North America* (Norman: University of Oklahoma Press, 1995).

■ WILMA MANKILLER

SEE ALSO Native American Women, Northeast.

≋ Islam

Although Islam began in 610 A.D. in Mecca, Muslims and Arabs are not one and the same. It is estimated that only 18 percent of Muslims are Arabic-speaking people living in the Arab world. The other 82 percent live in areas ranging from the southern Philippines to Nigeria; the world's largest Muslim community is in Indonesia. In the United States, scholars agree that by the year 2015, Islam will be the second-largest religion in the country after Christianity. The growing presence of Islam in the United States requires that any serious look at the history of U.S. religion must include an understanding of Islam and Muslims, not as a group foreign to the U.S. culture but as part and parcel of its diversity.

The Arabic word "Islam" means submission—in a religious context, it means the submission to the will of God. Islam's prophet is Muhammed, who received his first revelation from God through the angel Gabriel in about 610 C.E. Muslim beliefs include the oneness of God; the angels created by Him; the prophets through whom His revelations were brought to humankind; the Day of Judgment and individual accountability; God's complete authority over human destiny in life and in death; the directives of the Quran; and the devotional services of prayer, fasting, alms giving, and making a pilgrimage to Mecca.

Islam in the United States is divided mainly between Muslim immigrants, who make up two-thirds of the Muslim population, and African

American Muslims. Muslim women are part of the Islamic creed and have religious duties and responsibilities. The Quran addresses them sometimes specifically as women believers, *mo'minat*, and other times includes them with gender-neutral terms such as *insan*, human, and *nas*, people.

Islam as a religion views both men and women as equal creatures of God. The Quran states "O humankind! We created you from a single soul, male and female." (49:13) The idea of the same soul is repeated elsewhere in the Quran. Islam preaches not a sameness between women and men, but rather that they are equal but different. This "difference" has been subject to debate and interpretation. Some traditional patriarchal practices have been justified on the basis of an Islamic directive that women and men are different: men are allotted economic responsibilities and women are expected to play a primary role in childbearing and rearing. Thus women have been relegated to secondary positions. Quranic verses that proclaim women's rights to buy and sell, contract and earn, inherit, seek education, and manage their own property are often silenced or reinterpreted. Numerous Quranic verses justify asymmetrical sex roles and include directives on polygamy, divorce, veiling, birth control, and abortion. For example, Islam permits men to marry two, three, or four women, "but if you fear that ye shall not deal justly [with them] then only one" (4:3). The issue of polygamy is resolved later in the Quran by stating that men will not be able to be just with co-wives, even if they tried (4:119). Only the first part of the verse is repeated, however, to establish Islam as a religion that permits polygamy.

A debate about the dress of Muslim women also exists. The Quran mentions the notion of "covering" in three instances (2:53; 24:31; 33:59). Covering refers either to the prophet's wives or the calling for Muslim converts to use their dress (a scarf) to mark such conversion. Covering the head and wearing the black garb (known as the *Shador*) is the law in some Islamic countries and is now more common in places such as Egypt and Jordan.

Regarding abortion, which became an explosive issue at the 1994 U.N. Population Conference held in Cairo, Islam clearly informs the practice of first- and second-trimester abortions. The Quran dictates that life—or the soul—does not begin until the 120th day of gestation. As a result, abortion to ensure the well-being of the mother, or to enable her to care for elderly parents or other children, is permitted.

U.S. Muslim women, like all U.S. women, struggle to achieve in patriarchal institutions such as academia, law offices, research institutions, and so on. In addition, U.S. Muslim women face two other dilemmas. The first is a mainstream society that is hostile to Islam and Muslims. Islam is generally portrayed in the media as a bloodthirsty, sexually obsessed culture in which women are no more than cheap objects of trade. Such portrayals create defensive and antagonistic reactions from Muslim women who abide by stringent Quranic interpretations in response to society's hostility.

The second dilemma, faced by two-thirds of the Muslim women in the United States, is the need to preserve one's heritage as an immigrant community. Immigrant populations often isolate themselves from the larger society to preserve their identity. Such isolation leads to perpetuating practices and traditions that mother cultures have long abandoned. Thus Muslim American women in some communities still practice local traditions simply as a result of their isolation.

Said Ashmawi, "Al-Hijab lays farida Islamia" (Arabic text) (Trans: Al-Hijab is not an Islamic duty.) *Rose El Youssef* June 1994: 22–25; Yvonne Y. Haddad, "A Century of Islam in America," *The Muslim World Today*, Occasional paper no. 4 (1986), Washington, D.C.: Islamic Affairs Programs, The Middle East Institute; Jack G. Shaheen, *The T.V. Arab* (Bowling Green, Ohio: Bowling Green State University Popular Press, 1984).

■ NAWAL H. AMMAR

SEE ALSO Religion.

≋ Jacksonian Period

The Jacksonian period (1820–40) saw important changes in the status and perceptions of women. The prevailing rhetoric—celebrating democracy, mobility, and the attainability of economic independence for the "common" man—encouraged a restructuring and redefinition of political citizenship. By the 1830s, suffrage reforms first achieved universal white male suffrage by systematically disfranchising free Blacks and extending a formal political voice to unpropertied white men by abolishing property requirements for voting and holding office. The resulting increase in the size of the electorate, the rise of the two-party system, and the political culture that followed gave white men in the Jacksonian era a common identity as political actors and citizens. "Manly democracy" incorporated the belief that politics was best left to the economically self-reliant and independent, traits that women and Blacks purportedly lacked.

The exclusion of women from electoral politics helped cement an ideological demarcation between a public, political "male" world and a private, domestic "female" realm. In practice, a separate female sphere disconnected from public and political life was more of an illusion than a reality: female slaves and Northern factory hands did not have the luxury of domestic confinement; immigrant outworkers participated in the market economy from within their homes; and middle-class women reformers, although shunned at the ballot box, found other avenues for articulating their views. Women's political engagement during the Jacksonian period can be seen in the example of the Seneca Falls Convention in 1848, the first women's rights conference in the United States, which met to demand measures that would secure equal economic, social, and political equality for women, including female suffrage.

Although the latter demand would not bear fruit until 1920, the Jacksonian period included significant strides in the improvement of European American women's property rights. Strictures of common law had long discriminated against married women, requiring women to transfer ownership of real and private property to their husbands upon marriage, among other restrictions. By 1860 fourteen states had passed some type of Married Women's Property Act, which gave married women a measure of economic independence. Significantly, legislative reforms did not always reflect a newfound respect for married women or women's rights. A chief impetus for change was the desire to protect *men's* estates from determined creditors and ambitious sons-in-law. Indeed, the Mississippi Act, the first in the nation, protected a married woman's property from seizure for the purpose of repaying her husband's debt but did not give her the power to manage or sell her property independently. Nevertheless, the property acts, like the burgeoning women's rights movement, established an important foundation for future initiatives.

■ ANDREA TONE

SEE ALSO Republicanism; Seneca Falls.

≋ Japanese American Citizens League

The largest and most influential Japanese American civil rights organization, the Japanese American Citizens League (JACL) had twenty-four thousand members and one hundred fourteen chapters in 1994. Founded in 1930 by second-generation professionals to promote Americanization, JACL cooperated with World War II internment policies. After the war JACL leaders successfully campaigned against alien land laws, immigration restrictions, the denial of naturalization rights for immigrants, and antimiscegenation laws. The JACL led lobbying efforts for the 1988 Civil Liberties Act, which provided surviving internees with a public apology and a redress payment of $ 20,000.

Since the 1970s women activists have urged the organization to combat gender as well as race discrimination. In the 1980s women activists criticized sexism within the JACL, denounced Asian mail-order-bride catalogues, and condemned JACL's endorsement of beauty pageants. In 1992 the JACL elected Lillian Kimura as its first female national president and passed resolutions condemning sexual harassment, supporting family leave legislation, and affirming women's abortion rights. In 1993 and 1994 the organization supported gay and lesbian individuals' right to military service and opposed antigay initiatives in Colorado, Oregon, and Washington. Despite opposition from members who declared homosexuality immoral, the 1994 national council voted fifty to thirty-eight to endorse same-sex marriages. The vote was influenced by Congressman Norman Mineta's tribute to Barney Frank, a gay congressman who fought for redress for internees, and an account by Lia Shigemura, a former JACL program director, of the discrimination she faced as a lesbian. The JACL thus became the first nongay national civil rights organization to officially support same-sex marriage as a constitutional right.

■ ALICE YANG MURRAY

SEE ALSO Japanese American Internment.

≋ Japanese American Internment

During World War II, 120,000 Japanese Americans—two-thirds of them U.S. citizens by birth—were uprooted from communities in the U.S. West and interned in concentration camps. In the 1970s and 1980s, Japanese Americans mounted a political movement seeking a governmental apology and reparations. The Congressional Commission on the Wartime Relocation and Internment of Civilians concluded in 1981 that the incarceration was "not justified by military necessity" and had instead resulted from "race prejudice, war hysteria, and a failure of political leadership." The passage of the Civil Rights Act of 1988 authorized the issuing of a formal apology and monetary compensation to the survivors of the camps.

The bombing of Pearl Harbor on December 7, 1941, unleashed war between the United States and Japan and triggered a wave of hostility against Japanese Americans. On December 8, the financial assets of the *Issei* (immigrant Japanese) were frozen and the Federal Bureau of Investigation began to seize community leaders suspected of pro-Japanese sentiments. The press, politicians, and some military heads called for restrictions on the Japanese Americans. On February 19, 1942, President Franklin Delano Roosevelt signed Executive Order 9066, arbitrarily suspending the civil rights of American citizens by authorizing the removal of the Japanese and their American-born *(Nisei)* children from the western half of the Pacific coastal states and the southern third of Arizona.

The euphemistically termed "evacuation" was a time of chaos and trauma for Japanese Americans. Families had scant time to dispose of homes, businesses, pets, and belongings before they were taken to one of sixteen makeshift detention camps, called "assembly centers." They were told to furnish bedding, clothes, eating utensils, and toilet articles, but were allowed to bring with them only what they could carry.

The internees endured primitive living conditions at the assembly centers, hastily established at fairgrounds, racetracks, and Civilian Conservation Corps camps. They lived in tar-papered barracks; some families moved into stalls that had

Japanese Americans arrive at the Santa Anita Assembly Center in Arcadia, California, on April 5, 1942, before being sent to internment camps inland.

been recently vacated by horses. Life in the assembly centers, run first by the army and then by a civilian agency, the War Relocation Authority (WRA), required adjustment to mess-hall dining, long lines for the latrines and laundry facilities, and no privacy.

By November 10, 1942, the Japanese Americans were interned at ten permanent concentration camps, called "relocation centers," in desolate areas and usually ringed by barbed wire and sentry towers manned by armed guards. The camps included Manzanar and Tule Lake in California; Minidoka in Idaho; Topaz in Utah; Poston and Gila River in Arizona; Heart Mountain in Wyoming; Granada (Amache) in Colorado; and Rohwer and Jerome in Arkansas. As in the assembly centers, life was communal. Families resided in crudely constructed barracks; because of the cramped quarters and the disruption of previous routines, family members spent more and more time in the company of their peers, according to gender and age. The WRA ran each camp through a series of departments headed by European American administrators and staffed by the Japanese Americans. Most adults worked, earning meager wages.

In spite of the trauma of their uprooting and losses, as well as the unpredictable duration of their stay, these Japanese Americans tried to make life bearable, organizing religious services, adult education classes, recreational activities, and cultural events. And, as soon as possible, they sought to leave the stifling, artificial world of the camps. Despite the WRA's unwieldy and problematic leave-clearance process, by the end of 1942, women and men departed for work and higher education in the Midwest and East, and for military service. As American men went off to war, Black, white, and Mexican American women moved from domestic work into more lucrative jobs in industry; consequently, many of the positions initially available to *Nisei* women were in domestic service. As the Japanese Americans settled in unfamiliar regions of the country, many relied on networks of friends and kin for support. And, though far from home, most continued to contribute to the family economy.

In 1945, with the end of their exclusion from the West Coast, the majority of the *Issei* and *Nisei* began to return. Like the initial uprooting, the rebuilding of community was an arduous process marked by fear and uncertainty, requiring sacrifice and strength.

Commission on Wartime Relocation and Internment of Civilians, *Personal Justice Denied: Report of the Commission on Wartime Relocation and Internment of Civilians* (Washington, D.C.: Government Printing Office, 1982); Roger Daniels, *Concentration Camps: North America, Japanese in the United States and Canada During World War II* (Malabar, Fla.: Robert E. Krieger Publishing Company, Inc., 1981); Michi Weglyn, *Years of Infamy: The Untold Story of America's Concentration Camps* (New York: Morrow Quill Paperbacks, 1976).

• VALERIE MATSUMOTO

SEE ALSO Japanese American Citizens League; World War II Period.

≋ Japanese American Women

The first Japanese women to immigrate to the United States in the late nineteenth century called themselves *Issei*, the "first generation," for they envisioned themselves as the first generation of many Japanese Americans in the United States. They called their U.S.-born citizen children *Nisei*, the second generation. Subsequent generations are called *Sansei*, *Yonsei*, and *Gosei*, respectively.

The immigration of Japanese women to Hawaii and the mainland United States started in 1885 with the beginning of government contract labor importation from Japan to the kingdom of Hawaii, later annexed by the United States in 1898. These women were married and accompanied or joined their husbands who worked on the Hawaiian sugar plantations. Within five years of their arrival, *Issei* women comprised the majority of wage-earning women in Hawaii, where most worked as field hands in the sugar industry. Although the sugar industry remained the most important employer for Japanese women until 1920, *Issei* women gradually moved into other occupations. They played a major role in such fields as domestic and personal service, clothing trades, and the new pineapple industry. Many developed income-producing jobs in their homes, using their skills of cooking, washing, and sewing.

Issei women who first labored in Hawaii often lived in rural, isolated areas with few Japanese, helping their husbands till the soil. In urban areas, they worked in small businesses operated by their husbands, such as boardinghouses, stores, restaurants, and laundries, or became domestic servants, seamstresses, or cannery workers. Many of the women cooked for the workers employed by their labor contractor husbands, who worked for railroads, lumber mills and camps, and in agriculture.

The entry of *Issei* women into Japanese immigrant society was an integral part of the process

The Kubota family,
Mountain View,
California, in 1940
or 1941.

by which Japanese immigrant society sank its roots into U.S. soil. The arrival of women guaranteed that community and family life could be established. With the birth of the second generation, *Issei* began to identify their children's future in the United States. The Japanese American community developed a family orientation focused on schools, churches, clubs, and associations. But with the start of families, child care was also a critical issue for Issei working mothers, whose labor was vital to supplement their husbands' incomes.

Exclusion was a central force in the early history of Japanese American women. In 1907–08, under pressure by the United States and hoping to halt anti-Japanese agitation in the United States, the Japanese government agreed to prohibit the immigration of Japanese laborers to the United States. This was called the Gentlemen's Agreement. However, the Japanese government continued to allow wives, children, and parents of Japanese settled in the United States to emigrate. After 1908, many were "picture brides," whose marriages had been arranged by their families through the exchange of pictures with Japanese male immigrants, and married through proxy. After 1921, most grooms returned to Japan to marry and brought their wives back with them.

Between 1924 and the post–World War II period, restrictive legislation precluded further Japanese immigration. Following the war, however, women married to U.S. servicemen, known as "war brides" or *shin Issei* (new *Issei*), began to arrive. Still, because the Japanese males had been able to send for wives from 1908 to 1924, the Japanese community continued to grow as a generation of Japanese American citizens, *Ni-*

sei, were born in this country. Clearly defined generation and gender cohorts developed as a result of discriminatory U.S. immigration laws that halted new Japanese immigration early in the century.

The denial of naturalization rights led to the political weakness of the Japanese immigrant community during the first half of this century. Japanese immigrants were permanently disenfranchised in the United States by their status as "aliens ineligible to citizenship." This also served as the basis for further discriminatory laws, such as the anti-alien land laws passed in various West Coast states, which prohibited ownership, leasing, renting, or sharecropping of land. Furthermore, discriminatory legislation and social practices limited job opportunities for *Nisei* women before World War II.

The culmination of a century of racist discriminatory public policy came on December 7, 1941. Japanese immigrants, who had been denied the right of naturalization, suddenly were enemy aliens. They and their citizen children were subject to a myriad of restrictions, following Executive Order 9066, issued February 19, 1942, by President Roosevelt. More than 110,000 Japanese Americans were forcibly removed from their homes on the West Coast and interned in inland concentration camps. Two-thirds of them were U.S.-born.

After the war, there had been a dispersal of Japanese Americans on the mainland and many moved to more urban jobs and residences. *Issei* women, now nearing retirement age, with all their prewar assets and capital taken from them by internment, had to begin their lives over again as seamstresses in garment factories or as domestic servants. But their *Nisei* daughters were able to get higher education and better jobs in the postwar years.

There were many postwar reforms of discriminatory immigration and naturalization legislation. "War brides" marked the first significant number of Japanese women immigrating to the United States since 1924, a fact made possible by their marriages to U.S. servicemen. In 1952, Congress passed the McCarran-Walter Act, which ended the total exclusion of Asian immigration to the United States by giving every country a quota and made all races eligible for naturalization. However, this act still perpetuated a discriminatory barrier to Asian immigration by giving only a token quota to Asian countries (for example, Japan had an annual quota of 185). It was only after the passage of the 1965 Immigration and Naturalization Act that Asian countries were given quotas equal to those of other nations. Partly as a result of the strength of the Japanese economy since 1965, few Japanese immigrants, *shin Issei*, have come to the United States. With little new immigration, low birthrate, and increasing outmarriage, some observers question the viability of the Japanese American ethnic group. But Japanese American ethnic and community identity persists, despite predictions of its demise that date back to the 1920s. In the postwar years, Japanese American women have succeeded in an array of fields, including *Sansei* Patsy Takemoto Mink, the first woman of color in Congress, and *Yonsei* Kristi Yamaguchi, the 1992 Olympic gold medalist in ice skating.

▪ GAIL M. NOMURA

SEE ALSO Asian Pacific Women; Japanese American Citizens League; Japanese American Internment.

≋ Jazz and Blues

Mamie Smith, in February 1920, was the first woman to record the blues. She set into motion a partnership between blues and jazz that continues today. That collaboration altered for all time the vocal and instrumental styles of the blues and jazz artists as they experimented with new and innovative ways of using the voice and the instrument, sometimes effortlessly interchanging musical lines and roles. Thus began the era of wailing trombones, mournful cornets, and shrill clarinets keening like high voices in the wind. The inimitable Bessie Smith slid into phrases and attacked her lines at times as if they were too heavy for her to lift, adding tension to the lyrics and emotional content. Edith Wilson and Ivy Anderson took their soprano voices into the clarinet's range with the tremulous quality of nervous, fluttering birds. Later, Billie Holiday, with her uncanny sensibility, blended blues and jazz into a melange of sensuous and sometimes painful artistry.

In their own way the blues queens of the 1920s established an approach to singing and performing that influenced Holiday and nearly every other singer who succeeded them. Their theatricality, sense of audience, recognition of their ties to their listeners, and respect for the music are evident in the quality and emotional power of their recordings. These artists and the venues where they garnered fame and popularity illustrate how they became influential prototypes in U.S. popular music. When Bessie sang "Any Woman's Blues" she tapped into the reality of many women who suffered from the ambivalence of a relationship that had a powerful but distressing hold on them. What made Bessie and other blues singers unique was their superb musicianship, which matched the artistry of rising and already-arrived instrumentalists of the 1920s. The power of the word juxtaposed with the instruments' imitative sounds of nature, trains, funeral dirges, knocks on doors, and so on, created a visual image for the listener that was elaborated upon by the dramatics of the women singers. Words were infused with additional expressivity when they entered the stage from victrolas, clung to the stage curtains, or moaned and wailed in deep despair, emoting like the actresses of stage and screen.

Singers carried the blues into jazz and formed an entirely new approach to vocal performance, raising the question, What is singing? For the jazz singer, just as for the instrumentalist, there were no rules that were sacred. Bend a note, extend a phrase, insert an obbligato, employ a vocalise, throw away the words and scat in any nonlexical mode that suited the mood of the moment and the flavor of the piece. Ella Fitzgerald, Sarah Vaughan, and Sheila Jordan represent the finest performers of this art form. Bessie Smith's incredible timing and phrasing gave her melodic lines a tension that heightened the interplay between her vocals and the solo cornet or piano. She influenced singers—male and female—and instrumentalists in jazz, swing, and gospel. For example, Bix Beiderbeckc, Frank Sinatra, Billie Holiday, and Mahalia Jackson each acknowledged her impact on their performance styles.

The epitome of the jazz woman was reflected in the astounding International Sweethearts of Rhythm, led by Anna Mae Winburn. This group proved that jazz or, for that matter, music in general was not only a male bastion. Yet, the Sweethearts' success and popularity were based more on the fact that it was an all-female band. Interestingly, it was not the only all-female group operating during those or subsequent years. Ina Ray Hutton distinguished herself with a fine group of women musicians, as did Vi Burnside, Edythe Turnham, and, for a short while, Lil Armstrong. Other all-female groups performed throughout the 1930s and early-1940s, but few of the women, Black or white, were accepted as sidepersons in the swing bands that proliferated during that era. Although there were women bandleaders, arrangers, and composers, such as Lovie Austin and Her Blue Serenaders, as early as the 1920s, they constantly struggled to prove to the men in their ensembles or in the studios that they were "good enough." Being a pianist or singer was and remains acceptable as a woman's role although women have excelled as drummers and as string and horn players. Additionally, from the turn of the century until after World War II, women on stage, especially traveling groups, were considered outside the mainstream of social norms. Nevertheless, they endured racial and sexual hostilities because they had to sing, perform, and compose the music they loved. This tenacity informed their music in subtle and not so subtle ways, for example, Smith's "Poor Man Blues," which addresses poverty and racism, and Holiday's rendition of "Strange Fruit," a commentary on lynching. Mary Lou Williams was one of several pianists from Kansas City who played with jazz groups before going solo. Melba Liston also had a successful career as a horn player and arranger-composer.

Women contributed to the enhancement, development, and creation of jazz and blues in the United States. Their participation and presence were not as mere decorative appendages but as active innovators and creators of new approaches to sound, melody, rhythm, text, and performance style. They brought a voice that was not previously heard and presented a different perspective and posture when they addressed the stuff that makes blues and jazz. They employed intelligence, wit, intense sexuality, and expressivity. The women's collaboration and interaction with their male counterparts changed the music for the better, despite the social and sexual politics that prevailed. Women jazz and blues singers loved the music and its people too much to shut up and go away quietly.

▪ DAPHNE DUVAL HARRISON

SEE ALSO Music.

≋ Jewish Women

From the time of Jewish settlement in the Americas more than 350 years ago, women have played a vital role in the maintenance of Jewish tradition and have helped other immigrant Jews accommodate to the United States. Through their economic, philanthropic, political, and cultural contributions, they helped shape Jewish communal life as well as emerging patterns of U.S. womanhood.

In every epoch, Jewish women's economic activities have been central to family survival. In the Sephardic era (1654–1820) and the period of Germanic and central European emigration (1820–1880), Jewish women helped run shops and family businesses, peddled door to door, and took in boarders. From 1880 to 1920, when nearly three million Eastern European Jews immigrated to the United States (over 40 percent of them women), most Jewish women who worked outside the home were employed in factories or sweatshops. Clara Lemlich sparked the 1909 "Shirtwaist Strike," which unionized the garment industry and helped shape the course of the modern labor movement. Although marriage ended the labor-force participation of most immigrant daughters, many remained union loyalists and became active in housewives' consumer struggles and political actions. From their base in immigrant unionism, Jewish women labor leaders, including Rose Schneiderman and Pauline Newman, joined U.S.-born feminists in leading the campaign for social welfare legislation.

While Jewish families traditionally encouraged the education of sons, immigrant daughters took advantage of educational opportunities in public schools, evening schools, and settlement houses. Increasing numbers went on to college, particularly to tuition-free city universities. As the numbers of Jewish women and men at private colleges also increased, many colleges instituted discriminatory quotas to deal with their "Jewish problem." Even at Barnard College, founded by Annie Nathan Meyer, a Jew, admission of Jewish women was restricted. Jewish women attending Seven Sister schools experienced opportunities to widen their horizons coupled with pressures to assimilate.

Jewish women immigrants at Ellis Island, 1890s, part of the wave of nearly 3 million Jews who immigrated to the United States from the 1880s until legal quotas were imposed in 1924.

For second-generation college-educated daughters, schoolteaching supplanted factory and clerical work as a route to economic security and independence. Despite the oral exams often used to deny teaching licenses to those with unsatisfactory "foreign" pronunciation, Jewish women composed nearly half of all new teachers in New York public schools by 1930; schoolteaching became known as "the Jewish profession."

Although Jewish tradition emphasized women's responsibilities to family and home, Jewish women's extensive organizational networks brought their influence into the public arena. Nineteenth-century Jewish American women established societies to aid the poor, orphan asylums, hospitals, homes for the aged, Sabbath schools, and Hebrew Women's Benevolent Societies. The National Council of Jewish Women, formed in 1893, emphasized aid to immigrant women and children, and social services and legislative reform.

The NCJW was only one of a number of Jewish women's groups concerned with religious, civic, or political issues; by 1910 so many Jewish women's organizations had formed that a conference of Jewish women's organizations was created to coordinate them. In 1912 Henrietta Szold established Hadassah, a women's Zionist organization, to promote health and welfare services for women in Palestine and to provide a special home for U.S. women that did not exist in general Zionist organizations. Hadassah became the largest Jewish women's group in the United States. Other Jewish women's groups that provided support for the Jewish homeland were Pioneer Women (Na'amat) and Women's American ORT.

Several Jewish women's groups were formed in response to the Holocaust, including the left-wing Emma Lazarus Federation of Jewish Women's Groups, once affiliated with the Jewish People's Fraternal Order of the International Workers Order. This group, like the more centrist Women's Division of the American Jewish Congress, devoted itself to fighting anti-Semitism and securing civil rights and social justice for all Americans.

While Jewish women were excluded from the rabbinate and positions of lay leadership, they played active roles in congregational life through the Sunday-school movement, founded by Rebecca Gratz in 1838, and later, through temple sisterhoods. The National Federation of Temple Sisterhoods, affiliated with the Reform movement, was established in 1913; the Women's League of United Synagogues, a branch of Conservative Judaism, in 1918; and the Women's Branch of the Union of Orthodox Congregations in 1923.

Public activism of Jewish women has been reflected in their contributions to many social movements, including the international peace movement, socialism, and feminism. Among the most influential activists and rebels were Maud Nathan, a New York–born Orthodox Jew, who initiated suffrage campaign tactics; Eastern European immigrant Rose Pastor Stokes, a founder of the American Communist Party; and Russian-born anarchist Emma Goldman, who pioneered the American birth-control movement and led the call for greater sexual freedom for women. Nearly six decades later, Betty Friedan helped inaugurate the contemporary women's movement with her groundbreaking examination of the "feminine mystique." While neither Goldman nor Friedan maintained religious traditions, both acknowledged that their social visions were influenced by Jewish values and by their personal experiences of anti-Semitism.

Jewish women have played active roles within the contemporary U.S. feminist movement and have pioneered many areas of women's studies' scholarship. Although most secular feminists who were Jewish initially did not identify themselves as "Jewish" feminists, for many, a newfound Jewish identity came in response to anti-Zionist and anti-Semitic resolutions that emerged at the United Nations International Women's Conferences in Mexico City and Copenhagen in 1975 and 1980. In addition to organizing caucuses to protest anti-Semitism within the international women's movement, Jewish feminists have targeted the continued representation of Jewish women as self-centered "princesses" or as manipulative, monster mothers. *Lilith*, an independent Jewish women's magazine that began in 1976, has played a leading role in raising awareness of such issues and charting the growth of Jewish feminism.

Since the 1970s a vigorous Jewish feminist movement aimed at developing more egalitarian practices within religious life has effected numerous changes. The Reform movement ordained its first female rabbi, Sally Preisand, in 1972. Sandy Sasso later became the first Reconstruction rabbi and Amy Eilberg received Conservative ordination; change within the Orthodox community is reflected in increased opportunities for women to study Torah. Women within all branches of Judaism have engaged in revisions of liturgy and ritual.

Another strand of contemporary Jewish women's rights is represented by lesbian feminism. Refusing to remain invisible within the majority culture, these women have forcefully acknowledged their compound identities and created a powerful voice in literature, the arts, and community and religious affairs.

Numerous Jewish women have achieved prominence in professional and political life. In 1993 Ruth Bader Ginsburg became the second woman, and first Jewish woman, justice of the Supreme Court. In 1994 California elected two Jewish women, Dianne Feinstein and Barbara Boxer, to the U.S. Senate.

Jewish women have also made notable contributions in the areas of fiction, poetry, drama, film, and other popular arts. From the ghetto stories of Mary Antin and Anzia Yezierska to the pioneering modernism of Gertrude Stein, from the romances of Edna Ferber and Fannie Hurst to the biting critiques of Tillie Olsen and Grace Paley, from the intense spirituality of Cynthia Ozick to the secular feminism of E. M. Broner and Kim Chernin, Jewish women novelists and short-story writers have probed the changing meanings of the Jewish female experience in this country. Their linguistic inventiveness is paralleled in the poetry of Muriel Rukeyser, Adrienne Rich, Marge Piercy, and Irene Klepfisz; the plays of Lillian Hellman and Wendy Wasserstein; the radio scripts of Fannie Brice and Gertrude Berg; and the song lyrics and performances of Sophie Tucker and Barbra Streisand.

In each of these endeavors, Jewish American women blended elements of their heritage with specifically U.S. influences. Although they share many attributes with Jewish men and their non-Jewish U.S. sisters, Jewish women's historical patterns of engagement and achievement reflect a distinctive merger of gender-based and ethnic identities.

• JOYCE ANTLER

SEE ALSO Feminism, Jewish; Judaism; Lesbians, Jewish; National Council of Jewish Women.

≋ Journalism

SEE Magazines; Newspapers.

≋ Judaism

Judaism is traditionally defined as a religion based on divinely prescribed beliefs and rituals composed and interpreted almost exclusively by men, beginning with the Bible and Talmud, an extensive and wide-ranging discussion by rabbis of Jewish law and theology composed in Babylonia during late antiquity, and extending to medieval law codes and commentaries. These texts have not retained the memory of women's experiences and viewpoints. With the modern pressure to reshape gender roles, Jewish women have increased opportunities to express their identity as Jews inside and outside the religious framework. The women's movement has challenged the sexism of Jewish texts and institutions and led to defining a feminist Judaism.

Since women traditionally have been excluded from the central components of Jewish life, their experience of Jewish identity differs sharply from that of men. As secularism grew, new educational and professional opportunities arose for women, and women demanded comparable opportunities within Jewish life, in both religious and political spheres. By the beginning of this century schools opened to instruct women in Hebrew Bible and medieval commentaries, as well as limited instruction in Mishnah, a compilation from the first and second centuries of laws regulating Jewish religious practice, and Talmud, areas previously restricted to men.

Beginning in the nineteenth century women took a leading role in U.S. Jewish life, organizing the Sunday-school movement and a wide range of community-based charitable and social service organizations, many of which played a crucial role in settling vast numbers of new immigrants (about two million Jews arrived in this country between 1881 and 1914). Their philanthropic network was significant, but major control of the Jewish community's funds still remained in the hands of men.

At the turn of the century women played significant roles in U.S. political life, including the labor movement and various forms of socialism. Jewish women in the United States had not been particularly involved in the general suffrage movement during the nineteenth and early twentieth centuries for a variety of reasons, including anti-Semitism in the women's movement, the small number of Jewish women in the United States prior to the 1880s, and the concern of East European immigrant women with basic family and economic survival.

Since the 1960s Jewish women have been active in the women's movement and have created an important body of Jewish American literature reflecting their experiences. Jewish lesbians have created an especially important movement, questioning not only Jewish sexual ethics but also the motif of polar differences that marks many Jewish theological assumptions. Women with doctorates in Jewish studies have opened new areas of feminist studies in Judaism since the 1970s.

The most dramatic change in Judaism for many centuries is reflected in the increasing equality of women in synagogue worship, a movement led by U.S. Jewish feminists that has extended to Jewish communities around the world. Separate seating for women began to be abolished in non-Orthodox U.S. synagogues in the late nineteenth century and integrated seating was standard by this century. The public honoring of young women in the synagogue, the Bat Mitzvah, was widespread by the late 1960s, followed by decisions by Reform, Reconstructionist, and Conservative denominations of Judaism to include women in the prayer quorum, call women to the Torah (the scroll of the Pentateuch), and allow women to lead worship services.

Ordination of women as rabbis and cantors began in the United States in the 1970s and quickly was adopted by the non-Orthodox branches of Judaism. Over two hundred women rabbis and cantors have been ordained since 1972. Commissions within the Reform and Reconstructionist movements are currently revising the prayer books to use inclusive or gender-neutral language. New feminist rituals to mark occasions in women's lives have developed, including feminist Passover liturgies, ceremonies for naming baby girls (previously a male ritual only), and egalitarian wedding services for hetero- and homosexual couples.

Within the Orthodox community, women have called for changes in the traditional system of Jewish law and have won limited success. In recent years Orthodox women have established women-only prayer groups, institutions for study, and options for changing the religious marriage document to provide recourse for a woman whose husband refuses to grant her a Jewish divorce; without it, she is not permitted to remarry.

Efforts began in earnest during the 1970s to expose the sexism inherent in Judaism's exclusively male-authored texts and to reconstruct the lost voices of women. Jewish feminist theologians are redefining these texts and analyzing the male-centered Jewish understandings of God, as well as concepts such as revelation, evil, and the nature of prayer. Jewish feminism is resulting not merely in the inclusion of women in Jewish life but also in the ultimate creation of a new, feminist Judaism.

Judith Baskin, ed., *Jewish Women in Historical Perspective* (Detroit: Wayne State University Press, 1991); Charlotte Baum, Paula Hyman, and Sonya Michel, *The Jewish Woman in America* (New York: Dial Press, 1976); Susannah Heschel, ed., *On Being a Jewish Feminist: A Reader* (New York: Schocken Books, 1983).

▪ SUSANNAH HESCHEL

SEE ALSO Jewish Women; Religion.

≋ Knights of Labor

SEE Labor Unions.

≋ Korean American Women

Before the 1960s few Koreans immigrated to the United States. Only eight thousand Koreans sailed to Hawaii and the mainland before the Immigration Act of 1924 terminated Asian immigration to the United States. More than six hundred women first arrived as part of a group of seven thousand Korean laborers recruited by Hawaiian sugar planters between 1903 and 1905. After making Korea a "protectorate" in 1905, Japan barred male emigrants but allowed almost one thousand "picture brides" to leave for the United States before 1924. Nine-tenths of these women joined husbands in Hawaii while the rest went to the Pacific Coast. They fled Korea to seek economic, educational, and religious opportunities and to escape poverty, famine, heavy taxation, and Japanese colonial oppression. A few "warrior" women rebelled against husbands who had concubines and Confucian patriarchal ideals limiting women to the domestic sphere and a life spent serving male family members. Envisioning the United States as a land paved with gold, many picture brides were shocked to discover they had married poor laborers who were often twenty years their senior. A few returned to Korea or ran off with other men, but most of the women toiled beside their husbands as they raised the second generation. By 1945 sixty-five hundred Korean Americans lived in Hawaii and three thousand were scattered throughout the mainland.

Expanding slightly after the 1952 McCarran-Walter Act assigned Korea an annual immigration quota of one hundred, the Korean American population then grew rapidly after the 1965 Immigration Act, which granted Koreans twenty thousand annual visas and removed limits on the entry of immediate family members—spouses, minor children, and parents—of U.S. citizens. Only seventeen thousand immigrants arrived between 1952 and 1965, but more than six hundred twenty thousand Koreans arrived between 1966 and 1990. Seventy percent of all immigrants who arrived in the 1950s and 1960s were female. The percentage of women gradually leveled off in the 1970s and 1980s to approximately 55 percent by 1989. Before 1965 most female immigrants were "war brides" married to U.S. servicemen or children adopted by U.S. families. After 1965 many women left Korea to escape Park Chung Hee's military dictatorship and the economic instability produced by rapid industrialization and urbanization. Although a large number came as professional workers in the late 1960s, many women who immigrated between 1970 and the early 1990s were

working-class family members of citizens and permanent residents. These female immigrants helped the Korean American community grow from only forty-five thousand in 1965 to almost eight hundred thousand in 1990. In 1990 the median age of the more than four hundred forty-five thousand women of Korean ancestry in the United States was 30.3 years.

Korean American women have made vital contributions to the economic, social, and political development of the ethnic community. Denied naturalization rights until 1952, Korean Americans were excluded from white-collar and professional occupations before World War II. Relegated to low-paying jobs, women worked as agricultural laborers, cooks, laundresses, and boardinghouse keepers. Women's paid and unpaid labor helped families finance restaurants, laundries, retail groceries, and other small businesses. Women from the same village, province, and church also pooled their resources in *kyes*, traditional Korean mutual financing associations, to fund ethnic businesses and their children's education.

Despite working ten hours a day and seven days a week, women still found time to serve as Christian deaconesses, Sunday-school teachers, Korean language instructors, and activists in the campaign to liberate Korea from Japanese colonial rule. Between 1919 and 1945 separate women's groups, such as the Korean Women's Relief Society in Hawaii and the Korean Women's Patriotic Society on the mainland, organized protest rallies, trained emergency nurses, and raised funds for independence fighters in Korea. Illustrating how domestic roles can be politicized, women activists argued that they could not fulfill the Confucian ideal of the "good wife" and "wise mother" without fighting Japan's oppression of families in Korea. They urged patriotic women to raise independence funds by forgoing meat and soy sauce and by selling Korean foods and crafts. Before Korea was liberated from Japanese rule in 1945, women activists helped convince Korean Americans, most of whom were barely subsisting, to donate one month's wages every year to support the nationalist movement.

Women also assumed important economic, social, and political roles in the post–World War II community. Even immigrants who came after 1965 with advanced educations and professional training often started small businesses because of strict licensing requirements and because they lacked fluency in English and familiarity with American customs. In 1980 there were ninety Korean-owned businesses for every thousand Korean Americans. Many of these businesses were financed by women's *kyes* organized by female coworkers, neighbors, alumnae, and church members. Women also have maintained a tradition of serving multiple roles as wage earners or entrepreneurs, domestic caretakers, and community activists. Immigrant organizations, especially business and political groups, have tended to exclude women from leadership positions. Establishing their own organizations, immigrant women dominate nurses' associations, Christian deacon and missionary service, educational programs for immigrant children and adults, social service agencies, and the English-language sections of community newspapers. Numerous women mobilized to support the more than two thousand Korean small businesses that suffered losses of $350 million during the 1992 Los Angeles uprising. For example, women in the Association of Korean American Victims of the L.A. Riot helped stage midday marches at the Los Angeles city hall demanding that the government provide reparations for riot damage attributed to police negligence.

Almost fifty years separate the end of the movement to liberate Korea from Japanese rule and the campaign for victims of the 1992 Los Angeles uprising. Both groups of activists urged women to assume prominent roles in the public sphere to protect their families and the ethnic community. As women activists acquired political experience, some increasingly demanded recognition of women's leadership abilities and criticized gender discrimination in the ethnic and mainstream community. More recent activists, such as Angela Oh, president of the Korean American Bar Association, have been hailed as community spokespersons; these activists have maintained a long history of Korean American women's activism and assertiveness.

Haeyun Juliana Kim, "Voices from the Shadows: The Lives of Korean War Brides," *Amerasia Journal*, 17, no. 1 (1991): 15–30; Mary Paik Lee, *Quiet Odyssey: A Pioneer Korean Woman in America*, edited and with an introduction by Sucheng Chan (Seattle: University of Washington Press, 1990); Young Yu and Earl H. Phillips, eds., *Korean American Women in Transition: At Home and Abroad* (Los Angeles: Center for Korean-American and Korean Studies, California State University, 1987).

▪ ALICE YANG MURRAY

SEE ALSO Asian Pacific Women; Picture Brides.

≋ Ku Klux Klan

Women have been central in defining successive waves of the Ku Klux Klan (KKK) throughout its history. Women of color, Jewish women, and immigrant women have been particular targets of the Klan's brutality. White Protestant women have been important symbols—and at times activists—in the Klan's racist, nativist, and anti-Semitic doctrines.

The first KKK was organized in the South after the Civil War. Although the Klan did not include women as members at that time, it used images of white womanhood that were critical to its efforts to rally the defeated sons of the Confederacy. Charging that white widows living on isolated plantations were vulnerable to retaliation by their former slaves, the Klan used this as a rationale to threaten, flog, and murder countless African American men and women. Gangs of Klansmen

Klan members in Hartford City, Indiana, in the early 1920s.

also raped and sexually tortured numerous African American women as well as white women who were suspected of having had sexual relations with African American men.

Federal intervention and internal dissension caused the first Klan to collapse in the 1870s. But it reemerged in 1915 in response to massive immigration and grew rapidly in the northern and midwestern states. Within a decade it claimed approximately four million members, including women and children. Women's entry into the male bastion of the Klan, however, created a dilemma for the organization. Earlier, the Klan's identity had been that of a fraternity of "real men" in which women were only symbols for the men. The women who

joined the Klan's crusade of white Protestant supremacy in the 1920s, however, often had had prior experience in the women's suffrage, temperance, or morality movements. The Klan provided a way to safeguard these women's racial and religious privileges while also supporting the rights of white Protestant women. The Women's Klan thus used an agenda of women's rights to justify — even to require — vicious actions against African Americans, Catholics, Jews, immigrants, labor radicals, and others. As with its predecessor, internal scandal and external pressure undermined this second Klan and it virtually disappeared by 1930.

Between 1930 and 1980, the KKK emerged again and was based primarily in the South.

Women played no visible part in this Klan, which engaged in terroristic actions against organized labor, New Deal agents, Communist Party organizers, proponents of racial integration, and African Americans from the South. This KKK, like the first Klan, relied on images of white women's vulnerability and white male supremacy.

The fourth and current Klan arose in the early 1980s. Although small in number, this Klan has augmented its strength through alliances with other terrorist and paramilitary groups, including self-proclaimed Nazis and white-power survivalists. Women belong to these groups but, with the exception of some white-power Nazi groups, they play primarily supporting roles. Women's rights and lesbian and gay rights are antithetical to the agenda of most Klan groups, which affirm traditional gender roles, denounce affirmative action as curbing the rights of white men, and increasingly target lesbians and gay men for violent attack.

▪ KATHLEEN M. BLEE

SEE ALSO Civil Rights Movement; Lynching; Reconstruction.

≋ Labor Movement

W omen have contributed to the U.S. labor movement in a variety of ways. Like their male counterparts, they have participated in unions as members and leaders. But women have also engaged in many gender-specific labor-movement activities rooted in their distinctively female life experience. Among the organizational forms such efforts have produced are women's labor-union auxiliaries, which have played crucial roles in many key strikes; cross-class alliances like the Women's Trade Union League (WTUL); umbrella groups like the Coalition of Labor Union Women (CLUW); and "pre-unions" like Nine to Five and other working women's associations that

function outside of the formal collective bargaining system. In addition, the feminist movement has worked frequently in coalition with organized labor on mutual concerns.

The first factory workers in the United States were female, and women were also among the nation's earliest labor militants. But male workers' unions, especially in skilled craft occupations, often excluded women from membership. Most nineteenth-century unions stood for a "family wage," or pay sufficient to support a family, for male workers, and hoped that attaining this goal would allow working-class women to withdraw entirely from paid work. However, broader labor movement organizations like the Knights of Labor, which flourished in the 1880s, or the Industrial Workers of the World a few decades later, actively recruited women members. These organizations were short-lived. As long as craft unions dominated the labor movement, women remained a tiny minority of its members, despite ongoing efforts at self-organization. As more inclusive forms of unionism became the norm, beginning in the clothing industry in the 1910s, and growing more broad in the 1930s, women's involvement in unions increased dramatically. Today two out of every five union members are female.

Women's networks outside the workplace, rooted in family and community, have often helped galvanize women's labor activism. Native-born white women, women of color, and immigrant women have all participated in the labor movement, and indeed it has frequently brought together women workers from diverse ethnic and racial groups on the basis of shared employment conditions. Unions with strong grassroots community ties have generally had greater success in mobilizing women workers than more bureaucratic forms of labor organization. And women's union auxiliaries, comprised of the wives and other female kin of male workers, have recruited women into labor-movement struggles by appealing to their domestic roles as guardians of family welfare. The Women's Emergency Brigade, which was critical to the success of the United Auto Workers' 1936–37 strike against General Motors in Flint, Michigan, is the best-known case. Women's auxiliaries have played a major role in many other strikes as well, especially in communities dominated by a single industry, where the links between family welfare, community solidarity, and workers' rights tend to be most clear. Although women's auxiliaries have been less important in the post–World War II era, this organizational form persists to the present day—as illustrated by the 1983–85 Arizona copper miners' strike.

Women's community-based networks also have been central to another type of labor-movement organization predicated on alliances between elite and working-class women. In the early part of the twentieth century, the WTUL was the most important cross-class organization of this type, bringing upper-class maternalistic women into active support of poor immigrant factory women's struggles for improved wages and conditions and of union-building efforts among women workers. The WTUL's influence waned over the interwar period and then disappeared entirely in the aftermath of World War II. More recently, however, middle-class feminists and female professionals have allied with women clerical and service workers in the campaign for comparable worth. Here gender solidarity is as central as class solidarity in galvanizing labor-movement activity.

Starting in the 1970s, under the impetus of the second wave of feminism, a variety of women's organizations emerged that were devoted to advancing the specific interests of women workers within the labor movement. The most successful of such groups were CLUW and Nine to Five, each of which pursued a different strategy. CLUW took the existing structure of organized labor as a given and directed itself toward enhancing the power and status of women within that structure. Nine to Five sought instead to develop an alternative type of organization for women workers, implicitly challenging male-centered labor-movement traditions while working to expand the options for women within existing labor movement organizations.

Unlike CLUW, the working women's movement, of which Nine to Five is the best-known example, originated outside the established unions. In the 1970s young activists with roots in the women's liberation movement began to organize previously unorganized office workers into independent associations. At first, these groups deliberately avoided any formal links to established unions. Their founders believed that women clerical workers, unaccustomed to viewing themselves as powerful, would perceive unions as male-oriented and culturally alien. Instead the working women's movement concentrated on consciousness raising and other relatively unstructured, participatory organizational forms and on public dramatizations of specific issues affecting women clerical workers. To a degree, Nine to Five and similar groups functioned as "pre-unions," and over time they moved closer to the union model, devoting an increasing amount of their energy to unionization drives. Indeed, in the 1980s the highly democratic, bottom-up model of union organizing they developed was imitated by mainstream unions in efforts to recruit women clerical workers, most notably on university campuses.

Finally, the feminist movement itself has worked in coalition with organized labor on a variety of issues. Campaigns for pay equity, parental leave, child care, protection from sexual harassment, and other issues affecting working women have become a joint focus of lobbying, legal strategies, and grassroots organizing for both the feminist and labor movements, spilling over the traditional boundaries of union activity. More generally, feminist efforts to improve the pay, status, and working conditions of women have become an integral part of the contemporary labor movement.

Dorothy Sue Cobble, ed., *Women and Unions: Forging a Partnership* (Ithaca, N.Y.: ILR Press, 1993); Ruth Milkman, ed., *Women, Work and Protest: A Century of U.S. Women's Labor History* (Boston: Routledge and Kegan Paul, 1985); Nancy Seifer and Barbara Wertheimer, "New Approaches to Collective Power: Four Working Women's Organizations," in *Women Organizing: An Anthology,* edited by Bernice Cummings and Victoria Schuck, 152–83. (Metuchen, N.J.: Scarecrow Press, 1979).

▪ RUTH MILKMAN

SEE ALSO Coalition of Labor Union Women (CLUW); Protective Labor Legislation; Labor Unions; Women's Trade Union League.

≋ Labor Unions

Women workers have been consistently active in labor unions; but until the mid–twentieth century, relatively few women were in the work force, and unionism was concentrated in predominantly male industries and occupations. In recent years, that pattern has changed dramatically, so that many more women workers enjoy the higher pay, increased job security, and other benefits of union membership. Although overall union membership in the United States has declined, its composition has become increasingly female. In 1993 41 percent of all workers represented by unions were women—a record high. As recently as 1970, the figure was only 24 percent. And, in sharp contrast to earlier in this century, when women of color were underrepresented, today women of color are more likely than their white sisters to be unionized. In 1993 22 percent of African American and 15 percent of Latina women were represented by unions, compared with 14 percent of white women workers. Partly as a result of the growing presence of women within their ranks, labor unions have recently begun to embrace major feminist issues such as comparable worth and parental leave. Historically, however, women workers' concerns have been marginal to the agenda of labor unions.

Over the past two centuries, the steady feminization of the U.S. labor force has been accompanied by a parallel feminization of union membership, although the latter trend is less continuous. Organized labor today is the product of four major historical waves of unionization, each in a different sector of the economy and with a distinct relationship to women workers: the craft unionism of the nineteenth century, the "new unionism" of the 1910s, the industrial unionism of the 1930s and 1940s, and the public-sector and service unionism that began in the 1960s.

Craft unionism, which burgeoned in the late nineteenth century and the first decade of the twentieth, involved primarily skilled workers and produced only minimal organization among women. Except in such female-dominated trades as waiting tables, craft union members were overwhelmingly males who typically viewed women's labor as a threat to skill and wage levels. These unions, which banded together to form the American Federation of Labor (AFL) in the 1880s, often excluded women (as well as Blacks and many immigrants) from membership outright—until as late as the 1940s in some cases, though to this day informal exclusion sometimes occurs in these same unions. The craft unions that still exist—such as the construction trades "brotherhoods" and the machinists' union—are among those least receptive to women workers and their specific concerns and most faithful to their own past.

A second wave of unionism emerged in the 1910s, centered in the predominantly female garment industry. By 1920, 43 percent of the nation's women union members were clothing workers. This "new unionism" was both an outgrowth of craft unionism and a forerunner of the industrial unions of the 1930s. It generated a fivefold increase in the number of women union members between 1910 and 1920. While clothing union membership was almost entirely female, the leaders of these unions remained overwhelmingly

Women delegates to the 1886 Knights of Labor convention. At the time of this photograph, the Knights had an estimated female membership of 65,000.

male, and many viewed their women members paternalistically—as weak workers in need of special protection, not equal partners in the labor struggle.

The 1920s and early 1930s was an era of deunionization when the number of both female and male union members fell. Massive organizing drives of the Congress of Industrial Organization (CIO) unions in the late 1930s recruited both unskilled and skilled workers, bringing the number of women union members in the 1940s to twice the 1920 level. By 1944, the peak of the wartime economic boom, three million women were union members—nearly eight times the 1920 figure.

The new CIO unions targeted mainly male-dominated industries and had an almost exclusively male leadership, but their stance toward women workers was different from that of earlier unions. A shift in the larger political culture away from the former emphasis on gender difference (explicit in both patriarchal craft unionism and paternalistic "new unionism") and toward a new vision of gender equality followed the suffrage victory and the growth of women's employment in the 1920s and 1930s. The CIO unions embraced this change, explicitly opposing discrimination on the basis of sex, color, and creed, in a self-conscious break with craft union tradition. Theirs was a limited notion of gender equality, however, rooted in broader principles of class solidarity and opposition to employer efforts to divide workers by gender, race, or ethnicity. The CIO unions maintained their commitment to the abstract principle of equality in later years, and some were leading supporters of legislation against sex discrimination in the 1960s and 1970s. With the exception of the World War II era, however, women remained underrepresented in most of these unions, which were based in such heavily male industries as auto, steel, and other basic manufacturing.

Starting in the 1960s—precisely when overall unionization levels in the United States began to fall—a fourth group of unions emerged, mainly in the public sector but also in private-sector service industries such as health care. Now the gap between women's representation among union members and in the larger work force narrowed significantly. Indeed, almost all the growth in union membership in this period was among women workers. But it was rare for these public- and service-sector unions to organize women "as women." Rather, the feminization of their membership was an unintended consequence of organizing in occupations where women are particularly well represented: at one point, teaching; later, health care; and most recently, public-sector clerical and service work. Because this organizing occurred in a period of feminist resurgence and of broad changes in gender relations in the wider society, these unions have recruited women not only as members but also as leaders to an unprecedented extent. And the unions that emerged in the most recent wave of labor organizing have been particularly active in reformulating traditional labor issues to address better the concerns of women workers, most notably in the campaign for "comparable worth" in the 1980s. This offers a basis for optimism about the future if organized labor ever overcomes its present crisis and begins to grow in size and influence once again.

Ava Baron, ed., *Work Engendered: Toward a New History of American Labor* (Ithaca, NY: Cornell University Press, 1991); Ruth Milkman, ed., *Women, Work and Protest: A Century of U.S. Women's Labor History* (Boston: Routledge and Kegan Paul, 1985); Ruth Milkman, "Gender and Trade Unionism in Historical Perspective," in *Women, Politics and Change,* edited by Louise A. Tilly and Patricia Gurin, 87–107. (New York: Russell Sage Foundation, 1990).

■ RUTH MILKMAN

SEE ALSO Comparable Worth; Labor Movement; Needle Trades; Sweatshops; Women's Trade Union League.

Amalgamated Clothing and Textile Workers Union (ACTWU)

The ACTWU was formed in 1976 through the merger of two large garment unions, the Amalgamated Clothing Workers and the Textile Workers Union. In the 1970s the union came to national prominence through its campaign to organize workers at J. P. Stevens, then the second-largest textile manufacturer in the United States. The ACTWU publicized the harsh working conditions of the mostly female and heavily African American labor force in the southern garment industry through a nationwide boycott of J. P. Stevens' products. The consumer boycott, an example of the creative organizing strategies often employed by woman-dominated unions, fostered the cross-class participation of feminist, civil rights, and labor groups from both the North and South, in the J. P. Stevens organizing campaign. Triumphing over company efforts to divide Black and white workers, in 1980 the ACTWU won its seventeen-year battle when Stevens ratified a collective bargaining agreement. During the 1980s the ACTWU continued to focus on unorganized workers despite the negative impact of widespread plant closings and capital flight in the apparel, textile, and shoe industries. The union has established highly successful medical care and social welfare programs. Active in the Coalition of Labor Union Women, the ACTWU established its own civil rights department to address women's

Rally of the International Ladies' Garment Workers Union.

rights and racial justice. In 1995, ACTWU joined forces with the International Ladies' Garment Workers Union to found UNITE!, the Union of Needletrades, Industrial, and Textile Employees.

▪ BEATRIX HOFFMAN

SEE ALSO Needle Trades; Textile/Apparel Workers.

American Federation of State, County, and Municipal Employees (AFSCME)

The American Federation of State, County, and Municipal Employees (AFSCME), a public sector union, originated in the Midwest during the 1930s. Its emergence was part of the movement against patronage in government employment. Both growth in government employment and the extension of collective bargaining rights to those in public sector jobs boosted the union's membership. By the mid-1990s AFSCME, with over 1.3 million members, had become the largest public sector union and the second largest union in the AFL-CIO.

AFSCME has long been active on behalf of men and women of color. The union organized African American sanitation workers in Memphis, Tennessee. Their 1968 strike brought Martin Luther King, Jr., to the city, where he was then assassinated. African American women working in hospitals and as home health attendants also organized. By the end of the 1960s the composition of many AFSCME locals had shifted from predominantly white male workers to women of all races and men of color employed in hospital, school, and clerical jobs. AFSCME now organizes a large and growing number of Latinos/as in the Southwest, and Puerto Ricans are a significant proportion of members in New York City. Union policies favor a decentralized and democratic unionism that speaks to the working conditions as well as the family and community needs of these workers.

In the late 1960s AFSCME District Council 37 in New York City launched a pioneering career-ladder program for women in dead-end jobs, and other locals followed suit. In 1972 AFSCME was among the first unions to support the Equal Rights Amendment. The national union vigorously pursued pay equity in the 1980s. AFSCME locals actively negotiate work/family issues; and on the national level the union presses for legislation such as the Family and Medical Leave Act. By the 1990s half the membership and local leadership were women. Some consider AFSCME a model for a "new unionism" needed to revive the entire U.S. labor movement.

■ LINDA M. BLUM
and PEGGY KAHN

Association of Flight Attendants

Emerging from an almost exclusively female profession, the Association of Flight Attendants (AFA) is one of the few woman-led trade unions in the United States. From its beginnings as the Air Line Stewardesses Association (ALSA) in 1945, the AFA, along with other flight attendants' unions, has been a leader in the fight against sex discrimination. "Stewardesses," required to serve meals, calm passengers, master safety procedures, and project flawless femininity, were also faced with low pay, long hours, and dif-

ficult working conditions. Union officials increasingly realized that, in order to address these concerns, they also had to attack the airlines'—and society's—assumptions about women. Female airline workers achieved a significant victory in 1968, when the Equal Employment Opportunity Commission told the airlines to stop forcing stewardesses to retire upon marriage or at age thirty or thirty-five. During the 1970s, when the ALSA was renamed the AFA, the union fought for maternity leave from airlines that had traditionally fired flight attendants upon learning of their pregnancy. In the face of arguments that being female was a "bona fide occupational qualification" for the job of flight attendant because of women's superior ability to comfort passengers, the unions won a sex-discrimination case that compelled airlines to begin hiring male flight attendants in 1972. Throughout the 1980s and 1990s the AFA has fought, with increasing success, the airlines' imposition of age, weight, and appearance requirements for flight attendants.

■ BEATRIX HOFFMAN

Hospital Unions

Between 1920 and 1940, as the number of hospitals in the United States grew rapidly, changes in medical technology and practice transformed hospital care from the work of physicians assisted by nurse "hands," who were often student nurses, to work that required a large and specialized staff. This expansion of the labor force led to a hierarchy of workers, mostly women, who were subject to demanding work, low wages, long hours, and sometimes unreasonable conditions.

The first major hospital union drive occurred in the San Francisco Bay Area in the 1930s, bringing together engine room, dietary, and laundry employees as well as nurses' aides and orderlies. But the movement failed to spread. The 1947 Taft-Hartley Act exempted private hospitals from the requirement to recognize unions among their workers. This exemption—which was not removed until 1974—stymied organizing among all categories of hospital workers. By 1961, only 3 percent of hospitals had at least one labor contract.

Obstacles to unionization existed beyond the legal system. Hospital employers often had a near monopoly on jobs for nurses and other health care workers and set wages and working conditions so that few alternatives existed. Also, there were perennial questions of the appropriateness of unions for women. Hospital workers organized throughout the 1960s, mostly in public sector hospitals, which did little to prevent unionization. Beginning in New York City, links between unions and the civil rights movement facilitated organizing. The union 1199 and civil rights leaders worked together to unionize the mainly African American and Puerto Rican women working as aides, orderlies, and dietary staff in many major urban hospitals.

Organizing efforts slowed in the 1980s. Since 1990, changes in health care financing, cost containment, the growth of for-profit hospital chains, and the spread of managed care models of health insurance have resulted in hospital closings and downsizing. Women, who make up more than 80 percent of hospital workers, have been most affected. Job security and standards of care have been undermined, while families—often a euphemism for women—are expected to provide care at home. Pressure is building once again for a fundamental change in the health care system, accompanied by consumer demands for safe, affordable care.

■ ROSLYN L. FELDBERG

SEE ALSO Labor Unions: Nurses' Unions.

Hotel and Restaurant Employees International Union

Since 1890 the Hotel Employees and Restaurant Employees Union (HERE) has represented workers in high-turnover jobs that are typically sex- and race-segregated, casual, and low-wage. Bartenders and waiters founded HERE as an affiliate union of the AFL in 1891; waitresses joined after 1900, the majority of them in separate, autonomously run, and remarkably resilient locals. Craft or occupational identity was the prime element of their work culture and overall worldview.

Some craft locals enabled union members to govern their otherwise chaotic industry. Both male (waiters and bartenders) locals and female (waitress) locals limited membership to white workers, who performed only "skilled" jobs. "Menial"-labor jobs that they refused were fit for those racial and ethnic groups—African Americans, Native Americans, Asian Americans, and Jews—excluded from the union. Thus, occupational unionism unified workers across the hospitality industry at the same time as it deepened racial, ethnic, and gender divisions.

With the rise of mass-production unionism in the 1930s and 1940s, HERE organizers enrolled all classifications—including the hotel maids and kitchen workers formerly excluded from the craft locals—into mixed-sex and mixed-craft organizations that concentrated on providing worksite-centered protections and rights. In the 1970s legislation mandated the amalgamation of all the locals into industrial locals, in which, for the first time, the "menial" workers were in the majority. In their quest for leadership, they have launched a civil rights movement within HERE that is transforming anew the shape and meaning of U.S. trade unionism.

■ BETSY ARON

SEE ALSO Waitresses.

Industrial Workers of the World (IWW)

The IWW (or "Wobblies"), founded in 1905 by socialists and anarcho-syndicalists (including a lone woman, Mother Jones), envisioned organizing the U.S. working class, industry by industry, into "one big union" for a militant assault on capitalism. Unlike the AFL, the IWW welcomed women, Blacks, immigrants, and the unskilled.

The IWW had few women members, but it mobilized many working-class women in two major strikes in Lawrence, Massachusetts (1912), and in Paterson, New Jersey (1913).

The Lawrence strike, precipitated by a cut in wages already wretchedly low, involved twenty thousand textile workers, half of them women and children. The IWW dispatched its best organizers, including the young passionate orator Elizabeth Gurley Flynn, known as "the rebel girl." Police violence ensued and led to a woman striker's death and clubbing of women and children; the city became a scene of class warfare and labor solidarity, and produced the feminist anthem "Bread and Roses." National publicity forced the mill owners to grant all the strikers' demands, but the victory was short-lived; the next major strike in Paterson was defeated. At its peak in 1912 the IWW's strength (ca. 150,000) was among western migratory workers, miners, and loggers. It shunned labor contracts and, after 1908, all political action (including the struggle for women's suffrage), relying instead on strikes, slowdowns, and direct action, plus the revolutionary zeal of its crusading members. By 1920, after World War I repression, vigilante attacks, federal and state prosecutions, and internal dissension, the IWW was all but destroyed.

Although the IWW was a pioneer for birth control as a "working class necessity," women's issues were seen as disrupting class unity, to be addressed only "after the revolution."

■ MARGE FRANTZ

International Ladies' Garment Workers Union (ILGWU)

In 1900 male cloak makers organized the International Ladies' Garment Workers Union (ILGWU) to improve working conditions for employees manufacturing women's clothing. The founders promoted the union label, discouraged strikes, and endorsed socialism. Union leaders recruited the young immigrant women who composed 70 percent of the industry's work force, but did not trust women's ability to sustain constructive union membership.

The 1909 "uprising of the twenty thousand" among New York's female shirtwaist makers invigorated the union. This strike dramatized the plight of young Eastern European Jewish and Italian workers who received a meager three dollars for a fifty-four-hour work week. By withstanding freezing temperatures, strikebreakers' assaults, police brutality, arrests, and imprisonment, these women demonstrated their ability to act collectively to win improved working conditions and partial union recognition.

Inspired by the uprising, the ILGWU hired women organizers to convert picket-line heroics into union solidarity, including Rose Schneiderman, a Polish cap maker; Gertrude Barnum, a settlement-house resident who organized dressmakers; and Lithuanian-born Pauline Newman, a socialist. Several locals pioneered educational and social programs for their female members. By 1916 women composed 50 percent of the ILGWU's members, including eight women organizers and the educational director position.

After passage of the Wagner Act in 1935, the ILGWU recovered ground lost in the antiunion 1920s. After 1960 Latina and Asian women entered the industry in significant numbers, recruited by Katie Quan and other ILGWU organizers in California and New York.

The ILGWU utilized the courts to enforce health and safety regulations. Although some workers complained that the male-dominated leadership of the 90-percent female ILGWU neglected crucial "women's issues," union members receive health benefits, social and educational programs, paid vacations, and relative job security. In 1995, ILGWU merged with the Amalgamated Clothing and Textile Workers' Union (ACTWU) to form UNITE!, the Union of Needletrades, Industrial, and Textile Employees.

▪ CAROLYN D. MCCREESH

SEE ALSO Textile/Apparel Workers.

Knights of Labor

The Noble and Holy Order of the Knights of Labor, formed in 1869, sought to organize all members of the "producing class" into a single organization, rendering it broader than many other labor organizations, though it essentially performed the economic functions of a labor union federation. The first women to join the organization were Philadelphia shoe workers in 1881, who created the first known all-female Local Assembly of the Knights. The 1881 General Assembly of the Knights voted formally to admit women members. By 1886 approximately one hundred thousand women belonged to the Knights of Labor.

Many women joined the Knights of Labor, some as wage earners. As in other sex-segregated labor organizations, numerous women formed women-only local assemblies. Other local assemblies, especially in smaller towns, included both women and men. The Knights encouraged working-class women to join as housewives, since membership was based not on an individual's paid or unpaid status but on the usefulness of a person's work. Although the Knights' attention to women's domestic roles attracted many women to join, it also limited their participation by defining their "proper" role as being in the family. Unlike most organizations of the time, the Knights of Labor also included African Americans. The

Chinese, however, were specifically banned.

Membership in the Knights peaked in the spring and summer of 1886. By that fall membership began to decline, partly because of competition with the trade unions, which eventually formed the American Federation of Labor.

▪ ILEEN A. DEVAULT

Nine to Five (District 925 of SEIU)

For many working women, there comes a defining moment when they recognize the obstacles to fair treatment, decent pay, and respect on the job. As a clerical worker at Harvard in 1973, this author was asked by a student who poked his head in the door, "Isn't anybody here?" As a result, a number of fellow clerical workers in Boston built a new organization to change workplace conditions for women, called 9 to 5.

From that grassroots experience emerged several lessons: It is not enough to win power in the workplace over a specific issue; women must find ways to institutionalize and protect all changes, especially through unionizing.

In 1975 9 to 5 formed a sister organization to help office workers achieve economic gains and improved working conditions. This organization, District 925, joined the Service Employees International Union (SEIU), which represents about one million U.S. workers.

The benefits of unionization for women workers have been well documented. In 1992 union women earned an average of $3.07 more per hour than did nonunion women—a bigger differential than for men ($2.73). Unions have also decreased the wage gap between men and women. Union women earn an average of 82 cents for every dollar earned by union men, while nonunion women earn only 75 cents for every dollar earned by nonunion men.

Since 1975 District 925 of SEIU has helped more than ten thousand women and men win higher wages and improved working conditions—all as a result of the leadership and democratic participation of working women.

• KAREN NUSSBAUM

SEE ALSO Clerical Work; Labor Unions: Service Employees International Union.

Nurses' Unions

The leadership of formal nursing organizations historically has regarded labor unions and labor legislation with suspicion, if not outright distaste. During the early twentieth century, the American Nurses Association (ANA) stood firmly behind its vision of the discipline as a profession and its practitioners as professionals.

By contrast, practicing clinical nurses were somewhat more receptive to the idea of unions. During the 1920s and 1930s more and more nurses left the private-duty labor market to work in hospitals. They found the rhetoric of professionalization did not forward their struggle to control both the quality and the conditions of their day-to-day work. Gradually the idea of unionization made inroads among some hospitals' nursing staffs and helped nurses to secure contracts that improved wages and hours worked.

In the early 1940s state nurses' associations, frustrated by the ANA's opposition to formal organizing, began their own collective bargaining units. Finally, in 1946, the ANA formally sanctioned the idea of "professional" collective bargaining by its constituent state nurses' associations.

By the late 1960s the trade union movement had again resurfaced as a strategy for professional autonomy and economic security. Unions such as Local 1199 of the Hospital Workers Union reorganized to allow nurses separate guilds; and strikes, although deeply regretted, were no longer unthinkable tactics. Still, unionism remains only one of several options to ensure nurses' control over their practice. For nursing always has and always will need diverse organizing alternatives, whether through unions or specialized practice associations.

• PATRICIA D'ANTONIO

SEE ALSO Nursing Profession.

Service Employees International Union

The Service Employees International Union (SEIU) is unusual because it has always included some women among its ranks. Only in the 1960s, however, after SEIU began aggressively organizing public employees—many of whom were women—did women form a substantial portion of the union's membership. This influx of women recast the union into an important force on behalf of female workers.

SEIU began as the Building Service Employees International Union (BSEIU), which was chartered by the American Federation of Labor in 1921. It consisted largely of Chicago "flat janitors," building service workers who lived for free in the basements of the apartment buildings where they worked. Mostly immigrants and African Americans, flat janitors and other building service employees, such as office janitors, elevator operators, and window washers, were among the worst-treated workers, and BSEIU sought to represent them all.

Some of these workers were women. Among the BSEIU's seven founding locals was the Chicago School Janitresses, begun by Elizabeth Grady, who became the union's trustee. As a result, BSEIU can rightfully claim to be the first union to organize public employees.

Throughout the early decades, women were a minority in BSEIU, often organized in separate locals and barely represented among the union's leadership. But they were included in strike activities and their cases were pleaded at bargaining time. In the mid-1930s, New York's Local 32B launched huge strikes that resulted in pay increases for building service workers, including cleaning women.

During World War II, BSEIU janitors successfully fought against unequal pay for women janitors who performed the same work as men.

Although BSEIU did not set out in the 1960s to organize women per se, women became more prominent in the union when BSEIU stepped up its efforts to organize public employees, adding to its groundbreaking organization of health care workers. In 1968, the union dropped the word "building" from its name in recognition of the fastest-growing sector of the union, public workers. Despite the lack of a conscious strategy to fight for women workers, women employees benefited from the union's actions. In 1974, for example, SEIU won protection for nonprofit hospital workers, many of whom were women.

The increase in female participation in the union and the resurgence of the feminist movement transformed SEIU into a service-sector union with a special concern for women's issues. Women were targeted for organization just because they were women and SEIU activists joined in major fights for women's equality. In 1974, SEIU helped found the Coalition of Labor Union Women, an advocacy group for women unionists. The following year, SEIU chartered 9 to 5, an independent organization for working women. Together, SEIU and 9 to 5 started District 925, a nationwide local aimed at organizing clerical workers across the country. The structure of the new union was innovative as well; it was part of SEIU, but it was staffed by 9 to 5 members and had some autonomy. It was to be a union "for women and by women," in the words of SEIU president John Sweeney. In the 1990s, SEIU continued to organize nonunion women, focusing on home health care workers. By this time women made up a near majority of SEIU's one million members and were well-represented among the national leadership.

▪ ANNE KORNHAUSER

SEE ALSO Labor Unions: Nine to Five (District 925 of SEIU).

United Auto Workers (UAW)

Since its inception in 1936, the United Automobile, Aerospace, and Agricultural Implement Workers of America (UAW) has enjoyed a reputation as one of the most liberal and egalitarian labor organizations in the United States. Women historically have composed only a small proportion of the labor force in the automotive and aerospace industries—about 15 percent of UAW membership, except during World War II. Union efforts by and for women, however, have long been hallmarks of UAW's history. UAW's Women's Department, established in 1944, was the first of its kind. UAW began in the 1940s to compile a respectable record of collective bargaining in the interest of gender equity and has strongly supported federal legislation to eliminate sex discrimination in employment. Two UAW leaders were founders of the National Organization for Women, and Olga Madar, the first female vice president of the UAW, served as the first president of the Coalition of Labor Union Women. In 1970 UAW became the first U.S. union to endorse the Equal Rights Amendment. To diversify its membership and improve its prospects among predominantly female clerical workers, the UAW admitted District 65 as an affiliate in 1981 and gave it departmental status in 1987. Started in 1933 by dry-goods workers, District 65 has been a leader in organizing workers in technical, office, and professional fields. By integrating District 65 into its organization, UAW increased its strength and scope. The greater presence of women in the UAW has also prompted recent attention by the union to issues of sexual harassment and comparable worth.

▪ NANCY F. GABIN

United Cannery, Agricultural, Packing, and Allied Workers of America/Food, Tobacco, Agricultural, and Allied Workers of America (UCAPAWA/FTA)

Founded in 1937, UCAPAWA represented a model of democratic trade unionism and offered unprecedented opportunities for local leadership. The union made its greatest gains among Mexican cannery and African American tobacco workers. In 1939, led by veteran organizer and Communist Party activist Dorothy Ray Healey, over four hundred cannery operatives, the majority Mexican and Russian Jewish women, staged a successful strike at the California Sanitary Canning Company. Two years later, UCAPAWA's vice president, Luisa Moreno, expanded organizing campaigns throughout southern California. Los Angeles rank and file formed Local 3, the second-largest UCAPAWA affiliate. In 1943 twelve of the fifteen elected positions in Local 3 were held by women, eight by Mexicanas. They negotiated innovative benefits, such as a hospitalization plan, free legal advice, and at one plant, management-financed day care.

In 1944 UCAPAWA became the Food, Tobacco, Agricultural, and Allied Workers of America (FTA). In many respects, UCAPAWA/FTA was a woman's union. By 1946 66 percent of its contracts nationwide had equal pay for equal work clauses and 75 percent provided for leaves of absence without loss of seniority (e.g., maternity leave). Nationally, women held 44 percent of elected union posts in food-processing locals and 71 percent in tobacco units. After World War II, virulent red-baiting by rival unions, management, and politicians eviscerated the union. In 1950 UCAPAWA/FTA was one of ten unions expelled from the CIO for alleged Communist domination. UCAPAWA/FTA, however, has left a legacy of unwavering commitment to democratic trade unionism for people of color and for women.

• VICKI L. RUIZ

United Electrical Workers (UE)

The United Electrical, Radio and Machine Workers of America (UE), chartered by the Congress of Industrial Organizations (CIO) in 1936, drew its membership from machine and manufacturing workers in the electric light bulb, home-appliance, and automotive industries. Nearly 27 percent of electrical workers were women by 1940, but they were concentrated in the lowest-paying jobs and routinely made about half as much as men, who dominated the skilled and supervisory positions.

Influenced by the Communist Party, UE conducted a vigorous campaign to organize women and encourage them to lead union locals. Early UE contract agreements raised wages but continued to sanction different job and pay scales based on sex and to exclude married women from employment. During World War II, women entered new kinds of jobs and began to demand wages comparable to those of men. UE was one of the first large U.S. unions to advocate "equal pay for equal work," and in the late 1940s UE condemned the marriage bar and upheld women's rights to seniority and maternity leave. UE leadership attempted but failed to establish affirmative action policies to open more jobs to African Americans. Among the radical unions expelled from the CIO in 1949, UE lost many members to its rival, the more conservative International Union of Electrical Workers (IUE). It never regained its dominance in the electrical industry.

Still, UE pioneered feminist issues within the labor movement and produced an influential "Support Full Equality for Women" resolution at its 1979 convention, which endorsed reproductive rights, federally subsidized day care, the passage of ERA, and the national Coalition of Labor Union Women (CLUW). With a membership in 1994 of forty thousand, of whom about 35 percent are women, UE continues to advocate for what it calls rank-and-file unionism.

• SHARON HARTMAN STROM

United Farm Workers (UFW)

In 1962 in Delano, California, César Chávez, Delores Huerta, and Helen Chávez cofounded the Farm Workers Association, the precursor to the United Farm Workers Union (UFW). After nearly one hundred years of agrarian protests from Chinese, Japanese, Korean, Filipino, "Okie," and Mexican-heritage farm workers, postwar laborers mounted a sustained unionization drive.

Women and families were central to this grass-roots struggle for justice, dignity, equal wages, and a decent standard of living. Reflecting a gendered social activism, Mexican-heritage male workers joined strikes and picket lines for higher wages, while Mexicana and Chicana female workers supported strikes to improve opportunities for their children. Male laborers dominated ranch committees (union locals), but female union volunteers predominated in the campesino centers (social services offices). As men spoke at rallies, women cooked food for fundraisers. Entire farm-worker families moved from California to major cities across the nation to pursue the grape, lettuce, and Gallo boycotts, the UFW's nonviolent tactic to pressure growers to sign union contracts.

The boycotts of the late 1960s and 1970s were among the most successful cross-class and cross-cultural movements of the era. They united exploited Mexican-heritage, Filipino, Black, and white farm workers with middle-class supporters—religious groups, students, antiwar protesters, political and civil rights activists, labor unions, environmentalists, and consumer and women's organizations. Eventually, growers signed the historic 1970 grape contracts. In 1975 the Agricultural Labor Relations Act passed the first law to recognize the collective bargaining rights of farm workers in California. Farm laborers allied with female consumers distinguished this campaign from previous organizing attempts.

This movement brought together disparate groups and united Mexican-heritage peoples in support of their economic, social, and civil rights.

Experience in and exposure to the farm workers movement spurred parents and children to demand better educational opportunities and served as a training ground for many Mexican Americans to seek political empowerment and office.

- MARGARET ROSE

SEE ALSO Agriculture.

United Food and Commercial Workers International Union (UFCW)

The United Food and Commercial Workers Union (UFCW) has 1.4 million members in the United States and Canada. UFCW members, half of whom are women, work primarily in grocery stores, meat and food processing plants, department stores, and hospitals.

The UFCW maintains thirteen thousand collective bargaining agreements with employers that govern wages, working conditions, and workplace rights. All contracts guarantee equal pay for equal work, seniority rights, promotion opportunities, and dispute resolution procedures.

The UFCW was created in 1979 when the Retail Clerks (founded 1888) and Amalgamated Meat Cutters (founded 1897) merged. The Barbers and Cosmetologists, Boot and Shoe Workers, Packinghouse Workers, Fur and Leather Workers, National Agricultural Workers, Insurance Workers—and even Sheep Shearers—are among the unions that had previously merged into the Clerks and Meat Cutters. There were no exclusionary policies regarding women's membership in these unions, although some of the unions had few female members because of occupational segregation.

Women have influenced the union significantly and continue to shape policies as elected officials and through rank-and-file activism. Notable women include Mary Burke, elected first vice president, Retail Clerks (1888); Mary Anderson, Boot and Shoe Workers Union, named first head of the U.S. Labor Department's Women's Bureau (1920); and Addie Wyatt, first woman elected president of a Packinghouse Workers local union (1954), civil rights activist, and national officer.

The UFCW has six hundred local unions and supports an aggressive affirmative action policy that encourages women to seek leadership roles at all levels. The Women's Affairs Department educates members on sexual harassment, domestic violence, and other women's concerns. In 1988 the UFCW Women's Network was founded to assist local unions in political action, organizing, and community service activities.

> • SUSAN L. PHILLIPS

≋ Language and Power

Women have historically been excluded from participation in the communications of public institutions (e.g., universities, churches, medicine, government, and law). As a result, the forms of language found in the discourse of public institutions tend to be extreme versions of male communicative patterns.

Women and men engage in private communication for different reasons. Men tend to see communication as extrinsically useful for problem solving, while women see it as intrinsically valuable. Additionally, women and men come into conversations with differing amounts of power. Often men interpret conversational interactions in terms of hierarchy and competition, while women view their roles collaboratively. And finally, people enter conversations with stereotypes of how women and men typically engage in conversation. These implicit assumptions might become problematic in a scenario such as the following (loosely adapted from Deborah Tannen's *You Just Don't Understand*):

A woman tells her male partner of a disagreement with her boss at work, in the hope of getting sympathy from him ("Yeah, your boss is a jerk") and thus achieving solidarity in one relationship where it has failed in the other. But the man sees her story as a request for advice from someone wiser and more experienced in the ways of the outside world (that is, he perceives the situation hierarchically whereas she sees it as a move toward collaboration). She is hurt, feeling both put down and separated. She thinks: "Just like a man not to be caring!" He thinks, "Just like a woman to get hysterical over nothing!" Thus, the stereotypes about the communicative patterns of the opposite sex that each partner assumes play into their misinterpretations of each other's meanings and intentions.

These differences create divergences in male and female communication. Women seem more tentative, asking open-ended questions, and using hedges ("I guess" "maybe"), which to men suggest indecisiveness or illogic, but are intended to encourage the participation of others. Women find it easier to ask directions of strangers, as they are less apt than men to see this action as putting them in a "one-down" position.

In informal conversation, power tends to be associated with "holding the floor" and choosing a successful topic. In mixed-gender groups, men tend to have more and longer conversational turns than women. Many studies have found that men interrupt women more than women do men, for reasons that are unclear. The suggestion that women "invite" interruption is not empirically supported.

The habits of the private sphere transfer into the public. Men's private language becomes public discourse. Both are nonemotional, formal, hierarchical, and dependent on the verbal channel (versus gestures or vocal inflection) to carry meaning. Until recently, women entering public discourse could either learn men's speech patterns or risk not being taken seriously. But even when women become adept at public discourse, they

La Raza members in Houston during the 1972 presidential elections.

are not unequivocally rewarded. Often their competence in male speech is interpreted as "aggressive" or unfeminine.

School is the first public institution in which most people participate, and the message of the educational system about who may participate actively in communication carries over into later public encounters. Women are communicatively disadvantaged throughout their educational careers.

Despite these difficulties, women continue to work toward public communicative equality. Many professions, such as law and medicine, are increasingly aware of the ways in which they have excluded both women themselves and women's styles of communicating, and they are making changes. In business, women's communicative strategies (listening to the interlocutor; asking for suggestions) have proven effective. In medicine, both the form and content of women's communications (as doctor and patient) are being taken more seriously.

As women continue to gain in influence and numbers in public institutions, their styles will increasingly be integrated with traditional male patterns.

■ ROBIN TOLMACH LAKOFF

SEE ALSO Public Speaking.

≋ La Raza

The National Council of La Raza (NCLR) is one of the leading national Latino/a civil rights organizations in the country. The Council engages in policy analysis and advocacy for Latinos/as on national issues such as education, housing, immigration, and free trade. The Council also provides technical assistance and support to nearly 200 community-based affiliate organizations in the United States. Established in 1968,

the Southwest Council of La Raza, as it was originally called, promoted community development
projects in Mexican American barrios across the
Southwest. Today the Council serves Latinos/as
from all nationality groups in all regions of the
country.

Women have played important roles in the
Council's development, but their initial inclusion
in the Council involved a political struggle. In
1968, the original board of directors included only
one woman among its twenty-five members. At
the same time, only one of the Council's seven affiliate organizations was headed by a woman.
Three years later, only three women served on the
twenty-six member board.

The few but outspoken women in the Council
pushed for what became a controversial but ultimately successful cause: equal representation of
women and men on the board. They adopted this
policy in 1973 and it is still in effect. In the late
1970s, the first woman was elected chair of the
board of directors. Since that time, three of six
board chairpersons have been women.

NCLR's 1996 staff roster shows women to be
well represented throughout the organization's
corporate structure. Women in the Council have
called for increasing attention to women's concerns. As a result, NCLR has sponsored workshops on Latina empowerment at its annual conferences and in 1995 issued its first publication on
the status of Latinas. No doubt future changes are
ahead for the NCLR as women exert their influence in executive and policy-making positions
within the organization.

• CHRISTINE MARIE SIERRA

≋ Latina/Chicana Migration

From Chilean and Sonoran women migrating
between mining camps during the California
gold rush, to Mexicana farm workers crisscrossing
the country harvesting crops, to Puerto Rican garment workers traveling between New York City
and San Juan, Latinas responded to political and
economic conquest by moving. The confiscation
of the northern half of Mexico by the United
States following the Mexican War of 1846–48
transformed and degraded the political, social,
and economic status of Mexican women who remained in the region and became subject to U.S.
law. The 1848 discovery of gold in California drew
some Mexican women to the mining camps.
Women from the Mexican state of Sonora and
from as far away as Chile also joined the rush to
seek their fortune as sex workers, cooks, laundresses, and gambling house operators. When the
mining boom ended, many of these women migrated throughout the region in search of work,
while others returned to their homeland.

Meanwhile, Mexican women and men in the
former northern frontier of Mexico lost millions
of acres of land to Anglos in a few decades. Deprived of enough land to subsist, many entered
the wage labor force as seasonal workers. Although men dominated the migrant work force in
the second half of the nineteenth century, women
too left their homes in search of work. Migration
altered social and familial relations, while post-
poning ethnic Mexicans' complete dependence
upon wage labor: families could send away young
men and women to earn wages to supplement
farming, ranching, and shepherding, allowing
them to hang on to what was left of their land.

Puerto Rican and Cuban women and men
joined the migrant work force in the United States
as a consequence of U.S. imperial expansion into
the Caribbean in the 1890s. Millions of Puerto Ricans lost their land, and many migrated from
countryside to urban areas and from Puerto Rico
to the United States in search of wage labor. U.S.
employers transported thousands to the Northeast, the Midwest, and Hawaii in the early twentieth century. Following a similar pattern, most
Cuban workers migrated to Florida.

Latinas of this era worked for low wages on a
seasonal basis in sweatshops and tobacco factories

and on farms. They also labored in laundries and as domestic workers in the houses of mostly white, middle-class women. Latina workers responded to their status as cultural outsiders and to low wages and harsh conditions by organizing *mutualistas*, mutual aid societies, which provided them with death benefits, as well as an organizational base for a variety of activist projects, including educational reform and labor unions.

Central and South American immigrant women, who came in large numbers in the 1980s and 1990s to escape political oppression, joined a Latina labor force characterized by low wages and seasonal employment. Yet, some second- and later-generation Latinas have avoided migrant labor and moved into the primary labor market, along with numerous Latina immigrants who migrated in order to escape land-reform policies of revolutionary governments in Cuba and Nicaragua. Nevertheless, the pattern of low-wage labor and seasonal migration that developed in the late nineteenth and early twentieth centuries has continued to characterize the working lives of most Latinas in the United States.

• CAMILLE GUERIN-GONZALES

SEE ALSO Chicanas and Mexican American Women; Immigration; Latinas.

LATINAS

For more on the history of Latinas in the United States, see the following entries:

El Barrio
Chicana Civil Rights Organizations
Chicanas and Mexican American Women
Community Service Organization
El Congreso de Pueblos de Habla Española
Feminism, Chicana
Feminism, Latina
Feminism, Puerto Rican
La Raza
Latina/Chicana Migration
League of United Latin American Citizens
Lesbians, Latina
Maquiladora
Mujeres Activas en Letras y Cambio Social (MALCS)
Newyorican Women
Puerto Rican Women
Witchcraft on the Spanish-American Borderlands

≋ Latinas

From the East Coast to the West Coast, being Latina means coming from the racially mixed populations of North America, the Caribbean, Central America, and South America. That is, Latinas are a product of the cultures that unevenly combined as a result of the Iberian colonization of indigenous and African populations. This mixture suggests a racial designation different from—and much narrower than—merely having a Spanish surname. The latter is what the U.S. Bureau of the Census *officially* terms "Hispanic." Significant demarcations, painful historical realities, and persistent racial inequalities are glossed over when European and European American women are included with Latinas or "hispanas" (from *hispanoparlante*, or Spanish speaker) under the sanitized and deceptively simple rubric of "Hispanic." Latinas come in different races, classes, sexual identities, ages, levels of education, and nationalities.

Despite differences in specific origin, social position, and perception, racial mixture denotes a fundamental characteristic that historically has defined U.S. Latinas, that is, the common identity, burden, and condition of being racially oppressed women. Any claims to a European heritage and identity remain suspect for Latina women, no matter how fair their skin, how Castillian their Spanish, or how "American" their English. It is one of the ever present contradictions in how the national-cultural identity intersects with gender identity.

This tension not only unfolds against Latinas, oppressing them by constituting the group as racially subordinate women. It can also be mobilized in their favor as one of the ways to come together as Latina women, and as women of color—by structuring specific collective identities that will help them resist both racial domination and gender subordination. As women of color, Latinas share the common condition of racism, which brings together all women of Latin American and Caribbean descent, along with African American, Native American, and Asian American women in the United States. However, merely sharing the condition of oppression does not, in and of itself, guarantee the political consciousness of promoting common resistance, unity, and cooperation. This is evident in terms of racial categories, social classes, sexual identities, levels of education, political ideologies, age, physical ability, motherhood status, and/or national background and citizenship.

Such differences partially stem from how these populations were incorporated within U.S. control. Being occupied as part of mid-nineteenth-century land-grabs to secure the Pacific coast of North America (Tejanos, Californios, and Hispanos from Nuevo México after the Mexican War) was not the same as being occupied as part of turn-of-the-century land-grabs to secure the Panama Canal project (Puerto Ricans and Cubans after the Spanish-American War). After 1847 the United States territorially absorbed significant portions of Mexico's old rural aristocracy and middle classes and, since the 1940s, opened its doors to their Cuban counterparts. In contrast, the U.S. mainland has attracted mainly poor and unemployed Puerto Ricans.

Some Latinas arrived on U.S. shores to work as domestic servants, as field hands, and/or as cheap "sweatshop" laborers (Mexicans, Puerto Ricans, Dominicans, and Central Americans from the 1890s to the present). Others came as professionals and middle-class entrepreneurs (most Cubans before the Mariel exodus). Chicanas/Chicanos and Puerto Ricans (since 1917) are the only groups of Latin American descent under U.S. jurisdiction whose entire populations automatically are recognized as U.S. citizens.

Most U.S. Latinas/Latinos share a history of invasions and military occupation, the vagaries and needs of U.S. markets, and interimperial rivalries—with women among the most vulnerable to social and demographic dislocations. Perhaps for these same reasons, such women also have been in the forefront of struggles for political democracy and economic justice within U.S. jurisdiction and in the rest of the Americas.

According to the U.S. Bureau of the Census, the poverty levels of the Latina/Latino families in this country have been invariably higher than most of the U.S. population except for African Americans, who, as a group, are slightly poorer than Latinos. In 1974, for example, 10.5 percent of the entire population in this country lived below poverty level; specifically, 8.2 percent of whites, 28.6 percent of Blacks, and 21.9 percent of Latinas/Latinos. By 1992 11.7 percent of all U.S. families were below the poverty level: 8.9 percent of whites, 30.9 percent of Blacks, and 26.2 percent of Latinas/Latinos.

Further analysis of the "Hispanic" category by ethnic origin reveals stark contrasts among the people who are lumped together in this fashion. For the past three decades the largest groups are Mexican Americans (about two-thirds), Puerto Ricans (8 to 11 percent), and Cubans (4 to 5 percent). In a 1981 study spanning the 1950–80 period, Marta Tienda and others found that Puerto Ricans who had come to the U.S. mainland between 1950 and 1969 were not better off than those who had arrived during the 1970s. Cubans who had migrated to the United States between 1965 and 1970 had incomes that were 17 percent higher than those Cubans migrating between 1970 and 1979, while those who left for the United States between 1960 and 1965 had income levels that were 33 percent higher.

The disparities among income levels and, hence, among the various characteristics of each migration and the corresponding postwar Latina/

Latino populations, were later confirmed by the U.S. Bureau of the Census. In a 1990 study, this agency discovered that although U.S. Mexican and Puerto Rican families had similar average income levels, Puerto Ricans had the lowest incomes within the entire Latina/Latino population. The report indicated that Puerto Rican families in the United States had poverty levels comparable to those of African Americans (29 percent of all U.S. Puerto Rican families have incomes below $10,000), whereas Cubans had the largest ratio of families (25 percent) with incomes of $50,000 or more.

Historically, as in the present, the majority of Latina mothers have not fared very well. Latina-headed households constitute the demographic categories with the greatest economic need and the lowest income. During the past decade, Latina women under the age of eighteen have tended to be more than four times as likely to have children as are white women, and twice as likely as Black women. For this same period, the number of Latina female-headed households has increased twice as much as the number of Black and white female-headed households. Several studies have established that the percentage of female-headed households within the two largest Latina categories (U.S. Mexicans and Puerto Ricans) has been consistently rising over the past three decades. For Mexican American families headed by females, these figures changed from 11.9 percent in 1960 and 13.4 percent in 1970 to 19 percent in 1989. Puerto Rican families headed by females increased even more dramatically: from 15.3 percent in 1960 and 24.1 percent in 1970 to 39.6 percent in 1989.

Other indicators of the deteriorating economic conditions affecting most U.S. Latinas are the interrelated proportions of labor participation, occupational access, and education levels. A 1981 study by Marta Tienda and others reported that the labor participation rates of Mexican American and Puerto Rican females (legally employed and/or registered as searching for employment) were consistently at least 20 percent below those of

Mexican and Puerto Rican males between 1970 and 1992. During the past decade, the position of Latinas within the job hierarchy has not changed meaningfully vis-à-vis the general U.S. female population. For instance, in 1983, women of all races constituted 40.9 percent of the managerial and professional occupations, 2.6 percent of whom were Latinas; whereas, in 1992, women in general made up 47.3 percent of such occupations, 3.9 percent of whom were Latinas. As recently as 1992, only 10 percent of Latinas between the ages of twenty-five and thirty-four had attended four-year-plus colleges, as compared to 24 percent of white women of the same age group.

There is a third aspect that is usually avoided when constructing a profile of U.S. Latinas, namely, sexual identity, including the ways in which their individual and collective identities—desire, affection, and sensuality—have been historically and culturally constructed, as well as the institutionalization of compulsory heterosexuality. Latina sexual identities can bring women together as Latinas but also tear them apart. This issue needs to be discussed, problematized, and studied further to promote the emancipation of women of color.

Latina lesbians are among the most sexually oppressed, but they are still Latina. Since these forms of sexual oppression are predicated on the basis of socially enforced anonymity, there is a dearth of data on this matter. Nevertheless, some Latina lesbians have been in the forefront of much of the reconceptualization and problematization of identity politics within the struggles against sexism, racism, and colonialism in this country (e.g., Gloria Anzaldúa).

Latina lesbians have taken a leading role in building bridges across national-cultural lines among women of color regarding scholarship and literary production. Here the role of women such as Cherríe Moraga, who helped to form the Kitchen Table: Women of Color Press, is important as is her role in putting together, with Gloria Anzaldúa, one of the first anthologies of writings by women of color, *This Bridge Called My Back,* published in 1981. Another recent example of this kind of work is the 1990 anthology *Making Face, Making Soul, Haciendo Caras,* edited by Gloria Anzaldúa. These women have contributed significantly to rethinking and critiquing the historically and still hegemonically white/Anglo foundations of what is popularly known as the "women's movement" in the United States.

During the past decade, Latinas have organized around issues such as homelessness, AIDS, domestic violence, popular education, improving working conditions for farm workers, child care, gay and lesbian rights, and feminism. Some examples of organizations in which this work has been carried out are the Escuela Popular Norteña, the Center for Immigrant Rights, the Centro para el desarrollo de la mujer dominicana, and Mujeres Activas en Letras y Cambio Social.

A number of Latinas have risen to prominence within these groups. María Lugones, Argentinean, became an important activist and cofounded the Escuela Popular Norteña. A founder and principal leader of the most important radical, Puerto Rican community-based organization, the Young Lords Party (during the late 1960s and early 1970s), was Denise Oliver, who is now a writer and social activist.

Clara Rodriguez et al., *The Puerto Rican Struggle* (New York: Puerto Rican Migration Research Consortium, Inc., 1980); Marta Tienda et al., *Hispanic Origin Workers in the U.S. Labor Market* (Washington, D.C.: Employment and Training Administration, U.S. Department of Labor, 1981).

■ GLADYS M. JIMÉNEZ-MUÑOZ

≋ Latter-Day Saints

SEE Mormons.

≋ Lavender Menace

The "Lavender Menace" was coined in 1969 by members of the National Organization for Women (NOW) to describe what they felt was a public relations threat to the emerging women's movement: lesbians. Betty Friedan may have uttered "lavender menace" first although she may not wish to take credit for it.

Purged from NOW and banned from other feminist groups, lesbians by 1970 also understood that gay men didn't want them in their groups either. Deciding to use the term as a source of pride rather than a badge of shame, lesbians wore lavender T-shirts emblazoned with "Lavender Menace" across the chest to the Second Congress to Unite Women held in New York City in 1970.

Filling the aisles and the stage, they spoke of their negative experiences with their straight sisters. This simple act of telling the truth as opposed to pointing the finger was one of the pivotal moments in the feminist movement. Women began to realize that they could not claim exclusion and mistreatment from men and then turn around and hand out the same to other women.

■ RITA MAE BROWN

≋ Lawyers

In 1869 Arabella Mansfield was admitted to the Iowa state bar, becoming the first woman in U.S. history to gain admission to practice law. In 1873 the Supreme Court declared women unfit for the law but naturally suited for the home.

Between 1869 and 1872 white women were rejected from a number of elite law schools. Yet, in 1870 Ada Kepley graduated from Union College of Law (later Northwestern) to become the first woman to earn a law degree in the United States.

White women were also admitted to the University of Iowa, University of Michigan, and Boston University. African American women, as well as white women, could study at Howard University in Washington, D.C., where, in 1872, Charlotte Ray became the first African American woman to graduate from law school.

Throughout the nineteenth century and well into the twentieth, women were a distinct minority at sexually integrated law schools. Only seventeen women and over nine hundred men graduated from Boston University in the late nineteenth century, while, as late as 1910, barely forty women had graduated from the University of Michigan among thousands of men. To overcome their isolation and loneliness, six white female students and graduates of the law school at Michigan organized the Equity Club in 1887, a correspondence club open to all women lawyers and law students in the country and the first national organization of women lawyers in U.S. history. Though the Equity Club had only thirty-two members and lasted just four years, its members identified the professional issues for women lawyers of their era.

For the Equity Club members the dilemma of balancing the notion of "femininity" with their new professional identity shaped every aspect of their lives, including whether to practice in the courtroom with men or remain in the privacy of an office, how to dress, and whether working for profit was "ladylike." The tension between femininity and professional identity also affected women lawyers' personal lives as they struggled with the question of whether to marry and, if so, how to balance work and family.

By 1920 the legal profession was significantly more open to women. Every state bar and most law schools admitted women. Two women's law schools, Washington College of Law (1898) and Portia Law School (1907), provided legal education to immigrant, working-class, and middle-class women.

In the 1920s a number of African American women attended some of the most elite law schools in the country, gained admission to state bars, and practiced law nationwide. During this era Jane Bolin was the first African American woman to graduate from Yale Law School, in 1931, and became the first African American woman judge in the country. However, by 1940 only thirty-nine African American women were lawyers, compared with 4,146 white women lawyers.

Women gained admission into the American Bar Association in 1917 and joined all areas of legal practice, including the courts, especially the newly founded juvenile courts. Some women lawyers, such as Florence Allen, appointed in 1934 as the first woman judge on the United States Court of Appeals, and Mabel Walker Willebrandt, assistant United States attorney general in the 1920s, surpassed the accomplishments of all but the most successful male attorneys.

At the same time, women lawyers still encountered severe sexual discrimination following graduation from law school. Elite corporate and financial institutions were closed to them. Many went into general office practice, focusing on domestic relations and real estate. Often they tried solo practice or found positions in banks, real estate offices, and insurance agencies. Some considered themselves lucky if they found a job as a stenographer, while others were unable to find legal work at all. Women lawyers continued to find the task of balancing work and family extremely challenging. Solidly in place by 1920, this profile of women lawyers remained unchanged for the next fifty years and confronted a new generation of women lawyers in the 1970s.

Virginia G. Drachman, *Women Lawyers and the Origins of Professional Identity in America: The Letters of the Equity Club, 1887 to 1890* (Ann Arbor: University of Michigan Press, 1993); Cynthia Fuchs Epstein, *Women in Law* (New York: Basic Books, 1981); Karen Berger Morello, *The Invisible Bar: The Woman Lawyer in America: 1638 to the Present* (New York: Random House, 1986).

▪ VIRGINIA G. DRACHMAN

≋ League of United Latin American Citizens (LULAC)

The League of United Latin American Citizens (LULAC) was the first national Mexican American civil rights organization, founded in 1929. Cuban Americans, Puertorriqueños, and Filipinos joined in the 1980s and 1990s. Since 1929 LULAC has been a major desegregationist force in southwestern and midwestern schools, public housing, and employment.

Ladies' LULAC chapters were founded in 1933. By 1940 more than twenty ladies' chapters existed in Texas and New Mexico. Before 1965 LULAC women were typically Mexican Americans, U.S. citizens, middle class, and often worked as teachers or clerks. Some single women and widows belonged.

Women founded Junior LULAC (youth chapters) in the 1930s, a protective service program for the elderly, and the LULAC Information and Referral Center. They helped Mexican immigrants and the poor and sold poll taxes, registered voters, raised funds, organized women's leadership conferences, sponsored *LULAC News*, and fought for social change.

LULAC women have experienced sexism and heterosexism. In the 1930s Alice Dickerson Montemayor of Laredo, Texas, condemned sexism in her writings in *LULAC News*. From the 1960s to the 1980s men formed voting blocs to prevent the election of women to LULAC offices. Although LULAC does not officially exclude lesbians and gay men, like much of U.S. and Latino society, LULAC is homophobic.

Women were barred from Texas state directorship until 1969 because of a male bloc vote. Dolores Adame Guerrerro, Rosa Rosales, and Angie García served as the only Texas state directors, in 1969, 1990, and 1995. In 1994 feminist Belen Robles was elected national president.

■ CYNTHIA E. OROZCO

≋ League of Women Voters

The League of Women Voters (LWV) of the United States was founded in 1919 as the National League of Women Voters, a successor organization to the National American Woman Suffrage Association. The LWV had dual goals of preparing enfranchised women for their new responsibilities and of working for social legislation that suffragists had long supported. The first goal was called "Voters Service," still one of the principal activities of LWV's local and state branches. Voters Service disseminates nonpartisan information to help citizens make up their minds about candidates or issues and sponsors public forums in which candidates can present themselves to voters. The goal of supporting legislation has also continued to shape the league's activities; its members have taken stands on local, state, and national issues ranging from sewage systems to international peace.

The LWV has never been a mass organization. Its membership reached one hundred fifty thousand in the years just after the Second World War, and there are now fewer than one hundred thousand members nationwide. On May 6, 1974, the biennial convention voted to change the bylaws to permit men to join the league. Its influence has been much greater than its numbers would suggest. In many communities the league is the most trusted source for objective data on voter registration, candidates' views, and on the structure of local government. Nationally, LWV has been chosen to sponsor presidential debates. Two defining characteristics of the league have been its constant emphasis, from the beginning, on research as a basis for action and its effort to develop policy positions from the grassroots level rather than imposing them from the top.

The structure of local, state, and national boards permits a variety of adaptations to fit local and regional conditions. The national office provides information and guidance to local and state leagues, but in the end these groups make their own choices about where to focus their energies.

Over the years the league has remained principally a white, middle-class organization. Repeated efforts to broaden the membership to include working-class women and women of color have not had much success. Since the 1950s membership has been racially integrated; early conflicts over integration in southern leagues faded during the civil rights movement. Like most women's voluntary associations the league has changed with changing times. In its first four decades its white, middle-class members were not working for pay and formed the backbone of its leadership. In recent years more white, middle-class women are becoming professionals in the work force, and the changing nature of "women's issues" has forced the league to rethink issues of program and structure. The league has managed to adapt to social and political change and to fill a niche in many communities not filled by any other group.

However, the future is not necessarily bright. It is difficult to find women with the time and ability to devote to the league's demanding work. Recently an excellent branch of the league in North Carolina had to shut down when no one was available to be president. And like nearly every other voluntary association with a national office, the league has become increasingly bureaucratic over the years. Despite these difficulties, the value of the league's local work will probably keep the organization active for many years.

• ANNE FIROR SCOTT

See also Suffrage Movement.

≋ Legal Status

From the Constitutional Founding to the late twentieth century, the legal status of women has been inferior to that of free men. Until the 1970s women constituted a distinct legal caste: laws subordinated women to men in the family, restricted women's access to public life, attached women's obligations to the domestic sphere, and denied women independent personhood.

Although all women have been legally inferior to free men throughout much of U.S. history, women's inequality has not been uniform. Even today, class and race inflect gender inequality. For example, middle-class white women fare better under rape laws than do women of color, and heterosexual women are recognized under family law while lesbians are not. During the first half of the nineteenth century, married women could not own property. However, not all women could even marry; enslaved women could not enter legally recognized marriages—they also could not own property because they were themselves property. Nor were the marriages of all free women honored under law: into the 1950s, most states prohibited marriages between whites and non-Caucasians; sixteen states did so until 1967 (*Loving* v. *Virginia*). Meanwhile, under nativist immigration laws of the early twentieth century, U.S.-born women who married foreign nationals lost their citizenship. So did American women who married "aliens ineligible to citizenship"—a status inflicted on Asian immigrants until mid-twentieth-century naturalization reforms.

The original Constitution did not speak of women at all, leaving it to the states to prescribe and adjudicate gender relations. The states accumulated this power from the Tenth Amendment. Its "reserve clause" gave authority to the states over matters not specifically assigned to the federal government. The claim of "states' rights" flows from the Tenth Amendment, which also permitted states to order communities through property law (including slave law), family law, and criminal law, as well as through electoral law that deprived women of suffrage. Hence, women's specific legal disadvantages depended on where they resided. Only Native American women were excepted from the absolute rule of states' rights—

but only because their tribes were the objects of both federal and local terror and because their status was mediated by tribal governments and federal Indian laws.

Although gender-based laws varied across states, the English common law supplied many basic principles for civil codes. The most significant inheritance from the common law for women was the concept of *coverture*, in which married women were held to be represented in civil affairs by their husbands. Coverture assumed "spousal unity," meaning that legally, partners in marriage became united in the husband: wives could not execute wills, enter into contracts, or control their own wages.

During the 1830s and 1840s state legislatures began to chip away at the fiction of marital unity. Wives were permitted to be property holders in some states. However, especially in southern states, reformed property laws were not designed to give wives proprietary independence but rather to protect family property—especially slaves—from creditors. Reforms in northern states did give married women some redress but did not yield an inexorable flow of rights to women. Early victories remained incomplete and the federal government reinforced the subordination of women under state laws with constitutional principles. Late-nineteenth-century judicial interpretations of the Fourteenth and Fifteenth Amendments gave national legitimacy to women's inferior legal status.

The Fourteenth Amendment brought gender explicitly into the Constitution for the first time by specifically tying the number of *male* inhabitants to the apportionment of congressional districts in its enforcement clause. The Fourteenth Amendment also changed the constitutional arrangement, giving the federal government the power to prohibit state-level actions that violated equality, liberty, and due process principles. The federal government began to nationalize some rights and curtail states' control over social relations during the late nineteenth century. However, the rights singled out for protection by the

Supreme Court before the 1930s were the liberty and property rights of business rather than the equality and due process rights of persons. Moreover, the Court refused to extend Fourteenth Amendment rights to women.

The Fourteenth Amendment spoke of "persons" when it spoke of rights. So when she was barred from practicing law by the state of Illinois in 1869 because she was a woman, Myra Bradwell appealed to the Supreme Court to restore her vocational "privileges and immunities" of citizenship. The Court rejected her claim, holding that the states retained the authority to determine who could practice law. Still more damaging, a concurring opinion argued that women were "unfit" for many occupations, that they "properly" belonged in the domestic sphere, and that it was the right of states to regulate women's vocational choices (*Bradwell* v. *Illinois*, 1873).

The Fifteenth Amendment failed to extend the franchise to women, but it did not explicitly deny women the vote, either, for it guaranteed the right to vote to all *citizens*. Several suffragists attempted to exercise voting rights in the elections of 1872. Barred from voting by the state of Missouri, Virginia Minor took her case to the Supreme Court, which rejected her claim. The Court effectively formalized women's secondary status as the law of the land. Conceding that women are citizens, the Court argued that not all citizens have the right to vote. The Court explained that the suffrage question had been settled by state electoral laws depriving women of the ballot; notwithstanding the Fifteenth Amendment, national citizenship did not necessarily confer the right of suffrage, and states retained the power to withhold voting rights from women.

The Court's refusal to extend Fourteenth and Fifteenth Amendment rights to women anchored the prevailing "separate spheres" gender ideology in constitutional jurisprudence, reserved national citizenship for men, and fixed women's citizenship at the state level. The Court reasserted its view of women's different and lesser citizenship in

1908. *Muller* v. *Oregon* involved a state labor policy limiting the length of women's work day to ten hours. Defending the Oregon law, the Court reasoned that "the physical well-being of women" is "an object of public interest" and that woman "is properly placed in a class by herself." Validating Oregon's power to regulate women's working conditions in the name of motherhood, this decision subjected women to a separate system of labor law and reserved the fundamental, national contract rights announced by the Court three years earlier (*Lochner* v. *New York*) to men.

Women remained the wards of state governments for the next seventy years. Women did win one national right of citizenship with the Nineteenth Amendment, which granted them suffrage (1920). However, racial laws and practices in southern states deprived African American women of access to the ballot box.

Equally important, the Nineteenth Amendment theoretically conferred formal political citizenship on women, but it did not guarantee women formal political equality. For example, jury rights and obligations contained in the Sixth Amendment continued to be withheld from women in many states until 1976 (*Billy Taylor* v. *Louisiana*). As recently as 1961 the Supreme Court upheld a Florida statute exempting women from jury duty unless they explicitly volunteered (*Hoyt* v. *Florida*).

Federal deference to the states made onerous the work of improving women's legal status. Patriarchal biases had to be challenged on a state-by-state basis either through new legislation or through amendments to state constitutions. Even in states that improved women's legal status, women's citizenship would remain inferior to men's because it was still fixed at the state level. Only federal legislation and constitutional recognition could win full national legal equality for women.

Beginning with the Equal Pay Act of 1963, the federal government began to nationalize key rights for women. The most significant legislative initiative was the Civil Rights Act of 1964, which included in its employment provision a ban on sex discrimination targeted at the private sector. During the 1970s legislative initiatives ended many other private sector practices—in banking, credit, and housing—that limited women's participation in economic life. But these statutory changes did not resolve the problem of women's constitutional status, and therefore did not break the patriarchal control of state governments over women's lives.

Although the national government, too, is inscribed with patriarchal gender ideology, the equality clause of the Fourteenth Amendment suggested a means to combat the effects of that ideology. Once the Court revived the equal protection clause and deployed it against racist laws and practices beginning in the 1950s, feminists urged the Court to apply equality principles to women. This gave rise to two strategies: one, a revived Equal Rights Amendment, which would have added a gender equality guarantee to the Constitution; and the other, litigation based on the Fourteenth Amendment, which, if successful, would extend the equal protection clause to women. Either strategy would open the way to contesting the myriad state laws that treated women differently from men.

As the ERA movement mobilized to amend the Constitution during the 1970s, feminist lawyers —most notably future Supreme Court Justice Ruth Bader Ginsburg—brought cases before the Supreme Court claiming rights for women on equal protection grounds. Although the ERA was never ratified, litigation secured several pathbreaking decisions that reverberated across lower courts and legislatures to change many laws that harmed women. By the late 1970s the Court had announced new constitutional principles to bring gender discrimination by federal and state governments under equal protection scrutiny (*Reed* v. *Reed*, *Frontiero* v. *Richardson*, *Craig* v. *Boren*). As a result, for example, women can now manage estates and cannot be excluded from governmental jobs merely because they are women. Still, the Court has never read the Fourteenth Amendment to forbid all sex-based classifications. Meanwhile, state laws and practices continue to govern important aspects of women's lives, such as who may be sexually intimate, who may marry, and who may raise children, as well as whose rape "matters" and how it will be prosecuted.

The Court has often declined to find discrimination in laws it explains by "real differences" (linked to biology) rather than by stereotypes (based on social roles). It also has not understood that women experience inequality differently, sometimes uniquely, depending on race, culture, class, or sexuality. Generally, the Court notices discrimination only when it affects (or could affect) all women. Thus, it has been difficult to secure judicial redress for practices that harm distinct groups of women—Black women, Latinas, Asian women, and lesbians—who endure differential treatment based on stereotypes and biases against them as simultaneously raced, sexualized, and gendered people.

If Fourteenth Amendment litigation won constitutional standing for gender equality claims, that standing is precarious. Although even the conservative Court remains suspicious of laws that single out women for distinctive treatment because they are women, it is less suspicious of neutral practices that have unequal gender effects (*Personnel Administrator of Mass. v. Feeney*, 1979). The Court also refuses to see that if women's rights are to have real meaning, they must be available to all women. Hence, even though it now understands the connection between reproductive choices and gender equality (*Planned Parenthood of Southeastern Pa. v. Casey*, 1992), it sustains policies that restrict many women's exercise of those choices. For example, the Court upheld the Hyde Amendment's ban on most Medicaid financing for abortion (*Harris v. McRae*, 1980), sustained parental notification requirements (*Hodgson v. Minnesota*, 1990), and permitted waiting periods and mandatory counseling *(Casey)*.

Where the meaning of the Fourteenth Amendment is at issue, the Court has the last word. Neither Congress nor the president can direct the Court's interpretation of the Constitution. Nor, had the ERA prevailed, would it have yielded predictable and secure outcomes, as the Court would have adjudicated its meaning in relevant cases. Statutory innovations, although subject to judicial review, can give firmer guidance to the Court about how the legal aspects of gender relations should proceed. Well-defined legislation can rein in judicial discretion; Congress and the president can correct the judicial misapplication of statutes by amending them; and federal laws can counter the prerogatives of states. Thus, for example, the Congress enacted the Pregnancy Discrimination Act in 1978 to check the Court's unwillingness to extend to pregnant women workers the protection of employment discrimination law. So too did Congress amend the Civil Rights Act in 1991 to reverse the Court's erosion of antidiscrimination principles during the 1980s. Further, the Congress enacted the Violence Against Women Act of 1994, offering incentives to states to take rape and domestic violence and their effects more seriously. But just as the point of view of judges guides their decisions affecting women, the point of view of elected officials determines their willingness to legislate gender equality: a conservative Congress can undo many of the legislated improvements in women's legal status.

The 1970s supplied women with legal weapons to combat discrimination. So, even though women are still subordinated by the law and though the law still tolerates society's subordination of women, the law also now supplies tools for helping women.

Women's legal agenda remains full: reproductive choices—both to control and to enjoy fertility—are not available to all women; poor women and women of color are burdened by economic and welfare policies that deprive them of options, opportunities, and dignity; pregnant women are often subject to invasive scrutiny and regulation when they come into contact with criminal justice systems; raped or sexually harassed women are often not believed, especially when they are women of color; welfare laws intervene in women's intimate relationships, requiring recipients to identify their children's father; custody and adoption laws in most states measure a parent's fitness by her sexual orientation. We are each differently positioned in the law, but the promise of equality still commonly eludes us.

■ GWENDOLYN MINK

SEE ALSO Citizenship; Civil Rights Act of 1964; Constitution, Coverture, Equal Credit Opportunity Act; Equal Pay Act; Equal Rights Amendment (ERA); *Muller v. Oregon*; *Roe v. Wade*; Title VII.

≋ Legislature

SEE Congress.

≋ Lesbian Herstory Archives

The Lesbian Herstory Archives (LHA) was founded in New York City in 1974 and since 1993 is housed in a three-story townhouse in Brooklyn's Park Slope district. The LHA is part of a grassroots lesbian and gay history movement and was one of its earliest manifestations. The LHA is defined on its newsletter masthead as archives that exist "to gather and preserve records of lesbian lives and activities so that future generations of lesbians will have ready access to materials relevant to their lives. The process of gathering this material will also serve to uncover and collect our herstory. These materials will enable us to analyze and re-evaluate the Lesbian experience."

The LHA is the oldest and largest archives in the world dedicated to the history of lesbians. Co-founders Joan Nestle and Deborah Edel were joined by Judith Schwarz in 1978 who, along with a coordinating committee and countless volunteers, work to collect, maintain, and preserve over ten thousand books, twelve thousand photographs, two hundred special collections, fourteen hundred periodical titles, one thousand organizational and subject files, film, video, art and artifacts, musical scores, records and tapes, posters, T-shirts, buttons, and personal memorabilia. The LHA is a library and research center, museum, and cultural center. All women are welcome to use the collections at no charge, with the promise that the archives will never be sold or become a part of either a public or private mainstream institution. As Joan Nestle confirms on a videotape distributed to raise monies for the current building, "The Archives transform a people's secret into a people's herstory, which is for us a life-saving act of self-inheritance."

■ JANICE L. DEWEY

SEE ALSO Lesbians.

≋ Lesbianism

Throughout history some women have engaged in sexual acts with other women and/or desired other women, but only since the late nineteenth century have such women been categorized as a distinct type of person, a lesbian, by virtue of their sexual interests. The evidence suggests that emotional/sexual life has taken various forms in different periods of history and in different cultures. For example, in some societies women have erotic relationships with other women while living a married life with men. Such women are not labeled as lesbian or different. Their desire is accepted as part of the normal range of human intimacy. It is not easy to define who is a lesbian or what is lesbianism or to determine its etiology.

Whether there is a biological determinant to lesbianism is fiercely debated by scholars. Those who assume the constants in all historical manifestations of woman's desire for another woman, tracing them to biology or nature, are called essentialists, while those who see the dissimilarities in cultural forms of lesbianism and heterosexuality are called social constructionists. Like all debates between nature and nurture the two are not mutually exclusive.

Information on sex or desire between women in the colonial period of North America is scant. The traditions of Native American nations were attacked and disrupted by colonization and are being reclaimed by Native Americans in the late twentieth century. Paula Gunn Allen suggests that Native society had at least two types of relationships between women, neither of which was stigmatized. One was spirit-directed in the sense that a woman was summoned by the spirits to take on a male role. She also may have developed relationships with women; however, she was characterized as different not on the basis of her sexual relationships but on her spiritual powers. The other form of lesbianism grew out of the deep attachments that self-reliant women developed with one another. In many instances, such relationships did not interfere with heterosexual marriages.

Among European settlers, colonial court cases indicate that some women had sexual relations with other women. The evidence suggests that such women were not labeled as distinct kinds of people because of their sexual interests, but rather as sinners, along with all other sinners who could not control their appetites. Women's sexual relations with women were not classed as sodomy and therefore not punishable by death. The serious breach of conduct occurred in challenging women's appropriate role in marriage and procreation. Such transgression might, in the extreme, lead to a trial for heresy, which was a crime punishable by death.

Throughout U.S. history some women have passed as men, particularly to join the army. According to Jonathan Katz, in nineteenth-century United States an increasing number of women did so to improve their lives in a gender-polarized society that prevented women from adequately supporting themselves outside of marriage. Some "passing" women developed sexual and emotional intimacy with other women, and in a few cases they even married women. In no case did "passing" women see themselves as a distinct kind of person, nor did they congregate together. Many, such as Murray Hall, were not discovered to be women until their death. Some were discovered during their lifetime—Milton B. Matson, Cora Anderson—and were not criticized for being deviant sexually but for transgressing gender roles and taking on male privilege.

Intense romantic friendship developed between middle-class women in the homosocial environments created by the gendered division between home and work in the nineteenth century. Marriage did not disrupt these ties because husband and wife spent little time together. We know of these friendships from the passionate letters friends and family members wrote to one another as analyzed by the historian Caroll Smith-Rosenberg. In most cases female friends did not eschew marriage and live with one another. History shows that similar romantic friendships existed in Europe from the sixteenth century on. The prevalence of romantic friendship among women raises questions about what lesbianism is. Although these relationships were unquestionably intimate and erotic, were the romantic friendships genital as well? Do relationships have to be genital to be lesbian?

The period between 1880 and 1920 was one of significant transition in sexual relations in the United States. The early women's movement had made it possible for women to hold jobs and act autonomously. The developing consumer society promoted sexual pleasure and leisure to sell products and created a culture that separated sex from reproduction and valued the pursuit of sexual interests. Intellectuals of this period also made sex basic to their interpretive and artistic frameworks, as exemplified by Freud's claim that erotic interest was central to a person's being. At that time the cultural categories of heterosexuality and homosexuality were born in the United States, and soon came to name particular kinds of people according to their sexual dispositions.

In this context women's emotional/sexual lives were transformed. In large industrial centers, many European American working-class families "lost control" of their daughters' sexuality. After work and on weekends, working girls adorned themselves for fun in dance halls, movie houses, and amusement parks. Their social life created the prototype for twentieth-century heterosexual dating. Some bourgeois European American women also pursued sexual independence, aiming to form enduring, close, intimate sexual relationships with men. The popular image of this new woman was the flapper. Many of these sexually radical women were part of the bohemian movement in Greenwich Village, New York. Some of these "sex-radical" women continued the nineteenth-century tradition of friendships among women as well, while others, particularly in the 1920s, took on the designation of "bisexual" through entering physical relationships with women and men.

Certain "new women," as the European American bourgeois women were known, chose not to marry. They developed strong supportive communities of women defined by work, politics, or school. Their relationships with women were intensely passionate but not consciously sexual. Some women lived together for life in what were called Boston marriages. These independent women, such as Mary Woolley, president of Mt. Holyoke College, or Jane Addams, the famous settlement-house worker, did not label themselves and were not labeled by society as lesbian or deviant because of their emotional attachments with other women. They saw themselves as women who lived outside of marriage, not as women who had a different form of sexuality. Because of the stigmatization of lesbianism in the later twentieth century, biographers and historians have overlooked or in some cases even hidden these women's deep attachments to other women.

The lack of economic resources in the African American community as a result of slavery and Reconstruction, combined with white society's stigmatization of African American women as sexually loose, made marriage and moral character important to African American women at the turn of the century. They already carried the burden of proving the respectability of their race. Nevertheless bourgeois African American women who were respectably married also developed deep attachments to other women in the context of their civic work. Alice Dunbar-Nelson, for instance, recorded in her diary several significant romantic/erotic attachments with women with whom she worked in the Black Women's Club Movement.

Another manifestation of the "new woman" was the mannish lesbian, a woman who took on masculine attributes in part to break through the Victorian assumption of the sexless nature of women. She became the "modern" lesbian in that she identified herself as "different" because of her erotic, sexual interest in women. In literature she is immortalized by Stephen Gordon in Radcliffe Hall's *The Well of Loneliness*, and in the blues, by Lucille Bogan's "B.D. [bull dagger] Women Blues." The masculine lesbian was stigmatized as abnormal both by the medical profession and by popular culture. Her difference often led her to look for others like herself. She was key in building working-class lesbian communities in most racial/ethnic groups in the United States.

The meaning of lesbian and lesbianism has changed quite dramatically during the twentieth century. In the late nineteenth and early twentieth century the mark of a lesbian was gender inversion, that is, a woman who had male inclinations for dress and behavior and an interest in women. Feminine women of the time who were interested in "masculine" women were not considered lesbians. Gender was such a powerful determinant of behavior that they were considered normal by most sexologists because of their feminine attraction for a more masculine being, or in some cases they were defined as bisexual. In the first half of the twentieth century there was a gradual and uneven shift in the definition of lesbianism, from gender inversion to object choice, that is, to the idea that a homosexual is a person who is attracted to someone of the same sex. By the 1950s Kinsey's *Sexual Behavior in the Human Female* unequivocally assumed homosexuality to be a sexual relationship between people of the same sex.

Buoyed by a new understanding of women's oppression, lesbian feminists of the late 1970s attempted to redefine lesbianism. Their new definition emphasized passionate and loving connections over specifically sexual relationships and explicitly separated lesbian history from gay male history. Adrienne Rich established a "lesbian continuum" that included woman-identified resistance to patriarchal oppression throughout history. The lesbian, thus understood, transcends time periods and cultures in her common links to all women who have dared to affirm themselves as activists, warriors, or passionate friends. The place of sexuality in this construction was not specified.

In the 1980s a feminist, sex-radical position reemerged that validated sex as a source of pleasure as well as danger for women and identified sexuality as central to women's entrance into modernity. Those who have adopted this theory interpret the masculine lesbians of the turn of the century and the working-class butch-femme lesbians of the midcentury as key players in having shaped lesbian consciousness and identity, which eventually made lesbian feminism and gay liberation possible. In the late twentieth century some scholars and activists have taken this position to its extreme and linked women's sexual history completely with men's, categorizing lesbians, gay men, and all other outsiders to heterosexual norms as "queer." The study of lesbianism has yet to settle upon a single appropriate framework that acknowledges women's repression by male supremacy and at the same time recognizes women's agency in expanding and controlling their own lives.

Harry Abelove, Michele Aina Barale, and David M. Halperin, *The Lesbian and Gay Studies Reader* (New York: Routledge, 1993); Gloria Anzaldua, Borderlands, *La Frontera: The New Mestiza* (San Francisco: Spinster's/Aunt Lute, 1987); Martin Bauml Duberman, Martha Vicinus, and George Chauncey, *Hidden from History: Reclaiming the Gay and Lesbian Past* (New York: New American Library, 1989).

■ ELIZABETH LAPOVSKY KENNEDY

SEE ALSO Lesbians; Sexuality.

≋ Lesbian Organizations

The first lesbian organization in the United States, the Daughters of Bilitis (DOB), was founded in San Francisco in 1955 as an alternative to the multiracial, predominantly working-class world of the bars. The very existence of lesbian organizations depended on the growth of a lesbian subculture, which had taken root during the Second World War. DOB originated as a social group and developed into a primarily white and middle-class political organization devoted to winning acceptance within U.S. society. By sponsoring discussion groups, publishing a magazine, *The Ladder*, and supporting research on lesbians, DOB sought to show that what they called the "sex variant" was no different from anyone else except in the choice of a sex partner. DOB, like the mixed-gender but mostly male Mattachine Society, and ONE, Incorporated—the other major organizations that composed what was known as the homophile movement—took a cautious approach to political organizing. DOB was never able to mobilize large numbers of women in the hostile climate of the 1950s.

The resurgence of the women's movement and the flowering of the gay liberation movement in the late 1960s created a radically transformed context for lesbian organizations. Although DOB became increasingly feminist and responded to the new militance of the 1960s, by the 1970s white, middle-class lesbians flocked instead either to women's movement organizations, where they were welcome as women but often invisible as lesbians, or to the burgeoning gay movement, where they often found themselves subordinated to men and male interests. As a result lesbian feminist groups such as Radicalesbians and The Furies sprang up in the early 1970s to represent the interests of radical, militant, and young white lesbians.

These new lesbian organizations shared political perspectives and tactics with the radical or women's liberation branch of the women's movement and embraced consciousness raising and dramatic "zap actions" designed to expose practices oppressive to lesbians. In one of the most famous actions, lesbian participants in the 1970 Congress to Unite Women in New York reacted to National Organization for Women founder Betty Friedan's characterization of lesbianism as a "lavender menace" by taking over the stage, baring their Lavender Menace T-shirts, and articulating their demands that the women's movement affirm lesbians and accept the notion that "Women's Liberation is a lesbian plot." By this they meant that lesbianism, redefined as a political choice to be "woman-identified," was central to feminism.

As more women came out within the predominantly white radical branch of the women's movement, by the 1980s groups comprised primarily of lesbians formed in a variety of communities, including small towns with major colleges and universities. These local lesbian organizations included groups organized to support women coming out, to fight rape and domestic violence, to publish newspapers and books, to record and distribute women's music, to support women in recovery from substance abuse, to explore women's spirituality, and to run restaurants, coffee houses, and other women's businesses.

Groups such as the Lesbian Mothers National Defense Fund, founded in 1974, and the National Center for Lesbian Rights, which originated in 1977 as the Lesbian Rights Project, fought for basic civil rights for lesbians. The National Organization for Women, which had played such a crucial, if negative, role in the emergence of the early radical groups, became increasingly supportive of lesbian rights in the 1970s and by the 1990s had earned the designation of a "gay front group."

In different lesbian organizations, criticism of the dominance of white and middle-class individuals and values evolved with increasing urgency by the late 1970s. Sparked by criticism from women of color, working-class women, and Jewish women, primarily white, middle-class lesbian organizations attempted to confront their racist, elitist, and other exclusionary attitudes and practices. By recognizing the theoretical linkages among different forms of oppression, expanding "women's culture" beyond its original white and middle-class character, and addressing issues of access for women with disabilities, lesbian organizations struggled, not always successfully, to shed their own oppressive ideologies and procedures. At the same time, new organizations representing diverse constituencies formed, including the Combahee River Collective (1974), Senior Action in a Gay Environment (1977), the National Coalition of Black Lesbians and Gays (1978), African American Lesbian and Gay Alliance (1986), Education in a Disabled Gay Environment (1986), and the National Latino/a Lesbian and Gay Organization (1987).

In the 1980s and 1990s, the outbreak of AIDS and frustration over the conservative political tide gave birth to direct-action groups that engaged in what came to be known as "in-your-face" tactics. ACT-UP (AIDS Coalition to Unleash Power), founded in 1987, consists of largely autonomous local chapters that engage in "die-ins," in which members lie down in the streets to represent those who have died of AIDS, and other dramatic confrontations designed to call attention to the AIDS crisis. In 1990 members of New York's ACT-UP chapter formed Queer Nation; local Queer Nation groups staged "kiss-ins," plastered neighborhoods with confrontational stickers, and advocated a strategy of physical response to violence against lesbians and gay men, billed as "Queers Bash Back." Women members of the male-dominated ACT-UP and Queer Nation formed separate women's caucuses. Along the same lines, the Lesbian Avengers formed in New York in 1992 and committed themselves to "creative activism: loud, bold, sexy, silly, fierce, tasty and dramatic," according to their 1993 "Dyke Manifesto." In their first action, they marched into a Queens, N.Y., school and handed first graders lavender balloons inscribed with the words "Ask about Lesbian Lives" to protest the board's refusal to allow a multicultural curriculum that included discussion of lesbians and gay men. Lesbian Avengers groups quickly popped up around the world.

Through forty years of history, lesbian organizations have ranged from mainstream to radical, moderate to militant, national to local, general to special interest, and they have grown out of and worked in conjunction with both the women's movement and the gay and lesbian movement.

Alice Echols, *Daring to Be Bad: Radical Feminism in America 1967–1975* (Minneapolis: University of Minnesota Press, 1989); Lillian Faderman, *Odd Girls and Twilight Lovers: A History of Lesbian Life in Twentieth-Century America* (New York: Columbia University Press, 1991); Verta Taylor and Leila J. Rupp, "Women's Culture and Lesbian Feminist Activism: A Reconsideration of Cultural Feminism," *Signs: Journal of Women in Culture and Society* 19 (Autumn 1993): 32–61.

■ VERTA TAYLOR
and LEILA J. RUPP

SEE ALSO Gay, Lesbian, and Bisexual Organizations; Gay Women's Alternative; Lesbian Herstory Archives; National Center for Lesbian Rights.

≋ Lesbians

"**W**e are everywhere" was a popular slogan used by lesbians to boost pride and challenge invisibility at 1970s marches. Research has since confirmed that indeed lesbians are omnipresent in the twentieth-century United States. Women who had sexual relations with other women and/or had masculine interests and inclinations have been called lesbians or female homosexuals in the medical literature since the late nineteenth century; however, different class and ethnic/racial cultures also have developed their own terms: for example, *butch, fem, stud, gay girls, bull dagger, dyke, koskalaka, entendida, loca, marimacha*. Since, for most cultures, except Native American ones, women loving women was an anathema, many of these terms are derogatory. As part of the process of claiming power, lesbians have positively redefined many of these epithets.

In the early twentieth century, lesbian communities existed in the major metropolitan centers of Western culture, including New York, Chicago, Paris, and Berlin. These communities primarily formed around bars, salons, and/or house parties. For most of the twentieth century, bars were the only public places where lesbians could congregate. Stigmatized as degenerates, the women met in the seedier parts of towns, where other "sexual deviants" such as gay men and prostitutes (many of whom were lesbians) were also welcome.

Despite the difficulties, lesbians attained some visibility in U.S. culture. Expatriate U.S. writers and artists in Paris, such as Natalie Barney, Gertrude Stein, and Margaret Anderson, explored in their lives and art what it meant to be erotically attracted to women and began to develop a lesbian consciousness. During the Harlem Renaissance — 1920 to 1935 — Black artists and working-class Black lesbians and gay men socialized at house parties, speakeasies, drag balls, and entertainment clubs. The relative visibility of lesbians in Black culture at the time is indicated by references to them in popular blues songs.

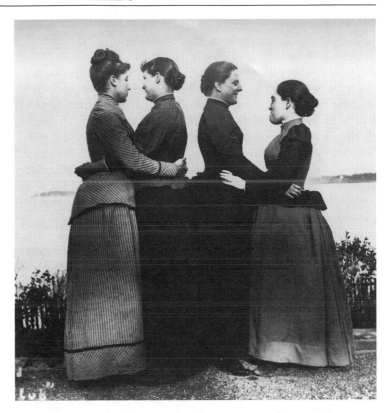

"The Darned Club," by lesbian photographer E. Alice Austen, October 29, 1891.

In the 1930s lesbians had less of a public presence than in the Roaring Twenties. Most lesbians lived private lives; however, they were no longer limited to metropolitan centers. Lesbians were now in small cities and towns throughout the country. In rural western New York a group of lesbian friends socialized together on weekends. In the world of women's sports during the 1930s, 1940s, and 1950s, lesbians formed hidden networks.

World War II had profound effects on lesbians. Increasing numbers risked socializing in bars and house parties, for a variety of reasons. First, more work was available to women, affording them more opportunities for independence. Second, the Women's Army Corps openly discussed the undesirability of lesbians in the armed services, making lesbians a common subject of conversa-

tion. Third, and by far the most important reason, was the absence of men on the home front, making it easier for women to socialize together in public. Risking exposure, lesbians in the bars and at house parties served as a beacon for those migrating to cities from rural America. But there were many others who continued to live discreetly. They could not take the risk of associating publicly with other lesbians because they anticipated negative repercussions at work, within the family, or in their neighborhoods.

The thriving public communities in bars and house parties were primarily working class and racially segregated. They were characterized by butch-fem culture in which the butch projected the masculine image of her particular time period—at least regarding dress and mannerisms—and the fem, the feminine image. Almost all members of the culture were exclusively one or the other. Although on the surface butch-fem roles appear to be simply an imitation of heterosexual roles, in fact they have been transformed by lesbians into a method for resisting oppression. Before the gay liberation movement, the only way that lesbians could announce themselves to the public was by a butch appearance, or by the butch-fem couple. Butch-fem roles not only shaped the lesbian image but also lesbian sexuality: the butch was the more active partner, the pleaser of the fem, and the fem was the more receptive partner.

Despite the McCarthy era witch-hunts of lesbians and gays, the 1950s was a pivotal time for emerging lesbian politics. The homophile movement began with the predominantly male Mattachine Society in 1951, and Del Martin and Phyllis Lyon founded the all-lesbian Daughters of Bilitis in 1955. Their primary concerns were to educate the public that lesbians and gays were no different from other people and to help homosexuals adjust to mainstream society. These groups specifically tried to dissociate themselves from bar culture. During the 1950s bar lesbians became more explicitly defiant; butches wore butch clothes in as many situations as possible and fought back when attacked. These acts of resistance, although very different from those advocated by the homophile movement, also challenged the repressive social order.

Throughout the twentieth century lesbian culture has manifested a national dimension as well as marked regional and ethnic/racial variations. There is remarkable similarity among bar cultures in cities such as New York, San Francisco, New Orleans, Denver, and Buffalo, and between homophile organizations in different cities as well. Yet at the same time there is unquestionably significant regional and ethnic/racial variation in lesbian culture. Lesbians of color document that the meaning of lesbianism and the way it is expressed vary from culture to culture. Their lesbianism can't be separated from their ethnic/racial identities and the ongoing reality of racism affects their experience of lesbianism. Southerners argue that

their lesbian culture is different from that of the Northeast or the West on the basis of religion, race, and the proportion of rural inhabitants.

During the 1960s lesbians increased their public presence either through participation in bar culture or in homophile organizations. Mythology has it that in June 1969, a butch lesbian started the Stonewall rebellion, the event that marks the beginning of the gay liberation movement, by swinging at the police. Lesbians have been active in all the gay liberation and lesbian feminist organizing that has followed.

Lillian Faderman, *Odd Girls and Twilight Lovers: A History of Lesbian Life in Twentieth-Century America* (New York: Columbia University Press, 1991); Elizabeth Lapovsky Kennedy and Madeline Davis, *Boots of Leather, Slippers of Gold: The History of Lesbian Community* (New York: Routledge, 1993); Barbara Smith, ed. *Home Girls: A Black Feminist Anthology* (New York: Kitchen Table/ Women of Color Press, 1983).

■ ELIZABETH LAPOVSKY KENNEDY

SEE ALSO Lesbianism; Lesbian Organizations; Marches, Lesbian and Gay.

Asian American Lesbians

The 1987 March on Washington for Lesbian and Gay Rights was a watershed event in the political history of Asian American lesbians. For those who lived outside large urban centers on the East and West coasts, where support groups such as Asian Lesbians of the East Coast (New York City) and Asian Women United (San Francisco Bay Area) had been active since the late 1970s and early 1980s, the moment was especially poignant and empowering because it was the first time that they met other women like themselves; their isolation was lifted forever. The following year, aided by a grant from the March on Washington Committee, the Asian Pacific Lesbian Network (APLN) was formed.

In 1989 APLN organized the first-ever national retreat for Asian Pacific Islander (API) lesbians, bringing together over 140 women from different parts of the United States and Canada. The retreat was a lesson in coalition and community building for the participants; it embodied not only the power of identity politics but also the dangerous consequence of ignoring difference within commonality. Many participants voiced their anger at their marginalization by organizers of the retreat. Recalling her experience at the retreat, Ann Uri Uyeda wrote, "In essence, we created ourselves as queer API women in a culture that otherwise would ignore or erase our contributions, identities, and our very presence. We were also angry. Women who felt excluded—bisexuals, those from Canada and Hawaii, foreign-born and immigrant, South Asian, those with mixed heritage—said so."

This struggle was perhaps inevitable, given the invisibility of bisexual women within the lesbian community and the convention of lumping all Asians in this country together into one undifferentiated group, thus denying the diverse histories and experiences of "Asia" and "Asians." This twin historical burden took time to shed, and it was only in 1993, at a West Coast retreat, that Asian Pacific Lesbian Network was renamed Asian and Pacific Islander Lesbian and Bisexual Women's Network. At the same retreat, women of native Hawaiian descent and their allies challenged participants to reexamine and reaffirm their commitment to the struggles of "Pacific Islanders" and educated them about the realities of coalition politics. In the words of J. Kehaulani Kauanui and Ju Hui "Judy" Han, "'API' must be based on coalition politics, not identity politics. . . . We must re-open, redefine, and continuously question the boundaries of 'Asian Pacific Islander' because a coalition is a temporary unity. And 'API' can work only as a coalition."

The issue of marginalization is not strange to Asian and Pacific Islander lesbians and bisexual women because of their experience with the larger lesbian community. As Jee Yeun Lee, a graduate student, put it bluntly, "[We] often find ourselves marginalized, tokenized, and/or exoticized. . . . When white women make a serious effort to work through issues of racism and cultural

sensitivity, it is usually a precarious balancing act between inclusion and tokenism." Insensitivity to racism and ethnocentrism in the gay and lesbian community allowed Lambda Legal Defense and Education Fund, a national lesbian and gay rights organization, and the New York City–based Lesbian and Gay Community Services Center to choose *Miss Saigon*, a racist and misogynist Broadway musical, for their fundraiser in 1991. When members of Asian Lesbians of the East Coast and Gay Asian and Pacific Islander Men of New York and their allies protested the choice and urged the two organizations to drop *Miss Saigon*, the Community Services Center canceled their fundraiser, but Lambda Legal Defense and Education Fund did not.

The struggle against Lambda Legal Defense and Education Fund over *Miss Saigon* mobilized antiracist lesbians, bisexuals, and gay men around the twin issues of Orientalism and sexism. In speeches and press releases, protesters educated the public about the insidious tradition of Orientalist representations of Asian women in operas such as *Madame Butterfly*, in films such as *The World of Suzie Wong*, and in other Broadway musicals. On April 11, 1991, a second protest was organized against the official opening of *Miss Saigon*. This time, API lesbians, bisexuals, and gay men organized coalitions with the larger Asian and Pacific Islander community.

Given the commercial success of *Miss Saigon* and the continued indifference of Broadway and Hollywood producers to the issues raised by the protesters, it is clear that the demonstration had had very little impact on American mass cultural production. On the other hand, although the second protest was smaller than the first and attracted less attention, it was an important development because it signaled the possibility of a significant collaboration of Asians and Pacific Islanders—regardless of sexual orientation—working together for a common political cause.

▪ VIVIEN W. NG

SEE ALSO Asian Pacific Women.

Black Lesbians

Documenting the history of Black lesbian, bisexual, and transidentified women in the United States poses a particular set of challenges. The most significant is that women (and men) whose sexual orientations or sexual practices differed from mainstream heterosexuals often took great pains to hide their sexual, emotional, and social lives. The survival strategy of the closet, especially before the 1969 Stonewall Rebellion, discouraged visibility and the preservation of useful evidence.

European Americans' sexual exploitation and sexual stereotyping of Blacks, especially Black women, which originated in slavery, is another factor that makes the expression and revelation of same-gender desire a volatile act within the Black community. Because racist whites have viewed the range of Black sexuality as deviant and pathological, some Blacks have made great efforts to censure and repress any but the most conventional sexual mores and behavior.

The problems of naming and definition challenge all historians of sexuality, because currently used identifiers became widespread only in the twentieth century and do not necessarily mirror how women would have conceptualized their sexual orientation in earlier eras. For example, Mary Fields (1832?–1914), a former slave and frontierswoman, wore men's attire and could fight and shoot like a man. She devoted herself to working for an order of Catholic nuns in Montana and as a stagecoach driver was the second woman to drive a U.S. mail route. She is sometimes included in discussions of Black lesbians because she never married and did not fit gender stereotypes, but her actual sexual orientation is not known.

Despite these challenges, by the early twentieth century there are specific examples of Black women who did not conform to heterosexist expectations. The Great Migration created vital centers of Black populations in northern cities. By the 1920s, Harlem, especially, had become a focal point for Black culture, politics, and social life.

Black gay men, lesbians, and bisexuals played important roles in the intellectual and artistic movement known as the Harlem Renaissance as well as in the popular entertainments and nightlife that characterized the Jazz Age. Heiress A'Lelia Walker (1885–1931), daughter of cosmetics millionaire Madame C. J. Walker, held salons and parties attended by major figures of the Harlem Renaissance, many of whom were gay or bisexual. Some neighborhood clubs and speakeasies were known as places where same-gender couples could socialize and dance. Private parties and "buffet flats," where customers paid to watch or participate in a variety of sexual exhibitions, provided settings with even more freedom for lesbians and gay men to interact.

Blues songs of the period, such as Lucille Bogan's "B. D. (bull dagger) Women Blues," Bessie Smith's "Foolish Man Blues," and Ma Rainey's "Prove It on Me Blues," made specific references to "mannish" women who went with other women. These songs indicate that lesbians and gay men were a visible part of the urban Black scene. Gladys Bentley (1907–60), one of the most popular entertainers of the period, dressed in men's suits both on and off stage and married another woman in a well-publicized ceremony. The playwright, poet, and teacher Angelina Weld Grimké (1880–1958) wrote love poems to women which were never published. Writer and activist Alice Dunbar-Nelson (1875–1935) documented her relationships with women as well as men in her diaries written from 1921 to 1931.

Although most Black lesbians during the first half of the twentieth century were not public figures, oral histories confirm that Black lesbians formed their own social networks in which house parties played a vital role; established families with partners and friends; sometimes raised children; maintained ties with their birth families; and actively participated in the civic and social life of Black communities.

Since the growth of lesbian and gay liberation in the early 1970s, Black lesbian lives have be-

Marchers for lesbian and gay rights demonstrate in Washington, D.C., 1979. Poet Audre Lorde (center, wearing hat) helps hold the banner.

come much more visible and Black lesbians have made significant contributions to the lesbian, gay, women's, and Black feminist movements. Black lesbians were among the first African American women to critique the sexual oppression of Black women. They played major roles in building Black feminist organizations in the early 1970s such as the National Black Feminist Organization and Boston's Combahee River Collective. Black lesbian organizations also formed during this period, most notably New York's Salsa Soul Sisters (now African Ancestral Lesbians United for Societal Change), the oldest ongoing Black lesbian group in the United States.

Black lesbian feminist writers and activists have done crucial work to challenge Black lesbians' isolation and to build community. Authors Audre Lorde, Pat Parker, Cheryl Clarke, Jewelle Gomez, and Barbara Smith, and organizers Tania Abdulahad, Mandy Carter, Pat Hussain, and

Kathleen Saadat, among others, have done groundbreaking work to make links among multiple oppressions and to bring together various constituencies to struggle for progressive political and economic change.

In the 1990s, however, many Black lesbians still do not come out for fear of the very real homophobic reprisals they might face. Ironically, the pseudo-Christian right wing has targeted homophobic hate campaigns at churchgoing Blacks and other people of color, communities they previously had attacked. The mainstream white-dominated gay movement has been ill equipped to counter the Right's race-specific attacks. The closet, especially in the case of Black women who are highly visible public figures, continues to hamper historical accuracy. Nevertheless, more research is being done in this challenging and exciting field.

■ BARBARA SMITH

European American Lesbians

The history of European American lesbians is many histories, united by the privilege of race but divided by class and region. The result is a past whose shape is far from being defined, but whose boundaries have overlapped with the history of heterosexual and bisexual women, other European Americans, working-class people, gay men, lesbians of color, and others.

In colonial America females brought to trial for sexual acts with other women received punishment far less harsh than did men under similar circumstances, who were regularly sentenced to death. Lesbian behavior was prosecuted under laws forbidding adultery and sex outside marriage. Women of the servant class reportedly received harsher penalties—beating and fines—than did women of higher status, who were made to acknowledge their transgressions publicly.

During the Victorian era middle-class women gained increased freedom in expressing romantic devotion to other women. As the century ended, relationships between "romantic friends" were institutionalized and formed the basis for political networks and close-knit female communities. Were these relationships sexual and therefore "lesbian" as it would come to be defined (and pathologized) by doctors and later defended by a political movement? This question has been debated by historians. Though these women may or may not have been sexual with each other, they lived openly as partners.

Working-class white women of the nineteenth century faced other choices. What contemporary society would call "lesbian" behavior was exhibited through the phenomenon of the "passing" or "crossing" woman. Numerous working-class white women and women of color chose to pass as men; for some, their gender was discovered only upon death. They tried to obtain better-paying jobs, to serve in the military, to vote, to travel safely, and, undoubtedly, to marry other women. Their actions challenged the understanding of gender and sexuality at the time.

As the emerging field of sexology began to describe lesbians, pathologizing theories of gender and sexuality emerged. The punishment for female or male "homosexual behavior" shifted from prisons to mental institutions. The stigma of illness and depravity affected European American lesbians regardless of their economic and social status.

World War II was a turning point for white lesbians. The war provided job opportunities for single, self-supporting women. The sex segregation of the war and the first women's branches of the military provided environments where lesbians could meet. Lesbians developed institutions and norms that weathered cultural emphasis on strict gender roles and traditional family life that began during the cold war era. Lesbian bars appeared in urban areas and near military bases. The Daughters of Bilitis, the first lesbian organization, formed in 1955, reflected the class and race of its middle-class white founders just as the bars reflected their working-women clientele.

The women's movement of the 1960s and the gay liberation movement of the early 1970s greatly catalyzed European American lesbians to organize. By the early 1980s communities of lesbians, some inspired by back-to-the-land and separatist beliefs, developed lesbian-feminist politics. These communities nurtured a culture with its own music, art, publications, and other institutions dedicated to living outside a patriarchal, capitalist society.

Splits within the lesbian-feminist movement around class, race, and sexual politics, along with the difficulty of creating an entirely woman-centered society, caused the movement to wane in the mid-1980s. Lesbians of color were the most vocal critics of this movement. They pointed to the reluctance of the movement to address, or to recognize, the racial privilege enjoyed by white women. They also criticized the basic tenets of lesbian feminism, especially separatism. Nevertheless, many lesbian-feminist communities still thrive. A new wave of lesbians, including young women who became activists as a result of the AIDS crisis, challenged this vision and reclaimed their ties with gay men and the butch-femme roles of the earlier lesbian bars, both of which had been rejected by lesbian feminists.

Media exposure increased in the 1990s. Some was sympathetic; some was part of a right-wing onslaught against homosexuals. Rising numbers of women lived openly lesbian lives. The question remains: Will the movement bridge the gap between those who have been its chief beneficiaries—educated, white, middle-class, urban lesbians and gay men—and those whose lives more closely resemble those of their predecessors?

Lillian Faderman, *Odd Girls and Twilight Lovers: A History of Lesbian Life in Twentieth-Century America* (New York: Columbia University Press, 1991); Jonathan Ned Katz, *Gay/Lesbian Almanac: A New Documentary* (New York: Harper and Row/Colophon, 1983); Elizabeth Kennedy and Madeline Davis, *Boots of Leather, Slippers of Gold: The History of a Lesbian Community* (New York: Routledge, 1993).

■ ROCHELLA THORPE

Jewish Lesbians

Hey look at me, do you know who I am?
Look at all of me, I'm a Jewish lesbian . . .
Two hands pulling me in different directions
But you cannot tear me apart
I am one woman

Abbe Lyons, "Jewish Lesbian"

This song was performed at a 1982 program entitled "Jewish Lesbians: A Cultural Celebration," one of many celebrations that marked the publication of *Nice Jewish Girls: A Lesbian Anthology. Nice Jewish Girls* was the first full-length book to document the voices and experiences of Jewish lesbians. Its publication was experienced as a profound relief, for it broke the silence of lesbians within Jewish communities and created a space for Jewish lesbians to speak freely as Jews

among lesbians. The title's juxtaposition of *nice Jewish girls* with *lesbians* challenged the traditionally restrictive definitions of Jewish womanhood and stimulated Jewish lesbian creativity, as evidenced by the publication of *Tribe of Dinah* and the founding of *Bridges*, both of which provided significant outlets for Jewish lesbian material. Jewish lesbian work is marked by its broad range of interests, which is Jewish and lesbian even when not focused directly on lesbian experience. "We are not wholly like other Jews. Our experience as lesbians makes our expression of Jewish identity distinctive, just as our experience as Jews influences our feminist visions," wrote Faith Rogow.

Although Jewish lesbians had been extremely active in the creation of all aspects of feminist (and lesbian feminist) institutions in the early years of the second wave, most were not "out" as Jews in these movements, possibly because they feared being overly visible and subject to stereotyping as Jews. As a result, their contributions as *Jewish* lesbians were often not recognized, much as lesbians' contributions to feminism frequently have remained unnamed. For example, lesbian visibility in the Jewish community was a major theme of the Jewish Feminist Conference held in San Francisco in 1982. Although nine of the ten organizers of that conference were lesbians, in the press and in the public eye, their lesbianism was subsumed under Jewish feminism (presumed to be heterosexual).

Before 1982 only a few lesbians had written as Jews in small-circulation lesbian publications, and considerably fewer had written as lesbians in Jewish publications. As a result, the pioneering work of these women did not gain recognition until after the publication of Evelyn Torton Beck's *Nice Jewish Girls*, a culmination of work done in the 1970s and a beginning for grassroots organizing. New groups took names that had Jewish meanings, such as *Di vilde chayes* (Yiddish for "the wild beasts"), the *Balebustehs* (Yiddish for "the perfect housewives"), and *Di yiddishe shvestern* (Yiddish for "the Jewish sisters"). These groups focused on topics ranging from Israeli-related politics, transformations of religious practices, issues of socioeconomic class, the meaning of conversion (a number of Jewish lesbians were converts to Judaism), relationships among Jewish women and women of color, and parenting children as Jews in a lesbian feminist context.

Over time, common themes have remained central to Jewish lesbian writings in all genres: foremost, the desire to be whole—to bring all the disparate parts of oneself together; to fight homophobia in Jewish institutions and families; to fight anti-Semitism in lesbian communities and personal relationships; to understand the meanings of the Holocaust; to grapple with the complexity of supporting Israel's right to exist while struggling with the painful realities of Israeli foreign and domestic policies, especially the treatment and land rights of Palestinians; to recognize differences among Jews, especially between Ashkenazi Jews (of European origin) and Sephardic Jews (descendants of Jews who lived in Spain or Portugal until their expulsion in 1492).

The same forces that have kept lesbians hidden in Western historiography have affected their visibility and inclusion in research on Jewish history, but in recent years the work of writers such as Muriel Rukeyser and Jo Sinclair (a pseudonym for Ruth Seid) has been newly understood as the work of Jewish lesbians. However, it is in the contemporary period that Jewish lesbian creativity has fully flowered in the arenas of poetry (Irena Klepfisz and Adrienne Rich); fiction (Elana Dykewoman, Jyl Lynn Fellman, Ruth Geller, Judith Katz, Sarah Shulman, and Nancy Toder); essays (Irena Klepfisz, Elly Bulkin, Melanie Kaye/Kantrowitz, and Alice Bloch); films *(Chicks in White Satin, When Shirley Met Florence,* and *Complaints of a Dutiful Daughter);* music (Linda Shear, Alix Dobkin, and Lynn Lavner); comedy (Robin Tyler and Maxine Feldman); cultural history and the reclaiming of Yiddish (Sarah Shulman and Irena Klepfisz). Jewish lesbians have also been involved in political activism, organiz-

ing for the Lesbian, Gay, and Bisexual Marches on Washington, and launching protests against the Israeli occupation of the West Bank. They have reinterpreted biblical narratives and created new rituals and ceremonies. Such awareness has been central to Jewish lesbian feminist work through the 1990s.

Evelyn Torton Beck, *Nice Jewish Girls: A Lesbian Anthology* (1982. Revised edition, Boston: Beacon Press, 1989); Evelyn Torton Beck, "Naming is not a Simple Act: Jewish Lesbian Community in the 1980s," in *Twice Blessed: On Being Lesbian, Gay and Jewish,* 171–81. (Boston: Beacon Press); Faith Rogow, "The Rise of Jewish Lesbian Feminism," *Bridges: A Journal for Jewish Feminists and Our Friends,* 1, no. 1 (Spring 1990): 67–79.

■ EVELYN TORTON BECK

SEE ALSO Jewish Women.

Latina Lesbians

Latina lesbians are those lesbians whose ancestors come from Latin America. In their efforts to identify themselves, Latina lesbians utilize a diversity of terms regarding both their ethnicity and their sexuality. Latina is a general term that includes women from the Caribbean, Central America, South America, as well as Mexican/Chicana women from both sides of the U.S.-Mexican border. Women from Puerto Rico often identify not as Latinas but as Puertorriqueñas (Puerto Ricans). Yolanda Leyva asserts in her research that Latina lesbians refer to their sexuality in various ways depending on such variables as geography, age, economic status, and immigration status. Because of the negative stigma attached to the word "lesbian" many Latinas will use alternate terms such as *amigas* (friends), *compañeras* (companions), or *tortilleras* (a derogative Spanish slang term for lesbian, which is sometimes reclaimed as a positive self-identification).

Historically, many races and ethnicities mixed

in Latin America, and Latina lesbians reflect this diversity. A Latina lesbian might be light-skinned, blonde with blue eyes, as dark as her African ancestors, or a mixture of these, along with indigenous features. Latina lesbians in the United States might be fourth-generation Mexican Americans or recent refugees from Central America or Cuba, or they might be undocumented. Class differences vary from poor to working-class to well-educated entrepreneurs. Consequently, their politics vary as do their religious backgrounds. Since degrees of patriarchy vary from country to country as well as regions, historians must be cautious about categorizing Latinas as being "traditionally" family-oriented or Catholic. They share the experience of being transcultural in the United States and they encounter the sexism, racism, and homophobia of not one but two cultures.

History has largely neglected the subject of Latina lesbians. One might find it challenging to isolate historical texts referring specifically to Latina lesbians. Scholars such as Yolanda Retter and Yolanda Leyva are presently working on studies on the subject.

With the advent of the civil rights movement, the growth of feminist research, and the increasing participation of women of color in academia, issues related to lesbians of color began to emerge in the mid- to late 1970s. As a result of the growing visibility of this population, by the mid-1980s, interest and research on the subject appeared in various fields such as social work and psychology. In this period of activism, Latina lesbians created networks and organizations such as Lesbianas Latinas Americanas (LLA) in Los Angeles, in 1978; lesbians joined Gay Latinos Unidos (GLU) in Los Angeles, in 1984, forming the lesbian task force that became Lesbianas Unidas; Las Buenas Amigas in New York, in 1986; and Ellas of Texas; Latina Lesbianas de Tucson, in Arizona; and Ellas en Accion in San Francisco.

Members of these groups and other U.S. Latina lesbians participated in organizing on both sides of the U.S.-Mexican border. It is important to note that the feminism that influences these groups is from Latin America as well as the United States. In the mid-1980s lesbians from the United States and Latin America met in a series of conferences. According to Mariana Romo-Carmona, the First Encuentro de Lesbianas de Latino America y El Caribe was held in Cuernavaca, Mexico, in 1987. In 1990, the second Encuentro occurred in Costa Rica, and the third in Puerto Rico, in 1992. At these conferences, lesbians from throughout Latin America and the United States celebrated one another, hotly debated issues of class and diversity within their international community, and held workshops on issues such as leadership and culture.

In 1987, during the weekend of the second Gay and Lesbian March on Washington, activists formed the first gay, lesbian, bi, and transgender Latino/a organization, National LLEGO, headquartered in Washington, D.C. In 1994, LLEGO funded Latina Lesbianas de Tucson to hold the first national leadership conference, where writer Cherríe Moraga gave the keynote address. Participants attended workshops on community organizing, spirituality, sexuality, lesbian health, creative writing, and continued establishing national networks.

These organizations exist to promote positive images of Latina lesbians and to provide culturally affirming environments. They have funded projects and events toward this objective. The groups have participated in local and national marches, organized workshops, conferences, rap or support sessions, held retreats, and published newsletters. As a result, Latina lesbian organizations have created vehicles for their members to be politically active in their communities. They have developed relationships with many politicians and educated them to recognize issues of homophobia, sexism, and racism in society. As a result, some politicians now advocate on their behalf at the local, state, and federal levels. Individuals and groups have participated in policymaking and service delivery on AIDS issues and

Latina lesbians have been involved in the area of immigration policy for persons with AIDS. They have also worked in coalition with non-gay-specific Latino organizations and issues, such as immigrant rights, labor, human rights, education, and housing.

Researchers in this subject area need to look in a variety of sources including and beyond the field of history. Resources for primary documents can be found in the lesbian archives in Los Angeles, San Francisco, Tucson, and New York. Located at the Latina Lesbian Archive in Tucson, historian Yolanda Leyva has compiled numerous interviews with Latina lesbians from throughout the United States. Leyva's interviews include women's life stories and issues of race and gender in the late twentieth century. The archives are a crucial resource for historians as well as for background information for magazine articles, art, poetry, and newsletters produced by regionally based Latina lesbian organizations, and for photographs, personal, and professional papers.

Another crucial resource is the substantial body of literature and theory produced by Latina lesbians, beginning with the 1981 publication of *This Bridge Called My Back: Writings by Radical Women of Color*, edited by Cherríe Moraga and Gloria Anzaldúa. The first-person narratives in this anthology and in later anthologies such as Juanita Ramos's *Compañeras* and Carla Trujillo's *Chicana Lesbians: The Girls Our Mothers Warned Us About* provide an important context for historical research and offer personal descriptions that challenge traditional historical analysis. Through their work, Moraga and Anzaldúa relate experiences of family, politics, sexuality, and gender roles in a manner that illustrates not only the complexities of being a woman of color but also of being a lesbian in the late twentieth century.

Gloria Anzaldúa and Cherríe Moraga, eds. *This Bridge Called My Back: Writings by Radical Women of Color* (Watertown, Mass.: Persephone Press, 1981; Rpt. New York: Kitchen Table/Women of Color Press, 1983); Juanita Ramos, ed. *Compañeras: Latina Lesbians, An Anthology* (New York: Latina Lesbian History Project, 1987. Rpt. New York: Routledge, 1994); Carla Trujillo, ed. *Chicana Lesbians: The Girls Our Mothers Warned Us About* (Berkeley: Third Woman Press, 1991).

▪ ANTONIA VILLASEÑOR

SEE ALSO Latinas.

Native American Lesbians

Reference to lesbianism among American Indian women in historical and anthropological literature is almost nonexistent. Because of nineteenth-century taboos against speaking about sexuality, Victorian notions of "proper" sexual behavior, and an androcentric bias, little information is available about women's roles among Indian tribes. Where information exists, it must still be recontextualized to eliminate misconceptions and erroneous beliefs about Native women. Can we equate a Western cultural category, such as lesbian, with any of the numerous roles practiced by preconquest indigenous women? This remains a question. Nevertheless, the Native world seems to offer to women, in pre- and post-contact times, roles that resemble modern-day lesbianism. Lesbian is defined here as a woman who forms affectional and/or erotic bonds with another woman or women. From the information available, it seems lesbianism probably occurred in indigenous America in specific and socially sanctioned ways.

Some have conjectured that lesbianism was practiced through female cross-gender identification. Cross-gender females, while biologically female, behaved like men in their actions, dress, talk, work, and so on. Girls who became cross-gendered often showed this proclivity as children. They chose to play with boys, learned male activities such as hunting, and refused to perform female tasks or engage in female play. Indian parents did not discourage this behavior. Although their daughter was "different," this was not cause for denigration or shame.

Parents may have accepted their daughter's choice to follow cross-gender pursuits because such choices were spiritually sanctioned. Tribal people believe that dreams or visions provided by spirits often direct individuals' life choices. Among the Mojave, a Southwestern tribe, it was thought that the *hwame* dreamed of becoming cross-gendered while still in her mother's womb. The Maricopa believed that a girl became a *kwiraxame* because as a child she was said to "dream too much."

Among the Mojave, a ceremony was performed when the cross-gender girl reached puberty. She was given a male name and the right to marry another woman. Thus, a cross-gendered woman received validation not only within her own extended family, but from the tribe as well.

Among Plains groups, idealized female behavior included modesty, chastity, and marital fidelity. Nevertheless, other socially sanctioned models of behavior allowed women to become self-sufficient and achieve special status. While the aggressive woman was probably more the exception than the rule, it was possible for Plains women to make names for themselves as hunters and warriors. Not all of these women were cross-gendered, nor were they necessarily lesbian. Some women who accompanied war parties went only once, usually for the purpose of revenge. Early in the nineteenth century, a young Gros Ventre woman was captured by the Crow. At twelve years of age, she already showed interest in manly pursuits and so was trained in a number of male skills by her adopted father. Though this woman did not dress in male attire, she seems to have practiced cross-gender behavior. She became an accomplished hunter, a brave warrior, and was much respected among the Crow. She eventually married four women, to whose families she gave horses. The number of wives she took indicates this warrior's high status and shows she was capable of providing for a large and productive household.

Many changes took place in indigenous cultures as a result of conquest and colonization. Native people were seen as savage and immoral. Rather than completely exterminate Indians, white America decided to "assimilate" them. This would be achieved by destroying tribal ties, reducing the Native land base, and forcing Indian children into boarding schools where they would be indoctrinated with Christianity and American patriotism. Indians were expected to embrace the rigid sex- and gender-identifications of white, middle-class America.

To an extent, European American sexual ideology succeeded in effacing evidence of cross-genderism and any attendant nonheterosexual behaviors. But it did not wipe out entirely these cultural variations. Today, Native American lesbians, homosexuals, cross-gender, and transgendered individuals exist. Many identify as "two-spirits" whose lives reflect a balance of female and male energies and interests. Many are mixed-bloods with diverse cultural influences, but it is likely there are gay and lesbian full-bloods too. Lesbian Native Americans are active in groups such as Gay American Indians (GAI), an organization cofounded by Barbara Cameron, which has been active in gay history projects, human rights activism, and AIDS education. Other Native American lesbians, such as Chrystos and Beth Brant, are among the foremost poets and writers of Native American literature. Though the record is sparse, the lives of the extraordinary Indian women who came before serve as poignant and powerful reminders of the capacities of their hearts.

Paula Cunn Allen, "*Hwame, Koshkalaka,* and the Rest: Lesbians in American Indian Cultures," in *The Sacred Hoop: Recovering the Feminine in American Indian Traditions* (Boston: Beacon, 1986); Evelyn Blackwood, "Sexuality and Gender in Certain Native American Tribes: The Case of Cross-Gender Females," *Signs: Journal of Women in Culture and Society* Vol. 10 (1984): 27–42; Beatrice Medicine, "'Warrior Women'—Sex Role Alternatives for Plains Indian Women," in *The Hidden Half: Studies of Plains Indian Women* (Washington, D.C.: University Press of America, 1983).

■ JANICE GOULD

SEE ALSO Native American Women.

≋ Liberalism

liberalism is a strange and powerful political term because it is continuously used but rarely defined. In Western societies liberal often connotes "open-minded." It is also used as a synonym for radical. Elsewhere, liberalism is equated with welfare-state politics; that is, the idea that the state has a responsibility for ensuring the social welfare of its people, as in the New Deal or the Great Society. The actual history of liberalism explains pieces of each conception yet differs somewhat from any of these readings.

Liberalism is a theory about individual rights, freedom, choice, and privacy. It articulates the differentiation between church and state, family and economy, public and private; it conceptualizes a sphere of separateness for the individual. This new notion of individualism developed with the rise of capitalism and the bourgeois revolution and it was exclusive to white, property-owning men.

John Locke (1632–1704) was one of the first theorists to embrace the concept of private property. His theory articulated an independent, rational individual with free choice who no longer could be confined by absolutist feudal authority. Locke's vision of the newly self-contained individual was promissory of a new politics.

Mary Wollstonecraft (1759–97) expanded this promissory to include women. She wrote of women's right to education, which would allow them to take part in the developing bourgeois society. The woman she envisioned—the rational mother—was also the middle-class woman, not the wage-laboring woman. Wollstonecraft's demands for education were later used by liberal feminists who called for the enfranchisement of all women.

J. S. Mill and Harriet Taylor discussed equality of opportunity and individual rights and critiqued the "subjection of women" in nineteenth-century England. They articulated and demanded that women be full citizens and fought for women's right to vote. Although Mill assumed most women would choose to be wives and mothers, he argued that women should be able to decide for themselves whether they wanted a career.

By the end of the nineteenth century Western liberalism had more fully articulated the autonomy of the individual and the importance of freedom of choice, equality of opportunity, and equality before the law. The idea that individualism related to anyone, regardless of sex, race, or economic class, brought to light the fact that individual rights were actually limited to white men. Liberalism promised freedom and equality (of opportunity) to all but gave it to only some. The inherent inequity of liberalism was uncovered and societal debate about the subject began.

Liberalism is more a theory about freedom of the individual than it is a theory about equality. The key commitment is to freedom of thought and expression. Much less is said about equality among individuals. As such, the problem of inequality—whether economic, racial, or sexual—is sidestepped. Opportunity, meaning "a chance," displaces the concept of equity.

The promissory aspect of liberalism arose during the latter half of the twentieth century. The premise of the civil rights movements in the United States, as well as various dissident movements internationally, supports the Western liberal notion of individual freedom of expression and equality before the law. Worldwide feminist movements are also based on this notion—the right to vote, to abortion, to equal pay, and so on.

As we enter the twenty-first century, many people are criticizing the supposed excesses of liberalism, citing too much freedom, too much equality, too much identification with the self. These reactions against liberalism, often termed *neoconservatism*, are viewed as an attempt to return liberalism to its intended "original" meaning. Neoconservatives, who are most often revisionist liberals, argue that liberalism was never meant to guarantee equality; rather, it would offer an opportunity to compete.

According to neoconservatives, competition presumes a system of losers and winners. They declare that liberalism was never meant to provide for everyone and reject the ideals of civil rights and feminist politics of the 1960s and 1970s, which they believe instigated a crisis for liberalism. Neoconservatives blame people of color and white women in particular for expecting too much from the government, rather than being "self-sufficient."

The challenge of neoconservatism is still one of the greatest threats to the progressive promises of liberalism today. Liberalism ideally applies to every individual; therefore it remains unclear how its theory and practice will be shaped in twenty-first-century society. It is clear, however, that liberalism will continue to adapt and change.

Zillah Eisenstein, *The Radical Future of Liberal Feminism* (Boston: Northeastern University Press, 1981); C. B. MacPherson, *The Theory of Possessive Individualism, Hobbes to Locke* (New York: Oxford University Press, 1962).

▪ ZILLAH EISENSTEIN

SEE ALSO Civil Rights Movement; Feminism and Feminisms; Great Society/War on Poverty; Labor Movement; New Deal; Progressive Era.

≋ Librarianship

L ibrarians acquire, organize, and make permanently accessible the world's recorded knowledge. The first library school class in the United States (1887) was 85 percent women. Eighty-five percent are still women. Most of the 150,000 librarians are public servants. In 1933 women's clubs were credited with initiating 75 percent of existing public libraries.

Established as standard in 1948, the master's degree in librarianship still fetches lower wages than masters' for historically male professions. The professional librarian evolved from the male keeper of the scholarly books in a single university room

(mid-1600s) to the female instrument of the people's right to know anything public (mid-1900s).

Around the turn of the century, librarians recognized that caging books in closed stacks was counterproductive. They gradually identified and continue to tear down barriers to access: gender, age, religion, nationality, race, ethnicity, sexuality, interests, beliefs, income, disability, region, and various levels of literacy. Equal access to uncensored expressions requires librarians to honor these distinctions in collections that vary in form, content, and sophistication. Since the early 1960s librarians of color have promoted services reflecting the linguistic and cultural needs of their communities. The first avowedly homosexual group within a profession in the United States formed in 1970 to make gay and lesbian literature accessible.

Beginning in the 1970s tax "revolts," disrespect for feminized professions, and unwarranted faith in technology's capacity to replace books, librarians, and libraries undermined professional fee-free service and library schools. Higher salaries of (mostly male) administrators, computer experts, and those serving prestigious or paying "customers" were bolstered, while the number and status of (mostly female) librarians directly serving children and those who lacked information declined. In the 1990s enlightened communities increased support for endangered libraries, valued as commons of knowledge nurtured by librarians who open access to the world of information, whether in high technology or in print.

▪ MELISSA RILEY

≋ Literature

U .S. literature is unimaginable without the contributions of women writers. Though often critically neglected, their work has been strong, original, and diverse.

Some of the sources of this literature are this country's various indigenous cultures, in many of which both women and men were storytellers. Women also had powerful roles in Native myths, legends, songs, chants, and sacred rituals. Settlement of the Americas by Europeans (English, Spanish, French, Dutch) both subordinated these cultures and provided new literary sources. Colonial literature drew from European traditions and models. Colonial women writers—largely from the more affluent and educated families—explored religious, moral, historical, social, and domestic questions in a variety of genres: poetry, meditations, travel writing and journals, captivity narratives, plays, letters, and autobiography.

Anne Hutchinson (1591–1643) was known for her charismatic oratory, religious doctrines, and "ready wit and bold spirit." She was too bold, for the Puritans banished her for heresy from newly settled Boston in 1637. Anne Dudley Bradstreet (1612–72), the daughter and wife of Puritan leaders in the Massachusetts colony, was the first poet published in the British colonies. She was self-conscious about the audacity of a woman taking up the pen, declaring in the prologue to her *The Tenth Muse, Lately Sprung Up in America* (1650) that she is "obnoxious to each carping tongue / Who says [her] hand a needle better fits." Mary Rowlandson (c. 1636–c. 1678), taken by Indians from her Massachusetts home in 1676, returned to write her story of these events, one of the earliest and most popular examples of the captivity narrative. In the eighteenth century Judith Sargent Murray (1751–1820) wrote fiction, plays, and essays on religion, the meaning of the new American nation, and women's issues. Phillis Wheatley (1753–84), forcibly brought to the colonies as a slave for whom English was a second language, was the first Black person to publish a volume of poems, in which she explored religious, moral, racial, and elegiac themes.

In the years between the founding of the United States and the Civil War, some women gained professional success as writers, editors, and journalists. The scholar Nina Baym estimates that women produced almost half of U.S. literature between 1812 and 1860. From 1826 to 1833 Lydia Maria Child (1802–80), a feminist and abolitionist, edited *Juvenile Miscellany*, the first children's monthly in the United States. Emily Dickinson (1830–86) was born during this period, though her poems and letters were not widely published until the 1890s. Although their incomes were often precarious, some professional women writers became best-selling authors and celebrities. In 1791 Susanna Haswell Rowson (1762–1824) wrote *Charlotte Temple*, the first best-selling U.S. novel. Other successful women writers of this period included poet Lydia Huntley Sigourney (1791–1865); novelists Catharine Maria Sedgwick (1789–1867) and Susan Warner (1819–85); columnist Sara Payson Willis Parton ("Fanny Fern," 1811–72); and expert domestic adviser Catharine Beecher (1800–78).

Didactic and melodramatic as pre–Civil War literature frequently was, it is also culturally revealing, dramatizing great national issues such as education, abolition, the impending war, women's rights, the growth of industrialization, and, to a degree, racial relations. Margaret Fuller (1810–50), a New England transcendentalist, wrote the passionately feminist *Woman in the Nineteenth Century* (1845). Catharine Sedgwick's *Hope Leslie* (1827) told the story of the Pequod heroine Magawisca, who challenges her colonial captors, "I deny your right to judge me . . . not one of my race has ever acknowledged your authority." In 1852 Harriet Beecher Stowe (1811–96) published *Uncle Tom's Cabin*, the extremely influential antislavery novel of protest and prophecy. Abraham Lincoln pronounced Stowe "the little lady who made this big war." Free Black Frances Ellen Watkins Harper (1825–1911) was a lecturer and organizer as well as author of fiction and poetry, and Harriet E. Wilson (1807?–70) published the first novel by an African American woman, *Our Nig*. African American women such as Harriet Jacobs ("Linda Brent," 1813–97) wrote or dictated slave narratives, accounts of the cruelties of the U.S. slave experience that also described the sexual exploitation of Black women by white men. Jane Johnston Schoolcraft (1800–41), of Irish and Ojibwa descent, recorded Ojibwa history, customs, legends, and speeches.

After the Civil War, the United States was transformed into a modern nation. As women such as the reformer Jane Addams (1860–1935) became more acceptable as public figures, some of their books and articles took on the status of public wisdom. Social subjects included women's rights, reproductive rights, labor, racial justice and civil rights, the poor, the ill, children, peace, and, increasingly, the environment. Reform impulses also motivated women's utopian writing, a genre exemplified by *Herland*, an imaginary world of women governed by the principle of cooperation, written in 1915 by Charlotte Perkins Gilman (1860–1935).

The growth of literacy and the rise of modern popular genres increased women's opportunities as professional writers. Editor and journalist Louisa May Alcott (1832–88) wrote poetry, thrillers and sensation stories, a novel about work, and, most famously, *Little Women* (1868). In this era women shaped the genres of mysteries, detective stories, and private eye novels. In 1866 Metta Victor, writing as Seeley Register, published *The Dead Letter* in a periodical. In 1878 Anna Katherine Green (1846–1935) became the first woman to publish a best-selling mystery, *The Leavenworth Case*. Later creating both male and female detectives, Green was a forerunner of today's popular women mystery writers. Women also excelled in regional or "local-color" writing, a genre popularized after the Civil War by such influential periodicals as *The Atlantic Monthly*. Sarah Orne Jewett's (1849–1909) luminous *The Country of the Pointed Firs* (1896) is often hailed as the masterwork of the genre. Kate Chopin's (1851–1904) *The Awakening* (1899) was for years controversial because, in addition to its descriptions of Louisiana's Creole culture, it frankly explored a married woman's journey of erotic and socially critical self-discovery.

Published according to Act of Parliament, Sept. 1. 1773 by Arch.ᵈ Bell, Bookseller Nᵒ 8 near the Saracens Head Aldgate.

An engraving depicting eighteenth-century poet Phillis Wheatley at her desk. This image originally appeared in the frontispiece of her book, Poems on Various Subjects, Religious and Moral *(1773).*

The plurality of voices among women writers was an emerging force, if grudgingly recognized by men and women alike in the dominant culture. Native American authors such as Gertrude Bonnin/Zitkala-Ša (1876–1938) helped to establish a movement that based literature in histories, materials, and cultures that the European invasion had shattered but not erased. In 1927, Mourning Dove/Christine Quintasket (1884?–1936) published *Cogewea: The Half-Blood*, the first known novel by a Native American woman. Its structure and history exhibit the tensions of writing from and about one culture within a dominant, destructive younger one.

The early twentieth century saw great vitality among African American women writers, especially during the Harlem Renaissance of the 1920s. Jessie Redmon Fauset (1882–1961) wrote about the emerging Black middle class; Nella Larsen (1891–1964) wrote about women of mixed Black and white heritage. Among the most original and versatile was the anthropologist, fiction writer, and autobiographer Zora Neale Hurston (1891–1960).

Immigrant women began to tell their stories during these years. Edith Maud Eaton ("Sui-Sin Far," 1865–1914) wrote fiction and nonfiction about East-West cultural conflicts and about Chinese immigrants and Eurasians. Central and southern European immigrants, many of them Jews and Catholics, arrived in great numbers in the 1880s. Their experiences of the journey, discrimination, work, urban life, and assimilation became raw material for such texts as *The Promised Land* (1912), by Mary Antin (1881–1949), and *Bread Givers* (1925), by Anzia Yezierska (1881–1970). Later in this century, African American authors chronicled the internal migration of Blacks from south to north, and immigrant literature encompassed the movement of Caribbeans, Mexicans, Central Americans, South Americans, and Asians to the United States.

Among the profound changes of the modern era was women's increased access to higher education. College, which usually meant leaving home, supplemented families as a literary woman's source of education, friendship, and support. Elizabeth Bishop (1911–79), Mary McCarthy (1912–89), Eleanor Clark (1913–96), and Muriel Rukeyser (1913–80)—significant writers all—met at Vassar College, which the poet Edna St. Vincent Millay (1892–1950) had earlier attended. The college experience became a central element in the female *bildungsroman* and in the exploration of the character of the New Woman as women writers grappled with expanded opportu-

nities made possible by education as well as lingering patterns of discrimination and dependence.

Inseparable from the rise of educated women was the rise of literary modernism, characterized by bold, experimental styles and audacious subject matter. Gertrude Stein (1874–1946), for instance, radically rewrote every genre; much of her work, including her erotic lesbian writing, was published after her death. Hilda Doolittle ("H.D.," 1886–1961), novelist and poet, created fragmented Imagist poems, epics such as Helen in Egypt (1961), and autobiographical fiction. Marianne Moore (1887–1972) wrote intricate, incisive poetry.

Other women writers in these years, though not as formally experimental, created complex works that were intellectually challenging, aesthetically pleasing, and revisionary in their engagements with society and history. Edith Wharton (1862–1937) wrote devastating critiques of the affluent New York society into which she was born. Willa Cather (1873–1947) combined elements of the American realistic, regionalist, and romantic traditions.

Subsequent generations have drawn from the legacies of both the avant-garde and the revisionists to create new forms and traditions. Fiction writers Eudora Welty (b. 1909) and Flannery O'Connor (1925–64) broadened the literary range and accomplishments of the American South. The new formalist Amy Clampitt (1920–94) used thick, precise description to engage the metaphysics of objects in the world, while the poet Susan Howe (b. 1937) has engaged the poem as a visual and verbal icon. Susan Sontag (b. 1933) has developed a unique body of fiction, film, and cultural criticism that is both intellectual and sensory. Joyce Carol Oates (b. 1938) has worked in a host of genres to carry out a searing analysis of the socio- and psychopathologies of American life.

World War II irrevocably changed the United States. A greater candor emerged in literature as a result of cultural developments, feminism, and the influence of the "confessional poetry" of writers such as Anne Sexton (1928–74) and Sylvia Plath (1932–63). After World War II, women began to write openly about sexuality. Today, lesbian writers have proven that lesbian love and sexuality may be the stuff of prize-winning poetry, while writers such as Erica Jong (b. 1942) and Rita Mae Brown (b. 1944) have gained popular success for their work in liberating the erotic word.

With the rising influence of science on modern life, women increasingly wrote modern science fiction and fantasy, though the genre had been initiated long before by the English writer Mary Wollstonecraft Shelley (1797–1851) with her novel *Frankenstein* (1818). This genre has benefited from the contributions of women writers born in the mid–twentieth century, including Judith Merril (b. 1923), Ursula LeGuin (b. 1929), Marion Zimmer Bradley (b. 1930), Patricia Haden Elgin (b. 1936), Joanna Russ (b. 1937), and Octavia Butler (b. 1947). Often adventurous with form and unafraid of vital women characters, these writers have been architects of new worlds with their own social structures, values, and language.

Beginning in the 1960s, two linked developments influenced U.S. women's literary history. The first was a renewed interest in gender and the rebirth of feminism. The 1950s had tended to marginalize women but their voices began to be heard again in the 1960s. In the world of theater, women such as Clare Boothe Luce (1903–87) and Lillian Hellman (1905–84) gained popular and critical acclaim in the 1930s and 1940s. These accolades virtually disappeared for women until the late 1960s and 1970s, when Maria Irene Fornès (b. 1930), Wendy Wasserstein (b. 1950), and Ntozake Shange (b. 1948) proved again that women were vital playwrights. In addition, the growth of modern media such as film, radio, television, and video created new opportunities for women writers. The novelist and essayist Joan Didion (b. 1934) has written film scripts; Jane Wagner, perhaps best known for her work with comedian Lily Tomlin, has written one-woman plays for Broad-

way as well as material for film and television.

Beyond theater and film, feminism has deeply influenced the form, the content, and the reception of women's writing. Writers, editors, and publishers such as Betty Friedan (b. 1921), Marilyn French (b. 1929), Gloria Steinem (b. 1934), Kate Millett (b. 1934), Robin Morgan (b. 1941), Barbara Smith (b. 1946), and Gloria Watkins/bell hooks (b. 1952) reenergized the genre of the defense of women as well as feminist theory and feminist polemic. Feminist insights have been interwoven with personal vision by writers such as Elizabeth Janeway (b. 1913), essayist, social analyst, novelist; Grace Paley (b. 1922), activist and short story writer; Adrienne Rich (b. 1929), poet, critic, essayist; Audre Lorde (1934–92), poet, essayist, autobiographer; Alix Kates Shulman (b. 1932), novelist, children's writer, anthologist; Marge Piercy (b. 1936), poet, novelist; June Jordan (b. 1936), poet, essayist; and Marilyn Hacker (b. 1942), poet, editor. Editors and publishers established feminist magazines, journals, and presses. The development of multicultural women's studies and the areas of women's history and feminist criticism offered new methods for reading women writers.

Alongside feminism, the second major development in U.S. women's literary history was the increasing acceptance of the pluralism of U.S. writing by both women and men and the growing diversity of their audience. In 1950 Gwendolyn Brooks (b. 1917), who first published at the age of eleven, became the first Black person to receive the Pulitzer Prize, for her volume of poetry *Annie Allen* (1949); by the late 1960s her belief in Black nationalism precipitated a commitment to Black publishing and eventually to the establishment of her own house, The David Company. In 1982 Alice Walker (b. 1944) won the Pulitzer Prize for *The Color Purple*. In 1993 Toni Morrison (b. 1931) became the first African American to win the Nobel Prize for literature.

Women of Native American, Asian, and Latina descent are also writing in increasing numbers: Maxine Hong Kingston (b. 1940), Mitsuye Yamada (b. 1923), Louise Erdrich (b. 1954), Leslie Marmon Silko (b. 1948), Cherríe Moraga (b. 1952), Ana Castillo (b. 1953), Sandra Cisneros (b. 1954). They speak at the point where race, ethnicity, and gender meet. Their works are often marked by stylistic and cultural hybridity, mingling languages and genres in an effort to negotiate boundaries and to articulate the complex situation of double and even triple marginality. They ask what it means to be alive and to write in a United States that has not always wanted a woman of color to write or to be alive.

In the 1990s many Americans began to describe society as "postmodern" rather than "modern" and their environment as "cyberspace" rather than a "landscape" or a "place." In this United States, the fate of writing by women, men, or computers with artificial intelligence has still to be determined. Yet as long as the human species uses language, it will compose narratives, tell stories, crack jokes, cast spells, and sing out lyrically. In new genres, through new media, the various voices of literary women in the United States will mingle in what Emily Dickinson called a "Titanic Opera" of language.

Sandra M. Gilbert and Susan Gubar, *The Norton Anthology of Literature by Women: The Tradition in English* (New York: Norton, 1985); Emory Elliott, ed., *The Columbia Literary History of the United States* (New York: Columbia University Press, 1988); Paul Lauter, ed., *The Heath Anthology of American Literature,* 2 vols. (Lexington, Mass.: D. C. Heath, 1990); Cathy N. Davidson and Linda Wagner-Martin, eds., *The Oxford Companion to Women's Writing in the United States* (New York: Oxford University Press, 1995).

> • CATHARINE R. STIMPSON,
> with MARILEE LINDEMANN
> and MARTHA NELL SMITH

SEE ALSO Autobiography; Feminist Literary Criticism; Feminist Presses, Publications, and Bookstores; Harlem Renaissance; Romance Novels.

≋ LULAC

SEE League of United Latin American Citizens.

≋ Lynching

Mob violence and vigilantism or "establishment violence" are deeply entrenched traditions that began in the eighteenth-century Western frontier in the United States. Rosenbaum and Sederberg defined the latter as "the use of violence by established groups to preserve the status quo at times when the formal system of rule enforcement is viewed as ineffective or irrelevant." *Lynch Law* was a term used during the Revolutionary War, when Virginian Charles Lynch organized a group of vigilantes to eliminate invading British from the region. Following the war, Lynch's extralegal actions were deemed justifiable by the Virginia legislature on the grounds that the Tories were a clear and present danger and law and order needed to be restored by any means necessary.

During the antebellum era the primary victims of lynching or mob violence were rebellious Black slaves and, to a lesser extent, abolitionist white men. Since lynching records were not kept before 1882, it is difficult to ascertain the incidence of racially motivated violence. Lynching reached its peak, however, in the South between 1880 and 1900, when African American men, stereotyped as savage criminals, became the primary victims. Southern whites also wanted to halt "negro domination" and intimidate Black men attempting to exercise their newly gained right to vote. Between 1882 and 1923 over five hundred Blacks were lynched in Georgia, the largest number of lynchings in the United States. The myth of the Black male rapist who harbored an insatiable lust for white women was a contrivance and the most frequently cited reason for lynching, though not the major cause of the Lynch Law. Lynchings were a public ritual that included men, women, and children as witnesses; they also saw bodies being burned following a hanging or shooting and the distribution of portions of the body for souvenirs among those gathered.

Contemporary discussions of racial violence, particularly lynching, focus primarily on Black men, though individual women and their organizations were critical in efforts to expose the horrors of lynching during the late nineteenth and early twentieth centuries. Seventy-six Black women were lynched between 1882 and 1927; sixteen white women were lynching victims during the same period.

African American women's antilynching activity, largely overlooked by scholars, began with Ida Wells-Barnett, who was motivated to conduct a systematic investigation of the real reasons why Blacks were lynched following the 1892 killings of three innocent businessmen (one of whom was a close friend) by angry white mobs in Memphis, Tennessee. The mobs resented the men's economic success and whisked them away from jail in the middle of the night. Wells-Barnett described the brutal lynchings in her newspaper *The Free Speech* and urged Blacks to leave Memphis and settle in the West. Six thousand people did relocate within two months. One inflammatory editorial suggested that white women engaged in voluntary liaisons with Black men; the article aroused enormous anger and her newspaper offices were destroyed as a result. Wells-Barnett was also threatened with lynching if she returned to Memphis from her vacation in the North. In 1893 she chronicled lynchings from January 1882 to January 1892 and identified the charges for which the 728 Black men were killed. She also indicated that women were also victims of mob rule and described the lynching in 1886 of one Black woman in Jackson, Tennessee, accused of poisoning her white mistress. The woman was dragged from jail, "every stitch of clothing torn from her body, and was hung in the public court house square in sight of everybody," according to Wells-Barnett.

Women played a significant role in the antilynching movement on a number of fronts. The Black women's club movement, which began in the 1890s, fought against lynching. Clubwomen also supported Wells-Barnett morally and financially in her efforts to publish two antilynching pamphlets, *Southern Horrors: Lynch Law in All Its Phases* (1892) and *The Red Record* (1895). Antilynching strategies accounted for a major part of the reform work of the National Association of Colored Women (NACW), founded in 1896; they also worked with other civil rights organizations, such as the National Association for the Advancement of Colored People (NAACP), in support of the 1918 Dwyer Bill, which would have made lynching a federal crime, although the bill never passed the Senate.

African American women, as part of their strategy, enlisted and encouraged white women to join the antilynching movement. White U.S. women were slow to respond. Black clubwomen, including Mary Church Terrell, Wells-Barnett, and others, persisted, however. They appealed to Southern white women and accused them of being complicit in the national crime of lynching for not speaking out against the rape of Black women by white men and for supporting arguments that lynching protected white womanhood. In the 1920s and 1930s white women began to heed the call from Black women, initially in organizations such as the Commission on Interracial Cooperation and the National Council of Women. Perhaps the most well-known public antilynching effort by white women was the white-only Association of Southern Women for the Prevention of Lynching (ASWPL), founded in Atlanta in 1930 by Jessie Daniel Ames, who underscored the relationship between lynching and the sexual control of white women. According to Ames's biography, Ames felt that "lynching was not just a punishment for forcible assault; it was also a severe sanction against voluntary sexual relations" between white women and Black men, and enforced the notion of white supremacy.

The definitive narrative of the role of Black and white women in the antilynching movement that spanned half a century remains to be written. Although Black women were important pioneers in one of the most important reform movements in the United States, they have been largely invisible; the men of the NAACP and Southern white women received greater attention. Until this narrative is rewritten, lynching will continue to be perceived primarily as a crime against Black males and the violence to which Black women have been subjected—rape and lynching—will remain unseen.

Paula Giddings, *When and Where I Enter* (New York: William Morrow & Company, 1984); Jacquelyn Dowd Hall, "'The Mind That Burns in Each Body': Women, Rape and Racial Violence," in *Powers of Desire, The Politics of Sexuality*, edited by Ann Snitow, Christine Stansell, and Sharon Thompson (New York: Monthly Review Press, 1983); H. Jon Rosenbaum and Peter C. Sederberg, eds., *Vigilante Politics* (Philadelphia: University of Pennsylvania Press, 1976).

■ BEVERLY GUY-SHEFTALL

SEE ALSO Interracial Cooperation Movement; Pedestal.

≋ Magazines

Women in the United States have been valued magazine readers ever since periodicals appeared in this country in 1741. The first published specifically for women was the *Lady's Magazine and Repository of Entertaining Knowledge* (1792–93). It sought an elite audience, as did the famous *Godey's Lady's Book* (1830–98), which sold 150,000 copies monthly at its peak in the 1850s. In *Godey's*, readers found some discussion of women's rights and employment amid the sentimental fiction and elaborate fashion plates offered by editor Sarah Josepha Hale.

For an entirely different readership, Massachusetts mill workers presented a sometimes ideal-ized picture of factory life in *The Lowell Offering* (1840–45), and the Park Hill Female Seminary produced *Cherokee Rose Bud* (1848). Amelia Bloomer's *The Lily* (1849–56) promoted temperance and dress reform and, in 1868, Elizabeth Cady Stanton and Susan B. Anthony founded *The Revolution*, a sixteen-page weekly that branched out from women's rights to such topics as land and labor reform. In the 1890s an early magazine published by African American women, *The Woman's Era* (1894–1903), appeared, and Rosa Sonnenschein founded *The American Jewess* (1895–99).

Of course, women's journalistic contributions over the years were not limited to magazines for women. Margaret Fuller, for example, edited the influential transcendentalist journal *The Dial* (1840–44). Ida Tarbell's 1903 series on Standard Oil Company abuses helped *McClure's Magazine* claim its place in muckraking history. Women's periodicals, however, had led the way when readership began to increase dramatically after the Civil War. Encouraged by the Postal Act of 1879, which facilitated nationwide communications with low second-class rates, the number of magazine titles grew overall from 700 in 1865 to 4,400 by 1890. In 1904 the *Ladies' Home Journal* was the first to reach one million in circulation.

Some of the new crop of magazines directed at women were mail-order catalogues that ran barely enough editorial material to qualify for the low postal rates. Others, such as *McCall's* (1876) and *The Delineator* (1873–1937), began as dress-pattern books after domestic sewing machines had become available to middle-class women. They offered a democratic alternative to the designs that experienced seamstresses copied from *Godey's* cover engravings and plates, hand-colored by a staff of 150 women, and to the fashion shown in the newer *Harper's Bazaar* (1867) and *Vogue* (1892).

Of the new magazines, the *Ladies' Home Journal* was poised to take maximum advantage of a confluence of high literacy, increased availability of consumer goods, and a population whose migrations cut them off from familial sources of information. Founded in 1893 by Cyrus Curtis as a supplement to his farm journal, it was first edited by his wife, working under her birth name, Louisa Knapp. Knapp's son-in-law, Edward Bok, later opposed woman's suffrage and wrote disapprovingly of club activity. But most of his audience disagreed with him and did not hesitate to say so, both in reader surveys and in letters to the editor.

In the twentieth century, women's fashion magazines were as innovative visually as Curtis's *Journal* was commercially. In the 1930s Carmel Snow began to edit *Harper's Bazaar*, where she worked with brilliant artists and photographers to create a cinematic flow of illustration and words. Her pages accommodated fiction and poetry by Colette, Virginia Woolf, and Marianne Moore. In 1936 Snow hired Diana Vreeland who, at *Bazaar* and later at *Vogue*, became a legendary fashion editor. Also in the 1930s *Family Circle* (1932) and *Woman's Day* (1937) began as weekly giveaways at food stores. At the end of the decade, the first issue of *Glamour* appeared, promising the "Hollywood way to fashion, beauty, charm" for fifteen cents.

During World War II the propaganda potential of women's magazines was well appreciated. Geraldine Rhoads, who edited a number of women's magazines including *Woman's Day*, attended one meeting in which federal officials "literally laid out plots" for magazine fiction to manipulate attitudes toward servicemen and Rosie-the-Riveters on the homefront.

Although few new titles appeared in the 1950s and 1960s, women's magazines were becoming so financially successful that they were derisively referred to as the "cash cows" of the industry. Something of a sea change was prefaced in 1965 when Helen Gurley Brown remade *Cosmopolitan* after the success of her bestseller *Sex and the Single Girl*. *Essence*, founded in 1970 as an alternative for Black women, was implicitly feminist because it spoke to an audience that, for example, found it natural for women to work both inside and outside the home. Two years later *Ms.* magazine

The October 1965 cover of The Ladder, *featuring a photograph of an early march for lesbian and gay rights.*

reached out to readers so hungry for an explicitly feminist message that three hundred thousand copies of the preview issue sold out in eight days. In the context of a vibrant new feminist and lesbian-feminist press, Gloria Steinem worked collectively with a group of editors who introduced the fiction and poetry of Alice Walker and Erica Jong and, in language that readers embraced, Jane O'Reilly's feminist "clicks."

Other publications sought out women readers who were transforming their lives. In the 1970s the Jewish feminist magazine *Lilith* began; a quarterly newsletter *Ohoyo* ("woman" in Choctaw) was founded for Native American women and survived for four years; and the progressive Asian

American magazine *Bridge* put out a number of special issues by and about women. The Latina community has produced *Encuentro Feminil* and *Revista Mujeres. Working Woman* (1976), founded to support women challenging male preserves in the workplace, achieved the fastest-growing advertising revenues in the entire industry in 1982. *Lear's* (1988–93) and *Mirabella* (1989) broke ground by daring to address women older than those presumably coveted by advertisers.

Under pressure from feminism, the more traditional women's magazines also began to evolve. In 1976 and again in 1979, more than thirty women's magazines simultaneously published articles about the Equal Rights Amendment—most of them positive though some merely informative—and in 1992 *Glamour* won a National Magazine Award for its abortion coverage. The fact that Ms. had to stop competing for ads in 1989 and rely only on subscribers indicates how difficult it is to achieve institutional change. In 1994, when *Good Housekeeping* editor John Mack Carter stepped down, women then held the editor-in-chief positions for all the major women's magazines in the United States.

> Helen Damon-Moore, *Magazines for the Millions: Gender and Commerce in the "Ladies' Home Journal" and the "Saturday Evening Post," 1880–1910* (Albany: State University of New York, 1994); Gloria Steinem, "Sex, Lies, and Advertising," in *Moving Beyond Words* (New York: Simon & Schuster, 1994); Mary Ellen Zuckerman, *Women's Magazines and the American Woman* (New York: Columbia University Press, forthcoming).

     ▪ MARY THOM

SEE ALSO Feminist Presses, Publications, and Bookstores; Newspapers.

≋ Mail-Order Brides

Mail-order bride buying and selling usually involves marketing women from underdeveloped countries to men in highly developed countries, especially Europe, the United States, Australia, and Japan. Men select wives through mail-order catalogues and videos or they take sex tours that are arranged by mail-order bride agencies. Women in poverty who see no chance to improve their condition within their home country may make themselves available for these arrangements. Mail-order bride buying is both racist and sexist because it is promoted as an "opportunity" for First World men to find wives in other cultures who are less influenced by the women's movement, who are less independent, and who will serve their every need. Women who immigrate through mail-order arrangements are then trapped in a marriage without their own income and by immigrant laws that require their deportation if they leave the marriage. Mail-order bride agencies and schemes exploit desperate labor migration policies in poor countries whose leaders encourage immigration to other countries to find work. Women leaving their native lands for marriage abroad is generally an additional relief to their country's labor force. Under President Corazon Aquino, the Philippines became the first country to ban mail-order bride buying and selling as a human rights violation. The patriarchal culture base for mail-order bride trafficking lies in traditional family-arranged marriages—the transfer of daughters from father to husband, usually involving a payment in the form of dowry by the bride's family.

     ▪ KATHLEEN BARRY

≋ Manners and Etiquette

Mentioning "manners and etiquette" to progressive women of the late twentieth century is a little like yelling "Veal!" in a crowd of vegans. Of all the conventions that helped keep women in their place, etiquette may be the most proscribed: There were, after all, *rules*. And these rules placed women in the kitchen and men in the Cabinet. But there are misconceptions as well.

One distortion is that women wrote all the rules that imprisoned them. Though women such as Emily and Elizabeth Post, Letitia Baldridge, and Judith Martin have gained fame as arbiters of taste, in the early years of the Republic, the enormous question of what would be appropriate etiquette in this new "classless" society was the province of men. In European society men had as great an interest in etiquette as women and this carried over to the colonies. George Washington, Thomas Jefferson, Benjamin Franklin, and Ralph Waldo Emerson all wrote about it. It was the scarcity of women and men's need to impress them that improved men's manners.

Another misconception is that the rules of etiquette encroached on a woman's freedom, when in fact some were designed to provide them safety. The United States is a country born from conflict, its raucous entry into the community of nations marked by colonial conquest, revolution, domination, and manifest destiny. And women often were among those most buffeted by the peculiarly violent winds of U.S. expansionism.

The written history of U.S. etiquette has virtually ignored people of color, as well as Jews, lesbians, and gays, while the operation of etiquette in society has also worked both subtly and overtly to marginalize and exclude. That the rules of etiquette may differ among classes and cultures is also largely absent from the written discourse on manners. Etiquette expert Judith Martin, known to her millions of readers as "Miss Manners," notes that stringent etiquette may originally have protected white women from rough treatment in the early nineteenth century. Needless to say, the weight of manners has never been enough to stifle brutality toward "the weaker sex."

The rise of the middle class and the Industrial Revolution gave birth to the division of labor between women and men, thrusting women into the private realm, not just of child rearing but also of social, cultural, civic, and philanthropic activities. It was in these areas that women wrote the rules. To a greater or lesser extent the women who created rules abridging their own rights and freedoms had internalized the misogyny that swirled around them. For example, Mrs. H. O. Ward, whose *Sensible Etiquette of the Best Society* was published in 1878, wrote: "What do women want with votes, when they hold the scepter of influence with which they can control even votes, if they wield it right?" Her little treatise against woman's suffrage is tucked between a discussion of "bad society" and instructions on how to proceed from the drawing room to the dining room for a formal dinner party.

In a curious proscription that has been passed down in various forms since the earliest U.S. settlements, "talking" by women was considered impolite and in some cases cause for punishment. Gerald Carson in the *Polite Americans* reported that in seventeenth-century America, "Women in Maine whose tongues wagged maliciously were gagged. In East Hampton, New York, cleft sticks were slipped over too-busy tongues." This, while men gabbed incessantly in taverns and town halls throughout the colonies. In modern times the talking prohibition has been applied to women activists who are "strident," women politicians who are "tough," and feminists who are "shrill" in their efforts to be heard.

While etiquette, much like baseball fanaticism and sexual openness, ebbs and flows with the times—waxing in the froufrou 1890s and waning in the turbulent 1960s—a late-twentieth-century phenomenon has again brought etiquette to the fore. That phenomenon is the flood of women who entered the work force in the early 1970s and sent the etiquette gurus racing back to their drawing boards. Elizabeth L. Post, in *Business Etiquette* (1990), offers a chapter, "Especially for Men," in which she advises men not to stand up when a woman enters a conference room: "Only the man seated in the chair next to her should rise, to pull out her chair." Letitia Baldrige's massive 1993 tome, *New Complete Guide to Executive Manners*, features the chapter heading, "The Executive Faces Problems in Today's Working World Which Never Existed Before." Among the problems addressed: "An older woman who sees a young male executive trying unsuccessfully to hail a cab (because he's laden with luggage, briefcases, and an umbrella) should find and hail the cab for him."

While the history of U.S. etiquette written by whites has virtually ignored Latinas, Asian Americans, Native Americans, African Americans, Jews, lesbians, and gays, the modern etiquette experts all devote space in their most recent work to the impolitesse of racism, anti-Semitism, and homophobia. And an issue that many would assume to be a point of law has also been a point of etiquette—sexual harassment. "A well-known politician," Martin says, "tried to make the claim that the rules kept changing. There didn't used to be anything wrong with grabbing women by the hair and shoving your tongue in their mouths. But of course there was a rule of etiquette against it. No decent man would do this."

Martin is of course talking about Senator Bob Packwood (R., Oreg.) who was accused in 1994–95 of sexual harassment by some thirty women. These accusations, along with Supreme Court Justice Clarence Thomas's alleged sexual harassment of Anita Hill, made the issue a hallmark of the 1990s.

"The etiquette we're working on enforcing now," writes Martin, "is the one that requires men to treat women respectfully in the workplace. Men shouldn't be able to use the excuse that women really have no business in certain places when they engage in behavior ranging from the merely rude to the now illegal. A tremendous history of prejudice has hampered professional women."

■ KATE ROUNDS

≋ Maquiladora

Since 1965, under the Border Industrialization Program (BIP), the Mexican government has granted licenses to foreign companies, mostly U.S.-owned, for the temporary importation of duty-free machinery, raw materials, parts, and components. After being assembled in Mexican plants, they are exported, primarily to the United States. Duties levied for export are based solely on the value added by the actual cost of wages and related costs in Mexico.

Many U.S. companies have not simply opened new facilities in Mexico but have also taken advantage of low costs by relocating. They are attracted by labor costs that in 1990 were one-eighth the U.S. minimum wage, by loose environmental protection laws, by unions that make few demands on companies, and by unenforced safety regulations. The number of these runaway U.S. factories—*maquiladoras* or *maquilas* as they are called in Mexico—has now risen to an estimated two thousand. They are the fastest-growing sector of the Mexican economy. Although Mexico's interior is now open to *maquiladoras*, over 85 percent of these operations remain along the border between Tijuana and Matamoros, employing nearly 500,000 Mexican workers. Seventy percent are young women between the ages of sixteen and twenty-four.

Young women are considered the ideal maquiladora workforce. They can be paid less than men; they are not only outside the labor organizing tradition because of gender but are often too burdened by home responsibilities to be easily organized; and as this work is usually a first job they are unlikely to know their own rights.

Although the *maquiladoras* mean new jobs for desperate people, mostly women, they also mean poor working and living conditions. Tens of thousands of workers are now packed into shantytown *colonias*, living with no electricity, sewers, potable water, or garbage service.

■ TANI TAKAGI

Marches

Since the early part of this century, activist U.S. women have used marches to champion important issues. As early as 1903 labor reformer Mary Harry ("Mother") Jones organized children working in factories to parade in front of city hall in Kensington, Pennsylvania, with their maimed fingers and hands held high in the air. A suffrage parade in 1913 helped to integrate the movement; members of the Black sorority Delta Sigma Theta marched as a delegation, while Black activist Ida B. Wells-Barnett marched side by side with white women from Illinois. In 1913 and 1914 African American activist Lucy Parsons led mass demonstrations of homeless and unemployed people in San Francisco and Chicago. In 1917 Black women in white dresses were prominent in the front lines of a fifteen-thousand-person march in New York protesting lynchings and racial discrimination.

In the latter half of the twentieth century, Latina women in the United Farm Workers Union movement marched to gain improved working conditions. Women activists also marched on behalf of tenant farmers. Black women were among the thousands of protesters arrested during civil rights marches throughout the south, and they heard Dr. Martin Luther King, Jr.'s "I Have a Dream" speech during the enormous August 1963 march on Washington. Women joined in Vietnam-Era antiwar marches and protests. And women participated in Solidarity Day marches with men in the labor movement.

On August 26, 1970, on the fiftieth anniversary of woman's suffrage, the National Organization for Women (NOW) organized a "Women's Strike for Equality." Hundreds of thousands of women marched or participated in demonstrations and rallies throughout the country. In 1978 feminist activists organized the first "Take Back the Night" marches around the country, protesting sexual assault and other violence against women. Feminists joined in a 1979 antipornography march and helped organize the first national gay and lesbian rights march, which drew one hundred thousand people.

Marches on behalf of the Equal Rights Amendment (ERA) began in May 1976, when NOW brought sixteen thousand supporters to Springfield, Illinois. In August 1977 four thousand people marched down Pennsylvania Avenue to demand that President Carter take a more active role in efforts to ratify the ERA. In 1978 one hundred thousand people again marched on Washington to press for an extension of the time limit on ratifying the ERA, and the extension was granted.

After the defeat of the ERA in 1982, feminist activists did not organize major marches again until the late 1980s and early 1990s. NOW organized a record-breaking crowd of six hundred thousand people for an abortion rights march in 1989, then broke its own record during another march in 1992. Lesbian and gay rights marches on Washington in 1993 and New York in 1994 each drew crowds estimated at three hundred thousand to one million. A far smaller crowd marched on Washington in 1993 and helped increase appropriations for breast cancer research by $100 million.

Marches have built and rejuvenated various movements for women's rights. Marches have forced issues into the forefront of political debate and provided strong new networks of activists and contributors. Efforts to mobilize local participants have turned inexperienced activists into community leaders working together to wage the ongoing struggle for women's equality.

• PATRICIA IRELAND

Marches, Lesbian and Gay

Three lesbians in skirts and seven gay men in suits picketed the White House on April 17, 1965. Those ten lonely protesters never imagined that thirty years later one million people would march for lesbian and gay rights. In a society where homosexuals were expected to hide, visibility was strength. "Out of the closet and into the streets!" became both a chant and a key strategy in the struggle for equality.

The first official national March on Washington for Lesbian and Gay Rights was held on October 14, 1979. The established national organizations had feared that people would not risk coming out, but over one hundred thousand marchers, "gay and proud," followed the lesbians of color who carried the lead banner down Pennsylvania Avenue.

The second national March on Washington for Lesbian and Gay Rights brought out almost six hundred fifty thousand people on October 11, 1987. Chanting "For love and for life, we're not going back," the angry marchers protested the lack of AIDS funding and the Supreme Court's 1986 *Hardwick* decision, which criminalized gay sex. Among the eighty events that took place that weekend were the inaugural unfolding of the NAMES Project Quilt, a morning rally organized by the People of Color Caucus, and the largest civil disobedience action ever held at the Supreme Court. Although the major media ignored the march, the participants went home inspired and empowered. People used this energy to create many new lesbian and gay organizations.

The National March on Washington for Lesbian, Gay and Bi Equal Rights and Liberation on April 25, 1993, attracted some eight hundred thousand people and extraordinary media coverage. The marchers were hopeful and called on President Clinton to keep his promise to lift the ban on gays in the military. Allies from the civil rights and women's movements joined elected officials and celebrities at the speakers' podium. The "Dyke March" for lesbian visibility was one of hundreds of related events.

The twenty-fifth anniversary of the Stonewall Rebellion was marked on June 26, 1994, when about one million lesbian, gay, bisexual, and transgender people and their families, friends, and allies marched in New York City. The Stonewall Rebellion commemorates events that resulted from a routine raid at a gay bar, the Stonewall Inn, on June 28, 1969. Lesbians and drag queens, many of them people of color, led the fight against police. Their resistance sparked a three-day rebellion generally regarded as the birth of the modern lesbian and gay rights movement. By 1995 people in three hundred cities in twenty countries celebrated Stonewall's anniversary with annual Pride Day marches and parades.

Marches provide visibility, support, safety in numbers, and a sense of joy and celebration that lesbian and gay people need to continue the fight for justice and equality for all Americans.

▪ JOAN E. BIREN

≋ Marriage

Throughout U.S. history, marriage has been deemed a social good, especially for women. If marriage rates for a specific group of women diminished—as happened for college-educated women in the late 1800s—this was generally treated as cause for concern. Unlike divorce rates, the marriage rates for women have remained fairly consistent. Allowing for some deviations, it has been true since nationhood that less than 10 percent of women eligible to marry never marry during their lifetime.

While marriage has significant social, psychological, religious, and cultural dimensions, these have often been overshadowed by legal definitions. The historical trajectory of marriage is often described as a shift from marriage as a status to the notion of marriage as a contract, but both status and contract coexist in conceptions of marriage. The law has traditionally constructed marriage as limited to two people, one man and one woman, whose marriage creates a legal unity represented in the public sphere by the male partner. Thus, until the Married Women's Property Acts of the 1840s, married women were not able to own property or enter into contracts because their legal existence had been extinguished by the status of marriage. Rooted in the theory of the legal unity of marriage are more recent laws, including state statutes that attempted to require spousal notification before a married woman could obtain an abortion. The Supreme Court has declared that these spousal notification laws violate constitutional privacy (*Planned Parenthood of Southeastern Pennsylvania v. Casey*). Perhaps ironically, the notion of constitutional privacy itself springs from the notion of marriage as a legal unity; the first case recognizing a privacy right to obtain contraception identified the right in relation to the sanctity of the marital relation (*Griswold v. Connecticut*).

Whether marriage is viewed as status or contract, it is pervasively regulated by state law. Since colonial times, state laws have governed marriage, including who was qualified to perform the ceremony. At first, only justices of the peace were so qualified, but this soon was expanded to include clergy certified by the state, despite objections that such authority violated the separation of church and state. Now most states require some sort of ceremony and the registration of a marriage certificate. A handful of states recognize common-law marriage, meaning that the state will deem a relationship a legal marriage even if there is no ceremony and registration if the couple can meet certain other requirements, such as living together for a certain period of years and defining themselves as married.

In the slave states before the Civil War, slaves could not enter into any contracts, including the marriage contract. After the Civil War, one of the first issues to be considered by legislators in states of the former Confederacy was the legalization of slave unions. While this may have partially been a recognition of the humanity of former slaves, there are some arguments that the state interest in marriage was a mechanism to deem children the financial responsibility of freedmen rather than of their former masters or of the state itself. A vestige of the slave codes persisted in miscegenation laws, which disqualified and often criminalized marriages between nonwhite persons and white persons. Many states began to repeal their miscegenation laws after World War II, but it was not until 1967 that the Supreme Court held that miscegenation laws were unconstitutional (*Loving v. Virginia*).

State laws have historically regulated, and continue to regulate, the degree of permissible relation between the parties, prohibiting, for example, marriages between brothers and sisters or between first cousins. The rationale for such laws is based upon questionable notions of genetics and supports prohibitions of all such marriages, even when the couple would not or could not procreate. Although such marriages are usually not criminal, the state generally views such marriages as void and refuses to recognize them.

State laws also regulate the minimum age for marriage, usually legislating differently for females and males. For example, the legal age for marriage with parental consent ranges from twelve years for females and fourteen years for males in some states and without parental consent the ages range from sixteen to twenty-one for females and eighteen to twenty-one for males. The courts have generally rejected arguments that the differential ages for men and women constitute gender discrimination, concluding that the state's goal of preventing unwed teenage pregnancy is a sufficiently important reason for the differential.

All states now prohibit a person who is already legally married from entering into another marriage; however, this has been a controversial issue in U.S. history because of the Mormons' acceptance of polygamy. Although marriage is supposedly within the province of state rather than federal regulation, the federal government conditioned Utah's entry into the Union upon abolishment of its laws permitting polygamy, causing the delay of Utah's statehood until 1896, more than forty years after the initial application.

Echoes of the federal-state conflict regarding polygamy are found in the contemporary controversy surrounding same-sex marriage. Although during the 1970s many courts had rejected challenges to the limiting of marriage licenses to couples consisting of a male and a female, in 1993 the Hawai'i Supreme Court ruled that such treatment might constitute sex discrimination (*Baehr* v. *Levin*). The court relied upon its state constitutional provision prohibiting sex discrimination and held that unless the state could demonstrate a compelling interest for the limitation of marriage to male-female couples, the practice must be discontinued and same-sex couples must be allowed to avail themselves of legal marriage. When the case was remanded for trial, the trial court found that the state did not satisfy its burden of demonstrating a compelling reason and most observers expect that the Hawai'i Supreme Court will affirm this ruling. Such an affirmation would legalize same-sex marriages in Hawai'i, although opponents plan to amend the state constitution to prevent such a decision from taking effect.

Whether same-sex marriages in one state would be valid in other states is unclear. In response to the Hawai'i litigation, in 1996 Congress passed the Defense of Marriage Act (DOMA), which attempts to clarify that states need not recognize same-sex marriages. Many states have passed similar statutes providing that the state will not recognize same-sex marriages even if such marriages are legally valid in other states. These state laws as well as DOMA contradict the general practice of states recognizing as valid marriages that are valid in other states, a practice that is possibly mandated by the full faith and credit clause of the Constitution.

The controversy over same-sex marriage not only implicates laws and legislators but feminist theorists have also divided over the issue. In one feminist view, legalizing same-sex marriage has the potential to erode the gendered configuration of marriage and to liberalize and perhaps even liberate the institution of marriage from its patriarchal roots. In the opposite view, legalizing same-sex marriage will mean merely that same-sex couples will be assimilated into the institution of marriage with all its defects, including its current construction as a civil contract among three parties, one of which is always the state.

▪ RUTHANN ROBSON

SEE ALSO Coverture; Divorce and Custody; Families; Legal Status.

≋ Maternity Homes

Maternity homes had their origins in the late nineteenth century, when white, middle-class, evangelical Protestant women—many of whom were Woman's Christian Temperance Union members, teachers, or missionaries—established "rescue homes" in a dual effort to redeem what they saw as desperate, powerless female victims of urbanization and industrialization, and to assert their own female moral authority, grounded in piety and sexual purity. Rescuers cast themselves as doing "women's work for women," and believed that their charges, often prostitutes, would embrace the values of late-nineteenth-century middle-class womanhood after receiving prolonged training in domestic skills and Christian virtues.

Rescue homes were first established in the 1880s, including the first Crittenton homes for prostitutes (1882) and the first Salvation Army Home (1887). By 1909 there were seventy-eight Crittenton homes all over the country, and in that year, Kate Waller Barrett took charge of the National Florence Crittenton Mission and began to shift the organization's mission from rescuing prostitutes to providing refuge for unwed mothers. Over the next twenty years, many rescue homes followed suit, partly because these facilities never attracted enough prostitutes. Also, in most cities, prostitution had become a criminal offense handled by the police.

The women who founded the homes carried their evangelical purposes into their work with the new clientele, mostly working-class unwed mothers with few resources or alternatives. Home matrons and staff generally construed the origins of the pregnant woman's plight as a matter of seduction and abandonment. They did not perceive unwed mothers as "bad girls," exactly; but they believed that the women's unwed pregnancies proved that they were morally vulnerable as well as untrained in religious and domestic life. Maternity home staffs aimed to ameliorate these deficiencies by keeping unwed mothers in the home for a year or more, imbuing every aspect of life with religious fervor, and training their charges to be domestic servants (considered appropriately submissive and educative employment for ruined but spiritually redeemable daughters of the working class).

A key principle in all homes in this era claimed that only by becoming a mother to her child would the unwed mother overcome the degradations of seduction, abandonment, and out-of-wedlock pregnancy and achieve redemption. The sins of seducers were beyond the province of the homes; unwed mothers alone were expected to bear the consequences of illicit sex and maternity and take full responsibility for the child as well as for their own renewal.

Between 1910 and 1930 the authority of the evangelical founders was compromised, first by newly minted "experts"—academically trained social workers and social scientists who became interested in the diagnosis and treatment of unwed mothers. These professionals explained female sexual deviance, including illegitimate pregnancy, as the result of the poisonous interaction between negative sociological or environmental conditions—the immigrant urban slum, for example—and negative biological conditions—the innate degeneracy of the lower classes, where illegitimacy was judged to occur frequently. The new experts prescribed a shortened stay in the home and stressed the importance of learning practical maternal and vocational skills. The revamped diagnosis and program were championed as well by the Community Chest, which began to supplant religious-based giving as the main source of financial support for maternity homes. The secular, community-based funders, along with the Children's Bureau, credited their professional peers as modern, credentialed experts and pressured evangelical maternity home matrons to cede authority accordingly.

In the 1940s, as the white illegitimacy rate rose sharply, homes continued to professionalize treatment, a process that often involved a struggle between evangelicals and the social work professionals. From 1940 to 1970 social workers, psychologists, and psychiatrists forcefully insisted that the home resident—now likely after World War II to be a white, middle-class girl—was a maladjusted individual whose out-of-wedlock pregnancy was proof of psychological disturbance that could be cured, if and only if she submitted to treatment under the auspices of the home. The experts recommended that first the girl and her family must arrange her disappearance from family and community. Then the unwed mother must undergo intensive psychological treatment; and most important, she must agree to relinquish her illegitimate child to a married couple, for without a husband, the young woman was not a mother, according to the ideology of the era. Having cooperated, the unwed mother could ostensibly deny the entire episode and resume development toward normative, middle-class womanhood. This program was considered a reform over the days when fallen women were forever stigmatized. The new, professionalized home staff rarely imagined, however, the devastating, lifelong consequences many unwed mothers of that era suffered for having been shamed and coerced into relinquishing their babies.

From the advent of the homes in the late nineteenth century through the post–World War II period, most homes were for whites only. This practice reflected segregation policies governing most institutions in the United States until well after midcentury and also reflected the determination of white authorities to treat white unwed mothers differently from unwed mothers of color, whether they were Black, Latina, or Native American. White authorities argued that illegitimate pregnancy was not a shameful event in these communities, so unwed mothers of color needed neither refuge nor relinquishment-oriented services; in fact they supposedly needed no services at all, since the African American community and other communities of color could always absorb another baby. Nevertheless, a handful of Black urban communities across the country sustained small, Black-only homes for several decades between the 1920s and 1960s. These homes were established and supported variously by coalitions of church and secular leaders. By the early 1960s, unable to support themselves financially, the few that remained were folded into newly integrated Salvation Army or Crittenton homes, all of which received Community Chest backing.

In the late twentieth century, maternity homes still exist, but in two radically different forms. Some, like the Florence Crittenton Home in San Francisco, serve a multiracial, multicultural, generally youthful, indigent population of teenage mothers and their babies, who receive support services, supervision, and sometimes residence on the premises. Other, newer homes, ironically, have revived the evangelical mission of the original founders as they aim to rescue unwed mothers from exercising the option of abortion and protect them from the dangers that face vulnerable young women in this society.

Regina Kunzel, *Fallen Women, Problem Girls: Unmarried Mothers and the Professionalization of Social Work 1890–1945* (New Haven: Yale University Press, 1993); Rickie Solinger, *Wake Up Little Susie: Single Pregnancy and Race Before Roe v. Wade* (New York: Routledge, 1992).

▪ RICKIE SOLINGER

SEE ALSO "Illegitimacy"/Single Pregnancy.

≋ Medical Research

Early health practices in the United States grew out of a long tradition of home-based health maintenance, disease prevention, and self-help "cures" for illnesses. Women's roles had long been to enhance health through dietary means and to aid those who were ill. Although some homemakers and midwives were literate, domestic care was often part of an oral tradition. Women learned by assisting other women.

Less is known about early health beliefs and lay-doctoring practices among Native Americans, Blacks, and Latinos. Particularly in the South, self-help cures were based more in notions of magic, prayer, and spirituality than in what modern physicians would consider science. Ethnically diverse folk practices were nonetheless based on careful observation, were transmitted orally and, in some cases, required an apprenticeship. Like other "recipes," these methods were "kitchen-tested," albeit not rigorously proven. Folk methods were thus subjected to at least a modicum of scrutiny and, perhaps more importantly, were contemporaneously believed to work.

From 1740 through 1860, written domestic health guides often challenged the professional authority of physicians. In the 1700s both physician- and lay-authored manuals existed in the colonies. Some were written by women and combined cooking and medicinal advice in a single volume, stressing proper diet, exercise, fresh air, dress reform, and cleanliness.

Throughout the 1800s increasing conflict existed among competing trained practitioners and their theories. Without a dominant paradigm, there was no orthodoxy against which to judge treatments and identify quackery. By the mid-1800s, a variety of medical groups arose: traditional and nontraditional. Traditional, or regular, medicine was the precursor to modern "scientific" medicine. It was characterized by treatments such as bleeding, purging, and inducing vomiting. In 1809 modern surgery was introduced in the United States by a Kentucky surgeon, Ephraim McDowell, who successfully removed an ovarian cyst. Nontraditional approaches to medicine included homeopathy and, later, osteopathy, chiropractics, and hydropathy. Spiritual and homeopathic approaches to health were often combined with dietary and other lifestyle recommendations.

Women were leaders of several charismatic religions that diverged from what became modern medicine. Mary Baker Eddy, founder of Christian Science, published her textbook on mind healing in 1875. She had earlier been influenced by homeopathy. Ellen White, cofounder of the Seventh-Day Adventist Church in 1963, advocated abstention from meat, alcohol, tobacco, tea, and coffee.

Although women found it harder to gain admission to regular medical schools, they nonetheless participated in both traditional and nontraditional areas of the field. Leaders in the feminist movement did, however, often support nontraditional medicine. For example, Susan B. Anthony's physician was a homeopath, Julia Holmes Smith. Anthony and Amelia Bloomer later helped found the Vegetarian Society. Elizabeth Blackwell, a leading feminist supporter, criticized regular (interventionist) medical science as well as germ theory. The schism between traditional medicine and the various nontraditional groups, as well as the popularity of patent medicines, can be attributed to dissatisfaction with increasingly professionalized medicine.

Some misogynist claims about women were framed in the language of science. In the sixteenth century anatomical drawings and systematic observation of childbirth in France gave rise to "scientific midwifery." Between 1800 and 1840 research was being conducted by relating clinical signs and symptoms with lesions observed at autopsy. Unfortunately, this approach offered little relief in the short run. Advances in anesthesia in the mid-1800s hastened the use of surgical interventions, including those for childbirth. The British later developed surgical tools, such as for-

ceps, which could save lives, giving physicians, in comparison to midwives, a claim to special expertise in childbirth. By 1852 the Alabama physician J. Marion Sims published a method for repairing vaginal tearing sustained during childbirth. Sims is known to have "experimented" surgically on Black female slaves, a form of torture.

In London during the 1860s, sexual surgery on women was practiced briefly, including the removal of healthy ovaries and the clitoris. These practices quickly came into disrepute; still, the practice continued in the United States until the early 1900s.

Women health care providers also used the "scientific" method. Based on her work in the 1850s during the Crimean War, Florence Nightingale provided data supporting the need for sanitary reforms. She kept careful records, contributing to analyses of data on outcomes. For example, she pioneered the use of pie charts to illustrate the percentages of research subjects with different outcomes.

Other women used science to more directly address images of female frailty. In 1873 Dr. Edward Clarke published the influential *Sex and Education*, which popularized the notion that education was physiologically draining for young women and that it was physically damaging to the development of reproductive organs. He concluded that higher education for women produced "monstrous brains and puny bodies."

In the mid-1870s Dr. Mary Putnam Jacobi interviewed 268 women about their menstruation-related experiences and found that those who were generally in poor health or under stress, or who did not exercise enough, had the greatest risk of menstrual pain.

In the early 1900s Henry Hollingworth asked his wife, Leta, to assist him in an experimental study of the effects of caffeine on mental and motor abilities. The women subjects recorded their menses over the six-week study period. The menstrual cycle had no striking relevance and Hollingworth ignored these data in his report. His wife, however, examined the data more carefully and, given recurrent negative stereotypes about menstruation, was much more interested than he in the "negative" finding. She went on to obtain her doctorate and published a study about her research in 1914. In this study, women performed twenty-four tasks at two times during the menstrual cycle, demonstrating that learning and performance were not affected by timing in the cycle.

More generically, notable medical findings made by women around the turn of the century included those of Augusta Klumpke (who won the Academy of Medicine prize for her article on brachial plexus injury); Florence Rena Sabin (on the origins of lymphatic vessels); Dorothy Reed (on the cell type in lymphoid tissue that is pathognomonic for Hodgkin's disease); Alice Evans (on Brucellosis, which was transmitted in untreated milk); Winifred Ashby (who determined red-blood-cell survival time); Maude Slye (who proposed that cancer has a hereditary basis); and Helen Taussig (whose heart research contributed to saving "blue babies"). There were fewer Black than white women physicians. An early Black researcher was May Chin, who believed that her patients were harmed by society as well as by disease. She obtained a public-health degree and worked in cancer research. Women's scientific contributions generally tended to be lost or buried. Women researchers are not as commonly credited or cited in scientific literature as are men.

In the 1800s female physicians specialized mainly in obstetrics and gynecology, pediatrics, public health and education, and counseling. Women activists, including women physicians, played important roles in the public-health movement of the late 1800s and early 1900s. The women's movement of the Progressive Era sought to improve the health of women, especially women as mothers. For example, women were active in the fight to establish infant and prenatal clinics and to distribute milk to the needy.

Women also founded the field of occupational or industrial health. In 1912 Congress banned the use of phosphorus in the match industry. Toxic exposure to phosphorus resulted in jaw necrosis in some workers. Alice Hamilton studied toxic hazards among women workers, ranging from lead poisoning to jaundice caused by TNT poisoning in munitions factories to jaw necrosis caused by radium exposure in watch-dial painters to psychosis as a result of exposure to carbon disulphide among rayon workers. Others who contributed to the field of public health during the 1920s and 1930s were Josephine Baker, Connie Guion, Leona Baumgartner, and Margaret Barnard.

The status of women in medical science diminished after the 1920s. Appeals to "science" were increasingly used to help justify the medicalization of childbirth and, by the 1920s, childbirth was removed from women's homes and brought into the professionally dominated hospitals. To the extent that "women's health" continued to be studied and taught, it survived largely in schools of nursing and in public health and the social health sciences, including psychology.

In the 1960s women initiated widespread, activist concerns about environmental health issues, echoing earlier themes. The Women's Strike for Peace led fifty thousand women in a march against nuclear testing. Thalidomide-related birth defects were recognized in 1962. And Rachel Carson's *Silent Spring* focused public attention on the negative health effects of environmental toxins, such as pesticides.

In the 1970s pregnant women were increasingly excluded from participation in clinical experiments and research, ostensibly because of fears of untoward effects on their unborn offspring. Ethicists and policymakers then were oddly blind to inadequate testing of oral contraceptives and inappropriate use of DES (diethylstilbesterol) in presumably pregnant women. Women's health activists responded to these and other crises by forming groups such as the National Women's Health Network, an important advocacy organization. There was increasing diversity among scientists. Noted Black women researchers since the 1950s have included Jewel Plummer Cobb, a cancer researcher, and Effie Ellis, a parasitologist known for her work on the health and nutrition of the poor. Black physician-scientists have also made their mark in recent years—Janice E. Green Douglas, who has studied mechanisms of blood pressure regulation; Jane C. Wright, who has studied chemotherapy; Joycelyn Elders, who has studied cancer and served as surgeon general of the United States. The next critical step was to directly confront the gaps in scientific knowledge about women's health.

By the mid-1980s women physician-scientists and other health professionals began to work with advocacy and public policy experts in Washington, D.C., to heighten public and professional awareness of research issues pertaining to women's health. This collaboration moved beyond a reactive, crisis-to-crisis approach toward a proactive plan. Interest was galvanized by the public revelation that as little as 13 percent of the budget for government-financed research at the National Institutes of Health went to women's health issues. In particular, there was concern that research on breast cancer, a leading killer of women, was underfunded. Knowledge was lacking about cardiovascular illness among women (compared with the abundance of such knowledge about men) even though it was the leading killer of women. In addition, the negative effects of policies that excluded women from early phases of drug testing were documented. For example, men were found to respond better to some antidepressants than women, even though women were depressed and were treated with antidepressants twice as often as men.

Recent studies have addressed gaps in knowledge about women's health. Current leaders in women's health research include Elizabeth Barrett-Connors, Maureen Henderson, Margaret Chesney, Nancy Woods, Hortensia Amaro, and Vivian Pinn. Barrett-Connors has directed a postmenopausal trial to determine which type of postmenopausal hormone replacement treatment has the best effect on cardiovascular health outcome measures. Early findings will help to guide treatment for many postmenopausal women.

Maureen Henderson, a cancer researcher, originally planned the Women's Health Trial, which was later undertaken by the NIH. This is the largest single study related to midlife women's health. Margaret Chesney, a health psychologist, has studied behavioral factors related to HIV infection, as has Hortensia Amaro. Nancy Woods is a nursing researcher who obtained funding for the first NIH-sponsored Center for Research on Women's Health. One of the most important leaders in women's health research is Vivian Pinn, a physician-scientist specializing in pathology. Pinn has served as the first director of the Office for Research on Women's Health at the NIH. A Black woman, Pinn has worked to ensure the inclusion of people of color in clinical trials.

Current themes in women's health continue to echo those of the 1800s. The present focuses on "alternative" and more humane approaches to health maintenance and disease prevention are strikingly similar to the concerns of social and health reform movements led by women over a hundred years ago. What may distinguish the present revival is that women are increasingly in a position, as medical researchers, to create and define knowledge. Since "women's health" can be considered "applied women's studies," there is also reason to hope that the explosion of feminist knowledge in the humanities and social sciences can be transferred to medical centers and other health institutions in a way that will help institutionalize advances and improve women's lives.

Rima D. Apple, ed., *Women, Health, and Medicine in America: A Historical Handbook* (New Brunswick, N.J.: Rutgers University Press, 1992); G. Kass-Simon and Patricia Farnes, *Women of Science: Righting the Record* (Bloomington: Indiana University Press, 1990); Eileen Nechas and Denise Foley, *Unequal Treatment: What You Don't Know About How Women Are Mistreated by the Medical Community* (New York: Simon & Schuster, 1995).

▪ JEAN A. HAMILTON

See also Cancer.

≋ Men's Movement

Although some would argue that to speak of a "men's movement" in a male-dominated society is redundant and even absurd, the term is commonly used to describe the organized efforts of men to champion, explore, or challenge either traditional notions of masculinity or the feminist movement. Some conservative men's groups have denied that their efforts relate to feminism at all, yet the popularity of such groups throughout U.S. history seems inevitably to follow periods of women's advancement; that is, the late nineteenth century, the mid-1900s, the mid-1940s, the mid-1970s, and from the late 1980s to the early 1990s.

In each period, the men's movement, which is usually comprised of white, middle-class males, falls into three categories. The *antifeminists* defend the "natural law" of male supremacy, warn that higher education for women inhibits fertility, and argue for the exemption of women from public responsibilities due to their higher moral duty to curb the antisocial male. The *masculinists* insist that men themselves suffer gender oppression and seek to protect their virility by establishing preserves against feminization, such as the Boy Scouts and fraternal orders. Robert Bly, author of *Iron John*, led "wild man" retreats for men to recover "essential masculinity" which, in his view, waned during the second wave of U.S. feminism. The *pro-feminists* support suffrage and reproductive rights, work to extend women's influence beyond the home, challenge male violence against women, and lobby to enact feminist principles, believing feminism benefits men by creating a gender-just society.

▪ KAY LEIGH HAGAN

≋ Mental Health and Illness

The diagnosis and treatment of women's mental health and illness in the United States have been shaped by cultural values about what constitutes a good and acceptable woman and have been used to punish women who fall outside the norm. In particular, a woman's body and its cycles as well as her adaptation to social roles have been implicated as factors that cause mental illness. As a result of these formulations, specific treatments have been designed "for women only." Generally, these clinical interventions have been directed at women's bodies or have taken the form of verbal prescriptions aimed at helping a woman live a more "feminine" life.

In the mid-nineteenth century, women were judged by the standard of True Womanhood. The True Woman was a faithful wife, a pious servant, and, above all, a good mother. Ironically, biological mothering, so central to a woman's identity as a True Woman, was considered in the nineteenth century to be a cause of insanity. One hypothesis linked insanity to prolonged lactation. One in eleven women diagnosed as "insane" in the 1850s reportedly suffered a nervous breakdown either during or after pregnancy. The emphasis on "good mothering" posed additional problems for poor and African American women. Poor women had more children and felt more acutely the strain and burden of caring for them. For African American women, motherhood was tainted by the legacy of slavery, in which women were valued for their "breeding" potential and were often forcibly separated from their children.

Women who strayed too far from the domestic sphere were also considered to be at risk for psychic distress. A woman who overtaxed her delicate sensibilities by engaging in too much intellectual work was subject to "brain strain." Not surprisingly, this same work was not considered to be crazy-making for men, who were felt to have the natural endowments to engage in active intellectual efforts.

At the end of the nineteenth century, medicine began to adopt a more scientific approach, but medical literature about women's mental illness remained unscientific. Failing to fulfill the roles of wife and mother and pursuing occupations and professions for which they were "not suited" were considered to cause insanity. Researchers postulated that unfeminine activities caused uterine derangement which in turn caused mental illness.

During this period, two separate treatment approaches were developed specifically for female patients. The belief that an insane woman had something wrong with her "female organs" resulted in treatments such as electrical stimulation of the uterus, clitoral cauterization, and prescribed weight gain to prevent the ovaries from slipping out of place. Women diagnosed with psychological problems were subjected to a form of paternalistic behavior modification. S. Weir Mitchell, the chief proponent of what was called the rest cure, recommended that women who were suffering from emotional exhaustion take to their beds for a period of six weeks to two months. This solution served to make being ill sufficiently aversive so that women would readily return to their roles as wives and mothers. Indigent women, by contrast, who received all of their care in state-run asylums, were prescribed "work therapy," laboring as unpaid servants, performing many of the domestic chores required to keep the institution functioning.

First-person accounts by women who were institutionalized in insane asylums in the nineteenth century suggest that incarceration in a mental hospital was used as one means of forcing conformity onto women. These women felt that the reason they were declared insane was that they held religious beliefs contrary to those of their families and husbands, owned property coveted by relatives, or held controversial opinions not shared by members of their family. In some states, husbands had the legal authority to commit a wife to an asylum without a doctor's order; thus "unwanted" wives found their way into mental hospitals.

By the beginning of the twentieth century, women began to see themselves not only as wives and mothers but also as sexual beings. Not surprisingly, this new awareness of female sexuality and reproductive independence was implicated as a cause of mental illness. Excessive masturbation by intellectual women was considered a cause of divorce in later life. Interrupted coitus (used to prevent conception) was deemed a cause of excessive nervousness and irritability.

By the 1930s, psychoanalytic theory was a vital force in U.S. psychiatry. Early Freudian theory identified the castration complex and penis envy as core elements in female development. Even her eventual desire to bear a child was seen as a compensation for her lack of a penis. Early theorists speculated that the sexually assertive woman was really a frustrated man, a woman uncomfortable with her own inherently passive position. Lesbianism, which was linked to feminism, was also declared deviant. Freudian psychology defined both narcissism and masochism as particularly feminine disorders. Some psychoanalysts concluded that feminism threatened a woman's happiness, because a woman could not be herself when she was "imitating a man," that is, being assertive. These psychoanalytic explanations of a woman's psyche served to stigmatize and condemn independent and professional women at the time. Despite attempts to modify some of its elements, Freudian theory remained a largely antifemale force in U.S. psychiatry for almost fifty years.

Psychiatric diagnosis and treatment historically have been used as means of social control in the lives of women. Women who deviate from the cultural norm in terms of role, sexual orientation, demeanor, appearance, or race are more likely to be labeled deviant and to receive psychiatric treatment. As late as 1986, in the Revised Diagnostic and Statistical Manual of Mental Disorders published and developed by the American Psychiatric Association, two disorders linked to a woman's demeanor and to her female body were still under consideration for inclusion: Late Luteal Phase Dysphoric Disorder (characterized by anxiety, irritability, depression, and affective lability during a specific phase of the menstrual cycle) and Self-defeating Personality Disorder (a variant of the old female "masochism").

Women clearly have suffered because of the labels and diagnoses assigned them—some accurate, some not. By the late 1980s, researchers and practitioners began to recognize and acknowledge that a large number of women being treated for mental illness were in fact experiencing symptoms as a result of sexual abuse trauma perpetrated by a trusted family member, male or female, or by a teacher, baby sitter, or clergy member. In the past, a woman's accusations of sexual abuse, rather than being considered as an accurate report of her experience, were thought to be fantasies, delusional or "hysterical" thinking, or the result of suppressed and forbidden desires. Some women repressed the memory of their trauma involuntarily, thus retaining their role as good daughters within the traditional family structure. Throughout history, treatment and diagnosis of mental illness for women has been confounded by cultural norms of what constitutes acceptable "feminine" behavior.

Phyllis Chesler, *Women and Madness* (San Diego: Harcourt Brace Jovanovich, 1972); Jeffrey Geller and Maxine Harris, *Women of the Asylum* (New York: Anchor Books, 1994).

▪ MAXINE HARRIS

SEE ALSO Depression.

≋ Mexican American Women

SEE Chicanas and Mexican American Women.

≋ Midwifery

Probably the oldest women's profession in the United States, midwifery is the practice of assisting women during childbirth. As such, it evokes strong and contradictory images. Some people condemn midwives as ignorant and superstitious women whose unsanitary practices risk mothers' lives, while others glorify them as sensitive, highly skilled health practitioners who have been unfairly victimized by a misogynistic medical establishment. In reality, midwives were and are a varied group. They include highly skilled women who have delivered thousands of infants over long careers, and those who have attended a birth only occasionally. They include the formally educated and the empirically trained, women who regard their work as a profession, and those who see it as a religious calling. They include nurse-midwives who work as part of an obstetric team, and independent practitioners who reject the medical model of birth. The diversity among midwives reflects the changes and variety in women's economic status and of religious and cultural views of childbirth and labor.

Before the mid–eighteenth century virtually all babies in North America were delivered by midwives. Native American midwives and female helpers gave physical support and, sometimes, herbal medicines to women in labor; they also performed other rituals, such as preparing the birth location, dancing, and bathing or naming the baby, depending on the traditions of the tribe. In most Native communities, women also attended the sick, laid out the dead, and led the mourning ceremonies.

African American midwives were both spiritual and medical advisers to their communities. Religious women whose skills were passed down between generations, they were esteemed members of their communities, delivering the babies of plantation whites as well as slaves. In addition to catching babies, "granny" midwives provided herbs to heal the sick and comfort the dying, advised parents about child rearing, and took care of children while their mothers worked in the fields. In the process, they helped maintain West African culture and traditions.

Like their Native and African American counterparts, colonial English midwives also understood their work in a religious context and served their communities through births, illnesses, and deaths with the help of other women. They used herbs to speed up labor and ease its pains, examined the cervix to assess the progress of labor, and, if necessary, turned the baby. They also prescribed herbal treatments for burns and minor illnesses, helped patients with housework and child care, visited the sick, and prepared the dead for burial.

While Native and African American traditions persisted well into the twentieth century, among Anglo Americans the medicalization of birth began prior to the American Revolution. Physicians, or "men-midwives," entered the field of obstetrics in the 1760s. By the mid–nineteenth century, most middle-income women looked to science and medicine for safer and easier births, choosing doctors to deliver their babies.

The influx of immigrants at the turn of the twentieth century led to a revival of midwifery: midwives delivered about one-half of all babies born in the United States in 1910. Immigrants from Europe, Mexico, and Asia still viewed childbirth as a domestic, female event, not a medical one. Most wanted their babies to be delivered by midwives who, in addition to preparing teas and massaging the mother, cooked the meals, cleaned the house, looked after older children, and provided emotional support. Midwives also cost less than doctors; most worked in exchange for crops or services, or for nothing at all. And they attended births that doctors would not because of racial or ethnic prejudice, difficult access, or the patient's inability to pay.

Between 1910 and 1930 the proportion of midwife-attended births dropped from 50 to 15 percent. The decline of midwifery was due to a variety of factors, including immigration restriction, assimilation, a falling birthrate, and a vigorous medical campaign against midwives. Obstetricians, seeking to advance their professional status by depicting obstetrics as a complicated medical specialty, blamed midwives for childbirth-related deaths and called for the elimination of midwifery. Midwives, a diverse group without any central organization, were unable to defend themselves. Their only supporters were public health advocates who promoted training and licensing programs similar to those in Europe. The 1921 Sheppard-Towner Act provided federal matching funds for midwife training programs in thirty-one states.

By 1930 80 percent of practicing midwives were in the South, where Black and Mexican American women were denied equal access to medical care. Midwifery remained an important part of the health care system until the 1950s. Black and Mexican American midwives continued to use herbs and traditional birth positions and followed established rituals, such as the African American practice of placing a knife under the bed to "cut the pain." At the same time, they worked with state health departments, providing immunizations and health education in rural communities. Strict licensing policies, however, combined with urban migration, led to the decline of traditional midwifery in the 1950s. By the early 1970s, the number of midwife-attended births nationwide reached an all-time low of 0.5 percent.

While midwifery was dying out in the South, middle-class women dissatisfied with medicalized birth revived interest in woman-centered birth. A product of the 1970s women's health movement, modern midwifery has gone in two directions. The first, nurse-midwifery, provides professional, woman-centered care for low-risk mothers within the framework of a medically directed health service. The second, lay or "independent" midwifery, grew out of the home birth movement. Mostly empirically trained, independent midwives explicitly reject the medicalization of birth and have thus provoked considerable opposition from the medical profession. Currently, in the Native American community, there is a large movement to restore midwifery to its traditional role in the birthing process. Although midwives will probably never regain their former status, the revival of midwifery has increased women's options and strengthened their chances for a woman-centered birth.

Linda Janet Holmes, "African American Midwives in the South," in *The American Way of Birth*, edited by Pamela S. Eakins (Philadelphia: Temple University Press, 1986); Judy Barrett Litoff, *American Midwives, 1860 to the Present* (Westport, Conn.: Greenwood Press, 1978); Laurel Thatcher Ulrich, *A Midwife's Tale: The Life of Martha Ballard Based on Her Diary, 1785–1812* (New York: Vintage, 1990).

● MOLLY LADD-TAYLOR

SEE ALSO Childbirth; Sheppard-Towner Maternity and Infancy Protection Act.

≋ Military

SEE Armed Forces.

≋ Miscegenation

Sexual liaisons that cross the color line have been intertwined in American history with issues of gender, race, politics, and law from the colonial period onward. The word "miscegenation" was invented during the 1864 presidential campaign (from the Latin *miscere*, "to mix," and *genus*, race) when Democrats claimed that Lincoln's Republican Party advocated sex and marriage across the color line. Like "mulatto," probably derived from the concept of mules and hybridity, "miscegenation" was pejorative in its historical context.

Europeans and Africans reproduced together from the time of earliest contact in the colonial South, where white indentured servants and Black slaves lived and labored in the same households. White authorities wrote the first laws against such mixtures in the late seventeenth century; white women and Black men were threatened with the harshest consequences among the possible mixtures. Under the institution of racial slavery, such laws were intended to prevent the growth of a free African American population. One's legal status as slave or free was based on the *mother's* status as slave or free; thus when white women had children with Black men, those children would be free but of partial African ancestry, thereby threatening racial slavery. When Black women bore the children of white men, however, those children would be slaves and usually remain enslaved throughout their lives, thereby benefiting the institution of racial slavery.

Black women and their families in the South suffered continuous sexual exploitation, or the threat of it, by white masters. Historical documents testify to the anger and humiliation female slaves experienced in the face of their masters' cruelty. Although the women's resistance remained constant, their efforts often proved futile in a patriarchal slave society. Southern courts did not recognize the rape of Black women by white men as a crime.

Under slavery it was much less frequent, though not impossible, for white women to have sexual liaisons with Black men. Dominant ideology deemed these white women, especially the poorer ones, as depraved agents of illicit actions, and they were usually treated as outcasts; elite white women were more likely to exercise social power and remain out of the public eye if their cross-racial relationships were discovered. Planter-class white women in the slave South also commanded power over Black men, including the power of sexual coercion.

In the antebellum North, liaisons between African Americans and whites were socially taboo at least until the Civil War ended, despite the fact that not all Northern states had laws against intermarriage. Voluntary cross-racial liaisons did occur, though many others were exploitive, usually occurring in the context of poverty. As members of the laboring poor, Black women were subject to exploitation from white employers, and Black and white women who were struggling economically might temporarily or permanently engage in prostitution, serving Black and white men alike.

After emancipation, white Southerners viciously targeted white women and Black men who engaged in sexual liaisons together. These Southerners wished fervently to retain their place at the top of the racial hierarchy. They conflated the new political power and economic independence of Black men with sexual transgressions against white women, ignoring the long history of sexual assault of Black women by white men under slavery. As part of this process of countering African American freedom, Black women were also subject to assault and rape by Klansmen and their allies, and white women who consorted, or allegedly consorted, with Black men were also vulnerable to white violence. Thus full-fledged, racist white rage about sex between Black men and white women developed in the Reconstruction years, commencing an era of terrorism and lynchings which ultimately spread north and west. By the early twentieth century, marriages across the color line were rendered explicitly illegal in the South, as well as in parts of the North and West. The consequences of interracial marriages ranged from simply declaring such unions null and void to imposing fines or imprisonment. Such laws were most frequently enforced against white women and Black men.

Beginning in the late nineteenth century, Black women began to organize nationally. Journalist and activist Ida B. Wells-Barnett candidly called attention to the newfound, intense white anxiety about sex between white women and Black men.

She demonstrated that lynching was part of a political campaign to suppress Black male suffrage and economic independence. She noted also that fears of sexuality had not existed when white Southern men had deserted their households when they went to fight in the Civil War, leaving their wives, daughters, and male slaves at home. In 1930 a group of white, middle-class Southern women formed the Association of Southern Women for the Prevention of Lynching, which asserted that white women suffered also under an ideology that cast Black men as rapists and white women as victims in need of protection from white men. Over the next decades, small numbers of those who lived in Northern and Western states married across the color line, especially after World War II. In the South, liaisons still took the form of concubinage between Black women and white men, though to a much lesser degree than during the slavery period.

The 1967 case of *Loving* v. *Virginia,* involving the marriage of a Black woman and a white man, reached the United States Supreme Court after nine years of trials and appeals. The Court ruled unanimously that laws prohibiting marriages between Blacks and whites were unconstitutional; at that time, sixteen Southern states had such laws. While the number of mixed couples has increased in the second half of the twentieth century, the percentage is still small. White women and Black men make up the majority of mixed couples; this phenomenon caused considerable tension between Black and white women during the civil rights movement of the 1960s. Many African Americans, while recognizing legal sanctions against intermarriage as racist and a violation of rights, have looked down on other Blacks who consorted with whites. Many white Americans have continued to respond to mixed couples with racist attitudes.

The ongoing legacies of the legal and social history of miscegenation are apparent in issues ranging from the influence of racist ideology in sex crimes or alleged sex crimes, to ambivalence or antagonism on the part of both white and Black communities toward marriages and relationships across the color line.

Karen A. Getman, "Sexual Control in the Slaveholding South: The Implementation and Maintenance of a Racial Caste System," *Harvard Women's Law Journal* Vol. 7 (1984): 115–52; Jacqueline Dowd Hall, *Revolt Against Chivalry: Jessie Daniel Ames and the Women's Campaign Against Lynching* (New York: Columbia University Press, rev. ed., 1993); Nell Irvin Painter, " 'Social Equality,' Miscegenation, Labor, and Power," in *The Evolution of Southern Culture*, edited by Numan Bartley (Athens: University of Georgia Press, 1988).

▪ MARTHA HODES

SEE ALSO Colorism; Rape; Whiteness.

≋ Misogyny

Misogyny has its roots in the Greek *miso-*, meaning hatred, and *gyne-*, meaning woman; it means the hatred of women. In patriarchal culture the word is used to designate an extreme abhorrence of women, a pathological antipathy not shared by ordinary or normal men, not expressed in laws or social policy or in the presumed humanism of art, literature, and philosophy.

Friedrich Nietzsche, a German philosopher (1844–1900), and August Strindberg, a Swedish playwright (1849–1912), for instance, are recognized as misogynists by the male-supremacist culture. In an 1888 letter to Strindberg, Nietzsche wrote of the "deathly hatred of the sexes." This "deathly hatred" included the convictions that women are filthy (especially genitally), sluttish, and whorelike; and that physical love is a war in which the woman must be vanquished by physical force, not excluding beating, rape, and murder. The woman is regarded as a provocateur who, by her nature and will, initiates combat. In Nietzsche's and Strindberg's view, feminists were an even worse "enemy," an "army of whores and would-be whores—professional whores with ab-

normal inclinations," wrote Strindberg. Denunciation, humiliating insult, and a degrading sexualization of women characterize misogyny, which is bitter, passionate, and often tormented.

U.S. feminists recognize a more normative woman-hating that is institutionalized in a broad and, except for feminist challenges, uncontested social devaluation of women, second-class citizenship for women, and systematic violence against women. Across different cultures, this misogyny is organized and institutionalized to different degrees and in different ways.

In the United States, legitimized woman-hating has its origins in European and Anglo-Saxon institutions of ownership: married women were defined as chattel, or property, of their husbands, with no rights to independent civil existence; the majority of the African American population was held in captivity as slaves, and women were worth half the price of men and subjected to forced sexual intercourse by white owners. Indentured women, often white, often single, were owned for a fixed period of time, which was extended if the woman gave birth to a "bastard," a legal designation that meant the child was not owned by a man but by the mother and therefore was in permanent exile from civil society.

These institutions of domination—marriage, slavery, and indentured labor—denied legal and social personhood to women. Men, especially white men, had rights over women and children that permitted physical brutality, invasion of the body, indifference to health and well-being, and coerced reproduction.

Marriage, slavery, and indentured servitude were fundamental institutions of dominance in a European and British culture of conquest built on the genocide of the indigenous people of this continent. Thomas Jefferson wrote that the native population could be "extirpated from the earth" or vacate the land. He was committed to killing Native American women and children in particular. This bloodsoaked land, then, was fertile ground for despotic, not democratic, institutions that wiped out personhood through ownership, domination, and civil invisibility, with a sadistic underbelly of physical assault and control.

Many misogynist violations of women were once rights of men over women and children. These rights were protected by custom, law, and force of arms: battery, marital rape, child rape and incest, acquaintance rape. Male access to women through prostitution and pornography was protected even when illegal. Stranger rape was virtually immune from prosecution and nearly always considered the victim's fault; it was a crime only insofar as it robbed a father of a pure daughter, or a husband of the exclusivity of physical possession of his wife. Women and children also lacked individual sovereignty, civil rights, and human status. The state's protection of male dominance had strong support from religions with Jewish and Christian imperatives. The theology and practices of Protestants, Catholics, and Jews upheld patriarchal power by positing a male godhead; androcentric authority; and a female nature, either depraved or submissive.

The contemporary women's movement has opposed traditional sex-role arrangements and challenged the conjunction of hierarchy and hate. Women activists have exposed intimate aggression and violation, dominance and invasion, and insult and humiliation as intolerable expressions of contempt. Women have repudiated the colonial rights of men over their reproductive and sexual capacities and resisted the industrial and technologized packaging and selling of women and children as sexual commodities. The dehumanization of women, women's civil inequality, continuing economic marginality, and ongoing exclusion from political power are manifestations of woman-hating: plain old misogyny. The war against women is not love. Nietzsche's "deathly hatred of the sexes" is not fundamental law. That hatred is the inevitable contempt a master feels for the slave he exploits. Woman-hating will end when women's subordination is ended, however (or wherever) it is imposed.

Andrea Dworkin, *Woman Hating* (New York: Dutton, 1974); Kate Millett, *Sexual Politics* (New York: Avon, 1971); Julia Cherry Spruill, *Women's Life and Work in the Southern Colonies* (New York: W. W. Norton, 1972).

■ ANDREA DWORKIN

SEE ALSO Violence Against Women.

≋ Missionaries

Missionary work provided U.S. women an opportunity to combine religious belief and spiritual concern with work that was thought to be socially useful. This was especially true in the nineteenth century, which saw a proliferation of Protestant women's mission organizations. When this movement peaked in the early twentieth century, it counted three million members who were drawn from mission organizations in every denomination. Thousands of women served as foreign and home missionaries. Being a missionary was a way for women to become unofficial "ministers." Ordination was closed to women in most Protestant denominations until the latter part of the twentieth century. It offered a rare opportunity to combine travel and adventure with work deemed "respectable."

Although the Protestant women's mission movement was predominantly white, Black women were involved, as well as women of color—including Chinese Americans, Native Americans, and Latinas—who had been "clients" of the mission organizations. Among home missions, the fields included work among the African Americans and poor whites of the South, Native Americans, Hispanics, Asian immigrants, and Mormons. Home missionaries also opened settlements among European immigrants in industrial cities, from New York to Chicago. Overseas, they went to China, Japan, Korea, the Philippines, Turkey, India, and various parts of Africa.

Grace Roberts, a U.S. missionary, teaches the Bible to women in Manchuria, in 1903.

In the early nineteenth century, the movement also was intended to provide aid to the wives of male missionaries. As women in Protestant churches lobbied to expand their work, single women were assigned to mission stations to work specifically among women. The Civil War served as a turning point, legitimizing, extending, and lending new power to women's benevolent activities. Drawing on this experience, Protestant women demanded that informal mission societies be recognized as part of the Church. Women did gain official recognition and used these organizations to increase the numbers of women hired as missionaries, to raise money for their support, and to expand the social services of the Church.

▪ SUSAN M. YOHN

SEE ALSO Protestantism.

Black Missionaries

At the beginning of the nineteenth century, U.S. Protestant missionary societies began mission activities in Africa. The first white foreign missionary society was formed in 1810. In 1822 the African Methodist Episcopal Church became the first U.S. Black church to appoint an official foreign missionary to Africa. The last Black church to enter mission work in Africa was the Baptist Foreign Mission Convention of the United States, which was established in 1880 and sent six missionaries to Liberia in 1883.

By the mid–nineteenth century, some women formed church groups for women only, including home and foreign mission societies, which sent out female workers. Often wives accompanied their husbands who had been appointed as missionaries, and eventually church officials appointed single women as missionaries. Women missionaries, both Black and white, were designated assistant missionaries and were teachers or principals at day, industrial, and Sunday schools; supervised or worked in nurseries, orphanages, or boarding schools; made house-to-house visitation; did evangelistic work; conducted Bible classes; prepared vernacular literature; and provided medical care for women and children as nurses or physicians.

The largest number of U.S. Black missionaries were sent to Africa during the period from 1880 to 1920. During that time almost eighty U.S. Black women traveled to Africa as assistant missionaries. These women were trained as teachers, nurses, and deaconesses. Almost half of the Black American missionaries sent to Africa from 1820 to 1980 were women. Two-thirds of these were unmarried commissioned missionaries and one-third were married to male missionaries.

• SYLVIA M. JACOBS

≋ Mississippi Freedom Democratic Party

Founded in 1964 to protest racial segregation in mainstream political parties, the Mississippi Freedom Democratic Party (MFDP) was a racially integrated alternative Democratic political group. At the Democratic National Convention that year, it challenged the seating of the regular all-white Mississippi delegation, which officially excluded Blacks.

The noted civil rights activist Fannie Lou Hamer, who took part in its founding, spoke at the convention. In her eloquent testimony Hamer described her attempt to register to vote in August 1962 and the harassment that followed, as well as the permanently disabling brutal beating that she, along with two middle-aged Black women and a young Black girl, had suffered while returning from a voter registration workshop in South Carolina in 1963.

These efforts did not unseat the all-white delegation, despite two compromises offered by Democrats Hubert Humphrey and Walter Mondale, which stated that: 1) MFDP delegates could participate in party proceedings without any vote, and 2) Two nonvoting MFDP members selected by Humphrey—African American Aaron Henry, president of Mississippi NAACP chapters, and Anglo-American Ed King, chaplain at the historically Black Tougaloo College—could have at-large seats. Acting on principle, the MFDP completely rejected both offers.

The MFDP's actions, however, resulted in an unprecedented pledge from the national Democratic party not to seat any delegate groups that excluded Blacks at the next convention in 1968. Moreover, the publicity about Black disenfranchisement generated by the MFDP was a factor in President Lyndon Johnson's introduction of voting rights legislation, which was enacted in the summer of 1965. The MFDP helped transform Mississippi politics locally and the Democratic party nationally.

• LINDA REED

SEE ALSO Civil Rights Movement; Mississippi Freedom Summer.

≋ Mississippi Freedom Summer

Mississippi Freedom Summer refers to the summer of 1964 when a large contingent of white supporters, largely college students from various parts of the country, joined the ongoing Black-led civil rights movement in Mississippi.

They assisted with voter registration efforts and other projects throughout Mississippi, including setting up fifty Freedom Schools to continue community organizing. Through the support of various local people in communities in the state, volunteers worked with the Student Non-Violent Coordinating Committee (SNCC) and other civil rights workers to teach African American youth and adults basic educational subjects such as reading, writing, and arithmetic. For adults, these skills increased the possibility of registering to vote because potential voters were required to pass literacy and "understanding" tests. For youth, these Freedom Schools helped boost confidence and self-esteem.

The summer is most remembered, however, for the horrific attacks of white extremists who opposed racial equality and the civil rights movement in general. In June, national and international attention centered on three missing civil rights workers—Andrew Goodman, James Chaney, and Michael Schwerner. On August 4, their bodies were found buried under an earthen dam at a Neshoba County farm. The search for them made clear that whites in Mississippi held no regard for the safety—and the lives—of Blacks and sympathetic whites who interfered with the status quo.

We now know what members of the civil rights struggle suspected—that local authorities acted in concert with white racists. After this summer, doubts increased among some Blacks about whether racial equality could be achieved through peaceful means.

By the end of the summer an estimated one thousand volunteers had contributed to the movement in Mississippi. Women's participation was difficult because of additional sexist dangers and fear of violence or sexual assault by white opponents of the freedom struggle. Nonetheless, women made up approximately 40 percent of the group of volunteers for Mississippi Freedom Summer.

■ LINDA REED

SEE ALSO Civil Rights Movement.

≋ Montgomery Bus Boycott

When, on December 1, 1955, Rosa Parks refused to give up her seat to a white man on a segregated transit bus, she sparked the needed action that tested the segregation policy on Montgomery buses and symbolically raised the nation's consciousness of the civil rights movement. Parks's act embodied the pivotal role of women in the movement. The Montgomery Bus Boycott that followed brought together organizations that resulted in forty-two thousand African American men and women staying off the buses for thirteen months. Subsequently, the U.S. Supreme Court ruled that segregation on city buses was unconstitutional. ■

Parks, who had been secretary of the local NAACP chapter, had the support of the Black community, particularly the support of other women. Jo Ann Gibson Robinson, president of the Women's Political Council (a group that promoted voter registration and activism among Black women), duplicated the fliers calling for the boycott. WPC members and many others had long deplored segregated busing and had anticipated for years the activity that would end such practices. In May 1954, within days of the *Brown* v. *Board of Education* decision, Robinson wrote to the mayor, threatening a boycott if conditions did not improve on the segregated bus system.

Constituting 56 percent of the city's Black population, women usually suffered more abusive treatment related to segregated busing than did men. The majority of Black women worked as domestics in white homes across town and relied on public transportation to reach their workplaces. Their sacrifices and commitment were central to the success of the boycott, which became not only the symbolic beginning of the Black civil rights movement but a model for Black protests in that movement.

■ LINDA REED

SEE ALSO Civil Rights Movement.

≋ Moral Reform

Moral reform, a belief that women were sexually pure and men sexually dangerous, was the joint product of eighteenth-century sentimentalism and nineteenth-century evangelical religious enthusiasms. It played a key role in middle-class representations of "True Womanhood" and in middle-class men's efforts to constrain women's sexual and social autonomy and their political activism.

The term also refers to a specific mid-nineteenth-century women's movement to end urban prostitution and enforce a national sexual standard to protect women. The American Female Moral Reform Society, founded in New York City in 1834, was one of the largest and most active women's reform organizations in the nineteenth century, its members representing a broad spectrum of the population—fashionable bourgeois matrons, small-town housewives, farm women, New England mill girls and schoolteachers, and newly freed African American women. By the 1840s it boasted over 450 auxiliaries. Its bimonthly journal, *The Advocate of Moral Reform and Family Guardian,* claimed twenty thousand subscribers and a far larger number of actual readers.

To understand the Society's complex sociosexual and political vision and the ways it differed from a more conservative male moral reform view, it is important to examine two stories that appeared repeatedly on the pages of the *Advocate.* The first was a realistic depiction of the lives of poor rural women new to the cities. Sweatshop-like working conditions and exploitive wages transformed these women into an impoverished urban underground of beggars and prostitutes. Paralleling, indeed preceding, this economic narrative was a second drama that told of vulnerable farming daughters who were seduced by urban merchants and lawyers and carried off to the city to face prostitution and sometimes death. By interweaving these two stories, the Society's sexual rhetoric bespoke the women's economic anxieties. Male *sexual* avarice became a symbol for male *economic* avarice; women's sexual vulnerability for women's economic vulnerability; prostitution (e.g., commercialized sex) for commerce itself. The powerless prostitute stood for the image of helplessness all women felt within the new economy. The Society used its representations of male sexual license and female vulnerability to legitimate middle-class matrons' entrance into the public and political arena to denounce men's sexual and economic exploitation of women. Members signed political petitions, edited and printed reform journals, managed respectable employment agencies for women—all in the name of protecting women and the home.

Increasingly politicized, many members joined the abolitionist movement, where, defending their sexually vulnerable enslaved "sisters," they publicly denounced slavery for empowering lascivious male slaveholders to rape and claim innocent women for prostitution. Well into the twentieth century, African American churchwomen continued moral reform and advocated "politics of respectability" to counter racist stigmatization of African American women as oversexed and unworthy of respect or legal protection.

Feminist historians draw parallels between feminist moral reform and contemporary feminism. Some evaluations are negative. "The feminist movement has played an important role in organizing and even creating women's sense of sexual danger in the last one hundred fifty years," Linda Gordon and Ellen DuBois have argued. "Mainstream feminists," they continue, "ceding the area of sexuality to men, addressed primarily the dangers and few of the possibilities of sex." Representing men as sexually powerful and unrestrained and good women as asexual victims of male sexual appetites, moral reformers reinforced Victorian sexual power relations.

Other historians see strong similarities between moral reform concerns and contemporary feminist rage against sexual harassment in the workplace and on campuses. Still others praise moral reform for successfully challenging eighteenth- and nineteenth-century theories that excluded women from the political and public sphere because women were considered incapable of civic virtue and would corrupt men's politics. Handmaidens of the Lord, these reformers made it women's right, indeed their duty, to drive out lascivious men and seize public and political space for God, virtue, and pure womanhood. So inspired, middle-class matrons worked closely with working-class women as early as the 1850s, becoming experts on urban poverty, homeless children, and the problems of women in the needle trades. Male moral reform, associated with Progressive public-health attacks upon prostitution and venereal disease, was far more restrictive of women's autonomy.

Evelyn Brooks Higginbotham, *Righteous Discontent: The Women's Movement in the Black Baptist Church, 1880–1920* (Cambridge, Mass.: Harvard University Press, 1993); Harriet Jacobs, *Incidents in the Life of a Slave Girl: written by herself*, edited by L. Maria Child with an introduction by Jean Fagan Yellin (Cambridge, Mass.: Harvard University Press, 1987); Carroll Smith-Rosenberg, *Disorderly Conduct: Visions of Gender in Victorian America* (New York: Oxford University Press, 1986).

▪ CARROLL SMITH-ROSENBERG

SEE ALSO Cult of Domesticity; Social Hygiene.

≋ Mormons

The Church of Jesus Christ of Latter-day Saints, also known as the LDS or Mormon Church, is a self-proclaimed patriarchal order that strongly supports traditional sex roles. Paradoxically, the church's female members tend to be high achieving and well educated. Female members of the church in the United States are more likely to obtain some university education than are non-Mormon U.S. women, and they enter the work force at approximately the same rate.

This apparent contradiction arises from the fact that LDS theology does not support a merely subordinate position for females. This theology is a synthesis of Judeo-Christian tradition and the egalitarian philosophy of nineteenth-century United States. Both were incorporated into the doctrines of Mormonism by Joseph Smith, who founded the church in 1830. Since these two ideological traditions often contradict each other, Mormon doctrine paradoxically supports both equality and inequality.

For example, the LDS *Book of Mormon* states that "black and white . . . male and female . . . all are alike unto God." Mormons believe that God the Father has a cocreator, God the Mother. Women and men are considered interdependent, since neither can attain the highest salvation without being "sealed" in marriage. In the church's early history, Joseph Smith attributed spiritual gifts to women such as receiving revelation, faith healing, and giving blessings. Smith's successor, Brigham Young, encouraged women to learn economic management and obtain higher education and was a strong proponent of women's enfranchisement. Utah was the second state to grant women the vote. When Susan B. Anthony visited Salt Lake City during the 1860s, the Mormons greeted her and many of her ideas enthusiastically.

Nevertheless many of Mormonism's policies subordinate women. Females are not given the priesthood, as are all "worthy males" over the age of twelve. Women therefore have never wielded much power within the church. Another now-defunct LDS policy that many see as discriminatory was polygamy. Research suggests that up to two-thirds of Mormon wives living in the Utah Territory before 1880 were in polygamous marriages. In 1894, after the U.S. Congress legislated against polygamy (thus barring Utah from statehood), prophet Wilford Woodruff announced a divine revelation that resulted in rescinding the practice.

Mormon women with their children and husband, circa 1868.

Mormonism's contradictory philosophy has fueled controversy both inside and outside the church since the rise of the women's movement. In 1979 a housewife named Sonia Johnson was excommunicated for disobeying church leaders by publicly supporting the Equal Rights Amendment. In 1987 prophet Ezra Taft Benson proclaimed that Mormon mothers should not hold jobs, creating considerable distress among the majority of LDS women who were already in the work force. In 1993 leaders prohibited the practice of praying to the "Heavenly Mother." The same year, six Mormon writers were excommunicated for heresy; all but one had published works criticizing the church's stance on women's roles. One of the church's Twelve Apostles identified the major enemies of Mormonism as homosexuals, feminists, and intellectuals—three groups that tend to share nontraditional views on gender.

Some Mormons believe that activism may lead to a "revealed" change in discriminatory policies. Precedents exist for such "revelations of convenience," the most famous being the rejection of polygamy and, much later, of race discrimination. Until 1978 people of African descent were denied the Mormon priesthood on the grounds that, according to Melvin Ballard, they were "cursed" with "a skin of blackness" for "some act committed by them before they came into this life." That doctrine has never been rejected or revised, but in 1978 the LDS prophet announced he had received a revelation allowing all worthy male Mormons to be ordained, regardless of race.

This change ameliorated heavy political pressure from the civil rights movement and facilitated a missionary effort that has made Mormonism one of the world's fastest-growing religions. The exclusion of African Americans (all other races were ordained) from the priesthood historically limited the LDS church's growth in Black populations and contributed to a low percentage of African American migration to Mormon-dominated regions during the settling of the

American West. Since 1978 Black conversion to Mormonism has climbed steadily. Black LDS women are now probably more disempowered by their sex than by their race. For example, in the early 1980s, a Nigerian matriarch read *The Book of Mormon* and single-handedly created a small band of African believers. When this group contacted LDS headquarters, they were officially baptized and the men ordained—making the group's founder organizationally subordinate to her male converts.

Despite the precedent of "revelations of convenience," it seems doubtful that Mormonism's ambivalent approach to women's roles will change much in the near future. Present leaders perpetuate the ambivalence, repeatedly affirming women's doctrinal equality while simultaneously moving to quash structural enactments or public proclamations of equal status.

Melvin R. Ballard, *Melvin J.—Crusader for Righteousness* (Salt Lake City: Bookcraft, 1966); Sonia Johnson, *From Housewife to Heretic: One Woman's Spiritual Awakening and Her Excommunication from the Mormon Church* (Albuquerque, New Mexico: Wildfire Books, 1989).

▪ MARTHA N. BECK

SEE ALSO Religion.

≋ Motherhood

Families in the United States have experienced a series of far-reaching "domestic revolutions" that have fundamentally transformed family structure and organization, family dynamics, reproductive choices, and the spaces occupied by women. But the myth has persisted of the white Eurocentric family as a stable, nuclear, heterosexual unit, with mother at center stage in a specific domestic and social position in relation to fathers, children, and the state. Although families have always been ethnically diverse structures in which women as mothers have played multiple roles, "normalized" motherhood has been framed against the contours of whiteness and social class.

The Puritans who escaped to the New World sought to establish the godly family, "a little commonwealth." Both church and legal doctrine required wives to submit to the authority of their husbands. Obedience, rather than maternal bonds of affection, was promoted, and it permitted physical abuse toward children—the "better-whipt-than-damned" approach—as moral training. Within their domestic units, Puritan mothers followed the widespread custom of their Western European sisters, fostering out their newborns for long periods of time to wet nurses. Women who transgressed the sexual and religious boundaries of the "little commonwealth" were apt to meet a fate such as that of Hester Prynne in Hawthorne's *The Scarlet Letter*—forced to the outer margins of the moral universe in which neither single motherhood nor illegitimate childhood was tolerated.

Early industrial capitalism saw a change from a familial domestic economy to an industrial one in which the social forms of the family underwent dramatic shifts. As the separation of the workplace and the dwelling place became institutionalized, the sentimental image of the family as haven in a heartless world was born, placing mother as domestic monarch at center stage, buttressed by a rapidly growing cult of womanhood and tied to an expanding science of childhood.

These ideals of domesticity and the separation of spheres—public and private—were embraced by the leading domestic feminists of the nineteenth century. Catharine Beecher elevated motherhood to a glorious temple of self-sacrifice "whose summit shall pierce the skies, whose splendor shall beam on all lands." In this mid-nineteenth-century discourse motherhood became a sacred calling in which the "true woman," the white woman, emerged as desexualized, indifferent to intellectual life, imbued with Christian piety (and not a little class privilege) and devoted to home and church.

By the late 1800s these ideals led to vastly different outcomes for mothers of different social classes and of different racial ethnic heritage. Anglo women of affluence and privilege became child savers and protectors of the nation's families. Poor mothers became eligible either for salvation or condemnation, depending on their color, their class position, and their moral adherence to norms of domesticity—norms difficult to meet since many worked long hours outside the home.

By the turn of the century, middle- and upper-class mothers had made the "science" of motherhood a central organizing principle of Progressive Era politics. Influenced by the child study movement founded by G. Stanley Hall, who decreed child study as "preeminently the women's science" and accentuated its importance for the progress of the white race, the National Congress of Mothers played a key role in the expansion of child welfare, parent's (mother's) education, and the development of mothers' pensions, but they opposed suffrage. While sentimental maternalism characterized the National Congress of Mothers, progressive maternalism led to the creation of the Children's Bureau in 1912, the first federal agency headed and staffed primarily by women. Like the sentimental maternalists, the progressive maternalists emphasized the special capacity of women to nurture; but they linked this to an explicit social and political agenda, arguing that maternal and infant welfare and child labor reforms were the public responsibility of women of privilege and the cornerstone of democracy. The rise of the famous settlement houses—New York's Henry Street and Chicago's Hull House—were founded by women social reformers, promoting motherhood as the "most universal and essential of employments."

Motherhood rhetoric had now shifted from the private to the public sphere as the progressive maternalists attempted to rouse the nation to the desperate plight of infants and children. This culminated in the national baby-saving campaign during the 1920s and the short-lived maternity and infancy protection legislation—the 1921 Sheppard-Towner Act. Maternalist and suffragist agendas coexisted during the first two decades of the century, but this alliance broke down after suffragists, led by Alice Paul of the National Women's Party, challenged motherhood rhetoric, arguing instead for personal, economic, and political emancipation in the public sphere.

However, the ideological durability of "normalized" nuclear motherhood rhetoric held sway, only to be supplanted during the 1940s by a psychological determinism influenced by Freud's patriarchal images of the family, and buttressed by attachment ideology, which gained popular prominence at a pivotal moment in the political economy. After the Second World War, mothers were evicted from the workplace, wartime daycare centers closed down, and suburban isolation grew. Post–Freudian theories, in particular John Bowlby's theories about exclusive maternal care and attachment, recast infant bonding as mother bondage—urging the "provision of constant attention day and night, seven days a week and 365 days in the year" as the cornerstone of infant mental health. The mother-infant separation research of Mary Ainsworth in the 1970s, followed by John Kennell and Marshall Klaus in the pediatric literature, elevated maternal-infant bonding to a scientific fetish, which further trapped mothers in a medical and psychological dogma of exclusive mother-infant care. Despite the widespread impact of motherhood and attachment discourse, white Anglo-American women of privilege were its central agents. Working-class women, immigrant women, and women of color were largely excluded from the discourse as they struggled through the double-day, working, taking care of children, and confronting racial, ethnic, and class discrimination.

For women of color, motherhood has historically been linked to dual oppressions: gender as well as racial and ethnic discrimination. The conquest and genocide of Native American women, brutal ownership and sexual and labor exploitation of African American women under slavery, exclusionary immigration policies and discriminatory domestic practices applied to Latina and Asian American women all created forms of motherhood that were uniquely different from white maternal images. Survival of the family and survival of the community were interwoven in such a way that the traditional separation of spheres was not a widespread phenomenon among women of color as family survival generated a need for "motherwork" both at home and outside.

Historically, Native American family and kinship systems diverged sharply from those of the conquering colonists. Kinship practices were diverse — both patrilineal and matrilineal societies existed; in some, child rearing was exclusively a woman's province, but in others, fathers and male relatives played a key role. Thus motherhood emerged as distinctly different from the dominant colonial ideology. Chief Wilma Mankiller of the Cherokee nation has argued that sexism was imposed by white men on Indian culture. The Cherokee were a matrilineal society in which women actually chose the chiefs and clan mothers shared political power with men.

African American motherhood also differed radically from white norms. Under slavery African American mothers' reproductive labor was a crucial factor in maintaining the slave economy; however, their own families were under constant threat of forced disruption and women lived under the terror of master rape. While motherhood under slavery was an experience of pervasive brutal assaults on self and family, African American mothers maintained unique kinship practices, family ties, and naming patterns that served to sustain the durability of their dispersed families. After emancipation, they continued to work in the fields of Southern agriculture and in domestic service; by the 1920s newly migrated women had moved into manufacturing. Black married women far outnumbered white married women in the work force during this period. A long history of enforced racial and economic subser-

vience had created quite a different set of maternal images for African American families; as mothers worked long hours to ensure the survival of their children, grandmothers and other female relatives often functioned as primary caretakers of their children.

Clear cultural differences existed among women of color, but they shared a common struggle to mother in the face of racism and discrimination. For Latina and Asian American women, family survival and the collective effort to maintain family life against the onslaught of discrimination and exclusionary immigration policies long characterized their realities of motherhood. In addition to domestic service, Latina women have continued to labor in the fields as exploited migrants with their children; Asian American mothers have also worked in domestic service and labored in sweatshops as undocumented aliens. The daily struggles of women of color have frequently focused on their powerlessness in the social and economic institutions that structure their lives and those of their children. Mothering has variously involved struggles against master rape, sterilization abuse, enforced maternal separation from one's own children, and the maintenance of family in a racist society, in which high infant mortality and widespread poverty have decimated the lives and futures of millions of children of color.

Although women of color who were mothers often did not conform to mainstream images of family, neither did single mothers. Historically portrayed as moral deviants, failing to fulfill their marital obligations, their children have supposedly carried multiple forms of social pathology, while the roots of state-constructed poverty for single mothers and their children have been concealed. Fifty-nine percent of poor children now live in female-headed households. Poor, single mothers have become a central feature of the larger motherhood discourse. The "stop favoring unwed mothers" political rhetoric continues to cast the contemporary single mother as a moral deviant, endlessly reproducing criminals at tax-payer expense. Behind the political rhetoric lie savage politics of distribution that structure and maintain single-mother poverty.

While single motherhood has been perceived as deviant, embedded in underclass myths and coded racial and class attacks, lesbian mother-hood has been framed as abnormal and a clear threat to the patriarchal power structure of the family. Prior to the civil rights movement of the 1960s, and the women's and the gay and lesbian movements of the 1970s, lesbian motherhood had been largely shrouded in secrecy, amid fears of the legal system's power to disenfranchise lesbian mothers in relation to child custody. While moth-ers' custody rights are still imperiled in the 1990s, lesbian mothering, comothering, and lesbian families are increasingly visible in the United States. At present between seven and fourteen million children are living in gay or lesbian households. An entire generation of children raised by lesbian mothers are part of a growing co-hort of nontraditional children whose socializa-tion in an alternative family structure has yet to be acknowledged and validated by educational, le-gal, and social institutions. A slow shift has oc-curred in favor of biological lesbian and gay par-ents' custody rights in a few states, but lesbian mothers continue to struggle against pervasive so-cial and family laws that target their parenting and their children.

As wider alternative family structures continue to gain visibility, the meanings of motherhood and the family are expanding. Grandmothers are increasingly caring for their children's children; many become primary caregivers in cases of abuse and neglect, teen pregnancy, substance abuse, and the AIDS crisis. In 1993 2.1 million grandmothers were raising grandchildren in their own households, and over six hundred thousand grandmothers were raising grandchildren with no parent present in the household at all.

But dominant ideologies of motherhood have served effectively to rationalize public policies of indifference to employed and nonemployed mothers. With 60 percent of married women with children under six in the work force, and millions of single mothers working and struggling to serve as nurturers and providers for their young chil-dren, it is significant that in 1997, the United States stood alone as the only Western industrial-ized democracy with no paid parental/maternity leave, no nationally subsidized child-care system, no system of child allowances, and no national health care system. This stands in stark contrast to the universal family entitlements of Western and Northern Europe, whose primary beneficiaries are mothers and their children.

Evelyn Nakano Glenn, Grace Chang, and Linda Rennie Forcey, *Mothering: Ideology, Experience, and Agency* (New York: Routledge, 1994); Molly Ladd-Taylor, *Mother-Work: Women, Child Welfare, and the State 1890–1930* (Urbana/Chicago: University of Illinois Press, 1994); Va-lerie Polakow, *Lives on the Edge: Single Mothers and Their Children in the Other America* (Chicago: University of Chicago Press, 1993).

■ VALERIE POLAKOW

SEE ALSO Families; Maternity Homes; Mother's Day; Mothers' Pensions; National Congress of Mothers; Sheppard-Towner Maternity and Infancy Protection Act; Single Motherhood.

≋ Mother's Day

On May 9, 1914, President Woodrow Wilson signed a proclamation establishing Mother's Day, a national holiday to be celebrated annually on the second Sunday of May. Wilson's action represented success for what had been a fairly brief campaign to give the holiday official status. Anna Jarvis, of Philadelphia, had lost her own mother and had begun the observance in 1907. She launched a vigorous letter-writing drive to es-tablish Mother's Day. She quickly found adher-ents, especially in the Protestant churches, and several states acted in advance of the federal proclamation.

The story of Mother's Day is larger, however, than just the energetic organizing efforts of Anna Jarvis. It cannot be understood apart from the heroic stature that home and motherhood enjoyed in Protestant American culture in the nineteenth century. Historians have delineated a remarkable saga of women who seized on the reverence for home to advance claims for influence both within the home—"domestic feminism"—and in the outside world. Using their credentials as mothers, the women organized to combat slavery, to control male drinking behavior, and to fight against other social evils. Many of the women who founded settlement houses, most notably Jane Addams, saw themselves and were seen by others as "social mothers." The maternal role, whether real or fictive, thus provided a major, if not *the* major, justification for white middle-class Protestant women's activism in the nineteenth century.

Within this context, one of the century's outstanding reformers, Julia Ward Howe, author of "The Battle Hymn of the Republic," first suggested a Mother's Day observance in 1872. She suggested setting aside June 2 as a day dedicated to peace and in honor of mothers, and she held an annual Mother's Day meeting for several years.

At the time Jarvis began her campaign in 1907, U.S. mothers had their highest peak of influence upon U.S. public policy. Many scholars of the welfare state contend that women reformers created a "maternalist" argument for social policy in the course of working—successfully—for the establishment of mothers' pensions in more than forty states and for the creation of the U.S. Children's Bureau, among other achievements. Thus the context could not have been more favorable for a drive to honor the nation's mothers.

And yet change was in the air. Stiff competition for the home was beginning to appear in nickelodeons and in dance halls. Mothers would soon have to contend with the freedom their children obtained by using an automobile. According to a contemporary account, Anna Jarvis had come to "a realization of the growing lack of tender consideration for absent mothers among worldly-minded, busy, grown-up children. . . ." Jarvis was prescient about the devaluation of domesticity that would occur in the twentieth century. Mothers, it seems, got their "day" just as the sun was about to set on their cultural heyday.

▪ GLENNA MATTHEWS

SEE ALSO Motherhood.

≋ Mothers' Pensions

The mothers' pensions laws enacted in a number of states in the 1910s formed the basis for Aid to Families with Dependent Children, now known as welfare. Also known as widows' pensions or mothers' aid, mothers' pensions provided financial assistance to widows and other women without employable husbands so that they could support their children at home. (Poor children in the nineteenth century were frequently placed in institutions.) The first statewide law was enacted in Illinois in 1911; by 1919 thirty-nine states provided some form of mothers' aid. In 1935 the Social Security Act nationalized the program, then called Aid to Dependent Children.

One of the most successful reforms of the Progressive Era, mothers' pensions laws were supported by a broad coalition of women's organizations, labor and civic groups, and juvenile court judges. Supporters endorsed aid as a way to prevent juvenile delinquency and the breakup of poor families, and to dignify motherhood. Distinguishing mothers' aid from charity, they claimed that mothers were entitled to pensions because they performed a service—child rearing—that benefited the nation.

In reality, mothers' pensions were underfunded and administered as charity. Many states denied aid to divorced and deserted women, required mothers to supplement their grants by working outside the home, and had a "suitable home" provision that limited aid to "deserving" women and frequently discriminated against Black and immigrant mothers. Despite these limitations, mothers' pensions recognized the state's responsibility for the welfare of poor women and children and provided many families with much-needed aid.

■ MOLLY LADD-TAYLOR

SEE ALSO Social Security Act; Welfare and Public Relief; Welfare State.

≋ Movies

SEE Film.

≋ Ms.

Ms. (pronounced MIZ), a form of address introduced into popular use by feminists in the 1970s, indicates female without reflecting marital status. It is intended to be the equivalent of *Mr.*, and to provide an alternative to *Miss* or *Mrs.*, wherever titles are chosen or required.

Contrary to assumption, Ms. was not invented by modern feminists. Mario Pei, in his 1949 *The Story of Language*, attributed the term to the women's movement of the nineteenth and early twentieth centuries. Its first recorded use in the United States was on the tombstone of Sarah Spooner, who died in Plymouth, Massachusetts, in 1767. This and other early uses in England have led to speculation that Ms. originated as an abbreviation for *Mistress*, a fourteenth-century adaptation of the French *maîtresse*. Like Master, it denoted sex without regard to marital status and was used when addressing any powerful or respected person, including a child of a respected family.

In the late 1960s, feminists discovered the term Ms. in secretarial handbooks that were published from the 1930s to the 1950s. The appellation was recommended to address a woman whose marital status was not known. In 1971 the term became the title of the first national feminist monthly, Ms. magazine, which gained extensive media attention and introduced this form of address to a wider public. In 1972 Congresswoman Bella Abzug of New York sponsored the "Ms. Bill," which forbade the federal government from using prefixes indicating marital status in any official document or publication of the U.S. Government Printing Office.

Ms. was popularized in daily use by millions of women of all races and classes, married and unmarried, who often braved resistance and ridicule in order to subvert the patriarchal practice of identifying females by their status—or lack of status—as male property. To oppose that result, many antifeminist women, fundamentalist religious groups, and other antiequality organizations refused to use Ms. In addition, some women of color preferred not to be addressed as Ms. because of their long struggle to be addressed respectfully, as white women were, as Miss and Mrs. Nonetheless, they usually supported Ms. as an option for others. For Native American women, Ms. was an echo of indigenous traditions that referred to both men and women by individual name, clan name, and position of respect—but not by marital status. By the 1980s, public opinion polls showed that about one-third of U.S. women supported the use of Ms.

In the 1990s, antiabortion, religious fundamentalist, and other groups opposed to feminist goals—plus some upper-class women whose wealth and status derived from their husband's name—still disagreed with the use of Ms. However, most resistance retreated into interpretation. In movies and television, the term Ms. was sometimes said with derision and/or used to indicate a character of unwelcome ambition and aggressiveness, or to imply lesbianism. According to Australian feminist and scholar Dale Spender, in her 1980 study, *Man Made Language,* "The (unstated) reason for the undesirability of Ms. is that it is of no assistance in the maintenance of the patriarchal order and it can even be problematic for males. . . . This is why I think it extremely important that all women should make use of it as a title—if we are to persist with titles."

■ GLORIA STEINEM

≣ Mujeres Activas En Letras Y Cambio Social (MALCS)

Chicana/Latina women were an integral part of the activities collectively recognized as the *Chicano Movimiento,* most active and visible from 1964 to 1975. By the early 1980s their contributions were barely acknowledged. Sensing this collective loss of voice, feeling highly isolated, eager to extend their knowledge to other women, and desiring to change society's perceptions, a group of Chicana/Latina academic women gathered at the University of California, Davis, in spring 1982. Mujeres Activas En Letras Y Cambio Social (MALCS) (Women Active in Letters and Social Change) was established at this first meeting. The MALCS declaration, written one year later at the Berkeley campus, formally established the organization and affirmed the membership's dedication to the unification of their academic life with their community activism.

MALCS hosts a summer research institute (established in 1985), publishes a newsletter and *Trabajos Monograficos* (a working paper series changed in 1991 to the *Series in Chicana Studies*). The series is in its second volume and soon to become the Journal of *Chicana/Latina Studies.* MALCS members also helped establish a perma-

nent research center at the University of California, Davis, in March 1991, to develop Chicanas/Latinas as scholars. It was to be a center for knowledge by, for, and about Chicanas/Latinas. MALCS is an academic organization that articulates Chicana/Latina feminist perspectives.

■ ADALJIZA SOSA-RIDDELL

SEE ALSO Chicana Civil Rights Organizations.

≣ *Muller v. Oregon*

The 1908 U.S. Supreme Court case *Muller v. Oregon* stands as a landmark—though a rather ambiguous one—in the history of both female reform and constitutional jurisprudence. The case arose from the criminal prosecution of a laundry owner who violated an Oregon statute limiting the hours of women's employment to ten per day. The question before the Court was whether the statute conflicted with the guarantee of the Fourteenth Amendment that bars states from depriving any person of liberty or property without due process of law.

The Oregon law at stake in *Muller* typified the gender-based, protective labor legislation central to reform in the Progressive Era. The crusade for such enactments was led by a cross-class alliance of women reformers in the National Consumers' League and the Women's Trade Union League.

The *Muller* case upheld the constitutionality of the hours law. Paradoxically, it arrived at a ruling quite radical in its day through thoroughly conventional patriarchal reasoning. The Court recognized the legitimacy of legislation restricting labor exploitation, contravening the free market and abridging fundamental individual rights of liberty of contract. But it did so in the name of woman's physical frailty, traditional dependence, and reproductive destiny—what the justices termed "inherent" sexual difference. The ruling sharply distinguished between protective laws for women and men. In the Court's eyes, the sex-specific "burdens of motherhood," which made women unequal to men as economic competitors, together with public interest in procreation, afforded women a unique entitlement to special legal protection as wage earners.

The *Muller* decision represented a triumph for female reform. Yet its legacy remains troubling, for it etched female dependence into constitutional doctrine, enshrined gender as a legitimate legal category, and defined women as a distinct and unequal class of citizens.

■ AMY DRU STANLEY

SEE ALSO Protective Labor Legislation.

≋ Multiculturalism

Most of the early work in U.S. women's history paid little attention to race and assumed instead a universal women's experience, defined in contrast to "man's" history. In this essentially uniracial model, race and gender could not be brought into the same theoretical field. White women appeared "raceless," their historical experiences determined solely by gender. By contrast, the distinct historical experiences of women of color, to the degree that they were acknowledged, were credited solely to race. Working within the uniracial framework, women's historians, even when they were eager to expand their range and include different women's experiences, found themselves appending women of color to the main story. They fell right into the trap of "women and minorities," a formula that accentuates rather than remedies the invisibility of women of color.

From many quarters has come the call for a more complex approach to women's experiences, one that explores not only the conflicts between women and men but also the conflicts among women; not only the bonds among women but also the bonds between women and men. This new approach, for which we use the label "multicultural," attempts to reconceptualize U.S. women's history as a series of relations among and across races and classes of women, representing diverse cultures and unequal power.

Multicultural women's history is best understood as an umbrella term that encompasses everything from elementary school "rainbow" posters for National Women's History Month to cultural studies tomes on the deconstruction of race, sexuality, and power. Nor is there a single political agenda, goal, or pattern to this research. It can express an expanded appreciation of U.S. democracy or provide withering critiques of white privilege and power, celebrations of minority cultures or heartbreaking accounts of painful legacies of oppression, slavery, dispossession, and humiliation. Multicultural history can concentrate on the discrete nature of various historical experiences, or it can build on the multiplicity of separate histories to create comparative frameworks. But what unites all these seemingly discordant aims is a commitment to a fully inclusive history of women in the United States.

At its best, multicultural women's history can contribute substantially to a new, complex, and more satisfying synthesis of the past. Multicultural history opens up social categories including gender, race, class, culture, region, generation, and sexual orientation; it also brings them together through comparative analyses, studies of unequal power dynamics, and explorations of intercultural borders. Shading U.S. history with overlapping narratives, such as those rooted in region, helps bring out the range of women's experience without unduly sacrificing coherence. Because of the confluence of many cultures and races in the region, Western women's historians provide a particularly good example of the compatibility of multiculturalism and regional narratives. Even the term "the West" reflects only one of several historical perspectives; the Eastern homesteaders'

"West" is also the Mexican "North," the Native American "homeland," and the Asian "East."

The expanding literature on multicultural women's history has developed despite (or perhaps because of) the intense debate over its legitimacy. Like multiculturalism its critiques vary in tone and substance and occupy different places along the political spectrum. To conservatives, for whom universal cultural values are already dangerously under assault, multiculturalism so fragments the narrative as to make a coherent account of U.S. history impossible. They argue that multiculturalists discount the uniquely American capacity to absorb and transform generations of immigrants into full citizens and fragment a common national legacy into the stories of individual groups. For some critics, a triumphant national history becomes a collection of victims' tales.

The conservative opposition to multiculturalism is not merely an intellectual position but also an important component of the Right's political agenda. Indeed, right-wing groups have organized against attempts for a more inclusive curriculum. For instance, conservatives orchestrated a campaign against the Children of the Rainbow Coalition curriculum in New York City because it included positive information on gays and lesbians. Debate over the moderate national U.S. history standards has been reduced to counting how many times specific historical actors are mentioned, with conservatives lamenting the perceived privileging of Sojourner Truth over Robert E. Lee.

Those on the Left, who have no problems with critiques of U.S. history, nonetheless have their own qualms about the conceptual utility of multiculturalism. They argue that multiculturalism pays too little attention to power and domination rather than too much. They claim that multiculturalism boils down to a celebration of "diversity," a kind of updated cultural pluralism, which functions as a salve to a liberal consciousness guilty about continuing racial inequality. Another aspect of the critique holds that so much attention is given to race that the deeper and more enduring inequalities of class, always a problem for U.S. historians, are ignored. Rather than propelling change, they argue, multiculturalism forestalls it. Indeed, some scholars have characterized multiculturalism as a kind of postcolonial racism.

The continuing vitality of multiculturalism probably depends on how well its practitioners meet two sets of analytical challenges. The first of these is the building of bridges across the conceptual territories of race, class, and gender. It seems quite clear that at this point research on both gender and race relations has permanently altered concepts of class in U.S. history. Discussions of "working class" now have to feature domestic service and agricultural labor along with industrial work, and they must explore family economies rather than simply subsume women and children under male workers. Perceptions of "middle class" have similarly been expanded by reconceptualizing "female domesticity" as a crusading middle-class culture advanced by those who espoused a belief in female moral authority.

The second set of issues facing multicultural history comes from the new scholarship in literary criticism and cultural analysis. Multicultural history is a way to establish the context within which voices long ignored can be heard. And yet, what constitutes historical "voice" and how we, from our own positions in the present, can hear all the women of the past is a complex matter. "Experience" is the fundamental category of all social history; yet these other disciplines have alerted us to the importance of systems of expression—of discourse and representation. As a result, historical "experience" no longer seems simple and unmediated. We can no longer avoid analyzing the languages, attending to the silences, and decoding the symbols by which people place themselves in history.

In addition, inasmuch as these representational systems reflect power inequalities in any given society, we must acknowledge them and yet continue to hear what has been so invigorating in multicultural women's history—the independent voices of those furthest from the centers of power. We can never lose sight of differential power relations as we reclaim, reconstruct, and interpret women's voices and women's choices. In the words of sociologist Evelyn Nakano Glenn, "Unless we consciously bring these systems of power into our analysis, the multicultural paradigm can lead to a depoliticized, and therefore incomplete, account of women's lives." This involves recognizing the fact "that the kinds of lives some women lead depends on the kinds of lives other women lead."

At the risk of overreaching, it does seem that a multicultural approach, one in which many pasts can be explored simultaneously, may be the only way to organize a genuinely national and truly inclusive history of women. To allow for overlapping narratives and to recognize multiple forms of power is both an old populist dream and a postmodern challenge.

As educators committed to a more inclusive U.S. women's history, our politics must reverberate in our teaching and in our scholarship. We would do well to heed the words of author and civil rights activist Elizabeth Martínez in her article "Campus Racism: Tip of an Iceberg." Martínez forthrightly declares, "In defending and affirming the multicultural vision, we can never forget the need to teach that nasty word 'racism'— white supremacy—which diversity alone will not eradicate. A multicultural education is an anti-racist education, or it's *nada.*"

Gloria Anzaldúa, *Making Face, Making Soul/Haciendo Caras: Creative and Critical Perspectives by Women of Color* (San Francisco: Aunt Lute Foundation, 1990); Valerie Matsumoto, "From Silence to Resistance," *Women's Review of Books* Vol. 8 (November 1990); Vicki L. Ruiz and Ellen Carol DuBois, *Unequal Sisters: A Multicultural Reader in U.S. Women's History,* 2d ed. (New York: Routledge, 1994).

▪ VICKI L. RUIZ
and ELLEN CAROL DuBOIS

SEE ALSO Education; History and Historians.

≋ Music

The earliest women's music in the United States, that of Native American women, continues to be vital during the twentieth century. Among the various tribal cultures, their music reflects gender-differentiated but equally valued functions. Women not only have their own genres of music but also take specific roles in mixed-gender ceremonies. Although women do not play the drums or serve as masters at these ceremonies, they exert much authority through their memories of traditions and song words. Women have been and still are known as creators/composers of songs, and their performance practices, such as high-pitched ululations, add essential aesthetic elements to musical events. Although most of their music remains unknown to people outside the culture, the popularity of Native American spirituality in the new age and women's movements has promoted musicians including Brooke Medicine Eagle (Crow), Lisa LaRue (Cherokee), Joanne Shenandoah (Oneida/Iroquois), and Medicine Heart Woman (Cherokee/Ojibwa), who were preceded by the Native American activist and singer Buffy Sainte-Marie in the 1960s and 1970s.

With the arrival of Europeans in the 1600s, different gender values dominated the history of women's music in the United States: music by males was accepted in the public sphere and considered more professional, serious, and advanced than women's music, which was restricted to the musical sphere of the home.

The colonizing settlers and slaves brought women's traditions from their homelands: songs about love, loss, and betrayal, as well as lullabies and children's songs. Folksongs that evolved in this country include "O, Bury Me Beneath the Willow," "Careless Love," and "Hello Girls" ("Don't you never marry no good-for-nothing boys"). Contributions by African American women include "Go to Sleepy" or "All the Pretty

Horses," which reveal the bitter feelings of slave mothers who had to watch over their white charges while their own children went untended.

The church offered another acceptable outlet for women's music making. In colonial times, women participated in male-led psalm singing and family prayer. The religious revivals of later periods encouraged more input by women, especially in the Sunday-school movement. The 1835 collection *Southern Harmony* contains several hymns by women, notably "The Promised Land," by Mrs. M. T. Durham. The best-known children's hymn, "Jesus Loves Me," by Anna B. Warner, was published in 1860. Phoebe Palmer Knapp (1893–1908) was one of the most prolific composers. Her songs included "Blessed Assurance," with words by Fanny Jane Crosby (1823–1915). Another hymn and anthem composer was Clara H. Scott (1841–97). Her *Royal Anthem Book* (1882), which contained "Open My Eyes, That I May See," was the first such volume published by a woman. Music was also associated with the woman suffrage and temperance movements.

As the nineteenth century came to a close, amateur dabbling on the parlor piano gave way to the more serious, educated efforts of girls headed for careers in the professions. Ladies' seminaries and normal schools offered rigorous musical training. More women entered the formerly male domain of classical music as performers, teachers, and composers.

In popular music before 1920, women were active as amateur composers and players of sheet music. Hundreds of middle-class white (but not Black) women at the turn of the century composed and published ragtime parlor pieces. With the advent of radio and recordings after 1920, more women became professional musicians. Singers were more recognized although instrumentalists made significant contributions. In mainstream Tin Pan Alley music, Patti Page, Ella Fitzgerald, Rosemary Clooney, Dinah Shore, and Peggy Lee were among the reigning queens from the 1940s to the 1960s, followed by Barbra Strei-

sand and Linda Ronstadt. In country music, the Carter Family women were early influences, inspiring Kitty Wells, Patsy Cline, Loretta Lynn, and Dolly Parton. In Black gospel music, the female choir was an early tradition and women composers and singers were strong influences: Lucie Campbell, Sallie Martin, Roberta Martin, Willie Mae Smith, Rosetta Tharpe, and especially Mahalia Jackson. A civil rights era outgrowth of gospel and rhythm and blues, soul music found its chief interpreter in Aretha Franklin; Motown "sequin" soul was exemplified by Diana Ross and the Supremes and other female singing groups. Urban folk music of the 1960s and 1970s was epitomized by singer/composers Carole King, Judy Collins, and Joni Mitchell. Janis Joplin and Grace Slick were the female superstars of rock music then. In the 1980s and 1990s, music video and cable TV's MTV rock channel helped to catapult Madonna into a modern icon.

The music of U.S. Latina musicians includes durable folk-activist Joan Baez, Cuban American Gloria Estefan, and Mexican Americans Lydia Mendoza, Tish Hinojosa, and the late Selena, who was tragically murdered in 1995. The new women's music ranges from the growing worldwide popularity of the group Sweet Honey in the Rock (begun in 1973), which combines African, gospel, and human rights and feminist themes, to Black female rap groups and singers such as Salt 'n' Pepa, Queen Latifah, Yo Yo, and Sister Souljah, to alternative white, all-female bands labeled "foxcore."

Specifically woman-identified music emerged in the late 1960s. This genre sought to create not only woman-centered music and environments at all-female music festivals including the National Women's Music Festival begun in 1974 and the lesbian-oriented Michigan Womyn's Music Festival but also to establish woman-controlled enterprises such as Olivia Records (1973), Women's Independent Label Distributors (1978), Ladyslipper Distributors (1976), and others. Malvina Reynolds and Ronnie Gilbert were pioneers in woman-identified music, followed later by Meg Christian,

Cris Williamson, Holly Near, and groups such as the Anna Crusis feminist choir. Lesbian concerns are addressed by many of these women as well as by newer lesbian artists such as the Indigo Girls, k. d. lang, and Melissa Etheridge, who also have been popular with general audiences.

S. Kay Hoke, "American Popular Music," in *Women and Music: A History*, edited by Karin Pendle (Bloomington: Indiana University Press, 1991); Karen E. Petersen, "An Investigation into Women-Identified Music in the United States," in *Women and Music in Cross-Cultural Perspective*, edited by Ellen Koskoff (Westport, Conn.: Greenwood Press, 1987).

▪ HELEN WALKER-HILL

SEE ALSO Classical Music; Jazz and Blues.

≋ National Abortion and Reproductive Rights Action League (NARAL)

The National Abortion and Reproductive Rights Action League (NARAL) was formed in 1969 at the first national gathering of grassroots activists advocating repeal of state abortion laws. Originally named the National Association for the Repeal of Abortion Laws, its mission was to provide an information clearinghouse for efforts to repeal restrictive state laws. In 1973, when the Supreme Court decriminalized abortion by passing *Roe* v. *Wade*, NARAL changed the words for which its acronym stood and opened a Washington, D.C., government affairs office. Five years later, it formed a tax-exempt educational operation called the NARAL Foundation, and an electoral arm called the NARAL Political Action Committee.

NARAL has 500,000 members and thirty-six state affiliates. It tracks legislation, lobbies for reproductive rights at the state and federal levels, and compiles annual guides to inform voters of their congressmember's record. The NARAL Foundation is supported by individuals and foundations. It conducts public opinion polls, researches legal issues, funds public education efforts, trains activists, and produces an annual publication, *A State-by-State Review of Reproductive Rights*. NARAL PAC, like all membership-connected political action committees, can solicit only members of NARAL for support. The group collaborates with its affiliates in state and local elections and provides financial support and endorsements for both Republican and Democrat pro-choice candidates at all levels of government.

▪ JULIE BURTON

≋ National Association for the Advancement of Colored People (NAACP)

The National Association for the Advancement of Colored People (NAACP) was founded in 1909 in response to a 1908 race riot in Springfield, Illinois. William English Wallins, a southern socialist journalist, issued a challenge to anyone interested in coordinating their efforts to fight racism and injustice. Sixty women and men responded to "the call," issued by Oswald Garrison Villard, editor of the *New York Evening Post*, which invited interested persons to form a national organization dedicated to justice. Two of the original signers of "the call" were Black women, Mary Church Terrell and Ida Wells-Barnett. Many of the white women signatories included social activists and reformers such as Jane Addams and Mary White Ovington.

Through the decades, women such as Frances Blascoer, a white socialist, and Kathryn Johnson, a Black activist, have held significant if not always prominent positions in the organization. In 1919 W. E. B. Du Bois hired Jessie Fauset as literary editor of *The Crisis*, the NAACP's official monthly news organ.

Throughout its history the NAACP has been involved in numerous key civil rights cases with women at the helm, including the Montgomery, Alabama, bus boycott and the Little Rock, Arkansas, Central High School desegregation crisis. Since 1909 a variety of proud and confident women continued to serve the NAACP with resolute dedication. The most recent example of competent female leadership within the NAACP at the national level is Myrlie Evers-Williams's appointment as the chairperson of the association's board in February 1995. Evers-Williams is the third woman to hold that position.

▪ LISA BETH HILL

SEE ALSO Civil Rights Movement; Montgomery Bus Boycott.

≋ National Association of Colored Women

The National Association of Colored Women (NACW), the oldest secular, national African American organization, was incorporated in Washington, D.C., in 1896, with the merge of the National Federation of Afro-American Women, founded in Boston in 1895 and headed by Margaret Murray Washington, dean of women at Tuskegee Institute, and the National League of Colored Women, established in Washington, D.C., in 1895, with educator and activist Mary Church Terrell as president.

The NACW addressed many of the social issues facing African American communities at the turn of the century, including the pseudoscientific ideologies that relegated Blacks to second-class citizenship. Widespread media attacks upon their character outraged educated Black women, and founding the NACW was, in part, their response to these negative charges. The NACW also reflected the tradition of mutuality and the recognition that the new century required a national body to mount a sustained, professional assault to improve Black people's social, economic, and political conditions.

The NACW was a federation comprised of state and local affiliates. It published *National Notes* to inform members and to maintain a national identity. It established settlement houses with classes in cooking, sewing, child care, and crafts. Members founded YWCAs, working girls' homes, reformatories, hospitals, and schools. It also promoted woman suffrage, Prohibition, and the civil rights agendas of the NAACP and the National Urban League.

The NACW's presidents were among the most highly educated women in the country, including Mary Church Terrell, an Oberlin College graduate, Josephine Silone Yates, Margaret Murray Washington, Elizabeth Brooks, Mary Burnett Talbert, and Mary McLeod Bethune. Their pragmatic leadership yielded success. With a membership in excess of one hundred thousand in 1915, the NACW was an increasingly important force for those who hoped to gain access to the Black community.

During the 1930s and 1940s the NACW supported the National Recovery Act, protested racial bias in the judiciary system, and asked the government to end its policy of discrimination in employment and in the distribution of services. The NACW forged ties with such social and political groups as Planned Parenthood, the AFL-CIO, and the Democratic and Republican national committees. It established the National Council of Girls' Clubs, Inc., to continue its policies. With the ascendancy of the National Council of Negro Women, founded in 1935, the NACW's visibility waned. Nevertheless, it continues to advocate on behalf of women and children, and its members remain important spokespersons for the Black community.

▪ LILLIAN SERECE WILLIAMS

SEE ALSO Black Clubwomen's Movement; National Council of Negro Women.

National Black Feminist Organization

In May 1973, approximately thirty African American women held an all-day gathering, using the donated offices of the New York chapter of the National Organization for Women (NOW). Their politics were diverse and they met with no specific agenda other than to bond, honor, and recognize one another, and to share histories. Participants who called themselves feminists decided to organize a conference to reach out to other Black feminists. It was the media, however, that propelled those twenty women into forming an organization.

The male-dominated media continued to portray the women's movement as the exclusive property of white, middle-class females, overlooking the presence, activism, and accomplishments of women of color. The conference organizers agreed upon the need to speak out to declare that 1) there was indeed a Black feminist politic, 2) racism and sexism needed to be addressed by the Black community and the larger women's movement, and 3) there was a need for an organization to address those issues, led by those who were victimized by those dual oppressions.

In August 1973, they formed the National Black Feminist Organization (NBFO). NBFO became an active part of feminist coalitions in New York City, confronting media stereotypes, fighting for minimum wage for domestic workers, raising consciousness about rape and sexual abuse, and working with political candidates who supported NBFO issues.

In November 1973, the first Eastern Regional Conference on Black Feminism was held in New York City, drawing over five hundred African American women from across the country. Later, chapters were founded in numerous major U.S. cities.

By 1977 independent chapters continued to work on local and regional issues, but the national structure dissolved. The National Black Feminist Organization affected the feminist movement by proving that feminist issues were survival issues for all women.

- MARGARET SLOAN-HUNTER

SEE ALSO Feminism, Black.

National Center for Lesbian Rights

The National Center for Lesbian Rights (NCLR) is a lesbian feminist public-interest legal resource center that provides litigation support and technical assistance on behalf of lesbians and gay men. NCLR was established in 1977 as a sponsored project of Equal Rights Advocates, a feminist-based organization. NCLR grew out of the efforts of lesbian feminists in the 1970s; its co-founders articulated the need for an organization that would explicitly and openly address issues that affect lesbians and gay men. Before there was an AIDS legal referral service in San Francisco, NCLR was the primary provider of legal services to gay men. NCLR successfully litigated the first case in California and in the nation involving HIV discrimination and child custody.

NCLR's litigation program includes advocating on behalf of lesbians and gay men in the areas of family law, sex discrimination, employment discrimination, sexual harassment, immigration law, and custody issues. NCLR's Public Policy Project drafts legislation and policies that provide lesbian-centered analyses of issues such as health care, adoption, and employment discrimination. One of the most significant influences NCLR has had on the lesbian/gay movement and public-interest law has been the articulation of lesbian issues as civil rights issues. NCLR initially took on lesbian mother custody cases at a time when other segments of the law profession did not view them as civil rights cases. Lesbian mother custody cases affect more individual lesbians than any other legal case. NCLR's Lesbians of Color Project provides legal assistance to lesbians of color, develops analyses of how racism and homophobia affect lesbians of color, designs educational programs, and provides technical assistance to lesbians of color organizations.

NCLR has had a significant impact on creating a forum for the larger legal community to become acquainted with lesbian leaders. Cofounder Honorable Donna Hitchens was appointed the first open lesbian judge on the California Superior Court in 1990. Former NCLR legal director Honorable Abby Abinanti was the first Native American to be appointed commissioner in the California Superior Court in 1994. Former NCLR executive director Roberta Achtenberg was the first openly lesbian San Francisco city supervisor, and in 1993 was appointed as assistant undersecretary for fair housing and equal opportunity in the Department of Housing and Urban Development.

▪ SKYE WARD

SEE ALSO Lesbian Organizations.

The Congress's greatest success was the nationwide campaign for "mothers' pension" legislation, which afforded small stipends to "deserving" single mothers, usually white widows, and formed the basis for the Aid to Dependent Children program of the New Deal. The pensions, however, reflected the group's racial and class politics: The Congress's rhetoric extolled the virtues of universal motherhood but viewed Anglo-American middle-class mothers as the ideal and others as needing to assimilate to "American" norms. Despite its emphasis on Anglo-American motherhood, rightwing leaders found the Congress's gender politics threatening; in the early 1920s the Congress was listed as one of fifteen "socialist-pacifist" women's groups indicted in an "international socialist conspiracy," prompting the leaders to redirect their activities away from explicit support of "mothers" and toward "parents" and professionals. It was renamed the National Congress of Parents and Teachers in 1924.

▪ MAUREEN FITZGERALD

SEE ALSO Mothers' Pensions.

☰ National Congress of Mothers

The National Congress of Mothers, now known informally as the PTA, was established in 1897. Founded as a traditional "maternalist" organization, the Congress depended for its legitimacy on the simultaneous avowal of mothers' rights to influence public policy and disavowal of women's rights leading to sex "equality." Founder Alice McLellan Birney, wife of a Washington, D.C., lawyer, expanded the group from the top down, seeking "women of position" in communities throughout the nation and then incorporating local groups into the National Congress. This organizational method predetermined the group's elite membership and discouraged nonwhite, nonelite women from participation.

☰ National Council of Jewish Women (NCJW)

Founded in 1893 by Hannah Greenebaum Solomon at the Jewish Women's Congress, held at the Chicago World's Fair, the NCJW emerged as an organization of primarily middle-class German-Jewish women devoted to the study of Bible and Jewish history and to the provision of social services to Jewish immigrants. By 1920 the council emphasized social welfare issues almost exclusively.

The NCJW directed its primary efforts toward helping new arrivals with housing, education, and vocational services; it also sponsored Americanization programs and lobbied for legislative reform. Although the council's leadership of the campaign against forced prostitution allied it with feminists worldwide, the organization was slow to support suffrage, preferring to focus on issues related to women's familial roles.

In 1923 the NCJW convened the first World Council of Jewish Women and organized the International Council of Jewish Women, with several European affiliates. In the 1930s and 1940s, NCJW's immigrant aid services helped refugees from fascism. In the postwar period, the council expanded its mandate to include services for children and senior citizens, campaigns for civil rights and against anti-Semitism, and, more recently, women's issues such as the ERA, domestic violence, and pay equity. The NCJW somewhat belatedly backed the ordination of women rabbis.

Melding voluntarism with increasingly complex programmatic expertise, the NCJW provided an early training ground for Jewish women leaders and a forum for Jewish women's concerns within and outside the Jewish community.

■ JOYCE ANTLER

SEE ALSO Jewish Women.

≋ National Council of Negro Women

The National Council of Negro Women (NCNW), the first Black organization of organizations and the first national coalition of Black women's organizations, was founded by Mary McLeod Bethune in December 1935. Its structure was similar to the National Council of Women, which for years admitted only one Black women's organization, the National Association of Colored Women (NACW).

As past president of NACW, Bethune was aware of the pervasive sexism that Black women faced within the Black community and the racism and sexism they confronted in the larger society. She envisioned a new organization that could "harness the great power of nearly a million women into a force for constructive action" and would represent all Black women. After 1980 insiders and observers acknowledged that the national council concept had become difficult to implement. The growth in numbers and power of the major Black sororities and the powerful National Coalition of 100 Black Women challenged NCNW's goal of unification.

The council has worked actively with the national board of the YMCA, the NAACP, the National Council of Women, the National Women's Political Caucus, the National Urban League, and numerous women's groups to implement educational programs working to eliminate racism and sexism.

The NCNW's recent international division has maintained a strong program in Africa. Its domestic program has focused mainly on Black Family Reunion celebrations, an event launched to address prevalent negative images of the Black family. The Black Family Reunion consists of workshops, forums, exhibits, demonstrations, and entertainment and has led to the NCNW's highly visible public presence.

■ BETTYE COLLIER-THOMAS

SEE ALSO Black Clubwomen's Movement; National Association of Colored Women.

≋ National Federation of Business and Professional Women

The National Federation of Business and Professional Women of the United States (BPW/USA) was founded in 1919 to advance the status of wage-earning women. The organization offers to its approximately eight hundred thousand members legislative advocacy on issues such as economic equity, health, and civil rights, a legislative hotline, personal and professional development workshops, opportunities for networking, a quarterly magazine, a benefits package that includes business loans and medical insurance, and annual national conventions and lobby days.

The BPW/USA has had an extensive legislative program over the years and the organization has supported historic legislation such as the Women's Business Ownership Act of 1988, the Equal Credit Opportunity Act of 1974, the Civil Rights Act of 1964, the Equal Pay Act of 1963, and Title IX. Moreover, in 1937, BPW/USA became the first women's organization to endorse the Equal Rights Amendment. More recently, BPW/USA promoted the Child Care Act of 1991. To advance its legislative priorities, a political action committee (BPW/PAC) offers contributions and endorsements to supportive candidates.

In 1956 the Business and Professional Women's Foundation, a nonprofit research, education, and grant-making organization, was created to further women's educational and career status. The foundation has awarded over $5 million in loans, grants, and scholarships to over seven thousand people. Of particular note are the Lena Lake Forrest Fellowship and related research grants that support those women who study issues relevant to working women; and the Sally Butler Memorial Fund for Latina Research, which supports research promoting equity for Latinas and assists Latina scholars. Members of BPW/USA also have access to the Marguerite Rawalt Resource Center, in Washington, D.C., a library of information on working women's issues.

■ SUE THOMAS

SEE ALSO Businesswomen and Corporations.

≋ National Organization for Women (NOW)

Founded in 1966, the National Organization for Women (NOW) was the first national post–World War II feminist group to combat sex discrimination in all spheres of life: social, political, economic, and psychological.

Although laws such as the 1963 Equal Pay Act and Title VII of the 1964 Civil Rights Act (which included sex in its discrimination prohibitions) were on the books, they were not taken seriously by legislators. In response, a small group of women formed NOW during the third National Conference of State Commissions on the Status of Women. According to Betty Friedan, one of NOW's twenty-nine founders, "it took only a few of us to get together to ignite the spark—and it spread like a nuclear chain reaction." Within a year, there were three hundred charter members and a "Bill of Rights for Women," which became the basis for feminist action everywhere. It called for an Equal Rights Amendment to the U.S. Constitution; enforcement of Title VII; maternity leave rights; home and child-care tax deductions for working parents; child-care centers; equal education and job-training opportunities; and reproductive rights.

By 1973 NOW had grown to fifteen thousand members in 365 chapters. Its first major successes included the elimination of sex-segregated want ads and protective labor legislation. NOW also put some muscle into the enforcement of Title VII and pressed for such landmark laws as the Equal Credit Opportunity Act. Over the past two decades, NOW has campaigned to stop violence against women and sexual harassment.

Even though NOW's legal challenges and successes affected all women, and even though more than one of its founders and its second president were African American, NOW's early membership was almost entirely white and middle class. To some degree it still is, but NOW has expanded its base by frequently joining forces with other civil rights organizations to strengthen support for issues common to all women.

In the 1970s, the defining issues of women's equality began to include not only the economic and legal but also the sexual and psychological.

NOW's lesbian members had become a major force and added lesbian issues to NOW's agenda. In 1971 NOW declared lesbian rights a feminist issue, arguing on ideological grounds that if sex roles were irrelevant, then sexual orientation was equally irrelevant. That stance caused many NOW members to resign.

NOW lost still more members in the late 1970s and early 1980s as a result of its hotly debated decision to support the Equal Rights Amendment (ERA) ratification drive to the exclusion of almost every other issue. ERA opponents cast both the amendment and the NOW membership as antimale and antifamily. This contributed to the defeat of the Equal Rights Amendment in 1982 and to lingering public skepticism about feminism.

Disagreements over issues and priorities as well as internal power struggles common to any maturing organization reduced NOW's effectiveness in the 1980s and early 1990s. So, too, did a general backlash against women's changing roles and rights. If NOW's national clout had diminished by the 1990s, its political and legislative influence at the state and local level had increased considerably due to the activism of its more than six hundred chapters.

▪ JUDITH HOLE

≋ National Organization for Women Legal Defense and Education Fund (NOW-LDEF)

Founded in 1970 by the National Organization for Women as a separate, tax-exempt organization, NOW Legal Defense and Education Fund (NOW-LDEF) pursues equality for women and girls in the workplace, the schools, the family, and the courts through legal, education, and public information programs. Headquartered in New York City since its inception, NOW-LDEF currently maintains a Washington, D.C., office as well. Staff size, which peaked at approximately forty in the mid-1980s, has stabilized at twenty-four, including eight attorneys.

Significant projects of the 1970s and 1980s included the ERA Impact Project, which monitored implementation and participated in litigation under state ERAs; the Project on Equal Education Rights, which monitored implementation of Title IX and advocated for women's educational equity nationwide; and the Media Project, which used innovative communications techniques to educate the public about women's fight for equality. In addition, NOW-LDEF's National Judicial Education Program, now in its fourteenth year, has been responsible for the creation of task forces to address gender bias among judges, lawyers, and other court personnel in forty states and five federal circuits.

NOW-LDEF's docket includes over seventy-five direct and *amicus* cases at all levels of the federal and state court systems. Priority areas for the 1990s include litigation and legislation to ensure women's access to abortion services; litigation and public education to help eradicate sexual harassment in the workplace and in schools; efforts to end violence against women through the Violence Against Women Act and other legal strategies; and litigation and legislation to help alleviate women's poverty and make welfare work more effectively for women.

▪ MARTHA F. DAVIS

≋ National Origins Act

The National Origins Act was a discriminatory U.S. immigration law passed in 1924. It established admission quotas and was designed to curtail immigration from new source countries such as Russia, Poland, and Italy by allocating them small quotas; it allowed immigration from older source countries, such as England, by allocating them large quotas. Initially the quotas were set at 2 percent of a country's foreign-born residents in the United States in 1890. In 1929 quotas were apportioned according to the national origins or roots of the total U.S. population, enlarging England's quota. The legislation included a clause that completely barred immigration for all those prohibited from attaining U.S. citizenship, specifically, Asians.

Racist arguments permeated the debates over the act. Potential East European Jewish immigrants were characterized in some government documents as "abnormally twisted." The most racist part of the act was the clause barring Asian immigration. It was aimed at potential Japanese immigrants — Chinese laborers had already been barred by the Chinese Exclusion Act of 1882. The 1924 legislation, often known as the Japanese Exclusion Act, blocked growth of the Japanese community in the United States by banning immigration and freezing the gender imbalance. Japanese immigrants had initially been almost all men, but an increasing number of Japanese women had migrated to the United States as wives and picture brides in the 1910s, enabling community growth through procreation. Further correction of the gender imbalance through immigration of women was blocked by the act.

The national origins quota system was abolished in 1965. Since then countries in the Eastern Hemisphere have been allocated equal quotas. Since 1976 countries in the Western Hemisphere have been limited to the same per-country quotas as those applied in the Eastern Hemisphere.

■ LEAH HAUS

SEE ALSO Immigration.

≋ National Urban League

Founded in 1911 as an amalgamation of social service agencies to protect women and improve conditions in cities, the National Urban League became the premier African American employment and social service agency for northern migrants. The organization provided jobs, housing assistance, health and birth-control clinics, recreation, and general relief. League staff members dispensed advice to help rural migrants assimilate to the mores of middle-class northern life. The league was organized along the well-tooled networks of Black philanthropy created by clubwomen and advocated the ethic of self-help.

The National Urban League was an interracial organization and, although its ties to white philanthropists may have modified a potentially more radical social agenda, African Americans nevertheless made significant financial, administrative, and policy contributions.

Women figured prominently among the league's rank and file as volunteers, staff members, and directors, although they did not contribute significantly to national policy until the 1940s. The Urban League grew simultaneously with the profession of social work and adopted the scientific research methodology of that discipline as its model.

The Urban League's official journal, *Opportunity*, also spawned the careers of literary artists and playwrights through literary contests, especially during the Harlem Renaissance. Aiding migrants and promoting the careers of middle-class professionals, the Urban League has been an important part of the larger movement among African Americans throughout the century to attain social and political equality.

■ JESSIE M. RODRIQUE

SEE ALSO Social Work.

≋ National Welfare Rights Organization

In 1967 groups of welfare mothers from Boston to Los Angeles confederated into the National Welfare Rights Organization (NWRO). Voting members were poor—most were mothers receiving Aid to Families with Dependent Children (AFDC). The multiracial organization drew heavily from urban areas, so although white women constituted more than half the nation's AFDC population, the majority of NWRO leaders and members were African American. Johnnie Tillmon, a welfare mother from Los Angeles, was elected chair. Former college professor and civil rights leader George Wiley, who had raised the money for the founding convention, became executive director.

Local WROs—founded and run directly by welfare mothers (such as Tillmon's) or established by paid organizers (usually white, male, middle-class professionals)—sprouted everywhere. NWRO became the largest and most influential national organization of welfare recipients to exist in the United States.

NWRO strove to include poor women's voices in public policy debates, particularly to counter the mass of misinformation surrounding welfare. Members sought dignity for welfare recipients and fought for individual and collective rights under the law. They advocated a universal guaranteed income to support child rearing, or *productive*, choice (whether and when to work outside the home). Their efforts resulted in the overall extension of welfare benefits, particularly to eligible families who were not receiving benefits, and to a short-lived but important expansion of consciousness of welfare as a women's issue and the value of women's work in the home. NWRO also indirectly rekindled an international debate on "wages for housework."

NWRO's style (often confrontational and angry) and tactics (often direct action) created the conditions for its existence—media attention, guilt money, and so on—and for its demise. The organization required funding and support from members of upper classes, whose vested interests were ultimately perceived to contradict NWRO's own. External pressures, including FBI and IRS intrusion, were daunting. Internal strife between the mothers and paid staff, including Wiley, over issues, power, politics, and funding resulted in his resignation and the defection of most of the staff by the end of 1972. One hundred thousand dollars in debt and left with few funding contracts, the AFDC leaders never recouped. In 1975 the national office closed.

Still, NWRO continued to influence subsequent activist welfare mothers. The Downtown Welfare Advocate Center in New York, for instance, a group of welfare mothers guided largely by the philosophy of NWRO and infused with a more consciously feminist agenda, evolved into a statewide organization of more than five thousand paid members by 1980—the largest since NWRO. Other indigenously organized welfare rights groups continue and new ones surface, often exerting influence for several years before succumbing to many of the same forces that felled NWRO. None has achieved the prominence, the numbers of participants, the level of influence, or nearly the funding that NWRO garnered at its peak. Unfortunately, over time, the history of welfare rights as AFDC mothers defined it is more obscured and less available to those who would best learn from it.

• THERESA FUNICIELLO

SEE ALSO Welfare and Public Relief.

≋ National Woman's Party

The National Woman's Party, a nonpartisan group devoted to equal rights for women, grew out of the National American Woman Suffrage Association in 1913. Alice Paul, the group's charismatic founder, organized militant public demonstrations on behalf of a federal amendment to grant women the right to vote. Taking at first the name "Congressional Union," a small group of predominantly young, white, middle- and upper-class women took to the streets to demand suffrage and, during the First World War, outraged the authorities, the public, and mainstream suffragists by picketing the White House and, when arrested, going on hunger strikes.

After the suffrage victory, the Woman's Party turned its attention to what it saw as the next step toward equality: the Equal Rights Amendment, first introduced into Congress in 1923. This single-issue focus alienated African American women, working-class women, and socialist women who had rallied to the cause of militant suffragism in the last years of the struggle.

Because the ERA threatened to eliminate the special labor legislation that reformers hoped would protect vulnerable working women, the amendment found little support. Liberals and labor leaders feared that "equality" would mean further exploitation, and they accused the Woman's Party of callousness toward women working in industrial jobs.

After 1920 membership dropped off and the Woman's Party remained a small, exclusive group that attracted little new blood, although its aging members continued to carry the banner of feminism. In the 1970s, as legislative gains made the conflict over special labor legislation increasingly moot, a more progressive women's movement took up the ERA as a central goal. The National Woman's Party, headquartered in Washington, D.C., lives on as a remnant of earlier struggles and continues to work solely for women's equality.

▪ LEILA J. RUPP

SEE ALSO Suffrage Movement.

☰ National Women's Political Caucus

The National Women's Political Caucus (NWPC) is a national, multipartisan organization dedicated to increasing the participation of women in U.S. political life—as elected and appointed officials, judges, delegates to national party conventions, lobbyists, campaigners, and voters.

NWPC was founded during a July 1971 meeting in Washington, D.C., attended by 320 women from all over the United States, a group including elected women officials, feminists, community activists, Democrats, Republicans, radicals, union women, homemakers, students, women of color, and lesbians. The group approved a "statement of purposes" to oppose sexism, racism, institutional violence, and poverty through the election and appointment of women to political office; the reform of party structures to give women an equal voice in decision making; the selection of particular candidates who would increase the numbers of registered women voters; and to support women's issues and feminist candidates across party lines. The participants elected a national policy council, initially cochaired by former Democratic Congresswoman Bella Abzug, an NWPC initiator, and Republican Virginia Allen, former chair of President Nixon's Task Force on Women's Rights and Responsibilities.

Since its founding, NWPC chapters have been organized in forty-five states, with a total membership of more than thirty-five thousand. National Democratic and Republican task forces plan electoral activities. A major activity of the NWPC is recruiting, training, holding public meetings, and fundraising for women candidates who support the Equal Rights Amendment and women's rights, including abortion. Its Minority Women Candidates Training Program began in 1987.

In 1971 women numbered 362 in the state legislatures and 15 in Congress. By 1992 the numbers rose to 1,517 women state legislators and 54 in Congress: 22.2 percent of statewide elected offices; 20 percent of state legislators; 11 percent of the House of Representatives; and 7 percent of the Senate. Two of the nine Supreme Court justices are women. The NWPC in 1992 supported five of the seven winning Senate candidates and 37 of 47 successful women House candidates.

> ▪ MIM KELBER

SEE ALSO Electoral Politics; Politicians.

≋ Native American Cultures

The values of Native American cultures have always been rooted in an association with land. Native men hunted wild game rather than domesticating animals for food. Female sexuality affected male hunters. On the Northwest Coast, young women were taught that the wives of Makah whale hunters must lie very still in bed while their husbands hunted, since their movements influenced whales' behavior. In a Navajo story, Black God had all the animals penned up until his wife opened the gate. The animals escaped, and thereafter men had to hunt them.

Women gathered wild plants and domesticated them by systematic selection of wild varieties that had desirable characteristics. Communities often attributed the origin of their major crops—corn, beans, and squash—to female spirits. The Iroquois tribes in the Northeast referred to them as the three sisters. They structured their societies around rich and complex explanations of the world in which plants, animals, and humans interacted on an equal basis. In a story common to agriculturalists who depended upon the triad of corn, beans, and squash, a woman fed her family with a delicious but mysterious grain. Her son or sons wondered about the source of the grain and followed her as she gathered it. They found her

rubbing skin from her body and forming the grain from it and accused her of witchcraft, to which she responded that they must kill her and bury her body. They did so, and the next year, corn grew from her grave. Such stories are metaphors for the interconnections of female fertility and the productivity of nature, the relation of cycles of human birth and death with the seasonal cycles of the year.

Time was measured by these cycles—constantly repeating events essential to human survival—the growth of crops, the rutting seasons of game animals, the gathering of the great buffalo herds on the Plains, the spawning of salmon in the rivers of the Northwest Coast. On the Northwest Coast, the salmon swam up rivers to their spawning grounds in the spring. The Makah in the state of Washington and the Hupa on the Trinity River in California, among other tribes, had a ceremony when the first salmon was caught. The first fish was cooked, and everyone in the village had a piece, except pregnant and menstruating women, whose conditions bespoke their power to give birth. This power could affect the future salmon runs.

Pueblo peoples in the Southwest held ceremonies at the times of the summer and winter solstices. They believed the sun was a male spirit who had two houses in the sky, one at the far north on the horizon, and one at the far south, in each of which he rested during his journey through the sky. Their ceremonies gave the sun the power to rise from his rest and return back across the horizon to his other house. In the ceremonial cycle of many Pueblo peoples, men's societies conducted certain ceremonies, and women's societies conducted others. The complementary nature of male-female relationships was maintained throughout.

Because people know what has happened in the past, they can anticipate the future, if they act in appropriate ways. The Hopi language expresses the future in terms of humans anticipating events, which then occur. The Navajo language has over three thousand conjugations of the verb "to go." Indian languages generally emphasize verbs (action) rather than nouns (things).

The world depends upon relationships—between humans and other beings—that are based on power. In many societies, men seek understanding of the spirit world through vision quests, dreams, and ceremonies. Women's power comes through their ability to give birth, a power demonstrated in the menstrual cycle.

Spirits in the natural world demonstrate their power in their ability to move and to exercise volition and choice. Wind, storms, and running water all have power. A basic dichotomy exists between things that are alive and things that are not. Rocks may have power, if they demonstrate the ability to move, or to speak, or to assume a form other than that which they ordinarily have. But power does not exist as an absolute in and of itself. It is manifest in the actions of beings—spiritual and human. The relationships between human and spiritual forces stem from their mutual dependence. Humans require food, shelter, clothing. A Havasupai song from the Southwest asks the sun for the energy to work in the fields. People are recognized for individual abilities that are based on relationships with spirits.

Human and spiritual beings interact and acknowledge one another's powers. The Medicine Arrow ceremonies of the Cheyenne tribe restore their relationship with the spiritual world. They include sexual relations between men and women as a form of renewal. Navajo chants intend to bring the world back to a state of perfection through the power of speech. The major deity of the Navajo is Changing Woman, who created the Navajo clans out of skin rubbed from different parts of her body. The chants all include some part that describes the origins of the Navajo world, including the story of Changing Woman's impregnation by the sun and by running water and the birth of her twin sons, who slew monsters that threatened humans.

In societies where writing does not exist, people control events by speaking. Songs and ceremonial speeches determine relationships of power among individuals, which are dynamic and involve the constant exchange of power. In some languages, such as Koasati in the Southeast, men's and women's speech are distinct. In all tribes ceremonial speech is primarily men's domain, since they generally conduct ceremonies, but women as healers can exercise the power of speech to cure their patients.

Men and women demonstrate power by speaking in different arenas—men in the public sphere of making decisions about community actions, and women in their influence over their children and husband. In societies where descent patterns and inheritance of property are dictated through the female line, women control their children's futures and the products of their work.

With the advent of European explorers, adventurers, missionaries, and traders and colonists, Native Americans were confronted with sudden and rapid changes. Whole villages were destroyed by diseases introduced by Europeans—smallpox, cholera, and syphilis. New relationships had to be established with European invaders. Guns, iron cooking utensils, woven cloth, and glass beads became available, changing men's hunting patterns and altering women's work. Guns and metal traps made warfare and hunting more efficient for men. Women found new marriage partners with European traders.

With the relatively rapid introduction of new elements into traditional cultures, the sense of time began to change. Hunting for skins for trade changed traditional patterns of Natives' relationship with animals. They had to adapt to the sudden imposition of linear, historical change on the cyclical nature of their lives. Communities resisted change in some respects, adapted newly introduced elements to their own needs in others, and despite the loss of much knowledge of the past, persist in contemporary society.

History has changed the way in which American Indians are identified. The Constitution gives special status to Indians, and treaties between groups and government agents have become the basis for political recognition by the U.S. government. Government policies to educate Indians took many children from their communities and put them in boarding schools, where they were taught in English. There are over three hundred tribes currently recognized by the Federal government, as well as some one hundred fifty more seeking recognition. The majority of tribal languages are no longer spoken. Women have assumed roles as tribal chairpersons, and in economic systems that depend on wage labor, their work is as important to their families as that of men. Women's crafts, such as pottery, basketry, and weaving, have become important to museums and private collectors. Reservations, however, still constitute a distinguishable land base for Indian communities and allow a continuing relationship with nature that sustains ceremonial activities. Indian people living outside of these areas still find in these activities a source of identity.

Ruth Fulton Benedict, "The Concept of the Guardian Spirit in North America," *Memoirs of the American Anthropological Association*, No. 29 (Menasha, Wisconsin: The American Anthropological Association, [1923]); Murray Wax, "The Notions of Nature, Man, and Time of a Hunting People," *Southern Folklore Quarterly*, 26, no. 3 (September 1962): 175–86; Benjamin Whorf, "An American Indian Model of the Universe," *Language, Thought, and Reality* (Cambridge, Mass.: Massachusetts Institute of Technology Press, 1970).

■ CLARA SUE KIDWELL

SEE ALSO Native American Religions; Native American Women.

≋ Native American Religions

Native American religions have been a major conundrum both historically and contemporarily for both Natives and non-Natives. For the former, it is an ongoing reality; for the latter, it is derision, or a searching, as in the New Age movement toward indigenous beliefs. The term *religion* has been used to describe the varied belief systems of North American aboriginal peoples, but this term reflects a concept superimposed by European conquerers. The core values and sentiments are often expressed in Native terms such as *wakan* (Lakota), meaning a universal force or power. The English term *gloss*, or spirituality, may be a more functional means for examining the complexities of Native epistemologies. European concepts of gods, hierarchical arrangements of spirits, and codified systems of reward and punishment such as heaven and hell are not categories that encompass the integrated whole of Native beliefs. Moreover, the emphasis upon medicine men, shaman, and male ceremonial leaders has served to obscure the dyadic relationships between males and females in the maintenance of spiritual well-being and in the performance of rituals that provide harmony and equilibrium within the larger social group.

Women were part of the natural and supernatural world, as were men and children. Most beliefs and rituals fostered proper transitions from childhood to adulthood, and the rites of passage—birth, puberty, marriage, and death—were regulated by appropriate ceremonies to allow for personal development and a smoothly functioning social system. The Navajo (Diné) term *hozho*, or beauty, indicates everything is in place, in balance.

Balance and harmony were important existential features of many indigenous "religions." Many societies equated "Mother Earth" and "Father Sun" as symbolic girders. To Tanoan-speaking pueblos of New Mexico "the mother earth navel is the *source* of all these blessings, so they are directed *outward* in all directions," according to Alfonso Ortiz, the Pueblo anthropologist. The Tewas' primordial past originated in an underworld where their first mothers were Blue Corn Maiden and White Corn Maiden, who symbolized summer and winter respectively. ("Tewa" is a name for a group of pueblos.) This female duality is seen in the binary social organization in this horticultural, matrilineal society. A complex ritual system of yearly and life-cycle events was necessary to regulate life in the natural and spiritual world of Tewa males and females. Feminine metaphorical symbols such as the "earth navel" are equated with the *sipapu* in the *kiva* (ceremonial center) in many Pueblo villages. The emergence of Pueblo peoples from a creature-peopled underworld is related to this concept in a rich and complex seasonally directed pattern that is carefully guarded from intrusion by "others."

The "Father Sky" imagery is widely prevalent. Ake Hultkrantz, in his 1980 book *The Religion of American Indians*, indicates that "everywhere in North America, except among the Eskimos [*sic*] and some eastern tribes, the sun is perceived as a male being." Eskimos themselves prefer to be called Inuit. Other nations prefer their own linguistic appellations, such as Diné for Navajo, Lakota for Sioux, and so forth. This may indicate an enhanced self-awareness and negation of such terms as American Indian and Native American.

In many prevalent dualities of sacred and secular, the moon was important as an indicator of the monthly cycle of some aboriginal women. It marked the time of menstruation. Some ethnographers, for example, Thomas Buckley, predicated a synchronicity of "being on the moon" for women in villages such as the Yurok in northern California. Because of the use of so-called *menstrual huts*, which isolated women in many tribal groups, the notion of pollution was prevalent in anthropological literature. From an emic, or Native, standpoint, the awesome power of creation by women was recognized and celebrated in ceremonies marking the menarche of young girls in such groups as the Apache where the "Changing Woman" ritual indicated to all the creative power of women.

Life-crisis events demonstrated the underlying beliefs and values that were cogently contrived and delicately intertwined in the philosophical, linguistic, and behavioral aspects of daily life in all Native societies. Native epistemologies, rituals, and expected behavioral norms were integrated into holistic frames that regulated daily lives. Each cultural group of the some three hundred fifty extant tribes must be apprized to understand traditional, changing, and contemporary beliefs.

Because Native belief and ceremonial systems were such a part of daily life, so functional, and so cherished, these philosophies were seen as detriments to the colonizing and Christianizing forces of European immigrants. These cohesive patterns of worship were seen as pagan, heathen, and barbaric. Christians attempted to "civilize" the Natives and destroy them in a "superior and ethnocentric manner." Christianization and education were forced upon aboriginal peoples to guarantee conformity to European religion. Repression by legal means was initiated by the federal government in the 1880s. Vine Deloria notes that "by the time of the Allotment Act, almost every form of Indian religion was banned on the reservations. In schools the children were punished for speaking their own language." As the core of traditional beliefs was embedded in Native languages, this stricture cut at the heart of aboriginal life. Political, social, and economic spheres were intricately interwoven with Native values. It is only since the passage of the American Indian Freedom of Religion Act (1978) that tribal peoples may worship freely in their traditional ways. Because the eradication process had been so extreme, many tribal groups are now revitalizing ceremonies and expressive elements of culture such as art, language, and songs, which were dormant or lost. Critical in the process are women as reservoirs of and transmitters of aboriginal cultures.

Because each nation values the integrity and reality of its unique belief system and often resents intrusion into them, and because this author is Lakota, the following discussion emphasizes Lakota beliefs and rituals and the undergirding premises of their lifeway.

The Lakota (Sioux), a Siouan-speaking, buffalo-hunting, and nomadic nation of the Northern Great Plains, epitomized the dominant society's notion of a "Warrior Society." This designation clearly obliterates the complementarity of genders in the economic, social, and ritual life of this group who battled for their land and way of life. Men, women, and *winkte* (Lakota term for male gender-crossing individual) all had designated and appreciated social roles in this society. The defeat of General Custer and the acceptance of the Ghost Dance, a Native movement that promised a re-union with deceased kinfolk, bountiful buffalo, and the disappearance of the immigrant *Wasicu* ("White" or European peoples), held great hope for a demoralized nation.

The aboriginal belief system was brought to the Lakota nation by the White Buffalo Calf Woman in the mythic past. The pipe she brought is symbolic of the union of the catlinite (red stone) bowl and the wooden stem, which represented male and female. The offering of the sacred pipe to an all-encompassing power *(wakan)*, which permeated all things—known and unknown—of the Lakota universe, was a powerful act. Along with the sacred pipe, the White Buffalo Calf Woman instructed the Lakota people in the seven sacred rites. These consist of the Pipe Offering, the Sun Dance, the Sweat Lodge, Spirit-Keeping (Mourning), Puberty Ceremony (girls), Vision Quest (boys), and Making of Relatives. These ceremonies correlated with the life cycle of males and females and were beautifully presented with music, dance, and recitation of oral traditions that fostered integration with the four cardinal virtues of the Lakota: generosity, fortitude, bravery, and wisdom. When each ceremony is viewed in context with the Native milieu, one can easily comprehend its affiliation with the cardinal virtues and the normative patterns of behavior. For example, young Lakota females who were virgins were chosen to chop the cottonwood tree in a ceremony that symbolized the unity of earth and sky while bringing honor to the extended family *(tiospaye)* and upholding womanly ideals (such as generosity) for emulation. Conversely, young Lakota males who pledged to dance—with thongs through their chest muscles and attached to the sacred SunDance tree—brought good blessings and good welfare to their nation as well as fulfilling their own wishes and exemplifying bravery and fortitude. Aged men and women (who were chosen to enact the White Buffalo Calf Woman) displayed wisdom in intellectual knowledge and cultural transmission. The supreme Siouan prayer, *Mitaku Oyasin*, offered that "all my relatives" may live.

The girl's puberty rite and the boy's vision quest were rituals that transformed youth into fulfilling adult roles and functioning members of Lakota society. Rituals and beliefs in this society engendered equity and complementarity.

This brief description is somewhat denuded of detail. However, an examination of any ritual or ceremony in the cultures of native North America can highlight the fully integrated aspects of a world-view that regulated daily life in coexisting natural and supernatural worlds. Indigenous spirituality illuminated both.

Thomas Buckley and Anna Gottlieb, *Blood Magic* (Berkeley: University of California Press, 1988); Vine Deloria, *God Is Red* (New York: Dell Publishing, 1973); Alfonso Ortiz, *The Tewa World: Space, Time, Being, and Becoming in a Pueblo Society* (Chicago: University of Chicago Press, 1969).

• BEATRICE MEDICINE

SEE ALSO Native American Women; Religion.

Native American Women

There are over 450 Native nations in the United States, each with its own distinct language, culture, history, and political structure. Tribal populations range from over 250,000 in the great Navajo Nation to less than one hundred in some Native nations. Land bases range from California rancherias smaller than five acres to millions of acres of land held by some tribes. The roles of Na-

A young woman wrapped in an upside-down flag was one of five hundred West Coast Native Americans to occupy the Bureau of Indian Affairs for a week in 1972 to protest broken treaties and other injustices.

tive American women, therefore, are extremely diverse, but some similarities prevail.

Creation, power, and sexuality are integrally related concepts in Native American societies. The world is shaped by powerful beings like Wenebojo, the offspring of a woman impregnated by the wind (a Chippewa tradition). The Iroquois world was shaped by twin brothers, one creative and one destructive. A woman was impregnated by the breath of a spirit in the world above this one. She fell to this world through a hole and gave birth to a daughter who in turn gave birth to twin sons. One was born in the normal way. He created the good things of the world, such as food and medicine. The other burst out of his mother's side, killing her. He created weeds, disease, and harmful animals

and insects. Among the Keresan-speaking Pueblo people of the Southwest, the creation of the world is the work of Sus'sistinako, or Thinking Woman, whose thoughts became reality.

Power can be defined as the ability to influence events by maintaining proper respect and relationships with beings who have certain attributes. It is based on notions of reciprocity. Power manifests itself in things that are unusual, beyond the ordinary experience.

The roles of men and women are based on both the biological characteristics of sexuality and the maintenance of complementary and reciprocal relationships. The role of men was to hunt, to defend their lands and families, to deliberate in public forums, and to lead the community's religious life. The role of women was to gather and prepare food, provide clothing and shelter, bear and raise children, and maintain the home.

Depending on the amount of food that women produced, their status in their society was greater or lesser, but women's work complemented that of men. On the Plains, women gathered a fair portion of food in berries, seeds, and roots, but men as hunters provided an equal or greater portion. The highly mobile lifestyle of nomadic plains groups also placed a higher premium on male activity. Inuit and Yupik (Eskimos) depended almost exclusively on meat for subsistence, and the custom of wife sharing among Eskimo hunters was a way of bonding men together in joint activities, creating an extended family.

Men and women also had access to power through contact with the spiritual world. For Native Americans, spiritual beings are one category, human beings another. Humans are able to communicate with those spiritual beings who are the reality of the physical world, and they can thus establish relationships with them and gain influence or control over them and affect the outcome of events in their own lives or those of others.

The experience of vision seeking was characteristic of many but not all tribes. The seeker was sent out after having been instructed on what to expect. The person was often purified with a sweat bath and told to fast and pray for four days. The nature of vision questing differs among tribes. In some areas vision quests were expected of all males; in some areas females were also expected to go on quests, as among the Winnebagos and the Ojibwas in the Northeast. In those societies, the quest put an individual in direct contact with spiritual powers.

Women's most obvious source of power was to bear children, a power manifest in the menstrual cycle. Where men had actively to seek power, it came upon women as a matter of course. The vision quest was the most widespread rite for men, while a girl's first menses was an occasion for her seclusion, during which her dreams held special significance for her future, followed by a ceremony that was either a familial or tribal acknowledgment of her new status as a marriageable woman. Men feared the power of menstrual blood, hence the ritual of seclusion. Women's blood could destroy the power of a man's weapons in hunting. Men even avoided traveling paths that might be trod by menstruating women. The fear came from the fact that men had no way of controlling or influencing menstruation. It was a uniquely female experience, and the power of birthing that it represented was greater than the power of the spiritual beings who were men's guardians.

Women were also the source of identity in terms of descent and inheritance in many tribes. As a general rule, descent and inheritance of property rights were matrilineal in those societies where women played the most significant role in subsistence, that is, in agricultural societies where women were the farmers. Among the Iroquois and the Cherokees, and Creeks and Choctaws in the Southeast, matrilineal clans were the sources of identity.

The power of women in matrilineal societies included that of selecting men for positions of leadership and adopting captives taken in warfare. The *owichira*, the extended matrilineage among the Iroquois, was the unit of decision making, for example. Navajo matrilineal clans were ostensibly headed by men, but males married into their wives' families and were always outsiders. Their primary obligations were to their own matrilineages.

Men played the public roles in Native American societies. They governed, even if they were selected by female lineages, as with the Iroquois. They controlled the performance of ceremonial cycles, although women might have their own parts of the cycles to perform, as among the Pueblos. They were war leaders, responsible for decisions to make war or for the protection of the tribe against enemies, although sometimes bravehearted women joined them in battle, as among the Blackfeet on the Plains.

Cow Creek Seminole women, circa 1917.

Standards for women's behavior were strict. They applied in the less public domestic sphere in which women operated. Women bore and raised children. Public praise focused on their reputations for hard work, productivity in tanning hides, making pottery or exquisite quillwork, or constructing buffalo-skin tepees, and, most important, from the actions of the children they raised. These were the most lasting contributions that women made to society and those that reflected most favorably on them as individuals. Men could take on women's roles and women men's—this reciprocity was recognized and sanctioned. Men as "wives" could work harder and be more productive. Women could be recognized for exploits in war or hunting. Such reversal was, however, unusual.

Marriage relationships in Indian societies were generally based on economics more than emo-tion. Marriages were arranged between family groups, and the two individuals involved might have little say in the matter. Alliances were made to ensure cooperative relationships among family groups. As Black Elk said in his description of High Horse's courting when High Horse was so sick with love that he could not eat or sleep, "True love is a sickness that people get over." Love was sometimes the basis for marriage, but the practical implications of family relationships made it the exception, not the rule. In raising children, kinship structures favored the extended family for child rearing. In matrilineal clans, for instance, it was not the child's biological father who was the most important male figure in a child's life, but the maternal uncle.

Men and women in Indian societies spent considerable time apart. Men went to war, to hunt, or spent significant amounts of time together preparing for and taking part in ceremonial activities. Kivas in Pueblo communities were underground ceremonial chambers that were male enclaves, although women might enter them for certain ceremonies.

Women gathered food in groups; they had their own societies for ceremonial activity. They raised their children together until the children were about six or seven, at which point boys generally were sent to spend time with male relatives to learn their roles in life. Girls remained with their mothers.

The one sphere of activity that was open to both men and women was in curing. The realm of spiritual power is beyond the realm of ordinary human activity. Some spiritual powers were associated with healing, and special efforts would allow a person to have access to those powers and to become a healer. Women did not use such powers during their childbearing years, but when the power of the menstrual cycle ended, the latent power of curing that they might have acquired became fully active.

The role of healer is dangerous. If illness is the result of malevolent or uncontrolled powers that affect a person, the healer must stand beyond the normal social order, confront the powers directly, and have the ability to overcome them through his or her own powers.

Sanapia, a Comanche woman who was born in 1895 in Oklahoma, practiced as an eagle doctor after menopause. Her mother and her maternal uncle were eagle doctors who acquired power through instruction from other relatives who had the power of eagles. Sanapia acquired the power through a period of ceremonial blessing and instruction from her relatives during which she handled hot coals and fasted on a mountaintop for four days to encounter the eagle spirit. Although she did not remain on the mountain and thus failed the final test of eagle power, she became recognized as a healer.

Mountain Wolf Woman, a Winnebago, learned about herbal medicines from an elderly man who taught her in exchange for a favor. Esoteric knowledge allowed women and men to exercise unusual power. A woman might go to a curer to learn about specific plants that had curing power. As in contemporary pharmaceutical education, such knowledge was passed on by the initiated to those who wished to learn, for a fee. In some cases this was done in ceremonies such as that of the Midewiwin of the Ojibwe. In other cases it was done within family groups.

The association of women with knowledge and power in Indian societies is widespread. Thought Woman created the Pueblo world. White Buffalo Calf Woman gave the Lakota people the sacred pipe and ceremonial knowledge. Whether the social structure of a tribe is patrilineal or matrilineal, the mythology usually includes a female figure as a source of knowledge.

In the process of cultural change that Indian tribes have been undergoing since the first European contact, women have been cultural intermediaries. Marina, the woman who became the mistress of Cortez, and Sacajawea, the Shoshone woman, wife of a French trader, who led the Lewis and Clark expedition through the West,

played that role. But women are also powerful forces for conservatism. Because they are the mothers of new generations, they are also the conservators of culture.

With the coming of Europeans, Indian people encountered new, predominantly male, influences in their lives. The nature of warfare changed with the introduction of guns; game disappeared, and with it men's ability to hunt. Leadership revolved around treaty negotiations, in which men bargained away land, the rights to which were often controlled through matrilineal descent. Men's roles were changed and often undermined as Indian people were reduced to dependency upon the U.S. government for food, clothing, and shelter on much-diminished reservations. Women's roles were more covert and less affected by cultural change, although they were sometimes forced into servitude to white traders.

The change from a subsistence economy to a wage economy among Indian tribes as a result of white contact was more disruptive to men than to women. Men's roles as hunters changed dramatically when reservations were established. When they were forced to work for others, they were reluctant to adapt to wage labor. Men have had to deal to a greater extent than women with the demands of white employers, and their lack of success in doing so is reflected in high unemployment rates on Indian reservations. Women, although they contributed to their tribes' subsistence, were less affected by the shift to a wage economy, but the disruption of the traditional family relationship changed their status and the ways in which they influenced their communities.

The most potentially destructive element for contemporary Native American communities is the generational gap that often develops. Many people in younger generations have lost interest in traditional medicine and cultural practices. Although great variation existed, all tribes shared the idea that the forces of nature were spiritual. They had will to act, and they made choices as a result of their actions. The changes that have taken place in American Indian societies have eroded the sense of power that once prevailed. The older generations in Indian societies find that many in the younger generations do not want to carry on the traditions of tribal life or learn the languages. As a woman in Minnesota said, "The young people, they don't want to learn. They don't believe anymore." Where traditions and language do persist, however, elderly women of a tribe are respected for their wisdom and knowledge. They still retain their roles as culture bearers and are respected as such.

Indian women have become public and political advocates for their people. They were active in the Society of American Indians, founded in 1912. The North American Indian Women's Association is one of the oldest organizations. Groups such as Women of All Red Nations have addressed issues of involuntary sterilizations at Indian health service hospitals. Women have found ways to organize politically to promote the interests of Indian people.

David E. Jones, *Sanapia: Comanche Medicine Woman* (New York: Holt, Rinehart & Winston, 1972); Mountain Wolf Woman, *Sister of Crashing Thunder: The Autobiography of a Winnebago Indian*, edited by Nancy Oestreich Lurie, 63–64 (Ann Arbor: University of Michigan Press, 1961); Hamilton A. Tyler, *Pueblo Gods and Myths* (Norman: University of Oklahoma Press, 1964).

■ CLARA SUE KIDWELL

SEE ALSO Feminism, American Indian; Lesbians, Native American; Native American Cultures; Native American Religions.

Alaska

Indigenous peoples everywhere have suffered immensely from subjugation, domination, and exploitation since the time of first contact with non-Natives. Like indigenous women worldwide, Alaska Native women have been fighting against the legacy of outside control and discrimination. The history of Alaska Natives includes the stories of indigenous women who have tried to right the wrongs of colonialism. This brief essay highlights three Alaska Native women and the critical issues that they championed in an effort to protect and promote the rights of Alaska Native people.

Sadie Neakok (b. 1916), an Inupiat elder from the north coast village of Barrow, became the first Alaska Native woman magistrate in 1960. She recalls the many changes in the legal system during a period of transition from traditional Inupiat laws to those of the newly formed state of Alaska: "Everything changed and we had to go by rules then—not our own rules, outside rules."

One of her early cases went to the heart of the traditional hunting and gathering rights of the indigenous residents of the Arctic. A hunter was arrested for taking a duck in violation of federal regulations, which allowed for hunting of waterfowl only after they had flown south. Neakok saw the absurdity of this law and urged members of the entire village to go duck hunting and each return with a duck, overwhelming the government's administrative capacities with the possibility of jailing the whole village. Recognizing the impossibility of this, the state and federal governments were forced to change the regulations. Neakok's famous "duck-in" is an example of activism toward gaining respect for and recognition of Native peoples' rights and lifeways.

Though international human rights instruments state that "no peoples shall be deprived of its means of subsistence," the hunting and fishing rights of Alaska Native peoples were purportedly "extinguished" by federal legislation in 1971. Both Native women and men continue to fight for recognition or restoration of that right.

Elizabeth Wanamaker Peratrovich (1911–58), a Tlingit Indian, organized a campaign to end racial discrimination against Alaska Natives. Like the discriminatory policies toward African Americans, Alaska Natives faced discrimination and gross inequality. Many storefronts and businesses displayed signs stating "No Natives Allowed" and "No Dogs, No Natives."

Some Alaska Native tribes were labeled "civilized tribes," but their members were not considered citizens and were subject to policies of segregation and discrimination. Peratrovich, as Alaska Native Sisterhood grand president, successfully lobbied the Alaska Territorial Legislature for the passage of the Anti-Discrimination Act in 1945. However, true equality for Alaska Native women remains elusive. Like women worldwide, Alaska Native women suffer from sexual discrimination and inequality. In the 1990s the struggle for equality of opportunity and rights, with a cultural context, continues for Alaska Native women.

Anfesia Shapsnikoff (1900–73), an Unangan (Aleut) tradition bearer, combined both the importance of Aleut culture and caring for Aleut children in her day-to-day work. Shapsnikoff was an artist, nurse, church reader, teacher, and community leader. She not only raised her own children but she also adopted several others and even became a licensed foster parent at the age of seventy-two.

During the Second World War, the Aleutian Chain fell under U.S. military command and later was attacked by the Japanese. Unangan people were removed to internment camps in southeast Alaska, which caused family disruption and the loss of one-fourth of the Aleut population. Unangan homelands remained under the control of the military, who felt it was best to remove Native children from their homes. Shapsnikoff protested this policy, long before the Indian Child Welfare Act was adopted to ensure the nonremoval of Native children from their homes and communities. She succeeded in gaining an investigation of this government policy by social scientists. In addition to her lecturing on Aleut history and basket weaving, she worked to establish a local organization to care for neglected or abused children. Shapsnikoff's work demonstrates the inseparable nature of the various dimensions of the social, cultural, spiritual, political, and economic rights of Alaska Native peoples.

These three women exemplify the aspirations and struggles of all Alaska Native women. Their struggles for basic human rights, dignity, and equality need to be continued by present and future generations of Alaska Native women and men.

Thomas R. Berger, *Village Journey: The Report of the Alaska Native Review Commission* (New York: Hill & Wang, 1985); Virginia Brelsford, *Profiles in Change: Names, Notes & Quotes* (Juneau: Alaska State Women's Commission, 1982).

■ DALEE SAMBO DOROUGH

Great Plains

The aboriginal nations of the Great Plains in North America conform to the common stereotype of the American Indian. These groups are often referred to as "warrior societies" in historic and ethnographic literature. The prevailing imagery presented in movies—tall male warriors with commanding countenances, wearing fringed clothing as they ride atop horses, women following meekly behind them—has diminished women's roles, giving the image that the women are drudges—timid, tireless toilers.

Plains peoples' lifestyles were egalitarian and satisfying. In their social worlds, the aspects of kinship, views of the supernatural and natural worlds, and the underlying values of the tribal groups stressed responsibility, respect, and reciprocity among all people, and encouraged a smoothly functioning and rewarding life. This life was not easy and the social and economic roles of men and women, including gender-crossing males known as *Winkte*, were deemed essential for the continuation of the Plains Indians, including the Lakota and Cheyenne.

The origin stories and the sanctioned values that provided a rationale for the existence of

Plains tribes historically have included a cultural heroine who brought ritual and ceremony to the nation. For instance, the White Buffalo Calf Woman brought the seven sacred *Wakan* rites to the Lakota people. This formed the belief system that has sustained the Lakota people since mythic times and has given a mandate to care for and protect women. In addition, the four cardinal virtues—generosity, bravery, fortitude, and wisdom—have been cornerstones of behavior between genders. In such important rituals as the Sun Dance, the roles of the Pipe Woman and the young maidens who ceremoniously cut the sacred tree validate the importance of women. The virginity of the maidens was the expected norm. This valued behavior was complemented by the stringent adherence to sexual continence for a year by the male pledgers. This, and the supernaturally sanctioned continence during the long lactation period of children (four or five years), indicated a respect for women.

Generally, a strong complementarity of gender roles and egalitarian relationships has existed between men and women. Historic inferences often have distorted and misinterpreted cultural practices. For example, Plains Indian women often were attributed low status because men traded horses for them in marriage arrangements. The aboriginal view was different: Their behavior assumed that only when a man proved his courage and ability by going against the enemy to capture their horses could he ensure his capability to provide for a woman. She, in turn, provided the tepee, the home. Because "good, honored, and beloved" virgins of families were highly desirable, fathers and brothers of the bride-to-be were concerned about the future of their kin. This practice was an honorific way to establish marriage bonds in the social and economic institution of marriage.

It is important to understand the historical role of power shifts within the Plains tribes. Men's role as hunters and providers for their family was destroyed along with the destruction of the bison herds in the 1880s. Men felt demasculinized and many women were sympathetic. The role of women as caretakers and nurturers has continued with their increased responsibilities to provide for the family.

Informal networks of Native women have existed throughout history. These networks evidence class considerations and often form the basis for allegiances. The degree of native blood or adherence to native tradition is a perennial issue. Class differences are a new phenomenon. Some Indian women wear designer clothes; others wear polyester clothes, and still others wear denim jeans. Many women wear more traditional clothes such as "camp" dresses (Lakota) and "fiesta-style" dresses (Comanche). Many levels of education and lifestyles are evident among contemporary Plains Indian women. Some are fluent in their ancestral languages. Others speak only English. Women's educational achievement ranges from those who attain doctorates to those who complete eighth grade. Tribal values and expectations represent a wide diversity in cultural background, both individually and as a group.

Some women are based in tribal enclaves such as reservations or in border towns close to reservations. Some women who are urban residents often maintain a connection with their natal reservations by returning periodically for ritual events, powwows, and other ceremonies. Maintaining contact with their original communities is an important way of ensuring cultural continuity for the next generation.

All of these social and political variables play an important part in the status of contemporary Plains Indian women. As the primary socializers of children, these diverse tribal women are the "carriers of Plains aboriginal cultures" who will continue the varied and vibrant cultures of the Plains tribal groups of North America.

• BEATRICE MEDICINE

Inland Northwest Plateau

For perhaps thousands of years, the women of the Plateau have participated in societies shaped through the way peoples coexist with their environment. The tribes of the Inland Plateau live in and care for their lands as large permanent gardens. Their highly developed knowledge of earth sciences, seen in the practice of natural permaculture, is a unique aspect and sets them apart from the nomadism and the agriculture-based economies of other indigenous tribes in North America.

The region of the great Northwestern Inland Plateau, between the Rocky Mountains and the coastal Cascade Range, sustains an extremely fragile ecosystem. Climate and altitude create a mix of dry sparse alpine and semiarid subalpine grassland surrounding the arid drainage of small streams into lakes and narrow river valleys. The plateau peoples travel extensively through these systems, harvesting foods at various levels and at different times of the year. The seasonal growth cycles of all species are carefully studied and customs and traditions center around such knowledge. The women of the plateau tribes were instrumental in maintaining these traditions. They are the principal keepers of such knowledge and they teach the young. Gathering root and berry crops is still practiced among all tribes; however, fishing harvests have seriously diminished as a result of limits on Indian access to traditional fishing sites, environmental problems, and large dams, which have caused major fisheries to flood.

The cultures of the various plateau tribes reflect the complexity of applying ecologically sound principles of coexistence to all aspects of their lives. It is evident in the peaceful systems of governance common to these tribes. The governance systems, fundamentally based on regional and village autonomies, coexist within an intricate system of shared resources and territories, within larger units bordered by common language and cultural practice.

The plateau peoples' nonviolent philosophies are most apparent in the religious practices that underlie laws governing interaction with other species on the land. Religion in all plateau tribes centers on a sophisticated pattern of observances and celebration of creation in the natural order. Village-wide and regional first-food feasts and ceremonies are common to all plateau peoples. Individualized observances to all life forms and seasonal occurrences in the natural order are incorporated into the everyday lifestyle and economic strategy in an overall social order implemented by the individual, the family, and the community. Love for life and compassion for the needs of all living beings are an inherent precept in social process, in which the interdependence of life forms is so fragile. The plateau peoples are recognized for their deep ecological principles.

The principles of true egalitarianism resonate in their societally cooperative customs and familial constructs. Ethnographers who have documented various plateau customs have commented widely on various outstanding aspects of social order unique to the plateau peoples. Although there were and are recognized male and female leaders, there seems to be no noticeable class distinction among the plateau communities. The leaders act as speakers and carriers of the responsibility to "remind" their community. The reminders are about responsibilities that each person willingly carries out without enforcement, because implementing is considered gratifying in a practical as well as economic and spiritual sense. Division of labor is related to the social order in a system of social and family responsibilities that observes and honors the physical challenges inherent in age, sex, and individual talents and at the same time encourages choice and challenge.

Plateau social customs esteem women in all roles. Women are natural leaders in conservation practice carried in the customs and rituals observed in gathering plant species. Headwomen are appointed and their knowledge of permaculturing to preserve and conserve the harvest crops is respected. In addition, women's extensive knowledge of climatic, seasonal, and geographic factors is necessary to regulate gathering quantities of root and berry crops. They regulate even down to counting the exact numbers of roots to be dug in given areas in given seasons. Women are considered the most knowledgeable herbalists and healers in all plateau tribes. Elder women as spiritual leaders are sought by both men and women for healing and counseling because of the great wealth of societal, spiritual, and ecological knowledge they possess. Women chiefs and leaders are common to the Inland Plateau in the present and traditional cultures. Indeed, the natural liberation of women is customary in the traditional and contemporary cultures of the Inland Plateau tribes of the Northwest and is a necessary principle in the practice of deep ecology.

Jeannette C. Armstrong et al., *We Get Our Living Like Milk From the Land* (The Okanagan Rights Committee and The Okanagan Indian Education Resource Society, 1994); Christopher L. Miller, *Prophetic Worlds, Indians and Whites on the Columbia Plateau* (Rutgers University Press, 1985).

▪ JEANNETTE C. ARMSTRONG

Northeast

Native American women of the Iroquois Confederacy of the Northeast—the Cayuga, Mohawk, Oneida, Onondaga, Seneca, and Tuscarora nations—are fortunate to share a cosmology that has its genesis in the woman. The primordial, spiritual character is female, a pregnant woman called Iotsitsisonh (Mature Flowers), or Sky Woman, the first being to inhabit the earth. As Sky Woman fell through a hole in the floor of the Sky World, which was created by the upheaval of a great tree, she grasped at the roots of the tree and the edges of the opening. Embedded under her fingernails were seeds of sacred plants and bits of things that are today traditional foods and medicines. With the as-

sistance of the winged ones and the sea creatures, Sky Woman set in motion on the back of a great turtle the cycles of continuous creation and the cycles of continuous birth.

The oral tradition that describes the establishment of the Iroquois Confederacy is called the Kaienerekowa, or Great Law of Peace. This peacemaking epic recalls that around 1142, Jigonhsaseh (New Face), a woman chief, brought the Nations to unity by putting the deer antlers of chieftainship on the Great League's first chief, an act that represents the power of women in Iroquois governance. Jigonhsaseh, a cultural daughter of Sky Woman, has been called the Peace Queen or the Mother of Nations. To this day, clan mothers continue to hold the power to appoint or impeach a chief.

Iroquois society is matrilineal and matrifocal. Clan groups are composed of families associated through their female members. And women have long been the main producers of food: traditionally, after men cleared the fields, women planted, harvested, and distributed crops.

Contemporary Iroquois women are herbalists, toxicologists, traditional farmers and agronomists, artists and educators, clan mothers, former tribal chiefs, traditional practitioners, and medical care personnel. Today, Sky Woman is chief administrative officer for her community organization. She attends to the improvement of her people's skills. Sky Woman is a skilled medical care provider who uses traditional medicine and ceremonies to sustain wellness in her community. She is an herbalist and midwife who provides community-based well woman and baby care. She continues to nurture the sacred plants. Sky Woman has many faces.

Many daughters of Sky Woman are part of an emerging network of Iroquois women dedicated to the work of cultural and ecological preservation. Prominent women include Branda LaFrance, Wolf Clan Mohawk, curriculum developer for the Seventh Generation; Jan Longboat, Turtle Clan Mohawk herbalist, who eloquently describes the centrality of healing to individual and community development; Iowne Anderson, Tuscarora agriculturalist, who is dedicated to improving the quality and quantity of indigenous foods available to her community; Dr. Mary Fadden, Wolf Clan Mohawk veterinary toxicologist, who discusses the limitations of science and the use of the tools of science as they relate to community matters; Tonya Frichner, Snipe Clan Onondaga, lawyer with the American Indian Law Alliance, who champions indigenous property rights and is concerned about genetic mining; and Dr. Jane Mt. Pleasant, Tuscarora agronomist and director of the American Indian Program at Cornell University, who focuses on the potential of institutional partnering with indigenous communities.

From the seeds and sacred things that Sky Woman brought to Turtle Island grew Earth's capacity for continuous creation and birth. Iroquois women's leadership, as individuals and as representatives of their communities and societies, continues to manifest the power that the daughters of Sky Woman still share as centers of families in significant, surviving matrilineal societies. The glue that continues to bind the group is female. Working in partnership with the men in the communities, women anticipate the perpetuation of the celestial mother's enduring vision.

■ KATSI COOK

SEE ALSO Iroquois Confederacy.

Northwest Coast

The Northwest Coast is characterized by the most extensive temperate rain forest in the world, reaching from Oregon to Kodiak Island, and this environment has shaped the lifestyle of its residents. Native American culture of this region has captured the imagination of explorers ever since first contact in the late 1700s. These are the people of totem poles, elaborately carved wooden hats, headdresses, bowls and bentwood boxes, plank houses, oceangoing canoes, spruce root and cedar bark weaving, Chilkat weaving, beaded button blankets, and many other well-known features, especially the ceremony known in English as potlatch (the single most important vehicle for validation of life passages such as marriage, death, and inheritance, where, through family- and clan-owned songs, dances, and visual art designs, social identity and encounters with the spirit world were manifested).

Many of the groups are matrilineal. Kinship, descent, inheritance, and the entire social organization follow the mother's line rather than the father's. Women were not rulers traditionally, although they have played important roles as community leaders, counselors, and advisers. Recognizing the leadership ability of individual women, male elders in positions of authority could (and did) publicly empower these women to assume leadership responsibilities.

As diplomats and peacemakers, women traditionally "make things right" (although they may also be responsible for helping things go wrong). Key elements in the traditional story "The Woman in the Ice" include the importance of right thought, right speech, and right action; the social and cosmic impact of error; and taking responsibility for one's actions. The land's fertility and the people are connected spiritually and physically, and women are responsible for maintaining the balance.

Many of today's elders were raised in a traditional lifestyle. Some families lived on fishing boats and in tents. Women still play a vital role in subsistence economy, where survival depends on the labor of all. More women fished commercially from the 1930s to the 1950s than do now. They jigged for halibut and hand-trolled for salmon, rowing their own skiffs in dangerous waters, where they had to know how to read the weather and tide. Women married to fishermen routinely ran the larger fishing boats as well. At

Yakutat, women still do setnet seining at the river mouths. Some fish with their husbands, others with their daughters, often in separate boats. When the cash economy entered Native life on the Northwest Coast in the 1880s (but especially in the early twentieth century), women worked in the canneries and cold storage plants while the men were employed in commercial fishing. Women also earned supplemental wages as cooks, waitresses, domestic and hotel maids, secretaries, beauticians, and laundry workers in urban areas.

Today, Native women of the Northwest Coast are entering new professions formerly closed or otherwise inaccessible to women and ethnic minorities. There are Native women lawyers, health and social workers, school and college teachers, dentists, writers, actors, and civil engineers. Over 90 percent of the Native language teachers in bilingual programs of the last twenty-five years have been women. Where aunts and grandmothers did emergency surgery and saved lives in remote camps, now Native people of southeast Alaska run their own hospital, and the director is a Tlingit woman. Women serve on boards of directors, in positions of tribal and corporate leadership, and as magistrates in tribal courts.

Native women of the region are world-famous for their visual art, especially beading and weaving. Wood and silver carving, traditionally a male domain, is now done by some women. Many Native women are known for their skill in verbal art, especially storytelling, history, ceremonial oratory, and singing.

For over a century, Native women have been involved with church work. In Alaska, the Presbyterian sodalities, along with the Orthodox brotherhoods, led to the creation in 1912 of the Alaska Native Brotherhood (ANB), the oldest Native American organization still in existence and a prime mover in political efforts for Native sovereignty and land claims settlements. After playing a major role in founding the ANB, the women formed the Alaska Native Sisterhood a few years

later. Elizabeth Peratrovich fought a long and bitter struggle that led to the passage of the Anti-Discrimination Act of February 1945, the first civil rights act of its kind not only in Alaska but in the United States.

Just as the different groups of the region share similarities in traditional world-view, material culture, and artistic expression, so was the impact of Western contact on these cultures sadly similar. From the 1880s on, white economics exerted pressure on Native land and use of resources, and white missions and schools suppressed Native languages and traditional practices such as puberty seclusion for women, and potlatching.

Native women today work in modern offices and receive salaries their grandmothers could not imagine. They have black belts in karate, run in the Boston Marathon, and race in downhill skiing at speeds that are illegal in a car. "Getting up before Raven calls" was a traditional ideal. It is easy to romanticize the past and forget that it is now "no big deal" for women to be up before Raven in the dark, wet midwinter Northwest Coast, getting kids off to school and themselves off to jobs. Maybe this will also seem remote and romantic to the great-granddaughters of the future.

Nora Marks Dauenhauer and Richard Dauenhauer, *Haa Kusteeyí, Our Culture: Tlingit Life Stories* (Seattle: University of Washington Press, 1994); Ruth Kirk, *Tradition and Change on the Northwest Coast* (Seattle: University of Washington Press, 1986); Wayne Suttles, *Northwest Coast* (Volume 7 of Handbook of North American Indians), (Washington, D.C.: Smithsonian Institution, 1990).

▪ NORA MARKS DAUENHAUER

Southeast

Despite four centuries of decimation of their numbers, languages, and cultures, some descendants of the historic matrilineal nations of the Southeast—among them the Powhatan, Cherokee, Muskogee (Creek), Seminole, and

Choctaw—have remained in the region, where they constitute the major Native presence. Since the mid–nineteenth century, the Native cultural definition of the region extends to the eastern parts of Texas, Arkansas, and Oklahoma.

During the Jackson administration in the 1830s, the majority of people from the southern Indian nations that lay east of the Mississippi River were forcibly removed to Indian Territory, which is now part of Oklahoma. Thousands died on this forced march, commonly known as the "Trail of Tears."

By this time, the gender roles of Native women had been profoundly altered, both by patriarchal federal policies and by some Native women's intermarriage with European or African Americans. However, even after the nineteenth-century removal and revitalization of some tribes in Indian Territory, women were critical to the resurgence of tribal governments in the new land, as well as in the old. For example, when the Oklahoma Cherokee decided to build an educational system, the Tribal Council created schools for women also. The Cherokee Female Seminary was modeled after the Mount Holyoke Female Seminary, and several teachers from Mount Holyoke helped with the seminary's development. Among its graduates were many women, including Choctaw, Creek, and Chickasaw women, who had great influence in Cherokee life and in the larger society well after statehood in 1908.

For tribal members who had remained in the devastated ancestral homelands, however, recovery of their own cultural values was slower. Many were folded into European or African American cultures. Others, such as bands of Seminoles in Florida, and of Cherokees in North Carolina, were able to maintain relatively intact tribal communities. But even these communities were beleaguered by federal and state governments and their policies. In Mississippi, for example, the Choctaw were forced to sharecrop land that had once been part of their nation. Their public school system, which in the early 1800s had been the finest in the mid-South, was destroyed. Choctaw children were denied education in public schools.

Thus, from the Removals onward, Native women in the old and new lands faced the daunting task of sustaining the recovery and reorganization of their individual families and of their people. Then, as now, they drew courage and stamina from the strength and traditions of their foremothers.

Traditionally (before European immigration), most tribes in the Southeast were matrilineal. Although their status differed significantly from tribe to tribe, women had central roles in family, agriculture, trade, healing (medicinal), arts, education, and ceremony. Seminole women, along with other women adopted or held captive by their nation, even developed a trade language of their own, vestiges of which exist to this day. In some cultures, women were chiefs and warriors. In the Cherokee nation, which at its zenith encompassed parts of eight southern states, women had such a prominent place in the councils that some historians referred to the eighteenth-century Cherokee government as a "petticoat government."

In at least one of the other Southeastern tribes, women were discouraged from participation in politics or public discourse of the tribe, and their roles were more narrowly defined. But in many tribes, women had equal rights in marriage, divorce, and family planning. Name and inheritance passed through the mothers, who held the land in trust for future generations. Both genders were taught principles of respect, strength, assertiveness, and nurturing, principles that sustained the intricate balance of the people and their nations.

To conquer indigenous peoples and take their land, the patriarchal colonists had to destroy this balance between the sexes, just as they took away the balance between Native peoples and the land. For three centuries they used a combination of methods: trade, treaties, war, rum, slavery, education, law, and religion. This strategy gradually eroded the strength of the Southeastern nations and simultaneously undermined the powerful place of women, a place that was anathema to most European males. Nonetheless, through many cycles of peace and war, women played a vigorous role in negotiating, fighting, and adapting.

Southeastern Native women have sustained that role in coping with the tribes' personal and societal challenges of the twentieth century. The traditional "mother-roots" have remained staunch and strong, as exemplified in national leadership by three Southeastern chiefs: Betty Mae Jumper of the Seminoles, Wilma Mankiller of the Oklahoma Cherokee, and Joyce Dugan, recently elected to lead the Eastern Band of Cherokees in North Carolina.

Marilou Awiakta, *Selu: Seeking the Corn-Mother's Wisdom* (Golden, Colo.: Fulcrum Publishing, 1993); Rayna Green, *Women in American Indian Society* (New York: Chelsea House Publishers, 1992).

• MARILOU AWIAKTA

Southern Plains

Native American women are diverse and historically have lived in every part of this island country. For some the earth rests in the water upon the back of Grandmother Turtle, and they consequently know the earth as grandmother or mother. The Native American woman of the southern plains is the beloved descendant of many generations of mothers and grandmothers who were Kiowa, Comanche, Apache, Wichita, Caddo, Pawnee, Osage, Sac and Fox, Arapaho, Cheyenne, Creek, and Cherokee, to name but a few.

The Grandfather Great Spirit planted them upon their Road of Life at the time of creation and gave them their unique cultural ways, which generally included the tradition of democratic self-government. This sovereign status of nations was acknowledged through the negotiation of treaties, of which approximately four hundred were ratified by the United States Senate. As a result, many tribes eventually were forced to move away from their familiar homelands.

The reservation policy, which consisted of Indians' "reserving" specific land areas for their use, followed treaty making and Oklahoma became a microcosm of the southern plains. "Oklahoma" is a Choctaw word that means "home of the red people." Had the political thinking of the late 1800s prevailed, it eventually would have been admitted into the Union as an Indian state.

Other tribes have differing histories. For example, the Five Civilized Tribes were militarily forced over their tragic "Trail of Tears" from their ancestral homes east of the great Mississippi River pursuant to the Removal Act of 1830. A deeply spiritual people, the Cherokees carried their sacred fire before them and their collective cultural memories in their hearts.

As was her traditional role, the Cherokee woman, called "Beloved," wisely counseled all her children about reestablishing their strong cultural ways in their new motherland. Uprooted but resilient, they recreated their towns, communities, academies, and schools. In the mid–nineteenth century, after Sequoyah developed the Cherokee alphabet, the Cherokees became more literate than their white neighbors in Arkansas and Texas.

Land hunger was the rationale behind federal Indian policy such as treaties, reservations, and the breaking up of those reservations into small land allotments. These policies were the result of the long-standing trust relationship between the various Indian nations and the United States federal government.

The Southern Plains Indian woman has withstood the arbitrary policy vacillations of the U.S. government and her strength of spirit has helped her survive into the twentieth century. She historically belongs to a self-reliant people. As a member of basically egalitarian societies, she has been free to pursue her vision. Through the development of skills and knowledge, she could qualify to become a member of a select women's society, a healer, or warrior. She also could become a keeper of sacred knowledge and ways. Her various roles as mother, wife, keeper of the family, home, culture, and nation, as well as the first teacher of her children were clearly delineated.

Many of the western Oklahoma tribes' way of life revolved around the buffalo, with which they lived in respectful interdependence. The completion of the railroad, however, brought buffalo hunters, who slaughtered the buffalo for sport or only for their hides or tongues. The buffalo's disappearance posed a direct threat to Indian cultural and spiritual survival.

For example, the Cheyenne Sun Dance cannot be held without a woman, who is a spiritual offering in this ceremonial prayer for the renewal of life and the continuing blessings of tribal well-being and prosperity. The buffalo represents this well-being, the good life. Consequently, the extermination of the buffalo was culturally threatening and the Cheyenne woman believed the tribal prophecy that the buffalo had returned into the vast womb of the earth from which they had come initially.

From her specific cultural frame of reference, the Southern Plains Indian woman explained the disappearance of the buffalo. She, accordingly, had to make adjustments so that her children could continue to walk the medicine wheel of earth. Her very survival was threatened by brutal and externally enforced changes. She not only had to maintain her family, but the strength of her nation as well. She also had to maintain a strong sense of identity and direction in a dramatically altered world, which she has demonstrated over time. Today the Native American woman of the southern plains is a symbol of the American Indian spirit and cultural continuity.

Gretchen M. Bataille, ed., *Native American Women: A Biographical Dictionary* (New York: Garland Publishing, 1993); Rayna Green, *Women in American Indian Society*

(New York: Chelsea House Publishers, 1992); Carolyn Neithammer, *Daughters of the Earth: The Lives and Legends of American Indian Women* (New York: Collier Books, Macmillan Publishing Company, 1977).

● HENRIETTA MANN

Southwest

The term *cultural diversity* has been a key concept in studying all aspects of American Indian societies. The concept is useful in examining the role of women in southwestern Indian societies. However, the term *diversity* in the English language also means *unlike in character or qualities*. The inherent concept in the culturally defined word *diversity* does not capture the "finer" meaning of Indian culture and societies, and thus the role of Indian women. Indian societies traditionally have not emphasized differences but sameness.

Throughout the Southwest, which refers to the current states of New Mexico, Colorado, Utah, and Arizona, there are at least four major cultural groupings (Uto-Aztecan, Yuman, Athabascan, Shoshonean) of Indian tribes, representing fifty-two modern-day Indian tribes. These tribes live in different environments consisting of mountains, valleys, plateaus, deserts, and plains. They have varied histories, religions, social organizations, economic systems and practices, beliefs, and customs.

Environmental and ecological factors have greatly influenced the lifestyles of Indian people of the Southwest. The old adage that Indians are the original environmentalists takes on true meaning when studying Indian societies and religion. Religion is a part of life and nature, not an entity to be categorized, diversified, or institutionalized. The Pueblos of the Southwest exemplify the idea of wholeness in relation to nature. Their religious and secular lives are integrated; their religious beliefs and practices are key to political and social behavior and to a large extent affect their economic activities. Men and women are seen to coexist in the circle of life; thus they are not separate within Indian societies.

Compared to Western cultures, where men have dominated all aspects of society, in southwestern Indian societies, women have historically played important roles in the life of the tribe. The popular portrayal of warriors and chiefs as sole leaders of Indian societies was created by the dominant society. Among the Apache and Navajo people, the influence and role of women are more respected than in Western society, and the political power among women has equaled that of the men, at least until the U.S. political system was imposed on Indian societies. The decline of the political leadership role of Indian women may be related to the political structure established by Europeans, because Indians were not allowed to vote until 1921 and men were considered the head of household. In traditional Indian societies, important political decisions were made with the consent of all adult members of the tribe. Today, Indian women serve in tribal governments, courts, on school boards and enterprise boards, and in numerous other decision-making capacities.

Economically, women have played a large role in Indian communities. Agriculture is key to the economies of Indian tribes in the Southwest. By examining the area of agriculture alone, we may gain important insights about the changing role of Indian women throughout history. Indian women have been involved in growing crops, including plant genetics for variety, soil selection, insect control, yield of crops, irrigation, and preparation and uses.

Religion and philosophies have defined the role of women in Indian societies of the Southwest. Some significant religious deities are female, and numerous ceremonies are staged to celebrate womanhood. Indian women have served as medicine women, experts in administering medicine from nature's pharmaceutical abundance, and as keepers of religious songs.

Ironically, the contemporary dominant society has just begun to extol the virtues of what Indian societies had achieved before the arrival of Europeans: living in harmony with nature; the importance of the family structure; the wisdom of a healthy diet and exercise, all of which make for a clean and healthy environment, a less stressful and conflict-ridden society, and an egalitarian political system. All of these values had characterized Indian societies and are illustrated in the role of Indian women in their native societies.

■ VERONICA E. VELARDE TILLER

West Coast

Before the arrival of the Europeans on the West Coast, no written records existed about the Indian peoples who occupied the several thousand miles of coastline. Even after the arrival of Europeans, written records about Indians remained scarce. But the Indian people who lived in what is now California, Oregon, and Washington made account of their own presence by means of oral tradition. Indian people occupied the shores of this continent as long as ten thousand or eleven thousand years ago in California, perhaps longer. In Oregon and Washington there is evidence that Indian peoples had entered the area by 3,000 B.C.

The history of American Indian women on the West Coast is marked by tragedy and grief. Early historians did not take much notice of Indian women, thus there is a paucity of records about them. Women's work and their social and religious functioning seem to have been of little interest to male anthropologists, who typically associated with Indian men.

We do know that indigenous women engaged in activities that were essential to daily subsistence. The typical division of labor made women responsible for many gathering activities. In California, women collected seeds, pine nuts, berries, clover, and various tubers. While men, women, and children gathered acorns, the main subsistence crop in California, women were responsible for pounding acorns into meal that could be used for making mush or bread. All along the West Coast, women dressed skins, produced clothing and baskets, and cared for the young. In Oregon and Washington, and along the northern coast of California, women were responsible for drying fish, the staple food of northwest tribes, for winter storage.

Throughout the West Coast generally, women became shamans, or healers. In some tribes this was a hereditary post, but in many tribes women became healers through dreams, visions, or other extraordinary feats.

Contact with Europeans proved to be utterly devastating for the aboriginal people of the West Coast. The Spanish entered California for purposes of colonization and missionization in 1769. Many thousands of people died after their removal to the missions, but even people who escaped the cruelty of the Padres died as a result of a number of highly communicable diseases. Within one hundred years, over 80 percent of the population in the area died from smallpox and other epidemics.

It was not just disease that decimated Indian populations in the West. Starvation took many lives, as did warfare. The extermination policies of white people both before and after statehood in the three states also took many hundreds of lives. What the decimation of home and family, clan and tribe meant for American Indian women was doubtless serious social and psychological upheaval and disorganization. Traditional living patterns were disrupted and the gathering of food sources severely constrained.

Another effect of the rapid influx of Anglos during the gold rush period in California was that by 1852 men outnumbered women by nearly seven times. Many Anglo pioneers and soldiers saw Indian women as sexually available and exploitable. Indian attitudes toward sexuality were different from those of Anglo men. Indian women's demeanor was usually modest and reserved, even chaste; and as Cole and Darling point out, "prostitution was alien to native society." Nevertheless, women in some tribes could and did offer their sexual favors, or those of their slaves, to foreigners. In the Northwest, where wealth and social status were important, they did it for payment. Also just as typically, Anglos interpreted this behavior as licentious and amoral.

As the Anglo male population grew, and as Indians became more vulnerable through dispossession of their lands and homes, violence against women increased. In California, "apprenticeship" laws allowed for the indenturing of Indian laborers and provided a cover for white men who kidnapped Indian girls and made them into concubines or slaves.

While Indian women were denigrated, forced into concubinage, prostitution, and "marriages of convenience," intermarriage also occurred among whites and Indians who hoped to form stable families. Most of these marriages were not approved of socially by whites, but they may have protected women to some extent against sexual molestation and rape carried out by white men against Indian women living in traditional communities.

As the social fabric of traditional life unraveled, women had to find employment to take care of themselves and their families. Women's education in federally run boarding schools was geared toward training them to be good domestics: they became servants, cooks, and washing women for white families. As shifts in regional economies took place, Indians sought work on ranches and farms, in towns and factories. By the twentieth century, Indian women could be found working not only as domestics but also in the hop fields, orchards, and the fruit and fish canneries. Employment tended to be seasonal, migratory, and poorly paid.

While no tribe underwent exactly the same historical pressures, it is clear that many Indian women on the West Coast found ways to adapt to the demands of catastrophic colonization. Even under conditions of genocide, Indian women managed to construct useful and interesting lives and to hold on to much of their culture and traditions. The spiritual and material practices of healing, dancing, singing, storytelling, basket weaving, and the making of religious regalia, like Indian women themselves, have survived and endured.

Albert L. Hurtado, *Indian Survival on the California Frontier* (New Haven and London: Yale University Press, 1988); Malcolm Margolin, ed., *The Way We Lived: California Indian Reminiscences, Stories and Songs* (Berkeley, Calif.: Heyday Books, 1981); Greg Sarris, *Mabel McKay: Weaving the Dream* (Berkeley, Los Angeles, London: University of California Press, 1994).

▪ JANICE GOULD

Woodlands

The "Woodlands" refers to a vast geographic region in the upper Midwest. Historically, tribes with ancestral ties to the Woodlands include the Algonquin-speaking Ojibwe, Menominee, Ottawa, Potawatomi, Sauk, and Fox, among others from the western Great Lakes. The Siouan-speaking Dakota people long resided near the Mississippi River in what would become the state of Minnesota, and the Ho-Chunk lived in the southern areas of Wisconsin. Oneidas, part of the Iroquoian Confederacy of the Northeast, arrived in Wisconsin in the early nineteenth century, as did the Stockbridge-Munsee. Woodlands peoples, though sometimes divided by language, shared many commonalities, including a subsistence system that combined farming with seasonal hunting and fishing; the autumnal practice of gathering wild rice; and the springtime activity of making maple sugar. Although hunting was primarily the domain of men in the northern forests, Ho-Chunk women took part in communal bison-hunting trips to the prairies, and the work of women was central to the economic well-being of all Woodlands tribes. Historical evidence suggests that wild ricing was traditionally a female activity, although in the twentieth century, men and women continue to gather and finish rice. Recent work by anthropologists and historians working in the field of Great Lakes tribal history has shown that many activities of Woodlands peoples were far more gender neutral than previously thought.

The arrival of Europeans to the western Great Lakes brought many changes to the region and had significant consequences for Woodlands women. American Indians were drawn into the fur trade and women contributed to that venture by outfitting traders for winter work, tanning animal skins, providing food, and often marrying Euro-Americans, thereby cementing ties between traders and Native communities. The missionary agenda of Europeans accompanied the arrival of the fur trade to the western Great Lakes. Missionaries called for Native conversion to Christianity as well as changes in marital practices, family life, and gender roles. When the Euro-American population of Minnesota swelled in the mid-nineteenth century, Dakota women were expected to retire from farming in favor of spinning and sewing. In all regions of the Woodlands, thousands of Native people died as a result of European diseases. During the years of Euro-American expansion into Michigan, Wisconsin, and Minnesota, struggles frequently emerged among missionaries, settlers, and Indians, as smallpox epidemics ravaged tribes and treaties that called for extensive land cessions were forced on Indian nations. The Dakota Conflict of 1862 erupted in Minnesota after missionaries, corrupt traders, and settlers invaded Dakota lands. Mountain Wolf Woman, a Ho-Chunk woman from Wisconsin, detailed in her life history, related during the 1950s, the harrowing experiences of her people, who were forcibly moved to reservations in South Dakota, Nebraska, North Dakota, and Minnesota.

As Mountain Wolf Woman's biography eloquently testifies, Woodlands women have been remarkably resilient throughout the struggles of the reservation era. Reservations were drastically reduced in size after the allotment of communal landholdings called for in the Dawes Act of 1887. The allotment of reservations, promoted by policymakers, missionary organizations, and other so-called friends of the Indian in the late nineteenth century as the solution to the "Indian problem," also sought to impose a new model on American Indian families that emphasized the nuclear, patriarchal structures of the dominant culture. In a further blow to American Indian family life, off-reservation boarding schools were established and compulsory attendance laws passed, allowing for the removal of children from their homes and families for long periods of time to assimilate Indian children into the language, values, and religion of Anglo-Protestant society. By the turn of the century, thousands of Indian boys and girls were being educated in government-operated residential schools.

In the twentieth century, American Indians have made population gains and become increasingly urbanized. Most Indian people in cities such as Milwaukee and Minneapolis strongly identify with their rural reservations and maintain ties to the community, both spiritual and familial. Indians sometimes vote in tribal elections at polling stations in the city, and tribes often extend their social services to the urban community. Native women have participated actively in tribal life in both regions. Ada Deer, the Menominee leader, began her career in politics when the U.S. government followed a disastrous policy in the postwar years calling for the "termination" of federal services and reservation status of tribes. Ada Deer and other Menominee tribal members worked tirelessly for the restoration of tribal land to reservation status, which finally came about in the 1970s. During the Clinton administration, Deer was appointed assistant secretary for Indian Affairs after a long career in Wisconsin as social worker, tribal chairperson, educator, and political activist. In addition to the Menominee Nation, other tribes have had strong tribal political leaders who are women. Marge Anderson (Mille Lacs Ojibwe), JoAnn Jones (Ho-Chunk), and Deborah Doxtator (Oneida) have each been elected as chairpersons of major tribes in the western Great Lakes.

Brenda Child, "Homesickness, Illness and Death: Native American Girls in Government Boarding Schools," in *Wings of Gauze: Women of Color and the Experience of Health and Illness*, edited by Barbara Bair and Susan E. Cayleff, 169–79. (Detroit: Wayne State University Press, 1993); Maude Kegg, *Portage Lake: Memories of an Ojibwe Childhood* (Minneapolis: University of Minnesota Press, 1993); Nancy Lurie, *Mountain Wolf Woman, Sister of Crashing Thunder* (Ann Arbor: University of Michigan Press, 1966).

• BRENDA CHILD

≋ Native Hawaiian Women

The popular image of Native Hawaiian women as beautiful, graceful, voluptuous hula maidens has been promoted by the tourist industry to market the romantic lure of the Hawaiian Islands.

The day-to-day reality of the average Native Hawaiian woman seldom resembles the poster-girl image. Native Hawaiian women span a broad spectrum of political involvement, socioeconomic status, physical features, and sexual orientation. Native Hawaiian women have also suffered uncommonly high rates of lung cancer, breast cancer, and obesity since the introduction of a Western diet. Nevertheless, Hawaiian women continue to assume the strong physical, social, and spiritual roles played by their ancestresses.

In Hawaiian cosmology, female forces of nature play an equal role in creation. Native Hawaiians trace their ancestry to earth mother Papa, who mated with sky father Wakea to give birth to the Hawaiian Islands. Ho'ohokulani, the maker of stars in the heavens, mates with father, Wakea, and gives birth to Haloa Naka, a stillborn fetus. When buried in the earth, Haloa Naka grows into taro, the primary food plant of the Hawaiian people from generations past to present. Their second-born child, Haloa, becomes the progenitor of the Hawaiian people.

One of the most awesome and magnificent forces of nature is acknowledged to be a female force—Pele, deity of the volcano. Of all the Hawaiian deities, she alone has continued to be publicly worshiped, respected, and honored at all levels of society throughout time. Hula and chant have also continued, largely inspired by Pele's eruptions and activities.

The core Hawaiian culture established between the years 600 and 1100 was organized around the 'ohana, or extended family. Responsibilities and roles within the 'ohana were distinguished by gender under the Hawaiian kapu, or sacred rules of behavior. Men cultivated food plants, did the deep-sea fishing, and prepared the food. Women's work, although less physically demanding, was nevertheless arduous and required planning. Women gathered and then beat and wove materials used for thatching, clothing, rope, mats, sails, and so on. They also gathered resources from the land, streams, and reefs. Men and women ate separately. Women were restricted from eating certain choice foods and from engaging in some religious ceremonies.

Between 1100 and 1400, new influences were introduced through the Tahitian migration of men and women to Hawai'i. The cultures merged both through intermarriage and as a result of battles and conquest.

Between 1400 and 1778 (the opening of Hawai'i to continuous European contact), chiefs emerged as rulers of the Hawaiian social system. Women also assumed sacred and chiefly roles in the hierarchy. The lives of the men and women of the 'ohana remained stable but now involved regular labor service and tribute to the chiefs.

With European and American contact, the development of a capitalist social system in Hawai'i led to the redefining of gender roles. In 1819 the Hawaiian kapu system was abolished by the Hawaiian chiefs and chiefesses. The division of labor and restrictions on the consumption of resources according to gender ceased. Women as-

sumed a greater role in production for the households of 'ohana, including cultivating and preparing food. Men, freed of the household duties, were increasingly drawn into wage labor outside of the household as merchants and as workers on whaling ships, ranches, and plantations.

The Hawaiian monarchy, established in 1810, was overthrown in 1893 by the U.S. government. Women chiefs played important roles with their husbands in the new political, economic, and social system. High Chiefess Kaahumanu succeeded her husband, King Kamehameha I, as a co-ruler with his heirs Kamehameha II and Kamehameha III (sons of the king with his sacred wife, High Chiefess Keopuolani). High Chiefess Manono was killed in battle, fighting alongside her husband, Kekuaokalani, defending religious beliefs and social order. Hawaiian queens looked after the educational, health, and social welfare of their people during their lifetime and in the establishment of their estates. The Kamehameha Schools Bishop Estate of Princess Bernice Pauahi Bishop has already educated five generations of Hawaiian children. The Queen Emma Foundation provides health care to native Hawaiians. The Queen Lili'uokalani Children's Center provides social services to Hawaiian orphan and indigent children. Daughters of landed Hawaiian chiefs married wealthy American and European merchants and businessmen and established plantations, ranches, and banks.

The women of the 'ohana bore the burden of social and economic change under the monarchy. Disease decimated the Hawaiian population. The unprecedented establishment of a Western system of private property left the majority of 'ohana landless. Some of the women in the burgeoning port towns of the islands were drawn into prostitution. However, in the main, the women remained with the families and households of 'ohana and held them together, day to day. The men periodically left to engage in the market economy in wage labor or trade. Women continued to cultivate the taro and sweet-potato fields. Toward the end of the nineteenth century, Hawaiian women began to intermarry with Chinese and Portuguese men as they left the plantations.

At the beginning of the twentieth century, after the annexation of Hawai'i to the United States, urbanization increased and Hawaiian women also entered the work force. In the tourist industry they worked part-time as hula dancers, lei makers, greeters, waitresses, and hotel workers. Hawaiian women also worked in the pineapple canneries, as clerical workers and telephone operators, and they entered the professions of teaching and nursing. After suffrage, Hawaiians were the first women to become attorneys and to serve in the legislature. Throughout the twentieth century, women have also played important roles as the keepers of the culture as *kumu hula* (hula teachers and chanters) and *kupuna* (elders), even as intermarriage of Hawaiians with non-Hawaiians increased in the twentieth century. As Hawai'i moves into the twenty-first century, Hawaiian women are in the forefront of the movement for Hawaiian sovereignty and self-determination.

▪ DAVIANNA POMAIKA'I MCGREGOR

≋ Nativism

Nativism, a blend of ethnocentric nationalism and antiimmigrant, antiforeign sentiment, has been a persistent undercurrent in U.S. society since the founding of the Republic. Whether expressed as anti-Catholic, antiradical, racist, or anti-Semitic prejudice, it reflects fears that this country's professed mission to serve as a haven for the world's oppressed could undermine the distinctive national character that allegedly sustained free government. During three periods (1830–60, 1890–1920s, and 1980–90s), when the volume of immigration made assimilation problematic, and the religious, ethnic, and racial composition of immigration threatened Protestant Anglo-American cultural and racial hegemony, nativistic sentiment erupted with special intensity. These outbursts had important consequences for women and demon-strate the complex interplay of ethnicity, race, religion, class, and gender in U.S. society.

For immigrant women, nativism compounded the liabilities of sex. Relegated to the least desirable, most onerous of the limited jobs available to women, they suffered both economic and sexual exploitation. Single migrants and illegal immigrants were especially vulnerable. When gender barriers in higher education, the professions, and white-collar jobs weakened, racial and ethnic barriers continued to marginalize most immigrant women. Non-Europeans and the alleged "inferior races" of Europeans (the Irish and the Southern and Eastern Europeans) experienced the greatest prejudice, particularly those who were also Catholic or Jewish.

Nativism also affected native-born women. Nativist sentiment has often stymied advances in women's rights and progressive reforms. Antisuffragists warned that woman suffrage would endanger the Republic by doubling the number of ignorant foreign voters. Citing high fertility rates among immigrant women and raising the specter of "race suicide," conservatives fought anything that they believed led U.S. women to abdicate their reproductive responsibilities, whether the pursuit of higher education or careers, a single lifestyle, "voluntary motherhood," abortion, or contraceptives. Since 1920 opponents have attacked feminism; reforms such as child labor, child care, peace, and unionization they labeled radical, foreign, and un-American.

Whether out of frustration, strategic considerations, or ethnocentrism, Anglo-American women's rights advocates and reformers sometimes exhibited nativistic inclinations. Some offered woman suffrage as a way to counter the power of male immigrants and African American men and championed citizenship and literacy requirements for voting. Margaret Sanger advanced eugenics arguments to win middle-class support for birth control. Many reforms advanced by Anglo-American women, notably compulsory school, vice and Sabbath laws, municipal reform, and temperance, sought to control and "Americanize" immigrants.

Thousands of native-born Protestant women enlisted in the three major nativist crusades. Antebellum white women joined mobs that attacked convents, participated in anti-Irish riots, and organized three networks of female patriotic-benevolent organizations, one of which thrived again after 1880. In the 1920s they flocked to white supremacist, nativist women's organizations. White women have been major participants in the most recent wave of nativism, championing English-only laws, immigration restriction, and welfare reforms aimed primarily at women and children of color.

In each crusade, nativist women were propagandists, fundraisers, lobbyists, and activists. Some sought to protect their jobs from foreign competition; others sought notoriety, power, and public office. Some championed women's rights, including access to education, jobs, and political power. Nativism enabled these women to expand their traditional gender roles as guardians of morality, Protestantism, patriotism, and the family to the public sphere. Distancing themselves from immigrant women and native-born women of color enabled them to preserve their own status and racial/cultural supremacy. Ultimately, nativism fostered divisions among women and helped perpetuate existing gender hierarchies.

• JEAN GOULD BRYANT

SEE ALSO Eugenics; Immigration; National Origins Act.

≋ Needle Trades

Encompassing garment sewing and ancillary processes like embroidery, the needle trades included by the mid–nineteenth century custom tailoring and dressmaking, and factory and home production. The transformation of these crafts came not from the invention of the sewing machine or the arrival of immigrant labor but from the development of the ready-made market for men's clothing, spurred on by the Civil War man-

ufacture of uniforms. Most women's and children's garments continued to be made in small shops or by mothers for their families until the early twentieth century.

Irregularity and seasonality characterized these trades, with work organization and labor composition varying among cities. Rochester and Cincinnati had more native-born and German workers in factories. Women constituted about 60 percent of the laborers in Chicago; Poles and Scandinavians primarily ran the machines. In New York, Jewish men predominated as cutters and machine operators; women composed about 40 percent of the menswear industry in 1900. Most places saw married women, especially Italians, engage in home handwork and finishing. Immigrant daughters, Jewish and Italian, dominated the female factory work force.

Ferocious competition among contractors led to poor working conditions and low wages. Labor conflict abounded from the 1880s to the 1930s; unions were unstable and took numerous forms prior to the formation of the International Ladies' Garment Workers in 1900 and the Amalgamated Clothing Workers in 1914. The Triangle Shirtwaist Fire of 1911, which killed 146 young women, intensified the reform campaign for further labor standards, which, along with unionization, would improve conditions in the needle trades. In 1995 the ILGWU and ACTWU formed one union, the United Needle and Industrial Textile Employees (UNITE).

• EILEEN BORIS

SEE ALSO Industrial Homework; Labor Unions; Textile/Apparel Workers.

≋ New Deal

Franklin Delano Roosevelt's First 100 Days energized the people of depression-ruined America. The New Deal transformed the relationship between government and business, workers and bosses, the public and the state. It firmly rooted the precept that government had a mandate to improve the quality of life for all citizens.

Between March and June of 1933, fifteen laws and a new bureaucracy anchored the New Deal: the Banking Act, Economy Act, Agricultural Adjustment Administration (AAA), Securities and Exchange Commission, Federal Deposit Insurance Corporation (FDIC), Civilian Conservation Corps (CCC), Civil Works Administration (CWA), Federal Emergency Relief Administration (FERA), Tennessee Valley Authority, and the National Industrial Recovery Act (NIRA), which launched both the National Recovery Administration (NRA) and Public Works Administration (PWA) and contained a far-reaching and controversial provision (7A) that guaranteed collective bargaining and independent unionism.

During the depression it was customary for married women to be fired. In several states, all married schoolteachers, university professors, and hospital workers were fired. Within two years, thousands of women in government service were dismissed. Home mortgages were foreclosed; life savings were lost. The formerly working wives and children of army and navy personnel went on relief.

FDR's First 100 Days did nothing for an estimated 140,000 homeless women and girls who wandered U.S. streets and railroad sidings. New programs ignored the needs of almost four million unemployed women. The plight of single, divorced, and widowed women was also ignored.

Dismayed that no specific program existed to alleviate the suffering of women, Eleanor Roosevelt sponsored a White House Conference on the Emergency Needs of Women in November 1933. Harry Hopkins estimated that over 400,000 women required immediate help from FERA or CWA. Only 50,000 women were actually on relief. Hopkins promised to increase that eightfold within twenty-five days. But he needed imaginative advice about available work and tasks suitable for women's special needs. FERA projects could not compete with the private sector, and men had decided women were too "weak" to work outdoors or on construction projects. Women with families could not travel as men could and were limited to work in their own communities.

Within two months, under Ellen Sullivan Woodward's direction of the Women's Division of FERA, over 300,000 women were employed. By January 1934 every state relief administrator received sixty job descriptions and was ordered to hire a women's division coordinator to recruit women of all races and backgrounds. Projects were created in canning and gardening, public libraries, and schools. Desperately needed social services were provided across the economic spectrum. But women's reemployment was slow, sporadic, inadequate. By 1938, 372,000 women had WPA (Works Progress Administration) jobs, but over three million women remained unemployed; almost two million women suffered the insufficiency of part-time work.

Over 25 percent of the women employed by FERA and WPA agencies were professionals: teachers, athletic directors, artists, photographers, librarians, nurses, performers, musicians, technicians, and administrators. The vast majority were unskilled and reemployed in domestic services, mattress and bedding projects, surplus cotton projects, or sewing and craft projects. Wage differentials prevailed.

In the Civilian Conservation Corps, relief administrators refused to allow women "outside" work and prohibited them from reforestation and environmental projects. Discrimination in salaries and all benefits continued. CCC men received a wage of one dollar a day; camp women received "an allowance" of fifty cents a week. The camps were not racially segregated, although ninety percent of the campers were white. Arrangements to include widows and young married women with children were discussed but never materialized.

After the Supreme Court declared provisions of the NIRA and AAA unconstitutional in 1935, FDR introduced the "Second 100 Days." The Second New Deal included the National Labor

Relations Act (the Wagner Act); new taxes on inheritance, corporations, and large fortunes; the Fair Labor Standards Act; and the Social Security Act.

Social Security's most enduring provisions involved old-age and unemployment insurance programs that workers would pay for out of their own salaries. These provisions favored male workers and essentially limited coverage to white industrial workers. Agricultural and domestic workers were excluded from the coverage, as were workers in nonprofit organizations, self-employment, small businesses, and other sectors—including laundry workers, seamen, and educational and government workers. As a result, over 80 percent of Black women workers were not covered and only half the work force was included.

Excluded workers and the chronically poor became eligible for Old Age Assistance and Aid to Dependent Children. Both required a means test, "a demonstration of destitution."

Following the 1939 amendments to the Social Security Act, FDR's era of social reform ended. The lights dimmed on the New Deal even before the United States entered World War II. From the Fair Deal to the Great Society and beyond, the new military industrial complex confused the New Deal legacy. What had it achieved? Who was benefited? Did it contribute to the enhancement of democracy? Was there a redistribution of wealth and power?

For business owners and bankers, depositors and homeowners, farmers and ranchers, a new sense of security and action replaced years of anxiety and political torpor. With amazing unity, Congress, the president, and business leaders agreed: the government had a role to play to save the United States from fiscal disaster. But the halcyon days of innovation and change represented a grab bag of inconsistency: expansionist and reductionist; conservative and progressive; deflationary and inflationary. It did not end the Depression, unemployment, or poverty.

• BLANCHE WIESEN COOK

SEE ALSO Fair Labor Standards Act; Great Depression; Great Society/War on Poverty; Social Security Act; Welfare and Public Relief; Welfare State.

≋ Newspapers

Elizabeth Timothy published one of the earliest newspapers in colonial America. Mary Katherine Goddard, a publisher herself, printed and distributed the first official copies of the Declaration of Independence. Margaret Fuller sailed to Europe and covered the Italian uprisings of 1848 for the *New York Tribune*. Ida B. Wells-Barnett's newspaper office in Memphis was ransacked after she criticized the lynching of three Black grocery store operators in 1892. Nellie Bly, of the *New York World*, feigned insanity to report on harrowing conditions at a mental asylum, and Winifred Black was one of the first reporters on the scene after a devastating tidal wave hit Galveston, Texas, in 1900. Despite these women's journalistic undertakings, however, female reporters—and especially editors—remained rarities in U.S. newsrooms until well into the twentieth century. This absence not only inhibited women's professional opportunities but also limited the range of news covered.

Through the nineteenth and into the twentieth centuries, some women reported on "society" events, although even that job was initially handled by men. "Sob sisters," so called because of the emotion they generated through their stories, covered trials and other human-interest features; "stunt girls," like Nellie Bly, disguised themselves to get stories. In later years female reporters (and some of their male colleagues) might ride an elephant when the circus came to town or brush a hippopotamus's teeth to provide a feature story. These reporters, usually confined to writing for what were then called the women's pages, rarely covered war or politics, business, or sports.

Women's success stories in the newspaper world were individual achievements until at least the 1930s. Dorothy Thompson gambled that she could sell enough free-lance articles in Europe to stay afloat, eventually convincing the *Philadelphia Public Ledger* to hire her. She reported from Vienna and Berlin as Adolf Hitler rose to power and in 1934 became the first correspondent expelled from Nazi Germany. She was a leading columnist for the *New York Herald-Tribune*, while Anne O'Hare McCormick covered international affairs with distinction for the *New York Times*, winning a Pulitzer Prize in 1937.

First Lady Eleanor Roosevelt contributed to the first major breakthrough for women journalists when she decided that only women could cover her news conferences. One of her first briefings concerned the White House policy on serving alcohol—big news at the end of Prohibition. Roosevelt traveled extensively as an emissary for her husband's administration, so every major news organization covering Washington had to hire at least one woman or bring one to the capital from outlying bureaus.

World War II advanced the careers of women in journalism. Women became the reporters and editors, and even covered sports. During the war Mary Garber, originally hired as society editor of the *Winston-Salem Journal-Sentinel*, in North Carolina, became the sports editor on the all-female staff. After the war ended, however, many women lost their jobs when men returned from overseas.

By the 1960s newspapers found it increasingly difficult—and eventually illegal—to deny jobs to women simply because they were women. As more women entered newsrooms, however, they still found the way blocked to choice assignments and promotions to jobs as editors or bureau chiefs. In 1973 women at the Associated Press filed a complaint at the Equal Employment Opportunities Commission, charging discrimination in hiring, pay, and promotion; their case later became a lawsuit. In 1974 seven women at the *New York Times* sued their paper, making similar allegations of sex discrimination. Although both cases were settled out of court, the lawsuits against the lead-

ing wire service and newspaper put the entire industry on notice and helped open doors for women to advance within management and to receive better assignments.

Meanwhile, feminist groups founded their own newspapers to report events that they felt were being ignored. The first women's liberation newspaper was *off our backs* in Washington, D.C.

Racial as well as gender discrimination slowed the entry of women of color into the nation's white newsrooms and the women endured discrimination once there. Columnist Dorothy Gilliam of the *Washington Post* found that few restaurants in Washington would serve her lunch, and she had to stay at a Black mortuary instead of at a local motel when she covered James Meredith's entry into the University of Mississippi in 1962. Only a few women of color, whether African American, Latina, Asian American, or Native American, have become editors at daily metropolitan newspapers despite their growing numbers among reporters. Within the Black press, Charlotta Bass bought the *California Eagle* in Los Angeles in 1912 and was its publisher for forty years. Ethel Payne paved the way for many Black women in the press, both as the *Chicago Daily Defender*'s one-person Washington bureau starting in 1953 and later as a correspondent covering the civil rights movement, Black troops in Vietnam, and the Nigerian civil war

Newspapers lagged not only in hiring and promoting women but also in assigning them to the full range of stories covered every day. The usual excuse: combat or police or sports reporting was too dangerous or unsavory for women; and cameras were supposedly too heavy to carry. Marguerite Higgins helped break the barrier for women to report from war zones, arriving in Europe at the end of World War II and sharing a Pulitzer Prize for her coverage of the Korean War. A handful of women covered the Vietnam War. By the time of the Persian Gulf War women were as much—or more—a part of the press corps as they were of the military itself. Edna Buchanan of the *Miami Herald* showed she could cover crime with the best of them and won a Pulitzer Prize in 1986. And, although it took a lawsuit to allow female reporters in sports locker rooms, women now cover the World Series, women's tennis, and other sports, although they suffer occasional harassment from male athletes.

Charting the influence of women on news coverage is more difficult than mapping their progress as reporters and editors. The emergence of more women in business, politics, sports, and other fields, coupled with the advancement of women in the newspaper business, has, however, unquestionably affected the range of stories covered. In the 1990s, newspapers' front pages are almost as likely to carry stories about breast cancer research or sexual harassment as about war in Bosnia or increases in the prime lending rate. Women are also increasingly seen by reporters as sources of information and analysis on areas other than women's issues, whether economic policy or Middle East politics. But men still provide most of the commentary on the nation's opinion pages.

Maurine H. Beasley and Sheila J. Gibbons, *Taking Their Place: A Documentary History of Women and Journalism* (Washington, D.C.: American University Press, 1993); Kay Mills, *A Place in the News: From the Women's Pages to the Front Page* (New York: Dodd, Mead, 1988; Columbia University Press, 1990); Nan Robertson, *The Girls in the Balcony: Women, Men and The New York Times* (New York: Random House, 1992).

■ KAY MILLS

SEE ALSO Feminist Presses, Publications, and Bookstores; Magazines.

≋ The New Woman

The "New Woman" refers to successive generations of educated and self-supporting middle-class women who, between the 1880s and 1920s, demanded careers and public roles. Frequently unmarried, often living with other women, they were associated with the settlement-house movement, educational and political reform, the medical and legal professions, journalism, the arts, and literature. Examples include Jane Addams, Ida B. Wells-Barnett, M. Carey Thomas, Mary McLeod Bethune, Willa Cather, Gertrude Stein, Zora Neale Hurston, H. D., and Djuna Barnes. New Women bridged racial divisions. They were prominent as leaders of the National Association of Colored Women and, like Nannie Burroughs and S. Willie Layten, also initiated the Black women's church movement. The term rightly incorporates less visible women as well as stars— teachers, social workers, businesswomen, physicians, and nurses—who supported themselves and lived independently.

The first generation, attending the new women's colleges in the 1870s and 1880s, flourished professionally between the 1880s and the First World War. Many were outspoken feminists, addressing issues of industrial, racial, and sexual justice at home and promoting world peace. A second generation, educated in the 1890s, often by the first generation, came into their own in the years immediately before and after the First World War. They placed more emphasis on self-fulfillment, less on social service, and a great deal more on the flamboyant presentation of self. Moving easily within the bohemian world of Paris, Greenwich Village, or Harlem, they sought to appear as successful, as political, and as sexual as men.

■ CARROLL SMITH-ROSENBERG

≋ Newyorican Women

The term *Newyorican* or *Neorican* first emerged during the early 1970s to identify Puerto Ricans born or raised in the continental United States. Initially, the term carried some derogatory connotations in the way it was used by Puerto Ricans back on the island to differentiate themselves culturally from the Puerto Rican migrant population in the United States. However, the label was fostered by New York Puerto Rican writers as a way of defining their "straddling" position between two cultures and to give a name to their collective Puerto Rican identity based on the migrant experience (and cultural and linguistic contact with other minority cultures) as well as with the wider U.S. society. The "Nuyorican Poets' Cafe" was established in New York City during the mid-1970s to promote the work of emerging writers. Regardless of its implied geographical limitations, since not all U.S. Puerto Ricans are from New York, *Newyorican* is used primarily to refer to the generations of artists and writers born or raised in the United States who write in English or bilingually.

The literature by Puerto Rican women writers in the United States has grown significantly since the 1970s, though many of these writers live or were raised in places other than New York City. Nicholasa Mohr is one of the best-known writers of prose fiction for adults as well as young adults and children. Mohr's novels and short-story collections include *Nilda, El Bronx Remembered, In Nueva York, Felita, Going Home, Rituals of Survival: A Woman's Portfolio,* and *Growing Up Inside the Sanctuary of My Imagination.* Sandra María Esteves has achieved recognition as a poet, authoring the poetry anthologies *Yerba Buena, Tropical Rains,* and *Bluestown Mockingbird Mambo.* Outside of New York City, writers such as Judith Ortiz Cofer, Carmen de Monteflores, and Esmeralda Santiago have produced important autobiographical accounts of the migrant experience. Ortiz Cofer's *The Line of the Sun, Silent Dancing,* and *The Latin Deli* have received critical acclaim. Her poetry includes the collections *Terms of Survival* and *Reaching for the Mainland.* Monteflores's autobiographical novel *Cantando bajito/ Singing Softly* and Santiago's *When I Was Puerto Rican* have made their mark on readers, who are expecting more from these emerging talents. Aurora Levins Morales and her mother, Rosario Morales, have poignantly captured in their poetry and prose collection *Getting Home Alive* the multiple borderland identities and struggles experienced by Puerto Rican women, and their solidarity with other women of color.

The wide spectrum of Puerto Rican women's writing in the United States also includes those writers who write primarily in Spanish and who are frequently better known among Puerto Rican literary circles. In some cases their works have been translated into English. Names such as Julia de Burgos, Iris Zavala, Luz María Umpierre, Etna Iris Rivera, Rosario Ferré, Giannina Braschi, and Brenda Alejandro are also part of the complex dynamic that constitutes the Puerto Rican migrant experience.

U.S. Puerto Rican women writers share with other Latina writers a strong panethnic Latina consciousness that incorporates elements of solidarity with other women's struggles in Latin America and the United States. The adoption of the term *women of color* reflects a recognition of the diverse oppressions faced by women worldwide based on race, class, gender, or sexual orientation. A literary discourse has emerged as a result of the cultural subjectivity of being a Latina, which recognizes the shared experiences at individual, collective, and interethnic levels, but also transcends national origins in its solidarity with the liberation struggles of women and other oppressed groups.

■ EDNA ACOSTA-BELÉN

SEE ALSO Puerto Rican Women.

≋ Nineteenth Amendment

SEE Constitution and Amendments; Suffrage Movement.

≋ Nontraditional Jobs

Nontraditional jobs for women refer to those jobs historically dominated by men. Although the phrase can be used to refer to any occupation that has been virtually all-male (including certain professions, sales and business positions, and blue-collar jobs), most often in popular usage the phrase has referred to the blue-collar, manual-skilled trades.

Sex segregation of occupations has created a situation in which a number of occupations are either overwhelmingly female (for example, nursing or elementary school teaching) or overwhelmingly male (for example, carpentry and firefighting). "Nontraditional" entered the jargon in the late 1960s and early 1970s, especially as federal contractors attempted to attain compliance with federal affirmative action policies instituted after 1968. These government mandates led to the opening of a number of the skilled trades and their unions to women. Programs set up to facilitate women's entry into these jobs have met with limited success. For example, in 1975 women made up only 0.6 percent of all U.S. carpenters; by 1988 women still made up only 1.5 percent of carpenters. Over the same years, firefighters increased their proportion of women from virtually none to 2.1 percent, and women welders increased from 4.4 percent to 4.9 percent. Although unions have worked to open up apprenticeship programs to female applicants, women working in such jobs often continue to face sexual harassment in both training programs and at their job sites. Women of color in nontraditional jobs face an even more difficult challenge. Although employers and unions have made strides integrating men of color into skilled trades, women of color must deal with both sexism and racism when they attempt to break the barriers into nontraditional jobs. Skilled manual trades and their unions remain both male and white.

In recent years many activists and scholars concerned with the issues involved in nontraditional jobs for women have argued that "nontraditional jobs" is a misnomer. The key issue for these people is not whether jobs are traditional, but rather concerns the levels at which different sex-segregated jobs are remunerated. Thinking of nontraditional jobs for women as "high-wage" jobs instead helps clarify the need for some type of pay equity. In the past women who sought high-wage jobs were often accused of abandoning their femininity rather than acknowledged for seeking better wages for themselves and their families.

Using terminology such as "nontraditional jobs" also reinforces the impression that these jobs have always "belonged" to men and that the sex segregation of occupations is therefore "natural" and should not be disturbed. This makes it more difficult to change existing patterns of sex segregation and wage inequity.

▪ ILEEN A. DeVAULT

SEE ALSO Work.

≋ NOW

SEE National Organization for Women.

≋ Nuns

The history of North American nuns is one of women pursuing autonomy and justice—first within the institutional Roman Catholic Church and later, separate from it. Nuns (defined here as including both contemplative nuns and socially active sisters) are seen by ordinary Catholics as akin to the clergy, yet they are defined by the church as laypeople and excluded from power by the all-male ordained hierarchy. Until the twentieth century, most U.S. sisters were not even nuns in the Vatican's eyes—despite their vows of poverty, chastity, and obedience—because, as missionaries and women earning a living for their communities, they did not confine themselves to the cloister.

With the opening of one convent in Mexico in 1550 for the daughters of Spanish conquistadors and settlers, convents quickly spread in the 1500s and 1600s throughout Spain's North American territories. Religious and secular leaders looked to these nuns to exemplify for Native American women Christian ideals in the New World. The convent also offered women protection in a world with few marriageable men for the elite class. Similarly, women's religious communities developed and thrived in the late eighteenth and nineteenth centuries in heavily Catholic areas of the Midwest and Northeast, such as Baltimore and Boston.

Each convent was subject to the governance of either the Vatican or the local bishop. These officials often encroached on convents' self-governance in areas such as the admission and "formation" of new sisters, whom the bishops regarded as an essential labor force. Church officials and convent leaders were often in open conflict. Yet these women enjoyed otherwise unavailable levels of intellectual freedom and productivity, independence, social respect, and education—considered a tool of spirituality. They were not only teachers but financial managers, property owners, landlords, and litigants in cases over property and debts as well.

Nineteenth-century North American nuns' work was instrumental in overcoming anti-Catholic hostility. They ran hospitals and charitable institutions (such as homes for the aged and mentally ill, "delinquent" girls, and unwed mothers) and operated schools whose success attracted Protestants as well as Catholics. Nuns also nursed the victims of cholera and yellow fever epidemics so fearlessly that many patients thought them immune to disease. The most dramatic improvement in attitudes toward Catholics may have been a result of their nursing activities on both sides of the Civil War.

By the mid–twentieth century nuns' relative degree of autonomy and professional satisfaction began to fade. The United States was no longer a mission country and the Catholic Church was institutionalized and increasingly mainstream. A watershed for nuns' renewal and rebellion was the Second Vatican Council (1962–65), the century's major gathering of Roman Catholic bishops with the pope. Among other decisions the council told congregations to experiment with (and request Vatican approval for) modernizing their constitutions.

The personal and communal renewal unleashed by Vatican II far exceeded Rome's intent. Starting with abolishing regimented bedtimes and mail censorship, congregations began to question the church's very patriarchy, from wearing habits to the meaning of the obedience vow. By 1982 one-third of sisters no longer wore the habit and many moved out of convents. Professionally, they branched out from the classroom and became involved in everything from college administration to radical antipoverty and social justice work. As they left the convent, more sisters talked explicitly about their own sexuality for the first time; in 1985, two former nuns published *Lesbian Nuns: Breaking Silence*. Many nuns rejected the idea of subservience to a male hierarchy, reinterpreting their vows as a commitment to the work of God.

Some sisters challenged Vatican authority by supporting the legality of abortion. During the 1980s the National Coalition of American Nuns and the National Assembly of Religious Women opposed efforts to outlaw abortion. In 1983 the Vatican hierarchy drove from her order Sister Agnes Mary Mansour, director of social services for the state of Michigan, because the agency funded abortions. In 1984 two dozen nuns signed a *New York Times* ad declaring that the Church contains a diversity of legitimate opinions on abortion. The Vatican responded with protracted threats and negotiations, attempting unsuccessfully to silence the signers. Many of the signers continue to speak out on the abortion issue.

The population of U.S. nuns has declined sharply. By 1987 their average age was sixty-two. Even as their numbers dwindle, nuns pose a huge financial challenge to a Church that, in exchange for their virtually free labor, implicitly agreed to support them as they aged. Church authorities estimate that they must raise several billion dollars to support nuns in or approaching retirement.

Not only are fewer women becoming nuns but in recent decades many nuns have returned to secular life, often continuing to work for social justice, with greater autonomy. The nuns who remain include both the most traditional as well as those who assert their independence in their dress, residence, work, and, often, public statements challenging the religious hierarchy.

James K. Kenneally, *The History of American Catholic Women* (New York: Crossroad Publishing, 1990); Rosemary Radford Ruether and Rosemary Skinner Keller, eds., *Women and Religion in America*, 3 vols. (San Francisco: Harper & Row, 1981, 1983, 1986); Mary Jo Weaver, *New Catholic Women: A Contemporary Challenge to Traditional Religious Authority* (San Francisco: Harper & Row, 1985).

• FRANCES KISSLING

SEE ALSO Catholicism.

≋ Nursing Profession

Modern nursing, a predominately although not exclusively women's field, began during the Civil War, when those women who volunteered to nurse sick and wounded soldiers proved that careful attention to proper sanitation, nourishing diets, cleanliness, and comfort dramatically cut shockingly high morbidity and mortality rates. After the war the volunteers spearheaded a movement for formal nurses' training. Simultaneously, hospitals also recognized a need for more skilled,

disciplined, and competent nurses to improve the quality and efficiency of care.

By the early twentieth century women wishing to nurse "bartered" two or three years of service to hospitals in exchange for a diploma that promised entry into a respectable, autonomous form of work, free from the constraints that accompanied other "women's" occupations, such as teaching, factory labor, or domestic service. But it was not always a fair exchange. Hospitals quickly recognized student labor as a cheap and easily exploited commodity. They structured training around their own staffing needs. Upon graduation, nurses found themselves in sex-stereotyped, overcrowded, and isolated practice, competing for jobs with poorly trained women and also with new nursing graduates.

Leaders among nurses—most often the directors of large, prestigious, urban schools—addressed these problems by attempting to professionalize nursing education and practice. By the early 1920s, nurses created the American Nurses Association (ANA), and successfully lobbied for strict registration credentials. However, the initial registration laws were voluntary.

It was not until the 1930s that registration became a legal prerequisite to practice. By that time, nurses themselves had actively proved their worth. Public health nurses, in particular, had moved aggressively to carve an independent domain of responsibility for the health care of immigrants and the working poor in urban areas. Funded by both private and public monies, these women brought health care to those people whom other clinicians were unable or unwilling to serve.

African Americans similarly supported their own community's nurses. Barred by racist custom and often by law from working in the U.S. health care system, Black communities established hospitals for their sick and offered nurses' training schools for Black women. These activities strengthened the reciprocal bonds between Black nurses and the people they served, despite the nurses' continued exclusion from the white-run

A visiting nurse in New York City, circa 1910.

health care system. African American nurses established an ongoing commitment to care for people of color, particularly in the South, where doctors were scarce and health care limited. These nurses garnered respect and a status within the Black community often denied their white sisters, although they earned less and worked under much harsher conditions.

In 1908 African American nurses, excluded from many of the state nurses' associations, organized the National Association of Colored Graduate Nurses (NACGN) to represent their interests and to push for full integration into nursing's social and professional life. Their moment came at the end of World War II when, in 1945, the army and the navy nurse corps opened their doors to African American nurses. In 1948 the ANA followed suit and in 1951 the NACGN disbanded. In 1971 the National Black Nurses Association

formed, both out of concern that the ANA had failed to recognize the contributions of African American nurses and out of a vision to increase the numbers of and the opportunities for all nurses of color.

In the postwar era, rapid changes occurred in health care treatments, technologies, research, and financing. These changes redefined nursing practice. In the new intensive care units, for example, one's background and education (in nursing, as in other professions, code words for race and class) often mattered less than one's skill and competence. Nurses then began organizing in new ways. Clinical associations now promised to be a bridge of sorts among nurses from diverse backgrounds and with professional aspirations.

Darlene Clark Hine, *Black Women in White: Racial Conflict and Cooperation in the Nursing Profession, 1890–1950* (Bloomington: Indiana University Press, 1989); Susan Reverby, *Ordered to Care: The Dilemma of American Nursing, 1850–1945* (Cambridge: Cambridge University Press, 1987).

• PATRICIA D'ANTONIO

SEE ALSO Labor Unions: Nurses' Unions.

≋ Obscenity

Following common-law principles, colonial governments treated obscenity as an indictable offense when it was linked to other crimes, such as blasphemy and sedition. By the early nineteenth century, however, states enacted obscenity laws, viewing obscenity as *per se* harmful to public morality. Congress passed a federal obscenity statute barring the importation of obscene books in 1842. Under pressure from anti-vice reformers, most notably Anthony Comstock, in 1873 Congress banned circulation of obscene materials through the U.S. postal system.

Nineteenth-century obscenity laws broadly defined obscenity as filthy, disgusting to the senses, and grossly repugnant to social norms and principles. This definition permitted obscenity laws to regulate individuals' sexual and reproductive conduct. The Comstock laws included bans on contraceptive information and devices along with bans on material about abortion, and they directly affected the reproductive health and choices of women.

In the twentieth century obscenity law has targeted sexual representations and conduct. In 1957 the Supreme Court defined obscenity as "material which deals with sex in a manner appealing to prurient interest" and "utterly without redeeming social importance" (*Roth* v. *United States*). Thus, the Court does not consider obscenity speech within the protection of the First Amendment. In 1973 the Court strengthened the standard set out in *Roth* by rejecting the requirement that sexually explicit materials must be *utterly* without social value to be considered obscene (*Miller* v. *California*). Since 1973 courts have applied three criteria to determine obscenity: 1) Does it offend local community standards? 2) Is it "patently offensive"?, and 3) "Taken as a whole," does the work lack serious literary, artistic, political, or scientific value?

Critics of obscenity law find these criteria arbitrary. For example, "community standards" vary widely depending on the attitudes of local majorities and reflect biases not only about sex but about race and sexual orientation as well. This may permit the selective application of obscenity law against artists who are considered "different" or "deviant" because of their race and/or sexuality.

The core issue in obscenity law is whether the sexual description/depiction appeals to "prurient interest." Under this definition, "obscenity" is a problem because it purportedly harms consumers (that is, men) by stimulating lustful thoughts. Many contemporary feminists dispute this doctrine because it ignores the harm to the subjects (that is, women) of violent and degrading sexual representations.

• GWENDOLYN MINK

SEE ALSO Pornography.

≋ Painting

Although it is possible to name U.S. women who have contributed to most major painting styles—from portraitist Sarah Miriam Peale to color-field theorist Alma Thomas to abstract expressionist Lee Krasner—folk, or self-taught, art is the only tradition in which women have participated in great numbers. Noteworthy folk painting displays an innate sense of design, color, and pattern, but its idiosyncratic perceptions of space and time have been depreciated by an elite Western artistic record that narrowly defines art and isolates

The award-winning 1935 painting Thanksgiving *by Doris Lee (1905–1983) depicts the energetic prep-aration of a Thanksgiving feast in a farmhouse. It was so controversial when first hung at the Art Institute of Chicago that its detractors formed the anti-modernist Society for Sanity in Art, dedicated to promoting the representation of "sweetness and light." Lee, renowned for her paintings of U.S. folkways, also illustrated children's books and painted murals.*

it from everyday life. As a result, self-taught art, without acceptance or patronage, is often lost. Because education is necessary to master perspective, line, and form, most renowned painters owe their success in part to apprenticeship or higher learning, which historically has been restricted, legally and culturally, by sex, race, and class. In 1848, the Pennsylvania Academy of Fine Arts became the first arts institution to accept women, almost all of them white and middle- or upper class. The gendered institution of the family also has been historically important to artistic development: Before the twentieth century, many male painters were sons of painters, and most women painters were daughters of painters, although daughters were often relegated to subordinate positions in the studio. Furthermore, limited options meant that most women would marry young, bear children, and spend their lives engaging in other unpaid work.

It is not surprising, then, that women who did devote themselves to painting had lives that were in some way unusual. Most trained women painters had familial support, wealth, and connections, as well as education; many never married or had children; some, especially folk artists, began painting late in life, when they had fewer responsibilities. Mary Anne Wilson (dates unknown) settled with her female companion in rural New York, around 1800. She made a living selling her folk paintings (the novel *Patience and Sara* was based on her life). Sarah Miriam Peale (1800–85) was born to a family of artists and trained by her father and male cousins before moving to Baltimore, where relatives ran a museum and introduced her to wealthy Baltimore residents and Washington, D.C., politicians, of whom she ultimately painted more than one hundred full-scale commissioned portraits. Lilly Martin Spencer (1822–1902), the daughter of reform-minded intellectuals, was taken by her father to study painting with artists in Cincinnati. Although Spencer married and had seven children, her husband gave up his work to help her execute and sell her domestic genre paintings and to devote himself to managing their household.

Impressionist Mary Cassatt (1844–1926), from a wealthy Pittsburgh family, studied painting at the Pennsylvania Academy of Fine Arts and then in Paris, where she became the only U.S. painter accepted by French impressionists. Cassatt is most celebrated for her intimate mother-child portraits. Black folk artist Clementine Hunter (1886?–1988) painted scenes of life on the Louisiana plantations, where she spent her 102 years. At age fifteen she started work in the fields of Melrose plantation, an arts colony, where she eventually began to paint with materials discarded by Melrose's artists. She attracted the attention of art promoters there who organized exhibits and introduced her work to collectors. Marguerite Thompson Zorach (1887–1968), born to a wealthy New York family, went to live with an aunt in Paris, where she met and was influenced by Gertrude Stein, Picasso, and Matisse. After taking time out to raise children, she became a successful landscape painter.

Georgia O'Keeffe (1887–1986) studied at major art schools before teaching in Texas, where the light and landscape helped shape her artistic vision. Her paintings abstract and sometimes magnify nature: flowers, desert landscapes, and animal bones. Like many other Black folk artists, Minnie Evans (1890–1987) began painting at a mature age after being inspired by a series of visions. Her combinations of religious and floral motifs are resonant of Caribbean imagery although she spent her life in Pender County, North Carolina, where she worked as a gatekeeper at botanical gardens that may have inspired the images. Alma Thomas (1891–1978), who in 1924 was the first graduate of Howard University's art school, devoted herself to painting after forty years of teaching art in the Washington, D.C., public schools. Thomas was in her eighties when she painted her most important color-field works: mosaiclike, brilliantly colored shapes arranged in abstract forms. Lois Mailou Jones (b. 1905) grew up in Boston, where on scholarship for six years she took classes at the Museum of Fine Arts. Denied a graduate assistantship because she was Black, Jones taught art at a segregated secondary school in North Carolina before joining the faculty of Howard University, where she taught art for forty-seven years and focused her own painting on African and African American themes.

Portraitist Alice Neel (1900–84) was one of many women artists who received a stipend from the New Deal federal art programs. Choosing to work outside conventions necessary to commissioned work, Neel is known for exacting portraits of people from diverse socioeconomic classes and for an unromantic series of pregnant nudes. The abstract expressionist work of Lee Krasner (1908–84) was overshadowed by the fact that she was married to noted painter Jackson Pollock. It was Krasner, however, who introduced Pollock to the possibilities of divisionist patterning. Surrealist Dorothea Tanning (b. 1910) painted images of women pregnant, or isolated with their children, or in vaguely threatening situations. Margaret Herrera Chavez (b. 1912) grew up in northern New Mexico, the subject of most of her landscape paintings, done in clear light colors and broad distant views that emphasized vertical as well as horizontal elements. Abstract expressionist Helen Frankenthaler (b. 1928) painted large-scale landscapes in her bright and luminous "soak-stain" technique, created by thinning paint with turpentine.

Social changes in the 1960s and 1970s provided new subjects and support for women artists at a time when the art world was moving away from painting toward mixed-media, installations, and other nontraditional forms. The mid-1960s paintings of Faith Ringgold (b. 1930) vividly depicted the turmoil of the civil rights movement; Ringgold went on to do explicitly feminist multimedia work. Multimedia artist Judy Chicago (b. 1934) started the first feminist art course at Fresno State College and founded, with artist Miriam Schapiro (b. 1923), a feminist art program at the California Institute of the Arts. Women-of-color artists, inadequately supported by the feminist art movement and by cultural arts movements, formed groups such as Mujeres Artistas del Suroeste (Southwestern Women Artists), which organized exhibitions for Latinas, and Where We At: Black Women Artists, which advocated for Black women artists. Some women eschewed traditional forms of painting, striving to break down distinctions between art and craft, working outside elite Western tradition in ways they believed were consistent with the work of their foremothers. Others, such as photorealists Janet Fish and Audrey Flack, and Elizabeth Murray and Hung Liu, who experiment with canvas form, continued to focus on painting—and, for the first time, these women were among those recognized as artistic leaders.

• HOLLY HARTMAN

See also Art and Crafts.

≋ Peace Movement

Acting both as concerned citizens and as "the mother half of humanity," U.S. women have played a central role in movements against militarism and for peace since the early nineteenth century. Confined almost entirely to the role of foreign policy outsiders, women nevertheless have petitioned, lobbied, demonstrated, and participated in individual and collective acts of nonviolent civil disobedience to oppose this country's wars and military interventions.

Although white, elite, Christian women made up the majority of the members of the national peace societies in the nineteenth century, they were never the spokespersons or policymakers. For the most part, they were wives and mothers of the growing middle class, Quakers and evangelical Protestants who were sufficiently removed from household drudgery to devote their free time to charitable works. Many also were abolitionists—they perceived slavery, like war, to be morally indefensible. By the end of the century, these women and their daughters were experienced organizers and dissenters.

The first autonomous woman-led peace action was organized by Julia Ward Howe, who wrote "The Battle Hymn of the Republic," the rousing Civil War song that had sent tens of thousands of Union soldiers into battle. By 1870 Howe was so distressed by the "human cost" of the Civil War and by the bloody Franco-Prussian War then raging, that she traveled to Europe to call upon mothers "to prevent that waste of human life which they alone bear, and know the cost." At her first stop in London, she failed in her attempt to found a European-American women's peace organization because the male leaders of British peace societies refused to allow a woman to address their meetings. Discouraged but undeterred she returned home to organize a Mothers' Peace Day, held in 1873 in eighteen U.S. cities. Celebrations of Mothers' Peace Day ended after only a few years, probably because Howe and her followers had turned their efforts to the woman suffrage movement.

By the end of the nineteenth century, a network of women's clubs, female benevolent societies, temperance groups, and suffrage organizations included peace advocacy as an integral part of their social agendas. Although the women's club net-

Peace activists in the 1980s.

work, representing hundreds of thousands of U.S. women, was overwhelmingly white and Protestant, it did include the National Council of Negro Women and the National Council of Jewish Women.

Women's organizations opposed the Mexican War of 1846, called for arbitration of the Venezuelan border conflict with England in 1895, urged President McKinley to avoid war with Spain in 1898, and supported the 1899 Hague Conference on international disarmament. U.S. feminist pacifists were among the small group of dissenters who protested sending U.S. marines to Haiti in 1914, but it was not until 1915 that the first independent women's peace organization, the Women's Peace Party (WPP), was founded.

Outraged by the outbreak of World War I and appalled by the silence and passivity of male leaders, a group of nationally prominent women reformers, including Jane Addams and Carrie Chapman Catt, brought thousands of women together to demand immediate negotiations for an end to the war, the limitation of military preparedness in the United States, and the nationalization of the arms industry. In 1915 representatives of the WPP joined women from the belligerent nations of Europe who had crossed their own national boundaries to take part in the historic International Congress of Women, in The Hague, Netherlands. The Hague Congress called for continuous mediation to end the war. Looking to the future, the Congress demanded that women of all nations be consulted on issues of war and peace. When, despite the continued protests of the WPP, the United States decided to enter World War I, suffragist-pacifist Jeannette Rankin, the first woman elected to Congress, after much soul-searching, voted against the declaration of war. In one of the strange twists of women's history, Rankin later was elected to a second term in Congress after a hiatus of twenty-four years, just in time to be the only member of the House of Representatives to vote against U.S. entry into World War II.

The majority, but not all of those women who had opposed the war in Europe in 1915 and 1916, abandoned the peace cause once their own country had become a belligerent. Those who did not support militarism turned to war relief, the defense of civil liberties, and the founding of a movement to protect the rights of conscientious objectors. However, at the conclusion of World War I, and after woman suffrage had been achieved, the leaders of prewar suffrage and social reform movements turned once again with vigor to the fight for peace.

They established four peace groups: 1) the Women's International League for Peace and Freedom, organized in 1919 to promote international cooperation among women for world peace based on social justice; 2) the Women's Peace Society, founded in 1919 to support total nonresistance and spiritual pacifism; 3) the Women's Peace Union, which campaigned steadily throughout the 1920s and 1930s for a constitutional amendment that would declare war illegal; and 4) the National Committee on the Cause and Cure of War (NCCCW), founded in 1924 as a coalition and clearinghouse of twelve women's organizations. NCCCW engaged millions of U.S. women in an ongoing campaign for U.S. membership in the World Court and for ratification of the Kellog-Briand Peace Pact, which would have made war an international crime.

After World War II, in the wake of the atomic bomb and during the promilitarist atmosphere of the cold war, U.S. women were among the most notable citizens calling for nuclear disarmament. Women Strike for Peace (WSP), founded in 1961, campaigned for a nuclear test ban treaty and opposed the Vietnam War. WSP focused on the draft, counseling over one hundred thousand young men on their legal rights, supporting draft resisters, and signing their own statement of complicity with draft resisters. Another Mother for Peace, a small, brilliant group of women peace publicists, created invaluable lobbying materials for nonaffiliated women and coined the most memorable and persuasive peace slogan of the Vietnam Era: War Is Not Healthy for Children and Other Living Things.

On January 15, 1968, the opening day of the Ninetieth Congress, a coalition of five thousand women gathered on Capitol Hill to demand that Congress refuse to participate in an insatiable military-industrial complex and use its power instead to meet social needs at home. This occasion has been recognized by most historians of the women's liberation movement as the moment when the "second wave" of women's rights activism became a national force. It was a turning point in the consciousness of traditional women peace protesters of the Vietnam Era, as the radical feminists from New York and Chicago argued passionately that the women of the Jeannette Rankin Brigade had come to Congress as mourners and supplicants—"merely" wives, mothers, sisters—instead of full citizens and taxpayers. Unless women challenged the age-old cultural construct that men make war and women weep, the feminists warned, wars would go on forever, and women remain powerless.

Since the end of the Vietnam War, women's peace groups have also addressed the issue of social justice, stressing the connections among racism and sexism, and domestic and state violence. Women's peace action groups of the 1980s reflected the insights of the feminist movement, built on female cultural values and feminist notions regarding the sharing of leadership and power.

In 1980 the Woman's Pentagon Action, using guerrilla theater and traditional female symbols, wove a lace chain across each door to the Pentagon and later surrounded the building with a ring of women carrying placards shaped like gravestones, in memory of victims of domestic violence. In the 1980s grassroots peace groups across the country developed new forms of protest, such as peace camps that were established adjacent to military bases. The Seneca peace encampment and the Puget Sound peace encampment experimented with inclusive forms of group interaction, shared leadership, and empowerment in the interest of class and racial equality.

The 1980s were marked by protests against nuclear proliferation. Women established encampments at missile-base sights in the United States and Europe. New women's peace efforts emerged globally in the early 1990s to protest military conflicts in the Persian Gulf, the former Yugoslavia, Rwanda, and Chechnya.

Worldwide women's peace and environmental organizations of the era affirmed that only cooperative international approaches to peace and widespread education on conflict resolution could lead to the diminution of escalating global instability and military violence. At mid-decade peace groups called for a critical mass of women to be involved in deliberating issues of peace, war, development, and the environment. The Women's Environment and Development Organization (WEDO), led by former U.S. Congresswoman Bella Abzug, carried to the Fourth World Congress on Women, held in Beijing, China, in August/September 1995, a call for 50-50 percent participation of both sexes in all governmental bodies, elected or appointed, including the United Nations. Abzug reflected the conviction of the attending women peace activists when she declared, "The time has come to challenge the male military mystique, and only a worldwide effort of women can do the job."

■ AMY SWERDLOW

≋ Pedestal

Two paradoxical constructs of U.S. womanhood emerged during slavery in the United States and continued to coexist for decades—Black women as immoral, promiscuous, and sexually insatiable, and white women as innocent, chaste, and inaccessible. According to myth, virginal southern white women occupied a metaphorical pedestal that distanced them from sinful Black women. Contemporary historian James McBride Dabbs, in his book *Who Speaks for the South?*, asserted that "the height of the pedestal for the white woman was equal to the depth of the furrow in the high cotton for the Negro woman," and that the white woman became "an angelic being hovering high above the earth."

These twin images became more entrenched during the post–Reconstruction South, when lynchings of African Americans reached epidemic proportions—235 in 1892 alone. Lynchings were used as a major form of racial control and the requisite punishment for Black men who allegedly raped white women because of their supposed out-of-control sexual impulses.

Ida Wells-Barnett, journalist and legendary antilynching crusader, was the person most responsible during the late nineteenth century for enlightening the nation about the powerful connection between lynching and cultural notions of white womanhood. She also aroused extreme rage among southern whites after her May 1892 editorial in *Free Speech* (a Memphis newspaper, which she co-owned), which suggested that white women voluntarily engaged in interracial sexual unions with Black men. Her painstaking investigative journalism also named "race prejudice," not rape, as the reason why Black men were lynched. Wells-Barnett debunked the myth of the pure southern white lady and the brutish Black male rapist and also asserted the inappropriateness of the pedestal metaphor for white women's place in the world.

The rise of lynchings in the 1930s resulted in a similar crusade on the part of white women, marked by the founding of the Association of Southern Women for the Prevention of Lynching, by Jessie Daniel Ames. Undoubtedly the group had been inspired by Mary McLeod Bethune, founder of the National Council of Negro Women (1929), who admonished white women to assume responsibility for the eradication of racial violence, particularly since crimes against Black people continued to be perpetrated in defense of white womanhood. Members of the association renounced their pedestal status and the fact that they received chivalrous treatment, when such privileges were not extended to Black people. By 1936 this exclusively white organization had 35,000 southern women supporters.

Ida Wells-Barnett's insightful analysis of lynching as both a women's and a race issue underscores the role Black feminists historically have played in discourse about the intersection of race, gender, and sexuality. Wells-Barnett's treatises on the connection between lynching and the alleged purity of southern white womanhood provided a major catalyst for white women to climb down from their pedestals and engage in important antiracist work.

• BEVERLY GUY-SHEFTALL

SEE ALSO Lynching.

≋ Philanthropy

Women in the United States have been active philanthropists since the colonial era. Beginning in the late–eighteenth century, middle- and upper-class white women (and to a lesser extent, women of color) fostered the development of a wide array of charitable services and social reform movements for women and children, creating parallel power structures that resembled, but rarely precisely replicated, the political and economic functions of men. Most of these organizations were built on a foundation of voluntarism rather than cash. Until recently, U.S. women tended to reserve their largest monetary donations for institutions that bolstered the professional aspirations of men.

Unlike white women philanthropists, when women of color had enough disposable income to make donations it was as a result of their own tenacity and hard work. Although women of color have lacked upper-class access to unearned fortunes, historically they have been generous monetary donors and volunteer workers in the institutions they have created and supported such as churches, schools, colleges, hospitals, sororities, and civic and social service organizations. Many of these institutions have specifically served women and girls.

Harvard University was one of the earliest institutions to receive sizable donations from women. The university was created in 1638, when John Harvard bequeathed half of his estate and his library to found the first college in the North American colonies. Five years later, Anne Radcliffe (for whom Radcliffe College is named) added £100 sterling, the first in a string of munificent gifts from women. In the eighteenth century, Mary and Dorothy Saltonstall were among the female patrons who set aside donations for scholarships for male students and to educate men for the clergy. More scholarship funds poured into Harvard's coffers from women in the nineteenth century, as well as gifts for the library and for professorships. The figures continually rose, encompassing multi-million-dollar donations from women, such as Eleanor Elkins Widener's $3.5 million gift for the Widener Library.

Often, the male-dominated institutions that were the objects of feminine largess openly discriminated against women. Harvard barred female students from its classes until 1943 and female professors from its faculty until 1919. Seventy years later, women still held only 23 of the university's 364 tenured positions. Even the main reading room of Widener Library, which Eleanor Widener so liberally endowed, was officially off limits to women until the late 1940s.

Occasionally, female donors earmarked their gifts as a means of breaking down the barriers of discrimination. One of the most famous examples of this kind of "creative philanthropy" was Mary Garrett's $307,000 donation to the medical school at Johns Hopkins University in 1893, which carried the proviso that the medical school would be opened to women students and that they would receive the same training as the men. Harvard was more recalcitrant concerning these sorts of "strings." When Marion Hovey offered the university's trustees $10,000 to open their medical school to women in 1879, her gift was resoundingly rejected.

While male-dominated foundations, universities, think tanks, and museums prospered through the combined generosity of men's and women's gifts, many of the most influential women's organizations operated on shoestring budgets. For example, Hull House, one of the country's leading social settlements, which was created by the future Nobel laureate Jane Addams in 1889, survived primarily through the generosity of Addams and two close friends, Mary Rozet Smith and Louise de Koven Bowen, and never received a donation on the scale of Widener's gift during Addams's lifetime.

There were, of course, exceptions. Mrs. Frank Leslie bequeathed $2 million to the suffrage movement in the 1910s, and Katherine Dexter McCormick donated several million dollars to back the scientific research that produced oral contraceptives. One of the nation's first African American female entrepreneurs, cosmetics executive Madame C. J. Walker, donated part of her fortune to provide scholarships for female students at Tuskegee Institute in the 1910s. But for much of the twentieth century, women donors with the cash and the inclination to fund feminist agendas accounted for only a fraction of the country's philanthropists.

Part of this pattern is traceable to the ways in which U.S. women historically gained control of large fortunes. Mrs. Leslie and Madame Walker were exceptions, in part, because both were highly successful entrepreneurs. Because they had made their fortunes themselves through publishing and cosmetics, they undoubtedly had a freer hand in the distribution of their gifts. However, the majority of rich women inherited rather than created their fortunes. Often, these inheritances were hemmed in by legal restrictions and tied up in trusts controlled by male executors.

Even when widows did control the fortunes they inherited, many continued to consider the money their husband's rather than their own. As a result, women frequently have given their largest gifts to the institutions in which their spouses had been involved, often in their husband's name. The Russell Sage Foundation was created by Sage's widow, Olivia, not by Russell; and the extraordinary H. O. Havemeyer collection of impressionist paintings was donated to the Metropolitan Museum of Art, in New York City, by Havemeyer's widow, Louisine, who had amassed most of the collection that bears his name.

These patterns began to change in the 1980s, with the emergence of women's funds, which are designed to channel money into organizations that focus on women and children, and to do so in ways that involve the recipients as well as the donors in the allocation of grants. In effect, they are designed to cut across the barriers of class and race.

One of the innovators in this area was the *Ms.* Foundation. Created in 1972, *Ms.* was the first national, multi-issue public women's fund. Since its inception, *Ms.* has funded a variety of efforts, providing funds to prevent sexual abuse, to aid battered women, to curb sexual harassment in the workplace, to promote the passage of pro-choice legislation, to develop income-generation programs for poor women, and to train women at all levels of society to assume more visible leadership roles. In 1993 the foundation launched a $10 million endowment campaign, nearly half of which was raised within the first year.

Other feminist organizations adopted different fund-raising strategies and programmatic priorities. Women's Way of Philadelphia initiated a program of workplace efforts to raise funds for feminist social service and advocacy groups, successfully competing for donations with more established organizations such as the United Way. The Global Fund for Women raised over $3 million during its first six years, providing grants to women's organizations to combat domestic violence, increase literacy, and provide birth-control counseling (as well as other initiatives) in over 90 countries.

EMILY's List took a more political tack, raising $6.2 million in 1992 alone to help Democratic, pro-choice women candidates win election. Grounded in the idea that "early money is like yeast—it makes the dough rise," the group garnered funds from a formidable roster of 63,000 donors, capitalizing not only on the generosity of women with inherited fortunes but the earnings of women within the paid labor force as well. EMILY's List, although of recent vintage (founded in 1985), has made a considerable impact. Backed in part by its donations, the number of Democratic women holding seats in the House of Representatives trebled between 1985 and 1993.

The number of women's funds has skyrocketed since 1980, when only eight were in existence. By 1990 there were over sixty members in the recently created National Network of Women's Funds, accounting for over $50 million in assets. In 1993 Wellesley College successfully topped off its $167 million fund-raising campaign, tallying one of the country's highest rates of per capita donations from graduates of any college: male, female, or co-ed.

Wealthy individuals also began to assume more public roles as feminist donors to feminist causes. In 1991, for example, Peg Yorkin donated $10 million to the Feminist Majority Foundation, which she helped found. Backed by a new genre of more aggressive feminist fundraising, these entrepreneurs and donors are beginning to recast the contours of U.S. philanthropy to empower in new ways women at all levels of society.

■ KATHLEEN D. McCARTHY

≋ Photography

In 1839, when the process of photography was introduced, no one realized the profound effect it would have on people's concepts of reality. Women—as professionals, amateurs, and artists—have made major contributions, using the medium as a means of social exploration and personal expression, and revealing it as a form of sexual exploitation.

Information on women's early involvement in photography in this country is scarce. The heavy equipment, dangerous chemicals, and prevailing social climate created barriers in the new field. Women commonly assisted with poses and with retouching images in portrait studios usually owned by their male relatives. As technology and society made the process easier, more women became photographers.

Toward the end of the century, the introduction of "The Kodak" amateur camera encouraged many women to create family photo albums. Others, like Alice Austen (1866–1952), used fifty pounds of camera equipment to show the intimate side of her women friends' lives and their mockery of Victorian convention. Frances Benjamin Johnston (1864–1952), an unconventional and successful documentarian and portraitist, published "What a Woman Can Do with a Camera" in the *Ladies' Home Journal*. As Johnston photographed women factory workers, Gertrude Käsebier (1852–1934) and others in the fine arts used the soft-focus pictorialist style to represent women idealized as mothers.

After World War I women photographers became more noticeable as technical innovators, critics, and historians. Berenice Abbott (1898–1991), a realist who helped define architectural and scientific photography, struggled for years to fund her work and achieved recognition only at the end of her life. Consuelo Kanaga (1894–1978), who photographed for the *Daily Worker*, believed that photography could change the world by exposing the reality of social conditions. Dorothea Lange (1895–1965), best known for her work with the Farm Security Administration, documented the plight of the rural poor, stirring the conscience of both the public and the decision makers.

In 1936 *Life* magazine ushered in the era of the picture story with a cover photograph by Margaret Bourke-White (1904–71). During World War II she and others showed that they could photograph war, industry, and other areas usually identified with men. Elizabeth "Tex" Williams (b. 1924) was one of a number of Black women who moved beyond portraiture and worked as a photographer in the Women's Army Corps. At the same time, Louise Dahl-Wolfe (1895–1989) was the premiere fashion photographer for *Harper's Bazaar*.

The 1950 census showed that 52,890 people were photographers; 8,550 were women and 240 of those were Black. As the decade advanced, women were pushed into documenting more domestic areas. Ruth Orkin's (1921–85) photography is a twenty-three year record of what she saw through her window while working as a wife and mother.

In the 1960s African American Elaine Tomlin (n.d.) covered contemporary racial and social upheavals and was the official photographer for the Southern Christian Leadership Conference. Although they were discriminated against within educational institutions, many women photographers also were teachers. As feminism rose to challenge all aspects of the culture, women in photography worked to reverse their exclusion from history books, galleries, and museums. They confronted the objectification of women in pho-

tographs and changed existing ideas of representation. The work of Anne Noggle (b. 1922) exemplifies the use of portraits and self-portraits to explore women's ideas of themselves. Women created visibility for groups that rarely had been represented in mainstream media. Native American Carm Little Turtle (n.d.) incorporated the signs and symbols of her culture in her work. Carrie Mae Weems (b. 1953) used African American narrative forms in her photography. JEB (Joan E. Biren) (b. 1944) documented the emergence of lesbians from hiding into full view. Seeing themselves reflected increasingly in authentic, nonexploitive images helped all women to reclaim the power to define themselves.

By the 1980s the number of women press photographers equaled that of men. Female photojournalists still fought to be taken seriously in the male-controlled photo establishment. But the work of some women, like Mary Ellen Mark (b. 1940), gained acceptance as both documentation and art. Women photographers challenged the source and the presentation of cultural images. Barbara Kruger (b. 1945) superimposed phrases such as "I shop therefore I am" over appropriated images. She and other postmodernists use images to reexamine the construction of power, gender, and sexual difference. Women photographers have expanded the idea of vision, allowing both women and men to see themselves and others in vital new ways.

Jeanne Moutoussamy-Ashe, *Viewfinders: Black Women Photographers* (New York: Dodd, Mead & Co., 1986); Naomi Rosenblum, *A History of Women Photographers* (New York: Abbeville Press, 1994).

▪ JOAN E. BIREN
with PEGGY A. FEERICK

SEE ALSO Art and Crafts.

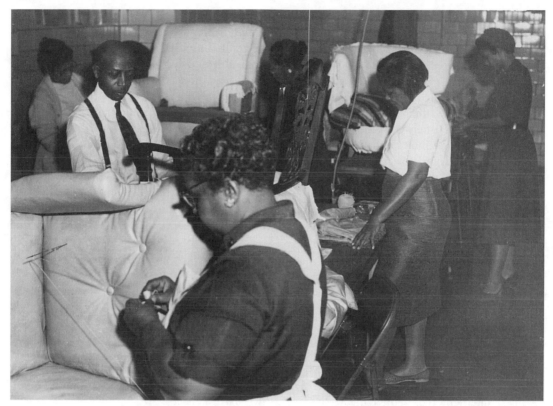

A 1950s upholstery class at the Phillis Wheatley Association in Cleveland, Ohio.

≋ Phyllis Wheatley Clubs and Homes

For Black women, the young slave girl Phyllis Wheatley came to symbolize intellect and resourcefulness, particularly as race relations deteriorated during the latter part of the nineteenth century and the first half of the twentieth century. Wheatley's rise from illiteracy to become the nation's first published Black woman poet inspired a group who were relegated to society's bottom rung by custom and law because of their race and gender. Thus, as groups began to organize and to build institutions, her name (correctly spelled Phillis, but most often updated to Phyllis) became almost synonymous with residences and clubs for Black women, young and old.

Although there are no records to indicate when or where the first Phyllis Wheatley Club was organized, the first institution to use the name was probably established by a Black women's club as a home for aged Black women in Detroit in 1897. However, the most popular use of the name referred to residences and clubhouses for young Black women. For the most part, these facilities were operated under the auspices of local branches of either the National Association of Colored Women (NACW) or the Young Women's Christian Association (YWCA). As a result of much negotiating between the two organizations, as well as the considerable overlap in membership among Black women, the YWCA opened segregated branches with residences in most major cities where there was a sizable Black population. In cities where there was no Black YWCA, the NACW organized residences and/or clubs. Although records are incomplete, by the mid-1930s at least thirty-three affiliated Phyllis Wheatley YWCA branches existed across the nation. Likewise, NACW records indicate that their affiliated clubs reached into numerous cities and towns.

• ADRIENNE LASH JONES

SEE ALSO Black Clubwomen's Movement; National Association of Colored Women; Social Work; YWCA.

≋ Physicians

"**E**very woman," observed the nineteenth-century physician Ella Flagg Young, "is a born doctor. Men have to study to become one." Dr. Young's statement represented the feelings of many of the early women physicians, Black, white, and Native American, who, from the mid–nineteenth century through the early decades of the twentieth, braved prejudice, poverty, social convention, professional hostility, and sometimes family opposition in order to join the medical profession. They believed that they belonged in medicine by virtue of their natural gifts as healers and nurturers.

In 1849 Elizabeth Blackwell became the first woman to receive a medical degree in the United States and emerged as a leader of the movement to train women in medicine. Her writings helped convince many doubters that medicine was especially suited to women because it combined the alleged authority of science with an inherently "female" dedication to alleviating suffering. Blackwell and others insisted that, in a rapidly industrializing society unprepared for the burgeoning problems of poverty and disease, women physicians were well suited to teach the practical tenets of family health and hygiene. In theory, these dedicated practitioners would not be motivated by selfish concerns and would be sensitive to the wives, mothers, and children who would be their primary constituency. In addition, women doctors supported preventive medicine at a time when other physicians did not consider it a high priority. The few African American women who managed to receive medical training particularly took to heart their role as community health educators. Dr. Rebecca J. Cole, for example, who received her degree in 1867 from the Woman's Medical College of Pennsylvania, worked with Elizabeth Blackwell and her sister Emily Blackwell (also a physician) in New York, visiting the sick in slum neighborhoods and teaching the fundamentals of health and hygiene. Cole later performed critical health education and treatment in the African American communities in Philadelphia and Washington, D.C., and was recognized well into the 1920s as an authoritative spokesperson.

Female medical educators had worked valiantly in the nineteenth century to provide young women with first-rate medical education. After they failed to gain admittance for women at the best male schools, they founded several women's institutions to train female students. The three most outstanding were the Woman's Medical College of Pennsylvania, the Woman's Medical College of the New York Infirmary, and the Chicago Female Medical College. Students benefited not only from an educational policy that kept abreast of the latest developments but also from female mentors who provided an otherwise unattainable example. Gradually other schools opened their doors to women, following the University of Michigan's example in 1871. Women doctors also established hospitals and dispensaries that offered clinical experience to women graduates. As a result, female physicians comprised close to 5 percent of the profession by 1900, a figure that remained relatively stable until the 1960s.

At the turn of the century, then, there was cause for optimism regarding the woman physician's future. Women were first admitted to the prestigious Johns Hopkins Medical School in 1892. A few were training in surgery, and others had begun to publish extensively in medical journals. They had joined medical societies, including the American Medical Women's Association, founded in 1915, and started *The Medical Woman's Journal*. Between 1900 and 1930 women physicians were active and visible in the new specialty of public health, staffing positions at the state and local level and providing crucial lobbying support for a new government agency, the Children's Bureau, established in 1910. Women had become the "conscience" of the profession.

But other forces were at work that eventually kept women's numbers and position in the profession static. Twentieth-century medicine was professionalizing, promoting individualism, scientific objectivity, rationality, personal achievement, and careerism, forming a new ethos that was distinctly different from traditionally held "female" values. This trend toward professionalism created subtle tensions for older women physicians who still viewed their role from a nineteenth-century perspective.

The first generations to come of age after 1920 found themselves maneuvering in a medical world bereft of female-run institutions, support systems, and a viable feminist movement. Younger women physicians learned to accept the traditional male values of the profession, subsuming their power within it. Not until the feminist movement in the 1960s did women critique the elitism and masculine orientation that had prevailed in medicine. In doing so, they generated a new appreciation for the "female" qualities of nurturing and cooperation in patient care and revived an interest in medicine as a female occupation. Today women compose almost one-third of the profession and close to half of the students, and the numbers are rising.

Virginia Drachman, *Hospital with a Heart: Women Doctors and the Paradox of Separatism at the New England Hospital, 1862–1969* (Ithaca: Cornell University Press, 1984); Regina Morantz-Sanchez, *Sympathy and Science: Women Physicians in American Medicine* (New York: Oxford University Press, 1985); Mary Roth Walsh, *"Doctors Wanted: No Women Need Apply": Sexual Barriers in the Medical Profession, 1835–1975* (New Haven: Yale University Press, 1977).

■ REGINA MORANTZ-SANCHEZ

≋ Picture Brides

Picture brides were Japanese and Korean women who immigrated to the United States during the first two decades of the twentieth century due to the Gentlemen's Agreement of 1907–8, which prohibited the further emigration of Japanese laborers but allowed wives and families to join Japanese already in the United States. Based on the *omaiai-kekkon*, or arranged marriage custom, women in Japan and Korea exchanged photographs with prospective husbands in the United States, had their names entered into their spouse's family registers, and then applied for passports to join husbands they had never met. (Korea was annexed by Japan in 1910 and remained under Japanese domination until the end of World War II.) In this way, twenty thousand Japanese women and 1,000 Korean women immigrated to the United States until 1920, when the Japanese government voluntarily prohibited female emigration because of anti-Japanese sentiment in the United States. As a result of the picture-bride system (*shashin kekkon* or "photo-marriage"), women composed 35 percent of the Japanese American population and 21 percent of the Korean American population in 1920. Many picture brides, misled by visions of wealth and photographs of younger versions of their new husbands, were sorely disappointed upon arrival in the United States. Unprepared

A congressional committee examines the passports of Japanese picture brides at Angel Island, California, July 25, 1920.

for the back-breaking labor, the primitive living conditions, and the cultural adjustments, some deserted their husbands and ran away with lovers. Most, however, stayed and made the best of the situation, working alongside their husbands in the fields or in small businesses while helping to establish family life in their new country.

▪ JUDY YUNG

SEE ALSO Japanese American Women; Korean American Women.

≋ Pink Collar Ghetto

The words "pink collar ghetto" entered the feminist vocabulary in 1977 with the publication of Louise Kapp Howe's *Pink Collar Workers*, which vividly portrayed the lives of women in tradition-ally "female" jobs like beautician, waitress, sales clerk, and secretary. Howe argued that the concept of equal pay for equal work could do little to allevi-ate wage inequality between men and women be-cause of the prevalence of occupational segrega-tion by sex. The majority of women workers are in "pink collar" occupations—clerical, service, and sales jobs. Pink collar workers have, on average, more years of education than their male counter-parts in blue collar jobs but make considerably less money. Jobs in the pink collar ghetto are usually low paying, nonunion, and offer few or no benefits and no chance of advancement; commonly, they are part-time, seasonal, or temporary. To address the low pay for women in the pink collar ghetto, feminists and labor experts have advocated equal pay not only for equal work but also for jobs of com-parable worth. In the 1980s attention shifted to the problem of the "glass ceiling," which describes the barriers to job advancement faced by mainly white, educated women in managerial positions.

Concern for the far more restricting limitations of the pink collar ghetto has revived with the concept of the "sticky floor" that traps women, particularly women of color, in the lowest-paid job categories of government bureaucracies and large corporations.

• BEATRIX HOFFMAN

SEE ALSO Clerical Work; Comparable Worth.

≋ Planned Parenthood

In 1942 the Birth Control Federation of America, operator of 350 contraceptive clinics, changed its name to Planned Parenthood. The new name signaled the end of women's dominance in a birth-control movement built by and for women. Three years earlier, when the formation of the federation united the major birth-control organizations, men for the first time dominated top leadership positions. By 1942 many longtime women workers resigned with disdain for the new masculine leadership. With their departure, the movement's commitment to women's reproductive self-determination was muted. In addition, the new leadership cut back the federation's activities in the Black community.

African American women, including Mabel Staupers, May Chinn, and Dorothy Ferebee, were involved in birth-control projects throughout the 1930s. Like white women, African American women saw birth control as a way to reduce maternal and infant deaths as well as the number of abortions. Yet they had to struggle to have their concerns recognized by the larger movement. In particular, they had to fight to get African American staff in Black community clinics. Black women, they knew, would (and did) shun white-run clinics, fearing genocide. With limited success, African American women did influence the organization. The Birth Control Federation's Division of Negro Service organized several clinics in the South, where segregated state-run clinics refused service to Blacks. Apart from the Division of Negro Service, the particular concerns of women of color went unrecognized at the national level of Planned Parenthood. However, Asian American women and Latinas participated at the state and local levels, especially in the West and Southwest, where birth-control organizations had thrived since the 1920s. Shidzue Ishimoto, a leader of Japan's birth-control movement, frequently spoke at California birth-control leagues when she came to the United States. In fact, the birth-control activism of U.S. women of color was often connected to the birth-control movements in Mexico, Puerto Rico, Japan, China, and Korea.

Although Planned Parenthood prohibited segregation within its affiliated chapters, and required chapters to hire ethnically diverse staff, it did not expand on the work of its predecessor. Thus, the contraceptive needs of African American women also fell victim to the organization's internal restructuring, while the concerns of other women of color continued to be ignored.

The shift to Planned Parenthood mirrored changes in the wider historical context. As with other charitable organizations, the depression put enormous strain on the movement's resources: funding plummeted but demand for birth control soared. Through Roosevelt's New Deal, men took over the historically female domain of social welfare, while a return to traditional family values assuaged anxieties stirred by the depression and reaffirmed traditional sex roles. With these changes, feminism became a liability and politically active women were compelled to respond to charges that they were antimale. In this context, birth control appeared both to limit support to women and to undermine family values. The rhetoric of *planned parenthood* was intended to broaden the movement's financial appeal, to include men, and to confirm traditional family values. Yet, the new rhetoric ultimately failed. During the baby boom years, Planned Parenthood languished and the number of its clinics declined.

By the 1970s the resurgence of feminism, concern about overpopulation, and the legalization of birth control and abortion revitalized Planned Parenthood. Again, women's perspectives came to the organization's forefront. The influence of women of color continued to be muted by racism, but under former Executive Director Faye Wattleton, they emerged among the leaders of the renewed organization. Independent African American and Latina women's health organizations have also joined in coalition with Planned Parenthood and other organizations to fight for women's reproductive rights. As in the 1930s, however, the future of this women's institution is again jeopardized by antifeminist politics that are shrouded in the guise of family values.

■ CAROLE R. MCCANN

SEE ALSO Birth Control.

≋ Plantation System

From the founding of European colonies on the North American continent, women played a central role in the growth and expansion of the plantation system. Although settlers in Massachusetts Bay and other northern colonies called their enterprises plantations, the plantation system was refined and came to be associated primarily with southern land holdings. The Virginia House of Burgesses declared in 1619, "in a newer plantation it is not known whether man or woman be the most necessary." Females were viewed as essential domesticating elements in these colonial communities.

During the seventeenth century white and Black men and women labored in the fields, but by the early eighteenth century fewer white indentured servants were engaged in agricultural production, and those were primarily male. Increasingly slaves were brought from Africa to undertake arduous work in tobacco and hemp fields. The slave population increased dramatically in the lower South during this period, from 650 in 1685 to 31,000 in 1730 and 187,000 in 1775, as the sex ratio of the slave population (which had been disproportionately male) evened out. The expansion of the slave population corresponded with the rapid exponential growth and development of the plantation system. Plantations extended farther southwest from 1750 to 1850, adding more and more slaves.

Planters (estate owners who held twenty slaves or more) not only enjoyed the golden age of tobacco in the upper South, but by mid–eighteenth century rice was a profitable crop in the lush Carolina low country, sugar in the Mississippi Delta, and sea-island cotton was cultivated along the Atlantic coast, creating an increasing demand for slave labor. With the invention of the cotton gin in 1793, cotton could be grown profitably away from coastal plains, and plantations spread into western Georgia, Alabama, and Mississippi. By 1820 the introduction of "Mexican cotton" doubled planters' output per acre and again required more workers. The expansion of the plantation system and the natural increase of the slave population (to replace external importation of slaves, banned by federal law in 1808) created a dynamic economic force by mid–nineteenth century; the cry "Cotton is King" was proven by the spectacular trade figures, which made the crop America's top export.

Black and white women were central to this enterprise. From the visionary Eliza Lucas Pinckney, who introduced indigo in South Carolina during the 1740s, to the dynamic Catharine Greene, who introduced Eli Whitney to the problem of ginning cotton in the 1790s, white plantation mistresses were critical to the extension of the plantation system. White women's work roles were mainly supervisory, although they did undertake some chores that belied their iconographic roles as symbols of gentility and leisure. For example, white women were involved in the slaughter of stock and the salting of beef and pork, and many other unglamorous tasks. The labors of Black women on plantations were essential to production of crops and profit on the estate.

Slave women not only had to perform harsh and exacting labor in the field but they were also expected to serve all the needs of the master class. For this reason, African American women were encouraged to become pregnant and reproduce as often as possible to meet the demands of the expanding plantation system. The 1839 journal of Fanny Kemble lists women who begged for assistance on her husband's Georgia estate. The journal offers tragic testimony about Black female slaves: Fanny, six children (all dead but one); Nanny, three children (two dead); Leah, six children (three dead); Sophy, ten children (five dead); Sally, two miscarriages, three born (one dead); Charlotte, two miscarriages; Sarah, four miscarriages, seven born (five dead). African American children as young as seven were sometimes assigned duties on the plantation tending toddlers. By age ten they were put into the fields, working reduced loads, along with pregnant and nursing women. A healthy adult woman was expected to complete three-quarters of the labor assigned to an adult male, although many women could and did outperform male comrades. Slave women were not assigned supervisory roles as drivers on the plantation, but within the slave community many African American women were granted status based on their skills as midwives, healers, or religious leaders.

The sexual double standard among the planter elite pitted Black and white women against one another. The exultation of white women's purity kept most on a pedestal, while most African American women were restricted to the auction block. This pattern of racial discrimination persisted well past the decline of the plantation system, which effectively ended after the Civil War.

Catherine Clinton, *The Plantation Mistress: Woman's World in the Old South* (New York: Pantheon, 1982); Elizabeth Fox-Genovese, *Within the Plantation Household: Black and White Women of the Old South* (Chapel Hill: University of North Carolina Press, 1988); Deborah Gray White, *Aren't I a Woman? Female Slaves in the Plantation South* (New York: W. W. Norton, 1985).

• CATHERINE CLINTON

SEE ALSO Agriculture; Colonial Period; Slavery.

≋ Poetry

SEE Literature.

≋ Police Forces

Police include overlapping public forces at all levels of government and private forces funded by corporations, neighborhood associations, and shopping malls. Responsible for maintaining order, responding to reported crime, and repressing civil disorder, police sustain the unequal distribution of wealth and power by protecting property and selectively enforcing the law.

The earliest police in the United States were the slave patrols, bands of white men who pursued runaway slaves and administered summary whippings. City police started in the 1840s. Native-born white women were arrested infrequently, but African American and Irish women were arrested routinely, usually for misdemeanors such as vagrancy, public drunkenness, or prostitution.

Poor, working-class, and women of color historically have been frequently subjected to police violence. For example, police clubbed entire families during the unemployed demonstration in New York's Tompkins Square in 1874, and women strikers in the Chicago garment workers' strikes of 1910 and 1915 were savagely beaten. In direct violation of tribal sovereignty, an Indian Agent created the first Native police force in Nebraska in

1869. Its duties included determining which families were working hard enough to deserve food rations. Farther south, the Texas Rangers pushed Mexicans and Native Americans off land coveted for cattle ranching. Both the militia and the state police throughout the country considered immigrant women strikers, especially Slavs and Italians, the most difficult to restrain.

Police cooperated in protecting white vigilante violence against people of color. Police in California towns stood aside as whites attacked Chinese people in the 1870s. Both the police and National Guard were ineffective against the lynching of African Americans. In early-twentieth-century race riots, during which white men and women attacked Blacks, police refused to protect Blacks, or, as was true in New York in 1900 and East St. Louis in 1917, led the rioters. In Los Angeles in 1943, off-duty policemen joined servicemen in beating Latinos and Latinas during the "zoot-suit" riots. Police arrested, beat, and spied upon civil rights workers and the Black Panthers in the 1950s and 1960s, and only mass pressure forced the FBI to investigate.

Police brutality in the context of extreme poverty and racism ignited the race riots of the 1960s, which destroyed entire neighborhoods and left many dead. Police beat and tear-gassed white student antiwar protesters in the late 1960s, but police in Los Angeles killed at least five Latino demonstrators. Continuing a long tradition of resistance by people of color to police brutality, Celia Luna created the Barrio Defense Committee, which helped victims and organized protests.

Police harassment and violence against lesbians, especially working-class and Black lesbians, were common in the 1950s and 1960s. Lesbian or gay bar owners often had to pay bribes to the police or criminals to operate, and when politicians demanded a crackdown, the bars' patrons were nevertheless arrested and humiliated. Before an election in San Francisco in 1956, police arrested thirty-six women in one night at the lesbian Alamo Club. The Daughters of Bilitis and other groups worked with American Civil Liberties Union (ACLU) lawyers in many cities to reduce harassment.

Police political surveillance work has targeted women. In the 1920s people in military intelligence stated that the activities of all women's organizations should be regarded with suspicion, and the Women's International League for Peace and Freedom was under FBI and Office of Naval Intelligence surveillance for at least fifty years. The National Organization for Women and the National Welfare Rights Organization were but two of the thousands of groups infiltrated and under surveillance in the 1960s and 1970s.

Although women have always been subject to policing, they have by contrast had difficulty in securing police services. Both the law and the male bias of many police officers undermine effective response to wife battering. It required a political movement for rape to be taken seriously as a crime.

Women are arrested at a much lower rate than men, but women of color are arrested at a rate far out of proportion to white women. Larceny and victimless crimes such as drug addiction account for most female arrests. Although the proportion of women arrested has not increased compared with that of men, the numbers of women arrested have increased dramatically since the 1970s because of harsher laws against drugs, drug abuse, and welfare fraud.

The police expanded in the 1960s in response to the rise of social movements and the decay of cities, but it has done little to reduce the level of crime and violence. Despite large criminal justice budgets, for instance, police urge women to take personal responsibility for avoiding violence by residing in "safe" neighborhoods or by exercising similar options available only to the wealthy.

The police historically have strongly resisted opening their ranks to women. Even in 1991 only 9 percent of public police officers were women, compared to one-fourth of lawyers, judges, and law faculty. White middle-class female reformers won the appointment of police matrons for female detainees in at least twelve cities by 1885, but the first woman with arrest authority was Lola Baldwin, in Portland, Oregon, in 1905. Called a "safety worker," she and others in similar positions considered themselves social service workers rather than policewomen and were mainly responsible for the supervision of recreation for working-class women and juveniles. Many white women entered policing during World War I, when men joined the army. In order to protect the soldiers' health and morals, antivice reformers called for strict policing of the young women who flocked to the outskirts of army camps for socializing and prostitution. By the end of the war, more than 220 cities had policewomen, whose duties were distinct from those of policemen. Organized in separate women's bureaus, the policewomen escorted females, did clerical work, and patrolled as plainclothes women to prevent vice and juvenile delinquency. Although policemen were overwhelmingly from a working-class background, the first policewomen were often middle or upper class and had college degrees and experience as social workers or teachers. Despite their education and experience, these women received lower salaries than did policemen and had very limited opportunities for promotion.

In 1956 women formed the International Association of Women Police to change the stereotype of policewomen as social service workers. Organizing and individual lawsuits in the changed context of federal law in the 1960s enabled women to gain access to promotion, despite the concerted legal and bitter personal opposition of male-dominated police departments. The Justice Department helped to force legal compliance by responding to women's demands that it withhold federal money from police departments practicing sex discrimination. The proportion of female sworn officers rose from 1.5 percent in 1972 to 3.38 percent in 1979 to 8.8 percent in 1986. Police work, despite the often difficult working conditions, offers the opportunity for secure employ-

ment, pensions, and civil service protection. Proportionately more women of color enter policing than do white women. It is unclear why women of color are proportionately more likely to enter police work than are white women. The higher representation of women of color among female officers compared with that of men of color among male officers may be due simply to the long dominance of the occupation by white males. (Since police forces were overwhelmingly made up of white men until the 1960s, many men of color will need to join before they constitute a significant percentage of the men as a whole.) By contrast, very few white women belonged to the force at the time that the recruitment of both women of color and white women began.

Women, and especially women of color, continue to be underrepresented at the supervisory level and within state and federal forces. In 1986 only 3.3 percent of the supervisory positions were held by women; of them, less than a third were women of color. Women composed only 5.3 percent of all sworn officers in state police agencies in 1991. FBI head J. Edgar Hoover's ban on hiring women did not end until his death in 1972. As of March 1994 women represented only about 11 percent of all FBI agents. Women have had an easier time entering the lower-paid, less-prestigious, but fast-growing field of private policing. More private police than public exist and, as of 1994, women made up about 18 percent of the employees of the five largest private security firms.

Women's roles within policing now range from firearms instructors to prostitution decoys. As an occupation traditionally characterized by a high degree of institutional autonomy and white male privilege, policing poses special hurdles for white women and all people of color. Sexist stereotypes about women's physical strength and emotional self-control contribute to a working environment in which men have considerable latitude to harass, undermine, and discriminate against women, especially women of color and lesbians.

Clarice Feinman, *Women in the Criminal Justice System* (Westport, Conn.: Praeger, 1994); Lawrence M. Friedman, *Crime and Punishment in American History* (New York: Basic Books, 1993); Tony Platt, et al., *The Iron Fist and the Velvet Glove: An Analysis of the U.S. Police* (Berkeley, Calif.: Center for Research on Criminal Justice, 1977).

■ GERDA W. RAY

≋ Political Parties

Political parties, since their formation in 1789, have dominated U.S. politics within a system of two-party electoral competition. Most voters identify with a political party. The vast majority of U.S. elected officials have been party-affiliated nominees, and their parties influence policymaking through platforms and officeholders. Despite some ambivalence, U.S. women have generally acceded to Elizabeth Cady Stanton's original belief that women must be involved with parties "inasmuch as our demands are to be made and carried, like other political questions, by the aid of and affiliation with parties." To illustrate, in 1996 only 17 of 1,541 elected female state legislators were not members of either the Democratic or Republican parties.

The barbershop and saloon settings of nineteenth-century political clubs excluded women from many party activities. But in the presuffrage era, women were party workers. Women participated in political torchlight parades by lighting their windows or even by marching as "Miss Liberty."

Neither major party was an ally in the suffrage campaign after the Civil War. Democrats opposed woman suffrage on states' rights grounds. The mostly Democratic political machines feared women's support of Prohibition and resisted woman suffrage as contrary to expected immigrant sex roles. Republicans urged that the post–Civil War era be used to advance the rights of the newly enfranchised Black male, a constituency that the party needed to control national government. Stanton and Susan B. Anthony (and the National Woman Suffrage Association) broke with the Republican Party over this stance, while Lucy Stone (and the American Woman Suffrage Association) remained loyal. The association in the minds of white southerners between feminism and the abolitionist movement brought strong opposition to woman suffrage. White southern suffragists argued that because of literacy and property qualifications only white women should be enfranchised and thus assure the survival of white supremacy. This viewpoint was embraced in ugly racist rhetoric by most Northern suffragists, including Stanton, Anthony, Carrie Chapman Catt, and Alice Paul. African American women, excluded from white suffrage groups, organized their own clubs and vigorously worked for the vote.

In 1872, the Republican Party became the first to mention women, blandly recognizing women's broader role in society and promising to respectfully consider women's demands for additional rights. Not until 1916 was woman suffrage mentioned in a major party platform, when both parties endorsed suffrage adopted on a state-by-state basis. At best, both parties ceased obstructing the constitutional amendment.

It was the hope of National Woman's Party president Mrs. O.H.P. Belmont that the two parties would merge to oppose a unified women's party. However, women joined the two major parties after 1920 in proportions mirroring those of men. Although the more affluent and well-educated women who were the first to vote, between 1920 and 1932, probably leaned toward the Republican side, poorer and immigrant women entered the electorate as Democrats beginning in 1932.

A large gender gap existed in voter participation, which favored men well into the 1960s. Since 1980 women as a group have been slightly more likely to vote than men; among African Americans and Latinos this gender gap is even more pronounced. Until the 1970s no distinct gender gap in party identification and candidate choice was noticeable. Since 1976 women have supported the Democratic Party and its candidates more strongly than have men. The gender gap is largest among younger voters, the college-educated, African Americans, and Latinos. Although no information is available on gender gap trends among Asian Americans and Native Americans, both groups have been more likely to be independent or lean slightly to the Democratic Party. Among Native Americans, voting data vary in each nation, and are influenced by current party and reservation residence stances on federal Indian policies. Among Asian and Latino groups, voter choices vary by country of origin, with those from Cuba, Vietnam, and Cambodia being largely Republican.

Both major parties have used their control over party rules to require women's equality as party officers and convention delegates and to symbolically affirm women's policy goals in platforms. The Democratic National Committee (DNC) in 1920 and the Republican National Committee (RNC) in 1924 mandated equal representation for women on the national committees, and by 1928 eighteen states had adopted the same rule for state party executive committees. This formal equality was illusory in that only compliant women were appointed by male party leaders; for decades women served in a dual hierarchy as coleaders and vice-chairs, but never as chairs.

Today, women at the state and local levels are increasingly moving into positions as county and state party chairs and executive directors. In the 1970s Jean Westwood and Mary Louise Smith became the first (and still only) women to head the DNC and RNC, respectively. Women activists no longer continue to be the "hidden hands" of the party, working extra hours on the less visible tasks, with no expectation of future elected office. Women party leaders are now as ambitious for political rewards and recognition as are their male colleagues.

Historically, African American women were targeted by both major parties through the DNC's Colored Women's Activities office and the National League of Republican Colored Women. Mary McLeod Bethune, Crystal Fauset, Daisy Lampkin, and Mary Church Terrell are among the notable Black women once active in these groups. In the 1990s, more than half of Democratic state party officials are African American women. The interests of other women of color have been addressed through women's caucuses and organizations such as the DNC's Latino Caucus and the National Democratic Council of Asian Pacific Americans. In 1985 all ethnic and women's caucuses were abolished by the DNC, and in 1988 the RNC rejected a request for similar groups.

Until the 1960s the Republican Party was the leading advocate of equal rights for women, and the Democratic Party continued to endorse the protective legislation supported by its labor-reform constituency. In 1940 the Republican platform was the first to include the equal rights amendment, and in 1956 the party endorsed a ban on sex discrimination. But neither party worked toward legislating these policies, even after both parties converged in support of women's equality in the 1960s. In the 1970s the Republican Party began to withdraw support from legal equality and abortion rights, and in the 1980s and 1990s antifeminists have in effect written the women's planks, as the new Christian right has gained power. In contrast, liberal groups (women, people of color, and lesbians and gays) have dominated the Democratic platform, producing extensive proposals in support of the feminist agenda.

The most dramatic shift in women's party roles involves the quadrennial presidential nominating conventions. Earlier women served most visibly as hospitality room hostesses, members of escort committees, readers of a platform section, and presenters of seconding speeches for nominees. Beginning in the 1970s women frequently have served as convention chairs and keynote speakers.

Equally impressive has been the upsurge in the numbers of female delegates. From the appearance in 1900 of the first women delegates, the percentage of female delegates remained a fairly steady 10 to 15 percent (1920–68), although a larger percentage attended as nonvoting alternates. According to the rules of the McGovern-Fraser Commission on Party Structure and Delegate Selection for the 1972 Democratic convention, each state delegation was to include representatives of people of color, women, and young people in reasonable relationship to their population in the state. In 1979 the DNC mandated equal division for the sexes in national convention state delegations. To balance the white male bias of the Democrats' at-large and superdelegates, more than half of the Latino, Native American, and African American delegates have been female. In 1972 the Republican national convention passed an advisory Rule 32 declaring that each state should try to have equal representation of men and women in their delegations. Since then Republicans have had female representation ranging from 30 percent (1972) to 44 percent (1984). More women usually attend the Republican conventions when an incumbent is renominated, which suggests that those presidential candidates are interested in projecting a misleading television image of gender equity.

Women's rights advocates have often viewed parties as hostile to female candidates by withholding resources and nominating women only in hopeless contests. Women were excluded from national tickets until Democrat Geraldine Ferraro's nomination for vice president in 1984. The only deviations from this pattern were the symbolic nominations of women for vice president at the 1924 and 1928 Democratic conventions (and the feminist-led nomination of Frances Farenthold for vice president at the 1972 Democratic convention, which garnered 13 percent of the delegate votes), and the underfunded presidential candidacies of Republican Margaret Chase Smith in 1964 and Democrat Shirley Chisholm in 1972.

It is generally conceded that parties have become more responsive to women candidates. In 1988 both platforms endorsed women candidates' access to elective office with party support. Parties recruit women candidates, train them, provide services, and introduce them to potential contributors. Party donations to women candidates are evenhanded, if not slightly more generous.

In the post–suffrage era, female officeholders were more likely to be Republicans. In 1996 the majority of women in Congress and state legislatures were Democrats. However, Republican women hold significant numbers of these positions and constitute a majority of those women officials elected statewide, including the nation's only state governor, Christine Todd Whitman, of New Jersey. Elected women of color, however, are strongly Democratic: 14 of 15 in Congress, all but one of the five statewide officials, and all but 12 of the 221 state legislators. But of the nationally elected female officials who are Native American, Asian Pacific, Latina, or African American, at least one woman within each group is Republican.

U.S. third parties have been in the vanguard in embracing the feminist goals of suffrage and national officeholding. At least six parties, including the Populist, Progressive, and Prohibition parties, preceded the major parties in support of suffrage and equal-pay legislation. Of the female candidates for president (12) and vice president (46) appearing on a national ballot since 1920, all but one were nominated by third parties. Parties of the Left, in particular the Socialist Workers Party, have been most open to a woman on the ticket. More than a dozen women of color were nominated between 1980 and 1992.

Exclusively women's parties have also been formed or considered. The Equal Rights Party offered the presidential candidacies of Victoria Claflin Woodhull (1872) and Belva Ann Bennett Lockwood (1884, 1888) as a means of raising gender and ethnic issues. For example, the platform of 1884 advocated equality and justice for all regardless of sex, color, or nationality and supported full citizenship for Native Americans. In 1989 the national conference of the National Organization for Women (NOW) agreed to explore the possibility of forming a new political party that would be more responsive to the issues of women's rights, racism, homophobia, the environment, peace, and social justice. The resulting Commission for Responsive Democracy, after two years of regional hearings and meetings, announced in 1992 the 21st Century Party, the Nation's Equality Party, with Dolores Huerta as its chair. The national NOW conference has endorsed the concept of the party, but it is unclear whether this group would operate as a political party by contesting elections or act as a social movement/interest group as has the National Woman's Party.

With the founding of the National Women's Political Caucus in 1971, the new feminist movement successfully pressured political parties to change rules on delegate selection and adopt numerous planks on women's issues. But with a gender gap clearly favoring the Democratic Party, debate has emerged over women being one of that party's core constituents and thus foregoing interparty competition for women's votes. A final problem is that U.S. parties are inherently "weak" because they are powerless to require the nomination of women for elected office. Party nominations are made in direct primaries open to all party voters, who do not appear to discriminate but too infrequently find women on the ballot.

Barbara C. Burrell, "Party Decline, Party Transformation and Gender Politics: The USA," in *Gender and Party Politics* (London: Sage, 1993); Anne N. Costain, "After Reagan: New Party Attitudes Toward Gender," *Annals* 515 (May 1991): 114–25; Jo Freeman, "Feminism vs. Family Values: Women at the 1992 Democratic and Republican Conventions," *PS: Political Science and Politics* 26 (March 1993): 21–28.

• JANET K. BOLES

SEE ALSO Electoral Organizations; Electoral Politics; Gender Gap.

≋ Political Prisoners

In every country, the category of political prisoner is defined by the interests of government. Legitimate protest is often classified as a crime and those who engage in it as criminals. The United States is no exception. International watchdog organizations such as Amnesty International (AI) have been extremely conservative in their definitions. AI now recognizes one, perhaps two, U.S. political prisoners, neither of them women. The advocacy and outreach group Freedom Now, however, recognizes approximately 100 political prisoners, 25 percent of whom are women. Women compose about 5 percent of the total U.S. prison population— 32,691 in state and federal facilities by the end of the 1980s. The trend is toward larger numbers of female prisoners as well as higher percentages of women of color.

Evelyn Williams, a lawyer famous for representing Assata Shakur (discussed below), defines the category of political prisoner as "someone who has been illegally convicted of a crime, is brutalized while in prison because of his or her political opinions or who is convicted of committing a crime for political reasons." She also believes "all African American prisoners are political prisoners, whether or not they label themselves as such, because of the circumstances that got them into jail as well as the harshness of sentencing applied only to them."

The poor and people of color are greatly overrepresented in the prison population. The largest number of women political prisoners in this country today are Puerto Rican and white women supporters of Black liberation forces. In 1988 an international protest campaign succeeded in closing the infamous Lexington Control Unit in Kentucky, a high security pavilion that used sensory deprivation and other methods of torture on six women held for two years within its underground walls. The prison system, however, has moved the former inhabitants of Lexington to other maximum security institutions.

Gender has been a factor in imprisonment throughout history. Institutionalized violence against women was especially dramatic in the case of the witch-hunts of sixteenth- and seventeenth-century Europe; these hunts were reenacted in the Americas (particularly in New England) in the late-1600s. At least thirty-six, possibly many more, women were executed. Some historians believe that issues of inheritance and property were at the root of the hysteria; overwhelmingly, the women accused and tried were widowed, single, over forty, or otherwise a threat to the male-controlled economy. Today hundreds of women are in prison for standing up to ongoing battering and some for lashing out at—sometimes killing—husbands or others who perpetrated abuse. It might be argued that in a patriarchal system these too are political "crimes."

Women political prisoners serve long sentences. Haydee Beltrán, Dylcia Pagán, Alicia Rodríguez, Ida Luz Rodríguez, Alejandrina Torres, and Carmen Valentín and others call themselves Puerto Rican prisoners of war; they are serving sentences ranging from thirty years to life. They were inspired by women like Lolita Lebrón, who spent twenty-seven years at Alderson Women's Prison for her 1954 standoff with the U.S. Congress, demanding freedom for her native Puerto Rico. Assata Shakur and other African American women have been imprisoned under the most brutal of conditions. Shakur managed to escape and has been living in Cuba for the past decade. Joan Little was freed by a massive popular protest after she killed a male guard who raped her. Kathy Boudin, Marilyn Buck, Judy Clark, Susan Rosenberg, and Laura Whitehorn are women imprisoned for what may be the rest of their lives for their involvement in the revolutionary movements that sprang up in the early 1970s. Native American women were also imprisoned for their activism in the 1970s after Wounded Knee. History shows that Mildred Cleghorn, chairwoman

of the Oklahoma Apache Tribe, was a U.S. "prisoner of war" as an infant.

All these women suffered or suffer the degradation of an overcrowded and unjust prison system, compounded by patriarchy's abuse of them as women. They are frequently subject to sexual harassment or abuse—by prison authorities, guards, and in some cases by male prisoners.

Women political prisoners have not remained passive victims. They resist by studying, teaching, organizing, and sometimes organizing protests. From 1915 to 1920, women at New York State's Bedford Hills Correctional Facility protested cruelty to inmates. In 1971 the women at Alderson staged a work stoppage simultaneous with the better-known Attica rebellion of that year.

Ward Churchill and J. J. Vander Wall, *Cages of Steel* (Washington, D.C.: Maisonneuve Press, 1992).

▪ MARGARET RANDALL

≋ Politicians

"**I**f you don't run, you can't win," admonished Geraldine Ferraro, former member of Congress and the unsuccessful 1984 Democratic vice-presidential candidate. Ferraro, the first woman to be nominated by a major political party for the vice presidency, was correct; yet until the past few decades, few women ran for elective office and even fewer won. Historically, women have faced several barriers to participating in electoral politics, including public attitudes, family demands, and sex discrimination. These barriers have deterred women from running for office. Historically, for example, unlike men, women with small children have postponed running for office until their children were older. Similarly, nearly a quarter of the electorate believes that "men are better suited emotionally for politics" and that Americans are not "ready to elect a woman to higher office." Nevertheless, studies show that when women do run against nonincumbent men, they win just as frequently. The incumbency factor, in particular, has posed problems for women candidates. The successes of women candidates in 1992, often hailed as the "Year of the Woman," can, in part, be explained by the high number of available electoral seats. Despite the glaring underrepresentation of women in electoral politics and continued negative attitudes, women do have a long history of activism in electoral system politics.

Although women did not gain the national franchise until 1920, women could vote in some local school-board elections far earlier and some even won office. This apparent political acceptance of women reflects public attitudes toward women's proper role in society; school-board activity was seen as local and within women's domestic sphere of interest. Other local electoral activity for women soon followed. For example, in Illinois in 1906, women were nine of one hundred two elected county superintendents, even though women in that state were not yet enfranchised. Until the 1960s women candidates tried to capitalize on public sentiments that considered women to be more moral than men and thus properly interested in politics as an extension of their maternal roles. Women who did seek elective office often were older than their male counterparts and, if married, no longer had young children at home. Throughout history, parenthood and politics have often been viewed as incompatible female roles.

As more women gained experience in local elective office and entered professions such as the law, the number of women in state Houses increased dramatically by the mid-1970s. By 1997 women were elected to 21.3 percent of state legislative seats, a fivefold increase since 1969. The number of women who ran as well as who won increased at a steady rate until 1993.

Women of color have also made significant inroads. In 1997, 14.1 percent of women in state legislatures were women of color. Of the sixty women in the 104th Congress, 27 percent were women of color, and two more women served as delegates to the U.S. House. (In the past decade Native American women have also made significant gains in elective leadership of tribal governments.) In 1990, African American women represented 22 percent of the nation's Black mayors. In that same year, women constituted 16 percent of the mayors of the 100 largest U.S. cities.

The picture for openly lesbian candidates is not nearly so positive. Although San Francisco has elected lesbians to its city council, and Roberta Achtenburg ran for mayor in 1995, few out lesbians have been elected to local office elsewhere in the United States.

Public acceptance of women governors has not fared much better. Through the 1960s public opinion polls revealed that a majority of Americans objected to the idea of a woman mayor or governor. Not surprisingly, few women have been elected to head state governments. Since Nellie Tayloe Ross was elected in 1925 to replace her deceased husband, only thirteen women have served as governors. In 1994 thirty-four women sought their political party's nomination for governor; ten won those primaries but none won the general election. Consequently, in 1995, Christine Todd Whitman of New Jersey, elected in 1993, was the country's sole woman governor.

Although national-level polls reveal that nearly 20 percent of the electorate would not vote for a woman for president, the public appears to be more accepting of women in the U.S. Congress. Since Jeannette Rankin became the first woman to serve in the U.S. House of Representatives in 1917, few women were elected until 1992. Throughout the 1970s the proportion of women in the House never reached more than 5 percent. By 1990 that proportion rose to only 6 percent. In the 1992 election, however, women were elected in record numbers. The proportion of women elected to the House jumped to 11 percent, where it remained after the 1994 elections. As of 1995, the women in the House included thirteen women of color: nine African Americans, three Latinas, and one Asian American.

The presence of women in the House clearly illustrates the importance of prior local and state elective office holding. Elective experience was extremely important for the eight women who served in the U.S. Senate as of 1995. Paralleling women's success in House elections in 1992, women's ranks in the Senate also increased dramatically. From 1991 to 1997 the number of women in the Senate doubled. Although only twenty-five women have served in the U.S. Senate throughout history, nine are in the 105th Senate, including Carol Moseley-Braun (D., Ill.), the first African American woman senator. Two states, California and Maine, are represented by two women in the Senate.

Today many commentators believe that being a woman is no longer as negative as it once was in the public's eye. The public's perception that women are more honest in an era of continued public scandals and general distrust of government makes women more appealing to many voters and just as likely to win when they actually run for office. Many women continue to face the problems of reconciling marriage, family, and a career in electoral politics, especially at the national level. Women's skills are increasingly valued as the country turns from international to domestic priorities. Studies show that most Americans see women in public office doing "a better job than men" in a wide range of domestic affairs including dealing with the poor, education, health care, homelessness, aging, and the environment.

R. Darcy, Susan Welch, and Janet Clark, *Women, Elections, and Representation* 2d ed. (University of Nebraska Press, 1994); Nancy E. McGlen and Karen O'Connor, *Women, Politics, and American Society* (Englewood Cliffs, N.J.: Prentice Hall, 1995); Sue Thomas, *How Women Legislate* (New York: Oxford University Press, 1994).

▪ KAREN O'CONNOR
and BERNADETTE NYE

SEE ALSO Congress; Electoral Politics.

≋ Populism

During the presidential campaign of 1892, thousands of U.S. women worked to elect Populist presidential and vice-presidential candidates James Weaver of Iowa, and James Field of Virginia. Women worked for countless other local People's Party candidates even though they themselves could not vote in most states.

The Populist Party, comprised primarily of southern and midwestern white farmers who were members of the National Farmer's Alliance, began at a convention in Kansas in 1890. In 1892 the People's Party convention in Omaha nominated presidential and vice-presidential candidates and drafted a platform. Although the new party, the most successful third party since 1856, lost the 1892 presidential election, it nevertheless elected governors, other state officeholders, and sent members to Congress.

The party argued for agrarian reform; railed against the scarcity of western land, the gold standard, and the monopoly of the railroads; and espoused woman suffrage and temperance. At the party's Omaha convention, women who were voting delegates, caucused with like-minded politicians, argued about the party platform, and spoke from the podium. Kansan Mary Elizabeth Lease, a favorite and controversial Populist orator and founder of the party, gave the seconding speech nominating Weaver. Other women performed valuable political work and earned modest incomes from lecture fees, editorial salaries, book royalties, and spoils jobs.

Ultimately, the national Populist conventions omitted suffrage and temperance from later platforms, arguing that women's issues were not expedient to winning elections. Despite their disappointment, most Populist women continued to support the party, believing that if the Populists could win, temperance and suffrage victories would soon follow.

▪ MARY JO WAGNER

≋ Pornography

Prior to the 1980s pornography generally referred to sexually explicit material. Obscenity is the legal definition of pornography that appeals to the prurient interest, offends, and lacks serious artistic, political, or scientific value. To date, the legal argument for limiting pornography is based on the notion that its degree of sexual explicitness is associated with harm. Research indicates that it is the violence toward and degradation of women in some pornography, not sexual explicitness alone, that cause harmful effects. Such depictions of women are presented as sexually pleasurable; the problem, however, is that the mistreatment of women is classified and sold as *entertainment.* Sexual activity shown in pornography is not harmful per se.

The feminist movement of the mid-1970s redirected the focus of attention and research, asserting that pornography was one cause of violence against women. Robin Morgan stated, "Pornography is the theory, rape is the practice." Since then, feminists such as Diana E. H. Russell have redefined pornography as "material that combines sex and/or the exposure of genitals with abuse or degradation in a manner that appears to endorse, condone, or encourage such behavior." The literal definition of pornography is taken from the ancient Greek *porne,* meaning female sexual slaves, and *graphos,* meaning writings or graphic depictions thereof. In 1984 feminist legal scholar Catharine A. MacKinnon and author Andrea Dworkin suggested a legal definition of pornography as the graphic, sexually explicit subordination of women through pictures and/or words that includes women dehumanized, objectified, enjoying pain, humiliation, or rape in a context that makes these conditions sexual. This definition of pornography as the systematic practice of sexual exploitation that violates women's civil rights by undermining women's equality formed the basis of the 1983 model antipornography ordinance in Minneapolis.

Social science research has examined in laboratory experiments the content of pornography and its effects on men. Content analyses of pornography conducted by Gloria Cowan between 1976 and 1985 demonstrated increases in violent, degrading, and racist representations of women. Neil Malamuth's research found that exposure to eroticized rape scenarios increased males' self-reported likelihood of rape, rape fantasies in male college students, and males' acceptance of rape myths and violence against women. Men's exposure to degrading pornography, studied by Dolf Zillman and Jennings Bryant, was found to increase sexual callousness toward women, decrease support for the women's movement, and decrease recommended jail sentences for rapists. Based on these findings, Russell developed a model of pornography as a cause of rape, in which exposure to pornography 1) predisposes men to rape through conditioning of their sexual arousal to rape, 2) undermines men's internal inhibitions and social inhibitions against acting out rape desires, and 3) undermines potential victims' abilities to avoid or resist rape or sexual abuse. Even nonviolent degrading pornography was found to increase rape-supportive attitudes in some studies. In 1989 James Check identified two types of pornography: violent pornography and degrading/dehumanizing (nonviolent) pornography. In contrast, erotica (based on the root word *eros,* meaning sexual love) depicts mutual, egalitarian, consensual sexual interactions.

Until the mid-1980s little research on the effects of pornography on women had been conducted. In response to standard, nonviolent pornography, women had increased levels of anxiety, feelings of disgust, and numbing, according to Donald Mosher and Irene Greenberg. Wendy Stock found in 1990 and 1992 that women were distressed, depressed, hostile, and confused in response to pornography. Charlene Senn in 1985 found that women who viewed both violent and nonviolent/degrading pornography became more anxious, hostile, and confused. Scientific research has detected no negative effects of erotica.

Feminist researchers also have raised concerns about how pornography affects women. In 1980 Russell found that 10 percent of 930 women reported that they had been upset by someone trying to get them to enact behaviors depicted in pornography. Similar response rates have been found among female university students. Of 6,100 women respondents to a 1986 *Woman's Day* magazine survey, 21 percent said they had been sexually abused as a direct result of their attacker's access to pornographic materials. Much legal testimony and autobiographical documentation exists indicating that many women are underage, coerced, abused, raped, and tortured in the process of making pornography.

Although research has accumulated in support of the feminist theory that pornography causes harm to women, a division known as the "feminist sex wars" has developed over the quality of evidence of harm and what action to take regarding pornography. Antipornography feminists have defined pornography as a form of hate speech. They advocate for awareness about the effects of pornography, boycotts, and feminist civil rights–based legislation, and have organized groups such as Women Against Pornography, Organizing Against Pornography, Media Action Alliance, and Action Watch. Self-proclaimed "pro-sex feminists" have formed the Feminist Anti-Censorship Task Force (FACT), advocating for unrestricted freedom of speech and the right of women to develop as sexual beings, including participating in and consuming pornography.

This ongoing debate may be placed within the larger social context of hate speech and freedom of expression. Some argue that when speech causes harm to any group of individuals, then limitation of such expression is necessary. Others fear that any limitations of freedom of speech are more harmful than the speech itself. Hate speech likely will continue to be a much-debated topic as U.S. society struggles toward balancing the right to equality with freedom of expression.

Gloria Cowan et al., "Dominance and Inequality in X-rated Videocassettes," *Psychology of Women Quarterly* Vol. 12 (1988): 299–311; Andrea Dworkin, *Pornography: Men Possessing Women* (New York: Perigee Books, 1979); Diana E. H. Russell, "Pornography and Violence: What Does the New Research Say?" in *Take Back the Night: Women on Pornography*, edited by Laura Lederer, 218–38 (New York: William Morrow, 1980).

• WENDY STOCK

SEE ALSO Antipornography Activism; Censorship.

≋ Poverty

Poverty has long been a women's issue. In the 1990s, two out of three poor adults are women; one in three female-headed families live below the poverty line; one in two poor families is headed by a woman. Most explanations of poverty, limited by sexism and ignoring the significance of women's traditional role in the home, ignore women's plight or blame poverty on women themselves. Feminist theories, however, link female poverty, powerlessness, and oppression to the gender division of labor and women's economic dependence on marriage, markets, and the state. The poverty of women cannot be separated from the wider context in which women live: the capitalist system of production in which profits depend heavily on the availability of cheap labor; patriarchal power relations in the home and on the job; and racism that leaves women of color particularly vulnerable to the adverse effects of class, gender, and racial discrimination.

Marriage is often promoted as an antipoverty strategy for women, but it is not an effective one. Access to male income through marriage historically has sheltered many women—especially those who are white and middle class—against privation. But many women do not marry and others are divorced or abandoned. As a result of a declining standard of living as well as changes in marriage patterns, tying the knot today shields fewer and fewer women from poverty. Regardless of its other benefits, marriage has a downside: women's economic dependence on men underpins their subordination at home and on the job.

Today's falling standard of living weakens marriage as a poverty buffer for women by lowering a male breadwinner's wage. From 1945 to 1970 family income adjusted for inflation rose about 4 percent a year. Since the mid-1970s, international competition, the loss of high-paying manufacturing jobs to low-paying service jobs, and an economic recovery plan based on cheapening the cost of labor has dramatically reduced the average paycheck. By 1990, while corporate profits soared, 18 percent of fully employed workers earned too little to keep a family of four out of poverty (up from 12 percent in 1979). Many more two-parent families would have faced impoverishment if three out of four married mothers had not gone to work and increased family income by 30 to 40 percent. So much for a return to the traditional one-earner nuclear family called for by the New Right!

In a sagging economy, marriage shelters fewer women from poverty. But for those who lost or never gained access to male income, indigence is a constant threat. Elderly women who outlive male partners are at high risk of penury. Twenty-seven percent of all women over age sixty-five living on their own (but only 17 percent of the men) suffer too little income because of widowhood, women's low wages, inadequate pensions, and lack of government support. Reflecting their larger numbers, poor elderly women outnumber their male counterparts five to one.

Single mothers also lose out. Single motherhood is on the rise among women of all classes and races due to higher divorce rates, increased violence against women, and the overall trend toward fewer and later marriages: in the 1990s, one in six women is a single mother. Marriage to avoid destitution is also less available to more women of color who, if they seek to marry men of their own race, often face a shrinking pool of potential partners. Racism and the imperatives of capitalist production have left too many men of color poor, jobless, dead, or in jail. In 1992 an astounding 46 percent of mother-only families with children under eighteen lived in poverty compared to only 8 percent of husband-and-wife families with children. Family poverty appears to increase with a woman's "distance" from male income: In that same year, 29 percent of persons living in households where the female head was widowed were poor compared to 35 percent in those where she was divorced, 55 percent in those where she was separated, and 62 percent in those where she was never married. Race also makes a difference. Poverty devastates 38 percent of white, 56 percent of Black, and 58 percent of Hispanic female-headed families every day.

Single motherhood would be less devastating economically if society did not stigmatize mother-only families; if the labor market and the welfare state came through for women; and if more non-custodial fathers supported their children. In 1989 40 percent of absent fathers paid no child support at all, while only 25 percent of the custodial mothers received the full court-ordered award. Middle-class and previously married women fared better than the rest because poor women tend to pair with poor men, but even they did not do well. At fifty-seven dollars a week, the average child support payment fell below three thousand dollars a year. If the gender division of labor did not assign women near exclusive responsibility for children or if men, markets, or the state did not leave single mothers to bear the emotional and economic costs of child rearing alone, far fewer single mothers would be destitute.

Another reason for questioning marriage as an antipoverty strategy is that it limits women's choices and autonomy. Marriage promotes the economic dependence of women on men that keeps women at home, where they serve society by bearing and raising children, maintaining the family, and ensuring employers a healthy and fit labor force. The need for women's unpaid domestic work restricts their chances in the job market, opens the door to male violence, and otherwise reinforces the subordination of women to men. Locking women into unpaid labor in the home has reinforced the unequal treatment of women in the workplace. The latter is justified by the argument that women's real place is in the home. The economic inequality derived from sex discrimination in the labor market encourages women to turn to marriage or the state for support. This arrangement is upheld by defining non-marriage, homosexuality, and single motherhood as "deviant" behavior, thereby penalizing women's autonomy and self-determination.

The labor market also fails to protect women from poverty. Women over age 25 averaged 72 percent of the wages paid to men in the early 1990s, up from 60 percent in 1979. But the improvement reflects falling male wages more than female gains. Women, especially women of color, also endure especially high unemployment rates. Some 5 percent of white, 9 percent of Black, and 10 percent of Hispanic women over age 20 sought but could not find work in 1994. Nine percent of single mothers faced joblessness compared with only 4.6 percent of wives living with their husbands — a fact to be considered by welfare reformers eager to force single women on welfare to work outside the home.

Education helps women out of poverty, but their earnings are still not equal to those of men. In 1990 a woman with eight or fewer years of schooling earned an average of $13,222 a year compared with $19,188 for a similarly educated man (whose earnings also exceeded those of a woman with a high school diploma: $18,954). A male high school graduate secured the same salary as a woman with a college degree. Young women with limited education have an especially hard time. Their average wage ranges from five dollars an hour for younger high school drop-outs to eight dollars an hour for older women with high school diplomas. Between 1979 and 1989, these already low wages plummeted 20 percent and continue to fall, which explains the need for and importance of adequate welfare benefits.

Women's market-induced poverty reflects not only the demand for cheap female labor but also the male-dominated job hierarchies that "gender" the labor market. These forces crowd large numbers of women into a small number of sex- and race-segregated jobs whose tasks parallel women's work at home. Professional and managerial women face reduced occupational segregation. But in 1991 women still represented over 90 percent of the workers in the occupations in which they were heavily clustered ten years ago. Located in the secondary labor market, most of these dead-end but expanding "women's" jobs create high profits for business but leave women with low wages, few fringe benefits, and little or no union protection.

Women are also disadvantaged because they are assigned near-exclusive responsibility for family matters. Despite the mounting rhetoric about "family values," caretaking does not "play well" on the job. First, caretaking keeps women from paid work. In 1992 27 percent of married mothers did not work and only 37 percent of those who did worked full-time, year-round. Second, child care is in short supply. In one of the few detailed studies on this topic, the Bureau of Labor Statistics (BLS) reported that in 1986 child-care problems kept about 1.1 million young mothers ages twenty-one to twenty-nine from working, especially poor, single, women of color, and less educated women. This pattern still prevails. Child-care costs also cut into women's disposable income. The Institute for Women's Policy Research found that after paying child-care costs for one child, 45 percent of all women working full-time all year earned too little to bring a three-person family out of poverty. Since many low-paid jobs lack health coverage women often turn to government programs for medical care. Finally, many working mothers withstand the burdens of balancing work and family responsibilities, or what sociologist Arlie Hochschild calls "second shift." If the double-day fatigues middle-class married women and places them on the "mommy track," it exhausts single mothers and dumps them into poverty's "bottomless pit." Perhaps this is why half of all poor single women apply for welfare. Their plight represents the worst case of the caretaking crisis faced by *all* women.

Although the state is a major source of income for women, its gendered programs reinforce the traditional nuclear family, uphold women's economic dependence on men, and bolster patriarchal work and family patterns that keep women poor. Social security, unemployment insurance, Aid to Families with Dependent Children, and most other public income-support programs reinforce the traditional male as breadwinner/female as homemaker family unit by defining women as "deserving" or "undeserving" of aid based on their compliance with prescribed wife and mother roles. Married women and previously married women whose lack of a male breadwinner is perceived to be through no fault of their own, such as widows, or wives of sick, disabled, or temporarily unemployed men, are treated far better than single mothers, abandoned wives, and women whose breadwinners do not provide adequate support.

This invidious distinction that rewards marriage and penalizes single mothers enables more white, married, and middle-class women to qualify for the most generous social insurance benefits than poor women, single mothers, and women of color, who are consigned to the deeply stigmatized public assistance program. Meager benefits, bureaucratic harassment, and forced work punish women for departing from assigned gender roles. The monthly AFDC stipend averaged $377 in 1994. As a result of inflation, cutbacks, and the failure to raise benefits since 1975, its real value dropped 37 percent nationwide. In no state does the combination of AFDC and food stamps lift a family of three out of poverty.

Social insurance programs also keep women poor because their benefits—based on wage level and length of employment—reflect male work patterns and thus discriminate against women. Women's lower wages, interrupted work histories, and part-time jobs result in lower social security benefits. The social security pension lifts some people over the poverty line, but not if the benefits are the retiree's or survivor's sole source of income. Women's employment patterns, based on gender division of labor, also disadvantage them in the unemployment insurance system.

Welfare reform legislation promises to make things worse. The 1996 Personal Responsibility Act included two key changes. 1) Time limits would force women on AFDC to work by restricting the number of years during which they can receive aid despite high unemployment, lack of child care, and the fact that 70 percent of AFDC recipients leave the rolls within two years without coercion. 2) Block grants would strip AFDC of its entitlement status, which means less money for AFDC and the loss of federal protections for the poor.

The repeal of AFDC is but the leading edge of the coming attack on the entire welfare state. It meshes well with an economic recovery strategy based on redistributing income upwards, cheapening the cost of labor, and shifting the costs of caregiving from the state back to families. Meager as they are, cash benefits increase the economic leverage of women struggling against exploitation on the job and subordination (and in some cases violence) at home. By providing a floor under market wages and an alternative to marriage, social benefits have the potential to subvert the imperatives of capitalism and patriarchy. No wonder they are under attack!

Women's poverty reflects the failure of the labor market to provide jobs and adequate income for all those available for work; the subordination of women by marriage, markets, and the state; and the decision to promote economic recovery by distributing income from the have-nots to the haves. Better pay, child care, and health care, along with less family violence and higher cash benefits, would go a long way toward reducing poverty among women. For these reforms to make a lasting change, the gender division of labor that underlies women's oppression in all spheres of life must be transformed.

Mimi Abramovitz, *Regulating the Lives of Women: Social Welfare Policy from Colonial Times to the Present* (Boston: South End Press, 1992); Teresa Amott, *Caught in the Crisis: Women and the U.S. Economy Today* (New York: Monthly Review Press, 1993); Chris Tilly and Randy Albelda, *Glass Ceilings and Bottomless Pits: Women, Income and Poverty in Massachusetts* (monograph produced in 1994 for Women's Statewide Legislative Network, 37 Temple Place, Boston, MA 01222).

■ MIMI ABRAMOVITZ

SEE ALSO "Culture of Poverty"; Great Society/War on Poverty; Single Motherhood; Welfare and Public Relief; Welfare State.

≋ Pregnancy

In U.S. society pregnancy has had and continues to have very different meanings: a rite of passage to "adult woman" status; a normal and expected condition for much of a married woman's life; a sign of sin; a contraceptive failure; the successful outcome of infertility treatment; a medical condition requiring professional management; a diseaselike or "disabling" condition; a public-health drain and bid for increased welfare payments; a public service that produces workers and soldiers; a purchased service under so-called *surrogacy* contracts. In various times and places in U.S. history, pregnancy has been a sign of health, a sign of illness; a sign of purity, a sign of damnation.

Pregnancy in contemporary times is usually thought of as leading to the birth of a healthy child from a healthy mother—and that is indeed the typical outcome. But pregnancy also results in miscarriage, infant death, premature births, elective abortions, selective abortions to avoid the birth of a child with disabilities, premature births, sick newborns, adoptions, occasional maternal mortality, and not infrequent maternal illness— the last is especially notable as approximately one-fourth of U.S. births result in the major abdominal surgery that is the caesarean section. The chance of a given pregnancy leading to any one of these results depends primarily on the social situation of the pregnant woman: her class, race, ethnicity, education, occupation, age, and marital status. This is generally true worldwide, but particularly true in the United States, where women's access to all kinds of services, including medical and midwifery services and essential social services (including housing and food), varies enormously.

Because pregnancy outcomes in the United States are rather dismal in comparison with those in other developed countries, discussions of this subject have tended to group women into broad racial/ethnic categories, that is, "Hispanics" or "African Americans" or "Native Americans." Then, according to one approach, since poor pregnancy outcome is primarily a problem among women of color, it need not reflect poorly on the U.S. medical care system. In other words, since white, middle-class women fare well enough, the system "works," and the only problem is a woman's access to services. The situation, however, is more complex, and more medically based prenatal care is not the solution.

For example, since 1978 increasing numbers of states have been identifying "Hispanic" parents on birth certificates, making national data collection possible. About one in eight babies born in the United States is the child of an identified Hispanic woman. But generalizations are difficult: in 1988 teenage mothers accounted for 17 percent of all births among Mexican Americans, 21 percent among Puerto Ricans, but only 6 percent among Cuban Americans. Unfavorable pregnancy outcomes are more common because of greater poverty among Latinas compared with Anglo women. Looking specifically at low birth weight, a generally reliable indicator of poor maternal circumstances and a critically important measure of birth outcome, one expects and finds for most babies born to Latinas, high rates of low birth weight. Yet, Mexican American women, who often have high rates of poverty, limited education, high birthrates, and limited access to medical prenatal care, have birth weight outcomes that approximate that of white, non-Latina women. Smoking rates, attitudes toward weight gain, familial support, cultural meanings of pregnancy, and other factors, known and unknown, all contribute to outcome and cannot be generalized across groups.

More careful examination of the data shows how misleading racial categorization can be. Recent Jamaican immigrants are quite differently situated than are the descendants of African American slaves; Navaho are not Cree; and Hmong American women and Japanese American women do not face the same life circumstances any more than Mexican American women are interchangeable with Cuban or Puerto Rican women.

One accurate generalization is that the more resources a group of women has available, the better the expected pregnancy outcomes. The more stresses women face, the higher their chances of unfavorable outcomes. Resources include financial position, education, social support, and good general health. Stresses include not only poverty but also domestic violence, substance and alcohol abuse, extreme youth or age, and ill health, some of which are considered here:

One in fifteen pregnant women are physically or sexually assaulted by their partners during pregnancy, and battered women have twice as many miscarriages as pregnant women who are not bat-

tered. Data on the rates and consequences of battering have come not from providers of prenatal care services, where evidence of domestic violence has been systematically overlooked, but from workers who serve battered women. Research has shown clearly that pregnancy increases a woman's vulnerability to domestic violence.

Much has been discussed about alcohol use among pregnant women, culminating in the well-publicized warnings against using alcohol during pregnancy. The data, however, are complex. Even women who are alcoholic and drink to excess during pregnancy give birth to infants with fetal alcohol syndrome at rates ranging from a high of 40.5 percent to a low of 2.7 percent, depending on the population. This research strongly suggests the existence of other factors beyond the use of alcohol. In spite of all the concern, data does not show harmful effects of low-level alcohol use among healthy women. The epidemiology of fetal alcohol syndrome has tended historically to cluster along racial lines; for example, among certain Native American women living on government reservations and among poor, urban Black women. These findings point to poverty and class status as strong predictors for fetal alcohol syndrome in the offspring of alcoholic women. However, alcohol and drug abuse are also problems in the general population.

It is important to note that an effective argument can be made regarding alcohol and drug use by men, which is highly correlated with violence against women and poses a greater threat to fetal outcome than does alcohol and drug use by pregnant women.

Similar to the data on ethnicity or on drug and alcohol use, the data on early pregnancy are also complex. Much contemporary concern is currently being voiced about teenage pregnancy. The U.S. rate of adolescent pregnancy actually has stabilized in recent years, but the tendency for teenage mothers to remain single and keep their babies has increased substantially. That fact has generated a great deal of social furor. Poverty is linked with adolescent childbearing and its negative outcome: youth itself apparently is not the problem. Poor teenagers are two-and-one-half times more likely to become parents than are teenagers who are not poor. Poor teenagers may be sexually active at younger ages, particularly in urban, impoverished areas. Even more significantly, poor teenagers are less likely to use contraception than are other teenagers and more likely to carry pregnancies to term rather than to abort when compared with middle- and upper-income teenagers. Significantly, receiving public assistance does not appear to increase pregnancy rates—a study of thirty-six developed countries, for example, found that all had more generous welfare programs than did the United States, and all had lower rates of teenage pregnancies and births.

The decisions of unmarried women to become pregnant and/or to continue a pregnancy to term (and not place the child for adoption) has been the subject of much public debate, even in the popular media, as seen recently in former Vice President Dan Quayle's objections to the television character Murphy Brown becoming a single mother. Adult women who are not economically dependent on men have, in recent years, increasingly chosen motherhood. Some of these women are lesbians who have chosen donor (sometimes called "artificial") insemination, either with or without medical assistance. Others are unpartnered heterosexual women, some of whom have used self-insemination, some of whom have sought medical assistance and some of whom have chosen not to terminate "accidental" pregnancies.

Because most of the variation in pregnancy outcome is a result of social factors, medical services are of limited value. Medical prenatal care involves a series of "risking" evaluations, indicating the likelihood of pregnancy problems. Although some conditions can be medically diagnosed and managed with some success (for example, early detection of diabetes in pregnancy, or recognition of blood-clotting disorders), most cannot. Prenatal diagnostic testing, the focus of much contemporary prenatal care, can only inform the pregnant woman about the condition of her fetus; it cannot itself improve fetal outcome. The extraordinarily difficult decision the woman faces when given such information is whether to continue the pregnancy to term once a given fetal condition, such as Downs Syndrome or neural tube defects, is diagnosed. Here, too, the resources the woman has at hand in terms of family, economic, or community support may say as much as the medical condition of the fetus about the quality of its life should the pregnant woman choose to continue the pregnancy.

For all of these reasons, the women's health movement has focused greater attention on larger social concerns. Sheryl Ruzek, one of the major historians of the women's health movement, has pointed out that the movement has broadened its scope beyond the white, middle-class participants of its earliest days to focus more on the needs of women of color. The National Black Women's Health Project has over one hundred fifty self-help groups in twenty-five states. The groups address race and gender-specific aspects of infant mortality, teenage pregnancy, AIDS, and so on. The Native American Women's Health Education Center began as a community-based health project offering programs on fetal alcohol syndrome, diabetes, and other health issues; the project now helps women across the country and Canada. The National Latina Health Organization distributes information nationally about the reproductive health concerns of Latinas.

In sum, any understanding of the role of pregnancy in U.S. women's history must place it in the larger context of women's lives—in the social, political, economic, and familial circumstances in which we live and work.

Barbara Katz Rothman, ed., *Encyclopedia of Childbearing: Critical Perspectives* (Phoenix, Ariz.: Oryx Press, 1993).

• BARBARA KATZ ROTHMAN

SEE ALSO Childbirth; "Illegitimacy"/Single Pregnancy; Reproductive Technology; Surrogacy.

≋ Prisons

During the eighteenth century, the use of prisons spread in the United States and Europe as an alternative to physical punishment and hanging. These institutions were primarily custodial and were built for and around the needs of male prisoners. Women were housed in separate, smaller units within these prisons, and their specific needs were for the most part ignored.

Prior to the Civil War, the racial division of criminal prosecution was quite pronounced. Slaves were disciplined by their owners; only free Blacks were eligible for public punishment. In the Northeast and Midwest, African American women entered prison in grossly disproportionate numbers. Native American women, however, were considered members of enemy or colonized nations and were excluded from the United States criminal justice system. Small numbers of white women were incarcerated in jails and prisons.

"Reformatories" established by middle-class white women in the late nineteenth century were designed to provide separate facilities for women. Reformatories promoted the twin theories of innate sexual differences and the need for appropriately separate spheres for women prisoners. The reformatory movement was ultimately a widespread success and led to the establishment of separate women's institutions in twenty-three states by 1940.

The women's reformatories were run by white women and served primarily young, white, native-born women. Their theme was refuge and reformation, with an emphasis on domestic life and a concept of sisterhood among all women. However, the reformatories were a challenge to male control in two ways: they had removed women from the mixed institutions and they were run by

women. To meet challenges to their legitimacy, many wardens emphasized strict discipline similar to the male-dominated prison system.

Custody and confinement dominated approaches to both women's and men's incarceration in the twentieth century. Early in the century every state maintained at least one custodial unit for women, often located on the grounds of a men's medium or maximum security prison. They provided minimal education, training, recreation, visiting, health care, and maternal services for women. The populations of the custodial institutions also reflected existing class and race biases, with poor women and African Americans predominating.

Women's reformatories took on more wards during the 1930s and 1940s, which led to overcrowding and to an increase in the numbers of African American and foreign-born inmates. Overcrowding set the stage for a more custodial and disciplinary atmosphere, with less emphasis on education and job training. African American women were placed in racially segregated units in both women's prisons and mixed institutions until the 1960s.

The legacy of the reformatory movement has included the retention of women-only prisons and the maintenance of women's units within co-correctional facilities. The reformatory philosophy continues to affect the lives of female inmates. The goal of providing a domestic atmosphere has been retained in much correctional theory. In both reformatories and custodial settings, women tend to form more familial attachments.

In many single-sex institutions lesbian and other very close relationships are tolerated by authorities. Mixed institutions generally emphasize heterosexual behavior and are less tolerant of female-to-female bonding.

Currently about ten percent of jail inmates and five percent or less of state and federal prisoners are women. The majority of women prisoners are incarcerated for nonviolent property or economic crimes or for drug-related offenses. Those women who are serving time for crimes against persons are most likely to have been involved in domestic violence, particularly self-defense against a male partner. Women of color continue to be overrepresented in prisons. Approximately 70 percent of women in U.S. prisons are mothers of children under eighteen, and most are single parents.

During the 1970s and 1980s, the combined effects of the feminist and prison reform movements led to the reassertion of some of the principles of the reformatory movement, including the need for special health and maternity services for women. Visiting centers, in-prison maternity units (where children could stay with their mothers for weeks or months), and other parent-child services spread. Women obtained legal access to the educational and training programs available to men. Services were later curtailed or abandoned in the 1980s and early 1990s in the face of significant budget cuts, vastly increased prison populations, and a general rise in custodial and punitive philosophies of criminal justice.

The feminist movement also led to some deleterious changes in women's prison conditions. Just as female prison guards gained the right to work in male prisons, more male guards were assigned to women's institutions. In addition, women had usually served shorter sentences than men, but equalization in sentencing produced lengthier terms for women.

Near the end of the twentieth century, the conditions for women in prison remain bleak and include longer sentences, the reimposition of capital punishment, severe overcrowding, and the application of a basic custodial and punitive philosophy of management.

Karlene Faith, *Unruly Women: The Politics of Confinement and Resistance* (Vancouver: Press Gang Press, 1993); Estelle B. Freedman, *Their Sisters' Keepers: Women's Prison Reform in America, 1830–1930* (Ann Arbor: University of Michigan Press, 1978); Nancy Stoller Shaw and Judith Resnik, "Prisoners of Their Sex: Health Problems of Incarcerated Women," *Prisoners' Rights Sourcebook: The-ory, Litigation, and Practice* Vol. 2, edited by Ira Robbins (New York: Clark Boardman, Inc.: August 1980).

▪ NANCY E. STOLLER

≋ Privacy Rights

The due process clause of the Fourteenth Amendment prohibits a state from denying individuals liberty without due process of law. Throughout history the Supreme Court has interpreted the due process clause to protect certain basic liberties from state interference, for example, parents' rights to make choices about the education of their children.

In the early twentieth century, the Court read the due process clause broadly to strike down child labor laws and minimum wage and hour laws, in effect protecting the "liberty" of bosses to pay subminimum wages and the "liberty" of workers to work long hours. During the period when the Court used the concept of liberty to strike down laws protecting workers, the Court also allowed protective laws that applied only to women. *Muller* v. *Oregon* in 1908 relied on sex-stereotyped, paternalistic ideas about women to uphold a law fixing the maximum number of hours that a woman could be required to work. Women-only protective laws encouraged sex-segregated wage labor markets in which women were paid less than men and excluded from more desirable jobs. This chapter in our constitutional history ended during the New Deal era and is widely regarded as an unwise assertion of constitutional protection against democratic legislative choice. That history has made the Court cautious about giving broad meaning to the liberties protected by the Fourteenth Amendment.

In addition, the Ninth Amendment provides that "the enumeration in the Constitution, of certain rights, shall not be construed to deny or disparage others retained by the people." The idea behind this amendment is that historic rights, in addition to those specifically mentioned in the Constitution, deserve protection. The question of which rights are fundamental has always been controversial. Some judges look to rights that were historically recognized, such as the right to pursue a common occupation or to travel from place to place. Others would read the Ninth Amendment to protect a broader range of rights that are of central importance to individuals, such as reproductive freedom and choices about family formation.

In 1964 the right to privacy was expanded in *Griswold* v. *Connecticut,* in which the Court held that a state law prohibiting doctors from prescribing contraceptives to married people violated the right to privacy. For fifty years Connecticut women and physicians had sought without success to repeal the law. Ultimately, the law was enforced only against clinics that served low-income women.

In 1972 *Eisenstadt* v. *Baird* extended the privacy right to protect the freedom of single people to use contraceptives. The Court said, "The marital couple is not an independent entity with a mind and heart of its own, but an association of two individuals each with a separate intellectual and emotional makeup. If the right of privacy means anything, it is the right of the *individual,* married or single, to be free from unwarranted governmental intrusion into matters so fundamentally affecting a person as the decision whether to bear or beget a child." Most important for women, in *Roe* v. *Wade* (1973) the Supreme Court held that the right to privacy protects a woman's right to choose abortion.

These cases emerged as a product of vast changes in U.S. consciousness about reproduction and sexuality. Women who are wealthy and sophisticated have always been able to gain access to abortion and contraception, albeit in ways that were sometimes expensive, dangerous, and demeaning. Laws limiting access to reproductive services have always had the greatest impact on the poor, the young, and the vulnerable. Thus formal legal protection of rights of privacy is of even greater practical importance to women of color

because they are more likely to be disadvantaged.

These cases, particularly *Roe* v. *Wade,* produced a powerful backlash from the Catholic Church, fundamentalist Protestants, and others who believe that it is always wrong to break the link between sex and procreation and that unplanned motherhood is women's paramount destiny. Furthermore, the Reagan and Bush administrations appointed Supreme Court justices who were believed to be opposed to constitutional protection of reproductive choice.

Privacy rights shield individuals from state oppression, but they do not require the state to help people exercise those rights. The constitutional right to reproductive privacy does not require the state to pay for contraception or abortion, just as the right to free speech does not require the state to provide public halls and television time to all who wish to speak. The equal protection guarantee of the Fourteenth Amendment does require that the state make public services available on a nondiscriminatory basis. Nonetheless, in 1980 *Harris* v. *McRae* approved the federal Hyde Amendment excluding payment for medically necessary abortion from the otherwise comprehensive Medicaid program, which finances health care for the poor. In 1984, in a sharply divided 5-4 decision, the Court held in *Bowers* v. *Hardwick* that the right to privacy does not prohibit the state from prosecuting lesbians and gay men for having voluntary sexual relations. In 1992 the Court's *Casey* v. *Planned Parenthood of Southeastern Pennsylvania* decision formally reaffirmed *Roe* v. *Wade.* However, the Court articulated a new standard for evaluating state laws, which makes it more difficult for women to obtain an abortion. The Court approved biased counseling requirements, designed to discourage women from having abortions; waiting requirements; and parental notification rules for teenagers.

At this time, the constitutional right of privacy provides the strongest protection for the people who are best able to protect themselves in the legislative process, that is, heterosexual, married peo-

Pro-choice and antiabortion groups confront each other on the steps of the U.S. Capitol.

ple with income and resources. Constitutional protection has not yet been extended to the disenfranchised, who most need it—lesbians and gay men, the poor, and the young.

■ SYLVIA A. LAW

SEE ALSO Constitution and Amendments; Legal Status; *Roe* v. *Wade*.

≋ Pro-Choice and Antiabortion Movements

By the 1960s, almost one hundred years had passed since women had lost the right to legal abortion, and much had changed. Women had won the vote in 1920, and the development of antibiotics and the vacuum aspiration abortion technique made abortion medically safer. A landmark case, *Griswold* v. *Connecticut*, established for the first time that married couples had a right to use contraception—and it established a right to privacy that would set the stage for a test case to decriminalize abortion. Significantly, whereas abortion had not been a common topic of conversation, there was a growing public consciousness of the dangerous choices faced by women who wished to terminate a pregnancy. Before 1973, it has been estimated that as many as 1.2 million illegal abortions happened each year, with thousands of women dying or getting injured in the process.

National women's and pro-choice organizations began forming in the late 1960s. The Alan Guttmacher Institute was formed to provide accurate statistics, research, and public policy information to activists and legislators across the country; Planned Parenthood Federation of America took a public stand supporting abortion rights in 1969, adding its network of birth-control clinics and advocates to the grassroots efforts; and the National Association for the Repeal of Abortion Laws (NARAL) was formed in 1969 to be an information clearinghouse for grassroots groups advocating the reform of state abortion laws.

Leading the opposition was the Catholic Church, which has largely been credited with running and/or bankrolling the early development of the anti-choice movement's political organizations, including the National Right to Life Committee. Other women-led organizations emerged, including Phyllis Schlafly's anti-feminist Eagle Forum, which focused on electoral politics and advocacy, and Feminists for Life, a "pro-woman, pro-life" educational organization.

Meanwhile, lawyers across the country searched for the right test cases to challenge abortion laws in their states. In Texas, two young female lawyers filed one such case on March 3, 1970. That case, *Roe v. Wade*, was decided on January 22, 1973. The immediate effect of *Roe* was far-reaching: Abortion laws in forty-nine states and the District of Columbia were declared invalid, and the back-alley, illegal locations for abortion were replaced by a national network of clinics and hospitals providing safe, affordable, and accessible abortion. Within thirty days of the *Roe* decision, conservatives came together and established goals to take away the right to choose: 1) elect an anti-choice president, 2) stack the Supreme Court with anti-choice justices, and 3) pass a Human Life Amendment banning abortion.

The Catholic Church called for massive civil disobedience (launching its own thirteen-page *Pastoral Plan for Pro-Life Activities* in 1975, a political agenda by another name). Energized anti-choice forces created new organizations to forge the way. The National Right to Life Committee spun off of the National Conference of Catholic Bishops and became a significant nationwide political operation; the Christian Action Council was founded to create anti-choice educational materials and films; Concerned Women for America was formed to serve as a conservative alternative to the National Organization for Women; and the American Life League was started to fight for passage of the Human Life Amendment.

The conservative New Right movement, which opposed a range of social issues, identified abortion as the key to mobilizing its support and resources. Paul Weyrich, founder of the Heritage Foundation and the Committee for the Survival of a Free Congress, was the first leader to make opposition to abortion a litmus test for candidates. Richard Viguerie, the fund-raising and direct-mail pioneer, used the abortion issue to raise millions of dollars for conservative efforts. Kevin Phillips, who founded the Conservative Caucus, mobilized the conservative grassroots.

As abortion became a political issue, the National Right to Life Committee pioneered the use of fliers and ads featuring aborted fetuses. In one of the early candidate's uses of this tactic, 1974 Kansas Senate candidate Bob Dole gave the NRLC permission to distribute fliers depicting aborted fetuses in garbage cans and equating abortion with euthanasia by showing skulls and crossbones.

Abortion was a prominent presidential issue for the first time in 1976, when candidates were asked whether they would support a constitutional ban on abortion and the Republican Party passed a plank advocating banning abortion.

The 1980 elections were a tour de force for the anti-choice and New Right movements. Ronald Reagan was elected president. Vice President George Bush earned his spot on the ticket by switching to an anti-choice position. Republicans took control of the Senate with anti-choice ideologues. With only 52.4 percent of all eligible voters voting, roughly 25 percent of the country gave the New Right a "mandate."

Shortly after *Roe v. Wade*, anti-choice forces pushed for Congress to pass constitutional amendments that would overturn the decision. Over the next decade, variations of the Human Life Amendment, declaring the fetus a person at conception (and giving fetuses, but not women, equal protection under the Fourteenth Amendment), were introduced and rejected. The anti-choice movement worked to restrict as many abortions as possible and succeeded in eliminating federal financing of the vast majority of abortions, affecting poor women; government employees; and women in the military, the Peace Corps, and in the District of Columbia. State referenda to ban Medicaid funding for abortions passed in Colorado and Michigan. Domestic and international family planning were assailed, research denied, and importation of the early abortion drug RU-486 (mifepristone) banned through a series of executive and legislative measures.

State legislation was pushed to create barriers to abortion and to launch court challenges, including restricting state funding, parental and spousal notification and consent laws, waiting periods, and so-called "informed consent" laws.

In the early and mid-1970s, anti-choice activists adopted tactics of "sidewalk counseling," that is, picketing and prayer at abortion clinics. By 1977, activists directly disrupted services and intimidated providers. In addition, their tactics included stalking clinic workers, bombing and arson attacks, blockades, picketing at clinic workers' homes, tracking and identifying clinic patients, making death threats, and even kidnapping. Joe Scheidler's Pro-Life Action League led the way with his book *Closed: 99 Ways to Stop Abortion*. Later, he was joined by the violent direct-action groups, the Army of God and Operation Rescue.

In 1990, there were 100 violent attacks on clinics. By 1992, that number had risen to nearly 700, and the war on clinics escalated to include shootings, chemical bombs, and acid attacks.

"Wanted" signs advertising the names, addresses, and phone numbers of abortion providers—a virtual death warrant for physicians—were distributed throughout the United States. Drs. David Gunn and John Britton, two physicians featured on these signs, were murdered in Florida, as were clinic escort James Barrett and two clinic workers in Massachusetts, Leeann Nichols and Shannon Lowney. The Army of God published and distributed step-by-step instructions on how to assault clinics with bombs, chemical agents, and other violent means.

At a time when 84 percent of the counties in the United States did not have abortion providers, insurance rates for clinics skyrocketed, and they were forced to spend thousands of dollars hiring armed guards, constructing fences, installing video surveillance equipment, and purchasing bulletproof vests.

From 1973 on, pro-choice forces worked to deliver abortion and contraception services, pushed for federal funding of family planning, and fought the onslaught of anti-choice initiatives. Many new groups formed as the community previously scattered throughout fifty different states developed a national legislative, legal, and political base. Important new organizations included the Religious Coalition for Abortion Rights, Catholics for a Free Choice, Reproductive Freedom Project, and Voters for Choice.

In April 1989, the pro-choice majority marched on Washington. Between 500,000 and one million supporters filled the Mall in protest of anticipated cutbacks on the right to choose. In Congress, pro-choice lawmakers attempted to deny the courts and state legislatures the ability to whittle away reproductive rights by codifying the principles of *Roe*. These efforts failed, but Congress did pass laws protecting clinics and patients. Still, the Supreme Court continued to uphold anti-choice restrictions affecting abortion counseling as well as access to abortions for young women and poor women.

The Supreme Court was poised to overturn *Roe* by the early 1990s, and anti-choice and pro-choice forces battled to elect lawmakers—from the White House to all fifty states—who pledged their support to their respective sides.

Polling, media, phone-bank, and voter outreach campaigns required substantial resources, and donors on both sides opened their wallets to help put the abortion issue front and center. In every state, candidates' media campaigns and persuasion mail included abortion positions, and organizations rallied to identify their supporters and deliver them to the polls. Anti-choice tacticians added to their arsenals fetus ads, misleading fliers, and push polls—contacting voters as "survey research organizations" and spreading lies and innuendo impugning the character and positions of pro-choice candidates.

A reinvigorated Religious Right—a collection of conservative national, state, and local fundamentalist churches, radio ministers, and televangelists—expanded its reach. The Christian Coalition, launched by Christian Broadcasting Network founder and 700 *Club* host Pat Robertson, was built out of the ashes of his 1988 presidential campaign. With millions of identified activists, 134,000 donors, a seed grant of $67,000 from the Republican National Committee, and the direction of Ralph Reed, a young Republican activist and organizer, the preeminent political organization in the Religious Right gained a foothold.

While pro-choice organizations focused on Congress, state legislative, and gubernatorial elections, the Christian Coalition focused its initial activities on school board and county commission elections. Increasing its membership through a network of conservative churches, the Coalition distributed voter guides and backed candidates running "Stealth Campaigns," in which candidates espoused "moderate" political leanings, did not reveal any affiliation with the Religious Right, showed no signs of major contributions from right-wing organizations, and did not have a record in campaigns or in elected office that could invite criticism. These candidates had church-based field operations and the ability to raise money late in the campaign.

In 1992, the Supreme Court declined to overturn *Roe*. That same summer, the Religious Right gripped the public's consciousness during the Republican National Convention. With one-third to two-fifths of the delegates identified with the Religious Right, rhetoric calling for the imposition of conservative Christian morality and vows to ban abortion dominated the party platform and convention speeches.

An anxious pro-choice community mobilized and provided the winning margin to elect pro-choice President Bill Clinton, the first president in U.S. history proudly and publicly to endorse freedom of choice for all women. Within days of taking office, and with the stroke of a pen, President Clinton eliminated a host of anti-choice policies, including: rules "gagging" health workers in federally supported domestic and international family planning programs from discussing abortion; a ban on fetal tissue research—research with potential for developing treatments for diseases like Parkinson's syndrome; and a ban against importation of RU-486. He also improved prospects for choice by appointing two pro-choice justices to the Supreme Court, Ruth Bader Ginsburg in 1993, and Stephen Breyer in 1994.

At the same time, the Christian Coalition diligently continued to build its national operations. By 1994, and with the help of a complacent pro-choice majority that didn't believe the right to choose was in danger, the Christian Coalition played a major role in helping conservative Republicans take the House and Senate by distributing seventeen million Congressional Scorecards, placing three million get-out-the-vote phone calls, and distributing thirty-four million voter guides through a national network of conservative churches.

The 1994 elections were a disaster for the pro-choice movement and led to a conservative drive to roll back the right to choose, leaving it far more limited than most Americans know. Congress limited medical training, access for poor women, access for women in the military, forbade discussion of abortion on the Internet, and came within twenty votes of eliminating the national family planning and contraception program. Anti-choice leaders in Congress announced their intention to eliminate abortions procedure by procedure. They grossly distorted the facts involving a rarely used late-trimester procedure, and President Clinton vetoed their action to criminalize it.

The effort to outlaw late-term abortions was used prominently in the 1996 elections. Distortions of the procedure were used in ads, some including Catholic priests, in persuasion-mail fliers, and in candidate debates across the country. Despite these tactics, the Religious Right did not win the White House in 1996. Voters re-elected President Clinton, and more pro-choice representatives were elected to Congress.

                                        ▪ JULIE BURTON

SEE ALSO Abortion; National Abortion and Reproductive Rights Action League (NARAL); Voters for Choice.

≋ Progressive Era

Stretching from the 1890s to at least World War I, the Progressive Era was characterized by a profusion of public activism. Since the 1930s scholars have debated the scope and significance of the movements that flourished in this period. Some focused on the efforts of political parties and legislative bodies to rationalize government and regulate corporations, workplaces, the environment, and public morals. Others emphasized voluntary and collective activities by groups concerned as much with social justice as social control.

Many advocates for social justice also envisioned an activist state. Armed with professional expertise, social science data, and moral commitment, they campaigned for protective labor legislation, civil rights, social purity, and suffrage; they sought to outlaw lynching, alcohol, and prostitution; and they established kindergartens, settlement houses, public health associations, and missions to "heathens" at home and abroad. These Progressives sought to expand the meaning of citizenship and to establish institutions to educate and uplift the less fortunate.

Throughout this period, all women were denied the right to vote in all federal and most state elections. Nonetheless, many women were in the vanguard of social change. The prototypic woman Progressive is Jane Addams, founder of Hull House, a charter member of the National Association for the Advancement of Colored People, and a supporter of the Progressive Party. She campaigned for social welfare legislation, educational reform, suffrage, and world peace. Ida B. Wells-Barnett, who led the antilynching crusade, was not merely committed to progressive change, but as a Black woman militantly challenged white supremacy in all of its manifestations. Other leading Progressives include Frances Willard of the Woman's Christian Temperance Union; Josephine Goldmark of the National Consumers League; and Rose Schneiderman, of the Women's Trade Union League.

It was women at the grassroots level, however, who formed the real army of social activists. Many local efforts were directed by as well as at workers, African Americans, and immigrants. Eastern European Jewish women organized kosher meat boycotts in New York City; native-born workers' wives led union label campaigns in Seattle; African American women battled segregated facilities in Memphis and Washington, D.C.; evangelical Christians established missions to the Chinese in San Francisco and Mexicans in El Paso; immigrant women led strikes in Lawrence, Massachusetts, and Tampa, Florida; and middle-class white women established pure milk and public-health projects and campaigned for child labor legislation and prohibition.

The range and diversity of women's activism illuminates the complex relations among gender, class, race, region, ethnicity, and sexuality in this era. Affluent women Progressives, especially those who were also white, native-born, and from the North and West, typically focused on legal and judicial reform and the establishment of social welfare institutions. They often worked through all-female associations. Many national leaders remained single throughout their lives, preferring to depend on women for emotional and financial as well as political support. Some even embraced the newly available and controversial lesbian identity. Less affluent women activists, including wage earners and immigrants, were more likely to organize within their own communities, often alongside male relatives, coworkers, and neighbors. They formed permanent organizations, including unions, mutual aid societies, and day-care facilities, but they were just as likely to engage in spontaneous actions that meshed more easily with domestic obligations, such as food boycotts, rent strikes, and refusals to accept segregated seats on public transportation. African American women were central in efforts at community uplift and racial justice across the country, including in the Jim Crow south.

Women developed different definitions and visions of social progress and those differences led to conflict. Affluent, native-born women often ignored the cultural values and maternal needs of those they sought to uplift, and thus exacerbated rather than eradicated problems faced by their poorer "sisters." For poorer women, then, uplift often translated into intrusion, purity into coercion, and protection into domination. Child labor and compulsory education laws, for example, made it impossible for some families to survive economically. Moral purity crusades reinforced sexualized stereotypes of African American, Asian, and Appalachian women. Even woman's suffrage was often supported on the basis of racist, nativist, and elitist arguments that enhanced the power primarily of white, native-born, educated women.

These divisions multiplied the forms of women's activism and thereby expanded women's influence in the public sphere. Studies of the Progressive Era now make clear that women were as central to the social movements that ushered in the twentieth century as in those emerging at its close, and they were just as clearly divided in their visions of social order and social justice.

Noralee Frankel and Nancy Shromm Dye, eds., *Gender, Class, Race and Reform in the Progressive Era* (Lexington: University Press of Kentucky, 1991); Paula Giddings, *When and Where I Enter: The Impact of Black Women on Race and Sex in America* (New York: William Morrow, 1984); Nancy A. Hewitt and Suzanne Lebsock, eds., *Visible Women: New Essays on American Activism* (Urbana: University of Illinois Press, 1993).

■ NANCY A. HEWITT

SEE ALSO Mothers' Pensions; National Association of Colored Women; New Woman; Protective Labor Legislation; Settlement House Movement; Woman's Christian Temperance Union; Women's Trade Union League.

≋ Prohibition and Temperance

The movement to reduce or ban the consumption of alcohol is one of the largest and most enduring in U.S. history and has been one in which women have been consistently active. The Woman's Christian Temperance Union (WCTU), begun in the early 1870s as a series of women's "praying bands," quickly became thoroughly political. The WCTU was deeply dedicated to gaining the vote for women so that they could use it to defend cherished home and family values against the aggressions of "King Alcohol." Alcohol abuse was also associated with rising levels of domestic violence, of which women and their children were the victims. Frances Willard, the WCTU's second president and greatest leader, was one of the most well known and influential U.S. women in the late nineteenth century.

An early-nineteenth-century temperance flier shows the peacefulness and order of a home free of alcohol. The harmony surrounding the male figure reflects the emphasis that temperance activists placed on achieving family and community stability through the control of male behavior.

In the early twentieth century, the Anti-Saloon League, a male-led organization, redirected the temperance drive from state-level reform toward a constitutional amendment that would ban legal commerce in alcohol throughout the country. Because of the WCTU's long history, this "Prohibi-

tion Amendment" was closely associated with women's political power and became intertwined with the drive for the Woman's Suffrage Amendment. Prohibition was passed in 1919 as the Eighteenth Amendment. The Nineteenth Amendment for woman's suffrage was ratified the next year. By this time, the temperance ethic had become an artifact of a bygone Victorian generation. Almost immediately a movement developed to repeal the Prohibition amendment and, astonishingly, many women were involved. In 1933 the Twenty-first Amendment was passed to repeal Prohibition, the only constitutional action to be so undone.

■ ELLEN CAROL DuBOIS

SEE ALSO Alcoholism; Woman's Christian Temperance Union.

≋ Prostitution

Prostitution is the exchange of sex for money, a practice that for the most part involves men buying sex from women, boys, or girls. Patriarchy has mislabeled prostitution the "oldest profession" to suggest that it is an inevitable practice. In fact, it developed during historical periods that excluded women from public life. Women who were not confined by either slave labor or domestic labor in the home were assumed to be prostitutes and/or had no alternative means of survival. Prostitution persists in this form in underdeveloped countries today, where there are few possibilities for economic survival for women who labor in the informal domestic sector. With industrialization, sex industries transform local, indigenous prostitution into major commodity markets.

During U.S. industrialization in the nineteenth century, and in the late twentieth century in newly industrializing economies in the Third World, sex industries procure large numbers of rural girls and women for urban brothels, thus relieving the developing labor force from employing them. Men, enjoying the first advantages that come as a result of developing economies, turn part of their new incomes to buying prostitution. Although economic destitution is one factor in the proliferation of prostitution, only in the past decade has research revealed another major factor that contributes to the prostitution of women: childhood sexual abuse. Systematic sexual abuse can cause harm to one's identity and selfhood, convincing girls (and some boys) they have only a sexual value. Sometimes sexual trauma can result in the victim's developing a multiple personality disorder or other debilitating psychiatric problems, which often leaves them vulnerable to becoming prostitutes.

Customers (or "johns" or "tricks") are men from all walks of life, across cultures, who have the economic means to buy the services of prostitutes and search the market according to their interests, child or adult, homosexual or heterosexual, white or Black or Asian or Latino. They are the least known in the prostitution triangle of pimp, prostitute, and customer because they expect and require their identity to be kept secret as part of the prostitution exchange, which both intensifies their sexual desire and protects them from exposure.

It is estimated that over 90 percent of the prostitution industry is pimp controlled. Pimps acquire women and children for prostitution (procuring) and put them into prostitution (pandering). They generally live off the earnings of prostitution (pimping), taking all or most of the prostitute's money. Pimping includes individual operators, agencies, brothels or prostitution hotel operators, and pornographers.

Sexually transmitted diseases are one of the principal health consequences of prostitution. Female prostitutes, who often have multiple sex partners daily, are in the highest risk category for AIDS. Even in the face of the increased threat of death from AIDS, prostitution has massively increased globally. Some health agencies have encouraged the use of condoms among prostitutes, but condoms are not totally effective to protect against AIDS. Because many customers refuse to use condoms despite the prostitute's insistence, they often pay the prostitute more money as a form of "compensation." Fear of AIDS has also caused men to seek younger, more "virginal" girls for sex.

Drug abuse is another common consequence of prostitution. Women often report needing something to numb their feelings to get through many anonymous sexual contacts daily. Pimps frequently traffic in drugs as well as prostitutes and pacify the prostitutes with the drugs. However, the notion that all prostitutes are completely strung out on drugs is false. Usually addictions are sufficient to help them distance themselves emotionally from the sex exchange and the customer, but such drug effects do not prevent them from providing prostitution altogether.

Prostitution laws in the United States, as elsewhere in the world, reflect the sexual double standard of misogyny, which honors women as wives and condemns them as whores, making sure that the market always supplies men with prostitutes. Whether state laws prohibit prostitution, making prostitutes criminals (as they do in most of the United States), or they legalize it, thus making them functionaries of the state, or they decriminalize it, female prostitutes are the ones who are arrested, fined, and imprisoned for *street* prostitution. Thus, these women are expected to be available as commodities but are punished for being visible. Rarely are customers or pimps punished.

In response to this legal double standard, some women in prostitution have organized. Either not seeing any way to get out of prostitution or not wanting to, they are demanding better treatment under the law and from society. Other women who have left prostitution have formed programs such as WHISPER, Women Held in Systems of Prostitution Engaged in Revolt, to help women get out. They consider prostitution a sexual exploitation that harms women's health and identity, and they have developed self-help approaches, including shelters, health services, counseling, and job training programs. A small group of women in prostitution and other parts of the sex industry have organized to promote prostitution as a right over one's own body, a viable form of work for women, and a legitimate mode of sexual expression. They created the International Whore's Congresses in the Netherlands, where they have also influenced legislative changes to reflect a pro-prostitution policy, and sex workers' groups in the United States.

Their organizing has captured media attention and researchers and many agencies take them to be representative of all women in prostitution. As a result, these women become a powerful pro-prostitution lobby. Their claim that prostitution is a woman's right, a profession, and a form of sexual freedom has reintroduced a nineteenth-century debate about "forced" versus "free" prostitution. They oppose trafficking in women as a way of demonstrating that when prostitution is not forced by traffickers, it is freely chosen. This position removes prostitution from the context of women's economic subordination and detaches it from the context of sexual exploitation in society. In opposition, human rights groups and feminists, including former prostitutes, have called for new international standards of human rights that would protect women from sexual exploitation, rape, prostitution, and pornography via a proposed United Nations Convention Against Sexual Exploitation.

• KATHLEEN BARRY

SEE ALSO Sexual Slavery.

≋ Protective Labor Legislation

For the past century the issue of sex-specific protective labor legislation has divided proponents of women's emancipation and generated debates that have shaped the meaning of feminism, equality, rights, and public welfare. The laws have varied from state to state and over time. But all have designated women a distinct legal class, adopting the notion of fundamental sex difference as their premise. Historically the legislation has derived from the theory that women's unique capacity to be mothers renders them unequal to men in the work force and therefore specially entitled to legal protection. Protective legislation throws into relief the dilemma of equality and difference that has haunted the feminist movement since its advent.

Working women's quest for labor legislation dates from the 1840s, when Massachusetts textile workers unsuccessfully petitioned the state for a ten-hour work day. Over the next few decades, a handful of states imposed such rules. Some of the early laws used gender-neutral language. But the dominant trend was for legislatures to regulate only the hours, wages, and working conditions of women and children.

This trend peaked in the Progressive Era, chiefly as a result of the efforts of female reformers in the Women's Trade Union League (WTUL) and the National Consumers' League (NCL). Founded in 1903, the WTUL aimed to promote female union membership and to educate the public about the needs of women workers. The NCL, created in 1899, sought to organize consumer protest against unsafe and oppressive conditions of labor. Contemporary investigations showed that such work conditions fell hardest on women—especially immigrant women—who were segregated in unskilled, poorly paid jobs and much less likely to belong to trade unions than were men. Cooperating across lines of class and ethnicity, wage-earning women and female reformers lobbied legislatures and provided crucial support when protective laws were challenged in court. As the union leader Pauline Newman declared, in the absence of protection, women "were 'free' and 'equal' to work long hours for starvation wages."

The paradoxical proposition that women could gain genuine equality only through special legal protection was most fully developed by Florence Kelley, the NCL's leader and author of an Illinois statute. Kelley denounced "the cry 'Equality, Equality,' where Nature has created Inequality." Focusing on women's needs as mothers, emphasizing their frailty and dependence, she argued that innate difference justified sex-based legislation.

In the landmark 1908 case *Muller* v. *Oregon*, the U.S. Supreme Court affirmed the constitutionality of a ten-hour working day law for female workers. Carving out a gender-based exception to its 1905 holding in *Lochner* v. *New York* (which struck down an hours law covering male workers as an unconstitutional interference with individual rights of contract), the Court set its imprimatur on the notion that a "woman's physical structure" and public interest in her "maternal functions" justified protection. No less noteworthy in *Muller* was the legal brief defending the Oregon law that was jointly written by Josephine Goldmark, of the NCL, and her brother-in-law, Louis Brandeis, soon to be appointed to the Supreme Court. Introducing a new sociological jurisprudence, the famous "Brandeis Brief" presented only two pages of abstract legal reasoning, but over one hundred pages of excerpts from so-cial-scientific studies documenting the perils of overwork for women's "special physical organization." Buoyed by *Muller*, the NCL led the campaign for an extended web of sex-based labor laws. By 1925 all but four states limited women's work day, sixteen states banned female night work in certain jobs, and thirteen states fixed minimum wages for women.

If arguments for protection on grounds of sex difference held sway with lawmakers, by the 1920s they clashed with the agenda of the National Woman's Party, which championed an Equal Rights Amendment. This wing of the women's movement eschewed maternalist rhetoric, insisting that special legal treatment obstructed the hir-ing of women and reinforced their inequality in the labor market—that difference meant discrimination. As Harriet Stanton Blatch argued, women were "ready for equality." But to the ERA's opponents, this was "hysterical feminism with a slogan for a program." The controversy intensified with the Supreme Court's 1923 decision in *Adkins* v. *Children's Hospital*, which declared a minimum wage law unconstitutional in the name of women's equal rights of free contract. Though both sides claimed to represent all women, neither addressed the exclusion of domestic and farm workers—the great mass of working women of color—from the laws' protection.

Today, gender-neutral labor laws have displaced many sex-based precedents. The legal revolution of the New Deal culminated in the Supreme Court's validation of the 1938 Fair Labor Standards Act, which set national wage and hour rules for men and women alike. The 1993 Family and Medical Leave Act, abandoning a special treatment model based on female physiology, guarantees workers of both sexes unpaid leave to care for a new child or a sick family member. Yet the underlying conundrum of equality and difference—of formal rights and special needs—remains at the heart of feminist debate.

• AMY DRU STANLEY

SEE ALSO Equality and Difference; *Muller* v. *Oregon*; Women's Trade Union League.

≋ Protestantism

Since the U.S. colonial period, the emphasis of the Protestant movement on the primacy of scripture gave religious women new opportunities for expression, despite the male domination of institutional structures within church and society.

The Puritan vision of man as head and woman as helpmate was challenged by white women such as Anne Hutchinson, who believed that grace came directly from God. She opened her home to teach others but was banished in 1637.

Black women also challenged the Christian social order. Elizabeth (surname unknown), born a slave in Maryland in 1766, began a preaching career at age thirty that called attention to "spiritual wickedness in high places."

Quakers believe Christ is revealed directly to the soul, deemphasizing the need for ordained clergy, liturgy, and sacraments. Inspired by this vision, Quaker women spoke out with authority in response to public issues such as slavery and universal suffrage. Shakers also allowed leadership roles for women. Mother Ann Lee (1736–1784), founder of the Shaker religion, claimed that Christ's second coming would be as a woman. The communities she started believed they were living as though the millennium had already arrived and felt there was no need to produce a new generation. Shaker communities gradually faded as the nineteenth century wore on.

Early-nineteenth-century Protestantism was marked by revivals that awakened religious fervor and the growth of denominationalism on the frontier. Despite the early success of evangelists such as Jarena Lee (1783–185?) and Phoebe Palmer (1807–1874), women needed sanctioned access to the pulpit. The struggle became visible with the full ordination of Antoinette Brown in 1853 at the Congregational Church in South Butler, New York. Some groups with a polity that did not emphasize hierarchy, such as the Congregationalists, Unitarians, and Disciples, ordained women much sooner than others, such as the Methodists, who licensed women to preach but did not admit them to full membership as clergy until many years later.

As women pushed the boundaries within the church for ordination, their response to God's call to be in mission and ministry was also seen in increasingly public ways. Frances Willard, a Methodist laywoman, helped found the Woman's Christian Temperance Union to wipe out drunk-

enness and promote family life. Other women worked in the inner cities, where the increasing numbers of immigrants were changing the urban landscape. Caroline Bartlett Crane, a Unitarian minister, was part of the Social Gospel movement, which interpreted the Bible in response to the fracturing of Victorian culture and the growing industrialization. Some groups even connected across racial lines, bound together by a common commitment to Christ. Following the Civil War, for example, women from the Northern Baptist and Black Baptist churches made joint mission efforts. Still other women answered the call to evangelize in foreign lands, particularly China, India, and Africa.

Missionary training schools were key to the empowerment and training of women for these roles. Support for the mission work was provided throughout local churches by women's groups who raised money and educated women about the world and its needs. Most Protestant churches had separate women's societies by the late nineteenth century.

Women's service within the church expanded in the twentieth century. Volunteerism became a profession in itself. Helen Barrett Montgomery and Lucy Waterbury Peabody, two Northern Baptist women who combined marriage and family with careers, led ecumenical efforts such as World Day of Prayer and union schools of higher education for women overseas. Montgomery was elected president of the Northern Baptist Convention in 1921, becoming the first woman to head a national governing body for a Protestant denomination.

Georgia Harkness was the first woman to teach theology in a Protestant seminary. Appointed to the faculty of Garrett Theological Seminary in 1939, she worked for international peace and the elimination of racism and sexism in the church.

The battle over women's ordination that had begun a century before reached fruition for the Lutherans, Methodists, Episcopalians, and Presbyterians in the latter half of the twentieth century. The few who entered ordained ministry in the 1950s grew into a swelling stream by the 1970s, leading to the election of the first woman bishop, Reverend Marjorie Matthews, in 1980. In mainline denominations and ecumenical organizations, women sit on boards and agencies, teach at and head seminaries, and provide leadership at all levels of the ordained and lay ministry of the churches.

Janet Wilson James, *Women in American Religion* (Philadelphia: University of Pennsylvania Press, 1980); Rosemary Radford Ruether and Rosemary Skinner Keller, *In Our Own Voices: Four Centuries of American Women's Religious Writings* (San Francisco: Harper, 1995); Rosemary Radford Ruether and Rosemary Skinner Keller, *Women and Religion in America*, 3 vols. (San Francisco: Harper and Row, 1981).

▪ LINDA J. GESLING

SEE ALSO Evangelicalism; Puritanism; Religion.

≋ Public Speaking

Public speaking traditionally is seen as part of the art of persuasion. In theory, this art is judged in relation to the resources available to a speaker on a particular occasion, for a certain audience, and for a specific end. In practice, other criteria are involved: the speaker's "importance," the "significance" of their actions to historical events, their evident position in a group, the language they use, the setting for speaking, and their gender. Understandably, then, the history of women's public speaking is relatively short.

Throughout the eighteenth and well into the nineteenth century, all U.S. women were barred from speaking "in public," that is, from the pulpit, in the courtroom, or on the Senate floor. Many women had little access to these forums in any case (for example, most African American women, because of slavery, and most Native American

women, because they did not speak English). But general prescriptions for women's silence were enforced so emphatically that when Emma Hart Willard, a white woman, addressed the New York legislature in 1819, she remained seated to avoid any suggestion that she was engaged in public speaking. At a Boston meeting of abolitionists in 1832, Maria B. Miller Stewart, a free African American woman, became the first U.S.-born woman to stand and speak publicly before an audience of women and men.

In the twentieth century, dramatic increases in the numbers of women in "public" arenas have led to increased recognition of some women as public speakers. Equally important, the changes have led feminists to question whose speech is likely to be regarded as "important" and "historically significant" (that is, privileged white men who speak English), and to recognize why most women's speech is not.

▪ CANDACE WEST

SEE ALSO Language and Power.

≋ Puerto Rican Women

Since before the twentieth century, Puerto Rican women have played key roles in facilitating migration, building community, and shaping institutions on U.S. shores. The earliest Puerto Rican enclaves in New York City included women who were exiled for their political persuasions and militant actions in the struggles for Antillean independence, which took place from 1868 until 1898, when the islands became U.S. possessions.

The second migratory phase, predominantly comprised of working-class individuals, unfolded under U.S. occupation. Between 1900 and 1901 eleven expeditions carrying approximately five thousand contract workers, almost half of whom were women and children, set sail for Hawaii

The Brooklyn, New York, chapter of the Liga Puertorriqueña e Hispana circa 1927.

from Puerto Rico's southern ports. The U.S. and Puerto Rican presses noted the gender balance in those prearranged labor movements, forecasting the likelihood of steerage romances and impending unions. Hawaiian planters favored family groups that they felt would provide greater stability and length of service. As family members, or on their own, women were critical to these expeditions although contractual work arrangements sanctioned gender-based salary differentials that placed them at a distinct disadvantage.

Migration to the continental United States continued, particularly to New York City, which received the bulk of the migrant flow until the 1960s. Profiles of migrant women in the 1920s and 1930s indicate that the average Puertorriqueña was a woman in her reproductive years — usually fifteen to thirty-four years old — and a resident in the city for less than five years. Among this group, most women upheld traditional values and identified themselves as housewives even though some were heads of households or were self-employed. Such homebound activities included piecework, needlecrafts, child care for working mothers, provision of room and board, and sale of home-prepared foods.

The late 1940s and 1950s set the stage for the "Great Migration," a massive, economically motivated relocation from Puerto Rico. More women came; daughters accompanied parents, single women followed siblings, wives joined trailblazing husbands, and some came on their own. All wanted a better life than was available in Puerto Rico, and although each held personal reasons for emigrating, their decision generally was rooted in the island's impoverished conditions as well as public policies that sanctioned emigration.

A few women came to study or pursue careers in teaching or other professions, but the majority took jobs as domestics, or worked in manufacturing, laundries, restaurants, hospitals, or the garment industry. Even as they confronted economic exploitation, discrimination, racism, and the insecurities inherent in the migration process on a daily basis, women fared better than did men in the job market, and Puertorriqueñas left the home for the factory in record numbers.

By the end of the 1960s Puerto Rican women increasingly lost jobs in New York City and other urban centers in the economically depressed Northeast because of technological, industrial changes, including the relocation of factories to the sunbelt region. Nonetheless, more Puerto Rican women entered white-collar and professional positions.

Women had always been involved in the organizational life of their communities. Before 1898 women's associations in New York cut across class and color lines as they marshaled support for Cuban and Puerto Rican independence from Spain. Clubs like *Hijas de Cuba*, *Hijas de Libertad*, and *Cespedes y Marti* raised migrant consciousness as they engaged in promoting revolutionary propaganda and fundraising. To support liberation, women held rallies, sponsored cultural events, and performed charitable work. After 1898, when Puerto Rico officially became a U.S. colony, Puerto Rican organizations continued to represent the interests of predominantly working-class, racially diverse communities. These groups built a sociocultural, political agenda targeting conditions in U.S. communities, but maintained relations with Puerto Rico. Some groups, including the Home Town clubs, fostered *Hispanidad* language, customs, traditions, and identity, while others provided social services for the indigent, affirmed culture, protested against imperialist interventions by the United States in Latin America, and denounced its colonial posture in Puerto Rico. Still others reflected island struggles over statehood, autonomy, and independence.

Women were also instrumental in the organizations that peaked following the Great Migration, for example ASPIRA (1961) and the Puerto Rican Family Institute (1963). ASPIRA projected a national image centered on education as the vehicle for advancing diaspora communities. It founded chapters in secondary schools for Puerto Ricans, aided in preparing students for college, and helped to procure the ASPIRA Consent Decree, which guaranteed bilingual education in New York City public schools. The Puerto Rican Family Institute catered to the special needs of migrant families in transition, offering a wide array of social services.

Women continue to contribute much to the progress, history, and education of Puerto Ricans in the United States. Feminists such as Luisa Capetillo; writers Lola Rodriguez de Tio, Pura Belpre, and Julia de Burgos; journalists including Josefina Silva de Cintron; the Reverend Leoncia Rosado, and Sister Carmelita helped pave the way for their followers. Today's writers, including Judith Ortiz Coffer, Aurora Levins Morales, Rosario Morales, and Nicholasa Mohr; grassroots organizers such as Evelina Antonetty, founder of United Bronx Parents; and perhaps the best-recognized, Antonia Pantoja, founder of the Puerto Rican Forum and ASPIRA, are joined by contemporary politicians like Nydia Velasquez, the first Puerto Rican woman elected to the U.S. Congress; Olga Mendez, New York State legislator; and many others committed to advancing Puerto Rican communities at all levels.

The roll call of Puerto Rican women leaders and activists in feminist and gender politics, sociocultural organizations, commercial enterprises, professional associations, and the performing and creative arts is impressive. Women's leadership in U.S. Puerto Rican communities enjoys a long historical tradition measured and celebrated by the work that women perform daily —collectively and individually—in the home, barrios, boardrooms, public schools, and universities.

Edna Acosta Belén, *The Puerto Rican Woman* (New York: Praeger, 1986); Virginia Sánchez Korrol, *From Colonia to Community: The History of Puerto Ricans in New York City* (Berkeley: University of California Press, 1994); Altagracia Ortiz, ed., *Puerto Rican Women in the Twentieth Century: New Perspectives on Gender, Labor and Migration* (Philadelphia: Temple University Press, 1995).

■ VIRGINIA SÁNCHEZ KORROL

SEE ALSO Feminism, Puerto Rican; Latinas; Newyorican Women.

≋ Puritanism

Puritanism began as a religious reform movement in late-sixteenth- and seventeenth-century England. Its advocates hoped to "purify" the Protestant Church of England of all Roman Catholic influences. They called for the elimination of church ritual and all extraneous elements, including images, candles, vestments, holy days, even homiletic elegance. Followers of Calvinist theology, Puritans believed that all humanity was innately depraved but that God had chosen a few, the elect, for salvation through the offer of divine grace; the rest were predestined for damnation.

One group of Puritans turned toward the colonization of New England. The first immigrants landed in 1630, and during that decade, some twenty thousand more English immigrants arrived. Determined to establish a biblical commonwealth, Puritans based their government upon biblical law. They envisioned themselves as the new chosen people and New England as the promised land. Native Americans were sometimes viewed as missionary opportunities, sometimes as obstacles, but always as heathens who must be transformed or removed so that the creation of the New Israel could move forward.

Puritan leaders saw themselves as patriarchs. They established a rigidly hierarchical society with a family system that arranged all members into dichotomous power relationships: master-servant, parent-child, husband-wife. The father assumed the central role as head of household, and women spent their lives under the control of their fathers, then husbands. Even single women and widows generally turned to brothers, uncles, or adult sons for guidance and assistance. Within a climate that demanded submission, deference, and silence from women, those who assumed agency on their own behalf might have found themselves alienated from their community, excommunicated from the church, and, in extreme cases, accused of witchcraft.

Spiritually, however, Puritans affirmed that all souls were equal before God. The elect included women as well as men, and every soul was perceived to have a personal relationship with God. Salvation came through grace, and Puritans longed for and embraced conversion—the experience of that grace in their lives. Through this experience all believers discovered a close communion with God. Such mystical phenomena affected and empowered both male and female Puritans of all ranks and vocations, and it became a powerful force for political upheaval, colonization, and social revolution.

In the nineteenth and twentieth centuries, Puritans were stereotyped as an intolerant and moralistic community, whose members publicly rejected all physical pleasures, including sexual ones, and then hypocritically indulged themselves. While this reputation was grounded in the admittedly harsh treatment of supposed witches, sexual deviants, and dissidents, it owes more to such literary imaginations as that reflected in Nathaniel Hawthorne's *The Scarlet Letter* or Arthur Miller's *The Crucible*. Puritans rejected asceticism in any form, enjoyed good food and drink (in moderation), and encouraged all persons toward love and marriage. In fact, their writings decried celibacy, acknowledged human sexual drives, and countenanced sexual satisfaction in marriage as a divine gift. Like all English people of that time, they did not tolerate extramarital sexuality; homosexuality, bestiality, rape, and adultery were all capital offenses. Puritans, however, were lenient in cases of premarital fornication. Puritans did espouse the Protestant ethics of hard work, frugality, sobriety, and chastity, but they also understood that class and rank were matters of providence, and that wealth and virtue were not synonymous.

Puritanism as reconstructed in U.S. literature more closely resembles the writers' Victorian and post-Freudian cultures than seventeenth-century New England. Puritanism, however, began as a sincerely religious culture whose spiritual radicalism clashed with its social conservatism. Puritan leaders often found themselves enmeshed in irreconcilable conflicts between their commitment to patriarchy and the egalitarianism of their religiosity. The most prominent illustrations of conflict were the trial of Anne Hutchinson in 1637 and the response to the Quaker missionaries in the 1650s and 1660s.

■ MARILYN J. WESTERKAMP

SEE ALSO Religion; Salem Witchcraft Trials.

≋ Quilting

Women have always made art, but for most women of the past, the arts most highly valued by male society, such as painting, sculpture, and architecture, were closed to them. Women instead created needlework, a universal female art that transcends race, class, and national borders. Needlework is the one art in which women controlled the education of their daughters, the production of the art, and were also its audience and critics. Before the Civil War quilting was the main form of needlework in the United States, practiced in most households by females old enough to hold a needle. Later, girls were taught to sew even before they learned to read (if they even were taught to read). Quilts as they were first made were products of necessity as well as tradi-

tion. Factory-made blankets were largely unavailable until the mid–nineteenth century and fabric was scarce and expensive. To provide bed coverings, women reused every scrap from worn-out clothing, lining their quilts with old homespun blankets, wool, cotton, or rags, and backing them with muslin or homespun.

Quilts were made in three ways: pieced, appliqué, or by quilting stitches alone on a solid-color background. For economic reasons a majority were pieced: small bits of fabric joined edge to edge made a top single layer, called patchwork. Appliqué quilts, however, had a double top layer. Besides the designed top, quilts had two other layers, the padding for warmth and the backing layer. The layers were held together by fine quilting stitches that went through all three layers and contributed light and rhythm of their own design. Solid-color quilts were usually white, their beauty coming from the low relief of the top created by thousands of tiny stitches, flattening out some areas, puffing out others.

Piecing, appliqué, and quilting can be traced to ancient Syria, Egypt, India, and China. Flags are piecework (remember Betsy Ross?) and quilted bed coverings were made by Chinese and East Indian women in the seventeenth century as well as by European women. The tradition came to the United States with early female immigrants; several of the first American designs are identical to those from England. The mixture of design traditions resulted in the creation of even more quilt designs here than had previously existed. The European tradition continued with numerous variations and inventions; in addition, African slave women brought their needlework traditions to the American South, where they produced highly valued appliqué quilts. The design influence of Native American tribes is notable for a variety of saw-tooth patterns. The most well-known Native American pattern is the *Lakota Star*, or *Morning Star*, which represents life and new beginnings. The repeat patterns characteristic of appliqué quilts became particularly American, as did the quilting bee and the custom of creating presenta-

Appliqué quilt by Harriet Powers, circa 1900, depicting biblical tales and local folk legends. Born a slave in Georgia, Powers used a traditional appliqué technique of the Fon people of Dahomey in West Africa.

tion quilts for special occasions, such as weddings.

Although quilts served functionally as bed coverings, their display was equally important. Early bedrooms frequently possessed only one piece of furniture, the bed, and its quilt was the central motif. Good quilt makers were known and envied throughout their area, and the exhibition of exceptionally fine craftswomanship at regional fairs, churches, or grange halls influenced other women and spread ideas about color and design.

The history of American quilt making has been distorted by prejudices against women's creativity; the quilting bee, for example, has been popularly understood as a site where women collaborated on designing and producing quilts. Bees were actually organized to assist an individual in the tedious work of quilting the top, which she had already designed and made. Even the design of the stitches was chosen in advance by the quilt maker, who functioned much as a traditional male artist directing studio assistants. Interestingly, Susan B. Anthony delivered her first speech to women at a church quilting bee in Cleveland.

There are hundreds of names for quilt designs,

and often women changed the names, discarding the old ones as the visual image evoked became irrelevant to their lives. For example, a design known in England as *Prince's Feather* became *Princess Feather* on arrival in the United States and afterward became *California Plume*. The names are generic, however, for a quilt's design elements are so complex (color, pattern, size, rhythm, borders) that duplication is virtually impossible; yet the belief continues that quilts had "patterns" that anonymous women followed. In fact, U.S. women became artists in a society in which their efforts were likely to be the only art that most of the populace saw and frequently the only art possessed.

Patricia Mainardi, *Quilts: The Great American Art* (San Pedro, Calif.: Miles and Weir Ltd., 1978); Patricia Mainardi, "Quilts: The Great American Art," in *Feminist Art History: Questioning the Litany,* edited by Norma Broude and Mary D. Garrard (N.Y.: Harper and Row, 1982); Patricia Mainardi, "Quilt Survivals and Revivals," *Arts Magazine* Vol. 62 (May 1988): 49–53.

▪ PATRICIA MAINARDI

SEE ALSO Art and Crafts.

≋ Racial Discrimination

Racism is an enduring and integral part of U.S. history. From the earliest European incursion to the present, discriminatory practices and ideologies have informed state and institutional structures and have framed national popular consciousness and culture as well as social, economic, and political discourse. Examples of discrimination are abundant in our everyday lives: median income for whites is far greater than for nonwhites, while some of the widest income gaps are between white men and women of color; people of color are consistently discriminated against in employment; they are disadvantaged in the criminal justice system, whether because of race biases in sentencing or in prosecutions or on juries. Meanwhile, the 1996 repeal of affirmative action in California impairs people of color's access to higher education and jobs, and may become a precedent for other states.

Nonetheless, many Americans neither accept nor understand the centrality of race in U.S. history. Indeed, Americans tend to think of race as a residual problem, rather than as a core element of politics, institutions, and culture. This is in part because the category "race" and practices considered "racist" have changed over the centuries. It is only in the twentieth century that racial inequality has been mostly freed from a definition rooted in biology and blood. Until the early twentieth century, white people thought that biological distinctions among groups explained differences in character and culture. Correspondingly, the practice of ranking people by race and subordinating groups based on their ranking (racism)—for example, under slavery, colonialism, and imperialism—was viewed as a natural and justifiable consequence of the biological superiority of whites.

During the twentieth century, rigid notions of race have given way to more liberal, cultural, and academic understandings that offered such concepts as assimilation and racial formation in opposition to biological and genetic theories. New ideas contesting the significance of race to human differentiation changed the way institutions, including government, viewed racism. After a century of political struggle, the shift from biological theories of race also propelled a shift from government-sponsored discrimination against some individuals based on their racial classification toward government-endorsed equal treatment of all individuals. Remaining categorization by race was generally aimed at compensating for past discrimination; that is, affirmative action.

The period of formal, legal discrimination stretched roughly from conquest and colonization to the Civil War, Reconstruction, and the era of Jim Crow. Discrimination, or the formal practice of racism, was manifest in discourses on nationhood, citizenship, and individual rights. Sequestration, exile, exclusion, and antimiscegenation laws were favored methods of discrimination. By the middle of the seventeenth century, British colonists had already begun a reservation system whose main purpose was the acquisition of Native American lands by white men. Through the eighteenth and well into the nineteenth centuries, colonization and the dispossession of Indian lands were grounded in the conviction that whites were the superior race and were fueled by faith in the manifest destiny of white Americans to settle the West. Paternalism mixed with brute force governed encounters between whites and indigenous peoples, 90 percent of whom were eliminated by a combination of military force and imported diseases.

The enslavement of Africans by British colonists and Americans from the seventeenth century to the mid–nineteenth century also presumed that whites were the inherently superior race. While slavery as an institution was abolished first by the Emancipation Proclamation of 1863 and then under the Thirteenth Amendment at the end of the Civil War, *de jure* racial subordination continued. For example, many Southern states passed so-called "Black Codes," which were designed to limit the rights of newly freed slaves, including rights to travel or resettle. Even after passage of the Fourteenth Amendment (equal protection) and the Fifteenth Amendment (voting for Black adult males), lynchings, poll taxes, wide use of racial epithets and slurs, white-enforced racial segregation, and white resistance to the very idea of Black equality persisted. For African American women, the practices of racism during this period included the spread of myths about their dangerous sexuality, their immorality, their fecundity. Such stereotypes set Black women in stark opposition to the ideals and virtues of white womanhood, and did so by locating Black women's difference from white women in their biologically determined nature.

Conquest and dispossession characterized the transfer of lands in the West and Southwest from Mexicans to whites. The Mexican War, the Treaty of Guadalupe Hidalgo, and a system of taxation and review of land grants during the second half of the nineteenth century ensured economic, political, and cultural isolation of Chicanos, Hispanos, and Californios, as well as the establishment of a near-colonialist relationship between them and white Americans.

In the eighteenth and nineteenth centuries, immigrant laborers from China, Japan, and Korea settled in the U.S. West. Discrimination against Asian immigrants followed nineteenth-century legal and political understandings of race, understandings that were primarily defined by Black-white experiences. However, the treatment of Asians was not strictly analogous to that of other races considered inferior: Asian immigrants were the only group excluded from the United States on racial grounds. Among Asian immigrants, the Chinese were the only group whose female members were disproportionately disqualified from immigrating both because they were Chinese and because they were women. The 1882 Chinese Exclusion Law, the 1908 Gentlemen's Agreement with Japan, the 1924 National Origins Act, and the 1934 Tydings-McDuffie Act specifically targeted and limited Chinese, Japanese, and Filipino immigration to the United States. In addition, because the Naturalization Law of 1870 deemed only whites and African males eligible for naturalization, foreign-born Asians were generally excluded from citizenship until federal legislation permitted the naturalization of Chinese in 1943 and of all Asians in 1952.

Discrimination came under increasing challenge during the twentieth century. Antilynching campaigns early in the century, along with the NAACP's challenges to discriminatory laws, blossomed into a mass civil rights movement by the 1950s. This movement led to the historic 1954 *Brown* v. *Board of Education* decision and the 1964 Civil Rights Act. National governmental actions to prohibit discrimination by state governments, schools, and employers were notable during the 1960s. The federal government explicitly outlawed racial classifications designed to harm people of color, initiated affirmative action programs, and recognized additional racial categories in the federal census.

A reaction to the rights revolution of the 1960s set in during the Reagan-Bush presidencies (1980–92), a reaction that continues to drive much of contemporary politics. The backlash, which occurs amidst globalization and shrinking economic opportunities for the middle classes, is directed against social programs developed by the national government to compensate for some of the effects of centuries-long racial discrimination. Attacks against "big government" and the welfare state often express white resentment toward people of color, whom whites see as receiving "special privileges" from government.

It is important to point out that the granting of formal equality under law has not spelled an end to discrimination in and by the institutions that determine our opportunities and govern us. For example, biased or bigoted thinking continues to affect hiring, promotion, and admissions decisions. Intentional discrimination may be strictly monitored now, but actions and habits that produce discriminatory effects continue to constrain the life chances of people of color. One of the most vexing late-twentieth-century debates about discrimination concerns how we define the problem. What exactly is discrimination? Should it be measured by outcomes, access, or opportunity? Two principal perspectives have emerged. One, chiefly associated with liberals, has tended to assess progress against discrimination by outcomes. That is, has a school or employer or government program promoted the inclusion of underrepresented groups where they have been historically excluded? Conservatives and neoconservatives, meanwhile, argue that policies should never take race into account, and if they do, color-blind opportunity should be their goal rather than positive outcomes for people of color.

Another set of debates has centered on the relationship of racial discrimination to other forms of inequality—especially class, gender, and sexual inequalities. Feminists of color in particular have developed theories of intersectionality, stressing the ways in which gender and class are braided with race in each of our experiences with one another and with institutions.

What is clear from existing historical research and contemporary case studies is that discrimination based on race may have independent effects but also interacts with other forms of discrimination. Likewise, while gender is a distinctive basis for discrimination, it is not a singular basis—it is always racialized. For example, racially discriminatory practices in employment create racial hierarchies among women workers, resulting in vast differences in income among women of different racial backgrounds. Also, racism and sexism function together both to maintain women's oppression and to divide women of color from white women.

In the late twentieth century, discrimination flourishes in public and private arenas. As we venture into the twenty-first century, our key challenge is to forge a common comprehension of racism so that we can commonly work to extin-guish it. To meet this challenge we will have to understand better how racism is concealed and encoded in discourses about other contemporary social problems such as welfare and crime.

■ DANA TAKAGI

SEE ALSO Civil Rights Movement; Legal Status; Racism.

≋ Racism

Students seldom hear the word "racism" in U.S. history classrooms, yet racism—the ideology that whites are superior to people of color, and the practices arising from that ideology—is as fundamental to the creation of the United States as are Enlightenment notions of liberty, such as religious freedom. Further, actions that challenge racism, beginning with slave rebellions, have always been part of this country's history. The failure or refusal to address racism in school curricula contributes to the reproduction of racism not only in the schools, but also in society as a whole, because it reinforces the view already widely held among whites that racism is a thing of the past, having ended with the demise of legally enforced segregation.

From that perspective, racism has no explanatory power for the contemporary social situation in which people of color are disproportionately poor, overrepresented in the prison population, and underrepresented in universities. Such persistent inequalities, when not flatly denied or deliberately ignored by those who consign racism to an ever-more-distant past, tend to be blamed on people of color themselves, thereby exonerating whites from all responsibility. Without understanding how racism reproduces itself and acknowledging its deep roots and continued presence in U.S. culture, it is impossible to understand our social system or to act effectively to change that system to a more equitable one.

Although the civil rights movement of 1955–1970 succeeded in pressuring a reluctant federal government to end the formal encoding of racism in the law, no Supreme Court decisions or federal statutes could root out racism—nor, indeed, was that their intent. Racism, like race itself, is fundamental to the U.S. power structure and is an invention of culture, not simply of the law.

Perhaps the most useful way to examine racism is first to distinguish it from prejudice and then to consider its two chief aspects: personal and institutional. Prejudice—a judgment (usually adverse) formed beforehand without considering facts or evidence—can often do harm and certainly contributes to racism. Racism differs from prejudice, however, in its power to affect its targets' life chances: where one lives, where (or if) one works, where (or if) one goes to school, whether one has access to health care, how long one lives, what one thinks of oneself and of one's group. One widely used equation is Prejudice + Power = Racism, which exposes the fallacy of "reverse racism" (bias against whites). While individual people of color may indeed be prejudiced against whites, this prejudice does not find the systemic reinforcement inherent in white racism; in short, it lacks power.

Personal racism finds affirmation in the ordinary practices of businesses, schools, and government; in popular culture, including advertising, films, television, music, and magazines; and in common forms of speech ("Indian giver," "denigrate," etc.). Racism is institutionalized. Most institutions in the United States were formed by whites to serve the perceived needs and desires of whites, as was the government itself. The legal changes brought about by the civil rights movement have greatly reduced open discrimination in employment and in schools by providing for the entry of people of color into previously all-white domains. However, antidiscrimination legislation has had less impact on institutions themselves, which for the most part have treated affirmative action as a matter of adding people of color to existing structures without altering these structures. For instance, most school curricula still focus on the history and cultural productions of European Americans, with Americans of color ignored or relegated to the margins. In education, as in society, people of color are not seen as constitutive of U.S. history and culture. Similarly, the movement of people of color into corporations has not altered most corporations' systems of rewards, which favor those who have mastered the nuances of a white-defined way of being in the world and which reserve the highest positions for white males. Further, most people in the United States live highly segregated lives, with neighborhoods, schools, and churches seldom fully integrated. People of color still face discrimination caused by racism on the job, in housing, and in schools. Blacks and Latinos, in particular, are still met with police harassment and brutality throughout the United States, racial epithets on the street, and rudeness and suspicion in stores. People of color in general must still deal with racist jokes and remarks at work and in school, and distorted, stereotypical images in the mass media. One measure of the gulf racism creates between whites and people of color is the depth and breadth of the gap between these two groups in their attentiveness to racism: Many whites deny racism's existence, while most people of color recognize racism's permeation into every element of their lives.

This gulf is not surprising, considering that racism is integral to U.S. history. It arrived in what is now the United States with the first European attempts to settle here. In 1526, approximately five hundred Spaniards and one hundred enslaved Africans arrived in what is now South Carolina. Within a few years, the slaves rebelled, and the Spaniards attempted to put down the rebellion. The African survivors escaped to join local Native Americans, while the Spanish survivors fled to what is now Haiti. The early part of the following century saw more permanent colonies established by British settlers, followed in short order by laws that bound Black people to be enslaved for life, and their descendants to be subjected to inherited slave status, a unique set of circumstances in the history of world slavery. At approximately the same time as they enacted laws meant to preserve the enslavement of Blacks, British colonists began a reservation system to aid their theft of Native American lands. In these two events—the systematic destruction of Native Americans and theft of their land, and the enslavement of Africans to work that stolen land—are the intertwined historical roots of contemporary racism, roots that reveal unbridled economic exploitation to benefit white middle and upper classes as racism's first cause.

Modern popular understandings of race originate in slavery, with Black and white seen as the fundamental (and opposing) categories, and slavocracy's "one drop" rule, which held that even one drop of "colored" blood meant that a person was "colored." Although modern science has debunked race as a legitimate biological category, society continues to function as if race is biologically determined and hierarchical. In general, other "minority" groups in the United States have been treated in the context of Black-white opposition, and the treatment afforded such groups has been socially determined by their placement in relation to the color gradations between Black and white. For example, laws limiting the immigration of Asians followed the logic of the 1790 Naturalization Law that reserved citizenship for whites and was drafted mainly in response to the "problem" of free Blacks and Native Americans. The very language used to describe Chinese people in a California Supreme Court decision echoes the racist language describing Blacks in federal Supreme Court decisions of the same period. In *People* v. *Hall* (1854), the California Supreme Court asserted that a state statute barring Blacks and Indians from testifying in court cases involving whites logically extended also to Chinese people: "a race of people whom nature has marked as inferior, and who are incapable of

progress or intellectual development beyond a certain point."

Every gain made by people of color has been achieved only through long and arduous struggle, and has often been met by white violence and inventive new ways of legally reproducing and enforcing white supremacy. For example, as the doctrine of the "universal rights of man" caused some whites to turn against slavery and to support Black rights, and as increasing numbers of Northern states barred slavery, some Blacks began to succeed against the odds in farming and in small businesses. In response, beginning with the Ohio legislature in 1804, most Northern states passed "Black Laws," restricting the rights of free Blacks. The constitutions of three states went further, banning Black settlers outright.

The Civil War and its aftermath changed the legal expression of racism, but had little effect on either the ideology itself or the many practices growing from it. In 1865, Southern states enacted Black Codes designed to relegate former slaves to virtual slave status. In response to such codes, Congress passed the Civil Rights Act of 1866 over President Johnson's veto, giving Blacks citizenship and the same rights "enjoyed by white citizens." In 1867 Congress passed a series of Reconstruction Acts, providing for political reforms such as the federal military oversight of the former Confederate states and the requirement of constitutional conventions in those states. That same year saw the first national meeting of the Ku Klux Klan, an organization dedicated to the ideology of white supremacy and to preserving white power by illegal means, most notably campaigns of terrorism against Blacks. These racist campaigns intensified after the passage of the Fourteenth (equal protection) and Fifteenth (voting for Negro male adults) Amendments. Race riots, lynchings, and massacres of Blacks were common throughout the South as many whites resisted Black progress during the Reconstruction period. Schools and churches established by Blacks were frequently burned. Between 1890 and 1920, virtually all Black progress was violently halted, segregation increased in both the South and the North, and Blacks were forced back into pre-Reconstruction status. During this same period, civil rights groups remained active, and new campaigns against racism were begun, including many led by Black women, such as Ida B. Wells-Barnett's anti-lynching campaign, and the activist National Association of Colored Women, with Mary Church Terrell as president.

In modern times, the years 1955 to 1970 marked the end of formal, legal segregation in the United States, with all credit due to the unremitting hard work and painful sacrifices made by participants in the civil rights movement. Protest by protest, legal decision by legal decision, the framework of Jim Crow was dismantled. Large-scale, coordinated actions, such as the Prayer Pilgrimage, Freedom Riders to register Black voters in the South, sit-ins at lunch counters across the South, the Poor People's March on Washington, and many others, brought so much pressure to bear on the government that laws similar to those passed during Reconstruction improved the legal standing of people of color. Each gain—school desegregation, voting rights, housing antidiscrimination legislation, restaurant and public accommodation desegregation—was met by renewed white racist attacks, including murder.

During the same period, the Black Power, Black Nationalist, and Black Liberation movements were more committed to empowering self-sufficient Black communities than to attaining government concessions and integration. These more militant strategies posed significant challenges to white supremacy and racism.

From 1965 to 1980, employment, education, and income gaps between whites and people of color narrowed. Since 1980, however, those gaps have been widening as the Reagan and Bush administrations failed to enforce antidiscrimination regulations. The 1990s have seen a renewed onslaught of overt, unashamed racism that has prompted anti–civil rights legislation in several

states, led to a turning away from affirmative action, fueled an increase in hate crimes, pushed the federal government to reduce aid to the poor (although welfare programs serve more whites than any other group, welfare wears a Black face in the popular, racist imagination), increased the amount of spurious "research" that attributes inequalities to "natural" differences, and widened divisions both between whites and people of color and among different "minority" groups (e.g., Koreans and Blacks). Even though white women have been the primary beneficiaries of affirmative action programs, these programs are depicted in the media as "unfairly" favoring people of color, especially Blacks, over whites and are increasingly under attack.

Given this history, racism may seem entirely intransigent and actions against it doomed. The civil rights, Black Power, and Black Liberation movements, however, proved that racism is mutable. It is learned, not natural, and therefore can be unlearned and undone. The first step to ending racism lies in seeing it clearly.

■ MAUREEN T. REDDY

SEE ALSO Civil Rights Movement; Japanese American Internment; Ku Klux Klan; Lynching; Racial Discrimination; Racism in the Women's Movement; Slavery; Whiteness.

≋ Racism in the Women's Movement

Racism has significantly undermined feminist organizing over the past two centuries. Despite the fact that campaigns for women's rights in the United States have been initiated by women of all racial and ethnic backgrounds, and that various women's organizations have fervently struggled against racist hierarchies and institutions, racism has persisted both within and beyond the movement.

Consternation and denial about racism in the women's movement stem from the political principle that a movement struggling for the empowerment of women must, by definition, oppose all systems of oppression that affect women's lives. Women of color who have committed themselves to the women's liberation struggle have long done so from the standpoint that movements against sexism must also address racism if they are to have any real impact upon their lives. If the women's liberation struggle pertains to *all women*, rather than to white women exclusively, then it must work to achieve an end to pervasive racism both in institutional forms and in personal dynamics. Although various women's organizations have cited countering racism as a priority, it is not surprising to find racist hierarchies within the movement that are both the reflection and the result of the racism of the larger culture.

When John Adams failed to heed the advice of his wife, Abigail Adams, to "remember the ladies" in the drafting of the Declaration of Independence, women, as well as free Blacks, indigenous peoples, and other residents of non-European origins, were legally and politically excluded from the Revolution and the creation of this country. This disenfranchisement resulted in the marginalization of women in the new nation and in the total repression of Black participation in the new society, except as slave laborers. Two movements eventually grew out of this context: 1) the abolitionist movement that sought to abolish slavery, and 2) the movement for full suffrage for *all* residents, from which the woman's suffrage movement emerged. Advocates of these causes often joined forces to strengthen one another's efforts. Many feminist activists were birthed through these movements and although organizations allied across race to resist slavery, their efforts were largely segregated because of the overwhelming racial segregation of U.S. society as a whole.

Women of color were discouraged from taking part in the first women's rights convention in 1848, in Seneca Falls. Although the great Black abolitionist Frederick Douglass participated, not a single woman of color was recorded to be in attendance. Moreover, with the passage of the Fifteenth Amendment, which extended the right to vote to Black men, white women suffragists resorted to aggressively racist tactics, undermining their fragile alliances with Black women who were working for the women's vote. When women finally achieved the vote in 1920, some fifty years later, most Black women were functionally disenfranchised following the rise of Jim (and Jane) Crow segregation in the South. Some whites who perceived rights for Blacks as a threat to white supremacy encouraged the belief among whites that Black men were likely to rape white women. This belief led to an era of lynchings of Black men for allegedly assaulting white women, many of whom had become fearful for their safety. These conditions exacerbated tensions between white women and women of color.

Another barrier to alliances was created by the theft of lands long occupied by Native Americans in the southeast and midwest and by Mexicans in the southwest. The status of white women was often tied to the success of their men in establishing land claims and developing communities based in white culture.

What is commonly referred to as the second wave of the women's movement began in the 1960s, when great numbers of women activists who were involved in the Black civil rights and antiwar movements reacted against their exclusion from significant leadership and decision-making bodies by organizing for change. Once again an alliance for the empowerment of women and Blacks (later expanded to include other people of color) gained momentum and stirred passions. Black, Latina, and Asian American women were elected to public offices and appointed to executive positions for the first time in the nation's history. Women acted as critical forces in eliminating barriers to fuller participation in society, including Vilma Martinez's leadership in securing the passage of the Voting Rights Act, Gloria Richardson's community organizing to end segregation, and Lillian Sing's achievement of being the first Asian American woman to be appointed a judge. The women's movement grew both in terms of individual activism and many newly formed grassroots and national organizations (the National Organization for Women, the National Abortion Rights Action League, the Center for Women Policy Studies, and the Women's Legal Defense Fund).

Some of the strongest antiracist voices within the movement emerged from the grassroots feminist, and especially lesbian feminist, organizing of the second wave. The early 1970s, for instance, saw the establishment of the Black lesbian feminist Combahee River Collective in Boston, whose mission statement proposed that racism, sexism, class oppression, and homophobia were linked systems of oppression that must be addressed together. Lesbian poets such as Pat Parker and Audre Lorde articulated a clearly feminist, powerfully antiracist political point of view that challenged many white feminists' views of women's liberation. Radical feminists of color claimed a space at the center of the dialogue on women's rights for perhaps the first time in U.S. history. The reverberations of their work remain a dynamic force for change in feminist organizing today.

Among progressive white women, a tradition of resistance to racism continued to grow. It had its earliest origins in the Deep South, with abolitionists such as the Grimké sisters and white women who opposed lynching in the early twentieth century, and it carried into the 1950s in the work of women such as the writer Lillian Smith. In the 1970s white lesbian poet Adrienne Rich created both a literature and a practice of resistance to racism that emerged from her southern predecessors and was hewn out of substantive alliances across race with women-of-color writer/activists.

In the 1990s southern lesbian feminists Suzanne Pharr and Mab Segrest carried this work to its next level in their writing and organizing.

Alongside the more radical wing of the movement, the mid-1970s to mid-1980s saw several mainstream women's organizations focus intensely on challenging racism, such as the YWCA, whose mission was "to eliminate racism wherever it exists and by whatever means necessary." Heightened awareness of the double jeopardy of racism and sexism led in some sectors of the movement to new and more substantive alliances among women across race. Women of color actively formed coalitions that addressed the myriad forces influencing their lives.

Despite consistent efforts to educate white women about the interconnectedness of oppressions and their impact upon women's lives, few women of color were provided the opportunity (by white feminists in power) to serve in the leadership of second wave organizations, and many experienced a new kind of marginalization. Scholar and writer bell hooks wrote of this period in her book *Ain't I a Woman:* "Black feminists found that sisterhood for most white women did not mean surrendering allegiance to race, class, and sexual preference, to bond on the basis of the shared political belief that a feminist revolution was necessary so that all people, especially women, could reclaim their rightful citizenship in the world." As disillusionment set in for women of color, hooks noted, "We dropped out of groups, weary of hearing talk about women as a force that could change the world when we had not changed ourselves."

This disillusionment that many women of color experienced in the second wave was most apparent in the clash between purported "feminist" goals (largely defined by white activists) and the actual needs of women of color. Accordingly, as white women demanded ratification of the Equal Rights Amendment, women of color argued that economic equity was meaningless to people without jobs. As white feminists at the helm of the domestic violence and antirape movements organized for mandatory arrest of batterers and an intensified police presence to deter rape, they did so with no heed to the pervasiveness of police brutality in communities of color. While white women developed a reproductive rights agenda that prioritized abortion rights, women of color argued that *access* to basic health care (including abortion and contraception) along with issues such as forced sterilization, the marketing of experimental and unsafe contraceptives in communities of color, and economic justice were at the crux of a woman's right to choose motherhood. Finally, as white women emphasized the creation of women-only space and institutions, women of color saw their fate inextricably bound to the fate of men of color.

Strengthened by progress in breaking down racial barriers in society, and often frustrated by attempts to overcome racism in women's organizations, women of color revitalized and/or continued to create their own organizations to combat both the limitations of the women's liberation movement and the oppression of racial degradation within the context of the second wave. Some declined to call themselves "feminists" and chose instead Alice Walker's "womanist" term; they demanded that white women support their efforts to organize and to secure funds; and in a remarkable alliance of purpose, women of color demanded that organizations seeking their endorsement and/or participation address the needs of racial/ethnic populations as represented in this country. With heightened consciousness about the link between racism and sexism, new national women-of-color advocacy organizations emerged, including the Organization of Pan Asia American Women (1976), the Organization of Chinese American Women (1977), the National Black Women's Health Project (1981), the National Institute for Women of Color (1980), the Mexican American Women's National Association (1974), the National Conference of Puerto Rican Women Inc. (1972), and the North American Indian Women's Association (1970).

As white women proposed to change the system to allow women the opportunity to reap the same benefits as men, they often failed to recognize the complex realities embedded in this simple statement. Over the course of more than a century of organizing for equality, white women consistently have failed to acknowledge the widely different historical, material, and cultural realities between themselves and women of color; they have thus presented white women's experiences and agendas as representative of all women. Moreover, when challenged by women of color, white women often have faltered at examining the racist underpinnings of their analyses and practices—whether personal or organizational. Women of color have experienced these denials as a deep betrayal. Accordingly, fragile alliances among white women and women of color frequently have not survived frank discussion of the various issues presented here.

Fundamentally, the motives of white women and women of color for organizing for equality coincide: the elimination of oppression that limits any woman's access to full participation in the larger society. However, women of color generally have sought broad institutional transformation in the dismantling of policies, practices, and structures that perpetuate oppression on the basis of race/ethnicity, class, *and* gender, while white women generally have sought to gain access to male power structures and then to transform gendered hierarchies from the inside. White feminists have named "male power" as the root cause of sexist practices, while women of color have long recognized that men of color are not the equals of white men in U.S. society and thus not fundamentally culpable in the perpetuation of existing hierarchies.

Because women of color continue to gain visibility and leadership strength in conventional political organizations as well as women's movement groups, white women and women of color are working together in greater numbers, forming new alliances, and struggling to address substantive differences. Such alliances will continue to challenge the primacy of white, middle-class, reformist viewpoints within the mainstream women's movement. White women's involvement in antiracist movements is anticipated to increase, as understanding between women across race foments new strategies and new visions for change.

• JAIME M. GRANT
and SHARON PARKER

SEE ALSO Racism.

≋ Radicalism

To be a "radical" is to advocate extreme or drastic change in society, literally to go "to the root or foundation" to solve social problems. By this definition, many women in U.S. history have been radicals. As individuals and as members of organized social movements, women have advocated fundamental changes in the economy, in the nature of politics in the public sphere, and in the equally political relationships and power dynamics within families and households. Although radicals are commonly associated with left-wing politics, radicalism can also occur in support of right-wing or antifeminist causes. On the left, women radicals have been active in a variety of anticapitalist, antiimperialist, socialist, communist, and feminist groups and in numerous movements for liberation of people of color and colonized peoples. On the right, women have engaged in efforts to restrict citizenship rights, to reduce the political power of women, and to outlaw nonconventional sexual and familial relationships.

It is also the case, however, that women often are labeled "radical" for supporting even moderate or gradual reform measures. Because women's proper role has been viewed historically as tied to a male-dominant family and household, any woman who dared to press in public for social change ran the risk of being viewed as a radical.

Historically, feminist ideas have been denounced as challenging the foundations of family life and upsetting social arrangements rooted deeply in conventional gender roles. Even the most moderate advocates of woman suffrage in the nineteenth century and women's legal equality in the twentieth century were castigated as "radicals" by those unwilling to admit women as full members of society. In both the suffrage movement and the contemporary feminist movement, however, there were those who advocated more fundamental measures. The tactics and demands of these radical suffragists and radical feminists were to some extent key in securing the movement's more moderate demands. As radicals pressed for basic social transformation, more temperate calls for gender parity seemed less threatening to established institutions, resulting in some political concessions and modest social change.

In the nineteenth century, most suffragists were careful not to stray far from conventional morality and respectability. Yet some did push beyond reformist visions. Emboldened by the militant tactics of British suffragists and drawing from the examples of the International Workers of the World and other labor radicals, radical suffragists struggled to end discrimination against women in the family, religion, the polity, and the workplace.

Radicals in the second wave of the women's movement similarly have refused to restrict their demands for change—or their visions of alternative ways to organize families, intimate relationships, the economy, or politics—to those sanctioned by mainstream political organizations. Radical feminists reject compromise in the quest for gender equality and struggle to create alternative, feminist-inspired ways of living. Through women's culture, women-owned cooperative workplaces, and women-only households, radical feminists have fashioned highly participatory and egalitarian institutions separate from and opposed to the hierarchical, male-centered institutions of mainstream society, with the goal of their eventual transformation.

Until recently, those who insisted that women possessed sexual desires equal to those of men or that women should be permitted sexual fulfillment without fear of unwanted pregnancy were decried as sex radicals. In the early twentieth century some feminists proclaimed the erotic needs of women and urged greater (heterosexual) freedom for women, even outside the bounds of marriage. At the same time, working-class and socialist women championed birth control as the means to liberate women from unwanted pregnancies and intolerable marriages.

Currently, radical challenges to traditional norms of sexual desire and sexual behavior are continuing, including questioning the rigid dichotomies of male/female and heterosexual/homosexual, opening possibilities for bisexual, transgendered, and transsexual erotic attraction.

Women have been active, if often invisible, in almost every U.S. radical movement for civil rights, peace politics, and economic justice. In the early nineteenth century, African American and European American women fought to end slavery. Women also fought for unionized, racially egalitarian, and participatory workplaces in many sectors of the economy—from agriculture and automobile production to service and clerical work—often while struggling for recognition within their own male-dominated unions. They also have infused the civil rights struggles of African Americans, Chicanos and Latinos, Native Americans, the disabled, welfare recipients, and persons with AIDS with passion, commitment, and a vision of social equality and democratic politics. Women environmentalists and self-proclaimed "peaceniks," together with radical feminists, have been in the forefront of struggles to abolish nuclear weapons, eliminate wars internationally, reduce military expenditures domestically, protect natural resources, and decrease reliance upon nonrenewable energy resources. Radical women of color in the U.S. have been particularly active in movements for Puerto Rican independence, Black liberation, American Indian and Native land rights, and farmworkers' rights.

Not all radicalism by women has been progressive or feminist. Women have also been active, as leaders and followers, in a number of right-wing movements. These include movements favoring gender inequalities; opposing reproductive freedom in general and abortion in particular; supporting restrictions on the rights of immigrants and/or people of color; and favoring white, Christian, and heterosexual supremacy. Many of these radical right-wing movements originated to oppose progressive or feminist social change efforts.

Ruth Milkman, ed., *Women, Work and Protest* (Routledge and Kegan Paul, 1985); Carroll Smith-Rosenberg, *Disorderly Conduct* (Oxford University Press, 1985); Nancy Whittier, *Feminist Generations* (Temple University Press, 1985).

■ KATHLEEN M. BLEE

SEE ALSO Abolitionist Movement; Anarchism; Black Nationalism; Conservatism and the Right Wing; Feminism, Radical; Labor Movement; Peace Movement; Socialism; Suffrage Movement.

≋ Rape

SEE Violence Against Women.

≋ Reconstruction

Although many mark the end of the Civil War with the surrender at Appomattox on April 9, 1865, the beginning of Reconstruction predated the war's end and might well be said to have begun with the Emancipation Proclamation (January 1, 1863). The dramatic restructuring of the political economy in the South from 1863 to 1877 began with the dismantling of slavery and followed with the establishment of statewide constitutional conventions that included newly franchised Black male delegates. White political elites, used to tyrannical influence over African Americans, were hamstrung by the presence of federal troops, and white racists were driven underground; they formed the Ku Klux Klan and other secret organizations.

These enormous upheavals created unprecedented transformations for women in the North and South. Activists such as Elizabeth Cady Stanton and Susan B. Anthony tried to push through female suffrage, as Congress rapidly enacted the Thirteenth (1865), Fourteenth (1868), and Fifteenth Amendments (1870), which abolished slavery, extended citizenship to former slaves, and protected male voting rights. Even such a staunch supporter of women's rights as Frederick Douglass was unwilling to compromise what he called "the Negro's hour," and thus feminists' bid for suffrage failed. Despite limited advances (for example, in education when states established land grant, coeducational colleges) feminists lost ground during Reconstruction. Women pioneers in the treasury office, the U.S. Sanitation Commission, and within private industry found their services no longer required once the war ended. At the same time, many Yankee women, Black and white, undertook a noble adventure, traveling south to establish schools for freedpeople, despite hostile and dangerous conditions, an effort dubbed "the tenth crusade" by W.E.B. Du Bois.

Most Southern women were consumed with the struggle for economic survival, as the war resulted in unprecedented poverty within former Confederate states, particularly for recently freed Black women who had been slaves. Widows of Confederate veterans (over 80,000, for example, in Alabama alone), orphans, and others seeking relief found that their appeals to the government confounded the white leadership, which was literally and metaphorically bankrupt.

The Civil War dramatically reshaped opportunities for Native Americans. The war left the Cherokee Nation devastated—libraries, schools, churches, public buildings, and private homes were destroyed. By the surrender at Appomattox, at least seven thousand Cherokees had lost their lives. So many Cherokees died that one of the main priorities of the Cherokee Nation was to provide housing and care for their children.

Southern Blacks sought assistance from the Freedman's Bureau, a government agency established to serve the needs of refugees and former slaves, but a bureaucracy overwhelmed by the prospect of redistributing lands, settling interracial disputes, and, most significantly, protecting the freedpeople from violence and injustice. Many former masters sought to reinstitute patterns of slavery. Indeed Southern lawmakers passed Black Codes, which reproduced patterns of expropriation and discrimination. These laws were struck down only by federal intervention.

Black male leaders, eager to distance themselves from slavery's legacy, fought hard to protect freedpeople's rights and especially to safeguard other African Americans. White sexual coercion and rape of Black women, all too common before the Civil War, continued to be a threat. Black working women struggled for economic justice in the worsening economy. In Jackson, Mississippi, in June 1866, washerwomen petitioned the mayor, demanding better, more uniform wages. Labor militance and increasing defiance typified Black discourse during this era. White women, for example, reported that former slaves, now working for wages, were no longer willing to soak and clean menstrual rags, and many jeered at their ex-mistresses' demands.

The former master class was devastated by postwar conditions. One Georgia white woman complained, "There is nothing for us to do but bow our heads in the dust and let the hateful conquerors trample us under their feet." Planter pride was only temporarily acquiescent, as Confederate diehards embraced and promoted the Cult of the Lost Cause. White women fashioned memorialization into a fine art, creating the United Daughters of the Confederacy, dedicated to preserving defeated values. "The suffering South" became the battle cry and by the mid-1870s many Northerners were won over, resulting in widespread erosion of the commitment to Black equality.

African Americans fled in the wake of federal retreat, like the "Exodusters," who pioneered all-Black settlements in Kansas beginning in 1879. Those who remained behind agonized over the introduction of "Jim Crow" legislation (writing segregation into law, beginning in Tennessee in 1881) and over the racial terrorism and lynching that followed. Nevertheless, the status quo of antebellum life in the United States was never restored.

Catherine Clinton and Nina Silber, eds., *Divided Houses: Gender and the Civil War* (New York: Oxford University Press, 1992); Ellen DuBois, *Feminism and Suffrage* (Ithaca: Cornell University Press, 1978); Eric Foner, *Reconstruction* (New York: Harper & Row, 1988).

• CATHERINE CLINTON

SEE ALSO Constitution and Amendments: Emancipation Proclamation and Thirteenth Amendment; Ku Klux Klan; Lynching; Plantation System; Slavery.

≋ Religion

B roadly defined, religion is the process by which individuals and groups create meaning and affirm values. A shared understanding about human origins, ends, and ethical practice distinguishes one belief system from another. As a universal human endeavor that is historically and culturally defined as well as limited by human finitude, religion is contingent and ambiguous.

Religious organizations have used their beliefs to justify and legitimate practices that have caused evil and suffering on a massive scale. Religious beliefs have also inspired selflessness and sacrifice. With regard to women's history, religions have been the source of insight and power as well as the cause of arbitrary violence and destruction in the name of divine authority.

The religious history of the United States is shaped by the culturally diverse experiences of women. In spite of their diversity, women's lives are affected by the patriarchal assumptions embedded both in this country's normative cultural value system and in the foundational principles of many traditional religions. Confronted by the choice between conforming to patriarchal values and choosing to define their own religious identities, some women accept traditional beliefs without question. For others, the choice to remain committed to religious traditions that are fundamentally sexist may be predicated on the idea that it is possible to create the conditions for change from within. Those who reject sexist religious traditions turn to alternative forms of spirituality, or to political activism or secular humanism.

During the formative period of U.S. religious history in the seventeenth and eighteenth centuries, Protestant Christianity was established as the dominant religion. Although the constitutional separation of church and state exists, Protestant Christianity continues to have a powerful impact on U.S. politics and culture. Informed by both patriarchal assumptions and a Western European cultural predisposition, Protestant Christianity defined Native Americans, Africans brought as slaves, and women as "other." Native Americans and African slaves were considered subhuman and, as a group, women were considered to be less significant than their male counterparts. These attitudes were reflected in the paternalism, infantilization, and abusive practices suffered by these marginalized groups.

The colonization of the United States resulted in the destruction of Native American peoples, their cultures, religions, and traditions. Little written evidence exists about the religious life of Native American women, because of the oral tradition of tribal narratives. Written documentation was primarily the work of European male missionaries who paid little attention to the religious experiences of Native women, which varied from tribe to tribe. Most tribes had a creation myth that included a female creator and an Earth Mother figure, both of whom provided justification for women to be healers and shamans. Many Native American women were converted to Christianity, in which rituals of fasting, mortification, prayer, and visions were similar to those of Native American spirituality. Kateri Tekakwitha, from the Mohawk tribe of the Iroquois Nation, converted to Christianity in the middle of the seventeenth century. After her death, miraculous events that occurred on the reservation were attributed to her and she was venerated by the tribe.

In the early colonial period, Puritan women were encouraged to participate in their churches. Some of those who challenged male authority by desiring radical equality and the right to preach the gospel were excommunicated, hanged, or burned at the stake. Anne Hutchinson (1591–1643), a midwife and healer, believed that grace and salvation were gifts from God given directly to individuals. She claimed that her theology and her role as a teacher of younger women conformed to the teachings of the Scriptures. Hutchinson was excommunicated and banished, as was her friend, Mary Dyer, who shared her theological beliefs. Dyer returned to England and became a Quaker. A year after the Bay Colony passed a law forbidding the profession of Quaker beliefs, Dyer returned to Boston. Defying the law, she preached and was expelled on three occasions. Refusing to be silenced, she returned for the fourth time and was hanged in Boston on June 1, 1660.

Hutchinson, Dyer, and hundreds of other women were accused of practicing witchcraft. Nearly thirty women hanged between 1620 and 1725 were perceived to be a threat to the "natural" order. Their "crimes" ranged from preaching and healing to disobeying their husbands, ministers, and magistrates. Historically, "woman" named the discursive rupture in the his-story of patriarchal authority. The natural order ascribed to women was subordination and silence. Those who opposed it were seen as threats to the divinely ordained harmony within the community.

In spite of the cultural, ethnic, religious, and economic diversity that defined the eighteenth century and the Enlightenment vision of democracy and equality, the position of women in New England and the southern colonies remained unchanged. Considered intellectually and morally inferior to men, women were instructed to restrict their piety to the home. Some women, particularly in the South, extended the religious instruction they offered their children to their slaves. In general, slave owners feared that Christianization would lead to emancipation. Therefore, they taught slaves a version of Christianity that emphasized their sinfulness and the importance of obeying the masters.

Although the religious life of African slave women was in sharp contrast to their experience in Africa, where in some tribes women were religious leaders, Christianization offered a degree of empowerment. In the 1760s Phillis Wheatley was accepted as a member of Boston's Old South Meeting House. Her zealous Congregationalist beliefs inspired her to write poetry and essays. Katherine Ferguson, a freed slave influenced by her Christian beliefs, opened the first Sabbath School for orphaned children in New York City in 1793.

From the middle to the late eighteenth century, opportunities for women to exercise greater religious freedom increased. Events that contributed to the changes included the Great Awakening (1720–70), which revived interest in piety, and the nascent antislavery movement, the emergence of new religious groups, and the disestablishment of Protestant Christianity after the Revolutionary

A woman rabbi reads the Torah. Traditionally, only men were permitted to touch the Torah, which contains the first five books of the Hebrew Scriptures.

War, which, at least in principle, separated church and state and made religion a matter of personal conscience. Furthermore, the Enlightenment established the philosophical foundations for religious tolerance, social justice, abolition, and woman suffrage.

The individualization of religious experience during the Great Awakening emphasized personal salvation. Both Black and white women benefited from this shift. Their piety and fervor were valued by revivalist preachers and their testimony of conversion provided legitimation of their experience as religious women. Although neither Black women nor white women were permitted to preach in most Christian churches, they could become missionaries or work for social causes. In spite of the fact that the Great Awakening is asso-

ciated with the name of Jonathan Edwards, it was his wife, Sarah Edwards, who was the source of his inspiration and his ideas about spiritual cleansing.

With the growth of Quakerism, German Pietist sects, and evangelical revivalism, the religious experience of women was enriched. Opportunities for leadership expanded and made it possible to displace the traditional hierarchy of male authority over women worshipers. Women founded religions such as the Shakers, Christian Science, and Spiritualism, led the revival of Voodoo cults, and became leaders in Pentecostal churches. For Quakers, the theological basis for permitting women to preach was first established by Margaret Fell, who supported the rights of women to participate fully in the life of the Society. Therefore, Quaker women had administrative and supervisory roles within the Society and developed and managed social justice projects in their communities. Among the better-known Quaker women was Lucretia Mott (1793–1880), minister, abolitionist, and, with Elizabeth Cady Stanton, coorganizer of the Seneca Falls Convention, which marked the beginning of the woman suffrage movement. Sarah Moore Grimké (1792–1873) joined the Society of Friends in 1823, having rejected the privileges of her southern aristocratic upbringing. She was reformer, abolitionist, and woman suffragist. Although she admired Mott, she left the Society over its reluctance to support the antislavery bill. In her crusade against slavery she was joined by her sister, Angelina Grimké.

During the revolutionary period and throughout the nineteenth century, many new religions were founded, including some by women, offering a wide range of alternatives. The growing cultural secularism, emerging socialism, and the perception that religion was within the sphere of the feminine changed the country's religious landscape. The claim that women were by nature religious and the new scholarly interest in the Scriptures both justified the subordination of women and underscored their equality with men. The scriptural justification for human freedom and equality empowered women to live their religious beliefs in the public arena as supporters of abolition, woman suffrage, women's ordination, and changes in divorce laws.

Ann Lee (1736–1784), the founder of Shakerism; Mary Baker Eddy (1821–1910), the founder of Christian Science; and the Fox sisters—Margaret (1836–1893) and Kate (1839–1892)—who founded the Spiritualist movement all recognized in different ways the feminine as a higher form of divine consciousness. All represented powerful models of women in religious leadership positions as visionaries, prophets, preachers, and writers. The growing understanding of human perfectionism and the value placed on individual experience encouraged women to develop new religious insights.

Some women turned their attention to social issues. Jewish women, such as Rebecca Gratz (1781–1869) of Philadelphia, organized the Female Association for the Relief of Women and Children in Reduced Circumstances in 1801, established the Hebrew Sunday School in 1818, and worked to create the Jewish Foster Home and Orphan Asylum in 1855. Catholic religious women were committed to improving education and health care. Owing to the culture's anti-Catholic bigotry and suspicion of celibate women, the work of nuns historically has been underestimated. Three notable women were Elizabeth Seton, who founded the order of the Sisters of Charity in 1809; Frances Cabrini, who, as a Missionary of the Sacred Heart, established schools and orphanages in New York's Little Italy in 1889; and Katherine Drexel, who founded the Sisters of the Blessed Sacrament for Indians and Colored People in 1891. In 1915 Drexel also founded Xavier University in New Orleans, the first and only Catholic university for Black students.

Another woman who devoted her life to improving the social conditions of people affected by industrialization was Jane Addams (1860–1935), a committed pacifist. She founded Hull House in Chicago in order to meet the needs of the community. In 1915 she became chair of the Women's International League for Peace and Freedom and in 1931 was the corecipient of the Nobel Peace Prize, the first U.S. woman to be so honored.

Evangelical revival meetings were an outgrowth of Protestant Christianity and the emphasis on individual salvation. They offered women opportunities for preaching and leadership that was not available within traditional churches. Among the best-known Black visionaries was Sojourner Truth (1797?–1883), who, beginning in the late 1820s, was a street preacher in Manhattan and worked for social reform. After 1843, she preached throughout New England, supporting abolition and woman suffrage. Lay preacher Phebe Palmer (1807–1874), of the Methodist Episcopal Church, distinguished herself as the leader of the Holiness Movement. In 1859 she wrote an impassioned defense of women's ordination. Amanda Smith (1837–1915), of the African Methodist Church, and an internationally acknowledged Black evangelist, was influenced by Palmer. Despite ministers' resistance, she preached from Maine to Tennessee in the 1870s and in England, India, and Africa from the late 1870s to 1890.

Although not an evangelist herself, Ellen Gould White (1827–1915) was strongly influenced by Methodist evangelism. She was a member of the William Miller's adventist sect, which believed in the imminent second coming of Christ. By the 1860s the sect renamed itself the Seventh-Day Adventists, and White became their spiritual leader. Health reform was part of her Christian commitment; therefore, she established the Western Health Reform Institute in Battle Creek, Michigan, which became a model sanatarium. Aimee Semple McPherson (1890–1944), founder of the International Church of the Foursquare Gospel; and Kathryn Kulhman (1907–1976), faith healer and radio and television evangelist, were two of the best known and widely acclaimed charismatic leaders of Pentecostal and Holiness movements.

Within traditional Protestant churches, support for women's ordination met with a great deal of resistance. The first woman to be ordained was Antoinette Brown, who became a Congregationalist minister in 1853. Anna Howard Shaw was ordained a United Methodist minister in 1880 but her ordination was revoked four years later because of her gender. At the end of the twentieth century, women ministers and bishops exist in several Protestant denominations, including Anglican, Lutheran, Episcopalian, and United Methodist. There are also women in the rabbinate of Conservative and Reform Judaism. However, the Roman Catholic Church continues to refuse to ordain women.

By the end of the nineteenth century and the beginning of the twentieth, women contributed significantly to reshaping religious self-understanding in the United States. Abolition, woman suffrage, temperance, reform of divorce and child labor laws, education and health care reform were all within the purview of women's commitment to social justice. Elizabeth Cady Stanton (1815–1902) founded the woman suffrage movement in collaboration with Lucretia Mott and Susan B. Anthony. She also worked to change divorce laws that impoverished women. Between 1895 and 1898, with a committee of international women scholars, Stanton published *The Woman's Bible*, a commentary on the parts of the Hebrew and Christian Bible that either demean women's experience or are silent about the subordination and abuse of women. Frances Willard (1839–1898), a prominent educator, Dean of Women at Northwestern University, and supporter of woman suffrage, worked with the Woman's Christian Temperance Union and served as its president from 1891 to 1898. Henrietta Szold (1860–1945) tried to preserve Jewish culture in the United States and supported the restoration of the state of Israel. In 1912 she founded and was the first president of Hadassah, a women's organization committed to providing and supervising medical services to Jews in the Middle East. Dorothy Day (1897–1980), a Catholic and socialist, established *The Catholic Worker*, a monthly publication to which she contributed for over fifty years, supporting social causes and speaking on behalf of women, the poor, homeless, and unemployed. Combining faith and charity, she created houses of hospitality and rural communes for the needy.

Throughout the twentieth century the tension between conformity to patriarchal norms and religious self-determination persists and continues to shape the nature of women's religious experience, authority, and power. In Native American religions, mainstream Protestant denominations, Conservative and Reform Judaism, as well as within African American churches, women's participation and leadership was circumscribed by male authority. As a means of self-empowerment, women formed auxiliary organizations that focused on teaching, social work, and fundraising. In general, institutional religions remain patriarchal, permitting women to participate only in subordinate positions. Among those that ordain women very few allow women to hold high positions of authority.

There are more than sixteen hundred religions practiced in the U.S. today, including Mormonism; Unification Church; Scientology; Hinduism; Buddhism; Islam; and Yoruba, Voodoo, and Santaria, which are of African origin. There are also alternative religions, particularly women's religions such as Wicca, African Spiritual churches in New Orleans, and the Roman Catholic nonseparatist Women-Church, which provide women with the greatest opportunities for leadership because they do not replicate patriarchal hierarchy. They attract charismatic women with a heightened sense of spirituality. Whereas their nineteenth-century predecessors focused on the spirit, currently, these movements focus on the body as well as the spirit in their attempt to recover women's wisdom and power. They have replaced male gods and the Jewish-Christian rhetoric that blames Eve with goddess and nature worship, and have reclaimed their sensuality and sexuality as an integral part of their religious experience and practice. Alternative women's religions tend to be participatory, emphasize interconnectedness among the members and the community, affirm the spiritual journey as a human endeavor of self-discovery and self-transcendence, and provide a place where women can be free to determine their own spiritual realities.

Rosemary Radford Ruether and Rosemary Skinner Keller, *Women and Religion in America*, 3 vols. (San Francisco: Harper and Row, 1981); Rosemary Skinner Keller, "Women and Religion," in *Encyclopedia of American Religious Experience* Vol. 3 (New York: Charles Scribner's Sons, 1988); Catherine Wessinger, ed., *Women's Leadership in Marginal Religions: Explorations Outside the Mainstream* (Urbana and Chicago: University of Illinois Press, 1993).

■ IRENA S. M. MAKARUSHKA

SEE ALSO Buddhism; Catholicism; Evangelicalism; Feminist Theology; Fundamentalism; Hinduism; Islam; Judaism; Missionaries; Mormons; Native American Religions; Protestantism; Puritanism; Spirituality; Wicca.

≋ Reproductive Rights

Only during the last quarter century has the concept of "reproductive rights" come into common usage in this country. The legal recognition of the right to decide whether, when, and how to have children, reproductive rights encompasses a range of decisions concerning reproductive health, including family planning, contraception, abortion, pregnancy, and childbirth.

Although fertility regulation has been a part of women's lives throughout the past two centuries, it wasn't until the late nineteenth century that birth control ascended as a political and legal issue. In 1873 Congress made it a crime to distribute via mail or to import information about contraception and abortion. During the same period, the notion of "voluntary motherhood" and other tenets of a woman's right to control her own fertility began to gain momentum among feminists.

The contemporary movement for birth control blossomed in the early 1900s, as advocates of family planning spoke out and wrote on the issue, distributed pamphlets, and established birth-control clinics. Although the early feminist movement sought to provide women with the means to control their own fertility, legislators and some members of the medical profession sought to impose fertility control on certain "undesirable" elements in society. Criminals, who at one time were believed to be genetically predisposed to "antisocial" behavior, and persons with supposedly low mental faculties were involuntarily sterilized under state laws and court orders. In 1927, in one of its most reprehensible decisions, the U.S. Supreme Court defended involuntary sterilization in *Buck*

v. *Bell*. A decade and a half later, however, the Court recognized as fundamental the right to procreate in its 1942 *Skinner* v. *Oklahoma* decision.

Sadly, this constitutional guarantee did not protect countless low-income women, especially women of color, from being involuntarily sterilized by government programs and clinics well into the 1990s. Recently, long-lasting, hormone-based contraceptives such as Norplant and Depo-Provera have raised similar concerns about coercion, as their use is advocated for teenagers and women receiving public assistance.

During the past thirty years, the Supreme Court has decided a number of cases involving the right of individuals to control their fertility. In a landmark 1965 case, *Griswold* v. *Connecticut*, the Court found that the right of married couples to use contraception is protected by the fundamental right of privacy found in the Fourteenth Amendment and the other guarantees of the Bill of Rights. The Court subsequently extended this right to unmarried couples and individuals (*Eisenstadt* v. *Baird*, 1972) and to minors (*Carey* v. *Population Services*, 1977). Legislative action has also influenced access to contraceptives and family planning services. In 1970 Congress enacted Title X of the Public Health Service Act, which provides direct federal grants to thousands of family planning providers that collectively serve more than five million low-income clients annually. The statute authorizing Title X, however, bars the use of funds "in programs where abortion is a method of family planning."

From colonial times in this country, abortion was legal prior to "quickening," the point in pregnancy when fetal movement is detectable. Prior to the rise of the medical establishment in the mid-1800s, pregnancy terminations were performed by people, primarily women, who usually were not physicians, and only a handful of states passed measures restricting abortion. Beginning in the mid–nineteenth century, however, state legislatures enacted statutes criminalizing virtually all abortions.

A broad-based movement of women's rights activists, health care providers, and members of the clergy worked in the 1960s to find competent abortion providers for women seeking to terminate unwanted pregnancies. By the early 1970s, one-third of the state legislatures had liberalized their abortion laws. Against this backdrop, in 1973 the Court issued rulings in *Roe* v. *Wade* and *Doe* v. *Bolton*, which recognized for the first time that the fundamental constitutional "right of privacy is broad enough to encompass a woman's decision to terminate a pregnancy" in consultation with her physician. The Court struck down criminal abortion statutes from Texas and Georgia, severely limiting states' ability to restrict abortions during the first two trimesters of pregnancy or after viability when the procedure is necessary to protect a woman's life or health.

Immediately following *Roe*, abortion opponents pressured state legislatures and the federal government to impose restrictions on abortion services. From the mid-1970s to the mid-1980s, legal advocates for women challenged restrictive state laws, ultimately obtaining Court review. Finding that certain laws imposed unconstitutional limitations on a woman's right to privacy, the Court struck down:

- husband consent for a married woman's abortion (*Planned Parenthood* v. *Danforth*, 1976)
- mandatory counseling and a twenty-four-hour waiting period for abortion (*City of Akron* v. *Akron Center for Reproductive Health*, 1983; *Thornburgh* v. *American College of Obstetricians & Gynecologists*, 1986)
- requirements that post-first-trimester abortions be performed only in hospitals (*City of Akron* v. *Akron Center for Reproductive Health*, 1983)
- mandatory use of techniques most likely to result in a live birth when a fetus is or may be viable (*Colautti* v. *Franklin*, 1979)
- requirements that physicians performing postviability abortions use the method most likely to preserve the life of the fetus and have a second

physician present to "save" the fetus (*Thornburgh* v. *American College of Obstetricians & Gynecologists*, 1986)

Still, abortion opponents succeeded early on in restricting the right to choose abortion, particularly for low-income women and young women. Beginning in 1977, the Court found that the right to privacy does not extend to women who rely on state programs for their health care or to those obtaining abortion services at public hospitals (*Maher* v. *Roe, Beal* v. *Doe*, and *Poelker* v. *Doe*, 1977). Three years later, the Court found constitutional the Hyde Amendment, a prohibition on the use of federal funds for abortions under Medicaid—the joint federal/state program established in 1965 to provide comprehensive health care to low-income individuals (*Harris* v. *McRae*, 1980).

Every year since 1976, the Hyde Amendment has been reenacted, barring federal reimbursement for low-income women's abortions except in extremely limited circumstances. Similar restrictions have been attached to a wide range of federal programs, at times affecting millions of U.S. citizens. Following the cutoff of federal coverage for abortion services, more than two-thirds of the state legislatures adopted similar limitations on state Medicaid funds. As a result, low-income women, particularly women of color, have been forced to postpone abortion, thus exposing themselves to the risks associated with later abortions, or endangering their lives and health trying to self-abort.

The right and ability of young women to obtain abortions also have been weakened by the Court. The Court held that states may require a young woman to obtain the consent of, or notify, one or both parents prior to an abortion, so long as there is an "alternative" for waiving the requirement, such as a judicial bypass procedure, in which she must demonstrate to a judge that she is mature enough to choose abortion or that the procedure is in her best interests.

During the 1980s the antiabortion movement was bolstered both by its success in the courts and legislatures and by support from Presidents Reagan and Bush, both of whom opposed abortion and used the power of the executive office to restrict federal funds provided to domestic and international health organizations; skew government research and reporting on abortion; and prohibit personal importation of the pill RU486, a method of nonsurgical abortion. Reagan and Bush also had an enormous impact on the federal judiciary, appointing at least 60 percent of the nation's sitting federal judges—the majority of whom espoused antiabortion philosophies and have ruled in favor of abortion restrictions.

Until 1989 the Supreme Court appeared to support the right to choose abortion so long as an adult woman was seeking the procedure with her own funds. That year, however, in *Webster* v. *Reproductive Health Services*, the Court upheld a number of Missouri abortion restrictions, which bar the use of public facilities and public employees in abortion procedures and create a presumption of fetal "viability" beginning at twenty weeks' gestation. Women's rights advocates and antiabortion forces were certain that the Court was ready and able to overturn *Roe* v. *Wade*, if the right case arose.

In 1992, in *Planned Parenthood of Southeastern Pennsylvania* v. *Casey*, the Court reaffirmed that women have a constitutional right to choose abortion and made clear that states cannot ban abortion or give another person veto power over an adult woman's choice. However, the justices adopted an "undue burden" standard, under which states may impose abortion restrictions so long as they do not have "the purpose or effect of placing a substantial obstacle in the path of a woman seeking an abortion." Applying this standard, the Court struck down Pennsylvania's mandatory husband notification provision, but a plurality upheld the state's mandatory waiting periods, biased counseling, and parental involvement requirements.

In 1993, President Clinton took office and quickly reversed some of the antiabortion policies of the previous administrations—lifting the ban on federal funding for research using fetal tissue; reversing the "Mexico City Policy," which prohibited nongovernmental organizations receiving federal funds from administering international family programs that encouraged or supported abortion "as a method of family planning"; and urging review of the import ban on RU486.

Antiabortion forces continued to push the limits of the right to choose abortion. Although barring bans on abortion, the Casey ruling created ambiguity about the constitutionality of many abortion restrictions. Some federal courts have upheld antiabortion measures identical to those struck down by the Court during the 1970s and 1980s. Meanwhile, the Republican majority in the 104th Congress has imposed additional restrictions on abortion services and family planning programs.

Some opponents of abortion advocate illegal, violent tactics to prevent women from obtaining medical services. Since the mid-1980s, abortion providers and women seeking their services have reported thousands of incidents of harassment and violence. Between March 1993 and December 1994, two abortion providers, two clinic workers, and a volunteer security escort were killed by antiabortion demonstrators; others were wounded. Faced with such extreme pressure, some physicians have stopped performing abortions, adding to an already critical shortage of these providers.

By the early 1990s fear of reprisal, lack of medical-school training, and the fact that many older physicians had retired left at least 84 percent of all U.S. counties without an abortion provider. In the early 1990s, legislative bodies and the federal and state judiciaries responded to antiabortion harassment and violence by passing laws and imposing court orders designed to protect physicians as well as women obtaining abortions. From 1990 to 1995, the Court heard three cases involving antiabor-

tion harassment and violence and returned mixed opinions. In early 1994, Congress and President Clinton adopted a new federal statute—the Freedom of Access to Clinic Entrances Act—creating federal jurisdiction over antiabortion violence and allowing criminal federal prosecution for violent actions directed against abortion providers and women seeking their services.

Unfortunately, some of the earliest Court decisions on pregnancy set troubling precedents, finding that disability plans could treat pregnancy differently from other disabilities without violating the Equal Protection Clause of the Fourteenth Amendment or Title VII of the Civil Rights Act of 1964. Responding to pressure from the women's movement, the legal community, and civil rights advocates, in 1978 Congress adopted the Pregnancy Discrimination Act, repudiating the Court's decision in *General Electric* v. *Gilbert*, 1976, and amending the definition of sex discrimination to include pregnancy discrimination. In 1987 the Court upheld a law guaranteeing maternity leave to pregnant women, finding that employment practices *favoring* pregnant women are not discriminatory. The statute's protections, however, extend only to employment decisions and benefits such as employer-provided health insurance; the law explicitly excludes discrimination on the basis of abortion. Neither the federal courts nor Congress has yet overturned the 1974 holding in *Geduldig* v. *Aiello* that pregnancy discrimination does not violate the Constitution.

Beginning in the mid-1970s, the antiabortion movement's agenda included efforts to regulate women's behavior during pregnancy. Legal opponents developed a strategy to expand "fetal rights," hoping that establishing such rights would help to reverse *Roe* v. *Wade*.

Courts have consistently held that it is unconstitutional to compel a person to undergo a medical procedure for the benefit of another. Nonetheless, doctors and hospitals still seek court orders to force pregnant women to undergo caesarean sections and other procedures against their will. The fetal rights argument also has led to other punitive measures against pregnant women, including prosecution for drug or alcohol use, or for not following doctors' orders.

David J. Garrow, *Liberty and Sexuality: The Right to Privacy and the Making of Roe v. Wade* (New York: Macmillan, 1994); Linda Gordon, *Woman's Body, Woman's Right: Birth Control in America* (Revised and Updated) (New York: Penguin Books, 1990); James Mohr, *Abortion in America: The Origins and Evolution of National Policy, 1800-1900* (New York: Oxford University Press, 1978).

■ KATHRYN KOLBERT
and ANDREA MILLER

SEE ALSO Abortion; Birth Control; Eugenics; Fetal Rights; Pregnancy; Privacy Rights; Pro-Choice and Antiabortion Movements; *Roe v. Wade*; Sterilization and Sterilization Abuse.

≋ Reproductive Technology

Since the late 1970s, clinicians developed numerous techniques, with expansions and permutations, to assist conception. On July 25, 1978, in Oldham, England, the first laboratory-conceived baby, Louise Brown, was born. From 1954 to 1969 attempts had been made to fertilize human eggs from ovaries removed in surgery. The 1970s saw the development of the technique of laparoscopy: seeing the eggs with a thin, lighted telescope inserted at the navel. For standard in vitro fertilization (IVF) and embryo transfer (ET), eggs are aspirated through a needle inserted near the laparoscope, and sperm are added in a culture dish. If fertilization and cell division succeed, resulting embryos are inserted into the potential mother's uterus. To become a baby the embryo must then successfully implant in the uterus.

After Louise Brown's media-event birth, IVF clinics sprang up worldwide; by 1994 some eight world congresses on assisted reproduction had taken place. Australia emerged early as a leader; France and Israel have the most clinics per capita; the United States by 1988 had more than one hundred sixty clinics. Until 1981 only three IVF babies had been born; in that year twelve more arrived, including the first U.S. baby, Elizabeth Jordan Carr, conceived at the Jones Institute in Norfolk, Virginia. But even by 1995 success rates remained below 15 percent.

Since a woman usually releases only one egg per menstrual cycle, and since more eggs increase the chance of success, most clinics inject fertility drugs to cause multiple ovulation. Usually a drug like Clomid® or Pergonal® is followed by the pregnancy hormone to trigger ovulation. Since 1986 many clinics have suppressed menstrual cycles beforehand with contraceptive pills or an imitation hormone that disables the pituitary gland. Risks to women from these fertility drugs include ovarian hyperstimulation syndrome, ovarian cysts, menstrual irregularities, premature menopause, and ovarian cancer. As with other drugs, regulation of fertility drugs is loose: effectiveness and safety have not been ascertained; private physicians sometimes prescribe unapproved drugs; approved drugs sometimes get used for other conditions or at incorrect dosages.

Laparoscopy requires a highly skilled surgeon; for the patient, the procedure is stressful and may cause hemorrhage, gas embolism, or coma from anesthesia. Between 1982 and 1985, European clinicians invented egg-retrieval procedures that use ultrasound to find eggs without surgery, and manufacturers devised ultrasound transducers to fit in the vagina. Although these procedures also require skill and are not pain- or risk-free, by 1990 most clinics had adopted an ultrasound method in which the egg-retrieval needle punctures the vaginal wall next to the cervix.

One outcome of IVF may be multiple pregnancy if several embryos are transferred. In Australia, from 1979 through 1986, 38 percent of surviving IVF babies were twins, triplets, or quadruplets. Multiple pregnancy risks include toxemia and gestational diabetes for the mother; congenital anomalies, reduced survival, growth retardation, and premature birth for the babies; as well as socioeconomic problems for parents raising triplets and quadruplets. Hence some clinics restrict the number of embryos transferred, and some use techniques for "reduction in number," in which a surgeon locates fetuses by ultrasound and then terminates all but one or two.

As IVF attempts became widespread, expansions and variations burgeoned. In 1984 in Texas, Ricardo Asch invented gamete intrafallopian transfer (GIFT), in which eggs retrieved by laparoscopy are mixed with sperm and inserted into the anesthetized woman's fallopian tubes. Although most Catholic hospitals will not carry out IVF/ET, many permit GIFT because egg and sperm unite inside the woman's body. From the early 1980s, donor sperm had been used when male partners had few functional sperm. Then, in 1983, a Melbourne team reported the first donor-egg baby, an event that soon became commonplace. Donor eggs are used when a potential mother's eggs are at risk for a chromosome anomaly or defective gene or when she is past menopause or cannot ovulate. First reported in 1993, postmenopausal pregnancy immediately became controversial—even forbidden in some countries. Another fad (also sometimes restricted) is obtaining eggs from ovaries of aborted fetuses.

IVF-surrogacy, or gestational surrogacy, occurs when a woman incubates an embryo—from an egg and sperm united in the laboratory—to produce a baby for others, usually the couple who provided those gametes. The first reported U.S. IVF-surrogacy baby was born in 1986; in 1987 a South African mother bore triplets for her daughter. In 1984 a Melbourne team produced the world's first baby from a frozen embryo. Freezing excess embryos has since become routine; most clinics offer or require it. Since the late 1980s many laboratories have tried injecting sperm through the egg's coating but with limited success.

Experiments with embryos of domestic animals have motivated many countries to prohibit certain procedures in humans, for example, fertilizing human eggs with nonhuman sperm (cross-species fertilization) or splitting embryos in two (cloning).

In the 1990s other expansions of IVF included embryo biopsy and genetic screening. After removal of one or two cells (biopsy) to test them, the rest of an eight- or sixteen-cell embryo (if successfully implanted) can become a complete baby; in 1989 the first sex-checked baby was born after such testing. In the 1990s, after pinpointing genes for numerous genetic disorders, many geneticists are trying to screen biopsied cells for "bad" genes in order to select embryos without disabilities. Beyond mere detection, many researchers hope to replace or cure defective genes in eggs or embryos.

Artificial or assisted insemination (AI) is the oldest, simplest, and most widely used reproductive technology. In its basic form, the doctor inserts sperm (from a partner or a donor) into a woman's upper vagina at the time of ovulation. Freezing of sperm started in the 1940s; after the 1960s sperm banks proliferated. With the spread of the AIDS epidemic in the late 1980s, freezing often became mandatory to keep sperm until a donor had a second HIV test six months later. Since lesbians and single women were often excluded from AI clinics, they used self-insemination with known donors or anonymous ones recruited by friends or by feminist sperm banks. A major social issue with AI is the conflict of secrecy to protect the donor versus the right to know one's genetic parentage: often clinics either keep no records or refuse to reveal names of donors to grown AI children.

Historically many parents have wished to choose their children's sex, because of preferred family configurations or cultural devaluation of females. Although folk methods and unproven theories predominate, certain new techniques can indeed select sex. Technologies such as amniocentesis and chorionic villus biopsy, that diagnose genetic anomalies in a fetus, can also give accurate sex detection. Both procedures are invasive and have risks. Ultrasound, a much less invasive technology, improved rapidly through the 1980s until machines could depict genitalia in midpregnancy with 95 percent accuracy. In India amniocentesis and ultrasound for sex selection are widespread even though prohibited; in Western nations a pregnant woman with access to health care is routinely told her fetus's sex after ultrasound.

Most couples with a sex preference wish to avoid abortion. Do-it-yourself folk methods for sex selection of sperm have appeared in scientific guise but produce sex ratios no better than chance. These methods include timing of intercourse or of orgasm, position during intercourse, acidity level in the vagina, and salt content in the diet. In 1986 ProCare of Colorado marketed a kit ("Gender Choice"), based on a timing theory, but in 1987 the Food and Drug Administration labeled it "a gross deception," and in 1988 ProCare went bankrupt. Another unverified procedure, the "Ericsson method," uses an albumen column to separate male- and female-determining sperm before AI; it allegedly produces over 75 percent boys. Most who attempt sex detection and sex preselection (except for sex-linked diseases) seek males.

Although few feminists study reproductive technologies, lively—sometimes heated—debate has occurred. Some have questioned safety, efficacy, and informed consent; many have criticized lack of access. In the United States reproductive technologies (RTs) often are unavailable to lesbians, single women, disabled persons, the poor, or women of color: prejudice may motivate doctors to refuse treatment or avoid suggesting RTs. Poverty may limit access to any medical service: by 1995 only two states required all health insurers to cover IVF.

In the 1990s almost no feminists supported the views of Shulamith Firestone, who, in 1970, rec-

ommended that technology be developed to free women from the burden of childbearing. Yet many liberal feminists believe that the new RTs offer options to women—that any woman fully informed about risks and success rates should decide whether to use them. Many radical feminists, however, maintain that RTs separate reproduction from the body and give doctors too much power over women's bodies. This relatively ineffective service to infertile women may be economically advantageous to the medical profession and to drug companies. For example, Serono Pharmaceuticals (which has the monopoly on Pergonal® in the U.S.) funds RESOLVE, a patient advocacy/education group for infertile couples, which endorses all RTs.

With these technologies now available to the educated middle class, friends and family may pressure an infertile woman to keep trying new variants of IVF. Inevitably, RTs reinforce the cultural stereotype that procreation is women's primary role.

Andrea L. Bonnicksen, *In Vitro Fertilization: Building Policy from Laboratories to Legislatures* (New York: Columbia University Press, 1989); Helen Bequaert Holmes, "In Vitro Fertilization: Reflections on the State of the Art," *Birth* Vol. 15 (1988): 134–45; Helen Bequaert Holmes, "Choosing Children's Sex: Challenges to Feminist Ethics," in *Reproduction, Ethics and the Law*, edited by Joan Callahan (Bloomington: Indiana University Press, 1995).

▪ HELEN BEQUAERT HOLMES

SEE ALSO Infertility; Pregnancy; Surrogacy.

≋ Republicanism

Between the fifteenth and eighteenth centuries, the classical republican ideal of a virtuous citizenry and an active public life was recovered and refashioned in the context of growing national societies. Originally the outlook of Renaissance civic humanists, republicanism came to influence such broad political developments as the establishment of parliamentary rule in seventeenth-century England; the wars for independence and the establishment of new republics in the Netherlands and colonial America; the claims of popular sovereignty and radical republicanism during the French Revolution; the emancipation of slaves and the fight to preserve the Union during the American Civil War; and struggles to democratize politics and widen the suffrage to include propertyless men, women, and former slaves during the nineteenth century.

Early modern republicans developed a theory that arms were essential to liberty and the defense of the republic. They also tied property ownership to virtuous citizenship. The republican community was committed to the *vita activa*, according to which citizenship was not merely a role performed by individuals but the very definition of what it means to be human. In the republican view, citizens were conscious, autonomous participants in a free, self-governing community. The republican conception of liberty was positive not negative. Virtue signified a devotion to the public good as well as relations of equality among those citizens who were actively engaged in ruling and being ruled.

The modern republican revival also invested public action with a decidedly masculinist ethos. Active citizenship in the republic was deemed to be the explicit province of men, since only men possessed the prerequisites of citizenship—the capacity to soldier and own property. From constitutional monarchists to democratic populists, republicans agreed on the necessity and propriety of female domesticity. Modern republicanism accorded the domestic sphere a civic importance. Though private, the modern republican family assumed a decidedly political function within the larger commonwealth and women's freedom was associated with their domestic roles.

Jean-Jacques Rousseau (1712–1778) articulated

forcefully the gender dimension of modern republicanism, placing the "woman question" at the center of an argument for political and social reform. He posited woman as a new kind of political and moral subject, curiously lacking in formal political rights. He praised virtuous women's domesticity and "chaste power," which allowed them to "govern" men, if only in the realm of the family. However, others inspired by republican convictions sought to expand on women's role. The British author Mary Wollstonecraft (1759–1797), the Americans Benjamin Rush (1746–1813) and Judith Sargent Murray (1751–1820), and the French philosopher and revolutionary the Marquis de Condorcet (1743–1794) all advocated for women's education.

In the nineteenth century in the United States, the doctrine of republican motherhood helped to consolidate the class interests of an emerging white middle-class elite in much the same way that republicanism remained an expression of the world view and interests of white middle-class men, despite the strong appeal of its broadly universal principles of liberty, free labor and equality to working men. Middle-class white women were empowered by a new ideal of companionate marriage, a shared belief in women's education, and a view of motherhood as vital to the transmission of civic virtue. By the 1830s and 1840s, numbers of white northern, middle-class, Protestant women moved beyond the domestic sphere to swell the ranks of moral reform and abolitionism. White antislavery women drew upon the language of republicanism to condemn slavery but divided over whether to endorse association with Black antislavery women. The issue of racial equality proved far more intractable than that of antislavery, and female republicans, like their male counterparts, disputed the concrete meanings of legal and political equality for Blacks. After the failure of her experiment for racial amalgamation and slave emancipation, feminist, abolitionist, and labor reformer Frances Wright transported former slaves from her community in Nashoba, Tennessee to

Haiti out of concern that color would preclude their equality in the United States. Similarly, republican doctrines did not wholly alleviate class and ethnic divisions in the new nation, such as those between native women and immigrant newcomers.

It was white middle-class women who most effectively seized upon republican rhetoric, as in the new women's rights movement born at the Seneca Falls Convention of 1848. Supporters of republican motherhood saw education as bringing about a progressive future, though one still anchored in the force of natural sexual distinctions. They believed that an improved education would raise women's natural virtues up to the level of reason, and that a republican mother's major political task was to instill her children with patriotic duty. As citizens, women would be educated beyond their limited horizons and wholly self-oriented concerns in order to serve their families and the republic, but would leave to men the foremost political task of governing the nation. Beginning in 1848, however, feminists would claim that women had a special contribution to make as active citizens in the public sphere. Like moral reformers and abolitionists, they challenged the overwhelmingly masculinist construction of the republican political tradition.

Eric Foner, *Free Soil, Free Labor, Free Men: The Ideology of the Republican Party Before the Civil War* (New York: Oxford University Press, 1970); Linda Kerber, *Women of the Republic: Intellect and Ideology in Revolutionary America* (Chapel Hill, N.C.: 1980); Nancy Woloch, *Women and the American Experience* (New York: McGraw-Hill, 1994).

• JOAN B. LANDES

SEE ALSO Citizenship; Liberalism.

≋ Revolution

SEE Wars: Colonization to 1900.

≋ Roe v. Wade

On January 22, 1973, the U.S. Supreme Court issued its 7-2 decision in *Roe v. Wade*, which recognized for the first time that the constitutional right to privacy encompasses a woman's right to decide to terminate her pregnancy. Striking down Texas's criminal ban on abortions not necessary to save a woman's life, this ruling marked a critical moment in this nation's history—an intersection of the demands of a burgeoning grassroots movement for women's liberation and the efforts of legal scholars and advocates seeking to use the courts to guarantee equal rights for all Americans. Written by Associate Justice Harry A. Blackmun, *Roe v. Wade* also reflects the perpetual tension in the law between the need for the U.S. Constitution to evolve to protect vulnerable members of our society and the need to adhere to precedent. Finally, the case—which had been argued before the Court twice prior to this decision—highlighted the intense divisions in the United States over the issue of abortion.

The Court's task "is to resolve the issue by constitutional measurement, free of emotion and of predilection," wrote Justice Blackmun. He dispassionately reviewed the history of abortion from ancient times, noting that "the restrictive criminal abortion laws in effect in a majority of States today are of relatively recent vintage." Noting that pregnancy and childbirth implicate a woman's physical and mental health, the majority specifically recognized the stigma of "unwed motherhood" and the difficulties of families unable to care for an additional child. However, the many tragedies caused by the criminalization of abortion—scores of women died from illegal or self-induced abortions; many others were left scarred and maimed—were not detailed in the Court's opinion.

As former counsel to the prestigious Mayo Clinic in Rochester, Minnesota, Justice Blackmun recognized the importance of positioning the right to choose abortion as, at its base, a decision resting on a physician's best medical judgment. As a result, the opinion detailed the stance of the American Medical Association—as an advocate for criminal abortion laws in the mid– to late nineteenth century and a supporter of liberalized abortion statutes beginning in the late 1960s—and cited the American Public Health Association's 1970 standards for abortion services. The majority opinion also noted that criminal abortion statutes often sought to protect pregnant women from the severe health risks of terminating a pregnancy and emphasized that medical advances made abortion a safer option for women, with mortality rates for early abortions as low or lower than for childbirth. *Roe*'s companion case, *Doe v. Bolton*, which struck down a Georgia statute criminalizing most abortions, underscored the Court's emphasis on physicians, stating that *Roe* "sets forth our conclusion that a pregnant woman does not have an absolute constitutional right to an abortion on her demand." In that ruling, the 7-2 majority opinion stated that a physician's professional judgment regarding when an abortion may be performed "may be exercised in the light of all factors—physical, emotional, psychological, familial, and the woman's age—relevant to the well-being of the patient."

The majority opinion in *Roe* was careful to acknowledge the need to strike a balance between a pregnant woman's right to privacy and the state's interests in potential human life, stating that "[t]he pregnant woman cannot be isolated in her privacy." To that end, the Court established a framework under which the state's interest in potential life did not become "compelling" until after the point of viability—the point in pregnancy when the fetus is capable of independent survival; even then, protection of potential life could not be promoted at the expense of a woman's life or health. During the first trimester, restrictions on abortion (other than a requirement that the procedure be performed by a licensed physician) would be unconstitutional. After the first trimester

but prior to viability, a state could only impose measures that represented the least restrictive means for protecting a woman's health. Moreover, the Court stated that the question of whether the fetus is a "person" is fraught with political and religious controversy, which should not be decided by the judiciary.

The legal foundations for the *Roe* decision were formed in Supreme Court decisions dating from the 1890s. Although the term *right to privacy* does not exist within the text of the U.S. Constitution, the Court had long recognized that citizens have a fundamental right against governmental intrusion in such intimate family matters as procreation, child rearing, and marriage. The Court relied particularly on the Fourteenth Amendment's explicit guarantee of individual liberty, which it has repeatedly found to encompass privacy. In the mid-1960s, a 7-2 majority of the Supreme Court recognized that this "zone of privacy" protects the right of married couples to use contraceptives. The year before *Roe* was decided, the Justices extended this protection to unmarried couples and individuals, stating, "If the right of privacy means anything, it is the right of the *individual*, married or single, to be free from unwarranted governmental intrusion into matters so fundamentally affecting a person as the decision whether to bear or beget a child." Rather than creating a new affirmative right, Justice Blackmun drew on the historical constitutional tradition of limited government to protect "a woman's decision whether or not to terminate her pregnancy." To find otherwise would have signaled a radical departure from legal precedent.

Roe by no means put to rest the political conflict over abortion and the judicial debate over the scope and contours of constitutional protection for individual liberties. However, the decision heralded a new era and forever changed the face of this nation. Although the language in *Roe* did not tout the decision's truly momentous nature, the Supreme Court's ruling nearly twenty years later to reaffirm the landmark case stated it clearly: "[F]or two decades of economic and so-cial developments, people have organized inti-mate relationships and made choices that define their views of themselves and their places in soci-ety, in reliance on the availability of abortion in the event that contraception should fail. The abil-ity of women to participate equally in the eco-nomic and social life of the Nation has been facil-itated by their ability to control their reproductive lives." Indeed, as Justice Blackmun himself stated upon his retirement from the High Court, *Roe* was "a step that had to be taken as we go down the road toward the full emancipation of women."

■ JANET BENSHOOF

SEE ALSO Abortion; Privacy Rights; Pro-Choice and Antiabortion Movements; Reproductive Rights.

≋ Romance Novels

No genre of women's writing is more ma-ligned—or more popular—than romances: stories reflecting the interests, conflicts, and de-sires that animate women. A romance is tradition-ally defined as a love story between a woman and a man who meet, struggle, and end up happily together. But women's fiction—stories from a woman's point of view—dates back only to the eighteenth century in the United States, when the growth of capitalism and women's literacy first made it profitable to write and publish stories for women. Throughout the eighteenth and nine-teenth centuries, most bestsellers were by women, and most contained elements of romance: Harriet Beecher Stowe's *Uncle Tom's Cabin* (1852), for in-stance, includes several love stories between slaves.

Modern romances, in which strong women truly choose their destinies, could not be created until women had much more power in the world—in the twentieth century. With Harlequin romances, introduced by the English publisher Mills and Boon in 1954, the contemporary series ("category") romances were born. The Harlequin romances were small, professionally written nov-els of uniform length (about two hundred pages), with relatively simple one woman–one man plots. Sold by mail and in nonbookstore outlets, Harle-quins reached readers who might never enter bookstores. Also popular by the 1960s were gothic romances and romantic suspense stories by such writers as Phyllis A. Whitney, whose resourceful heroines triumph over mysterious or arrogant men. Yet the white women in pre-1970s Harle-quins and gothics tended to be young, fairly uned-ucated, and naive; some accepted violence from men. Sexual intercourse was unmentionable in these books.

By the 1970s the women's liberation movement spurred discussions and protests among women about jobs and equal pay, reproductive and sexual freedom, and getting men to be nurturers. New stories were needed, and the first was Kathleen Woodiwiss's *The Flame and the Flower* (1972), a historical romance delivering what modern ro-mance readers wanted—passionate and sensual (but not graphic) sex scenes; a strong, beautiful heroine with a sense of purpose; and an arrogant hero whose love for her transforms him. After Woodiwiss, such writers as Rosemary Rogers (*Sweet Savage Love*, 1974) wrote "bodice rippers," historical romances about repeatedly raped women who survive—but readers eventually re-jected such violent stories of women as victims.

In 1980 Silhouette Books (Simon and Schuster) became Harlequin's first U.S.-based competitor. In 1981 Dell series romances opened the bedroom door: as in real life, unmarried heroines were hav-ing sex. In the 1990s, because of AIDS, the women in romance novels were more apt to wait for sex. Publishers have created multiple lines of category romances, many with "tip sheets" advis-ing would-be authors about characters' preferred ages, occupations, secondary plots, and level of explicit sex. Different lines now vary in length and emphases (mystery, second chances, historicals). The Regency historical novels, modeled after Jane Austen and Georgette Heyer, take place in the early nineteenth century and feature clever word play and romantic comedy. In 1994 Pinnacle's Arabesque line was founded to publish romances for women of color, especially African American women.

Noncategory historical romances have also flourished, as have contemporary mainstream women's novels and family sagas by such writers as Belva Plain and Danielle Steel (although their work is not strictly "romance"). Some authors who began as category writers—notably Sandra Brown, Janet Dailey, Jayne Ann Krentz, and Nora Roberts—have now moved into writing mainstream bestsellers. Romances still depict women's professional and personal power and pleasure, yet romance readers and writers are often wrongly accused of being dupes of capitalist patriarchy. Even feminist critics writing about romance (Tania Modleski, Kay Mussell, Janice Radway) disparage the genre and its readers. Few academic critics mention the numerous lesbian romances published by Naiad Press, for example, whose best-selling author is Katherine Forrest.

In Jayne Ann Krentz's book about romance literature, *Dangerous Men and Adventurous Women*, however, nineteen romance writers note their work's impact (47 percent of mass-market paperback sales are romances); their typical readers (college-educated, full-time workers); and their books' most appealing features (verbal sparring, sensually coded language, sexual tension, and intriguing plots in which the woman always wins). Most romance authors are members of the Romance Writers of America (RWA), the largest writers' organization in the world and a strong lobbyist for authors' rights. Through local chapters, RWA also provides critique groups to teach members to write publishable romances. Romance writers are the only authors who train their own competition and pride themselves on sharing what they know.

The world of romances involves women's traditional values: love, family, relationships—but also the empowerment of women to control their own destinies. Most romance writers call themselves feminists, part of an ancient sisterhood of women telling and sharing stories.

Jayne Ann Krentz, ed., *Dangerous Men and Adventurous Women: Romance Writers on the Appeal of the Romance* (Philadelphia: University of Pennsylvania, 1992); Romance Writers of America, *Romance Writers' Report* (13700 Veterans Memorial, Suite 315, Houston, TX 77014), bimonthly journal; Emily Toth, "Labors of Love," *Women's Review of Books* Vol. 10 (January 1993): 10–11.

● EMILY TOTH

SEE ALSO Literature.

≋ Rosie the Riveter

Largely because of the exodus of over twelve million men into the armed services during World War II, the employment of women in the U.S. industrial labor force increased from twelve million to nineteen million between 1941 and 1945. In this most striking labor-market development of the war, white women and women of color entered industries previously reserved almost exclusively for white men. After the soldiers returned, in 1945–46, women were bumped from their skilled, well-paying industrial jobs. But they never really left employment. They couldn't afford to.

This is the true story. But truth at the time was shrouded in the mythic figure of "Rosie the Riveter," invented by the government's poster-making crews and popularized by the press. The "Rosie the Riveter" so depicted had never worked before the war and had entered industrial employment only out of patriotic duty, loneliness for her soldier husband, or boredom. Although the nation admired her willingness to exchange her

A teenage girl in Salem Village, Massachusetts, accuses George Jacobs of witchcraft at the trials in 1692. The painting, made by T. H. Matteson in 1855, conveys the centrality of the young women accusers.

kitchen apron for overalls, people assumed that her industrial work was temporary and that she (the mythic "Rosie") would be happy to relinquish her job to a returning soldier so that she could resume her role as homemaker.

The myth reflected both the nation's desire to romanticize wartime work and its continuing unwillingness to see women as equal earning partners with men. Industrial employment was good employment from working people's point of view; it provided job security, union membership, and wages unavailable in the laundries, piecework manufacturing, and in the domestic work that working-class women had done before the war. It

was to reinstate that occupational gender and racial segregation after the war that the myth of wartime "Rosie the Riveter" was perpetuated.

　　　　　　　　　　　　■ SHEILA TOBIAS

SEE ALSO World War II Period.

≋ Salem Witchcraft Trials

During the colonial period, nearly three hundred women were accused by their neighbors of performing witchcraft. Although those accusations spanned approximately the first century of English settlement in North America, about half were voiced during one ten-month period in 1692. This episode is commonly known as the Salem witchcraft crisis, although it began in Salem Village (now Danvers), Massachusetts, a small settlement on the outskirts of Salem Town, and although most of the accused were from nearby Andover.

The crisis began when a group of girls and young women connected to the household of the Reverend Samuel Parris began to suffer from convulsions and hysterical fits. By the end of February 1692 the afflicted young people had accused various local women of having bewitched them. Others in the surrounding area then also claimed to be the objects of sorcery, and the jails were soon crowded with accused men and women. A special court handled the trials, and by the time prosecutions ceased in May 1693, twenty-six people had been convicted and nineteen (including sixteen women) executed by hanging. Fifty more people confessed to being witches.

Historians have had great difficulty explaining this puzzling episode, which was one of the last two witch-hunts in the English-speaking world. It does seem, however, to have been generated in part by divisions within Salem Village that were magnified because local institutions were unable to resolve the conflicts satisfactorily. Still, current interpretations have not yet adequately accounted for women's prominent role in the crisis.

■ MARY BETH NORTON

SEE ALSO Puritanism.

≋ Science and Gender

For many years, questions about the differences in mathematical, scientific, and technical ability between boys and girls have been staple features of newspaper and magazine articles. The articles suggest that boys make better grades in math than girls because mathematical ability and, more generally, scientific ability are biologically based. They also claim that that's why most scientists are male. In the mid-1970s female scientists in the United States began to address the question of why so few women were scientists.

Despite the efforts of female scientists since the 1920s to improve the status of women through a number of strategies—the development of educational programs designed to encourage more young women to enter the sciences in elementary and high schools; summer research programs for undergraduate women in leading university and industrial laboratories; increased support and funding for graduate education; wider recognition for the contributions of senior female scientists and more visibility for women in science at every level—some female scientists felt that little significant progress had been made and identified the need for different approaches to understand the persistent underrepresentation of women in the sciences.

Instead of asking why so few women were becoming scientists, they asked what it was about science that had prevented women from participating more and from advancing to the field's highest levels. Feminist scientists challenged the notion that biologically based gender differences were responsible for women's lack of achievement in the sciences and began to reevaluate the validity of the notion. They exposed flaws in research design, subject choice, data interrelation, and theoretical constructs that purported to demonstrate a biological basis for female inferiority. Much of this literature attempted to explain observed gender differences in social roles or socially recognized achievements. The scientists demonstrated that much of the research on sex differences had flaws in both experimental design and interpretation, including sociobiology, brain lateralization, psychology, and primatology.

The biologists also urged caution in assigning behavior to any single root cause. Biology, they argued, both shapes and is shaped by interactions in society. While much of this research claimed to study differences between males and females, that is, sex differences, they concluded that what was actually being studied was gender differences—those masculine and feminine behaviors which are actually social meanings and values assigned to sex differences. Gender differences are shaped by social behaviors that are considered appropriate for girls and boys. Therefore, the differences in mathematical ability between boys and girls must be influenced by biology *and* the fact that, until recently, girls in many societies were restricted from participating in certain activities to the same extent as boys.

Science has been historically represented as quintessentially masculine: abstract, depersonalized, objective, authoritative. Feminists involved in the study of gender and science have tried to discover how certain notions of gender shape the theory and practice of science. Their goal is to provide a fuller account of the natural world by not devaluing the influence of the feminine and by explaining how scientific knowledge is shaped to some extent by scientists' practices and beliefs. For example, the standard textbook description of human reproduction has been revised. This discussion typically emphasized that an "active" sperm comes in contact with a "passive" egg. Feminist biologists argued that this explanation was not supported by fact—indeed, fertilization is an active process that requires the participation of both egg and sperm. The traditional version relied on cultural stereotypes of male and female behavior rather than on scientific facts. This productive and evolving field of freeing science from gender includes topics such as studies of new reproductive technologies and women; the social behavior of primates; genetic theories of gender and behavior; biographies of women scientists; ecology, environmentalism and concepts of nature and women crossculturally; computer technologies and women; and many other issues that reveal the place of gender in the theory and practice of science.

■ EVELYNN M. HAMMONDS

≋ Sculpture

The achievements of U.S. women sculptors have never been adequately recognized. Since early times women have executed large-scale works that stand in parks, plazas, and public buildings. Long before the arrival of white settlers, Native American women among the Anasazis of the Southwest, the Mississippi tribes, and others were creating three-dimensional objects in basketry, ceramics, and other materials.

Just before the American Revolution, a Quaker widow, Patience Wright, became the first professional white U.S. sculptor. Beginning her career with a waxworks tableau, she later won acclaim in London for wax portraits of prominent Britons.

During the mid–nineteenth century a small number of women studied sculpture in Rome and became professionals. Among them, Harriet Hosmer achieved international fame for works based on mythological and literary themes. Edmonia Lewis drew inspiration for marble sculptures from her mixed Black and Native American heritage; Emma Stebbins created the *Bethesda Fountain* in Central Park, and Vinnie Ream completed a marble portrait, *Lincoln,* for the U.S. Capitol.

By the early twentieth century, sculptors such as Anna Hyatt Huntington and Evelyn Longman were members of the National Sculpture Society, completing equestrian statues and other commissions. At the same time, others began to challenge the academic tradition of glorified realism and allegory. Abastenia Eberle, a member of the ashcan school, modeled sensitive, lively bronze studies of poor immigrants as early as 1908. Around 1917 Alice Morgan Wright and Adelheid Roosevelt created some of the earliest U.S. cubist and abstract sculptures. Augusta Savage and other Black women sculptors, inspired by the Harlem Renaissance, employed themes drawn from African American culture.

During the Great Depression of the 1930s,

women hired by federal art agencies carried out commissions for post offices and public buildings around the country. After World War II the abstract movement swept through U.S. art, and Louise Nevelson, Lee Bontecou, and others created a variety of powerful works. Osage artist Yeffe Kimball studied at the Art Students League and in Paris, paving the way, with her abstract and expressionist forms, for Native American artists to enter the mainstream. In the 1960s Marisol and Niki de St. Phalle developed their own distinctive figurative approaches, related to pop art.

Despite the emerging freedoms of the feminist movement in the 1970s, women artists still were largely shut out of museums, galleries, and textbooks. In protest of all chauvinistic aspects of the art world, they picketed museums, formed their own organizations, and, led by innovators such as Miriam Schapiro and Judy Chicago, explored new forms based on female sexuality, spirituality, and other aspects of women's experience. Embracing the long women's tradition of crafts, they broke down the boundaries between sculpture, weaving, ceramics, and other three-dimensional forms. Feminist critics discovered depths of meaning in the work of such innovative sculptors as Louise Bourgeois and Eva Hesse. Women of color, such as Elizabeth Catlett, Betye Saar, and Latina artist Amalia Mesa-Bains, moved into the forefront.

Today, although sexism is far from eradicated, women like Louise Bourgeois and Nancy Graves are major figures in the mainstream art world. Mary Miss, Athena Tacha, Ann Hamilton, and many others are creating large site works and installations. Perhaps the work that best exemplifies the expanding position of women in U.S. sculpture is Maya Lin's *Vietnam Veterans Memorial Wall* (1982) in Washington, D.C. Conceived and executed by this young Asian American, the wall is one of the greatest war memorials ever created and brings new meaning to the concept of a public monument.

Charlotte S. Rubinstein, *American Women Artists: From Early Indian Times to the Present* (Boston: G. K. Hall & Co., 1982); Charlotte S. Rubinstein, *American Women Sculptors: A History of Women Working in Three Dimensions* (Boston: G. K. Hall & Co., 1990).

■ CHARLOTTE STREIFER RUBINSTEIN

SEE ALSO Art and Crafts.

≋ SDS

SEE Students for a Democratic Society.

≋ Senate

SEE Congress.

≋ Seneca Falls

The Seneca Falls Convention met in Seneca Falls, New York, from July 19–20, 1848. It was the first convention in the world held specifically to discuss women's rights. Attended by 240 people (including forty men), the meeting was organized by Lucretia Mott and Elizabeth Cady Stanton. Mott and Stanton, both Quakers, had met in 1840 at the World's Anti-Slavery Convention in London, where Mott had been denied a seat because of her sex. The event encouraged Mott and Stanton to join forces to work for abolitionism *and* women's rights.

The Seneca Falls Convention issued the "Declaration of Sentiments," a comprehensive enumeration of the many ways U.S. women were oppressed. It asserted that "all men and women are created equal," and discussed women's exclusion from higher education, the professions, and the pulpit. The document also lamented female disfranchisement and the absence of married women's legal and property rights, among other issues. It demanded, finally, that women be granted "immediate admission to all the rights and privileges which belong to them as citizens of the United States," including the right to vote. The suffrage demand was the only resolution not unanimously supported by the convention; many, including Mott, worried that its inclusion would weaken public support for other demands.

Two weeks after Seneca Falls, an even larger women's rights convention was held in Rochester, New York. From that point forward, annual meetings would become an important component of the women's movement.

■ ANDREA TONE

SEE ALSO Jacksonian Period.

≋ Separate Spheres

Separate spheres embodied the vision of a social order based on a polarity of roles and personalities rooted in presumed biological and sexual differences between the sexes. Men were rational, instrumental, independent, competitive, and aggressive; women were emotional, maternal, domestic, and dependent. England's nineteenth-century emerging bourgeoisie, idealized and popularized by the sentimental novel, advice books, and medical and religious writings, emphasized the concept of a society structured around supposedly "natural," God-ordained distinct male and female spheres.

Western political theories, both republicanism and liberalism, inscribed the concept, pronouncing the political sphere, civic virtue, and citizenship exclusively male preserves, and excluding women from political subjectivity. Feminist political theorists argue that the social contract established women's political and legal inferiority to

men. The concept of separate spheres was also central to common-law doctrines, which, until reforms in the mid- and late nineteenth century, severely restricted married women's legal rights and independence. It also underlay that key feminist-sponsored Progressive economic reform—protective labor legislation that sought to protect women workers as the future mothers of America.

The philosophy of separate spheres was also closely tied to emerging medical and scientific theories. The assumptions of biologically determined separateness thus shaped physicians and scientists' visions, and biological determinism presumed and reaffirmed this vision.

Alice Paul introduced the Equal Rights Amendment in the 1920s, one of the movement's first formal challenges. Feminists continued the attack in the 1970s. Nevertheless, a belief that innate differences distinguish men and women remains central to some current feminist thought.

■ CARROLL SMITH-ROSENBERG

≋ Service Sector

The service sector, which accounts for ninety percent of the jobs created in the past decade, has expanded far beyond the traditional consumer or institutional service industries and currently includes distributive services, such as transportation, communications, and utilities; the rapidly expanding producer services, such as finance, insurance, real estate, and advertising; wholesale and retail trade and sales; the nonprofit sector, including health, philanthropy, and education; and government. Institutional service work, which includes food production, laundry and dry cleaning, cleaning and building services and janitorial work, child care, health care service, teaching, the manufacture of clothing, and personal services, is the sector in which women of all races and ethnic

The expanding service sector of the 1920s opened the job market for many women, such as these telephone operators, photographed on April 7, 1927. Their fashionably bobbed hair and silky dresses illustrate the influence of consumer culture on young women and the increasing importance of female appearance in the workplace. Although opportunities grew for white women, racism limited women of color to domestic employment and the least desirable factory jobs.

groups first constituted an unprecedented majority of the work force.

Service industries employ relatively large numbers of low-paid workers and high-paid professionals, and distribute wages more unequally than goods-producing industries. Over one-quarter of workers in the service sector are hired on a temporary, subcontracted, or leased basis, without benefits or job security, in small decentralized work sites. Technological advances provide professionals with greater labor-saving flexibility, and many men are for the first time sharing the menial

tasks of their job with a computer instead of a secretary. The use of technology in the service sector promotes deskilling, that is, automation, routinization, and punitive supervision.

The division of labor in the service industries highlights the pervasive gender and racial stratification built into organizational structures through lines of authority, job descriptions, rules, and spatial and temporal segregation. Jobs have been and continue to be segregated by race as well as class: women of color are disproportionately employed as service workers in institutional settings while white-collar, supervisory, and lower professional positions are filled by white women. White women are more frequently hired for positions requiring physical and social contact with the public, that is, as waitresses, transportation attendants, and dental assistants. Women of color typically do the heavy, dirty, "back-room" chores of cooking in restaurants and serving food in cafeterias, cleaning hotel rooms and offices, and caring for the elderly and ill in hospitals and nursing homes.

Clear patterns of racial specialization in the structure of institutionalized service work often follow the racial-ethnic caste lines of the local economies, in which distinct racial and ethnic groups of workers gravitate toward "niches" that become distinct homogeneous occupational communities. These occupational/ethnic niches often reflect the tight social structures and status of various ethnic communities as well as the flow of recent immigrant patterns. In Los Angeles, one scholar found that "the pattern of niching is most evident in the hotels, where Mexicans and Central Americans dominate housekeeping and the kitchen; blacks are likely to work in security, parking, and the front office; Filipinos are employed as accountants, night managers and clericals; and whites work as waitresses in the restaurants and bars." In one Los Angeles hotel, "the Hispanics were so strong that they successfully refused to work with Filipino and other Asian workers." Only the "Russian ladies" in housekeeping had the stamina to stand up against them and survive.

Management's hiring strategies often lead to the displacement of African American and other native-born groups: instead they recruit people from those immigrant groups that are perceived to be more productive and more tractable, such as Asians and Latinas, and they expel those groups they consider to be troublemakers and/or those groups whose members' career ambitions lie beyond the secondary labor market.

Finally, the interaction of the racial and gender division of labor in the service sector aggravates conflicts among women as well as ethnic and racial tensions that present a challenge to a just, civil society.

Karen Brodkin Sacks, *Caring by the Hour: Women, Work, and Organizing at Duke Medical Center* (Urbana: University of Illinois Press, 1988); Dorothy Sue Cobble, ed., "Introduction," in *Women and Unions: Forging a Partnership* (Ithaca: ILR Press, 1993); Roger Waldinger, *Still the Promised City? African Americans and New Immigrants in Postindustrial New York* (Cambridge, Mass.: Harvard University Press, 1996).

▪ BETSY ARON

SEE ALSO Waitresses.

≋ Settlement House Movement

The settlement house movement flourished in the United States from the late 1880s through the Great Depression. Middle-class women and men volunteers lived and worked in settlement houses, which were often converted residential buildings in poor urban neighborhoods. The volunteers hoped to improve the lives of poor families by providing amenities and services not then extended by government agencies, beginning with clubs, classes, and social gatherings, and extending to playgrounds, arts programs, sports and summer camps, clean-milk stations, well-baby clinics, and other innovative programs. Early settlement leaders saw their mission as social reform, and the settlements became "laboratories" for developing new techniques and offering training in the rapidly professionalizing field of social work. By World War I the settlements had become the most important setting for the honing of a U.S. philosophy of social work and social services, with ties to universities, city governments, and other agencies.

The settlement house movement originated in England in the early 1880s as a quasi-religious middle-class response to industrial poverty. Lon-

A basket-weaving class at Denison House in Boston, Massachusetts, circa 1915. Denison was one of many settlement houses where young girls learned traditionally female arts and crafts, activities that were believed to alleviate the stresses caused by Americanization and urban life. Note the Renaissance art on the walls, intended to be a positive influence.

don-based reformers collaborated with university dons and students to substitute "personal service" to the poor for the alms so distasteful to bourgeois sensibilities on both the Left and the Right. Several years after the founding of the first English settlement in 1884, the idea reached the United States and appeared almost simultaneously in New York (the Neighborhood Guild and the College Settlement on Rivington Street), Boston (Andover House), and Chicago (Hull House). Dozens of settlements would be founded over the next three decades by middle-class activists with different religious and institutional affiliations.

Shortly after 1910 the new National Federation of Settlements listed over four hundred settlement houses concentrated in the urban East and Midwest.

The U.S. settlement movement took on its own priorities and rhetoric, centered on the cultural issues arising from the concentration of European immigrants and their children in U.S. cities by 1900. While they prided themselves on the "democratic" flavor of their work, the mostly Protestant settlement workers often showed insensitivity toward Catholic and Jewish immigrants, which stemmed from the chauvinism of their own cultural, racial, and class backgrounds. Jane Addams, of Hull House, typifies the most liberal of the settlement philosophers, as she called on native-born Americans to appreciate "immigrant gifts" in the form of ethnic arts and artisans' skills. Yet she may be seen as more of an assimilationist than a pluralist because she believed the future would reveal the essential commonality of all peoples. Many settlements based their programs on rapid "Americanization" of immigrants' language, work habits, family life, and ideals. The simplest form of immigrant resistance to settlement programs was failure to attend them. Jane Addams admitted ruefully that her experiment with a public kitchen (modeled on Ellen Richards's New England Kitchen), which sold nutritious prepared foods to overworked laboring families, flopped because immigrants preferred their own food choices.

With few exceptions, the white settlements and settlement workers replicated the racism of the Progressive Era by distinguishing between native-born Blacks and immigrant whites. European Americans were deemed good candidates for acculturation, while African Americans were seen as a degraded group with special rehabilitative needs. Settlements for Blacks were segregated from those for whites; moreover, most settlement-like experiments in Black communities, such as rural, school-based settlements and YWCA-affiliated houses, have been overlooked by historians because they appeared different from the "mainstream" settlements. Although whites often were involved in staffing these settlements, Blacks, particularly women, were central in launching and maintaining Black settlement work.

The U.S. settlement movement's virtual gender parity was unique among U.S. institutions during the Progressive Era. At least half of the prominent U.S. settlement houses were headed and staffed largely by women. The roster of influential women settlement leaders includes Jane Addams, Lillian Wald, Mary K. Simkhovitch, Mary McDowell, and Helena Dudley. Further, the settlements offered an urban immersion to thou-

sands more middle-class women, including Hull House's Florence Kelley, Alice Hamilton, Julia Lathrop, and Grace and Edith Abbott, who moved rapidly into government service and advocacy for children, workers, and immigrants.

Mina Carson, *Settlement Folk: Social Thought and the American Settlement Movement, 1885–1930* (Chicago: University of Chicago Press, 1990); Ruth Hutchinson Crocker, *Social Work and Social Order: The Settlement Movement in Two Industrial Cities, 1889–1930* (Urbana: University of Illinois Press, 1992); Elisabeth Lasch-Quinn, *Black Neighbors: Race and the Limits of Reform in the American Settlement House Movement, 1890–1945* (Chapel Hill: University of North Carolina Press, 1993).

▪ MINA CARSON

SEE ALSO Progressive Era; Social Work.

≋ Sex Education

Sexuality education ideally would encompass sexual knowledge, beliefs, attitudes, values, and behaviors. Included would be anatomy, physiology, and biochemistry of the sexual response system, gender roles, identity and personality, and thoughts, feelings, behaviors, and relationships. In addition, moral and ethical concerns, group and cultural diversity, and social change would be addressed. Unfortunately, sexuality education classes in the United States fall far from this ideal. In 1992 Debra Haffner found that less than 10 percent of U.S. children "receive comprehensive sexuality education from kindergarten through adulthood." Although most students are exposed to some type of sexuality education before they complete high school, they usually study only biology, reproduction, and virology. Sexuality education classes often focus on disaster prevention. In elementary grades, sexual abuse is presented; HIV/AIDS is introduced by junior high school; and in high schools, date rape is addressed. Although these areas are all crucial and essential components of sexuality education, omission of more positive aspects of sexuality conveys a powerful message that sex is dangerous. Most programs in the United States promote abstinence from sexual behaviors without offering equal attention to a presentation of safe sex. The official curriculum focuses on heterosexual reproductive sexuality, excluding discussion of gender politics, sexual violence, and pleasure.

Parallel to the "official curriculum" in sexuality education in the typical U.S. high school exists the "hidden curriculum," which teaches teenagers that popularity requires one to be attractive, physically fit, able-bodied, and heterosexual to conform to gender-role expectations and to dress according to school norms. For males, social status depends on "scoring" the sexual conquests of females; for females, social status requires a sexually attractive appearance based on highly unrealistic standards, paired with denial of desire and sexual agency. The double standard continues to exert great influence on the sexuality of adolescents and remains largely unaddressed and uncontested by standard sexuality curricula. Sexuality educators in James Sears's 1992 *Sexuality and the Curriculum: The Politics and Practices of Sexuality Education* critique sexuality education as "an instrument of social control, often reinforcing patriarchal, antisexual norms." Although politically conservative forces have lost the battle to prevent sexuality education, opposition groups promote the teaching of moral absolutes, sexual abstinence, and withholding information in an attempt to prevent adolescents' sexual behavior.

According to Sears, the abortion controversy, AIDS, and teenage pregnancy have resulted in the mandating of sexuality education in twenty-two states, compared to three in 1980. Two-thirds of the nation's largest school districts require sex education. What the classes include, however, varies considerably. For example, South Carolina prohibits teaching about abortion or homosexuality, and in Utah it is a misdemeanor for school personnel to discuss condoms with students without parental consent. Only three states (New Jersey, New York, and Wisconsin) and Washington, D.C., have a program on sex education and AIDS education. The most common sexuality-related topics covered in schools are anatomy and physiology (e.g., changes at puberty, physical differences), sexually transmitted diseases, and sexual decision making with particular emphasis on abstinence. Topics least discussed are homosexuality, gynecologic examinations, birth control, abortion, and masturbation and other safer sex practices.

Treatment of sexuality in the curriculum does not meet students' needs and concerns. Given that a substantial number of youth are sexually active *before* they encounter sexuality education, it is clear that the timing of sexuality education is generally too late to have an impact on adolescents' decisions to engage in sexual activities. However, adolescent females who have had exposure to sexuality education are more likely to seek birth-control services when available. Unfortunately, this holds only for *white* women; for African Americans and Latinas, studies find no relationship between sexuality instruction and contraceptive behavior. This may indicate that even at best, the sexuality curriculum fails to help many students of color.

In addition to inappropriate timing of sexuality education, a gap exists between topics of interest to adolescents and content of such courses. One Chicago-based survey found that teens were most concerned about birth control, abortion, and how to handle sexual feelings while 75 percent of sexuality teachers believed that students should be taught *not* to have sex. Given a social context in which the former U.S. Surgeon General, Dr. Joycelyn Elders, was dismissed for acknowledging the normalcy of masturbation, it is not surprising that sexuality educators may feel constrained in their choice of material.

The dominant sexuality conveyed in curriculum materials, according to Sears, presents sexuality as a "natural human drive to be held in abeyance through self-control, self-management, and postponement of sexual gratification. As a result, these curricula are poorly timed in presentation and prove irrelevant and damaging by omission of crucial information. Michelle Fine argues that the naming of desire, pleasure, or sexual entitlement, particularly for females, barely exists in the formal agenda of public schooling on sexuality. When spoken, it is tagged with reminders of "consequences." Fine cites the approved discourses on adolescent female sexuality as discourses of victimization, disease, and morality. She suggests that the missing discourse of desire may result in girls' failure to know themselves as the subjects of their own sexuality.

Deborah Tolman notes, "If girls could conceive of themselves as sexual *subjects*, they could then potentially make decisions about their sexual behavior and experience that would be healthy for them." The importance of social context has also been acknowledged by some sexuality educators, suggesting that having just more sexuality education, or earlier is not enough, and that sexuality education will be more effective when accompanied by efforts to improve social conditions, decrease poverty, and train people in life skills.

Debra W. Haffner, *Sex Education in 2000: A Call to Action* (New York: Sex Information and Education Council of the U.S., 1990); James Sears, ed., *Sexuality and the Curriculum: The Politics and Practice of Sexuality Education* (New York: Teachers College Press, Columbia University, 1992); Deborah Tolman, "Adolescent Girls, Women and Sexuality: Discerning Dilemmas of Desire," *Women and Therapy, Women, Girls, and Psychotherapy: Reframing Resistance,* 11, no. 3/4 (1991): 55–70.

■ WENDY STOCK

SEE ALSO Sexuality.

≋ Sexism

Sexism is the cultural assumption that men are superior to women and deserve preference and power over them. The term *sexism* was coined in the 1960s by feminists working in the civil rights movement to dramatize the parallel between the negative stereotyping of women and Blacks. The parallel was discussed in the nineteenth century by abolitionists and suffragists and in the early twentieth century by sociologists studying race relations.

The resonance between the words "sexism" and "sexist," and the common words "racism" and "racist," occurred to a number of feminists at about the same time. In a mimeographed speech of 1965, Pauline Leet, then director of special programs at Franklin and Marshall College, charged that historians had been sexist in ignoring women poets, just as historians had been racist in "ignoring the contributions of Negroes."

In 1967 Caroline Bird had trouble getting permission to use the phrase *sexist and racist job assignments* in her 1968 book, *Born Female*, because the terms weren't in the dictionary. Asked for a definition, she said that it meant "going by sex where it doesn't matter" and repeated that definition on September 25, 1968, in an appeal for sex equality to the Episcopal Church Executive Council.

The most influential early use of the term was in a position paper for the Southern Student Organizing Committee, demanding that women working to enfranchise Blacks be treated as the equals of the men in the movement. "Freedom for Movement Girls Now," a document dated 1969 and signed only with the gender-neutral last name "Vaughan," asserted that "the parallels between *sexism* and *racism* are sharp and clear." The manifesto was mentioned in the February 1969 issue of the early feminist publication *No More Fun and Games*, with the suggestion that "we use the word sexism rather than male chauvinism or male supremacy."

The premise of female inferiority and subordination runs so deep and affects so many customs that it is hard to recognize and uproot, so although the premise has faded from mainstream rhetoric, many of its results still remain.

In employment, for instance, childbearing and family duties are no longer used to justify paying women less than men for the same job. Jobs once confined to males have been redesigned to specify the physical ability required, such as upper-arm strength for firefighters, but the cultural funneling of women into subordinate "women's jobs" still depresses women's pay relative to men.

In education single-sex institutions founded on the presumption that women need the protection of segregation and special training for feminine roles at home have all but disappeared, but cultural conditioning still discourages females from the "hard" sciences and from leadership in extracurricular affairs on college campuses.

In sports the presumption of female weakness has been challenged by the records of women granted access to competitions such as marathon racing, but when the sexes are segregated, women's athletics still aren't funded as well as men's.

▪ CAROLINE BIRD

SEE ALSO Stereotypes, Sexual.

≋ Sexology

The late nineteenth century was an important era in the history of sexuality. Rapid social changes, such as the shift from the household economy and the intensification of industrialization and urbanization, facilitated a shift in dominant sexual ideologies away from a family-centered, reproduction-oriented sexuality. This new era, described by historians as "sexual liberalism," marked the emergence of patterns familiar to us today—the growing separation of sex and reproduction; the expansion of commercialized sexuality; and the affirmation of sex as central, not just for a solid marriage but for personal fulfillment. The medical profession, most specifically the field of sexology, played a crucial role in both supporting and helping to effect some of these changing dynamics.

"Sexology" is loosely defined as the scientific study of sex. It is an umbrella term denoting the activity of a multidisciplinary group of researchers, clinicians, and educators concerned with sexuality. Over the last century, sexologists have endeavored to establish themselves as a viable profession with cultural authority over issues of sexuality and gender. Sexual scientists are concerned with sexual functioning, sexual variation, and gender development and dysfunction. They have invented interpretive systems, categories, and languages to describe sexual experience. Sexology has played a complex role in identifying, challenging, and perpetuating cultural imperatives about sex and gender.

Sexology arose indirectly in Europe as a result of public concerns about such issues as prostitution and venereal disease. In addition, the eugenics movement, which sought to create a "superior race" by regulating sexual behavior and limiting reproduction of supposedly inferior groups such as immigrants, Blacks, and Jews, prompted support among many officials for the scientific study of sex.

By the beginning of the twentieth century, major figures such as Richard von Krafft-Ebing and Havelock Ellis had written significant texts on sexuality. Early sexology was centered in Germany. In addition to housing two professional organizations, Berlin was the home of the first sexological institute, the Institut für Sexualwissenschaft, founded in 1919 by Magnus Hirschfeld. Although by the early 1930s there were approximately eighty sex-reform organizations, their efforts were cut short by Hitler's rise to power. In May 1933 Nazis raided Hirschfeld's institute and burned much of their material.

While the progress of German sexology was largely destroyed, sexual science had emerged in other countries, most notably the United States. Among early U.S. sexologists, including Clelia Mosher and Robert Latou Dickinson, it was Alfred Kinsey's research that garnered the most visibility in the young field. *Sexual Behavior in the Human Male* (1948) and *Sexual Behavior in the Human Female* (1953) triggered enormous controversy but, along with the growing cultural discourse on sexuality, helped to establish the foundation for an explosion of sex research in the second half of the twentieth century. Masters and Johnson, Helen Singer Kaplan, and John Money are among the most recognized contemporary sexologists.

Sexologists have engaged in two major projects: the development and provision of sex therapy; and research and therapy concerning sex/gender variations, such as transsexualism and homosexuality. An assessment of these endeavors is complex, since sexologists have often been motivated by contradictory impulses. They have been dedicated to dispelling sexual myths and ignorance and to encouraging sexual knowledge and pleasure. Yet their progressive impulses have been mediated by society's conservative tendencies and hindered in their attempts to achieve professional credibility and to create financially lucrative markets for their services.

Sexology's complicated impact is clearly evident with respect to women. On the one hand, sexologists assert the importance of women's sexuality and sexual pleasure. Feminists have used sex research to address the myth of the vaginal orgasm and to implement self-help and sexual empowerment groups. Many sexologists have genuinely dedicated their work to the achievement of sexual and gender equality and to the support of lesbian/gay liberation. On the other hand, sexual science operates in some cases to reinforce many traditionally oppressive sexual values. For example, most of the categories of sexual dysfunction that sex therapists developed, such as impotence,

vaginismus (spasm and severe constriction of the vaginal barrel, which prevents penetration), and dyspareunia (difficult or painful coitus) privilege the norm of sexual intercourse. And although many sexologists support lesbian/gay rights, some have developed "therapeutic" programs that attempt to convert homosexuals into heterosexuals. Finally, sexology has attended largely to the concerns of well-educated, high-income European Americans. Although this bias is now shifting, much sex research has ignored diversity in sexual cultures based on influences such as race and ethnicity as well as social class.

There are two important methodological and theoretical weaknesses in sexology. First, there is an overriding emphasis on scientific objectivity. This affords sexologists the illusion that their work is neutral, rather than acknowledging that values infuse all scientific projects. Second, most sexologists view sexuality as a natural, internal drive rather than as socially constructed. In their view, sexual problems are individual rather than social issues. The insistence on objectivity, coupled with biological determinism, renders sexology ineffective in truly grappling with the profoundly social and political nature of sexuality and gender. The failure of sexology to address power and social relations and to explore diversity in the symbols, values, and meanings different groups may attach to sexuality has cleared a path for challenge and resistance by the feminist and lesbian/gay liberation movements. These social movements have demonstrated more successfully that sexuality is not just a product of our hormones or genes, but that it is deeply shaped by our varied social and cultural backgrounds.

Janice M. Irvine, *Disorders of Desire: Sex and Gender in Modern American Sexology* (Philadelphia: Temple University Press, 1990); Jeffrey Weeks, *Sexuality and Its Discontents* (London: Routledge & Kegan Paul, 1985).

■ JANICE M. IRVINE

SEE ALSO Sexuality.

≋ Sexual Harassment

Women were sexually harassed long before there was a word for it. Under slavery, African American women were sexually used by white masters. Women working in homes have long been targets of sexual abuse. Since industrialization, women working in factories and offices have had to endure sexual comments and demands by bosses and coworkers as the price for economic survival. As students, women and girls have been sexual prey to teachers for as long as they have been allowed to be educated. On the streets and in the home, sexual pressure that women are not in a position to refuse has been invisible but pervasive. The exchange of sex for survival under conditions of coercion that defines prostitution has also marked women and men's unequal relations throughout and across societies.

In the mid-1970s women began to speak in public for the first time about this form of sexual abuse. The Women's Center at Cornell University held the first Speak Out in May 1975; feminists in Boston and women workers in New York formed action groups; women students organized at Berkeley and Yale. In this political context, the words "sexual harassment" emerged to describe and give coherence, communality, and communicability to an experience that women previously had no choice but to consider just life.

The history of sexual harassment is, to an unusual degree, a legal history. Unlike most abuses of women, sexual harassment was established as a legal claim long before it was commonly accepted as harmful. In the early 1970s, before the law against sexual harassment existed, individual women, most of them Black, brought suits against perpetrators and institutions for acts amounting to sexual harassment under civil rights laws, arguing that they were victimized by sexual harassment *because* they were women, hence treated unequally on the basis of sex. In 1977, in the case of Paulette Barnes, an appeals court first agreed;

other courts soon followed. Sexual harassment was recognized as a legal claim for sex discrimination at work under Title VII of the Civil Rights Act of 1964.

In 1980, in Pamela Price's case, sexual harassment in education was found to violate women's rights to equal access to an education as guaranteed under Title IX of the Education Amendments of 1972. Universities were thereafter required to have grievance procedures through which victims could complain or the school could face a cutoff of federal funds.

Sexual harassment is illegal at work and school because that is where sex equality is legally guaranteed, not because there is no sexual harassment in other places in society. Activists, scholars, and legislators have begun trying to address sexual harassment by priests, lawyers, landlords, and passersby on the street, but the absence of a legal right to sex equality in these social relations has made this difficult.

Once it became possible to hold perpetrators publicly accountable for sexual harassment, it became possible to learn about it. Studies found that most victims of sexual harassment are women, although some are men, and most perpetrators are men in some position of power over the women (and men) they harass. Approximately 85 percent of working women have been or will be sexually harassed at some point in their working lives, and most never report the abuse. About one-third of women students are victimized. Almost no difference in incidence of sexual harassment has been identified on the basis of race, class, age, marital status, or income. Unwanted sexual incursions include threats, extortion, and rape, as well as leering and ogling, obscene gestures, misogynistic hate speech, groping and fondling, and pressure for dates. Often pornography is posted, circulated, or directly forced on women as part of the practice. Much sexual harassment sexualizes racism. Many perpetrators have had no idea they were doing anything wrong.

In the decade from 1976 to 1986, as hundreds of

cases were adjudicated, sexual harassment was legally divided into two types. The simplest, termed *quid pro quo*, demands sex in exchange for benefits to which a person is otherwise entitled. But sexual harassment can be oppressive and exclusionary in itself also, whether or not a measurable benefit or opportunity is lost. This second type is termed *hostile environment*. Sexualizing a job or school environment can poison it for anyone who wants to be accepted as an equal worker or student—something few men have to tolerate. Often the perpetrators are otherwise women's equals in formal hierarchies, or even their formal subordinates. Environmental sexual harassment can include sexual advances, epithets, and forced sex—all imposed forms of sexual behavior that a woman must either tolerate or leave where she is entitled to be, free of sex discrimination. When men are harassed sexually because they are men, the same prohibitions apply, although the hierarchy of men over women in society makes this rare.

Sexual harassment was recognized as a practice of sex discrimination, hence illegal, by the U.S. Supreme Court in 1986. The case that established this principle was brought by Mechelle Vinson, a Black woman who sued her supervisor for sexual harassment because she had been raped by him over a period of two-and-a-half years. She argued that having to tolerate forced sex to keep her job was environmental sexual harassment, hence sex discrimination in itself—whether or not she actually lost the job for this reason. The U.S. Supreme Court agreed, establishing freedom in the working environment from severe or pervasive sexual harassment as women's human right. In 1993, in Patricia Harris's case, the Court further specified that a woman need not be psychologically damaged by sexual harassment to sue; being disadvantaged by it because she is a woman is enough.

During twenty years of litigation, no perpetrator argued that he had a First Amendment right to say "Sleep with me and I'll give you an A" to a student, or "Fuck me or you're fired" to an employee. The argument has been raised recently that because sexual harassment can be verbal or expressive conduct, it should be legally protected speech, or, at least, word-only environmental sexual harassment should be. Since the First Amendment was written and has been interpreted largely in an equality vacuum, the outcome of this developing tension will measure progress in taking equality seriously.

The law against sexual harassment is the first law to be written on the basis of women's experience, as well as the first to recognize that sexual abuse can violate equality rights. When Professor Anita Hill charged now Supreme Court Justice Clarence Thomas, in his 1991 confirmation hearing, with sexually harassing her, national politics were also affected by women's enraged response to the extent of disregard and disbelief of Professor Hill. Justice Thomas was confirmed, but consciousness of sexual harassment soared worldwide; laws against sexual harassment were passed abroad; complaints to agencies skyrocketed in number.

Many women, seeking to keep their jobs but end their abuse, impatient with the delays and loss of control of being caught up in the legal system and apprehensive at its insensitivity, have created their own remedies. Some of the most effective and imaginative have been scripted "confrontations" with abusers, in which groups of supporters of the sexually harassed carry out a carefully planned encounter with the sexual harasser, during which he is pointedly educated.

The story of sexual harassment is a story of women's mobilization for accountability and change against one form of male dominance and gender bias. Law now exposes this practice of bigotry rather than colluding in silence. Sexual harassment has become less legitimate and less costly to resist. It remains to be seen whether the fact that sexual harassment is illegal and increasingly unacceptable means it will stop.

Martha J. Langelan, *Back Off! Confronting Sexual Harassment and Sexual Harassers* (New York: Simon and Schuster, 1993); Catharine A. MacKinnon, *Sexual Ha-*

rassment of Working Women: A Case of Sex Discrimination (New Haven, Conn.: Yale University Press, 1979).

• CATHARINE A. MACKINNON

See also Title VII.

≋ Sexuality

Throughout the course of U.S. history, the meaning of sexuality has been continuously reshaped by changing economic and social institutions. From a strong mooring in reproduction during the colonial era, sexuality later became associated with passion and marital intimacy. Today's consumer society has further elaborated an ideal in which sexual relations are expected to provide personal identity and individual happiness—apart from either reproduction or marriage. Increasingly, sexuality and its regulation have been politically contested by forces objecting to those changes, which reflect the realignment of gender, class, and race relations.

Among European settlers in the colonial era, sexuality was almost always organized within families. A scarcity of laborers encouraged a high rate of reproduction; white women bore an average of over eight children. Church and state ensured the familial and racial "legitimacy," or patriarchal ownership, of children, prosecuting those who committed fornication, rape, sodomy, adultery, or miscegenation. In contrast, neither sexuality nor reproduction could be owned within Native American cultures. Rape and prostitution were extremely rare, and some tribes allowed same-sex marriages.

In the nineteenth century, the growth of a market economy in which children were an economic liability rather than an asset as agricultural laborers encouraged a new reproductive strategy of family limitation as did a growing agitation for fertility control by women. White marital fertility

rates dropped by 50 percent, from over seven children in 1800 to under four in 1900; African American rates paralleled the drop one or two generations later. Although some couples limited family size through periodic abstinence, many couples began to use contraception, and when it failed, some turned to abortion. Sex thus became more associated with personal intimacy.

The meaning of sexuality, however, differed for men and women, and by race and class. Among the white middle class, a morally pure, domestic woman maintained her family's virtue and status, but men had access to nonreproductive sexual relations outside the home, including with women of color. Working-class women filled the ranks of prostitutes in Northern cities; Southern white men assumed the sexual availability of slave women and profited by owning the offspring of interracial rapes; imported Chinese slave prostitutes provided sex for Western male migrants. Men's extramarital relationships were condoned by a double standard that condemned and heavily penalized adulterous white women and defined most prostitutes as "fallen women." Some middle-class women opposed the double standard through moral reform and social purity campaigns. Physicians also claimed authority over sexual policies, attempting to regulate prostitution and successfully criminalizing abortion.

By 1900 a new sexual system emerged among working- and middle-class youth of both sexes. Educated women formed same-sex "Boston Marriages" or became "New Women" in search of sexual independence. A small male homosexual subculture began in some cities. Working women, including daughters of immigrants, dated men and engaged in sex not for pay but pleasure. These changes provoked political efforts to channel sexuality back into the home and reproductive arena through censorship of birth-control information, and antiprostitution and antivenereal disease campaigns. Sex became a political symbol, as seen in the Southern lynchings that relied on often false claims of interracial rape to intimidate the Black population and to keep white women immobilized on a pedestal.

Despite resistance to change, the commercialization of sex within the economy and popular culture paved the way for "sexual liberalism" in the twentieth century. This system separated sexuality from a purely procreative purpose, affirmed the value of heterosexual pleasure, and defined sexual satisfaction as critical to personal happiness. By the 1950s birth control, once a radical cause, became less controversial; as women increasingly entered the labor market, fertility control became critical, as evidenced by the decriminalization of abortion and extensive use of oral contraceptives. By the 1980s the separation of sexuality and reproduction deepened further as new reproductive technologies—such as artificial insemination and in vitro fertilization—made possible reproduction outside of the family and even apart from heterosexual relationships.

The "science" of sexology and the widespread use of sex to market consumer goods helped make sexuality a primary form of identity. A key feature of sexual liberalism became the removal of older constraints—the deregulation of birth-control information, the liberalization of abortion, and the reduction of censorship. By the 1960s sexuality had been channeled into acceptable patterns of pleasure seeking, including marital heterosexual relations, "going steady" among U.S. teenagers, and commercialized fantasies, including *Playboy* magazine and clubs. Homosexuality was subject to closer scrutiny and social stigma, which in turn strengthened lesbian and gay identities and political resistance. Women's fear of pregnancy, society's fear of "illegitimate" children, and ongoing racist practices continued to mark the boundaries of female sexuality.

In its demand for "control over one's own body," the feminist movement of the late 1960s sought to extend the ideal of reproductive and sexual autonomy from men to women. In the process feminists exposed subtle and direct means by which women's bodies had been appropriated by men, whether through advertising or the use of vi-

olence against women. Lesbian feminism and gay liberation extended sexual liberalism to include previously outcast groups. Some feminists emphasized sexual exploitation by men, others insisted on greater sexual expression for women, and still others focused on the sexual nexus of racism and sexism.

A backlash in response to modern sexual politics represented opposition to the separation of sexuality and procreation. After Roe v. Wade, conservative women and men in particular called on the state to restore the earlier reproduction-centered system by limiting or cutting off women's access to abortion and denying rights to lesbians and gay men. In the wake of the AIDS epidemic, conservative politicians rallied support for a narrow, reproductive view of sexuality by calling for a return to "traditional" sexual morality. In response to right-wing political attacks and slow government response to the AIDS crisis, lesbian and gay activists demanded funding for medical research and greater sex education. By the end of the twentieth century, debates about sexuality had become central to U.S. politics, just as sexuality had become central to personal identity.

John D'Emilio and Estelle B. Freedman, *Intimate Matters: A History of Sexuality in America* (New York: Harper & Row, 1988); Kathy Peiss and Christina Simmons, with Robert A. Padgug, eds., *Passion and Power: Sexuality in History* (Philadelphia: Temple University Press, 1989); Ann Snitow, Christine Stansell, and Sharon Thompson, eds., *Powers of Desire: The Politics of Sexuality* (New York: Monthly Review Press, 1983).

▪ ESTELLE B. FREEDMAN

SEE ALSO Bisexuality; Celibacy; Gender; Heterosexuality; Lesbianism; Sex Education; Sexology; Sexual Revolution, The.

≋ The Sexual Revolution

It is ironic that the birth-control pill, first developed to regulate irregular menstrual cycles and thus enhance women's ability to conceive, became a powerful weapon that gave women greater control of their fertility and thus of their sexuality. Until the 1960s, girls were indoctrinated with the idea that no "good" girl had (or admitted to having) premarital sex, as it was delicately called. A typical edict decreed that no man would respect her, much less marry her, if she did. The specter of "unwed motherhood" or of a "back-alley abortion" was enough to cause some women to consider suicide.

While mainstream culture (through such youth-oriented films as *Where the Boys Are* directed by Henry Lievin, 1960) reinforced the idea that girls who "went all the way" were doomed, *Playboy* magazine was enthusiastically repackaging and promoting "free love" for men. This was the one reputedly communist precept to be openly espoused at a time when anything smacking of the "Red Menace" was rejected. Along with pictorials of women, the magazine promulgated the findings of the second Kinsey report; it trumpeted the news that women did enjoy sex, i.e., were virtually always orgasmic when properly stimulated, and perhaps most liberating of all, that men no longer considered virginity in women important or even desirable.

As the 1960s progressed and the establishment-challenging student movement gained momentum, the idea that women were now as readily available for guilt-free sexual intercourse as men began to be taken for granted, even foreordained. If prior to this male-oriented sexual revolution women who had sex before marriage were considered degenerate, now those who resisted sex on demand were vulnerable to having their mental and political health questioned. Fashions, as usual, reflected the changing sexual mores and attitudes: stiff, teased, and straightened hair, cinched waists, panty girdles and high heels were replaced by long, flowing or naturally curly hair; Afros; flat, comfortable footwear, jeans, loose garments, and miniskirts or hot pants. Brassieres became optional. Required intercourse flourished, as this phase of the sexual revolution moved into full swing. The Pill and the I.U.D. (intrauterine

device) created a false sense of security; there was no dearth of unwanted pregnancies when these and other contraceptives, ever more widely and legally available, failed. Abortion was still not federally sanctioned, so the consequences of slip-ups were still dire and/or expensive.

With the founding of the National Organization for Women in 1966, the feminist movement began to push the pendulum of sexual mores toward the center, from the extremes of sex-never and sex-always. Masters and Johnson published their landmark study of sexuality in 1966, but it was a feminist theorist, Anne Koedt, who popularized and interpreted the study's findings: 1) female orgasms do not vary in kind, but in intensity; 2) all orgasms originate in the clitoris, whether it is stimulated directly or indirectly; and 3) women are in the main multiorgasmic; when stimulated immediately after orgasm, most women can experience an orgasmic chain reaction.

Another major contribution to the feminist sexual revolution was Betty Dodson's insufficiently recognized work on the demystification of gynecology and masturbation. Dodson organized workshops to familiarize women with their sexual and reproductive organs, using a slide show of dozens of vaginas, which through repetition took on an iconic value; and through the distribution and use of transparent plastic specula. Dodson contended that masturbation was the last frontier, branded as lonely, antisocial, and second-best. Vibrators were utilized as a way for women to control their own orgasms and set sexual standards for themselves: speed of response, frequency, intensity, duration.

The reproductive rights movement gained impetus and strength from the women's movement in the 1960s. Thanks to feminist involvement, the legal thrust was changed from reforming laws limiting pregnancy termination to repeal of all laws limiting access to abortion. Success was achieved on a federal level with the Supreme Court's *Roe* v. *Wade* decision of 1973, allowing women who could afford it the right to voluntary maternity. While the importance of this legislation cannot be overestimated, it places a heavy responsibility on women. Safe medical pregnancy terminations and reliable contraception are basic requirements for sexual equality, and feminists pointed out that all these methods, with the exception of vasectomy and condoms, involve exclusively women's bodies. In the early blooming of feminist consciousness, and since responsibilities were more available than rights, many women, primarily white middle- and upper-class women, considered it a point of honor to assume the full emotional (and often financial) burden for abortion.

Whatever the effects of the sexual revolution upon white middle- and upper-class women, its impact upon and meanings to women of color were vastly different. Historically all groups of women of color in the United States often have been sexually exploited and brutalized by white males; for example, the organized and sanctioned rape of Black women during and after the era of slavery. This exploitation was justified by the most virulent racist sexual stereotypes and myths. Since most women of color, especially African American women, are still widely viewed as sexually amoral, the sexual revolution supposedly has had little impact upon their already "promiscuous" sexual values and behavior.

In reality there is a complex range of sexual mores and practices among different racial, ethnic, and nationality groups of women of color; there is also a variety of sexual attitudes and practices among individual women of color, influenced by such factors as upbringing, personality, economic opportunities, education, religious beliefs, and cultural values. Access to effective contraception and legal abortion positively affected women of color during the sexual revolution. But they carried with them a history of racist sexual exploitation and vicious stereotyping of their sexuality. In some cases, more liberated views of women's sexuality in communities of color that predated the 1960s greatly affected how women of color perceived and experienced the so-called sexual revolution.

Also part of the feminist sexual revolution was the recognition that the lack of free or inexpensive contraception and abortion is most onerous for poor women, the working poor, and women on welfare (a disproportionate number of whom are women of color). They regularly found themselves caught between the Scylla and Charybdis of dangerous, illegal abortions or enforced, serial, single motherhood. Added to this were pressures in the Black and Latina communities to see recourse to abortion and birth control by women of color as collusion with the white power structure, to contain and limit their demographic increase, thus equating the attempt to control one's reproductive destiny with the betrayal of one's own people.

During the 1960s the prevailing atmosphere of sexual experimentation, the challenging of new ideas, and sexual hedonism, as well as a context in which other oppressed groups were fighting for the right to exist, created the conditions for lesbians and gay men to come forward and denounce discrimination based on sexual preference. On June 29, 1969, the patrons of a gay bar in New York's Greenwich Village resisted a police raid for the first time. The Stonewall Inn riots, as they came to be known, led to the founding of the gay liberation movement. During the early years of the second wave of the feminist movement, there was opposition in some quarters to the open acceptance of lesbians. This was vigorously contested and effectively defeated within the feminist movement (though not in society at large) by a vote at the Second Conference to Unite Women in New York City in 1970. A popular British film released that same year (*Saturday Night and Sunday Morning*, directed by Karl Reisz) is an example of the glamor that bisexuality had assumed by the end of the decade. This applied especially to the androgynous male, at least until the advent of AIDS.

During this tumultuous era many advances were made toward sexual equality. However, the controversies surrounding sexual harassment, reproductive rights, antipornography, and gay antidiscrimination legislation testify that contradictions, especially for women, persist, and that issues of sexual politics raised during and by the sexual revolution are far from resolved.

Betty Dodson, *Sex for One: The Joy of Self-Loving* (New York: Crown Publishers, 1986); Anne Koedt, Ellen Levine, and Anita Rapone, "The Myth of Vaginal Orgasm," in *The Anthology of Radical Feminism* (New York: Quadrangle Books, 1973); Gloria Steinem, *Outrageous Acts and Everyday Rebellions* (New York: Holt, Rinehart, and Winston, 1983).

■ ANSELMA DELL'OLIO

≋ Sexual Slavery

Female sexual slavery is present in all situations where women or girls cannot change the immediate conditions of their existence; where regardless of how they got into those situations, they cannot get out; and where they are subject to sexual violence and exploitation. It takes the form of systematic wife abuse; incest; and prostitution, pornography, and trafficking of women in the sex industries. Shelter programs provide refuge for victims of wife abuse and new laws now frequently result in the removal of sexually abusive fathers from homes, rather than removing the child or children.

In the sex industries, sexual slavery results from the trafficking in women from one country or region to another. Pimping is considered a form of sexual enslaving. It is known as the exploitation of the prostitution of others, in brothels and through other marketing outlets, such as the pornography industry. Studies show that once a pimp has control of a woman for prostitution or pornography, he rarely allows her to leave.

Sexual slavery is imposed individually through a "seasoning" process that breaks down the will and ego of its victims. Systematic subjugation to debasing practices and derogatory comments steadily erodes women's or girls' sense of self-worth. Beatings and rape from spouses, pimps, or traffickers secure the enslaving conditions until, eventually, the pimp can leave the victim alone at home or out on the street to prostitute without fear she will flee.

Trafficking in women for the purposes of prostitution from one country or region to another often involves fraudulent contracts. Women are kidnapped or promised jobs abroad and then forced into prostitution when they arrive. In their country of origin, they sign a contract for other work, which enables traffickers to clear them through immigration and customs without question. Upon arrival, their passports and airline tickets are confiscated so that they have no means of escape. Traffic routes often include transfer of women from Latin America and Southeast Asia to Australia, Europe, Japan, and the United States.

Sexual slavery includes forcing women into prostitution to provide sex for men in the military, sometimes known as military prostitution. For example, during the Vietnam War, an estimated 250,000 Vietnamese women and girls were prostituted to serve the military, primarily U.S. forces.

Sexual slavery is culturally based in the devaluation of women and girls, which in the First World takes the forms of economic and political discrimination as well as sexual exploitation in pornography and in the media, which promote a normalization of prostitution, the base for trafficking and sexual enslavement. In the United States, although prostitution is illegal and women are frequently arrested for prostitution, few cases that involve actual trafficking of women are brought to the criminal justice system. Periodic raids in brothels, however, reveal the existence of underground sexual slavery, especially among women from Southeast Asia or Latin America. In some areas of the Third World, the devaluation of women and girls exists in belief systems and practices such as the dowry, which effectively makes girls economic liabilities for their families. The sale of girls for slave labor or to traffickers for prostitution takes place under these conditions; sex industries are organized to exploit that market.

Laws against sexual slavery include local laws in certain regions that ban pimping, the United Nations Convention Against the Exploitation of the Prostitution of Others, and, in the United States, the more narrowly construed Mann Act.

▪ KATHLEEN BARRY

SEE ALSO Prostitution; Violence Against Women.

≋ Sheppard-Towner Maternity and Infancy Protection Act

The Sheppard-Towner Maternity and Infancy Act of 1921 was the first federally funded social welfare measure in the United States. Sponsored by Texas Senator Morris Sheppard and Iowa Congressman Horace Towner, it distributed federal matching grants to the states for prenatal and child health clinics, information on nutrition and hygiene, midwife training, and visiting nurses for pregnant women and new mothers. It did not provide any financial aid or medical care.

Infant and maternal mortality rates were very high in the 1910s, and women's organizations made passage of the Sheppard-Towner Act their first priority after winning the right to vote. The "maternity bill," written by U.S. Children's Bureau chief Julia Lathrop and introduced into Congress by Jeannette Rankin, the first woman in the House of Representatives, was supported by virtually every women's organization. It was vigorously opposed by right-wing groups and by the American Medical Association, whose members called it a threat to the home and a step toward state medicine. Congress, appealing to the new "women's vote," passed the bill by a wide margin. Sheppard-Towner programs were administered

by the women-led Children's Bureau, with the assistance of volunteers from women's clubs and parent-teacher organizations. They were popular with mothers and contributed to a significant drop in infant mortality. Still, opponents of the Sheppard-Towner Act managed to force the bill's repeal in 1929. Although federal funds for maternal and infant care were restored in the 1935 Social Security Act, public health services were no longer available for women and children of all classes. Instead, the services were needs-based and limited to the poor.

▪ MOLLY LADD-TAYLOR

SEE ALSO Children's Bureau; Welfare and Public Relief.

≋ Single Motherhood

The term *single motherhood* became popular about 1970, replacing "unmarried" or "unwed" mother. The new term was intended to mute emphasis on the relation of "mother" to marriage. But public discourse had firmly established the stigma of unmarried maternity—a woman was not a mother without a husband—so the new descriptor, especially in the conservative, misogynistic political climate after 1980, incorporated and extended the assumptions of the older terms.

In the late 1930s, when the marital status of pregnant women became a public policy concern, and not simply a familial or community dilemma, policymakers began to treat unwed mothers in racially specific ways and to use unwed motherhood to prove theories of racial inferiority and gender subordination. White single mothers were considered mentally ill and a source of babies for childless married couples. Unmarried African American and other girls and women of color who gave birth were reviled by the same policy analysts as the source of all problems in communities of color, including unwanted babies for whom white taxpayers were alleged to pay the levy.

Under the dictates of racialization, white single mothers were coerced into giving up their babies to married, middle-class couples, while single mothers of color, including Native Americans, Asian Americans, Puerto Ricans, and Mexican Americans as well as Blacks, generally kept their babies but were threatened with legislative efforts mandating sterilization, incarceration, and denial of welfare benefits.

In the late 1960s, in the context of the struggle for abortion rights, many women asserted the right to decide whether and when to become a mother and also the right to decide *who was a mother.* Consequently, thousands of white single mothers each year kept their babies, and many single mothers of color participated in the civil rights, welfare rights, and antisterilization movements, declaring that reproductive autonomy was key to female self-determination. In the somewhat liberalized political climate between 1965 and 1980, single mothers demanded that their legitimacy as mothers be recognized, although individuals of various races often lacked the material and political resources to secure the cultural legitimacy of single mothers.

After 1980 the disintegration of the industrial base in the United States and the surge of political conservatism fostered a new hostility toward poor, single mothers and a renewed willingness to level punitive sanctions against them. In the 1990s approximately 65 percent of African American babies and nearly one of four white babies were born to single mothers. This phenomenon reflects, among other causes, unprecedented levels of unemployment and incarceration of men of color, reduced job opportunities and wages in cities, persistence of male domination and sexual coercion, inadequate access to and resources for birth control and abortion services, as well as the determination of many women to decide on their own terms about childbearing. Nevertheless, "single mother" became code for insubordinate woman—sexually self-indulgent and fiscally irresponsible. Despite the demonstrable vulnerability of single mothers, politicians of every stripe ascribed extraordinary power to them, assigning them responsibility for the degradation of the large structures of society, for example, the family, and the educational, taxation, and welfare systems.

▪ RICKIE SOLINGER

SEE ALSO "Illegitimacy"/Single Pregnancy; Motherhood; Poverty.

≋ Single Women

Different categories of single women became socially and demographically prominent at different times in U.S. history. Widows, divorcées, and never-married women varied in numbers, depending on contemporary economic and cultural circumstances. Before 1800 most single women were widows. The proportion of never-married women rose steadily in the nineteenth century, cresting around 1900. In the twentieth century the percent of never-married women declined and widowhood occurred more frequently toward the end of the life cycle, while the numbers of divorced or separated women increased dramatically.

Between 1607 and 1807, it was difficult for U.S. women to choose to remain unmarried. Except in New England, men predominated among migrants to the New World. Economically, the family served as the chief mode of production before 1830, making it hard for single women (or single men) to support themselves. Under these conditions, fewer than 5 percent of women did not marry. A widow might choose not to remarry if she could perpetuate the economic base that she and her husband had previously established, or if she could draw upon the labor of her children, or if she succeeded at one of the few trades open to mature women, such as innkeeping. But unmarried daughters could not establish an economic base unassisted, and patriarchal cultural patterns of inheritance prevented most of them from inheriting land. To remain unmarried was to forfeit even the modest degree of independence that married women achieved by running their own households. Unable to support themselves, "spinsters," as never-married women came to be called in the seventeenth century (referring to their work at the spinning wheel), had to accept a place in a relative's home, where, in exchange for services, they customarily were supplied with shelter and food.

Although free Blacks formed legal marriages in both the North and South, the marriages of slave women and men were not legally recognized. Nevertheless, most slave women formed lasting unions and considered themselves married. Marriages and visiting privileges across plantation boundaries were common. Between 1800 and 1860, however, when slavery expanded westward, many slave couples were separated through forced migration. After emancipation in 1865, former slaves sought legal recognition of their unions.

Two new populations of never-married women appeared in the nineteenth century. The first occurred after 1830 in New England and the mid-Atlantic states in connection with the extensive out-migration from that region that populated the Northwest Territory, the upper Midwest, and the Pacific Northwest between 1800 and 1850. Although most of that migration took place in family units, more women than men stayed behind.

This growing population of single women often exercised a disproportionate influence in the lives of other women in their communities. Because single women retained civil rights that married women did not have, especially the right to make contracts or open bank accounts, they served dis-

proportionately as treasurers of many women's organizations that developed during the surge of voluntarism and social reform in the antebellum era.

A second, larger, group of single women emerged between 1880 and 1920 with the expansion of women's access to higher education. Although few persons obtained a college education then, by 1880 women constituted one of every three students enrolled at institutions of higher learning, and many remained single. Of eight thousand female college graduates in 1880, only five thousand were married. Many of these women had access to meaningful professional employment, which was one alternative to marriage. In 1890 the proportion of women doctors was greater than it was to be in 1960, and the proportion of women in other professions was twice that of those in the work force as a whole. In 1890, for example, when women composed about 17 percent of the labor force, 36 percent of all "professionals" were women.

After 1920 the proportion of never-married women declined dramatically. "Companionate marriage," involving the use of contraceptives, recognized women's sexual needs as similar to those of men, and many women continued to work after marriage, although usually not after the birth of children. Personal satisfaction replaced economic need as the chief basis for marriage. Soaring divorce rates accompanied this change. In 1880 one divorce was recorded for every twenty-one marriages; in 1900, one for every twelve marriages; and by 1916, one for every nine marriages. About two-thirds of these divorces were sought by women.

By the 1990s a new pattern had emerged. Many women chose not to marry. About 19 percent of women age eighteen and over in 1990 had never married—a proportion roughly equivalent to that of 1890. Although a smaller proportion of women age 35 and older in 1990 remained unmarried than was the case in 1890, the proportion remaining unmarried was larger than at any previous time in the twentieth century. Some of these un-married women lived alone. Some lived with het-erosexual partners. Some lived with partners of the same sex. Many lesbians preferred to marry, but the state refused to sanction their unions. Women of color found their marital options re-duced by the rising rates of imprisonment that kept men of their racial and ethnic group behind bars.

Perhaps the most important difference between unmarried women in the 1890s and the 1990s was the high proportion of single mothers in the 1990s. Being single and having children was no longer a contradiction in terms. In 1970 the pro-portion of single mothers among white women was about 9 percent; by 1991 that proportion had grown to 19 percent. Among African American women the proportions were 33 percent in 1970 and 58 percent in 1991. Comparable statistics for Latinas show that 24 percent were single mothers in 1980 and 29 percent in 1991. One important cause for this unprecedented increase in the numbers of single mothers was the economic gains made by women wage earners. In 1939 the average wages of full-time, year-round employed women were not sufficient for a woman to support herself and two children. In 1970 such wages were sufficient. Patterns of remarriage or serial monog-amy reveal women's desire to supplement their own income with that of another wage earner, but by 1990 the twentieth-century pattern of single motherhood was well established as an alternative to marriage.

Lee Virginia Chambers-Schiller, *Liberty, a Better Hus-band: Single Women in America: The Generations of 1780–1840* (New Haven: Yale University Press, 1984); Nancy Cott, "Divorce and the Changing Status of Women in Eighteenth-Century Massachusetts," *William and Mary Quarterly* 33 (1976): 586–614; Kathryn Kish Sklar, *Cath-arine Beecher: A Study in American Domesticity* (New Haven: Yale University Press, 1973; pb Norton, 1976).

■ KATHRYN KISH SKLAR

SEE ALSO Marriage; Single Motherhood.

≋ Slavery

The story of female slavery is the story of sur-vival of Black women and their construction of a definition of womanhood that made sense to them. In some ways it is the story of the phoenix. Faced with misery and suffering that many suc-cumbed to, African American women as a group proved resilient enough to triumph against the odds.

Despite their common bondage, men and women did not experience slavery the same way. Slave women experienced sexual exploitation, childbearing, motherhood, and the slaveholder's sexism. Slave women were exploited for their re-productive as well as productive capacities.

Stereotypes were devised to justify the sex-ual exploitation of Black women. Unlike white women, who were viewed as prudish, pious, and domestic, Black women were considered sensual and promiscuous, an idea used to sanction the rape of African American women.

The conditions under which slave women lived and worked only confirmed these stereotypes. In the United States, slavery after abolition of the for-eign slave trade in 1807 depended upon reproduc-tion rather than continual transatlantic importa-tions; the burden of slave increase was on the slave woman's shoulders. Since causal correla-tions were drawn between sensuality and fertility, the increase in the slave population served as "ev-idence" of the slave woman's lust.

Slave women were no more or less lustful than other women but in slavery their bodies did not command respect. Unlike white women, Black women did not dress in layers of clothes. Black women often worked with their dresses lifted up around their hips to keep the hems out of the water, dirt, and mud in which they worked. Women's bodies were also exposed during whip-pings. Indeed some whippings had sexual over-tones. Few utterances are as revealing as those of ex-slave Henry Bibb's master, who declared that "he had rather paddle a female than eat when he was hungry."

Female slavery was also distinguished and structured by childbearing and childbirth. Each year between 1750 and the Civil War more than one-fifth of the Black women in the 15 to 44 age group bore a child. It was no accident of nature that caused the average slave woman to begin motherhood two years before the average white Southern woman.

Slaveholders, both men and women, manipulated Black women to have children early and frequently. First they used verbal prodding, then subtle practices such as giving pregnant women more food and less work. Some slaveholders used an outright system of rewards such as a new dress, or silver dollar, or Saturday afternoons off. For women who resisted these "positive" incentives coercion always existed—the threat of a whipping, sale, or both.

Medical care was usually unavailable or inadequate for pregnant slave women. Black women were neglected because of the common assumptions that they were less fragile, gave birth more easily, and therefore needed less care than white women. They were thus more likely to have a midwife deliver their child than a more costly doctor. Midwives, many of whom were slaves, were usually competent, but they could do little for women who had severe complications or for women who suffered from illness resulting from the brutality and callousness of masters, mistresses, and overseers. Women who had been whipped, forced to perform heavy tasks, or sent back to fieldwork too soon after delivery ran a high risk of death.

Motherhood structured a woman's life as much as planter manipulation of reproduction. On plantations where there were nurseries, women were constantly running back and forth between the field and the quarters to nurse their children. On farms where there was no central place for the children, women had to take their children to the fields with them and either work with them on their backs or put them down somewhere. Mothers risked a whipping if they attended their children too often; their children risked harm if left unattended. House servants were not always better off. Often they were not allowed to keep their children with them, and they too ran back and forth to the quarters caring for their children.

Childbearing and child rearing structured the slave woman's pattern of resistance. Most runaways were between sixteen and thirty-five years old. Most slave women this age were either pregnant, nursing an infant, or had at least one small child to care for—male runaways could be more assured that their children would be cared for, but slave women had no such assurance. This is why all of the 150 fugitive women advertised for in the 1850 New Orleans newspapers ran away with their children.

Escaping with children only made an already hazardous undertaking all the more risky. "Females," wrote William Still, the head of the Philadelphia Underground Railroad, "undertook three times the risk of failure [to escape] that males are liable to." Truancy, running away for short periods of time, seems to have been the way many slave women reconciled their desire to flee and their need to stay.

Slaveholder sexism also made female slavery different from male slavery. That sexism played a role in structuring the female slave's workload and day-to-day existence is somewhat ironic since slaveholders so often treated Black women like men. Not surprisingly, however, Black women were denied most of the so-called "rewards" of womanhood while they suffered all of the restrictions and performed all the "woman's work."

There is no question that slave women worked as hard as men. They worked as lumberjacks and turpentine producers in the forest of the Carolinas and Georgia. They hauled logs by leather straps attached to their shoulders. They plowed using mule and ox teams, and hoed, sometimes with the heaviest implements available. They dug ditches, spread manure fertilizer, and piled coarse

Several generations of slaves at a plantation in Beaufort, South Carolina, 1862. Women formed the center of the slave family.

fodder with their bare hands. They built southern roads and railroads, and they cultivated rice, cut cane and tobacco, and picked cotton. Besides all this exhausting labor, slave women also did "woman's work." For instance, in the Sea Islands, sorting cotton lint according to color and fineness and removing cotton seeds that the gin had crushed into the cotton and lint was woman's work. Men usually shelled corn, threshed peas, cut potatoes for planting, and platted shucks. Grinding corn into meal or hominy, however, was woman's work, as was spinning, weaving, sewing, and washing, work done on Saturday or at night, after a long day at other backbreaking work.

Besides making women's days especially long, slaveholder practices restricted female slave movement. Slaveholders usually chose their male slaves to assist in the transportation of crops to market and the transport of supplies and other materials to the farm or plantation. More male

than female slaves were artisans and craftsmen, so when slaveholders had a chance to hire skilled slaves from other plantations, they usually hired males. Fewer bondwomen, therefore, had a chance to vary their work experience.

Therefore women, more than men, were tied to the immediate environment of the plantation or farm. Like motherhood, this decreased the likelihood that women would run away. The would-be female fugitive had to consider her unfamiliarity with the surrounding countryside before fleeing. She also had to consider how conspicuous a lone Black woman or group of Black women would be in the predominantly white-populated countryside. Some female fugitives like the celebrated Ellen Craft overcame this last impediment by disguising themselves as males. However, the small number of female fugitives indicates that few slave women could match the legendary exploits of Harriet Tubman, who not only ran away but returned over and over to rescue more than 300 slaves.

Self-protection and individual resistance were necessarily part and parcel of the female slave's definition of womanhood. Women could not rely on men for protection, and they had no recourse in any formal justice system. Therefore, they had to protect themselves against whites and Black men the best they could. Some women were overtly aggressive. Some murdered their masters and mistresses, some were arsonists, and still others refused to be whipped. Although those who resisted whippings usually were strong enough to fight off their master, mistress, or overseer, those bold enough to commit murder usually used poison rather than outright violence.

Since slaves could not ignore the reality of the overwhelming power and authority of whites, most women dissembled and feigned illness to get their way. As did men, women pretended to be ignorant of a job in order not to have to do it. Some pretended to be mentally unbalanced and regularly insulted whites and refused to do their bidding. The most common form of female self-defense was feigning illness. This form of resistance proved effective for slave women because they were expected to have children, and slaveholders could never be sure that the women's aches and pains would not impair their ability to have children. Since the eighteenth and nineteenth centuries still found women's diseases shrouded in mystery, as long as slave women did not overdo it, the clever could feign illness and get away with it.

While resistance demonstrates the resourcefulness and self-reliance of the slave woman, these traits were learned from other women. On large southern plantations Black women usually worked together in single-sex work gangs. Women also attended at childbirth and helped with postpartum care. Much of the medical care for women and children was in the hands of slave women who served as nurses for Black and white alike. Self-reliance and self-sufficiency, therefore, were not just functions of what the slave woman did for herself but what the female community did for itself.

Slave women shared child-rearing responsibilities. They depended on the elderly women who ran plantation nurseries, midwives, nurses who mixed folk and contemporary medical techniques to heal the sick, and other female relatives and friends to provide food, clothing, and supervision. Communal motherhood helped slaves cope with one of the most difficult of predicaments—who would provide maternal care for a child whose mother was either sold or deceased? Fathers sometimes served as both mother and father, but when slaves, as opposed to the master, determined child care it was usually someone from the female community who became a child's surrogate mother.

In this way they helped structure their world. Good cooks and seamstresses were admired, as were midwives and "doctor women." Occasionally women were put in charge of female work gangs, and these women, if not admired, were at least respected. The same could be said of conjure women and women thought to be witches. Along with respect there was fear. Old women, though, were in a class apart. Absolute age was important, but for women, age also corresponded to the number of children one had, and one's stage in the childbearing cycle. By virtue of their greater experience, wisdom, and number of children, old women commanded the respect of the young.

To consider the cooperative aspect of female slave life is to understand one of the ways that Black women provided a buffer against the depersonalizing regime of plantation work and the dehumanizing nature of slavery. Men were more likely to be sold than were childbearing women. Add to this the facts that women were much more confined to the plantation than men; that some women were part of "abroad" marriages, where husbands visited infrequently; and that slave women generally outlived men by two years, and we find that on a given plantation the male presence was more tenuous than the female presence. We also find that outside of their forced dependence on whites for food and shelter, women were more dependent on one another than they were on men.

The female community also schooled its members on survival under slavery, helped and protected them when possible, but most of all gave its women the opportunity to forge independent ideas about womanhood.

In the slave woman's definition of womanhood, motherhood was more central than marriage. This is because mothers were the least likely to be separated from their children, and mothers were the crucial link between a child and his or her separated father. Since nonprolific women were sold, childbearing was a way to anchor oneself to a given plantation for an extended period of time and thus maintain enduring relationships with family and friends. Childbirth also secured somewhat the nuclear family against breakup by sale because stable, childbearing families were an asset to slaveholders.

Beyond this, giving birth was a life-affirming action. It was, ironically, an act of defiance, a signal to the slaveowner, that no matter how cruel and inhuman his actions, African Americans would not be utterly subjugated or destroyed. For these reasons motherhood, not marriage, was a Black girl's most important rite of passage. So central was motherhood to womanhood that unmarried mothers were not stigmatized; neither were their children deemed illegitimate.

This did not mean of course that male-female relationships were of no consequence, just that they were subject to many uncertainties. Because white men and women could and did make cruel and life-threatening decisions, their power and influence not only shaped the nature of male-female relationships but also molded the role that women assumed in slave families.

Without a master's interference courtship and marriage looked very familiar. Women appreciated male attention and did what was necessary to

An enslaved woman, Louisa, holds a baby, who legally owns her, as evidenced by this bill of sale.

get it. On Sundays they fixed their hair and dressed in clothes that had sat in sweet-smelling flowers all week. They responded to flattery and made men vie with one another for their attention. Although marriage was not legally binding, and masters treated slave unions casually, slaves held their marriage vows sacred.

However, the oppressive hands of white men and women seldom failed to touch male-female relationships. Husbands and wives were often separated. They could not protect each other nor their children from whippings. Although enslaved males could sometimes retaliate against the Black men who abused their daughters, wives, and mothers, when white men assaulted Black women, raped them, and made them bear their children, they could do nothing. The violence done to the Black woman's body was not recognized as a crime. Few relationships survived this brutal assault.

Slavery, therefore, made it impossible for women to be overly dependent on their husbands. Like their men they had to hunt, fish, grow, and steal extra food for their family. They had to survive, with and without the help of men or the female community.

And the women did survive, generation after generation. The slave system tried to beat them down but African American women survived conditions that were debilitating to body and mind, all the while inventing a womanhood with its own meaning.

■ DEBORAH GRAY WHITE

SEE ALSO Abolitionist Movement; Constitution and Amendments: Emancipation Proclamation and Thirteenth Amendment; Pedestal; Plantation System.

≋ SNCC

SEE Student Non-Violent Coordinating Committee.

≋ Social Hygiene

Emerging after 1900, social hygiene recast the issues of social and sexual order in the secular and technical terms of the twentieth century. Its adherents offered a pragmatic approach to social reform based on applying scientific research methods and organizational efficiency to the problems of vice and disease. Although dispas-

sionate social scientists rhetorically distanced themselves from moral reformers, ultimately the movement bolstered conservative moral precepts while vastly expanding the reach of social and state intervention.

Hygienists established new rationales for social action, placing issues that had been viewed as religious, spiritual, and personal into the secular, physical, and civic framework of public health. Social hygienists argued that prostitution spread venereal disease; illegitimate infants had high mortality rates and drained the public purse; and the unfit reproduced, weakening the national stock. Considering health the basis for social stability and the good society, hygienists believed that solutions to such problems were in the public interest. Public health advocates thus demanded breaking the Victorian code of silence on sexual matters, presented a critique of laissez faire, and provided a key rationale for an activist, disciplinary state.

As researchers in the fields of medicine, social work, education, law, sociology, and criminology replaced the concept of sin with the concept of sickness, they simultaneously established themselves as society's doctors, disseminating scientifically sound data on social and sexual matters and demonstrating the efficacy of their methods through experimental social programs. Cultural authority shifted from female voluntary reformers and mothers to trained, usually male, experts.

Despite social hygiene's claim to scientific authority, hygienists were as concerned with moral cleanliness as with physical vigor. Teaching the values of sexual continence and self-discipline was as important as teaching the biology of reproduction. In the name of public health rather than morality, professionals took responsibility for the sanctity of the family and for securing conservative values. Thus, social hygiene drew together two poles of social reform: health and morality—those seeking a technocratic vision and those seeking a homogeneous moral order.

Concern about unrestrained sexuality and its

consequences often brought female moral reformers together with social hygienists, yet such alliances were uneasy because of the groups' differing gender politics. To moral reformers, sisterhood demanded that women protect one another from male exploitation. In contrast, social hygienists argued that sexually transgressive women were not victims but culprits.

Understanding the causes of vice and disease in individual, often hereditarian terms, social hygienists relied on physical and psychological testing to identify those who would benefit from rehabilitation. Their solutions were thus therapeutic, instructional, or eugenic, transforming individuals or populations rather than social conditions, and expanding the authoritarian scope of experts and the state to intervene in individual and family life.

The social hygiene movement gained strength in a period of extensive immigration and changing gender roles. In these new social contexts social hygiene reinforced racism and gender stereotypes, grounding them in alleged biological truth and historical necessity.

• ELIZABETH FEDER

SEE ALSO Moral Reform.

≋ Socialism

Women of all races, classes, and sexual orientations have played a major role in the development of socialism in the United States, both in officially socialist parties and ideologies, and in the wealth of movements for social and economic justice that have shaped the socialist movement. Socialism, in turn, has had an impact on a wide range of movements and issues that have affected women.

Socialism is the theory and practice of replacing capitalism with a political, economic, and social system believed to be more just and equitable. According to socialist theory, private ownership of the means of production is replaced with collective, cooperative, or public ownership. Government policies protecting private wealth are changed to promote more equal ownership and distribution of resources. International aggression to secure raw materials, markets, and labor is replaced with international working-class solidarity. In practice, countries and movements calling themselves socialist have had a wide variety of structures and policies, from egalitarian to elitist.

In the development of U.S. capitalism, the wealth of some was inextricably tied to the poverty of others, and race and gender largely determined which were which: Native American land, Black slavery, Latin American resources, and the underpaid labor of women and children factory workers formed the pillars of capital accumulation. Thus race, gender, and class, as interrelated factors in oppression and resistance, are at the core of the history of U.S. socialism.

Socialist and nonsocialist movements for fundamental social change are historically interconnected; together they constitute the "left," or progressive, forces of the political spectrum. They include various socialist parties and organizations; the labor movement; organizations for the rights and survival of Native Americans, African Americans, Asian Americans, and Latinas/os; the suffragist, women's liberation, feminist, and lesbian feminist movements; anti-imperialist, antiwar, and international solidarity movements; and community-based groups fighting for economic and social justice.

Modern socialism was brought to the United States by European immigrants in the 1870s. It was a movement of workers that defined the primary moving force in history as a class struggle between workers and owners. The early socialist immigrants brought with them a history of women's participation and of debates on "the woman question"—the sexual division of labor, the family, women wage workers, and sexuality.

The first socialist party in the United States was the Socialist Labor Party, formed in 1876. Its charter read, in part, "The emancipation of women will be accomplished with the emancipation of men, and the so-called women's rights question will be solved with the labor question. All evils and wrongs of the present society can be abolished only when economical freedom is conquered for men as well as for women." This position was challenged as more women entered the socialist movement; it formed the starting point for a still-ongoing debate about the relationship between class and gender oppression.

Women first made their mark on U.S. socialism through strikes and trade union activism, and the first prominent U.S. women socialists, in the early 1900s, were labor leaders such as Elizabeth Gurley Flynn and Mother Jones. From 1900 to 1919, challenges to traditional gender roles in the United States often involved women who were both feminist and socialist. These challenges were precursors to later feminist and lesbian feminist movements. Emma Goldman, Charlotte Perkins Gilman, Crystal Eastman, and Margaret Sanger advocated birth control, suffrage, economic reform, and nontraditional sexuality.

Turn-of-the-century labor and socialist organizations included few Black men, and even fewer Black women. Lucy Parsons (1853–1942), legendary labor leader, anarchist, journalist, orator, and communist organizer, was a notable exception. Because of white workers' fear of Black competition, socialist and labor movements often failed to support Black rights. Early socialist ideology did not recognize African slavery as an indispensable pillar of international capitalism. During the following decades, the pivotal political impact of the struggle for African American rights and freedom forced changes in these policies.

African American women in the early 1900s organized women's clubs, church groups, and civic organizations; addressed the needs of their communities; advocated for justice; and campaigned against lynching. This continuous tradition of ac-

tivism built the foundations for the Black resistance movements that would redefine social justice for socialists and other progressives later in this century.

Native American movements usually have not considered themselves socialist. Nevertheless, early socialists drew inspiration from indigenous cultures characterized by equality and communal property ownership. The relatively independent and equal status of women in most Native American nations has been particularly important in developing a socialist vision of women's rights. However, socialists often failed to support the rights and survival of indigenous nations. During the battle for Indian rights at Wounded Knee in 1973 and the protests in 1992 surrounding the five-hundredth anniversary of Columbus's landing, Native American activists for justice and others, including socialists, began to forge links.

After a period of severe repression and decline in the 1920s, the socialist movement in the United States reached its greatest strength during the 1930s and 1940s. Propelled by the Great Depression, the Communist Party of the United States formed Unemployed Councils, published journals, ran candidates for public office, protested evictions, led labor union activity, and created popular organizations. Women of all races were involved in socialist and socialist-led activities. This was also a period of confluence between socialism and the movement for Black freedom. The influential Harlem Communist Party included dynamic women leaders, such as Claudia Jones, Maude White, and Audley (Queen Mother) Moore. The courageous Sharecroppers' Union in Alabama had substantial Black women leadership.

An onslaught of anticommunist repression in the 1950s devastated the alliances forged among socialists, trade unionists, feminists, and Black rights activists. The reconvergence of these forces during a period of international revolutionary ferment in the 1960s and 1970s posed for a time a formidable threat to "the system": capitalism, imperialism, patriarchy, white supremacy, and the established order of power.

In China, Vietnam, Cuba, Mozambique, Angola, and Nicaragua, liberation movements with socialist leadership won national independence. Internationally, socialism was no longer the property of Europeans but was being implemented by people of color—many of them women. Women and men in the new societies reexamined and reconstructed traditional sexual roles and relationships.

In the United States, the civil rights movement of the 1950s and 1960s and the Black liberation movement of the 1960s and 1970s, which included socialist and nonsocialist forces, irrevocably changed the definition of justice to include racial justice. Inspired by liberation movements around the world and by the civil rights movement at home, a vast array of movements for social change flowered in the United States in the 1960s and 1970s. A new breed of activists, including many socialists, defined a different sort of challenge to capitalism, one in which race, gender, nation, class, and sexual orientation were linked.

The Mexican and Chicano/a farmworkers' movement, which rose under the banner of the United Farm Workers in the early 1960s, expanded the concept of union organizing to include health, housing, immigration, and education as they impacted not just individual workers but whole communities. Women were vital leaders in this movement.

The history of Puerto Rican socialism since U.S. occupation in 1898 has been intertwined with the movement for independence. Puerto Rican activists in the 1960s, 1970s, and 1980s called the attention of international progressives and socialists to continuing U.S. colonial exploitation in Puerto Rico. Many independentistas captured in the 1980s, including Alejandrina Torres, are still serving long prison terms.

Asian American women, excluded for eight decades by racially biased immigration laws, began to enter the United States in large numbers only after the Immigration Act of 1965. Some joined the movements of the day. Many were, and are, employed in the garment industry. Their resistance has exposed the existence of 1800s sweatshop conditions in the 1990s.

A generation of youth threw itself into campus uprisings, the Vietnam antiwar movement, Black power, peace, student rights, community organizing, and anti-apartheid and anti-imperialism efforts. As they increasingly questioned a society that could produce so much injustice, a plethora of socialist, communist, and anarchist parties and youth groups appeared, along with scores of other organizations.

The women's movement emerged from women's involvement in all of the social justice movements of the time, especially the civil rights movement. Women of color and white women, lesbians and heterosexual women, organized together and separately in caucuses and independent women's groups. Lesbian feminists, the historic bedrock of the women's movement, came out both as individuals and as an organized force.

Women began to articulate an ideology of social change from women's point of view, rewriting history and theory to include themselves. Much of this rewriting was influenced by socialism. Socialist and feminist women, divided by the question of whether class or gender is primary in the history of human oppression, influenced each other powerfully, overlapped, and changed both movements. Women of color and lesbians analyzed the intersections of class, race, gender, and homophobic oppression.

In the 1980s and 1990s, the fall of the state-centered regimes of Eastern Europe and serious defeats to the socialist countries and movements of the Third World opened a period of profound change for socialism. Its opponents pronounce it dead; its proponents engage in extensive reevaluation and reflection, examining the relationship of socialist practice to the ideals of democratic participation, women's rights, and racial justice. At the same time, the conditions that produced socialism have intensified: the domestic and international concentration of wealth and power, predominantly along lines of race; the persistence of interconnected oppressions of class, race, sexuality, and gender; international economic aggression and military violence; and the tendency of capitalism to produce fascist and right-wing forces. As a new generation of justice seekers confronts these conditions, it will need to draw on the experiences, contributions, and lessons of its predecessors, including those of socialism.

· NAOMI JAFFE

See also Feminism, Socialist.

≋ Social Security Act

The Social Security Act of 1935 initiated a national old-age pension for wage workers. Under the Old Age Insurance program (OAI), workers and employers each paid a tax of 1 percent on the first three thousand dollars of wages. At age sixty-five workers could retire with a modest benefit. Because agricultural laborers and domestic servants were excluded from OAI coverage, three-fifths of African American workers were ineligible for these benefits, as were most Native Americans. Also excluded were teachers, nurses, hospital employees, librarians, and social workers—all predominantly female occupations. Of the 22 percent of women employed in 1930, 52 percent were not covered by Social Security.

In 1939 amendments to the Social Security Act added benefits for spouses and widows. The spouse benefit granted wives a portion of the full benefit if they were at least sixty-five and living with their husbands. Women separated from their husbands, even if they were still married, were ineligible for Social Security. Working wives were also ineligible if their own earned benefit was more than one-half the spouse's benefit. Divorced

women, regardless of how long they had been married, were ineligible for a spouse benefit if their former husbands retired. Widows were only eligible for benefits if they were at least sixty-five, living with their husbands at the time of his death, and had never remarried. Like wives, widows were ineligible for benefits in their own names. Thus, the eligibility rules for benefits rewarded women in stable marriages who were supported by their husbands but penalized women who became separated or divorced or worked outside the home. Subsequent reforms have corrected some of these inequities.

· JILL QUADAGNO

See also Mothers' Pensions; Welfare and Public Relief; Welfare State.

≋ Social Work

Social work in the United States reflects the stresses and strains of modern liberalism, which is committed to developing policies that alleviate human suffering without fundamentally altering the economic structures that create unemployment, poverty, and persistent social inequalities. Taking a woman-centered look at the history of social work highlights the dual role of the social work profession as a source of progressive social policy and a supporter of a social order characterized by hierarchies of race, ethnicity, class, and gender.

Although more women than men are and have been social workers, their status and image, like those of people of color and poor people, reflect the Eurocentric, androcentric priorities of the dominant culture. In 1990 women social workers, constituting 67 percent of the profession, earned less money and held fewer doctoral degrees and senior administrative and academic positions than did their male peers. Social work practice that promotes feminist objectives is impeded in the late twentieth century by increasingly conservative policies that limit women's access to education, employment, child care, mental health services, and medical care.

The social work profession has, however, continuously supported women's causes and needs. Social workers have played a large role in policymaking and social welfare activism. Currently, social workers are focusing their attention on "vulnerable populations" and supporting feminist activities such as rape crisis centers, battered women's shelters, and therapeutic programs that treat women who have suffered sexual abuse, economic exploitation, and medical neglect and mistreatment.

Social work is one of the few professional fields that historically has recognized the existence of social classes in the United States. Professional social work emerged in the early twentieth century from a culture of voluntary and quasi-voluntary groups such as settlement houses and charity organization societies. Several generations of middle-class women, many with college degrees, provided staff and sometimes leadership in these organizations. The imperative for "service" promoted by religious groups motivated many volunteers of the late Victorian period—even those in the settlement movement, many of whom tried to honor the pluralistic, tolerant philosophy of Jane Addams, founder of Hull House in 1889. For these women pioneers who provided social service to an industrializing society, class divisions as well as gender commonalities were acknowledged in the relationships between them and their largely female, white, immigrant clients. "Civic housekeeping" justified women's contributions to urban reform movements in sanitation, education, health, and recreation. For example, in the Woman's Christian Temperance Union (WCTU) and the YWCA, women settlement workers advocated for clean milk stations, day nurseries, limited hours, and better working conditions for women laborers. Perhaps the best example of this philosophy of women's service to women's interests is

the creation of the federal Children's Bureau. The bureau's advocates, including Florence Kelley, Addams, and Lillian Wald, aimed to aid poor children without removing them from their homes. After Congress created the Children's Bureau in 1912, its promoters lobbied for Julia Lathrop as its first head, believing that a woman should administer an agency concerned with children and families.

Despite their relative progressivism in matters affecting women and labor, very few white social workers of the early twentieth century advocated for people of color, who experienced the so-called Progressive Era as a dangerous period of increased race-based lynchings and legal discrimination undergirded by pseudoscientific doctrines of the racial inferiority of non-Western European peoples. Social service organizations and institutions remained segregated into the 1960s. White settlement leaders were at best ambivalent about serving predominantly or increasingly African American neighborhoods. Some settlements segregated their activities; some excluded Blacks outright; some encouraged founding all-Black settlements; some followed migrating white populations to new locations. With a few exceptions, Black leadership spearheaded the vital institutions serving Black communities of the North and South in the first half of the twentieth century: the YMCA and YWCA movements, the Urban League, the school-settlement experiments in the rural South, and others. Among African American communities, as among white ones, there was a movement of middle-class women to serve poorer Blacks, children, and those with special needs. And perhaps even more than white social workers, many Black social workers were influenced by their observations to embrace social justice and civil rights objectives. The Black colleges that educated these workers as well as other Black professionals became functional centers of leadership training focused on social change as well as community service.

Social service providers attempted to construct

a "profession" of social work through adopting common goals and values and establishing common training curricula in schools that could credential their graduates. This fifty-year process culminated in the founding of the National Association of Social Work in 1955 and yielded mixed outcomes for the status of social work among U.S. professions and for the status of women within social work. Though many of the early theorists and educators of social work (such as Mary Richmond, Edith Abbott, and Sophonisba Breckenridge) were women, men were overrepresented in leadership ranks in proportion to their numbers in the occupation (about 30 percent in New York in 1915) and in social work schools (about 20 percent between 1912 and 1917).

Psychiatric social work, beginning during World War I, was perceived as an appropriate occupation for women. The defining aim of psychiatric social work—psychological "adjustment" of the individual—was an acceptable ideology that suited the times and the mores prescribed for middle-class young women. Prior to the 1960s, with the exception of the "rank-and-file" movement of the Depression years, social workers did little collectively to challenge the dominant U.S. political and social order. However, alone among professionals, they deliberately concerned themselves with the welfare of the poor, a group of little interest or potential for profit, as sociologist John Ehrenreich points out, to more fortunate Americans.

Like the civil rights and antiwar movements, the antipoverty programs of the 1960s Johnson administration planted seeds of feminist change by mandating "maximum feasible participation" of agency clients and neighborhood residents while empowering male agency heads, policymakers, and community leaders. Not until the mid-1980s did the social work literature reflect issues concerning the feminist movement, which responded angrily and assertively to an era of social-change movements that often excluded women. The "postmodern" movements of the 1980s—move-ments that recognize the social construction of gender and racial identities and highlight the persistence of social and economic hierarchies in modern democratic societies—have found their way into the social work theory of the early 1990s. The first phase of civil-rights-era feminism carried mostly middle-class white women's concerns into social work practice; in the 1990s, some activist social workers have begun to focus on feminism as a transformative ideology that addresses issues of race and class as well as gender.

Clarke A. Chambers, "Women in the Creation of the Profession of Social Work," *Social Service Review*, 60 (March 1986): 1–33; John H. Ehrenreich, *The Altruistic Imagination: A History of Social Work and Social Policy in the United States* (Ithaca: Cornell University Press, 1985); Roy Lubove, *The Professional Altruist: The Emergence of Social Work as a Career, 1880–1930* (Cambridge, Mass.: Harvard University Press, 1965).

▪ MINA CARSON

SEE ALSO National Urban League; Settlement House Movement; YWCA.

≋ South Asian American Women

Although a small segment of the population, South Asian women have made significant contributions to gender issues in the United States.

Before the 1960s, South Asian communities in the United States were male-dominated, consisting of agricultural laborers on the West Coast and Western-educated professionals and merchants scattered throughout the country. Women were few but stood out as strong individuals. Most South Asian women in the United States now are either post–1960s immigrants or their daughters. Large proportions of these immigrant women are highly educated and professional workers. According to the 1990 census, about 85 percent of Asian Indian women, the largest group among the diverse category of South Asians, had at least a high school level education.

Beginning in the 1980s, a series of South Asian women's organizations, such as Manavi in New Jersey, Narika in the San Francisco Bay area, and Sakhi in New York City, emerged. Their agendas ranged from providing specific services to South Asian women to advocating for general women's issues. Through these efforts, South Asian women have tried to establish the centrality of women's issues to the well-being of families and children and to contribute to the public debate about immigration and ethnic representation. Outside of these women's organizations, South Asian women are spearheading community mobilization efforts. To empower women of color and their communities, the leaders are forging links among activists from their South Asian communities and across cultures.

South Asian women face many challenges in the United States, not the least of which is fighting the stereotypical image of a weak woman who comes from a tradition-bound society. South Asian women have opened up the complex layers of human and social dynamics and intervened in the making and unmaking of cultural traditions. They have not soaked in feminism as passive receivers but have given it their own agency and color. Chandra Talpade Mohanty charts the contours of struggle of Third World women in her introduction to *Third World Women and the Politics of Feminism*. Naheed Islam points to the pitfalls of the callously constructed idea of ethnic diversity in her essay titled, "In the Belly of the Multicultural Beast, I Am Named South Asian." Shamita Das Dasgupta, a cofounder of Manavi, locates her feminist activism both in a local immigrant community and an international women's movement. Some of the leading contributions of South Asian women are their thought-provoking work on Third World feminism, on tradition and modernity, and on the place of gender at the intersection of forces of race, nation, ethnicity, and class.

In their respective fields of expertise—among others, Meena Alexander as a writer, Urvashi Vaid as the former director of the National Gay and Lesbian Task Force, and Mira Nair as a movie director—South Asian women are offering their distinct perspectives. Whether in their homes or workplaces, South Asian women are facing challenges of empowerment with tremendous fortitude and vigor. Their efforts are characterized in the title of an anthology edited by the Women of South Asian Collective, *Our Feet Walk the Sky: Women of the South Asian Diaspora*.

● MADHULIKA S. KHANDELWAL

SEE ALSO Asian Pacific Women.

≋ Spirituality

Women have always been spiritual leaders in society and in religious and occult groups. But around 1970 there began a movement, born of feminism, to identify and create a separate women's spirituality. Many women felt that the prevailing images of women in contemporary society were so tainted with patriarchal values that it was important to do research into history, archaeology, anthropology, and myth to find images of women that were stronger than those in the prevailing culture.

While some feminists do not believe spirituality is a part of feminism, and regard it as a diversion from the necessary political struggles at hand, the women's spirituality movement has engaged perhaps a hundred thousand U.S. women, and the ideas in the movement have influenced women's literature, art, and music.

The women's spirituality movement exists both within and outside mainstream religious institutions. In the consciousness-raising groups of the 1970s, small gatherings of women sat in a circle and spoke about their most personal and intimate concerns. They learned that what was seemingly peculiar and unique to them, since it had been unspoken, was often part of other women's lives. They gained a feeling of empowerment, political insight into the nature of women's oppression, and a belief that personal experiences were to be trusted and acted upon.

In later years, some women began to feel that sharing spiritual experiences, dreams, visions, and psychic phenomena could also be important. Using the consciousness-raising group as a model, women began to form small, nonhierarchical groups for religious and psychic exploration. Some women became interested in ancient history and began to research whether women in other times and societies had held more power or used power differently. In the last twenty years, hundreds of feminist scholars have written groundbreaking works in history, archaeology, and anthropology, examining these questions and also creating controversy.

Two principal controversies have emerged as a result of women's scholarship in these areas. First, they explored whether there was a previous matriarchal age when women had equal or superior power to men and when the primary deity was a goddess or goddesses. Second, they examined whether there is an "essential female nature." Some feminists believe that women are by nature more intuitive and peaceful. Other feminists disagree strongly and believe most differences between the sexes are cultural.

Many women both within and outside mainstream religions began to look into the question of God as female. Patriarchy seemed founded on the notion that God was male and men were fashioned in his image, with women as a lesser afterthought. Women began to write new liturgies and ceremonies. Since 1980 a veritable revolution has occurred in the liberal mainstream churches, with the production of revised versions of hymn books and prayers to include less male-centered language. Feminist Jewish women have rewritten the Seder. Catholic, Episcopal, and Jewish women have fought dynamic battles to enter the ministry.

Some women found their own religions too oppressive and opted to create new religious organizations. Groups of women chose to identify with the ancient archetype of the witch as a symbol for feminine power. While often depicted as ugly and evil, the witch was also seen as a woman who defined herself; claimed her own authority; was at home with nature and her own intuition; and was skilled in the ancient arts of healing, herbalism, midwifery, and magic. The witch, therefore, was a powerful symbol for thousands of women who opposed patriarchal ideas—particularly those in predominantly male medical and scientific establishments.

The images of ancient goddesses sparked interest as well. The idea of a goddess, one that stands simply for the creative force within, or an actual deity, is a difficult concept for some women to embrace, but for others it is an idea that for the first time freed them from the vestigial prejudices they may have held about their own body. No longer were they the daughters of Eve, the sinner, a mere bone of Adam; they were part of the divine cosmos. Certain women saw the goddess as the earth; others saw her as the creative force in the universe; and some saw her as the mystery of birth, life, death, and regeneration.

By the 1990s thousands of women's spirituality groups in North America existed, ranging from study groups within Jewish and Christian denominations to at least a thousand small goddess-oriented Wicca groups.

▪ MARGOT ADLER

SEE ALSO Feminist Theology; Religion.

≋ Sports

Throughout much of the past century, the woman athlete has been a controversial public figure. Noted for her muscular physique, her athletic virtuosity, and her bold entrance into a traditionally male arena, she has embodied soci-

A Chinese American girls' basketball team in Boston, Massachusetts, circa 1930.

ety's hopes, fears, and conflicts about ever changing definitions of womanhood. Sometimes celebrated as the quintessential modern woman, other times condemned as a repulsive aberration from proper femininity, the woman athlete has provided a focal point for larger cultural debates about gender relations and, specifically, the much disputed question of whether men are "naturally" or physiologically superior to women. As popular debates swirled around them, however, most women played sports simply for the pleasures and challenges of athletics. Through sport, they found opportunities to develop skills, win public acclaim, expand their social worlds, and push their physical and mental limits through competition and teamwork.

In the early 1800s women romped, skated, played Native American ball games, and sometimes entered road races and boxing matches. Not until the late nineteenth century did women enter organized sports in significant numbers. In the post–Civil War decades, wealthy white women took up country club sports like tennis and golf while middle-class girls and women rode bicycles, followed exercise regimens, and played basketball and baseball at their high schools and colleges. In the 1910s and 1920s young working-class women also took up sports in municipal athletic leagues, YWCAs, ethnic clubs, and workplace recreation programs. In Chicago, for example, African American women played basketball on the powerhouse "Roamer Girls" team while Jewish baseball players from the Hebrew Institute formed the "Hebrew Maidens" team.

Early-twentieth-century observers were fascinated by the "modern athletic girl," who seemed to thrive in every class, racial, and ethnic community. *Lippincott's Monthly* in 1911 glowingly described the modern athletic woman: "She loves to walk, to row, to ride, to motor, to jump and run . . . as Man walks, jumps, rows, rides, motors, and runs." Some doubted that the resemblance was a change for the better. In 1912 the *Ladies' Home Journal* published a piece whose title, "Are Athletics Making Girls Masculine?", signaled alarm at the very possibility. The article posed the question in its starkest terms: Would female athleticism turn women into masculine facsimiles of the opposite sex? Or might women "feminize" sport, eroding the boundary between male and female realms?

When women competed seriously as athletes, they threatened men's exclusive claim to "masculine" qualities of physical aggression, strength, speed, and power; women's participation in sports suggested that physical differences between the sexes might be an artifact of culture rather than a law of nature. Much of the debate about female athleticism focused on an area of undisputed physical difference—women's reproductive capacity. Although doctors had long recommended moderate exercise as a cure for menstrual irregularity and discomfort, women's enthusiasm for highly competitive sport pushed experts toward a revised view of athletics as dangerous. Doctors and physical educators warned that excessive exercise would damage reproductive organs, diminish fertility, and overstimulate female emotions to the point of nervous collapse. They warned as well that overindulgence in sport would reduce the sexual inhibitions, and thus the moral stature, of the "overzealous girl."

In response to such fears, medical experts and women physical educators agreed that the best policy was to recommend moderate competition under separately supervised female athletic programs. The policy of moderation sought to preserve the benefits of sport to the modern athletic girl while at the same time ensuring her physical safety and moral respectability. For women physical educators, "moderation" also served as a rationale for their separate control of women's sports in schools and colleges around the country. From the 1920s to the 1970s, school athletic programs typically limited female students to intramural competition among classmates, banning interscholastic competitions as too strenuous and "unladylike."

As the policy of moderate competition took hold in school and city recreation programs, commercial sport promoters and sympathetic journalists worked out another solution to the conflict between femininity and athleticism. Responding to the charge that sport made women ugly and unfeminine, promoters and journalists countered with the claim that an athlete's "masculine" skills were offset by her appealing femininity. The media, enraptured with aquatic stars like Helene Wainright and tennis "goddesses" like Helen Wills, promoted women athletes as exemplars of a new standard of beauty characterized by physical energy and a sassy vitality. Advertisers even hosted beauty pageants as sidelight events at athletic tournaments, featuring athletes as contestants. To their credit, sports promoters actively supported highly competitive sport for women. But by constantly contrasting women's "masculine" athletic talents with their "feminine" attributes, their strategy implicitly apologized for women's athletic skill and confirmed the essential masculinity of sport.

This strategy of promotion mixed with apology increased the popularity of women's sport in the years between World War I and World War II but did little to reduce the underlying tension between sport and womanhood. In fact the great popularity of sport in the 1920s led many journalists to view it as a site of women's larger challenge to male authority. Reporters described record-breaking female performances as "battle[s] won for feminism" by women athletes "who can meet the male upon even terms." Although few women competed directly against men, the press regularly reported on women-only events as if they were mixed competitions designed to dethrone men from their designated position of athletic and social superiority. Catch phrases such as "Men's athletic crown in danger" or "Who will be the weaker sex?" hinted that underneath the fascination with female athletic achievements lay a perception that women's athleticism did indeed challenge men's physical and cultural authority.

In the late 1930s and 1940s, the sense of imperiled manhood became more explicit. The playing fields were increasingly populated not by glamorous swimmers and golfers but by white working-class women, African American women, and other women of color, who competed on factory-based teams, at the renowned Tuskegee Institute track teams, or for ethnic clubs like the Polish Falcons. As the unsettled social relations of the Depression and war years sparked a renewed conservatism on matters of gender, the media's earlier tone of wondrous appreciation shifted to one of suspicion and hostility.

The career of Mildred "Babe" Didrikson illuminates the changing currents in women's sport. As a working-class teenager from Port Arthur, Texas, Didrikson was recruited in the late 1920s to play for a Dallas insurance company and soon became a national celebrity when she won two golds and a silver medal in track and field at the 1932 Los Angeles Olympics. With her slim, angular build, close-cropped hair, and baggy sweatsuit, Didrikson was a diamond in the rough who delighted the media with her homespun manner and razor-sharp wit. Yet because she excelled in the more controversial women's sports — track, basketball, and baseball — and failed to meet conventional standards of femininity or show any romantic or sexual interest in men, Didrikson's spot in the limelight faded quickly. By the late 1930s, if the press referred to her at all, it was as a freakish anomaly.

In the mid-1940s, however, Didrikson made a remarkable comeback in the sport of golf. To ensure her success, Didrikson muffled her earlier outspokenness and, like many midcentury U.S. women athletes, chose a path of compromise. She took up a more "respectable sport," began to wear skirts and makeup, and married professional wrestler George Zaharias. She successfully revived both her career and her image through a combination of astounding skill and accommodation to prevailing gender norms. The press commented less on the former and more on the latter; in 1947 *Life* magazine featured Didrikson under the headline "Babe Is a Lady Now: The World's Most Amazing Athlete Has Learned to Wear Nylons and Cook for Her Huge Husband."

The Midwest-based All-American Girls Professional Baseball League (AAGPBL), which drew over a half-million fans annually between 1943 and 1954, adopted a similar approach. The league employed what officials called the "femininity principle," a shrewd strategy designed to contrast athletes' "masculine skill" with their "feminine attractiveness." Dressed in pastel, skirted uniforms and forbidden by league rules to wear their hair in boyish bobs or to dress in masculine garb, AAGPBL players courted public approval with a wholesome girl-next-door image while thrilling their fans with stellar play. Although some players approved of the femininity principle and others found it ludicrous, all agreed that abiding by the rules was a small price to pay for the chance to pursue a dream — playing high-level professional sport before appreciative audiences. Women of color were denied this opportunity, since the all-white league management believed that African American players, in particular, might damage the league's "feminine" image. Outside of the Olympics, a de facto color bar prevailed until the 1950s, when Althea Gibson broke the racial barrier in women's tennis.

The near obsession with femininity in the postwar era spoke to a relatively new anxiety connected to women's sport — the matter of lesbianism. As mentioned earlier, previous fears about women's sexuality centered on the possibility that sport might remove sexual inhibitions and unleash women's heterosexual passions. But midcentury Americans more often suspected that the erotic desires released through sport might be those of women for other women. During the first half of the century, the recognition of active female desire, the acceptance of Freudian theories of sexual development, and a greater awareness of homosexuality combined to cast sexual suspicion on all women who did not appear appropriately feminine and heterosexual. Women athletes, long noted for their "masculine" skills and desires, became prime targets of the heightened sexual suspicion.

Although lesbians typically rejected the pernicious stereotype of the mannish lesbian athlete, by the 1940s and 1950s many athletically inclined lesbians had found sport to be a convivial and safe space to gather with other women. As a public activity that encouraged a certain amount of gender unorthodoxy—to "throw like a boy" was a *good* thing in sport—and nurtured close bonds among women, sport provided a social space in which lesbians could express themselves and create a sense of community.

By the 1960s the problematic image and limited popularity of women's sport had created something of a stalemate. Women continued to compete in school sport, industrial and community-based recreation, and high-level amateur competitions like the Olympics, but they did so with minimal financial support, scant media coverage, and damning suspicion about their sexual preference. However, the stasis soon gave way to change as a restless generation of young physical educators began to lobby for intercollegiate competition. Women within the Amateur Athletic Union (AAU) were also pressing for change, and after decades of rivalrous animosity physical educators and AAU leaders joined forces to promote women's athletics.

With the new wave of feminism in the early 1970s, women's athletics entered a watershed era in which long-standing barriers to full participation in sport seemed to fall almost as fast as women could push them over. Bolstered by the women's movement, advocates of women's sport began demanding equal access to athletic resources and training. They won their most important and controversial victory with the passage of Title IX of the 1972 Educational Act, which prohibited sex discrimination in any educational institution receiving federal funds. Although slow to be enforced, the act dictated that schools at all levels establish gender equality in their athletic programs.

Title IX and the momentum it generated ushered in two decades of significant athletic prog-

ress not limited to academic institutions. While professional athletes such as tennis player Billie Jean King organized women's tours and campaigned for increased prize monies, amateur women's sport blossomed at all levels, from elite Olympic competitions to community-based programs like youth soccer, aerobics, and adult softball. Girls' participation in interscholastic high school competition jumped from three hundred thousand in 1971 to more than two million in 1992. In women's college sport, the number of intercollegiate athletes rose from sixteen thousand to over one hundred sixty thousand between the early 1970s and late 1980s. Along with this dramatic increase in numbers, women athletes have also earned far greater acceptance and appreciation as women such as tennis star Martina Navratilova (who is now "out" as a lesbian), track champion Jackie Joyner-Kersee, speed skater Bonnie Blair, and figure skaters Debi Thomas and Kristi Yamaguchi became household names and national celebrities.

The recent popularity of women's sports also indicates its pivotal and controversial place in ongoing conflicts over gender and power in U.S. society. Within sport, issues of access and equity are by no means resolved. After more than two decades since Title IX, few colleges meet standards for gender equity in school sport, and women's athletics are typically governed by male-dominated athletic departments and national sports organizations. Some women's struggles around body image and sexuality suggest that the persistent tension between sport and womanhood continues to affect athletes on a personal level as well. For some, the pressure to meet ever shrinking ideals of thinness has turned athletic training into a punitive program of weight loss rather than a source of skill or enjoyment; for others, the continued stigma of the "mannish lesbian" creates pressure to leave sport, compete less vigorously, or remain closeted.

Far from being discouraged, women are approaching these barriers with a new sense of entitlement, energized by their own positive experiences in sport. In its fullest expression, the demand for meaningful leisure, unrestricted access to sport, and athletic self-determination involves more than simply forcing men to make room for women in the existing sports world. It demands that athletic attributes long defined as masculine—skill, strength, speed, physical assertiveness, uninhibited use of space and motion—become human qualities, not those of a particular gender. Ultimately, obtaining athletic freedom will be part of transforming the broader social relations of gender within which sporting life takes place.

Susan K. Cahn, *Coming on Strong: Gender and Sexuality in Twentieth-Century Women's Sport* (N.Y.: Free Press, 1994); Helen Lenskyj, *Out of Bounds: Women, Sport and Sexuality* (Toronto: Women's Press, 1986); Mariah Burton Nelson, *Are We Winning Yet? How Women Are Changing Sports and Sports Are Changing Women* (N.Y.: Random House, 1991).

▪ SUSAN K. CAHN

SEE ALSO Title IX.

≋ Standardized Testing

Standardized testing began in the United States in the early 1900s to determine one's individual intelligence quotient (I.Q.) and has generally benefited Northwestern European men while lowering the opportunities of women, Southern and Eastern European men, and people of color. This was unequivocally true until 1992, when Asian American males received higher average scores than white males on the major college admissions tests, the Scholastic Assessment Test (SAT) and the American College Testing Program's ACT Assessment (ACT). Many occupations also require standardized licensing tests, which has an adverse impact on the participation of women and people of color.

Standardized testing is used educationally from kindergarten through college to determine readiness for school; to track students into remedial, regular, or advanced classes; for admission to college or graduate school; and to place students in college English and math classes. Standardized I.Q. and achievement tests have restricted educational opportunities for African American, Latina/ Latino, and immigrant students by classifying them as "learning disabled" or slow learners and tracking them in special education classes in the earliest elementary school years. Frequently, the result is that they are never able to catch up to their peers and eventually drop out of school. In 1986 the U.S. District Court for the Northern District of California ruled in the *Larry P. v. Wilson Riles* case, a class-action suit brought by a group of African American parents, that standardized and other I.Q. tests could no longer be used to classify children as "educable mentally retarded."

The standardized tests that have the greatest impact on women's educational opportunities are the major gatekeeping college entrance examinations. The main purpose of these tests is to predict first-year college grades, not subsequent college grades or success in later life. Considerable documentation shows that women receive higher average grades than men in every course they take in high school and college. However their score averages on the SAT have been 50 to 60 points lower than men's since 1967. Since 1981 women have averaged approximately 10 points lower than men on the SAT-Verbal and 50 points lower on the SAT-Math despite equal training in math and nearly equal background in science.

The Educational Testing Service (ETS) has acknowledged that the SAT underpredicts women's college performance and overpredicts men's. It also admits that the single best predictor of college grades is high school grades. Many studies have corroborated this, including an ETS researcher's 1991 study of twelve thousand students, which found that the SAT substantially underpredicts women's college math grades at every level. Massachusetts Institute of Technology (MIT) accepts women with lower SAT-Math scores than men and finds they perform equally well throughout their college career. In 1989 a federal district court in the southern district of New York ruled that the

SAT could no longer be the sole criterion for determining merit scholarships in New York State because of its bias against women.

The ACT Assessment is also biased against women. In 1993 women averaged 20.5 points out of a possible 36 points while men averaged 21.0. The ACT is a test of acquired knowledge in English, math, reading, and science reasoning. Women traditionally score higher on the English and reading sections but lower in math and science.

Reasons for the differences on college entrance tests are complex but relate to the speed of the test; women's reluctance to guess if they aren't sure of the answer; and the content of the questions, which are more often about math, science, and politics, subjects that favor men's scores, rather than the humanities, the arts, psychology, and writing, in which women excel. Women have consistently outperformed men on tests of writing ability, including ETS's tests.

These biased tests diminish women's opportunities to obtain millions of dollars in merit scholarships that are awarded by the National Merit Scholarship Corporation—women receive only two-fifths of the National Merit Scholarships—and hundreds of private companies and foundations; gain admission to the nearly 1,600 accredited colleges and universities in the U.S., Canada, Mexico, and Europe; and enter many special education programs for "gifted and talented" high school students, which rely on these scores for admission. Lower scores also result in women being placed in less challenging college English and math courses.

These factors contribute to a real dollar loss for women in later life; they get less prestigious jobs, earn less money, and have fewer leadership opportunities than do men, which may affect their self-esteem.

Students of color, except for Asian American males, have much lower average scores than white males on both college entrance exams. Females of color are doubly penalized by the SAT because on average they have lower SAT scores than the males in their racial or ethnic group. (The ACT does not publish gender breakdowns of scores by ethnic group.) Students of color have problems with the tests because of differences in language usage, cultural experience, and quality of academic preparation. For women of all races, gender bias on the SAT is systemic and has occurred for more than twenty-five years.

▪ PHYLLIS ROSSER

SEE ALSO Education.

≋ Stereotypes

Age Stereotypes

The pairing of ageism and sexism creates stereotypes against older women that are among the most vicious in society. Even if stereotypes are false, they are powerful and can be harmful because they influence public opinion and action. Throughout history negative images of older women have resulted in dislike, denigration, and outright persecution. Older women are lumped together as if their only identity is age and as if age somehow disqualifies their sexuality and value. Because of these stereotypes men, employers, and younger women discriminate against older women.

Older women themselves internalize the negative stereotypes. As they age, some women have diminished self-esteem. Instead of being proud of their age, they deny their aging to others and even to themselves. Many try to hide the signs of aging, as if aging is shameful, and often lie about their ages. Stereotypes stigmatize older women at much earlier ages than men and result in what Susan Sontag first called the double standard of aging.

By contrast, in Native American cultures, older women are generally well-respected members of the community. They are listened to, their counsel on important matters is sought, and they are well incorporated into the community and family. In some tribes, women cannot become healers or medicine people until after menopause. Being called an Elder is an honorific word, not one that calls forth a negative image.

In medieval times, old women were stereotyped as witches and suffered cruel punishments. Fairy tales and other stories characterized old women also as nuisances, mean, selfish, and shrews. According to Jane Mills's research in *Womanwords: A Dictionary of Words*, the following stereotypes are often applied to old women: anile, bag, battle-axe, beldam, biddy, dame, dowager, girl, gorgon, gossip, hag, haggard, hen, jade, maid/maiden, mother, mutton, spinster, and witch.

"Anile," which comes from the Latin word *anus*, means old woman and, as Mills points out, the word "entered English in the mid 17th century with grotesque, misogynistic connotations. Dictionary definitions include a doddering old woman, old womanish, imbecile, a silly old woman." "Anile" was used more in England than in the United States, according to Mills, who lives in England. However, most of the other terms continue to be used in the United States. In the 1890s the word "bag" referred to a middle-aged or elderly slattern, notes Mills. In the United States "bag" has come to refer to a woman with an old uterus or to a postmenopausal, nonfertile older woman.

In the United States older women are also stereotyped as witches, bitches, nags, and crones. Older feminists are reclaiming the word "crone" as an honored appellation by creating croning ceremonies to celebrate the coming of maturity. Despite this, "crone" is still used to describe old women negatively. Numerous dictionaries, for example, define crone as "an ugly, withered old woman."

Even the seemingly neutral word "grandmother" also may be used as a stereotype. As Barbara Macdonald points out in her book with Cynthia Rich, *Look Me in the Eye: Old Women, Aging, and Ageism*, even women who never marry or who are childless are stereotyped as grandmothers once they are older and are often expected to serve and nurture others, including younger feminists whose feminism fails to embrace old women as worthwhile.

This author's research demonstrates that not only are older women stereotyped by others but also that many self-stereotype by adopting a peapod lifestyle characterized by the seven Ps: adhering to patriarchy, propriety, politeness, perfectionism, passivity, patterning, and mourning prettiness. The older women's movement has sought to substitute more positive Ps such as pride, power, passion, and proactivity.

When women become mothers-in-law, they suffer from cruel stereotypes claiming that all mothers-in-law are possessive of sons, manipulative, mean to daughters-in-law, and so on. Older mothers themselves are the butt of many jokes that stereotype them as demanding, whining, enveloping women who are unable to give up control. Such stereotypes can be most cruel to Jewish older women.

Many lesbians, now old, suffered terribly in youth from homophobic stereotypes. Now, in somewhat more accepting times, they suffer from the double stigmatization of being old women and being lesbians. Even within the lesbian women's community, young lesbians are not immune to the ageism that permeates society.

Despite some notable exceptions, movies, television, and the print media stereotype older women as silly, stupid, senile, screechy, and stubborn. For example, Sophia, the old mother in the long-running situation comedy *The Golden Girls*, had some endearing qualities but nevertheless perpetuated ageist stereotypes. Although many people loved the portrayal by Ruth Gordon of feisty eighty-year-old Maude in the film *Harold and Maude*, this film also stereotyped old women as useless. Maude committed suicide at age eighty because she saw no further role for herself.

The stereotype that older women are nonsexual has had profound consequences both for women, who have feared what would happen to them, and also for older men, who have eschewed older women to bed or have wed women much younger than themselves. Novelist Kurt Vonnegut has referred to the "new cookie syndrome" of men dropping their midlife and old wives for younger women.

Women who are unmarried at later ages are often called old maids and considered to be petty, peculiar, prudish, or pests. Married, single, widowed, or divorced older women are sometimes referred to as "girls," which infantilizes them and denies their wisdom and life experience.

Despite the marvelous new roles some older women are carving out, the stereotype of the old woman knitting in a rocking chair persists. According to this author's research, when people are asked to write anonymously what comes to mind when they hear "old woman," they generally write words such as cranky, lonely, sad, wrinkled, messy, poor, or infirm. Younger women fear aging because of these negative images and often fail to include old women in their friendship and organizational networks or relegate them to serving refreshments, as Barbara Macdonald has pointed out.

A leading opponent of ageist stereotypes has been Maggie Kuhn, founder of the Gray Panthers. This organization began when Kuhn and some of her friends were forced to retire because of the ageist stereotype that they could no longer function well after sixty-five. The myths about older women, embodied in stereotypes, were also combated as early as the 1970s by Robert Butler, M.D., in his book *Why Survive: Being Old in America*. Despite nearly twenty years of combating stereotypes by these and other leaders, ageist stereotypes remain prevalent in U.S. society.

In the 1990s, with the focus on the U.S. health care system, old women, who tend to live longer than do men, became stereotyped as costly consumers of health care, including long-term care. They were blamed for rising health costs and rationed services when the problems in the health care system obviously resulted from other causes.

Research also has demonstrated that many physicians discriminate against older women. Rather than spending time and effort for diagnosis, advice, and treatment, many physicians often rush older women out of the office or overmedicate them with psychotropic medications. Perhaps the negative stereotypes of older women in many physicians' magazines influence the doctors. For example, *Geriatrics*, a journal read by many physicians, is full of pharmaceutical companies' color advertisements that depict menopausal women and old women as cranky, depressed, frail, confused, and silly. Even when the women's illnesses, such as arthritis, were the same as men's, the old women were portrayed in the journal as unkempt, passive, and incompetent, while the men with the same diagnosis appeared neat, well dressed, and active.

Perhaps it was accurate that the 1994–95 television series *Chicago Hope*, in one of its first shows, portrayed a young male physician who overlooked appendicitis in an old woman, then yelled at a female intern for interrupting him and asking him to look at "an old woman with arthritis." The patient might have had terrible arthritis (his stereotype of old women), but she also ended up with a burst appendix because of his stereotypical thinking.

Stereotypes hurt old women and can even kill if old women are neglected as a result. There are homeless old women on U.S. streets who are pictured as senile when what really troubles them is poverty and the lack of affordable housing. One old woman in a housing project for the elderly keeps a basket of marbles outside her apartment. When asked why she does this, she explains, "I want to show I haven't lost my marbles," which is her joking way of counteracting the stereotype. However, on the whole, many old women in the United States feel powerless to counteract the stereotypes against them.

Ruth Harriet Jacobs, *Be An Outrageous Older Woman—A R.A.S.P. [Remarkable Aging Smart Person]* (Manchester, Conn.: K.I.T. Press, 1993); Barbara Macdonald, with Cynthia Rich, *Look Me in the Eye: Old Women, Aging and Ageism* (San Francisco: Spinsters, Inc., 1993); Jane Mills,

Womanwords: A Dictionary of Words About Women (New York: The Free Press, 1992).

■ RUTH HARRIET JACOBS

SEE ALSO Aging.

Class Stereotypes

Class stereotypes, which abound in all class-stratified societies, have always been a part of U.S. culture. The primary stereotypes have typically reflected the world views of the dominant classes—their self-satisfaction on the one hand and their contempt for underlings on the other. While women who belong to the social elite have been stereotyped as refined, accomplished, and virtuous, for example, women who belong to subordinate groups have been labeled ignorant, lazy, and depraved. Nowhere is this phenomenon more evident than in the numerous stereotypes that have disparaged the sexual morality of women at the bottom of class hierarchies.

A prime example is the "Jezebel" stereotype that has been applied to Black slaves. Building on transatlantic slave traders' derogatory descriptions of African mores, slave-holding households in the U.S. colonies excused men's sexual abuse of female slaves by labeling the victims instinctively promiscuous women. By the time of the American Revolution, images of lustful bondwomen suffused public discussion of chattel slavery. Such images became more pervasive in the nineteenth century, when antislavery movements demanded discussion of the rape evidenced by the significant numbers of slaves fathered by white men. The Jezebel stereotype was deployed by slavery's opponents as well as its defenders: abolitionists referred to Black Jezebels and white rapists alike to support arguments that slavery corrupted everyone it touched. At base, though, the Jezebel stereotype served slavery's defenders. It buttressed the master class's claims to respectability by excusing the men for rape and suggesting that women of the master class were paragons of chastity because males looking for illicit sex had to look no further than the slave quarters. When bondwomen were branded libidinous, the whole slave community was defined as unfit for freedom because its members supposedly lacked self-control.

Dichotomous thinking about the sexual standards of women on opposite sides of the color line has shaped other class stereotypes as well. In the late 1840s, when Anglo businessmen began to form financial and marital alliances with wealthy Mexican families in California, Anglo writers replaced blanket aspersions on Mexicanas' moral character with sharply color-conscious portrayals of lower-class mestiza hussies and upper-class "Spanish ladies." In the 1880s and 1890s, journalists associated with political movements that wished to bar Chinese immigrants from the United States stereotyped West-Coast prostitutes as "Chinese slave girls" and ignored the far greater numbers of white prostitutes. Contrasting images of vice-laden Black workers and innocent white working women in danger of contamination became key ideological props for excluding Black workers from factory jobs in the industrializing South. Stereotypes of Native American women as ignorant drudges clinging to backward ways of life have long gone hand in hand with romantic depictions of white women "civilizing the wilderness" as homesteaders.

Women of color who excel in their work sometimes have been condescendingly labeled "credits to their race," but only when their work has seemed valuable in capitalist terms. The dominant culture has disparaged or ignored their labors for people other than white employers: Native American women's contributions to tribal societies, Mexicanas' role in communal economies that antedated Anglo settlement and investment in the Southwest, Black women's domestic work for their own families as opposed to white households, and so on. This has fueled stereotypes that define women of color as virtually worthless unless they are working under white supervision.

White chauvinism has not been so inflexible,

however, as to preclude stereotypes that depict white working-class women as sexually loose. Members of stigmatized ethnic communities have often felt the sting of such insults. In the 1840s and 1850s, for example, Irish Catholic immigrants were widely portrayed as loose women, as were Russian Jewish immigrants in the early 1900s. Another especially vulnerable group has been white women who work in occupations in which people of color predominate—sharecroppers in the Southeast, for instance, and migrant agricultural laborers in the West. But ethnic prejudice and contempt for whites in jobs defined as "colored" have not by any means been the only forces at play.

Sterling testaments to that fact can be found in genteel literature on white "working girls" employed in the Northeast's factories and department stores in the late nineteenth century. Though these women held jobs exclusively reserved for whites and belonged in the vast majority of cases to ethnic groups well above the bottom of the heap, legions of writers defined the working girl as a woman prone to sexual vice. Some blamed her parents, portraying them as lowlifes incapable of imbuing their children with decent behavioral standards. Others argued that miserably low wages compelled working girls to engage in part-time prostitution in order to make ends meet. The image dominating the literature, however, was that of a woman corrupted by an unseemly taste for luxuries beyond her means. Working girls were most commonly vilified, in other words, for failing to accept their lowly station.

Stereotypes charging lower-class women with sexual misconduct have invariably promoted the idea that the communities these women represent deserve their lot in life. The underlying assumption in every case has been that a natural dominion of good people over bad people determines the community's place in the social order. Just how the line dividing the good people from the bad people is drawn has depended on the racial and ethnic identity of the particular target group

and on the specific historical circumstances that made the group a target.

One thing has remained constant, however; socially subordinate classes have been depicted as morally inferior beings. Bigotry on the part of the stereotypes' architects accounts to a large degree for this motif, but fears regarding the social order's stability enter the picture as well. Slaveholders and their sympathizers peddled the Jezebel myth with increased vigor, for instance, in response to a wave of antislavery agitation led by free Blacks after the American Revolution. Denigrating images of the late-nineteenth-century working girl came to the fore as her communities launched mighty challenges to employers' control of the workplace and to upper-class political clout. Charges that Russian Jewish women staffed a giant network of brothels established by their landsmen poured forth in the muckraking press of the 1910s as workers from that same ethnic group took the lead in a series of strikes and union-organizing drives in the garment industry. In similar fashion, today's stereotype of the immoral "welfare mother"—portrayed as an African American or Latina despite the fact that most women receiving welfare payments are white—emerged against the backdrop of social revolts by working-class people of color in the 1960s and 1970s.

As these patterns suggest, stereotypes that define oppressed populations as inherently base can also be interpreted as admissions that their subordination requires ideological props—that it is not, in fact, a law of nature but the result of social arrangements that might be overturned. If class hierarchies and the racial-ethnic inequities that interlace them were really natural phenomena, the elite would have no need to defend their privilege with specious images of the groups they dominate.

Antoñia I. Castañeda, "The Political Economy of Nineteenth-Century Stereotypes of Californianas," in *Between Borders*, edited by Adelaida Del Castillo (Los Angeles: Floricanto Press, 1989); Sarah Eisenstein, *Give Us Bread But Give Us Roses: Working Women's Consciousness in the United States, 1890 to the First World War* (London: Routledge & Kegan Paul, 1983); Deborah Gray White, *Ar'n't I a Woman?: Female Slaves in the Plantation South* (New York: W. W. Norton & Company, 1985).

• PRISCILLA MUROLO

Disability Stereotypes

Over the past several decades, the treatment of people with disabilities has been evolving from a charity model to a civil rights model, but societal attitudes have lagged far behind. Women and men with disabilities face pervasive negative stereotypes that call into question their ability to function as independent, competent, sexual adults. Women with disabilities face disability-based *and* gender-based stereotypes that are mutually reinforcing and further limit their roles and options.

According to available research, the attitudes of nondisabled people toward people with disabilities are predominantly negative. Typical assumptions are that disability is punishment for sin, that it is contagious, and that individuals with disabilities are sick, helpless, incompetent, and asexual. These stereotypes are reflected in the language used to describe people with disabilities, which is dehumanizing and emphasizes victimization, for example, "the blind," "suffers from polio," or "confined to a wheelchair." The disability rights movement favors language that puts the person first, and presents disability as a fact, not a tragedy. This movement has successfully fought for the passage of laws that prohibit discrimination against people with disabilities, such as the landmark Americans with Disabilities Act (1990).

In part, stereotypical attitudes reflect a lack of exposure to and realistic information about the lives of people with disabilities. Also, nondisabled people often use their own experiences with illness and temporary disability to make assumptions about the helplessness of disabled people. Finally, at the root of frightened and hostile feelings are unconscious anxieties regarding wholeness, perfection, loss, and weakness.

Women with disabilities face numerous stereotypes, including those based on disability, gender, race, and sexual orientation. Studies suggest they are perceived more negatively than are disabled men or nondisabled women. Stereotypes about disability tend to reinforce stereotypes about women. Both emphasize passivity, weakness, and helplessness, so that women with disabilities have few models for positive identification. In contrast, the positive male stereotypes of virility, assertiveness, and independence serve as a counterforce to negative disability stereotypes; thus men with disabilities have some affirmative imagery with which to identify.

Although stereotypes of women and disability overlap, women with disabilities are not perceived as the "ideal" female. Myths about their sexuality and nurturing capacities bring into question their ability to assume the traditional female roles of wife and mother. The power of these myths is suggested by the fact that women with disabilities are less likely to have partners and face more barriers to having children than do nondisabled women or disabled men. Because sexual attractiveness and desirability of women continue to be measured in terms of physical perfection, women who fail to meet traditional standards of beauty by virtue of disability are often perceived as asexual. Based on this narrow view of sexuality, such a perception fails to acknowledge the potential of every individual to be sexual. Existing simultaneously with the myth of asexuality is the myth that women with disabilities are oversexed and/or unable to control their sexuality, as though disability inevitably alters their impulses and judgment. This assumption is often used to restrict their sexual expression and childbearing, for example, through sterilization or placement in institutions or other confining environments, in the guise of protecting them from becoming victims of sexual exploitation.

Another stereotype limiting the access of women with disabilities to the social/sexual arena is that they "should stick with their own kind" and choose disabled partners, as though disability is their only defining characteristic. For lesbians with disabilities, a prevalent myth reflecting heterosexist bias is that these women have become lesbians by default, since they cannot attract a man. Partners of women with disabilities face their own set of stereotypes, including being "saints" for coupling with a disabled woman, or choosing to be with her as the result of psychological problems, such as a pathological need to rescue someone who is "helpless," or that they are with her because they have low self-esteem and feel they cannot attract anyone "better." Such stereotypes about partners are based on the false assumption that disabled women only take and have nothing to give in the relationship.

A variety of myths serve to deny women with disabilities the right to bear or raise children. These include the assumption that women with disabilities will invariably produce children with disabilities. While this is rarely the case—most disabilities are not hereditary—reproductive freedom should encompass the right of women to bear children like themselves, including children with disabilities. Another myth is that women with disabilities will be unable to care adequately for their children, disabled or not. Some of the misconceptions embedded in this myth are that women who may need disability-related help are also not capable of giving nurturance, and that there is only one "right" way to mother.

Negative assumptions about sexual desires and mothering capacities of women with disabilities have limited their access to sex education and information and to family planning services. Also, there have been widespread efforts to restrict their procreative activities through involuntary sterilization or other extreme birth-control methods, at times prescribed without the woman's consent; laws prohibiting the marriage of people with certain disabilities; and the use of legal means or family pressures to remove children from the care of mothers with disabilities.

While stereotypes about sexuality and nurturance limit the access of women with disabilities to partner and parent roles, stereotypes about their competence also limit their access to worker roles. It is typically assumed that women with disabilities need care, not jobs. In fact, women with disabilities are less likely to be employed than are men with disabilities or women without disabilities, and they are more likely to have lower-paying jobs when they are employed. Disabled women of color have even greater difficulty securing decent employment. Schools can be training grounds for unemployment: young women with disabilities are less likely than young men to participate in career-oriented courses or to receive training for high-paying jobs.

For women with disabilities, the limited access to the socially sanctioned roles of partner, mother, and worker can be debilitating. But some women are able to create new identities that move beyond stereotypes and negative societal expectations, taking pride in inhabiting and exhibiting their bodies exactly the way they are, disability and all. Women whose disabilities affect sexual expression, pleasure, and positioning invent new ways of doing that which is as old as time. Women whose capabilities are called into question are able to challenge the narrow-minded definitions of competence that focus on the male way and/or the able-bodied way of doing things. In addition to individual successes, women with disabilities have begun organizing as a movement committed to fighting oppression, confronting stereotypes, and translating their strengths into positive imagery that can benefit all women.

Susan E. Browne, Debra Connors, and Nanci Stern, eds., *With the Power of Each Breath: A Disabled Women's Anthology* (San Francisco: Cleis Press, 1985); Michelle Fine and Adrienne Asch, "Disabled Women: Sexism Without the Pedestal," *Journal of Sociology and Social Welfare* Vol. 8 (July 1981): 233–48; Jenny Morris, *Pride Against Prejudice: Transforming Attitudes to Disability* (Philadelphia: New Society Press, 1991).

■ HARILYN ROUSSO

Racial Stereotypes

Stereotypes—fixed, conventional notions of individuals and groups that suppress individuality and critical thinking—affect many people and groups in society. However, they have special significance for women, and for any other less powerful or marginalized groups, because the stereotypes applied to them are usually imposed and controlled by others and, as a result, are difficult to change.

Who are you? It's a simple question that demands a complex answer if any of us is to come close to describing ourselves. However, the stereotypes that society imposes usually have less to do with an individual's or a group's characteristics than with the assignment of preordained roles. This typecasting indicates what is expected from you: behavior, intellect, integrity, capabilities, as well as how others treat you. Individuality is overshadowed by negative judgments based on caste, class, sexuality, gender, and race.

Often passed from one generation to the next as indisputable truths, stereotypes become embedded within family and community belief systems and in turn are used to justify how society responds to those being labeled, and to advance specific policies or agendas. Not surprisingly, race has been central to the creation and perpetuation of stereotypes in the United States.

Racial stereotyping flourishes in the most virulent forms when race, more correctly the concept of racial groupings, is used systematically as a means of advancing nationalistic or economic goals, assuming and maintaining privileges, establishing apartheid systems, denying access, abridging rights, or fostering inequalities. Such racist stereotypes have been a key ingredient in the lethal mix of conquest, exploitation, oppression, and genocide that has defined this nation's history.

Sexuality and sexual behavior, mental capacity, moral and ethical beliefs, and physical characteristics are all ingredients of stereotypes that depict people of color in this country as abnormal and inferior. At their most hateful extreme, such labeling advances the dangerous libel that "they" are less than fully human. For example, the stereotyping of Native people as "dirty, thieving, bloodthirsty savages" has historically been used to justify punitive military policies, routine acts of atrocity, wholesale slaughter, and seizure of land. Stereotyping of African Americans that denied their humanity, intelligence, morality, and capabilities was similarly and routinely used in support of slavery and the subsequent limitation of their rights and freedoms.

Racial stereotyping not only disempowers and dehumanizes the targeted group as a whole, it is also gendered to place women and men outside society's ideal of femininity and masculinity, removing any possibility of privilege or protection. For women, regardless of color, gendered stereotypes tend to undermine self-esteem, while also pushing them to conform to socially set standards of speech, dress, and behavior, and to keep to their assigned secondary place in the sexual hierarchy. Racially gendered stereotypes of women of color are employed to confirm their greater subservience, deny them the respect and "protection" accorded to white women, and to sanction their use and abuse.

All too often these stereotypes reflect this society's obsessive and twisted fixation on female sexuality. If white women were once locked into tightly prescribed roles that deified their virtue, the stereotyping of women of color frequently has depicted them as virtueless, sexually available, and eager. Where some white women are labeled "sluts" and therefore made to seem like "acceptable prey," all women of color are often stereotyped in that way. In addition to being labeled sexually loose, women of color have also been characterized as lazy, irresponsible, childlike, and untrustworthy, among a host of other diminishing terms and images meant to justify their perceived lack of status. In popular culture, the colored "she" becomes nameless: "squaw," "nigger bitch," "mama san," "tamale."

Racially gendered stereotyping not only seeks to destroy women's worth to enhance the superiority of others but it also seeks to undermine women's value within their own group, and to distort women's collective and individual sense of esteem. How many stories and films, how many news reports have played to this theme by depicting women of color being abused, given away or traded by their own kin, or typically cast as addicts, prostitutes, derelicts, drug dealers, or abusive or negligent mothers?

Through the distorted lens of racial stereotypes, the woman on welfare almost automatically becomes beige or brown, and her mothering skills, state of need, sexual behavior, reproductive choices, ethics, and morals are immediately suspect in the public mind. She can be demonized and used to justify punitive policies. If you say "illegal immigrant," the imagined person's skin is immediately visualized as dark. Images of women of color as breeders dropping babies wherever they go, taking public resources, and giving nothing back in return fuel the fire of those who cry for a policy to close the doors and kick the "interlopers" out. Through this lens the woman on drugs is vilified and criminalization supersedes treatment; the issue of teenage sexuality is reduced to branding pregnant teenagers as shameless wantons in need of harsh supervision; poor women's sexual behavior and responsibility become even more suspect and in need of outside controls ranging from pushing contraceptive techniques to forced sterilization to denying funding for abortion. These racial stereotypes of "illegal immigrants" perpetuate their subjugation when, in reality, countless women without U.S. citizenship often perform menial, low-paying tasks, without job security, union protection, or other benefits afforded to women in mainstream U.S. society.

Stereotyping also leads to public indifference regarding issues ranging from women's increased rates of incarceration (because the majority of those behind bars are women of color) to the decline in public health or housing services (because it is assumed that women of color are the major beneficiaries). In a society where violence and poverty overshadow the lives of millions of women and children, these stereotypes are used to distance further those ugly realities, deaden the public's conscience, distort the debate, and stifle reform.

■ MARCIA GILLESPIE

SEE ALSO Images of Women.

Sexual Stereotypes

Sexual or gender stereotypes are structured inferences that link personal attributes to the social categories of women and men. Despite women's recent advances in nontraditional areas and occupations, certain sexual stereotypes persist. These stereotypes interact closely with racial, class, and sexual orientation stereotypes.

Stereotypes tend to form most representations of women in media. For example, the "Jewish American Princess" dominates the film *Clueless* (1995) and Black or Latina women often fill the roles of domestics, as in films such as *Forrest Gump* (1994) and *The First Wives Club* (1996). In some rap music, the stereotype of the Black woman as emasculating and manipulative is central to the message. Lesbians have had to watch as the pendulum of popular culture swings from the stereotype of man-hating and masculine, to chic and fashionable.

Stereotypes have been used both to define women and to control them. They limit the possibilities women envision for themselves and therefore damage women's self-esteem and deprive society of women's potential. Examples abound in literature and social reality of the damage sexual stereotypes have done to women's lives. Because of the limited options embedded in stereotypes, women have suffered alcoholism, drug addiction, self-hate, and suicide. Although men have been defined by their relationship to the outside world—to nature, to society, even to God—women have been defined in relationship to men. This fact—definition by relationship to men—holds true for all women, but women of color are defined not only by their relationship to white men but also by their relationship to white women and to men of color.

Nearly all the sexual stereotypes of women currently in operation were formed in the past century under racist and classist ideologies. Anglo-American women of the upper and middle classes were generally confined to the roles of wife, mother, and mistress. As white man's ideal companion and as the mother of his children, the Anglo-American woman was considered the "true woman." True womanhood was glorified and placed on a pedestal, especially in the antebellum and post–Civil War South. According to the "cult of true womanhood," white women possessed four cardinal virtues: piety, purity, submissiveness, and domesticity. The external, physical signs of true womanhood were delicacy, softness, and weakness. The true woman was to be protected by white men, and true womanhood was inaccessible to working-class, poor white women and to all women of color. It is difficult in this instance (indeed, in most instances) to separate ideology from stereotype: they work together like a hand and glove.

In the nineteenth century, enslaved women of African descent were expected to be strong—able to bear fatigue and reproduce "property" for the white master. African American women were everything that the white, "true" woman could not be. In terms of sexuality, they were viewed as promiscuous and overtly sexual. After emancipation, the stereotype of the strong, Black woman-slave fragmented into the controlling images of the mammy, matriarch, welfare mother, and jezebel. Each of these images is central to the interlocking systems of race, gender, and class oppression. The mammy, for example, is the faithful, devoted family servant. Although portrayed as physically sensuous, she is asexual, a surrogate mother devoted to the happy development of a white family. Lately, professional Black women have been hampered by this image more than any other. They are treated like mammies and penalized if they do not appear warm and nurturing.

A more recent image of Black women, that of the welfare mother, is an updated version of the "breeder" stereotype created during slavery. The welfare mother is categorized as a bad mother, content to sit around and live off the "dole," shunning work, passing on her bad values to her offspring, and having babies to receive more welfare.

Sexual stereotypes are also projected onto other women of color. The mammy stereotype is applied to the Latina/Chicana domestic in the western and southwestern United States but with a twist: she is assumed to lack intelligence because she does not speak English. Latinas are also seen as sexually aggressive in response to the cultural stereotype of machismo and sexually repressive, strict Roman Catholicism. This sexual aggression feeds stereotypes of Latinas' welfare dependency.

Asian women are stereotyped as quiet, delicate, and submissive, especially to men's desires. Of all women of color, Asian women are perceived as closest to the stereotype of true womanhood but with the discriminating marker of sexual availability. Stereotypes of the sexually available Asian woman range from the geisha to the mail-order bride. The crucial difference between this stereotype and the jezebel/whore image is that Asian women are not seen as aggressive, just available and malleable. According to the stereotype, Asian women make ideal wives because they make no demands, never complain, and exist only to serve. These stereotypes, because they limit roles and opportunities for Asian American women, are as controlling for Asian American women as the images of matriarch and welfare mother are for Black women. Also burdened by the label of "model minority," Asian women are exploited economically and politically.

Native American women are stereotyped as strong, spiritual "earth mothers." Because Native peoples have been effectively controlled by U.S. policies, the Native woman is not seen as a threat and has not been subject to stereotyping in recent years. In fact, she has been rendered invisible. But during the period of colonization and westward expansion of the United States, two dominant stereotypes of Native women existed. The first, a variant of the mammy stereotype, was represented by Pocahontas (Native name: Matoaka) and Sacajawea. Loyal, trusting, and trustworthy, these Native women "redeemed" themselves by being useful to white men. The other stereotype of Native women was the "squaw." They were seen as general servants to men — ministering to their sexual needs, mothering their children, and maintaining the culture, while the men were great hunters and warriors. Both these stereotypes dismiss the real power Native women had and have in many Native nations.

All the sexual stereotypes discussed so far are rooted in heterosexuality. Women who claim a lesbian or bisexual identity share a similar stereotype, with variations based on race or class. Until recently, popular culture, arguably, dismissed lesbians as social rejects — unattractive, unpleasant, and frustrated women. Current portrayals are less negative for lesbians, but more negative for bisexual women, who, especially in film, are stereotyped as dishonest, maniacal, murderous, promiscuous, and fearful of commitment. Lesbians of color and bisexual women of color have to contend with the perception in their broader communities that homoeroticism is a "white thing." Claiming a lesbian or bisexual identity is sometimes perceived as a rejection of ethnic and racial culture and community.

Hazel V. Carby, *Reconstructing Womanhood* (New York: Oxford University Press, 1987); Patricia Hill Collins, *Black Feminist Thought* (Cambridge, Mass.: Unwin Hyman, 1990).

■ SHELLEY P. HALEY

SEE ALSO Images of Women.

≋ Sterilization and Sterilization Abuse

In the early 1970s women created a movement to end sterilizations without proper informed consent. The movement arose in many parts of the country as a result of abuses that were then coming to light. Numerous community organiza-tions, particularly the National Welfare Rights Organization, became alarmed at reports of forced sterilizations of women on welfare and of those receiving care in city, county, and other government hospitals.

Following the disclosures of the Relf case in 1973, leaders of Black organizations and civil libertarians raised outraged voices against what was increasingly recognized as sterilization abuse. Relf involved two sisters, Mary Alice, then fourteen, and Minnie Lee Relf, then twelve, who were sterilized in Montgomery, Alabama, in June 1973. As described in court, two representatives of the federally financed Montgomery Community Action Agency called on the girls' mother requesting consent to give the children birth-control shots. She consented by placing an X on a form that called for surgical sterilization. Presiding Judge Gerhard Gesell declared:

> Although Congress has been insistent that all family planning programs function purely on a voluntary basis there is uncontroverted evidence in the record that minors and other incompetents have been sterilized with federal funds and that an indefinite number of poor people have been improperly coerced into accepting a sterilization operation under the threat that various federally supported welfare benefits would be withdrawn unless they submitted to irreversible sterilization.

Native American women were also targeted. A General Accounting Office report in 1976 revealed that the Indian Health Services, a federal agency, had sterilized thousands of women between the ages of fourteen and forty-four between 1973 and 1976. As a result of the 1974 decision in the Relf case, government-funded sterilizations of individuals under twenty-one were no longer permitted. Nevertheless, the Indian Health Services had sterilized thirteen women and girls younger than twenty-one years.

Many other instances substantiated women's allegations that abuses were rampant. In Los Angeles County, Mexican American women were being sterilized at the County Hospital without much explanation or information. In South Carolina a white physician threatened women on Medicaid, white and Black, by refusing to deliver their babies unless they consented to be sterilized after giving birth.

Women and men organized to research, publicize, agitate, and to enact guidelines and legislation for informed consent. Organizations such as the Committee to End Sterilization Abuse on the East Coast and the Committee Against Forced Sterilization on the West Coast took on the campaigns and formed coalitions with other groups committed to reproductive and health rights.

The history of forced sterilization in the United States is long and tragic. The first of the laws empowering the state to sterilize unwilling and unwitting people was passed in 1907 by the Indiana Legislature. The act was intended to prevent procreation of "confirmed criminals, idiots, rapists, and imbeciles" who were confined to state institutions. Other states followed with what became known as the eugenics laws. It is shocking to learn that between 1907 and 1964 more than 63,000 people were sterilized under such laws in the United States and in the colony of Puerto Rico.

These infamous laws are no longer on the books, but their spirit lingers. By the late 1970s at least ten states had proposed compulsory sterilization of women on welfare. Similar proposals in the 1990s aim to limit welfare benefits of women who have more than the approved number of children or to mandate the use of long-acting contraceptives, such as Norplant, for poor women.

The movement against sterilization without proper consent accomplished great successes. One was the enactment of regulations for New York City hospitals and of a law in New York City requiring a thorough informed consent procedure that has become a model for the country. Another success was the establishment of new guidelines for the Department of Health, Education, and Welfare, based on those used in New York City.

The organizations involved in those struggles of the 1970s established a forum for dialogue among different groups of women. Initially, the New York coalitions working to establish guidelines in the city hospitals brought together representatives of hospital community boards, health care professionals, civil rights groups, and women's groups involved in securing abortion rights. Such diverse groups as the National Black Feminist Organization, the Lower East Side Neighborhood Health Center, Healthright, Health-PAC, the Committee to End Sterilization Abuse, the Center for Constitutional Rights, the Family Planning Division of the Human Resources Administration, the Puerto Rican Socialist Party, *Ms.* magazine, the National Council of Negro Women, and the National Organization for Women ensured that many experiences, opinions, and positions were shared. In the process, white middle-class women understood that women of color and women of low income experienced realities vastly different from their own. Women learned together that the male-dominated medical power structure could act differently toward them because of classist and racist attitudes. But the women also learned that the power structure viewed them with similar misogyny, infringing upon their rights to make choices.

Allan Chase, *The Legacy of Malthus: The Social Costs of the New Scientific Racism* (New York: Alfred A. Knopf, 1977); Betsy Hartmann, *Reproductive Rights and Wrongs: The Global Politics of Population Control and Reproductive Choice*, rev. ed. (Boston: South End Press, 1995); Helen Rodriguez-Trias, "The Women's Health Movement: Women Take Power," in *Reforming Medicine. Lessons of the Last Quarter Century*, edited by Victor W. Sidel and Ruth Sidel (New York: Pantheon, 1984).

■ HELEN RODRIGUEZ-TRIAS

SEE ALSO Birth Control; Eugenics; Reproductive Rights.

≋ Strikes

Strikes originated as collective employee work stoppages and, with accompanying picket lines and boycotts, became labor's chief weapons against employers. They proved effective for other

The famous shoemakers' strike in Lynn, Massachusetts, on March 7, 1860, was the largest labor uprising before the Civil War. The twenty thousand workers on strike included these eight hundred women, whose banner read, "American ladies will not be slaves. Give us a fair compensation and we labour cheerfully."

forms of social conflict, and women have used adaptations of the strategies in struggles of many different kinds, including the following illustrative (but not exhaustive) examples:

In 1852, Elizabeth Cady Stanton, president of the Women's State Temperance Association, probably inspired by *Lysistrata*, proposed a strike advising women to resolutely refuse conjugal rights to husbands who drank to excess. There is no evidence, however, of this strike's effectiveness.

Skyrocketing food prices led thousands of immigrant Jewish working-class housewives in New York City to organize boycotts of kosher butchers in 1902 and of chicken, fish, and vegetable sellers in 1917. Similar protests occurred in Philadelphia, Boston, Chicago, and other cities that year.

Women, desperate to feed their families, used mob violence against peddlers and market owners to enforce the boycotts.

In 1904 and 1907, spiraling rents led to mass rent strikes, again organized by working-class Jewish women. Further rent strikes occurred between 1917 and 1920 and again in the 1930s, all women-led. The latter led to the formation of the Consolidated Tenants League of Harlem, which organized a parade of over four thousand protesters.

Historians call these consumer actions, common in Europe, "communal strikes," in which working-class women, acting out of "female consciousness," mobilize to preserve their communities, rather than to fight for gender equality.

Similarly, using the slogan "Don't Buy Where You Can't Work," African American women organized boycotts of white businesses during the depression in Chicago, Baltimore, Washington, Detroit, Harlem, and Cleveland.

The following three mass protests involving largely middle-class white women, though not literal strikes, were called strikes to dramatize their militancy: After U.S. entrance into World War I, fought presumably to "save the world for democracy," the National Woman's Party, the militant wing of the suffrage movement, conducted a round-the-clock silent vigil, picketing the White House, their banners demanding democracy at home. Some women were arrested and jailed for up to seven months for "obstructing sidewalk traffic"; imprisoned women resorted to hunger strikes and were forcibly fed. Over five hundred women were arrested, one hundred seventy imprisoned, between 1917 and 1919. Courts invalidated the convictions in 1919; this nonviolent protest contributed to the victory of women's suffrage in 1920.

In 1961 an estimated fifty thousand women in sixty communities joined in an unprecedented strike for peace, demanding, "End the Arms Race, Not the Human Race," and later helping to achieve the ban on atmospheric testing.

The nationwide Women's Strike for Equality on August 26, 1970, the fiftieth anniversary of the Woman's Suffrage Amendment, was the largest protest for gender equality in U.S. history. Moderates and radicals joined to demand equal opportunities in employment and education, free abortion on demand, and twenty-four-hour child-care centers.

Clearly, the word "strike" has become a widely used name for many different kinds of mass struggle, which do not always involve work stoppages, the word's classic meaning.

■ MARGE FRANTZ

SEE ALSO Atlanta Washerwomen's Strike; Labor Movement; Labor Unions.

≋ Students for a Democratic Society (SDS)

Students for a Democratic Society (SDS) was the most important white, radical, New Left organization of the 1960s. It began as a primarily male youth group in a small, anticommunist leftist organization but became the central organizational vehicle for the student movement of the 1960s. In 1962 students from the University of Michigan produced the Port Huron Statement, which became SDS's manifesto. The group's founders articulated a political concept of participatory democracy in which individuals participate in decisions affecting their lives. SDS's ideas attracted thousands of college students, many influenced by the civil rights movement's efforts to practice direct democracy in the struggle against racial segregation.

The rejection by young, middle-class whites of their society's elite control and bureaucracy in favor of its democratic promise was one of the most dramatic developments of the postwar period. In the mid-1960s, SDS's opposition to the Vietnam War made it the actual and symbolic leader of the New Left. Thousands of students looked to SDS to articulate their discontent with U.S. society. The organization became popularly associated with the 1960s' generational and youth revolt.

As the decade progressed and young people became more frustrated and disappointed, particularly with the Vietnam War and the government's responses to the civil rights and Black power movements, violent demonstrations and tactics took their place alongside peaceful protests and community organizing. By the late 1960s SDS had split into a Marxist-Leninist group and a guerrillalike, underground vanguard organization (called Weathermen), which advocated a violent, Third World revolution. Although most of the attention in SDS focused on white male leaders of the organization, many white women were as active as the men and, in the movement, first comprehended the sexism they experienced in the larger society. Organizers and activists, women also found themselves providing support and service for male leaders. Much of what they learned they brought with them into the women's movement, most noteworthy, perhaps, skills, political ideas, and anger. SDS disappeared by 1970 as an important Left political force.

■ WINI BREINES

SEE ALSO Radicalism.

≋ Student Non-Violent Coordinating Committee (SNCC)

The Student Non-Violent Coordinating Committee (SNCC), created in 1960, was the brainchild of Ella Baker, a seasoned activist and former director of the NAACP's national branches. Although women rarely held positions on the executive committee, they were active leaders at the grassroots level. Ruby Doris Smith Robinson, Diane Nash, Muriel Tillinghast, Dorie Ladner, Prathia Hall, Donna Moses, Cynthia Washington, and Marian Wright are just a few of the women whose leadership proved critical to the successful mobilization of the civil rights movement.

SNCC's primary contribution to the movement was its mobilization of rural communities in the deep South. SNCC encouraged local leadership, and many of these leaders were women, including Fannie Lou Hamer, Annie Devine, Victoria Gray, Unita Blackwell, and Mama Dollie. These women facilitated the entry of SNCC workers into their communities. Work in these areas was extraordinarily dangerous and many of these women were jailed, threatened, and beaten.

Without SNCC's entry into these communities, the civil rights movement could not have succeeded.

SNCC developed a massive education program which was implemented through the Freedom schools. They educated the poor about their constitutional rights and began door-to-door voter registration drives. Much of this daily one-on-one work was done by African American women whose efforts persuaded the masses to join the movement despite widespread fear of reprisals. After the passage of the 1965 Voting Rights Act, SNCC began to question its goals and philosophies. The group began to dissolve and ended in 1970.

■ BELINDA ROBNETT

SEE ALSO Civil Rights Movement.

≋ Suburbanization

Suburbs developed early in United States history. By the 1830s a form of domestic architecture called the "cottage" encouraged families to construct homes outside the towns or cities that supplied their livelihood. Social reformers thought the countryside a better place for families than crowded, dirty cities. In the 1890s improved railways and trolleys expanded this trend, as did the abundance of cheap land and the invention of the balloon-frame house. But not until after 1945, when the federal government began subsidizing housing for the families of returning World War II veterans, did the suburban boom become the dominant trend in U.S. home ownership.

The movement to the suburbs was widespread but was not equal among all groups. In 1949 the Federal Housing Authority denied home loans to female-headed households and to people of color. The communities that prospered on the periphery of urban areas were racially segregated by design. After the beginning of the federal desegregation of schools in 1954, white, urban Americans moved to the suburbs by the millions to seek what they deemed superior educational opportunities for their children. The suburbs were not necessarily ideal, however. Women became more isolated within their homes, their domestic work increased in order to maintain the presumed higher standard of living, and they became more thoroughly identified by the domestic work they performed for their families. By the 1970s many suburban women, discontented with their circumstances, swelled the ranks of the National Organization for Women and joined the women's movement.

• KATHRYN KISH SKLAR

SEE ALSO Housing.

≋ Suffrage Movement

The first clear assertion of women's right to the vote was made in 1848 at the women's rights convention organized in Seneca Falls, New York. At that point, when many progressive people regarded the political arena with contempt for its collusion with slavery, woman suffrage was controversial even among women's rights advocates. Thus, it was not really until the constitutional upheavals of Reconstruction that woman suffrage became the chief women's rights demand.

The Fourteenth and Fifteenth Amendments expanded and federalized the franchise, legitimated the popular sense that suffrage was a fundamental right of citizenship, and then excluded women from the newly democratized electorate. In response, two organizations were formed in 1869, the National and the American Woman Suffrage Associations. Both were committed to winning the right to vote for women but disagreed on how. The American Woman Suffrage Association

(AWSA) conceded the federal arena to those defending the freedmen's right to vote and concentrated on the state level so as to minimize interference between Black and woman suffrage. AWSA also tended to focus exclusively on suffrage, again so as not to raise opposition to political equality for women. The National Woman Suffrage Association, led by Elizabeth Stanton and Susan B. Anthony, insisted on fighting for woman suffrage at the federal and constitutional level as the only way to establish women's political rights beyond challenge, and thus for a few years challenged the Fifteenth Amendment for excluding women. This led to a dramatic and painful break with former abolitionist allies and many defenders of Black suffrage. The association also linked votes for women to other aspects of emancipation, most notoriously to challenges to women's marital and sexual subordination. Unfortunately, the two organizations shared a strong tendency to argue for woman suffrage on the nativist and racist grounds that educated, white, native-born women should not be denied the franchise, when immigrant and ex-slave men were honored with it.

During the next two decades, both organizations reached out for new recruits across the country. By the late 1880s state woman suffrage associations had been formed almost everywhere, and woman suffrage was on its way to becoming a substantial, broad-based political movement. The original causes for the split now were less important and the two societies united in 1890, forming the National American Woman Suffrage Association (NAWSA), which remained the major organizational framework for the U.S. suffrage movement for the next thirty years.

Other developments and organizations also helped to build the woman suffrage movement from a tiny band of women's rights radicals into a mass women's movement by the early twentieth century. The Woman's Christian Temperance Union (WCTU), formed in 1874, carried the woman suffrage movement west and brought it to the attention of large numbers of native-born

Protestant white women. Frances Willard, second president of the WCTU, became convinced that the WCTU's mission to defend the values of home and church against the depredations of "King Alcohol" could be won only by women moving outside the domestic sphere and into politics. She established an approach to woman suffrage that would be pursued until equal political rights for women were secured in 1920: that women deserved political responsibilities on the basis of their traditional obligations as homemakers, wives, and mothers. African American women also began to form their own organizations, uniting in 1896 as the National Association of Colored Women, and they showed considerable eagerness for the vote to try to counter the accelerating de facto disfranchisement of their men.

Through the 1870s and 1880s U.S. women began to secure various "partial suffrages," such as the right to vote in municipal elections, for school boards, and on prohibition measures. But it was not until the 1890s that full-fledged enfranchisement began to be secured. Wyoming, which had enacted votes for women in 1869 when it was still a territory, entered the union in 1890 with its woman suffrage provisions in place. An even more important victory occurred in Colorado in 1893, when, for the first time, voters (all men) enfranchised the women of their state. The victory in Colorado reflected the influence of the Populist movement in the West, which was more supportive of woman suffrage than the Republican and Democratic parties.

The 1890s was also the period in which the woman suffrage movement went international. In 1893, New Zealand became the first country in the world to enfranchise women on the same terms as men, followed in 1902 by Australia, 1906 in Finland and 1913 in Norway. U.S. suffragists exported woman suffrage ideas around the world and drew on victories in other countries to make their own case. In 1912 Anna Howard Shaw marched down Fifth Avenue in New York under a banner that read, "Catching Up With China," be-

cause Chinese provinces had briefly authorized votes for women in 1911, and she was contending that New York State should be able to go as far.

Beginning about 1906 and 1907, the U.S. suffrage movement not only underwent a considerable revival but changed in many ways, becoming much more modern and politically sophisticated. The revival of suffragism was centered in the cities, and instead of arguing for woman suffrage as a way to defend traditional American values, supporters began to call for women's political involvement as a way to deal with new economic, political, and social conditions. Also, new classes were drawn into the movement. Wage-earning women in the cities were among the first of the "new" suffragists; they claimed that inasmuch as they labored outside the home and were subject to laws and government regulation, they needed the vote to gain control over their conditions and to protect themselves rather than to be protected by fathers and husbands. They argued for the vote less as an individual right than as a class tool. Wage-earning women were joined by college-educated, aspiring young professionals such as lawyers, teachers, and librarians. They too saw a link between political rights and their working lives. While wage-earning women helped to build the ranks of the suffrage movement, young professional women provided the organizers, publicists, and propagandists. Finally, extremely wealthy women, wives and daughters of gilded age millionaires, began to find suffragism "fashionable" and provided the money for full-fledged political campaigns to win the vote. These classes formed an uneasy but potent alliance that gave the cause new power and possibility. African American women, barred from full participation in many suffrage societies by the widespread racism of white suffragists, energetically continued to demand political equality nonetheless.

So much had suffragism changed by 1910 that it began to be known by a new name: "Votes for Women." The final decade of the movement in the United States was characterized by great tacti-

Suffragists march in Washington, D.C., April 7, 1913.

cal originality and bold political strategies. Suffragists moved out from their parlors and made their arguments before groups of working-class men on street corners, and to giant crowds of spectators lining the streets of the cities to watch their parades. They formed new organizations, including the Women's Political Union and Woman Suffrage Party, in New York; the Political Equality League, in Philadelphia; and the Wage Earners Suffrage League, in San Francisco. They issued tens of thousands of leaflets in many languages to reach voters of different nationalities. Their graphics were striking and modern and they made use of all the newest technologies—moving pictures, telephones, and automobiles.

Perhaps most important, suffragists began to learn the intricacies of the U.S. political system and to tackle the traditional enemies of women's reform activism, the mechanisms of party and partisanship. The lockhold that Republicans and Democrats had on state legislatures began to give way as third parties, particularly the Progressives and the Socialists, gained greater power in state legislatures, and suffragists learned how to exploit rifts in party loyalty. In 1910 the first successful referendum since Idaho's in 1896 occurred in Washington, and suffragism was on the march again. In 1911 California voters passed votes for women by a narrow four-thousand-vote margin. In 1914 Illinois became the first state east of the Mississippi in which women could vote in presidential elections, though this was done by clever legal maneuvering rather than by action of the voters.

At this point, the movement's energies, which had been building at the state level, began to move toward the national arena. It is important to understand how each of the state victories of the 1910s helped shift the movement's dynamic to the federal level. When the women of Colorado, Washington, and California were enfranchised by action of the electorate, they gained the vote, not just in state elections but also in federal elections. (One of suffragists' favorite arguments was that it was unfair for a woman who lived in Colorado and had full voting rights to lose them when she crossed the border and moved to Nebraska.) By 1916 women in twelve states had full voting power, and it became clear that these women voters were potent forces in fostering action at the federal level.

In the final phase of the suffrage movement, the giant NAWSA proved quite inadequate to the new energies coursing through the movement and to the intricate political maneuvering necessary to force reluctant national political parties to amend the Constitution and complete the enfranchisement of women. In 1913 a new organization, the Congressional Union, was formed, initially within the NAWSA and then as its rival, to bring modern methods and energies to the national campaign. Formed by Alice Paul and Lucy Burns, the Congressional Union was the dynamic center of the final campaign for political rights for women. Its debut was a stunning, disciplined national suffrage parade held in the nation's capital in March 1913.

By this time, British suffragists had gained international headlines for their dramatic acts of civil disobedience on behalf of the vote: by 1913 they were being arrested, undertaking hunger strikes, and being force-fed by the British police. The Congressional Union felt much allegiance with their militant British sisters, although U.S. women did not resort to such tactics for several years. Instead, what they borrowed from the British militants was a plan to force the party in power (the Democrats, who, after 1912, controlled the presidency and both houses of Congress) to enact woman suffrage. In 1914 and again in 1916, the Congressional Union worked to organize tens

of thousands of women voters to pledge to vote against the Democrats until they made woman suffrage law. In 1916 the Congressional Union became the National Woman's Party (NWP) in recognition of the importance of this strategy of organizing women voters on behalf of votes for women.

At this point, the Great War intervened, both complicating and accelerating victory. President Woodrow Wilson, the National Woman's Party's primary target, was now leader of a nation at war, moreover a war to end all wars. The women of the suffrage movement, like the rest of the American people, split over the war, the majority supporting Wilson and the minority opposing the war. NAWSA urged its members to undertake war-support work, hoping that such patriotic service would strengthen women's case for the vote when hostilities were over. However, the National Woman's Party insisted on maintaining its antigovernment stance, ignoring cries to put aside "lesser" issues for the duration. The NWP's dramatic picketing of the White House, which had been tolerated before, now appeared treasonous, and in May 1917 the first militants were arrested and imprisoned.

The NWP claimed it was these arrests and the trouble they caused Wilson that led to his decision to support the amendment and the successful January 1918 House of Representatives vote on woman suffrage. NAWSA argued that it was other factors, especially the successful November 1917 suffrage referendum in New York. Ratification seemed right around the corner, but it was not. The Senate, led by obstructionists from southern and eastern states, took another year and a half to pass the amendment, and the ratification process was also excruciatingly slow. Finally, in 1920, Tennessee became the thirty-eighth state to approve the amendment, and woman suffrage became constitutional law.

The story of woman suffrage conventionally ends here. But the Nineteenth Amendment was interpreted as not applying to U.S. territories, and separate campaigns had to be launched in Puerto Rico and the Philippines; nor did African American women gain full use of their franchise for many decades. From their perspective, the civil rights movement of the 1960s was yet another stage in the ongoing struggle for women's political equality.

Ellen Carol DuBois, *Feminism and Suffrage: The Emergence of an Independent Women's Movement in America, 1848–1869* (Ithaca: Cornell University Press, 1978); Eleanor Flexner, *Century of Struggle: The Woman's Rights Movement in the United States,* 2d ed. (Cambridge: Belknap Press, 1975); Aileen Kraditor, *Ideas of the Woman Suffrage Movement, 1890–1920* (New York: Columbia University Press, 1965).

▪ ELLEN CAROL DuBOIS

SEE ALSO Constitution and Amendments: Nineteenth Amendment; National Woman's Party; Seneca Falls; Woman's Christian Temperance Union.

≋ Superheroines

Diana Prince transforms herself in the Fall 1943 issue of Wonder Woman.

December 1941 saw America's entry into World War II, and the birth of Wonder Woman — "beautiful as Aphrodite, wise as Athena, stronger than Hercules, and swifter than Mercury" — in *All Star Comics.* Psychologist William Moulton Marston, creator of the world's first superheroine, had set out to design a heroine for girls in the hitherto all-male cosmos of comics. He succeeded, using a mixture of myth and feminism.

The traditional hero of European mythology is a child of a mortal mother (usually a virgin) and a godly father. But in Marston's version, Princess Diana, daughter of the amazon queen, Hippolyta, has as her other parent the goddess Aphrodite: Thus little Diana has two mommies.

Marston knew that children identify most strongly with their own gender, and Wonder Woman's world is comprised almost entirely of women; men play a marginal role. Even villains tend to be beautiful females who eventually see the error of their ways, though male villains, such as the Duke of Deception or Doctor Psycho, are often grotesque dwarves who remain evil. The pervading message is one of sisterhood and self-esteem: women can do everything men can do, and working together they can often do it better.

Wonder Woman was not the first costumed heroine in comics. *Miss Fury,* a newspaper strip by a woman, Tarpe Mills, beat her by eight months. Although beautifully drawn and reading like film noir, the strip's heroine lacked superpowers and seldom wore her panther costume after the strip's first year.

Scores of comics about superwomen followed Wonder Woman, but they were called *Sun Girl, Moon Girl, Hawk Girl, Bullet Girl, Super Girl,* and

Bat Girl and tended to be sidekicks of the male heroes (dubbed "man," not the equivalent "boy"): *Hawkman, Bulletman, Superman, Batman*. Most did not last very long. *Miss America* (1944) lasted exactly one issue, then the superheroine, whose patriotic costume was clearly inspired by Wonder Woman, was relegated to the back of Blonde Phantom's comic book. Blonde Phantom herself, fighting crime in a red evening gown and high-heeled pumps, lasted only ten issues.

Many of these costumed heroines did not really have superpowers, but one of the longest lived, Mary Marvel, had only to say the magic word "Shazam!" to become invincible. Bullets bounced off her, and she could fly. Perhaps best of all, Mary Marvel really *was* a girl—she was too young to have breasts. One can only guess how many ten-year-old girls in 1947 whispered "Shazam!" alone in their bedrooms, hoping to become like their idol. Mary lasted for twenty-eight issues in her own comic book, and also appeared in *Captain Marvel, The Marvel Family, Wow,* and *Shazam.*

The comics industry has made at least some attempt to change with the times. In 1974 Marvel comics introduced the first Black superheroine, Storm, in its popular series, the *X-Men.* But Storm, an African goddesslike figure, has always been portrayed with Caucasian features. It was up to the Black-owned company, *Milestone,* in 1993, to come up with African American superheroines who not only look Black but who reflect contemporary social problems. One of these characters, Flashback, is a crack addict, and another, Rocket, is fifteen years old, unmarried, and pregnant. But Rocket is just the sidekick of Icon, the real hero of the comic book, and Flashback belongs to a team of superheroes. Despite the rise of feminism in the real world, only rarely does a superheroine star in her own book today.

Television superheroines have not fared any better. A letter written by nine-year-old Alexandra Early of Arlington, Massachusetts, and printed in the *Los Angeles Times* on November 9, 1993, said, "There aren't enough girl superheroes on TV. On 'King Arthur and the Knights of Justice,' there are only princesses and they always need to be saved. . . . On 'X-Men,' there are some strong-seeming women, but they always need help and they always look sexy. They're very thin. They wear short dresses and funny bikini tops." Speaking for countless U.S. girls and women, Alexandra ended her letter, "I hope the people who make these shows know that girls like me are watching. We want fairness."

■ TRINA ROBBINS

≋ Surrogacy

First coined in 1981, "surrogacy" describes the arrangement in which a woman gestates a fetus for others after artificial insemination. Current terms include contract pregnancy, intrauterine adoption, or preconception arrangement. By the early 1990s, private agreements and some twenty agencies had arranged over four thousand births.

Although most surrogacy arrangements are successful, some go awry. In the widely publicized "Baby M" case, Mary Beth Whitehead contracted to carry a child for William and Betsy Stern, but then decided to keep the baby. William Stern's sperm was used to impregnate Whitehead. After a court awarded the Sterns temporary custody, the Whiteheads fled with Baby M to Florida, where police later found and removed the baby. In 1987 a New Jersey court gave the Sterns permanent custody and prohibited Whitehead's further contact. Upon appeal, a higher court sustained the custody award, but Whitehead gained visitation rights.

Feminists are divided on the question of surrogacy. Most feminist writers strongly oppose surrogacy's valorization of women's biological role and its potential for exploitation of low-income women who become surrogates because they need money. Others argue for surrogacy as a low-tech, woman-controllable method for alleviating

Apparel workers in a 1950s sweatshop.

infertility that enables alternative family structures and they oppose limiting women's freedom to choose how to use their bodies.

Since surrogacy is expensive, it is generally a white middle-class phenomenon, one that risks exploiting the poor. However, racism or elitism may also limit transactions since women of a given race are unlikely to buy eggs from women of another race or from malnourished or drug-addicted women.

■ HELEN BEQUAERT HOLMES
and LAURA M. PURDY

≋ Sweatshops

The late-nineteenth-century sweatshop — with its low wages, long hours, poor sanitation, and detrimental working conditions — symbolized the exploitation of immigrant women and child laborers. Characteristic of the ready-made garment industry, these tenement workrooms encouraged sweating, or a form of production under which "the worker is at the mercy of middlemen, where his [or her] life-blood is sweated out by the pressure of the profit-sucking contractors piled on top," the poet Edwin Markim explained in 1907. Under intense competition, contractors and subcontractors lowered piece rates so that individual earnings remained below the amount necessary to sustain life. Domestic life and wage earning merged as the employer's own living quarters turned into a place where employees of both sexes ran foot-powered sewing machines. Homes also became sweatshops when women and their children took in garments to finish or flowers to assemble. By 1900 nearly all clothing manufactured in Chicago and over four-fifths in New York came from these overcrowded, badly ventilated places.

Women reformers and trade unionists condemned sweatshops for spreading disease to the consumer, but also, as the middle-class periodical *The Outlook* asserted in 1895, for "destroy[ing] the home life of its victims," who were predominantly Jewish and Italian. From the state factory acts of the 1890s through the federal Fair Labor Standards Act of 1937, legislation outlawed sweatshop conditions and promoted minimum wages, maximum hours, and safe workplaces. During the 1980s sweatshops returned under intensified international competition, new immigration, weakened trade unions, and economic deregulation. Recent arrivals from Asia and the Americas today compose the sweatshop labor force, often working for compatriots as had the European immigrant women of the early twentieth century.

■ EILEEN BORIS

SEE ALSO Fair Labor Standards Act; Needle Trades; Protective Labor Legislation.

≋ Take Back the Night

The slogan *Take Back the Night* was first used in 1978 as a theme for a national protest march in San Francisco. The march took place at night following the first feminist conference on pornography. Conference participants heard testimony by women who had been harmed by pornography, research results asserting that pornography is harmful, and legal analysis of the First Amendment's protection of pornographers. Over ten thousand people marched down residential streets and in the area where strip joints, peep shows, pornography theaters, massage parlors, and brothels lined the streets. That event was the largest antipornography march in the history of the women's movement.

Thousands of similar marches have since occurred around the world. The slogan has become a symbolic statement of women's commitment to stopping not just pornography but also all violence against women. It reflects the realization that crimes against women are linked—including rape, domestic violence, child sexual abuse, incest, and sexual harassment. It represents the conviction that images of women being raped, tortured, or degraded for male sexual entertainment are related to and contribute to a culture of violence against women. Until Take Back the Night, only two sides to the pornography issue existed: the conservative approach that pornography is immoral because it exposes the human body; and the liberal approach that pornography is just another aspect of human sexuality. A third and feminist perspective holds that pornography is part of a cultural ideology that promotes and condones violent crimes against women.

■ LAURA J. LEDERER

SEE ALSO Antipornography Activism; Marches; Violence Against Women.

≋ Talk Shows

This relatively unscripted format—a host plus interviewees, letters or phone calls from listeners, and/or audience participation—has brought entertainment, advice, consumerism, education, and shared experience into the daily lives of women since the 1920s and 1930s, when two-thirds of U.S. homes acquired radios, more than had telephones. As television arrived in the 1950s, these inexpensive-to-produce shows became the "bread and butter" of programming. By the 1970s, 97 percent of homes had a TV. TV talk shows often became platforms for the personal experiences from which feminism sprang, as well as for activist information. Radio was more likely to feature women psychologists who gave personal advice or suggested activism. By the 1980s, however, the numerous TV talk shows, in a ratings competition, often focused on the most bizarre experiences rather than the most shared ones, and offered escape rather than help. This trend became known as "freak TV." The 1980s backlash against social change also created radio call-in shows with combative male hosts who invented terms like "feminazi," and who opposed efforts toward racial equality, gay rights, environmental protection, and other challenges to the traditional status quo. In the 1990s, the advent of personal computers and the World Wide Web had created "chat rooms" and other participant-controlled, specialized talk formats. Though mostly white, male, and class-bound, this new technological link to communities of interest, local and international, motivated many women and girls to gain access to the high-tech revolution.

From the beginning, talk show subjects have been almost as diverse as talk itself, ranging from Hollywood gossip to foreign policy, from cooking to national politics. By making this wide range of experience and information available without regard to sex, race, class, geography, literacy, or access to anything other than a radio or television, talk shows have had a disproportionate impact on homemakers; rural women; domestic workers; immigrants learning English; women seeking ethnic, racial, or language communities; and housebound or otherwise isolated women.

In rural America, Native American women have innovated the use of radio talk shows as a way of bridging long distances, furthering consensus building in the tradition of "talking circles," and teaching Native languages and practices that were discouraged or forbidden by the dominant culture.

In general, women of color have been voices in their communities, especially those large enough to have their own radio stations. Mainstream talk shows began to diversify only in the 1960s, with pressure from social justice movements, and the Federal Communications Commission's affirmative action requirements for licensing both radio and TV stations. Now, Spanish-speaking Americans who once listened to shows originating in Mexico, Cuba, or Puerto Rico can hear daily Spanish-language programs, such as "Cristina Opina," hosted by veteran journalist Cristina Saralegui. Nevertheless, mainstream radio listeners still hear mostly male voices, and rarely even an accent.

With respect to TV talk shows, the technical, visual, and capital-intensive nature of the medium wiped out much of the progress women had made on radio. Age and appearance requirements discouraged the transfer of hard-won gains by women on radio, and ornaments became the order of the day for the predominantly young, thin, white, beautiful, and usually blonde personalities.

Feminist pressures of the 1970s for broader coverage and improved hiring policies wrought some progress. A major advance also came with a male host's talk show scheduled in the "women's ghetto." Phil Donahue—who was influenced not only by the issues being raised by the women's movement but also by the consciousness-raising style of leaderless feminist groups—became the first TV host to invite a mostly female audience to discuss social and political topics with a wide variety of guests. His talk show became the most popular in the nation and remained there for much of the next twenty-five years. As Donahue always explained, "If I succeed, the next major talk show host will be a Black woman." His prediction came true in the 1980s when Oprah Winfrey, an on-air journalist who had worked in Baltimore and Chicago, became the first nationally successful African American woman talk show host.

Other TV talk show hosts range from Sally Jessy Raphael, who makes activist suggestions at the end of programs, to Rolonda, to cable shows that pair a liberal/feminist with a conservative/antifeminist. On political talk shows, however, there are few female hosts, and none on the major late-night talk shows. Moreover, the choice and treatment of women interviewees on daytime shows give the frequent impression that they have power only to complain, not to act. Thus, an advertising-motivated, gender-polarized TV talk show world continues.

■ GLORIA STEINEM

≋ Teaching Profession

Women began to leave their homes and enter public school classrooms as teachers in the United States in the early nineteenth century. Three reasons explain this remarkable change in antebellum United States. One was the emergence of "republican motherhood" as an ideology. Concerned about how to educate boys for the responsibilities of citizenship, leaders turned first to mothers for instruction at home in the virtues of liberty. Before women could teach their sons, however, they had to be educated themselves. Second, school administrators recruited women as teachers because they could be paid half the salary men earned. Third, women were viewed as natural guardians of the young and better able to nurture learning among children. By the end of the Civil War white women were firmly entrenched in teaching and outnumbered men as teachers in public schools. In 1900 teaching ranked fifth in paid employment for women, clearly making it the most populous occupation that could be ranked as "profession."

By the late 1830s reformers in education, desiring a more proficient teaching force, instituted rigorous and standardized examinations and pushed states to build training schools to teach educational methods as well as to increase knowledge in subject areas. By the 1920s most northern and western states demanded at least a high school diploma and many required training beyond high school. In southern states, teacher training, like education in general, was segregated, and some African American women entered classrooms with little or no formal training.

Initially teaching was viewed as an occupation ideally suited to young women before they married. With the exception of western states, most teachers were young and single until the late 1930s. In the early twentieth century teachers initiated challenges to laws that ejected them from the classroom upon marriage but it was severe teacher shortages during World War II that prompted the repeal of such laws. As a result many more older women are presently teaching.

While both age and marital status of women teachers has changed, social class has remained consistent. Most who entered teaching grew up in middle-class white families. For immigrant women and women of color, teaching was a route to the middle class. Not until the end of the nineteenth century were teaching jobs available in large numbers to them.

Wages were a crucial reason young women entered teaching. Many preferred teaching to factory, agricultural, or domestic work. For nineteenth- and early-twentieth-century women, teaching was also a means to gain advanced education. Teaching offered women a sense of independence and autonomy and, until recently, was one of only a few professions besides social work and nursing accessible to them. Through the 1940s those women who completed postbaccalaureate work found employment in colleges and universities, but after World War II those opportunities declined. African American women sought professional training as well, often at institutions founded specifically for them.

Teaching provided women access to the political arena in the early twentieth century. Many white women were elected to school boards and positions as superintendents of education. But as superintendency became appointed rather than elected and required advanced training, men reclaimed those slots. Since the 1960s, however, women increasingly have been hired as superintendents.

Activism has also emerged from the teaching profession. Classroom teachers were the first to advocate equal pay for equal work. In their deter-

Public school in Valdez, Colorado, October 1902. Because schools in most rural areas at this time did not have school boards, teachers—most of them young women—essentially ran the schools.

mination to exert influence on educational bureaucracies and to have a voice in structuring the teaching profession, teachers began to form unions in the 1890s. The Chicago Teachers Federation was the strongest and most active. The American Federation of Teachers was created in 1912, and it formally joined the American Federation of Labor in 1915. In the 1890s white women teachers also claimed a place in the male-dominated National Education Association, the largest educational organization in the United States. At the same time African American teachers formed the National Association of Teachers of Colored Students.

Today, as they did a century ago, women compose more than 70 percent of the elementary and secondary teaching force but hold only 30 percent of the principalships. Three-quarters are married,

their median age is about forty, and more than half hold a graduate degree. Women of color make up roughly 12 percent of the female teaching corps. Teaching has been a profession of central importance to women over the past one hundred sixty years, allowing them a socially acceptable means of working outside the domestic arena. Although it is not the best-paying occupation, teaching has served historically as one way to autonomy and higher education for U.S. women.

Nancy Hoffman, *Woman's "True" Profession: Voices from the History of Teaching* (New York: The Feminist Press, 1981); Donald Warren, ed., *American Teachers: Histories of a Profession at Work* (New York: Macmillan, 1989).

▪ KATHLEEN UNDERWOOD

SEE ALSO Education.

≋ Temperance

SEE Prohibition and Temperance.

≋ Temporary Work

SEE Contingent Work.

≋ Terrorism

The term *terrorism* traditionally has described acts of violence against civilians meant to draw attention to the political demands of the terrorists. It is a tactic sometimes used to exact revenge against the state or against an enemy. It is also used symbolically to demonstrate the power to cause destruction as well as the inability of society to prevent it. For example, bombs set off in marketplaces, government offices, or railroad stations are usually followed by a statement or demand from the organization responsible. The devastating 1995 Oklahoma City bombing of the Alfred P. Murrah federal office building is an example of terrorism directed against the government by right-wing extremists. The word "terrorism" connotes senseless violence directed at innocent people by uncaring zealots.

During the civil rights movement and the protest movements of the 1960s and 1970s the often violent and repressive tactics used by federal and state authorities against protesters and political activists increased public awareness of the state's power to use force against its citizens. Radical thinkers began to see aspects of state repression as terrorism. Examples of state-sponsored terrorism include the repression of leftists during the 1960s and 1970s in Chile and Argentina; in both cases many innocent people were killed at the whim of the state. In the United States terrorism directed primarily against people of color, such as police brutality or white supremacist violence, is sometimes condoned or tolerated by forces of the state.

In recent years the definition of terrorism increasingly has been expanded to include bias-motivated hate crimes. A bias-motivated hate crime, such as the killing of an African American by white supremacist youths, shares many of the characteristics of the classic definition of terrorism. A crime such as this evokes the lynchings and burnings of the past and both reflects and is intended to incite hatred of Black people. Bias-motivated hate crimes can be seen also in the contemporary murders and beatings of lesbians and gay men and immigrants, simply for being who they are. Given this new understanding of the shared characteristics of bias-motivated hate crimes and terrorism, it is logical that women, who are killed by their spouse or boyfriend at the rate of four per day in the United States, are increasingly beginning to see this unrelenting violence as an epidemic of hate crimes. The ongoing use of terror tactics such as rape, beatings, and stalking, combined with the position of dominance occupied by men in the larger society, is considered by many to be an impressive fit with the expanded definition of terrorism.

Within the debate over the collection of statistics on bias-motivated hate crimes, a prominent issue has been, and continues to be, whether or not to include crimes against women. To define a crime as bias-motivated one must positively answer the question, Did the act reflect a bias against the victim for his or her innate characteristics? Experts agree that statistics should be kept on hate crimes based on racism, anti-Semitism, and homophobia, but as yet no consensus exists about whether crimes motivated by misogyny and directed against women also should be considered motivated by bias.

▪ JEAN V. HARDISTY

Skirtmakers in an engraving from Harper's Weekly, *February 19, 1859. The industrial revolution transformed the traditional textile work of young rural white women by moving it from the home into the mills.*

≋ Textile/Apparel Workers

Lucy Larcom, a Lowell, Massachusetts, mill worker, recalled that when she was a small child she believed that the "chief end of woman was to make clothing for mankind." In her Western world the distaff, used to spin, had long symbolized the female sex; in time "spinster" came to mean a single woman. Not all women were spinners and weavers, but in virtually every culture women have prepared the clothing. In the early nineteenth century an Indian agent concluded that teaching Native American women, proficient at curing animal skins, the arts of carding, spinning, and weaving was essential to their becoming "civilized." Enslaved African women commonly worked as field laborers, but some, including two advertised as "Wenches about 16 or 17 Years of Age, who Understand Spinning and Knitting," were considered especially valuable. Most white women in the North and South did their own spinning. A white colonial diarist observed that "all spin, weave, and knit, whereby they make good shift to cloath the whole family; and to their credit . . . many of them do it very completely." Eventually women who previously produced apparel at home were hired to work in the textile factories, which was considered work still in keeping with a woman's central "domestic" role.

The transition to a market economy in textiles and apparel was gradual and uneven. Some women continued spinning at home and traded their yarn for woven goods while others bought factory yarn to weave. The putout system, paying women for home production, continued throughout the nineteenth century.

In 1813 the first large, integrated textile factories were built in Lowell, Massachusetts, and young women were hired. The Lowell system of strict supervision was widely heralded as a model for organizing female labor. Young women typically worked for several years and controlled their own wages until they married. The resulting sense of independence sometimes prompted protest, including several strikes to demand less control and better conditions. As the textile industry spread south, so did the preference for hiring female workers, although a system utilizing family labor ultimately became more common than the Lowell system.

After they gave up spinning and weaving, women still continued sewing at home. By 1860 the number of working women who were seamstresses ranked second only to domestics. Seamstress work was transformed in the 1850s as a result of the invention of the sewing machine, which allowed women to stop laborious hand sewing but, according to one study, also "provided closer control of workers in the industry and additional opportunities for contractors to cheat them."

The garment industry grew in the Northeast through the late nineteenth century, hiring large numbers of immigrants, especially Italians and Jews, for its female work force. By the turn of the century most women garment workers were employed in sweatshops or small factories, including the Triangle Shirtwaist Factory in New York City. In 1909 its workers went on strike to demand better working conditions. Owners made minimal concessions but continued such practices as locking fire escape doors. When a fire erupted there in 1911, 146 women died.

Polish and Slavic women often worked in textile factories in the Northeast. In the South, white women and children made up a majority of the textile industry's work force. Throughout the United States, however, women were denied access to the highest-paying jobs or leadership positions in the unions, including the National Textile Workers Union and the International Ladies' Garment Workers Union, which sought to represent them. Women often played key roles in strikes. In 1929 Ella May Wiggins was killed during a textile workers' strike in Gastonia, North Carolina, and became a martyr for the struggle to unionize.

Although New Deal legislation somewhat improved the conditions in mills and sweatshops, the Women's Bureau of the Department of Labor documented that poor conditions continued. The proportion of females in the textile industry dropped in the twentieth century until the 1960s, when it rose to nearly 50 percent; the number of African American female textile workers, who had previously been denied employment because of racism, grew almost fourfold. Since World War II the rise of imports from Asia has profoundly affected the textile and apparel industries. The apparel industry, particularly, has looked to female Hispanic immigrants in the Southwest to compete with the low-paid Asian work force. In the early 1970s garment workers at Farah Manufacturing Company in El Paso, Texas, virtually all of them Chicanos and 85 percent of them women, successfully struck for a union contract.

In the 1970s the popular film *Norma Rae* dramatized the plight of nonunionized textile workers as well as their determination to fight for improvement. The movie ends with their victory; but the reality for the many women today who "make the clothing for mankind" is a continuing struggle.

Thomas Dublin, *Women at Work: The Transformation of Work and Community in Lowell, Massachusetts, 1826–1860* (New York: Columbia University Press, 1979); Jacquelyn Dowd Hall, "Disorderly Women: Gender and Labor Militancy in the Appalachian South," *Journal of American History* Vol. 73 (1986): 354–82.

■ BESS BEATTY

SEE ALSO Industrial Revolution; Labor Unions: Amalgamated Clothing and Textile Workers Union

(ACTWU); Labor Unions: International Ladies' Garment Workers Union (ILGWU); Needle Trades.

≋ Thalidomide

In 1960 the widespread use of the drug thalidomide in nearly twenty countries later yielded a tragic epidemic of limbless babies born to mothers who thought they were using a mild sedative.

Food and Drug Administration medical officer Dr. Frances Oldham Kelsey refused approval of thalidomide for distribution in the United States, despite early news of the drug's success and pressure from its U.S. manufacturer, The Merrell Company. While the drug's effects on animals tested negative to malformation, Dr. Kelsey mistrusted the sleeping pill that did not cause sleepiness in animals.

She was not told that her suspicions were correct when, in November 1961, West Germany reported to the FDA that thalidomide had been associated with birth defects. Told instead was The Merrell Company, which had furnished nearly 1,100 doctors (almost 250 obstetricians and gynecologists) with samples of the drug. Disbelieving West German evidence, The Merrell Company wrote only a brief letter of warning to just 10 percent of the physicians to whom thalidomide was distributed. They were still hoping for the drug's FDA approval and promising prescription sales.

Thalidomide's danger to pregnant women was not made public in the United States until 1962, a year after it was recognized abroad. The *Washington Post* broke the story about Dr. Kelsey's good judgment, and President Kennedy ordered a crash program to retrieve all samples of thalidomide. For her role in preventing thalidomide distribution, Dr. Kelsey received the President's Award for Distinguished Federal Civilian Service in 1962.

In that same year, Sherri Finkbine, a thalidomide-exposed pregnant woman, was denied the U.S. abortion she sought for medical reasons, but did obtain one in Sweden. Her harrowing, well-publicized odyssey helped arouse sentiment for abortion law reform.

Although widely banned, thalidomide remained available for limited use as a leprosy treatment. It was controversially revived in the 1990s as an experimental treatment for tuberculosis and certain AIDS-related wasting illnesses.

▪ BARBARA SEAMAN

≋ Theater

The development of the theater in the United States had a difficult beginning, mainly because of the influence of various religious groups that regarded theater as sinful and frivolous. Also, much of early U.S. theater was based on male-dominated European traditions and participation by women was limited. From the early Greeks to Shakespeare, women's roles were performed by men. Women slowly took to the stage during the late eighteenth century, primarily as actresses. Some of the first performers were Anne Merry, Olive Logan, and Charlotte Cushman; the twentieth century produced such great actresses as Eva Le Gallienne, Katherine Cornell, Uta Hagen, and Helen Hayes.

Despite women's historical lack of recognition, until recently, women have and continue to play a significant role in the American theater both on and off the stage. Anna Mowatt was one of the first female playwrights—in 1845 she authored *Fashion*. The first female writer to affect the theater was Harriet Beecher Stowe, author of *Uncle Tom's Cabin*. While Stowe neither authorized the countless dramatic adaptations nor received royalties from the hundreds of "Tom shows" that resulted from the novel, productions of *Uncle Tom's Cabin* were the most-produced plays during the latter part of the nineteenth century and into the twentieth.

The early part of the twentieth century witnessed women writers on Broadway. Rachel Crothers, best known for *A Man's World* (1910) and regarded by scholars as the first U.S. feminist playwright, had twenty-five plays produced on Broadway between 1906 and 1937. Other writers of the time included Alice Gerstenberg *(Overtones)*, Zona Gale *(Miss Lulu Bett)*, Sophie Treadwell *(Machinal)*, and Susan Glaspell *(Trifles)*. These women focused primarily on female protagonists who struggled for autonomy and often threatened male authority. From the 1930s through the 1950s, writers such as Lillian Hellman *(The Children's Hour)*, Carson McCullers *(Member of the Wedding)*, and Ketti Frings *(Look Homeward Angel)* came to the fore. Alice Childress *(Trouble in Mind)* was the first African American to receive the Obie Award, in 1955; in 1959 Lorraine Hansberry's *A Raisin in the Sun* was the first play written by an African American female to be produced on Broadway. With the women's movement of the 1960s and 1970s, many more women playwrights wrote about issues relevant to women including Wendy Wasserstein, winner of the 1989 Pulitzer Prize for *The Heidi Chronicles*; Beth Henley; Marsha Norman, who won the 1983 Pulitzer Prize for *'Night, Mother*; and Wendy Kesselman. Women-produced plays emerged, along with a growing number of female producers and feminist theaters, including companies like The Women's Project in New York City, and At the Foot of the Mountain in Minnesota.

Women historically have often taken the lead as theatrical producers or directors since the late nineteenth century. Susan Glaspell cofounded the Provincetown Players in 1915, which promoted dramatist Eugene O'Neill. When the Federal Theatre Project (FTP) was organized in 1935, Hallie Flanagan was appointed national director. In 1950 Zelda Fichandler created Arena Stage in Washington, D.C., currently one of the leading regional theaters in the nation.

While white women faced sexual discrimination, women of color encountered—and still do—the double burden of racial and sexual discrimination. Women of color were barred from playing dramatic roles in early mainstream U.S. theater. Roles for Blacks were confined to the musical stage or vaudeville, while whites "blackened up" and stereotypically portrayed Black characters and other people of color. In 1916 African American actress Anita Bush organized the Anita Bush Players, the first major Black professional company, as an alternative to Broadway, which later became the Lafayette Players. Her group became the oldest Black professional theater company of its time, producing some of the greatest dramatic performers. One of the earliest Broadway African American actresses, Rose McClendon, produced plays during the 1930s; when the Negro Unit of the FTP was organized, she was appointed its director, although she died shortly afterward.

The civil rights movement of the 1960s spurred the Black theater movement, in which African American women participated in all areas of dramatics. Prominent companies included Ellen Stewart's La Mama, Vinnette Carroll's Urban Arts Corp, Hazel Bryant's Richard Allen Center, and Barbara Ann Teer's The National Black Theatre. Inspired by the vitality of the Black theater movement, other women of color organized groups. Some included Tisa Chang of the Pan Asian Repertory Theatre, Miriam Colon of the Puerto Rican Traveling Company, and the Native American companies of Spiderwoman and the Colorado Sisters. Other outstanding producers of color include Marsha Jackson, Abena Brown, Rosalba Rolon, Roberta Uno, and Pearl Cleage, to name a few. Many of these women, who had started their careers as performers, created these companies to provide a platform for people of color.

Several women-of-color playwrights came into prominence during the 1960s and 1970s, for example, Maria Fornes, Adrienne Kennedy, and Ntozake Shange. A new generation of writers now includes Elizabeth Wong, Jessica Hagedorn, Endesha Holland, Velina Houston, Cheryl West, Cherrie Moraga, Marga Gomez, and Migdalia Cruz. These women address an array of issues dealing with universal female themes and experiences in addition to confronting racial issues.

One of the most difficult areas for women to break into has been design. Those who have succeeded include Theoni Aldredge, Judy Dearing, Florence Klotz, Patricia Zipprodt, and Willa Kim for costumes; Jean Rosenthal, Peggy Clark Kelley, Tharon Musser, Jennifer Tipton, Shirley Prendergast, Dawn Chiang, and Marcia Madeira for lighting; and Marjorie Kellogg, Heidi Landesman, and Franne Lee for set design.

Helen Krich Chinoy and Linda Walsh Jenkins, eds., *Women in American Theatre* (New York: Theatre Communications Group, 1987).

▪ KATHY A. PERKINS

≋ Thirteenth Amendment

SEE Constitution and Amendments.

≋ Title VII

Title VII of the Civil Rights Act of 1964 is the centerpiece of efforts to end discrimination in the workplace. It prohibits discrimination in hiring, firing, promotion, and terms and conditions of work based on race, color, religion, sex, or national origin. Ironically, the ban on sex discrimination was added to the act by amendment during the House floor debate by enemies of its passage, who believed that some members of Congress would vote against the bill if its protections were extended to women.

The place of women in the work world had been the product of an ideology that assigned man the role of breadwinner and woman the role of childrearer. Underlying this ideology was the belief that women and men are fundamentally different. Early Title VII litigators sought to dismantle sexual inequality in the workplace by attacking the assertion that men and women are fundamentally different. They argued that the antidiscrimination principle required that women and men similarly situated must be treated equally with respect to ability to perform a particular job.

Title VII enables employers to defend practices and policies that discriminate on the basis of sex where sex is found to be a bona fide occupational qualification. In the 1991 groundbreaking decision of *International Union, UAW v. Johnson Controls,* for example, the Supreme Court held that an employer must prove that a sex-based job qualification is related to the essence of the employer's business. The Court required the employer to prove that substantially all women are unable to perform the job's duties safely, efficiently, and without discrimination.

The Court also has sent a strong signal that sexual harassment is a serious violation of the law and that lower courts should cease putting legal roadblocks in the way of success. Title VII undoubtedly has improved the condition of women in the workplace. Much remains to be accomplished to "break the glass ceiling," including improving women's wages, providing job settings that accommodate work and family needs, and fully integrating women into traditionally male-dominated occupations.

▪ JANE DOLKART

SEE ALSO Sexual Harassment.

≋ Title IX

Sponsored by feminists in Congress, including Edith Green and Patsy Mink, Title IX of the Education Act Amendments of 1972 offers women a legal weapon with which to contest discrimination in education, including admissions, athletics, financial aid, extracurricular activities, and academic programs. The provision parallels Title VI of the Civil Rights Act of 1964, which bars race discrimination in education.

When first debated in Congress, Title IX met furious opposition from the educational establishment. Prestigious schools, athletic directors, and male congresspersons charged that the measure would require unisex locker rooms and integrated football teams; would destroy sororities and fraternities; and would shrink the pool of generous alumni contributors. Title IX withstood a vicious and often misogynist assault, however, and remains the most important policy affecting women in education today.

Title IX put schools in a contractual relationship with the federal government: to receive federal funds they must not discriminate. In 1991 the Supreme Court expanded the financial incentives for Title IX compliance when it permitted victims of discrimination to seek monetary damages.

The federal government has not always enforced Title IX consistently. Under the Republican administrations of the 1980s, Title IX's enforcement agency (headed for a time by Clarence Thomas) pursued few complaints and rarely initiated compliance reviews. In addition, the Supreme Court restricted the meaning of Title IX in its 1984 decision in *Grove City College* v. *Bell*. In 1988 the Congress reversed the Court in the Civil Rights Restoration Act, enacted over President Reagan's veto. This created new possibilities for Title IX enforcement during the Clinton administration. In 1994 an invigorated Office for Civil Rights conducted a pivotal "hostile environment" investigation of the University of California at Santa Cruz.

Women have secured important new opportunities since Title IX's enactment. Title IX expanded athletics programs, tore down inequitable admissions policies, broadened women's vocational education choices, permitted women to en-

ter professional schools in unprecedented numbers, reduced discrimination against pregnant students and teen mothers, and provided women with a means to fight sexual harassment. As a result of Title IX, women's participation in school sports has increased more than tenfold since 1971, women's enrollment in law schools has risen from 6.9 percent in 1971 to nearly 50 percent at many institutions today, pregnant students are now entitled to remain in school, and many colleges and universities have developed sexual harassment policies.

■ GWENDOLYN MINK

SEE ALSO Education.

≋ Trashing

During the first few years of the women's liberation movement, women who stood out in any way, particularly those who were achievers or had assertive personal styles or who received too much publicity, were often attacked, both privately and publicly, by other feminists. Known as "trashing," this phenomenon went far beyond criticism; it was the woman herself, not her deeds or words, that was targeted.

These attacks were usually quite vague, marked by name-calling and character assassination. Although occasional confrontations arose, most accusations were made behind a woman's back so she was never able to defend herself to her accusers, or even know exactly who they were. Her activities were interpreted in the most negative light. Reports would be circulated that anything she did was for personal gain rather than for the benefit of the movement.

A woman being trashed was shunned, but no one would admit what was going on. She would be ignored in meetings, removed from mailing lists, left out of delegations, not notified of changes in meeting dates or places, and generally treated like a nonperson. If she questioned this treatment, it was usually denied, though she would be told that "others" thought she was too aggressive, too masculine, too ambitious, "elitist," or some other bad thing.

Trashing was a *group* phenomenon. It was much more common in the small rap groups or service projects that claimed to operate on consensus or without structure than in the large organizations which relied on parliamentary process. It was rare for more than one woman in any given group to be trashed at a time. Isolation was part of the process. Eventually the woman would drop out and no one would ever ask her why.

Exposing trashing did not have any effect on its pervasiveness. Anselma Dell'Olio gave a speech on this topic at the 1970 Congress to Unite Women. In June 1970 a small group of women from around the country dubbed themselves the "feminist refugees." Joreen wrote about "Trashing: The Dark Side of Sisterhood" in *Ms.* in 1975. The response from readers was so great that *Ms.* devoted several pages to the letters in a subsequent issue.

The effects of trashing are best summed up by Ti-Grace Atkinson, herself an object of some very vicious attacks: "Sisterhood is Powerful: It Kills Sisters." Despite the fact that trashing helped destroy part of the movement, it was never adequately analyzed, explained, or understood.

■ JO FREEMAN

≋ Unemployment

U nemployment occurs when and where rigid market structures, imperfect information, or incorrect expectations of the economy prevent workers and employers from adjusting their behavior so that all individuals willing to work at prevailing wages are able to do so. Unemployment caused by market rigidity includes, for example, the case when workers do not leave an economically depressed area in sufficient numbers to lower unemployment rates there. Alternately, employers may not hire available white women or people of color, preferring to pay a higher wage to white males and creating more unemployment than would exist in the absence of discrimination. Unemployment generated by imperfect expectations or information would include cases where employers overestimate the future rate of inflation or the productivity of employees and, as a result, pay wages that are too high relative to other components of production. Unexpected external shocks, such as oil price increases, can diminish demand for what firms produce, causing them to reduce production and their need for workers.

Most economists believe that removing imperfections in the market and improving information and the accuracy of expectations would result in lower unemployment rates. There is, however, debate as to whether policies aimed at lowering unemployment by stimulating the economy can reduce unemployment in the long run.

In data collected by the U.S. government for most of the twentieth century (the only period for which data have been methodically collected), a person is considered unemployed if she or he does not have a job *and* is actively seeking employment. The labor force is defined as the sum of employed and unemployed individuals. Given these definitions, the unemployment rate is:

$$\frac{\text{number of persons unemployed}}{\text{total number of persons in the labor force}}$$

This measure is commonly said to underestimate unemployment because it fails to capture those unemployed workers who become "discouraged" and stop looking for work. It also fails to capture "underemployed" workers who have jobs but would like to work more hours or at higher skill levels. Women are especially likely to be "discouraged" or "underemployed" since they are more likely to leave the labor force or accept reduced hours during economic downturns in order to work in the home. Therefore this traditional measure of unemployment may understate the female unemployment rate more than it understates that of men. And because unemployment statistics are based on self-reporting, the resulting data fail to capture the experiences of those who are difficult to locate, such as the homeless and the poor, or those who participate in the underground economy.

Unemployment has become an increasingly important issue as Americans have become more dependent on wage labor. In the antebellum period, land was plentiful and most Americans engaged in agriculture either as self-employed farmers or as slaves. In this context, unemployment was not a significant issue. Throughout the nineteenth century, the proportion of the population engaged in wage labor increased with industrialization and urbanization.

Until the 1980s female unemployment rates were usually higher than male rates, but women's rates have also generally been less susceptible to economic downturns than men's, at least since World War II. The unemployment rates of women of color have generally been higher than those of white women, although they have at times been lower than the rates of men of color. Mothers of all races tend to have higher rates of unemployment than childless women. Women's relatively high rates of unemployment have been attributed to many factors, including statistical artifact, the inconsistency of a woman's labor-force participation over her lifetime, the limited ability of women to change occupations or geographic locations, and discrimination.

During economic downturns, women's—like men's—unemployment rates typically rise; not all women, however, are affected equally. Many women work in occupations such as clerical work, areas where employment is not very sensitive to economic downturns. Other women, working in industries such as manufacturing, historically have experienced higher unemployment rates than their male counterparts, as they were more likely to be laid off or fired during recessions. Workers at the bottom of the employment hierarchy, often women of color, also face increased risk of unemployment during recessions as the downward mobility affecting all workers pushes them out of the work force altogether. During the Great Depression, many Black women pushed out of service jobs were not able to find alternative sources of employment. Immigrant women, particularly immigrant women of color, also have particularly high unemployment during recessions. For instance, during the Great Depression, only 28 percent of Mexican-born families were able to find employment for at least two able-bodied workers compared to 39 percent of all white immigrant families.

Since the Great Depression, the federal and state governments have attempted to ameliorate unemployment through targeted job development strategies, fiscal and monetary policies, and social insurance. Women have traditionally benefited less from these programs. Since its inception in 1935, women have been less likely to qualify for Unemployment Insurance (UI) because they have been overrepresented in industries not required to provide UI (such as domestic service) and because their hours and earnings are often insufficient to meet eligibility requirements. Women are also underrepresented in industries such as construction and defense, typical targets of government efforts to increase aggregate demand during recessions. Government programs to reduce unemployment in particular geographic areas through job creation, such as the 1930s' Works Progress Administration or more recent community reinvestment programs, may be more likely to reach women who are identified as unemployed since they typically target all unemployed workers in a given community.

Teresa L. Amott and Julie A. Matthaei, *Race, Gender, and Work* (Boston: South End Press, 1991); Francine D. Blau and Marianne A. Ferber, *The Economics of Women, Men, and Work*, 2d ed. (Englewood Cliffs, N.J.: Prentice-Hall, 1992); *The Economic Report of the President* (Washington, D.C.: United States Government Printing Office, 1992).

■ STEPHANIE AARONSON
and HEIDI HARTMANN

≋ United Farm Workers

SEE Labor Unions.

≋ Urbanization

Urban places within the present boundaries of the United States include sixteenth-century Spanish cities, and English, Dutch, and French colonial towns and ports. The process of urbanization that involved the creation of large industrial-era cities was a nineteenth-century phenomenon. Urban U.S. growth occurred simultaneously with the incorporation of distinctive regions and peoples. Eastern seaboard towns began to grow as early as 1820 as a result of the expansion of internal trade, industry, and transportation. Southern towns also grew and were the frequent destination of Black women emancipated from slavery. Slavery created a complex community of women in southern cities, but significant urbanization did not begin there or in the West until after the Civil War. Towns expanded into industrial cities in the Midwest and Northeast between 1880 and 1920. These years overlapped with the period of enormous immigration from Europe, Asia, and Mexico. In the former Mexican and Indian territories of the West, new U.S. cities created the urban and financial structures to support the growth of industrialized agriculture, mining, and cattle ranching. Some western U.S. towns grew out of former colonial and Mexican pueblos, whose histories, as inscribed in the physical structure of town space, were often reduced to only traces of the past in the new urban order.

Nineteenth-century urbanization coincided with the rise of new social classes and gender relations. As industrialization began, land became an increasingly important way to accumulate capital through rent and speculation. Renters, in turn, sought a wage to pay for their lodging. Urban working-class wives and mothers bought, sold, traded, and shared goods among neighbors. They created close-knit communities for their survival. The city offered women greater economic independence than did the countryside, but women who worked as domestic laborers, cooks, laundresses, seamstresses, boardinghouse operators, and working girls in the textile and garment trades earned meager wages that improved only slightly with the growth of jobs in the clerical and retail sectors.

The middle class shaped the city into socially differentiated communities after 1820 by creating neighborhoods built around an ideology of domesticity that removed middle-class wives and daughters from places of production and exchange to the private space of the home, where they were expected to attend to the family. The middle class created the urban structures that separated work and residence and developed a language of housing that defined residential conditions as manifestations of individual or collective morality and ethics rather than relating housing issues to structures of urban power and wealth. This language of housing relied on polarized categories of private and public, respectable and immoral, home and workplace. City governments' role in urban planning was formalized in the twentieth century, but their earlier decisions tended to protect the property values of middle-class neighborhoods and provide better services and public works.

The housewife's work removed most middle-class married women from public life until the end of the twentieth century, but unmarried women commonly worked outside the home, and those who remained single often worked as "social housekeepers" in professions that included teaching, nursing, social work, and urban reform. Their initiatives attempted to regulate industry; end political corruption; extend the vote to women; and improve housing, education, and public health. As settlement-house workers, urban reformers built educational and social welfare institutions in immigrant neighborhoods across the nation. Many of their ideas influenced the urban and social policy of the welfare state that emerged during the 1930s.

Northern cities promised work and a cultural renaissance for southern Black women whose large-scale migration began when industry expanded and jobs opened up as male workers went to fight during World War I. Northern and midwestern cities became cultural meccas with their innovative music, artistic, and dance scenes, epitomized by the Harlem Renaissance of the 1920s. In her novel *Jazz*, Toni Morrison describes what New York City offered to rural women of all backgrounds: "Even if the room they rented was smaller than the heifer's stall and darker than a morning privy, they stayed to . . . hear themselves in an audience, feel themselves moving down the street among hundreds of others who moved the way they did. . . . Part of why they loved it was the specter they left behind." The specter, of course, was that of southern racism and extreme poverty.

But an ideology of white superiority cut into the utopian vision of the city. The systematic segregation of persons identified as racial minorities began as early as the 1850s with the creation of restricted areas for Chinese residents in western towns. Public institutions and places of leisure, commerce, and entertainment also segregated persons of Mexican, Native American, Black, and Asian descent, even though the white majority's right to do so was contested frequently in the courts at the time.

Ethnic neighborhoods historically preceded segregation in U.S. cities. They are generally comprised of more than one ethnic group, though one group, with origins in a common area of migration, typically predominates. Neighbors commonly develop close ties, and the neighborhood offers a commercial and cultural life that responds to the tastes and social practices of its residents.

In the post–World War II era, suburbs and shopping malls were built across the nation in such massive proportions that they began to replace the prominence and function of the city. Federal and state governments supported suburban sprawl by funding roads and highways in lieu of supporting mass-transit systems and centralized urban growth. A slow deindustrialization coupled with suburbanization left cities with high unemployment because of the decline in job opportunities. The loss of a tax base led to a decline in the quality of local services. City governments and planning agencies have developed policies to bring capital investment, jobs, and commerce back into the cities. Grassroots community organizations similarly have organized since the 1960s to contest urban decay and redevelopment policies they consider unfavorable to their neighborhoods. These urban movements often are led by women who draw upon strong community ties. Despite the importance of these movements and of urban policy initiatives, the future of U.S. cities remains unclear at the close of the twentieth century.

▪ LISBETH HAAS

SEE ALSO Housing; Immigration; Industrialization; Settlement House Movement; Suburbanization.

≋ Vietnam Era

The era of the Vietnam War (1964–1975) was a time of breathtaking change for women in the United States. New patterns, long in the making, reshaped most women's lives. Women participated in and frequently led the social movements we associate with the era and initiated a massive second wave of feminism. Since the American Revolution, wars have been times of accelerated change in gender roles. In such times daily life takes on intensified political meaning, and labor shortages created by mobilization open up new economic opportunities for women. Historians of women, however, have challenged the tendency of political, military, and diplomatic historians to frame historical narratives around wars as turning points.

The Vietnam War was a different kind of war. It lasted longer than any other war. It was not a "total war," which required the mobilization of the entire population, and it was ultimately very unpopular, ending in defeat. One of the key characteristics of this era is the breakdown of an American consensus on many levels. Women, without question, led the way in this breakdown and opened up for subsequent generations a new world of possibilities for relations between the sexes.

When President Johnson asked Congress for authorization to "take all necessary measures" (Gulf of Tonkin Resolution, August 1964), a careful look at American women might have predicted that this war would not be fought on the same gender terrain as previous wars. The meaning of womanhood was under challenge (which meant, of course, that manhood was also an unstable ideal). The baby boom was over. Birthrates plummeted; marriage ages rose; and, in an expanding economy, women's education levels as well as men's skyrocketed. Middle-class women's employment patterns had shifted decisively during the previous decade away from the norm of marriage and full-time domesticity toward greater labor force participation for mothers and individualistic (often sexual) self-expression for younger single women. Thousands of Black women in the South were mobilizing in their communities, challenging political authorities, and providing grassroots leadership to the civil rights movement. In California, Latinas like Delores Huerta were beginning to mobilize migrant farm workers in the campaign led by César Chavez. These momentous changes were well under way by the mid-1960s. As the war began to escalate, early signs of the second wave abounded: Betty Friedan had issued her salvo against traditional domesticity in *The Feminine Mystique*, in 1963; in February 1964, an amendment to Title VII of the Civil Rights Act had added "sex" to the categories of people protected from discrimination in employment. On college campuses a new mobilization of students was well under way. In October 1966, the National Organization for Women was founded at a conference of state Commissions on the Status of Women. By the fall of 1967, women's liberation groups began to emerge among student activists across the country.

The rebirth of feminism provided a counterpoint to the cynicism and despair generated by the conduct of the war (including official lying about "body counts," and so on) and later by the Watergate scandal. The first national gathering of radical feminists took place at an antiwar march in January 1968, the Jeannette Rankin Brigade. Later that same year, after the assassinations of Martin Luther King and Robert Kennedy and street riots at the Democratic Convention in Chicago, women's liberationists made the national news with a demonstration at the Miss America Pageant, where the protesters crowned a live sheep.

The years between 1970 and 1975 were filled with female activism. A national women's strike for equality on the fiftieth anniversary of woman suffrage brought thousands of women into city streets to make good-humored but firm demands for change. "Don't Iron While the Strike Is Hot," they said. While radical feminists formed consciousness-raising groups, liberals created new structures to address policy issues and public inequities: the Women's Equity Action League (WEAL), the National Women's Political Caucus

(NWPC), the NOW Legal Defense Fund, and the Coalition of Labor Union Women (CLUW). Lesbian and gay liberation groups formed across the country.

In 1972, Shirley Chisholm was the first African American woman to run for president in a major party's primaries. Congress passed an equal rights amendment to the Constitution and sent it to the states for ratification (which was never completed). Consciousness-raising groups also gave birth to the first shelters for battered women, rape crisis hotlines, and a self-help health movement. They founded dozens of journals, presses, coffeehouses, clinics, bookstores, day-care centers, and women's studies programs. *Ms.* magazine competed with *McCall's* and *Redbook* at grocery checkout lines. Despite ridicule even words began to change: fireman gave way to firefighter; hymns about "brotherhood" were revised to be more inclusive.

The mobilization of women for greater equality evoked an opposing response in which women also played important roles. Phyllis Schlafly founded STOP ERA in 1972, as soon as the amendment passed Congress. When the Supreme Court ruled in *Roe* v. *Wade* (1973) that abortion in the early months of pregnancy was a private decision to be made between a woman and her doctor, a pro-life movement emerged as a powerful force in the New Right.

Women were also among the Vietnam War vets who returned home to a country that wanted to forget the experience. Still excluded from combat duty, women served extensively in the armed forces and especially in military hospitals. Their service was rendered invisible both by the presumption that soldiers (and war) are male and by the debates then raging about whether an ERA would make women subject to the draft. Not until the 1990s was their service recognized and memorialized.

In the aftermath of the Vietnam War era, American politics incorporated a range of issues previously considered private. The old consensus was gone, and women and men faced a long process of renegotiating the meanings of womanhood and manhood. For better or worse, the personal had become political.

▪ SARA M. EVANS

SEE ALSO Wars: 1900 to the Present.

≋ Vietnamese American Women

The flow of refugees from Vietnam to the United States began in 1975, the year that marked the end of the long war and the reunification of the country under communist forces. As part of the evacuation effort designed to aid South Vietnamese associated with the U.S. military presence in Vietnam, about 130,000 Vietnamese were flown to the United States. Since then, thousands of other Vietnamese have fled Vietnam to escape political and economic persecution by the new government. From 1975 to 1985, nearly half a million Vietnamese settled in the United States.

For Vietnamese American women, the process of migration has been accompanied by important life changes. Vietnamese women in the United States are of course not a monolithic group, but one that is differentiated by such variables as social class and age, each of which shapes the form and extent of the change caused by migration in women's lives.

Although migration to the United States has resulted in greater gender equality, it has also involved important gender-role changes for Vietnamese American men and women. The ideal traditional Vietnamese family, modeled on Confucian principles, is one in which women are subordinate to men in all phases and aspects of their lives. According to Confucian teachings, women are expected to obey their fathers when they are young, their husbands when they are married, and their sons when they are widowed. The ideology of male dominance is expressed in sayings such as "A hundred girls aren't worth a single testicle."

The reality of traditional Vietnamese gender relations deviated from this normative model in many ways. Despite all appearances, women in traditional Vietnamese society had not been bereft of power and respect. One of the most famous historical Vietnamese revolts against Chinese domination (in A.D. 40) was led by women—the Trung sisters—who are widely revered by the Vietnamese as national heroines. Certain systematic avenues of authority and power for women existed in traditional Vietnamese life. Older women tended to have considerable power in the household. As part of their domestic caretaking role, women often controlled the family budget and exerted influence over the family economy. Although men controlled key economic institutions, Vietnamese women did have access to economic resources through their extensive involvement in small business and trading.

A recent ethnographic study of low-income, newly arrived Vietnamese refugees suggests a movement toward greater equality in the relations of men and women who migrated to the United States. The rise in women's power resulted from the complex interaction of many factors. Perhaps most importantly, the income of women had become more critical to the survival of their families. Unlike the situation in pre-1975 Vietnam, the Vietnamese men were unable to find jobs that paid enough to comfortably support their families. Families were thus more dependent on the income generated by women through their employment, which usually consisted of low-paying and unstable jobs such as housecleaning, waitressing, and assembling garments.

Besides economic conditions, changes in Vietnamese American gender relations reflected the male-dominated sex ratio of the Vietnamese American population. Young unmarried women in particular experienced greater power in their sexual relationships with men because of the "shortage" of Vietnamese women in the United States. Migration to the United States had also expanded the Vietnamese immigrant women's homemaking activities beyond such traditional work as child care and housework to include negotiation with social institutions located outside the household, such as schools, hospitals, and welfare agencies. Despite the fact that negotiating with bureaucratic institutions on behalf of the household was onerous work, it was a process that ultimately equipped women with valuable skills that were a resource in women's efforts to exert control over household affairs.

One arena in which Vietnamese American women collectively and actively used the resources that they had gained in the migration process was in situations of domestic violence against women. Women often used informal networks of women friends and kin to intervene on behalf of other women who were the victims of domestic violence. Using such mechanisms of social control as gossip and ostracism, the women's networks were sometimes able to influence positively men's behavior toward women in the family.

Along with these gains, Vietnamese American women also associated migration to the United States with important losses, including the decline in their authority as mothers over children. Many Vietnamese American women felt that U.S. society impinged on their rights as parents, and they were ambivalent about the protection from domestic violence offered to them by the U.S. legal system. The women were extremely concerned that the intervention of the law into family life detracted from the authority and rights of parents to discipline their children as they chose. These attitudes highlight the complexity of women's position within the patriarchal family order, which assigned women to a position of subordination to men but also gave power and authority to women in their relations with children.

Besides a decline in their authority as mothers, Vietnamese American women also associated migration to the United States with a general deterioration in the quality of family life and relations. That is, what had been lost or at least threatened by the move to the United States were the traditions of obligation, cooperation, and caring that had marked their family life in Vietnam.

Nazli Kibria, *Family Tightrope: The Changing Lives of Vietnamese Americans* (Princeton, N.J.: Princeton University Press, 1993).

■ NAZLI KIBRIA

SEE ALSO Asian Pacific Women.

≋ Violence Against Women

Western society identifies gender, class, race or ethnicity, and sexual orientation as significant social categories. These categories, which often overlap, serve to locate individuals in hierarchically ordered groups within the social structure. Depending on their place in that structure, the groups are valued or devalued and consequently are differentially advantaged or disadvantaged. For example, white women are privileged by their race, penalized for their gender, and may be further disadvantaged if they are members of the "lower" class; Black women, who form a disproportionate share of the poor, are penalized for their race *and* gender.

Despite differences of class, race or ethnicity, or sexual orientation, many women still share certain similarities. One similarity is that women are targets for specific forms of violence: incest, battering, sexual harassment, and rape. Whether pornography is a form of violence against women remains a matter of serious contention and disagreement among feminists. Each form of violence is a manifestation of societally organized, supported, and condoned or "naturalized" arrangements of power and control based on the combi-

nation of gender, race or ethnicity, class, and sexual orientation.

The interrelationship among the forms of violence is widely acknowledged. Each form of violence supports the others; together they create systemic and pervasive constraints on women. The infliction or threat of violence and abuse is a means of keeping women silent, and thereby controlling them. Despite guarantees of legalized equality between men and women, this silencing often compromises the possibility of women's full and active participation in society and their rights as citizens in a democracy.

Violence against women has occurred for centuries within a historical and cultural context. The infliction of violence has varied in its extent and incidence over time. For example, during the nineteenth century non-slave women who worked in domestic service were the targets of rape and sexual harassment regardless of their race and this violence went unpunished. Young white women who worked in New England textile mills suffered the same experience. Prior to the divorce-law reforms of the second half of the twentieth century, women seeking a divorce from an abusive husband were required to demonstrate ongoing serious abuse before a court would grant a divorce on the grounds of cruelty.

Punishment for offenders is often divided along racial lines in the United States. Research shows that Black men accused of raping white women were and still are more likely to be charged and convicted than Black men accused of raping Black women. Moreover, compared with the rate of conviction for white men accused of raping white or Black women, Black men are still more likely to be convicted. Men from the lower class or men of color are commonly stereotyped— when accused, they are assumed to be guilty of battering their wives or partners, while white men from the middle or upper classes are far less likely to be accused or convicted for battering. Privileged white men serve less time in jail; and in communities where there are alternative sen-

Marchers in 1978 symbolically reclaim the streets as safe for women.

tences, such as mandatory participation in batters' reeducation groups, economically privileged white men frequently are allowed to seek private therapeutic help in lieu of attending publicly subsidized reeducation programs.

In rape cases, lawyers often use rules of evidence or other means to undermine the credibility of a woman who alleges rape. This test of the accuser's credibility predominates in the legal system and perpetuates the sexist belief that women are likely to lie or misrepresent the facts when they accuse a man of rape. Skepticism regarding women's motivation for alleging rape occurs on the civil side of the law as well. When women claim that they have been sexually harassed or have been the victim of incest, society's message is remarkably similar. A woman's word is subject to

distortion and bias. Regardless of the formal law, there is a strong likelihood that she will be viewed as a liar, provocateur, or fantasizer until proven otherwise under intensive and often demeaning courtroom scrutiny.

In the past twenty years, women's rights groups have uncovered and documented the epidemic nature of all forms of violence against women. Researchers have questioned the disparity between the aggressive pursuit by police and prosecutors of virtually all crimes and their lack of similar tactics in cases of battering and rape. The increased interest in recent decades regarding violence against women has underscored the failure of public officials and social agencies to act responsively and responsibly toward and on behalf of women who are targets of violence.

Widespread systemic problems and gaps exist in the formal law, its implementation, and the policies and practices of concerned agencies. In many jurisdictions police officers fail to answer in a timely fashion emergency calls from abused women, or they may treat domestic violence as a "private" matter. The police may also fail to enforce court-ordered protective or "stay-away" orders against a perpetrator. Police officers are sometimes insensitive to the emotional needs of a woman who has been raped. Prosecutors often subject women who allege rape to demeaning and confusing procedures or fail to prosecute batterers or family members alleged to have committed incest. Criminal court judges frequently "warn" batterers rather than mandate treatment or incarceration. Family court judges are often overwhelmed with cases and may be cynical about the prospects for successful interventions aimed at preventing future family violence. In many cases, social workers lack the resources to provide adequate follow-up services for abused or raped women, and some health care providers may not recognize or report incidents of violence. Women who are the targets of violence may be too frightened or intimidated to report the violence or to pursue available legal remedies such as a court order of protection.

Dramatic events such as the recent case of alleged rape against Kennedy-family member William Smith, the Anita Hill–Clarence Thomas hearings, or the charges of domestic violence raised in the O. J. Simpson trials, as well as less notorious incidents of violence against women, fuel public awareness and concern.

Research documenting the incidence, frequency, and severity of domestic violence has helped to strengthen calls for reform in laws and policies addressing violence against women. As a result of pressure from grassroots activist organizations, significant reforms have been initiated at different levels of government. In many states laws have been amended to require mandatory arrest of batterers. Special training and education about domestic violence and rape has been mandated for police, prosecutors, and judges. Various case disposition and punishment regimes such as incarceration, a combination of jail plus work release, and required counseling and reeducation programs for batterers are being developed or evaluated. Some states have passed legislation extending the statute of limitations for bringing a charge of incest; some have included marital rape in their criminal code. At the federal level, judges have recognized sexual harassment as a civil rights violation. Recent congressional legislation (such as the 1994 Violence Against Women Act) underscores the seriousness of violence against women and the need for additional federal efforts to reduce such crimes.

Within Native American communities, women confront unique issues when assaulted. If they live in a tribal community or on a reservation, they may experience racism or cultural insensitivity by some outside service providers. In addition, laws created by predominantly male tribal officials have often ignored the problem of violence against Native American women. An increase in such violence has occurred as tribal cultures have begun to adopt the values of the world around them, but many communities continue to view this type of violence as not only an assault against an individual woman but also an assault against the larger community, family, and tribal culture. In response, some tribal governments have adopted extensive protective codes and strict sanctions for those who perpetrate violence against women.

Some of the most innovative and creative programs addressing the needs of all women who have been the targets of violence have been and continue to be developed and implemented by women's rights activists. They have organized rape and domestic violence crisis hotlines; battered women's shelters; support groups for women who have experienced rape, battering, or incest; and "Take Back the Night" marches, designed to call attention to women's right to walk the streets safely. These women-centered institutions and activities also have attempted, though not always successfully, to address the many complexities regarding racial, ethnic, or class issues.

Federal legislation recognizes the special vulnerability of immigrant battered women, whose lack of access to police and social services may be exacerbated by their lack of fluency in English, and whose legal residence is often dependent on the citizenship status of the abusive spouse. Asian Pacific and Latina organizations have been crucial to the development of culturally sensitive services for battered women in their communities. They have also challenged some batterers' "cultural defense" theory that wife or partner beating is an integral part of their culture.

Women-oriented social services recently have begun to receive public funding and support. The funding is an acknowledgment that there exists a gap in services for female victims of violence, though many programs are ready targets for a right-wing fiscal retrenchment. There remains a pronounced need for expanding services and developing new programs. For example, battered women who are divorced custodial parents often risk further violence from their perpetrators during the men's visits with their children. To protect divorced women, supervised visitation programs for noncustodial parents must be developed and monitored. Moreover, family violence has a strong negative impact on children. As a result there is a clear need for greater sensitivity on the part of educators and other adults in identifying children who observe or are targets of abuse. School programs are being created that are devoted to the issue of family violence.

Neither the conventional category of "victim" nor the identification of "learned helplessness" as a dominant mode of abused women's behavior fully encompasses or recognizes the many strategies for survival and resistance developed by women confronted with violence. Although the categories of victim, survivor, and resister are not mutually exclusive in experiential terms, they are often classified as distinct within the larger society and may generate different responses. For example, societal presumptions regarding "appropriate" roles for women may create more sympathy and support for a "victim" than for a "resister" who readily strikes back. Women who appear to be "helpless" in a violent situation are stereotyped as women who demonstrate "acceptable" sex-specific behaviors and responses.

Existing assumptions in the law are open to question and revision regarding what constitutes "reasonable" behavior, or self-defense, on the abused woman's part in response to rape, battering, sexual harassment, or incest. Scholars disagree about the desirability and utility of developing a sex-specific standard for "reasonableness" or relying on gender-neutral standards. Whether a sex-specific or sex-neutral standard is used, the legal system's failure to understand the complexity of women's responses in violent situations often results in a double penalty for women: first as the actual target of violence and again as a plaintiff in the courts. For example, women who recognize that there is little or no possibility of avoiding rape in a particular situation may encourage the rapist to reveal information that could later lead to his identification and arrest; her "complicitous" behavior should not be misconstrued as "consent." Or, a battered woman may remain with her male partner because she believes that by staying she can best protect her children from abuse. In such circumstances the woman's behavior should not be considered child neglect, which could lead to termination of her parental rights. Lesbian battered women are rarely able to use existing intervention systems because their relationships are not legally sanctioned. Battered lesbians are rarely treated seriously by police, prosecutors, or courts.

During the 1990s recognition in the United States and other countries that violence against women is a cross-cultural and cross-national phenomenon has led to an understanding that all forms of violence against women are violations of women's human rights internationally. The amended International Convention on the Elimination of Discrimination Against Women (CEDAW) and other worldwide campaigns that focus on violence against women reflect this emerging consciousness.

Kerry Lobel, ed., *Naming the Violence* (Seattle: Seal Press, 1986); Susan Schechter, *Women and Male Violence* (Boston: South End Press, 1982); Kersti Yllo and Michele Bograd, eds., *Feminist Perspectives on Wife Abuse* (Newbury Park, Calif.: Sage Publications, 1988).

■ ISABEL MARCUS

Abuse

Violence against women cuts across cultures and time, extending through the entire life cycle from abortion of unwanted female fetuses and rites of female circumcision to beating deaths or forced suicides of elderly women. Age, color, religion, and socioeconomic status do not protect against becoming the target or victim of abuse. No group of women is safe.

In research based on behavioral observations of family violence in ninety societies worldwide, David Levinson (1989) recorded more than forty categories of family violence. Wife beating occurred in seventy-six societies and was rare in only fourteen. Forty-two societies recorded fatal incidents of wife beating. Husband beating occurred in twenty-four cultures. Where husband beating was found, the frequency and severity was less than with wife beatings.

Abuse is not confined to the home, however. Woman abuse ranges from personal crimes of violence such as muggings and rapes, to work-related exploitation and harassment, to system-embedded bias against all women. Further, in many parts of the world, including the United States, at least some forms of woman abuse are considered normal and are reinforced by the prevailing culture and institutions.

Because psychology, history, anthropology, sociology, medicine, and law all have documented the frequency, severity, and forms of abuse of girls and women, a standard definition of abuse is needed that will be useful to researchers across disciplines and account for a spectrum of violent acts. Richard Gelles and Murray Straus have conducted and analyzed national surveys of violence in U.S. families and define violence as "an act carried out with the intention, or perceived intention, of causing physical pain or injury to another person."

Feminists have criticized this definition because 1) it gives scant attention to psychological techniques of terrorism that may not involve physical injury but that have devastating impact on victims, and 2) it can lead to simple tallies of violent behaviors that insufficiently differentiate less violent forms of abuse (more often used by women) from more dangerous acts (disproportionately used by men). Such a definition can lead one to conclude women and men are equally violent.

Nonetheless, the Conflict Tactics Scale (CTS) developed by Gelles and Straus for use in their surveys has become a standard instrument to measure interpersonal violence. Hundreds of researchers have used it since the late 1970s. The CTS remains a valuable tool for comparative purposes.

A further complication is that findings from one discipline may negatively affect efforts by another. For example, medical researchers have linked brain chemistry changes in abused children to the children's aggressive behavior. Social scientists, victim advocates, and prosecutors are concerned that such findings could be utilized by batterers who were abused as children to avoid accountability and responsibility for their criminal acts.

Contradictions occur not only across disciplines but also within professions. Feminist psychotherapists work in the context of a profession that initially validated women's reports of sexual abuse; Freud then labeled such reports the products of fantasy and wish fulfillment. Anna O., treated and abandoned by Joseph Breuer and subject of one of Freud's best-known case studies, fortunately survived. As Bertha Pappenheim, she accomplished her own recovery, then became an early contributor to feminist social theory in Germany.

Similar contradictions occur within the legal arena. The attorney general's Task Force on Family Violence final report (1984) stated, "The legal response to family violence must be guided primarily by the nature of the abusive act, not the relationship between the victim and the abuser. . . . Many segments of the population are unaware that beating one's wife or children is a crime."

Lawyers used this report to craft innovative laws to improve community response to violence against women and to extend protection under family violence legislation to never-married partners, including same-sex couples. Despite these efforts, ten years later the task force findings are neither universally understood nor consistently accepted and applied. The legal system remains a dangerous place for women. For example, women are severely criticized for remaining with abusive partners. Mothers are threatened with termination of their parental rights by a legal system that holds her responsible for neglect even if she is not the child's abuser. Laws do not protect her from medical insurers who deny her coverage because treating her injuries from assaults represents risk to the company, or from employers who fire her because she misses work as a result of assaults.

Yet when women leave abusive partners, they also risk losing custody of their children. Domestic violence is not considered relevant to custody decisions in some states. Judges may grant custody to the batterer because he is economically superior or seems the friendlier parent in court. State welfare agencies may label survivor mothers neglectful instead of addressing their poverty. Professional women may lose custody because their success is interpreted as proof that they are less effective parents than are fathers with similar careers.

Poor women are threatened with losing custody for having too many children or for being teenagers. Older women whose financial security frequently depends upon male wage earners are particularly vulnerable to poverty following divorce or widowhood. Elder abuse is emerging as a particular hazard for older women who have lost their independence and must rely upon relatives, home health aides, or institutions for care.

No single theory explains all forms of violence against women. The fact that violence against women is both traditional and normative in much of the world creates significant barriers to naming abuse, documenting its frequency and severity, and finding ways to prevent, reduce, and eliminate it.

Judith L. Herman, *Trauma and Recovery* (New York: Basic Books, 1992); Mary P. Koss, Lisa A. Goodman, et al., *No Safe Haven: Male Violence Against Women at Home, at Work, and in the Community* (Washington, D.C.: American Psychological Association, 1994); David Levinson, *Family Violence in Cross-Cultural Perspective* (Newbury Park, Calif.: Sage, 1989).

■ MARTHA L. DEED

Battered Women

By tradition, law, and religious prescription, men in most societies throughout most of recorded history have been entitled to discipline their wives and to inflict physical punishment. That some men routinely beat their wives or girlfriends for "bad" behavior was regarded as a fact of life. The first thoroughgoing protest against this violence was published in England in 1879 by Frances Power Cobbe, who urged legislation to prevent "Wife Torture in England." Protest continued in the United States. Susan B. Anthony and other leaders of the nineteenth-century women's movement often spoke out against the brutality of men who coerced their wives through physical and sexual violence. After 1964, the year

Al-Anon women in Pasadena, California, opened the first shelter for women victims of physical abuse, the term *battered women* gradually began to come into widespread use.

The term has proved problematic in several ways. First, it suggests that "battered" is the woman's constant condition—that she exists in an unremitting state of victimhood—a description few battered women would accept. On the contrary, most battering is intermittent or occasional, and most battered women see themselves not as victims but as strong women working hard to get on with life while coping with a difficult situation. Second, by focusing attention on victim rather than perpetrator, the term battered woman encourages the persistent public habit of blaming *her* for what the perpetrator does to her.

For the past twenty years battered women (but not batterers) have been a popular research subject for psychologists seeking to explain why some women are battered. Many "experts" still maintain that battered women are masochists. Feminist researchers, on the other hand, note that battered women generally try to prevent, defuse, or flee violence, and recent studies have found battered women to be extraordinarily resourceful and resilient in escaping violence. Recent feminist analysis focuses not on battered women but on men who perpetrate assault and on social institutions that look the other way.

One widely publicized and generally misunderstood psychological concept colors public perceptions of battered women: the concept of the battered woman syndrome. The syndrome is said to include extreme passivity or "learned helplessness," a condition that results from repeated battering and impairs the woman's ability to take constructive action on her own behalf. Expert witnesses at the murder trials of battered women who kill their batterers in self-defense use this theory (originally developed by Lenore Walker) to explain to jurors why the woman was unable to leave the man before the fatal confrontation. Yet battered woman syndrome is commonly—and

wrongly—thought to be a legal defense that gives any battered woman an excuse to kill. The term also unfortunately suggests that a woman who defends herself against a batterer is somehow mentally defective. Originally intended to help battered women, the concept is now often used against them and is often rigorously applied by prosecutors to disqualify a woman's claims of self-defense: if a woman was not utterly passive and "helpless," as most battered women are not, then she may be disqualified as a "real" battered woman and portrayed as a cold-blooded killer. The standard is used particularly against women of color and poor women who cannot afford expert help. In addition, in civil divorce proceedings, some women are deemed unfit mothers and lose custody of their children when the court determines they are impaired by battered woman syndrome.

During the 1970s women who identified themselves as "formerly battered" and their feminist allies organized the battered women's movement to stop violence against women by providing emergency shelter, raising awareness, and influencing legislation and public policy. This grassroots movement marked an extraordinary moment in U.S. history: never before had there been such an organization of crime victims who, when denied redress, established a de facto system of protection for themselves and other crime victims. By 1978 the movement had established a National Coalition Against Domestic Violence. In the following decade, in addition to providing shelter and support for battered women and their children, the movement effected legal changes giving battered women the right to obtain orders of protection, maintain residence (while batterers are evicted), and receive child custody and support. Facing enormous resistance from the criminal justice system, the movement brought lawsuits and influenced police, prosecutors, and judges to enforce laws against domestic assault just as they would in nondomestic cases.

The movement also emphasized public education and in-service training for people who come in contact with battered women, including criminal justice, social work, and medical personnel. Working at local, state, and national levels, the movement caught public attention and made "private" violence against women in the home a public social issue of great importance. This achievement prompted several foundations and professional organizations, including the American Medical Association and the American Bar Association, to initiate programs to combat violence against women and children in the home. The movement's achievements are also reflected in the Violence Against Women Act passed by Congress in 1994, legislation that includes provisions to aid battered women.

Despite these remarkable accomplishments, battering remains the most frequently committed crime in the United States. Law enforcement is still inadequate and erratic, and shelters and services for battered women are increasingly institutionalized, staffed primarily by professionals in mental health and social work rather than by formerly battered women and feminists. These conditions reflect the persistence of age-old attitudes—that wife beating is an individual psychological and marital problem, that it cannot be stopped, that it is normal behavior bound to happen when women "ask for it," and that victimized women have only themselves to blame.

Ann Jones, *Next Time, She'll Be Dead: Battering & How to Stop It* (Boston: Beacon, 1994); Susan Schechter, *Women and Male Violence: The Visions and Struggles of the Battered Women's Movement* (Boston: South End Press, 1982); Lenore E. Walker, *The Battered Woman Syndrome* (New York: Springer, 1984).

▪ ANN JONES

Domestic Violence

In 1978 feminists of the grassroots battered women's movement lobbied Congress in support of civil rights legislation for battered women. They devised the phrase *domestic violence* to overcome congressional resistance to a "women's" issue. This euphemism became the common term for criminal acts of assault and battery committed by a person against a current or former intimate partner, most often at home. Responsibility for such assaults is usually, but erroneously, assigned to the woman, who is thought to provoke, invite, and enjoy violence. Feminist analysis assigns responsibility for violence to the perpetrator and sees violent acts as part of a pattern of deliberate coercive control designed to compel the victim to comply with the victimizer. Domestic violence occurs in heterosexual, lesbian, and gay relationships, and men are sometimes the victims of either their male or female partner.

Men batter four million women a year, according to the National Clearinghouse on Domestic Violence, and battering is the leading cause of injury to women in the United States. Untold numbers of women suffer permanent disfigurement and disabilities. Approximately twenty-five hundred domestic violence homicides occur every year; some fifteen hundred women die violently at the hands of current and former husbands and boyfriends, while about one thousand battered women defend themselves by killing batterers.

▪ ANN JONES

Incest

Although there is no consensus regarding the best definition of incest, most researchers include sex acts between blood and nonblood relatives (whether of the same or opposite sex) ranging from vaginal and anal intercourse to milder acts of sexual contact such as sexual kissing. Some researchers also include noncontact experiences such as genital exhibition or sexual propositions. The term *incestuous abuse* is used here to distinguish exploitive incest from normal sex play between relatives of approximately the same age.

With the emergence of the second wave of feminism in the United States, increasing numbers of incest survivors began to talk about their abuse. For example, in 1978 a random multiethnic sample of San Francisco's women residents conducted by this author found that approximately 16 percent, or one in every six women, admitted having experienced at least one incident of incestuous abuse before the age of eighteen.

This study contradicted the widely held myth that incestuous abuse is more prevalent in the lower classes and among people of color. When focusing on father-daughter incest, however, significant differences in prevalence emerged. Although the number of Native Americans in the sample was unreliably small, 36 percent of them had been sexually abused by a father compared with 7.5 percent of Latina women, 5.4 percent of non-Jewish white women, 4.4 percent of African American women, and 0 percent of Asian, Filipina, and Jewish women. These findings merit further research.

Studies invariably show that the overwhelming majority of female incest survivors are abused by male relatives and that most male incest survivors are *also* abused by males. The prevalence of incestuous abuse for boys, however, consistently has been found to be much lower than for girls. For example, in the largest national epidemiological study conducted in the United States (n = 2,626), only 1.8 percent of boys reported having been incestuously abused. Eight percent of girls in this study reported such abuse—a rate more than four times that of the boys.

Incestuous abuse is an important social problem because of the trauma and long-term damage that frequently result. Research, such as that reviewed by David Finkelhor and Angela Browne in 1986, repeatedly has found a history of incestuous abuse to be associated with adult mental health impairments, including "depression, self-destructive behavior, anxiety, feelings of isolation and stigma, poor self-esteem, a tendency towards revictimization, and substance abuse." Sexual maladjustments and difficulty in trusting others also are widely reported. Acting-out behavior by females—for example, running away from home, prostitution, alcoholism, drug addiction, and delinquency—also is common.

Feminism has revolutionized our understanding of violence and sexual abuse of females, including incestuous abuse. Besides helping incest survivors to disclose their experiences without fear of being blamed, the feminist movement recognizes how gender inequality, embedded in patriarchal institutions like the traditional family, promotes incestuous abuse. In her groundbreaking 1981 book on father-daughter incest, for example, Judith Herman wrote, "a frankly feminist perspective offers the best explanation of the existing data [on incestuous abuse]. Without an understanding of male supremacy and female oppression, it is impossible to explain why the vast majority of incest perpetrators . . . are male, and why the majority of victims . . . are female." Herman goes on to indict the patriarchal family as the structural context that fosters incestuous abuse.

Efforts to combat incestuous abuse therefore require a radical transformation of the patriarchal family into a family based on equality—whether the adult caregivers are heterosexual, bisexual, lesbian, or gay. To achieve such a shift is a mammoth and daunting task.

Recently, a movement has emerged that denies the validity of retrieved memories of forgotten incestuous abuse reported by many adults. This movement has become a serious threat to incest survivors because their experiences once again are being discredited and their voices silenced. Although many convincing cases exist in which false memories of incestuous abuse have been induced by authority figures, particularly therapists, the false memory movement grossly exaggerates their prevalence. Its supporters—including many accused child molesters—appear to be trying to turn back the clock to the "good old days" when incestuous abuse was a secret between perpetrator and victim. Just as Freud maintained that most of his female patients' reports of incestuous abuse were fantasies, most future reports of incestuous abuse may come to be dismissed as instances of false memory. The lack of an organized and politically militant incest survivor movement increases the likelihood of this tragic outcome.

David Finkelhor, *A Sourcebook on Child Sexual Abuse* (Beverly Hills, Calif.: Sage Publications, 1986); Judith Herman, *Father-Daughter Incest* (Cambridge, Mass.: Harvard University Press, 1981); Diana E. H. Russell, *The Secret Trauma: Incest in the Lives of Girls and Women* (New York: Basic Books, 1986).

• DIANA E. H. RUSSELL

SEE ALSO Child Abuse.

Medical Response to Violence Against Women

Authorities in public health have come to recognize that "wife beating" is not only a crime, but also a major cause of death and injury to women. An estimate accepted by the American Medical Association (AMA) states that more than half of female murder victims are killed by their partners, and that eight to twelve million women in the United States are at risk of abuse.

While many battered women fear informing the police and courts, they do access health facilities, where, until recent years, professionals have been ill-equipped to treat victims of domestic violence. The AMA estimates that "75 percent of battered women first identified in a medical setting will go on to suffer repeated abuse," and that a majority of women who are murdered by intimates had previously sought medical help.

The vast number of unaided and unidentified victims of spousal abuse was discovered during the 1980s by a handful of women physicians, including Drs. Anne H. Flitcraft and Carole War-

shaw. At New York's Bellevue Hospital, Dr. Mary Zachary discovered that while 40 percent of female emergency patients were presently or previously battered, only one in twenty-five are so recorded. When in 1985, Surgeon General Everett Koop confirmed that more women are injured by battery than by rape, muggings, and accidents combined, domestic violence reached the forefront of public health reform. Government, public health, and organized medical authorities have since developed a blueprint for new medical response to domestic violence.

In 1990, the American Medical Women's Association became the first major medical group to pass resolutions regarding physicians' responsibility toward victims of domestic violence. Their example was followed by several state health institutions, and the U.S. Public Health Service, which announced as its objective for the year 2000 that at least 90 percent of hospital emergency departments would have procedures for routinely identifying, treating, and referring victims of spouse abuse.

The Joint Commission on Accreditation of Healthcare Organizations (JCAHO), which can close down a hospital or portion thereof for non-compliance, in January 1992 required that ambulatory departments and emergency rooms attend to domestic violence and elder abuse with procedures similar to those used to address victims of child abuse and rape.

Ultimately, a shift in responsibility from the police and courts to the *educated* healthcare provider as the first intervening authority in the lives of battered women will occur in healthcare reform. The AMA's Council on Ethical and Judicial Affairs has concluded that the principle of "beneficence" requires physicians to intervene in cases of domestic violence, and warns that the physician who does not inquire about abuse or who accepts an unlikely explanation for injuries could be held liable for any subsequent injuries suffered by the victim.

Often, the simplest and least expensive efforts in public health reform bring the greatest results.

If on every intake form issued to emergency room patients the question "Did anyone hurt you?" was added, and a social worker was present to treat battered victims, thousands of lives could be saved. Furthermore, a good record (photographs and medical prognosis) of the victim's injuries would help victims in court.

A four-step intervention strategy is suggested for use by all healthcare providers who treat female patients: identify battered women by interviewing all female patients apart from their partner; validate her experience by believing what she tells you; advocate for her safety and help her expand her options; and support the battered woman in her choices.

It is sad, however, how frequently a "backlash" phenomenon occurs when women begin to make progress to correct injustices. As more physicians follow protocols to identify and document domestic abuse, some insurance companies use these medical records as an excuse to deny coverage (health, life, and even property) to victims of abuse, considering battered women to be at "high risk" and to have made a "voluntary lifestyle choice." Some insurers also get information from legal records such as orders of protection. Starting in the mid-1990s some state legislatures as well as the federal government began considering proposals to stop insurance discrimination against battery survivors. At this writing, in 1996, only one company, State Farm, has voluntarily eliminated domestic violence as a reason to rate or deny insurance.

■ BARBARA SEAMAN

Rape

From a legal standpoint, rape laws have their origins in laws about property, since women were considered to be property under Anglo-Saxon law. Transplanted from England, the law traditionally defined rape as "intercourse between a man and a woman not his wife, against the woman's will and without her consent."

The history of rape and rape law in the United States is full of contradictions. "On paper," for hundreds of years, rape has been illegal and subject to severe penalties. Yet it has been effectively legal, because it has been almost impossible to prove in most circumstances. One type of rape charge historically has been easy to prove, namely that involving a Black man and a white woman. From slavery through the post–Civil War period and to some extent to the present, when a Black man/white woman rape has been claimed, the legal system and society generally have come down with full force on the alleged offender. The most common "justification" for lynching Black men was the claim that they had raped a white woman.

When a white woman claimed that a Black man raped her, the legal system treated her with much less suspicion than when a white woman claimed that a white man raped her. The courts historically provided Black men virtually no protection from false rape charges, yet they protected white men even if the charges were true.

Rape of Black women during slavery was *legal* for white men. Rape of slaves by slaves was legal. The KKK and white mobs used rape of Black women as a weapon of terror during Reconstruction. Following Reconstruction, and to some extent to the present, rape of Black women by white and Black men was ignored and/or minimized by the legal system. Several recent studies have found that historical patterns still continue. For example, a 1990 Texas study found that average prison sentences for men convicted of raping Black women were only one-fifth of average sentences for men convicted of raping white women. Some scholars conclude that of all racial combinations of rape charges, the legal system still treats accusations by Black women of rape by Black men the least seriously and accusations by white women of rape by Black men the most seriously.

Scholars have not conducted much historical or analytical work on rape of female Native Americans, Asian Americans, or Latinas and other groups. Rape of Amerindian women by colonizing Spanish soldiers in what is now California was frequent. Whites also raped Native American women but the incidence is impossible to estimate, as it is for rapes of white women by Indians.

Before the 1970s rape was widely seen as a sexual act of uncontrollable lust, not an act of violence. Critical to the concept of rape was the concept of women's "chastity." In traditional rape ideology, an "unchaste" (sexually experienced) woman lacked credibility and/or must have "wanted it" or consented. Only white women could be "chaste"; the law presumed that Black and probably other women of color were "unchaste." The historical treatment of rape charges often stemmed from men's extreme distrust of women (when the alleged perpetrator was white). Freudian theory posited that women fantasized rapes and fueled the legal system's suspicious attitude.

Police and prosecutors frequently have been hostile to women alleging rape. They threw out charges if the woman reported the rape too soon, or not soon enough after the event. Rape charges had to be supported by physical evidence, while other crimes did not.

Until recently it was impossible to gather meaningful estimates of the incidence of rape; incidence is still hard to gauge. The 1990 FBI statistics show a total of 102,560 reported forcible rapes (including attempted rapes). Rape is statistically underreported, but the extent to which it is underreported is unknown. By comparing the 1990 FBI rape statistics cited above with statistics from studies of victims by the Justice Department, it is estimated that in 1990, 54 percent of forcible rapes were reported. Susan Brownmiller, in *Against Our Will: Men, Women and Rape* (1975), estimated that between one in five and one in twenty rapes were reported. It appears that reporting rates for rape have increased over the past twenty years.

Rape became widely recognized as a public policy issue in the 1970s, sparked in part by *Against Our Will.* Feminists criticized society's treatment of rape, although they often did not challenge the racist aspects of the culture's attitude toward rape. Feminists reconceptualized rape as a crime of violence and as part of a range of violence against women. This approach gained wide acceptance, although some feminists believed that the specifically sexual aspect of rape should be emphasized more.

In the 1970s and 1980s rape reform efforts spread around the country. Activists sought to improve the treatment of victims, expand the definition of rape, and increase the conviction rate for offenders. Feminists set up rape crisis centers and rape hotlines that helped women deal with the legal system and supported rape victims. Almost every state passed rape reform laws. Many laws shielded victims from being forced to reveal their sexual histories during cross-examination, a change from traditional tactics. Activists also tried to change the definition of rape so that it would focus more on the defendant's behavior and less on the victim and whether she resisted sufficiently. Marital rape, previously legal, was outlawed in many states although it still remains legal in some circumstances. Police training programs to raise awareness were initiated. Increased numbers of women became prosecutors, defense attorneys, and judges.

In the late 1980s society increasingly recognized the act of forced sex in social situations, which came to be known as "date" or "acquaintance rape." Researchers at several college campuses found that one in five women reported being forced by a male companion to have intercourse. Activists made efforts to deal with the problem. Others attracted publicity in the early 1990s by claiming that feminists were exaggerating the problem.

It is not clear what difference the changes since the 1970s have made overall. Some argue that the legal system treats rape the same way that it did, although the written laws have changed. Indeed, several empirical studies have found that rape law reforms have made no difference in the arrest, prosecution, or conviction of rapists. The criminal justice system retains race-based, gender-based, and other inequities. Yet, the work that has been done brings society closer to the recognition that women have an absolute right to be free from forced sex.

Susan Brownmiller, *Against Our Will: Men, Women and Rape* (New York: Simon & Schuster, 1975); Susan Estrich, *Real Rape* (Cambridge, Mass.: Harvard University Press, 1987); Jennifer Wriggins, "Rape, Racism and the Law," *Harvard Women's Law Journal*, 6, no. 3 (1983): 104–41.

▪ JENNIFER WRIGGINS

SEE ALSO Pedestal.

≋ Vocational Education Act (1917)

When the National Commission on Federal Aid to Vocational Education convened in 1914 to shape policies and define programs in vocational education, the range of vocational choices for most young women was clear and limited. Courses in women's trades prepared them for industry, and courses in typing, stenography, and bookkeeping prepared them for office work. The legislation that resulted from the commission's work and was approved by Congress was the Smith Hughes Act of 1917. This landmark legislation that became law followed the lead of conservative women's groups in the United States by focusing on home economics as the definitive vocational coursework for young women. The implementation of the legislation gave rise to the development of a large bureaucratic structure that sustained home economics departments in public schools. Moreover, a broad-based campaign to increase funding for women's vocational education in the late 1920s resulted in a substantial increase in federal monies expended on "vocational home economics." By 1930 home economics had a permanent and federally assisted place in public junior and senior high schools in the United States.

Office work, teaching, social work, and nursing were occupations in which women dominated the labor market, yet it wasn't until the 1960s that the federal government expanded the scope and definition of vocations for young women by formally recognizing and funding business courses.

▪ JANE BERNARD-POWERS

SEE ALSO Education; Title IX.

≋ Voters For Choice

Voters For Choice was founded in 1979 by Gloria Steinem and board members of Planned Parenthood as the only independent, bipartisan political action committee devoted exclusively to electing pro-choice candidates. It offers contributions and assistance to candidates running for the U.S. House of Representatives and Senate, state governorships, and state legislative seats during each election cycle.

In addition to contributions, Voters For Choice provides in-kind technical assistance to candidates related to polling, media, fundraising, and general political strategy. One element of the group's services is their publication, *Winning With Choice*, a guide to candidates. In its eighth edition, it has been distributed to nearly 10,000 candidates.

Voters For Choice assisted more than 240 federal candidates in the 1996 election. The organization directly contributed $360,000 to federal candidates and conducted voter identification and informational campaigns in California, Illinois, Massachusetts, New York, and Washington, D.C. Evidence of its success may be seen in the fact that of the 25 close races targeted by Voters For Choice for priority attention, 21 of those candidates endorsed won. Fund-raising efforts have included rock concerts on the East and West Coasts and nationwide fund-raising and publicity tours.

■ SUE THOMAS

SEE ALSO Pro-Choice and Antiabortion Movements.

≋ Voting

SEE Civil Rights Movement; Suffrage Movement.

≋ Wage Gap

The wage gap refers to the difference in earnings between female and male workers and between workers of different races and ethnicities. One statistic commonly used for studying the gender wage gap is the wage ratio, the female wage rate divided by the male wage rate. The wage gap is one minus the wage ratio multiplied by 100. For instance, a wage ratio of 0.56 signifies a wage gap of 44 percent.

Historically, men have had higher wages than women, and white male workers have had the highest wages of all. Economic studies offer different explanations about why white men are paid more than other workers. Some portion of the wage gap is due to differences in education, skills, and other individual endowments between the groups whose wages are being compared. Portions of the wage gap that cannot be attributed to individual characteristics may be due to employer discrimination. Many argue that differences in education and skills also may be the result of discrimination.

The first surveys of earnings and individual characteristics in the late nineteenth century indicate that men were paid more than women upon hiring but that the wage gap closed over time. Analysis of these data suggests that the nineteenth-century wage gap can be explained largely by differences in experience, productivity, and expected lifetime workforce participation. The fact that women were paid low wages may have encouraged them to leave the workplace, creating a self-perpetuating cycle of low employer expectations, low wages, and low lifetime female workforce participation.

Starting in the mid-twentieth century, the proportion of the wage gap accounted for by individual characteristics began to shrink. Surveys show that women and men receive similar wages at young ages in the same fields but that a gap develops with experience. The portion of the wage gap not due to personal characteristics grew during this time as employers increasingly barred women from higher wage jobs. However, occupational segregation does not account for the entire gap. Employers may also pay women less for the same or comparable jobs. One study found that discrimination increased from no more than 20 percent of the wage gap in manufacturing jobs around 1900 to 55 percent of the wage gap among office workers in 1940. Studies of recent data find that the unexplained proportion of the wage gap is between 23 and 72 percent with studies including more detailed variables on education and experience finding a smaller unexplained gap.

Just as the causes of the wage gap have changed over time, so too has the size of the wage gap. During the early nineteenth century, the wage gap fell rapidly in manufacturing and agriculture as industrialization increased the productivity of women relative to that of men. Between 1820 and 1885, the wage ratio for full-time employees in manufacturing increased from approximately 0.35 to 0.56.

Between 1885 and 1970, the wage ratio for full-time manufacturing workers rose slightly, to 0.59. The wage ratio did fluctuate, rising during recessions and falling during expansion. This pattern may result from employers substituting cheaper female labor for expensive male labor in hard times or because women may work in more recession-proof industries.

The wage ratio for full-time workers across all occupations increased from approximately 0.463 around 1900 to 0.603 in 1970. Professional women experienced the greatest growth in the wage ratio (from 0.236 to 0.710). Clerical workers also experienced an increase in the wage ratio. The wage ratio in agriculture, service, and manufacturing stayed relatively constant, between 0.53 and 0.598, while female sales workers experienced a decrease in relative earnings from 0.595 to 0.438.

One factor contributing to the generally slow improvement in the wage ratio between 1885 and 1970 was the enormous growth of the female labor force and the consequent entrance of women with lower levels of experience into the job market. At the same time, a greater proportion of men than women entered the higher-paying professions.

Between the mid-1970s and the early 1990s, the wage gap closed by about one percent a year, with the female/male wage ratio for all full-time workers reaching a historical high of 0.715 in 1993. Black, Latina, and white women saw an increase in their wages relative to those of white men, though white women's wages are consistently above those of Latina and Black women. Furthermore, white women's earnings rose more quickly relative to white men's earnings than did the earnings of women of color.

Three factors are generally credited with the increase in the wage ratio during this period. First, the gap in skills, education, and experience between women and men closed as women gained college education and increased their time in the workforce. Second, women began to be paid more similarly to men for their experience and skills. Third, men's real wages declined, because they were heavily represented in the depressed industry of manufacturing. In contrast, women tended to work in growing occupations and industries. Women also increasingly trained and became employed in occupations not traditionally open to them, such as law, medicine, and various skilled trades. Another factor enabling women's entry into these formerly segregated occupations is the array of civil rights legislation and regulations including the Equal Pay Act of 1963, Title VII of the Civil Rights Act of 1964, the Higher Education Act of 1965, the Federal Contract Compliance program, and the Civil Rights Act of 1991.

Francine D. Blau and Marianne A. Ferber, *The Economics of Women, Men, and Work,* 2nd ed. (Englewood Cliffs, NJ: Prentice-Hall, 1992); Claudia Goldin, *Understanding the Gender Gap: An Economic History of American Women* (New York: Oxford University Press, 1990).

■ STEPHANIE AARONSON
and HEIDI HARTMANN

≋ Waitresses

Waitressing is the quintessential female job, revealing the deeply gender-based expectations in the world of work. It is also the prototypic job of the modern service work force: sex-segregated, low wage, part-time, and contingent. Before the 1920s the majority of commercial food and lodging establishments employed men. Two historical transformations rapidly feminized the trade: eating became a widespread commercial phenomenon rather than a home event; and the presence of women in public became socially acceptable. Other forces—such as Prohibition (it was much more acceptable for women to work if liquor was not served), economic crisis, immigration restrictions, and the two world wars—played important roles. In addition, consumer preference for attractive young white women played a role in the feminization of the waiting occupation.

As waitressing emerged in the twentieth century as one of the principal jobs for women, it began as a job largely reserved for white women drawn from the "old" Northern European immigrant groups: English, Irish, German, Scandinavian. Although this racial and ethnic homogeneity enabled waitresses to sustain a culture of solidarity, it reinforced their racial and ethnic prejudices—as well as those of the proprietors—and showed the real limits of "sisterhood." In unions, the majority of waitress locals excluded Black and Asian women from membership until the 1930s and 1940s. A similar lack of Southern and Eastern European immigrants also existed. Even after legal racial barriers fell, women of color continued to be relegated to the lowest-paid, least-desirable positions in the industry and remain underrepresented in the occupation. Whites monopolized employment at higher-priced restaurants while women of color worked in fast food chains or neighborhood restaurants that served people of color.

Despite the larger societal view of their work as unskilled, the quality of waitresses' service was central to their consideration of themselves as skilled craftswomen. Before the advent of self-service buffets and cafeterias, food service required both highly choreographed teamwork and individual enterprise to ensure that hundreds of individual multicourse meals were correctly and contemporaneously dispatched. Verbal and mental agility as well as emotional and physical stamina were demanded of waitresses, who often worked long hours at a frantic pace; yet their low wages were not complemented by health or other benefits. Instead, they faced unsanitary conditions, capricious management, threatening customers, and the highest rates of sexual harassment of any occupation. Especially because most waitresses lived apart from a family setting and were therefore primarily self-supporting, they could not resign themselves to withering work conditions but actively created a supportive work culture and militant organizations.

Beginning in 1900 waitresses joined mixed culinary locals of waiters, cooks, and bartenders; they also formed all-female union locals, which enjoyed a degree of institutional independence and autonomy experienced by few other groups of organized women. Although they were affiliated almost exclusively with a male-dominated international union (the Hotel Employees and Restaurant Employees International Union, HERE), the waitresses' separate craft- and sex-based locals remained among the most powerful organizations within HERE until the 1970s, despite the official mixed-sex and mixed-craft organizing strategy endorsed by HERE in the 1930s. At the height of their influence in the 1940s and 1950s, over one-fourth of all women in the trade were organized. Most waitresses today do not belong to unions.

Separate-sex craft organizations were informed by the distinctive experiences of wage-earning women. Waitresses advocated for a feminism that stressed "difference" and "separateness" rather than for the similarity of the sexes stressed by the dominant middle-class ideology. They endorsed sex-based legislation, sex-based organizational structures, and a separate "female sphere" within the work world. They sought economic justice and "equal opportunity" through collective advancement and unionization of jobs traditionally held by women, rather than focusing on individual upward mobility. They also created a social identity and solidarity centered on a quest for respect and for rights that are otherwise not a characteristic feature of service sector work. These women's historic struggles and achievements are critically relevant to the new majority of service sector workers.

Dorothy Sue Cobble, *Dishing It Out: Waitresses and Their Unions in the Twentieth Century* (Urbana and Chicago: University of Illinois Press, 1991); Robin Leidner, *Fast Food, Fast Talk: Service Work and the Routinization of Everyday Life* (Berkeley: University of California Press, 1993); James P. Spradley and Brenda J. Mann, *The Cocktail Waitress: Woman's Work in a Man's World* (New York: Alfred A. Knopf, 1975).

■ BETSY ARON

SEE ALSO Service Sector; Labor Unions: Hotel and Restaurant Employees International Union.

≋ War on Poverty

SEE Great Society/War on Poverty.

≋ Wars: Colonization to 1900

The peoples who inhabited the North American continent before the arrival of Europeans were varied in their attitudes toward war making. Some were nomadic and assigned high value to the role of warrior. Others, for instance the Iroquois, appear to have developed cultures that bestowed fewer privileges on warriors, looking instead upon agricultural cultivation as more integral to collective security than warfare. It was the latter communities that were less likely to imagine that masculinity was a precondition for community authority. On the other hand, when the British, Dutch, French, and Spanish arrived in the sixteenth and seventeenth centuries, they brought with them not only advanced war-making technology—the stirrup, the rifle, gunpowder—they also imported notions of state administration, land ownership, and conquest that rapidly spread across the continent, along with the presumption that making national-security decisions was "men's work."

Warfare in North America tended to bolster the idea that men, particularly white Christian men, were the principal protectors of the nation's well-being and the ones in whom public trust could be invested. U.S. warfare was never merely an all-male affair, however. As in Europe, Asia, and Africa, male soldiers did not live on weapons alone. To conduct wars—first against the Indians, the French, and the British; later to take Texas from the Mexicans and the southern white secessionists; and finally, at the end of the nineteenth century, against the Caribbean Spanish colonists—the government had to mobilize U.S. women of different ethnic and racial groups to support war.

During wartime crops had to be planted or gathered and meals prepared; uniforms had to be sewn and laundered; boys had to be raised and taught to accept soldiering as manly; wounds had to be bandaged and healed; rifles had to be assembled and ammunition had to be packed with gunpowder; heroism had to be valorized and emotional scars tended; and imperial visions had to be portrayed as Christian and civilized. All of these war-supporting activities depended on women's participation. U.S. women of all classes and races were excluded from voting and holding public office during these years. Women were not subject to military conscription, and they were not enlisted as volunteers into the regular uniformed ranks of the U.S. military before the twentieth century. Yet without the physical labor and moral support of at least a majority of U.S. women, none of these wars could have been waged successfully.

Although there is evidence that women disguised as men (the most celebrated being Deborah Sampson) served in the revolutionary army and that General George Washington mobilized a group of women to water down overheated cannons when he ran short of men, by the end of the Revolutionary War male constitution writers were imagining citizen soldiers as men and soldiering as the duty of vote-endowed citizens. While the existence of a standing army was hotly contested in the new nation and male conscription continued to be widely resisted throughout the nineteenth century, the founding assumption persisted: only men could soldier and only men (free, unenslaved men) who soldiered for the federal government had the right to cast a ballot.

An estimated 3,200 white and Black women served as volunteer nurses without pay in both the Confederate and Union armies during the Civil War. These women were not deemed genuine soldiers, though they served at great risk often in the midst of gunfire and their skills allowed the commanders to send scarce troops back into battle. Their presence was resisted by some male officers; but others, including the press, regarded the volunteer nurses as feminized patriots. Women also served as spies, the most famous being former slave and Underground Railroad activist Harriet Tubman. Like nursing, spying was treated as marginal to "real" soldiering and thus consistent with the male-only suffrage principle.

Contemporary and subsequent commentators paid less attention to the scores of women who worked in armories along the Connecticut River between Hartford and Springfield, the precursors of the modern defense industry. These women came from the same backgrounds—often literally the same families—as the women who supplied the majority of labor for the textile and garment factories that produced the Union army's uniforms. Women's increasing importance to U.S. industrialization during the mid–nineteenth century meant that they had also become essential to U.S. war making.

Also overlooked in most histories of the Civil War were the Black and white women who farmed and grew needed crops while men were off at war, as well as those white women who began to take over clerical jobs from white men in Washington's expanding civil service. Ignored altogether were those women, often destitute, who decided to follow the troops, providing services ranging from cooking to laundry to sex, in exchange for subsistence. Those women who followed the Union soldiers commanded by General Joe Hooker were disparagingly labeled "hookers," a term that has survived in the parlance, though its roots in warfare have been forgotten.

Euro-Americans' military assault on the continent's Native American women and men is perhaps one of the central themes of seventeenth-, eighteenth-, and nineteenth-century U.S. history. In the thirty years following the Civil War, these assaults reached their zenith. Sometimes they took the form of engagement between Euro-American (and some African American) male soldiers and Native male warriors. But very often these military attacks pitted the U.S. army against un-

armed Native women, men, and children. Native women were displaced from their lands, often raped, and frequently taken prisoner by U.S. troops.

Military wives have received scant attention in the history of U.S. wars. Yet women as wives helped to sustain the armed forces as they supported expansion westward into the regions controlled by Native peoples, by independent Mexico, and by the Hawaiian monarchy. White U.S. women married to U.S. army officers sent to fight and then constrain Indians left behind letters and diaries that described their work as assisting their government's territorial expansion. They were their husbands' helpmates but also the representatives of East Coast, European-defined civilization. They, along with white pioneering women, often set themselves up as role models for the Indian women, now confined to reservations. Indian women were active in developing their own strategies for supporting resistance to a kind of warfare that increasingly targeted civilian populations in the name of pacification and for developing survival strategies subsequent to their peoples' defeats at the hands of the U.S. cavalry. Thus the relationships between white military wives, white pioneer women, and Indian women during the latter half of the nineteenth century were complex and dynamic.

The image of U.S. society as not only a beacon of civilization but also as an active exporter of civilization was a crucial building block for the popular support of the government's western, Pacific, and Caribbean military operations. Central to that image was the notion that U.S. womanhood was somehow more advanced, more enlightened, and more free than that of other cultures, especially those societies resistant to U.S. government annexation or paternalistic control. In this sense, nineteenth-century U.S. debates over feminine respectability and women's rights helped legitimize or undercut U.S. warfare.

U.S. peace activism became a prominent movement during the 1890s. Many of the spokespeople and organizers critical of imperialist expansion were Black and white women, who challenged the ideas that U.S. society was a model of enlightenment and that U.S. women in particular were its beneficiaries. While, for instance, journalists and congressmen who urged U.S. intervention in Cuba's war of independence expressed horror at the rapes of Cuban women by Spanish colonists, actions that allegedly violated U.S. values, anti-imperialist women contended that women in this country in fact routinely were treated merely as the property of men. Not only were wives often the property of husbands, slave women were, by definition, property. For centuries, Black women had been raped, a right of white male ownership.

On the other hand, it was precisely because soldiering remained for men a litmus test of societal acceptance that some African American women antiracist activists saw the government's overseas operations as a chance for Black men to prove their trustworthiness and courage. Thus in 1898, Ida B. Wells, a leader of the antilynching movement, lobbied Washington officials to stop lynchings of Black people. She found that members of Congress were so swept up in the excitement over the war with Spain that they scarcely had time to think of anything else. She decided, therefore, that her antilynching cause would be furthered if the Illinois state's Black regiment were sent to Cuba. She was successful and went to the Springfield train station to see off the men.

Throughout the nineteenth century women could be found on both the pro-imperialist and anti-imperialist sides of the emerging public debate about when and where U.S. military operations were justified. By the time of the Spanish-American War, the debate was as much about gender as it was about commerce. While the United States supposedly had a model of womanhood to carry to the far reaches of the world, there was rising anxiety over what industrialization, city life, and office work were doing to

once-rugged U.S. white manhood. As the century came to a close military intervention in the Caribbean and the Philippines was being promoted by many as a formula for reinvigorating the wilting image of U.S. masculinity. Theodore Roosevelt and others were trying to persuade their compatriots that soldiering abroad would roll back the "softening" effects of urban life and office work that threatened to feminize the country's men. Insofar as U.S. women accepted this argument, they aided in the promotion of overseas warfare and imperialism as guarantors of the nation's security.

Amy Kaplan and Donald E. Pease, eds., *Cultures of American Imperialism* (Durham: Duke University Press, 1993); Linda K. Kerber, "May All Our Citizens Be Soldiers and All Our Soldiers Citizens: The Ambiguities of Female Citizenship in the New Nation," in *Women, Militarism and War*, edited by Jean Bethke Elshtain and Sheila Tobias, 89–104. (Savage, Md.: Rowman and Littlefield Publishers, 1990); Susie King Taylor, *A Black Woman's Civil War Memoirs* (New York: Marcus Wiener Publishing, 1988).

■ CYNTHIA ENLOE

≡ Wars: 1900 to the Present

The U.S. war against independence forces in the newly annexed Philippines was its first of the new century (1901–1902). As in past wars, U.S. women were involved (even though they were still denied the vote) as supporters, as critics, as wives and mothers of male soldiers, as laborers who helped support the war effort, and especially as civilian missionaries and teachers who helped to consolidate the U.S. colonialization process after the Filipino nationalists were defeated. Had they had the means to make contact with their Filipino counterparts, one could speculate that Native American women might have aided the pro-independence insurgents' efforts.

First-generation Japanese American women in Chicago sell Liberty Bonds to help finance the war effort, 1917.

During World War I, factories for war preparations became a home-front business, in which women participated. Some suffragists were concerned about women's entry into war industries and saw the war as a contest between imperialist, male elites driven by notions of masculinized honor. Other suffragists contended that if women contributed to the war effort against Germany, they would prove that women deserved the right to vote.

Jane Addams and Alice Paul, among other U.S. women pacifist feminists, helped found the Women's International League for Peace and Freedom (WILPF) in 1915 to sustain female reformers' connections internationally and to organize opposition to U.S. entry into World War I. WILPF, with its headquarters in Geneva, and its U.S. main office in Philadelphia, remains active today.

Once the government decided to enter the war in 1917, women were of explicit concern to U.S. policymakers—as mothers and wives of soldiers, as workers, and as threats to the health of male soldiers. One concern related to venereal disease, which was designated a major threat to U.S. male soldiers who hired prostitutes. Local public health officials and police officers worked with federal authorities to control and often to shut down brothels frequented by soldiers.

Although a brief conflict for Americans, World War I spawned stiffer rules against labor activism. A new African American women's organization, the Women Wage-Earners Association, tried to support the demands of poorly paid Black women employees at the American Cigar Company in Norfolk, Virginia. The association was investigated by government agents on the grounds that its members were subverting the war effort. While many Black women did increase their income during the war, their gains proved short-lived; when the war ended, returning male soldiers reclaimed their pre-war jobs, and by 1920 almost 90 percent of all employed Black women were working in domestic service or agriculture; only 6.7 percent retained jobs in industry.

During the World War I period, the armed services were scarcely prepared to wage the sort of battles being fought against Germany. One early decision made by U.S. male military planners to bolster the country's military resources was to mobilize women to serve in the armed forces. The Army Nurse Corps had already been created in 1901, and the Navy Nurse Corps began in 1908. While even the idea of women serving as volunteers far from the battle-front contravened Victorian notions of feminine respectability, the navy department convinced Congress that hiring women would meet the needs of the personnel-short military and allow more men to go into battle. By the end of World War I, approximately 10,000 American women had served as army and navy nurses, more than 1,000 American women had served as "Yeomen (F)" in the navy and marines, and another several thousand civilian women became army employees in France.

Women won the vote in 1920, but they were quickly demobilized after the war. The U.S. military was once again an overwhelmingly male institution. The nursing corps remained one of the few female units, but it too became smaller: within the corps a handful of Black women nurses had gained entry into the military in the last months of World War I, but they were excluded at war's end — military nursing became once more an all-white affair.

In the late 1930s, World War II began to loom in Europe and the Pacific. U.S. women activists drew upon the lessons of World War I and tried to prevent a repeat of the post–World War I rollback of women's wartime gains. For the first time in U.S. history, this war would be fought in a domestic political context partially shaped by women, who now had the right to vote. While pacifist Congresswoman Jeannette Rankin was vocal in opposition to a declaration of war, in 1941 Massachusetts Republican Congresswoman Edith Nourse Rogers, backed by several women's organizations, notified the War Department that she planned to introduce a bill to establish a women's army unit. In the face of this pressure, the department eventually created the Women's Army Corps (WAC).

Racial discrimination in the military and the struggles to overcome it became an integral part of World War II politics. Several hundred Native American women enlisted in the regular armed forces, though most had a hard time resisting demobilization after the war. Black women activists such as Mary McLeod Bethune effectively lobbied to ensure not only that Black women could serve in the armed forces but also that they would be assigned duties that matched their skills and educational credentials. Nonetheless, while the WAC recruited more than 4,000 Black women, more than one hundred of whom became officers, the WAC's membership was never less than 94 percent white. Black women nurses were allowed to care for white soldiers only later in the war after Bethune, the Black nurses association, and Eleanor Roosevelt together had exerted pressure on President Roosevelt. Virtually all U.S. ethnic and racial communities faced controversies over whether enlisted women were jeopardizing their feminine respectability in the still largely masculinized military. The women in charge of recruiting thousands of women into the armed forces, consequently, invested considerable energy into ensuring that women in uniform would not be portrayed in the press either as "promiscuous" or "unfeminine."

Policies designed to define and control sexual behavior were deemed crucial in World War II also. For many women, joining the military provided an unprecedented opportunity to define their sexuality. The U.S. military, however, was increasingly bureaucratizing and psychologizing its fears of homosexuality. Lesbians in the service also felt pressured to hide their sexual orientation from their women superiors. Government personnel debated over whether contraceptives should be distributed to heterosexual women troops, just as condoms were being distributed to male soldiers. Hawaiian brothels were allowed to operate smoothly despite the military's own anti-prostitution guidelines.

In Britain, white British women choosing to

date American Black soldiers provoked a dispute between officials in London and Washington. When some British officials called on their wartime allies to send over more African American armed forces women to serve as social partners of African American men, General Dwight Eisenhower refused.

The government vastly expanded its facilities in the Caribbean and the Pacific. Puerto Rican, Aleut, and Eskimo women gained access to jobs at the new civilian bases. The enormous increase in women of color's economic dependency on military bases would raise difficult questions in the 1990s, when many of the bases were closed. "Rosie the Riveter" had come to symbolize opportunities for women in higher-paying industrial jobs as the government drafted more and more men into the military. As in the military itself, the actual processes by which these well-paying jobs were distributed and maintained, however, were fraught with racist overtones. It took concerted organizing by African American women's groups to open up the most highly skilled, best-paying jobs to Black women in war factories. Opposition to Black female workers came not only from white male managers but also from white male industrial workers and white women as well.

For Japanese American women on the West Coast, World War II brought profound losses, not gains. While Japanese Americans in Hawaii were seen by federal officials as too valuable a part of the labor force to intern, those in California, Oregon, and Washington were forced to abandon their homes and businesses and to travel to remote and barren internment camps. Later, Japanese American young men in these camps were offered release if they enlisted in the U.S. military, while most women were compelled to stay in the camps.

In the postwar years from 1946 to 1973, civilian women had to struggle to hold on to the economic gains made during World War II. The military kept its Waves and WAC and largely female nursing units, but they reverted to small and mostly white units. Even the battles in Korea and

Vietnam did not cause Congress to lift the post-war 2 percent ceiling it had imposed on women's membership in the active duty military. The Defense Department used the draft to fill its ranks. Neither the Korean conflict nor the Vietnam War was an all-male U.S. operation. Women held medical posts, including those in "MASH" (Mobile Army Surgical Hospital) units, and they filled clerical, administrative, and communications positions. The very nature of the war in Vietnam, in which the boundaries, purposes, and goals were often blurry, undermined the presumption that women would be safely confined to "noncombat" jobs. Almost unnoticed was the role many American women played during the Korean conflict and the Vietnam War as emotional supports for male soldiers. As wives, mothers, and girlfriends, U.S. women were expected to help returning veterans reenter civilian life and overcome their psychological wounds.

Korean American women were directly engaged in the 1951–54 conflict, especially because they often had family members living in South Korea and because some came from families in which political commitments—whether to the resistance to Japanese colonialism, to communism, or to the imposition of U.S. control—infused the war with ideological significance. Similarly, the U.S. war against nationalist and communist forces in Vietnam between 1965 and 1975 had distinctive meanings for Asian American women. Many Asian American women watched the prostitution industry flourish in South Vietnam, where it was designed to service U.S. male soldiers. The women connected such prostitution directly with the perpetuation of stereotypes of Asian American women as passive, sexually available "Susie Wongs." Korean and Filipino women who, in the early 1990s, uncovered evidence of the Japanese Imperial Army's forced recruitment of "comfort women" made the point that this World War II Japanese practice was not so far removed from the U.S.-Asia prostitution policies in the 1970s, 1980s, and 1990s.

By the 1980s Congress had ended the male military draft and lifted the 2 percent ceiling on women in the military. Many women inside and outside the military saw the invasions of Grenada (1982) and Panama (1989) as tests of the military's commitment to women. The press gave increasing coverage to women soldiers, and polls showed that a rising proportion of the American public acknowledged the right of women to serve in combat posts. Some feminists, however, especially those active in the 1980s' peace movement, warned that women on battleships or piloting jet fighters would only give new credibility to an institution that remained imperialistic and patriarchal.

The Gulf War, though it lasted only from August 1990 to the spring of 1991, perhaps most persuaded the majority of Americans that the reality of women as soldiers was now normal, even when those women were subject to capture and death. The press and television coverage portrayed U.S. women soldiers as "liberated," especially when contrasted with Muslim women, who were depicted by journalists as veiled and subservient. Seven percent (41,000) of the U.S. troops sent to Saudi Arabia to battle and defeat the Iraqi forces in Kuwait were women. Incidences of rape and sexual harassment of U.S. women soldiers by their own male superiors were not reported during the war, though they were later the subject of senatorial hearings. By the early 1990s the performance of women in the Gulf War and the favorable media coverage, together with the legislative strategizing by women House members, seemed to push forward Congress and the Defense Department to lift nearly all bans on women holding combat posts.

The militarization of women's lives occurs whenever women are pressed to adopt attitudes, values, and roles intended to bolster a military's smooth operation. Not all women, however, are pressed to play the same part: some are needed by the military to be loyal wives, others to be prostitutes, still others (a few) to be uniformed personnel. It is during wartime that these roles are most visible. But militarizing pressures shape women's self-perceptions long before and long after the guns are fired.

Paula Giddings, *When and Where I Enter: The Impact of Black Women on Race and Sex in America* (New York: William Morrow and Company, 1984); Judith Hicks Stiehm, *Arms and the Enlisted Woman* (Philadelphia: Temple University Press, 1989); Yoshiko Uchida, *Desert Exile: The Uprooting of a Japanese American Family* (Seattle: University of Washington Press, 1982).

• CYNTHIA ENLOE

SEE ALSO Armed Forces; Rosie the Riveter; Vietnam Era; World War I Period; World War II Period.

≋ Wealth and Its Distribution

To economists, personal wealth consists of assets that have a market value. Wealth can take the form of real property (as in buildings, land, or machinery) and financial assets (as in stocks or bonds, which imply a share of ownership in real wealth or a claim on income). Wealth also includes, in theory, assets such as education or job training that produce income. Measures of wealth and property focus on market values and thus ignore women's unpaid work in reproduction. Slavery constitutes an appalling exception to this general lack of attention to women's reproductive role: the value of a woman slave depended in large measure on her capacity to bear and raise children.

Although most Americans own some personal property, ownership of income-producing assets is far more highly concentrated. Ownership of wealth that produces income also conveys power, both because the wealthy are not required to work for others and because they have privileged access to political power. The distribution of wealth, therefore, is a measure of the distribution of power in a society. Measurement of wealth poses a number of conceptual problems. Since 1962, the Federal Reserve Board has surveyed households regularly to determine their assets and debits and a measure of their net worth. Historical studies have imputed wealth through indirect means such as probate and estate tax records. Since data on wealth are collected by household, no studies exist that measure the real distribution of wealth between women and men. The available data suggest that men own substantially more wealth than do women in the United States; only recently, for example, have divorce settlements accorded to women equal shares in marital property upon the dissolution of a marriage. Ownership of wealth, however, does not necessarily imply control over that wealth (freedom to sell the asset or to control the income it produces). A worker who has a pension fund does not control that wealth but, nonetheless, will have a claim on the income it produces in her retirement years. To avoid taxes, wealth owners may sign over assets to family members who hold legal title to the wealth but have no actual control over its disposition or over the income it produces. A woman whose husband is the legal heir to a family fortune is likely to have a higher standard of living than a woman whose husband has no property, even though neither woman may actually have property in her own name. Thus, it is difficult to separate out issues of legal ownership, control, and consumption in assessing the gender distribution of wealth.

The distribution of wealth is far more highly concentrated in the hands of the very few than is the distribution of income. Data from the 1989 *Survey of Consumer Finances* conducted by the Federal Reserve Board suggest that the richest 0.5 percent of families hold as much wealth as the bottom 90 percent. For most households, the family home is the most important asset. Subtracting residential assets, the distribution of wealth becomes even more concentrated: the top 10 percent hold 79 percent of nonresidential wealth.

Prior to industrialization, most wealth consisted of productive land and slaves and was held by white men. To the extent that indigenous peoples were pushed off the land through armed force, genocide, trickery, and other means, and that slaves constituted "wealth," the distribution of wealth starkly illustrated Proudhon's famous statement that "property is theft." In the tradition of British common law, married women ceased to exist as independent legal agents and were subsumed under their husband's legal identity. Thus, married women were barred from holding property. Widows and daughters could, however, inherit property, and there are records of property ownership among both white and free African American women in the seventeenth and eighteenth centuries. Slaves were themselves property and thus could not own property. With the abolition of slavery and expansion of married women's property rights, property ownership became more common for groups other than white men. Still, white men continue to monopolize wealth ownership. In 1989, the most recent year for which data are available, white families had median net worth 20 times greater than families of color.

Historical studies of the distribution of wealth in the United States suggest that the distribution of wealth was relatively equal and stable for free people during colonial times, but the studies show that inequality rose sharply in the first half of the nineteenth century. The Civil War era brought some leveling in the wealth distribution, but the first two decades of the twentieth century were again marked by sharply rising inequality. From 1929 to midcentury, there was some movement toward equality, and the distribution of wealth has been essentially stable since.

Conservatives typically argue that inequality in the distribution of wealth serves as an important incentive for capital accumulation and economic growth and that the income from wealth serves as a reward for risk taking and saving. Liberals argue that inequality in the distribution of wealth creates undesirable barriers to mobility, leaves families without wealth vulnerable to any interruption in income, and concentrates political power in the hands of the wealthy. Thus, they favor estate taxes and other forms of progressive taxation aimed at wealth. Radicals agree with these criticisms, arguing that ownership of certain forms of wealth, particularly ownership of the means of production, is illegitimate because it represents, in the first instance, the equivalent to an outcome of theft, and, in subsequent form, the appropriation of value produced by labor. Radical economists favor more sweeping changes in property rights along with progressive taxation of wealth.

Lawrence Mishel and Jared Bernstein, *The State of Working America 1994–1995* (Armonk, N.Y.: M. E. Sharpe, 1995); Andrew J. Winnick, *Toward Two Societies: The Changing Distributions of Income and Wealth in the U.S. Since 1960* (New York: Praeger, 1989); Jeffrey G. Williamson and Peter H. Lindert, *American Inequality: A Macroeconomic History* (New York: Academic Press, 1980).

▪ TERESA L. AMOTT

SEE ALSO Economic Growth; Poverty; Unemployment.

≋ Welfare and Public Relief

The organization of public assistance has had particular import for women because women have been overrepresented among the poor and because public welfare systems have enforced and constructed particular family and gender systems. For centuries public assistance has been stigmatized; hostility toward the poor, toward relief, toward women without male support, and more recently toward racial/ethnic minorities created an escalating spiral of ill will. That stigma has been so embedded in language that the history of welfare cannot be understood without examining its terms.

Welfare is stigmatized only when it is given to the poor. The U.S. government was constructed around "giveaways"—starting with land grants to European settlers and developing into massive tax deductions and aid to corporations. The idea of a welfare state developed in the mid-twentieth century as governments became more active in promoting public health, safety, education, and well-being. But by the 1960s in the United States, "welfare" referred only to stigmatized forms of assistance—primarily Aid to Families with Dependent Children (AFDC), which provided support for poor single mothers and their children and was the main program people meant when they spoke of "welfare" until the Personal Responsibility Act of 1996 repealed the program. By contrast, aid programs which benefit the nonpoor, such as Social Security old-age insurance, are not considered "welfare." Yet 80 percent of direct government aid goes to citizens who are not poor.

In the early British North American colonies, relief for the poor was governed by the traditions of the English poor laws dating from 1597. Poor relief was the responsibility of local governments, usually towns or cities, which might provide both "indoor" (institutional) and "outdoor" (aiding the poor in their own homes) assistance. Government aid at this time did not so much substitute for as supplement women's familial responsibility. Kinfolk (mainly female) were expected to care for relatives, even rather distant ones; those among the needy who lacked helpful relatives and could not care for themselves were often placed in the households of others (again female) who, for a small stipend, provided caretaking services. The 1662 English law of settlement was also influential in the United States, creating legal residency requirements for obtaining relief. Since men were the primary citizens and property owners, women left on their own could find it difficult to prove legal settlement.

Early poor relief was guided by assumptions that continue to shape our welfare system today. One was the distinction between the "deserving" and the "undeserving" poor, the belief that relief should go only to the morally worthy, and the fear that relief might encourage immorality if too easily or generously allocated. These moral distinctions heightened discrimination against women, especially since women's sexual activity outside of marriage as well as single motherhood were always morally suspect. Another assumption was the principle that public assistance should always provide less than the lowest local wages. Here the justification was that public assistance should not make it more difficult for employers to hire help, but the effect was to increase poverty and push down wages by pressuring workers to accept what they were offered.

The U.S. Constitution's Tenth Amendment assigned responsibility for the public welfare to the states and local governments, explicitly removing this function from federal jurisdiction—an assignment that created a major legal obstacle to the development of a national welfare state during the early twentieth century.

In the nineteenth century both poverty (understood as a relative concept) and the stigma of relief intensified. Industrialization, urbanization, and immigration together worsened some aspects of poverty and made it more visible. Private charities multiplied. Progressive reformers began to understand that a capitalist industrial economy by its nature produced unemployment and economic distress and responded with public investigations to establish the "facts" of poverty. Women and feminists were disproportionately influential in this social welfare movement. But simultaneously the Horatio Alger mythology, that those who worked hard would succeed, insisted that poverty was in itself a sign of character defect. This myth fed resentment among the prosperous about money spent on "paupers." Such punitive attitudes expanded the institutionalization of the needy in poorhouses, where their characters could be "reformed."

In the midst of the nineteenth century two federal welfare programs developed. The first was the Freedmen's Bureau, a multifaceted federal agency devoted to advancing the welfare of for-

mer slaves; its promising work ended with the defeat of Reconstruction and the resurgence of southern states' autonomy. Most southern Blacks were recaptured into a sharecropping system that deprived them of political and economic rights. The second was the most massive federal program before the New Deal—Civil War pensions. By the 1890s 40 percent of the annual federal budget, about $106 million, went to support needy soldiers and their relatives; by 1912 it covered two-thirds of nonsouthern white native-born men. These recipients, although most were distant from those who actually fought the war, were not screened for their moral respectability, and the pension program was in this respect a precursor of today's honorable, non-"welfare" welfare programs. At the same time the administration of the pensions was partly shaped by political patronage, which led many reformers to suspect that all government provision would necessarily be corrupt.

By the Progressive Era (approximately 1890–1917), the problems of poverty and the horrors of large asylums had become so visible that a renewed campaign for public "outdoor" aid developed. The first victory was won by women who organized and designed state programs of aid to single mothers, the Mothers' Aid laws, passed in forty-one states between 1911 and 1920. Their objectives were to prevent children from being separated from their mothers and to stop child labor by providing stipends for poor single mothers, primarily widows; it was also important to them to demonstrate that public aid could be administered efficiently. To win support for their programs the mothers'-aid reformers argued that they should serve only the "deserving," using rhetoric that required maligning some of the poor as morally undeserving. During the same period forty-three states passed workmen's compensation laws, requiring employers to compensate employees for workplace injuries; and although most relied on private insurance companies, the laws nevertheless set the precedent that government could require employers to provide certain benefits. Workmen's compensation and mothers' aid both supported the then-dominant view of women as economic dependents of men; both ignored the increasing numbers of wage-earning women.

Resistance to a federal government welfare role was broken by the Great Depression of the 1930s. With one-third of the nation in poverty, the usual conservative, corporate, and states'-rights oppositions to national welfare programs were temporarily weakened and President Roosevelt was able to inaugurate the foundations of today's welfare system. The most dramatic New Deal initiatives provided emergency aid and public jobs through programs such as the Works Progress Administration, the Civilian Conservation Corps, and the Federal Emergency Relief Administration. These programs effectively relieved suffering, but they also discriminated against women and minority men by excluding them from jobs and/or offering them inferior work and stipends. Despite the great popularity of these direct federal projects, Roosevelt, whose inclinations were fiscally conservative and antifederal, insisted that they remain temporary and that the states should reassume responsibility for emergency relief.

The Roosevelt administration's permanent welfare legislation was the Social Security Act of 1935. Its centerpiece was two social-insurance programs—old-age insurance and unemployment compensation—which were intended to prevent the need for relief by compensating unemployed men for lost wages, thus also taking care of their dependents. The programs were not means-tested (earmarked for the poor) and in fact benefited the nonpoor much more; and they were not morals-tested (covering only the "deserving") and thus carried no stigma. But these programs excluded the majority of Americans. Most women were not covered, except in an inferior way—as dependents of covered men. Entitlement to the programs derived from employment in certain categories of jobs and again most women and minority men were excluded.

Social Security also contained one modest program, AFDC, intended to help single-mother families not covered by the social-insurance programs. The designers of the program, adopting the mothers'-aid model, envisioned it as small and temporary because they believed that single motherhood would decline as a growing welfare state reduced poverty. Even this program originally excluded most minority and most unmarried single mothers. It was inferior to the social-insurance programs in a number of ways: it was means-tested and morals-tested; its benefits were below the lowest prevailing minimum wages; it was funded primarily by the states through property and sales taxes; and it was not an entitlement but a public charity. As a result, the one program specifically aimed at women and children gradually became stigmatized, scapegoated, and vulnerable to tax-cutting rhetoric, while the programs that benefited primarily prosperous white men and their dependents were considered honorable and politically immune from challenge.

Simultaneously several other welfare programs that New Dealers expected to pass, such as medical insurance and a permanent program of public jobs during times of high unemployment, were blocked. Their absence contributed to worsening inequality in the years since, as those who had good wages got steadily better public and private benefits while those who most needed public help got less. Women were also becoming more stratified among themselves, as a large middle class of employed women began to receive good benefits, separating their interests from those of poor women.

In the 1950s and 1960s, poor minority single mothers began asserting their rights to be included in and decently treated by the welfare system. In 1961 Congress extended AFDC eligibility to two-parent families with unemployed parents. AFDC rolls grew dramatically and recipients formed the National Welfare Rights Organization (NWRO)—an organization that was part of both the civil rights and women's movements and won major legal changes. It had been regular state practice for social workers to conduct surprise, late-night visits to welfare recipients' homes where, without warrants, they searched for extra toothbrushes, men's clothing, or gifts that had not been reported and deducted from a stipend. Using the "substitute father" rule, state welfare administrators regularly held that *any* man in a recipient's life should be considered responsible for the support of the mother's children. Protesting these and other forms of harassment, the NWRO mobilized lawyers, who won considerable legal victories. The Supreme Court held in *Goldberg* v. *Kelly* in 1970 that welfare benefits could not be cut off without a prior hearing, challenging a tradition of arbitrary use of welfare as a weapon to control women. In other decisions the Court defended recipients' right to privacy (outlawing "midnight raids") and to freedom of travel (outlawing residency requirements) and abolished the "man-in-the-house" rule.

As AFDC grew and took in more minority and unmarried mothers, so legislative and administrative attempts to shrink it also grew. For forty years, starting in the 1950s, attempts to "reform" welfare have emphasized fraud and the "undeserving-ness" of recipients and have used primarily punitive measures to try to cut costs rather than to alleviate poverty among mothers and children. AFDC recipients were caught in the middle of a historical contradiction: their program had been designed in the 1930s to keep mothers out of the labor force and its rules penalized wage earning; but as more women became employed, including mothers of young children, the alleged "idleness" of welfare recipients became a target of resentment. Several welfare reform campaigns, starting with Nixon's Family Assistance Plan, tried to induce or coerce recipients into relying exclusively on wage work. These campaigns almost all failed, largely because the low wages of unskilled women did not enable most recipients to support themselves and their children even with full-time work.

Although the NWRO captured the imagination of the left wing of the newly reviving feminist movement in the late 1960s, it rarely gained much support from middle-class or working women, many of whom shared the view that "welfare" recipients were collecting often undeserved charity at the expense of hardworking taxpayers. Thus the two-tier American welfare system—in which the benefits of the more prosperous are considered entitlements and those going to the poor are considered "welfare"—helped shape the values of a predominantly middle-class feminist movement, which has not made welfare rights a priority.

In 1992 Bill Clinton was elected president on a platform that included a promise to "end welfare as we know it." He too used "welfare" to refer only to AFDC and his administration made no threats to entitlement programs that benefited the middle class or the wealthy. The Clinton proposal combined major cutbacks with promises to help single mothers earn through job creation and training. In the 1994 Congressional campaign, the Republicans competed by escalating threats to "welfare" still further: dropping any assumption of obligation to help single mothers and children out of poverty, they fully resurrected the nineteenth-century conservative view that "welfare" created only laziness and dependency. In the summer of 1996, President Clinton signed legislation into law that ended AFDC, repealed the federal guarantee of economic assistance to poor mothers and children, block granted welfare funds to the states, and imposed strict conditions and time limits on welfare eligibility.

Mimi Abramovitz, *Regulating the Lives of Women: Social Welfare Policy from Colonial Times to the Present* (Boston: South End Press, 1988); Linda Gordon, *Pitied but Not Entitled: Single Mothers and the History of Welfare* (New York: Free Press, 1994); Linda Gordon, ed., *Women, the State and Welfare* (Madison: University of Wisconsin Press, 1990); Michael B. Katz, *In the Shadow of the Poorhouse: A Social History of Welfare in America* (New York: Basic Books, 1986).

▪ LINDA GORDON

SEE ALSO Great Society/War on Poverty; Mothers' Pensions; National Welfare Rights Organization; New Deal; Poverty; Social Security Act; Welfare State.

≋ Welfare State

Welfare states—systems of public social provision in all the Western industrial capitalist democracies—modify the play of market forces and family arrangements and/or provide security against risks of income interruption due to retirement, disability or accident, widowhood, single parenthood, unemployment, and sickness. (The term itself was coined only in the 1940s in Britain but is commonly used to refer to all modern social programs.) These interventions vary greatly cross-nationally; states may create greater equality among their citizens but may also reinforce or alter gender norms, market discipline, and racial/ethnic distinctions. Modern social programs give assistance as a right of citizenship, in contrast to the earlier system of public provision, poor relief, which forced able-bodied workers to sell their labor power by conditioning assistance on entering a semipenal workhouse. Mothers were not treated consistently; sometimes they were exempted from paid labor and given relief in their homes under strict supervision, other times forced to work and to institutionalize their children.

Social-scientific research challenging individualistic analyses of poverty, the support of working class, social reform, and women's organizations for nonpunitive assistance to the elderly, widowed, and jobless, and the spread of new views of the importance of mothering for children undermined poor relief. The initial programs of the welfare state were gendered, reflecting the realities of the sexual division of labor, with men as breadwinners and most women as primary caretakers and domestic workers (and sometimes as secondary wage earners).

In the 1910s women's voluntary groups, such as the National Congress of Mothers and the General Federation of Women's Clubs, campaigned for mothers' pensions—cash public assistance to allow widowed mothers to stay home to care for their children. Despite the resistance of private charities, by the 1920s most states had county-optional mothers' pension programs, although inadequate funding meant that not all eligible families received aid. African American widows, despite their poverty, were underrepresented among pensioners, reflecting discrimination and the absence of pension programs in the rural counties where most African Americans lived. Maternalist reformers and others were also instrumental in passing the Sheppard-Towner Act (1921), which gave federal funding to states to establish infant and maternal health programs and initiated protective labor legislation for women workers (e.g., hours laws, minimum-wage statutes and safety legislation). Protections for male workers such as old-age pensions or health insurance were unsuccessful, despite the backing of the American Association of Labor Legislation, trade unions, and some politicians; only workmen's compensation legislation, requiring employers to insure their workers against industrial accidents, was passed in most states. Private "welfare capitalism"—corporations offering programs for their employees—was celebrated instead. The Sheppard-Towner program, despite its successes, was allowed to lapse.

The Great Depression ushered in a political crisis that gave new openings for policy reform in the 1930s. The Social Security Act, the "charter legislation" for the current U.S. version of the welfare state, was passed in 1935, backed by President Franklin Roosevelt, Democratic politicians, the organized elderly, and unions. Women's political mobilization was at an ebb. Indeed, women's issues were not prominent on the political agenda, despite participation of women social scientists and officials in the Committee on Economic Security, headed by Labor Secretary Frances Perkins, that drafted the Social Security Act. Rather, concern focused on the plight of unemployed and forcibly retired wage earners. The Social Security Act established contributory social insurance programs against the risks of income loss due to retirement and unemployment for wage earners, disproportionately white men, as well as giving federal funding to state-level, non-contributory old-age assistance programs (OAA) and to the mothers' pensions programs, renamed Aid to Dependent Children (ADC). Conservative and southern political forces excluded agricultural and domestic workers—meaning most African Americans and Latinas/Latinos—from social insurance coverage and permitted states to set benefit levels and eligibility requirements for OAA and ADC. In the 1939 amendments to the Social Security Act, the actuarially strict contributory old-age insurance program was fundamentally altered by the addition of dependents' and survivors' benefits for spouses and widows of covered wage earners, leaving only divorced, deserted, and never-married mothers dependent on ADC. Health coverage was considered but excluded from the bill due to fears that doctors' opposition would scuttle the entire package. Labor standards legislation was extended to all workers with the passage of the Fair Labor Standards Act in 1938.

As in the earlier period, these social programs assumed a traditional sexual division of labor, with women responsible for caretaking and domestic work. Yet views of women's work were racialized—while white women were expected to stay at home to care for their children, some state-level officials, particularly in the South, enforced paid work on Black single mothers.

The social security approach of the New Dealers was premised on government economic planning and the provision of public jobs to deal with unemployment, but both were ended after World War II. Through the 1950s and early 1960s privately provided welfare in the form of fringe benefits was increasingly offered to many wage earners in the primary labor market, leaving non-workers and those outside the primary labor market with inferior coverage. When the buoyant economic conditions of the post–World War II era vanished after the 1960s, the combined lack of public employment and planning capacities and employment-dependent coverage impeded antipoverty efforts.

The next burst of activity related to the welfare state was initiated with President Lyndon Johnson's "War on Poverty" of the 1960s, encompassing efforts (e.g., job training) to help those left behind by the expanding economy, especially African American, Latino, and poor rural white male breadwinners. A series of political and legal challenges, notably by the National Welfare Rights Organization, also led to changes in AFDC. AFDC assumed more the character of an income-tested entitlement, which could be combined with paid work. Old-age provision became nearly universal, and old-age poverty was reduced by legislated benefit increases and the replacement of sometimes-discriminatory state old-age pensions by the fully federal Supplemental Security Income program in 1972. The expansion of the U.S. welfare state led to historically low poverty levels in the late 1970s.

The U.S. welfare state was made formally gender-neutral in the 1960s and 1970s, but women who do not have the typical male worker's pattern of uninterrupted, full-time work are still at greater risk of poverty if single or widowed. Civil rights laws invalidated protective legislation and discriminatory hiring practices for women only. But labor market and family "failures" are still covered by different programs. Wage earners are treated differently from those who do primarily unpaid domestic work; thus, men's and women's different locations within the labor force and the household division of labor mean they are not treated equivalently.

Reforms that would have brought welfare provision to larger segments of the population were unsuccessful. Jobs and training programs never went beyond the hard-core unemployed; a Nixon administration proposal to replace AFDC with a national Negative Income Tax for all the working poor was scuttled when experiments correlated payments with increased marital breakups and reduced work effort. Universal medical insurance proposals failed; instead, in 1965 health coverage was provided for the elderly and the very poor (Medicare and Medicaid).

The division among groups of single mothers resulting from the 1939 amendments proved especially significant for the racial and ethnic composition of different social programs in the wake of social policy changes of the 1960s and 1970s. Widows covered under social security, disproportionately white, benefited from the expansion of survivors' insurance. As eligibility barriers to AFDC fell, increasing proportions of the single mothers depending on AFDC were African American and Latina due to demographic differences and their greater vulnerability to poverty. "Welfare" (i.e., AFDC) became a racialized term at just the historic conjuncture when women of color were able to claim the right to domestic motherhood through AFDC.

Thus, rather than a coherent system of protection affording welfare for all citizens, Americans were left with a "two-tier," residual system—"welfare" for the poorest single mothers and their children, largely people of color, and "social security" for most wage earners and their families. Universal programs for working-aged people and their children—health insurance, family allowances, job training, or child care—are lacking, and U.S. citizens tend to rely on private, market-based forms of welfare provision. The residualism of U.S. public provision, except for that targeted toward the elderly, and the racialized character of AFDC, help to explain the political support for welfare cutbacks in the 1980s and 1990s and the political isolation of welfare recipients.

Increasingly stringent requirements for work on the part of single-parent welfare recipients and more rigorous attempts to collect child support from noncustodial parents of children on welfare (mostly fathers) also date from the 1960s; but they were stepped up considerably under the Reagan and Bush administrations. The 1988 Family Support Act, passed with bipartisan support, required all AFDC parents with children three years of age and above (one or above at state option) to work or undergo training. In the mid-1990s, almost all proposed changes to welfare would limit recipients to a fixed, lifetime term of welfare eligibility. Enacted in 1996, these and other changes will further limit full-time caregiving as an option for poor mothers. The United States, then, is moving in the direction of making welfare more similar to unemployment insurance—a short-term benefit to help claimants "get on their feet" after the crisis of job loss, divorce or birth of a child outside of marriage, but then requiring paid work, perhaps with some support services. The policy pendulum has swung 180 degrees from the intentions expressed in the Social Security Act—women are to be treated as workers rather than as mothers.

        ▪ ANN SHOLA ORLOFF

SEE ALSO Fair Labor Standards Act; Great Society/ War on Poverty; New Deal; Sheppard-Towner Maternity and Infancy Protection Act; Social Security Act; Welfare and Public Relief.

≋ Western Women

W omen and their menfolk have inhabited places we now think of as western for tens of thousands of years. When Europeans invaded what became the West, the women who descended from these first peoples lived in a variety of cultural, spiritual, and natural worlds, from Arctic Alaska and the coastal Northwest, to the Great Plains and desert Southwest, to the lush Hawaiian islands. Native women's relations with European newcomers depended on the historical moment of contact, which ranged from the sixteenth to the eighteenth century, and the provenance and purposes of the colonizers, who were Spanish, French, English, and Russian. Relations were shaped too by the decisions Native women and men made as the European presence forced changes in subsis-

Polly Bemis, born in China in 1853, became a highly respected homesteader in Warrens, Idaho.

tence—for example, as a decline in animal populations altered the relative importance of women's gathering or farming and men's hunting; or as European introductions, such as horses or iron kettles, engendered new cultural practices. Also key was the disproportionate number of men among the newcomers, which brought both intermarriage between Native women and European men and sexual violence against Native women. Then, too, as European women arrived in western places, Native wives and their mixed-blood offspring often lost status. But separate Métis and Mestizo communities also took root.

In the nineteenth century the West emerged as an identifiable region when the United States took title to the former hinterlands of European empires. Native claims to use of the land still existed, and multiracial and mixed-blood communities flourished too. But territorial aggrandizement spelled an unprecedented migration of Euro-Americans, as easterners came to terms with industrialization and the commercialization of agriculture. Women and men sold farms, loaded wagons, and headed to Oregon; merchants set out

to profit from the Santa Fe trade; young men answered the call of gold and silver that beckoned them to the Sierra Nevada or Rocky Mountains or Klondike; young women followed these men—or those who herded cattle on the plains—hoping to earn their keep selling domestic or sexual services in western boomtowns.

Some westering women followed different paths: In the 1830s, for example, the U.S. government forced southeastern peoples such as Choctaws and Cherokees to resettle in present-day Oklahoma as part of a policy of removing Indians from the East to the West. This policy was forsaken when white westward movement by the 1860s precipitated Native resistance and, in turn, a new practice of restricting Native peoples to reservations. White women who joined the Church of Jesus Christ of Latter-Day Saints (the Mormons) back east faced persecution; they followed their leaders west in the 1840s to present-day Utah. There, some engaged in the church-sanctioned practice of plural marriage.

All of these newcomers wrought changes in the lives of women resident in the West. Spanish-

Mexican women in New Mexican villages, for example, took on new responsibilities as men entered a wage economy, while some in Santa Fe decided to profit from Anglo intruders by working in saloons or dance halls. In California, Miwok women assimilated gold digging into their customary gathering activities, thereby enabling Indians to purchase food as miners trampled plants and killed off game.

New women became westerners as well; Chinese women, for instance, sailed east to the West. A few were married to merchants, but most, like many white women migrants, did sex work in heavily male communities. In 1875 the U.S. government all but ended the immigration of Chinese women with passage of the Page Law, which targeted prostitutes. The moral panic that occasioned its passage coincided with an influx of middle-class white women to the West, as railroads reached the Pacific and cities and towns proliferated.

This suggests a central theme of western women's history: that white women, though subjugated to white men, were nonetheless linchpins in establishing racial and economic dominance in the West. They did this by supplanting with "respectable" gatherings popular recreations that catered to men and provided work for polyglot women; by casting themselves as moral guardians of women led astray by western men (prostitutes and plural wives, for example); by constricting the meaning of "woman" to the habits and values that ruled their own lives.

Not all white women benefited equally from this dominance, and class privilege was not unique to Euro-Americans. As mining industrialized, for example, multiethnic working-class communities emerged in western gold, silver, and copper towns. White women in these communities enjoyed fewer perquisites than their affluent sisters, and they often joined their menfolk in contesting the power of employers over working people. Nonetheless, given western demographic diversity and interlocking ideas about white supremacy, sexual propriety, and female morality, race privilege was readily available to white women who upheld norms of chastity outside of marriage and fidelity within. Notions of "respectability" involved with class meanings also structured the all-Black towns that emerged on the Great Plains, as African Americans fled the post–Reconstruction South. But, as elsewhere in Black communities, the western emphasis on morality and propriety emerged from a southern context in which white men forced sex on Black women with impunity.

At the turn of the century, ideas about women and women's habits were changing: mothers had fewer children, more women demanded a voice in politics, and more worked outside their homes. It was in the West that women first won full voting rights; the trend began in Wyoming Territory in 1869, and by 1914 almost all far western states plus Kansas had granted women suffrage (no eastern state had done so). And since the West was becoming the most urban of U.S. regions, and women's job opportunities expanded most quickly in cities, it appears that national trends in women's employment got a strong western regional push. Urbanization and expansion of the female labor force offered unmarried women the chance to live apart from conventional families. Meanwhile, sexual desire between women entered the vocabulary of everyday life, and people began to think of such desire and its practices as constituting a lesbian identity. By midcentury recognizable lesbian communities thrived in cities such as Denver, Los Angeles, and San Francisco.

Western urbanization was linked to a larger transformation of the regional economy from one dominated by extractive and agricultural pursuits to one in which manufacturing gained a foothold, while the service sector grew exponentially. Farming itself industrialized, most notably in California, where the shift from wheat to fruit and vegetable growing also gave rise to large-scale food processing ventures. If women's work, often understood as reproductive in nature, had been largely invisible in the agricultural economy that glorified men's productive activity, in the new economic order it was harder to obscure the labor of women. And by midcentury, the number and kinds of women who lived in the West had multiplied.

Economic change drew unprecedented numbers of women to the West from around the globe and elsewhere in the United States and encouraged migration within the region too. Mexican, Japanese, and Filipino immigration all exploded in the early twentieth century, and some Koreans and South Asians arrived as well. California was the destination of disproportionate numbers of these peoples. But many new Asian immigrants traveled first to work on Hawaiian plantations, while some moved to the Pacific Northwest or Alaska. And many Mexicans crossed the border into Texas or other southwestern states. What characterized the labor of these western women of color—whether as field hands or cannery workers or domestics in the homes of affluent white women—were low wages, high turnover, and seasonality with attendant migration. What characterized their lives at home and at work was participation in new ethnic communities as family members, labor activists, and community organizers.

World War II introduced another shift as the federal government poured capital into the West and built a manufacturing base there. For the first time since Blacks had migrated to the Great Plains, large numbers of African American women moved west, especially to far western cities where defense industries burgeoned. Native Americans, too, left reservations to work in urban factories, part of a larger trend of wartime rural to urban migration. While Japanese American women and their families were interned in remote western camps by a hysterical U.S. government, other women in the region were allowed—indeed, encouraged—to break with a past of labor segmentation by sex for the duration of the war. Many left or lost traditionally male jobs when the troops returned, but patterns of high female labor-force participation in the West, as elsewhere, continued. Women increasingly found work in the expanding service sector.

Since World War II this trend has accelerated, as suburbanization and then the growth of multi-centered, postsuburban metropolises have altered the landscape of western women's lives. The late twentieth century has also seen heightened consciousness of how powerful gender, race, class, and sexuality are in defining women's life chances. Such consciousness is not a distinctly western phenomenon—indeed, much inspiration came from the southern movement for Black civil rights. The Chicano and Asian American movements began in the West, with strong student contingents in the universities, where Third World strikes could bring academic business to a halt. Women have been active participants, some advancing separate women's agendas that have challenged male domination in ethnic movements for social change and white domination in the concurrent resurgence of feminism. Similarly, much of the renaissance in Native American activism occurred in the West, both on and off the reservations. Native women have been central to this activism, and many also have worked in tribally based women's organizations or pan-Indian women's groups.

Perhaps the best introduction to this new western landscape—a landscape created by conquest, capitalism, migration, accommodation, and resistance—can be found in the women's literature that has blossomed in the late twentieth century. We are blessed by many such writers, including Betty Louise Bell, Mary Clearman Blew, Octavia Butler, Ana Castillo, Sandra Cisneros, Louise Erdrich, Gretel Ehrlich, Alicia Gaspar de Alba, Teresa Jordan, Cynthia Kadohata, Maxine Hong Kingston, Valerie Miner, Cherríe Moraga, Fae Myenne Ng, Leslie Marmon Silko, and Amy Tan—westerners all.

▪ SUSAN LEE JOHNSON

≋ Whiteness

Whiteness emerged in the seventeenth century in the British colonies as a common identity across class lines among Europeans in opposition to African slaves and Native Americans. The first shipment of "negars" to the British colonies debarked in Virginia in 1619, only twelve years after the first settlement at Jamestown. By 1640 Africans were being subjected to lifetime servitude and inherited slave status, the twin characteristics of slavery and both very different from the indentured servitude of Europeans and the "tendency toward liberty" of English common law. Discriminatory laws and practices against Africans accompanied the consolidation of chattel slavery. By 1671 the British began encouraging the naturalization of Scots, Welsh, and Irish to enjoy the "liberties, privileges, immunities" of natural-born Englishmen. In 1676 Bacon's Rebellion in Virginia showed the danger of cross-racial alliances when indentured and unemployed European workers joined slaves in an uprising against the planter aristocracy. Historian Winthrop Jordan commented, "From the initially most common term *Christian*, at midcentury there was a marked drift toward *English* and *free*. After about 1680, taking the colonies as a whole, a new term appeared—*white*."

The emergence of the term white for the various hues of European pigmentation was shaped, probably, by the existing dichotomy between light and dark in Elizabethan culture, which led the English (one of the most light-skinned peoples) to see Africans (one of the darkest-skinned peoples) as both "Black" and "heathen" and to link their physical appearance with barbarity, animalistic behavior, and the devil. Color and culture were dangerously conflated. The decision to allow African slaves to become Christian (the Virginia legislature decided in 1670s that "the conferring of baptism doth not alter the condition of the person as to his bondage or freedome") removed the "heathen" part of the equation, so that biology came to stand for culture. Ironically, miscegenation (often through the rape of Black slave women by white masters) was lightening skin pigment below the color line. In the British colonies, policy regarding the racial identity of the offspring of interracial unions was much more rigid than the Spanish policy, categorizing anyone with any African parentage as belonging to the subordinated race to ensure property rights of slaveholders, a practice historian Marvin Harris calls the "law of hypodescent."

The expansion of democracy for Europeans would continue to occur at periods of contraction of freedom for people of color. White identity became a fluid concept which, over the centuries, would allow various European nationalities access to relative privilege, with the ultimate privilege and most secure whiteness reserved for Anglo-Saxon Protestants. The administration of Andrew Jackson (1828–36) brought a frontiersman into the White House, displacing the Virginia aristocracy that had ruled during previous presidencies. Constitutional changes in a number of states widened suffrage, in some cases giving the vote to all adult white males. These votes brought Jackson to the White House. Jackson, who had risen to prominence in the Indian Wars of the Southeast, removed the five southern tribes to the Midwest, in spite of the fact that Supreme Court Chief Justice John Marshall found the removal unconstitutional. The Indian removals, which destroyed one-quarter of the Cherokee tribe, were actually conceptualized by Jefferson and then extended and carried out by Jackson. There were great debates about whether the "redskins" were human and whether they had souls.

After the Civil War new waves of immigrants from eastern Europe entered a work force during the Industrial Revolution that suddenly skewed the distribution of wealth. These immigrants were often viewed as different "races" from Northern Europeans; however, they eventually battled their way into the white working class through a burgeoning union movement in the twentieth century.

By the nineteenth century, ideologies of white supremacy had evolved to justify several centuries of white supremacist practice. Opposition to the slave trade at the end of the seventeenth century prompted European and United States scientists to consolidate the theory of race, drawing on anthropology and evolution. In 1843 the English Ethnological Society grew out of the need to understand "the whole mental condition of the savage . . . so different from ours" in the various domains of the British Empire. Charles Darwin did not himself assign superiority to particular traits or place races in positions on the evolutionary scale, but his followers did. They used the doctrine of natural selection or survival of the fittest to explain the superiority of the conquering European (in the United States read "white") culture. Various tests were devised to classify humanity into racial groups in a highly subjective process that always placed the European/white person in a superior position and in the United States justified the decimation of indigenous people, the enslavement of Africans, the appropriation of Mexican territory in the Southwest, and the use of Asians, African Americans, and Latinas/Latinos as a superexploited class. The belief that European cultures were more evolved also undergirded U.S. imperialism, as President McKinley explained in his decision to keep the Philippines after the Spanish-American War: "They were unfit for self-government. . . . There was nothing left for us to do but take them all."

The same hierarchy locked women into seemingly biologically determined roles: as breeders and mothers, as guardians of public morality, and as sexually determined beings (virgins or whores). Men of color were often also viciously sexualized (leading, among other things, to an epidemic of lynching in the South), and white women (feminists included) often identified politically and emotionally with white power. Like the "cult of true womanhood," which worked to draw the line around who was a "real woman," race ideology created a highly elastic cult of "true whiteness," both of these seemingly biological categories drawing power in part from their volatility and their ability to exclude.

■ MAB SEGREST

SEE ALSO Colorism; Miscegenation; Racism.

≋ Wicca

Wicca is the term commonly used to describe several different traditions of contemporary Paganism—an earth-centered religion that reveres nature; celebrates seasonal and lunar cycles; and worships a goddess, or many goddesses, or sometimes a goddess *and* a god. Although people involved in Wicca often call themselves witches, their religion has nothing to do with the historical accounts of witchcraft during the fourteenth through seventeenth centuries. It also has nothing in common with the popular notions of witches in film or fiction, nor does it relate to Satanism.

The modern Wiccan movement began in England in the 1920s and 1930s, inspired by the writings of folklorists, including Margaret Murray and Gerald Gardner, who described Wicca as the "old religion," the pre-Christian religion of Europe. Contemporary practitioners of Wicca draw on the ancient traditions of Europe and the rest of the world: herbalism, midwifery, and the healing arts. Within Wicca, the many different traditions include those from the Celtic, Italian, Greek, and Norse cultures.

Beginning in the 1970s many women in the United States became interested in Wicca and other outgrowths of women's spirituality associated with the feminist movement. Searching through history, anthropology, archaeology, and myth, women found evidence of goddesses, witches, and matrilineal societies to counter patriarchal ideas and connect women to the sacred. Wicca was attractive not only because its primary deity was a goddess but also because men and women had equal leadership roles. Although the witch was often depicted as ugly and feared, she was a powerful woman, skilled in folk wisdom, and at home with nature and herself. She defined her own reality, clear that her reality existed outside the predominantly male scientific and medical establishments.

Wicca in the United States is a decentralized religion; each group is autonomous. Wiccans worship in small groups, often in people's homes or in an outdoor environment. They also worship on the date of a full or new moon and during eight seasonal festivals. The basic tenets of Wicca include a reverence for nature and ecological principles and a code of ethics known as the Wiccan Rede: "An ye harm none, do what ye will."

> • MARGOT ADLER

SEE ALSO Religion.

≋ Witchcraft

SEE Salem Witchcraft Trials; Witchcraft on the Spanish-Mexican Borderlands.

≋ Witchcraft on the Spanish-Mexican Borderlands

From the mid–sixteenth to the mid–nineteenth century, *brujería* (witchcraft) and *hechicería* (sorcery) on the Spanish-Mexican borderlands were defined as heresy and criminal acts. As throughout Christendom, individuals accused of witchcraft on the borderlands were mainly women. Rooted in the religious, political, and gender history of medieval and early-modern Spain, the gendering and the criminalization of witchcraft were fixed at the end of the Middle Ages. During the late fifteenth century, Roman Catholicism and the new Spanish nation-state initiated a Christian order and a nationalism rooted in the reinscription of misogyny and the violent extirpation of the religious, political, racial, linguistic, and cultural "other," specifically Jews and Muslims, from the body politic.

To accomplish this, the church and state initiated the Inquisition (1478), a terrifying political institution designed to "cleanse" Spain of heretical non-Christian beliefs and practices. While targeting Judaism and Islam, the Inquisition also sought to abolish all residual "paganism," especially witchcraft and sorcery. In 1487 two Dominican Inquisitors published *Malleus Maleficarum*, the misogynist theological treatise that laid the theoretical and ideological foundation for criminalizing and persecuting witchcraft. Calling witchcraft a "vast and vile conspiracy against the Faith, a treason against God, and the most horrible of all crimes deserving the most exemplary punishment," this work linked the *maleficium* of popular sorcery with heresy through the agency of the Christian concept of the Devil. It also placed the blame for sorcery on women and created the popular view of the witch as a woman. Witchcraft was subsequently sexualized and eroticized, and women who practiced it were represented as cannibalistic child murderesses.

Some of these events occurred during the Counter Reformation, a period in which church and state further inscribed misogyny by centering on women's powers to lead men's souls to hell and by condemning all women as inherently dangerous to men. Accordingly, men's salvation depended upon the control of women—in particular, control of the female body, of women's sexuality. The gender ideology that required control of women on the basis of their sex was thus conceptualized and institutionalized. It was fixed at the time when the Spanish Inquisition was ridding the nation of Jews, Muslims, and all other "heretics" and when European powers were imposing colonial hegemonies, including enslavement, on the religious, racial, cultural, and linguistic "other"—the non-Christian peoples of the Americas and Africa.

While all women on the Spanish-Mexican borderlands were suspect of being witches on the basis of gender, women of colonized groups were suspect on multiple grounds. Amerindian women, African-origin women, and racially mixed women, whether Indo-mestizas or Afro-mestizas, were automatically suspect by virtue of being female, of deriving from non-Christian religions and cultures, and of being colonized or enslaved peoples. In the Christian imperialist gaze, non-Christian women and their mestiza daughters were thereby sexualized, racialized, and demonized.

With few exceptions, women charged with witchcraft between 1525 and 1817 in Mexico were Black or mulatta and women accused of witchcraft on the borderlands were Mexican Indian, Indian, mestiza, or mulatta. The borderlands' denunciations focused on "sexualized magic" such as using women's menstrual blood, wash water, pubic hair, and ensorcelled food to attract, tame, or tie men into submission, or, sometimes, to harm or kill a physically abusive, often unfaithful husband or lover.

In this way women used "magical" power to resist gender oppression and subvert the male order. Amerindian women who participated in rebellions and resistance movements against Spanish colonial oppression were invariably accused of witchcraft, sorcery, or diabolism. By attributing Amerindian women's visible and active rebellion to witchcraft or other supernatural phenomena, their Spanish-Mexican captors effectively dismissed women's agency and their conscious, political action, which, in addition to armed rebellion, included planning strategy, poisoning priests, and serving as decoys. From the mid–sixteenth to the mid–nineteenth century on the Spanish-Mexican borderlands, the criminalization of witchcraft can best be understood within the context of the gendered, sexualized, and racialized ideologies, politics, and policies of colonialism.

Ruth Behar, "Sexual Witchcraft, Colonialism, and Women's Power: Views from the Mexican Inquisition," in *Sexuality and Marriage in Colonial Latin America*, edited by Asunción Lavrín, 178–206. (Lincoln and London: University of Nebraska Press, 1989); María Helena Sánchez-Ortega, "Woman as a Source of 'Evil' in Counter-Reformation Spain," in *Hispanic Issues: Culture and Control in Counter Reformation Spain*, edited by Anne J. Cruz and Mary Elizabeth Perry, 196–215. Vol. 7 (Minneapolis and Oxford: University of Minnesota Press, 1992); Marc Simmons, *Witchcraft in the Southwest: Spanish and Indian Supernaturalism on the Rio Grande* (Lincoln and London: University of Nebraska Press, 1980).

■ ANTONIA I. CASTAÑEDA

≋ Womanism

Womanist and *womanism* are culture-specific and poetic synonyms for *Black feminist* and *Black feminism*. Though *womanism* appears in the *Oxford English Dictionary* as a nineteenth-century term for "advocacy of or enthusiasm for the rights, achievements etc. of women"—and *womanist* as a synonym for "womanizer"—their current U.S. usage has been redefined by Alice Walker, African American novelist, poet, essayist, and activist. In her 1983 collection of essays, *In Search of Our Mothers' Gardens: Womanist Prose*, she traced the populist origin of these terms to such usage as "the black folk expression of mothers to female children, 'You acting womanish,' i.e., like a woman. Usually referring to outrageous, audacious, courageous or *willful* behavior . . . as in: 'Mama, I'm walking to Canada and I'm taking you and a bunch of other slaves with me.' Reply: 'It wouldn't be the first time.'"

As Walker explained to the *New York Times Magazine* in 1984: "I don't choose womanism because it is 'better' than feminism . . . Since womanism *means* black feminism, this would be a nonsensical distinction. I choose it because I prefer the sound, the feel, the fit of it; because I cherish the spirit of the women (like Sojourner) the word calls to mind, and because I share the old ethnic-American habit of offering society a new word when the old word it is using fails to describe behavior and change that only a new word can help it more fully see." Walker added in an interview for this article, "I dislike having to add a color in order to become visible, as in *black feminist*. *Womanism* gives us a word of our own."

Welcomed by some for having a stronger sound because the word's root is not shared with *feminine*—as Walker put it in 1983, "Womanist is to feminist as purple to lavender"—womanist and womanism bring a racialized and often class-located experience to the gendered experience suggested by feminism. These terms have helped give visibility to the experience of African American women and other women of color who have always been in the forefront of movements against sexual and racial caste systems yet have often been marginalized in history texts, the media, and feminist movements led by white feminists or civil rights movements led by men of color. Thus, womanism reflects a link with a history that includes African cultural heritage, enslavement in the United States, and a kinship with other women, especially women of color. As Walker told the *Times*, "Feminism (all colors) definitely teaches women they are capable, one reason for its universal appeal. In addition to this, womanist (i.e. black feminist) tradition *assumes*, because of our experiences during slavery, that black women *are* capable." Her 1983 definition also included any "feminist of color . . . *Also:* A woman who loves other women, sexually and/or nonsexually. Appreciates and prefers women's culture, women's emotional flexibility (values tears as natural counterbalance of laughter), and women's

strength. Sometimes loves individual men, sexually and/or nonsexually. Committed to survival and wholeness of entire people, male *and* female. Not a separatist, except periodically, for health. Traditionally universalist . . . Loves music. Loves dance. Loves the moon. *Loves* the Spirit. Loves love and food and roundness. Loves struggle. *Loves* the Folk. Loves herself. *Regardless.*"

By the late 1980s, the terms *womanist* and *womanism* had been adopted in many Women's Studies and Black Studies courses as well as by many of Walker's readers. In addition to identifying as womanists, for example, some historians felt better described as womanist historians, religious scholars called themselves womanist theologians, activists felt more included and inclusive by talking about womanist theory, and critics traced a womanist creative tradition that extended from quilts made by anonymous Black women during slavery to modern films such as *Daughters of the Dust*; from the timeless patterns of Ndebele women's wall paintings to the timely references in Emma Amos's paintings. Perhaps the most thoughtful extensions of Walker's definition have taken place among womanist theologians who do not offer *Black feminist* or *feminist of color* as synonyms but prefer *womanist* to stand alone, describing a woman of African descent, strong in her faith (not necessarily Christian) and concerned about the multiply oppressive impact of race, class, and gender.

Unlike *feminist* and *profeminist*, however, the definitions of womanism and womanist rarely included men who were also working for equality: thus some feminists, male and female, were still reluctant to use them. Others preferred *Black feminism* because retaining the adjective made racial experience visible, because the noun was better understood, or because failing to use *feminism* might have been seen as deserting its controversies; for instance, the notion that feminism is synonymous with lesbianism.

By 1993, however, the new usage of these terms was wide enough to be included in *The American*

Heritage Dictionary, which defined *womanist* as: "Having or expressing a belief in or respect for women and their talents and abilities beyond the boundaries of race and class; exhibiting a feminism that is inclusive esp. of Black American culture." As Alice Walker made clear, *womanist* and *womanism* were not popularized to narrow or criticize existing terms, but to shed light on women's experience by increasing the number and richness of words describing it.

- GLORIA STEINEM
  and DIANA L. HAYES

SEE ALSO Feminism, Black.

≋ Woman's Christian Temperance Union

O rganized in 1873–74, the Woman's Christian Temperance Union (WCTU) quickly became the largest U.S. women's organization in the nineteenth century. The WCTU built on social traditions of Protestant women's activism that had developed between 1830 and 1860. The union achieved national scope, appealing to both white and African American women, and offering a wide range of activities. When Frances Willard was elected president in 1879, the WCTU shifted its focus from closing saloons to an ambitious and multifaceted campaign, "Do Everything." The union endorsed woman suffrage when it was still considered radical.

By 1896 the WCTU served as an umbrella organization for social activism for temperance as well as for prison reform, public health, suffrage, and improved working conditions for wage-earning women. The strength of the union rested on its decentralized practice of allowing locals to select which departments their members would pursue. Through lobbying and petitioning, the WCTU

gave numerous middle-class, native-born women the opportunity to participate in U.S. civic and political life long before the passage of the 1920 woman suffrage amendment to the Constitution. By 1900 the WCTU's heyday had passed.

The WCTU reflected racial and class boundaries of contemporary society. Black women participated actively but usually within their own locals, partly because they focused on "the Negro question," and partly because they were not welcome in most white locals. Similarly, WCTU activists were more interested in "saving" immigrant communities from their foreign ways than in empowering immigrant women. The white, Protestant, middle-class traditions that originally led WCTU members into activism also limited their ability to form coalitions with Black, working-class, or immigrant women.

- KATHRYN KISH SKLAR

SEE ALSO Prohibition and Temperance.

≋ Women's Bureau

T he U.S. Women's Bureau, established in 1920, remains the only federal agency specifically devoted to the advancement of women workers. Created as a temporary agency during World War I, the bureau developed the first U.S. standards for the employment of women workers. After the war, women's organizations successfully lobbied Congress to establish the bureau permanently. Mary Anderson, a member of the Chicago boot and shoe union and a founder of the Chicago Women's Trade Union League, was the first director. Her long term of leadership (1920–45) cemented the bureau's ties to (white) middle-class women's organizations and (white) working-class women in the trade unions and stamped it with a firm commitment to "maternalist" ideas about women workers.

The Women's Bureau was a relatively small, ineffective agency during its first forty years. Anderson's weak leadership, the battle among women reformers over the ERA, and the inhospitable climate for a federal labor agency during the 1920s consigned it to the margins of the federal government. During the New Deal era and World War II, the bureau provided data on women workers to the National Recovery Administration and the National War Labor Board and lobbied ceaselessly for more equitable treatment of women workers. But the bureau was unable to benefit permanently from the great expansion of governmental authority that took place at this time. The rationale for an agency devoted specifically to women workers seemed to disappear when the Supreme Court upheld labor legislation for men as well as women. From 1937 on, the Women's Bureau was bypassed, as federal authority over employment was placed in new agencies responsible for both male and female workers.

The Women's Bureau remained active during the postwar years. Hoping to build on wartime regulations, the bureau campaigned unsuccessfully for congressional enactment of an equal pay law. The bureau also led the campaign within the federal government to oppose the Equal Rights Amendment, which the bureau believed would jeopardize the legal status of the special labor legislation passed for women in the early twentieth century. Even after the Supreme Court upheld the Fair Labor Standards Act in 1941, establishing the legality of wage and hours laws for men and women, the bureau maintained that women workers needed additional legal protection. The Women's Bureau did not drop its opposition to the ERA until the 1970s.

The bureau's height of influence occurred during the Kennedy administration. Under the leadership of Esther Peterson, a savvy former lobbyist for the American Federation of Labor and the Congress of Industrial Organizations (AFL-CIO), the bureau achieved many of its long-standing goals. The Women's Bureau finally convinced Congress to approve the Equal Pay Act in 1963. It also persuaded Kennedy to establish the President's Commission on the Status of Women (1961–63), the first national committee to review the position of women in U.S. society. Though the bureau never again achieved a similar degree of influence, it has continued to be an important voice for women workers within the federal government.

▪ HELENE SILVERBERG

SEE ALSO Commissions on the Status of Women; Equal Pay Act.

≣ Women's Colleges

Throughout the nineteenth century, a fierce debate raged concerning the wisdom of allowing women to attend colleges and universities. Proponents argued that women were the intellectual equals of men and their cultural superiors, and that the fulfillment of women's duties as mothers and elementary school teachers necessitated the best education available. Those opposed maintained that higher education would "unsex" women, rendering them physically and emotionally unfit for traditional roles.

In the midst of these arguments, women gradually gained access to advanced secondary and higher education, sometimes in coeducational schools, but also in a nationwide network of single-sex institutions, beginning in the 1830s and 1840s with the creation of women's seminaries, academies, and normal schools. The first women's colleges were Georgia Female College (1839) and Mary Sharp College in Tennessee (1851). In the post–Civil War era, pressure from tax-paying parents who wanted their daughters to have a means of self-support led to the admission of women to newly created state universities in the West and the Midwest. In the South and the East, neither the well-established prestigious men's colleges nor the state universities would ac-

Spelman Seminary students, 1893. The varied ages of the students and the pregnant student (front) reflect the institution's wide appeal.

cept women students. In 1870 only one-third of existing colleges and universities were coeducational. Thus, between the 1860s and the 1930s, many more women's colleges were founded by different individuals and organizations.

New women's colleges included the institutions of the "women's Ivy League" or the "Seven Sister" schools—Barnard (a coordinate college with Columbia), Bryn Mawr, Mt. Holyoke, Radcliffe (the women's college of Harvard), Smith, Vassar, and Wellesley. Six of the Seven Sisters were founded either by individual philanthropists (Matthew Vassar, Sophia Smith, Wellesley's Henry Durant) or by groups of wealthy and influential women determined to provide high-quality education for girls (Barnard, Radcliffe, Bryn Mawr). In the South, individual philanthropy and church support led to the establishment of Goucher (the Women's College of Baltimore), Sophie Newcomb (the women's college of Tulane University), and Agnes Scott, among others. Catholic orders of sisters founded nineteen women's colleges between 1900 and 1930; many more followed. White women missionaries established Spelman Seminary for African American girls and women in 1881, and it became a college in 1923. Other historically Black institutions—Bennett, Barber-Scotia, and Huston-Tillotson—have been women's colleges at various times.

The demographic features of women's colleges remained relatively constant until the 1970s. Some, particularly the Catholic institutions, had a diverse student population, but most restricted their admissions to accept only those who could pay their own way. However, most excluded or restricted nonwhites and Jews.

Women's colleges have always prided themselves on offering an education fully as rigorous as that provided by the best men's colleges, but they never slavishly reproduced the Amherst, Notre Dame, or Morehouse curricula. They pioneered in offering laboratory science and fine-arts courses; some also offered but did not require vocational subjects. Others have established special opportunities for "returning" older students, and programs (e.g., the Bunting Institute at Radcliffe) designed to encourage women scholars and professionals. A few, such as Mt. Holyoke, Bryn Mawr, and Smith, offer graduate work. Motivated by the need to demonstrate their respectability, women's colleges placed numerous social restrictions on their students and many did not support political activities such as the feminist or civil rights movements. Women's studies programs originated at coeducational institutions and were not initially welcomed by women's colleges.

Nevertheless, women's colleges were hardly conservative institutions. They hired women scholars who encouraged their students to attend graduate school and enter the professions. The student culture at women's colleges was assertive and socially progressive. Many alumnae became career women, participated in politics, remained single, had smaller families, and in other ways defied middle-class feminine norms. Recognizing this, the public has periodically attacked women's colleges for producing spinsters (1890–1920), encouraging lesbian relationships (1920s and 1970–90), or educating women to be discontent with domesticity (1930–60).

Since 1960 women's colleges have seemed anachronistic to many in an era when even Harvard and West Point are co-ed. Their numbers dropped rapidly—from 233 in 1960 to 90 in 1986. In 1960, 10 percent of women college students attended single-sex institutions; by 1986 less than 2 percent did. And yet recent social science research demonstrates that alumnae of women's colleges, even those from less prestigious and wealthy institutions, include a greater percentage of "achievers," especially in nontraditional fields, than do graduates of coeducational schools, possibly because of mentoring and the supportive environment. Although it seems unlikely that new women's colleges will be established, it seems equally unlikely (as well as undesirable) that the remaining ones will disappear.

Lynn D. Gordon, "Race, Class, and the Bonds of Womanhood at Spelman Seminary, 1881–1923," *History of Higher Education Annual* Vol. 9 (1989): 7–32; Helen Lefkowitz Horowitz, *Alma Mater: Design and Experience in the Women's Colleges from Their Nineteenth Century Beginnings to the 1930s* (New York: Alfred A. Knopf, 1984); Patricia A. Palmieri, "Women's Colleges," in *Women in Academe: Progress and Prospects*, edited by Mariam K. Chamberlain, 107–31 (New York: Russell Sage Foundation, 1988).

■ LYNN D. GORDON

SEE ALSO Education.

Black Women's Colleges

With the founding of colleges for African American women during the nineteenth century, much debate ensued on the philosophy of Black women's education, especially on the role of Black women's education for the betterment or "uplift" of the race. Educators also focused on the differences between the role of higher education for Black women and for white women.

Notable among the institutions that were once Black women's colleges but that became coeducational are the following: 1) Barber-Scotia College, Concord, North Carolina, founded in 1867 as Scotia Seminary, a preparatory school for African American women. Scotia merged with Barber Memorial College, Anniston, Alabama, in 1930, adopted the name Barber-Scotia College in 1932, and became coeducational in 1954; 2) Bethune-Cookman College, Daytona Beach, Florida, is the result of the merger in 1923 of Daytona Normal and Industrial Institute for Girls, founded in 1904 by Dr. Mary McLeod Bethune, and the Cookman Institute for Boys, Jacksonville, Florida; and 3) Huston-Tillotson College, Austin, Texas, which is the result of the merger in 1952 of Andrews Normal School, founded in 1876, Dallas, Texas, and Tillotson Collegiate and Normal Institute, founded in 1875, which was a women's college from 1925 to 1935.

Only two U.S. institutions remain exclusively Black women's colleges: Bennett College, Greensboro, North Carolina; and Spelman College, Atlanta, Georgia. Bennett was founded as a coeducational institution in 1873 and was reorganized as a college for women in 1926. Spelman was founded in 1881 and has always been a women's college.

Bennett College began in 1873 in the basement of St. Matthew's Methodist Episcopal Church in Greensboro. The school was named Bennett Seminary in recognition of its first large donor, Lyman Bennett. In 1926, with society turning more attention to the educational needs of women, the Methodist Board of Education and the Methodist Woman's Home Missionary Society began the joint enterprise of overseeing Bennett College for Women with an academic program ranging from the seventh grade through the first year of college. By 1932 the school offered a full four-year college program. Of historically Black colleges and universities that award bachelor's degrees, Bennett College is among the top ten in graduating African Americans who earn the doctorate degree.

Spelman College is the nation's oldest undergraduate liberal arts college for Black women. Founded in 1881 by two white women from New England, Sophia Packard and Harriet Giles, Spelman first opened in the basement of Friendship Baptist Church in Atlanta. The initial class at the Atlanta Baptist Female Seminary, as it was known at that time, consisted of eleven pupils of all ages, girls and women newly freed from slavery. In 1884, in recognition of John D. Rockefeller's fi-

nancial support, which allowed the school to prevent its merger with the Atlanta Baptist Seminary (later Morehouse College), the school's name changed to Spelman Seminary, after his wife's maiden name. In 1924 the name became Spelman College.

Spelman, along with Clark Atlanta University, Interdenominational Theological Center, Morehouse College, Morehouse School of Medicine, and Morris Brown College, together compose the Atlanta University Center. Spelman benefits from access to and cooperation with these five other institutions, while still offering special opportunities for the education of women. In 1988 Spelman was named one of the nation's best colleges or universities in *U.S. News & World Report*. In 1993 Spelman was listed in *U.S. News & World Report* as the number one liberal arts college in the South.

▪ JOHNNETTA B. COLE

SEE ALSO Education.

≋ Women's Educational Equity Act (WEEA)

The Women's Educational Equity Act was introduced in Congress by Representative Patsy T. Mink in 1973 as a complement to the Equal Rights Amendment (ERA) and to Title IX of the Education Act Amendments. The ERA would have required equal treatment for women and Title IX struck down barriers to women's educational opportunity. But neither addressed the social and cultural structures of gender inequality. The persistence of gender stereotyping, gender tracking, and sexism in schools and society would not be rooted out by the ERA and Title IX. In fact, continued sex bias in the curriculum would undermine the promise of both.

Enacted in 1974, the WEEA provided federal funds for projects designed to promote gender equity in the curriculum, in counseling and guidance, in physical education, and in the development of classroom materials. The measure also supported activities for reentering women students, expanded vocational and career education for women, and funded women's resource center initiatives.

Although the WEEA was never generously funded, it was a successful program during its early years. WEEA stimulated projects across the country that challenged the restrictive messages given to women and girls. During the 1980s, however, Republican administrations substantially weakened the program through funding cuts.

A 1992 report published by the American Association of University Women showed that gender bias against girls and women continues to pervade our educational system; teachers pay more attention to boys than to girls; textbooks ignore or stereotype women; and vocational education programs continue to channel women into traditionally female-dominated, low-wage jobs. Since 1993 feminists in Congress have worked to revive and expand the WEEA to more intensively combat gender bias in instruction, career advising, and the educational climate.

• PATSY T. MINK

SEE ALSO Education; Title IX.

≋ Women's Environment and Development Organization

The Women's Environment and Development Organization (WEDO) was founded in 1990 to put analytic and activist clout behind its two guiding themes: Women must have an equal say in fate-of-the-Earth decisions, and healthy communities make a healthy planet.

In focusing on women's roles, needs, and ca-

pacities in movements to restore the environment to sustainable health, WEDO is committed to empowering women. But in both industrialized and developing nations, policymakers, who are overwhelmingly male, have largely ignored the needs and concerns of women. From the grassroots level to the international arena, women are challenging that exclusionary view. Based in New York City, WEDO has a global information and advocacy network of more than twenty thousand.

In 1991 WEDO held the World Women's Congress for a Healthy Planet in Miami, Florida. Attended by 1,500 women from 83 countries, with about one-third coming from developing countries, the conference was designed to bring women's perspectives to the process leading up to the 1992 United Nations Conference on Environment and Development (UNCED), also known as the Earth Summit.

WEDO has since organized a women's caucus meeting at every major international conference affecting women, including the International Conference on Population and Development, held September 1994 in Cairo, Egypt, the World Summit for Social Development held March 1995 in Copenhagen, Denmark, and the Fourth World Conference on Women held in September 1995 in Beijing, China.

• BELLA ABZUG

SEE ALSO Environmentalism.

≋ Women's Health Movement

Born unmistakably out of feminism's second wave in the late 1960s, the Women's Health Movement's (WHM) values derived from feminism's broad commitment to equality and nondiscrimination. It came alive out of the protest climate of the 1960s, inspired by "the movement" for social justice then sweeping the land.

Unique to the WHM of the second wave was its insistence on placing female sexuality, sexual self-determination, and sexual identity at the center of women's health concerns. This analysis exposed the blame-the-victim moral tyranny, prejudice and health neglect underlying so many of the reproductive laws and medical practices of the day.

The WHM started spontaneously in different parts of the country through different activities, with varied leadership, and raising multiple issues; there was never any single individual or group founder of the WHM. Contrary to popular assumptions, however, women of various ages, women of color, and working-class women did participate in the WHM from its beginnings, although not in great numbers. Latinas, Black women, and Native American women knew first-hand about clinic care, illegal abortions, infant mortality, sterilization abuse, and population control. For the WHM, these scandals rapidly became core knowledge for every advocate in the ongoing class, race, and gender analysis of the health system.

"Consciousness-raising" and "know-your-body" group experiences gradually changed thousands of women's outlooks on their private lives and on the meaning of personal bodily and medical experiences, allowing them to see these events for the first time in political terms.

In women's groups across the country, and eventually the world, activists introduced personal gynecological self-examination via plastic speculums, along with alternative remedies, fertility awareness, and basic body wisdom, called *self-help* groups. Menstrual Extraction (ME) or Menstrual Regulation (MR) (withdrawing the uterine lining in a simple, sterile, mechanical procedure) was unquestionably the most precedent-shattering achievement of "lay" women working in advanced self-help groups. Their development of the flexible cannula was and is revolutionary. This innovation established a higher worldwide standard for abortion care, acknowledged by the medical establishment itself. The full potential of this technology for returning abortion control to women, however, has yet to be realized.

The era of citizen and journalist health investigations was at its height. Harmful drugs were on the market; contraceptive experiments such as the birth-control pill involved deaths that were concealed; unnecessary hysterectomies, ovariectomies, and mastectomies were widespread and ignored; poor women were used as guinea pigs in government-approved experiments.

WHM writers and researchers began producing a prolific flow of books, pamphlets, films, and articles. These works provided an enraging history of women's health, a platform for protest, and, eventually, a solid base of accurate knowledge on which ordinary women and the oncoming movement were nourished and could begin to pursue their advocacy and action efforts.

Ordinary women, "lay" women, suddenly felt entitled to conduct their own research, to challenge publicly the presumed scientific authority of doctors' pronouncements about female sexuality, women's proper roles in society, and their health and diseases. These attitudes and behaviors were considered extremely deviant at the time. As with sexuality, women patients challenging medical and scientific expertise in public discourse was shocking. Women began to listen to and trust other women. The WHM thus was considered "revolutionary."

The movement came early to its international, "global" outlook. Outraged by experimental birth control for poor women—mostly women of color—activists quickly took up the issue of population-control practices. In the 1970s the United States Agency for International Development's (USAID) policies made aggressive, high-technology birth-control programs a precondition for loans and economic aid to Third World countries.

When U.S. WHM activists realized their efforts were effective in protecting U.S. women by keeping dangerous or questionable drugs and devices off the U.S. market (e.g., the "high-dose" pill; the

Dalkon Shield IUD; Depo-Provera), they saw these products simply "dumped" or widely available as bargains for financially strapped Third World governments. Without benefit of warnings, millions of women could be harmed by these rejects. The WHM protested, demanding action on behalf of women overseas. A global view thus became essential.

Much of the WHM's early focus was concerned with women's need for sexual self-knowledge, self-determination, and reproductive rights, but the WHM's vision was broader, including addressing the impact of DES and its iatrogenic effects, unnecessary surgery, damaging childbirth practices, and violence against women. Long before HIV/AIDS was identified, women's health advocates took the lead in educating women about the risks of undiagnosed sexually transmitted diseases and pelvic inflammatory disease. Menstruation was demystified and PMS alternative remedies discovered. Others founded Feminist Women's Health Centers in several U.S. cities, providing women-controlled settings for self-help programs, and, once abortion became legal in 1973, early abortion care. Simultaneously, other women's communities across the country launched their own well-woman health and abortion centers as "alternatives" to conventional care.

By 1975 the National Women's Health Network (NWHN) was formed, the nation's first and only public-interest membership organization devoted exclusively to all women's health issues, especially those related to federal policy. The NWHN helped to strengthen the FDA's Patient Package Insert (PPI) program, improving the quality of warnings, especially to healthy women, about the risks and side effects of the Pill and powerful menopausal estrogens. It supported class-action suits against drug companies that manufactured DES. The WHM monitored the federal budget for amounts spent on barrier methods of contraception as opposed to more experimental hormonal or device methods. The WHM also helped initiate the study and approval of the cervical cap as an alternative. It launched Citizen Petitions to the FDA, established registries for women given drugs or devices not approved for the purpose, and developed model informed consent forms so women could become more aware of potential health risks. Working with women scientists, it challenged research protocols and raised ethical issues concerning the use of healthy women in studies. It organized letter-writing campaigns to force the FDA to establish uniform labeling of tampons to prevent Toxic Shock Syndrome and helped expose corporate negligence related to the Dalkon Shield IUD and silicone breast implants.

By the mid-1970s, U.S. women and the WHM saw both setbacks and gains. The rise of the New Right and antiabortion religious groups had begun. The Hyde Amendment passed in 1977, eliminating federal Medicaid funding for abortions, forcing all states to decide whether or how to fund this service. Beginning in the 1970s and continuing through the 1980s, resisting right-wing and antiabortion efforts to roll back gains consumed the efforts of most activists. Despite this struggle, the WHM was now established.

Growing out of an NWHN project, incorporating WHM values, the National Black Women's Health Project (NBWHP) was ignited by a highly successful 1983 conference. It has become one of the country's major women's health groups advocating for the needs of women of color. Other groups, the National Latina Health Organization, the Native American Community Board's Women's Health Education Project, Asian American Sisters in Action, and the National Asian Women's Health Organization, also were formed. New national coalitions of women of color organized around reproductive rights, population and environment issues, violence, and AIDS. Women of color transformed the WHM by leading organizations drawn from their own communities and by participating in the leadership of multicultural women's health organizations such as the National Women's Health Network. Focusing on health issues in the context of racism, coercion and violence, and economic discrimination, these diverse voices have strengthened the movement at all levels.

The public became increasingly aware of the dearth of woman-centered medical research or health-care provisions. Many women found it difficult to demystify health-related concerns or to challenge doctors; instead, they pinned their hopes for better care on finding a sympathetic woman doctor. The results have been mixed. Although studies show that most women are pleased, many women bring inappropriate expectations to women doctors, whose ability to be flexible or question traditional medical practice often is more constrained than that of most male physicians. Most women doctors collaborate with the drug industry, just as male doctors do, and tend to disparage alternative therapies. Nevertheless, women physicians are mobilizing to change teaching programs in medical schools to include more about women's health. The WHM has always worked with progressive women professionals and supported women's struggle to become a critical new force in medicine and health care.

The WHM continues debate on the potential of women professionals' leadership to improve medicine or health and medical care for women. Some argue for a women's health medical specialty, while others agree with experts who conclude that the system needs fewer, not more, specialists. Opponents believe obstetrics and gynecology, as a surgical specialty that excludes primary care, needs either to be abolished altogether or drastically revamped to meet women's needs rather than those of doctors and surgeons. Many WHM activists feel that there are too many physicians, as much public-health research suggests. Recognizing the justice in women having equal access to a medical career, reformers promote increased use of midlevel nurse practitioners and

nurse-midwives. They see nurses as the best possible providers of more satisfying and equitable care at far less cost—even as these health care workers become increasingly tied to the insurance and drug industries and to the medical profession.

The WHM continues to include all reproductive rights as a central part of its agenda, believing that a woman's right to control and express her fertility is a basic precondition for exercising other rights. Many believe that without improvements in fundamental economic conditions for women, family planning alone cannot cure poverty. Most continue to feel that women's reproductive options are best exercised within the framework of all women's right to optimum economic survival, comprehensive health services, and sexual self-determination.

The WHM remains concerned with the broadest range of health and disease issues affecting women as well as with the safety and efficacy of touted technologies and therapies. But it is also concerned with women's paid and unpaid relationship to the service-delivery and caregiving systems, which profit handsomely at women's expense. In addition to women-of-color concerns, the movement has also broadened since its beginnings to include older women; differently abled women; and the issues of working women facing occupational health hazards, reproductive rights violations, and harassment problems.

The WHM's strongest focus remains on issues of accountability to citizens/users/consumers/patients/clients. This includes making government more accountable for the impact on women of its health policies and regulations, more forthcoming to all citizens with health and medical care information it collects through taxpayers' money, and more vigorous in policing researchers and corporations. The WHM challenges conventional medical ethics and medical education or training to include feminist values, working to keep alive issues of patients' rights, informed consent, experimental treatments, and Patient Package Inserts in pharmaceutical products. In effect, feminist health activists have become a new breed of ethicists.

Citizen-led women's health organizations continue to play the major role in defining the WHM and producing its leadership, although many outstanding individuals contribute. The public interest initiative in women's health—community women's control and input, accountability from the medical establishment, government and corporations—will remain with the WHM for the foreseeable future. In some ways, these "lay" spokeswomen have themselves become experts in health, developing perspectives that have scientific validity but are frequently at odds with the medical establishment's opinion or practice. One original dream of the WHM, that all women would eventually be able to evaluate critically the entire realm of health and medicine for women, has remained elusive.

However, women's groups across the United States are now coming to the realization that health reform is overwhelmingly a women's issue. In a few states, women's health activists are now forming state-level coalitions, planning for the long haul to become a force with which their state legislatures and state regulators will have to reckon. Many observers feel that the WHM remains one of the most vibrant, active, leading edges of the women's movement.

Barbara Ehrenreich and Deirdre English, *For Her Own Good: One Hundred Fifty Years of Experts' Advice to Women* (New York: Doubleday/Anchor Books, 1989); Betsy Hartmann, *Reproductive Rights and Wrongs: The Global Politics of Population Control* (Boston: South End Press, 1994); Nancy Worcester and Marianne H. Whatley, *Women's Health: Readings on Social, Economic and Political Issues*, 2d ed. (Dubuque, Iowa: Kendall-Hunt, 1994).

• NORMA SWENSON

SEE ALSO Abortion Self-Help Movement; Alternative Healing; Boston Women's Health Book Collective; Diethylstilbestrol (DES); Medical Research.

≋ Women's Liberation

Women's Liberation was the early term for the feminist movement that began in the 1960s. The popularity of the term declined after a few years because some used it to ridicule the movement.

No one person coined the term. The word "liberation" was in common use, having been adapted from Third World movements that were attempting to liberate themselves from colonial occupation. In particular the National Liberation Front in Vietnam was instrumental in "liberation" becoming part of the popular lexicon, but it was also used in this country by many different organized efforts to reject traditional roles, restraints, and expectations.

The phrase *women's liberation movement* first appeared in March 1968 as the tag line of the first issue of the movement's national newsletter. When the second issue came out in June, it was called the "voice of the women's liberation movement." The newsletter's first editor, Joreen, picked this name because she wanted to refocus the debate from the "woman problem" or "woman question," as it had been called in previous decades, to the question of women's liberation.

The new movement had two origins from two different strata of society, with two different styles, orientations, values, and forms of organization. In many ways there were two separate movements that only began to merge in the mid-1970s. Although the composition of both branches was predominantly white, middle class, and college-educated, initially the median age of the activists in the "older branch" of the movement was about twenty years greater.

Early descriptions of the movement called the two branches "women's rights" and "women's liberation." The implication was that those espousing women's liberation were more radical than those seeking merely women's rights. However, the primary difference was structure and style.

The "older branch" consisted of national organizations with a formal structure, and the "younger branch" was made up of small groups, loosely linked by the newsletter and subsequent publications. The latter borrowed the idea of participatory democracy from the New Left, and expanded it to include the idea that groups should deemphasize structure and leadership.

Over time the press turned the words "women's liberation" into "women's lib" and began to refer to active participants as "libbers," "libbies," and "libbists." The use of the diminutive was not neutral. As if to highlight the intended disrespect, one article was even entitled "Black Liberation and Women's Lib." Because of this ridicule, the phrase women's liberation slowly went out of common use, to be replaced by the more generic term *feminist*. The name's intended goal, of defining the debate as one of how to liberate women, was never achieved.

▪ JO FREEMAN

SEE ALSO Feminism and Feminisms.

≋ Women's Studies

Women's studies has its roots in the social ferment of the late 1960s and 1970s. The continuing movement for civil rights among people of color, the anti–Vietnam War movement, and the women's liberation movement criticized both the structure of educational institutions and the content of scholarship. For feminists the former critique led to the development of affirmative action programs, while the latter led to the founding of the field of women's studies.

"Women's Studies" became an established academic field within twenty years, one of the most remarkable accomplishments of the second wave of feminism. Before 1969 no women's studies programs and few courses were available at universities or colleges in the United States. But by the early 1990s over five hundred formal women's studies programs existed, most of which offered a major, minor, and/or certificate; over fifty offered some type of graduate degree. Many campuses also created research institutes for the study of women and gender.

The early goals of women's studies were to transform higher education by including the history and culture of women in most courses and research and by developing new forms of pedagogy that were more cooperative and gave women a more active role in their education. Soon the goals became more complicated. The content of women's studies came to include identifying and criticizing male bias in research and curriculum; encouraging teaching and research about women and gender; and using this new knowledge to develop women-centered but inclusive frameworks for understanding the world. Such a comprehensive definition of women's studies encouraged its development in social sciences, natural sciences, education, the law, and the humanities.

The formation of the National Women's Studies Association (NWSA) in 1977 was influential in developing the field. Its annual conventions brought together women's studies scholars and students from around the nation to share their research and teaching and to formulate strategies for the institutionalization of women's studies. Unlike most academic organizations, the NWSA affirmed its political roots, placing social change for women on the agenda. It experimented with forms of governance that fostered solidarity among feminists yet also encouraged dissent. Third World women and lesbian caucuses played a prominent role from the beginning, the former making the fight against racism integral to women's studies, the latter supporting the visibility of lesbians in academe. Other caucuses include preschool educators, Jewish women, and poor, working-class women. Over the years the NWSA has been resilient despite crises brought on by lack of resources and political differences.

Despite a verbal commitment to represent the voices of all women, most women's studies scholarship has focused on European American, middle-class heterosexual women as a result of racism, elitism, and heterosexism in the society as a whole as well as the restrictive traditions of academic scholarship and hiring. Just as women's studies has continuously criticized the academy for its male bias, women of color, working-class women, and lesbians have actively criticized the biases of women's studies. Although such reevaluation is ongoing, it has already had some results; feminist scholarship has begun to explore differences among women and examine the social hierarchies that divide women, as well as their similarities. Women of color have also taken the lead in developing links between women's studies and ethnic studies programs.

An early issue facing scholars in the field of women's studies was whether to become a separate department or a network of feminist faculty hired in different departments. It became clear that both approaches had advantages. If the goal was to change the content of research and teaching throughout the university, it would be useful to have feminist faculty fully integrated into departments. At the same time an independent resource base and a focused intellectual group would also help. To prevent their ghettoization, women's studies programs developed curriculum transformation projects that offered faculty development for all those interested in including women and gender in their research and teaching. This model also has been used to foster the inclusion of women of color in the curriculum.

Most universities and colleges resisted the development of women's studies, and in many cases women's studies has not yet gained full respect and support. Faculty and students have had to expend enormous political energy to shepherd women's studies through educational bureaucracies. In the process, the support of the feminist movement nationwide was essential. In addition, the high quality of feminist research was helpful in winning over hostile or indifferent faculty.

Cherríe Moraga and Gloria Anzaldúa, eds., *This Bridge Called My Back: Writings by Radical Women of Color* (Watertown, Mass.: Persephone Press, 1981); Gloria T. Hull, Patricia Bell Scott, and Barbara Smith, eds., *All the Women Are White, All the Blacks Are Men, But Some of Us Are Brave: Black Women's Studies* (Old Westbury, N.Y.: Feminist Press, 1982); Ellen Carol DuBois, Gail Paradise Kelly, Elizabeth Lapovsky Kennedy, Carolyn W. Korsmeyer, and Lillian S. Robinson, eds., *Feminist Scholarship: Kindling in the Groves of Academe* (Urbana: University of Illinois Press, 1985).

▪ ELIZABETH LAPOVSKY KENNEDY

SEE ALSO Education; History and Historians.

≣ Women's Trade Union League

Founded in 1903 during the Boston convention of the American Federation of Labor, the Women's Trade Union League (WTUL) was a unique organization of wage-earning women and their middle- and upper-class supporters. Like its British counterpart, the WTUL pursued the dual goals of unionizing female workers and advocating labor legislation for women. The cross-class nature of the WTUL was exemplified by its first two presidents: Margaret Dreier Robins, the daughter of a wealthy and influential New York family; and Rose Schneiderman, a Russian-Polish immigrant and former factory worker. The WTUL was most active in New York and Chicago and played a major role in the garment workers' strikes of 1909–10 and in the response to the Triangle Shirtwaist fire disaster. The league was also instrumental in developing working-class support for women's suffrage.

The WTUL's union-organizing efforts were met by indifference or hostility from the male-dominated American Federation of Labor. Lack of support from male trade unionists, combined

A woman airs bedding outside her home in Green Lake, Washington, 1890.

with the difficulties inherent in organizing women whom society perceived as only temporary members of the labor force, led the WTUL to focus increasingly on protective legislation. After World War I, the WTUL abandoned much of its union-organizing work in favor of campaigns for the eight-hour day, a minimum wage, and child labor legislation. WTUL members strongly opposed the Equal Rights Amendment because it would overturn protective laws for women workers, leading to a bitter rivalry with the National Woman's Party. Membership began to decline during the 1920s, and the WTUL disbanded in 1950.

▪ BEATRIX HOFFMAN

SEE ALSO Labor Movement; Labor Unions; Protective Labor Legislation.

≋ Work

Since the nineteenth century women in the United States have been caught in a bind: much of the daily labor they perform is not directly compensated with wages, and yet the dominant ideology defines "work" as waged labor only. Thus many women have had to struggle against the notion that they "don't work" while trying to achieve recognition for the labor they do perform.

This dominant, narrow definition of work has been historically constructed. Pre- and postconquest Native American tribal communities conceptualized work in dramatically different terms, integrating it into spiritually understood sexual divisions of labor bound to the natural world. In the European colonies of the seventeenth and eighteenth centuries, waged labor itself was rare. Most women and men worked in differing forms of bound labor—whether enslaved or as indentured servants—or as subsistence farmers, none of whom received cash compensation and all of whom were acknowledged to be "working." The concept of the skilled "goodwife" captured the high value placed on European American women's domestic labors, which were viewed as complementary to men's skills.

Only with the triumph of "free labor" and industrial capitalism in the nineteenth century did new ideologies emerge that devalued much of women's labor. As markets in both labor and commodities spread to dominate economic life, only those activities rewarded through cash—whether wages, salary, or entrepreneurial profits—were viewed as "work." Unwaged labor in the home, now called "housework," was newly invisible. Most of the labor performed by men now was considered "work," while the women's labor in the home was transposed into "leisure." The ubiquitous presence of domestic servants performing housework for wages failed to undermine this ideology, since working-class women, often women of color, were not considered "women."

In the twentieth century women are still struggling with this legacy. Wage-earning women are seen as "working women," but women who perform full-time domestic labor are asked "Do you work?" and often respond "No." The rapidly rising labor-force participation of all groups of women has only heightened the tension between waged and unwaged work, without a greater recognition of women's "double day" of waged work plus cleaning, shopping, child care, and the emotional labor involved in kinship and nurturance. Feminist theorists are only beginning to rethink the definition of work and how to take all of women's labors into account.

Yet popular, alternative conceptualizations of work have always thrived among women, countering the dominant ideology. Women have been well aware that their reproductive labors are indeed work, hard work. At the same time, much of what others might view as drudgery has imparted value: the pleasure of producing a clean house, a delicious dinner, or a cherished holiday ritual. For much of women's labor, traditional notions of the line between work and leisure have not applied. Cut off from the social valuation some men obtain through achievement in the labor force, women have built their own cultures valuing one another not by their wage-earning capacities but by their centrality in providing love, sustenance, and survival for their communities.

• DANA FRANK

SEE ALSO Contingent Work; Double-Day; Household Workers; Indentured Servitude; Labor Movement; Nontraditional Jobs; Service Sector; Slavery; *and entries for specific professions.*

≋ World War I Period

Although the United States was formally at war for only a year and a half, World War I profoundly affected many American women. It opened new job opportunities in industry, commerce, and public service to women white and Black. Volunteers produced huge quantities of food and supplies for European war victims. Sculptor Gertrude Vanderbilt Whitney built and ran a hospital in France; novelist Edith Wharton depleted her fortune assisting European orphans and refugees; others spent their life's savings to sail to Europe to nurse or work in the motor corps. Even before the United States entered the war, American nurses thronged to battlefields, where they did heroic work.

Some women agitated against the war. Some created pacifist organizations like Lilian Wald's and Crystal Eastman's American Union Against Militarism. Anarchist Emma Goldman warned against the militarism that was already fostering a repressive atmosphere in the United States. When the United States entered the war in 1917, three years after fighting began in Europe, draft resisters demonstrated across the country. Goldman encouraged them: troops broke up her meetings and arrested dissenters, and Goldman was sentenced to two years in prison.

Suffrage organizations differed in strategy. Mainstream feminists swarmed into war work. Carrie Chapman Catt, leader of the National American Woman Suffrage Association (NAWSA), felt that assisting the war effort would improve the suffragists' position afterwards. NAWSA and Women's Trade Union League leaders took government posts. The National Woman's Party, however, with many Quakers in its leadership, continued to picket the White House. When Alexander Kerensky, briefly the premier of Russia (which granted women suffrage after the revolution), visited the White House, suffragist banners declared that Woodrow Wilson could not make the world safe for democracy since his own country was not democratic. Male onlookers and soldiers violently attacked the women; the police imprisoned nearly one hundred women. The suffragists' various war-related activities ultimately led President Wilson to support the Nineteenth Amendment.

While some women protested the war, some women participated in it. In 1916, worried about maintaining sufficient clerical staff if the United States entered the war, the Secretary of the Navy decided that law did not say yeomen must be male, and accepted 13,000 women in the navy and 300 in the Marine Corps. None were permitted to remain in service when the war ended in 1919. Women everywhere were fired from their jobs. The one positive aftermath of the war for women was that in 1920, after seventy-two years of struggle, they won suffrage for women of all races—though poll taxes, literacy tests, and other racial barriers prevented the majority of Black women from voting until the civil rights movement of the 1960s.

■ MARILYN FRENCH

SEE ALSO Wars: 1900 to the Present.

≋ World War II Period

Historians often claim that women benefit from the upheaval that accompanies war because economic, political, and social opportunities open up for women as men are called into battle. Women's economic gains were indeed dramatic during World War II but tended to be short-lived. Overall female labor-force rates rose from 23.6 percent in 1930 to 27.9 percent in 1940, peaking at 37 percent in 1944. The sharpest increase was for married women, who composed 3 million of the 6.5 million new female workers. This trend affected white and Native American women more than Black, who had higher rates of prewar employment. Black women also experienced marked discrimination in wartime hiring, although the war also provided Native and other women of color an opportunity to work in nonservice, higher-paying occupations. Japanese American women, interned during the early part of the war, were later released to work in defense plants.

As women shifted into manufacturing and other sectors previously reserved for men, they encountered hostility from male workers; trade unions offered only sporadic protection. Lack of adequate housing and transportation, long shifts and erratic hours, and a scarcity of quality child care intensified the double burden of wage work and family care. Nevertheless, many female workers planned to remain employed after the war; male veterans, however, received priority in postwar hiring.

Women's efforts to participate in the military were similarly constrained by both racial and gender prejudice. Sixty thousand nurses were recruited into the Army Nurse Corps, including unprecedented numbers of Native American nurses, but the pool of trained Black nurses was underutilized despite severe shortages. Black women also were excluded from the Women's Airforce Service Pilots (WASP) and segregated in other service branches. Native American women, however, were largely integrated into white-led units. Partially as a result of opposition by the predominantly male American Medical Association, female doctors were barred from military service until 1943. All branches scrutinized recruits for suspected lesbians. Women in the military shared in many of the men's entitlements, including veterans' benefits and the GI Bill, but their pay was lower, and their dependents were denied allotments. The various female corps attracted hundreds of thousands of volunteers, including the

Mexican American women workers on the South Pacific Rail Road during World War II.

Women's Army Corps, 140,000; WAVES (Navy), 100,000; and the Marine Corps Women's Reserve, 23,000, among others.

Gender ideology permitted women's entry into nontraditional employment but stressed that their new economic and social roles were "for the duration only." Women were encouraged to retain their "femininity"; the iconic "Rosie the Riveter" was depicted wearing overalls and nail polish. Postwar "prescriptions for Penelope" urging women to defer to returning male loved ones and resume their domestic roles led to the "baby boom." After a brief dip in 1945, employment rates for both single and married women resumed their climb, slowly changing U.S. family patterns (but hardly disturbing occupational stratification by gender). Lesbians and gay men benefited from wartime opportunities and began forming strong communities despite severe repression during the McCarthy era. Many historians believe that women's expanded opportunities and often contradictory experiences during the 1940s led to the flowering of a feminist women's movement two decades later.

■ SONYA MICHEL

SEE ALSO Rosie the Riveter; Wars: 1900 to the Present.

≋ YWCA

The Young Women's Christian Association (YWCA) is one of the largest and most influential world organizations of women, providing educational and recreational services and leadership training opportunities for women and girls. First organized in London in 1855, the YWCA opened in New York City in 1858. Women organized YWCA associations in many U.S. cities to provide housing and religious instruction to young single women who were flooding into urban areas. In 1906 city organizations and college-based student associations that had been inspired by the Protestant evangelical movement joined together to form the YWCA of the USA. Originally a Protestant lay movement, it is now open to women of all religious persuasions. The YWCA of the USA is associated with the World YWCA, first organized in 1894, a federation of YWCA associations from over seventy nations.

The YWCA of the USA was influenced by the Social Gospel movement of the early twentieth century and adopted a social reform program, focusing first on the needs of working women. The YWCA organized the Industrial Clubs in the first decade of the twentieth century to provide a forum for working-class women to discuss wages, safety and health standards, and protective legislation. During the 1920s and 1930s the YWCA advocated protective labor legislation and encouraged trade union organization for women.

During the 1920s and 1930s the YWCA gradually moved toward a more progressive stance on race relations as well. The group was composed of women from many different racial and ethnic groups from the 1890s on, but women of color were organized into segregated facilities and programs. By the 1940s approximately 10 percent of the YWCA's membership was African American. In addition, the YWCA had programs for Native American girls in Indian schools, as well as for Chinese American, Japanese American, and Mex-ican American girls and women. During the 1920s and 1930s increasing pressure was mounted within the YWCA, particularly from the Student Division, to end the practice of segregation.

In 1946 the National Convention of the YWCA endorsed an "Interracial Charter," pledging the YWCA to racial integration. The YWCA provided support for the civil rights movement during the 1960s; the Student YWCA contributed participants to sit-ins and sponsored voter registration projects, while the National Board lobbied for civil rights legislation. In 1970 the Y's national convention endorsed the elimination of racism as its "one imperative."

The YWCA supported liberal internationalist positions in the postwar world, urging the United States to support the United Nations both to adjudicate disputes and to provide aid to developing nations. The YWCA's internationalist perspective flowed partly from the international connections women made; members of the YWCA of the USA often served as advisory personnel to YWCAs in other nations.

The YWCA continued to work to advance women's interests after World War II. In the face of post–World War II demobilization, the YWCA defended the right of women to work for wages and pushed for equal opportunities with men in education, training, and employment. The YWCA encouraged debate about women's roles in families and fostered women's leadership development. From the 1930s onward it advocated the dissemination of birth-control information. Several prominent members of the YWCA served on President Kennedy's Commission on the Status of Women. In 1973 the YWCA endorsed the Equal Rights Amendment, indicating its support for the revival of feminism. During the 1970s national conventions called for an expansion of child-care services, and maternal and child health services. The YWCA also supported repeal of all laws restricting abortions and greater involvement of women in governmental positions.

■ SUSAN LYNN

INDEX OF CONTRIBUTORS

GENERAL INDEX

ILLUSTRATION CREDITS

Index of Contributors

General Index

NOTE: Page numbers in **bold** refer to main entries (articles) for a subject. Page numbers in *italics* refer to illustrations.

Illustration Credits

Abolitionist Movement, Sophia Smith Collection, Smith College

Advertising, Scott Paper Company, Philadelphia, Pennsylvania

Aging, © Freda Leinwand

Agriculture, National Archives and Records Administration

Art and Crafts, Courtesy of the Museum of Fine Arts, Boston

Aviation, courtesy of Elizabeth Amelia Hadley Freydberg

Beauty Culture, Denver Public Library, Western History Department

Birth Control, Library of Congress

Chicanas and Mexican American Women, Rio Grande Historical Collections, New Mexico State University Library

Chinese American Women, National Archives and Records Administration

Civil Rights Movement, UPI/Corbis-Bettmann Archive

Clerical Work, Brown Brothers

Communism, UPI/Corbis-Bettmann Archive

Consciousness Raising, © Bettye Lane

Cooking, The University of Pennsylvania, Center for Judaic Studies

Cross-Dressing, Courtesy of the Trustees of the Boston Public Library

Decorative Arts, Courtesy of the Santa Fe Railway

Disability, © JEB (Joan E. Biren)

Dress Reform, Library of Congress

Education (Oberlin College), Oberlin College Archives

Education (Cherokee Young Ladies' Seminary), Denver Public Library, Western History Collection

Fashion and Style, Library of Congress

Film, Courtesy of Ally Acker

Great Depression, National Archives and Records Administration

Household Workers, State Historical Society of Wisconsin

Immigration, Library of Congress

Indentured Servitude, Historical Society of Pennsylvania

Japanese American Internment, National Archives and Records Administration

Japanese American Women, National Japanese American Historical Society

Jewish Women, Brown Brothers

Ku Klux Klan, Indiana Historical Society Library

Labor Unions (ILGWU), © JEB (Joan E. Biren)

Labor Unions (Knights of Labor), Library of Congress

La Raza, Alfonso Vazquez Collection, Houston Metropolitan Research Center, Houston Public Library

Lesbians (E. Alice Austen), Staten Island Historical Society Library

Lesbians (Washington, D.C., march), © JEB (Joan E. Biren)

Literature, Smithsonian Institution, National Portrait Gallery, Washington, D.C.

Magazines, Sophia Smith Collection, Smith College

Missionaries, ABCFM photographs, by permission of the Houghton Library, Harvard University

Mormons, Courtesy of the Oakland Museum History Department

Native American Women (BIA occupation), UPI/Corbis-Bettmann Archive

Native American Women (Seminole), Smithsonian Institution, National Anthropological Archives, Washington, D.C.

Nursing Profession, Brown Brothers

Painting, Courtesy of the Art Institute of Chicago

Peace Movement, © JEB (Joan E. Biren)

Phyllis Wheatley Clubs and Homes, Courtesy of the Phyllis Wheatley Association, Cleveland, Ohio

Picture Brides, UPI/Corbis-Bettmann Archive

Pro-Choice/Antiabortion Movements, © JEB (Joan E. Biren)

Prohibition and Temperance, Archive Photos

Puerto Rican Women, The Jesús Colón Papers, Center for Puerto Rican Studies Library and Archives, Hunter College, City University of New York

Quilting, Courtesy of the Museum of Fine Arts, Boston

Religion, © JEB (Joan E. Biren)

Salem Witchcraft Trials, The Essex Institute, Salem, Massachusetts

Service Sector, National Archives and Records Administration

Settlement House Movement, The Schlesinger Library, Radcliffe College

Slavery (family), Library of Congress

Slavery (Louisa), Missouri Historical Society, St. Louis

Sports, The Schlesinger Library, Radcliffe College

Strikes, Library of Congress

Suffrage Movement, Library of Congress

Superheroines, Courtesy of Trina Robbins

Sweatshops, Courtesy of the Women's Bureau

Teaching Profession, National Archives and Records Administration

Textile/Apparel Workers, Library of Congress

Violence Against Women, © JEB (Joan E. Biren)

Wars: 1900 to the Present, National Japanese American Historical Society

Western Women, Idaho State Historical Society

Women's Colleges, Courtesy of Spelman College Archives

Work, University of Washington Libraries

World War II Period, Arizona Historical Society, Tucson